Urban America
a historical bibliography

Clio Bibliography Series No. 7

Gail Schlachter, Editor
Pamela R. Byrne, Executive Editor

Users of the Clio Bibliography Series may refer to current issues of
America: History and Life *and* Historical Abstracts
*for continuous bibliographic coverage of the subject areas
treated by each individual volume in the series.*

Urban America

a historical bibliography

Neil L. Shumsky

&

Timothy Crimmins

editors

Santa Barbara, California
Oxford, England

ISBN 0-87436-038-2

American Bibliographical Center—Clio Press, Inc.
2040 Alameda Padre Serra
Santa Barbara, California

European Bibliographical Center—Clio Press
Woodside House, Hinksey Hill
Oxford OXI 5BE, England

Printed and bound in the United States of America.

Cover design and graphics by Lance Klass, after a
painting by Glenn Coleman.

TABLE OF CONTENTS

PREFACE

Urban America: A Historical Bibliography contains 4,068 abstracts of articles concerned with the development of, and life in, American cities from prehistoric times to the present. These abstracts originally appeared in volumes eleven through seventeen of *America: History and Life* published by ABC-Clio Information Services of Santa Barbara, California.

The database of *America: History and Life* contains abstracts of articles appearing in more than two thousand journals printed in 42 languages. Of these, about seven hundred are published in the United States and Canada, and they include journals of state and local historical societies, as well as those dealing with history in general, the humanities and the social sciences. The historical journals range in scope from very narrow to very broad, from the *West Tennessee Historical Society Papers* to the *American Historical Review.* The foreign journals are surveyed on a regular basis to discover any articles about the history and life of the United States and Canada. Thus, the database for the present volume is tremendous—the largest history database in the world.

In order to select the abstracts for *Urban America,* we each read every abstract contained in volumes eleven through seventeen of *America: History and Life* and independently selected those which seemed appropriate. Afterwards, we reconciled our lists. This task was even more difficult than it seems. Obviously, it consumed an extraordinary amount of time just to do the reading. But, more than that, selecting the abstracts to use meant devising some rigid criteria which we could apply systematically. We were very strongly tempted, at an early stage in the work, to include only those articles which satisfied our own individual definitions of urban history. We abandoned this criterion for two reasons. First, we could not agree on a working definition of urban history. Second, and much more important, we feel that this bibliography should be as inclusive as possible. We want it to be a basic reference tool which will be consulted regularly by everyone studying American cities. Therefore, we want researchers to feel confident that, for the years and journals covered, this volume is definitive and that no further searching need be done. We have therefore included all abstracts which have as their primary focus some aspect of urban life or which concern events which have occurred in cities. Thus, there are a large number of abstracts which neither of us would actually classify as urban history but which might nonetheless be useful to some scholar. For example, if we had found the abstract of an article titled "The Presidential Election of 1856 on Staten Island" we would have included it. While many would argue (and we would agree) that the article deals simply with national politics in a specific urban setting, it might still be important to someone preparing a general history of New York City or a study of presidential politics in American cities. Basically, our primary criterion for inclusion is potential utility. Do we think that a particular abstract has a reasonable chance of being valuable to someone studying cities? If the answer to that question is "yes," we have included the abstract.

Effective use of this bibliography requires utilizing both the Table of Contents and the Subject Index. The Table of Contents reflects the classification scheme we devised before reading the abstracts and revised after reading them. In general, it reflects the major divisions of the volume: American Urban History from 1607 to 1945; Contemporary American Urban Life Since 1945; Canadian Urban History and Life; American Indian Urban Settlements; and Historiography, Methodology, Bibliography, and Teaching. While most of these categories are self-explanatory, a few useful points might be made. First, the section of American Indian Urban Life contains only abstracts about cities founded and inhabited by native Americans. Abstracts about native Americans in other urban settings will generally be found in appropriate subject sections, much like other ethnic groups. Second, the section on historiography contains abstracts of articles dealing exclusively with urban subjects. More general articles about Teaching, Bibliography, and Methodology have been excluded, just as they have throughout the book.

Within the major divisions of the volume, a secondary level of categorization has been made. In trying to determine how best to organize the 4,068 abstracts, we initially considered categories of chronology and geography but ultimately decided that these systems would be very difficult to apply and much less useful than classes based on concepts. Therefore, the abstracts are organized around the two major questions of urban history. "How have cities grown, developed, and, in some cases, declined?" and "What has been the nature of life in cities?" The abstracts concerned with life in cities have also been categorized according to major aspects of urban life: politics, economics, society, ethnicity, health, physical structure, and attitudes toward cities. When the number of articles within a particular subtopic has been sufficient, these categories, too, have been broken down.

The Table of Contents thus serves as an excellent introduction to the way in which urban history has been written and as an initial entry to this bibliography. For someone seeking general information on subjects like "Voluntary Associations" or "Communications," it provides a good starting point.

But for someone seeking more specialized information, or making an all-inclusive literature search, or trying to research a subject which is not one of our categories, the analytical Subject Index is critical and must be consulted. Using the American Bibliographical Center's Subject Profile Index, editors expertly index each abstract, selecting key words not only from a list of preferred subject headings and the article title but from the text itself. Therefore, abstracts which might, on the basis of their titles alone, appear to be irrelevant to a particular topic, can be identified.

The subject index is also important because of the basic problem involved in any attempt to classify—almost any item can be classified in more than one way. An article like William R. Hutchinson's "Disapproval of Chicago: The Symbolic Trial of David Swing" could be categorized as either "Religion" or "Attitudes Toward Urban Life," or, John B. Myers' "The Freedmen and the Labor Supply: The Economic Adjustments in Post-Bellem Atlanta, 1865-67" could be located in either "Blacks" or "Work and the Work Force." Since each abstract is printed only once, the subject index serves as the basic cross-referencing tool which allows a thorough literature search to be made. More comprehensive than conventional indexes, ABC-SPIndex is uniquely designed to increase access to the bibliographic entries. The subjects of each entry are indexed as a set of terms (an index string) that provides a complete profile of the subject matter of the cited article—in effect giving the user an abstract of the abstract. By perusing the index profiles, the researcher should be able to find all relevant articles. See the explanatory note at the beginning of the index for more information about ABC-SPIndex.

Pamela R. Byrne, Executive Editor of the Clio Bibliography Series, directed and participated in every phase of the project, from the initial planning stage through the complex editorial processes of the computer-assisted indexing system and machine-readable database, to the final design and production of the book. Managing Editor Suzanne Robitaille Ontiveros and Assistant Editors Robert DeV. Brunkow, Paula May Cohen, David J. Valiulis, and Lance Klass provided editorial support at crucial stages of the project. The Data Processing Services Department under the supervision of Kenneth H. Baser, Director, Deborah Looker, Production Supervisor, and Cathy Clements, Applications Programmer, provided the technical expertise required to tap the *America: History and Life* database and reprocess the material according to editorial specifications. I especially want to acknowledge the contribution of all those individuals in the academic and library communities who prepared the abstracts used in this volume. Their names are listed at the end of the volume.

Neil L. Shumsky
Virginia Polytechnic Institute
    and State University
Blacksburg, Virginia

Timothy Crimmins
Georgia State University
Atlanta, Georgia

INTRODUCTION

If the urban crisis of the 1960s brought the city and its problems before the American public, it also generated a great deal of activity in the academic world that has produced an extraordinary literature on city life. Indeed, the quest for understanding of complex metropolitan issues led scholars in the 1970s to explore entirely new dimensions of the American experience. The mutual concern for the urban environment of historians, anthropologists, sociologists, political scientists, and economists provided the opportunity for interdisciplinary cross-fertilization and cooperation. The result of all of this ferment has been a rapid development of the subfield of urban history, a topical area that seeks to place present problems in perspective and to explain how our cities came to be what they are. The field of urban history, which is as diverse as the city that it seeks to illuminate, also has a past that is important for an understanding of the contents of this volume in the Clio Bibliography Series.

Until the 1940s there was not a great deal of interest in cities on the part of historians; rather, politics, diplomacy, the Revolution and Civil War, and the frontier occupied their attention. In 1940 there were three significant events which set the direction of historical inquiry over the next twenty years. First, Arthur M. Schlesinger, Sr. called for an urban interpretation of the American experience in his seminal essay, "The City in History." Schlesinger's students and others who responded to his challenge went on to reinterpret national history by arguing that city life had been critical to the development of our civilization. Secondly, the American Historical Association sponsored the publication of *The Cultural Approach to History* to demonstrate the diversity of the newer techniques of historical inquiry. This volume contained two articles that featured the industrial city; the particular place, however, was Birmingham, England, because American historians had yet to begin serious study of the city. There was also another important essay titled "The Value of Local History" by Constance McLaughlin Green, who was later to win a Pulitzer Prize for her history of Washington, D.C. The Green contribution began with the premise that "for any true understanding of American cultural development, the writing and study of American local history is of primary importance." Yet at the same time that the attention of academics was being called to cities and to local history, a third event was taking place: the formation of the American Association for State and Local History (AASLA).

The AASLA was formed to attract those practitioners interested in local history who worked outside of academia in historical societies and museums and who felt that their work was not appreciated by the existing historical associations. Constance Green offered the prevailing scholarly judgment of the non-academic "antiquarian" in her 1940 article: "The lack of perspective, the inability to see his own town as part of a larger community, has often made the local biographer's labors nearly sterile. Determination to paint his home town as a Garden of Eden, to enlarge upon the virtues of its leading citizens, and to portray its achievements as unparalleled, has rendered his work unsound and generally dull." But while academics were rendering such judgments and arguing for more scholarly city studies, local historians continued to conduct their research and publish the results. There developed two distinct traditions in the writing of city history: an academic variety, preferring the title, urban history; and another strain in state, county, and community historical societies called local history. These two traditions have also influenced the division of periodical literature, with state and city historical journals featuring articles of more local interest and university- and professional-association-sponsored publications selecting those studies that use city growth to represent larger patterns.

Since 1940 the two varieties have moved closer together as local studies have begun to add a larger context for their descriptions and urban histories have delved into the details of everyday city living. When Constance Green assessed the state of local history for academic historians, she concluded that they "supply the raw materials which, digested and presented in connection with other data as part of a pattern, can tell a story of deeper social import." In 1980 when the American Historical Association again sponsored the publication of a volume assessing the variety of approaches to the study of history, the merging of local and urban history was signaled in a contribution by Kathleen Neils Conzen, "Community Studies, Urban History, and American Local History." While noting that we have nothing yet to compare to Britain's Leicester University school of local history, Conzen asserted that the locally-oriented studies of the 1970s "provided the common ground on which the profession may be reunited with a local readership."

In addition to the growing relationship between urban and local history, city studies have also been influenced by perspectives offered by a variety of disciplines, some of which had longer standing concern with the urban environment than did historians. Thus, in the late 1960s and early 1970s when urban studies curricula proliferated on university campuses, historians began to establish a common set of reference points with geographers, sociologists, economists, and political scientists. These contacts, as well as an interest in new approaches to the study of cities, led to a number of interdisciplinary urban analyses.

The abstracts from the periodical literature of the 1970s which are included in this volume and selected from seven volumes of *America: History and Life* capture the diversity in the writing of urban history in the last decade. Section V— Historiography, Methodology, Bibliography, Teaching— offers numerous explanations of the currents in the field. Section II—Contemporary American Urban Life: 1945 to the Present—provides a selection of articles from a variety of disciplines that focus on modern city development. So too, the large number of case studies that appear in the Regional, State, and Local History section of *America: History and Life* can be found classified here in the more precise category that makes them relevant to urban history. In this respect,

Urban America: A Historical Bibliography actually contributes to the bridging of the gap between urban and local history.

This bibliography should be of value to historians studying any aspect of urban life, to urban historians who are looking for materials in the areas of their specialization, to students who are scouting potential research areas, and to practitioners who want to locate studies of neighborhoods, buildings, schools and other urban institutions that will illuminate current needs. It should be a standard reference for assessing the breadth of community studies in the 1970s, the developments in the field of urban history, and the advances in interdisciplinary city studies. Because of the value of this work as a research guide and as a compendium of the diversity of urban history over the last decade, we hope to regularly update it.

Timothy Crimmins
Georgia State University
Atlanta, Georgia

Neil L. Shumsky
Virginia Polytechnic Institute
and State University
Blacksburg, Virginia

LIST OF ABBREVIATIONS

A. . . . . Author-prepared Abstract
Acad. . . . . Academy, Academie, Academia
Agric. . . . . Agriculture, Agricultural
AIA . . . . Abstracts in Anthropology
Akad. . . . . Akademie
Am. . . . . America, American
Ann. . . . . Annals, Annales, Annual, Annali
Anthrop. . . . . Anthropology, Anthropological
Arch. . . . . Archives
Archaeol. . . . . Archaeology, Archaeological
Art. . . . . Article
Assoc. . . . . Association, Associate
Biblio. . . . . Bibliography, Bibliographical
Biog. . . . . Biography, Biographical
Bol. . . . . Boletim, Boletin
Bull. . . . . Bulletin
c. . . . . century (in index)
ca. . . . . circa
Can. . . . . Canada, Canadian, Canadien
Cent. . . . . Century
Coll. . . . . College
Com. . . . . Committee
Comm. . . . . Commission
Comp. . . . . Compiler
DAI . . . . Dissertation Abstracts International
Dept. . . . . Department
Dir. . . . . Director, Direktor
Econ. . . . . Economy, Econom-.
Ed. . . . . Editor, Edition
Educ. . . . . Education, Educational
Geneal. . . . . Genealogy, Genealogical, Genealogique
Grad. . . . . Graduate
Hist. . . . . History, Hist-.
IHE . . . . Indice Historico Espanol

Illus. . . . . Illustrated, Illustration
Inst. . . . . Institute, Institut-.
Int. . . . . International, Internacional, Internationaal,
         . . . . Internationaux, Internazionale
J. . . . . Journal, Journal-prepared Abstract
Lib. . . . . Library, Libraries
Mag. . . . . Magazine
Mus. . . . . Museum, Musee, Museo
Nac. . . . . Nacional
Natl. . . . . National, Nationale
Naz. . . . . Nazionale
Phil. . . . . Philosophy, Philosophical
Photo. . . . . Photograph
Pol. . . . . Politics, Political, Politique, Politico
Pr. . . . . Press
Pres. . . . . President
Pro. . . . . Proceedings
Publ. . . . . Publishing, Publication
Q. . . . . Quarterly
Rev. . . . . Review, Revue, Revista, Revised
Riv. . . . . Rivista
Res. . . . . Research
RSA . . . . Romanian Scientific Abstracts
S. . . . . Staff-prepared Abstract
Sci. . . . . Science, Scientific
Secy. . . . . Secretary
Soc. . . . . Society, Societe, Sociedad, Societa
Sociol. . . . . Sociology, Sociological
Tr. . . . . Transactions
Transl. . . . . Translator, Translation
U. . . . . University, Universi-.
US . . . . United States
Vol. . . . . Volume
Y. . . . . Yearbook

Abbreviations also apply to feminine and plural forms.
Abbreviations not noted above are based on *Webster's Third New International Dictionary*
and the *United States Government Printing Office Style Manual*.

1. AMERICAN URBAN HISTORY (1607-1945)

General

1. Abrahamson, Mark and DuBick, Michael A. PATTERNS OF URBAN DOMINANCE: THE U.S. IN 1890. *Am. Sociol. Rev. 1977 42(5): 756-768.* Macroanalyses of urban social organization have unduly exaggerated the importance of trade and commerce as the foundations of a division of labor among cities. This division of labor and the capacity of cities to influence each other differentially are examined as resting upon a convergence among fiscal-commercial activities, plus intellectual, cultural and organizational activities, and transportation and communication. This multifaceted conception of urban dominance stresses how different kinds of activities are associated with different geographical spheres of influence, resulting in three distinct types or dimensions of dominance: national-international, regional, and local. Examination of US cities in 1890 indicates two different functional and geographical distributions of regional and national dominance. They are associated with different patterns of regional integration and with variations in the economic development of regions. The types of dominance are also seen to exhibit substantial historical continuity between 1890 and 1970, with the multifaceted measure providing much better predictions than the financial measure.   J

2. Alexander, John K. URBAN AMERICA IN THE REVOLUTIONARY ERA: STUDIES IN THE NEGLECTED PERIOD OF AMERICAN URBAN HISTORY. *J. of Urban Hist. 1979 5(2): 241-254.* Review article prompted by four works in the "neglected" period of urban history, the Revolutionary Era. All of the works have an urban setting to a greater or lesser degree, but none purports to be urban history. Rather they are histories of the revolutionary activities of certain social-economic groups that resided in cities. The works covered are Stephen E. Lucas, *Portents of Rebellion: Rhetoric and Revolution in Philadelphia,* Edward C. Papenfuse, *In Pursuit of Profit: The Annapolis Merchants in the Era of the American Revolution,* Charles S. Olton, *Artisans for Independence: Philadelphia Mechanics and the American Revolutin,* and Philip S. Foner, *Labor and the American Revolution.* 14 notes.
                                                    T. W. Smith

3. Bernard, Richard M. A PORTRAIT OF BALTIMORE IN 1800: ECONOMIC AND OCCUPATIONAL PATTERNS IN AN EARLY AMERICAN CITY. *Maryland Hist. Mag. 1974 69(4): 341-360.* Using the federal assessors' boundary lines for districts in 1798, analyzes the physical evidence of early Baltimore, showing the largest, most fireproof buildings near the heart of the city. Population study is based on Warner and Hanna's city directory for 1800-01, although its coverage is far from thorough. "The general economic pattern . . . resembled that of Philadelphia, Boston, and Charleston, with the wealthy established downtown and poorer people generally away from the city's core," or the opposite of a modern city. Middle-income groups were almost evenly spread throughout the city, while upper and lower groups congregated in districts. No occupational grouping was drastically segregated, but political representation definitely favored the rich mercantile districts. Only about one-fifth of the families owned slaves, so Baltimore was not "a typical slave city." A ranking order according to wealth would read: merchants, government-professionals, artisan-mechanics, sea captains, other maritime workers. Based on primary and secondary sources; 4 illus., 4 maps, 5 tables, 48 notes.   G. J. Bobango

4. Blumin, Stuart M. ECONOMY AND SOCIETY: PHILADELPHIA AND ITS HINTERLAND: A COMMENTARY. *Working Papers from the Regional Econ. Hist. Res. Center 1979 2(3): 107-112.* Comments on the relationship between economy and society in Philadelphia during the 18th and 19th centuries as presented in articles in this issue by Claudia Goldin, Diane Lindstrom, and David Dauer.

5. Breen, T. H. TRANSFER OF CULTURE: CHANCE AND DESIGN IN SHAPING MASSACHUSETTS BAY 1630-1660. *New England Hist. and Geneal. Register 1978 132(Jan): 3-17.* Describes and documents how towns founded by colonists who immigrated to New

England in the mid-17th century were influenced by traditional patterns of life in their communities in Great Britain. "Localism" was an inherent quality, but it was strengthened by a wariness of intervention by the King and other factors such as environment, homogeneity, and longevity. A different pattern of settlement based on plantation economy developed in the southern colonies. A version of this essay was presented at "A Conference on Local Life, Public Policy," Greenville, North Carolina, 28 January 1977. 38 notes.   A. Huff

6. Bryan, Charles F., Jr. NASHVILLE UNDER FEDERAL OCCUPATION. *Civil War Times Illus. 1975 13(9): 4-11, 40-47.* An account of the Federal occupation of Nashville during the Civil War.   S

7. Butler, Jon. A BICENTENNIAL HARVEST: FOUR STUDIES OF THE EARLY AMERICAN COMMUNITY. *J. of Urban Hist. 1978 4(4): 485-497.* Review article on early American communities, prompted by: Thomas J. Archdeacon, *New York, 1664-1710: Conquest and Change,* Edward M. Cook, *The Fathers of the Towns: Leadership and Community in Eighteenth-Century New England,* Estelle F. Feinstein, *Stamford from Puritan to Patriot: The Shaping of a Connecticut Community,* and Stephanie Grauman Wolf, *Urban Village: Population, Community, and Family Structure in Germantown, Pennsylvania, 1683-1800.* Feinstein's and Wolf's works are community studies in the traditional mold, Archdeacon's book is a political history, and Cook's study is a New England-wide analysis of political leadership. Among the common themes are: 1) the failure of religion to harmonize communities, 2) the early rise of modern social thought, and 3) the role of elites in shaping communities. 6 notes.   T. W. Smith

8. Clark, Dennis. INVENTION AND CONTENTION IN THE QUAKER CITY. *J. of Urban Hist. 1979 5(2): 265-271.* Review article prompted by Richard G. Miller, *Philadelphia—The Federalist City: A Study in Urban Politics, 1789-1801,* Bruce Sinclair, *Philadelphia's Philosopher Mechanics: A History of the Franklin Institute, 1824-1865,* Michael Feldberg, *The Philadelphia Riots of 1844: A Study of Ethnic Conflict,* and Philip S. Benjamin, *The Philadelphia Quakers in the Industrial Age, 1865-1920.* These books examine three great city-shaping forces: politics, religion, and technology. Their limitation is that they describe and explain the particular rather than the overall structure and complexity of the city. 9 notes.   T. W. Smith

9. Corwin, Margaret. MINNA SCHMIDT: BUSINESSWOMAN, FEMINIST, AND FAIRY GODMOTHER TO CHICAGO. *Chicago Hist. 1978-79 7(4): 226-235.* Minna Moscherosch Schmidt (1866-1961) was a German immigrant to Chicago in 1886; she owned a school of dance and later a wig and costume shop, was a devout feminist and a philanthropist to the fine arts and higher education in Chicago.

10. Cullen, Joseph P. RICHMOND FALLS! *Am. Hist. Illus. 1974 8(9): 10-21.* Details city life in Richmond, Virginia, immediately prior to, during, and after the Union conquest of this Confederate capital, 2 April 1865; includes several photographs and sketches.   S

11. Frisch, Michael H. MODELED CITIES AND WEARY THEORY. *Rev. in Am. Hist. 1979 7(1): 85-91.* Review article prompted by Alan D. Anderson's *The Origin and Resolution of an Urban Crisis: Baltimore, 1890-1930* (Baltimore: The Johns Hopkins U. Pr., 1977) and Carl V. Harris's *Political Power in Birmingham, 1871-1921* (Knoxville: The U. of Tennessee Pr., 1977).

12. Furer, Howard B. "HEAVEN, HELL, OR HOBOKEN": THE EFFECTS OF WORLD WAR I ON A NEW JERSEY CITY. *New Jersey Hist. 1974 92(3): 147-169.* Discusses industrial-commercial expansion experienced by Hoboken at the outbreak of World War I, the patriotic spirit which infused its citizens, and the events of the war which brought about food shortages and housing shortages.

13. Gildrie, Richard P. SALEM SOCIETY AND POLITICS IN THE 1680'S. *Essex Inst. Hist. Collections 1978 114(4): 185-206.* The

history of Puritan Massachusetts can be characterized as the "tension between the ideal and the real, between aspiration and performance." By the 1660's the reality (individualism) was clearly different from the ideal (organicism), but the leadership would not surrender the ideal and instead tried to reconcile organicism to individualism. The chief arena for this struggle was the towns, and in particular Salem in the 1680's. Tension for Salem resulted from its regional economic specialization that created three societies: a farming region that participated in town affairs but whose influence was decreasing, a maritime society excluded from Salem life but tolerated as an essential labor force, and a commercial Salem made up of merchants and artisans who controlled the town's financial and political leadership. The merchant elite met the ideal of Puritan leadership and tried in the 1680's to reconcile organicism with commercial ethos. In the process a different definition of community appeared. Disrupted by the Dominion of New England and the Glorious Revolution, the leadership accepted the Lockean triad of life, liberty, and property as a new ideological basis for society. They reconciled themselves to a transient population within the town that would exist outside the social and political community. Examines assessments, occupations, voters, and elections in Salem in the 1680's. Primary and secondary sources; 5 tables, 30 notes.
R. S. Sliwoski

14. Goldfield, David R. FRIENDS AND NEIGHBORS: URBAN-RURAL RELATIONS IN ANTEBELLUM VIRGINIA. *Virginia Cavalcade 1975 25(1): 14-27.* Discusses the roles of slavery, agriculture, industrialization, and railroads 1840's-60.

15. Gragg, Larry. "A MOST CRITICAL TIME": PHILADELPHIA IN 1793. *Hist. Today [Great Britain] 1979 29(2): 80-87.* The summer of 1793 in Philadelphia, Pennsylvania, proved to be a devastating one with public violence (often between French and British soldiers following France's declaration of republicanism), political division between Republicans and Federalists, disdain for the actions of President George Washington, and an outbreak of yellow fever which killed many people and virtually halted trade and government.

16. Greene, Jack P. AUTONOMY AND STABILITY: NEW ENGLAND AND THE BRITISH COLONIAL EXPERIENCE IN EARLY MODERN AMERICA. *J. of Social Hist. [Great Britain] 1974 7(2): 171-194.* Reviews John Demos's *A Little Commonwealth; Family Life in Plymouth Colony* (New York: Oxford U. Pr., 1974), Philip J. Greven, Jr.'s *Four Generations: Population, Land, and Family in Colonial Andover, Massachusetts* (Ithaca: Cornell U. Pr., 1970), Kenneth A. Lockridge's *A New England Town: The First Hundred Years; Dedham, Massachusetts, 1636-1736* (New York: W. W. Norton, 1970), and Michael Zuckerman's *Peaceable Kingdoms: New England Towns in the Eighteenth Century* (New York: Alfred A. Knopf, 1970). These books suggest new interest in early New England society. They share a shift of the focus of inquiry from the intellectual and the political to the social and thereby "bring the search for the nature of colonial New England to a new and deeper level of analysis." They record a behavioral revolution in the direction of increasing autonomy of action. 26 notes.
R. V. Ritter

17. Groth, Philip. PLANTATION AGRICULTURE AND THE URBANIZATION OF THE SOUTH. *Rural Sociol. 1977 42(2): 206-219.* It is widely recognized that the South has been and remains the most rural region of the nation. Two divergent historical interpretations of the rurality of the South have been offered—one which focuses on the political economy of the South and one which stresses a variety of socioeconomic, topographical, and climatic features of the region. In this research the author derived and tested several hypotheses in which the level of urbanization of counties and economic subregions of the South were related to their plantation, political economic, character. The tests of these hypotheses suggest that neither the political economic nor the eclectic theory offers a sound explanation of the rurality of the South. J

18. Haffner, Gerald O. ASHBEL P. WILLARD'S TOWN. *Indiana Hist. Bull. 1975 52(2): 15-18.* Describes New Albany, Indiana, as it was when Governor Ashbel P. Willard lived there, 1840's-60. S

19. Harris, Neil. AMERICA'S COMING OF AGE: IN PURSUIT OF MODERN TIMES. *Social Educ. 1977 41(6): 500-504.* Discusses trends in the 19th century which caused it to be one of social change,

including urbanization, industrialization, and commercialism; highlights the birth of materialism and political unrest throughout the country.

20. Henretta, James A. AN ANTHROPOLOGY OF AN ELITE. *Rev. in Am. Hist. 1979 7(3): 362-368.* Review of Anthony F. C. Wallace's *Rockdale: The Growth of an American Village in the Early Industrial Revolution* (New York: Knopf, 1978) discusses the effects of changes in social order, technology, religion, and industrialization in Rockdale, Pennsylvania, 1825-65.

21. Howard, Brett. BOSTON, THE ATHENS OF AMERICA. *Mankind 1973 4(3): 10-15, 54-57.*

22. Hurst, Harold W. THE MARYLAND GENTRY IN OLD GEORGETOWN: 1783-1861. *Maryland Hist. Mag. 1978 73(1): 1-12.* Surveys the economic conditions causing Georgetown to replace Annapolis as the commercial and social center of Maryland's tobacco counties north of the Potomac after the Revolution, and the leading St. Marys, Charles, Calvert, Montgomery, and Prince Georges county families which dominated the tobacco, flour, lumber, and retail goods enterprises. The progeny of Robert Peter, Washington Bowie, Francis Lowndes, William Magruder, Thomas Corcoran, Charles Worthington, *et al.,* not only controlled the bulk of Georgetown's economic life, but produced a plethora of lawyers and judges, stood out in local politics, and made the city a Whig stronghold in national affairs. St. John's and Christ Church were bastions of the Southern gentry, and Fort Sumter found Georgetown still an essentially Southern community with a regional rather than national outlook. Primary and secondary sources; 50 notes.
G. J. Bobango

23. Johnson, Paul E. SOCIETY, SOCIABILITY, AND POWER IN A NINETEENTH-CENTURY CITY. *Hist. of Educ. Q. 1977 17(1): 75-80.* Review article prompted by Stuart M. Blumin's *The Urban Threshold: Growth and Change in a Nineteenth-Century American Community* (Chicago: U. of Chicago Pr., 1976), which studies Kingston, N.Y., during the transportation revolution, and the new urban and commercial world of the latter 19th century. The book also is valuable for an understanding of the political and institutional responses to urban growth.
L. C. Smith

24. Krog, Carl. MARINETTE: THE ORIGIN AND GROWTH OF A COMMUNITY, 1850-1870. *Old Northwest 1977 3(4): 389-407.* Relates the complete domination of Marinette, Wisconsin, by lumber companies who organized all phases of the community in its early years. Lists the net worth of settlers, cites immigration statistics, and describes the social life in Marinette. There was considerable disparity of wealth, the lumbermen being rich; but democratic institutions thrived. Typical of a frontier community, the population was youthful. After the Civil War more skilled workers arrived so that when lumbering was over the community could become industrialized. Based on U.S. Census statistics, newspapers, memoirs, and secondary works; 4 tables, 21 notes. J

25. Lawson, Michael L. OMAHA, A CITY OF FERMENT: SUMMER OF 1919. *Nebraska Hist. 1977 58(3): 395-417.* Examines the tensions and frustrations accompanying peacetime adjustment in Omaha. Mentions inflation, the lifting of a wartime strike ban, ethnic and racial tensions, prohibition, woman suffrage, municipal corruption, and returning veterans. This places the September race riot in a meaningful context.
R. Lowitt

26. Main, Gloria L. THE DUTCH "IN DUTCH" IN OLD NEW YORK. *Rev. in Am. Hist. 1976 4(3): 379-384.* Review article prompted by Thomas J. Archdeacon's *New York City, 1664-1710: Conquest and Change* (Ithaca, New York: Cornell U. Pr., 1976) which discusses the social structure of New York City, as well as ethnic tensions which arose over the British rule of Dutch inhabitants.

27. Mason, Bill. THE GARRISONS OF SAN DIEGO PRESIDIO: 1770-1794. *J. of San Diego Hist. 1978 24(4): 399-424.* Gives data and anecdotes regarding soldiers and employees in San Diego during the Hispanic period, discussing names and activities and their role in the development of the pueblo of Los Angeles.

28. McKelvey, Blake. BICENTENNIAL URBAN ESSAYS. *J. of Urban Hist. 1798 4(4): 477-484.* Review article prompted by Milton M. Klein, ed., *New York: The Cennnenial Years, 1676-1976,* Dennis J. Clark, ed., *Philadelphia, 1776-2076: A Three Hundred Year View,* and Philip W. Porter's *Cleveland: Confused City on a Seesaw.* The essays in the New York and Philadelphia volumes are generally solid pieces by leading scholars; they often lack a single theme, but individually add significantly to the literature. Porter's book is a journalist's personal remembrance of Cleveland and as such is primary source material rather than a scholarly work. T. W. Smith

29. Messmer, Charles. LOUISVILLE DURING THE CIVIL WAR. *Filson Club Hist. Q. 1978 52(2): 206-233.* Despite occasional guerrilla raids, Louisville, Kentucky, was able to survive the Civil War without major disruption. Business did suffer when the Mississippi River was closed during 1861-62, but by the end of 1865, the city's economy had expanded beyond 1861 levels. Generally, political and editorial sentiment opposed the Lincoln administration and was sympathetic toward the Confederacy. Social and cultural life continued to develop. Based on contemporary newspapers; 52 notes. G. B. McKinney

30. Messmer, Charles. LOUISVILLE ON THE EVE OF THE CIVIL WAR. *Filson Club Hist. Q. 1976 50(3): 249-289.* In 1860-61 Louisville, a rapidly growing commercial center, suffered a severe economic decline after the secession crisis began. Newspaper editor George Dennison Prentice was the leading spokesman for the Union during this period, and the city's voters followed his lead and supported the Constitutional Union Party in the 1860 presidential election. Based mainly on contemporary newspapers; 131 notes. G. B. McKinney

31. Milnor, Mark T. and Derone, William E. WARRENSVILLE IN THE EIGHTEEN NINETIES AND EARLY NINETEEN HUNDREDS. *Now and Then 1973 17(7): 281-289.* Describes mills, trades, school, recreation, and citizens of this Pennsylvania town. S

32. Moon, Elaine L. DETROIT, THE CITY OF WHEELS. *Mankind 1975 4(12): 10-19.* Despite its negative reputation, Detroit, capital of the automobile industry, has overcome great obstacles since its founding in 1701 and is moving to meet challenges.

33. Morse, Richard M. THE DEVELOPMENT OF URBAN SYSTEMS IN THE AMERICAS IN THE NINETEENTH CENTURY. *J. of Interam. Studies and World Affairs 1975 17(1): 4-24.* A fertile field for the urban historian is a comparative study of urbanization in the United States and Latin America in the 19th century. The US population began the move to urban centers earlier than their Latin American counterparts and had a lower degree of urban movement. The student of urban history can also gain insight into the economic development of both regions through his work with urbanization. Secondary sources; 4 tables, 6 notes, biblio. J. R. Thomas

34. Neeley, Mary Ann. MONTGOMERY, 1885-1887: THE YEARS OF JUBILEE. *Alabama Rev. 1979 32(2): 108-118.* Civic improvements —street lights, paved streets and sidewalks, trolley line, piped water, telephone service—came to Montgomery with a rush in the 1800's. President Grover Cleveland's stopover there on 20 October 1887 coincided with a sense of fulfillment and post-Civil War satisfaction. Primary and secondary sources; 27 notes. J. F. Vivian

35. Nodyne, Kenneth Robert. A VIGNETTE OF WHEELING DURING THE EARLY REPUBLIC, 1783-1840. *West Virginia Hist. 1978 40(1): 47-54.* Details the political, economic, and social life of Wheeling, West Virginia, 1783-1840. Primary sources; 29 notes. J. H. Broussard

36. Osborne, Alice. NOME'S EARLY YEARS. *Alaska J. 1974 4(1): 10-16.* Discusses Nome, Alaska's, social, economic, and political affairs during 1898-1915.

37. Pessen, Edward. FRUITS OF THE NEW URBAN HISTORY: THE SOCIOLOGY OF SMALL NINETEENTH-CENTURY CITIES. *J. of Urban Hist. 1978 5(1): 93-108.* Review article prompted by Kathleen Conzen's *Immigrant Milwaukee, 1836-1860;* Alan Dawley's *Class and Community: The Industrial Revolution in Lynn;* Michael B. Katz's *The*

People of Hamilton, Canada West; Eric H. Monkkonen's *The Dangerous Class: Crime and Poverty in Columbus Ohio 1860-1865;* and Michael P. Weber's *Social Change in an Industrial Town: Patterns of Progress in Warren, Pennsylvania, From Civil War to World War I.* Includes detailed critiques of each work and considers their shared features. All tend to embrace some form of "new urban history" usually either of the Thernstrom or Thompson mold and all tend to neglect or to subordinate politics. Sadly for comparative purposes all use sufficiently different techniques so that their precise findings are not easily comparable. 7 notes. T. W. Smith

38. Prior, Moody E. LOST (AND FOUND) CITIES. *Am. Scholar 1976-77 46(4): 506-513.* Uses Chicago as a model of the American city. Traces architectural and ethnic epochs since its beginning. With all of its problems, city fathers are currently planning a new Chicago. F. F. Harling

39. Schnore, Leo. BEYOND THE VEIL OF URBAN HISTORY: THREE GLIMPSES. *Rev. in Am. Hist. 1975 3(1): 129-136.* Review article prompted by Blake McKelvey's *American Urbanization: A Comparative History* (Glenview, Ill.: Scott, Foresman and Co., 1973), Zane L. Miller's *The Urbanization of Modern America: A Brief History* (New York: Harcourt Brace Jovanovich, 1973) and Sam Bass Warner, Jr.'s *The Urban Wilderness: A History of the American City* (New York: Harper & Row, 1972), which cover urbanization since the mid-1860's.

40. Schumacher, Alan T. 19TH CENTURY NEWPORT GUIDE BOOKS. *Newport Hist. 1978 51(4): 73-94.* Guidebooks of Newport, Rhode Island, 1819-96, introduced visitors to the business, historical, and tourist aspects of the community.

41. Schweitzer, Jeffrey. AMADOR CITY, 1907. *Pacific Historian 1974 18(3): 36-54.* Reviews life in Amador City, California, a gold mining boom town in 1907. 16 photos. C. W. Olson

42. Smith, Suanna. WASHINGTON, MISSISSIPPI: ANTEBELLUM ELYSIUM. *J. of Mississippi Hist. 1978 40(2): 143-165.* Discusses Washington, Mississippi, as a political, cultural, and educational center during the late territorial and early statehood period. Some of the town's prominent inhabitants described include Judge Thomas Rodney, Benjamin L. C. Wailes, John Wesley Monette, and W. C. C. Claiborne. Jefferson College, opened in Washington in 1811, was the first institution of higher learning in the Mississippi Territory. The removal of the territorial capital from Washington, however, accounted for much of the community's political and economic decline, though it continued as a social and educational center into the antebellum period. M. S. Legan

43. Snell, Joseph W. TRAIL CITY: A NOTE FROM THE RECORD. *Kansas Q. 1974 6(4): 37-42.* Examines the social customs and economic conditions (1883-87) in Trail City, Kansas—a little-known cattle town. S

44. Snyder, Perry A. CIVIL WAR SHREVEPORT. *North Louisiana Hist. Assoc. J. 1974 6(1): 1-8.* In 1861, Shreveport's economy was based on supplying manufactured items to the planters and farmers in surrounding areas, its inland port, and manufacturing. The city supplied a large number of troops to the Confederate Army during the Civil War, and those who remained at home made many contributions to the Confederate war effort. For most of the war, "life in Shreveport was . . . exciting, comfortable, and relatively safe. . . . Nor was there any suffering for the necessities of life." How to cope with the thousands of refugees from occupied south Louisiana was perhaps the main problem which faced the city after mid-1862. The war in the west ended 26 May 1865 and by 6 June 1865 Shreveport was occupied by federal forces. The city "had benefitted economically from the struggle" and "Reconstruction was not to be a period of rebuilding and repair." Reprint of an address given by the author on 20 April 1974 at the annual meeting of the North Louisiana Historical Society in Shreveport; 14 notes. A. N. Garland

45. Still, Bayrd. MILWAUKEE REVISITED: A REVIEW ESSAY. *Wisconsin Mag. of Hist. 1977 60(4): 330-333* Review article prompted by *Immigrant Milwaukee, 1836-1860: Accommodation and Community in a Frontier City* (1976) by Kathleen Neils Conzen, *Technology and Re-*

form: *Street Railways and the Growth of Milwaukee, 1887-1900* (1974) by Clay McShane, *Milwaukee: A Contemporary Urban Profile* (1971) by Henry J. Schmandt, John C. Goldbach, and Donald Vogel, *Yesterday's Milwaukee* (1976) by Robert W. Wells, and an article, "Housing and Services in an Immigrant Neighborhood: Milwaukee's Ward 14," by Roger D. Simon in the *Journal of Urban History,* 1976. Conzen's book is a study of the Germans, while Simon's article analyzes the Poles. Wells's is a pictorial history.   N. C. Burckel

46. Thomas, Emory M. WARTIME RICHMOND. *Civil War Times Illus. 1977 16(3): 3-50.* Traces the history of Richmond, Virginia, during the Civil War years. Covers early resistance to the Confederacy, the establishment of the city as the new nation's capital, the beginning of the war, and citizen moods and activities during the hostilities. Factories, entertainments, hospitals, prisons, protests, food shortages, prominent persons, and military preparations are described. A brief summary of critical battles is included, especially as they related to moods and events in Richmond. Map, 82 photos.   V. L. Human

47. Tobin, Eugene M. A "NEW" LOOK FOR THE "OLD" URBAN HISTORY. *J. of Urban Hist. 1979 5(4): 530-541.* As the recent works by Estelle F. Feinstein, *Stamford in the Gilded Age,* Brenda K. Shelton, *Reformers in Search of Yesterday,* E. Kimbark Maccoll, *The Shaping of a City,* and J. Kirkpatrick Flack, *Desideratum in Washington,* testify, the old urban history is not dead but alive and well. Despite the recent upsurge of interest in social structure, mobility, and the masses, these works make clear that much effort is still being spent on traditional topics such as politics, elites, institutions, and, in general, history from the top down. The common major theme that seems to emerge from these diverse works is that to stabilize the social dislocations created by industrialization it was necessary for an educated urban elite to lead a struggle for order through reform. 23 notes.   T. W. Smith

48. Travis, Anthony R. ESSAYS ON ETHNIC HISTORY. *Mid-America 1978 60(1): 43-48.* Review article prompted by three works on minority and ethnic groups in New York City and Chicago. *The Golden Door,* by Thomas Kessner, compares Italian and Jewish immigrants in New York City and concludes that Jewish immigrants were better skilled to show upward social mobility than were their Italian counterparts. *The Education of an Urban Minority,* by James W. Sanders, investigates public education and its impact on Catholic Church members in Chicago. To most Catholics of the past 150 years, Chicago public schools showed an anti-Catholic and anti-European bias. *Culture and the City,* by Helen Horowitz, analyzes cultural philanthropy in Chicago from 1880 to World War I, and shows the relations of the business and financial elite to culture and philanthropy.

J. M. Lee

49. Unsigned. THE MARKS BROTHERS OF LOS ANGELES, A PICTURE STORY. *Western States Jewish Hist. Q. 1979 11(4): 311-317.* Joshua H. Marks (1884-1965) and David X. Marks (1891-1977) were brought to Los Angeles by their parents in 1902. Joshua entered their father's brick business and became a building designer and contractor. Among his better known works are Grauman's Chinese and Egyptian theaters, and the Santa Anita Race Track. He also built several shopping centers, churches, business offices, and movie studios. David entered the insurance business and was active in civic affairs. He helped establish the Los Angeles Civic Light Opera Association, and contributed financially to developments at the University of Southern California, and other educational institutions. Family records and published sources; 7 photos, 8 notes.   B. S. Porter

The Growth and Decline of Cities and Suburbs

50. Abbott, Carl. BOOM STATE AND BOOM CITY: STAGES IN DENVER'S GROWTH. *Colorado Mag. 1973 50(3): 207-230.* The growth of Denver reflects a pattern different from that usually suggested by American urban historians. Rather, "national economic patterns and business cycles have had little influence on the stages of growth. Instead the town has responded directly to the rise and decline of local booms within Colorado." Based on primary and secondary sources; illus., maps, 74 notes.   O. H. Zabel

51. Abbott, Carl. BUILDING URBAN-INDUSTRIAL AMERICA. *J. of Urban Hist. 1976 2(3): 369-372.* Review article prompted by two studies of 19th-century American communities, Blake McKelvey's *Rochester on the Genesse: The Growth of a City* and Carol E. Hoffecker's *Wilmington, Delaware: Portrait of an Industrial City, 1830-1910.* McKelvey's work, a condensation of his four-volume history of Rochester, reflects a deep knowledge of the city but fails to make the transition from local history to urban history. Hoffecker's work frames itself in the urban history perspective but lacks sufficient analytical rigor and evidential support.   T. W. Smith

52. Abbott, Carl. INDIANAPOLIS IN THE 1850S: POPULAR ECONOMIC THOUGHT AND URBAN GROWTH. *Indiana Mag. of Hist. 1978 74(4): 293-315.* The depression of the 1840's ended in 1848 and the citizens of Indianapolis, and of other western cities, fervently desired industry and growth. The advent of the railroad inspired them with optimism, for Indianapolis found itself at the hub of regional railroad development. Moreover, the city was centrally located and well-situated as a shipping point for products coming from east or west. The new economic ideas were more practical than flamboyant; the citizens' concepts were clear, cohesive, and provided for orderly economic development. Development did come, although less than expected, primarily because of Cincinnati's commercial competition which Indianapolis never entirely overcame. 2 photos, 79 notes.   V. L. Human

53. Abbott, Carl. NORFOLK IN THE NEW CENTURY: THE JAMESTOWN EXPOSITION AND URBAN BOOSTERISM. *Virginia Mag. of Hist. and Biog. 1977 85(1): 86-96.* Norfolk's sponsorship of the Jamestown Tercentennial Exposition in 1907 reflected both the city's boosterism and a commitment to the New South. The sponsors hoped that the resulting publicity would help make Norfolk a thriving industrial city. Though they generally failed in their goals, the sponsors developed a unique form of southern boosterism in the early 20th century. Drawn largely from newspapers and public documents; 43 notes.   R. F. Oaks

54. Adkins, Howard G. THE GEOGRAPHIC BASE OF URBAN RETARDATION IN MISSISSIPPI, 1800-1840. *West Georgia Coll. Studies in the Social Sci. 1973 12: 35-49.* One of seven articles in this issue on "Geographic Perspectives on Southern Development."   S

55. Anderson, Gary C. MOORHEAD *VS.* FARGO: A STUDY OF ECONOMIC RIVALRY AND URBAN DEVELOPMENT IN THE RED RIVER VALLEY OF THE NORTH. *North Dakota Q. 1974 42(4): 60-77.* Discusses the rivalry between Moorhead, Minnesota, and Fargo, North Dakota, in the 1870's and the role of the railroad in their development.   S

56. Bach, Ira J. PULLMAN: A TOWN REBORN. *Chicago Hist. 1975 4(1): 44-53.* History of Pullman, Illinois, from its creation as a model company town by George Pullman to its designation as a national landmark.   S

57. Barnes, Joseph W. THE ANNEXATION OF BRIGHTON VILLAGE. *Rochester Hist. 1973 35(1): 1-24.* The city of Rochester sought to annex adjoining villages when the Kodak Company established a plant there and additional housing was needed for Kodak employees. The annexation of Brighton Village in 1905 was by no means the largest addition. Annexation raised problems such as whether the two sewage systems should be connected. Many residents of Brighton feared that annexation would increase their taxes.   J. H. Krenkel

58. Barnes, Joseph W. THE ANNEXATION OF CHARLOTTE. *Rochester Hist. 1975 37(1): 1-28.* Discusses the history of Charlotte, New York, from 1792 to its incorporation into Rochester, New York, in 1915.

59. Barnes, Joseph W. THE CITY'S GOLDEN AGE. *Rochester Hist. 1973 35(2): 1-23.* In Rochester's Golden Age, 1900-30, the population did not quite double but the assessed valuation increased from about $115 million in 1900 to about $650 million in 1930. The cost of municipal services increased more rapidly than the population. The most serious problem was the shortage of low-cost housing. As industry increased, there was a change from a rural to an urban atmosphere.
                                                                    J. H. Krenkel

60. Barrett, Glen. P. J. QUEALY: WYOMING'S COAL MAN AND TOWN BUILDER. *Ann. of Wyoming 1975 47(1): 31-44.* Kemmerer, an independent coal town, thrived ca. 1900. Details the town's founding by Patrick J. Quealy and Mahlon S. Kemmerer, and its subsequent development. Based on area newspapers, correspondence from company records, minute books of the Kemmerer town council, and other sources; 2 illus., 21 notes.   S. S. Sprague

61. Batman, Richard Dale. ORANGE COUNTY, CALIFORNIA: A COMPREHENSIVE HISTORY: PART I: "ANAHEIM WAS AN OASIS IN A WILDERNESS." *J. of the West 1965 4(1): 1-20.* Covers 1850's-90.

62. Bertoch, Marvin J. SALT LAKE CITY: THIS IS THE PLACE. *Mankind 1973 4(4): 10-16, 58-59.*

63. Bishop, Joan. A SEASON OF TRIAL: HELENA'S ENTREPENEURS NURTURE A CITY. *Montana 1978 28(3): 62-71.* The Helena Board of Trade, formed in 1877, worked to promote Helena, Montana, transforming it from a crude mining camp to a stable, urban community; a political and economic center. Several disastrous fires, the national financial depression, and a regional mining lull during the 1870's served as a season of trial for Helena. Such problems spurred local businessmen to take action. Among the leading proponents of unified effort was *Helena Daily Herald* editor Robert E. Fisk. Once formed, the Board of Trade led development of the city, including fire prevention, incorporation, and the promotion of overland and railroad transportation. Based on editorials in the *Helena Daily Herald,* Fisk Family papers in the Montana Historical Society, Helena, and secondary works; 14 illus., 17 notes.   R. C. Myers

64. Bitton, Davis. THE MAKING OF A COMMUNITY: BLACKFOOT, IDAHO, 1878-1910. *Idaho Yesterdays 1975 19(1): 2-15.* Blackfoot was established on the Utah and Northern Railway line as the railroad crept across southeastern Idaho. The town grew steadily in its early decades, built a toll bridge across the Snake River and a regional insane asylum. Once Blackfoot became the county seat, it acquired the land office and fairgrounds for southeastern Idaho. Based on primary sources; 2 illus., graph, 47 notes.   B. J. Paul

65. Booth, Larry and Booth, Jane. A GLIMPSE AT NINETEENTH CENTURY SAN DIEGO. *Am. West 1979 16(5): 20-29.* With the promise of a railroad, San Diego began a period of some growth in 1867. Slowed by the panic of 1873, the California city did not boom until 1885-88, when railroad construction began. 14 photograph portfolio from the San Diego Historical Society-Title Insurance and Trust Collection.
                                                                    D. L. Smith

66. Bosley, Donald R. COBURG: A MONTANA TOWN THAT IS NO MORE. *Montana 1975 25(4): 38-51.* The village of Coburg, in north-central Montana, dated from the coming of the railroad in the 1880's. It flourished briefly, then declined as the dryland farming experiment in the area failed because of unsuitable soils. A few determined families survived as ranchers in the neighborhood, but the town ceased to exist by 1940, although shown on official maps until 1974. Illus.
                                                                    S. R. Davison

67. Bowling, Kenneth R. "A PLACE TO WHICH TRIBUTE IS BROUGHT": THE CONTEST FOR THE FEDERAL CAPITAL IN 1783. *Prologue 1976 8(3): 129-139.* Owing to unstable conditions in Philadelphia, Congress in 1783 debated possible alternative sites for the

federal capital, including a location near Trenton in either New Jersey or Pennsylvania; Williamsburg, Virginia; Annapolis, Maryland; and several locations in New York State. Although no final decision was reached at this time, the debate resulted in the congressional determination that when a federal capital was built it would be independent of local and state jurisdiction. Based on primary sources.   N. Lederer

68. Brook, Anthony. GARY, INDIANA: STEELTOWN EXTRAORDINARY. *J. of Am. Studies [Great Britain] 1975 9(1): 35-53.* Traces the development of Gary, Indiana during the 25-year period since the United States Steel Corporation chose it as the site for a steel-making complex in 1905. Corporation leaders preferred a "regulated and well-ordered community" at Gary but limited the corporation to minimal involvement in the city's affairs. Effective city planning and orderly development, therefore, were absent. Gary was beset by the same housing, environmental, and ethnic problems that other industrial cities encountered and avoided only the serious racial violence which afflicted other American cities during the 1910's. Secondary sources; 3 maps.
                                                                    H. T. Lovin

69. Brown, Marion Marsh. THE BROWNSVILLE STORY: PORTRAIT OF A PHOENIX, 1854-1974. *Nebraska Hist. 1974 55(1): 1-141.* Brownsville was important at first, but was bypassed by the end of the 19th century as transportation and marketing found other outlets in the state. Recently the community has become a summer tourist attraction.   R. Lowitt

70. Brown, Richard D. THE EMERGENCE OF URBAN SOCIETY IN RURAL MASSACHUSETTS, 1760-1820. *J. of Am. Hist. 1974 61(1): 29-51.* Urban society emerged in Massachusetts and elsewhere in the United States before large scale industrial and commercial development. The American Revolution encouraged supra-local civic consciousness and political parties. Newspaper printing presses and improved postal service stimulated cosmopolitanism. Diverse voluntary associations grew up, many across local lines, all involving townsmen in conscious choices and resulting in an increasingly heterogeneous society. With town populations ranging from 1,000 to 2,000, more occupational choices were available. The result was that diverse loyalties grew up along side of, and often conflicted with, loyalties to family, church, and town meeting. Table, 45 notes.   K. B. West

71. Brumgardt, John R. TEA, CRUMPETS, AND SAN JACINTO GOLD: THE SHORT-LIVED TOWN OF KENWORTHY, CALIFORNIA, 1897-1900. *Pacific Historian 1976 20(3): 277-285.* One town has been overlooked by scholars of the 19th-century California gold-hope phenomenon. Kenworthy has physically disappeared, was economically insignificant, and has left few details of its existence during 1897-1900. It was a racially diverse community with corporate backing, and was largely free of boomtown crime and violence. Its backers hoped the town would prosper as a gold field and resort town, but neither prospect was successful and the town failed. Primary and secondary sources; 2 illus., 17 notes.
                                                                    G. L. Olson

72. Bufkin, Donald H. PHOENIX AND THE SALT RIVER VALLEY: A CARTOGRAPHER'S VIEW. *J. of Arizona Hist. 1977 18(3): 295-298.* A series of three maps delineates the beginnings of Phoenix. Early settlements, the plan of the original townsite, and surviving historical buildings are indicated in the context of modern survey lines, street names, dams, Indian reservations, national forests, and urbanized areas.
                                                                    D. L. Smith

73. Cahill, Helen Kennedy. CAPTAIN WEBER AND HIS PLACE IN EARLY CALIFORNIA HISTORY. *Pacific Hist. 1976 20(4): 425-460.* Captain Charles M. Weber came to California in 1841. He founded the city of Stockton in 1847 on a large grant of land. Under his influence, Stockton became a planned city with provision for orderly growth. Provides brief biographies of Weber's descendants. Primary and secondary sources; 8 illus., 40 notes.   G. L. Olson

74. Campbell, Leon G. THE SPANISH PRESIDIO IN ALTA CALIFORNIA DURING THE MISSION PERIOD 1769-1784. *J. of the West 1977 16(4): 63-77.* Examines presidial development and society in Alta California. Stresses the construction of the 11 missions at the expense of the four presidios which were built at the same time—San Diego

(1769), Monterey (1770), San Francisco (1776), and Santa Barbara (1782). Discusses the tensions between the soldiers and the missionaries. 14 illus., 2 maps, 37 notes.   R. Alvis

75. Capen, Dorothy. BODIE: SMALL NUGGET OF CALIFORNIA'S GOLDEN PAST. *Early Am. Life 1977 8(4): 54-56, 59.* During 1859-88, Bodie, California, was a goldmining town turned ghost town in the Sierra Nevada Mountains.

76. Cardona-Hine, Alvaro. MINNEAPOLIS & ST. PAUL: A TALE OF TWO CITIES. *Mankind 1976 5(6): 12-14, 52-57.* The quality of life in the Twin Cities is enhanced by their active cultural and artistic endeavors as well as by pleasant natural surroundings. The growth of Minneapolis was engendered by the establishment of Fort Snelling and the fur trading industry, followed by lumbering and flour processing. St. Paul profited from the fur trade and stimulated railroading by its position as the state capital.   N. Lederer

77. Carr, Lois Green. "THE METROPOLIS OF MARYLAND": A COMMENT ON TOWN DEVELOPMENT ALONG THE TOBACCO COAST. *Maryland Hist. Mag. 1974 69(2): 124-145.* Describes the birth and death of St. Mary's City which was Maryland's capital during 1634-95. Never becoming an actual "town," it had at most 18 structures by 1678, spread over 100 acres. Neither court nor probate records show any activity unconnected with government. St. Mary's thus provided no centralized economic functions, and stimulated little production or sale of local products. Population never grew enough to stimulate the erection of major public buildings, and the financial base of the town disappeared when the public offices were removed. Self-sufficiency of the planter classes, the convenience of the inland waterway system, and the decentralized system of collecting tobacco and distributing the goods it paid for account for lack of town development, although when port towns did appear they were minor compared to other colonies. Primary and secondary works; 2 illus., 2 maps, 64 notes.   G. J. Bobango

78. Cashin, Edward J. SUMMERVILLE, RETREAT OF THE OLD SOUTH. *Richmond County Hist. 1973 5(2): 44-59.* Founded in the early 1800's, this popular residential village near Augusta grew rapidly after the Civil War, largely because of its healthy location on "the Hill." Summerville lost its identity in 1911 when residents voted for annexation to Augusta. One of six articles in this issue on Augusta. Based on manuscript collections, including those of the Georgia Historical Society Collections, and on newspapers; 60 notes.   H. R. Grant

79. Cebula, James E. KENNEDY HEIGHTS: A FRAGMENTED HILLTOP SUBURB. *Cincinnati Hist. Soc. Bull. 1976 34(2): 78-101.* History of Kennedy Heights, a suburb of Cincinnati, Ohio, 1880-1976.

80. Cook, Nancy. CLEARY. *Alaska J. 1976 6(2): 106-112.* Details the short history of Cleary, Alaska, emphasizing the development of gold mining in the surrounding area and in the town. Describes social life in the community. The town declined following two fires in 1907. Map, 6 photos, 8 notes.   E. E. Eminhizer

81. Crockett, Norman L. THE OPENING OF OKLAHOMA: A BUSINESSMAN'S FRONTIER. *Chronicles of Oklahoma 1978 56(1): 85-95.* Historians have long stressed the agricultural impetus to Oklahoma's settlement and the disorderly nature of the land rushes. Yet equally important was the orderly urban development due to the efforts of small businessmen. A heavy influx of businessmen paralleled each land rush and made towns the center of Oklahoma business and social life. Primary and secondary sources; 5 photos, 29 notes.   M. L. Tate

82. Crowther, Simeon J. URBAN GROWTH IN THE MID-ATLANTIC STATES, 1785-1850. *J. of Econ. Hist. 1976 36(3): 624-644.* Analyzes aspects of secular urban growth in two systems of cities in the mid-Atlantic states. One system centers on New York City; the other on Philadelphia. The growth of New York's hinterland was an important factor in explaining that system's relatively rapid expansion through the War of 1812. In subsequent years, this situation changed; the relatively simple patterns of development gave way to complex situations shaped by the differential impacts of transportation, manufacturing, and commerce on these two urban systems.   J

83. Crutchfield, James A. THE SETTLEMENT OF NASHVILLE. *Early Am. Life 1977 8(2): 50-52.* Chronicles early settlement of Nashville, Tennessee, 1780-99, by two hunter/trappers, John Donelson and James Robertson.

84. Cunniff, Jeffrey L. A TALE OF TWO TOWNS: GILMAN AND AUGUSTA. *Montana 1976 26(2): 42-53.* The village of Gilman, Montana, founded in 1912, survived briefly in constant rivalry with the older town of Augusta, two miles away. Existing only because it had the railroad terminus, Gilman acquired a bank, schools, and a few business houses. Doomed by the extension of the railroad to Augusta in 1922, Gilman held its post office until 1942 and the school until 1955. The bank building still stands, amid crumbling foundations and sidewalks. Illus., 14 notes.   S. R. Davison

85. Curry, Leonard P. URBANIZATION AND URBANISM IN THE OLD SOUTH: A COMPARATIVE VIEW. *J. of Southern Hist. 1974 40(1): 43-60.* Challenges "the myth of the plantation (or, at least, rural) Old South," seeking "a quantitative and qualitative comparison of southern and nonsouthern" urbanization during 1800-50 to determine whether the southern urban experience differed from that of the rest of the country. In addition to analyzing urban population data, compares the public services of northern and southern cities such as fire and police protection, garbage disposal, public health inspection, and consumer protection. Developes a Comparative Urban Rate of Increase index which suggests that "urban development in the Old South was neither massively different from nor consistently inferior to that in the rest of the United States." Based on published primary and secondary sources; 2 figs., 26 notes.   T. D. Schoonover

86. Curtis, Allan. IDITAROD'S NEWSPAPERS: *OPTIMIST, NUGGET, PIONEER. Alaska J. 1976 6(2): 78-83.* Details the history of Iditarod, a gold rush town, through the history of its newspapers. When the Yukon district opened in 1908 with the discovery of gold, the community grew rapidly at first but fell into decline by 1911. During the brisk growing days, three papers were published: *The Optimist,* which ceased in 1910; *The Nugget,* which ceased in 1911; and *The Pioneer,* which lasted until 1919, by which time most of the people were gone. The post office closed in 1929 and the town of Flat, seven miles away, became the center of activity. 17 notes.   E. E. Eminhizer

87. Danforth, Brian J. HOBOKEN AND THE AFFLUENT NEW YORKER'S SEARCH FOR RECREATION, 1820-1860. *New Jersey Hist. 1977 95(3): 133-144.* Experiencing failure before 1820 in promoting Hoboken, New Jersey, as a vacation and leisure time center, John Stevens finally met with success when he organized the town as a fashionable resort for affluent New Yorkers. During the 1830's Hoboken's character changed as an amusement park, merry-go-round, and tin pan alley attracted a more diverse group of people. As the 1840's progressed industrialization occurred; a foundry and shipbuilding were established. The 1850's brought services considered prerequisites for city life. In forty years Hoboken had changed completely from a rural retreat for the elite to a busy commercial center. Primary and secondary sources and the Stevens family papers; 3 illus., 22 notes.   E. R. McKinstry

88. Daniels, Bruce E. EMERGING URBANISM AND INCREASING SOCIAL STRATIFICATION IN THE ERA OF THE AMERICAN REVOLUTION. *West Georgia Coll. Studies in the Social Sci. 1976 15: 15-30.* Traces the transition from ruralism to urbanism in British North America, 1740's-70's, and notes the effects of the Great Awakening and the American Revolution on social status.

89. Davies, Edward J., II. ELITE MIGRATION AND URBAN GROWTH: THE RISE OF WILKES-BARRE IN THE NORTHERN ANTHRACITE REGION, 1820-1880. *Pennsylvania Hist. 1978 45(4): 291-314.* By the 1880's, Wilkes-Barre became the dominant city in the northern anthracite coal region. Much of this success can be attributed to the city's ability to attract wealth, talent, and leaders from competing communities in that area. In 1870, 40% of the city's elite were migrants. Based on manuscript census returns and other materials; photo., map, 9 tables, 22 notes.   D. C. Swift

90. Doyle, Don Harrison. NINETEENTH-CENTURY CITIES: EVOLUTIONARY AND INSTANTANEOUS. *J. of Urban Hist.*

1978 5(1): 109-118. Review article prompted by Gunther Barth's *Instant Cities: Urbanization and the Rise of San Francisco and Denver,* and Roger W. Lotchin's more detailed *San Francisco, 1846-1856: From Hamlet to City,* and one work on the slow, limited urbanization of a rural community, Stuart M. Blumin's *The Urban Threshold: Growth and Change in a Nineteenth-Century American Community.* Admittedly this is an apples to oranges comparison, but one well worth making for these show urbanization in its most rapid and dramatic fashion and its slowest and most evolutionary manner. Somewhat surprisingly similarities are found as often as differences.   T. W. Smith

91. Druzhinina, E. I. VOZNIKNOVENIE GORODOV NA IUGE UKRAINY I V SSHA: OBSHCHEE I OSOBENNOE [The emergence of towns in the south of the Ukraine and in the South of the United States: common and specific features]. *Novaia i Noveishaia Istoriia [USSR] 1976 (2): 69-76.* The emergence of towns in the south of the Ukraine had much in common with the rise of towns in the South, due to similar economic and social conditions. The author also notes substantial differences. The Russian government was interested in the speedy settlement and economic development of the strategic frontier area and encouraged the agricultural, commercial, and industrial development of southern provinces.   J/S

92. Earle, Carville V. THE FIRST ENGLISH TOWNS OF NORTH AMERICA. *Geographical Rev. 1977 67(1): 34-50.* The first English towns in 17th-century North America are interpreted according to a monopolist-migration model. Companies and proprietors, operating as territorial monopolists, channeled resources into a chief colonial port, located near the center of their coastal colonial boundary. Once established, the initial growth of these towns hinged on the timing and destination of immigration flows. The astounding growth of Boston, Philadelphia, and Charles Town resulted from heavy family migration occasioned by long-swing European depressions that recurred at 50-year intervals. Elsewhere, urban growth was frustrated by bad timing and poor location, with respect to immigration. Components of the monopolist-migration model appear to be applicable to other frontier regions and their initial urban pattern.   J

93. Earle, Carville and Hoffman, Ronald. URBAN DEVELOPMENT IN THE EIGHTEENTH CENTURY SOUTH. *Perspectives in Am. Hist. 1976 10: 7-78.* A close correlation exists between the development of major agricultural products and the development of urban systems in the South during the 18th century. Although the three major export crops, wheat, rice, and tobacco, had expanding markets throughout the century, they traveled through coastal cities via different routes. Each required a different system of handling and packaging. Each fostered the growth of related industries and brought about the elimination of nonrelated industries. The effects of the relationship between agriculture and industry are reflected in the scattered, nonuniform patterns of Southern urbanization. These patterns laid the foundations and "predisposed production regions to divergent trajectories of [the South's] long run economic development." Table, 111 notes, appendix with 21 notes.
                                                                W. A. Wiegand

94. Ermisch, John. A NOTE ON THE DAVIS-SWANSON MODEL OF URBAN GROWTH. *Econ. Development and Cultural Change 1974 22(4): 691-697.* Examines the validity of the Davis-Swanson model of urban growth by applying it to several US cities during 1890-1910. Substantial disconfirming evidence was found, but the model might prove valid for other regions in other time periods. Based on the Davis-Swanson model and published sources; 4 tables, 17 notes.
                                                                J. W. Thacker, Jr.

95. Ernst, Joseph A. and Merrens, H. Roy "CAMDEN'S TURRETS PIERCE THE SKIES!": THE URBAN PROCESS IN THE SOUTHERN COLONIES DURING THE EIGHTEENTH CENTURY. *William and Mary Q. 1973 30(4): 549-574.* Disputes the traditional theory that southern urban centers were not important. The significance of urban places is measured by contemporary criteria of number of dwellings, population, and function. Small urban centers in the South performed urban functions of exchange, collection, storage, and distribution of commodities. A case study is made of origins and rise of Camden, South Carolina, which is related to a general discussion of the urban process in North Carolina, Virginia, and Maryland. Southern towns and cities formed a hierarchical arrangement and an urban system that fitted into a regional economy. Based on contemporary travel literature, original documents, and monographs; 55 notes.   H. M. Ward

96. Fairbanks, Robert B. CINCINNATI AND GREENHILLS: THE RESPONSE TO A FEDERAL COMMUNITY, 1935-1939. *Cincinnati Hist. Soc. Q. 1978 36(4): 223-242.* Rexford G. Tugwell's Greenbelt Towns during 1935-39 affected the establishment of Greenhills as a bedroom community outside Cincinnati which was to remove tenement and slum areas and replace them with city parks.

97. Farrell, David R. ANCHORS OF EMPIRE: DETROIT, MONTREAL AND THE CONTINENTAL INTERIOR, 1760-1775. *Am. Rev. of Can. Studies 1977 7(1): 33-54.* After the conquest of New France, Great Britain attempted to insure the military defense, political stability, and economic exploitation of the interior by direct imperial control through regional garrison towns. These outposts were subject to strict military and economic regulations which prevented their developing into urban centers. By 1770, changing trade patterns and unrest in the eastern colonies altered British policy, concentrating interest in the Great Lakes. Some garrison towns were abandoned and the fur-trading centers of Detroit and Montreal became the logical anchors for the realigned empire. Primary and secondary sources; map, 37 notes.
                                                                G.-A. Patzwald

98. Finger, John R. THE SEATTLE SPIRIT, 1851-1893. *J. of the West 1974 13(3): 28-45.* Focuses on the urban development of Seattle in the second half of the 19th century. Seattle had a favorable location for development and eventually acquired vital transportation connections which allowed the city to extend its economic ties to the eastern Washington coal fields. The "Seattle Spirit," the aggressive support of Seattle citizens, worked successfully for the growth of the city with the help of outside markets and investors. Based on contemporary newspaper reports, US Census reports, and primary and secondary sources; map, 67 notes.   N. J. Street

99. Flesher, Dale L. and Ross, Richard L. GAS BOOM TOWN. *Indiana Hist. Bull. 1973 50(6): 65-69.* Deals with the rise and fall of Albany, Indiana, following the discovery of natural gas there in 1886. Gas attracted many industries to Albany, principally glassmaking. Albany's population grew from 241 in 1880 to more than 3,000 in 1907 at the peak of the boom. Late in 1907 or early in 1908 the boom ended; and the population fell to 1,289 by 1910. Albany was too dependent upon one resource. Newspapers, census reports, and secondary accounts; 8 notes.
                                                                J. F. Paul

100. Foley, William E. ST. LOUIS: THE FIRST HUNDRED YEARS. *Missouri Hist. Soc. Bull. 1978 34(4): 187-199.* Residents and outside observers predicted a rosy future for St. Louis after its founding in 1764. The city never achieved all of its asserted potential before the Civil War, but it grew and prospered from the fur trade and its location central to the US agricultural domain developed after the 1790's. The War of 1812 hurt, but postwar recovery was rapid. The city increasingly became a commercial, light manufacturing, and transportation center for the Mississippi River basin. Based on manuscript and secondary sources; 3 photos, 61 notes.   H. T. Lovin

101. Folger, Fred. TRILBY: AN EARLY HISTORY, 1835-1919. *Northwest Ohio Q. 1978 50(2): 43-55.* Trilby, an unincorporated town in northwest Ohio, was eventually annexed by Toledo, as that city grew.

102. Foster, John R. and Morton, Glenn C.. KENDALL: TWENTIETH CENTURY GHOST TOWN. *Montana 1974 24(2): 68-84.* Between 1900 and 1920 Kendall, in Fergus County, boomed as its low-grade gold ore responded to the cyanide process, then collapsed as the mines played out. The ghost town is reviving as the site of a Boy Scout camp. 27 illus.   S. R. Davison

103. Fuller, Justin. BOOM TOWNS AND BLAST FURNACES: TOWN PROMOTION IN ALABAMA, 1885-1893. *Alabama Rev. 1976 29(1): 37-48.* Describes the methods and devices typically employed to promote Alabama's more than 23 boom towns when mining, industry, and rising prices were ascendant. No boom-town experience equalled the growth of Birmingham; however the steady decline in pig iron prices after

1890 undercut promoters' efforts. Peak activity was reached during 1888-89. Primary and secondary sources; 23 notes.   J. F. Vivian

104. Galphin, Bruce. ATLANTA: CITY OF TRADITION AND PROGRESS. *Americas 1974 26(3): 50-55.* Brief history of the city of Atlanta, Georgia.   S

105. Garofalo, Charles Paul. THE SONS OF HENRY GRADY: ATLANTA BOOSTERS IN THE 1920S. *J. of Southern Hist. 1976 42(2): 187-204.* The Atlanta Chamber of Commerce was deeply interested in the urbanization and industrialization of both Atlanta and Georgia. Henry Grady (1851-89) was their model, "the spirit of Atlanta," whom all southern businessmen sought to emulate in elevating the South. In an effort to attract northern capital and further industrialization, the Atlanta Chamber of Commerce boosted and published information about the labor force, particularly its skill, cleanliness, and docility, observing that the Blacks knew their place. They also became interested in agricultural growth, improvement in productivity, in the cultural and economic value of the state education system, and the talent of its businessmen. Based on primary and secondary sources; 55 notes.

T. D. Schoonover

106. Garr, Daniel J. A FRONTIER AGRARIAN SETTLEMENT: SAN JOSE DE GUADALUPE, 1777-1850. *San José Studies 1976 2(3): 93-105.* Offers a short history of California's first civilian settlement. 2 maps, 61 notes.

107. Garr, Daniel J. LOS ANGELES AND THE CHALLENGE OF GROWTH, 1836-1849. *Southern California Q. 1979 61(2): 147-158.* Traces efforts by the pueblo of Los Angeles to meet the problems of growth and to plan for the future. The pueblo's regional dominance was recognized in 1835 by an attempt to make it the capital of the province. Problems of the pueblo included faulty demarcation of its municipal limits, the need for street realignment, regulating the Indian population, development of lots, improvement and maintenance of houses, and the beginnings of a city beautiful movement. The *ayuntamiento* (town council) enacted ordinances during 1836-49 attempting to solve these and other problems. The pueblo thus displayed civic consciousness and a growing belief in the future grandness of Los Angeles. Primary and secondary sources; 44 notes.   A. Hoffman

108. Gates, Grace Hooten. ANNISTON: MODEL CITY AND RIVAL CITY. *Alabama Rev. 1978 31(1): 33-47.* Anniston, Alabama, founded in 1872, was less successful as a model town than as a rival to Jacksonville for the Calhoun County seat. Land speculation, random growth in the area, and the superiority of coke over charcoal-produced pig iron gave Birmingham large advantages after 1883. Anniston's prosperity, however, and a fortuitous political combination enabled the city to win the county seat referendum in 1889. Primary and secondary sources; 39 notes.   J. F. Vivian

109. Gilb, Corinne Lathrop. INSTANT CITIES: MIRROR FOR AMERICANS. *Rev. in Am. Hist. 1975 3(4): 429-432.* Spontaneous, rather than planned, urbanization in two western towns in the 19th century where "people interested only in getting rich quick accidentally also built stable, permanent cities" is the story told by Gunther Barth in *Instant Cities: Urbanization and the Rise of San Francisco and Denver* (New York: Oxford U. Pr., 1975).

110. Goheen, Peter G. INDUSTRIALIZATION AND THE GROWTH OF CITIES IN NINETEENTH-CENTURY AMERICA. *Am. Studies [Lawrence, KS] 1973 14(1): 49-66.* Growth of cities and industrialization were major themes in 19th-century America. Surveys the societal impact and interrelationship of these two forces. Urban society reflected industrialization, although the mere presence of factories did not effect fundamental social change. Based on secondary sources; 63 notes.   J. Andrew

111. Goodman, Mark. BUFFALO'S BLACK ROCK: A NEIGHBORHOOD AND THE CITY. *J. of Urban Hist. 1979 5(4): 447-468.* Finds in the history of Buffalo's neighboring community, Black Rock, one of the most important characteristics of urbanization. In charting the growth of Buffalo, its annexation of Black Rock, and the further decline of the former community from neighborhood to nonentity, the author

sees a general tendency of urbanization to destroy the distinctiveness of local neighborhoods and to redirect popular attention toward the city as a whole. Covers 1850's-90's. Map, 32 notes.   T. W. Smith

112. Grauman, Melody Webb. KENNECOTT: THE PRESENCE OF THE PAST. *Am. West 1979 16(5): 14-15, 58.* Kennecott, Alaska, was built as a company town to exploit what was probably the world's highest grade copper ore. During 1906-38, the mines supported an international copper conglomerate, dramatically advanced mining technology, and figured prominently in the Ballinger-Pinchot controversy which rocked Republican presidential politics. Today the small deserted town is a monument of abandoned technology framed by the scenic grandeur of an Alaskan mountain which overlooks the merging of two glaciers. Illus.   D. L. Smith

113. Greer, Edward. MONOPOLY AND COMPETITIVE CAPITAL IN THE MAKING OF GARY, INDIANA. *Sci. and Soc. 1976-77 40(4): 465-478.* Gary, Indiana, was not a company town in the historically accepted definition of the term. The planners of US Steel Corporation tried to create a community in which labor unrest would be subdued owing to the position of dependency on the corporation by its skilled workers. The corporation preferred control of Gary by respectable middle class elements rather than direct company control. The growth of an urban bourgeois class, of many ethnic origins, caused the corporation to compromise its position on at least peripheral matters in regard to events in Gary in order to maintain its basic pervasive and immensely influential position in the city.   N. Lederer

114. Guerard, Albert J. A VIEW FROM THE PERSIMMON TREE: HOUSTON 1924-72. *Southern R. 1974 10(2): 286-306.*

115. Guest, Avery M. ECOLOGICAL SUCCESSION IN THE PUGET SOUND REGION. *J. of Urban Hist. 1977 3(2): 181-210.* Looks at the timing, location, and rate of urban growth in western Washington, 1850's-1920's, and studies the causes and structure of urban development within the region. The development and location of towns in the extrametropolitan area were influenced decidedly by the railroad, but they were not influenced similarly by the introduction of the automobile. The automobile did not lead to the decline of the central city within metropolitan areas, but in turn led to the expansion of metropolitan influences within the greater region. Refers to the work of Roderick D. McKenzie in the 1920's. 6 tables, fig., 34 notes.   T. W. Smith

116. Haase, Carl L. GOTHIC, COLORADO: CITY OF SILVER WIRES. *Colorado Mag. 1974 51(4): 294-316.* Describes the development of the Copper Creek silver wire mines, 1878-79, and the resultant growth of the settlement at Gothic.

117. Haeger, John D. CAPITAL MOBILIZATION AND THE URBAN CENTER: THE WISCONSIN LAKEPORTS. *Mid-America 1978 60(2): 75-93.* A study of the formation of cities and towns in the Old Northwest, especially in Wisconsin, during the 1830's. Towns such as Green Bay, Racine, and Kenosha, among others, are the primary examples. Large capital resources and expenditures were needed to form cities, in contrast to agricultural areas. Eastern capitalists, such as John Jacob Astor, were the sources for much of the capital from outside the region. The towns did not spring up automatically, but were planned with the use of eastern capital and funds. This pattern held true for almost all the Wisconsin Great Lakes ports. 49 notes.   J. M. Lee

118. Hamilton, Kenneth Marvin. THE ORIGIN AND EARLY DEVELOPMENTS OF LANGSTON, OKLAHOMA. *J. of Negro Hist. 1977 62(3): 270-287.* Although it was an all-black town, Langston, Oklahoma, followed the general pattern of most new towns in the west. White hostility had made the haven of an all-black community seem attractive to Negroes in the 1890's. By 1891, the community had a population of 600. In 1897, the Oklahoma Territorial Legislature made Langston the seat of "The Colored Agriculture and Normal University of Oklahoma" (later renamed Langston University). Secondary materials; 88 notes.

N. G. Sapper

119. Hamilton, Kenneth Marvin. TOWNSITE SPECULATION AND THE ORIGIN OF BOLEY, OKLAHOMA. *Chronicles of Oklahoma 1977 55(2): 180-189.* Founded in 1904, Boley, Oklahoma has long

symbolized the achievements of America's black cities, yet its origins rested on economic rather than humanitarian motivations. Located on the Fort Smith and Western Railroad Company line, Boley became an important station after a 160-acre allotment was transferred from Choctaw ownership. The town's promoters recognized that since blacks dominated the surrounding area, lots could be more easily sold if directed solely at black ownership. Primary and secondary sources; 3 photos, 41 notes.

M. L. Tate

120. Hammon, Neal O. EARLY LOUISVILLE AND THE BLUE-GRASS STATIONS. *Filson Club Hist. Q. 1978 52(2): 147-165.* Describes a number of incidents about the early settlement of Louisville, Kentucky. Starting with surveys by Thomas Bullitt in 1773, John Floyd in 1774, and the Transylvania Company in 1776, Louisville grew rapidly during the American Revolution because of protection afforded by a garrison led by George Rogers Clark. Despite continual harassment by the Indians, Louisville's population grew and the city became a commercial center. Based on the Draper Collection at the University of Wisconsin and public records; 73 notes.

G. B. McKinney

121. Hammond, Charles. CONCORD'S "FACTORY VILLAGE": 1776-1862. *Old-Time New England 1975 66(1-2): 32-38.* Gives the history of the Assabet River in Concord, Massachusetts, and the "Factory Village" which was built on its banks, from 1776, when Roger Brown bought some land on the east bank of the river for building a fulling mill, until 1862, when the mill building burned down.

122. Handley, Lawrence R. SETTLEMENT ACROSS NORTHERN ARKANSAS AS INFLUENCED BY THE MISSOURI AND NORTH ARKANSAS RAILROAD. *Arkansas Hist. Q. 1974 33(4): 273-292.* The railroad shaped the pattern of settlement and economic growth of northern Arkansas towns between 1880 and the 1920's. thirty-three new settlements arose, five disappeared and several small towns and industries grew rapidly as the railroad passed along a 303-mile route between Seligman, Missouri, and Helena, Arkansas. Maps illustrate the alteration of village residence, road, and commercial growth patterns to take advantage of the railroad. Based on newspaper accounts, interviews and secondary sources; 7 maps, 62 notes.

T. L. Savitt

123. Harris, Carl V. ANNEXATION STRUGGLES AND POLITICAL POWER IN BIRMINGHAM, ALABAMA, 1890-1910. *Alabama Rev. 1974 27(3): 163-184.* Examines the three-way struggle among city, suburban, and corporate interests over urban annexation and taxation. The city promoted "Greater Birmingham" between 1893 and 1908, when a modest majority of suburbanites were persuaded to the advantages of annexation. The steel industry successfully resisted annexation until 1910. A coalition of reform groups enacted state legislation in 1908 providing no local tax exemptions for businesses. Corporate annexation broadened the city tax base, but another decade passed before the disparity between tax receipts and public expenditures was equalized. Primary and secondary sources; 36 notes.

J. F. Vivian

124. Hodgson, Edward R. EARLY SPOKANE'S 150,000 CLUB: MISSED 1910 POPULATION GOAL BY 31 PER CENT. *Pacific Northwesterner 1977 21(2): 17-22, 24-32.* Examines a city-wide immigration drive, 1905-10, in Spokane, Washington, so that by 1910 the population might be 150,000.

125. Hofsommer, Donovan L. TOWNSITE DEVELOPMENT ON THE WICHITA FALLS AND NORTHWESTERN RAILWAY. *Great Plains J. 1977 16(2): 107-122.* During 1900-20, businessmen Joseph A. Kemp and Frank Kell of Wichita Falls, Texas, built the Wichita Falls and Northwestern Railway some 305 miles into the panhandle of Oklahoma. The railroad and townsite developments "promoted the settlement of one of the country's last frontiers." 6 illus., map, 33 notes.

O. H. Zabel

126. Hollingsworth, J. R. TRIAL AND TRAVAIL OF AN EDITOR OR "I'LL DO ANYTHING FOR A BLOCK." *Panhandle-Plains Hist. Rev. 1975 48: 27-41.* During May, 1888, an experienced townsite promoter named J. T. Berry purchased 640 acres along the Fort Worth and Denver City Railroad in Potter County, Texas. His speculative venture came into conflict with Henry Sanborn, a prominent cattleman who owned land one mile east of Berry's townsite. Trying to

strengthen his claim, Sanborn lured newspaperman H. H. Brookes from Berry's location to his "new town" and the promotional battle began. Three years later Sanborn filed suit against Brookes' family for failure to surrender Block 88 as earlier promised by the newspaper editor. Despite the spectacular efforts of his attorney, Temple Houston, Sanborn lost the suit. By 1891, however, he had won the war when his townsite prospered over Berry's and became the main business district of Amarillo. Photo.

M. L. Tate

127. Holmes, Harry D. and Davis, Ronald L. ST. LOUIS: A NEW LOOK AT AN OLD WESTERN CITY. *J. of the West 1974 13(3): 5-16.* Discusses the urban rivalry between St. Louis and Chicago at the end of the 19th century and focuses on the urban growth and development of St. Louis. St. Louis was not "old and moribund" but dynamic and advanced in business and manufacturing, with a diversified and growing economy. Based on contemporary newspaper reports, US census reports, St. Louis trade and commerce reports, and secondary sources; illus., 37 notes.

N. J. Street

128. Horn, Kurt Van. TEMPTING TEMECULA: THE MAKING AND UNMAKING OF A SOUTHERN CALIFORNIA COMMUNITY. *J. of San Diego Hist. 1975 20(1): 26-38.* Describes the history of the southern California town of Temecula from its first Indian inhabitants in the 11th century, through its years as a Spanish town, ending with its agricultural development in the 19th century and economic death by 1890.

S

129. Hornbeck, David and Tucey, Mary. ANGLO IMMIGRATION AND THE HISPANIC TOWN: A STUDY OF URBAN CHANGE IN MONTEREY, CALIFORNIA 1835-1850. *Social Sci. J. 1976 13(2): 1-8.* Argues that the effect of Anglo immigration on developing California was not restricted to gold mining areas and that much urban change and expansion took place in Hispanic towns such as Monterey before 1850.

130. Horton, Loren N. RIVER TOWN: DAVENPORT'S EARLY YEARS. *Palimpsest 1979 60(1): 16-27.* A history of the establishment and early growth of Davenport, Iowa, 1833-50 as a river port and bridging area on the Mississippi River.

131. Hosack, Robert E. CHANUTE—THE BIRTH OF A TOWN. *Kansas Hist. Q. 1975 41(4): 468-487.* Most towns are established gradually, but Chanute was born on 1 January 1873, the offspring of four separate communities—New Chicago, Tioga, Chicago Junction, and Alliance. The four towns had emerged during the struggle between two railroads to qualify for a federal grant to build to Texas by reaching the southern Kansas border first. The original towns had grown up where the Missouri, Kansas & Texas was crossed by the Lawrence, Leavenworth & Galveston. After years of exhausting conflict the towns merged to form a new town named in honor of Octave Chanute, the chief engineer and superintendent of the Lawrence, Leavenworth & Galveston, whose later work in aviation was to inspire Orville and Wilbur Wright in the development of the airplane. Based on primary and secondary sources; illus., 101 notes.

W. F. Zornow

132. Jackson, Kenneth T. THE URBAN CRUCIBLE: AN AGE OF GREAT CITIES. *Social Educ. 1977 41(6): 504-506.* Examines the growth of cities, 1820-90, including the beginnings of city government, services offered, population booms, and housing problems; highlights difficulties unique to urban centers in the 19th century.

133. Jarrett, Walter. [FROM NEW AMSTERDAM TO THE BIG APPLE].
NEW YORK PART I: WHEN THE BIG APPLE WAS NEW AMSTERDAM. *Mankind 1975 5(3): 10-13, 52-55.*
NEW YORK PART II: FROM THE REVOLUTION TO FUN CITY. *Mankind 1975 5(4): 10-13, 60-63.*
The political, economic, and social history of New York City in the 17th-20th centuries includes the colonial governments of the Netherlands and Great Britain, the divided loyalties during the American Revolution, the impact of immigration, and the fortunes and innovations of businessmen.

134. Jarrett, Walter. [NEW ORLEANS].

NEW ORLEANS: THE CITY THAT CARE FORGOT. PART I: UNDER FRENCH AND SPANISH FLAGS. *Mankind 1974 4(7): 16-23, 48-51.* Traces the early history of New Orleans until the Louisiana Purchase.

DOWN THE RIVER TO NEW ORLEANS, PART II: UNDER AMERICAN AND CONFEDERATE FLAGS. *Mankind 1974 4(8): 18-25, 58-59.* Describes New Orleans from 1803, when Louisianna was purchased from France by Thomas Jefferson, to about 1900.

135. Jensen, Richard E. BELLEVUE: THE FIRST TWENTY YEARS, 1822-1842. *Nebraska Hist. 1975 56(3): 339-374.* Explores the founding and early growth of Bellevue, based on new data and reinterpretation of older material. Bellevue originally was a field headquarters and trading post of the Missouri Fur Company. In 1832 the Indian Agency for the Omaha, Pawnee, Oto, and Missouri tribes was transferred to Bellevue and was an important factor in the continued growth of Nebraska's oldest community.   R. Lowitt

136. Johnson, Richard Brigham. SWAMPSCOTT, MASSACHUSETTS, IN THE SEVENTEENTH CENTURY. *Essex Inst. Hist. Collections 1973 109(4): 243-306.* Highlights points of historical interest in the 17th century development of Swampscott, Massachusetts.   S

137. Jolley, Clyde W. THE GRANDEUR THAT WAS ROME. *Georgia Life 1977 3(4): 15-17.* Traces the history of Rome, Georgia, including establishment, economic growth, and social life, 1834-1976.

138. Jucha, Robert J. THE ANATOMY OF A STREETCAR SUBURB: A DEVELOPMENT HISTORY OF SHADYSIDE, 1852-1916. *Western Pennsylvania Hist. Mag. 1979 62(4): 301-319.* Traces the growth and planned development of Shadyside, a district in the East End of Pittsburgh, from the introduction of streetcars to the rise of automobiles.

139. Karsarda, John D. and Redfearn, George V. DIFFERENTIAL PATTERNS OF CITY AND SUBURBAN GROWTH IN THE UNITED STATES. *J. of Urban Hist. 1975 2(1): 43-66.* Annexation in many cases masked decentralization that occurred prior to 1920 in some older cities. Making allowance for annexation, in all regions the suburban ring increased more rapidly than the city by 1900. Actual decline in the central city's population occurred in the 1930's. 5 tables, 27 notes.   S. S. Sprague

140. Kelemen, Thomas A. A HISTORY OF LYNCH, KENTUCKY, 1917-1930. *Filson Club Hist. Q. 1974 48(2): 156-176.* The coal town of Lynch, Harlan County, Kentucky, was created in 1917 by the US Coal and Coke Company. The company, a subsidiary of US Steel, exploited the rich coal reserves in Harlan County to meet the fuel crisis caused by World War I. Management attempted to build an ideal company town, with well constructed houses, attractive churches, and a sewer and water system. Still, it was a company town where housing was only for workers, the company store dominated the local economy, and the workers were strongly encouraged to vote Republican. Documentation by contemporary newspapers; 93 notes.   G. B. McKinney

141. Kelsey, Harry. A NEW LOOK AT THE FOUNDING OF OLD LOS ANGELES. *California Hist. Q. 1976 55(4): 326-339.* Reappraises the circumstances surrounding the founding of Los Angeles. Governor Felipe de Neve was anxious to move the settlers onto their assigned lands as soon as possible in order to reduce the subsidy paid to them. Several families were located in the Los Angeles region as early as June 1781. Others were assigned building sites and fields during the summer months. 4 September 1781 marked the date of Neve's formal certification of the establishment of the pueblo. The version of Los Angeles' founding given by Franciscan missionary Francisco Palou, long discredited by most historians, may well be the most accurate. Primary and secondary sources; illus., photos, 83 notes.   A. Hoffman

142. Kimball, James L., Jr. A WALL TO DEFEND ZION: THE NAUVOO CHARTER. *Brigham Young U. Studies 1975 15(4): 491-497.* Discusses the success of the Mormon community in ascertaining a city charter for Nauvoo, Illinois, 1839-41, so that their sect might have a town of its own.

143. Kintrea, Frank. TUXEDO PARK. *Am. Heritage 1978 29(5): 69-77.* Tuxedo Park, New York, 40 miles from New York City, was developed in the 1880's by Pierre Lorillard IV as a refuge for wealthy New Yorkers. After decades of social exclusiveness, the Park Association has had to lower its standards in order to remain solvent. Pressures from land developers threaten the Park's integrity. 23 illus.   J. F. Paul

144. Kirkby, Dianne. GOLD AND THE GROWTH OF A METROPOLIS: A COMPARATIVE STUDY OF SAN FRANCISCO AND MELBOURNE, AUSTRALIA. *J. of the West 1978 17(2): 3-15.* The discovery of gold in California in 1848 and Australia in 1851 accelerated urban growth in the seaports of San Francisco and Melbourne. As a frontier outpost, San Francisco was unprepared for the influx of thousands of gold seekers and their requirements for city service. Fire protection, water, health care, and law enforcement were created in response to the emergency needs of the boom town. Melbourne, in contrast, was a large, prosperous city with the characteristics of an English town; basic city services were expanded to meet the needs of the newcomers. The most significant change brought by the gold rush in Australia was the overturning of the social structure, making Melbourne "the most American of Australian cities." Secondary sources; map, 11 photos, 50 notes.   B. S. Porter

145. Kleinmaier, Judith. SPRINGS MADE WAUKESHA A MOST FASHIONABLE RESORT. *Wisconsin Then and Now 1973 19(12): 4-5, 8.* The discovery of mineral springs in 1868 near Waukesha led to the development and promotion of the town as the "Saratoga of the West." Fashionable hotels were built and the springs were landscaped in the best Victorian manner. In addition to attracting ill people who hoped for restorative cures, the springs became fashionable resorts for the wealthy who sought refuge from the city heat. The springs were popular until the early 1900's. 4 illus.   B. J. Paul

146. Knight, Oliver TOWARD AN UNDERSTANDING OF THE WESTERN TOWN. *Western Hist. Q. 1973 4(1): 27-42.* Little is known of urbanization in its relationship to the westward movement. The types of urban studies already available cannot be used because they lack the necessary data and detail. A great deal more has to be known about western towns before generalization through synthesis can be made about the process and significance of western urbanization. Suggests areas and topics for investigation. 26 notes.   D. L. Smith

147. Kramer, Carl E. IMAGES OF A DEVELOPING CITY: LOUISVILLE, 1800-1830. *Filson Club Hist. Q. 1978 52(2): 166-190.* During 1800-30, Louisville, Kentucky, grew from a village of a few hundred inhabitants to a city of 10,000 people. Steamboats were primarily responsible for population growth after 1811, making the city a thriving center of river commerce. By 1830, the construction of the Louisville and Portland Canal insured continued success. Public health was generally poor, but cultural advances were significant. Based on contemporary newspapers and travel accounts; 87 notes.   G. B. McKinney

148. LaGory, Mark and Nelson, James. AN ECOLOGICAL ANALYSIS OF URBAN GROWTH BETWEEN 1900 AND 1940. *Sociol. Q. 1978 19(4): 590-603.* A study of 157 cities suggests that specialization theories, central to an ecological model of urban growth, require qualification. Contrary to expectations, specialization plays a limited role in urban growth, which appears to be most closely related to a city's inter-mural transportation system.   J

149. Larsen, Lawrence H. CHICAGO'S MIDWEST RIVALS: CINCINNATI, ST. LOUIS, AND MILWAUKEE. *Chicago Hist. 1976 5(3): 141-151.* Analyzes the rise of Chicago to dominance among the cities of the Midwest and suggests that financial leadership and economic strategy rather than location account for that rise.

150. Lee, Lawrence B. WILLIAM E. SMYTHE AND SAN DIEGO. *J. of San Diego Hist. 1973 19(1): 10-24.* Smythe, author of *The Conquest of Arid America* (Seattle: U. of Washington Pr., 1969), crusaded for the irrigation of the Imperial Valley through the Water and Forest Association. Closely connected to Senator Newlands and other national figures interested in irrigation, he became a new style of San Diego booster. Yet today he is locally best remembered for his *History of San Diego: 1592-1908* (San Diego, 1907), a standard work. Based on MS., the San Diego *Union,* and Smythe's writings; 3 illus., 84 notes.   S. S. Sprague

151. Ligibell, Ted J. TOLEDO MINUS PORT LAWRENCE EQUALS VISTULA: A RETROSPECTIVE LOOK AT TOLEDO'S OLDEST NEIGHBORHOOD. *Northwest Ohio Q. 1974 46(4): 123-130.* Discusses Vistula, an area of Toledo, Ohio, from its beginnings in 1832 until 1974. 5 photos, 22 notes.

152. Lindsey, David. THE WAY TO SAN FRANCISCO. *Am. Hist. Illus. 1976 11(6): 4-11, 44-48.* In 1775-76 Juan Bautista de Anza led a group of Spanish emigrants from Mexico to found the city of San Francisco, California.

153. Littlefield, Daniel F., Jr. and Underhill, Lonnie E. KILDARE, OKLAHOMA TERRITORY: STORY OF AN AGRICULTURAL BOOM TOWN. *Great Plains J. 1975 15(1): 28-54.* Discusses Kildare, Oklahoma, created when the Cherokee Strip opened to settlement, to present a case study of an agricultural boom town. Like many other boom towns, Kildare, founded in 1893, was "sustained for a time by the enthusiasm generated in land openings, but . . . ultimately lost out." Primary sources; 5 illus., 3 maps, 77 notes.   O. H. Zabel

154. Locke, Raymond Friday. MEMPHIS ON THE MISSISSIPPI. *Mankind 1975 5(2): 12-17, 52-55.* Covers the political and social history of Memphis, including its first European discovery by Hernando deSoto in 1539, the relations of colonial and US governments with the Chickasaw Indians, its 19th-century urbanization with the growth of the cotton industry, its fate in the Civil War, and its destruction and renovation in the wake of a yellow fever epidemic in 1878.

155. Locke, Raymond Friday. SAN DIEGO: FIGHTING TO STAY PRETTY. *Mankind 1976 5(8): 14-18, 44-45.* San Diego was visited by the Spanish as early as 1542. Its early history under Spanish control was uncertain because of Indian opposition as the settlement developed from a military outpost to a mission. The following period of American rule was turbulent. With the coming of the railroad, San Diego embarked on a period of growth based on tourism, coupled with commerce and the military development of its harbor.   N. Lederer

156. Locke, Raymond Friday. SAN FRANCISCO: LADY BY THE SEA. *Mankind 1973 4(2): 10-15, 62-64, 66.* The city's early history and eccentrics.   S

157. Locke, Raymond Friday. SANTA FE: THE DANCING GROUND OF THE SUN. *Mankind 1974 4(6): 12-19, 51-52.* Reviews Santa Fe's early history from 1540-1882, and focuses on the early settlement of Spaniards, Indians, and missionaries.   S

158. Love, Frank. POSTON AND THE BIRTH OF YUMA: THE FATHER OF ARIZONA INVENTS A STORY. *J. of Arizona Hist. 1978 19(4): 403-416.* Charles D. Poston, one of the founders of Colorado City (later known as Yuma), spread the story that Colorado City was founded so lots could be sold to pay for ferrying across the Colorado River. Poston's version of the founding of Colorado City has passed into Arizona history and been repeated countless times. Unfortunately, many of Poston's tales, including this one, have no basis in fact. Evidence indicates that Colorado City was founded at the Yuma crossing because 1) it was a traditional ford on the Colorado River, 2) the railroad was expected to cross the Colorado River at the Yuma crossing, and 3) the site was well suited as a trading location for Mormon settlements to the north and mining concerns in Sonora and New Mexico. Based on documents in the Library of Congress, Arizona Historical Society, newspaper accounts, and published secondary sources; 3 illus., 33 notes.

159. Luning Prak, N. PULLMAN. *Spiegel Historiael [Netherlands] 1977 12(4): 236-241.* George M. Pullman (1831-97) invented the famous sleeping car in 1858 and in 1880 established the city of Pullman near Chicago. Here his workers lived in company homes and sent their children to company schools. In 1885 and again in 1893 wages were reduced, but not rents. A strike in 1894 was supported by the American Railway Union. The strike was broken because President Cleveland called out federal troops, invoking the Sherman Anti-Trust act of 1890. Illus., biblio.   G. D. Homan

160. Maldonado, Edwin. URBAN GROWTH DURING THE CANAL ERA: THE CASE OF INDIANA. *Indiana Social Studies Q. 1978-79 31(3): 20-37.* Describes the relationship between urban growth and canal building in northern Indiana, from 1817 and the construction of the Erie Canal through the late 1840's.

161. Marsh, Margaret Sammartino. SUBURBANIZATION AND THE SEARCH FOR COMMUNITY: RESIDENTIAL DECENTRALIZATION IN PHILADELPHIA, 1880-1900. *Pennsylvania Hist. 1977 44(2): 99-116.* During 1880-1900, peripheral settlements in northwest Philadelphia began to become modern suburban areas. Reformers then considered suburbanization a panacea for many social problems. With the exception of Overbrook Farms, the area saw haphazard residential development. Overbrook Farms was a planned community for lower upper class families. In 1880, the typical resident of northwest Philadelphia was a laborer living near his place of employment. The area had relatively few churches and social institutions. By 1900, population had grown from 14,250 to 43,708, and mostly middle class and working class families had moved into the area. The many churches and social institutions provided cultural separation in a community that generally was not characterized by physical segregation. Primary sources; photo, map, 2 tables, 33 notes.   D. C. Swift

162. Mason, William and Mason, Roberta Kirkhart. THE FOUNDING FORTY FOUR. *Westways 1976 68(7): 20-23.* Supplies short biographies of the twelve founding families of Los Angeles, ca. 1781.

163. Mawn, Geoffrey P. PROMOTERS, SPECULATORS, AND THE SELECTION OF THE PHOENIX TOWNSITE. *Arizona and the West 1977 19(3): 207-224.* Camp McDowell was established on a branch of Arizona's Salt River in 1865. It was an important link in a string of military posts across the territory which controlled the Indians and protected mining districts and transportation routes. Farmers and businessmen were attracted to the Salt River Valley by the markets at Camp McDowell and the nearby mines. As early as 1867, land and trade speculators began to promote the area as a center of irrigated agriculture. The birth of Phoenix followed an evolutionary pattern typical of western towns, planned by successive groups of speculators and promoters vying to locate a formal town. John T. Alsap, land promoter and probate judge, guided Phoenix to its patent from the federal government in 1874. 6 illus., 2 maps, 40 notes.   D. L. Smith

164. McCarthy, Joe. THE MAN WHO INVENTED MIAMI BEACH. *Am. Heritage 1975 27(1): 64-71, 100-101.* Carl Graham Fisher, the builder of the Indianapolis Speedway, gambled millions of dollars on Florida long before the boom started. Heavy investments, completion of a bridge, and the end of World War I led to financial gains with peace, prosperity, and increased automobile travel. As money came in, more was spent on hotels, golf courses, and other attractions. The boom of the 1920's led to discouragement and Fisher turned his interests to Montauk, New York, a project overrun by the depression. Fisher died in 1939 leaving a meager estate of $40,000. 16 illus.   J. F. Paul

165. McCoy, Drew R. THE VIRGINIA PORT BILL OF 1784. *Virginia Mag. of Hist. and Biog. 1975 83(3): 288-303.* In an attempt to bring economic independence to Virginia after the Revolution, James Madison led a drive to restrict the state's trade to a few enumerated ports. Madison hoped to create port cities, ending Virginia's dependence on Philadelphia and Baltimore and reducing the influence of British merchants on the state's trade. Though his port bill passed the legislature, opposition from nonfavored areas of the state delayed its implementation and amended it to emphasize potential revenue. Madison, meanwhile, shifted his attention from the state to the national level in his attempt to achieve economic self-sufficiency. Based on published editions of the Madison and Jefferson papers, county petitions in the Virginia State Library, and secondary sources; 62 notes.   R. F. Oaks

166. McDonald, Russell. THE DEVELOPMENT OF LOVELOCK. *Nevada Hist. Soc. Q. 1976 19(4): 261-275.* Chronicles the growth and economic development of Lovelock, Nevada, since 1861. The town was named in honor of George Lovelock (1824-1907). It grew slowly but steadily as a trading center for nearby mining areas and for livestock raisers. It never achieved, however, the goal of its early boosters who envisioned Lovelock as a major population center. Based on newspaper sources; photo, 70 notes.   H. T. Lovin

167. McGinty, Brian. MONTEREY: CAPITAL OF OLD CALIFORNIA. *Early Am. Life 1979 10(1): 32-35.* History of Monterey through the Spanish, Mexican, and early American eras, 1770-1849.

168. McKelvey, Blake and Barnes, Joseph W. "BLAKE MCKELVEY'S ROCHESTER": SCRIPT FROM A ONE-HOUR FILM DOCUMENTARY. *Rochester Hist. 1976 38(1): 1-24.* Reprints a film script by the authors on the history of Rochester, New York, during 1811-1960's.

169. McKelvey, Blake. "CANALTOWN": A FOCUS OF HISTORICAL TRADITIONS. *Rochester Hist. 1975 37(2): 1-24.* Discusses the Canaltown district of Rochester, New York, during 1809-1924.

170. McLeod, Richard. THE DEVELOPMENT OF SUPERIOR, WISCONSIN, AS A WESTERN TRANSPORTATION CENTER. *J. of the West 1974 13(3): 17-27.* Studies the urban development of Superior, Wisconsin, in the late 19th century. Superior did not develop a diversified economy but remained a rail and shipping center dependent upon entrepreneurs including Jay Cooke, James J. Hill, and John D. Rockefeller. Competition from more diversified manufacturing cities such as Duluth, Chicago, and Milwaukee helped to bring about a decline for Superior. Based on contemporary newspaper reports and secondary sources; 46 notes.   N. J. Street

171. Meredith, Howard L. and Shirk, George H. OKLAHOMA CITY: GROWTH AND RECONSTRUCTION, 1889-1939. *Chronicles of Oklahoma 1977 55(3): 293-308.* Discusses population growth patterns and neighborhood development in Oklahoma City from its 1889 founding to 1939. Railroads provided Oklahoma City with its first boom period. This was sustained during the early 20th century by the oil boom and industrial-commercial expansion. This entrenched prosperity gained it the state capital and insulated it from the worst effects of the Depression. Primary and secondary sources; 7 photos, 50 notes.
                                                  M. L. Tate

172. Meyer, Carol Clarke. THE RISE AND FALL OF RUBY. *J. of Arizona Hist. 1974 15(1): 8-28.* Ruby, in southern Arizona, was settled in the 1840's but sputtered out during the Civil War. Resettlement began after the war encouraged by the discovery of a mine in the 1870's. Though it was believed to be an area rich in lead, silver, gold, zinc, and copper ore, water scarcity and unsatisfactory reduction methods minimized full development. Homesteaders and hard rock miners held on grimly despite the ever-present threat of Indian raids, reciprocal border cattle rustling, and the spillover from the revolutionary era in Mexico. Modern technology and capital of a new company reopened the Montana Mine in 1926 and Ruby became a boom town. For a few years the mine was the leading producer of lead and zinc in the state and the third in silver output. When the ore gave out in 1940, the mine was closed. Today, Ruby is a ghost town. 4 illus., 25 notes.   D. L. Smith

173. Miller, Zane L. CINCINNATI: A BICENTENNIAL ASSESSMENT. *Cincinnati Hist. Soc. Bull. 1976 34(4): 231-250.* Gives a short history of Cincinnati, Ohio, 1776-1976.

174. Mintz, Leonora Ferguson. THE WORLD'S ONE AND ONLY ROCKMART. *Georgia Life 1978 4(4): 16-19.* In 1849, Joseph G. Blance discovered slate at Van Wert, Georgia, which was founded in 1832; the town was renamed Rockmart in 1872 under Mayor Charles Taylor Parker; slate is still the town's chief product.

175. Muller, Edward K. SELECTIVE URBAN GROWTH IN THE MIDDLE OHIO VALLEY, 1800-1860. *Geographical Rev. 1976 66(2): 178-199.* Selective population growth among smaller towns and cities has been a neglected topic in the historical geography of North American settlement. A three-phased model of selective urban growth in a newly settling region emphasizes the nodality of towns within the evolving transportation network and the emergence of manufacturing activities. Examination of the middle Ohio valley from 1800 to 1860 confirmed that during the initial two periods of settlement and agricultural specialization urban growth was affected primarily by nodality with respect to local hinterlands and by concentration of processing industries. Regional integration with the national transportation network after 1850 shifted the basis of urban growth to the development of secondary manufactures, which emerged in the few towns of greatest regional nodality as well as in those close to the urban-industrial market of Cincinnati.   J

176. Muller, Peter O. THE EVOLUTION OF AMERICAN SUBURBS: A GEOGRAPHIC INTERPRETATION. *Urbanism Past and Present 1977 (4): 1-10.* Since the early 1800's, suburbanization has coincided with major transportation innovations, housing availability, and emigration rates of whites from big cities.

177. Myers, Raymond E. THE STORY OF GERMANNA. *Filson Club Hist. Q. 1974 48(1): 27-42.* Virginia's colonial Governor Alexander Spotswood was the driving force behind the organization of the town of Germanna in 1714. Owning land that was rich in iron ore, Spotswood contracted with German Protestants to immigrate and work the land. At first the project was successful, but religious differences among the Germans and the desire of the immigrants to own their own land brought an end to the experiment. Documentation from secondary works; 84 notes.   G. B. McKinney

178. Nadeau, Josephine E. RIPON: ETHNIC AND GENERAL DEVELOPMENT. *Pacific Historian 1976 20(1): 52-66, (2): 189-201, (3): 305-315.* Part II. Presents the history of Ripon, California, from the end of conflicts with Indians to the 20th century. Pays special attention to the arrival of representatives of various national and ethnic groups (the Americans Jedediah Smith and John C. Frémont, French Canadian trappers, "49er's," Irish, and Welsh). Also notes other important individuals. Primary and secondary sources; 4 illus., 35 notes. Part III. Narrates events which led to Ripon's claim to be the "Almond Capital of California," and to the annual Almond Blossom Parade and Festival. John P. Watkins is credited with the first commercial orchard, in 1909. Part IV. Provides brief biographies of prominent early settlers in Ripon. 38 notes.
                                                  G. L. Olson

179. Nelson, Howard J. THE TWO PUEBLOS OF LOS ANGELES: AGRICULTURAL VILLAGE AND EMBRYO TOWN. *Southern California Q. 1977 59(1): 1-11.* Contrary to the prevailing image of Los Angeles as an agricultural village at the time of American takeover, the pueblo had acquired the characteristics of an urban town at the beginning of Mexican rule in 1822. An 1836 census revealed a population of 1,000, who were tailors, shoemakers, merchants, carpenters, masons, clerks, and other urban types. The plaza area had been rebuilt, the church was dedicated in 1822, and homes of leading citizens had been erected in the downtown area. The image of self-sufficient ranchos in this era is inaccurate. Few ranchos had anywhere near the number of artisans and urban-skilled workers to be found in the pueblo. The arrival of American rule in 1848 marked "an evolutionary change in scale and spirit rather than a revolutionary alteration in economy and society." Primary and secondary sources; 31 notes.   A. Hoffman

180. Nichols, Roger L. A MINIATURE VENICE: FLORENCE, ARIZONA, 1866-1910. *J. of Arizona Hist. 1975 16(4): 335-356.* Discusses growth and development of Florence, Arizona, from Indian settlement to 1910. Anglo settlement was first established in 1866 and received its first boost through the efforts of an Indian agent, Levi Ruggles. Florence became the county seat in 1875 and continued to grow with the discovery of mineral resources in the vicinity.

181. Noel, Thomas J. ALL HAIL THE DENVER PACIFIC: DENVER'S FIRST RAILROAD. *Colorado Mag. 1973 50(2): 91-116.* Negotiations and financing by "Railroad Kings" such as John Evans and General William Jackson Palmer completed the Denver Pacific Railroad linking Denver with Cheyenne and the Union Pacific in 1870. Denver emerged as the regional banking and commercial center because of "the conscious, capable, courageous, if chicane, efforts" of these men.
                                                  O. H. Zabel

182. Olson, James S. and Byford, Liz. OASIS IN EAST TEXAS: CONROE AND THE DEPRESSION, 1929-1933. *Texana 1974 12(2): 141-148.* The Depression of 1929 was felt but shortlived in Conroe. After the community battled the economic crisis for two years, oil was discovered and it became a boomtown. The economy prospered and the town grew as never before. The same problems developed as in other boomtowns in Texas, and the town leaders were not able to cope successfully with them. Primary and secondary sources; 24 notes.
                                                  B. D. Ledbetter

183.   Pedersen, Elsa and Pierce, Richard A.   PORT AXEL.   *Alaska J. 1976 6(2): 113-117.* Port Axel was a paper town to be developed by the Alaska Colonization and Development Company headed by Axel Gustaf Hornborg (d. 1905). Describes the plans for the town, which was to house Finnish immigrants, and the activities of Adam Widenius, the company's agent at the town site. Discusses Widenius' suggestions for development of coal, oil, fishing, guano, and farming.   E. E. Eminhizer

184.   Pedersen, Walt and Pedersen, Elsa.   THE STORY OF STERLING.   *Alaska J. 1975 5(3): 179-187.* Chronicles the establishment of the town of Sterling on the Kenai Peninsula in Alaska, 1937-71; relates stories about early homesteaders and later inhabitants. 10 photos.

185.   Peebles, Robert H.   THE GALVESTON HARBOR CONTROVERSY OF THE GILDED AGE.   *Texana 1974 12(1): 74-83.* Focuses on the internal bickering and the engineering problems which had to be solved before Galveston harbor could be converted into a deep-water port. After much controversy in the 1880's, it was agreed that the cost would be so great that the federal government would be needed to underwrite the expense. It was also agreed that Galveston would be the best commercial harbor between the Rio Grande and the Mississippi River. With this settled, in 1890 Congress chose Galveston to receive federal funds for the project. Based on primary and secondary sources; 46 notes.   B. D. Ledbetter

186.   Pfeil, Don.   LAS VEGAS: THE SUDDEN CITY.   *Mankind 1973 4(1): 17, 62-64.*

187.   Piehl, Charles K.   THE RACE OF IMPROVEMENT: SPRINGFIELD SOCIETY, 1865-1881.   *Missouri Hist. Rev. 1973 67(4): 484-521.* Discusses the development of Springfield, Missouri, during 1865-81. Citizens of Springfield had hoped to control the future development of the town, but the post-war years failed to produce an adequately stable environment. Difficulties included transportation, the need for responsible businessmen, the physical structure and appearance of the town, and rivalry with North Springfield. During the first five years some progress was made, but economic depression in the 1870's caused a decline in both economy and society. Due to fragmentation and lack of unity, the town was unable to achieve the firm economic, social, and political stability necessary for orderly growth and improvement. Based on contemporary newspaper reports, primary and secondary sources; 17 illus., 2 photos, 111 notes.   N. J. Street

188.   Posadas, Barbara M.   A HOME IN THE COUNTRY: SUBURBANIZATION IN JEFFERSON TOWNSHIP, 1870-1889.   *Chicago Hist. 1978 7(3): 134-149.* Convenient transportation, relative economic prosperity, and profit-oriented land developers and real estate agents promoted population movement to Chicago's suburban areas, 1870-89.

189.   Powell, H. Benjamin.   ESTABLISHING THE ANTHRACITE BOOMTOWN OF MAUCH CHUNK, 1814-1825.   *Pennsylvania Hist. 1974 3(41): 249-262.* Discusses 10 manuscripts and two newspaper articles related to the establishment of Mauch Chunk, an early Pennsylvania coal boomtown. The materials were drawn from the Jacob Cist collections at the Wyoming Historical and Geological Society (W.H.G.S.), the Academy of Natural Science of Philadelphia (A.N.S.P.), the Isaac A. Chapman Collection at the W.H.G.S., and the Charles Fisher Wells Collection at the A.N.S.P.; illus., 26 notes.   D. C. Swift

190.   Powell, Lawrence Clark.   THE PHOENIX HAS RISEN: NOW WHAT?   *J. of Arizona Hist. 1977 18(3): 239-246.* Compares the emergence of Phoenix, Arizona, from the shadow of Tucson to the emergence of Los Angeles from the shadow of San Francisco. Phoenix has grown to master its environment and to take leadership in the state, and has potential and promise for future greatness.   D. L. Smith

191.   Price, Jacob M.   ECONOMIC FUNCTION AND THE GROWTH OF AMERICAN PORT TOWNS IN THE EIGHTEENTH CENTURY.   *Perspectives in Am. Hist. 1974 8: 123-186.* To illustrate the character of the principal 18th-century American port towns one must focus on two distinguishing features: their occupational structure, and the economic factors influencing their growth patterns. Occupational distribution in the ports shows remarkable consistency between the governmental, service, industrial and maritime sectors. Significant economic factors influencing growth patterns include geographic position and volume of export trade. But even more important is a less visible characteristic. To attract the maritime sector the port city had to be viewed as the "entrepreneurial decisionmaking center of a trade." 4 tables, 80 notes, 7 appendices.   W. A. Wiegand

192.   Rankin, Ernest H.   THE FOUNDING OF THE PORT OF MARQUETTE.   *Inland Seas 1976 32(1): 3-12, 42.* Although visited by French trappers and missionaries, the Carp River region of Michigan's northern peninsula was not widely explored until the 1840's. In 1845 Phil Marshall Everett discovered iron there and the following year his Jackson Iron Company established a furnace. In 1849 John Burt and Amos R. Harlow of the Marquette Iron Company purchased land which was later incorporated in Marquette. Illus.   K. J. Bauer

193.   Ratzlaff, Robert K.   LE HUNT, KAN.: THE MAKING OF A CEMENT GHOST TOWN.   *Kansas Hist. Q. 1977 43(2): 203-216.* During 1905-18, southeast Kansas experienced an industrial boom. The cement industry prospered at first. In 1905 the United Kansas Portland Cement Company built a plant at Le Hunt near Independence. While other cement companies prospered and survived, the Le Hunt mill and company town disappeared by the end of World War I. All the companies suffered from overproduction, discriminatory freight rates, and depletion of natural gas, but the Le Hunt mill was doomed by the absence of planning, unscrupulous promoters, and financial irresponsibility. Primary and secondary sources; illus., 39 notes.   W. F. Zornow

194.   Riefler, Roger F.   NINETEENTH-CENTURY URBANIZATION PATTERNS IN THE UNITED STATES.   *J. of Econ. Hist. 1979 39(4): 961-974.* By viewing urban areas in the northeast quadrant of the United States as a system of cities, this paper attempts to isolate the common factors precipitating the overall pattern of urbanization in the nineteenth century. For the antebellum period commercial activity, both interregional and especially intraregional trade, appears to be the driving force generating urbanization. During the post-bellum period manufacturing comes to the fore as the prime factor allowing cities to grow at a rate exceeding that of their hinterland. 2 tables, 33 notes.   J

195.   Riley, Mark B.   EDGEFIELD: A STUDY OF AN EARLY NASHVILLE SUBURB.   *Tennessee Hist. Q. 1978 37(2): 133-154.* Edgefield began as a community on the east side of the Cumberland River opposite Nashville's business district. In the late 19th century, with the introduction of streetcars, it became the suburban home of many of Nashville's most prominent citizens. Edgefield was annexed to Nashville during the civil booster movement in 1880. Beginning about 1900, East Nashville lost its attraction and began to fall behind West Nashville. In 1916 Edgefield was almost wiped out by a disastrous fire. Not until the 1960's did Edgefield begin to recover. In 1978 Edgefield became the first district in Davidson County to be given historic district status. Primary and secondary sources; 4 illus., 41 notes.   M. B. Lucas

196.   Rutman, Darrett B.   PEOPLE IN PROCESS: THE NEW HAMPSHIRE TOWNS OF THE EIGHTEENTH CENTURY.   *J. of Urban Hist. 1975 1(3): 268-292.* Analyzes New Hampshire's 198 towns. Concludes that populations sensed when towns exceeded their optimum density. Numbers of inhabitants would then overcome their reluctance to emigrate, and outmigration would be of sufficient magnitude to return densities to levels below the critical size for agricultural towns. Based on censuses, gazetteers and other sources; 3 tables, fig., 39 notes.   S. S. Sprague

197.   Sauers, Bernard J.   A POLITICAL PROCESS OF URBAN GROWTH: CONSOLIDATION OF THE SOUTH SIDE WITH THE CITY OF PITTSBURGH, 1872.   *Pennsylvania Hist. 1974 41(3): 265-287.* Eleven boroughs on the south side of the Monongahela River were consolidated with the city of Pittsburgh in 1872 by action of the Pennsylvania legislature. Efforts to accomplish this had begun in 1854 but were steadily resisted by the boroughs involved. With consolidation the population of Pittsburgh nearly doubled. Pittsburgh acquired a larger tax base to finance improvements and its existing debts, yet the consolidated boroughs retained separate responsibility for their existing debts. Illus., map, 8 tables, 53 notes.   D. C. Swift

198. Savage, Richard A. BAR HARBOR: A RESORT IS BORN. *New-England Galaxy 1977 18(4): 11-22.* Chronicles the transformation of Bar Harbor from a quiet seaport village in 1840 to a bustling resort patronized by wealthy businessmen and their families from New York and Boston during the 1850's-1860's. Notes the roles of Thomas Cole and Henry Pratt, well-known artists. 9 illus.   P. C. Marshall

199. Scamehorn, H. Lee. IN THE SHADOW OF CRIPPLE CREEK: FLORENCE FROM 1885 TO 1910. *Colorado Mag. 1978 55(2-3): 205-229.* Florence, a community between Pueblo and Canon City, Colorado, in 1901 seemed destined to become a major industrial center. It was a major source of crude oil and refined products and also boasted a smelter and numerous reduction mills for ore from Cripple Creek. In the first decade of the 20th century, however, inadequate transportation, declining investment capital, and changing reduction technology combined to prevent industrial greatness for Florence. Based on mining journals; 16 illus., map, 53 notes.   O. H. Zabel

200. Schnell, J. Christopher. CHICAGO VERSUS ST. LOUIS: A REASSESSMENT OF THE GREAT RIVALRY. *Missouri Hist. Rev. 1977 71(3): 245-265.* Wyatt W. Belcher in *The Economic Rivalry between St. Louis and Chicago, 1850-1880* (New York: AMS Press, 1947) attributed the rise of Chicago to more progressive entrepreneurial leadership. This author finds St. Louis business leaders equally progressive. St. Louis was doomed from the start because of sectional wrangling, legislative funding that encouraged inefficiency, negative geographic elements that prevented St. Louis from connecting with east-west transport routes, and the city's failure to attract eastern capital groups as Chicago had tapped the resources of the John Murray Forbes group. Illus., 52 notes.   W. R. Zornow

201. Schnell, J. Christopher. THE NEW WEST: THEMES IN NINETEENTH CENTURY URBAN PROMOTION, 1815-1880. *Missouri Hist. Soc. Bull. 1974 30(2): 75-88.* Analyzes "urban dreams" of western promoters. Three themes dominate these promoters' hucksterism: "geographic determinism" concerning the West's "natural advantages"; arguments keyed to technological advancement; and the concept of the West as America's ultimate center of economic and political gravity. Based on promotional tracts and secondary sources; 2 maps, 28 notes.   H. T. Lovin

202. Segal, Howard P. JEFF W. HAYES: REFORM BOOSTERISM AND URBAN UTOPIANISM. *Oregon Hist. Q. 1978 79(4): 345-357.* Jeff W. Hayes, a pioneer in the telegraph industry, settled in Portland, Oregon, in March 1882 and soon became one of Portland's most ardent supporters. Hayes' utopian views of Portland, as expressed in his essay "Portland, Oregon, A.D. 1999," stem from his boosterism. Many of Hayes's predictions have failed to materialize, but others have been suprisingly accurate. Hayes's essays provide a glimpse of life in Portland in the late 19th and early 20th centuries. Based on published, secondary sources; 6 photos, 25 notes.   D. R. McDonald

203. Sharpless, John. IN SEARCH OF COMMUNITY: A NEW THEME FOR THE OLD "NEW" URBAN HISTORY. *Rev. in Am. Hist. 1977 5(2): 215-222.* Review article prompted by Stuart Blumin's *The Urban Threshold: Growth and Change in a Nineteenth-Century American Community* (Chicago: U. of Chicago Pr., 1976), which diseusses Kingston, New York.

204. Shook, R. W. YEARS OF TRANSITION: VICTORIA, TEXAS, 1880-1920. *Southwestern Hist. Q. 1974 78(2): 155-182.* Contemporary Victoria is a product of late 19th- and early 20th-century technological, economic, and social forces, including agriculture, transportation, communications, road improvement, new commercial ventures, banking, and extended professional services. "The village which had begun as an empresario headquarters and cattle center prospered as a result of its distance from Gulf storms and direct connections with larger towns to the east and north." 23 photos, 34 notes.   R. V. Ritter

205. Silag, William. SIOUX CITY: AN IOWA BOOM TOWN. *Ann. of Iowa 1979 44(8): 587-601.* Describes the frenzied promotion and real estate speculation which followed the founding of Sioux City, Iowa, in 1855 by John Cook and James Jackson. A contraction of credit in 1857 burst the bubble and forced a retrenchment which lasted until well after the Civil War. The logic of the town's founders, who correctly perceived that Sioux City would become a commerce center for the upper Missouri Valley, was sound enough, but they began their "boosting" a decade too early.   P. L. Petersen

206. Sprague, Stuart Seely. ALABAMA AND THE APPALACHIAN IRON AND COAL TOWN BOOM, 1889-1893. *Alabama Hist. Q. 1975 37(2): 85-91.* Land speculation and the development of boomtowns were risky ventures. One of the most successful speculators in the latter quarter of the 19th century was W. P. Rice, who developed Fort Payne, Alabama. Describes his background and his method of operation. Compares the Fort Payne development with Sheffield, Piedmont, Bridgeport, Florence, Anniston, and seven other towns which were not as successful. 30 notes.   E. E. Eminhizer

207. Sprague, Stuart Seely. ALABAMA TOWN PRODUCTION DURING THE ERA OF GOOD FEELINGS. *Alabama Hist. Q. 1974 36(1): 15-20.* The town building boom following the War of 1812 in Alabama has been overlooked in past studies. The would-be Alabama towns were better advertised than any others of the period, and they were more successful, with four reaching urban status: Florence, Athens, Demopolis, and Marion. Muscle Shoals was the center for town promotion. The main outlets for advertising were newspapers in Tennessee and Georgia.   E. E. Eminhizer

208. Sprague, Stuart Seely. THE CANAL AT THE FALLS OF THE OHIO AND THE THREE CORNERED RIVALRY. *Register of the Kentucky Hist. Soc. 1974 72(1): 38-54.* Land speculation and urban rivalry complicated the struggle for development of a canal at the Falls of the Ohio River. When the Indiana Company was chartered in 1804, the Kentucky legislature chartered the Ohio Canal Company. The intense rivalry hindered stock selling and other development, but the financial success of the Erie reawakened interest in 1823. The first vessel passed through on 21 December 1830, thanks to extensive federal aid. Based on primary and secondary sources; 56 notes.   J. F. Paul

209. Sprague, Stuart Seely. TOWN MAKING IN THE ERA OF GOOD FEELINGS: KENTUCKY 1814-1820. *Register of the Kentucky Hist. Soc. 1974 72(4): 337-341.* Kentucky, like other states, was swept by a new-town fever during this period. Many of the new towns failed to survive, but some, like Owensboro, Newport, and Covington, did. The peak was reached in 1818 but the Panic of 1819 brought a halt to this movement. Based on primary and secondary sources; 24 notes.   J. F. Paul

210. Sprague, Stuart Seely. THE WHALING PORTS: A STUDY OF NINETY YEARS OF RIVALRY, 1784-1875. *Am. Neptune 1973 33(2): 120-130.* A consideration of economic competition between port cities during the whaling era. Cities rose and fell in importance as vessels, technology, and whaling grounds changed. The gold rush in California resulted in San Francisco being the dominant port for a time, a role traditionally played by New England cities. The whaling industry declined sharply after 1850, the result of a financial panic, the Crimean War, rising costs, and the introduction of kerosene and petroleum products. By 1875 the whaling industry was dead, and many formerly famous ports became inconspicuous hamlets. 16 photos, 10 tables, 18 notes.   V. L. Human

211. Spude, Robert L. SWANSEA, ARIZONA: THE FORTUNES AND MISFORTUNES OF A COPPER CAMP. *J. of Arizona Hist. 1976 17(4): 375-396.* Swansea was founded in 1908 in west central Arizona, and flourished as a copper mining town until 1923. There were subsequent attempts to reopen the mines, and there have been recent attempts to find copper ore in the region. Considers the mineral and human dimensions of the history of Swansea, "one of those overpromoted underproducing mining towns which sprang up and disappeared in so many places in the Copper State." 5 illus., 44 notes.   D. L. Smith

212. Stansfield, Charles. PITMAN GROVE: A CAMP MEETING AS URBAN NUCLEUS. *Pioneer Am. 1975 7(1): 36-44.* Analyzes Pitman Grove, New Jersey, a community which traces its origin to a combination of social and religious motives. Unlike most mid-19th-century settlements it evolved into a sizeable town, but currently does not

appear to be making the necessary urban adjustments. Primary and secondary sources and extensive field work; 3 photos, table, fig., 20 notes.
C. R. Gunter, Jr.

213. Stark, Lawrence R. A LOCAL FOLKTALE: THE FOUNDING OF PULLMAN. *Record 1977 38: 33-53*. Focuses on local folklore concerning the origins of Pullman, Washington. Challenges the contentions that Bolin Farr was Pullman's first settler, that Pullman was earlier named Three Forks, and that Chicago industrialist George Pullman had been associated with the community. Primary and secondary sources; 10 illus., 30 notes.
G. H. Curtis

214. Stelter, Gilbert A. THE CITY AND WESTWARD EXPANSION: A WESTERN CASE STUDY. *Western Hist. Q. 1973 4(2): 187-202*. Cheyenne, the commercial center and capital of Wyoming, furnishes a case study of the role of cities in westward expansion. Declining in size and importance as a terminal town along the first transcontinental railroad, Cheyenne could not expect to become great until it dominated a productive hinterland. Northeastern Wyoming Territory, with good soil and mineral resources, presented an exciting possibility for investment. In early 1870, Cheyenne prepared an expedition to wrest control of the area from the Sioux Indians, but the Army, policing the area, frustrated these efforts. Cheyenne's expedition typifies western community activity which promoted westward expansion. 49 notes.
D. L. Smith

215. Stewart, Peter C. RAILROADS AND URBAN RIVALRIES IN ANTEBELLUM EASTERN VIRGINIA. *Virginia Mag. of Hist. and Biog. 1973 81(1): 3-22*. Railroad construction provided a focus for the acceleration of economic rivalry between Richmond, Petersburg, and Norfolk from the 1830's through the 1850's. Richmond's place as a political center provided legislative leverage and attracted able promoters and sufficient capital. Richmond outdistanced its rivals handily, with Petersburg gaining little more than Norfolk. The rivalry left an enduring legacy. Based on railroad archives, manuscripts, and newspapers; 60 notes.
C. A. Newton

216. Strickler, Carolyn. A TOWN CALLED BODIE. *Mankind 1975 5(3): 42-55*. Bodie, California, was born in the gold rush bonanza of the 1860's, was deserted in the 1880's and is now a ghost town and a National Historic Site.

217. Sweig, Donald. A CAPITAL ON THE POTOMAC: A 1789 BROADSIDE AND ALEXANDRIA'S ATTEMPTS TO CAPTURE THE CHERISHED PRIZE. *Virginia Mag. of Hist. and Biog. 1979 87(1): 74-104*. Discusses the widely circulated and reprinted broadside's influence on the location of the national capital, and prints in an appendix the text, along with a draft by David Stuart, determined to be the author through handwriting and textual analysis. Gives factual and inferred connections between the broadside, and the Potowmack Company and George Washington. Washington, who was interested in Potomac navigation and Alexandria's development, chose the exact site of the Federal district, and included Alexandria. Map, 45 notes, appendix.
P. J. Woehrmann

218. Tanner, Ralph M. SOME CHARACTERISTICS OF EIGHT LAND COMPANIES IN NORTH ALABAMA, 1863-1900. *Alabama Rev. 1976 29(2): 124-134*. The experience of eight Alabama boom towns —Bridgeport, Cedar Bluff, Oxmoor, Anniston, Sheffield, Nottingham, Fort Payne, and Bessemer—indicates that iron and steel making commonly preceded the emergence of developed town sites. Yet, the promotion and growth of urban life determined the success of each enterprise, and only Bessemer lived up to original expectations. Based on secondary sources; biblio.
J. F. Vivian

219. Taylor, Morris F. THE TOWN BOOM IN LAS ANIMAS AND BACA COUNTIES. *Colorado Mag. 1978 55(2-3): 111-132*. Examines the short-lived boom conditions in southeast Colorado, especially Las Animas County (from which Baca County was carved in 1889), in the late 1880's. Encouraged by several years of good rainfall, speculators promoted founding of towns to serve an agricultural hinterland by often misleading advertising. Describes new boom towns with newspapers, hotels, and other businesses. Failure to attract a railroad and drought by 1894 had "collapsed all vestiges of the boom." Based on local newspapers and land records; 5 illus., 3 maps, 59 notes.
O. H. Zabel

220. Thomas, Ronald C. THE FOUNDING OF A HAPPY TOWN: MARTIN, TENNESSEE. *West Tennessee Hist. Soc. Papers 1973 (27): 5-17*. Martin, Tennessee, was founded as a result of the migration of William Martin to Weakley County in 1832, his diligent work in securing railroad connections, and the expansion of the Nashville and Northwestern Railway into the southeastern section of the country by 1873; in 1893 the population had reached 2000.

221. Ubrick, Doug. PORT COSTA. *Pacific Hist. 1978 22(4): 361-370*. An account of the history of Port Costa since its founding by George McNear of Maine in 1874 to service the needs of his grain ranches and grain shipping business and residences for his own employees and those brought in in 1878 to build a new line for the Central Pacific Railway (now Southern Pacific) to reach from Stockland to Oakland. Development of a ferry to carry the trains across the strait added to the business of Port Costa. Other warehouses for grain and docks for shipping, including oil, were built by other merchants. Fishing business and brick manufacturing added to the prosperity. When the wheat growing was reduced, what had been the greatest wheat shipping center in the west was much changed. Now Port Costa is primarily a quiet little tourist center. 11 notes, biblio.
R. V. Ritter

222. Unsigned. [URBANIZATION IN THE COLONIAL SOUTH]. *William and Mary Q. 1974 31(4): 653-671*.
Wellenreuther, Hermann. URBANIZATION IN THE COLONIAL SOUTH: A CRITIQUE, *pp. 653-668*. Criticizes Joseph A. Ernst and H. Roy Merrens's earlier article in this journal, especially for its definition of "town" and for too much reliance on descriptive features. 55 notes.
Siegel, Fred. FRED SIEGEL'S LETTER, *pp. 668-669*.
Ernst, Joseph A. and Merrens, H. Roy. JOSEPH A. ERNST AND H. ROY MERRENS REPLY, *pp. 669-671*. Calls for critics to eschew theoretical assumptions and to go to the sources.
H. M. Ward

223. Vitz, Robert C. GENERAL JAMES TAYLOR AND THE BEGINNINGS OF NEWPORT, KENTUCKY. *Filson Club Hist. Q. 1976 50(4): 353-368*. James Taylor, one of the founders of Newport, Kentucky, was a member of a prominent Virginia family and cousin of President Zachary Taylor. He first settled on his father's Kentucky land in 1793. He soon purchased this and other tracts of land and began to try to attract settlers to the region. Despite the presence of a military garrison, growth was slow until 1830. Based on Taylor MSS. at the Cincinnati Historical Society, the Kentucky Historical Society, and the Filson Club; 43 notes.
G. B. McKinney

224. Walker, Henry P. ARIZONA LAND FRAUD: MODEL 1880, THE TOMBSTONE TOWNSITE COMPANY. *Arizona and the West 1979 21(1): 5-36*. The Tombstone Townsite Company was formed in 1879 to promote a settlement near promising silver-mining claims in the southeastern corner of Arizona Territory. Tents, frame shacks, and adobe structures soon appeared. Although the company had only filed a claim without taking further steps to secure the patent it was soon engaged in a lively real estate business. Uncertainty concerning the legality of titles to town lots bred tension and violence by citizens prepared to defend their investments against claim jumpers. Further trouble was assured when it was discovered that there was some overlay of townsites and mineral claims. Legal entanglements, rumor, political intrigue, territorial and national government involvement, and fraud combined to create a situation that still clouds the title of unsold lots in the Tombstone townsite. 3 illus., 2 maps, 86 notes.
D. L. Smith

225. Warner, Sam Bass, Jr. and Fleisch, Sylvia. THE PAST OF TODAY'S PRESENT: A SOCIAL HISTORY OF AMERICA'S METROPOLISES, 1860-1960. *J. of Urban Hist. 1976 3(1): 3-118*. Looks at the 173 metropolitan areas into which the Bureau of Economic Analysis classified the country in 1960, and their population data. Matching the data variables according to similar patterns for each decade back to 1860, examines changes in the distribution of groups over time and across space. Discusses both regional and national trends. Extra detail is also given to the use of BEA units for other research interests. 9 maps, 10 tables, 25 notes, 3 appendixes.
T. W. Smith

226. Weaver, Robert. THE SUBURBANIZATION OF AMERICA. *New York Affairs 1977 4(3): 24-33.* Discusses economic, social, and racial aspects of the move toward suburbanization during 1900-76.

227. Weiher, Kenneth. THE COTTON INDUSTRY AND SOUTHERN URBANIZATION, 1880-1930. *Explorations in Econ. Hist. 1977 14(2): 120-140.* Using central place theory, shows that the hierarchy of central services associated with the cultivation and marketing of cotton and cotton byproducts shaped the pace and pattern of urbanization and were fundamentally responsible for the location, size, and growth of most southern cities through the 1920's. Published documents and secondary accounts; 2 fig., 5 tables, 27 notes, 14 refs.   P. J. Coleman

228. White, Dana F. and Crimmins, Timothy J. URBAN STRUCTURE, ATLANTA. *J. of Urban Hist. 1976 2(2): 231-251.* Discusses the urban structure of Atlanta during the late 19th and 20th centuries and the changes in residences followed by black club women and Colonial Dames. Analyzes shifts in black residential patterns and the impact of transportation. 9 maps, 9 notes.   T. W. Smith

229. Williams, James C. CULTURAL TENSION: THE ORIGINS OF AMERICAN SANTA BARBARA. *Southern California Q. 1978 60(4): 349-377.* Traces the evolution of Santa Barbara, California, from Hispanic pueblo to an American-European commercial center. At the time of statehood in 1850 Santa Barbara's population was predominantly Hispanic, its economic base agricultural, its buildings adobe, and its streets unaligned. Within a few years the pueblo dramatically changed; the cattle industry was eliminated by natural disasters in the early 1860's. The laying out of streets in a grid pattern resulted in an American-occupied business center south of *El Pueblo Viejo,* the original community, and the city exercised eminent domain over buildings located on the newly surveyed streets. A variety of businesses, brick homes, and increased immigration brought a cosmopolitan air to the community. By the 1870's the culture of Santa Barbara was transformed form its Hispanic origins to an American-oriented community, with the original *El Pueblo Viejo* section left to Spanish-speaking residents. Primary and secondary sources; 4 maps, 49 notes.   A. Hoffman

230. Wood, Jerome H., Jr. PHILADELPHIA: A VERY PERSONAL CITY. *Mankind 1974 4(10): 8-18.* Outlines the history of Philadelphia since 1681, including William Penn, Benjamin Franklin, the Continental Congress, industrialization, and aspects of city life.

231. Woods, H. Ted. COLUMBIA ESTABLISHED AS A PORT IN EARLY 1800'S. *North Louisiana Hist. Assoc. J. 1974 5(2): 73-76.* Caldwell Parish was carved from the original parishes of Ouachita and Catahoula and was established by an act of the state legislature on 8 March 1838. The settlement at Columbia had a fragmented early history. Its site was first settled in 1827 by Daniel Humphries. Its importance was as a river port and trading center. Destroyed by fire in 1876, 1900, and again in 1909, the city was rebuilt each time. Today Columbia has a population of 4,500. Note.   A. N. Garland

232. Zabriskie, George Olin and Kenney, Alice P. THE FOUNDING OF NEW AMSTERDAM: FACT AND FICTION, PART VI: THE GROWTH OF A MYTH. *Halve-Maen 1977 52(1): 11-14.* Concluded from a previous article. Examines the myth of the purchase of Manhattan Island from local Indians by Peter Minuit in 1624, and the founding of New Amsterdam.

Politics and Government

Institutions and Politics

233. Bloomfield, Maxwell. THE MUNICIPAL CORPORATION REVISITED. *Rev. in Am. Hist. 1976 4(1): 27-31.* Review article prompted by Jon C. Teaford's *The Municipal Revolution in America: Origins of Modern Urban Government, 1650-1825* (Chicago: U. of Chicago Pr., 1975).

234. Clotfelter, Charles. MEMPHIS BUSINESS LEADERSHIP AND THE POLITICS OF FISCAL CRISIS. *West Tennessee Hist. Papers 1973 (27): 33-49.* The ravages of Reconstruction, population flight due to an epidemic of yellow fever, stagnating revenue sources resulting from dependence on the cotton crop, and the onus of the loss of white control of the municipal government caused an economic depression, 1873-77, which spawned an angry taxpayers' revolt that resulted in municipal home rule and repudiation of the city's legal debts.

235. Daniels, Bruce C. CONNECTICUT'S VILLAGES BECOME MATURE TOWNS: THE COMPLEXITY OF LOCAL INSTITUTIONS 1676 TO 1776. *William and Mary Q. 1977 24(1): 83-103.* The unit of town government in the older towns was broken down with the emergence of proprietors, freemen, and ecclesiastical society as separate corporate units. Discusses the extent of democracy of each of the three units and the role of officials. Society government arose from the division of a town into two or more parishes. Throughout the period the authority of the selectmen expanded, not only in the town meetings, but also in influence upon the other deliberative bodies. Notes effects of government changes on townsmen. Based on Connecticut town and colony records; 64 notes.   H. M. Ward

236. Daniels, Bruce C. GOVERNING RHODE ISLAND'S METROPOLITAN: THE TOWN MEETING AND ITS OFFICERS IN COLONIAL NEWPORT, 1700-1776. *Newport Hist. 1979 52(4): 101-117.* The town meeting and its elected officers in Newport, Rhode Island, increased in importance during 1700-76 due to the town's rapid increase in population and trade.

237. Davis, Ronald L. F. COMMUNITY AND CONFLICT IN PIONEER SAINT LOUIS, MISSOURI. *Western Hist. Q. 1979 10(3): 337-355.* Saint Louis, Missouri, in the first part of the 19th century, is examined to determine how participatory government emerged as a problem solving mechanism in isolated communities. When economic development and growth characterize the context of a frontier settlement, a democracy of innovation, competition, conflicts, and compromise is likely to emerge. This was the experience of Saint Louis. 63 notes.   D. L. Smith

238. Ebner, Michael H. URBAN GOVERNMENT IN AMERICA, 1776-1876. *J. of Urban Hist. 1979 5(4): 511-520.* Review article prompted by Charles R. Adrian and Ernest S. Griffith, *A History of American City Government,* Leo Hershkowitz, *Tweed's New York,* and Jon C. Teaford, *The Municipal Revolution in America.* Teaford's and Adrian's and Griffith's contributions to the neglected topic of municipal government are worthwhile, but Hershkowitz's addition is "conjectural and at times downright circumspect."   T. W. Smith

239. Frank, Forest. THE DISESTABLISHMENT OF THE CHARTER COMMITTEE. *Cincinnati Hist. Soc. Bull. 1975 33(1): 27-47.* Discusses the Cincinnati City Council's political use of the Charter Committee 1933-36, emphasizing its alleged use as a force for political and social elitism.

240. Galvin, John T. THE DARK AGES OF BOSTON POLITICS. *Massachusetts Hist. Soc. Pro. 1977 89: 88-111.* During the 1880's women emerged as a political force, questions of corruption emerged, the park system developed, the parochial school system was debated, and Irish Americans became a force in local politics. Many of these issues' effects are still felt. Primary and secondary sources; 109 notes.   G. W. R. Ward

241. Goodstein, Anita S. LEADERSHIP ON THE NASHVILLE FRONTIER, 1780-1800. *Tennessee Hist. Q. 1976 35(2): 175-198.* A review of the men of leadership in the Nashville area during 1780-1800. Physical survival and clear land titles were tbe main problems. A temporary government was soon established whose members had all proven themselves in the cauldron of frontier survival. James Robertson, founder of the colony, was one of its early leaders. He was a capable Indian fighter and a tactful diplomat. A constant battle was waged with the established states to retain control of land, often purchased from questionable companies. The second generation of leaders were predominantly lawyers, because the court became the primary arena of local politics. By 1800, the Indians had been eliminated and the colony was firmly established. 49 notes.   V. L. Human

242. Grantham, Shelby. VOTED AND CHOSE. *Early Am. Life 1979 10(1): 11-14, 16, 20-21.* New England towns in the 18th century elected lesser officials including Hog Howards, Tithingmen, Viewers of Fish, Cullers of Staves, Sealers of Measure, Keepers of the Pound, and Fence Viewers.

243. Griffin, Richard T. SIN-DRENCHED REVELS AT THE IN-FAMOUS FIRST WARD BALL. *Smithsonian 1976 7(8): 52-61.* Details the events of the First Ward Ball, a social event held by Chicago's politicos, 1903; discusses the political camps in Chicago, 1880's-90's and anecdotes about political infighting.

244. Hays, Samuel P. THE CHANGING POLITICAL STRUCTURE OF THE CITY IN INDUSTRIAL AMERICA. *J. of Urban Hist. 1974 1(1): 6-38.* Using insights from geography and sociology, sees city politics as a continual tension between centralizing and decentralizing forces. Physical patterns, inventions such as the telephone and automobile, and the rise of experts all affect this tug of war. Primary and secondary sources; 43 notes.   S. S. Sprague

245. Hogan, Thomas E. CITY IN A QUANDARY: SALAMANCA AND THE ALLEGANY LEASES. *New York Hist. 1974 55(1): 79-101.* In 1850 the Erie Railroad leased a right-of-way in southern Cattaraugus County from the Seneca Nation, wherein the town of Salamanca developed. In February 1892, after a long and complex legal dispute, the Seneca Nation granted a 99-year lease to the town of Salamanca. Fears have been raised that the town might revert back to the Seneca Nation when that lease expires in 1991. The lease is renewable, but the Seneca and the Salamanca city government have been unable to agree on the terms of renewal. The Seneca receive $11,000 per year in rent from the city of Salamanca and are demanding an annual rental of $300,000. The city is prepared to offer $75,000 per year. The uncertainty of the leasing arrangement is depressing business in the Salamanca area and making mortgage loans difficult to secure. Primary and secondary works; 6 illus., 57 notes.   G. Kurland

246. Kilar, Jeremy W. COURTHOUSE POLITICS, LOUP CITY, SHERMAN COUNTY, 1887-1891. *Nebraska Hist. 1979 60(1): 36-57.* Examines factions, the Courthouse Gang and the Railroad Gang, in Loup City politics. By the end of the 1880's they merged into partisan party politics with the farmers casting aside urban factions for the Farmers' Alliance in search of honest, representative administration.   R. Lowitt

247. Kotter, Richard E. THE TRANSCONTINENTAL RAILROAD AND OGDEN CITY POLITICS. *Utah Hist. Q. 1974 42(3): 278-284.* Until 1869 Ogden city election procedures had no residency requirements and permitted election by acclamation. When a large group of railroad workers were to be in town on election day, the city council "passed a new and entirely different set of election ordinances intentionally designed to offset any railroad vote at the polls," including citizenship and residency clauses. Soon after, the ordinance was amended to require real estate and residency only. The Ogden City Council's purpose was to enable President Young to send his son to hold office. However with the rapid influx of non-Mormons into their city, the mayor and councilmen reinstituted the city residency clause. Illus., 14 notes.   E. P. Stickney

248. Leonard, Ira M. THE POLITICS OF CHARTER REVISION IN NEW YORK CITY, 1847-1849. *New-York Hist. Soc. Q. 1979 63(1): 6-23.* In 1846 a revision of the 1830 New York City charter, drawn up by the Democrats in power, was defeated. Subsequent reform attempts also failed, and the Whig Party captured the city government in the next year. Citing alleged Democratic corruption, the new administration under Mayor William V. Brady pushed through another charter revision, which was approved by the voters in 1849. However, changes were minimal and the municipal government was not modernized. The new document did not meet the needs of a growing metropolis. Primary sources; 3 illus., 47 notes.   C. L. Grant

249. Leonard, Ira M. THE POLITICS OF CHARTER REVISION IN NEW YORK CITY, 1845-1847. *New-York Hist. Soc. Q. 1978 62(1): 43-70.* By the 1840's the new professional politicians in both parties had taken over control of New York City politics from the more estab-lished families. The city charter of 1830 needed modernization to accommodate a city growing at the rate of almost five percent a year and rapidly becoming a cosmopolitan, industrial center. Thus, without firm direction from the charter, partisan city politics had produced a municipal government identified with political democracy yet characterized by corruption, patronage, and waste. During his first term as mayor, William Frederick Havemeyer, a Democrat and respectable sugar merchant, attempted to bring about reform without realizing how the city was changing. Soon it was obvious that neither the Whig Party nor the press was very interested in reform; thus, Havemeyer's party decided not to follow his lead. Nothing of significance was done. Primary sources; illus., 56 notes.   C. L. Grant

250. Mann, Ralph. NATIONAL PARTY FORTUNES AND LOCAL POLITICAL STRUCTURE: THE CASE OF TWO CALIFORNIA MINING TOWNS, 1850-1870. *Southern California Q. 1975 57(3): 271-297.* Examines political activity in two California gold camps, Grass Valley and Nevada City, 1850-70. Initially miners were a transient class, and political offices were held by local entrepreneurs. Successful miners later increased their participation, although businessmen and professionals continued to be overrepresented in political offices proportionate to their numbers. Foreign-born people held office less on their ethnicity than on their occupational success; Chinese were excluded from political participation. The Civil War was a factor in concentrating the Democratic Party in Grass Valley and the Republicans at Nevada City. Political offices and allegiances tended to follow practices in the East rather than ad hoc miners' institutions. Where a city was dominated by one party, occupational democracy was found in the minority party which was trying to build a larger political base. Based on census data, contemporary and secondary published works, and local newspapers; 14 tables, 13 notes.   A. Hoffman

251. Morazán, Ronald R. THE CABILDO OF SPANISH NEW ORLEANS, 1769-1803: THE COLLAPSE OF LOCAL GOVERNMENT. *Louisiana Studies 1973 12(4): 591-606.* Describes the function of the Cabildo, a Spanish colonial institution in New Orleans with administrative, legislative, and judicial functions.

252. Nash, Gary B. THE TRANSFORMATION OF URBAN POLITICS 1700-1765. *J. of Am. Hist. 1973 60(3): 605-632.* Political participation increased in Boston, New York, and Philadelphia among people normally considered ineligible for such activities: Germans, Dutch, and the "lower rank." The appeals of factions seeking victory through an expanded political base resulted in an increase in the percentage of actual voters, new organizational techniques such as the caucus, an increase in pamphlet literature and inflammatory rhetoric, extended involvement of religious leaders in political controversy, and use of the mob to intimidate partisans. These factors were all at work in the election of 1764 in Philadelphia, and generally predate the revolutionary struggles after 1765. 105 notes.   K. B. West

253. Noble, Richard A. PATERSON'S RESPONSE TO THE GREAT DEPRESSION. *New Jersey Hist. 1978 96(3-4): 87-98.* An already serious economic situation in Paterson, New Jersey, brought on by the exodus of its textile industry during the 1920's, was heightened by the Great Depression. By 1932, the city government finally had confronted the fiscal crisis by reducing the wages of its own employees, by not hiring new personnel, by cutting municipal improvements, and by appropriating fewer dollars for recreation. Relief programs included the use of state funds as well as private resources. While not fulfilling all the hopes of the unemployed, Paterson's record of public assistance on the eve of the New Deal was relatively good. Based on annual messages of the mayors of Paterson, census records, newspaper sources and secondary sources; 4 illus., 37 notes.   E. R. McKinstry

254. Oaks, Robert F. PHILADELPHIA MERCHANTS AND THE FIRST CONTINENTAL CONGRESS. *Pennsylvania Hist. 1973 40(2): 149-168.* By 1774, merchants still were the largest single group among the Philadelphia radical leadership, yet their influence had declined progressively. Compares the 1769 radical leadership with that in 1774 and notes that fewer Quakers were active in the patriot movement as time passed. Based on the papers of Henry Drinker, a conservative Quaker merchant, and of Thomas Wharton, a conservative-to-moderate merchant; illus., 49 notes.   D. C. Swift

255. Platt, Hermann K. THE JERSEY CITY WATER RIGHTS CONTROVERSY, 1845-1850. *New Jersey Hist. 1976 94(4): 141-154.* Jersey City's municipal government and the Associates of the Jersey Company, a private corporation that had once owned the land on which Jersey City was built, clashed concerning jurisdiction over the city's waterfront. The Associates argued that its charter granted it full ownership of the waterfront, but city government authorities hoped the state would cede underwater lands to the city and thereby weaken the Associates' territorial claim. The Court of Errors and Appeals, New Jersey's highest court, decided in favor of the Associates; and, when the legislature issued Jersey City a new charter in 1851, the Associates further secured a hold on the waterfront. If Jersey City's municipal government desired to expand its functions, it could not count on the waterfront as a source of power. Based on newspaper accounts, legislative minutes, charters, and secondary sources; illus., 2 maps, 31 notes.   E. R. McKinstry

256. Potts, James H. THE EVOLUTION OF MUNICIPAL ACCOUNTING IN THE UNITED STATES: 1900-1935. *Business Hist. Rev. 1978 52(4): 518-536.* Some early interest in state and municipal accounting procedures was evidenced in the 1880's and 1890's, but the movement really began about the turn of the century with the activities of the National Municipal League which appointed a committee on the subject in 1901. Over the next three decades municipal accounting principles passed through two stages. The first, lasting until about 1920, overemphasized the similarities between business firms and government operations. The second, lasting until 1935, represented a reaction to the first and too strongly deemphasized the same parallels. Based especially on periodical material; 41 notes.   C. J. Pusateri

257. Pusateri, C. Joseph. RURAL-URBAN TENSIONS AND THE BOURBON DEMOCRAT: THE MISSOURI CASE. *Missouri Hist. Rev. 1975 69(3): 282-298.* Republican victories in 1894 have been attributed to the depression of 1893, the inept response to it by Grover Cleveland, and the conservative (Bourbon) wing of the Democratic Party. The Bourbons have been regarded as businessmen, conservative in outlook, dedicated to laissez faire, and at odds with the rural wing of their party. This study of Governor David R. Francis and the Missouri Bourbons shows that they were consistently moderate and conciliatory toward the rural wing. However, they found it impossible to maintain the rural-urban alliance in the face of the farmers' desire to push the silver issue. Based on primary and secondary sources; illus., 44 notes.   W. F. Zornow

258. Reichard, Maximilian. URBAN POLITICS IN JACKSONIAN ST. LOUIS: TRADITIONAL VALUES IN CHANGE AND CONFLICT. *Missouri Hist. Rev. 1976 70(3): 259-271.* A local political crisis in 1833 ended traditional politics in St. Louis. Dr. Samuel Merry was denied the office of mayor by the aldermen because he held a federal job. The controversy which followed involved the right of the council to challenge the executive, the right of the people to elect the mayor, and whether the mayor was an officer of the state or of his community. The controversy also pitted Whigs against Democrats and the northside against downtown St. Louis. By 1838 the Democrats were well on their way toward breaking traditional political patterns by securing legislation that extended the suffrage and made more city offices elective. Primary and secondary sources; illus., 29 notes.   W. F. Zornow

259. Ryerson, R. A. POLITICAL MOBILIZATION AND THE AMERICAN REVOLUTION: THE RESISTANCE MOVEMENT IN PHILADELPHIA, 1765 TO 1776. *William and Mary Q. 1974 31(4): 565-588.* Calls for de-emphasis of ideological origins of the Revolution and more study of the translation of beliefs and anxieties into revolutionary action. Deals with one aspect of the mobilization of popular sentiment, leadership recruitment, attempting to identify patterns and impact. Examines the personnel who sat on the Philadelphia Resistance Committee, their persistence and continuity, age, wealth, occupation, ethnic origins, place of birth, and religion. Because of a new and more broadly-based elite, the resistance movement succeeded. Based on the author's unpublished Ph.D. dissertation, newspapers, and secondary sources; 2 tables, 3 figs., 42 notes.   H. M. Ward

260. Schutz, John A. THOSE WHO BECAME TORIES: TOWN LOYALTY AND REVOLUTION IN NEW ENGLAND. *New England Hist. and Genealogical Register 1975 129: 94-105.* The American Revolution had few overt effects on rural New England town life and government. Before the 1770's rural New England had had little contact with provincial government officials in Boston or the aristocracy of Salem and Newburyport, a situation that did not change as the war progressed. Town officials took the new loyalty oath as a matter of course, and the minority who were hesitant resigned office and were kept under watch but not unduly terrorized. Rural New England treated its few Tories as a local problem to be solved by the individual towns. Based on archival and published sources; 25 notes.   S. L. Patterson

261. Shepard, E. Lee. COURTS IN CONFLICT: TOWN-COUNTY RELATIONS IN POST-REVOLUTIONARY VIRGINIA. *Virginia Mag. of Hist. and Biog. 1977 85(2): 184-199.* Historians of Virginia's unique system of political and administrative independence of cities from counties trace its origin to the 19th century. Such an interpretation ignores the impact of the post-Revolutionary period when conflicts between urban and county officials led the legislature to increase the powers of city courts. As a result, the separation of towns and counties occurred by 1800. Based on legislative petitions in the Virginia State Library, published official records, and secondary sources; 51 notes.   R. F. Oaks

262. Stone, Clarence N. URBAN CONFLICT MANAGEMENT: OLD, NEW, AND EMERGENT. *World Affairs 1977 140(1): 78-89.* Reviews the patterns of conflict management from the preindustrial town where dissent was controlled by social coercion and consensus to the postindustrial metropolis where conflict resolution increasingly is being managed by scientific specialists and administrative technocrats.

263. Wright, Langdon G. LOCAL GOVERNMENT AND CENTRAL AUTHORITY IN NEW NETHERLAND. *New-York Hist. Soc. Q. 1973 57(1): 6-29.* A study of local government is the basis for comparison of popular participation and autonomy in Dutch and English colonial towns. Town patents were not identical, but all contained strict regulations concerning landowning and local government. The governor and council dominated, but even the autocratic Peter Stuyvesant gave the towns some freedom. Local government in New Netherland is best explained in terms of the "undefined and unstable balance" between the governor and local units. Based on colonial records; 2 illus., 45 notes.   C. L. Grant

The Distribution of Power

264. Daniels, Bruce C. DEMOCRACY AND OLIGARCHY IN CONNECTICUT TOWNS: GENERAL ASSEMBLY OFFICEHOLDING, 1701-1790. *Social Sci. Q. 1975 56(3): 460-476.* Examines 18th-century American society and politics by analyzing the elections of deputies from towns to the Connecticut General Assembly. Concludes that many variables such as location, age, and size of the towns affected their office holding patterns and that the patterns were sensitive to external events occurring in society such as war or political controversy.   J

265. Daniels, Bruce C. FAMILY DYNASTIES IN CONNECTICUT'S LARGEST TOWNS, 1700-1760. *Can. J. of Hist. 1973 8(2): 99-110.* Historiographical examination of theses on the nature of colonial American politics based on an analysis of office-holding patterns in three of the four leading towns of Connecticut, (Norwich, Hartford, and Fairfield, with New Haven excluded). Concludes that the same families dominated politics in these towns throughout the 18th century up to the American Revolution. Based on printed and MS. sources; 2 tables, 23 notes.   J. A. Casada

266. Daniels, Bruce C. LARGE TOWN OFFICEHOLDING IN EIGHTEENTH-CENTURY CONNECTICUT: THE GROWTH OF OLIGARCHY. *J. of Am. Studies [Great Britain] 1975 9(1): 1-12.* Analyzes the tenure of officials in several Connecticut towns between 1700 and 1780. Municipal offices fell into the hands of an increasingly smaller coterie of men from among Connecticut's wealthy elite. The oligarchs tightened their grip on municipal offices after 1760 and seemed best suited to deal with the "emergencies" of the Revolutionary era. Secondary sources; 8 tables and graphs, 13 notes.   H. T. Lovin

267. Eisinger, Peter K. ETHNIC POLITICAL TRANSITION IN BOSTON, 1884-1933: SOME LESSONS FOR CONTEMPORARY CITIES. *Pol. Sci. Q. 1978 93(2): 217-239.* Defines and describes (as an example for today's Detroit, Atlanta, Newark, and New Orleans) how Boston Yankees were forced into a political minority due to the consolidation of Irish political power.

268. Garrard, John A. THE HISTORY OF LOCAL POLITICAL POWER: SOME SUGGESTIONS FOR ANALYSIS. *Pol. Studies [Great Britain] 1977 25(2): 252-269.* Studies local politics by comparing the author's own work on Salford, England, since 1830 with the study of New Haven by Robert A. Dahl *Who Governs?* (New Haven: Yale U. Pr., 1961). Generalizations about the location of power in the past need to go beyond analysis of the background of office holders and the identifications of socioeconomic elites. The author's work on Salford suggests a framework for the comparative study of the political context within which the political leadership of 19th century cities operated. Graph, 36 notes.
R. Howell

269. Marger, Martin. ETHNIC SUCCESSION IN DETROIT POLITICS, 1900-1950. *Polity 1979 11(3): 343-361.* In tracing the changing ethnic patterns in the composition of the highest elective offices in Detroit from 1900 to 1950, the author distinguished three eras in the ethnic makeup of the city's political elite directly related to shifts in the economic and industrial structure. The relative ethnic balance during the first two decades of the century was displaced by Anglo-Saxon domination after the automotive industrialists, Detroit's new economic elite, had succeeded in instituting an electoral reform. The alliance of the Democratic Party with the United Automobile Workers restored the predominance of the non-Anglo-Saxon ethnics in the 1930's.
J

270. Pessen, Edward. WHO HAS POWER IN THE DEMOCRATIC CAPITALISTIC COMMUNITY? REFLECTIONS ON ANTEBELLUM NEW YORK CITY. *New York Hist. 1977 58(2): 129-155.* The trend toward universal manhood suffrage in antebellum New York City did not result in the achievement of political power by ordinary citizens. Substantial evidence suggests that power of every sort was exercised by the city's wealthiest men and that the enfranchised ordinary men were powerless. Several fields of research are needed to fill gaps in existing knowledge of the power imbalance in antebellum New York City. 3 illus., 50 notes.
R. N. Lokken

271. Ridgway, Whitman H. COMMUNITY LEADERSHIP: BALTIMORE DURING THE FIRST AND SECOND PARTY SYSTEMS. *Maryland Hist. Mag. 1976 71(3): 334-348.* Borrowing concepts of strategic elites (positional and traditional) versus decisional elites from modern community power studies, focuses on the changing power structure of Baltimore from the conservative merchant oligarchy of the postrevolutionary era down to 1806, to the younger professional-skilled artisan polyarchy of the Jacksonian era, 1827-36. Studies the decisionmakers in the salient local concerns of internal improvements and the creation of a water company in the first era, and internal improvements and political reform in the second. "The most important difference . . . was the opportunity for men without ties to the old elite to rise to power during the second party period." While still landed, the new elite was younger, held fewer slaves, and was increasingly drawn from nonmerchant ranks. Primary and secondary works; 4 tables, 36 notes.
G. J. Bobango

272. Snell, Ronald K. FREEMANSHIP, OFFICEHOLDING, AND THE TOWN FRANCHISE IN SEVENTEENTH-CENTURY SPRINGFIELD, MASSACHUSETTS. *New England Hist. and Geneal. Register 1979 133(July): 163-179.* Springfield was selected for this study because of the completeness and accuracy of its records. During most of the 17th century, affairs of the community were controlled by a few men of property and influence. The actual decline in numbers of freemen, who could vote and hold office, made it necessary to waive the rules frequently. Toward the end of the century, at the insistence of those desiring greater political rights, requirements for freemanship were relaxed. 13 tables, 48 notes.
J

273. Unsigned. THE FRANCHISE IN SEVENTEENTH-CENTURY MASSACHUSETTS. *William and Mary Q. 1977 34(3): 446-458.*

Ginsberg, Arlin J. IPSWICH, *pp. 446-452.* Compares the arguments and interpretations of sources by Thomas Franklin Waters and B. Katherine Brown in their treatment of the franchise in 17th-century Ipswich. Evaluates the several town lists used by these authors and notes the problems of duplication, nonresidency, and other discrepancies. Waters held that 28.4% adult males could vote, and Brown posited that 77.6% could. Ginsberg's analysis finds Waters' estimate nearly correct. Offers advice on quantitative investigation. 20 notes.

Wall, Robert E. DEDHAM AND CAMBRIDGE, *pp. 453-458.* Takes issue with B. Katherine Brown's criticism of his use of sources in his work on suffrage in Dedham and Cambridge. Objects to the accusation that he relied too heavily on vital statistics and not enough upon tax records. Lists 15 residents of Dedham who were not on tax lists and prints the names of 72 Cambridge residents who did not sign a petition of 1664. Defends his thesis that the franchise declined during 1647-66.
H. M. Ward

274. Warden, G. B. OFFICEHOLDING AND OFFICIALS IN BOSTON, 1692-1775. *New England Hist. and Geneal. Register 1977 131(Oct): 267-290.* Compares numerous social and economic characteristics of almost equal numbers of officials appointed by the governor and those elected to public office. Although differences are found, a majority of both groups shared characteristics which set them apart from the general population. There was no homogeneity within officialdom, however, and thus no interest to dominate the two political systems. Difficulties in perpetuating social or financial institutions created potentially revolutionary tensions.
S. Wheeler

275. Watts, Eugene J. PROPERTY AND POLITICS IN ATLANTA, 1865-1903. *J. of Urban Hist. 1977 3(3): 295-322.* Examines the property holdings of candidates for local office in Atlanta during 1865-1903. Political candidates had more wealth than the average citizen. Wealthier candidates enjoyed better electoral success than poorer candidates. Also favoring electoral success was long-term city residence, Southern birth, and youth. 8 tables, 23 notes.
T. W. Smith

276. Willingham, William F. DEFERENCE DEMOCRACY AND TOWN GOVERNMENT IN WINDHAM, CONNECTICUT, 1755 TO 1786. *William and Mary Q. 1973 30(3): 401-422.* Explores the relationship between political participation and elite direction of the political system. A small group dominated officeholding, and plural officeholding existed. Economic standing had little influence. Because of a communal consensus, voters tended to select their betters. Analyzes the town meeting. Compares Windham with other New England towns. Based on county court and other local records; 5 tables, 36 notes.
H. M. Ward

Parties, Elections, and Politicians

277. Alvarez, David J. and True, Edmond J. CRITICAL ELECTIONS AND PARTISAN REALIGNMENT: AN URBAN TEST-CASE. *Polity 1973 5(4): 563-576.* Ward-by-ward voting behavior in Hartford, Connecticut, during 1896-1940 indicates that support for the Democrats came from established middle-class, Protestant sectors of society, rather than from realignment of pro-Democratic Party ethnic groups in 1928.

278. Anderson, Elaine. WILLIAM KRAUS AND THE JEWISH COMMUNITY. *Northwest Ohio Q. 1977 49(4): 127-162.* Chronicles the demise of William Kraus, a leading member of the Jewish community in Toledo, Ohio, during 1869-76. A few unpopular acts during his administration as the city's mayor, compounded by the closing of his bank, and shady real estate dealings, led to his exile in Canada.

279. Bassett, Michael. MUNICIPAL REFORM AND THE SOCIALIST PARTY, 1910-1914. *Australian J. of Pol. and Hist. [Australia] 1973 19(2): 179-187.* Examines the mayoralty victories of Socialist Party candidates in the United States in 1910 and 1911 (e.g., Emil Seidel in Milwaukee, Lewis Duncan in Butte, George Lunn in Schenectady, Job Harriman in Los Angeles), and suggests that in each case local corruption caused voters to desert the main parties. In spite of urban reforms by the

Socialist mayors, the party could not maintain the impetus, and by 1913 most of the Socialists had been defeated. Documented from newspapers.

W. D. McIntyre

280. Baumann, Roland M. JOHN SWANWICK: SPOKESMAN FOR "MERCHANT-REPUBLICANISM" IN PHILADELPHIA, 1790-1798. *Pennsylvania Mag. of Hist. and Biog. 1973 97(2): 131-182.* Detailed biographical sketch of Democratic-Republican John Swanwick (1759-98) reveals that Philadelphia Republicans were supported by new entrepreneurial groups ("merchant-Republicans") as well as by persons with little or no property. These "merchant-Republicans" clashed with their Federalist counterparts over policy issues, "demanding greater protection of trade from foreign shippers, freer banking facilities, cheaper marine insurance, and a foreign policy that was immune from foreign domination." As spokesman at the national level for these "merchant-Republicans," Swanwick often was at odds with Jefferson on foreign and domestic issues. Swanwick's disagreements with Jefferson's policies sometimes reshaped Jefferson's thinking and are significant for revealing the strands of Democratic-Republicanism in the early National Period. Based on primary and secondary sources; 238 notes. E. W. Carp

281. Boxerman, Burton A. LOUIS PATRICK ALOE. *Missouri Hist. Soc. Bull. 1974 31(1): 41-54.* Louis Patrick Aloe (1867-1929), a St. Louis businessman, served the city of St. Louis in many public capacities, always seeking to make St. Louis a "progressive, dynamic" city second to none in the United States. In 1925, Aloe ran for mayor but lost the election. The embittered Aloe blamed his defeat upon anti-Semitism in the city. Based on newspaper sources; 43 notes. H. T. Lovin

282. Chalmers, Leonard. THE CRUCIAL TEST OF LA GUARDIA'S FIRST HUNDRED DAYS: THE EMERGENCY ECONOMY BILL. *New-York Hist. Soc. Q. 1973 57(3): 237-253.* The Emergency Economy Bill served as a test for Mayor Fiorello La Guardia (1882-1947) when he took office in January 1934. New York City was on the verge of bankruptcy, with 1,000,000 people on some form of welfare. The measure called for stringent economy because no federal aid would be forthcoming until the budget was balanced. When the bill was passed by the state legislature, it was a personal triumph for the mayor and attested to his great political skill. Based on newspapers and secondary sources; 6 illus., 16 notes. C. L. Grant

283. Chalmers, Leonard. FIORELLO LA GUARDIA, PATER-FAMILIAS AT CITY HALL: AN APPRAISAL. *New York Hist. 1975 56(2): 211-225.* Analyzes Fiorello La Guardia's term as mayor of New York during 1934-45, and his effect on New York City's government. Illus., 24 notes. R. N. Lokken

284. Chern, Kenneth S. THE POLITICS OF PATRIOTISM: WAR, ETHNICITY, AND THE NEW YORK MAYORAL CAMPAIGN, 1917. *New-York Hist. Soc. Q. 1979 63(4): 290-313.* The mayoral election in New York City in 1917 reflected the tensions, ethnic-aroused passions, and uncertainties in American life as the nation geared for war. The incumbent, John Purroy Mitchell, hoped for reelection on a Fusion ticket; instead he was opposed by a Tammany Democrat, a Republican, and a Socialist. In the bitter campaign which followed, Mitchell stressed patriotism and the cause of the Allies and thus alienated a large segment of the city's voting population, heavily weighted with second generation Irish and Germans. The result was a plurality for Tammany-backed John F. Hylan; Mitchell ran a poor second, barely beating the Socialist candidate, Morris Hillquit. Hylan's victory seemed to indicate that the American voter, in time of high tension or stress, tended to turn to a conservative leader who promised political security. It would happen again in 1952 on the national level. 7 illus., 40 notes.

C. L. Grant

285. Colley, Charles C. CARL T. HAYDEN—PHOENICIAN. *J. of Arizona Hist. 1977 18(3): 247-257.* Carl T. Hayden (1877-1972) was "one of the great forces in the development of the last untamed region of the American West." His active involvement in the Phoenix area began with his election to county sheriff in 1907 and continued through a 56-year congressional career. His primary concerns were land development, urban expansion, and environmental quality. Illus., 15 notes.

D. L. Smith

286. Daniels, Roger. DEPRESSION MAYOR. *Rev. in Am. Hist. 1976 4(1): 110-114.* Review article prompted by Sidney Fine's *Frank Murphy: The Detroit Years* (Ann Arbor: U. of Illinois Pr., 1975) which discusses Murphy's mayoral term in Detroit, 1930-33, emphasizing economic conditions in the city (as representative of many urban areas) and attempts to cope with the psychological effects of the depression.

287. deKay, Drake. THE ADMINISTRATION OF PETER STUYVESANT. *Halve Maen 1978 53(4): 1-2, 15-16; 54(1): 6-7, 11, (2): 7-9.* Continued from a previous article. Part IV. Discusses Peter Stuyvesant, the last governor of New Netherland, during 1650-51. Part V. Discusses his marriage in 1645 to Judith Bayard, violence at Fort Orange, and the growth, government, and management of New Netherland; covers 1645-53. Part VI. Chronicles events in the formation of municipal government in New Amsterdam during Peter Stuyvesant's administration, highlighting civic leaders and related events in Stuyvesant's personal life; covers 1643-54.

288. Falzone, Vincent J. TERENCE V. POWDERLY: POLITICIAN AND PROGRESSIVE MAYOR OF SCRANTON, 1878-1884. *Pennsylvania Hist. 1974 41(3): 289-309.* Terence V. Powderly served as mayor of Scranton during 1878-84. First elected as a Greenbacker, he found it necessary to run as a Democrat in 1882. Though an able mayor, he faced a variety of political problems, and in 1884 lost the fight for renomination to his long-time foe Frank A. Beamish. Powderly's political difficulties account in part for his belief that the Knights of Labor should avoid partisan political activity. Based on Powderly Papers, Scranton municipal records, and newspapers; illus., 78 notes. D. C. Swift

289. Filler, Louis. SOCIALISM LIVING AND DEAD. *J. of Urban Hist. 1978 5(1): 119-124.* Review article prompted by Bruce M. Stave, ed., *Socialism and the Cities,* a series of informative essays with a curiously missing common theme. Progressivism is generally omitted from the discussions. Telling the story of socialism or the cities without this element is like painting a landscape without a background.

T. W. Smith

290. Gaffield, Chad. BIG BUSINESS, THE WORKING-CLASS, AND SOCIALISM IN SCHENECTADY, 1911-1916. *Labor Hist. 1978 19(3): 350-372.* Analyzes the record of George Lunn, Socialist mayor of Schenectady, New York, and the voting patterns in the city. Socialism had its greatest strength in working-class wards, and business leaders were not unduly upset by the party victory. The demise of the Socialist Party may be more attributable to a hostile judicial system than to other factors. Based on city directories, census reports, and newspapers; 7 tables, 43 notes. L. L. Athey

291. Grothaus, Larry. KANSAS CITY BLACKS, HARRY TRUMAN AND THE PENDERGAST MACHINE. *Missouri Hist. Rev. 1974 69(1): 65-82.* Many writers have called Harry S. Truman a centrist, a moderate, and a man who failed to appreciate or take action on racial matters until forced to do so by political pressure. During 1922-34, when Thomas Pendergast's machine controlled Kansas City politics, both Truman and Negroes in the city learned to use the machine to advance their interests. Both Truman and the machine were not always correct in dealing with blacks, but they had better records than the city's reform groups. Truman's record as presiding judge of Jackson County and as state director of reemployment was good enough to win 88% of the black vote when he ran for the Senate in 1934. Based on newspapers, books, articles, and papers in the Harry S. Truman Library, the Western Historical Manuscripts Collection, University of Missouri-Columbia, and the Missouri Historical Society, St. Louis; Illus., 5 photos, 87 notes.

W. F. Zornow

292. Hoelscher, Robert J. THADDEUS STEVENS AS A LANCASTER POLITICIAN, 1842-1868. *J. of the Lancaster County Hist. Soc. 1974 78(4): 157-213.* Chronicles Thaddeus Stevens' political career in Lancaster, Pennsylvania, 1842-68, concentrating on his impact on local politics and his relations with constituents and political parties; touches on his community standing, personal relationships, activities as a philanthropist, and career in law.

293. Horowitz, Murray M. "THE MOST QUIET ELECTION": BEN BUTLER COMES TO NEW YORK. *Lincoln Herald 1973 75(4):*

148-151. November 8, 1864 was a crucial election day. Major General Benjamin Franklin Butler was dispatched to New York City to curb fraud at the polls in the Democrat stronghold. Butler insured order in the city with his troops so the election would be neither disrupted nor stolen. He accomplished his mission and the Empire State was safeguarded for President Abraham Lincoln. Based on Butler's *Private and Official Correspondence* and the Stanton papers in the Library of Congress; 6 notes.

A. C. Aimone

294. Johnson, Donald D. JOSEPH JAMES FERN, HONOLULU'S FIRST MAYOR. *Hawaiian J. of Hist. 1975 9: 74-100.* On 4 January 1909 Joseph J. Fern became the first mayor of the City and County of Honolulu. He held this office until his death in 1920. The years of his mayoralty were the formative years for municpal government in Hawaii. Fern, a native Hawaiian, often showed favoritism toward other native Hawaiians.

R. Alvis

295. McBride, Robert M. "NORTHERN, MILITARY, CORRUPT, AND TRANSITORY," AUGUSTUS E. ALDEN, NASHVILLE'S CARPETBAGGER MAYOR. *Tennessee Hist. Q. 1978 37(1): 63-67.* Augustus E. Alden (1837-86), a prototype of "carpetbaggers," was handpicked by Governor William G. Brownlow in 1867 in order to ensure his control of Nashville. A former "claims" agent who had only recently arrived in Nashville, Alden, in office 1867-69, began the Negro public schools and increased welfare programs. Nevertheless, he was hated by the citizenry and was ousted from office by a court injunction in 1869. Primary and secondary sources; 17 notes.

M. B. Lucas

296. Morse, W. Eugene. "JUDGE" WILLIAM HEMINGWAY, 1869-1937. *J. of Mississippi Hist. 1974 36(4): 338-351.* Sketches the legal and political career of Mississippian William Hemingway (1869-1937). Mayor (1901-05) and City Attorney (1904-10, 1912-21) of Jackson, Hemingway revised the city's municipal ordinances three times and edited the 1917 revised legal code for the state of Mississippi. Professor of law at the University of Mississippi beginning in 1921, he played a prominent role in developing football and other athletic programs there and in the Southeastern Conference athletics. Based on material in the Mississippi Department of Archives and History. Illus., 14 notes.

J. W. Hillje

297. Nord, David Paul. MINNEAPOLIS AND THE PRAGMATIC SOCIALISM OF THOMAS VAN LEAR. *Minnesota Hist. 1976 45(1): 2-10.* Thomas Van Lear's brand of socialism was flexible, reflecting his union background. He became mayor of Minneapolis in 1916 due to Mayor Nye's action against striking teamsters, franchise renewal, and the support for Wilson in the presidential contest. However, loyalty and civil rights issues during the Great War cost the local Socialist Party its standing and Van Lear his power base. Based on newspaper accounts and government documents. 4 illus., 37 notes.

S. S. Sprague

298. Pratt, William C. WOMEN AND AMERICAN SOCIALISM: THE READING EXPERIENCE. *Pennsylvania Mag. of Hist. and Biog. 1975 99(1): 72-91.* Reviews the role of women in building the Socialist Party in Reading, Pennsylvania. The party enjoyed considerable local electoral success during 1927-36, and much of this success depended on the women's vote. Women played a larger role in Socialist Party affairs than was the case with either of the majority parties, but this role was subordinate and supportive, as the Party was neither willing nor able to break through the prevailing philosophy of male dominance. 61 notes.

V. L. Human

299. Rabinowitz, Howard N. FROM RECONSTRUCTION TO REDEMPTION ON THE URBAN SOUTH. *J. of Urban Hist. 1976 2(2): 169-194.* Discusses the rise, operation, and fall of Republican Party government in Southern cities during 1865-75. Primary and secondary sources; 80 notes.

T. W. Smith

300. Rischin, Moses. SUNNY JIM ROLPH: THE FIRST "MAYOR" OF ALL THE PEOPLE. *California Hist. Q. 1974 53(2): 165-172.* James Rolph, Jr. (1869-1934), five-term mayor of San Francisco, was financially secure, politically honest, and a consummate politician. His fortune made in shipping and banking, Rolph was elected mayor in 1912. He loved his city and worked hard to modernize it. During his tenure the Panama Pacific Exposition was held, a civic center complex

was constructed, population grew, and schools, parks, and playgrounds were built. As the city's prime booster, Rolph supported the union movement, attended Catholic and Jewish services as well as Protestant, and involved himself in all phases of civic activity. He proclaimed himself "mayor of all the people" and made past polarizations a dim memory. The Rolph dynasty gave San Francisco an era of good feeling and metropolitan importance. Photos.

A. Hoffman

301. Saveth, Edward N. THE MOSES MODEL. *Rev. in Am. Hist. 1976 4(3): 451-457.* Review article prompted by Robert A. Caro's *The Power Broker: Robert Moses and the Fall of New York* (New York: Alfred A. Knopf, 1974); discusses Moses's brand of state government administration, his involvement with politics, and specifically, the Mugwumps, 1920's-40's.

302. Scharnau, Ralph William THOMAS J. MORGAN AND THE UNITED LABOR PARTY OF CHICAGO. *J. of the Illinois State Hist. Soc. 1973 66(1): 41-61.* In the 1880's the press depicted industrial strikers as lawless radicals and "reds." The Illinois General Assembly was particularly antilabor. Thomas J. Morgan, a socialist labor leader, favored political action to curb unfavorable political pressure. His United Labor Party worked as a labor coalition with local trade unions and Knights of Labor assemblies nationally. He helped write the 1886 national platform of the new party and made nightly speeches to workers to support the party ticket. Several state Labor Party legislature victories in Democratic districts in 1886 resulted in Democratic patronage lures to infiltrate Morgan's party. Women's suffrage, the eight-hour day for city employees, better school accommodations, and an equitable taxation system were popular party platforms. Morgan continued to spread socialist ideas through the early 1890's by his organizing genius, political interests, and speaking abilities. Based on the Morgan collection at the University of Illinois and on newspapers; 5 illus., 68 notes.

A. C. Aimone

303. Shover, John L. THE EMERGENCE OF A TWO-PARTY SYSTEM IN REPUBLICAN PHILADELPHIA, 1924-1936. *J. of Am. Hist. 1974 60(4): 985-1002.* Samuel Lubell has popularized the thesis that Al Smith's ethnic appeal in the 1928 election foreshadowed the urban, ethnic, "New Deal coalition" that Franklin D. Roosevelt put together so effectively after 1932. The evidence for Philadelphia voting patterns demonstrates that 1928 was *not* a critical election. Some major ethnic groups did vote Democratic in that year, but Jews, blacks, and Germans were not a part of the coalition till much later, and the Irish and Italian vote, heavily Democratic for Smith in 1928, did not persist in 1930 or even 1932. Furthermore, there was no great surge of voter protest against the Depression in 1932. Casts doubt upon the concept of a "critical election," emphasizing rather the importance of a critical, fluctuating period when new voter patterns start to crystallize. 4 tables, 43 notes.

K. B. West

304. Sullivan, Susan. JAMES MC COY: LAWMAN AND LEGISLATOR. *J. of San Diego Hist. 1977 23(4): 43-57.* Discusses James McCoy's political participation in San Diego, and the economic development of the area; includes his careers as county recorder, sheriff, and politico, 1850-95.

305. Tamplain, Pamela. PHILIP CROSTHWAITE: SAN DIEGO PIONEER AND PUBLIC SERVANT. *J. of San Diego Hist. 1975 21(3): 43-49.* Describes the life of Philip Crosthwaite (1825-1903), concentrating on 1845-74 when Crosthwaite held public office in San Diego.

S

306. Wyman, Roger E. AGRARIAN OR WORKING-CLASS RADICALISM? THE ELECTORAL BASIS OF POPULISM IN WISCONSIN. *Pol. Sci. Q. 1974-75 89(4): 825-848.* Populism in Wisconsin arose out of socialist-oriented labor radicalism rather than from agricultural distress. Urban workers, not agrarians, provided the largest component of Populist supporters. The findings thus challenge the commonly held belief that Wisconsin had a long tradition of agrarian radicalism in the late 19th century.

J

Inter-Governmental Relations

307. Abenheim, Daniel. NEVER A SHOT FIRED IN ANGER: THE COASTAL DEFENSES OF SAN FRANCISCO. *Military Collector & Hist. 1976 28(3): 100-110.* Examines the naval defenses in the San Francisco Bay area, 1776-1940's, concentrating on the period 1840's-90's; discusses fortresses of the American, Mexican, and Spanish governments and various military leaders who served in the Bay area.

308. Arnold, Joseph L. SUBURBAN GROWTH AND MUNICIPAL ANNEXATION IN BALTIMORE, 1745-1918. *Maryland Hist. Mag. 1978 73(2): 109-128.* Illustrates the rural-urban conflict as a central theme of American history by focusing on Baltimore City's annexations since the 18th century and the politics of intense belligerency which these generated in the surrounding counties for a century and a half. Baltimore County's political leaders were powerful in state politics and fought city fathers constantly seeking to expand the municipal tax base and political impact through population growth. Annexation proposals became central issues in statewide elections, and as late as 1968 during the debates on the new state constitution, Baltimore and Anne Arundel Counties helped defeat the new charter decisively by fighting its "regional government" features. Suburban sprawl today, however, has caused the "tool of annexation as a practical administrative device" to have been lost. Local archives, state legislative debates, secondary sources; 2 maps, 55 notes.
G. J. Bobango

309. Bateman, Herman E. ALBERT B. CUMMINS AND THE DAVENPORT "RIOTS" OF 1907. *Arizona and the West 1976 18(2): 111-124.* Progressive Republican Governor Albert B. Cummins of Iowa challenged a veteran incumbent US Senator. Most of the state was dry, but the river counties along the Mississippi were wet. The river counties were pro-Cummins. In the summer of 1907 a series of "riots" erupted in Davenport, a river town, over local enforcement of liquor regulations. As governor, Cummins was expected to act against the lawbreaking wets. He did, and consequently lost the river counties and was defeated in the primaries of 1908. The incumbent died before the election; the governor and the progressives pushed legislation through for a special senatorial primary election; and Cummins won the senate seat he was restricted from in the regular primaries. 2 illus., 25 notes. D. L. Smith

310. Burran, James A. THE WPA IN NASHVILLE, 1935-1943. *Tennessee Hist. Q. 1974 34(3): 293-306.* With the creation of the Works Progress Administration in Tennessee in 1935 Colonel Harry S. Berry was named administrator. First priority was given to construction, but service projects received considerable support. With the steady growth of projects, however, charges of misuse of money and power grew. Rumors of boondoggling led to a 1939 investigation which revealed numerous irregularities. Nevertheless, the WPA in Nashville no doubt did the best that might have been expected given the bureaucracy. Primary and secondary sources; 35 notes. M. B. Lucas

311. Chaput, Donald. LOS ANGELES AND THE DEPARTMENT OF ARIZONA. *Southern California Q. 1975 57(1): 17-26.* When the Department of War divided the Division of the Pacific into several military departments in 1870, the town of Prescott was designated as headquarters for the Department of Arizona, encompassing Arizona Territory, most of southern California, and, after 1885, New Mexico Territory. By 1886 Prescott had been bypassed by the railroads, and in January 1887 Los Angeles, because of its key rail connections, became headquarters for the Department of Arizona. Although few soldiers were stationed in California, Los Angeles merchants profited from the sale of supplies. In 1893 army reorganization abolished the Department of Arizona, created the Department of Colorado, and moved the headquarters to Denver. Los Angeles newspapers and the chamber of commerce protested the change, but the protests were to no avail. Primary and secondary sources; 35 notes. A. Hoffman

312. Coleman, Alan. THE CHARLESTON BOOTLEGGING CONTROVERSY, 1915-1918. *South Carolina Hist. Mag. 1974 75(2): 77-94.* The Dispensary Act made the liquor trade a state monopoly in South Carolina. For political and financial reasons it was not enforced. Richard Irvine Manning, governor, 1915-18, tried to enforce the act. His sustained and spirited clash with the mayor of Charleston left bootlegging unimpaired. 80 notes. D. L. Smith

313. Dorsett, Lyle W. FRANK HAGUE, FRANKLIN ROOSEVELT AND THE POLITICS OF THE NEW DEAL. *New Jersey Hist. 1976 94(1): 23-35.* Frank Hague was not pro-Roosevelt at the 1932 convention, but he enthusiastically supported him in the general election and helped deliver New Jersey's electoral votes to the Democratic ticket. Hague's political power was again demonstrated in his control of the New Deal's WPA and FERA programs in New Jersey. Abuses of the programs soon became common and the President's personal distaste for the Jersey City mayor grew. Roosevelt supported Charles Edison for governor in 1940, hoping to circumvent Hague with a friend in Trenton. As time passed it became evident that Hague could be embarrassed but not destroyed. Based on primary and secondary sources; 4 illus., 27 notes.
E. R. McKinstry

314. DuVall, Lucille Clark. WILLIAM KETTNER: SAN DIEGO'S DYNAMIC CONGRESSMAN. *J. of San Diego Hist. 1979 25(3): 191-207.* William Kettner (1864-1930) lived in San Diego after 1907, served in the House of Representatives from 1913 to 1921, and was responsible for bringing the US Navy to the city, with enormous financial benefits for San Diego.

315. Ebner, Michael H. "WINNING... IT'S THE ONLY THING": FDR VERSUS BOSTON. *Rev. in Am. Hist. 1978 6(1): 120-125.* Review article prompted by Charles H. Trout's *Boston, the Great Depression, and the New Deal* (New York: Oxford U. Pr., 1977).

316. Gordon, Martin K. CONGRESS AND THE DISTRICT OF COLUMBIA: THE MILITARY IMPACT ON FEDERAL CONTROL. *Capitol Studies 1978 6(2): 39-53.* Discusses the desire of Congress to retain control of the District of Columbia Militia for self-protection as one reason for its refusal since 1800 to grant the District full home rule.

317. Jones, Gene Delon. THE ORIGIN OF THE ALLIANCE BETWEEN THE NEW DEAL AND THE CHICAGO MACHINE. *J. of the Illinois State Hist. Soc. 1974 67(3): 253-274.* In 1932, the Chicago political machine had tried to shout down Franklin D. Roosevelt's nomination, but by 1940, Mayor Edward J. Kelly could refer to him as "our beloved President." The "politics of relief" had allied Roosevelt with the bosses, to the dismay of reformers. Kelly's overwhelming mayoral victory in 1935 put him in excellent position to demand a large share of New Deal relief funds for Chicago. It also convinced Roosevelt that machine support was necessary to carry Illinois in 1936. Primary and secondary sources; 2 illus., 3 photos, 76 notes. L. Woolfe

318. Kurtz, Michael J. EMANCIPATION IN THE FEDERAL CITY. *Civil War Hist. 1978 24(3): 250-267.* Senator Henry Wilson's District Emancipation Act of April 1862 provided opportunity to Abraham Lincoln in compensation and colonization provisions; problems in immediate emancipation. These provisions and even Congressional authority itself were hotly debated, but emancipation overrode all objection. Colonization and compensation principles were recognized, giving the act the broadest support in spite of local opposition. Lincoln appointed the three-man board administering the act in claims and monetary decisions. The board's work in trying circumstances won approval. It showed that immediate emancipation could work and bring a quiet social revolution nationwide. Primary and secondary sources; 57 notes.
R. E. Stack

319. Lotchin, Roger W. THE CITY AND THE SWORD: SAN FRANCISCO AND THE RISE OF THE METROPOLITAN-MILITARY COMPLEX, 1919-1941. *J. of Am. Hist. 1979 65(4): 996-1020.* Analyzes the relationship between militarization and urbanization in the San Francisco Bay area between the world wars. The coalition of local, military, and business interests became entwined over such issues as city planning, politics, employment, and metropolitan decentralization. The Navy's and the city's need for growth produced mutual dependence and cooperation. Federal policy encouraged a process of urban decentralization which the Bay Area willingly accepted. By 1941 the Navy alone had invested $1 billion in the San Francisco area. 2 maps, 96 notes.
T. P. Linkfield

320. Lowry, Charles B. THE PWA IN TAMPA: A CASE STUDY. *Florida Hist. Q. 1974 52(4): 363-380.* Deals with the efforts of Ernest

Kreher, founder of the Tampa Shipbuilding and Engineering Company, to secure a federal loan to build a dry dock in Tampa. Kreher first sought a loan in September 1932 from the Reconstruction Finance Corporation (RFC). By June 1933, with the RFC concerned only with the banking industry, Kreher shifted his attention to the Public Works Administration. Bureaucratic complications and political considerations produced a delay of more than two years before the loan contract was finally approved. The dry dock was almost completed by April 1937. Based on archival material from the University of Florida, newspapers, and secondary sources; 3 illus., 90 notes.

J. E. Findling

321. Macchiarola, Frank J. THE STATE AND THE CITY. *Pro. of the Acad. of Pol. Sci. 1974 31(3): 104-118.* Examines economic, social, political, and educational relationships between New York State and New York City, 1905-73.

S

322. Morris, Beau. THE POLITICAL ORIGINS OF BARKSDALE AIR FORCE BASE. *North Louisiana Hist. Assoc. J. 1977 8(3): 131-136.* During 1923-28 Shreveport citizens fought hard to convince the US War Department to locate the Third Air Attack Group at their city. The War Department finally approved the proposed Shreveport site, but a special session of the state legislature had to be called to clear certain property matters. Governor Huey Long was willing to accept the legislature's action only if Shreveport's civic leaders supported his free school textbook program, a program which they had publicly denounced. Eventually the governor and the city compromised. Barksdale Air Field was dedicated on 2 February 1933. Secondary sources; 37 notes.

A. N. Garland

323. Nelms, Willie. A DIVIDED CITY: BRISTOL'S BORDER DISPUTES AND THE WATER WORKS WAR OF 1889. *Virginia Cavalcade 1979 28(4): 172-179.* Discusses the dispute of the city of Bristol, divided down the middle of its main street by the Virginia-Tennessee border, over the Water Works War in 1889, the climax of antagonism among citizens of the divided city.

324. Patrick, Robert W. WHEN KANSAS CITY, MO., CAME CLOSE TO BEING A CITY IN KANSAS. *Kansas Hist. 1978 1(4): 266-277.* During 1855-84 the question of making Kansas City, Missouri, part of Kansas became a lively topic of discussion on several occasions. In 1855 the topic may have had a close link to the question of making Kansas a slave state; on later occasions it was often linked to the fact that it was unsound both economically and politically to have what was essentially a single urban unit shared by two states. The idea never got beyond the planning stage. Efforts to find support in alleged alterations of the Kansas and Missouri rivers added only an argument that could not be substantiated. Secondary sources; illus., 29 notes. W. F. Zornow

325. Ring, Daniel F. THE CLEVELAND PUBLIC LIBRARY AND THE WPA: A STUDY IN CREATIVE PARTNERSHIP. *Ohio Hist. 1975 84(3): 158-164.* The desire of the New Deal to substitute work for relief was embodied in several agencies, but it was the Works Progress Administration (WPA) that affected the Cleveland Public Library in two important categories: bibliographical service and fine arts. The Federal Writers' Project produced *The Annals of Cleveland*, the Union Catalogue, and the Historic Records Survey of Cuyahoga County. In the fine arts program, too, the main concern was to provide jobs for people, at the same time creating a cultural heritage for the community. 48 notes.

E. P. Stickney

326. Rouse, Parke, Jr. MOVING DAY AT WILLIAMSBURG. *Early Am. Life 1978 9(2): 14, 16-18, 20.* Chronicles the transfer of government from Williamsburg to Richmond in 1779; Virginians feared a British invasion of Williamsburg because of its proximity to the sea.

327. Ruffin, Thomas F. IT ALMOST BECAME SHREVEPORT, TEXAS. *North Louisiana Hist. Assoc. J. 1974 5(2): 50-55.* During the difficult Reconstruction days of 1873, talk began of the Shreveport area pulling away from Louisiana and joining Texas. This was the partial result of an intense dislike by the people of Shreveport for the governor of Louisiana, William Pitt Kellogg. As it turned out "it was not politics alone that killed the move; it was yellow fever." Politics temporarily subsided as the yellow fever epidemic of 1873 raged unchecked, for "the people cared not whether they lived in Shreveport, Louisiana or Shreveport, Texas. They just wanted to continue living." 28 notes.

A. N. Garland

328. Smith, David R. THE BEAST OF NEW ORLEANS. *Manuscripts 1979 31(1): 11-21.* Relates how New Orleans fell to the federal forces and how Benjamin F. Butler was given command of the city, where he was hated almost from the day he arrived. Butler earned the enmity of the city's women, which is shown in the letters written by them. Although Butler's administration of the city was in some respects enlightened and certainly efficient, he will always be known as Beast Butler in the South.

D. A. Yanchisin

329. Smith, Roland M. THE POLITICS OF PITTSBURGH FLOOD CONTROL, 1936-1960. *Pennsylvania Hist. 1977 44(1): 3-24.* In the 1930's, Pittsburgh's efforts to obtain federal funds for flood control continued; however, the characteristic unified leadership of upper class individuals disintegrated. This earlier pattern of unified elite leadership reemerged in 1943 when the Allegheny Conference on Community Development (ACCD) assumed responsibility for the overall economic development of the area. The Chamber of Commerce, operating as an arm of the ACCD, continued to lead the campaign for additional federal flood control money. There was a continuing relation between efforts to attract private capital for Renaissance Pittsburgh and the flood control program. In 1960, construction began on the Allegheny Reservoir, the largest and last of nine dams. 2 photos, 46 notes. D. C. Swift

330. Strobridge, William. SOLDIERS IN THE STREETS, 1906. *Pacific Hist. 1978 22(1): 3-8.* Analyzes the army's role in the aftermath of the San Francisco earthquake. General Adolphus Greeley commanded the army as it took on more than traditional functions—operating telephone and telegraph offices, running refugee camps, and maintaining sanitation services. Subsequently more formal policies were adopted to govern the army's role in disaster relief. Primary sources; 20 notes.

G. L. Olson

331. Teaford, Jon. CITY VERSUS STATE: THE STRUGGLE FOR LEGAL ASCENDANCY. *Am. J. of Legal Hist. 1973 17(1): 51-65.* Discusses the struggle between city governments and state governments for control of municipal affairs since the late 18th century.

332. Thompson, Neil B. A HALF CENTURY OF CAPITAL CONFLICT: HOW ST. PAUL KEPT THE SEAT OF GOVERNMENT. *Minnesota Hist. 1973 43(7): 238-254.* Congress directed in 1849 the establishment of territorial government in Minnesota with the temporary seat located at St. Paul. Numerous and persistent attempts were made to relocate the territorial and state capital. In the end tradition and increased costs determined that St. Paul would remain the permanent seat of government. 15 illus., 53 notes. D. L. Smith

333. Thurner, Arthur W. THE MAYOR, THE GOVERNOR, AND THE PEOPLE'S COUNCIL: A CHAPTER IN AMERICAN WARTIME DISSENT. *J. of the Illinois State Hist. Soc. 1973 66(2): 124-143.* Pulitzer Prize-winning correspondent Louis Paul Lochner organized the People's Council of America for Democracy and Peace. The council triggered a struggle between Chicago and Springfield (city and state) political forces in 1917 as the war effort was spurred on by the press, the ruling class, patriotic groups, and the government. The First American Conference for Democracy and Terms of Peace, organized by Lochner and other pacifists in New York City in May 1917, developed into the People's Council. A national meeting was scheduled in Chicago because of opposition in other states. Chicago Mayor William Hall ("Big Bill") Thompson countermanded Illinois Governor Frank Orren Lowden's order to lock out the peace delegates. Chicago police, Illinois state militia, and Federal troops were held ready. Whether Mayor Thompson had given aid and comfort to the enemy received national press and government attention. By December 1917 the pacifist movement as a strong force had died. Based on the Louis P. Lochner papers in the State Historical Society of Wisconsin Library and contemporary newspapers; illus., 39 notes.

A. C. Aimone

Machines and Bosses

334. Arnold, Joseph L. THE LAST OF THE GOOD OLD DAYS: POLITICS IN BALTIMORE, 1920-1950. *Maryland Hist. Mag. 1976 71(3): 443-448.* While Progressive-era reforms in Maryland did end classic-style bossism as embodied in the famous Rasin-Gorman machine, still the heirs of this machine continued to monopolize Baltimore city and county politics for 35 years, since "individual leaders and their relationships, not the total organizational structure, determine the continuing strength of machine control." Democrats successfully identified the Republicans with the voters' fear of black control during the 1920's, and both European and rural white immigrants registered heavily Democratic. Personal conflicts between Democratic bosses John J. (Sonny) Mahon and Frank Kelly, heirs of the two major machine factions, weakened their party's control at the center, and 15 years of battling between the forces led by William Curran and perennial mayor Howard Jackson splintered the party further. Local ward bosses were thus able to develop independent neighborhood machines, and control of city council and the mayoralty depended on shifting and temporary alliances of such local groups. Republicans, however, were never able to take advantage of such Democratic in-fighting. Primary and secondary sources; 13 notes.
G. J. Bobango

335. Bullough, William A. HANNIBAL VERSUS THE BLIND BOSS: THE "JUNTA," CHRIS BUCKLEY, AND DEMOCRATIC REFORM POLITICS IN SAN FRANCISCO. *Pacific Hist. Rev. 1977 46(2): 181-206.* The clash in San Francisco municipal politics during the 1890's between Democratic Blind Boss Christopher A. Buckley (1845-1922) and the Junta, an elite reform coalition, sheds light on the historiographic controversy concerning progressive reformers. Changed conditions had eroded Buckley's personal power by the 1890's, but his continued presence challenged the business and professional men who were seeking to establish their own authority and at the same time provided them with a moral issue to justify their manipulations. In reality, the reformers supplanted the Blind Boss by using more sophisticated versions of his political tactics. Based on newspapers; 71 notes.
W. K. Hobson

336. Bullough, William A. THE STEAM BEER HANDICAP: CHRIS BUCKLEY AND THE SAN FRANCISCO MUNICIPAL ELECTION OF 1896. *California Hist. Q. 1975 54(3): 245-262.* Describes the comeback attempt by blind politician Christopher A. Buckley in San Francisco's 1896 municipal election. Denied representation by opponents controlling Democratic party machinery, Buckley created the Regular Democratic Party, transforming it into the Anti-Charter Democrats when the former party was refused a place on the ballot. He also infiltrated the Populist party and managed to place candidates of his choosing on its ticket. Suspicion of collusion between Buckley and John D. Spreckels came to light but ended when the sugar heir lost power in the Republican party. During the campaign Buckley was actively opposed by Democrats as well as a hostile press, and in the election his candidates were roundly defeated, signaling the end of the political bossism that had dominated in the 1880's and marking the emergence of the professional man in politics, a product of changing urban conditions in cities across the country. Based on primary and secondary sources; 103 notes.
A. Hoffman

337. Colburn, David R. and Pozzetta, George E. BOSSES AND MACHINES: CHANGING INTERPRETATIONS IN AMERICAN HISTORY. *Hist. Teacher 1976 9(3): 445-463.* Discusses the literature dealing with the urban boss and the growth of American cities during the past century. The authors evaluate changing interpretations from the critical viewpoints at the turn of the century to the more favorable accounts of recent years. Urban bosses were not always inimical to reform; a number of them utilized reform movements to enhance the strengths of their own organizations. Based on primary and secondary sources; 4 illus., 18 notes.
P. W. Kennedy

338. Davenport, John F. SKINNING THE TIGER: CARMINE DE SAPIO AND THE END OF THE TAMMANY ERA. *New York Affairs 1975 3(1): 72-93.* Discusses the career of Carmine DeSapio, the last of the Tammany Hall bosses, emphasizing his activities during the 1950's and 60's.
S

339. Davis, John Kyle. THE GRAY WOLF: TOM DENNISON OF OMAHA. *Nebraska Hist. 1977 58(1): 25-52.* Sketches the life of Tom Dennison (1858-1934) who, for nearly 40 years, was boss of Omaha's third ward which was notorious for "saloons, gambling dens, street games, and brothels." By the 1890's Dennison became the middleman between the operators in his district and the police and politicians. He weathered all reform efforts and maintained close connections with administrations of all persuasions at city hall.
R. Lowitt

340. Gillette, Howard, Jr. PHILADELPHIA'S CITY HALL: MONUMENT TO A NEW POLITICAL MACHINE. *Pennsylvania Mag. of Hist. and Biog. 1973 97(2): 233-249.* Construction of a city hall for Philadelphia, an issue since 1830, eventually became the source of lucrative patronage and corruption. William Stokley, a Philadelphia councilman, was elected mayor in 1871 after publicly opposing the City Commission's recommendations for location and construction of a city hall. Once in office Stokley reversed himself and packed the city hall building commission with cronies who favored construction of the city hall at the disputed location. After political maneuvering and infighting Stokley secured the valuable contract for his friends and supporters. 60 notes.
E. W. Carp

341. Haslam, Gerald. *THE LAST HURRAH* AND AMERICAN BOSSISM. *Rendezvous 1973 8(1): 33-44.* Discusses the depiction of political bossism, ward heelers, and union leaders in Edwin O'Connor's novel *The Last Hurrah*, 1956.

342. Henderson, Thomas M. HARLEM CONFRONTS THE MACHINE: THE STRUGGLE FOR LOCAL AUTONOMY AND BLACK DISTRICT LEADERSHIP. *Afro-Americans in New York Life and Hist. 1979 3(2): 51-68.* Describes the relationship between the Democratic Party Tammany Hall machine and Harlem blacks during the 1920's in New York City politics.

343. Hoogenboom, Ari and Hoogenboom, Olive. WAS BOSS TWEED REALLY SNOW WHITE? *Rev. in Am. Hist. 1977 5(3): 360-366.* Review article prompted by Leo Hershkowitz's *Tweed's New York: Another Look* (Garden City, N.Y.: Anchor Pr., 1977), which argues William Tweed's innocence of corruption in the control of public works in New York City from 1869 to 1871.

344. Keller, Morton. A PASSION FOR POLITICS: THE POLITICAL MACHINE VS. THE POPULIST MOVEMENT. *Social Educ. 1977 41(6): 507-508.* Compares politics in urban and rural areas, highlighting animosities, 1860's-90's.

345. Kramer, Rita. "WELL, WHAT ARE YOU GOING TO DO ABOUT IT?" *Am. Heritage 1973 24(2): 17-21, 94-97.* Richard Croker (1843?-1922), better known as "Boss Croker," became the leader of Tammany Hall and usually dominated politics in New York City 1886-1901. He seemed immune to bitter satirical attacks against the graft and corruption of his reign, and his typical response to muckrakers' detailed charges of police corruption was, "Well, what are you going to do about it?" He lost bids to get control of the state and national Democratic Party mechanisms, and he retired to the splendor of his English, Irish, and Florida estates. 7 illus.
D. L. Smith

346. Kuepper, Stephen L. BOMBS, BULLETS AND BALLOTS: CHICAGO'S 'PINEAPPLE PRIMARY' OF 1928. *Mankind 1976 5(9): 12-16, 46-47.* The Republican city primary of 1928 in Chicago pitted the faction of Charles S. Deneen against the machine of William Hale Thompson. The primary electoral campaign was fraught with violence, murder, and irregularities; each faction relied considerably on gangster support. The Thompson faction upheld its own in the election for city ward committee positions but lost significant city-wide and state primary contests. Legal proceedings against persons for criminal actions during the campaign resulted in acquittals or lenient sentences.
N. Lederer

347. Lee, David D. THE TRIUMPH OF BOSS CRUMP: THE TENNESSEE GUBERNATORIAL ELECTION OF 1932. *Tennessee Hist. Q. 1976 35(4): 393-413.* After the death of Austin Peay in 1927 Edward Crump led an urban assault on Peay's successors who ran Tennessee politics until 1932. In a three-way primary campaign, Crump supported

State Treasurer Hill McAlister in a campaign which witnessed rampant fraud and appeals to racism. McAlister won a narrow victory over Lewis Pope, the independent candidate who protested fraud, bolted the Democratic Party, and ran in the general election. Once again in a three-cornered campaign, Crump's candidate won. This began the 16-year domination of Tennessee politics by the Shelby County boss. Primary and secondary sources; 7 tables, 77 notes.   M. B. Lucas

348.   McCarthy, Michael P.   ON BOSSES, REFORMERS, AND URBAN GROWTH: SOME SUGGESTIONS FOR A POLITICAL TYPOLOGY OF AMERICAN CITIES.   *J. of Urban Hist. 1977 4(1): 29-38.* Investigates why some cities have political machines and others do not. Argues that it depends on whether suburbanization resettled the middle class outside the political boundaries of the city or within it. When the middle class becomes overwhelmingly suburban then the nucleus for a reform movement is missing and bossism prevails. Argues this is what happened in Chicago, but not in New York City in the 20th century. Fig., 17 notes.   T. W. Smith

349.   Mushkat, Jerome.   MATTHEW LIVINGSTON DAVIS AND THE POLITICAL LEGACY OF AARON BURR.   *New-York Hist. Soc. Q. 1975 59(2): 123-148.* Closely associated with Aaron Burr and a practicing politician in his own right, Matthew Livingston Davis (1773-1850) has been generally characterized as opportunistic and not too scrupulous. However, Davis was important as a transitional leader of the political "machine" which evolved from the family system of colonial times, developing many of the political devices that would characterize Tammany Hall. He has remained an obscure figure because he consistently underestimated the political wisdom of the voters and never fully comprehended the political changes taking place or his contributions to them. Primary sources; 5 illus., 41 notes.   C. L. Grant

350.   Rorabaugh, William J.   RISING DEMOCRATIC SPIRITS: IMMIGRANTS, TEMPERANCE, AND TAMMANY HALL, 1854-1860.   *Civil War Hist. 1976 22(2): 131-157.* Discusses the emergence of a political coalition among the Irish, Germans, and Anglos in New York City during 1840's-50's. It turned the metropolis into a Democratic stronghold, while the rest of the North was becoming largely Republicanized. Although these groups differed on other matters, hostility to prohibition united immigrant Irish and German Catholics with enough native-born Protestants to control New York City. The corner saloon evolved from an unimportant neighborhood shop to a highly structured nerve center. It became the needed power base from which the coalition could effectively function.   E. C. Murdock

351.   Russell, Francis.   THE KNAVE OF BOSTON.   *Am. Heritage 1976 27(5): 73-80.* In an era controlled by ward bosses, one of Boston's worst was Daniel Coakley (1865-1952). A lawyer and friend of influential figures in state and local government, Coakley preferred dishonesty as the route to financial success. Fraudulent schemes and friendship with the right people (district attorneys, for example) led to great success, yet soon gained Coakley many enemies. Disbarred in 1922, he was acquitted of criminal charges; and in 1932 he was elected to the governor's council, where he worked hard getting easy pardons and the like until impeached from that office by the Massachusetts legislature in 1941. 4 illus.   J. F. Paul

352.   Stewart, John D., II.   THE DEAL FOR PHILADELPHIA: SIMON CAMERON AND THE GENESIS OF A POLITICAL MACHINE, 1867-1872.   *J. of the Lancaster County Hist. Soc. 1973 77(1): 41-56.*

353.   Thelen, David P.   URBAN POLITICS: BEYOND BOSSES AND REFORMERS.   *Rev. in Am. Hist. 1979 7(3): 406-412.* Reviews John M. Allswang's *Bosses, Machines and Urban Voters: An American Symbiosis* (Port Washington, New York: Kennikat Pr., 1977), Lyle W. Dorsett's *Franklin D. Roosevelt and the City Bosses* (Port Washington, New York: Kennikat Pr., 1977), Michael H. Ebner and Eugene M. Tobin, ed. *The Age of Urban Reform: New Perspectives on the Progressive Era* (Port Washington, New York: Kennikat Pr., 1977), and Kenneth Fox's *Better City Government: Innovation in American Urban Politics, 1850-1937* (Philadelphia: Temple U. Pr., 1977).

Reform and Reformers

354.   Aspinwall, Bernard.   GLASGOW TRAMS AND AMERICAN POLITICS 1894-1914.   *Scottish Hist. Rev. [Great Britain] 1977 56(161): 64-84.* Glasgow's municipalization of its tramway system created cheap and efficient public transportation and resulted in improved utilities, building, health, and educational services. American reformers considered Glasgow a model of progressive change, particularly because the Glasgow tramway paid reasonable wages and provided social benefits, hospital treatment, and recreational facilities. However, American interest shifted from city to state government because municipal ownership was considered a threat to capitalism, and because Glasgow labor became militant. Based on newspapers, government reports, and secondary sources; 141 notes.   R. A. Webb

355.   Bukowski, Douglas.   WILLIAM DEVER AND PROHIBITION: THE MAYORAL ELECTIONS OF 1923 AND 1927.   *Chicago Hist. 1978 7(2): 109-118.* Efforts of Chicago mayor William Dever to impose a reform-minded and prohibitionist city government following his election in 1923 led to discontent within the electorate, erosion of support from ethnic groups and blacks, and his defeat in 1927.

356.   Bulkley, Peter B.   TOWNSENDISM AS AN EASTERN AND URBAN PHENOMENON: CHAUTAUQUA COUNTY, NEW YORK, AS A CASE STUDY.   *New York Hist. 1974 55(2): 179-198.* Challenges the standard view that the Townsend Movement was primarily rural and Western, and supported by "Grant Wood type" native-born Americans. In New York's 43rd Congressional District (Chautauqua, Cattaraugus, and Allegany Counties), the Townsendites, in alliance with the minority Democratic party, came close to defeating the conservative Republican incumbent, Daniel A. Reed, in the 1936 elections. The pro-Townsend vote was strongest in Jamestown (the chief city of the district), which had a large immigrant population, and was weakest in the native American rural areas of the district. Townsendism, in this Eastern and highly industrialized region, had its greatest strength in urban areas with large immigrant populations. Based on primary and secondary works; 3 illus., map, table, 50 notes.   G. Kurland

357.   Burke, Padraic.   STRUGGLE FOR PUBLIC OWNERSHIP: THE EARLY HISTORY OF THE PORT OF SEATTLE.   *Pacific Northwest Q. 1977 68(2): 60-71.* Created as a municipal corporation in 1911 the Port of Seattle represented a victory for Progressives who opposed private ownership of port facilities by monopolistic shipping companies and railroads. The first two Port commissioners, Hiram Chittenden and Robert Bridges, continued resistance against businessmen who criticized public ownership of the lucrative institution. Bridges increasingly aligned the port's power behind liberal political causes but by 1919 more conservative commissioners outvoted him on major issues and he resigned. This signaled the Port's shift from control by liberal reformers to a domination by businessmen of the city. Primary sources; 4 photos, 51 notes.   M. L. Tate

358.   Capeci, Dominic J.   FROM DIFFERENT LIBERAL PERSPECTIVES: FIORELLO H. LA GUARDIA, ADAM CLAYTON POWELL, JR., AND CIVIL RIGHTS IN NEW YORK CITY, 1941-1943.   *J. of Negro Hist. 1977 62(2): 160-173.* Mayor Fiorello La Guardia and Councilman Adam Clayton Powell, Jr., were embroiled in political warfare during Powell's term as a councilman in New York City during 1941-43. Ironically, although both were liberals, their personalities, philosophies, and styles were so alike as to prove the physical law of magnetism that likes repel. Based on documents in the Fiorello H. La Guardia Papers and secondary sources; 92 notes.   N. G. Sapper

359.   Cerillo, Augustus, Jr.   THE REFORM OF MUNICIPAL GOVERNMENT IN NEW YORK CITY.   *New-York Hist. Soc. Q. 1973 57(1): 51-71.* New York City reformers turned after 1900 from attempts to appoint "good men" to attempts to improve administrative methods. Progressives led the shift after the 1903 defeat of reformist mayor Seth Low. The Citizens' Union (founded 1897) also participated. The movement culminated in the administration of Mayor John Purroy Mitchel (1879-1918), whose administrative reforms endured despite the return of Tammany Hall to power in 1917. Contemporary accounts and Oral History Memoirs; 4 illus., 32 notes.   C. L. Grant

360. Crooks, James B. POLITICS AND REFORM: THE DIMENSIONS OF BALTIMORE PROGRESSIVISM. *Maryland Hist. Mag. 1976 71(3): 421-427.* Today's history is rightfully paying more attention to the local and urban side of the Progressive era reforms. Reviews the efforts of Baltimore reformers to weaken Isaac Freeman Rasin's political machine and its boss rule. From the election of Alcaeus Hooper in 1895 to the formation of the New Charter Union in 1899, progressives such as Charles J. Bonaparte and William Keyser led members of the Baltimore Reform League and the Civil Service Reform Association to pronounced victories for good government candidates. The Municipal Art Society achieved urban renewal and beautification projects, and other reformers promoted bond issues for sewage systems, civic centers, parks, paved streets, and community centers. A Board of Awards began supervising city contracts and franchises. By 1910 a city-wide congress met to coordinate physical and social planning for Baltimore. Substantial improvements came in public health, but child labor laws were delayed by businessmen, and city funds for programs were always insufficient since politicians were reluctant to upset voters by raising taxes. Reform, then, was not just ousting a corrupt boss, but "a complex movement attempting to come to grips with the realities of a rapidly urbanizing and industrializing nation." Primary and secondary sources; 17 notes.
G. J. Bobango

361. Davis, Ronald L. F. and Holmes, Harry D. INSURGENCY AND MUNICIPAL REFORM IN ST. LOUIS, 1893-1904. *Midwest Rev. 1979 1: 1-18.* Examines this example of local reform movements, particularly local taxation, the street railway system, and politics.

362. Elenbaas, Jack D. THE BOSS OF THE BETTER CLASS: HENRY LELAND AND THE DETROIT CITIZENS LEAGUE, 1912-1924. *Michigan Hist. 1974 58(2): 131-150.* The thesis that the origins of Progressivism lay in the activities of the upper and upper middle classes finds support in the crusades of Henry Leland and the Detroit Citizens League. Leland thought that the upper class had a moral obligation to uplift society by freeing it from the tyranny of corrupt politicians and evil saloonkeepers. Supported by Detroit's business, professional, and Protestant religious communities, the League campaigned for a new city charter, an anti-saloon ordinance, and the open shop. Primary and secondary sources; 2 illus., 4 photos, 58 notes.
D. W. Johnson

363. Gerz, Richard J., Jr. URBAN REFORM AND THE MUSSER COALITION IN THE CITY OF LANCASTER, 1921-1930. *J. of the Lancaster County Hist. Soc. 1974 78(2): 49-110.* Analyzes the nature of the urban reform movement in Lancaster, Pennsylvania, 1921-30, drawing parallels to the national movement, 1900-16; chronicles and compares the concurrent Coalition Movement in which members of the Republican Party grew dissatisfied with the party machine and switched to the Democratic Party, forming a Coalition Party in order to bring about modernization and progressivism to Lancaster. 4 photos, 274 notes, 10 appendixes, biblio.
G. A. Hewlett

364. Gould, Alan B. WALTER L. FISHER: PROFILE OF AN URBAN REFORMER, 1880-1910. *Mid-America 1975 57(3): 157-172.* Walter L. Fisher, son of a West Virginia minister, began his career as reformer as special assessment attorney in Chicago. He became secretary and later president of the Municipal Voters' League, president of the Fisher-organized City Club of Chicago, and a founder of the Bureau of Public Efficiency. As special traction attorney, he accomplished his most significant reforms. Based on the Fisher Papers, Library of Congress, newspapers, official records, and secondary works; 43 notes.
T. H. Wendel

365. Grassman, Curtis. THE LOS ANGELES FREE HARBOR CONTROVERSY AND THE CREATION OF A PROGRESSIVE COALITION. *Southern California Q. 1973 55(4): 445-468.* Challenges the standard view of the Progressive movement in California as starting with the Lincoln-Roosevelt League in 1906. The origins of Progressivism can be seen in the efforts of Los Angeles in the 1890's to establish a free harbor at San Pedro instead of succumbing to the Southern Pacific's plan for a Santa Monica site. The key was the appropriation of federal funds for harbor construction. While Collis P. Huntington lobbied for funds for Santa Monica, newly elected Senator Stephen M. White campaigned on behalf of Los Angeles. White endured several reverses during 1893-99, but eventually succeeded in winning an appropriation for San Pedro. The free harbor controversy deserves credit for giving later Progressive campaigns their inspiration, organizational techniques, and many of the leaders. Based on unpublished materials at University of California (LA), Stanford University, and the Huntington libraries, newspapers, and secondary studies; 59 notes.
A. Hoffman

366. Greenberg, Irwin F. PHILADELPHIA DEMOCRATS GET A NEW DEAL: THE ELECTION OF 1933. *Pennsylvania Mag. of Hist. and Biog. 1973 97(2): 210-232.* In the 1920's Philadelphia "boss" William S. Vare, the local Republican leader, controlled the city's political affairs by dispensing patronage favors to his friend John O'Donnell, leader of Philadelphia's Democrats. In return O'Donnell did nothing to offend his GOP patrons. Reform-minded Democrats revolted against O'Donnell's leadership. Fielding its own candidates, the Independent Democratic Campaign Committee easily defeated O'Donnell's slate in the 1932 primary election. In the 1933 election the IDCC rode on the coattails of Franklin D. Roosevelt and the New Deal and defeated Vare and the Republicans. The election of 1933 signified the return of two-party politics to Philadelphia. Based on primary and secondary sources; 69 notes.
E. W. Carp

367. Henderson, Thomas M. IMMIGRANT POLITICIAN: SALVATORE COTILLO, PROGRESSIVE ETHNIC. *Int. Migration Rev. 1979 13(1): 81-102.* Describes the political career and attitudes of Salvatore Cotillo, an Italian American living in New York City during the rise of urban liberalism and reform in the early 20th century.

368. Henstell, Bruce. WHEN THE LID BLEW OFF LOS ANGELES. *Westways 1977 69(11): 32-35, 68.* In 1938 Clifford Clinton, a private detective, and an organization known as CIVIC (Citizens' Independent Vice Investigating Committee) succeeded in recalling Frank Shaw, the Mayor of Los Angeles and leader of a generally corrupt administration.

369. Holli, Melvin G. MAYOR PINGREE CAMPAIGNS FOR THE GOVERNORSHIP. *Michigan Hist. 1973 57(2): 151-173.* Hazen S. Pingree, wealthy shoe manufacturer, won four successive Detroit mayoralty elections. His administrations (1889-97) brought him national acclaim as the leading social-reform mayor in the country. He built a political machine, purged his opponents, and transformed Detroit from a Democratic into a Republican city. After the Republican-dominated state legislature voided reforms for which he was responsible, Pingree challenged the state political apparatus, won the gubernatorial nomination in 1896, and won the election, far outdistancing the GOP presidential candidate. 7 illus., 37 notes.
D. L. Smith

370. Isaac, Paul E. MUNICIPAL REFORM IN BEAUMONT, TEXAS, 1902-1909. *Southwestern Hist. Q. 1975 78(4): 413-430.* Reviews city government reform in Beaumont, Texas. Beaumont was not a victim of the usual political ills of the time; corruption was negligible and bossism was absent. A great oil strike swelled the city's population, rendering the current governmental forms obsolete. Businessmen desired to run the city effectively and efficiently. A series of gradual reforms seemed to achieve this objective. Poll taxes wiped out the purchasable Negro vote. Greater control was gained over utilities. The Commission plan was not adopted. In sum, Beaumont followed the political attitudes of the times. Photo, 58 notes.
V. L. Human

371. Issel, William. CLASS AND ETHNIC CONFLICT IN SAN FRANCISCO POLITICAL HISTORY: THE REFORM CHARTER OF 1898. *Labor Hist. 1977 18(3): 341-359.* The passage of the Reform Charter of 1898 in San Francisco revealed a political struggle divided by class and ethnic tensions that resulted in centralization of city government. The "business and professional elite" were victorious over labor and ethnic interests in city reform. Based on San Francisco newspapers; 51 notes.
L. L. Athey

372. Kaplan, Barry J. REFORMERS AND CHARITY: THE ABOLITION OF PUBLIC OUTDOOR RELIEF IN NEW YORK CITY, 1870-1898. *Social Service Rev. 1978 52(2): 202-214.* To reduce corruption in city government and the power of Tammany Hall, reformers in New York City government put public outdoor relief in the hands of private charitable organizations and subsidized it.

373. Kurtz, Michael L. DE LESSEPS S. MORRISON: POLITICAL REFORMER. *Louisiana Hist. 1976 17(1): 19-39.* Examines deLesseps S. Morrison's place as a political reformer. Much of his effectiveness as a reformer in New Orleans corrupt city government during his 14 years as mayor was due to his combination of idealism and practical politics. In public relations he projected an image of economic and social progress, racial moderation, and political reform. He secured home rule for New Orleans, leaving a last imprint on that city and on the entire South. Based on the Morrison Papers; 115 notes.   E. P. Stickney

374. McCarthy, Michael P. PRELUDE TO ARMAGEDDON: CHARLES E. MERRIAM AND THE CHICAGO MAYORAL ELECTION OF 1911. *J. of the Illinois State Hist. Soc. 1974 67(5): 505-518.* Charles E. Merriam, a progressive, intellectual professor, easily won the Republican mayoral nomination when the incumbent Fred A. Busse declined to seek reelection. Taking advantage of the new direct primary, the progressives broke the hold of downtown Republican bosses. But the Progressives could not stay in power without a victory on election day. This they failed to deliver. Merriam's overzealous campaign was wrecked by Democrat Carter Harrison II, who won the blue-collar vote, and by the opposition from regular Republicans on his own ticket. After Harrison became mayor, the machine politicians regained control of the battered Republican organization. Primary and secondary sources; 9 illus., 27 notes.   W. R. Hively

375. Miller, Grace L. THE ORIGINS OF THE SAN DIEGO LINCOLN-ROOSEVELT LEAGUE, 1905-1909. *Southern California Q. 1978 60(4): 421-443.* Traces the development of the progressive political reform movement in San Diego, California. Progressive Republicans opposed the control of their city by the Southern Pacific and by "Boss" Charles Hardy. Beginning with the 1905 municipal election, reformers sought an end to machine politics and boss rule. On 24 May 1906, the Roosevelt Republican Club was organized to support progressivism within the Republican Party framework. In 1907 progressive Republicans backed a Nonpartisan League, and under the leadership of Edgar Luce, George Marston, Ed Fletcher, and other reformers, the Roosevelt Republican Club was revitalized as the Lincoln-Roosevelt Republican League. A major test came in the mayoralty election of 1909; it marked a complete victory for the league. Whem Hiram Johnson opened his campaign for governor in March 1910, his first speech was in San Diego, a city that had been won over to the support of progressive goals. Primary and secondary sources; 73 notes.   A. Hoffman

376. Miller, Zane L. THE ETHNIC REVIVAL AND URBAN LIBERALISM. *Rev. in Am. Hist. 1974 2(3): 418-424.* John D. Buenker's *Urban Liberalism and Progressive Reform* (New York: Charles Scribner's Sons, 1973) studies the coalition of ethnic groups and middle-class reformers of the Progressive Movement who attempted political reform in metropolitan areas in the 1910's.

377. Nussbaum, Raymond O. "THE RING IS SMASHED!": THE NEW ORLEANS MUNICIPAL ELECTION OF 1896. *Louisiana Hist. 1976 17(3): 283-297.* Details New Orleans municipal elections of 1896, fought principally between Democratic Party "Regulars," a closely-knit machine, and a reform group calling itself the Citizens' League. After a spirited campaign, the League won a smashing victory, overturning the Regular machine and electing Walter C. Flower as mayor. The election represented a victory for Progressives, consistent with similar victories in other parts of the United States, at this time. Based on primary and secondary sources; 48 notes.   R. L. Woodward

378. Oster, Donald B. REFORMERS, FACTIONALISTS AND KANSAS CITY'S 1925 CITY MANAGER CHARTER. *Missouri Hist. Rev. 1978 72(3): 296-327.* Discusses where the city manager concept originated, who supported and opposed it, and why the voters of Kansas City accepted the innovation in 1925. There were several unsuccessful charter movements during 1905-22, as well as the successful attempt in 1908. Most of the reformers who pushed the plan through were native, white, Protestant, affluent, business and professional people. The system did not work as planned. Boss Thomas Pendergast had usually thwarted reform, but in 1926 he manipulated the new system to pick the city's first manager. Primary and secondary sources; illus., 71 notes.   W. F. Zornow

379. Pendergrass, Lee F. THE FORMATION OF A MUNICIPAL REFORM MOVEMENT: THE MUNICIPAL LEAGUE OF SEATTLE. *Pacific Northwest Q. 1975 66(1): 13-25.* Throughout the tenure of its existence, 1910-20, the Municipal League of Seattle presented a genuinely progressive, nonpartisan interest in the promotion of municipal improvements, the selection of competent civic officials, the preparation of citizens for active roles in urban affairs, and the dissemination of information about Seattle.

380. Reese, William J. THE CONTROL OF URBAN SCHOOL BOARDS DURING THE PROGRESSIVE ERA: A RECONSIDERATION. *Pacific Northwest Q. 1977 68(4): 164-174.* Traces the history of educational reform in Toledo, Ohio during the Progressive Era. The Niles Bill of 1898 reduced the city's school board to five members, nominated on nonpartisan ballots and elected on a city-wide basis rather than by wards. This produced a wave of progressive victories during 1898, but the victors were just as elitist as the group they replaced. Suggests that future studies should focus on members who dominated school boards and on outside forces which influenced policy. Primary and secondary sources; 3 photos, 32 notes.   M. L. Tate

381. Rice, Bradley R. THE GALVESTON PLAN OF CITY GOVERNMENT BY COMMISSION: THE BIRTH OF A PROGRESSIVE IDEA. *Southwestern Hist. Q. 1975 78(4): 365-408.* Reviews the origins and development of the Commission form of city government in Galveston, Texas. Historians generally argue that governmental reform was necessitated by the great hurricane of 1900, but citizen dissatisfaction and reform efforts were rife before that time. Reform was brought about by the business dominated Deep Water Committee. The Commission plan called for election of at-large delegates, who acted colletively as aldermen and individually as heads of various city departments. The city was elevated and a seawall was built. The Commission system was a great success and was widely adopted across the nation. 37 photos, 52 notes.   V. L. Human

382. Ritchie, Donald A. THE GARY COMMITTEE: BUSINESSMEN, PROGRESSIVES, AND UNEMPLOYMENT IN NEW YORK CITY, 1914-1915. *New-York Hist. Soc. Q. 1973 57(4): 326-347.* Disruption of trade and industry during World War I caused widespread unemployment in the United States, particularly in the Northeast and the Middle West. Most cities, some with Progressive administrations, began unemployment and relief programs. In New York City these efforts were led by Mayor John Purroy Mitchel and Elbert H. Gary, chairman of the Committee on Unemployment and Relief. The committee, composed of businessmen, promised much but never identified closely with the working class and failed to cope with basic problems. By 1917, prosperity and loss of confidence in the committee helped defeat Mitchel and bring in an urban reform movement identified with Alfred E. Smith. Primary sources; 6 illus., 45 notes.   C. L. Grant

383. Schiesl, Martin J. PROGRESSIVE REFORM IN LOS ANGELES UNDER MAYOR ALEXANDER, 1909-1913. *California Hist. Q. 1975 54(1): 37-56.* A study of progressive accomplishments and problems as Los Angeles moved into the status of a major metropolis. In an effort to rid the city of machine politics, reformers supported the election of George Alexander as mayor. But progressives disagreed over the goals of reform. Some supported honesty and efficiency in government, working for civil service reforms and "classless" politics. More radical reformers called for measures that promoted social welfare and economic reform. When business-oriented progressives merged their interests with the social welfare faction, the city enacted legislation creating a public utilities commission, a public power project, and other measures. However, some business-oriented progressives abandoned the reform movement, while labor leaders demanded leadership that went beyond middle-class values. Pursuing a middle course, the progressives defeated a Socialist bid for the mayoralty in 1911, and in Alexander's second term enacted additional measures benefiting the public welfare. Party regulars, however, defeated a proposed progressive city charter in 1912, and increased factionalism within progressive ranks ended progressive rule in 1913. Primary and secondary sources; illus., 65 notes.   A. Hoffman

384. Scott, George W. THE NEW ORDER OF CINCINNATUS: MUNICIPAL POLITICS IN SEATTLE DURING THE 1930S. *Pacific Northwest Q. 1973 64(4): 137-146.* With the advent of the New

Deal at the national level, the conservative burgher class, intolerant of radicalism and unruliness, organized a municipal party, the New Order of Cincinnatus, in August 1933, under the leadership of Ralph Potts, a young attorney. Interest groups posed a formidable opposition, and though three Cincinnatus members won seats on the city council, infighting greatly weakened the impact of the reform program. 49 notes.

R. V. Ritter

385. Silverman, Robert A. NATHAN MATTHEWS: POLITICS OF REFORM IN BOSTON, 1890-1910. *New England Q. 1977 50(4): 626-643.* Traces Nathan Matthews's (1853-1927) role in forming the Yankee-Irish alliance in the Democratic Party and his chairmanship of the Boston Finance Commission during 1907-09. Focuses on his four terms as the reform mayor of Boston during 1891-95 when he achieved his main goal of cutting expenditures through better management and established the Board of Survey which provided Boston with its first coordinated planning. Based on Matthews's correspondence and secondary sources; 42 notes.

J. C. Bradford

386. Stocker, Joseph. THE LITTLE FLOWER: GIANT AMONG THE MAYORS. *Mankind 1975 5(4): 22-27.* Fiorello LaGuardia, mayor of New York City 1933-45, "executed vast reforms, beautified the city, fought corruption, cleared slums, and improved sanitary conditions."

387. Teaford, Jon C. THE SEARCH FOR CIVIC EFFICIENCY. *Rev. in Am. Hist. 1978 6(2): 235-239.* Review article prompted by Martin J. Schiesl's *The Politics of Efficiency: Municipal Administration and Reform in America, 1880-1920* (Berkeley: U. of California Pr., 1977).

388. Tobin, Eugene M. THE PROGRESSIVE AND SINGLE TAXER: MARK FAGAN AND THE JERSEY CITY EXPERIENCE, 1900-1917. *Am. J. of Econ. and Sociol. 1974 33(3): 287-297.* The Progressives' failure is dealt with through the career of Mark Fagan, mayor of Jersey City during 1901-07 and 1913-17. Explores why he and other mayors adopted the single tax late in their careers. Secondary sources; 30 notes.

W. L. Marr

389. Tobin, Eugene M. THE PROGRESSIVE AS POLITICIAN: JERSEY CITY, 1896-1907. *New Jersey Hist. 1973 91(1): 5-23.* In tracing the career of Mark Fagan, mayor of Jersey City, the author relates the failure of Progressivism in one American city. Discusses Fagan's Republican Party affiliation, his program of equal taxation, his fight with the railroads and utilities, and his demise as a leader due to a lack of patience with the customary workings of party machinery. Based on primary and secondary sources; 7 illus., 39 notes.

E. R. McKinstry

390. Travis, Anthony R. MAYOR GEORGE ELLIS: GRAND RAPIDS POLITICAL BOSS AND PROGRESSIVE REFORMER. *Michigan Hist. 1974 58(2): 101-130.* George E. Ellis, mayor of Grand Rapids during 1906-16, was the most dynamic, innovative, and powerful chief executive in the city's history. Forging a coalition of ethnic working class and middle class voters, Ellis strove successfully to widen the spectrum of citizen participation in politics. Ellis' career as a left-wing progressive who was both machine politician and social reformer demonstrates that the "boss" versus "reformer" typology, advanced by Samuel P. Hays, James Weinstein, and others, inadequately describes the complexity of urban politics in the progressive period. Primary and secondary sources; illus., 7 photos, map, 2 tables, 45 notes.

D. W. Johnson

391. West, Elliott. DIRTY TRICKS IN DENVER. *Colorado Mag. 1975 52(3): 225-243.* Describes the voting fraud in the Denver mayoral election of 1889. Republican merchant Wolfe Londoner was elected only to face a lengthy trial which removed him from office in 1891. This seldom-mentioned episode reflects political reform sentiment well before the Progressive Era. Based on primary and secondary sources; 5 illus., 56 notes.

O. H. Zabel

The Economy

General

392. Abbott, Carl. POPULAR ECONOMIC THOUGHT AND OCCUPATIONAL STRUCTURE: THREE MIDDLE WESTERN CITIES IN THE ANTEBELLUM DECADE. *J. of Urban Hist. 1975 1(2): 175-187.* Chicago was reputed as being a commercial city, Cincinnati described as a manufacturing city, and Indianapolis a state capital city. Compares contemporary accounts with manuscript census data, which supports the generalizations. 2 tables, 20 notes.

S. S. Sprague

393. Babcock, Robert H. ECONOMIC DEVELOPMENT IN PORTLAND (ME.) AND SAINT JOHN (N. B.) DURING THE AGE OF IRON AND STEAM, 1850-1914. *Am. Rev. of Can. Studies 1979 9(1): 3-37.* Evidence for identification of a distinct Maritimes-New England international region can be drawn from a comparison of St. John, New Brunswick, and Portland, Maine, 1850-1914. The similar geographic features and economic interests of the two cities led to economic interaction, including a cooperative railroad development program promoted by Portland's John Poor. While Poor's endeavors achieved minimal success, both cities experienced similar economic development, demonstrated by examinations of the foundry and shoemaking industries, and comparable demographic change. While neither city reached its goal of becoming a dominant commercial or industrial center, both achieved substantial prosperity. Primary and secondary sources; 8 tables, 76 notes.

G.-A. Patzwald

394. Benson, Lee. PHILADELPHIA ELITES AND ECONOMIC DEVELOPMENT: QUASI-PUBLIC INNOVATION DURING THE FIRST AMERICAN ORGANIZATIONAL REVOLUTION, 1825-1861. *Working Papers from the Regional Econ. Hist. Res. Center 1978 2(2): 25-54.* Discusses the impact which various groups of elites and the Philadelphia Board of Trade had in promoting the economic development of that city, 1825-61.

395. Callahan, Helen. PATRICK WALSH: JOURNALIST, POLITICIAN, STATESMAN. *Richmond County Hist. 1977 9(2): 14-29.* Patrick Walsh, a newspaper editor, businessman, and political leader, urged the economic development and industrialization of Augusta, Georgia, during Reconstruction through 1899.

396. Ermisch, John and Weiss, Thomas. THE IMPACT OF THE RURAL MARKET ON THE GROWTH OF THE URBAN WORKFORCE: UNITED STATES, 1870-1900. *Explorations in Econ. Hist. 1973-74 11(2): 137-153.* The rural market had little effect on the acceleration of urban growth through the substitution of urban production of nonagricultural goods and services. A mathematical analysis based on published statistics and secondary sources.

P. J. Coleman

397. Ernst, William. THOMAS HICKS WYNNE: HORATIO ALGER IN NINETEENTH-CENTURY RICHMOND. *Virginia Cavalcade 1978 27(4): 186-191.* Recounts the business and political career of Thomas Hicks Wynne (1820-75), a leading citizen of Richmond, Virginia, 1840's-75.

398. German, Richard H. L. AUGUSTA ENTREPRENEURS, ARTISANS & POLITICIANS. *Richmond County Hist. 1973 5(2): 15-22.* Summarizes the relationship between the "commercial-industrial-financial tycoon" of post-Civil War Augusta and the textile millhand. The tycoons sought to maximize profits at the workers' expense, while the workers reacted by supporting union organizing drives. The union movement finally faltered; management here, as in much of the South, would reign supreme until the 1930's. One of six articles in this issue on Augusta. Based largely on newspapers and published accounts; 8 notes.

H. R. Grant

399. Greb, G. Allen. OPENING A NEW FRONTIER: SAN FRANCISCO, LOS ANGELES, AND THE PANAMA CANAL, 1900-1914. *Pacific Hist. Rev. 1978 47(3): 405-424.* The Panama Canal, even before its completion, was a major stimulant to the economic development of San Francisco and Los Angeles. Dominant commercial and financial interests

worked to improve port facilities, forestall possible railroad domination, and sponsor an international exposition for the West Coast. Their motives were self-centered and parochial, defined in terms of local ambitions. The experience is an episode in businessmen's increasing use of state and national government to achieve their ends. Based on newspapers, manuscript sources, published government documents, and secondary sources; 53 notes.   W. K. Hobson

400. Griffen, Sally and Griffen, Clyde. FAMILY AND BUSINESS IN A SMALL CITY: POUGHKEEPSIE, NEW YORK 1850-1880. *J. of Urban Hist. 1975 1(3): 316-338.* The extended family was used opportunistically in an unstable business environment. Financial arrangements were expedient and temporary. Relatives were used to fend off creditors. Fathers often set up sons in business. When fathers-in-law did so, it was usually in a different line of business. Based on Credit Ledgers, Dun and Bradstreet Collection, Baker Library, Harvard. 39 notes.
                                                  S. S. Sprague

401. Hearden, Patrick J. AGRICULTURAL BUSINESSMEN IN THE NEW SOUTH. *Louisiana Studies 1975 14(2): 145-159.* Argues that, contrary to other studies, in the last three decades of the 19th century Southern agricultural businessmen allied with urban entrepreneurs in calling for Southern economic independence which would be based primarily on large scale textile manufacturing. This was especially the case in South Carolina, North Carolina, Georgia, Alabama, and Mississippi. Such agrarian support for the New South of industrialization and manufacturing also came from major farm groups such as the Grange and the Farmers Alliance. Primary and secondary sources; 67 notes.
                                                  B. A. Glasrud

402. Hosler, Robert M. LEVI JOHNSON, A CLEVELAND PIONEER. *Inland Seas 1976 32(3): 200-202, 204, 211.* Levi Johnson (1786-1872) settled in Cleveland, Ohio, in 1809 and quickly became a builder of both houses and vessels. After service with the Navy in the War 1812 he operated a shipyard and sailed as a ship captain until 1831. He then devoted himself to lighthouse building, but after 1840 concentrated on his extensive real estate holdings. Illus.   K. J. Bauer

403. Inglesby, Charlotte. SAVANNAH AND THE CAROLINA PLANTERS. *Georgia Hist. Q. 1978 62(1): 24-31.* Brief biographies of some of the rice planters of the Savannah River area of South Carolina who had townhouses in Savannah. Included are the Longworths, James Proctor Screven (1799-?), William Coffee Daniell (1792-ca.1860), Langdon Cheves (1814-63), Joseph Alston Huger (1816-98), and James Heyward Lynah (1848-1933).   G. R. Schroeder

404. Kaufman, Burton I. NEW ORLEANS AND THE PANAMA CANAL, 1900-1914. *Louisiana Hist. 1973 14(4): 333-346.* Examines the economic growth in New Orleans (which had been beginning to experience a slight trade decline) after completion of the Panama Canal, 1900-14.

405. McQuaid, Kim. BUSINESSMAN AS SOCIAL INNOVATOR: N. O. NELSON, PROMOTER OF GARDEN CITIES AND THE CONSUMER COOPERATIVE MOVEMENT. *Am. J. of Econ. and Sociol. 1975 34(4): 411-422.* Describes Nelson O. Nelson's progressive business experiments around the turn of the century.

406. Miller, Zane L. SCARCITY, ABUNDANCE, AND AMERICAN URBAN HISTORY. *J. of Urban Hist. 1978 4(2): 131-156.* Examines the evolution of the American city from the perspective of relative economic surplus. During the 17th century, cities essentially were commercial communities. After the American Revolution cities began to expand their functions to include general sociowelfare responsibilities. Urban problems in the late 19th century led to an emphasis on efficient management. 25 notes.   T. W. Smith

407. Perkins, Edwin J. THE INTERSECTIONAL TRADE HYPOTHESIS REVISED: THE PHILADELPHIA REGION AS A TEST CASE. *Rev. in Am. Hist. 1979 7(2): 199-201.* Review article prompted by Diane Lindstrom's *Economic Development in the Philadelphia Region, 1810-1850* (New York: Columbia U. Pr., 1978).

408. Simon, Roger D. FOUNDATIONS FOR INDUSTRIALIZATION, 1835-1880. *Milwaukee Hist. 1978 1(1-2): 38-56.* Describes the development of industry and commerce in Milwaukee during 1835-80.

409. Smith, Merritt Roe. GEORGE WASHINGTON AND THE ESTABLISHMENT OF THE HARPERS FERRY ARMORY. *Virginia Mag. of Hist. and Biog. 1973 81(4): 415-436.* The selection of Harpers Ferry as the site for a federal armory resulted from President George Washington's desire to promote the economy of the Potomac River Valley. Advised by close friends who would benefit economically from the selection, Washington overrode adverse opinions and continued to press for Harpers Ferry, even in retirement. In the antebellum period the armory did promote the region's economy, but was not an efficient government installation. Based primarily on the published and unpublished Washington papers; 99 notes.   R. F. Oaks

410. Townley, Carrie Miller. HELEN J. STEWART: FIRST LADY OF LAS VEGAS. *Nevada Hist. Soc. Q. 1973 16(4): 214-244; 1974 17(1): 2-32.* Part I. Recounts ranching, land speculation, and mining in Nevada, 1879-94. Widowed by the murder of her husband, Helen Stewart (1854-1926) undertook the management of extensive properties near Pioche and Las Vegas which her deceased husband had acquired earlier. Based on newspaper and manuscript sources; 3 photos, 158 notes. Part II. Mrs. Stewart continued ranching in the Las Vegas Valley until 1903. Subsequently, her historical studies and many civic activities contributed notably to her reputation as "First Lady of Las Vegas." Based on primary sources; 3 photos, 159 notes.   H. T. Lovin

411. Walker, Joseph. LABOR-MANAGEMENT RELATIONS AT HOPEWELL VILLAGE. *Labor Hist. 1973 14(1): 3-18.* Traces the development of labor-management relations at the Hopewell Village iron furnace 1800-50. Relations were relatively stable with few wage changes. There were few strikes or lockouts, and no evidence of a trend toward unionism. A system of fines was used to keep workers in line, and paternalism and self-interest prevailed as a guide to relations. Based on the Hopewell Village recordbooks, documents, and other manuscript collections; 87 notes.   L. L. Athey

412. Wall, Bennett H. LEON GODCHAUX AND THE GODCHAUX BUSINESS ENTERPRISES. *Am. Jewish Hist. Q. 1976 66(1): 50-66.* Reconstructs the life and influence of Leon Godchaux (1824-99), New Orleans merchant, plantation owner, sugar refiner, real estate developer, and financier, who proved that hard work, canny business judgment and ingenuity made it possible for a poor immigrant boy to rise rapidly to wealth and importance. Based on papers and clippings of the Godchaux family. 29 notes.   F. Rosenthal

413. Williamson, Jeffery G. AMERICAN PRICES AND URBAN INEQUALITY SINCE 1820. *J. of Econ. Hist. 1976 36(2): 303-333.* Examines the forces that appear to have driven long-term trends in American urban inequality. The changing structure of consumer goods' prices is shown to have played a significant—but not dominant—role in every phase of increasing and decreasing nominal inequality from 1820 to 1929. The revealed symmetry in movement between the urban price and income structure suggests that a successful macro-distribution model must explain both historical phenomena. Technological imbalance was a crucial element in shaping peacetime patterns of income distribution.
                                                  J

Trade, Commerce, and Merchandising

414. Atwater, Edward C. HULBERT HARRINGTON WARNER AND THE PERFECT PITCH: SOLD HOPE; MADE MILLIONS. *New York Hist. 1975 56(2): 155-190.* Relates the promotional and advertising techniques employed by patent medicine businessman Hulbert Harrington Warner. Warner made Rochester, New York, "one of the world leaders in the manufacture of proprietary medicines" by 1890, but unsuccessful stock manipulations resulted in his bankruptcy in 1893. 8 illus., 41 notes.   R. N. Lokken

415. Barsness, Richard W. MARITIME ACTIVITY AND PORT DEVELOPMENT IN THE UNITED STATES SINCE 1900: A SUR-

VEY. *J. of Transport Hist. [Great Britain] 1974 2(3): 167-184.* Port development in the United States, especially in the 20th century, has been a neglected area of historical research. Surveys ports with particular reference to large scale growth in total commerce, fundamental technological changes in merchant vessels and cargo handling systems, the appearance of endemic industrial disputes since the 1930's, and the various factors which have led to increased port competition. Primary and secondary sources; fig., 51 notes.   R. G. Neville

416. Baumgarten, Linda R. THE TEXTILE TRADE IN BOSTON, 1650-1700. Quimby, Ian M. G., ed. *Wintherthur Conference Report, 20th, 1974: Arts of the Anglo-American Community in the Seventeenth Century* (Charlottesville: U. Pr. of Virginia, 1975), pp. 219-274. An inventory of the most important fabrics imported and used in Boston and its environs.   S

417. Bolding, Gary. CHANGE, CONTINUITY AND COMMERCIAL IDENTITY OF A SOUTHERN CITY: NEW ORLEANS, 1850-1950. *Louisiana Studies 1975 14(2): 161-178.* Notes that people in New Orleans developed a strong veneration for the Mississippi River, and that in the antebellum period this sentiment was largely responsible for the city's failure to adapt to technological change. By the latter 19th century New Orleans had lost its favored trade position, and its citizens began to search for a new commercial identity. Businessmen emphasized technological change while also advertising the city as the focus of world trade. The 20th century witnessed a further effort to stress both commercial and industrial activities and in the process the residents lost contact with the river that earlier made them so prominent. By the 1950's, however, the Mississippi River once more played a prominent role in the rhetoric and commercial mind of the business community which promoted New Orleans as an international city, transport center, and industrial port. Primary and secondary sources; 51 notes.   B. A. Glasrud

418. Bronner, Simon J. STREET CRIES AND PEDDLER TRADITIONS IN CONTEMPORARY PERSPECTIVE. *New York Folklore 1976 2(1-2): 2-16.* Discusses 12 cries which street peddlers employed during the 19th and 20th centuries, identifying them with urban, social, and ethnic elements.

419. Browne, Gary L. BUSINESS INNOVATION AND SOCIAL CHANGE: THE CAREER OF ALEXANDER BROWN AFTER THE WAR OF 1812. *Maryland Hist. Mag. 1974 69(3): 243-255.* Alexander Brown (1764-1834) of Baltimore, founder of Alexander Brown & Sons with its network of family firms in Liverpool, New York, and Philadelphia, was a forerunner of the later 19th-century businessman. Brown was a business innovator who observed social conditions carefully and was a transition figure to the era after 1819 when cash and short credits became the norms of business relations. By concentrating his capital in small-risk ventures and acquiring ships and Bank of the United States stock during the Panic of 1819, he came to monopolize Baltimore's shipping trade with Liverpool by 1822. Brown next expanded into packet ships, extended his lines to Philadelphia, and began financing Baltimore importers, specializing in merchant banking from the late 1820's to his death in 1834. The emergence of a money economy and the growth of the Anglo-American cotton trade allowed him to escape Baltimore's declining position in trans-Atlantic trade. His most important innovation was the drawing up of his own bills of exchange. By 1830 his company rivaled the Bank of the United States in the American foreign exchange markets, and the transition from the "traditional" to the "modern" merchant was nearly complete. Primary and secondary sources; 3 illus., 18 notes.   G. J. Bobango

420. Butler, Martin J. STEAMERS TO THE WHALEMEN'S PORT: THE NEW BEDFORD-NEW YORK LINES, 1853-1880. *Am. Neptune 1979 39(2): 83-108.* Discusses the development of steamship transportation between the ports of New York City and New Bedford, Massachusetts. The establishment of several such steamship lines reflected the desire to provide New Bedford with economic diversification and less dependency on whaling. Primary and secondary sources; 6 photos, 73 notes.   G. H. Curtis

421. Coerver, Don M. and Hall, Linda B. NEIMAN-MARCUS: INNOVATORS IN FASHION AND MERCHANDISING. *Am. Jewish Hist. Q. 1976 66(1): 123-136.* As innovative merchants and merchandiz-

ers Neiman-Marcus of Dallas, Texas, revolutionized the Southwestern approach to fashion. Relates the story of the store, its founders, and its progress until the present. 44 notes.   F. Rosenthal

422. Conzen, Michael P. and Conzen, Kathleen Neils. GEOGRAPHICAL STRUCTURE IN NINETEENTH-CENTURY URBAN RETAILING: MILWAUKEE, 1836-90. *J. of Hist. Geography 1979 5(1): 45-66.* Uses city directories, credit rating lists, and biographical sources to study numbers and types of businesses in the early phases of retailing. Milwaukee did not pass through the "general store" phase. Rather, the trend was toward specialization, even away from the city center, then department store consolidation. Thus, especially in working-class neighborhoods, specialty shopping was available before street cars. Evidence indicates that a basically "modern" retail structure had developed by the mid-19th century. Questions remain about the numerous decisions leading to the various patterns of retail development. Secondary sources; 8 maps, 2 tables, 2 graphs, 34 notes.   A. J. Larson

423. Darling, Sharon. ARTS AND CRAFTS SHOPS IN THE FINE ARTS BUILDING. *Chicago Hist. 1977 6(2): 79-85.* Discusses the shops located within Chicago's Fine Arts Building, 1898-1917, showing some of the pottery, china, silver, and glass objects sold there, many now museum pieces and remnants of the art nouveau tradition.

424. Egnal, Marc. THE CHANGING STRUCTURE OF PHILADELPHIA'S TRADE WITH THE BRITISH WEST INDIES, 1750-1775. *Pennsylvania Mag. of Hist. and Biog. 1975 99(2): 156-179.* Examines the profitability and structure of trade with the West Indies, especially during the 1750's. Most trade was on a speculative basis. The Philadelphia merchant supplied the capital, assumed the risks, and garnered the profits. After 1763 there were broad developments which transformed this commerce: 1) the change in the shuttle or direct trade from speculative voyages to commission business financed by the West Indies, and 2) the growth in the late 1760's of a triangular trade involving Great Britain, Pennsylvania, and the British West Indies, financed largely by the British commission agencies. The War for Independence brought it to an end. 56 notes.   R. V. Ritter

425. Eisterhold, John A. CHARLESTON: LUMBER AND TRADE IN A DECLINING SOUTHERN PORT. *South Carolina Hist. Mag. 1973 74(2): 61-72.* Traces the exploitation of the timber resources of South Carolina and its relationship to the development of Charleston as an important southern port during the colonial period. Charleston became preeminent among southern ports in the coastal and international exportation of lumber. After the peak in 1850 decline set in. A decade later Charleston was well below its rivals. 67 notes.   D. L. Smith

426. Eisterhold, John A. LUMBER AND TRADE IN PENSACOLA AND WEST FLORIDA: 1800-1860. *Florida Hist. Q. 1973 51(3): 267-280.* Deals with the main economic resource of early Pensacola, the lumber industry. Exploitation of abundant forest land in the Pensacola area, combined with a good harbor, ensured steady growth of the city during much of the 19th century. Beginning in the 1830's, use of steam power in saw mills greatly increased the amount of finished lumber that could be produced. The industry produced some of the most prominent civil and social leaders of Pensacola, including Alexander McVoy (a city alderman), Joseph Forsyth and E. E. Simpson (who jointly owned one of the largest operations in the state), and W. Main L. Criglar (also involved in shipping operations and with a personal fortune of more than $300,000). Based on primary and newspaper sources; 78 notes.

J. E. Findling

427. Eisterhold, John A. MOBILE: LUMBER CENTER OF THE GULF COAST. *Alabama Rev. 1973 26(2): 83-104.* Discusses the antebellum lumber industry and export market at Mobile. Large tracts of pine, cypress, and hardwoods in Alabama gave Mobile major importance by the 1820's, when steam sawmills were introduced along nearby rivers and streams. Production and exports rose steadily in the 1830's and 1840's; peak production came in 1854-55. Economic preferences for cotton, increased local and regional demand for lumber, and the mounting cost of shipping space later caused the export market to decline. The West Indies, France, and Spain were chief markets. Problems included a chronic shortage of skilled workers, racial tensions, and early attempts at unionization. Based on primary and secondary sources; 128 notes.

J. F. Vivian

428. Eisterhold, John A. SAVANNAH: LUMBER CENTER OF THE SOUTH ATLANTIC. *Georgia Hist. Q. 1973 57(4): 526-543.* Georgia was the leading lumber producing state in the antebellum South. Savannah, one of the busiest lumber markets and ports in the nation, received timber from back country plantations and processed it in sawmills and woodworking shops. Free Negroes and slaves dominated the skilled and semiskilled labor force. By the 1850's England was the dominant market for Savannah's lumber exports. 106 notes.

D. L. Smith

429. García, Mario T. MERCHANTS AND DONS: SAN DIEGO'S ATTEMPT AT MODERNIZATION, 1850-1860. *J. of San Diego Hist. 1975 21(1): 52-80.* Describes the economic development of San Diego after the Mexican War of 1846 from Spanish colonialism to Anglo-American industrial capitalism.

S

430. Goldenberg, Joseph A. THE *WILLIAM* AND *FAVORITE*: THE POST-REVOLUTIONARY VOYAGES OF TWO PHILADELPHIA SHIPS. *Pennsylvania Mag. of Hist. and Biog. 1974 98(3): 325-338.* The voyages of the two ships the *William* and the *Favorite*, owned by Stewart, Nesbitt & Co., demonstrate that the postrevolutionary search for new trade routes and the efforts to reestablish old ones were frustrated as much from the normal hazards of shipping, i.e. damaged vessels, uncollected debts, and rapidly changing markets, as from the obstacles set up by Great Britain and other European countries. Based primarily on the Stewart, Nesbitt & Company papers; 49 notes.

E. W. Carp

431. Hall, Linda. NEIMAN-MARCUS: THE BEGINNING. *Western States Jewish Hist. Q. 1975 7(2): 138-150.* On 10 September 1907 in Dallas, Texas, Herbert Marcus and Al and Carrie Neiman opened their first store, which specialized in fine clothes for women. They had operated a store in Atlanta for two years, but sold it to open their new store in Dallas. They developed new methods of merchandising ready-to-wear clothing. In 1913, the store was destroyed by a fire, after which it moved to larger quarters and continued to grow. The Neiman-Marcus Co. contributed greatly to the development of Dallas as the major fashion market in the Southwest. 36 notes.

R. A. Garfinkle

432. Harvey, Katherine A. WILLIAM ALEXANDER: A COMMISSION MERCHANT IN A NEW ROLE, 1837-43. *Maryland Hist. Mag. 1976 71(1): 26-36.* Surveys the activities of William Alexander, Baltimore commission merchant for the George's Creek Coal and Iron Company at Lonaconing. From his shop at Pratt and Light streets Alexander supplied the company store with clothing and dry goods, groceries, wines, and tobaccos, and his low prices enabled the store to make money. Seldom asking his principals for advice or recommendations, Alexander zealously promoted the company's interests along with his own, and his conscientious attention to packing, selecting wagoners, and acquiring scarce supplies, along with his willingness to do small favors for company personnel, made him invaluable and unique. Some evidence suggests he was preparing to be the marketer for the company's iron products, had it not fallen into hard times. Moreover, the advancing railroads eventually deprived the eastern factor of his position, as did the increasing numbers of traveling salesmen. Still, the contribution of the commission merchant to America's industrial development was considerable. Based on the author's *The Best-Dressed Miners* (Ithaca, 1969), and primary and secondary sources; 74 notes.

G. J. Bobango

433. Hattem, Maurice I. I. M. HATTEM AND HIS LOS ANGELES SUPERMARKET. *Western States Jewish Hist. Q. 1979 11(3): 243-251.* Hattem's Day and Night Drive-In Market, established in 1927, was the first of its kind in Los Angeles. Its owner, Isadore M. Hattem (1894-1966), was a cosmopolitan merchant, born in Constantinople, Turkey, and a world traveler by the time he was 20. He came to Los Angeles in 1913, found a job at a fruit stand, and expanded the business. His flair for showmanship was apparent in the Spanish mission style of his famous Drive-In Market. Hattem's career in the grocery business encompassed both the wholesale and retail outlets until his retirement in 1949. 4 photos.

B. S. Porter

434. Jordan, Jean P. WOMEN MERCHANTS IN COLONIAL NEW YORK. *New York Hist. 1977 58(4): 412-439.* Customs records and post-1730 newspaper advertisements reveal that there were numerous women merchants in New York City during the 17th and 18th centuries.

Women merchants were not allowed to participate in political decision-making. Economic opportunities for women declined after the American Revolution, and only now are women regaining the status in business they enjoyed in the colonial period. 2 illus., 68 notes.

R. N. Lokken

435. Kaplan, Marilyn. THE JEWISH MERCHANTS OF NEWPORT, 1740-1790. *Rhode Island Jewish Hist. Notes 1975 7(1): 12-32.*

436. Karsh, Audrey R. MANNASSE CHICO: ENLIGHTENED MERCHANT OF SAN DIEGO. *Western States Jewish Hist. Q. 1975 8(1): 45-54.* In 1853, Joseph Samuel Mannasse (1831-97) moved to San Diego, California, from New York. He started in the merchandising business and then purchased several rancheros along with his partner and brother-in-law Marcus Schiller. They were very successful until an 1870 drought ruined the ranches and a fire in 1872 destroyed their store. The partnership soon broke up. Mannasse served on the San Diego city council and was very active in civic affairs until his death. 2 photos, 45 notes.

R. A. Garfinkle

437. Killick, John. RISK, SPECIALIZATION AND PROFIT IN THE MERCANTILE SECTOR OF THE NINETEENTH CENTURY COTTON TRADE: ALEXANDER BROWN AND SONS 1820-80. *Business Hist. [Great Britain] 1974 16(1): 1-16.* Beginning in Baltimore in the linen trade in 1800, the firm Alexander Brown and Sons moved into cotton and, to a lesser extent, shipping. Branches were sited in Liverpool, Philadelphia, and New York. By mid-century it was the leading foreign exchange house in the United States. Late in the century it moved into investment banking. Based on primary sources; 2 tables, appendix.

B. L. Crapster

438. Kittell, Robert S. THE OMAHA ICE TRUST, 1899-1900: AN URBAN MONOPOLY. *Nebraska Hist. 1973 54(4): 633-646.* Delineates the brief history of the monopoly, how it operated, and how it was broken by legal action on the part of an aroused community.

R. Lowitt

439. Lahmeyer Lobo, Eulália María. O COMÉRCIO ATLÂNTICO E A COMMUNIDADE DE MERCADORES NO RIO DE JANEIRO E EM CHARLESTON NO SÉCULO XVIII [Merchants of Rio de Janeiro and Charleston and the Atlantic commerce in the 18th century]. *Rev. de Hist. [Brazil] 1975 51(101): 49-106.* In the 18th century, Rio de Janeiro and Charleston were two Atlantic ports with comparable economic structures and social development. Both had the same type of export economy based on African slave labor. Although both economies were subject to the fluctuations of the international market, cycles in South Carolina were of shorter duration than those in Rio de Janeiro. Both economies were at transitional stages between classic slave-plantation and capitalist economies. Based on archival and secondary sources; 64 notes.

C. A. Preece

440. LeFave, Don. TIME OF THE WHITETAIL: THE CHARLES TOWN INDIAN TRADE, 1690-1715. *Studies in Hist. and Soc. 1973 5(1): 5-15.* Studies the Indian trade in whitetail deer hides for local trade and shipment to England which centered in the Carolinas, the base camp being at Savannah Town (modern Augusta) for transport to Charles Town. For a time, trade in Indian slaves supplemented the take on the staple deer hides. The trade area was broad, extending from Pennsylvania south, concentrating in what is now North and South Carolina, Virginia, Georgia, and parts of Florida, Tennessee, Alabama, Mississippi, and Louisiana, involving several Indian tribes. The latter were often incited to war against each other to increase the quantities of hides and slaves. 43 notes.

R. V. Ritter

441. Lindsey, David. CHICAGO: FROM TRADING POST TO MERCHANDISING METROPOLIS. *Mankind 1974 4(9): 8-17.* Discusses the political aspects of merchandizing in the Chicago, Illinois area from the 17th to the 20th century.

S

442. Lutey, Kent. LUTEY BROTHERS MARKETERIA: AMERICA'S FIRST SELF-SERVICE GROCERS. *Montana 1978 28(2): 50-57.* Lutey grocery stores began in Butte, Montana, under Joseph Lutey, Sr., in 1897, and quickly became one of the largest retail, wholesale, and mail order groceries in the state. After Joseph Lutey's death in 1911, his sons Joseph, Jr., and William J., operated the firm as Lutey Brothers. In

1912, William applied the idea of cafeteria-style self-service to the grocery business and opened the "Marketeria" in Butte. He secured a trademark for this term and for "Groceteria" in 1913, and operated the nation's first self-service grocery store until business conditions in Butte forced an end to the operation in 1924. In 1916, Clarence Saunders of Memphis, Tennessee, modeled his Piggly Wiggly grocery chain after the Lutey operation. During World War I, William Lutey served as Federal Food Administrator for the Retail Food Industry in Montana, and contributed many Lutey products to aid European war victims. Based on material in the Montana Historical Society, Helena, and author's reminiscence; 9 illus.   R. C. Myers

443.   Moore, Jamie W.   THE LOWCOUNTRY IN ECONOMIC TRANSITION: CHARLESTON SINCE 1865.   *South Carolina Hist. Mag. 1979 80(2): 156-171.* Describes the economic plans for Charleston, South Carolina, which were drawn up and implemented in order to insure maximum prosperity and trade between Charleston and the Indians, France, Britain, Spain, and the rest of the United States following the Civil War in 1865.

444.   Moore, W. O., Jr.   THE LARGEST EXPORTERS OF DEERSKINS FROM CHARLES TOWN, 1735-1775.   *South Carolina Hist. Mag. 1973 74(3): 144-150.* Along with rice and indigo, deerskins were South Carolina's most valuable export commodities as late as 1769. From 1703 the colony levied export duties on deerskins. Surviving tax records, 1735-75, afford a measure of the trade; 664 firms or persons exported 3,621 consignments to 36 ports or colonies, principally to England. Lists the 176 most frequent exporters, years involved, number of entries, and duty paid. 15 notes.   D. L. Smith

445.   Ott, Joseph K.   RHODE ISLAND FURNITURE EXPORTS, 1783-1800, INCLUDING INFORMATION ON CHAISES, BUILDINGS, OTHER WOODENWARE AND TRADE PRACTICES.   *Rhode Island Hist. 1977 36(1): 3-13.* Newport and Providence continued to export large quantities of furniture and other wooden products after the Revolution. Based on MSS. in the R.I. Historical Society and the R. I. State Archives, Providence, the Newport Historical Society, and the U. of North Carolina, Chapel Hill, and on published documents and secondary accounts; 2 tables, 26 notes.   P. J. Coleman

446.   Paisley, Clifton.   TALLAHASSEE THROUGH THE STOREBOOKS: ERA OF RADICAL RECONSTRUCTION, 1867-1877.   *Florida Hist. Q. 1974 53(1): 49-65.* A study of the business records of hardware merchant William P. Slusser, merchant Alexander Gallie, and the City Hotel. Regardless of the common view that this period was one of "severe economic repression and hardship," the evidence indicates that it was possible to adjust to the times and enjoy a high level of prosperity by replacing the old plantation business with the expenditures of an expanding state government. 2 photos, 61 notes.   R. V. Ritter

447.   Platt, Virginia B.   "AND DON'T FORGET THE GUINEA VOYAGE": THE SLAVE TRADE OF AARON LOPEZ OF NEWPORT.   *William and Mary Q. 1975 32(4): 601-618.* Qualifies the findings of Gilman M. Ostrander's "The Making of the Triangular Trade Myth." Aaron Lopez, a Rhode Island merchant, sent 14 vessels to the slave coast during 1761-64. Each voyage and its shipment of slaves is analyzed. Contains information on prices of slaves, costs, and business organization. Slaving was not the main interest of the Lopez firm, but its activities along with that of other Newport firms demonstrate the triangular trade was not a myth. Based on Lopez' commercial papers; 45 notes.   H. M. Ward

448.   Quilici, R. H.   THE PORTSMOUTH MARINE SOCIETY: SOCIAL DIVERSITY IN A COLONIAL MARITIME COMMUNITY.   *Hist. New Hampshire 1975 30(2): 101-112.* Analyzes the 1765 membership of the Portsmouth Marine Society to explore the socioeconomic structures of colonial Portsmouth's maritime community. All the members who signed a 1765 petition were shipowners and/or shipmasters. Generally, those who became owners and managers had "the advantage of education and/or apprenticeship." But "beyond their common participation in maritime commerce and their joint non-participation in local government, the members of the Marine Society were a rather diverse social and economic collection of individuals." Their ages were mixed, they attended several different churches, and they did not all live in any one section of Portsmouth. 5 illus., 20 notes.   D. F. Chard

449.   Raymond, Robert S.   THE ECONOMIC HISTORY OF A MIDWESTERN RETAIL STORE, 1911-1934.   *Kansas Hist. Q. 1976 42(3): 308-328.* Scott Raymond and E. G. Green formed the Raymond-Green Furniture Company in Kansas City, Kansas. Patrons of their first store were the "dinner bucket brigade." Subsequently, stores on Grand Avenue attracted pedestrians and those who responded to advertisements. The partnership did not survive the Great Depression. The early success of the venture was due to environmental factors and to the business skills of the partners. Primary sources; illus., 8 notes.   W. F. Zornow

450.   Rowley, Dennis.   NAUVOO: A RIVER TOWN.   *Brigham Young U. Studies 1978 18(2): 255-272.* Examines the economic growth of Nauvoo, Illinois, especially the impact of the Mississippi River on its commercial development during 1839-46. While the steamboat era was in progress, the Mormons quickly took advantage of the maritime opportunities to improve their economic position. Whether constructing canals or dams, operating boarding houses for passengers, purchasing steamboats for the river trade, or developing wharves or sawmills, the Mormon leaders sought to improve the commercial position of Nauvoo for the Church's benefit.   M. S. Legan

451.   Rudd, Hynda.   AUERBACH'S: ONE OF THE WEST'S OLDEST DEPARTMENT STORES.   *Western States Jewish Hist. Q. 1979 11(3): 234-238.* Auerbach's Department Store was founded in Salt Lake City, Utah, in 1864. The Auerbach brothers had earlier stores in the mining camps of California. In the 1860's the Auerbachs operated tent stores along the route of the transcontinental railroad while it was under construction. The main store in Salt Lake City remained in the family from 1864 to 1977, although it had many changes of location. Published and archival sources; 7 photos, 3 notes.   B. S. Porter

452.   Schwartz, Henry.   THE LEVI SAGA: TEMECULA, JULIAN, SAN DIEGO.   *Western States Jewish Hist. Q. 1974 6(3): 161-176.* A biography of Simon Levi (1850-1918) and his brother Adolph Levi (1858-1943), who came to San Diego from Bohemia, set up stores in several locations, and became successful businessmen. Examines their many years of public service. Primary and secondary sources; 5 photos, 53 notes.   R. A. Garfinkle

453.   Segal, Beryl and Goldowsky, Seebert J.   JAMES JACOBS, EARLY JEWISH MERCHANT OF PROVIDENCE, RHODE ISLAND.   *Rhode Island Jewish Hist. Notes 1978 7(4): 461-470.* James Jacobs, possibly the first Jew to settle in Providence, was successful and prominent there, 1820's-30's and 1850's.

454.   Smith, David C.   COASTAL SHIPPING TRADE ON THE EVE OF THE RAILROAD: GARDINER, MAINE IN THE EARLY 1830S.   *Maine Hist. Soc. Q. 1974 13(3): 148-177.* Gardiner, a small Kennebec River port, handled nearly 500 vessels a year, mostly coasting schooners and sloops. These vessels exported wood products, agricultural goods, cloth, ice, imported flour, corn, and manufactures. Traffic was heaviest from mid-summer to late fall. The vessels usually sailed to Massachusetts, especially Boston. Many also sailed to the New England fishing and whaling ports, bringing supplies and provisions for the fleets. Newspapers and secondary sources; 7 tables, 47 notes.

E. A. Churchill

455.   Smith, Miriam Jane.   FORGOTTEN VIRGINIAN—FROM BRITISH MERCHANT TO PROMINENT CITIZEN: THOMAS RUTHERFOORD, 1755-1852.   *West Virginia Hist. 1974 36(1): 50-62.* Thomas Rutherford (1776-1852) was born in Glasgow, worked for his brothers' mercantile firm, and settled at Richmond, Virginia in the 1780's. In the business boom after 1790 he started his own firm, developed suburban land, speculated in tobacco, and later entered milling. A federalist, he feared war with Britain would be disastrous for America, and he opposed the 1807 Embargo. By 1811 he was the wealthiest man in Richmond, with assets over $110,000. After 1815 he made huge profits from land sales and retired, though continuing as a bank director and city councilman. Based largely on Rutherfoord's autobiography; 55 notes.

J. H. Broussard

456.   Somers, Dale A.   NEW ORLEANS AT WAR: A MERCHANT'S VIEW.   *Louisiana Hist. 1973 14(1): 49-68.* The Union blockade of New Orleans caused economic recession and failures there. One

firm that reflected this pattern was the cotton brokerage of Godfrey Barnsley. Barnsley was in Georgia during 1861-62 and was kept abreast of the firm's fortunes by his manager, Henry S. Gilmour. Gilmour's 12 letters to Barnsley, June 1861-April 1862, published herein, provide a clear picture of New Orleans, particularly of the cotton market and the defensive preparations, and suggest that many businessmen placed their financial interests above their southern sympathies. Based on Barnsley's Papers, in the Emory University Library; 22 notes.

R. L. Woodward

457. Springer, Kathleen M.; Springer, George W.; and Reichmann, Keith W.   AN HISTORIC PHARMACY: CENTRAL CITY, COLORADO.   *Pharmacy in Hist. 1974 16(3): 97-101.* Discusses the history of Best's Pharmacy (presently Springer's) in Central City, Colorado from 1861-1974, emphasizing its supplying of drugs and mill chemicals to Gold Rush miners in 1874.

458. Stern, Joseph S., Jr.   FINDLAY MARKET AND THE OVER-THE-RHINE REVISITED.   *Cincinnati Hist. Soc. Bull. 1976 34(1): 24-45.* History (1852-1976) of an open marketplace, Findlay Market, in the Over-the-Rhine section of Cincinnati, Ohio, and its redevelopment in the 1970's.

459. Stern, Norton B.   THE FRANKLIN BROTHERS OF SAN DIEGO.   *J. of San Diego Hist. 1975 21(3): 32-42.* Describes the lives of Lewis Abraham Franklin (1820-79) and his brother Maurice Abraham Franklin (1817-74), pioneer merchants of San Diego during the 1850's.

S

460. Stumpf, Stuart O.   IMPLICATIONS OF KING GEORGE'S WAR FOR THE CHARLESTON MERCANTILE COMMUNITY.   *South Carolina Hist. Mag. 1976 77(3): 161-188.* War between Spain and England, originally welcomed as a remedy for Spanish disruption of slaves, eventually caused economic depression and political uncertainty among South Carolina's merchants, 1739-54.

461. Teske, Robert Thomas.   ON THE MAKING OF *BOBONIERES* AND *MARTURIA* IN GREEK-PHILADELPHIA: COMMERCIALISM IN FOLK RELIGION.   *J. of the Folklore Inst. 1977 14(3): 159-167. Bobonieres* and *marturia* are the small, ephemeral artifacts that are given as commemorative tokens at Greek American marriage and christening rites. Tells of one young couple who manufacture and sell these traditional artifacts from their shop in Upper Darby, Pennsylvania. Their experiences reveal the conflicts inherent when a traditional folk art is adapted to a commercial context. Based on personal interviews; 8 notes.

J. L. White

462. Vinci, John.   CARSON PIRIE SCOTT: 125 YEARS IN BUSINESS.   *Chicago Hist. 1979 8(2): 92-97.* The 125-year-old Carson Pirie Scott and Company of Chicago was founded in 1854 by John T. Pirie and Samuel Carson, two Scotsmen who were joined in 1856 by two Scottish brothers, George and Robert Scott; presents photographs of the store's locations in Chicago during 1880's-1904.

463. Walker, Paul K.   BUSINESS AND COMMERCE IN BALTIMORE ON THE EVE OF INDEPENDENCE.   *Maryland Hist. Mag. 1976 71(3): 296-309.* "The economic foundations laid down in Baltimore between 1763 and 1776 were vital to the even greater expansion seen during the Revolutionary War." Though still behind Philadelphia, Baltimore merchants and enterprisers produced an expanding commercial community with family businesses and partnerships proliferating in shipping, the flour-milling and grain business, and the indentured servant traffic. Commerce concentrated in four areas: Britain, Southern Europe, the West Indies, and the North American coastal towns. Examines newspaper ads, cargo manifests, tonnage figures, wills, and inventories of Baltimoreans. Credit was the essence of the system and a virtual chain of indebtedness meant that bills remained long unpaid and little cash was used among overseas correspondents, merchant wholesalers, and retail customers. Bills of exchange were used extensively, often circulating as currency. Frequent crises of credit, and the wars with France kept prices and markets in constant flux, but men such as William Lux and the Christie brothers produced a maturing economy and a thriving metropolis by the 1770's. Largely primary sources; 41 notes.

G. J. Bobango

464. Wiener, Alfred D.   THE ELK STREET MARKET AND X-CEL FOOD MARKET.   *Niagara Frontier 1977 24(1): 20-28; (2): 45-50.* Continued from a previous abstract (see abstract 15A:2246). In two parts. Reminisces about his grocery markets in Buffalo, New York, 1917-65.

465. Wilkenfeld, Bruce M.   THE NEW YORK CITY SHIPOWNING COMMUNITY, 1715-1764.   *Am. Neptune 1977 37(1): 50-65.* During 1715-64, New York City shipowners became increasingly involved in the transatlantic trade. In the final decades of the colonial period the availability of positions in this social and economic elite appears to have been reduced. The changed patterns in this shipowning community suggest that by the close of the colonial period American shipowners may have become a source of tension within New York and the British empire. Merchant hostility developed because British merchants felt the transatlantic trade belonged to them, while New York colonials of middling and lower-class origin found fewer opportunities to advance economically. The patterns of development among colonial shipowners, therefore, may well have been a "possible factor in the proclivity towards violence and rebellion." Primary sources; table, 38 notes.

G. H. Curtis

466. Wohl, R. Richard.   THREE GENERATIONS OF BUSINESS ENTERPRISE IN A MIDWESTERN CITY: THE MC GEES OF KANSAS CITY.   *Westport Hist. Q. 1973 9(3): 63-79.*

Manufacturing and Industry

467. Adams, Donald R., Jr.   RESIDENTIAL CONSTRUCTION INDUSTRY IN THE EARLY NINETEENTH CENTURY.   *J. of Econ. Hist. 1975 35(4): 794-816.* Using census data and a detailed record from Philadelphia, 1785-1830, the author constructs a weighted cost index for the construction industry in the antebellum period. The findings indicate that for this industry costs have been stable over a very long time period, as has productivity. In the absence of technological change, the construction industry did not substitute factor inputs so as to lower costs. These conclusions can probably be applied to all eastern cities during the antebellum years.

J

468. Ames, Kenneth L.   GRAND RAPIDS FURNITURE AT THE TIME OF THE CENTENNIAL.   *Winterthur Portfolio 1975 (10): 23-50.* Three furniture companies—Berkey and Gay; Phoenix; and Nelson, Matter and Company—made Grand Rapids, Michigan an important furniture center during the 1870's. While quick to modernize, it was the skill, personality, and talents of manufacturers that accounts for the rise of Grand Rapids, their most important contribution being the establishment of the semiannual furniture market. Based on primary and secondary sources; 21 illus., chart, 57 notes.

N. A. Kuntz

469. Anderson, Harry H.   NORWEGIAN SHIPBUILDING IN EARLY MILWAUKEE.   *Milwaukee Hist. 1978 1(3-4): 81-104.* Traces the participation of Norwegian Americans in shipbuilding, ship ownership, and related industry during the 19th century in Milwaukee.

470. Becker, Carl M.   A "MOST COMPLETE" FACTORY: THE BARNEY CAR WORKS, 1850-1926.   *Cincinnati Hist. Soc. Bull. 1973 31(1): 48-69.* Much of Dayton's industrial well-being in the late 19th century was due to the Barney and Smith Car Company, which developed rapidly between 1850 and 1890. This company manufactured wooden railroad cars including freight, passenger, and private palace cars. After 1900 the company declined rapidly and was dissolved in 1926 due primarily to the failure of the company to produce steel cars. Additional causes were a lack of capital and the flood of 1913 which completely inundated its facilities. Based on primary and secondary sources; 11 illus., 60 notes.

H. S. Marks

471. Bergquist, H. E., Jr.   THE BOSTON MANUFACTURING COMPANY AND ANGLO-AMERICAN RELATIONS 1807-1820.   *Business Hist. [Great Britain] 1973 15(1): 45-55.* Founded in 1812, the Boston Manufacturing Company exemplifies the state of American industrial development during the period when war cut off English competition. Francis Cabot Lowell (1775-1817) went to England to learn the design of new machinery which, with improvements, was manufactured

in Massachussetts. The firm's heavy durable cotton sheeting survived the postwar reopening of international trade. Lowell was active in the movement leading to the mildly protectionist tariff of 1816. Based on unpublished dissertation. B. L. Crapster

472. Bixby, Arthur M., Sr. NORFOLK AND WESTERN'S ROANOKE SHOPS AND ITS LOCOMOTIVES. *Railroad Hist. 1977 (137): 20-37.* Discusses the Roanoke Machine Works during 1881-1976, in Roanoke, Virginia, which later became the Roanoke and Western's machine shop, a major center for the repair and production of railroad equipment.

473. Boland, S. M. SAN FRANCISCO AND WHALING ON THE WEST COAST. *Nautical Res. J. 1973 20(1): 15-17.* Examines the origin and development of the Pacific coast whaling industry in the 19th and 20th centuries, tracing its beginnings to the California Gold Rush. S

474. Candee, Richard. THE "GREAT FACTORY" AT DOVER, NEW HAMPSHIRE: THE DOVER MANUFACTURING CO. PRINT WORKS, 1825. *Old-Time New England 1975 66(1-2): 39-51.* Gives the history and describes the architecture and construction of the cotton mills built by the Taunton Manufacturing Company, the Merrimack Manufacturing Company, and the Dover Manufacturing Company between 1820 and 1825 to introduce and increase mechanical calico printing in New England; focuses on the Dover Manufacturing Co. Print Works built at Dover, New Hampshire in 1825.

475. Catalano, Kathleen M. ABRAHAM KIMBALL (1798-1890), SALEM CABINETMAKER. *Am. Art J. 1979 11(2): 62-70.* Describes Abraham Kimball (1798-1890), a prominent post-Federal period cabinetmaker from Salem, Massachusetts. During 1822-43 he worked in partnership with Winthrop Sargent producing a variety of pieces, although only one authenticated piece is known. The firm prospered and employed 17 journeymen. In 1844-45 Kimball worked alone and then retired. In 1843 he produced three pieces of Gothic Revival furniture in American black walnut for Henry Wadsworth Longfellow (1807-82). Kimball's career shows that furniture making continued to flourish in Salem after the Federal period. Primary and secondary sources; 11 illus., 26 notes. J. J. Buschen

476. Catalano, Kathleen M. FURNITURE MAKING IN PHILADELPHIA, 1820-1840. *Am. Art and Antiques 1979 2(6): 116-123.* Between 1820 and 1840, Philadelphia was the center of furniture manufacturing in the United States; describes the economic success of cabinetmakers, woodworking machinery, furniture style and decoration, and the market for Philadelphia-made furniture.

477. Champlin, Richard S. THE ART, TRADE, OR MYSTERY OF THE ROPEMAKER. *Newport Hist. 1973 46(4): 81-95.* Newport's long history of ropemaking began with Robert Taylor Freeman in 1655. The chief materials in the manufacture of rope were hemp and tar. In 1722 the General Assembly of Rhode Island began to pay bounties to encourage the growing of hemp. Much of the hemp, however, had to be imported from the Southern colonies and Russia. Ropemakers had to serve an apprenticeship before becoming journeymen ropemakers. Several disastrous fires plagued the Newport ropemakers. Deacon William Tilley was one of Newport's leading ropemakers in 1810. 29 notes. J. H. Krenkel

478. Clunie, Margaret B. FURNITURE CRAFTSMEN OF SALEM, MASSACHUSETTS, IN THE FEDERAL PERIOD. *Essex Inst. Hist. Collections 1977 113(3): 191-203.* The Reverend William Bentley's diary is only a starting point for a study of Salem's craftsmen, because he commented upon them as individuals and did not describe their work. The salient quality of cabinetmaking in Federalist Salem was the cooperative nature of the work. Furniture shops employed specialists whose pieces made up the final product. This symbiotic relationship was due to the nature of the apprenticeship system, family traditions, shop locations, and designs. Based on the diary (1784-1819) of William Bentley and on primary and secondary sources; 50 notes. R. S. Sliwoski

479. Cole, Glyndon. THE EASTMAN STORY. *York State Tradition 1974 28(3): 21-28.* Discusses the life and family home of George

Eastman (1854-1932), founder of the Eastman Kodak Company, in Rochester, New York. S

480. Dalzell, Robert F., Jr. THE RISE OF THE WALTHAM-LOWELL SYSTEM AND SOME THOUGHTS ON THE POLITICAL ECONOMY OF MODERNIZATION IN ANTE-BELLUM MASSACHUSETTS. *Perspectives in Am. Hist. 1975 9: 229-268.* Investors did not turn to industry in Massachusetts because of declining rates of return on capital in maritime commerce. The concept of modernization, provides a broader viewpoint linking social and political change with economic development. Boston merchants did not shift their capital from the sea to land simply to increase their profits. Rather, they shifted because they wished to maintain the existence of the New England leisure class by preserving fortunes already made. 76 notes. W. A. Wiegand

481. Destler, Chester McArthur. THE HARTFORD WOOLEN MANUFACTORY: THE STORY OF A FAILURE. *Connecticut Hist. 1974 (14): 8-32.* Mentions Jeremiah Wadsworth and covers 1788-95. S

482. Dibble, Ann W. MAJOR JOHN DUNLAP: THE CRAFTSMAN AND HIS COMMUNITY. *Old-Time New England 1978 68(3-4): 50-58.* Biography of cabinetmaker, house joiner, and farmer, Major John Dunlap (1746-92) of Goffstown and Bedford, New Hampshire; Dunlap's cabinetmaking accounts reveal his skills, employment patterns, trade, and farming in the Goffstown-Bedford area during colonial times.

483. Donnell, Robert P. LOCATIONAL RESPONSE TO CATASTROPHE: THE SHOE AND LEATHER INDUSTRY OF SALEM AFTER THE CONFLAGRATION OF 25 JUNE 1914. *Essex Inst. Hist. Collections 1977 113(2): 105-116.* On 25 June 1914 fire destroyed more than 250 acres of Salem's major shoe and leather industries. The catastrophe further stimulated migration underway by 1900 in the shoe industry. By the early 20th century most of Salem's industrial plants were outmoded and unable to compete advantageously with others in New England. Consequently, most did not rebuild in the burned out area, and moved their operations outside Salem. Salem was saved in the 1920's when lighting and electronics firms filled the industrial vacuum. Primary and secondary sources; 4 maps, photo, 14 notes.
R. S. Sliwoski

484. Donnelly, Gaylord. THE INFLUENCE OF STONE AND KIMBALL ON CHICAGO PRINTING. *Newberry Lib. Bull. 1978 6(9): 314-321.* Describes Chicago publishing and printing establishments in the 1890's, when the firm of Stone and Kimball established itself in the city. Illus. D. A. Yanchisin

485. Duggan, Edward P. MACHINES, MARKETS, AND LABOR: THE CARRIAGE AND WAGON INDUSTRY IN LATE-NINETEENTH-CENTURY CINCINNATI. *Business Hist. Rev. 1977 51(3): 308-325.* Tests H. J. Habakkuk's labor supply hypothesis which asserts that a labor shortage stimulated rapid technological change. Carriage and wagon producers in Cincinnati did not appear to suffer from such a shortage. They sought production techniques to increase output, not to save on labor costs. They also invested more capital in developing markets than in manufacturing, indicating a belief that there was more to gain from marketing innovations than from production. Based on governmental records and periodical sources; 30 notes.
C. J. Pusateri

486. Dunham, Bob. PROVINCETOWN'S BOAT BUILDING LEGACY. *New-England Galaxy 1978 19(3): 42-50.* Traces the rise and fall of the wooden fishing boat building industry in Provincetown, Massachusetts, during 1900-77. Describes the contributions of Manuel Furtago, Francis Santos, Frank Taves, Larry Meads, and Ted Box. 6 illus.
P. C. Marshall

487. Ellsworth, Lucius F. RAIFORD AND ABERCROMBIE: PENSACOLA'S PREMIER ANTEBELLUM MANUFACTURER. *Florida Hist. Q. 1974 52(3): 247-260.* Phillip H. Raiford and General Anderson Abercrombie formed a company in 1854 to manufacture bricks. Located in Pensacola, the company secured a government contract to supply bricks for the construction of Fort Taylor in Key West and Fort Jefferson on Dry Tortugas. Details problems encountered in making

satisfactory bricks and shipping them to Key West. A great step forward occurred with the hiring of John W. Creary as superintendent; his brick-making machine produced more bricks of consistently higher quality than those made by hand labor. Manuscript, newspaper and secondary sources; 7 illus., 56 notes.   J. E. Findling

488. Enders, Donald L. A DAM FOR NAUVOO: AN ATTEMPT TO INDUSTRIALIZE THE CITY. *Brigham Young U. Studies 1978 18(2): 246-254.* The geographic position of Nauvoo on the Mississippi River near the head of the Des Moines Rapids had long been extolled as being advantageous for industry. If the river could be harnessed for power, the populace could establish their community on a firm economic base. Traces Mormon attitudes and efforts to construct a dam during 1830-43 so that waterpower sites might be developed. However, the project proved too ambitious even for the hard-working Mormons. Not until 1913 was a hydroelectric dam completed to harness the Des Moines Rapids for waterpower.   M. S. Legan

489. Fey, Marshall A. CHARLES FEY AND SAN FRANCISCO'S LIBERTY BELL SLOT MACHINE. *California Hist. Q. 1975 54(1): 57-62.* A brief sketch of Charles Fey, inventor of the three-reel Liberty Bell slot machine. Fey invented the machine in 1895, superseding the cumbersome "Dewey" machine then in use. Rather than patent his invention or lease the machines, he operated and serviced them from his own business, serving the Bay area and central California. The attraction of the three reels brought customers to use them in saloons, gambling houses, and brothels. In 1905 a machine came into the possession of a competitor, the Mills Novelty Company, which then marketed its own Liberty Bell machine. Fey's slot machine business was ended by the 1906 earthquake and fire, which destroyed his establishment along with those businesses that carried most of his machines. The mechanism Fey developed is still found in modern slot machines. Primary and secondary sources; illus., 17 notes.   A. Hoffman

490. Frame, Robert M., III. MILLS, MACHINES AND MILLERS: MINNESOTA SOURCES FOR FLOUR-MILLING RESEARCH. *Minnesota Hist. 1978 46(4): 152-162.* Between the 1880's and the 1930's Minneapolis was the flour-milling capital of the world. Very few operating mills remain today in the city, although a few survive in other parts of the state. The history of the flour-milling industry in Minnesota has been largely unrecorded by the historian. Valuable sources for the compilation of this history exist in the files of the *Northwestern Miller,* a publication designed for the major elements in the industry, and in the records of this longtime business manager, William C. Edgar. The *American Miller* magazine concentrated on the interests of the smaller, largely rural millers. The technological side of the industry is worth investigation; sources exist for this research, although most of the early machinery of the industry has not been preserved.   N. Lederer

491. Gilbane, Brendan F. PAWTUCKET VILLAGE MECHANICS, IRON, INGENUITY, AND THE COTTON REVOLUTION. *Rhode Island Hist. 1975 34(1): 3-12.* Established in 1691, Pawtucket, Rhode Island, was well-established as a center of the iron industry by 1790 and was populated by a number of ingenious mechanics who were able to apply their knowledge to the cotton industry, 1790's-1810's.

492. Gould, Christopher. ROBERT WELLS, COLONIAL CHARLESTON PRINTER. *South Carolina Hist. Mag. 1978 79(1): 23-49.* Robert Wells (1754-81), worked at bookselling, printing, and bookbinding in Charleston, South Carolina; includes an annotated list of all publications printed by Wells.

493. Gumina, Deanna Paoli. THE FISHERMEN OF SAN FRANCISCO BAY. *Pacific Historian 1976 20(1): 8-21.* Brief history of Italian fishermen of San Francisco Bay, 1850's-1940's. Presents Gaetano Tarantino, a 92-year-old fisherman who has seen major changes in the industry, including change from sail to motors, creation of "Fisherman's Wharf," organization of fishermen, development of restaurants along the wharf, and alien restrictions during World War II. Based on primary sources; 5 illus., 41 notes.   G. L. Olson

494. Hart, Kenneth Wayne. CINCINNATI ORGAN BUILDERS OF THE NINETEENTH CENTURY. *Cincinnati Hist. Soc. Bull. 1973 31(2): 79-98.* As Cincinnati quickly developed into a major community,

that city experienced a remarkable expansion of churches. About 1850 a major influx of Germans made possible the development of organ building. Early organ builders were Adam Hurdus (the first), Luman Watson, and Israel Schooley. The premier early organ builder, however, was Matthias Schwab, who was succeeded by his principal apprentice, Johann Heinrich Koehnken. After Schwab retired, Koehnken and Gallus Grimm formed Koehnken and Company. In 1896 Koehnken retired and Grimm brought his son into the partnership and renamed it G. Grimm and Son, which lasted until 1900. Based on unpublished manuscripts, and on secondary sources; 8 photos, 65 notes.   H. S. Marks

495. Hekman, John S. AN ANALYSIS OF THE CHANGING LOCATION OF IRON AND STEEL PRODUCTION IN THE TWENTIETH CENTURY. *Am. Econ. Rev. 1978 68(1): 123-133.* Compares alternative explanations of the westward movement of steel production in the United States from Pennsylvania to Chicago, Cleveland, and Detroit between 1910 and 1972, using the results of an econometric model. Previous explanations have associated the change with geographical differences in the cost of production, but the econometric evidence indicates that cost differences had little or nothing to do with this movement. The crucial variable explaining the relatively greater growth of the western producers have been the differential growth of demand by steel-using industries. Based on official statistics and secondary works; 10 tables, 6 notes.   D. J. Nicholls

496. Hodge, Jo Dent. THE LUMBER INDUSTRY IN LAUREL, MISSISSIPPI, AT THE TURN OF THE NINETEENTH CENTURY. *J. of Mississippi Hist. 1973 35(4): 361-379.* Traces the development of the lumber industry in and around Laurel 1882-1916, when the town "grew from a crude lumber camp into an enterprising community around which centered the yellow pine industry of the nation." Laurel became "the lumber manufacturing center of the South" and by 1916 "was shipping more yellow pine lumber than any city in the world." The Eastman-Gardiner Company, headed by George and Silas Gardiner, "two of America's foremost lumber barons," and their brother-in-law, Lauren Eastman, furnished exceptional business and civic leadership after entering the area in 1890. Based largely on newspapers; 93 notes.
                                        J. W. Hillje

497. Hofsommer, Donovan L. RAILROADS AND RICHES: THE BURKBURNETT BOOM. *Great Plains J. 1974 14(1): 72-86.* The oil boom at Burkburnett, Texas, began in 1918 and ended by 1923. Oil had been produced in the area since 1902 and production continued after 1923, but for a short time the needs of thousands of workers, and the shipment of oil and equipment for new wells transformed the community and converted the Wichita Falls and Northwestern Railway into "an important artery of commerce." M.G.M.'s 1940 movie, *Boom Town,* was based on the Burkburnett boom. Based on primary and secondary materials; 12 illus., 15 notes.   O. H. Zabel

498. Jahant, Charles A. CHICAGO: CENTER OF THE SILENT FILM INDUSTRY. *Chicago Hist. 1974 3(1): 45-53.*

499. Knapp, Vertie. THE NATURAL ICE INDUSTRY OF PHILADELPHIA IN THE NINETEENTH CENTURY. *Pennsylvania Hist. 1974 41(4): 413-421.* Traces the development of the Philadelphia ice industry from colonial times to the 1870's. In the late 18th century, the rich stored ice for summer use and ice cream, and ice was also kept for medical purposes. The use of ice became more common in the early 19th century; suppliers cutting ice on the Schuylkill River or importing it from Maine. Discusses ice harvesting technology and the firms involved in the industry. By making it possible for the city to rely upon distant sources for food, the ice industry contributed to urban growth. Illus., 40 notes.
                                        D. C. Swift

500. Kuhm, Herbert W. THEN MILWAUKEE BEGAN TO BUILD ITS OWN SHIPS. *Milwaukee Hist. 1978 1(3-4): 58-66.* Shipbuilding in America. began ca 1520; traces the shipbuilding industry in Milwaukee, which was a prestigious Great Lakes shipbuilding center during the 19th century.

501. Kulik, Gary B. BIRMINGHAM. *Am. Preservation 1978 1(3): 20-23.* Discusses the Sloss Company, whose city furnaces produced pig iron until their close in 1970. The furnaces, rebuilt during 1927-28, are

a central element of the Birmingham, Alabama skyline and will be converted into an industrial museum by the city. Comments on the company's failure to innovate in laborsaving equipment. Rejects as inadequate, the explanations that Sloss Company iron works was a marginal producer and that Southern iron industries were backward. Covers 1881-1978. Illus.   J. Tull

502. Lamb, Blaine P. SILENT FILM MAKING IN SAN DIEGO, 1898-1912. *J. of San Diego Hist. 1976 22(4): 38-47.* Discusses the movie industry and the making of silent films in San Diego 1898-1912, emphasizing the productions of the American Film Manufacturing Co., the Essanay Western Co., and the Ammex Motion Picture Manufacturing Co.

503. Massouh, Michael. TECHNOLOGICAL AND MANAGERIAL INNOVATION: THE JOHNSON COMPANY 1883-1898. *Business Hist. Rev. 1976 50(1): 47-68.* Describes a manufacturing company established by Tom L. Johnson, the Progressive mayor of Cleveland, Ohio, in 1883. Established to meet the needs of the expanding street railway business, it was a pioneer in making a number of industrial innovations, including one of the earliest national marketing systems staffed by its own trained salesmen. Management ideas generated by the Johnson Company were later copied by such industrial giants as DuPont and General Motors. Based largely on periodical materials of the period and on private papers; 56 notes.   C. J. Pusateri

504. McKelvey, Blake. LUMBER AND WOOD PROCESSING IN ROCHESTER'S HISTORY. *Rochester Hist. 1978 40(1): 1-24.* Chronicles lumbering and wood processing in Rochester, New York, 1788-1880.

505. Muller, Edward K. and Groves, Paul A. THE CHANGING LOCATION OF THE CLOTHING INDUSTRY: A LINK TO THE SOCIAL GEOGRAPHY OF BALTIMORE IN THE NINETEENTH CENTURY. *Maryland Hist. Mag. 1976 71(3): 403-420.* Examines the nature, growth, location, ownership, and industrial organization of Baltimore's post-civil war clothing industry. Unskilled women predominated in the putting out (outside shop) system of the new ready-to-wear warehouses and factory enterprises. The wholesale manufacturer "became the central organizing force" in expanding the industry, and the contracting system not only met the expanding demands for ready-to-wear garments, but spawned the infamous "sweatshop" networks. The pedestrian nature of the employment linkage meant that residential patterning of workers as the industry expanded depended more on business organization and availability of intraurban transit networks allowing middlemen to move raw materials to the sweatshops than on ethnic groupings or the availability of housing. Urban historians need to consider the location of employment more than they have, even though essential sources of data such as census enumerations are problematic. 3 illus., 6 figs., 5 tables, 51 notes.   G. J. Bobango

506. Nelson, Daniel. SCIENTIFIC MANAGEMENT IN TRANSITION: FREDERICK W. TAYLOR AT JOHNSTOWN, 1896. *Pennsylvania Mag. of Hist. and Biog. 1975 99(4): 460-475.* Frederick W. Taylor is best known for his introduction of technological and organizational changes at the Midvale Steel Company at Philadelphia and the Bethlehem Steel Company. A third company, the Johnson Company at Johnstown, Pennsylvania, made rails and motors for the electric streetcar industry. Describes Taylor's 1896 work at the Johnson Company in new accounting methods, storekeeping systems, the differential piece rate, planning department, functional foremanship, and mechanical innovations. 54 notes.   C. W. Olson

507. Owen, Barbara. A SALEM CHAMBER ORGAN. *Essex Inst. Hist. Collections 1974 110(2): 111-119.* Traces the organ-making career of brothers Elias and George Hook in Salem, Massachusetts (1827-80's), and the history of an organ built by George in 1827.   S

508. Roppel, Patricia. LORING. *Alaska J. 1975 5(3): 168-178.* Discusses the history of the salmon packing industry in Loring, Alaska, 1883-1936. 11 photos, reproduction, 54 notes.

509. Russell, Jack. THE COMING OF THE LINE: THE FORD HIGHLAND PARK PLANT, 1910-1914. *Radical Am. 1978 12(3): 28-45.* Detroit became predominant in automobile making in the early

20th century due to its extensive industrial base and to the open shop environment that had been created through the Employer's Association of Detroit. The existence of many nonunionized workers and the destruction of previously significant craft unions in turn made the pre-World War I period a propitious time for the Ford Motor Company to introduce rationalization at its new Highland Park assembly plant. Ford engineers skillfully converted the previous hand assembly of the automobile and its parts into a continuous line assembly operation, with individual work contributions simplified and speeded up. The result was an automobile assembled far more quickly than ever before. Acute worker discontent arose over rationalization in 1913 and contributed to huge turnovers in the work force and to rising personnel costs. In 1914 Ford responded with the $5 minimum wage to quiet worker discontent and lessen turnover.
                                                                N. Lederer

510. Savoie, Ronald. THE SILK INDUSTRY IN NORTHAMPTON. *Hist. J. of Western Massachusetts 1977 5(2): 21-32.* Traces the history of the silk industry in Northampton, Massachusetts, during 1830-1930. Discusses the contributions of Samuel Whitmarsh, who began silk cultivation and weaving in the area in 1835. Focuses on the Corticelli Company, founded as Nonotuck Company, which absorbed many small firms and continued in business until 1930 when Northampton's silk industry ended. 101 notes.   W. H. Mulligan, Jr.

511. Schnell, J. Christopher and Stewart, Steven W. SEDALIA AS A CATTLE TOWN: THE LONG DRIVE. *Kansas Q. 1974 6(4): 15-21.* Discusses the economic growth of the cattle industry in Sedalia, Missouri, 1856-66.   S

512. Sharrer, G. Terry. FLOUR MILLING IN THE GROWTH OF BALTIMORE, 1750-1830. *Maryland Hist. Mag. 1976 71(3): 322-333.* Discusses the American flour and grain trade to Europe and the West Indies as affected by famines, crop failures, and the Napoleonic Wars abroad, and the Jeffersonian embargo at home. Waterloo and the British Corn Laws greatly diminished these markets and US consumption and the trade with South America replaced them. Baltimore dominated the flour trade in both periods due to the milling technology of Oliver Evans, the introduction of steam power in processing, and the merchant-millers' development of drying processes which greatly retarded spoilage. Still, by 1830 New York's competition was felt keenly, and Baltimoreans were hard-pressed to match the merchantability standards despite more rigorous inspection controls than earlier, nor could they match the greater financial resources of their northern rivals. Primary and secondary sources; 30 notes.   G. J. Bobango

513. Smith, Nancy A. PIANOFORTE MANUFACTURING IN NINETEENTH-CENTURY BOSTON. *Old-Time New England 1978 69(1-2): 37-47.* The first pianoforte maker, Benjamin Crehore, started his shop in Milton, near Boston, in 1792, making harpsichords, and finally in 1943 the Vose and Sons Piano Company auctioned off its stock and equipment; discusses the importance of pianos as a focus for family social gatherings.

514. Steffen, Charles G. CHANGES IN THE ORGANIZATION OF ARTISAN PRODUCTION IN BALTIMORE, 1790 TO 1820. *William and Mary Q. 1979 36(1): 101-117.* The artisan crafts of Baltimore had varied development: some held to the handicraft system while others changed substantially. Analyzes the distribution and kinds of wealth among members of different crafts. Emphasizes slaveholding and the uses of slave labor in certain crafts. Discusses problems of indentured and apprenticed service. Growing numbers of apprentices and slaves in some of the crafts threatened the status of journeymen. Based on account books, indenture contracts, and court documents; 9 tables, 42 notes.
                                                                H. M. Ward

515. Summar, Donald J. THE CENTRIFUGAL ROTARY ENGINE COMPANY OF LANCASTER, 1870-1871. *J. of the Lancaster County Hist. Soc. 1977 81(2): 101-112.* Based on papers of Alexander L. Hayes (1793-1875), chronicles his attempt to manufacture steam turbine engines in Lancaster in 1870, and attempts to organize the Centrifugal Rotary Engine Company in order to manufacture the machines.

516. Torrey, Kate Douglas. VISIONS OF A WESTERN LOWELL: CANNELTON, INDIANA, 1847-1851. *Indiana Mag. of Hist. 1977*

73(4): 276-304. Eastern industrialists who settled in the Ohio River Valley in the 1840's planned to transform Cannelton into an industrial city like Lowell, Massachusetts.

517.   Trimble, William F.   FROM SAIL TO STEAM: SHIPBUILDING IN THE PITTSBURGH AREA, 1790-1865. *Western Pennsylvania Hist. Mag. 1975 58(2): 147-167.*

518.   Unsigned.   THOSE WERE THE DAYS. *Idaho Yesterdays 1975 19(1): 16-17.* Photographic essay of John R. Atkinson's blacksmith shop in Boise, Idaho. Atkinson was also a wagon maker. 4 illus.
                                                                B. J. Paul

519.   Vlach, John Michael.   THE CRAFTSMAN AND THE COMMUNAL IMAGE, PHILIP SIMMONS: CHARLESTON BLACKSMITH. *Family Heritage 1979 2(1): 14-19.* Describes the philosophy and work of Philip Simmons, a 20th century blacksmith in Charleston, South Carolina, who was born a slave in 1855.

520.   Wade, Louise Carroll.   "SOMETHING MORE THAN PACKERS." *Chicago Hist. 1973 2(4): 224-231.* Chicago's meatpackers created a large industry by utilizing all parts of the animals and by controlling all aspects of the business, especially their employees. They created a dynasty by having their sons continue the family business. Establishment of the Union Stock Yards in 1865-66 and introduction of refrigerated railroad cars aided the rapid growth. In two short decades the Armours, Swifts, and Nelson Morris (d. 1907) became meat barons. 6 photos.   N. A. Kuntz

521.   Wallace, Anthony F. C.   A COTTON MANUFACTURING VILLAGE: ROCKDALE, PA., 1825-1865. *Working Papers from the Regional Econ. Hist. Res. Center 1977 1(1): 57-78.* Examines the economic conditions and industrialization of the cotton industry of Rockdale, Pennsylvania, and applies the findings to other manufacturing and production towns located in the Delaware Valley, 1825-65. With comments by Merritt Roe Smith, pp. 79-85.

522.   Walsh, Margaret.   BUSINESS SUCCESS AND CAPITAL AVAILABILITY IN THE NEW WEST: MILWAUKEE IRONMASTERS IN THE MIDDLE NINETEENTH CENTURY. *Old Northwest 1975 1(2): 159-179.* Strong capitalization was essential for survival to machinists and ironmasters on Milwaukee's industrial frontier in the mid-19th century. Hard work alone was not sufficient. E. P. Allis & Co., established by Edward P. Allis (1824-89), and the Cream City Iron Works, established by Delos Filer and John Stowell, succeeded. The Bay City Foundry, the Eagle Foundry, and others were not sufficiently capitalized to survive depression. Table, 24 notes.   J. N. Dickinson

523.   Walsh, Margaret.   PORK PACKING AS A LEADING EDGE OF MIDWESTERN INDUSTRY, 1835-1875. *Agric. Hist. 1977 51(4): 702-717.* Small pork-packing factories in the Midwest, during 1835-75, represented the beginnings of industry in what had been a frontier, rural society. Specialized goods and services, needed by these small entrepreneurships, could only be supplied in those areas that were beginning to experience rapid population growth, improved communications, and increasing urbanization. Based on primary and secondary sources; 2 tables, graph.   R. T. Fulton

524.   Walsh, Margaret.   THE SPATIAL EVOLUTION OF THE MID-WESTERN PORK INDUSTRY, 1835-75. *J. of Hist. Geography 1978 4(1): 1-22.* Processing of raw materials was the major industry in the Midwest. Pork processing illustrates the general pattern of development. The volume of pork packing in the Midwest rose steadily during 1835-75, but the major centers of this industry shifted as the dependence on river transportation declined and the railroads developed. Primary and secondary sources; 6 tables, 5 graphs, 29 notes.   F. N. Egerton

525.   Weinrott, Lester A.   THE SWEET, SWEET SCENT OF SOAP. *Chicago Hist. 1977 6(1): 44-52.* Discusses the soap industry in Chicago, 1870's-90's.

526.   Wolf, Stephanie G.   ARTISANS AND THE OCCUPATIONAL STRUCTURE OF AN INDUSTRIAL TOWN: 18TH-CENTURY GERMANTOWN, PA. *Working Papers from the Regional Econ. Hist.*

Res. Center 1977 1(1): 33-56. Through the case of Germantown, Pennsylvania, studies the basic economic conditions and occupational structure of the artisans of that community, 1767-91; manufacturing and preindustrial activity was greater than often suspected by historians, and required development of complex local production networks and economic infrastructures.

527.   Woodford, Arthur M.   BEFORE THE HORSELESS CARRIAGE: DETROIT'S EARLY INDUSTRIAL AGE. *Chronicle 1979 15(1): 4-13.* Describes the growth of industry in Detroit, Michigan, 1840's-90's, including the manufacture of railway equipment, ships, sawmills, and stoves.

Finance

528.   Alviti, John V. and Haller, Mark H.   LOANSHARKING IN AMERICAN CITIES: HISTORICAL ANALYSIS OF A MARGINAL ENTERPRISE. *Am. J. of Legal Hist. 1977 21(2): 125-156.* Loansharking involves both salary lending through a legitimate business operation with only the threat of law as means of collection, and a racketeer loanshark who relies on physical force and violence. The discussion of the first form takes the 1870's to the turn of the century as its formative period. The examples come largely from New York City and Chicago, and the loans were generally of small amounts, with the lenders comprising old stock American families who made their profits from a large-volume business. The racketeer variety developed during the 1930's-50's, especially in New York in the 1930's, and in Chicago in the 1950's. Based largely on newspaper reports; 61 notes.   L. A. Knafla

529.   Carosso, Vincent P.   A FINANCIAL ELITE: NEW YORK'S GERMAN-JEWISH INVESTMENT BANKERS. *Am. Jewish Hist. Q. 1976 66(1): 67-88.* German Jewish bankers began to assume an important role in American finance in the 1830's when public and private borrowing to pay for internal improvement increased rapidly and significantly. Men such as August Belmont, Rothschild's agent, Philip Speyer, Jacob Schiff, the Seligmans, the Lehman brothers, Jules Bache, and Marcus Goldman are some of the people whose careers illustrate this financial elite. As was true of their non-Jewish counterparts, family, personal, and business connections, a reputation for honesty and integrity, ability, and a willingness to take calculated risks were essential to recruit capital from widely scattered sources. The contributions of these investment bankers to American and Jewish life and society have been continuous, many sided, and substantial for over a century. 55 notes.   F. Rosenthal

530.   Conzen, Michael P.   CAPITAL FLOWS AND THE DEVELOPING URBAN HIERARCHY: STATE BANK CAPITAL IN WISCONSIN, 1854-1895. *Econ. Geography 1975 51(4): 321-338.* The urban system, notably in Milwaukee, contributed to the flow of capital in Wisconsin 1854-95.

531.   Conzen, Michael P.   THE MATURING URBAN SYSTEM IN THE UNITED STATES, 1840-1910. *Ann. of the Assoc. of Am. Geographers 1977 67(1): 88-108.* Examines the banking system in the US and its correspondence to the maturing of urban systems, concluding that banking integration of the urban network paralleled general economic trends in the 19th century.

532.   Dalin, David G. and Fracchia, Charles A.   FORGOTTEN FINANCIER: FRANÇOIS L. A. PIOCHE. *California Hist. Q. 1974 53(1): 17-24.* François L. A. Pioche (1818-72) was an important but historically neglected financier who contributed to San Francisco's development in the two decades following the gold rush. Pioche arrived in San Francisco in 1849. He made his fortune through general merchandise stores, followed by banking. With his partner, J. B. Bayerque, he purchased real estate in key areas of the city, built the Market Street Railway, and bought many large ranches throughout the state. He financed the Jackson Street Wharf Company, the San Francisco Gas Works, and the Spring Valley Water Company, as well as mining operations in Nevada and California, and the Sacramento Valley Railroad. A man of culture and taste, Pioche lent financial support to French restaurants, philanthropic causes, and cultural affairs. Financially overextended, Pioche took his own life, and his firm was liquidated in 1876. Despite his contri-

butions to San Francisco and the West, Pioche is remembered only on a small plaque on Clay Street and with a small, unpaved San Francisco street named for him. Illus., photos.   A. Hoffman

533. De Santis, Hugh S.   GEORGE S. BOWEN AND THE AMERICAN DREAM.   *Chicago Hist. 1977 6(3): 143-154.* Examines the investments and businesses of George S. Bowen, a resident of Chicago, 1849-1905, whose business ventures and reform-mindedness aided in the growth and modernization of the city; focuses on the failure of a foreign business venture with Japan.

534. Ellis, L. Tuffly.   THE NEW ORLEANS COTTON EXCHANGE: THE FORMATIVE YEARS, 1870-1880.   *J. of Southern Hist. 1973 39(4): 545-564.* Describes the formation and development of the New Orleans Cotton Exchange during 1871-80, established as a means to revive and regulate the cotton market in that city. By 1880 the Exchange was the leading cotton market in the world and had set up a futures market. It was able to restore order to the local market, curb further decline of trade, and help improve communication and transport between the city and other areas, developing a "spirit of mutual cooperation among New Orleans traders." Based on reports of the New Orleans Cotton Exchange, US government documents, contemporary newspaper reports, and primary and secondary sources; 56 notes.
N. J. Street

535. Forrey, Robert.   CHARLES TYSON YERKES: PHILADELPHIA-BORN ROBBER BARON.   *Pennsylvania Mag. of Hist. and Biog. 1975 99(2): 226-241.* Charles Tyson Yerkes (1837-1905) was one of the most notorious of those American financiers whose business methods earned them the name of "robber barons". Uses newspaper clippings and notes collected by Theodore Dreiser to piece together the little that can be learned of his career, from his first financial deal at age 10 to his death. Although of Quaker background, his methods in making his millions and dissipating them was appropriate subject matter for yellow journalists and foreshadowed lifestyles and values prevalent in the American society of the 20th century. 46 notes.   R. V. Ritter

536. Hinderliter, Roger H. and Rockoff, Hugh.   THE MANAGEMENT OF RESERVES BY ANTE-BELLUM BANKS IN EASTERN FINANCIAL CENTERS.   *Explorations in Econ. Hist. 1973 11(1): 37-53.* An econometric analysis of portfolio behavior in 82 banks of Boston, New York, and Philadelphia. Suggests that reserve positions reflected a careful decisionmaking process, that bankers were aware of the riskiness of both their investments and liabilities, that awareness varied from system to system, and that the traditional measures of banking conservatism provide an inadequate and often misleading basis for comparison. Based on official bank reports and secondary sources; 3 tables, 15 notes, appendix.   P. J. Coleman

537. Horstman, Ronald.   TRADE UNIONS IN THE BANKING FIELD: A FOOTNOTE ON THE HISTORY OF ST. LOUIS.   *Missouri Hist. Soc. Bull. 1978 34(2): 104-105.* Describes the Telegraphers National Bank in St. Louis during 1922-42. Owned by the Brotherhood of Railway Telegraphers, the bank flourished under the leadership of Edward J. Manion and Vernon O. Gardner. 2 photos.
H. T. Lovin

538. Horvitz, Eleanor F.   THE JEWISH WOMAN LIBERATED: A HISTORY OF THE LADIES' HEBREW FREE LOAN ASSOCIATION.   *Rhode Island Jewish Hist. Notes 1978 7(4): 501-512.* The Ladies' Hebrew Free Loan Association (LHFLA), which was established in 1931 to provide a loan fund for Jewish women in Providence, Rhode Island, to match the Hebrew Free Loan Association established in 1903 for male Jews, enabled Jewish women to maintain some element of independence; the LHFLA, no longer needed, disbanded in 1965.

539. Johnston, Patricia.   BENJAMIN FRANKLIN & FIRE INSURANCE.   *Early Am. Life. 1978 9(3): 30-33.* Discusses the history of fire insurance in the United States, 1666-1792, highlighting the research done by Benjamin Franklin in organizing and establishing the first fire insurance company, the Philadelphia Contributionship for the Insurance of Houses from Loss by Fire, 1752.

540. Jones, John Paul.   THE BIG MAN OF THE BIG FOUR.   *Cincinnati Hist. Soc. Bull. 1974 32(3): 78-103.* Chronicles the financial career of Melville E. Ingalls, a Cincinnati businessman and financier, including investments in railroads, local hotels, and business buildings, 1871-1914.

541. Lavender, David.   AN END TO INNOCENCE.   *Am. West 1975 12(6): 38-45.* Recounts the last days of William C. Ralston (1826-75) during which he tried desperately to salvage his Bank of California from disaster in the wake of the Panic of 1873. The bank's temporary collapse marked the conclusion to an unparalleled era of naive optimism for San Francisco and the West." Adapted from a recently published book. 7 illus.   D. L. Smith

542. Lurie, Jonathan   THE CHICAGO BOARD OF TRADE, THE MERCHANTS' EXCHANGE OF ST. LOUIS, AND THE GREAT BUCKET SHOP WAR, 1882-1905.   *Missouri Hist. Soc. Bull. 1973 29(4 part 1): 243-259.* The two major midwestern commodity exchanges, the Chicago Board of Trade and the Merchants' Exchange of St. Louis, normally cooperated in providing "a rationalized market framework" beneficial to producers, sellers, distributors, and consumers. To circumvent the rules and disciplinary powers of the two exchanges, "bucket shops" developed in Chicago and St. Louis. Bucket shops provided a less expensive outlet for commodity speculative activities on a smaller scale than was permitted by the two legitimate exchanges. The Chicago Board of Trade attempted to curb the bucket shops and sought the cooperation of its St. Louis counterpart. The St. Louis group responded warily and never cooperated fully in the war against the bucket shops. The Chicago Board of Trade ultimately prevailed over the bucket shops. Based on the records of the Chicago and St. Louis commodity exchanges, on government documents, and on secondary sources; 47 notes.
H. T. Lovin

543. McLear, Patrick E.   WILLIAM BUTLER OGDEN: A CHICAGO PROMOTER IN THE SPECULATIVE ERA AND THE PANIC OF 1837.   *J. of the Illinois State Hist. Soc. 1977 70(4): 283-291.* Considers the career of William Butler Ogden, "Chicago's most important nineteenth-century business leader." His success was due to his ability to serve the investment interests of Easterners while also providing long-term economic institutions for ambitious westerners. He was a land developer and also engaged in steamboat and brewing enterprises. 5 illus., 69 notes.   J

544. Olmstead, Alan L.   MUTUAL SAVINGS BANK DEPOSITORS IN NEW YORK.   *Business Hist. Rev. 1975 49(3): 287-311.* Describes the background of mutual savings bank customers in the first half of the 19th century, the distribution of deposits by amounts, and the attempts by bank operators to force wealthier depositors out of the clientele. Concludes that such banks attracted many middle and upper class depositors as well as laboring class customers. Based on bank records and other primary sources; 6 tables, 63 notes.   C. J. Pusateri

545. Olmstead, Alan L.   NEW YORK CITY MUTUAL SAVINGS BANK PORTFOLIO MANAGEMENT AND TRUSTEE OBJECTIVES.   *J. of Econ. Hist. 1974 34(4): 815-834.* Profiteering was an inconsequential motive among trustees of mutual savings banks. Types of investments in portfolios of four of New York City's oldest banks converged as legal restraints were removed. The trend suggested a similar purpose, to maximize profits, and rapid response to market forces. Continued observance of usury laws and balances between mortgage loans and government securities held reflected pursuit of depositors' welfare. Based on bank reports and secondary sources; table, 5 graphs, 36 notes.
J. W. Williams

546. Olson, James S.   THE BOISE BANK PANIC OF 1932.   *Idaho Yesterdays 1974-75 18(4): 25-28.*

547. Sandburg, Everett A.   RIGHT PLACE AT RIGHT TIME! 1889 SPOKANE FIRE LAUNCHED AN INVESTMENT BANKER.   *Pacific Northwesterner 1975 19(2): 17-25.* Examines Alonzo Miles Murphey's investment banking after a fire destroyed most of downtown Spokane, Washington, in 1889.

548. Shergold, Peter R. THE LOAN SHARK: THE SMALL LOAN BUSINESS IN EARLY TWENTIETH-CENTURY PITTSBURGH. *Pennsylvania Hist. 1978 45(3): 195-223.* Between 24 and 53 money lenders provided credit at very high interest to Pittsburgh laborers during 1900-13. The charges reformers leveled at these "sharks" were only partly valid, and reform legislation drove many legitimate lenders from the field and made possible the entry of criminal elements into the small loan business. 3 tables, 96 notes.   D. C. Swift

549. Simmons, Charles Willis. MAGGIE LENA WALKER AND THE CONSOLIDATED BANK & TRUST COMPANY. *Negro Hist. Bull. 1975 38(2): 345-349.* Maggie Lena Walker (1867-1934), Grand Secretary of the United Order of St. Luke, a Richmond, Virginia, black mutual-aid organization, urged the Order to establish a savings bank. In 1903 the Order opened the St. Luke's Penny Savings Bank with Mrs. Walker as president. The new bank flourished under Mrs. Walker's financial leadership. In 1930 the bank merged with two other banks, while Mrs. Walker continued as director. Notes.   M. J. Wentworth

550. Spreng, Francis. THE BIRTH OF THE PITTSBURGH STOCK EXCHANGE. *Western Pennsylvania Hist. Mag. 1975 58(1): 69-80.* Traces the history of stocks, securities, and the oil trade in Pittsburgh which led eventually to the establishment of the Pittsburgh Stock Exchange, 1896.   S

551. Story, Ronald D. "THAT DAMNED PACK OF SHARPERS": SAVINGS BANKS AND AMERICAN SOCIETY IN THE NINETEENTH CENTURY. *Rev. in Am. Hist. 1977 5(3): 335-341.* Review article prompted by Alan L. Olmstead's *New York City Mutual Savings Bank, 1819-1861* (Chapel Hill: U. of North Carolina Pr., 1976) and Carl R. Osthaus's *Freedmen, Philanthropy, and Fraud: A History of the Freedman's Savings Bank* (Urbana: U. of Illinois Pr., 1976).

Work and the Work Force

552. Baxandall, Rosalyn; Gordon, Linda; and Reverby, Susan. ARCHIVES: BOSTON WORKING WOMEN PROTEST, 1869. *Signs: J. of Women in Culture and Soc. 1976 1(3, part 1): 803-808.* Increasing numbers of women found employment in garment manufacturing in Boston during the Civil War because of the demand for military uniforms and the absence of male workers. But, by 1869, return of men and the end of war production reduced job opportunities for women despite increasing numbers of females who were dependent on their own earnings because of war casualties. Women, therefore, expressed anger at low wages and terrible working conditions, but they also railed against the degradation of their own labor and skill through the factory system's mechanization and division of labor. Primary sources.
                                                              S. E. Kennedy

553. Beeten, Neil. POLISH AMERICAN STEELWORKERS: AMERICANIZATION THROUGH INDUSTRY AND LABOR. *Polish Am. Studies 1976 33(2): 31-42.* The United States Steel Corporation in Gary, Indiana, manipulated immigrant workers under the guise of Americanization. In a final analysis, both immigrants and the employers profited from the corporation programs. Unplanned and unnoticed during the process, however, was a steady exposure of the immigrant workers to the merits of unionization, the potential benefits of organized strikes, and the necessary techniques of survival in a hard economic world. Covers ca. 1906-20. Based primarily on English newspaper accounts; 21 notes.   S. R. Pliska

554. Benson, Susan Porter. "THE CLERKING SISTERHOOD" RATIONALIZATION AND THE WORK CULTURE OF SALESWOMEN IN AMERICAN DEPARTMENT STORES, 1890-1960. *Radical Am. 1978 12(2): 41-55.* Unlike the contemporary trends in male-dominated crafts and skills, the impact of managerial involvement in department store sales work in the 20th century was to upgrade skills, enhance the position of the saleswoman, and contribute to the creation of a thoroughgoing work culture in the department store. The increasing emphasis on the selling skills of the work force on the part of management heightened the status of saleswomen and further impelled managers to find ways of enhancing the work setting to spur production. Saleswomen

in the various selling areas of the department store developed an *esprit d'corps* and sense of togetherness that managers ignored at their own peril.   N. Lederer

555. Berch, Bettina. THE DEVELOPMENT OF HOUSEWORK. *Int. J. of Women's Studies [Canada] 1978 1(4): 336-348.* The development of housework, 1840's-1970's, includes the "servant crisis," scientific management, technological revolution, and present-day task- and time-oriented housework.

556. Blackwelder, Julia Kirk. QUIET SUFFERING: ATLANTA WOMEN IN THE 1930'S. *Georgia Hist. Q. 1977 61(2): 112-124.* During the Great Depression of the 1930's, women in Atlanta, Georgia, suffered from poverty and unemployment. A caste system based on a woman's race, age, and (sometimes) marital status determined the type of job she was likely to have. Statistics indicate that, generally, black women had greater difficulty in the job market and were employed as domestics, while white women held clerical positions. Primary sources; 20 notes.   G. R. Schroeder

557. Blackwelder, Julia Kirk. WOMEN IN THE WORK FORCE: ATLANTA, NEW ORLEANS, AND SAN ANTONIO, 1930 TO 1940. *J. of Urban Hist. 1978 4(3): 331-358.* By studying women in three ethnically distinct communities (Atlanta—white, New Orleans—black, and San Antonio—Hispanic), compares the work experiences and motivations of different cultural groups of women. Matriarchy does not appear to be the main explanation for black women entering the labor force, and was actually higher among the supposedly close-knit Hispanics. 12 tables, 20 notes.   T. W. Smith

558. Davis, Susan G. WOMEN'S ROLES IN A COMPANY TOWN: NEW YORK MILLS, 1900-1951. *New York Folklore 1978 4(1-4): 35-47.* Traces the roles of the women (predominantly Polish) in New York Mills, New York, 1900-51, based on their personal reflections, including their roles as wife, mother, millworker, union member, landlady, etc.

559. Dawley, Alan and Faler, Paul. WORKING CLASS CULTURE AND POLITICS IN THE INDUSTRIAL REVOLUTION: SOURCES OF LOYALISM AND REVOLUTION. *J. of Social Hist. 1976 9(4): 466-480.* Discusses Lynn, Massachusetts, the center of the rapidly changing shoe industry, to study reactions to industrialization and changed behavior patterns called forth by factory work. Finds that radicalism was clear cut by the outset of the Civil War and was manifested by the rapid development of the Knights of St. Crispin after 1868. Previous students of the labor movement believe that the radicalism was muted by the particular character of the interaction between working class culture and politics.   M. Hough

560. Dublin, Thomas. THE HODGDON FAMILY LETTERS: A VIEW OF WOMEN IN THE EARLY TEXTILE MILLS, 1830-1840. *Hist. New Hampshire 1978 33(4): 283-295.* In the mid-19th century many young New Englanders migrated from rural areas to urban centers. Sarah and Elizabeth Hodgdon, whose letters are reproduced here, left Rochester, New Hampshire, to work in a Lowell, Massachusetts, textile factory. Typical of female mill workers of the period, they apparently migrated not from economic necessity but because of rural overcrowding. Their letters reveal their strong family bonds, adjustment problems, and their economic independence. 20 notes.   D. F. Chard

561. Dublin, Thomas. WOMEN, WORK, AND THE FAMILY: FEMALE OPERATIVES IN THE LOWELL MILLS, 1830-1860. *Feminist Studies 1975 3(1/2): 30-39.* Between 1830 and 1860 Lowell, Massachusetts, was a leading center of textile manufacture in the United States. From 1830 to 1845 women operatives formed a majority of the mill workforce. They were native-born and lived in company-owned boarding houses, which became centers of community life, and which provided the organizational base for the Lowell labor movement. After 1845 Irish immigrant men and women became an increased portion of the mill population. Immigrant women tended to live with their families (usually parents) rather than in boarding houses. Family dependence on the income of these female children meant greater caution in strike action and discouraged labor activity in Lowell during the 1850's. Primary and secondary sources; 33 notes.   S. R. Herstein

562. Dubnoff, Steven. GENDER, THE FAMILY, AND THE PROBLEM OF WORK MOTIVATION IN A TRANSITION TO INDUSTRIAL CAPITALISM. *J. of Family Hist. 1979 4(2): 121-136.* Using data from the payrolls of a Lowell, Massachusetts, factory and the 1860 federal manuscript census, studies the adaptation of the largely preindustrial labor force to the strictures of factory labor. Men were absent from work less than women and that family position influenced ones work orientation. 3 tables, 18 notes, biblio.   T. W. Smith

563. Gersuny, Carl. INDUSTRIAL CASUALTIES IN LOWELL, 1890-1905. *Labor Hist. 1979 20(3): 435-442.* Documents industrial accidents in Lowell, Massachusetts. Safety was not a major concern, and workers were held responsible. Based on Hamilton Co. records, Lowell Manufacturing Co. records, and the Lowell Hospital Register; 2 tables, 14 notes.   L. L. Athey

564. Glassberg, Eudice. WORK, WAGES, AND THE COST OF LIVING, ETHNIC DIFFERENCES AND THE POVERTY LINE, PHILADELPHIA, 1880. *Pennsylvania Hist. 1979 46(1): 17-58.* A family of five in Philadelphia in 1880 needed $643 per year for an adequate income. Even workers in most skilled trades could not earn that much, and unskilled laborers were far worse off. Children had to work and wives had to earn money, often through "home work." Male white Americans had the best prospects of earning nearly enough money. Germans held more skilled jobs than did Irishmen. Blacks encountered the most occupational difficulties. Based on Philadelphia Social History Project data and other materials; 2 photos, 10 tables, 87 notes.   D. C. Swift

565. Goldin, Claudia. HOUSEHOLD AND MARKET PRODUCTION OF FAMILIES IN A LATE NINETEENTH CENTURY AMERICAN CITY. *Explorations in Econ. Hist. 1979 16(2): 111-131.* Apart from the male head of household, urban families relied upon children as an important source of labor income. An examination of Philadelphia, Pennsylvania, in 1880 shows substitution between mothers and their daughters and the role of comparative advantage in family decisions concerning the allocation of their members' time. Ethnic differences were important only for daughters. Based on published documents and secondary accounts; 4 tables, 29 notes, 23 ref.   P. J. Coleman

566. Hareven, Tamara and Langenbach, Randolph. VOICES OF A VANISHED AMOSKEAG. *Am. Heritage 1978 29(6): 14-25.* Excerpted from the authors' book *Amoskeag: Life and Work in an American Factory-City.* Selections are illustrative of the varied reactions of workers in the Amoskeag textile mills in Manchester, New Hampshire, to life in such an environment, 1920's-30's. 11 illus.   J. F. Paul

567. Heavner, Robert O. INDENTURED SERVITUDE: THE PHILADELPHIA MARKET, 1771-1773. *J. of Econ. Hist. 1978 38(3): 701-713.* In the 1770's Philadelphia had a well developed indentured servant market which served the city and the surrounding region. This market had many attributes of rational labor and physical capital markets and provided a means for financing migration and education. This study is of indenture records which include prices, term lengths, employer-provided amenities, and servant attributes to test hypotheses based on a rational buyer model. Results indicate that in response to the riskiness of a servant, the buyer used indexes of servant productivity and reliability; that the servant paid for amenities offered by the master, such as general education; and that there was a seasonal pattern of prices corresponding to seasonal activities of agriculture.   J

568. Isserman, Maurice. INHERITANCE LOST: SOCIALISM IN ROCHESTER, 1917-1919. *Rochester Hist. 1977 39(4): 1-24.* Details the socialist movement among laborers in Rochester, New York, 1917-19.

569. Janiewski, Dolores. ARCHIVES: MAKING COMMON CAUSE: THE NEEDLEWOMEN OF NEW YORK, 1831-69. *Signs: J. of Women in Culture and Soc. 1976 1(3, Part 1): 777-786.* Women laborers in New York City's garment trades between 1831 and 1869 tried to deal with subsistence-level wages, exploitative homework, piecework, ruinous competition, and chronic unemployment by varying modes of organization and expression such as trade unions, producers' cooperatives dependent on public patronage, mutual aid societies, and feminist pressure groups. Some developed an analysis of class and sex oppression while others eschewed theory for publicity campaigns to at-

tract public support. All failed to change the economic and social system, but each group in its own way tried to resist oppression. Primary sources; 5 notes.   S. E. Kennedy

570. Murphy, Miriam B. THE WORKING WOMEN OF SALT LAKE CITY: A REVIEW OF THE *UTAH GAZETTEER, 1892-93.* *Utah Hist. Q. 1978 46(2): 121-135.* A review of Stenhouse's *Utah Gazetteer, 1892-93* indicates that almost 2,000 working women played important roles in Utah's economy as employees and employers. Factories, mills, and laundries provided jobs. Women created jobs for themselves as milliners, dress makers, and lodging house keepers. They worked at jobs requiring different levels of education, experience, mental and manual dexterity, management and leadership skills, business acumen, and physical endurance. A significant number entered the professions or owned or managed businesses. Primary and secondary sources; 8 illus., 20 notes.   J. L. Hazelton

571. Nash, Gary B. THE FAILURE OF FEMALE FACTORY LABOR IN COLONIAL BOSTON. *Labor Hist. 1979 20(2): 165-188.* Poverty, the escalating costs of poor relief, and the effects of war resulted in the first experiment in the American colonies, undertaken by Boston leaders in their organization of the United Society for Manufactures and Importation, to involve large numbers of women in a linen manufactory during the 1750's. Women resisted; officials were reluctant to use coercion; and the effort collapsed. Based on records of the Society for Encouraging Industry and the Employment of the Poor; 40 notes.   L. L. Athey

572. Pérez, Louis A., Jr. REMINISCENCES OF A *LECTOR*: CUBAN CIGAR WORKERS IN TAMPA. *Florida Hist. Q. 1975 53(4): 443-449.* Describes from personal experience the *lector's* (reader's) function and influence among the Cuban illiterate workers in a Tampa cigar factory. "A highly developed proletarian consciousness and a long tradition of trade union militancy accompanied the Cuban tobacco workers to the United States." They embraced a variety of radical ideologies. The *lector* often served as a disseminator of the proletarian tradition, as well as a broad variety of written materials. Conflicts arose between the workers and factory owners over the *lector's* pay and pro-labor materials. 13 notes.   R. V. Ritter

573. Shergold, Peter R. WAGE RATES IN PITTSBURGH DURING THE DEPRESSION OF 1908. *J. of Am. Studies [Great Britain] 1975 9(2): 163-188.* Assesses statistical and qualitative evidences to explain the phenomenon of wage rates declining less drastically in Pittsburgh during the depression of 1908 than in earlier recessions of considerably less severity. The depression of 1908 encouraged emigration from Pittsburgh, discouraged immigration from Europe to the United States, and produced "relative tightness" in the Pittsburgh labor market. Hence, wage rates remained higher than depression conditions otherwise warranted. Based on newspaper and secondary sources; 75 notes.   H. T. Lovin

574. Silvia, Philip T., Jr. THE POSITION OF WORKERS IN A TEXTILE COMMUNITY: FALL RIVER IN THE EARLY 1800S. *Labor Hist. 1975 16(2): 230-248.* Examines employer-dominance in the textile industry of Fall River, Massachusetts. Although a critique of labor conditions was led by Robert Howard, a muleskinner, the policies of the employers regarding grievances, wages, work conditions and company housing were maintained as a part of a laissez-faire philosophy hostile to organized labor in the 1880's. Based upon reports of the Massachusetts Bureau of Labor Statistics and Senate committees, newspapers and secondary sources; 32 notes.   L. L. Athey

575. Thompson, Agnes L. NEW ENGLAND MILL GIRLS. *New-England Galaxy 1974 16(2): 43-49.* Describes life in the woolen and cotton mills of Lowell, Massachusetts, in the 1840's and 1850's. Farm girls gained economic independence by working for a few years before marriage, but were closely supervised in the mill, boarding house, and community, and had to cope with long hours, low wages, and limited social and educational opportunities. By 1857 competition forced their replacement by a permanent industrial working class of Irish and French Canadians. 6 illus.   P. C. Marshall

Labor Organizations, Unions, and Strikes

576. Arroyo, Luis Leobardo. CHICANO PARTICIPATION IN ORGANIZED LABOR: THE CIO IN LOS ANGELES 1938-1950. *Aztlán 1976 6(2): 277-313.* During 1938-50 Chicanos were active leaders in the Los Angeles Congress of Industrial Organizations locals and the CIO Council. They worked in close association with community organizations to help solve *Mexicano* problems, among them the Sleepy Lagoon incident and the Zoot Suit Riots. After 1943 Chicano unionists lost an effective voice in the CIO Council but continued to work on the local level. Based on newspapers, oral interviews and labor union proceedings; 101 notes.   R. Griswold del Castillo

577. Asher, Robert. PAINFUL MEMORIES: THE HISTORICAL CONSCIOUSNESS OF STEELWORKERS AND THE STEEL STRIKE OF 1919. *Pennsylvania Hist. 1978 45(1): 61-86.* Most skilled steelworkers in the Pittsburgh district remained at work during the Steel Strike of 1919. Many factors influenced their defection, but none was more important than their recollection of earlier unsuccessful confrontations with the companies. Many of the skilled steelworkers had participated in those strikes, and others had been told of the events by "old timers" in the steel towns. The skilled steelworkers who did not support the 1919 strike doubted the ability of the union leadership, respected the power and wealth of the companies, and understood the relationship between paternalism and repression. Based on interviews undertaken by David Saposs and others in 1920, US Senate hearings, recent oral history interviews, and other materials; 3 tables, 56 notes.   D. C. Swift

578. Baughman, James L. CLASSES AND COMPANY TOWNS: LEGENDS OF THE 1937 LITTLE STEEL STRIKE. *Ohio Hist. 1978 87(2): 175-192.* Examines events in Canton, Youngstown, and Warren (Ohio) during the 1937 "Little Steel" strike, the first major strike since 1919. Discusses the relationship of the communities to the month-long labor-management conflict. After the strike of the Youngstown Sheet and Tube, Inland Steel, and Republic Steel, not solidarity but demoralization and internal division characterized the employees. The union never came close to victory—after four weeks the laborers began filing back into the mills and the managers had halted the impressive advance for CIO organization in the nation's basic industries. Through examination of the communities involved, discusses why the union lost. Based on primary and secondary sources; 3 illus., 48 notes.   N. Summers

579. Brody, David. WORKING CLASS HISTORY IN THE GREAT DEPRESSION. *Rev. in Am. Hist. 1976 4(2): 262-267.* Review article prompted by Peter Friedlander's *The Emergence of a UAW Local, 1936-1939: A Study in Class and Culture* (Pittsburgh: U. of Pennsylvania Pr., 1975), which documents the growth of a Detroit local of the United Automobile Workers of America.

580. Broyles, Glen J. THE SPOKANE FREE SPEECH FIGHT, 1909-1910: A STUDY IN IWW TACTICS. *Labor Hist. 1978 19(2): 238-252.* The free speech fight in Spokane, contrary to recent historical interpretation, was a victory not for the Industrial Workers of the World but for the city and Mayor Pratt. Based on Spokane newspapers; 27 notes.   L. L. Athey

581. Buhle, Mari Jo. SOCIALIST WOMEN AND THE "GIRL STRIKERS," CHICAGO, 1910. *Signs 1976 1(4): 1039-1051.* The 1910 Chicago garment workers' strike showed a new determined spirit in the American labor movement. The "new immigrants," especially young women, militantly opposed the United Garment Workers' conciliations with factory owners. Contemporary newspaper articles by Nellie M. Zeh and Mary O'Reilly represented Socialist women's responses to the strike and their efforts to publicize the implications of the struggle. Their perspective was rooted in their interpretation of the historic position of women workers. They themselves had given their girlhood to commodity production and felt a sisterhood with the young strikers. They saw the actions of the "girl strikers" as a symbol of the larger tendency in the industrial working class to determine their own destiny. Based on newspaper articles; 11 notes.   J. Gammage

582. Burran, James A. LABOR CONFLICT IN URBAN APPALACHIA: THE KNOXVILLE STREETCAR STRIKE OF 1919.

Tennessee Hist. Q. 1979 38(1): 62-78. In the period of demobilization and search for normalcy following World War I, a streetcar strike occurred in October 1919 in conservative, typically Republican, Knoxville, Tennessee. It was part of a larger movement of the American Federation of Labor which was aimed at organizing, among others, the Knoxville police. When violence broke out after strike breakers were hired, the governor called in federal troops. The presence of troops broke the strike. Primary and secondary sources; 35 notes.   M. B. Lucas

583. Carpenter, Gerald. PUBLIC OPINION IN THE NEW ORLEANS STREET RAILWAY STRIKE OF 1929-1930. Fink, Gary M. and Reed, Merl E., eds. *Essays in Southern Labor History: Selected Papers, Southern Labor History Conference, 1976.* (Westport, Conn.; London, England, Greenwood Pr., 1977): 191-207. Studies the New Orleans Street Railway Strike of 1929-30 as an illustration of the incorrectness of the usual stereotype of southern public opinion as united against trade unionism. This is seen both in company (New Orleans Public Service, Inc.) appeals which reflected the public's acceptance of unionism and in union (Street and Electric Railway Employees of America) appeals for support resting on "positive concern for the principles of organized labor and negative objections to outside control." The usual generalizations therefore must be examined more critically. 65 notes.   R. V. Ritter

584. Cook, Bernard A. and Watson, James R. THE SAILORS AND MARINE TRANSPORT WORKERS' 1913 STRIKE IN NEW ORLEANS: THE AFL AND THE IWW. *Southern Studies 1979 18(1): 111-122.* Two major types of divisions among workers in New Orleans, Louisiana, traditionally have prevented them from working together and improving their lot: racial differences and antagonism between skilled and unskilled workers. Although several attempts were made to unite the workers, and brief periods of cooperation took place, antagonism has been the general attitude. The dock strike of June-July 1913 by the Sailors' Union (American Federation of Labor) and the Marine Transport Workers (Industrial Workers of the World) against the United Fruit Company in New Orleans failed because of these antagonisms, lack of cooperation, scabbing by members, and betrayals by leadership. 47 notes.   J. J. Buschen

585. Corcoran, Theresa. VIDA SCUDDER AND THE LAWRENCE TEXTILE STRIKE. *Essex Inst. Hist. Collections 1979 115(3): 183-195.* During the 1912 Lawrence, Massachusetts, textile strike the Progressive Women's Club of Lawrence invited prominent speakers to address them on 4 March. No outsider stirred the conservatives more than Vida Dutton Scudder, professor at Wellesley College. A founder of the College Settlements Association and Denison House, a distinctively Boston settlement for women, a member of the Socialist Party in 1911, and author of *Socialism and Character* (1912), Scudder had moved into settlements in hopes that they might play their part in radical propaganda. In this she was discouraged, but later became convinced that Christianity offered the one solution to industrialized society, and after 1912 moved into various Christian groups for social reform. Examines Scudder's speech and the reaction to it, the Progressive Women's Club, and the textile strike. Primary and secondary sources; 30 notes.   R. S. Sliwoski

586. Cumbler, John T. LABOR, CAPITAL AND COMMUNITY: THE STRUGGLE FOR POWER. *Labor Hist. 1974 15(3): 395-415.* Discusses the eight-month leatherworkers' strike in Lynn, Massachusetts, in 1890. Although Lynn was a strong union town with a tradition of solidarity and close relationships with the community, the labor-community solidarity and community support was no match for an effectively organized group of employers, and the strike failed. Based on the Lynn *Daily Item* and other newspapers, and minutes of Lynn unions; 84 notes.   L. L. Athey

587. Dodd, Martin H. MARLBORO, MASSACHUSETTS AND THE SHOEWORKERS' STRIKE OF 1898-1899. *Labor Hist. 1979 20(3): 376-397.* The shoeworkers' strike of 1898-99 yielded a shift in Marlboro sentiment from support of labor to support for industry, thus forcing the shoeworkers to rely more on unions and less on support from other groups. The local unions were broken. Based on city directories and newspapers; 2 tables, 42 notes.   L. L. Athey

588. Doherty, William T., Jr. BERKELEY'S NON-REVOLUTION: LAW AND ORDER AND THE GREAT RAILWAY STRIKE OF 1877. *West Virginia Hist. 1974 35(4): 271-289.* During the Railway Strike of 1877, strikers seized the Baltimore and Ohio rail yard at Martinsburg, West Virginia, and halted service during July 16-19. Local militia were ineffective and federal troops were finally sent in to clear out the strikers. During and after the event, local newspapers took a moderate position, criticizing the actions of Governor Henry M. Mathews and the federal government as too pro-railroad. Local opinion sympathized with the strikers and thought the railroad was greedy, but objected to violence. Based chiefly on local newspapers; 56 notes.　　J. H. Broussard

589. Dublin, Thomas. WOMEN, WORK, AND PROTEST IN THE EARLY LOWELL MILLS: "THE OPPRESSING HAND OF AVARICE WOULD ENSLAVE US." *Labor Hist. 1975 16(1): 99-116.* The organization of work and the nature of housing in Lowell promoted the development of a sense of community among the women workers. The women relied upon the element of community in strikes in 1834 and 1836, and in the political action of the 1840's. The cultural traditions emergent involved preindustrial and industrial values. Based on records of the Hamilton Manufacturing Co. and on the *Lowell Offering;* 36 notes.　　L. L. Athey

590. Dunnigan, Kate and Quinney, Richard. WORK AND COMMUNITY IN SAYLESVILLE. *Radical Hist. Rev. 1978 (17): 173-180.* Describes the sense of community and worker solidarity in Saylesville village in Lincoln, Rhode Island, with excerpts from the cotton manufacturing company, Sayles Finishing Plants' company magazine, which contributed to the success of the 1934 strike.

591. Engelmann, Larry D. "WE WERE THE POOR PEOPLE": THE HORMEL STRIKE OF 1933. *Labor Hist. 1974 15(4): 483-510.* Narrates the formation of a union in the Hormel packinghouse in Austin, Minnesota, the conflict with the "benevolent dictatorship" of Hormel management and the violent strike of 1933. The union was sparked by an insurance proposal, issued as an edict, which would cost workers 20 cents per week. A strike ensued and peaked in November 1933 when workers seized the plant. The strike was successfully arbitrated after intervention by Governor Floyd B. Olson. Pay increases were granted, but union recognition was not achieved. The company shifted to a policy of "welfare capitalism." Based upon Austin, Minnesota, newspapers and personal interviews; 67 notes.　　L. L. Athey

592. Fink, Leon. "IRRESPECTIVE OF PARTY, COLOR OR SOCIAL STANDING": THE KNIGHTS OF LABOR AND OPPOSITION POLITICS IN RICHMOND, VIRGINIA. *Labor Hist. 1978 19(3): 325-349.* The Knights of Labor in Richmond turned to political action in 1886 by supporting a reform slate in municipal elections. A coalition with Negro Republicans threatened existing Democratic control, but racial divisions generated by the meeting of the l0th General Assembly of the Knights helped divide the coalition and ensured defeat. By 1888 the reform movement vanished, and Negroes steadily lost political influence. Based on newspapers; 50 notes.　　L. L. Athey

593. Foster, James C. AFL, IWW AND NOME: 1905-1908. *Alaska J. 1975 5(2): 66-77.* Describes the beginning of union organization in Nome. The first successful union was the AFL-Federal Labor Union, which had a strike for longshoremen in 1905. The Western Federation of Miners followed. Describes the conflict in the area between the American Federation of Labor and the Industrial Workers of the World. Reviews union interest and action in local politics. 11 illus., 37 notes.　　E. E. Eminhizer

594. Genini, Ronald. INDUSTRIAL WORKERS OF THE WORLD AND THEIR FRESNO FREE SPEECH FIGHT, 1910-1911. *California Hist. Q. 1974 53(2): 100-114.* After several victorious free-speech fights, the IWW clashed with authorities in Fresno, where there coexisted conservative agricultural interests and the most militant IWW local in the state. The free speech fight in Fresno consisted of confrontations from April 1910 to March 1911 between Wobblies and police over the issue of soap box speeches on street corners. Wobblies journeyed to Fresno from all parts of the country, answering the challenge of another free speech issue. More than 100 arrested Wobblies crammed the jails, demanded separate jury trials, and challenged prospective jurors. In De-

cember 1910, IWW leader Frank Little was freed after he pointed out that Fresno had no ordinance prohibiting street speaking. The city trustees instituted such a ban, but the impending influx of hundreds of additional Wobblies caused them to reconsider the move. On 2 March 1911 the ban was rescinded and all IWW prisoners were released. Most Wobblies went on to new battles elsewhere, losing the chance to build a labor organization in Fresno. Although the IWW had won its battle, the confrontations caused conservatives to view the IWW with growing concern, especially in agricultural regions. Based on contemporary articles and newspapers, interviews, and secondary sources; 61 notes.　　A. Hoffman

595. Gerstle, Gary. THE MOBILIZATION OF THE WORKING CLASS COMMUNITY: THE INDEPENDENT TEXTILE UNION IN WOONSOCKET, 1931-1946. *Radical Hist. Rev. 1978 (17): 161-172.* Gives the history and purpose of the Independent Textile Workers, an industrial trade union founded in 1931 by Belgians in Woonsocket, Rhode Island; during 1934-43 they organized Woonsocket's French-Canadian workers.

596. Glaser, Martha. PATERSON, 1924: THE A.C.L.U. AND LABOR. *New Jersey Hist. 1976 94(4): 155-172.* Loom assignments and low wages caused the Paterson silk strike of 1924. The American Civil Liberties Union (ACLU) involved itself on behalf of labor after the strike committee of the Associated Silk Workers Union asked for assistance. By taking legal action, by publicizing events in Paterson throughout the country, and by confronting the owners of the factories and local authorities who made it difficult to assemble for strike meetings, the ACLU demonstrated its tactics in handling the problems of free speech and assembly that arose from labor-management clashes. Although the owners were victorious in this instance, the ACLU won the right to assemble and to listen to any speaker desired for the union. Primary and secondary sources; 3 illus., 47 notes.　　E. R. McKinstry

597. Gordon, Michael A. THE LABOR BOYCOTT IN NEW YORK CITY, 1880-1886. *Labor Hist. 1975 16(2): 184-229.* The labor boycotts in New York City originated primarily in the previous agricultural experiences of Irish immigrants in their struggle for land reforms. Thus, the labor boycott was a pre-industrial mode of protection adapted to industrial conditions. The mass arrests and trials of immigrants during 1880-86 are examined. Based upon newspapers, reports of the New York Bureau of Labor Statistics and secondary sources; 79 notes.　　L. L. Athey

598. Headlee, Thomas J., Jr. THE RICHMOND STREETCAR STRIKE OF 1903. *Virginia Cavalcade 1976 25(4): 176-183.* Discusses trade unions' and streetcar workers' strike for higher wages against the Virginia Passenger and Power Company, including police and National Guard attempts to quell riots and violence.

599. Herring, Neill and Thrasher, Sue. UAW SITDOWN STRIKE: ATLANTA, 1936. *Southern Exposure 1974 1(3-4): 63-83.* Analysis of the labor strike at General Motor's Lakewood plant in Atlanta, one of a series of strikes that spread through the General Motors plants across the nation during 1935-37. Local conditions influenced the workers to strike while the United Auto Workers Executive Board played only a peripheral role. The workers and community cooperated to provide the necessities of life for the strikers. Job security resulted from the Atlanta strike. Based on oral interviews; 21 illus.　　G. A. Bolton

600. Hoffman, Abraham. THE EL MONTE BERRY PICKERS' STRIKE, 1933: INTERNATIONAL INVOLVEMENT IN A LOCAL LABOR DISPUTE. *J. of the West 1973 12(1): 71-84.* A detailed account of the 1933 berry pickers' strike in El Monte, California, which involved "Mexican laborers, Communist agitators, Japanese employers, Los Angeles Chamber of Commerce and business representatives, and state and federal mediators . . . over issues of wages, hours, and working conditions. The El Monte strike, however, claimed the distinction of direct involvement by the government of Mexico, in the form of diplomatic pressure, monetary assistance, and consular intervention. In contrast to the active assistance of the Mexican consuls, the Japanese consul maintained a low profile, probably because of his awareness that excessive publicity would raise questions about Japanese leasing of property in a state that had already endorsed two alien land laws." 44 notes.　　D. D. Cameron

601. Jebsen, Harry, Jr. THE ROLE OF BLUE ISLAND IN THE PULLMAN STRIKE OF 1894. *J. of the Illinois State Hist. Soc. 1974 67(3): 275-293.* On 29 June 1894 Eugene V. Debs delivered a strike appeal to the workers of Blue Island, a town 16 miles southwest of Chicago. The next day a striking switchman purposely derailed a Rock Island locomotive, blocking the main track out of the town and marking the first damage to railroad property in the Chicago region. Citizens, police, and town officials united behind the workers' boycott, responding to a federal injunction against the strike with jeers, violence, and the overturning of boxcars. Accounts of this incident by federal marshal John W. Arnold and a biased Chicago press convinced President Cleveland and much of the public that federal intervention was necessary in the Pullman Strike. Primary and secondary sources; 4 illus., 5 photos, 40 notes.

L. Woolfe

602. Keller, Kenneth W. THE PHILADELPHIA PILOTS' STRIKE OF 1792. *Labor Hist. 1977 18(1): 36-48.* Ship pilots in Philadelphia organized a work stoppage in 1792 which resulted in higher wages, but also a law which outlawed similar actions by any labor organization in Pennsylvania. The pilots were not motivated by radical social thought. Based on Pennsylvania statutes and newspapers; 18 notes.

L. L. Athey

603. Kilar, Jeremy W. COMMUNITY AND AUTHORITY RESPONSE TO THE SAGINAW VALLEY LUMBER STRIKE OF 1885. *J. of Forest Hist. 1976 20(2): 67-79.* In 1885 the community of Bay City, Michigan, supported striking lumbermen politically and legally against absentee millowners. The industrial diversification of the neighboring community of Saginaw precluded such community support. Industrial relationships in the two communities seemed similar, but social, ideological, and economic structures determined the different responses to the strike. 5 illus., map, graph, 65 notes. L. F. Johnson

604. Kritzberg, Barry. AN UNFINISHED CHAPTER IN WHITE-COLLAR UNIONISM: THE FORMATIVE YEARS OF THE CHICAGO NEWSPAPER GUILD, LOCAL 71, AMERICAN NEWSPAPER GUILD, A.F.L.-C.I.O. *Labor Hist. 1973 14(3): 397-413.* The Chicago Newspaper Guild spearheaded the drive toward unionization in a strike against the Hearst newspapers, the *Examiner* and the *American*. The strike (November 1938-April 1940) was initially successful as a result of an N.L.R.B. decision, but the effect was to shift union leadership to the A.F.L. The A.F.L. had hotly contested the guild, which was affiliated with the C.I.O.; so although the American Newspaper Guild was strengthened nationally, it was sharply weakened in Chicago. Based on oral interviews, C.N.G. files, and Chicago newspapers; 78 notes, appendix. L. L. Athey

605. Kulik, Gary. PAWTUCKET VILLAGE AND THE STRIKE OF 1824: THE ORIGINS OF CLASS CONFLICT IN RHODE ISLAND. *Radical Hist. Rev. 1978 (17): 5-37.* Describes the textile workers' strike of 1824 in Pawtucket, Rhode Island, in a discussion of the tradition of labor conflicts between mill owners and workers in Rhode Island.

606. Levi, Steven C. THE BATTLE FOR THE EIGHT-HOUR DAY IN SAN FRANCISCO. *California History 1978-79 57(4): 342-353.* From July 1916 to January 1917 the structural steel workers of San Francisco conducted a strike for the eight-hour working day. Fifty-four out of 64 companies agreed to the request; the 10 who refused, along with other members of the business community under the blessing of the San Francisco Chamber of Commerce, organized the Law and Order Committee to maintain the nine-hour day and recreate the open shop. The Committee employed a budget of $1 million against the union and conducted an anti-union propaganda campaign. However, several of the companies found it difficult to continue with nonunion labor and capitulated to the union. The union boycotted the remaining companies. Eventually Mayor James Rolph became exasperated by Law and Order Committee tactics and sided with the union. The companies admitted defeat and accepted the eight-hour day. The Committee lasted another two years before disbanding, having alienated much of its support through endorsement of extralegal measures. Primary and secondary sources; 4 photos, 37 notes. A. Hoffman

607. Levi, Steven. MINER CHIPMAN AND THE LAW AND ORDER COMMITTEE OF THE SAN FRANCISCO CHAMBER OF COMMERCE, 1917. *Pacific Historian 1974 18(4): 47-60.* Labor disputes in San Francisco led to the establishment of the Chamber of Commerce Law and Order Committee. Financed and supported by business interests, the Committee sought to destroy union power by instigating open-shop work policies. Miner Chipman, hired by the Committee to survey San Francisco industry, reported that both labor and management were responsible for the city's industrial problems. Chipman's report was never issued and the Committee was dissolved in 1919 after anti-union hysteria had dissipated. Table, 38 notes. S

608. Levi, Steven C. SAN FRANCISCO'S LAW AND ORDER COMMITTEE, 1916. *J. of the West 1973 12(1): 53-70.* A detailed account of the action taken by the Law and Order Committee in San Francisco following the first major longshoremen's strike on 1 June 1916. The International Longshoremen's Association (ILA) was in conflict with the Waterfront Employers Union (WEU). "The Law and Order Committee was originally established for a single purpose: open shop. Prior to July 22, 1916, the committee was a feeble power at best. Although its members represented both the Chamber of Commerce and San Francisco business and a substantial 'slush fund,' one million dollars by December, 1916, the committee did not have the support of great numbers of San Francisco businessmen. . . . By December the committee had effectively entered and ended, for better or for worse, most of the major strikes that had plagued the city six months earlier." 81 notes.

D. D. Cameron

609. LeWarne, Charles Pierce. THE ABERDEEN, WASHINGTON FREE SPEECH FIGHT OF 1911-1912. *Pacific Northwest Q. 1975 66(1): 1-12.* In an Industrial Workers of the World free speech fight in Aberdeen, Washington, 1911-12, IWW organizers carried on soap box harangues near hiring halls in the hope of being arrested, quickly replaced, and eventually overrunning local jails to promote their cause.

610. Marks, George P., III. THE NEW ORLEANS SCREWMEN'S BENEVOLENT ASSOCIATION, 1850-1861. *Labor Hist. 1973 14(2): 259-263.* The S.B.A. originated from a strike in 1850 and disappeared at the outbreak of the Civil War, when most members joined the Confederate Army. Based on New Orleans newspapers; 24 notes.

L. L. Athey

611. Marquart, Frank. FROM A LABOR JOURNAL: UNIONS & RADICALS IN THE DEPRESSION YEARS. *Dissent 1974 21(3): 421-430.* Discusses the development of labor organizations in Detroit during the 1920's-30's. S

612. McLaughlin, Doris B. THE SECOND BATTLE OF BATTLE CREEK: THE OPEN SHOP MOVEMENT IN THE EARLY TWENTIETH CENTURY. *Labor Hist. 1973 14(3): 323-339.* Assesses the career of Charles William Post, the cereal magnate, and his activities in promoting the open shop movement in Battle Creek, Michigan. Post fought for the open shop on local and national levels, and as Battle Creek grew in population he led the effort to maintain a nonunion industrial town by paternalism and "welfare capitalism." The A.F.L. unsuccessfully tried to organize in Battle Creek in 1910-12. The experience there was the historical forerunner of the resurgence of the open shop movement in the 1920's. Based on records of Post's companies, his official publication, *The Square Deal,* and the *American Federationist;* 33 notes.

L. L. Athey

613. Milden, James W. WOMEN, PUBLIC LIBRARIES, AND LIBRARY UNIONS: THE FORMATIVE YEARS. *J. of Lib. Hist. 1977 12(2): 150-158.* Presents histories of several of the unions which began and ended during 1917-20, including the New York Public Library Employee's Union and the Library Workers' Union of Boston Public. Discussion of the controversies of library employees over unionization. Primary and secondary sources; 24 notes. A. C. Dewees

614. Molloy, Scott. RHODE ISLAND COMMUNITIES AND THE 1902 CARMEN'S STRIKE. *Radical Hist. Rev. 1978 (17): 75-98.* Provides a brief history of transportation workers in Rhode Island, specifically discussing the streetcar workers' strike of 1902.

615. Morris, James M. NO HAYMARKET FOR CINCINNATI. *Ohio Hist. 1974 83(1): 17-32.* Discusses Cincinnati's general strike of 1886 which failed because both the press and the pulpits opposed strikes and violence. About 20% of the work force struck, but the city fathers remained calm. Lack of support by major unions and a 10% pay hike for freight handlers brought the strike to a close, although a Central Labor Union was formed. Primary and secondary sources; 4 illus., 33 notes.
S. S. Sprague

616. Moss, Roger W., Jr. THE CARPENTER'S COMPANY OF PHILADELPHIA. *Historic Preservation 1974 26(3): 37-41.* Despite attempts by Philadelphia craftsworkers to limit incoming craftsworkers, both state and city governments refused to set limitations on the number of craftspeople; though few guilds actually operated, the Carpenter's Company, an offshoot of an early London guild, provided protection for its members and quality control for the community of carpentry workers as well as the public, ca. 1700-74.

617. Musselman, Barbara L. WORKING CLASS UNITY AND ETHNIC DIVISION: CINCINNATI TRADE UNIONISTS AND CULTURAL PLURALISM. *Cincinnati Hist. Soc. Bull. 1976 34(1): 121-143.* Chronicles attempts of working classes, 1893-1920, in Cincinnati to unify along class rather than ethnic lines; discusses the labor union movement in Cincinnati, its pre-World War I domination by German and Irish Americans, and postwar ascendancy of Russian Jews, Orientals, and blacks.

618. Pacyga, Dominic A. CRISIS AND COMMUNITY: THE BACK OF THE YARDS, 1921. *Chicago Hist. 1977 6(3): 167-176.* Polish Americans living in the Back of the Yards district of Chicago, Illinois, though Catholic and conservative working class, were instrumental in labor organization and especially in organizing and carrying out a strike of the meat packing workers in 1921.

619. Piott, Steven L. MODERNIZATION AND THE ANTI-MONOPOLY ISSUE: THE ST. LOUIS TRANSIT STRIKE OF 1900. *Missouri Hist. Soc. Bull. 1978 35(1): 3-16.* As permitted by new state legislation passed in 1899, the United Railways Company took control of the transit lines serving St. Louis. That monopoly angered employees who organized a union, and the new corporation named the St. Louis Transit Company, signed an agreement with the union in March, 1900. The March pact only postponed a major transit employees strike for two months. The strike, accompanied by violence and killing, lasted two months and ended with reverses for the union. The strike also focused attention on the ills of monopolies. Manuscript and newspaper sources; 3 photos, 45 notes.
H. T. Lovin

620. Prickett, James R. COMMUNISTS AND THE AUTOMOBILE INDUSTRY IN DETROIT BEFORE 1935. *Michigan Hist. 1973 57(3): 185-208.* Traces the trade union activities of the Communist Party USA in Detroit automobile unionism before the formation of the United Automobile Workers in 1935. Such Communist leaders as Philip Raymond and Anthony Gerlach dominated the Automobile Workers Union in the 1920's and early 1930's. The AWU was particularly active in the wave of strikes of 1933. Communist rhetoric was tempered by pragmatism. 4 illus., 86 notes.
D. L. Smith

621. Reed, Merl E. THE AUGUSTA TEXTILE MILLS AND THE STRIKE OF 1886. *Labor Hist. 1973 14(2): 228-246.* Surveys the conditions of textile mills and workers before and during the 1886 strike. Working conditions in Augusta were among the best in the South, but wage cuts during depression generated union activity led by the Knights of Labor. The strike and lockout in the summer of 1886 were significant to the region and were part of the pattern of labor strife in the nation. The strike was broken largely because labor was in great supply. Based on newspapers and owner and labor publications; 35 notes.
L. L. Athey

622. Reilly, John M. IMAGES OF GASTONIA: A REVOLUTIONARY CHAPTER IN AMERICAN SOCIAL FICTION. *Georgia Rev. 1974 28(3): 498-517.* Six radical novelists wrote about the 1929 Gastonia textile strike with the intent of conveying Marxian revolutionary concepts. The strike had been called by a Communist organized union. To make the story fit the theme, however, inevitably led to a certain amount of predictability.
M. B. Lucas

623. Rich, David. THE TOLEDO MECHANICS' ASSOCIATION: THE CITY'S FIRST LABOR UNION. *Northwest Ohio Q. 1973-74 46(1): 25-31.* Austin Willey's Toledo Mechanics'. Association was a short-lived effort before the municipal elections of 1843 to unite local workingmen in an effort to protect them from exploitation and to assure a better reward for their labor. The union faded after the elections, because after the workingmen captured most of the positions they turned to regular political processes to achieve their ends. Based on newspapers; 25 notes.
W. F. Zornow

624. Rock, Howard B. THE AMERICAN REVOLUTION AND THE MECHANICS OF NEW YORK CITY: ONE GENERATION LATER. *New York Hist. 1976 57(3): 367-394.* Inspired by Revolutionary ideals, the mechanics of New York City a generation after Independence attacked the deferential system that excluded them from full political participation and equal status in American society. In their quest for recognition, the mechanics identified themselves with the Democratic-Republicans against the Federalists and sought to organize for protection against capitalist employers. Illus., 67 notes.
R. N. Lokken

625. Rock, Howard B. THE PERILS OF LAISSEZ-FAIRE: THE AFTERMATH OF THE NEW YORK BAKERS' STRIKE OF 1801. *Labor Hist. 1976 17(3): 372-387.* The 1801 bakers' strike in New York City arose from complaints about the city council's regulations of profits. The effect was to promote formation of a large manufactory of bread which endangered the economic existence of small bakeries. Based upon New York City newspapers and municipal archives; 35 notes.
L. L. Athey

626. Sale, Roger. SEATTLE'S CRISIS, 1914-1919. *Am. Studies [Lawrence, KS] 1973 14(1): 29-48.* Discusses Seattle in World War I and the General Strike of 1919. Local events reflected national developments, and Seattle newspapers developed strong support for President Wilson and Americanism. Organizing activity by the Industrial Workers of the World was cast as foreign subversion and German plots. The war (and productivity) gave Seattle labor leaders false hopes. These hopes collapsed with the failure of the General Strike in 1919. Based on primary and secondary sources; 13 notes.
J. Andrew

627. Schappes, Morris U. THE POLITICAL ORIGINS OF THE UNITED HEBREW TRADES, 1888. *J. of Ethnic Studies 1977 5(1): 13-44.* Details the origins, planning, and organizational meetings which produced the United Hebrew Trades (UHT) organization in New York City, a product of Branch 8 and Branch 17 of the Socialist Labor Party. The leaders were Yiddish-speaking workingmen such as Jacob Magidow, Lev Bandes, and Bernard Weinstein, who were products of the Jewish working class rather than the older middle-class composition of American Jewry. Demonstrates the close contacts and clearly imitative nature of the UHT and the older *Vereinigte Deutsche Gewerkschaften* (German Central Labor Union). The UHT faced opposition by Jewish middle class organs such as *The Jewish Messenger* and the *American Hebrew*, who called the Farein anarchistic. The opposition of Samuel Gompers, who objected to the socialist nature of the group's program and its religious basis, also took several years to overcome. Gompers' writings later falsely claimed him as one of the organizers of the UHT. For 25 years this union was a vital factor in organizing Jewish workers and bringing them into the American labor movement. Primary and secondary sources, 88 notes.
G. J. Bobango

628. Shanks, Rosalie. THE I.W.W. FREE SPEECH MOVEMENT: SAN DIEGO, 1912. *J. of San Diego Hist. 1973 19(1): 25-33.* During 1911 a "socialist army" dominated by the Industrial Workers of the World (I.W.W.) took over Tijuana, Mexico, for a time. Soon San Diegans feared violence and perhaps even pillage at the hands of the I.W.W. The city council prohibited free speech in a six-block area, resulting in mob action and arrests. To most people there was a tie between the red scare and the I.W.W., making restriction of civil rights respectable. Police brutality and vigilante tactics won the day and influenced laws to contain syndicalism. Based on interviews, San Diego newspapers, and secondary accounts; 3 illus., 78 notes.
S. S. Sprague

629. Snyder, Robert E. WOMEN, WOBBLIES, AND WORKER'S RIGHTS: THE 1912 TEXTILE STRIKE IN LITTLE FALLS, NEW YORK. *New York Hist. 1979 60(1): 29-57.* The 1912 textile strike in

Little Falls, New York, shows how immigrant women workers, Schenectady socialists, the Industrial Workers of the World, Helen Keller, and a visiting tuberculosis nurse overcame the hostility of Little Falls authorities and mill management and the indifference of native American labor to achieve reforms in wages, hours, and working conditions. 6 illus., 57 notes.   R. N. Lokken

630. Taft, Philip.   THE LIMITS OF LABOR UNITY: THE CHICAGO NEWSPAPER STRIKE OF 1912.   *Labor Hist. 1978 19(1): 100-129.* Analyzes the internal division generated by the strike-lockout of Chicago newspapers in 1912. Begun by pressmen in a dispute over crew reduction on Hearst newspapers, the strike led to sympathetic walkouts by stereotypers, delivery men, and newsboys. George L. Berry of the pressman's union attempted to obtain support from Chicago newspaper unions and to broaden the strike against the Hearst chain. His efforts failed as the limits of labor unity were reached when opposition to sympathy strikes and lack of support for a National Strike, led by typographers, split labor organizations in the newspaper industry. Based on union publications, conference proceedings, and newspapers; 92 notes.
L. L. Athey

631.   Ullmo, Sylvia.   THE GREAT STRIKES OF 1877.   *Rev. Française d'Etudes Américaines [France] 1976 (2): 49-56.* Studies the radical aspects of the massive railroad and industrial strikes of 1877 in Baltimore, Chicago, St. Louis, and Pittsburgh.

632.   Unsigned.   SEATTLE GENERAL STRIKE, 1919: CAN WE DO BETTER NEXT TIME?   *Progressive Labor 1973 9(2): 32-44.* The ability of Seattle workers to successfully carry out the duties of government without the "help" of the ruling class or its flunkeys in government and business proved the working class can run society and in fact will use their combined forces to seize power. This terrified the rulers. They defused the threat by relying on the weakness of the strike leadership, which lacked a communist core.   J

633.   Unsigned.   THE WORKINGMEN'S PARTY OF CALIFORNIA, 1877-1882.   *California Hist. Q. 1976 55(1): 58-73.* Presents a portfolio of 20 illustrations depicting the Workingmen's Party of California. Founded by Denis Kearney and others, the party opposed the competition of Chinese labor, called for regulation of banks and railroads, and demanded labor reforms. The Workingmen's Party participated in the framing of the 1879 State Constitution. Most of the reproductions are taken from the San Francisco *Illustrated Wasp*, which held a critical view of the movement.   A. Hoffman

634.   Walter, John C.   FRANK R. CROSSWAITH AND THE NEGRO LABOR COMMITTEE IN HARLEM, 1925-1939.   *Afro-Americans in New York Life and Hist. 1979 3(2): 35-49.* Frank R. Crosswaith (1892-1965), black socialist, labor organizer, and activist, founded the Negro Labor Committee in Harlem in 1935.

635.   Weaver, Bill L.   LOUISVILLE'S LABOR DISTURBANCE, JULY, 1877.   *Filson Club Hist. Q. 1974 48(2): 177-186.* On 24 July 1877, a small mob of disorganized workers caused some minor property damage in Louisville, Kentucky. Unlike the situation in other cities, Louisville's problems did not grow into a major conflict. Railway workers, the backbone of labor unrest in other areas in 1877, had just prevented a wage cut in Louisville and did not take part in the violence. In addition, Louisville had escaped the full force of the depression of the 1870's, which, combined with the prompt action of police, prevented continuation of the protest. Documentation from contemporary newspapers and memoirs; 54 notes.   G. B. McKinney

636.   Weisbord, Vera Buch.   GASTONIA 1929: STRIKE AT THE LORAY MILL.   *Southern Exposure 1974 1(3-4): 185-203.* The author, a labor organizer, views the textile workers' strike in which she was harassed, jailed, and tried on charges stemming from her participation in the strike. The National Textile Workers Union organized the strike which also was supported by International Labor Defense and the Young Communist League. Tension between white and black workers was exploited, while the National Guard were used as strikebreakers. The mills had not been unionized by 1974. Based on unpublished autobiography and oral interviews; 8 illus.   G. A. Bolton

637.   Wells, Dave and Stodder, Jim.   A SHORT HISTORY OF NEW ORLEANS DOCKWORKERS.   *Radical Am. 1976 10(1): 43-69.* Despite rigid segregation and racial antipathy, white and black longshoremen united at various periods since the 1850's to work together for mutual economic gain. Racial solidarity dissolved into hostility under outside pressures and the effort of each race to achieve gains for themselves. The recent history of the New Orleans longshoremen's unions has been characterized by extreme corruption which can only be eradicated through a socialist society.   N. Lederer

638.   Wollenberg, Charles.   WORKING ON EL TRAQUE: THE PACIFIC ELECTRIC STRIKE OF 1903.   *Pacific Hist. Rev. 1973 42(3): 358-369.* Discusses the pre-1910 migration of Mexican railroad workers and the Pacific Electric Railroad strike of 1903 in Los Angeles, California, which are largely ignored by scholars of Mexican American history. Mexicans were considered the most tractable workers by the railroads, primarily because they worked for lower wages than other ethnic groups, and with the aid of the railroads the Mexican-born population of Los Angeles reached nearly 20,000 in 1910. The Pacific Electric strike was "one of the first major labor disputes between Mexican workers and Anglo employers." Although the Mexican Federal Union was effective in organizing track workers to strike for higher wages, the strike was squelched when Anglo carmen affiliated with the Amalgamated Association of Street Car Employees failed to walk out, which would have shut down the entire electric railroad system owned by Henry E. Huntington. The railroad did raise wages on the Main Street line, which had highest priority, but did not rehire strikers. The tracks were completed in time for the Los Angeles fiesta, as planned, but the failure of the strike did not end conflict between Huntington and the workers on *el traque*. 47 notes.
B. L. Fenske

639.   Wolman, Philip J.   THE OAKLAND GENERAL STRIKE OF 1946.   *Southern California Q. 1975 57(2): 147-178.* Examines the causes and events concerning the general strike in Oakland, California, 3-5 December 1946. Part of a nationwide series of strikes in 1946, the Oakland incident involved most city workers whole-heartedly endorsing a strike which for 54 hours shut down most economic activity in the city. Essential facilities were maintained at minimum levels while city leaders and national union officials worked to end the strike, but its official termination neither resolved smoldering issues nor penetrated worker discontent. In the 1947 municipal election a labor slate of candidates defeated the incumbents. Suggests that the general strike was occasioned by an emotional outburst against business' failure to effect long-postponed social changes. Primary sources, including personal interviews, and secondary studies; 99 notes.   A. Hoffman

640.   Zeigler, Robert E.   THE LIMITS OF POWER: THE AMALGAMATED ASSOCIATION OF STREET RAILWAY EMPLOYEES IN HOUSTON, TEXAS, 1897-1905.   *Labor Hist. 1977 18(1): 71-90.* Studies the Amalgamated Association of Street Railway Employees and supports the thesis that a community often supported local labor organizations in opposition to corporations. The union failed in a lengthy, violent strike because of employer recalcitrance, not public hostility. Based on newspapers and union records; 44 notes.   L. L. Athey

Society and Culture

General

641.   Banit, Thomas F.   WAR: A TOOL FOR STUDYING SOCIETY: ANOTHER CASE FOR LOCAL HISTORY.   *New England Social Studies Bull. 1974/75 32(2): 11-16.* Examines the effects of World War I on Bridgeport, Connecticut.   S

642.   Bellow, Saul.   STARTING OUT IN CHICAGO.   *Am. Scholar 1974-75 44(1): 71-77.* Analyzes the social and cultural environment in Chicago during the late 1930's and the efforts of immigrants and their children to be "American," and discusses the way "being American" has developed since then. Our biggest enemy is "the Great Noise," the terrible excitement and distraction generated by the crises of modern life." Based on a commencement address delivered at Brandeis University, Spring 1974.   R. V. Ritter

643. Boucher, Ronald L. THE COLONIAL MILITIA AS A SOCIAL INSTITUTION: SALEM, MASSACHUSETTS 1764-1775. *Military Affairs 1973 37(4): 125-130.* The militia was one of the most enduring colonial institutions. That of Salem is a good example. The quarterly musters were secular holidays which provided both training and socializing. By 1770, however, many men escaped duty by paying a fine, and those who served were ill-trained. The officers represented wealth and the local political leadership, although provincial authorities controlled the granting of commissions. After 1774 the Salem militia mirrored the shifting political attitudes and began to reemphasize its purpose as the defense of Salem. Based on local records, newspapers, and printed memoirs; 19 notes.   K. J. Bauer

644. Bowie, Nancy. CLOUD CITY CAMEO. *Westways 1976 68(5): 18-21, 79.* Horace A. W. Tabor, an investor in silver mining in Leadville, Colorado, 1877-93, used his wealth to develop the town, build its opera house, divorce his wife, and marry Elizabeth McCourt "Baby Doe"; both died in poverty.

645. Clinton, Katherine. PIONEER WOMEN IN CHICAGO, 1833-1837. *J. of the West 1973 12(2): 317-324.* The women pioneers who came to Chicago were a hardy lot. "They played a leading role in civic life through their work in education and reform and through their humanitarian efforts." Unknowingly, they challenged the prevalent 19th-century social attitudes toward femininity—a stereotype which "scarcely fitted the rugged environment of frontier Chicago." 42 notes.
                                        E. P. Stickney

646. Deagan, Kathleen A. THE ARCHEOLOGY OF FIRST SPANISH PERIOD ST. AUGUSTINE, 1972-1978. *Escribano 1978 15: 1-22.* Discusses artifacts and excavations in Spanish St. Augustine, Florida, 1972-78, analyzing them as they reveal the town's social history.

647. Detweiler, Robert. SHIFTING PERSPECTIVES ON THE SALEM WITCHES. *Hist. Teacher 1975 8(4): 596-610.* Reviews the literature concerning witchcraft in Salem Village. Discusses historical interpretations of this phenomenon, and draws attention to studies in anthropology and psychology concerning witchcraft in other societies. Studies by anthropologists show fear of witchcraft to be a form of behavioral control especially in time of stress. Studies in psychology depict witchcraft as a form of revolt by young people against the restraints imposed by an older generation. Recent historians have built upon studies in both these disciplines. Based on primary and secondary sources; 57 notes.   P. W. Kennedy

648. Douglas, Paul H. THE MATERIAL CULTURE OF THE HARMONY SOCIETY. *Pennsylvania Folklife 1975 24(3): 2-16.* Uses material culture—specifically, town planning, buildings, and artifacts—to reinterpret social customs and living patterns in Harmony Society, a 19th-century communal society in Harmony and Economy, Pennsylvania and New Harmony, Indiana.   S

649. Doyle, Don Harrison. SOCIAL THEORY AND NEW COMMUNITIES IN NINETEENTH-CENTURY AMERICA. *Western Hist. Q. 1977 8(2): 151-165.* Uses data, principally from Jacksonville, Illinois, to establish a theoretical framework for understanding new communities as arenas of social change in 19th-century America. Examines demographic characteristics, social functions of conflict, and institutional mechanisms for social integration and social control. 23 notes.
                                        D. L. Smith

650. Faulk, Odie B. LIFE IN TOMBSTONE. *J. of the West 1972 11(3): 495-512.* Reproduces a chapter of the author's new book, *Tombstone: Myth and Reality*, which describes daily life in a frontier mining community. Despite primitive living conditions, the citizens were quick to establish churches, schools, theaters, and other civic improvements which competed with saloons and gambling halls for the miners' participation. Based on memoirs and secondary works; 31 notes.
                                        B. S. Porter

651. Fleming, Hartley G. THE EAST END, 1898-1915. *Western Pennsylvania Hist. Mag. 1977 60(4): 419-426.* Hartley G. Fleming reminisces about his boyhood in eastern Pittsburgh, 1898-1915.

652. Friedmann, Karen J. VICTUALLING COLONIAL BOSTON. *Agric. Hist. 1973 47(3): 189-205.* No records were found on everyday matters in colonial Boston, such as going to market or taking grain to the mill, but laws, ordinances, and other official records indirectly help fill this gap in information. Traces food distribution in Boston beginning in the 18th century, giving forms and channels through which the basic foods reached the consumer. Explains grist mills, meat packing, and the milk and cheese industry, and gives the rules of new markets and the functions of the huckster and the docks. New methods in the food marketing system may be attributed to population growth, an increase in cash purchasing power as barter declined, and the growth of a propertyless, wage-earning class. Based on printed documentary materials.
                                        V. B. Whitehead

653. Godfrey, Kenneth W. SOME THOUGHTS REGARDING AN UNWRITTEN HISTORY OF NAUVOO. *Brigham Young U. Studies 1975 15(4): 417-424.* Presents anecdotes about the Mormons in Nauvoo, Illinois, and thoughts regarding the possibility of writing a social history of the town, 1842-46.

654. Gordon, Dudley. CHARLES F. LUMMIS AND THE NEWMARKS OF LOS ANGELES. *Western States Jewish Hist. Q. 1974 7(1): 32-38.* The friendship of author-editor Charles F. Lummis and the Newmark brothers, leading merchants in Los Angeles, led to the preservation of several historical sites and a crusade for culture in Los Angeles. Lummis founded the Southwest Museum and edited *Land of Sunshine* for many years. He also wrote the foreword to Harris Newmark's *Sixty Years in Southern California*.   R. A. Garfinkle

655. Greven, Philip J., Jr. SALEM PROBED. *Rev. in Am. Hist. 1974 2(4): 513-518.* The content, methodology, sources, hypotheses, and significance of Paul Boyer and Stephen Nissenbaum's *Salem Possessed: The Social Origins of Witchcraft* (Cambridge, Mass.: Harvard U. Pr., 1974) are assessed in this laudatory review article which notes the book's important contributions to understanding Salem in particular and to understanding "processes of community development and social conflicts" in general.

656. Hunter, Albert. COMMUNITY CHANGE: A STOCHASTIC ANALYSIS OF CHICAGO'S LOCAL COMMUNITIES, 1930-60. *Am. J. of Sociol. 1974 79(4): 923-947.* Compares two different urban ecology perspectives, the static one emphasizing uniform spatial distributions, and the dynamic one emphasizing stages of community change and utilizes them to study census data for Chicago from 1930 to 1960. When community changes in the two dimensions of economic and family status were interrelated in a two-attribute stochastic model, the following were found: 1) rates of community change are increasing, but not uniformly; 2) society-wide and historically specific contexts must be considered in explaining different types and rates of community change; 3) four empirically derived stages of community change are delimited that show an ordering with respect to family and economic changes; 4) the four stages of change are arranged in concentric zones; and 5) the four stages of change are not mere spatial indicators of processes occurring over time but are sequentially ordered.   J/S

657. Johnson, G. Wesley, Jr. DWIGHT HEARD IN PHOENIX: THE EARLY YEARS. *J. of Arizona Hist. 1977 18(3): 258-278.* In 1895, Dwight Bancroft Heard (1869-1929) and Maie Bartlett Heard (1868-1951) went to Phoenix for a brief stay for his health. This evolved into a permanent move. The Heard estate became "an outpost of culture, refinement, and the arts in a city just emerging from the raw frontier." The Heards were involved in agricultural improvement, residential development, journalism, water, land, financing, and social welfare, as well as the arts and society. Their final legacy was the Phoenix Civic Center, home of the public library, museum, and little theater. 4 illus., 26 notes.
                                        D. L. Smith

658. Katz, Michael B. NOT THE LAST WORD. *Rev. in Am. Hist. 1977 5(2): 223-229.* Review article prompted by Alan Dawley's *Class and Community: The Industrial Revolution in Lynn* (Cambridge, Mass.: Harvard U. Pr., 1976).

659. Kusmer, Kenneth L. THE CONCEPT OF "COMMUNITY" IN AMERICAN HISTORY. *Rev. in Am. Hist. 1979 7(3): 380-387.*

Review article prompted by Thomas Bender's *Community and Social Change in America* (New Brunswick, New Jersey: Rutgers U. Pr., 1978) and Thomas Lee Philpott's *The Slum and the Ghetto: Neighborhood Deterioration and Middle-Class Reform, Chicago, 1880-1930* (New York: Oxford U. Pr., 1978) examines the development of the concept of community, ca. 1870's-1930's.

660. Lampman, Evelyn Sibley. AS IT WAS. . . . *Oregon Hist. Q. 1975 76(4): 368-378.* Describes family life and social conditions in Dallas, Oregon, during the early 20th century. One of the few nonwhites in the community was a Chinese, Ah Coe, whose family and activities are described. He ran a laundry. Illus.   E. P. Stickney

661. Lawson, Michael L. FLORA LANGERMANN SPIEGEL-BERG: GRAND LADY OF SANTA FE. *Western States Jewish Hist. Q. 1976 8(4): 291-308.* In 1875 Flora Langermann Spiegelberg (1857-1943) and her husband Willi (1844-1929) moved to Santa Fe. Willi and his five brothers operated a wholesale business that, along with new family enterprises, dominated the economy of the Southwest for several years. In 1893, the now wealthy Spiegelberg family moved to New York City. "Garbage Can Flora" became involved in the movement to clean up the city and she campaigned for investigations of war profits in the munitions industry during World War I. In 1914, she helped organize the Metropolitan Protective Association to work for improved wages for the city street cleaners. After Willi died she donated many family items to the Museum of New Mexico. Based primarily on Flora's manuscripts; 3 photos, 33 notes.   R. A. Garfinkle

662. Lowry, Charles B. "THE CITY ON A HILL' AND KIBBUT-ZIM: SEVENTEENTH CENTURY UTOPIAS AS IDEAL TYPES. *Am. Jewish Hist. Q. 1974 64(1): 24-41.* A sociological comparison of 17th-century Puritan New England towns and early 20th-century Kibbutzim in Palestine. The kibbutz is defined as a family, comparable to the Puritan family, and both societies are said to operate in a religious setting. Other similarities would include their agricultural character, position of women, and strong intellectual bent. 47 notes.   F. Rosenthal

663. Lynn, Kenneth S. THE REBELS OF GREENWICH VIL-LAGE. *Perspectives in Am. Hist. 1974 8: 335-378.* A biographical analysis of approximately 125 residents of New York's Greenwich Village during the Progressive era, challenging accepted beliefs concerning this "rebel" population. Their average age in 1912 was 31, and most were from established urban location in the East and Europe. Though all professed an aesthetic love of poverty, the majority were from middle to upper class backgrounds. 48 notes, appendix.   W. A. Wiegand

664. Lyon, Eugene. ST. AUGUSTINE, 1580: THE LIVING COM-MUNITY. *Escribano 1977 14: 20-33.* Describes the daily life, social organization, and civil-military relations in the town and presidio of St. Augustine, Florida, 1580.

665. McGinty, Brian. DOG DAYS IN SAN FRANCISCO. *Westways 1976 68(1): 40-43, 55.* Discusses life in San Francisco, California, during the 1860's, and the story of Bummer and Lazarus, who were among the first known dogs in that city.

666. Melbin, Murray. NIGHT AS FRONTIER. *Am. Sociol. Rev. 1978 43(1): 3-22.* While the settlement of some of the world's land areas was coming to an end, there began an increase in wakeful activity over more of the 24-hour day. This trend of expansion in time is continuing, especially in urban areas. The hypothesis that night has become the new frontier is supported by the premise that time, like space, can be occupied and is treated so by humans. A set of evidence, including results of several field experiments, show that nighttime social life in urban areas resembles social life on former land frontiers. The research data refers mainly to contemporary Boston and to the US West a century ago.   J

667. Petraitus, Paul W. HENRY RALPH KOOPMAN II: THE LIFE AND TIMES OF A NEIGHBORHOOD PHOTOGRAPHER. *Chicago Hist. 1978 7(3): 161-177.* Operating a small independent photography studio in Roseland, Illinois, 1884-1904, Henry Ralph Koopman II recorded the daily lives, and portraits of that community.

668. Quandt, Jean B. COMMUNITY IN URBAN AMERICA, 1890-1917: REFORMERS, CITY PLANNERS, AND GREENWICH VILLAGERS. *Societas 1976 6(4): 255-273.* Analyzes several categories of "communal experience and theory," especially community, a geographical concept and communion, a "commonality of feeling rather than a community of place." Although the two are by no means mutually exclusive, the latter, as in Greenwich Village, grew out of a rebellion against "stabilities of place" and local ties, a response to the throes of urbanization and industrialization. Based on the Edna Kenton Papers (Beinecke Library, Yale University), primary and secondary sources; 64 notes.   J. D. Hunley

669. Racine, Philip N. THE KU KLUX KLAN, ANTI-CATHOLI-CISM, AND ATLANTA'S BOARD OF EDUCATION, 1916-1927. *Georgia Hist. Q. 1973 57(1): 63-75.* The Ku Klux Klan became a power in Atlanta politics during and after World War I. Playing upon strong forces of religious bigotry and fundamentalism, the Klan yet failed to coerce the board of education into adopting anti-Catholic measures. Atlantans viewed the Klan's control of politics as a passing phenomenon, but interference in the education system was intolerable. 55 notes.
                                                              D. L. Smith

670. Radford, John. THE CHARLESTON PLANTERS IN 1860. *South Carolina Hist. Mag. 1976 77(4): 227-235.* Examines the impact which planters who came to Charleston in the nonplanting season for the social atmosphere had on the social history and social geography of the area.

671. Scott, Ann Firor. COMMUNITIES IN THE MAKING. *Rev. in Am. Hist. 1979 7(2): 209-214.* Review article prompted by Robert Doherty's *Society and Power: Five New England Towns, 1800-1860* (Amherst: U. of Massachusetts Pr., 1977) and Don Harrison Doyle's *The Social Order of a Frontier Community: Jacksonville, Illinois, 1825-70* (Urbana: U. of Illinois Pr., 1978).

672. Smith, Bruce R. BENJAMIN HALLOWELL OF ALEXAN-DRIA: SCIENTIST, EDUCATOR, QUAKER IDEALIST. *Virginia Mag. of Hist. and Biog. 1977 85(3): 337-361.* Benjamin Hallowell, who lived in Alexandria during 1824-60, influenced the development of education and other civic projects in that city. His *Autobiography* reveals much about his educational philosophy and his difficulties as a Quaker to grapple with such issues as slavery and the Civil War. Based largely on Hallowell's published *Autobiography;* 2 illus., 42 notes.
                                                               R. F. Oaks

673. Stringfellow, Nancy. AS IT WAS. *Idaho Heritage 1977 (8): 4-7.* Examines daily life in the mining town of Idaho City, 1865.

674. Tholl, Claire K. and Ward, Seely. SEELY WARD'S RECOL-LECTIONS OF THE SLOATSBURG AREA. *North Jersey Highlander 1973 9(2): 2-18.* Historically describes the Sloatsburg area in southeast New York. Many personal reminiscences and sites of the Sloatsburg-Ramapo area are related by the late Seely Ward. 10 illus., map.
                                                              A. C. Aimone

675. Tobey, Ronald C. HOW URBANE IS THE URBANITE? AN HISTORICAL MODEL OF THE URBAN HIERARCHY AND THE SOCIAL MOTIVATION OF THE SERVICE CLASSES. *Hist. Methods Newsletter 1974 7(4): 259-275.* Using Robert Wiebe's and Samuel Hay's views of Progressive reform as an upper middle class activity, the author concludes that the framework for a national generalization does not exist. Offers his mode, drawn from social structure theory, as the needed framework, emphasizing the characteristic value orientation by which society creates order.   D. K. Pickens

676. Topping, Eva Catafygiotu. CINCINNATI PHILHELLENISM IN 1824. *Cincinnati Hist. Soc. J. 1973 31(2): 127-141.* The Greek War of Independence began in March 1821. "Greek Fever," support for Greek independence, reached its zenith in Cincinnati in 1824. Its leader and chronicler was Moses Dawson, who raised funds successfully through a number of events held during the year. Based on a contemporary journal and newspapers; 8 illus., 22 notes.   H. S. Marks

677. Trotter, Margaret G.   A GLIMPSE OF CHARLESTON IN THE 1890S: FROM A CONTEMPORARY DIARY. *West Virginia Hist. 1974 35(2): 131-144.* Charleston, West Virginia, in the 1890's had 10,000 people but maintained its rural heritage. Houses were gas-lit but heated by fireplaces, window-screens had just arrived, and there was no telephone service. Air pollution was created by the coal industry and a local welfare problem was beginning. Based on the diary of Elizabeth Ruffner Wilson; 138 notes.   J. H. Broussard

678. Twombly, Robert C.   WHAT WAS IMPORTANT AND WHAT WAS NOT. *Rev. in Am. Hist. 1976 4(4): 526-532.* Review article prompted by Robert A. Gross's *The Minutemen and Their World* (New York: Hill and Wang, 1976); discusses local history and social history popular in New England chronicles, especially as it relates to the social history of Concord, Massachusetts, 1740's-1820's.

679. Viskochil, Larry A.   CHICAGO'S BICENTENNIAL PHOTOGRAPHER: CHARLES D. MOSHER. *Chicago Hist. 1976 5(2): 95-104.* Discusses the public-spirited and semi-philanthropic schemes 1870-97, of Chicago photographer Charles D. Mosher, including his plans for a Memorial Hall (in which to hang his own photography), a new sewage system, and a time capsule to be opened at the time of the national bicentennial.

680. Wilson, Laura Foster.   RICHARD BURTON VISITS THE CITY OF THE SAINTS. *Am. West 1975 12(1): 4-9.* English explorer and author Richard Burton (1821-90) traveled across the United States in 1860. His *City of the Saints and Across the Rocky Mountains to California* (1861) was the most complete and knowledgeable account written on the Mormons and Utah for several decades. The book was unique because of its favorable and sympathetic description of the Mormons and their institutions and its hundreds of pages of erudition. 5 illus., biblio.   D. L. Smith

681. Wrona, Christine.   WITCHCRAFT IN EARLY SPRINGFIELD: THE PARSONS CASE. *Hist. J. of Western Massachusetts 1977 6(1): 61-64.* Account of an episode of witchcraft accusation in 17th-century Springfield, Massachusetts. Illus., notes.
                    W. H. Mulligan, Jr.

682. Zochert, Donald.   HEINRICH SCHLIEMANN'S CHICAGO JOURNAL. *Chicago Hist. 1973 2(3): 173-181.* Schliemann (1822-90), later to be famous for his discovery of Troy, visited Chicago in November 1867. His journal observations reveal a rapidly growing city before the Great Fire. He visited the stockyards, water works, local schools, the University of Chicago, and other sites and was particularly impressed with the educational system and the grain trade. Based on primary sources; 9 illus.   N. A. Kuntz

Demography, Population, and the Family

683. Alexander, John K.   THE PHILADELPHIA NUMBERS GAME: AN ANALYSIS OF PHILADELPHIA'S EIGHTEENTH-CENTURY POPULATION. *Pennsylvania Mag. of Hist. and Biog. 1974 98(3): 314-324.* By using statistical formulas, provides estimates of Philadelphia's population from 1700 (4,389) to 1790 (42,535). Based on these estimates, Philadelphia's population increased 51.6% during 1769-90. Based on primary and secondary sources; 50 notes.
                    E. W. Carp

684. Ariés, Philippe.   THE FAMILY AND THE CITY. *Daedalus 1977 106(2): 227-235.* The 20th-century family is burdened with "the task of trying to satisfy all the emotional and social needs of its members." This phenomenon can be traced to "the decline of the city and the urban forms of social intercourse it had once provided" in institutions such as the cafe. The decline itself occurred during the 19th century in the process of decentralization, where the bourgeois and middle classes escaped to the privacy and rural surroundings of the suburb. Finally, with the advent of television and the automobile in the 20th century, the city's chief function as provider for social intercourse is now nonexistent and the balance between community life and family is destroyed, thus resulting in an all-inclusive family structure which can no longer fulfill all of its functions.   G. Fox

685. Auwers, Linda.   FATHERS, SONS, AND WEALTH IN COLONIAL WINDSOR, CONNECTICUT. *J. of Family Hist. 1978 3(2): 136-149.* Partible land inheritance was practiced in 17th and 18th century Windsor with a supplemental consideration frequently going to the eldest. When land was distributed in whole or in part before death of the parents, provisions were usually made for services and/or payments to be rendered to the parent. Parental control of inheritances appears to have had no demonstrable influence on age at marriage. 5 tables, 10 notes, biblio.
                    T. W. Smith

686. Bigham, Darrel E.   THE BLACK FAMILY IN EVANSVILLE AND VANDERBURGH COUNTY, INDIANA, IN 1880. *Indiana Mag. of Hist. 1979 75(2): 117-146.* Traditionally, sociologists have argued that slavery was the cause of the instability of Afro-American families. Analysis of the 1880 federal census for Vanderburgh County, Indiana, demonstrates that Afro-American family instability resulted from the urban experience rather than from the legacy of slavery. The census data offers considerable support for the integrity and strength of the Afro-American family in post-Civil War Indiana. 49 notes.   J. Moore

687. Blumin, Stuart M.   RIP VAN WINKLE'S GRANDCHILDREN: FAMILY AND HOUSEHOLD IN THE HUDSON VALLEY 1800-1860. *J. of Urban Hist. 1975 1(3): 293-315.* Troy, Kingston, and Marlborough represent industrial, commercial and agricultural towns respectively. Concludes that similarities in family characteristics among the three—household size, boarding houses as a transient experience, and four-fifths of the population living in nuclear families—outweigh the differences. 11 tables, 20 notes.   S. S. Sprague

688. Chudacoff, Howard P.   NEW BRANCHES ON THE TREE: HOUSEHOLD STRUCTURE IN EARLY STAGES OF THE FAMILY CYCLE IN WORCESTER, MASSACHUSETTS, 1860-1880. *Pro. of the Am. Antiquarian Soc. 1976 86(2): 303-320.* Links family history and urban history by examining family adjustment to change in a growing city. The nuclear family prevailed here, but living arrangements varied among families in different stages of development. Contextual factors, such as housing supplies, physical growth of the city, and economic change, caused household structures to fluctuate. Primary and secondary sources; 35 notes.   J. Andrew

689. Conzen, Kathleen Neils.   LOCAL HISTORY AS CASE STUDY. *Rev. in Am. Hist. 1978 6(1): 50-56.* Review article prompted by Stephanie Grauman Wolf's *Urban Village: Population, Community, and Family Structure in Germantown, Pennsylvania, 1683-1800* (Princeton, N. J.: Princeton U. Pr., 1976).

690. Corbett, Theodore G.   POPULATION STRUCTURE IN HISPANIC ST. AUGUSTINE, 1629-1763. *Florida Hist. Q. 1976 54(3): 263-284.* The population of 17th- and 18th-century St. Augustine generally followed a dependent community pattern, exhibiting late marriages, a high mortality rate, and a low number of births per marriage. This demographic study is based primarily on baptismal, marriage, and burial church records plus some census reports. 6 tables, 2 figs., 53 notes.
                    P. A. Beaber

691. Dubovik, Paul N.   HOUSING IN HOLYOKE AND ITS EFFECTS ON FAMILY LIFE 1860-1910. *Hist. J. of Western Massachusetts 1975 4(1): 40-50.* The poverty of the "Shanty Irish" of "The Patch," the financial difficulties of the Hadley Falls Company, inadequate transportation, and expensive land led to barracks-like tenements. High rental company housing was a method of exploiting the workers. Based on the Holyoke *Transcript*, Green's *Holyoke*, and state and local documents; 3 illus., 62 notes.   S. S. Sprague

692. Edmonston, Barry and Davies, Omar.   POPULATION SUBURBANIZATION IN THE WESTERN REGION OF THE UNITED STATES, 1900-1970. *Land Econ. 1976 62(3): 393-403.* Uses the negative exponential function to measure the degree of change in metropolitan population concentration in this century. Urban populations have become increasingly dispersed, and this trend has implications for planning policy. 3 tables, 19 refs.   E. S. Johnson

693. Goldin, Claudia.   FAMILY STRATEGIES IN LATE NINETEENTH-CENTURY PHILADELPHIA. *Working Papers from the*

Regional Econ. Hist. Res. Center 1979 2(3): 60-106. Analyzes the family decisionmaking process regarding economics in late 19th century Philadelphia households, based on a study of urban families from 1870 to 1880 United States Federal Population Censuses.

694. Graff, Harvey J. PATTERNS OF DEPENDENCY AND CHILD DEVELOPMENT IN THE MID-NINETEENTH CENTURY CITY: A SAMPLE FROM BOSTON 1860. *Hist. of Educ. Q. 1973 13(2): 129-143.* Statistical analysis of the growing-up process in urban areas which challenges previous studies of rural areas. The home and the market were "foci of opposite sets of values," thereby increasing dependency. Primary and secondary sources; 4 tables, 25 notes.

L. C. Smith

695. Grigg, Susan. TOWARD A THEORY OF REMARRIAGE: A CASE STUDY OF NEWBURYPORT AT THE BEGINNING OF THE NINETEENTH CENTURY. *J. of Interdisciplinary Hist. 1977 8(2): 183-220.* Studies remarriage in Newburyport in the early 19th century and explains why some people remarried. The data are compared with similar studies of European and North American communities. Remarriage was inversely related to age and less likely for women than for men of the same age. The effects of wealth and children on remarriage are also studied. There were variations in desire, need, and opportunity, which affected the likelihood of remarriage, and such variations can be measured in economic terms. Printed sources; 12 tables, 49 notes

R. Howell

696. Hareven, Tamara K. and Vinovskis, Maris A. ETHNICITY AND OCCUPATION IN URBAN FAMILIES: AN ANALYSIS OF SOUTH BOSTON MARITAL FERTILITY, AND THE SOUTH END IN 1880. *J. of Social Hist. 1975 8(3): 69-93.* Quantitative study of fertility in South Boston and the South End in 1880 "suggest that ethnicity was a major determinant of fertility differentials at the household levels." Occupation and location in the city also had an impact on fertility ratios. More work is needed on the relationship of fertility and women's work and also on evaluating the importance of the "level of education, religion, and income." 7 tables, 6 graphs, 29 notes, appendix.

L. Ziewacz

697. Hareven, Tamara K. FAMILY TIME AND HISTORICAL TIME. *Daedalus 1977 106(2): 57-70.* The family did not "break down" under the impact of industrialization and urbanization, but rather it contributed to both processes. Families aided in adapting their members to industrial work and to living in large urban settings. It is inaccurate to hold that the timing of family transitions was once more orderly than it is now. In fact, families are now less subject to sudden change. Some of the major problems facing the contemporary family arise from the demands placed on it by those who require that it be a haven and retreat from the outside world, which it has never been. Secondary sources; 27 notes.

E. McCarthy

698. Hareven, Tamara K. FAMILY TIME AND INDUSTRIAL TIME: FAMILY AND WORK IN A PLANNED CORPORATION TOWN 1900-1924. *J. of Urban Hist. 1975 1(3): 365-389.* Cumulative individual employee files 1910-36 of the Amoskeag Manufacturing Company of Manchester, New Hampshire, coupled with marriage and insurance records and oral histories, reveal a pervasive family influence in working. Vacancies were discovered via word-of-mouth, family members substituted for each other, family finances postponed marriages and caused babies to be dropped off so women could return to work. Young children found summer jobs in the mills, and many met their future spouses there. 45 notes.

S. S. Sprague

699. Hareven, Tamara K. INTRODUCTION: THE HISTORICAL STUDY OF THE FAMILY IN URBAN SOCIETY. *J. of Urban Hist. 1975 1(3): 259-267.* Considers "the family a critical variable" shedding "light on migration patterns which determine population change." This overview covers ca. 1750-1975 and introduces five papers in the same issue. 17 notes.

S. S. Sprague

700. Hynek, Paul. DEMOGRAPHIC STUDY OF EASTHAMPTON, MASSACHUSETTS 1850-1870. *Hist. J. of Western Massachusetts 1977 6(1): 6-22.* Analyzes population growth in Easthampton, Massachusetts, based on published US census reports, and considers the demands this rapid growth placed on the town. Illus., notes.

W. H. Mulligan, Jr.

701. Jacob, Kathryn A. THE WOMAN'S LOT IN BALTIMORE TOWN: 1729-97. *Maryland Hist. Mag. 1976 71(3): 283-295.* Examines the status of women in Baltimore based on primary records revealing births, marriage, and legal status, emphasizing that the quality of life, desirability as a marriage partner, and women's own self-image "were all determined by her place on the economic ladder." All free married women, rich or poor, were virtually legal nonentities and "all women were politically powerless," but single women and widows are shown by local court and land records to have "vigorously exercised all the rights and privileges to which they were entitled." Discusses high mortality rates in giving birth, frequent court appearances on charges of keeping disorderly houses, bastardy, and unlicensed liquor sales, women involved in land speculation, slaveholding, civil suits, and commercial enterprises, problems of dowries, and the nursing of infants. Distinguishes among the well-born, working-class women, and female indentured servants, who were most frequently before the courts. Baltimore primary records, and secondary sources; 77 notes.

G. J. Bobango

702. Laslett, Barbara. HOUSEHOLD STRUCTURE ON AN AMERICAN FRONTIER: LOS ANGELES, CALIFORNIA, IN 1850. *Am. J. of Sociol. 1975 81(1): 109-128.* Based on individual United States federal census schedules, this paper reports on the way in which economic and demographic variables relate to different types of household organization in Los Angeles in 1850. While the findings confirm the results of other recent research that the nuclear family predominated in preindustrial societies, they also emphasize the need to focus on variation rather than on modality in order to understand household organization. Methodological problems of working with this kind of data are discussed, as are the implications of the results for the study of social change.

J

703. Laslett, Barbara. SOCIAL CHANGE AND THE FAMILY: LOS ANGELES, CALIFORNIA, 1850-1870. *Am. Sociol. Rev. 1977 42(2): 268-291.* Using Marx's description of "the so-called primitive accumulation," which he associates with the development of capitalism in the West, explores the impact on the family of changes in the individual's access to actual and potential wealth. A multivariate analysis, based on the individual census schedules for the city of Los Angeles in 1850 and 1870, is used to explore the changing relationships between economic, demographic and other structural variables on household structure. The findings suggest that a dynamic, Marxian model can help explain the effects of social change on the family.

J

704. May, Elaine Tyler. THE PRESSURE TO PROVIDE: CLASS, CONSUMERISM, AND DIVORCE IN URBAN AMERICA 1880-1920. *J. of Social Hist. 1978 12(2): 180-193.* Compares and examines the effects of heightened material aspirations on white-collar and blue-collar Americans at the turn of the century. While a rising standard of living may have enhanced family life for some classes, it often wreaked havoc on those homes which could not afford the fruits of abundance. The emergence of an affluent society paralleled the skyrocketing of American divorce rate. A sample of 500 litigations in Los Angeles in the 1880's and another 500 from 1920 compared with a sample of 250 divorces filed throughout New Jersey in 1920 can show effects of economic change over time. Issues involving money became increasingly important. For the affluent couples tension arose over how the family's resources should be spent; for lower white-collar ranks status consideration clashed with limited incomes; and for working class couples, mass consumption remained out of reach thus contributing to a greater sense of economic insecurity and heightened frustrations. Primary and secondary sources; 5 tables, 22 notes.

R. S. Sliwoski

705. McIlwain, Josephine. TWELVE BLOCKS: A STUDY OF ONE SEGMENT OF PITTSBURGH'S SOUTH SIDE, 1880-1915. *Western Pennsylvania Hist. Mag. 1977 60(4): 351-370.* Examines population changes in the Twenty-sixth Ward of Pittsburgh, Pennsylvania, 1880-1915, due to changes in industrial focus from the iron and glass industries (requiring skilled laborers) to the steel industry (requiring unskilled laborers).

706. Merriam, Paul G. THE "OTHER PORTLAND": A STATISTICAL NOTE ON FOREIGN-BORN, 1860-1910. *Oregon Hist. Q. 1979 80(3): 258-268.* Portland has long been characterized as a transplanted New England commercial city. However, demographic statistics

convincingly shatter this myth and demonstrate that Portland was built and populated by numerous ethnic groups. By 1860, one-quarter of the city's population was foreign-born. The percentage rose to 31.1 by 1870. 3 illus., 4 tables, 12 notes.   D. R. McDonald

707.   Milan, Frederick A. and Pawson, Stella.   THE DEMOGRAPHY OF THE NATIVE POPULATION OF AN ALASKAN CITY. *Arctic [Canada] 1975 28(4): 275-283.* Examines the movement of Indians (primarily Athapaskans) and Eskimos into Fairbanks, Alaska, 1925-75; World War II attracted entire family units, but more recent migrations have consisted of single persons, women outnumbering men.

708.   Modell, John; Furstenberg, Frank F.; and Hershberg, Theodore. SOCIAL CHANGE AND TRANSITIONS TO ADULTHOOD IN HISTORICAL PERSPECTIVE.   *J. of Family Hist. 1976 1(1): 7-32.* It has been generally assumed that the industrial revolution changed the transition process from childhood to adulthood. Yet there is virtually no empirical data on what the maturation processes were in the 19th century, or how they have changed over the last 100 years. Drawing on evidence from the Philadelphia Social History project, the authors analyze the prevalence, timing, spread, age-congruity, and integration of the transition process. They find that over the last century the prevalence of the usual transition has increased somewhat, that the spread has narrowed, that there is much greater age-congruity, and that transitions are more contingent and integrated since formal institutions play a larger role. 2 tables, 6 graphs, 19 notes, biblio.   T. W. Smith

709.   Morgan, Myfanwy and Golden, Hilda H.   IMMIGRANT FAMILIES IN AN INDUSTRIAL CITY: A STUDY OF HOUSEHOLDS IN HOLYOKE, 1880.   *J. of Family Hist. 1979 4(1): 59-68.* From a sample of the census manuscript for 1880 studies the relationship between ethnicity and 1) household size, 2) household composition, and 3) family type in Holyoke, Massachusetts. Important differences are found among the major ethnic groups (native born whites, Irish, and Canadians). The native born had small household size, but included more non-relatives and non-immediate kin than the immigrant groups. As a result the native households were more frequently extended families than the immigrant households were. 6 tables, 8 notes, biblio.   T. W. Smith

710.   Nash, Gary B. and Smith, Billy G.   THE POPULATION OF EIGHTEENTH-CENTURY PHILADELPHIA.   *Pennsylvania Mag. of Hist. and Biog. 1975 99(3): 362-368.* Suggests that the ratio of people per house at the time the 1790 census was taken may not be applicable earlier in the 18th century. Family size, the decline of slavery and indentured servitude, and the rise of a free labor system in which large numbers of workers rented rooms in tenements, are variables that must to considered. Table, 15 notes.   C. W. Olson

711.   Smith, Billy G.   DEATH AND LIFE IN A COLONIAL IMMIGRANT CITY: A DEMOGRAPHIC ANALYSIS OF PHILADELPHIA.   *J. of Econ. Hist. 1977 37(4): 863-889.* This study analyzes the demographic characteristics of a previously neglected area in colonial America—the urban center. Growth, birth, and death rates in Philadelphia between 1720 and 1775 are estimated using a variety of sources. Immigration, smallpox, economic vacillations, and a skewed age structure are attributed primary responsibility in determining the level of and changes in Philadelphia's vital rates. The elevated level of these rates is evident in a comparison with vital rates in Andover and Boston, Massachusetts, and Nottingham, England.   J

712.   Smith, Judith E.   OUR OWN KIND: FAMILY AND COMMUNITY NETWORKS.   *Radical Hist. Rev. 1978 (17): 99-120.* Provides a study of immigrant family ties and traditions, particularly among southern Italian and eastern European Jewish immigrants as they experienced the urban industrial environment of Rhode Island during 1880-1940.

713.   Somerville, James K.   THE SALEM (MASS.) WOMAN IN THE HOME, 1660-1770.   *Eighteenth-Cent. Life 1974 1(1): 11-14.* Uses wills to explore the way the position of women in the home changed through generations.   S

714.   Swauger, John.   PITTSBURGH'S RESIDENTIAL PATTERN IN 1815.   *Ann. of the Assoc. of Am. Geographers 1978 68(2): 265-277.* The demography of Pittsburgh, Pennsylvania, in 1815 reveals that popu-

lation distribution and residential placement in the central city corresponded to lower social status.

715.   Unsigned.   [FAMILY STRUCTURE IN CONFRONTATION WITH SOCIAL CHANGE].   *J. of Social Hist. [Great Britain] 1974 7(4): 406-459.*
Yans-McLaughlin, Virginia.   A FLEXIBLE TRADITION: SOUTH ITALIAN IMMIGRANTS CONFRONT A NEW YORK EXPERIENCE,   *pp. 429-445.* Examines the way in which Italian immigrants transformed canning factories into communities where Old World social attitudes and behavior could continue and where kinship ties operated to maintain them. "Modern economic institutions were quite capable of incorporating such traditional needs." 61 notes.
Harris, Alice Kessler.   COMMENTS ON THE YANS-MCLAUGHLIN AND DAVIDOFF PAPERS,   *pp. 446-451.* The papers [including one by Leonore Davidoff on servants and wives in Victorian and Edwardian England, pp. 406-428] raise basic questions but do not go far enough in a number of questions or exploration of implications. 3 notes.
Tilly, Louise A.   COMMENTS ON THE YANS-MCLAUGHLIN AND DAVIDOFF PAPERS,   *pp. 452-459.* Familial rather than individualist values appear to be dominant. Consciousness of oppression did not come until individualist values replaced familial. We must view families in terms of their values, not ours. 18 notes.
                                                               R. V. Ritter

716.   Wilkenfeld, Bruce M.   NEW YORK CITY NEIGHBORHOODS, 1730.   *New York Hist. 1976 57(2): 165-182.* Analyzes New York City tax lists and other statistical records of 1730 and reveals that the city's population was clustered in socioeconomically, ethnically, and religiously differentiated neighborhoods in the early 18th century. The author suggests that the patterns of residential clustering in American cities, generally believed to be indicative of change in the late 18th and 19th centuries, had begun in the early colonial cities. Map, 3 tables, 27 notes.   R. N. Lokken

717.   Withey, Lynne E.   HOUSEHOLD STRUCTURE IN URBAN AND RURAL AREAS: THE CASE OF RHODE ISLAND, 1774-1800. *J. of Family Hist. 1978 3(1): 37-50.* Uses state and federal census manuscripts from 1774, 1782, 1790, and 1800 to study the household structure of Rhode Island. Analyzes differences in household structure by community types and finds: 1) household size varied inversely with urbanness, 2) black- and women-headed households were associated with urbanness, 3) mean household size declined as a result of fewer slaves and servants and lower fertility, and 4) the fertility decline was general, but it started in urban areas. 6 tables, 9 notes, biblio.   T. W. Smith

718.   Zunz, Olivier.   DETROIT EN 1880: ESPACE ET SÉGRÉGATION [Detroit in 1880: Spatial clustering and segregation]. *Ann.: Écon., Soc., Civilisations [France] 1977 32(1): 106-136.* This study examines the population of neighborhoods sampled in Detroit in 1880. It determines the different forms of spatial clustering when Detroit was developing into a metropolis. Ethnic and social groups are identified in their physical environments; their characteristics and their distribution in the city are examined. The respective roles of ethnic and social factors as they contributed to the formation of clusters in the urban environment are measured. The data were collected from the first real estate atlas of the city of Detroit in 1885 and the census manuscript of 1880. A chi-squared statistic approach was developed for measuring and testing geographic clustering.   J

719.   Zunz, Olivier; Ericson, William A.; and Fox, Daniel J.   SAMPLING FOR A STUDY OF THE POPULATION AND LAND USE OF DETROIT IN 1880-1885.   *Social Sci. Hist. 1977 1(3): 307-332.* One major problem of historical urban population studies has been that of sampling. To study the relationships of urban populations and space, either investigations of gross patterns of urban land use or intensive studies of neighborhoods or social groups have been undertaken. The goals of this study of Detroit in 1880 and 1885 were to represent the demographic, ethnic, and occupational make-up of Detroit, the geographic clustering in neighborhoods, and the interplay between various populations and land use. Presents a new sampling system they devised to overcome traditional sampling problems, and demonstrates its use in

a pilot study. Based on the 1880 manuscript United States Census, an 1885 city atlas, and secondary sources; map, 6 tables, 7 fig., 25 notes.

T. L. Savitt

Voluntary Associations

720. Betten, Neil. NATIVISM AND THE KLAN IN TOWN AND CITY: VALPARAISO AND GARY, INDIANA. *Studies in Hist. and Soc. 1973 4(2): 3-16.* A study of the Ku Klux Klan during the 1920's in two urban centers. Indicates that "The Klan grew in Gary and Valparaiso by fashioning its appeal to the concerns of its white Protestant citizens . . ." and focused on such "myriad enemies" as corrupt politicians, bootleggers, prostitutes, imagined radicals, and immigrants who would not or could not instantly assimilate.

J. O. Baylen

721. Breslaw, Elaine G. WIT, WHIMSY, AND POLITICS: THE USES OF SATIRE BY THE TUESDAY CLUB OF ANNAPOLIS, 1744 TO 1756. *William and Mary Q. 1975 32(2): 295-306.* Finds that the leading gentlemen's club in Maryland, the Tuesday Club of Annapolis, used satire in their deliberations in order to mute political conflict. Examines the role of Dr. Alexander Hamilton (1712-56) in founding the club, qualifications for membership, and the makeup of the membership, which included Virginians and New Yorkers. No subjects were allowed to be discussed in a serious vein. Debates and disputes, with excerpts showing the wit of the participants, are selectively discussed. Based on Tuesday Club records and other primary sources; 45 notes.

H. M. Ward

722. Bridenbaugh, Carl. PHILOSOPHY PUT TO USE: VOLUNTARY ASSOCIATIONS FOR PROPAGATING THE ENLIGHTENMENT IN PHILADELPHIA, 1727-1776. *Pennsylvania Mag. of Hist. and Biog. 1977 101(1): 70-88.* The Quakers were the first American group to publicize the ideals of the Enlightenment. Benjamin Franklin was influenced by them and began to establish organizations of his own. Practical applications of science and philosophy were emphasized, a trend that became stronger as the years passed. Inventions poured from the new societies, and Philadelphia became internationally famous. Revolutionary hostility toward Great Britain failed to diminish the Enlightenment's impact. 31 notes.

V. L. Human

723. Bushnell, George D. CHICAGO'S ROWDY FIREFIGHTERS. *Chicago Hist. 1973 2(4): 232-241.* Chicago's rapid growth in the 1830's created numerous fire hazards. Volunteers formed their own companies, purchased equipment and uniforms, and fought each other for the honor of fighting fires. By the late 1850's the coming of the steam fire engine and the rowdyism of the volunteers helped create a salaried fire department. 7 photos.

N. A. Kuntz

724. Carson, Gerald. IN CHICAGO: CRUELTY AND KINDNESS TO ANIMALS. *Chicago Hist. 1974/75 3(3): 151-158.*

725. Doyle, Don H. THE SOCIAL FUNCTIONS OF VOLUNTARY ASSOCIATIONS IN A NINETEENTH-CENTURY AMERICAN TOWN. *Social Sci. Hist. 1977 1(3): 333-355.* Jacksonville, Illinois, during 1825-70 contained a very transient population. Though the population constantly increased, the in- and out-migration was quite high. In so seemingly unstable a society voluntary associations such as the Masons, the Odd Fellows, temperance groups, and anti-slavery clubs filled several important roles. These organizations provided status and unity in an otherwise discordant, disorganized social community. They also enhanced opportunity for upward mobility, set modes of acceptable behavior, and acted as a means of social control. Based on census records, local family papers and newspapers, city directories, and secondary sources; 2 tables, 53 notes.

T. L. Savitt

726. Dykstra, Arlen R. ROWDYISM AND RIVALISM IN THE ST. LOUIS FIRE DEPARTMENT, 1850-1857. *Missouri Hist. Rev. 1974 69(1): 48-64.* During 1850-57 St. Louis moved away from the private fire companies on which it had relied for 50 years to a paid department. After failing to deal with the "Great Fire of 1849" the private companies became subjects of suspicion and ridicule, a trend further stimulated by acts of rowdyism, violence, and arson committed by lawless

elements that gained admission to the companies or loitered around the engine houses. Efforts at self-policing through a St. Louis Firemen's Association were not successful. The decline of the private companies was speeded by a shortage of funds, a trend that was not checked even when the city provided limited financial aid. Based on newspapers, books, and fire company records in the Missouri Historical Society, St. Louis; 7 illus., 61 notes.

W. F. Zornow

727. Farnam, Anne. A SOCIETY OF SOCIETIES: ASSOCIATIONS AND VOLUNTARISM IN EARLY NINETEENTH-CENTURY SALEM. *Essex Inst. Hist. Collections 1977 113(3): 181-190.* Discovers more than 25 social organizations and societies in Salem by 1819. Tension existed between the members of the societies and the community; the goals of the two groups were not always compatible. Societies were able to give their members an identity in a time of economic and political change, and associations could account for lost status. The character and motivation of the participants, as well as the purposes and methods of organization, are discussed in the Reverend William Bentley's diary. There he reflects upon his membership in the Union Fire Club and the Essex Lodge. Based on the diary (1784-1819) of William Bentley and on primary and secondary sources; 16 notes.

R. S. Sliwoski

728. Gale, Oliver M. THE QUEEN CITY CLUB—THE FIRST ONE HUNDRED YEARS. *Cincinnati Hist. Soc. Bull. 1974 32(4): 153-175.* Discusses the history of the Queen City Club for businessmen and civic leaders in Cincinnati, Ohio, 1874-1974.

729. Galey, Margaret E. ETHNICITY, FRATERNALISM, SOCIAL AND MENTAL HEALTH. *Ethnicity 1977 4(1): 19-53.* Examines 14 ethnic groups' fraternal organizations formed in Pittsburgh, Pennsylvania, 1900-70, in order to investigate the services offered, the alleviation of pains of assimilation, and implications of these health- and social-minded organizations for contemporary health care. Fraternal organizations helped immigrants from southern and eastern Europe assimilate early in this century, giving benefits for sickness, death, and disability, and helping socioculturally. The associations cemented ethnic feeling. They shared a lack of provision for mental health (due primarily to the stigma attached to mental illness), extensive self-help programs, focus on community benefit, and reinforcement of ethnic insularity through health care administered within ethnic communities.

G. A. Hewlett

730. Goldberg, Robert A. THE KU KLUX KLAN IN MADISON, 1922-1929. *Wisconsin Mag. of Hist. 1974 58(1): 31-44.* The stereotype of the Ku Klux Klan as violence-prone bigots who attacked blacks, Catholics, Jews, and immigrants is inaccurate for Madison Klansmen and for most Klans in the 1920's. Members were, instead, "ordinary men bewildered by changes that threatened to disrupt their lives and their city." Klan activity, aside from its similarity to other fraternal social organizations, concentrated on a law and order campaign and a drive to reassert American patriotism by stripping school textbooks of any negative remarks about American history or society. Internal dissension and the reform efforts of Dane County District Attorney Philip La Follette hastened their rapid decline. 7 illus., 58 notes.

N. C. Burckel

731. Granger, Frank. REACTION TO CHANGE: THE KU KLUX KLAN IN SHREVEPORT, 1920-1929. *North Louisiana Hist. Assoc. J. 1978 9(4): 219-227.* The new morality following World War I shook the foundations of moral standards. The revival of the Ku Klux Klan during 1915-44 appealed to those elements who desired to salvage them. The Klan revival was based not so much on racism and nativism as on moral authoritarianism: the preservation of premarital chastity, marital fidelity, respect for parental authority, obedience to state and national prohibition laws and the fight against crime and dishonest politicians. Shreveport was a boom town, rampant with bootlegging and prostitution, making it a good locale for Klan revival and growth. At first, the Klan attracted a large membership; but after two men were murdered allegedly by Klansmen in 1922, the Klan was accused of taking the law into its own hands, and its membership and influence began to wane. Assesses the moral contributions of the Klan and describes its gradual demise. Based on contemporary accounts in the *Shreveport Journal;* 54 notes.

H. M. Parker, Jr.

732. Greeley, Andrew M. LOOKING BACKWARD: COMMODORE BARRY COUNTRY CLUB IN TWIN LAKES, WISCON-

SIN. *Chicago Hist. 1979 8(2): 112-119.* Describes the prestigious and exclusive Commodore Barry Country Club, founded in the 1920's by members of the Commodore Barry Council of the Knights of Columbus in Chicago to provide a place for Irish Catholics to socialize; also gives the history of the Knights of Columbus in Chicago, 1907-20's.

733. Greenberg, Brian. WORKER AND COMMUNITY: FRATERNAL ORDERS IN ALBANY, NEW YORK, 1845-1885. *Maryland Hist. 1977 8(2): 38-53.* Describes the composition, history, and functions of the Independent Order of Odd Fellows in Albany, New York. Fraternal organizations in 19th-century America acted as "moral policing agents" reinforcing community solidarity while permitting interclass relationships. Based on IOOF membership data and on primary and secondary sources; 75 notes.   G. O. Gagnon

734. Greene, Michael. THE HANNAH SCHLOSS OLD TIMERS. *Michigan Jewish Hist. 1975 15(2): 34-39.* History of the philanthropic group, the Hannah Schloss Old Timers, active in the United Jewish Charities, headquartered in Detroit, Michigan.   S

735. Hux, Roger K. THE KU KLUX KLAN IN MACON 1919-1925. *Georgia Hist. Q. 1978 62(2): 155-168.* The Macon, Georgia, Ku Klux Klan of the 1920's, led by dentist C. A. Yarbrough, administered floggings primarily to punish moral offenders rather than to combat racial or foreign influences. Condemnation of violence, several trials of Klansmen, and political defeat brought about Klan decline. Newspapers and secondary sources; 30 notes.   G. R. Schroeder

736. Jenkins, William D. THE KU KLUX KLAN IN YOUNGSTOWN, OHIO: MORAL REFORM IN THE TWENTIES. *Historian 1978 41(1): 76-93.* The primary factor in the rapid growth of the Ku Klux Klan in Youngstown, Ohio, was not its white supremacy, anti-Catholicism, anti-Semitism, or nativism, but its desire to improve the morals of the community. An enforcement crusade, begun by the Mahoning County Dry Association, the Federal Council of Churches, and the Federation of Women's Clubs, soon fell under the control of the Klan and its leaders, who also met with surprising political success in local elections. Describes these leaders and Youngtown's attitudes toward other parts of the Klan platform. Speculates on causes of the decline of Klan influence in the area, and concludes that public confidence in the organization as the enforcer of community morals eroded as it proved unable to totally enforce the city's conservative moral code.
                        M. S. Legan

737. Kennedy, Michael. LA SOCIÉTÉ FRANÇAISE DES AMIS DE LA LIBERTÉ ET DE L'ÉGALITÉ DE PHILADELPHIE 1793-1794 [The French Society of the Friends of Liberty and Equality of Philadelphia]. *Ann. Hist. de la Revolution Française [France] 1976 48(4): 614-636.* Discusses those Frenchmen in Charleston, Alexandria, New York, Boston, and Philadelphia, whose sympathies with the French Revolution led them to establish Jacobin societies. Examines the vicissitudes of the Philadelphia society. This essentially middle class club, which soon admitted Americans to its membership, was greatly influenced by the participation of France's ambassador to Philadelphia: Edmond-Charles Genêt. On Genêt's resolution, the society officially forswore involvement in American politics; yet its tone was markedly anti-Federalist. Ultimately impaired by yellow fever, a schism, and Genêt's departure for New York, the society held its last recorded meeting on 4 June 1794. Based on archival, primary, and secondary sources; 44 notes.
                        P. T. Newton

738. Klein, Walter E. THE JEWISH COMMUNITY COUNCIL OF METROPOLITAN DETROIT: THE ORGANIZING YEARS. *Michigan Jewish Hist. 1978 18(1): 20-32.* The Jewish Community Council of Metropolitan Detroit was founded in 1937 after several meetings of prominent Jewish groups, formation of an organizing committee in 1935, and aid from the American Jewish Congress.

739. Krause, Joe W. LIBRARIES OF THE YOUNG MEN'S CHRISTIAN ASSOCIATIONS IN THE NINETEENTH CENTURY. *J. of Lib. Hist. 1975 10(1): 3-21.* A history of the Young Men's Christian Association's libraries, from the association's beginnings in London in 1844 to the present. Surveys the rise and fall of YMCA libraries in the United States with details on some of the larger ones, including the New

York YMCA library and its most outstanding librarian, Reuben B. Pool. Based on primary and secondary sources; 55 notes.
                        A. C. Dewees

740. Lewis, H. H. Walker. THE LAWYERS' ROUND TABLE OF BALTIMORE. *Maryland Hist. Mag. 1975 70(3): 279-285.* Baltimore lawyers' clubs date from 1852, when the Friday Club and later the Temple Club were organized to promote congeniality among mixed groups of lawyers and professionals, but they did not survive the strains of the Civil War. The modern "Lawyers' Round Table" began with Judge Alfred Salem Niles of the Supreme Bench of Baltimore City in 1911, when he gathered a group of colleagues for regular dinner meetings for the presentation of papers and legal discussion. The original membership was the core of the Baltimore Reform League, which fought to break the Gorman-Rasin political machine in the 1895 election. Niles's group was more diverse both in profession and age than earlier clubs, and its example spawned many similar groups within the Maryland bar, a progeny which often mixes gastronomic intensity with intellectuality as the age of the membership increases. Prohibition presented certain problems for the Round Table meetings, at which few members seem to have been devotees of the "great moral issue" being upheld. Based on minute books of the earlier clubs, correspondence, and secondary works; 1 photo, 13 notes.
                        G. J. Bobango

741. Luckingham, Bradford. BENEVOLENCE IN EMERGENT SAN FRANCISCO: A NOTE ON IMMIGRANT LIFE IN THE URBAN FAR WEST. *Southern California Q. 1973 55(4): 431-443.* From almost the inception of San Francisco as a booming urban center of gold rush California, various groups banded together for mutual assistance. Organized along national, religious, or occupational lines, these benevolent associations advised newcomers, provided information about friends and relatives, gave immediate financial aid, maintained clinics, obtained jobs for the unemployed, and provided transportation to the mines or back home. Typical organizations included the French Benevolent Society, Masons, Odd Fellows, Young Men's Christian Association, and the San Francisco Ladies' Protection and Relief Society. The benevolent associations resembled the efforts of groups in older American cities, with the groups attempting to provide for the welfare of their members. Based on primary and secondary sources; 21 notes.   A. Hoffman

742. Melching, Richard. THE ACTIVITIES OF THE KU KLUX KLAN IN ANAHEIM, CALIFORNIA, 1923-1925. *Southern California Q. 1974 56(2): 175-196.* The Ku Klux Klan in Anaheim was unlike the national organization in several respects; violence was at a minimum, Klan supporters endorsed prohibition, and their opponents were accused of favoring vice and gambling, thus presenting the Klan and their candidates as reformers. For a time, the Klan captured most of Anaheim's city offices, but a major blow against them occurred when the klavern's membership list was made public, revealing that the claimed membership of 1,400 did not match the reality of less than 300. Without its secrecy and with its true size revealed, the Klan went into decline, with the February, 1925 city election bringing about its complete defeat. For months afterwards resignations and firings purged the Klan from city hall, and despite a few subsequent attempts to resurrect it, the organization never regained its earlier power. Based chiefly on accounts in the Anaheim newspaper; 88 notes.   A. Hoffman

743. Moore, N. Webster. THE BLACK YMCA OF ST. LOUIS. *Missouri Hist. Soc. Bull. 1979 36(1): 35-40.* From 1877 to 1893, several YMCA organizations for blacks were established at St. Louis, but each of the fledgling organizations soon failed. New efforts to build a YMCA began in 1898 and, with outside financial aid and heavy contributions from Negroes in St. Louis, a lasting YMCA had been created by 1912. Since the 1920's, that YMCA has conducted innovative youth programs and offered leadership training opportunities. 2 photos, 9 notes.
                        H. T. Lovin

744. Moss, James E. FOR DISCOVERY, COLLECTION AND PRESERVATION: THE SAN DIEGO HISTORICAL SOCIETY. *J. of San Diego Hist. 1979 25(2): 136-150.* Though interest in the San Diego Historical Society waned from 1880 to the 1920's, in 1928 a movement to save historic buildings snowballed into an organized society dedicated to preservation, collection, and display of San Diego's artifactual history.

745. Myers, Rex C. THE MONTANA CLUB: SYMBOL OF ELEGANCE. *Montana 1976 26(4): 30-51.* Helena's Montana Club has survived since 1884, but only after constant struggles for membership and financial solvency. Erection of its own building in 1893 helped the former but not the latter; both problems increased when the structure burned in 1903. A replacement, designed by the architect Cass Gilbert, was erected in 1905 and still stands. Illus., notes.   S. R. Davison

746. Pearson, Ralph L. THE NATIONAL URBAN LEAGUE COMES TO BALTIMORE. *Maryland Hist. Mag. 1977 72(4): 523-533.* The Reverend Peter Ainslie and John R. Carey, founders of Baltimore's Interracial Conference, asked the National Urban League to conduct an in-depth sociological study of working conditions among Baltimore's black citizens in 1922, which led to the formation of a Baltimore branch of the League by 1924. Focuses on the League's interracial community achievements in its first decade and on the insights of "the first systematic . . . analysis of employment patterns among Baltimore's black(s)." Maryland's border-state location determined many aspects of the city's racial mores, with northern-style industrial development and southern-style segregation. High death rates, discrimination, physical degradation, and social maladjustment characterized the black community, mostly from lack of economic opportunity due to white unions and company hiring policies, all based on an emotionalism which sociological study could not overcome. Primary and secondary sources; 34 notes.
G. J. Bobango

747. Rader, Benjamin G. THE QUEST FOR SUBCOMMUNITIES AND THE RISE OF AMERICAN SPORT. *Am. Q. 1977 29(4): 355-369.* Sports clubs were an important form of voluntary association during the 19th century through which subcommunities of the American population established groupings based on ethnicity and social status. The sport club assumed some of the traditional functions of the church and the geographical community and also laid the groundwork for organized sports activities of more recent times. Ethnic groups such as the Scottish Caledonians and the German Turners, emphasized their ethnicity through sports. Upper class native Americans founded private sports clubs in such areas of activity as yachting and baseball, as well as establishing urban athletic clubs which combined recreation with status exclusivity. Primary and secondary sources.   N. Lederer

748. Renner, Richard Wilson. YE KORT MARTIAL: A TALE OF CHICAGO POLITICS, THEATRE, JOURNALISM AND MILITIA. *J. of the Illinois State Hist. Soc. 1973 66(4): 376-386.* During the mid-1850's Chicago joined in the military revival sweeping the nation in the form of "independent" militia companies. Until Elmer Ellsworth organized a crack drill unit of Zouaves in 1859, however, Chicago's militia companies suffered leadership squabbles, courts-martial, and newspaper lampooning. Stephen A. Douglas and James H. McVicker enjoyed attacking the militia courts-martial. Colonel George Pearson was court-martialed and removed for forging his commanding officer's signature. Based on newspaper accounts; illus., 42 notes.   A. C. Aimone

749. Rosen, Benton H. KING DAVID'S LODGE, A.F. & A.M., NO. 1 OF NEWPORT, RHODE ISLAND. *Rhode Island Jewish Hist. Notes 1974 6(4): 578-586.* A history of the King David's Masonic Lodge of Newport, Rhode Island (1780-90); includes copies of a letter from George Washington, ledger entries, and voting records.   S

750. Schwartz, Harry W. THE TUESDAY NIGHT CLUB. *Milwaukee Hist. 1979 2(2): 49-55.* The Tuesday Night Club in Milwaukee, Wisconsin, was begun in 1929 and functioned through the early thirties as a literary-political forum of interested local persons.

751. Schwartz, Joel. MORRISANIA'S VOLUNTEER FIREMEN, 1848-1874: THE LIMITS OF LOCAL INSTITUTIONS IN A METROPOLITAN AGE. *New York Hist. 1974 55(2): 159-178.* Morrisania, now a neighborhood in the South Bronx, was an independent township until its annexation by New York City in 1874. One of the primary factors in Morrisania's desire for annexation was that its volunteer fire department had degenerated into a rowdy and criminal element. Instead of fighting fires, Morrisania's Irish and German fire companies often fought each other in the streets of Morrisania. The appeal of New York City's professional and technologically modern fire department persuaded Morrisania's business community that merger with New York City was in

their economic interest. Based on primary and secondary works; 5 illus., 40 notes.   G. Kurland

752. Stern, Norton B. A NEW CLUB FOR LOS ANGELES. *Western States Jewish Hist. Q. 1978 10(4): 374-376.* About 40 Jewish men met in Levy's Cafe in Los Angeles, California, on 9 December 1908 to organize the Jewish Progress Club. Its object was to read papers and discuss current literary and scientific topics, especially those pertaining to Judaism. Those who founded and joined the club were a homogeneous group of civic and business leaders.   B. S. Porter

753. Sturdevant, Lynda M. GIRL SCOUTING IN STILLWATER, OKLAHOMA: A CASE STUDY IN LOCAL HISTORY. *Chronicles of Oklahoma 1979 57(1): 34-48.* Though first organized in 1927, Girl Scouting in Stillwater, Oklahoma, did not attach itself to the national organization until 1937. Fundraising projects dominated the following years as the local organizers attempted to attract new members and expand activities. Stillwater businesses contributed significant aid to the local chapter and helped build a lodge in the late 1930's. During the 1950's the Stillwater Council fought a losing battle with the national Girl Scout organization which merged several administrative districts. Still the local chapter was able to continue with its own goals and has been a major asset to the community. Newspapers and interviews; 5 photos, 50 notes.
M. L. Tate

754. Thomas, Richard. THE DETROIT URBAN LEAGUE, 1916-1923. *Michigan Hist. 1976 60(4): 315-338.* The Detroit Urban League, founded in 1916 and first headed by Forrester B. Washington, sought to alleviate problems of housing, recreation, and unemployment faced by blacks arriving from the rural South. Paternalistic and possessed of urban, middle-class values, Washington urged blacks to emulate northern white culture. Under Washington's successor, John C. Dancey, the League broadened and intensified its services and, by 1939, had become an established, recognized agency in the community. Primary sources; 8 photos, 72 notes.   D. W. Johnson

755. Thornbery, Jerry. NORTHERNS AND THE ATLANTA FREEDMEN, 1865-69. *Prologue 1974 6(4): 236-251.* Immediately following the end of the Civil War there were several federal agencies and northern religious organizations functioning in Atlanta to aid Negroes. The first and most extensive efforts were made by the Union Army. However, the Freedmen's Bureau, the American Missionary Association, and the Methodist Episcopal Church also offered limited assistance. A rudimentary school system was established, but a study of the activities of these organizations reveals considerable limitation because of northern attitudes toward race, work, and welfare. "Northerners as well as southerners shared a responsibility for Reconstruction's failure." 4 photos, 58 notes.   R. V. Ritter

756. Toll, William. VOLUNTARISM AND MODERNIZATION IN PORTLAND JEWRY: THE B'NAI B'RITH IN THE 1920'S. *Western Hist. Q. 1979 10(1): 21-38.* A case study of how ethnic groups and community development are related, addressing the issues raised by Moses Rischin, John Higham, and Kenneth Roseman. Examines the role of Jews in Portland, Oregon, in the 1920's in the local economy and their specific patterns of institutional adaptation to find out what their particular contributions were to the city's growth. Traces the effects of the particular region in which they settled on their internal patterns of change. Through its B'nai B'rith lodge, Portland Jewry "sorted out its social classes and allowed new spokesmen to coalesce." 3 tables, 37 notes.
D. L. Smith

757. Warsen, Allen A. THE ODESSA PROGRESSIVE AID SOCIETY OF DETROIT, MICHIGAN. *Michigan Jewish Hist. 1976 16(1): 39-42.* Reports on the operation, activities, and membership of the Odessa Progressive Aid Society, a charitable organization of Jews who assisted sick and disabled members and financially supported various associations, 1915-18.

758. Yearwood, Lennox. NATIONAL AFRO-AMERICAN ORGANIZATIONS IN URBAN COMMUNITIES. *J. of Black Studies 1978 8(4): 423-438.* In *The Negro in America* (1944) Arnold Rose reached two false conclusions about black voluntary associations—that they were "purely social" and "indicative of an unhealthy situation."

Formal, national, black voluntary organizations made major contributions to the economic, political, and educational progress of urban Negroes. The major associations were in the areas of religion, politics, education, professional, business, arts, women, and fraternal. Suggests areas for further research. Secondary sources; 2 tables, graph, biblio.

R. G. Sherer

Social Stratification and Class Culture

759. Alcorn, Richard S. LEADERSHIP AND STABILITY IN MID-NINETEENTH CENTURY AMERICA: A CASE STUDY OF AN ILLINOIS TOWN. *J. of Am. Hist. 1974 61(3): 685-702.* American 19th-century communities were, according to some historians, stable "island communities," while according to others massive population mobility made such stability impossible. A demographic study of Paris, Illinois, reveals the existence of a stable, older, wealthy elite maintaining control of the community through a period of rapid population change involving non-leader residents. A significantly high proportion of leaders in politics, boosterism, and temperance reform persisted as residents from 1840-60, lending an image of stable leadership flexible enough to meet local needs and to reflect local values. 8 tables, 23 notes. K. B. West

760. Averbach, Alvin SAN FRANCISCO'S SOUTH OF MARKET DISTRICT, 1850-1950; THE EMERGENCE OF A SKID ROW. *California Hist. Q. 1973 52(3): 196-223.* San Francisco's South of Market district long was recognized as an area which attracted single men employed primarily in seafaring jobs or as longshoremen and day laborers. A variety of cheap hotels, restaurants, clothing stores, houses of prostitution, pool halls, and saloons catered to them. With the Depression, the district became a skid row area. The hobo work force declined and missions provided food and offered spiritual aid to men ignored by social service agencies. Poor wages and lack of opportunity prevailed over attempts to unionize workers. In attempting to create the Yerba Buena Center, the San Francisco Redevelopment Agency has met increased opposition from the district's permanent residents. By the end of the 1960's, however, the "hotel society" South of Market was rapidly disappearing. Based on contemporary and secondary reports and on personal interviews; illus., 115 notes. A. Hoffman

761. Brobeck, Stephen. REVOLUTIONARY CHANGE IN COLONIAL PHILADELPHIA: THE BRIEF LIFE OF THE PROPRIETARY GENTRY. *William and Mary Q. 1976 33(3): 410-434.* Looks at 22 non-Quakers in pre-Revolutionary Philadelphia who had ties with the Proprietors. This Proprietary gentry held high office virtually for life. Notes organizations they belonged to and their commercial activity. Puts the group in the context of the assembly-led struggle against the Proprietary Party. By 1760 the non-Quaker gentry had developed into a cohesive group, aided measurably by ties of kinship. States reasons why this group resisted Independence. Based on secondary sources; 3 tables, 69 notes. H. M. Ward

762. Buettinger, Craig. ECONOMIC INEQUALITY IN EARLY CHICAGO 1849-1850. *J. of Soc. Hist. 1978 11(3): 413-418.* The wealth distribution in pre-Civil War America was "grossly unequal." An analysis of Chicago tax rolls of 1849-50 reveals that Chicago's unequal distribution of wealth was greater than eastern cities. In Chicago, 1% of the population owned 52% of Chicago's wealth while 10% owned 94% of the city's wealth. Thus, most of Chicago's economy in that period was controlled by a small group of men who had "arrived early and with capital." What is needed is a study of the economic and geographic mobility of these rich people. 19 notes. L. E. Ziewacz

763. Bushnell, Amy. THE EXPENSES OF HIDALGUÍA IN SEVENTEENTH-CENTURY ST. AUGUSTINE. *Escribano 1978 15: 23-36.* Hidalgos, the gentlemanly class, or those possessing the quality of *hidalguía,* were responsible for fair and efficient local government, public welfare, and hierarchical social organization in Spanish St. Augustine, Florida, in the 16th century.

764. Callahan, Helen C. UPSTAIRS-DOWNSTAIRS IN CHICAGO 1870-1907: THE GLESSNER HOUSEHOLD. *Chicago Hist. 1977-78 6(4): 195-209.* Discusses relationships between domestic servants and their employers in a prominent household.

765. Cowles, Karen. THE INDUSTRIALIZATION OF DUQUESNE AND THE CIRCULATION OF ELITES, 1891-1933. *Western Pennsylvania Hist. Mag. 1979 62(1): 1-18.* Applies the thought of Vilfredo Pareto in the area of social change and evolution to the industrialization of Duquesne, Pennsylvania, 1891-1933, assessing struggle among groups of elites for political, economic, and social hegemony.

766. Crandall, Ralph J. and Coffman, Ralph J. FROM EMIGRANTS TO RULERS: THE CHARLESTOWN OLIGARCHY IN THE GREAT MIGRATION. *New England Hist. and Genealogical Register 1977 131: (January): 3-27, (April): 3-7, 121-132, (July): 207-213.* Part I. During 1630-40, 273 householders settled in Charlestown, Massachusetts, but only 43 were influential in determining the direction of the town. Evoking a gentry image, these men (literate, older, militantly Puritan, experienced in government, and connected to the right families) controlled town government by 1634. Restriction of the franchise to church members followed. New immigrants who failed to secure the approval of this leadership class could either stay, relegated to a second-class status, or leave to found new communities. The oligarchy's success in banishing several Antinomians to Rhode Island in 1637 underlined its power to establish the religious and economic standards of citizenship for the first generation of immigrants. Based on primary and secondary sources; map, graph, chart of town inhabitants. 52 notes. Part II. Continues the list of names of these inhabitants and gives—where known—birth, marriage, and death dates, spouse's occupation, literacy, origin in England, town offices held, land owned, and other residences. Part III. Concludes the list. S. L. Patterson

767. Cumbler, John T. THE CITY AND COMMUNITY: THE IMPACT OF URBAN FORCES ON WORKING CLASS BEHAVIOR. *J. of Urban Hist. 1977 3(4): 427-442.* Compares the impact of industrialization on the working class in shoemaking Lynn and textile spinning Fall River, Massachusetts (1850-1930). In Lynn the shoe industry and the working class clustered together, while in Fall River centrifugal forces waxed. This arrangement led to significant differences in the formation of working-class institutions and behavior. Greater centralization of institutions created greater solidarity among the workers. Based on oral histories; 42 notes. T. W. Smith

768. Cumbler, John T. THREE GENERATIONS OF POVERTY: A NOTE ON THE LIFE OF AN UNSKILLED WORKER'S FAMILY. *Labor Hist. 1974 15(1): 78-85.* Reviews the need for more information and new methods of approach to the study of the life of the everyday laborer. The remnants of a case history of a family in Lynn from 1915-40 are published as an example of the types of material needed to understand poverty. Based on a case history from the files of the Associated Charities of Lynn, Massachusetts. 4 notes. L. L. Athey

769. Daniels, Bruce C. MONEY-VALUE DEFINITIONS OF ECONOMIC CLASSES IN COLONIAL CONNECTICUT, 1700-1776. *Social Hist. [Canada] 1974 7(14): 346-352.* Provides cutoff points for the 10th, 30th, 70th, and 90th percentiles of wealth in each of three types of communities in Connecticut, and for the colony as a whole for four 20-year intervals between 1700 and 1776. The three types are urban, medium-sized, and frontier communities. Corrections were made for changes in the type and value of money used in the evaluations. Based on probate inventories of real and personal estates; 5 tables, 12 notes. W. K. Hobson

770. Dehler, Katherine B. MT. VERNON PLACE AT THE TURN OF THE CENTURY: A VIGNETTE OF THE GARRETT FAMILY. *Maryland Hist. Mag. 1974 69(3): 279-292.* Describes the philanthropic and social activities of John Work Garrett (1820-84), dynamic president of the Baltimore and Ohio Railroad. In 1872 he bought the house at No. 11 Mt. Vernon Place in Baltimore for his son, Robert Garrett, and it became "the most magnificent and interesting private residence" in the city. Robert turned the house into a New York "brownstone" despite much opposition from his neighbors, with the renovation under Stanford White's direction. Robert's wife, Mary Frick Garrett (1851-1936), added an enormous art collection and became the social arbiter of Baltimore. The Garretts fully demonstrated the *noblesse oblige* of their class, creating endowments in their wills for numerous medical, educational, and cultural foundations, alongside their contributions to banking and commerce. Primary and secondary sources; 5 illus., 45 notes.

G. J. Bobango

771. Dodd, Jill Siegel. THE WORKING CLASSES AND THE TEMPERANCE MOVEMENT IN ANTE-BELLUM BOSTON. *Labor Hist. 1978 19(4): 510-531.* The working clases of ante-bellum Boston divided over temperance movements; some used "traditional" forms of collective violence to resist, others supported temperance. The evidence is analyzed in "pre-industrial" and "industrializing" terms which cut across class lines. Based on quantitative data from newspapers; 5 tables, 46 notes.
L. L. Athey

772. Faler, Paul. CULTURAL ASPECTS OF THE INDUSTRIAL REVOLUTION: LYNN, MASSACHUSETTS, SHOEMAKERS AND INDUSTRIAL MORALITY, 1826-1860. *Labor Hist. 1974 15(3): 367-394.* The Industrial Revolution was accompanied by a cultural revolution emphasizing an "industrial morality" which stressed self-discipline, work, and sobriety. Promoted by religious revivals, the changing economy, and the emergent manufacturing class who first accepted the industrial morality, the new value code was applied stringently to the poverty stricken, drunkards, and malingerers. Forms of recreation and leisure were modified, and three distinct responses appeared among workmen: traditionalists who clung to past customs, loyalists who accepted the new morality with deference to employers, and rebels who accepted the new morality but promoted collective self-help against employers. The division promoted discord and prevented the development of a class consciousness. Based on the Lynn *Mirror*, unpublished dissertations, and governmental reports.
L. L. Athey

773. Frye, John. CLASS, GENERATION, AND SOCIAL CHANGE: A CASE IN SALEM, MASSACHUSETTS, 1636-1656. *J. of Popular Culture 1977 11(3): 743-751.* Examination of the Essex County court records for Ipswich, a small Massachusetts Bay Colony town of 700-800 and one of several towns, such as Salem, in that county, reveals class-generational conflicts parallel in nature to those in the recent American experience. The records further reveal that the court was used as something of a class battlefield with conflicting social values. Primary and secondary sources; 24 notes, biblio.
D. G. Nielson

774. García, Mario T. THE CALIFORNIOS OF SAN DIEGO AND THE POLITICS OF ACCOMMODATION 1846-1860. *Aztlán 1975 6(1): 69-85.* The upper class *ricos* in San Diego hoped to accommodate themselves to the Anglo American conquest after 1848. In the numerical majority and owning most of the property, they were able to gain cultural and social recognition, but they failed to control the political process. By 1860 the Californios were on the decline economically as a result of political disfranchisement, economic depression, and high taxes. Based on US manuscript censuses, tax rolls, and newspapers; 89 notes, biblio.
R. Griswold del Castillo

775. Ghent, Joyce Maynard and Jaher, Frederic Cople. THE CHICAGO BUSINESS ELITE, 1830-1930: A COLLECTIVE BIOGRAPHY. *Business Hist. Rev. 1976 50(3): 288-328.* Attempts to determine whether the profile of a business elite, that of Chicago during 1830-1930, conformed to the national pattern found in previous investigations of this subject. Concludes that in education, religion, geography of birth, vintage of wealth, and family background, the commercial elite "had more privileged characteristics than did the national population." It became even less "Algeristic" with each succeeding generation. 32 tables, 19 notes.
C. J. Pusateri

776. Hareven, Tamara K. THE LABORERS OF MANCHESTER, NEW HAMPSHIRE, 1912-1922: THE ROLE OF FAMILY AND ETHNICITY IN ADJUSTMENT TO INDUSTRIAL LIFE. *Labor Hist. 1975 16(2): 249-265.* A case study of the Amoskeag Mills in Manchester, New Hampshire, which demonstrates the effect of ethnocentrism and family ties upon the modernization process. When the corporation introduced an efficiency and welfare system, the workers responded with attempts to control job mobility and hiring through their own ethnic and family affiliations. This was largely successful until the nine-month strike of 1922. Based on statistical family research, government reports and the *Amoskeag Bulletin*. Table; 25 notes.
L. L. Athey

777. Harring, Sidney L. CLASS CONFLICT AND THE SUPPRESSION OF TRAMPS IN BUFFALO, 1892-1894. *Law and Soc. Rev. 1977 11(5): 873-911.* Analyzes the origins, scope, and context of the Tramp Act (New York, 1885), focusing on its enforcement by the city of Buffalo in 1894. In a confrontation with a band of unemployed migrant laborers, the enforcement of tramp laws was intermingled with reforms and repressive strategies along with local police apparatus.
M. R. Mahood

778. Hershberg, Theodore et al. OCCUPATION AND ETHNICITY IN FIVE NINETEENTH-CENTURY CITIES: A COLLABORATIVE INQUIRY. *Hist. Methods Newsletter 1974 7(3): 174-216.* Examines employment and ethnicity in Philadelphia, Pennsylvania; Hamilton, Ontario; Kingston, New York; Buffalo, New York; and Poughkeepsie, New York, and concludes that property ownership was related to class considerations, but was substantially modified by ethnicity and culture. Based on primary and secondary sources; tables, graphs, and charts.
D. K. Pickens

779. Holli, Melvin G. FRENCH SEIGNIORIALISM AND THE SOCIAL STRUCTURE OF EARLY DETROIT. *Indiana Social Studies Q. 1975 28(2): 63-74.* Discusses the social, political, and cultural influence of French Seigniorialism in the development of Detroit, Michigan, 1701-1837.

780. Huffman, Frank J., Jr. TOWN AND COUNTRY IN THE SOUTH, 1850-1880: A COMPARISON OF URBAN AND RURAL SOCIAL STRUCTURES. *South Atlantic Q. 1977 76(3): 366-381.* Links of continuity between the Old and New South can be found in Southern towns. Athens, Georgia, achieved a mature and stable urban society before the Civil War which successfully resisted all the political and social upheavals of the period. Its flexible urban lifestyle provided better opportunities for all social classes and all races than the surrounding agricultural countryside. Primary and secondary sources; table, 18 notes.
W. L. Olbrich

781. Ingham, John N. THE AMERICAN URBAN UPPER CLASS: COSMOPOLITANS OR LOCALS? *J. of Urban Hist. 1975 2(1): 67-87.* Uses families of iron and steel magnates in Pittsburgh, Philadelphia, and Cleveland to test the idea that elites became cosmopolitan in the late 19th century through marriage to others of their class from other cities. Cleveland best approximates the theory, though even there a majority married within the community. 3 tables, 13 notes.
S. S. Sprague

782. Ingham, John N. RAGS TO RICHES REVISITED: THE EFFECT OF CITY SIZE AND RELATED FACTORS ON THE RECRUITMENT OF BUSINESS LEADERS. *J. of Am. Hist. 1976 63(3): 615-637.* Analyzes the backgrounds of 696 iron and steel manufacturers in six US cities, ca. 1874-1900. The pattern of social continuity presented by Frances W. Gregory and Irene D. Neu seems more applicable to this data than the "new elite" thesis of Matthew Josephson or Herbert G. Gutman. The typical manufacturer does not conform to the rags and riches stereotype. In the larger, established cities, industrialists belonged to antebellum upper social classes that had controlled the preindustrial economy. In smaller, more recently established cities, however, origins and social status were more complex. Primary and secondary sources; 9 tables, 12 notes.
W. R. Hively

783. Innes, Stephen. LAND TENANCY AND SOCIAL ORDER IN SPRINGFIELD, MASSACHUSETTS, 1652 TO 1702. *William and Mary Q. 1978 35(1): 33-56.* Unequal land distribution shaped Springfield's socioeconomic structure. Contrary to the findings of historians of other early New England towns, Springfield had its rich and poor, tenants and landlords, and debtors and creditors. The town's founding father, William Pynchon, wielded the chief patronage. Analyzes the size of tenant holdings and the obligations of dependent renters. Tenants were usually freemen, but not civic leaders. Discusses six classes of renters and the debtor relationship of tenants to landlords. Based on local records; 112 notes.
H. M. Ward

784. Jaher, Frederic Cople. OLD AND NEW ELITES AND ENTREPRENEURIAL ACTIVITY IN NEW YORK CITY FROM 1780 TO 1850. *Working Papers from the Regional Econ. Hist. Res. Center 1978 2(2): 55-78.* Gradual decline of preeminence among the aristocratic segment of New York City's social organization and the integration of commercial elites brought about economic development, 1780-1850.

785. Kipp, Samuel M., III. OLD NOTABLES AND NEW-COMERS: THE ECONOMIC AND POLITICAL ELITE OF GREENSBORO, NORTH CAROLINA, 1880-1920. *J. of Southern Hist. 1977 43(3): 373-394.* Studies of late 19th-century urban elites see a dichotomy of power between an older elite of wealth, intellect and status, and a newer, local political elite made up of lawyers, small proprietors, and professional politicians. Study of Greensboro, North Carolina's elite at the turn of the 20th century reveals some need for refinement and modification of the model. Greensboro was a rapidly urbanizing small town. Its elite was a relatively unified local group that dominated business, civic, religious, and fraternal organizations as well as political offices. Based upon manuscripts, printed primary and secondary sources; 5 tables, 28 notes.   T. D. Schoonover

786. Kleinberg, S. J. DEATH AND THE WORKING CLASS. *J. of Popular Culture 1977 11(1): 193-209.* Explores attitudes toward death in their social and economic context among working-class residents of Pittsburgh during the 1890's. Use of both quantitative and qualitative approaches in studies of popular culture overcomes in part the possibility of placing too much emphasis on the unusual or unrepresentative, as is the case where conventional sources alone are employed. Primary and secondary sources; 3 tables, 50 notes.   D. G. Nielson

787. Laurie, Bruce. "NOTHING ON COMPULSION": LIFE STYLES OF PHILADELPHIA ARTISANS, 1820-1850. *Labor Hist. 1974 15(3): 337-366.* Examines the life styles and changing social customs and ideologies of Philadelphia artisans from 1820-1850. Pre-industrial working-class culture with its equal emphasis upon work, leisure, and spontaneity slowly gave way to an emerging industrial culture emphasizing work, discipline, morality, and success. The depression of 1837-43, the temperance crusade, and the impact of evangelical Methodism conveyed a class identity and a modern work ethic to the increasingly diverse artisans. Assesses pre-industrial cultural activities centered in taverns, volunteer fire companies, circuses, and sports. Based on Philadelphia newspapers, census returns, organizational reports, and secondary sources; 106 notes.   L. L. Athey

788. Leinenweber, Charles. SOCIALISTS IN THE STREETS: THE NEW YORK CITY SOCIALIST PARTY IN WORKING CLASS NEIGHBORHOODS, 1908-1918. *Sci. and Soc. 1977 41(2): 152-171.* Socialism in New York City before World War I not only was politically oriented as part of an international radical movement but also was an integral part of the manifestation of working class culture, revealing cultural influences derived from ethnic and class traditions still vitally extant in urban neighborhoods. Socialism took to the streets through organized and spontaneous parades held to indicate neighborhood working class solidarity with striking employees, many of whom were residents of the areas of the parades. Socialist election campaigns were demonstrations of working class self-confidence and provided opportunities for neighborhood entertainment as well as being appeals for votes for radical candidates. The socialist street corner speaker provided a colorful addition to neighborhood street culture.   N. Lederer

789. Liebermann, Richard K. A MEASURE FOR THE QUALITY OF LIFE: HOUSING. *Hist. Methods 1978 11(3): 129-134.* Housing is a more dynamic measure of social class than occupation according to Libermann. Drawing on his research on the East Village of New York City in 1899, he demonstrates that housing data provides significant insight into social structure and the gradations of social class. The areas of religion and mobility can also be analyzed in the context of housing. 2 tables, 8 notes.   D. K. Pickens

790. Luria, Daniel D. TRENDS IN THE DETERMINANTS UNDERLYING THE PROCESS OF SOCIAL STRATIFICATION: BOSTON 1880-1920. *Rev. of Radical Pol. Econ. 1974 6(2): 174-193.* Both descriptive history and statistical analysis suggest that individual economic attainment became more significant in the process of Boston's social stratification after 1890; conversely the importance of ascriptive nativity and religious traits, which had increased during 1870-90, declined. By 1920 economic differences surpassed national origin and religion in determining stratified social outcomes within the city. Based on primary and secondary sources; table, 82 notes.   P. R. Shergold

791. Luria, Daniel D. WEALTH, CAPITAL, AND POWER: THE SOCIAL MEANING OF HOME OWNERSHIP. *J. of Interdisciplinary Hist. 1976 7(2): 261-282.* A statistical study of the relationships of capital and commercial social power based on Marxian theory, using data from the Boston Standard Metropolitan Statistical Area for 1890-1910. Argues that home ownership should not be considered capital and concludes that social power is even more unequally distributed than previous studies have concluded since they have included in their measures of property the value of owner-occupied housing. Home ownership has not gained relative to renters. Improvement for workers can come only through changing the relations of capitalist production. 16 tables, 17 notes.   R. V. Ritter

792. Main, Gloria L. INEQUALITY IN EARLY AMERICA: THE EVIDENCE FROM PROBATE RECORDS OF MASSACHUSETTS AND MARYLAND. *J. of Interdisciplinary Hist. 1977 7(4): 559-581.* Analyzes wealth distribution revealed in the probate records of Massachusetts, Connecticut, and Maryland as insight into the nature of inequality and its range of behavior. In rural areas of the pre-industrial Northeast there was a relatively egalitarian distribution, while in the early South, wealth distribution was far more unequal. Colonial cities in the North reveal greater inequality than the rural hinterland. However, it was prior to the Industrial Revolution and before the great growth of cities that distribution of wealth in Massachusetts made a sharp forward step in the degree of concentration. Printed sources; 7 tables, 29 notes.   R. Howell

793. McConachie, Scot. PUBLIC PROBLEMS AND PRIVATE PLACES. *Missouri Hist. Soc. Bull. 1978 34(2): 90-103.* Analyzes the development of exclusive enclaves in St. Louis since 1850. The wealthy built opulent residences and formed associations to purchase the streets. The associations protected enclave dwellers from unwelcome industrial and commercial intrusions and from association with the lower classes and Negroes until the 1920's. The associations wielded strong legislative and enforcement powers. Based on archival documents, newspaper material, and secondary sources; 5 photos, 51 notes.   H. T. Lovin

794. McPherson, Donald S. MECHANICS' INSTITUTES AND THE PITTSBURGH WORKINGMAN, 1830-1840. *Western Pennsylvania Hist. Mag. 1973 56(2): 155-169.* Economic pressures of industrialization broke down the mutuality of interests between workingmen and the rising entrepreneurial class in this social movement to popularize scientific knowledge.   S

795. Merriam, Paul G. URBAN ELITE IN THE FAR WEST, PORTLAND, OREGON, 1870-1890. *Arizona and the West 1976 18(1): 41-52.* Portland, Oregon, was still largely a frontier city in the 1870's and 1880's. Contrary to the conventional view that the urban West had a relatively open and egalitarian society, there emerged a class-conscious, stratified society in Portland. It was marked by its efforts to emulate the life-style and institutions of eastern cities rather than to be innovative and to adjust to the practicalities of the Far West. 8 illus., 30 notes.   D. L. Smith

796. Miller, Richard G. GENTRY AND ENTREPRENEURS: A SOCIOECONOMIC ANALYSIS OF PHILADELPHIA IN THE 1790'S. *Rocky Mountain Social Sci. J. 1975 12(1): 71-84.*

797. Morris, Richard J. WEALTH DISTRIBUTION IN SALEM, MASSACHUSETTS, 1759-1799: THE IMPACT OF THE REVOLUTION AND INDEPENDENCE. *Essex Inst. Hist. Collections 1978 114(2): 87-102.* Most historians of early America agree that wealth was becoming less equitably distributed and more concentrated in the hands of a few in the 18th century. The debate continues as to what impact, if any, the American Revolution had on wealth distribution. An analysis of wealth distribution in Salem between 1759 and 1799, particularly 1759, 1769, 1771, 1782, 1788, and 1799, based on Salem's tax valuation records, reveals patterns of wealth distribution that amend current historical interpretations. Utilizes both short-term and long-term analyses to support and/or challenge various aspects of Progressive, Consensus, and New Left historiography, and points to the pitfalls of adhering to either form of analysis. Primary and secondary sources; 2 tables, 25 notes.   R. S. Sliwoski

798. Nash, Gary B. URBAN WEALTH AND POVERTY IN PRE-REVOLUTIONARY AMERICA. *J. of Interdisciplinary Hist. 1976 6(4): 545-584.* Examines urban wealth and poverty, primarily in Boston, Philadelphia, and New York, in the years before the American Revolution and emphasizes their role in the onset of the revolutionary movement. While much work still needs to be done to define the linkages between the changing dynamics of urban society and the revolutionary movement, it appears that changing economic and social circumstances eroded the allegiance of many urban dwellers both to the British mercantile system and to their own internal social system. The changing conditions of colonial life and in future expectations make the creation and reception of revolutionary sentiments more comprehensible than does a purely ideological interpretation. 8 tables, 3 graphs, 66 notes, appendix.
R. Howell

799. Oaks, Robert F. PHILADELPHIA MERCHANTS AND THE ORIGINS OF AMERICAN INDEPENDENCE. *Pro. of the Am. Phil. Soc. 1977 121(6): 407-437.* The central political role of Philadelphia merchants before the American Revolution declined after their successful Stamp Act protests in 1765. By 1768 during the Townsend Acts protests, the wealthier merchants refused to sign agreements concerning the nonimportation of British goods. By 1770, artisans and radicals became more important to the resistance than merchants. With the Tea Act of 1774, more merchants united with the radicals to revive the languishing revolutionary movement. Although the radicals later succeeded in forcing the break with Britain in 1776, the merchants stepped in to manage the new governments. Primary and secondary sources; 14 tables, 163 notes.
W. L. Olbrich

800. O'Toole, Dennis A. DEMOCRATIC BALANCE—IDEALS OF COMMUNITY IN EARLY PORTSMOUTH. *Rhode Island Hist. 1973 32(1): 3-17.* Analyzes social and political structure from Portsmouth's formation in 1638 to the close of the 17th century. Despite efforts to democratize society by a more equitable system of land distribution, Portsmouth became a closed society which discouraged immigrants and preserved inequalities of rank and privilege. Based on manuscripts in Portsmouth and the State Archives, Providence, published documents, genealogical records, and secondary accounts.
P. J. Coleman

801. Pessen, Edward. THE LIFESTYLES OF THE ANTEBELLUM URBAN ELITE. *Mid-Am. 1973 55(3): 163-183.* Studies the lifestyles of the wealthy upper class of Boston, New York, Brooklyn, and Philadelphia during the second quarter of the 19th century, indicating that they rejected egalitarianism. Wealth married wealth, mingled socially with wealth, joined like clubs, formed socially purposeful voluntary associations, and established elite residential concentrations. The rich and eminent were a group apart, owning roughly one-half the wealth of the northeastern cities. Based on the Philip Hone diary in the New York Historical Society, published sources, and secondary works; 43 notes.
T. H. Wendel

802. Pessen, Edward. THE SOCIAL CONFIGURATION OF THE ANTEBELLUM CITY: AN HISTORICAL AND THEORETICAL INQUIRY. *J. of Urban Hist. 1976 2(3): 267-306.* Antebellum urban case studies have now grown to sufficient number that an empirical base for a general synthesis of the urban history and structure of the period has emerged. The author, whose intercity study of the antebellum rich already reaches beyond the narrow community study approach, now goes a step further by attempting a general overview of urban society. Concludes that size and not region is the more important difference between cities. Repeats his earlier criticism of occupation as the prime class indicator (he favors wealth), and places families and not individuals as the basic unit. Finds that wealth was becoming more concentrated and that classes were polarizing. To describe the political system he turns to C. Wright Mills' notion of a "ruling elite." 89 notes.
T. W. Smith

803. Pessen, Edward. THE SOCIAL NETWORK WOVEN BY AN ENTREPRENEURIAL ELITE IN THE INDUSTRIAL CENTURY. *Rev. in Am. Hist. 1979 7(3): 394-400.* Reviews John N. Ingraham's *The Iron Barons: A Social Analysis of an American Urban Elite, 1874-1965* (Westport, Connecticut: Greenwood, 1978) and discusses the myth of the self-made man as evidenced by the upper class social networks in the iron industry in Pittsburgh and Philadelphia (Pennsylvania), Youngstown, (Ohio), and Wheeling (West Virginia).

804. Ridgway, Whitman H. MARYLAND COMMUNITY LEADERS AND ECONOMIC DEVELOPMENT, 1793-1836. *Working Papers from the Regional Econ. Hist. Res. Center 1978 2(2): 1-24.* Traces political, propertied, and commercial elites in Baltimore City, Frederick, St. Mary's, and Talbot, Maryland, 1793-1836, to determine how individuals within the elite classes and communities were responsible for promoting economic development.

805. Rock, Howard B. A DELICATE BALANCE: THE MECHANICS AND THE CITY IN THE AGE OF JEFFERSON. *New-York Hist. Soc. Q. 1979 63(2): 92-114.* In the early 19th century, mechanics (skilled tradesmen) made up about 55% of the male population of New York City. They were the lower middle class, and thus were victimized by fluctuations in the economy, but also constituted a formidable political group. Their potential became obvious when they opposed efforts of the merchant-controlled city government to make reforms such as preventing pigs from roaming free. Since the pigs were often a mainstay of the mechanics, reform was opposed. Thus, a "delicate balance" came into being which made the mechanics appear to be reactionary and which resulted in a delay in many needed reforms in the area of health and cleanliness. Years later the city would still be referred to as "one huge pigsty." Primary sources; 34 notes, 5 illus.
C. L. Grant

806. Rudolph, Richard H. EIGHTEENTH CENTURY NEWPORT AND ITS MERCHANTS. *Newport Hist. 1978 51(2): 21-38, (3): 45-60.* Part I. Chronicles the social and political realities which led to the important position of the merchant classes (especially those associated with boatmaking, and the ocean trade) in Newport, Rhode Island, 1700-70. Part II. Discusses figures prominent in Newport's community, 1740's-60's.

807. Segesman, John. SKID ROAD BLANKET STIFFS. *Pacific Northwesterner 1973 17(1): 13-16.* The "Skid Road" area of Spokane was inhabited by many impoverished and often exploited transient laborers—miners, farm workers, and lumberjacks—who were attracted to the program of the Industrial Workers of the World. Laborers of this type, or "blanket stiffs," were frequently hired to work temporarily at "Waikiki," a farm on the Little Spokane River which was the summer home of millionare Jay P. Graves.
G. H. Curtis

808. Shade, William G. CLASS AND SOCIAL MOBILITY IN AMERICAN HISTORY: A REVIEW ESSAY. *Pennsylvania Hist. 1975 42(3): 248-251.* A review essay discussing Edward Pessen's *Riches, Class and Power Before the Civil War* (1973), Stow Persons' *The Decline of American Gentility* (1973), Stephan Thernstrom's *The Other Bostonians: Poverty and Progress in the American Metropolis, 1880-1970* (1973), and Frederick C. Jaher, ed., *The Rich, Well Born, and the Powerful: Elites and Upper Classes in History* (1973).
D. C. Swift

809. Shumsky, Neil L. FRANK RONEY'S SAN FRANCISCO—HIS DIARY: APRIL, 1875-MARCH, 1876. *Labor Hist. 1976 17(2): 245-264.* Presents a diary of an Irish immigrant iron molder. Poverty, unemployment, money problems, and part-time labor dominated his life struggle. 30 notes.
L. L. Athey

810. Shumsky, Neil L. SAN FRANCISCO'S WORKINGMEN RESPOND TO THE MODERN CITY. *California Hist. Q. 1976 55(1): 46-57.* Provides a reinterpretation of workingmen in San Francisco in the 1870's. Having come to California in search of opportunity and wealth, workingmen found neither. Skilled craftsmen found an industrialized economy operating machinery with unskilled labor and employing and exploiting Chinese immigrants. Workingmen labored long hours for low wages and lived in such areas as the district south of Market Street, where overcrowding, poor housing, and disease were part of everyday life. Tensions in home life, disillusionment with organized religion, and traditional support of the Democratic Party contributed to the frustration of workingmen. In 1877 the Workingmen's Party of California was organized, providing a new social and political outlet. The WPC proposed radical reforms from Chinese exclusion to creation of independent businesses. Although the WPC never fully grasped the fundamental changes created by modernization in their lives, it provided a new sense of vitality and meaning to the lives of workingmen. For a brief time they became a potent political force and were integrated into the new urban life through participation in social, religious, and political affairs. Based on primary and secondary sources; illus., photos, 43 notes.
A. Hoffman

811. Story, Ronald. HARVARD AND THE BOSTON BRAH-MINS: A STUDY IN INSTITUTIONAL AND CLASS DEVELOPMENT, 1800-1865. *J. of Social Hist. 1975 8(3): 94-121.* The development of Harvard University during the first half of the 19th century indicates that "the primary function of early institutionalized culture was 'internal' and allowed the formation of a 'coherent' upper class." Harvard provided the elite with: 1) protection against outside societal forces, and 2) supplied class identity which clearly differed from the middle class. Harvard's development spawned a college system which reflected class values. 2 tables, 86 notes.   L. Ziewacz

812. Story, Ronald. HARVARD STUDENTS, THE BOSTON ELITE, AND THE NEW ENGLAND PREPARATORY SYSTEM, 1800-1870. *Hist. of Educ. Q. 1975 15(3): 281-298.* Analyzes the increased enrollment of Boston's elite social classes in Harvard College, 1800-70, assessing the impact of the "Harvard experience" on securing the underpinnings of the economic, social, and cultural consolidation of Boston's elite.

813. Stout, Harry S. STATISTICS WITHOUT A STORY. *Rev. in Am. Hist. 1977 5(1): 36-42.* Review article prompted by Edward M. Cook, Jr.'s *The Fathers of the Towns: Leadership and Community Structure in Eighteenth-Century New England* (Baltimore, Md.: Johns Hopkins U. Pr., 1976).

814. Twombly, Robert C. CLASS CONSCIOUSNESS IN CHICAGO'S CULTURE. *Rev. in Am. Hist. 1977 5(3): 367-372.* Review article prompted by Helen Lefkowitz Horowitz's *Culture & the City: Cultural Philanthropy in Chicago from the 1880s to 1917* (Lexington: U. Pr. of Kentucky, 1976).

815. Vazsonyi, Andrew. THE *CICISBEO* AND THE MAGNIFICENT CUCKOLD: BOARDINGHOUSE LIFE AND LORE IN IMMIGRANT COMMUNITIES. *J. of Am. Folklore 1978 91(360): 641-656.* The predominantly male boardinghouse life of Hungarian immigrants in the steel towns southeast of Chicago, Illinois, produced a special triangular relationship often resembling a sub rosa and unsanctioned form of polyandry among landlord, landlady, and the *fóburdos* or starboarder. Covers 1899-1914. Primary and secondary sources; 51 notes.   W. D. Piersen

816. Walkowitz, Daniel J. STATISTICS AND THE WRITING OF WORKING CLASS CULTURE: A STATISTICAL PORTRAIT OF THE IRON WORKERS IN TROY, NEW YORK, 1860-1880. *Labor Hist. 1974 15(3): 416-460.* Provides a statistical profile of the iron workers of Troy, New York, as a vehicle for examining the relationship between class and culture. Census data can illuminate cultural and class configurations which shape working-class behavior, but it is necessary to integrate statistics with more traditional sources to encompass all dimensions of culture. Based on census schedules for 1860 and 1880 and secondary sources; 11 statistical tables, 66 notes.   L. L. Athey

817. Warden, G. B. THE DISTRIBUTION OF PROPERTY IN BOSTON, 1692-1775. *Perspectives in Am. Hist. 1976 10: 81-128.* An analysis of almost 10,000 deeds and more than 3,500 mortgages recorded in Boston during 1692-1775 reveals several characteristics of property distribution: 1) families who made Boston home often invested their capital by purchasing only parts of houses, 2) 50-66% of town's property owners purchased or sold 60-75% of Boston's real property on the average of every 10 years, 3) property was valued most highly as a medium of exchange, 4) no social class or group monopolized property transfer markets, and 5) property distribution was wide and frequent "among a majority of the adult population." 5 tables, 4 graphs, 25 notes.   W. A. Wiegand

818. Warden, G. B. INEQUALITY AND INSTABILITY IN EIGHTEENTH-CENTURY BOSTON: A REAPPRAISAL. *J. of Interdisciplinary Hist. 1976 6(4): 585-620.* Critiques the hypothesis that increasing inequality was characteristic of pre-Revolutionary America and that it explains the growth and acceptance of revolutionary ideology. The inequality argument is not persuasive because it is based on incomplete and inaccurate records, fails to take other quantitative information into account, and ignores other more familiar library sources. Quantitative methods do not make literary evidence and interpretation obsolete.

It was the instability, rather than the inequality, of society which accelerated the process of mistrust, extremism, and ultimately rebellion. 3 tables, 55 notes.   R. Howell

819. Waters, John J. PATRIMONY, SUCCESSION, AND SOCIAL STABILITY: GUILFORD, CONNECTICUT IN THE EIGHTEENTH CENTURY. *Perspectives in Am. Hist. 1976 10: 131-160.* An analysis of Guilford's tax records, genealogies and probate files reveals "high social stability," little poverty, and high social equality. Prevalent patrimonial lines reflect the fathers' strong desire for sons to continue their names and succeed them on Guilford land. Residents' wills consistently noted male heirs, cattle, and the distribution of wealth. 3 tables, 2 charts, 50 notes.   W. A. Wiegand

820. Wettan, Richard and Willis, Joe D. SOCIAL STRATIFICATION IN THE NEW YORK ATHLETIC CLUB: A PRELIMINARY ANALYSIS OF THE IMPACT OF THE CLUB ON AMATEUR SPORT IN LATE NINETEENTH CENTURY AMERICA. *Can. J. of Hist. of Sport and Physical Educ. 1976 7(1): 41-53.* Discusses detrimental aspects of social stratification in the New York Athletic Club on the development of amateur sports in the United States 1865-1900.

821. Willis, Joe D. and Wettan, Richard. SOCIAL STRATIFICATION IN NEW YORK CITY ATHLETIC CLUBS, 1865-1915. *J. of Sport Hist. 1976 3(1): 45-63.* The athletic club movement began in 1866 with the founding of the New York A.C. Before 1880 the clubs functioned to promote the athletic participation of their members, but soon they began to acquire social characteristics. As this happened, the clubs became more selective in terms of membership, and developed luxurious clubhouses and other trappings symbolic of wealth and success. In the 1890's many of the social clubs deteriorated, as a result of poor management and overextension of financial resources to develop the "proper" atmosphere of luxury. During 1900-15 the neighborhood athletic club developed, without facilities and without the social pretensions of earlier clubs. 60 notes.   M. Kaufman

822. Wright, Helena. THE UNCOMMON MILL GIRLS OF LOWELL. *Hist. Today [Great Britain] 1973 23(1): 10-19.* Describes the life and working conditions of women textile workers at the Boston Manufacturing Company at Lowell, an outgrowth of the Waltham experiment, 1813-50.

823. Zachary, Alan M. SOCIAL DISORDER AND THE PHILADELPHIA ELITE BEFORE JACKSON. *Pennsylvania Mag. of Hist. and Biog. 1975 99(3): 288-308.* Discusses the nature of Philadelphia's social elite of the 1820's who were determined to either eliminate or control the social forces which threatened their perception of society. "This perception was one of fundamental unity among social classes, of deference by lower orders, of responsibility by the well-born. Society was fluid enough to permit social mobility and rigid enough to protect privilege." Relates the views of several leading Philadelphians on poverty, education, tariffs, and slavery. 90 notes.   C. W. Olson

Social and Geographic Mobility

824. Bissell, Linda Auwers FROM ONE GENERATION TO ANOTHER: MOBILITY IN SEVENTEENTH-CENTURY WINDSOR, CONNECTICUT. *William and Mary Q. 1974 31(1): 79-110.* The social and community structure of Windsor determined geographic mobility. People left, regardless of status, usually because of little involvement in community affairs, lack of family ties, or deaths in the family. Those with institutional ties stayed longer. Migration from Windsor was heaviest before 1650. Settlers who stayed provided stability for the town. Compares family responses to stability on a generational basis and analyzes the economy and landholding. Chart, 10 tables, 25 notes.   H. M. Ward

825. Bracken, Alexander E. MIDDLETOWN BEFORE THE LYNDS: GEOGRAPHICAL AND SOCIAL MOBILITY IN MUNCIE, 1850-1880. *Indiana Social Studies Q. 1978-79 31(3): 38-45.*

826. Conzen, Michael P. LOCAL MIGRATION SYSTEMS IN NINETEENTH-CENTURY IOWA. *Geographical Rev. 1974 64(3):*

339-361. Two widely accepted generalizations about 19th-century settlement of the American interior, the westward movement and the urban frontier, have rarely been studied together as integral parts of a single circulation system. This study employs birthplace data by county-of-origin within Iowa for counties and urban settlements that provide a singular opportunity for testing the relative strengths of contemporaneous westbound and citybound migration in the state. A complex flow structure existed, explicable only in part by the pull of the West and of large cities. Other influences were more localized. In addition, despite the lack of urban primacy in Iowa, evidence indicates that incipient metropolitan dominance operated in rural-to-urban migration streams.   J

827. Dancis, Bruce. SOCIAL MOBILITY AND CLASS CONSCIOUSNESS: SAN FRANCISCO'S INTERNATIONAL WORKMEN'S ASSOCIATION IN THE 1880'S. *J. of Social Hist. 1977 11(1): 75-98.* Examines the social characteristics of the class conscious members of the International Workmen's Association revealing that they differ from the general working population of San Francisco because they were "both more stable and prosperous." This is because they were older and were more skilled workers which enabled them "to overcome ethnic differences within their own ranks." More research needs to be done, however, in regard to marital status and background of descent. 16 tables, 52 notes.
L. E. Ziewacz

828. Engerrand, Steven W. BLACK AND MULATTO MOBILITY AND STABILITY IN DALLAS, TEXAS, 1880-1910. *Phylon 1978 39(3): 203-215.* Blacks and mulattoes made up a large percentage (21.3% in 1900) of the population of Dallas, Texas, in the years 1880-1910. They tended to find work in semiskilled, service, or unskilled occupations, though a few, especially mulattoes, were professionals or proprietors. Despite this, the black and mulatto population tended to stay in Dallas during 1880-1910 at a greater rate (32% and 31.4%) than did the native white (22.2%) or white immigrant (18.8%) populations. This was especially true of those Afro-Americans in Dallas who owned property. 6 tables, 20 notes.
J. C. Billigmeier

829. Frisch, Michael. LADDERS, RACING, AND FOREST TRAILS. *Labor Hist. 1974 15(3): 461-466.* Reviews Stephan Thernstrom's *The Other Bostonians: Poverty and Progress in the American Metropolis, 1880-1970* (Cambridge: Harvard, 1973), praising the logic and precision of analysis in the work, but questioning its relationship to broader problems of meaning for the individuals involved, and the character of economic development and social-structural change.
L. L. Athey

830. Gottlieb, Peter. MIGRATION AND JOBS: THE NEW BLACK WORKERS IN PITTSBURGH, 1916-1930. *Western Pennsylvania Hist. Mag. 1978 61(1): 1-16.* Discusses the internal migration of 1.5 million job-seeking Negroes from the South to the Pittsburgh iron and steel mills during 1916-30; assesses job mobility, wage increases, and educational possibilities juxtaposed to preference for rural lifestyles.

831. Greer, Edward. SOCIAL MOBILITY IN THE U.S. WORKING CLASS. *Monthly Rev. 1975 26(9): 51-57.* Discusses Stephan Thernstrom's *The Other Bostonians: Poverty and Progress in the American Metropolis, 1880-1970* (Harvard U. Pr., 1973) in the context of social mobility in the United States.

832. Hardy, Melissa A. OCCUPATIONAL MOBILITY AND NATIVITY-ETHNICITY IN INDIANAPOLIS, 1850-60. *Social Forces 1978 57(1): 205-221.* Rates and patterns of occupational mobility in Indianapolis during the 1850's are analyzed using data from manuscript federal census schedules. Between 1850 and 1860, nearly half the working males who remained in the city were mobile, most of them within the nonmanual or manual categories. Analysis by age cohorts revealed that the young were more likely to be upwardly mobile and less likely to be downwardly mobile than older cohorts of workers. This differential mobility was almost totally a result of the different origin distributions of the cohorts. An analysis of nativity-ethnicity indicated that immigrant males occupied favorable positions in the occupational hierarchy in 1850, which led to considerable upward mobility. Once structural conditions were taken into account, however, differences between the mobility rates of native-born and foreign-born were small, with the native-born somewhat more likely to cross the manual-nonmanual boundary. Basic findings

from this study are compared with those from studies of Boston, Philadelphia, and Houston.   J

833. Hazelrigg, Lawrence E. OCCUPATIONAL MOBILITY iN NINETEENTH-CENTURY U.S. CITIES: A REVIEW OF SOME EVIDENCE. *Social Forces 1974 53(1): 21-32.* This paper reviews evidence concerning intracity trends in occupational status change among adult males from four studies of three cities—Boston, Philadelphia, and Poughkeepsie, New York—for the mid-nineteenth century. Rates of grossly defined vertical mobility and the transmission of status through adults' careers were stable among the nonmigrant male populations of the three cities for the periods of time in question. Data available for Boston indicate that the level of son's career beginnings had a substantial impact on his subsequent attainments and that the effect of father's occupation was largely interpreted by son's career-entry level.   J

834. Jackson, Susan. MOVIN' ON: MOBILITY THROUGH HOUSTON IN THE 1850'S. *Southwestern Hist. Q. 1978 81(3): 251-282.* Less than 1/6 of the free adults living in Houston, Texas, in 1860 had been there in 1850. The median age, male-female sex ratio, and percentage of unmarried men, foreign-born, unskilled workers, and adults without real property, all increased during the 1850's. Single young men, manual workers, and the propertyless, and the foreign-born left Houston at a greater than average rate after 1850. Most stayed within 200 miles of town, but increased their occupational status and amount of real property less than men who continued to live inside Houston. Primary sources; 13 illus., 4 tables, 35 notes.   J. H. Broussard

835. Katz, Michael B.; Doucet, Michael; and Stern, Mark J. MIGRATION AND THE SOCIAL ORDER IN ERIE COUNTY, NEW YORK: 1855. *J. of Interdisciplinary Hist. 1978 8(4): 669-701.* Illustrates a new method of calculating persistence (the proportion of the population remaining in a given place) for Buffalo and Erie County using the New York State census of 1855. While population movement varied with economic opportunity, a large number of factors affected length of residence. It is wrong to assume a relatively uniform rate of population persistence in different towns and regions; rates of population persistence and in-migration varied systematically with patterns of economic development. 7 tables, 24 notes from printed sources.   R. Howell

836. Kirk, Gordon W., Jr. and Kirk, Carolyn Tyirin. MIGRATION, MOBILITY AND THE TRANSFORMATION OF THE OCCUPATIONAL STRUCTURE IN AN IMMIGRANT COMMUNITY: HOLLAND, MICHIGAN, 1850-80. *J. of Social Hist. [Great Britain] 1974 7(2): 142-164.* A statistical study of three factors which alter the size and composition of a community's labor force—migration, natural or vital processes, and vertical social mobility. Explores especially the relationship among these three factors in meeting the occupational needs of a community and thus transforming its structure. Questions whether persistence or migration was the more viable avenue for upward mobility in the 19th century. At the same time the study becomes a check on varying methodologies in determining actual rates of vertical mobility. Concludes that "while certain relationships hold both in the nineteenth and twentieth centuries, others vary—implying that the relationships among structure and size of labor force, vertical mobility, migration, persistence and natural processes may depend on the historical period or period of economic development involved." 6 tables, 21 notes.
R. V. Ritter

837. Kocolowski, Gary P. STABILIZING MIGRATION TO LOUISVILLE AND CINCINNATI, 1865-1901. *Cincinnati Hist. Soc. Bull. 1979 37(1): 23-47.* Describes efforts to regulate urban migration patterns of immigrants to Louisville and Cincinnati.

838. Kopf, Edward. UNTARNISHING THE DREAM: MOBILITY, OPPORTUNITY, AND ORDER IN MODERN AMERICA. *J. of Social Hist. 1977 11(2): 206-227.* Most quantitative studies of 19th- and 20th-century communities have demonstrated that high levels of personal residential mobility have been common in American life. A study of Chelsea, Massachusetts, focusing on 1915, indicates a high degree of mobility, but much of it within ethnic neighborhoods. There was also substantial external migration, but Chelsea contained a highly stable adult population. This study indicates that more research is needed concerning how geographic mobility affected social integration, not social disintegration. 3 maps, 10 tables, 39 notes.   L. E. Ziewacz

839.   Lynch, Joseph P.   BLACKS IN SPRINGFIELD, 1868-1880: A MOBILITY STUDY.   *Hist. J. of Western Massachusetts 1979 7(2): 25-34.* Springfield's small black population experienced little upward occupational mobility during 1868-80, although the city was expanding rapidly. A few blacks did accumulate some real property and this economic mobility was more available than either residential or social improvement. Based on city directories and state censuses; 2 illus., 3 tables, 39 notes.   W. H. Mulligan, Jr.

840.   Matthews, Glenna.   THE COMMUNITY STUDY: ETHNICITY AND SUCCESS IN SAN JOSÉ.   *J. of Interdisciplinary Hist. 1976 7(2): 305-318.* A community study of social structure and social mobility in relation to ethnicity in San Jose, California, between 1860 and 1870. San Jose differed markedly from eastern cities in that there was a roughly equal mobility of Europeans and native-born Americans. Hence it can be concluded that there have been important regional variations in immigrant experience. 8 tables; 25 notes.   R. V. Ritter

841.   Monkkonen, Eric.   SOCIALIZING THE NEW URBANITES: HORATIO ALGER JR.'S GUIDEBOOK.   *J. of Popular Culture 1977 11(1): 77-87.* Often overlooked in the process of urbanization of America are the native-born migrants to the cities. This group enjoyed, in the form of Horatio Alger's novels, a distinct advantage over foreign immigrants, for one major theme in these works is how to cope with and exploit the new environment. Primary and secondary sources; table, 32 notes.
                                                        D. G. Nielson

842.   Nash, Gary B.   UP FROM THE BOTTOM IN FRANKLIN'S PHILADELPHIA.   *Past and Present [Great Britain] 1977 (77): 57-83.* From 1681 to about 1750 there was remarkable opportunity for new immigrants in Philadelphia. Marriage choices, business connections, and personal attributes determined who did well. In the 18th century, however, population growth was rapid (from 2,404 to 34,297). By mid-century, wealth had been redistributed to create a wealthy elite and an indigent poor. The moneyed elite of the early 18th century controlled shipping and urban real estate. This fact and the economic fluctuations and recessions of the late colonial period made it nearly impossible to emerge from poverty after the 1740's, and under these conditions militant radical artisan-laborer movements gained a major place in Philadelphian politics. Based on published works, documents, and manuscripts at the Historical Society of Pennsylvania, the Department of Wills, City Hall Annex, Philadelphia, City Archives, City Hall, and the Pennsylvania State Archives, Harrisburg; 6 tables, graph, 63 notes.   D. N. Levy

843.   Romo, Ricardo.   WORK AND RESTLESSNESS: OCCUPATIONAL AND SPATIAL MOBILITY AMONG MEXICANOS IN LOS ANGELES, 1918-1928.   *Pacific Hist. Rev. 1977 46(2): 157-180.* This quantitative study of Los Angeles Mexicanos during 1918-28 reveals a lower rate of upward occupational mobility and a higher rate of geographical mobility than found by historians of other groups in Los Angeles and other cities. Mexicanos worked primarily in transportation, manufacturing, and agriculture. Low wages, a high cost of living, discrimination, and excessive competition for jobs explain the high geographical mobility. Even second- and third-generation Mexicanos experienced little upward mobility. Based on Los Angeles marriage records and city directories, and on published primary sources; 7 tables, 54 notes.
                                                        W. K. Hobson

844.   Tank, Robert M.   MOBILITY AND OCCUPATIONAL STRUCTURE ON THE LATE NINETEENTH-CENTURY URBAN FRONTIER: THE CASE OF DENVER, COLORADO.   *Pacific Hist. Rev. 1978 47(2): 189-216.* Quantitative study of occupational and geographic mobility in Denver, 1870-92, finds that Denver resembled long-established urban communities in some ways and frontier communities in others. Like urban communities, Denver's occupational structure in 1870 favored native whites over immigrants and blacks and between 1870 and 1890 blacks and immigrants without skills were less likely to advance than similarly low skilled native whites. However, unlike urban communities, but like frontier communities, skilled and white-collar immigrants were able to experience considerable upward mobility. Geographical mobility was high in Denver and varied inversely with social status. Based on census manuscript schedules and city directories; 7 tables, 29 notes.
                                                        W. K. Hobson

845.   Unsigned.   [THE HISTORICAL STUDY OF SOCIAL MOBILITY]   *Hist. Methods Newsletter 1975 8(3): 92-120.*
Miller, Roberta Balstad.   THE HISTORICAL STUDY OF SOCIAL MOBILITY: A NEW PERSPECTIVE,   *pp. 92-97.* Criticizes Stephan Thernstrom's *The Other Bostonians and Progress in the American Metropolis, 1880-1970* (Cambridge: Harvard U. Pr., 1973) for being too narrowly focused and for having several conceptual problems such as overestimating occupational mobility. Further, the real poor do not appear in Thernstrom's figures.
Alcorn, Richard S. and Knights, Peter R.   MOST UNCOMMON BOSTONIANS,   *pp. 98-114.* The authors charge that Thernstrom used biased material. They find errors in six of the book's nine chapters to be based on bad methodology.
Thernstrom, Stephan.   REJOINDER TO ALCORN AND KNIGHTS, *pp. 115-120.* Provides a general defense of his work and acknowledges some minor errors.   D. K. Pickens

846.   Walsh, Margaret.   INDUSTRIAL OPPORTUNITY OF THE URBAN FRONTIER: "RAGS TO RICHES" AND MILWAUKEE CLOTHING MANUFACTURERS, 1840-1880.   *Wisconsin Mag. of Hist. 1974 57(3): 174-194.* Challenges the persistence of the "rags to riches" idea in American culture by looking at the business careers of Milwaukee's leading clothing manufacturers for a 40 year period. Emphasizes that, rather than any single factor, Jewish connections, German origins, technological innovation, previous business experience, substantial capital and credit, and good local market conditions, when combined in varying degrees, were the ingredients of a successful company. Instead of a spectacular leap from rags to riches, the Milwaukee clothing manufacturers' experience suggests that vertical mobility was possible, but "it was generally modest in both its claims and its end results." 12 illus., 5 tables, 51 notes.   N. C. Burckel

847.   Weber, Michael P. and Boardman, Anthony E.   ECONOMIC GROWTH AND OCCUPATIONAL MOBILITY IN NINETEENTH CENTURY URBAN AMERICA.   *J. of Social Hist. 1977 11(1): 52-74.* An analysis of the horizontal and vertical mobility of one Pennsylvania community in the 19th century reveals that "individual success was determined more by the structure of the city than by individual ethnic and cultural background." More importantly the "time one entered a city, the skill level of one's occupation at that time, one's industrial occupation and whether one switched occupations were crucial determinants of one's success in America." 5 tables, 29 notes, appendix.
                                                        L. E. Ziewacz

848.   Weber, R. David.   SOCIOECONOMIC CHANGE IN RACINE, 1850-1880.   *J. of the West 1974 13(3): 98-108.* Explores upward mobility in Racine, Wisconsin, in the 19th century. Considers studies of other cities in terms of Frederick Jackson Turner's thesis on the levelling effect of the frontier. Measures socioeconomic mobility by occupation and property ownership. Confirms Turner's thesis that greater egalitarianism and social change occurred in the rural West and adds to it the dimension of urban areas. Based on contemporary newspaper reports and secondary sources; 8 tables, 16 notes.   N. J. Street

Leisure, Entertainment, and Recreation

849.   Ahrens, Arthur R.   HOW THE CUBS GOT THEIR NAME. *Chicago Hist. 1976 5(1): 39-44.* Chronicles Chicago baseball, 1850's-1914, including the Chicago Cubs.

850.   Bain, Kenneth R.; Phillips, Rob; and Travis, Paul D.   BENSON PARK: SHAWNEE CITIZENS AT LEISURE IN THE EARLY TWENTIETH CENTURY.   *Chronicles of Oklahoma 1979 57(2): 164-170.* When the Interurban Railway Company created Benson Park in 1908, Shawnee, Oklahoma, citizens made it the focal point for community activities and individual entertainment. Benson Park—complete with swimming pools, canoe rides, picnic areas, opera house, baseball field, bandstand and botanical garden—survived for 24 years until it became a victim of the Depression. Includes 9 photographs of the park in its heyday.   M. L. Tate

851. Banks, Nancy. THE WORLD'S MOST BEAUTIFUL BALL-ROOMS. *Chicago Hist. 1973 2(4): 206-215.* The brothers Andrew (1881-1940) and William Karzas (d. 1963) built the famous Trianon (1922) and Aragon (1926) ballrooms. The popularity of ballroom dancing permitted the brothers to survive the depression. Their success was based on the lavishness of the ballrooms, an atmosphere of refinement, the use of radio, and sound business judgment. Social changes and the death of Andrew eventually brought about the decline of these ballrooms, the world's most beautiful. Based on primary and secondary sources; 6 photos, note.   N. A. Kuntz

852. Barnes, Sisley. GEORGE FERRIS' WHEEL: THE GREAT ATTRACTION OF THE MIDWAY PLAISANCE. *Chicago Hist. 1977 6(3): 177-182.* Discusses the first ferris wheel, invented by George W. G. Ferris and engineered with the assistance of Luther V. Rice for the World's Columbian Exhibition (Chicago, 1893).

853. Barney, Robert Knight. OF RAILS AND RED STOCKINGS: EPISODES IN THE EXPANSION OF THE "NATIONAL PAS-TIME" IN THE AMERICAN WEST. *J. of the West 1978 17(3): 61-70.* Professional quality baseball was brought to the West via the newly completed transcontinental railroad. In 1869 the Cincinnati Red Stockings played several exhibition games with the best amateur teams of San Francisco, Sacramento, and Omaha. Although no stop was made in Nevada, the citizens of Carson City became rabid fans and supporters of professional baseball. This western tour by an invincible professional team encouraged the western states to develop a strong interest in baseball in the 1870's. Published sources; 4 photos, 52 notes.   B. S. Porter

854. Calkin, Homer L. IOWA CELEBRATES THE CENTENNIAL OF AMERICAN INDEPENDENCE. *Ann. of Iowa 1976 43(3): 161-180.* Iowans celebrated the Centennial of American Independence with a great deal of enthusiasm. Contains descriptions of 1876 observances in several Iowa cities, especially Des Moines, where at least 40,000 spectators lining a parade route witnessed a procession three miles in length, an event then called "the grandest spectacle ever seen in Iowa". Based largely on newspapers; 2 photos, 23 notes.   P. L. Petersen

855. Carter, Gregg Lee. BASEBALL IN SAINT LOUIS, 1867-1875: AN HISTORICAL CASE STUDY IN CIVIC PRIDE. *Missouri Hist. Soc. Bull. 1975 31(4 part 1): 253-263.* In the post-Civil War competition between St. Louis and Chicago for "economic and cultural supremacy" in the Mississippi Basin, St. Louis fell behind. Thereupon, St. Louis boosters established two professional baseball teams in the city. Professional baseball became a symbol of the greatness claimed for the city. Based on newspaper sources; 29 notes.   H. T. Lovin

856. Chilman, C. William. THE FEEL OF FALL IN OLD BAR HARBOR. *New-England Galaxy 1977 19(2): 3-14.* Describes life in Bar Harbor, Maine, in the late 1920's. Notes the exodus of the summer visitors after Labor Day by train or steamboat to Boston or New York, and activities at the Eden Fair in celebration of the harvest season. 7 illus.   P. C. Marshall

857. Claereen, Wayne H. PITTSBURGH AND THE FIRST SHOW-BOAT: A NEW ANGLE ON THE CHAPMANS. *Western Pennsylvania Hist. Mag. 1976 59(2): 231-239.* Discusses the Chapman family of actors and actresses who left England in 1827 for the United States, where they settled in Pittsburgh, 1827-47, and invented and popularized a form of floating theater, the showboat.

858. Cohen, Arthur H. THE TROLLEY AND NEW CASTLE'S CASCADE PARK, 1897. *Western Pennsylvania Hist. Mag. 1978 61(2): 165-170.* In 1897 Pittsburgh, Pennsylvania's, New Castle's Cascade Park, complete with trolley, proved an excellent promotional item for electric railways and a new and popular concept in recreation.

859. Cookman, Aubrey O. CHICAGO'S EXCLUSIVE PLAY-GROUND: THE SOUTH SHORE COUNTRY CLUB. *Chicago Hist. 1976 5(2): 66-75.* Chronicles the South Shore Country Club from its inception in 1906 until it closed its doors in 1974.

860. Croak, Thomas M. THE PROFESSIONALIZATION OF PRIZEFIGHTING: PITTSBURGH AT THE TURN OF THE CEN-TURY. *Western Pennsylvania Hist. Mag. 1979 62(4): 333-343.* Traces the evolution of American boxing, using Pittsburgh as an example, stressing how boxing exemplified American social mobility, personal initiative, and regional identification, 1890's-1900's.

861. Damaris, Gypsy. THE COLUMBIA RESTAURANT. *North Louisiana Hist. Assoc. J. 1978 9(1): 43-46.* Discusses the Columbia Restaurant in Shreveport, Louisiana, from around 1900 until the restaurant was sold in 1969.

862. Daniel, W. Harrison. "THE RAGE" IN THE HILL CITY: THE BEGINNINGS OF BASEBALL IN LYNCHBURG. *Virginia Cavalcade 1979 28(4): 186-191.* A history of the beginnings of baseball in the 1830's and 1840's in Lynchburg, Virginia.

863. Davis, James M., Jr. THE COLONIAL COFFEEHOUSE. *Early Am. Life 1978 9(1): 26-29, 86.* Like most European institutions, the coffeehouse was adopted by the colonies in the 1700's, providing Americans an opportunity to exchange gossip, discuss social matters, and even do business. However, by the mid-19th century the true coffeehouse had disappeared, unable to survive the efficiency and specialization that the Industrial Revolution demanded.

864. deMetz, Kaye. DANCE DUELS ON NEW ORLEANS STAGES DURING THE NINETEENTH CENTURY. *Southern Speech Communications J. 1976 41(3): 278-289.* Discusses the social background of dance competitions in minstrel shows in New Orleans, Louisiana, in the 1840's and 50's, emphasizing their ideological relationship to traditional US individualism.

865. Dial, Scott. THE GOLD RUSH SALOON. *Alaska J. 1975 5(2): 81-88.* Saloons were a major part of the landscape and social life of any gold rush town. Describes the economic and social part Alaskan saloons played in gold rush days, and details the operation and appointments of some of the better known ones. 12 photos, 41 notes.
E. E. Eminhizer

866. Dobkin, J. B. TRAILS TO TAMPA BAY: A PHOTO ESSAY. *Tampa Bay Hist. 1979 1(1): 24-30.* Brief survey of tourism in Florida's Tampa Bay area; highlights steam transportation, overland travel, and railroad connections, 1876-1922, and includes 15 photos.

867. Drachman, Mose THE TUCSON GAMBLERS. *J. of Arizona Hist. 1973 14(1): 1-9.* As a young man in his uncle's cigar store in Tucson in the 1880's and 1890's, the author became acquainted with the gamblers who frequented the saloons and gambling halls. He recalls some of the leading gamblers, the saloon singers, gambling terminology, and how gambling was outlawed. 2 illus.   D. L. Smith

868. Duis, Perry. THE SALOON IN A CHANGING CHICAGO. *Chicago Hist. 1975-76 4(4): 214-224.* Describes the ups and downs of the liquor industry and Chicago saloons until prohibition (1920).

869. Engelmann, Larry. OLD SALOON DAYS IN MICHIGAN. *Michigan Hist. 1977 61(2): 99-134.* Michigan saloons, like their counterparts elsewhere, provided social services for the working class. By presenting an illusion of well-being, they also made labor organization more difficult. Small-town saloons, like those in urban areas, were lively, profitable, and ubiquitous. The saloons' political influence was a greater stimulant to reform than were social elements. Government taxing and licensing authority, competition, technological change, and economic disadvantages within the brewing industry, combined to destroy the saloon's prominence during the early 20th century. Based on primary and secondary sources; illus., 11 photos, 65 notes.   D. W. Johnson

870. Forman, William H., Jr. WILLIAM P. HARPER AND THE EARLY NEW ORLEANS CARNIVAL. *Louisiana Hist. 1973 14(1): 40-47.* William Poynot Harper played a major role in the development of the Mistick Krewe of Comus and celebration of Mardi Gras in New Orleans 1866-72. Based on the author's collection; 8 photos.
R. L. Woodward

871. Freedman, Stephen. THE BASEBALL FAD IN CHICAGO, 1865-1870: AN EXPLORATION OF THE ROLE OF SPORT IN THE

NINETEENTH CENTURY CITY. *J. of Sport Hist. 1978 5(2): 42-64.* The history of baseball in Chicago during 1865-70 provides an examination of the relation between sport and the social climate of the 19th-century American city. Baseball's most vigorous supporters were businessmen, educators, journalists, and social reformers who wanted to maintain widely-held middle-class values in a time of rapid social change. Baseball was seen as a healthy way to protect the players from the evil aspects of city life. Businessmen saw it as a way to extend the same benefits to their workers. The baseball clubs that were established were supported by the middle and upper classes. When Chicago's teams began to play against teams from other cities, however, the gentlemen-players had little chance against more agile and almost professional players on other teams. Pressure began to develop for Chicago to come up with a winning team. By 1869-70, all pretense of amateurism was abandoned with the establishment of the Chicago White Stockings. Now, baseball was a symbol of the success of the city and its business community in particular. 61 notes. M. Kaufman

872. Gale, Oliver M. THE CINCINNATI ZOO: 100 YEARS OF TRIAL AND TRIUMPH. *Cincinnati Hist. Soc. Bull. 1975 33(2): 87-119.*

873. Gomery, Douglas. MOVIE EXHIBITION IN MILWAUKEE, 1906-1947: A SHORT HISTORY. *Milwaukee Hist. 1979 2(1): 8-17.* Provides a history of movie exhibition in Milwaukee from 1906 and the opening of the first permanent theater, Thomas and John Saxe's Theatorium, until 1947, when television station WTMJ began regular broadcasting.

874. Gomery, Douglas. SAXE AMUSEMENT ENTERPRISES: THE MOVIES COME TO MILWAUKEE. *Milwaukee Hist. 1979 2(1): 18-28.* Traces the involvement of the Saxe brothers in the movie theaters business and related services from 1906 when they opened Milwaukee's first motion picture theater, until 1925, when they ran and controlled over 40 theaters in Wisconsin.

875. Good, L. Douglas. COLONIALS AT PLAY: LEISURE IN NEWPORT, 1723. *Rhode Island Hist. 1974 33(1): 9-17.* Describes early leisure activities, including tippling, processions, bonfires, hunting, horseracing, gambling, swimming, and sledding. Based on published documents, travel accounts, diaries, and secondary sources.
P. J. Coleman

876. Griffin, Al. CHICAGO'S CIVILIZED WORLD OF WILD ANIMALS. *Chicago Hist. 1975-76 4(4): 235-243.* Describes the successive stages of construction and improvement of the Chicago Zoo in Lincoln Park, 1874-1975.

877. Griffin, Al. THE UPS AND DOWNS OF RIVERVIEW PARK. *Chicago Hist. 1975 4(1): 14-22.* History of Chicago's amusement center, Riverview Park, describing famous rides, special attractions, and guiding policies. S

878. Griffin, Richard T. BIG JIM O'LEARY: "GAMBLER BOSS IV TH' YARDS." *Chicago Hist. 1976-77 5(4): 213-222.* Discusses the gambling enterprises of Jim O'Leary in Chicago, Illinois, 1892-1925.

879. Harris, Ira L. A LOS ANGELES POPULAR MUSIC DIRECTOR. *Western States Jewish Hist. Q. 1977 10(1): 62-67.* Abraham Frankum Frankenstein (1873-1934) began his musical career in Chicago, came to Los Angeles in 1897 with the Grau Opera Company, and remained to form the first permanent theater orchestra. During the 1920's Frankenstein conducted the Orpheum Theater orchestra for such stars as Jack Benny, Fanny Brice, George Jessel, the Marx Brothers, and Sophie Tucker. He organized the bands of the Los Angeles Police and Fire Departments. He served on the Los Angeles Fire Commission for most of the 1913-27 period. In collaboration with F. B. Silverwood he wrote the song, "I Love You California," in 1913; it became the official state song in 1951. Based on personal knowledge and published sources; photo, 18 notes. B. S. Porter

880. Horowitz, Helen L. ANIMAL AND MAN IN THE NEW YORK ZOOLOGICAL PARK. *New York Hist. 1975 56(4): 426-455.* Relates the development of the New York Zoological Park from the original suggestion by Madison Grant in 1894 to its completion in 1911. The original intention was to subordinate architecture to the natural habitat of wildlife, but architecture finally dominated the park. The original interest in wildlife conservation became subordinate to the desire to preserve American values against foreign immigration and commercialism. The park's leaders were also concerned about the relation of man to animal. 7 illus., 72 notes. R. N. Lokken.

881. Jable, J. Thomas. THE BIRTH OF PROFESSIONAL FOOTBALL: PITTSBURGH ATHLETIC CLUBS RING IN PROFESSIONALS IN 1892. *Western Pennsylvania Hist. Mag. 1979 62(2): 131-147.* Traces the professionalization of football in Pittsburgh athletic clubs, beginning in 1866 with the New York Athletic Club, which is considered a prototype; professional football first came to Pittsburgh in 1892, when the Allegheny Athletic Association recruited outside players for its football team.

882. Javersak, David T. LABOR DAY IN WHEELING. *Upper Ohio Valley Hist. Rev. 1979 9(1): 31-35.* Traces the history of Labor Day celebrations in the United States since the first was held in New York City in 1882, particularly the celebration of the holiday in Wheeling, West Virginia, beginning in 1886.

883. Javersak, David T. "WHEELING'S SUNDAY SENSATION: THE 1889 WHEELING NAILERS." *Upper Ohio Valley Hist. Rev. 1979 8(2): 2-6.* Controversy surrounded the Sunday baseball games of the Wheeling (Ohio) Nailers in 1889, because a city ordinance forbade all but absolutely necessary work on Sundays.

884. Kelly, Susan Croce. THE BEGINNINGS OF THE ST. LOUIS ZOO. *Missouri Hist. Soc. Bull. 1974 30(4): 268-278.* Treats the formation of the St. Louis Zoological Society in 1910 and subsequent crusading by society members for a city zoo. Despite citizen apathy and some opposition, the society persisted. By 1916, a first-rate zoo was being established. Based on newspaper and secondary sources; 8 photos, 42 notes. H. T. Lovin

885. Kingsdale, Jon M. THE "POOR MAN'S CLUB": SOCIAL FUNCTIONS OF THE URBAN WORKING-CLASS SALOON. *Am. Q. 1973 25(4): 472-489.* Turn-of-the-century saloons provided an all-male neighborhood social and political center for urban industrial and ethnic groups conserving and reinforcing working-class and ethnic values. Saloons retarded assimilation toward the Anglo-Saxon Protestant ideal and were, therefore, more than symbolic enemies to Prohibitionists concerned with conserving traditional American values and family life. Based on secondary sources; 65 notes. W. D. Piersen

886. Klein, Maury. SUMMERING AT THE PIER. *Am. Hist. Illus. 1978 13(2): 32-43.* Philadelphians boarded with residents of Narragansett Pier, Rhode Island, as early as the 1840's, but the heyday of summer vacationing was 1880-1914. Famous visitors included President Chester A. Arthur, industrialists James B. Duke, Pierre Lorillard, and John Wanamaker, and Varina Howell Davis, widow of Jefferson Davis. The Casino was the main social center. Major hotels were the Rockingham, the Mathewson, and the Imperial. Successive fads included roller-skating, roller polo, bicycling, and "lawn tempest." By the 1880's the upper classes began to build elaborate summer homes which, with improved transportation that made one-day excursions possible, soon put the hotels out of business. When a 1900 fire destroyed the Casino, it was replaced with a less elegant amusement center which charged modest admission fees and was open to all. By the 1920's the Pier had lost its glitter as a playground for the wealthy. Primary and secondary sources; 16 illus. D. Dodd

887. Kmet, Jeffrey. MILWAUKEE'S NICKELODEON ERA: 1906-1915. *Milwaukee Hist. 1979 2(1): 2-7.* Describes the nickelodeons in Milwaukee, small theaters charging five cents admission for slide presentations, short films, and variety shows, 1906-15.

888. Koziol, John A. RECREATION IN CHICOPEE, 1853-1857. *Hist. J. of Western Massachusetts 1978 6(2): 18-27.* Drawing on the *Chicopee Weekly Journal*, discusses the various types of entertainment available to residents of Chicopee, Massachusetts, during 1853-57. 5 illus., 55 notes. W. H. Mulligan, Jr.

889. Kramer, William M. and Stern, Norton B. SAN FRANCISCO'S FIGHTING JEW. *California Hist. Q. 1974 53(4): 333-346.* Joe Choynski (1868-1943) was American Jewry's first international sports figure. A professional boxer from San Francisco, Choynski contradicted the stereotype which excluded Jews from competitive sports. He fought 77 bouts, winning 50 of them during his 20-year career. Six of his opponents were or later became world champions, including Jim Corbett, Jim Jeffries, John L. Sullivan, and Jack Johnson. Known as a "scientific" boxer, Choynski fought at a time when matches could be declared illegal and the participants arrested. Bouts lasted for dozens of rounds and fighters used bare fists or two-ounce gloves. The sports press of the period praised Choynski's abilities, and his opponents held him in high esteem. Based on interviews, newspapers, and published works; photos, 73 notes.
A. Hoffman

890. Landis, Frank W. LANCASTER CITY KID BASEBALL LEAGUES. *J. of the Lancaster County Hist. Soc. 1976 80(3): 178-187.* Explores the beginnings of Lancaster City Kid Leagues, 1911-15, with the McCain League (later expanding to include the Sixth, Seventh, and Eighth Ward leagues); chronicles the competitions between leagues and the 50-year reunion held in 1965.

891. McArthur, Benjamin. SODOMS BY THE SEA. *Rev. in Am. Hist. 1979 7(3): 388-393.* Review article on Charles E. Funnell's *By the Beautiful Sea: The Rise and High Times of that Great American Resort, Atlantic City* (New York: Knopf, 1975) and John F. Kasson's *Amusing the Million: Coney Island at the Turn of the Century* (New York: Hill and Wang, 1978); discusses the creation of resorts as a reflection of accommodation to industrialized society, Victorian sensibilities, and the beginnings of present-day consumer society, 1890-1910.

892. McCarthy, Kathleen D. NICKEL VICE AND VIRTUE: MOVIE CENSORSHIP IN CHICAGO, 1907-1915. *J. of Popular Film 1976 5(1): 37-55.* Discusses nickel cinemas and nickelodeons in Chicago and the Progressive reforms which enforced censorship of the films of the era.

893. Noel, Thomas J. THE IMMIGRANT SALOON IN DENVER. *Colorado Mag. 1977 54(3): 200-219.* From the Civil War through Prohibition, Denver's immigrant population relied on saloons as haven for old world culture and introduction to the new home. German, Irish, Jewish, Italian, and Slavic immigrants relied on taverns as important community centers to stimulate social, political, and economic activities. Primary and secondary sources; 7 illus., 51 notes.
D. A. Hartford

894. Noel, Thomas J. THE MULTIFUNCTIONAL FRONTIER SALOON: DENVER, 1858-1876. *Colorado Mag. 1975 52(2): 114-136.* Argues that Denverites, before Colorado statehood, "had conducted government, gone to church, carried on business, cared for the sick and needy, and enjoyed social, cultural and recreational activities in saloon halls." As civilization arrived, various newly built private and public buildings replaced saloons for those purposes. Primary and secondary sources; 6 illus., table, 70 notes.
O. H. Zabel

895. Noel, Thomas J. GAY BARS AND THE EMERGENCE OF THE DENVER HOMOSEXUAL COMMUNITY. *Social Sci. J. 1978 15(2): 59-74.* Surveys the history of Denver's homosexuals, 1885-1976, the emergence during the 1970's of bars for homosexuals, and the functions (sociological, psychological, and sexual) of the bars.

896. Nolte, Linda M. Pearce. YACHTING: ITS HISTORY IN SAN DIEGO. *J. of San Diego Hist. 1975 20(4): 1-24.* Recounts the history of yachting and yacht clubs in San Diego, from the Pacific Pioneer Yacht Club in 1852 to the present day.
S

897. Northam, Janet A. and Berryman, Jack W. SPORT AND URBAN BOOSTERISM IN THE PACIFIC NORTHWEST: SEATTLE'S —YUKON—PACIFIC EXPOSITION, 1909. *J. of the West 1978 17(3): 53-60.* In the summer of 1909, Seattle, Washington, hosted its first world's fair, the Alaska-Yukon-Pacific Exposition (AYPE). The main purpose of the fair was to promote Seattle as a port and trade center by attracting the attention of the entire nation. To this purpose, the AYPE sponsored an extensive schedule of amateur and professional sporting events. In one major professional competition, the National Track and Field Championship, the Seattle Athletic Club defeated the best Eastern teams, thus doing more to advertise Seattle than any other AYPE event. Primary and secondary sources; 3 photos, 58 notes.
B. S. Porter

898. Nye, Russel B. SATURDAY NIGHT AT THE PARADISE BALLROOM: OR, DANCE HALLS IN THE TWENTIES. *J. of Popular Culture 1973 7(1): 14-22.* Discusses background, music, and atmosphere of dance halls, particularly in major cities during 1910-29.
S

899. O'Dwyer, Diane. PURVEYORS OF CLEVER AMUSEMENT. *Hawaiian J. of Hist. 1975 9: 60-73.* Traces the history of the Honolulu Community Theater since it began in 1915 as The Footlights Club. Mentions plays presented, the provision of a permanent home for the theater, and its organization through the years. Appendices include lists of the locations of the performances, cast of the first production, organization, and the cast of "The Last of Mrs. Cheyney."
R. Alvis

900. Oster, Donald Bright. NIGHTS OF FANTASY: THE ST. LOUIS PAGEANT AND MASQUE OF 1914. *Missouri Hist. Soc. Bull. 1975 31(3): 175-205.* Describes the elaborate and costly pageantry which was staged as part of St. Louis's sesquicentennial celebration in 1914. The pageant engendered civic pride in St. Louis and produced at least momentary cooperation among the customarily antagonistic social and political factions of the city. Based on Missouri Historical Society newspaper and manuscript materials; 89 notes.
H. T. Lovin

901. Post, Carl. EXIT LAUGHING: THE DEATH OF VAUDEVILLE. *Mankind 1975 5(1): 11-15, 54-59.* From its beginnings in England and France, vaudeville was transplanted to the United States, where it flourished from the 1870's until the advent of radio, motion pictures and (especially) television. The emergence of vaudeville as a major facet of the entertainment industry revolved to a considerable extent around the entrepreneurial talents of Tony Pastor, Benjamin Keith, Oscar Hammerstein, and Phineas T. Barnum. Besides bringing entertainment to areas that would have gone without, vaudeville served the purpose of allowing entertainers to obtain experience in a manner not available today.
N. Lederer

902. Potter, Beverly. MISSION CLIFF GARDENS. *J. of San Diego Hist. 1977 23(4): 1-11.* Chronicles the Mission Cliff Gardens, owned by the San Diego Electric Railway Company, which was located as an amusement park at the end of the line in San Diego, California, 1898-1942.

903. Reagon, Bernice. THE LADYSTREETSINGER. *Southern Exposure 1974 2(1): 38-41.* Portrays the life of Flora Molton, a black woman, who has sung her folk songs on the streets of the District of Columbia since the 1930's.
S

904. Ricards, Sherman L. and Blackburn, George M. A NINETEENTH-CENTURY WESTERN CIRCUS: VIRGINIA CITY, JULY 4, 1870. *Nevada Hist. Soc. Q. 1979 22(3): 199-208.* For the 4 July 1870 celebration at Virginia City, Nevada, civic boosters insisted upon elaborate and expensive entertainment and, accordingly, arranged performances by the Great Overland Circus, a major circus group quartered at San Francisco. The Great Overland Circus lost several star artists before arriving at Virginia City, but the residents there enthusiastically praised the entertainment offered. Based on US Census data and newspaper and secondary sources; 30 notes.
H. T. Lovin

905. Riess, Steven A. PROFESSIONAL SUNDAY BASEBALL: A STUDY IN SOCIAL REFORM 1892-1934. *Maryland Historian 1973 4(2): 95-108.* Examines the pattern of social changes in Chicago, New York, and Atlanta which converted Sunday to a recreation day. As America became more urban, bureaucratized, and industrialized, religious conservatism yielded. Baseball became a working-class entertainment and an inculcator of American middle class values. Periodical and secondary sources; 55 notes.
G. O. Gagnon

906. Riess, Steven A. THE BASEBALL MAGNATE AND URBAN POLITICS IN THE PROGRESSIVE ERA. *J. of Sport Hist. 1974 1(1): 41-62.* Baseball is supposed to exemplify the best in American society: competition, honesty, and diligence. During the Progressive era 17 of the

18 major-league teams were operated by men who "typified some of its worst aspects." They had political connections, and the owners included political bosses and friends of professional gamblers. Examines the situation in Atlanta, Chicago, and New York. 65 notes.   M. Kaufman

907. Ritchey, David. COLUMBIA GARDEN: BALTIMORE'S FIRST PLEASURE GARDEN. *Southern Speech Communication J. 1974 39(3): 241-247.* Examines the use of Baltimore's Columbia Garden as a pleasure garden setting for theatrical performances and other recreational uses, 1805-07.   S

908. Robbins, Peggy. WHERE CARNIVAL IS KING. *Am. Hist. Illus. 1979 13(10): 4-11, 46-49.* Discusses Mardi Gras celebrations in New Orleans, 1718-1978.

909. Senelick, Laurence. VARIETY INTO VAUDEVILLE, THE PROCESS OBSERVED IN TWO MANUSCRIPT GAGBOOKS. *Theatre Survey 1978 19(1): 1-15.* Describes the manuscript gagbooks which provided material for vaudeville performers during the 1790's-1890's, particularly the careers and gagbooks of J. C. Murphy and Jerry Cohan in vaudeville during the 19th century.

910. Shaw, Marjorie Betts. THE SAN DIEGO ZOOLOGICAL GARDEN: A FOUNDATION TO BUILD ON. *J. of San Diego Hist. 1978 24(3): 300-310.* Discusses the San Diego Zoological Society during 1916-21, the roles of its founders, and the recurrent financial problems.

911. Siegel, Adrienne. BROTHELS, BETS, AND BARS: POPULAR LITERATURE AS GUIDEBOOK TO THE URBAN UNDERGROUND, 1840-1870. *North Dakota Q. 1976 44(2): 4-22.*

912. Simpson, William S., Jr. 1908: THE YEAR RICHMOND WENT "BASEBALL WILD." *Virginia Cavalcade 1977 26(4): 184-191.* Sandlot baseball, extremely popular among the residents of Richmond, Virginia, was second place to the town's minor league baseball team, the Lawmakers, who won the state pennant in 1908, at the height of a local baseball craze.

913. Smith, Duane A. BASEBALL CHAMPIONS OF COLORADO: THE LEADVILLE BLUES OF 1882. *J. of Sport Hist. 1977 4(1): 51-71.* In the 1880's Leadville caught the national baseball craze. Local business leaders, to enhance the town's image, in 1882 set out to develop a championship team. They apparently paid high salaries, attracting high-quality players from across the country. They included Dave Foutz, who later was to win 41 games in one season for the St. Louis Browns and play for and manage Brooklyn. After winning the Colorado championship, the team went East to display its talents. In all, the Blues won 34, lost eight, and tied one. Illus., 22 notes.   M. Kaufman

914. Snow, Richard F. A GREETING FROM CONEY ISLAND. *Am. Heritage 1975 26(2): 49-55.* History of Coney Island, New York, as illustrated in the post card collection of the author. Experiencing its biggest growth around the turn of the 20th century, the park began its decline by the 1920's. 19 illus.   J. F. Paul

915. Snow, Robert E. and Wright, David E. CONEY ISLAND: A CASE STUDY IN POPULAR CULTURE AND TECHNOLOGICAL CHANGE. *J. of Popular Culture 1976 9(4): 960-975.* For most of the 19th and part of the 20th centuries, Coney Island mirrored popular attitudes toward recreation. In its first phase from 1829 to 1875, Coney Island was a beach resort; from 1876 to 1896, it became a popular escape for the masses of New York City; and from 1897 to 1910 it was an automated amusement park. Mechanization was vigorously protested by New Yorkers who wanted more rural spaces, but for the day laborers and workmen who patronized the park, solitude was foreign and machine-driven rides were familiar. Many reformers associated the roller coaster and ferris wheels with moral decline, but the rides increased in popularity. After 1910, Coney Island's mechanized rides had spawned too many rivals, and the park dropped more modern amusements. Primary and secondary sources; 43 notes, appendix.   J. W. Leedom

916. Sprague, Stuart Seely. MEET ME IN ST. LOUIS ON THE TEN-MILLION-DOLLAR PIKE. *Missouri Hist. Soc. Bull. 1975 32(1): 26-31.* Describes the atmosphere and some of the exhibits of the Louisiana Purchase Exposition, held in St. Louis in 1904. The promoters successfully made it more instructive than the previous World's Fairs. Based on primary sources; 8 photos, 28 notes.   H. T. Lovin

917. Starr, Stephen Z. PROSIT!!!!: A NON-COSMIC TOUR OF THE CINCINNATI SALOON. *Cincinnati Hist. Soc. Bull. 1978 36(3): 175-191.* Describes saloons in Cincinnati, Ohio, 1840-1920, and the growth of lager beer breweries.

918. Strozier, Robert. "YOU'VE GOT TO HAVE SOMETHING FOR EVERYONE": THE RADIO CITY MUSIC HALL PROCESS. *Audience 1973 3(1): 4-15.*

919. Terrie, Philip G. URBAN MAN CONFRONTS THE WILDERNESS: THE NINETEENTH-CENTURY SPORTSMAN IN THE ADIRONDACKS. *J. of Sport Hist. 1978 5(3): 7-20.* Recreational camping in the Adirondacks began roughly in the 1830's, when sophisticated New Yorkers and Bostonians went to experience the adventure of intimacy with the wilderness. The accounts of hunting and fishing indicate an implicit assumption of the inexhaustibility of nature. It was an escape from the commercial city life even then coming to typify American society. Ironically, although they came to the wilderness to escape from a society they perceived as sinister and spiritually empty, they brought with them their civilized ways and the tools of their society. 34 notes.   M. Kaufman

920. Unsigned. ICE FOLLIES. *Am. Heritage 1978 30(1): 60-63.* Brief history of St. Paul's (Minnesota) annual Winter Carnival begun in 1886. In 1979, more than 90 events were scheduled. 2 illus.   J. F. Paul

921. Wind, Herbert Warren. GOLFING IN AND AROUND CHICAGO. *Chicago Hist. 1975-76 4(4): 244-251.* Charles Blair Macdonald initiated golf in Chicago and won the first US Amateur Championship in the late 19th century.

922. Wolf, Edward C. THE WHEELING *SAENGERFESTE* OF 1860 AND 1885. *Upper Ohio Valley Hist. Rev. 1978 8(1): 6-17.* Recounts the Saengerfest of 1860 and of 1885 in Wheeling, West Virginia, involving German singing societies from the Upper Ohio Valley.

923. Yale, Andrew. OUR PLACE WAS BEALE STREET. *Southern Exposure 1978 6(3): 26-38.* Excerpts from oral interviews, musicians, street people, and storekeepers reveal aspects of Beale Street's existence in Memphis, Tennessee during the 1930's-40's when this street was the center of black entertainment and commercial life in the Mid South. Blues singers Furry Lewis and Booker White, hardware store owner Art Hutkins, and Casey Banks, promotions man, musician, and pool player, reflect on Beale Street activities, with special emphasis on the live entertainment and high quality food establishments once featured in the area which exerted considerable appeal for the white as well as the black community.   N. Lederer

924. Zimmerman, Mrs. James M., ed. THE SPORT OF KINGS: HORSERACING IN CINCINNATI. *Cincinnati Hist. Soc. Bull. 1973 31(2): 104-114.* For over a century horseracing has been part of the sporting scene in Cincinnati, beginning at Carthage. In the 1880's racetracks were opened at Latonia and Oaklaw. In this century, River Downs and the new Latonia track have been popular. 11 photos.   H. S. Marks

Communications

925. Barnes, Joseph W. OBEDIAH DOGBERRY, ROCHESTER FREETHINKER. *Rochester Hist. 1974 36(3): 1-24.* Obediah Dogberry fought for religious liberty and freedom of thought in Rochester, New York, through the *Liberal Advocate*, a newspaper published during 1832-34.

926. Bayard, Charles J. "ME AND MR. FINCH" IN DENVER. *Colorado Mag. 1975 52(1): 22-33.* Summarizes the newspaper war of the *Rocky Mountain News* and the Denver *Post* in the perspective of Pro-

gressive reform in the early 20th century. Senator Thomas M. Patterson, owner of the *News*, collected a remarkable staff: Edward Keating (later US Senator), George Creel, and, briefly, Alfred Damon Runyon and Frank Finch. During 1906-07 the latter two, writer and cartoonist, teamed up to attack corruption and the *News* carried the popular and influential "Me and Mr. Finch" column and cartoons. Primary and secondary sources; 10 illus., 36 notes.   O. H. Zabel

927. Beijbom, Ulf. THE PRINTED WORD IN A NINETEENTH-CENTURY IMMIGRANT COLONY: THE ROLE OF THE ETHNIC PRESS IN CHICAGO'S SWEDE TOWN. *Swedish Pioneer Hist. Q. 1977 28(2): 82-96.* By 1870 Swede Town, on Chicago's north side, was the largest Swedish urban settlement and a cultural capital of Swedish Americans. Outlines the character of the Swedish-language press in Chicago and its intellectual function. The press was instrumental in the creation of Swedish America. Based in part on the author's book, *Swedes in Chicago...* 34 notes.   C. W. Ohrvall

928. Bower, Donald E. THE FANTASTIC WORLD OF ORTH STEIN: MYTHICAL EXPLOITS OF A FRONTIER JULES VERNE. *Am. West 1973 10(3): 12-16, 61-63.* Stein wrote for the *Leadville Daily Chronicle* during the Colorado mining rush of the 1880's. His two-year stint as city editor made that newspaper vital and entertaining. He waged relentless and effective campaigns against the city's quack doctors and corrupt public officials. Besides his journalistic prowess, he soon became the leading science fiction writer on the frontier. His serials in the *Chronicle* were followed as avidly as the stories of Jules Verne. Stein left Colorado in 1882 and suffered a rapid and tragic decline, probably induced by a near-fatal beating. 5 illus.   D. L. Smith

929. Bronson, Kenneth C. THE LOCAL PRESS AND THE CHANGING COMMUNITY. *Kansas Hist. Q. 1976 42(1): 48-54.* Early Kansas editors were personal journalists. By engaging actively in politics they often made the news they reported. By 1930, as Kansas moved from an era of small-town to big-city journalism, the editors fought to stem the shift from local to federal government. Failing to do this, they turned to promotional journalism. They followed news instead of making it. They began trying to communicate with their readers, to cultivate cooperation, and to instill involvement in community affairs. Such editors keep debate centered on main issues and probably will play a larger role as people move to smaller towns. Paper read on 20 October 1975 at the Kansas State Historical Society.   W. F. Zornow

930. Crouthamel, James L. JAMES GORDON BENNETT, THE *NEW YORK HERALD,* AND THE DEVELOPMENT OF NEWSPAPER SENSATIONALISM. *New York Hist. 1973 54(3): 294-316.* Sensational (or yellow) journalism antedated Joseph Pulitzer and William Randolph Hearst by nearly 50 years. James Gordon Bennett, who founded the *New York Herald* as a penny paper on 6 May 1835, developed the art of appealing to a mass audience through human interest stories, especially those involving heinous crimes or scandals involving prominent people. By the Civil War, Bennett's journalistic formula had been copied in many American cities, freeing newspapers from financial dependence on political factions. By supporting his paper from advertising revenues geared to circulation increases, Bennett was able to develop new methods of news-gathering, and to improve news coverage in all areas. Based on primary and secondary sources; 6 illus., 77 notes.   G. Kurland

931. Culley, Margaret. DOROTHY DIX: THE THIRTEENTH JUROR. *Int. J. of Women's Studies [Canada] 1979 2(4): 349-357.* Traces the career of Dorothy Dix (Elizabeth Gilmer, 1870-1951), a crime reporter for the New York *Journal;* although best known for her syndicated advice column, she first gained fame reporting on crimes involving women, 1901-16.

932. Dornfeld, A. A. THE CITY NEWS BUREAU. *Chicago Hist. 1976 5(2): 76-84.* Discusses the operation of Chicago's City News Bureau, a central newsgathering agency for the city's numerous newspapers, 1891-1974.

933. Glauber, Robert H. THE NECESSARY TOY: THE TELEPHONE COMES TO CHICAGO. *Chicago Hist. 1978 7(2): 70-86.* Telephone service, first established in Chicago in 1877, quickly replaced the telegraph and monopolized communications there by 1900.

934. Hensher, Alan. "PENNY PAPERS": THE VANDERBILT NEWSPAPER CRUSADE. *California Hist. Q. 1976 55(2): 162-169.* Traces the first years of the Los Angeles *Illustrated Daily News*. Founded by Cornelius Vanderbilt, Jr., in 1923, the *News* was intended to counteract the image of eastern tabloids which focused on crime, sex and scandal. Vanderbilt stressed clean journalism, emphasizing honesty in government, better schools, improved rapid transit, and more parks. Although Vanderbilt's Los Angeles paper was the most successful of his small chain —other papers were started in San Francisco and Miami—it suffered from a lack of advertising revenue and inefficient management. By 1926 Vanderbilt was heavily in debt to his own family. The *News* went into receivership and, under a new editorial policy which included coverage of sex and scandal, lasted until 1954. But Vanderbilt's idealism had been much admired, and his competitors conceded his honesty while mocking his effort. Based on primary sources and published studies; 26 notes.   A. Hoffman

935. Keefe, Thomas M. THE CATHOLIC ISSUE IN THE CHICAGO TRIBUNE BEFORE THE CIVIL WAR. *Mid-America 1975 57(4): 227-245.* Blaming Chicago's troubles on Catholic immigrants, Henry Fowler's editorials began the Chicago *Tribune's* anti-Catholicism. However, he failed to defeat the Democrats in the 1854 municipal election. Editor Thomas Stewart followed Fowler's example, and with his editorial support the Know-Nothings won the next election. New owners of the *Tribune* Medill, Ray, and Vaughan carried on the Fowler-Stewart policy, which continued after the merger with the *Daily Democratic Press*, linking slavery and Catholicism, expressing sympathy for Italy's struggle for unity, and alleging that Stephen Douglas was a secret Catholic. Based on newspapers and secondary works; 83 notes.   T. H. Wendel

936. Klein, Maury. THE EARLY YEARS OF THE NEW YORK TIMES. *Am. Hist. Illus. 1975 10(5): 16-25.* Recounts the history of the *New York Times* from its founding by Henry J. Raymond in 1851 until its takeover by Adolf S. Ochs in 1896.

937. Lederer, Francis L., II. NORA MARKS, INVESTIGATIVE REPORTER. *J. of the Illinois State Hist. Soc. 1975 68(4): 306-318.* Eleanora Stackhouse, writing under the pen name of Nora Marks, published 80 pieces of investigative reporting in the Chicago *Daily Tribune* during August 1888-July 1890. Her exposés included coverage of the domestic servant situation, divorce mills, the Salvation Army, work conditions of peddlers and stockyard workers, Chicago's charity agencies, and delinquent and poor children's custodial care. Little is known of her life and career. Based on primary sources.   N. Lederer

938. Margavio, Anthony V. THE REACTION OF THE PRESS TO THE ITALIAN AMERICAN IN NEW ORLEANS, 1880 TO 1920. *Italian Americana 1978 4(1): 72-83.* Mirroring the national pattern of discrimination, the New Orleans press tended to use stereotypes of Italian Americans as criminals.

939. McDonald, Susan Waugh. EDWARD GARDNER LEWIS: ENTREPRENEUR, PUBLISHER, AMERICAN OF THE GILDED AGE. *Missouri Hist. Soc. Bull. 1979 35(3): 154-163.* Edward Gardner Lewis (1868-1950) came to St. Louis in 1893 and, as publisher of *The Women's Magazine,* shortly became one of St. Louis's most controversial journalists and established a banking institution whose transactions became suspect. Then he created other commercial establishments, struggled with US postal officials to keep his magazine afloat, encouraged the feminist movement, established a People's University, and was mayor of University City, Missouri, until 1912. Secondary sources; 18 notes.   H. T. Lovin

940. Montgomery, Harry. A SHIRTTAIL FULL OF TYPE: A THUMBNAIL SKETCH OF PHOENIX JOURNALISM. *J. of Arizona Hist. 1977 18(3): 357-366.* Traces Arizona journalism since the establishment of its first newspaper in 1859. Emphasizes the history of Phoenix newspapers and editors from the *Salt River Herald* (1878-99) to today's *Arizona Republic* and *Phoenix Gazette.* 4 illus.   D. L. Smith

941. Roff, Sandra Schoiock. THE CALIFORNIA GOLD MINES FROM BROOKLYN: AS VIEWED BY THE LOCAL PRESS. *J. of Long Island Hist. 1973 9(2): 6-22.* Uses four Brooklyn newspapers

1848-53 to evaluate press and community response to the gold rush. Initially skeptical of the reports of gold, the press soon acknowledged the truth but in news items and poetry cautioned seekers about the rigors of the journey and the probabilities of failure, frequently printing death notices. When the panning phase of the gold rush ended, the press intensified its cautioning but did acknowledge agricultural prospects and the growth of a settled society in San Francisco. Eventually, the press lost interest in California and turned attention to Brooklyn's own prosperity. 2 photos.   C. A. Newton

942. Saalberg, Harvey. DON MELLETT, EDITOR OF THE CANTON "NEWS," WAS SLAIN WHILE EXPOSING UNDERWORLD. *Journalism Q. 1976 53(1): 88-93.* Donald Ring Mellett (1856-1926) was shot after half a year of fighting corruption in Canton, Ohio, as editor of the Canton *Daily News.* His many enemies included the police department. Public good and increased circulation of his paper motivated him. His campaign and death had little effect on the corruption. Based on primary and secondary sources; 42 notes.   K. J. Puffer

943. Shankman, Arnold. JULIAN HARRIS AND THE KU KLUX KLAN. *Mississippi Q. 1975 28(2): 147-169.* Chronicles the efforts of Julian LaRose Harris, editor of the *Enquirer-Sun,* to expose the bigotry and racism of the Ku Klux Klan in Columbus, Georgia, during the 1920's.   S

944. Sim, John Cameron. 19TH CENTURY APPLICATIONS OF SUBURBAN NEWSPAPER CONCEPTS. *Journalism Q. 1975 52(4): 627-631.* The name suburban was applied to newspapers as early as the 1870's. The practice of printing newspapers for several communities in one plant also dates from the 1870's. This was aided by the popularity of readyprints. In this service, sheets printed with world and national news were supplied to publishers. The peak in suburban projects was undertaken in 1889-90 by Charles R. King & Co. in Chicago. Based on primary and secondary sources; 22 notes.   K. J. Puffer

945. Sternberg, Joel. TELEVISION TOWN. *Chicago Hist. 1975 4(2): 108-117.* Discusses the prominent role of the Chicago School of Television in the history of television, 1930's-53.   S

946. Taylor, George Rogers. GASLIGHT FOSTER: A NEW YORK "JOURNEYMAN JOURNALIST" AT MID-CENTURY. *New York Hist. 1977 58(3): 297-312.* Journalist George Goodrich Foster observed the life of New York City's poor during the mid-19th century. Discusses Foster's published work in the perspective of the urban revolution of the time and the publication by Foster's contemporaries of books about the urban poor. 3 illus., 43 notes.   R. N. Lokken

947. Weinrott, Lester A. CHICAGO RADIO: THE GLORY DAYS. *Chicago Hist. 1974 3(1): 14-22.* Recounts the "Glory Days" of Chicago radio, 1930-40.   S

948. Wolkovich-Valkavičius, William. THE IMPACT OF A CATHOLIC NEWSPAPER ON AN ETHNIC COMMUNITY: THE LITHUANIAN WEEKLY *RYTAS,* 1896-98, WATERBURY, CONNECTICUT. *Lituanus 1978 24(3): 42-53.* Father Joseph Zebris (d. 1915), editor and publisher of the Lithuanian weekly *Rytas,* used his newspaper to improve the welfare of his fellow countrymen in America. Zebris viewed preservation of the Catholic faith as his primary goal and did not hesitate to attack free thinkers in *Rytas.* He was also concerned with the immigrants' assimilation, commending citizenship, literacy, and voting. Through notices of available employment and encouragement of cooperative stores, Zebris aimed to improve the economic welfare of his readers. Health and social services were also a concern. Despite its brief life *Rytas* helped guide Lithuanian immigrants toward assimilation. 10 notes.   K. N. T. Crowther

949. Yodelis, M. A. BOSTON'S FIRST MAJOR NEWSPAPER WAR: A "GREAT AWAKENING" OF FREEDOM. *Journalism Q. 1974 51(2): 207-212.* During Boston's newspaper war in the 1740's between pro- and anti-revivalists, Thomas Fleet in the *Boston Evening Post* wrote and reprinted libertarian statements on freedom of the press.   S

Artistic and Intellectual Life

950. Abegglen, Homer N. THE CHICAGO LITTLE THEATRE, 1912-1917. *Old Northwest 1977 3(2): 153-172.* After failures in Europe, British Maurice Browne became a successful Chicago lecturer and married the talented Ellen Van Volkenburg. Together they began the Chicago Little Theatre in 1912. Browne, with no experience as a director, developed his own systems and experimented with stage lighting techniques. Their greatest artistic success was Euripides's *The Trojan Women* with Ellen in the role of Hecuba. However, Browne, a philanderer, was a poor money manager; and the theater went into debt. *The Trojan Women* was seen as a pacifist play, and the company closed in 1917. Based on Browne's autobiography and on secondary works; 13 notes.   J

951. Arrivi, Francisco. EL ANTIGUO SAN JUAN Y EL TEATRO TAPIA [Old San Juan and the Tapia Theater]. *Rev. del Inst. de Cultura Puertorriqueña [Puerto Rico] 1969 12(45): 40-44.* Historical résumé of theatrical life in Puerto Rico from the 16th century to the present, and of the Tapia Theater.   B. T. (IHE 80495)

952. Barnes, Joseph W. and Barnes, Robert W. FROM BOOKS TO MULTIMEDIA: A HISTORY OF THE REYNOLDS LIBRARY AND THE REYNOLDS AUDIO-VISUAL DEPARTMENT OF THE ROCHESTER PUBLIC LIBRARY. *Rochester Hist. 1974 36(4): 1-40.* Describes the history of the Reynolds Library, Incorporated, of Rochester, New York, 1884-1974, and the Reynolds Audio-Visual Department of the Rochester Public Library founded in 1948.

953. Berger, Morroe. FATS WALLER—THE OUTSIDE INSIDER. *J. of Jazz Studies 1973 1(1): 3-20.* Discusses the career and music of the jazz pianist Fats Waller in Harlem during the 1920's-30's.   S

954. Blair, Virginia K. THE SINGING SOCIETIES AND PHILHARMONIC ORCHESTRA OF BELLEVILLE. *J. of the Illinois State Hist. Soc. 1975 68(5): 386-395.* The heavily German population of Belleville, Illinois, engaged in organized vocal and instrumental musical activities as early as the 1850's. The Philharmonic Society was founded in November 1867 and has maintained its existence as a symphony orchestra to the present day. Despite anti-German feeling during World War I and economic difficulties in the 1930's, the Philharmonic and other Belleville musical groups managed to survive and even to expand their activities.   N. Lederer

955. Blazek, Ron. THE DEVELOPMENT OF LIBRARY SERVICE IN THE NATION'S OLDEST CITY: THE ST. AUGUSTINE LIBRARY ASSOCIATION, 1874-1880. *J. of Lib. Hist. 1979 14(2): 160-182.* Describes the development of the St. Augustine Library Association from its formation until its incorporation. The Association was a privately founded institution reflecting the late 19th-century interest in self-improvement and privatism. Much of the impetus for creating a library came from northerners who wintered in St. Augustine. 70 notes.   S

956. Bloomer, John W. "THE LOAFERS" IN BIRMINGHAM IN THE TWENTIES. *Alabama Rev. 1977 30(2): 101-107.* "The Loafers" was the name a group of aspiring fiction writers gave themselves in the 1920's. The leading personality was Octavus Roy Cohen in whose Birmingham apartment the group usually met. Most members were journalists, who concentrated on light stories and used the weekly gathering to hatch or develop plots and resolve literary problems. Several achieved national fame through major prizes or sensitive analyses of contemporary Southern themes. Primary and secondary sources.   J. F. Vivian

957. Braden, Waldo W. LECTURING IN NEW ORLEANS, 1840-1850. *Southern Studies 1978 17(4): 433-446.* Public lectures to spread culture, inform about science, educate, and entertain were a common phenomenon before the Civil War. In New Orleans between 1840 and 1850, lectures were sponsored primarily by the People's Lyceum and the Young Men's Free Library Association, although independent lecturers also appeared and there were occasionally other sponsors. Lectures were given by professional speakers, university professors, clergymen, and actresses on topics such as free trade, progress, the family, literature, science, pseudoscience, and history. Based on the New Orleans' *Daily Picayune* and on other newspaper accounts; 71 notes.   J. J. Buschen

958. Brazil, John R. AMBROSE BIERCE, JACK LONDON, AND GEORGE STERLING: VICTORIANS BETWEEN TWO WORLDS. *San José Studies 1978 4(1): 13-18.* Examines the literature of three San Franciscans, Ambrose Bierce, Jack London, and George Sterling, as examples of Victorian thought in an increasingly urbanized society; examines value changes in the contemporary society and the tendency toward social and cultural assessment (in Victorian terms) which characterized these authors.

959. Briggs, Martha Wren. SIGNBOARDS AND SIGN PAINTERS OF EIGHTEENTH-CENTURY WILLIAMSBURG. *Virginia Cavalcade 1977 27(2): 68-87.* Discusses the artists and artistry of signboards used by business proprietors in Williamsburg, Virginia, 1740's-70's.

960. Brown, Robert L. CLASSICAL INFLUENCES ON JAZZ. *J. of Jazz Studies. 1976 3(2): 19-35.* Examines the influence and use of classical music in traditional New Orleans jazz improvisations and composition, 1897-1970's.

961. Brubaker, Robert L. 130 YEARS OF OPERA IN CHICAGO. *Chicago Hist. 1979 8(3): 156-169.* Traces the history of opera in Chicago since 29 July 1850, when the first opera ever heard there, *La Sonnambula,* was performed in the Chicago Theatre; discusses operas, opera houses, and opera stars.

962. Brumbaugh, Thomas B. A PETITION OF PHILADELPHIA ARTISTS. *Pennsylvania Hist. 1974 41(2): 161-167.* Comments upon a petition of 29 Philadelphia artists to Pennsylvania state senator David McConaughy in 1868. The artists complained that federal tariffs on imported art works were too low while the tariff on imported art supplies was a burden upon native artists. Notes that the American market for domestic art eventually improved and that the federal tariff on foreign art was increased in 1883, while that on art supplies was reduced in 1890. Illus., 33 notes.   D. C. Swift

963. Bryan, George B. THE HOWARD OPERA HOUSE IN BURLINGTON. *Vermont Hist. 1977 45(4): 197-220.* Melodramas and musicals were most frequently produced at the $100,000 Howard Opera House, 1879-1904. Also shown were grand opera, Gilbert and Sullivan, Shakespeare, farce, pantomime, and amateur theatricals. Burlingtonian John Howard, a New York City innkeeper, hired fellow Vermonter Stephen D. Hatch to design the store block with a 1,300-seat theater. Howard gave the block to an orphanage, which leased it to three managers. Burlington citizens objected to suggestive posters and ticket policies. Health and fire inspection difficulties, the building of a rival theater, and a favorable offer from merchants occupying the block persuaded the managers to close. Provides a list of 41 shows produced. 5 illus., 62 notes.
T. D. S. Bassett

964. Buell, William A. THE GOLDEN AGE OF THE NEWPORT CASINO THEATRE 1927-1934. *Newport Hist. 1973 46(2): 29-35.* The first play at the Newport Casino Theatre was *Hamlet,* 26 July 1927. Many noted persons were present, including Will Rogers, Cornelia Otis Skinner, and Melvyn Douglas.   J. H. Krenkel

965. Callahan, John M. A HISTORY OF THE SECOND OLYMPIC THEATER OF ST. LOUIS, 1882-1916. *Missouri Hist. Soc. Bull. 1975 31(4 part 1): 231-252; 1975 32(1): 3-25.* Part I. Chronicles the growth of the Olympic Theater 1882-89. Mentions notable performers and performances. The theater presented many of the best classical and contemporary comedies and dramas. 9 photos, 82 notes. Part II. Traces the history of the Olympic Theater during 1889-1916. Under the management of Patrick Short and then Walter Sanford the theater remained the St. Louis home for high quality musicals and legitimate theater until 1916, when financial difficulties caused it to close. Based on newspaper sources; 92 notes.   H. T. Lovin

966. Calmenson, Wendy Cunkle. "LIKENESSES TAKEN IN THE MOST APPROVED STYLE": WILLIAM SHEW, PIONEER DAGUERREOTYPIST. *California Hist. Q. 1977 56(1): 2-19.* For more than half a century, William Shew (1820-1903) operated a photography studio in San Francisco. Born in New York, Shew came to California in 1851, after learning daguerreotyping from Samuel Morse. Conservative in technique and style, Shew preferred daguerreotypes and wet-plate methods of early photography and continued to use them long after more advanced techniques were developed. Unlike such contemporaries as Eadweard Muybridge who preferred landscapes and Carleton Watkins, who was known for Yosemite photographs, Shew was not a mobile photographer. His only moves were to change the location of his studio in San Francisco. Clients included such prominent people as David C. Broderick and William Tecumseh Sherman, but Shew's stock in trade were families, children, and babies. His best-known work is a five-plate panoramic view of San Francisco. After his death his negatives and records were lost in the 1906 earthquake and fire. Primary and secondary sources; photos, 84 notes.   A. Hoffman

967. Cavin, Susan. MISSING WOMEN: ON THE VOODOO TRAIL TO JAZZ. *J. of Jazz Studies 1975 3(1): 4-27.* Discusses the role of voodoo women and black magic cults in the evolution of jazz music in the 19th century, emphasizing the Negro culture of New Orleans.

968. Cohen, Blanche Klasmer. BENJAMIN KLASMER'S CONTRIBUTION TO BALTIMORE'S MUSICAL HISTORY. *Maryland Hist. Mag. 1977 72(2): 272-276.* Records the important role played by Benjamin Klasmer in bringing music to Baltimore for over 30 years, first as a cofounder of the Baltimore Symphony Orchestra, in 1916, and then as conductor of the Jewish Educational Alliance Symphony Orchestra in the 1920's. Throughout his career, Klasmer was the "leading musical director of pit orchestras" furnishing accompaniment to silent movies and vaudeville acts at the New Theater, the Garden and Rivoli Theaters, and the Hippodrome until his death in 1949. The tradition which he began is continued today by the Jewish Community Center and other groups. Perhaps his most popular renown, however, comes from his coauthorship of the theme song of the Baltimore Colts. 3 illus.   G. J. Bobango

969. Coiner, Miles W., Jr. THE GRAND OPERA HOUSE AND THE GOLDEN AGE OF THE LEGITIMATE THEATER IN KANSAS CITY. *Missouri Hist. Rev. 1973 67(3): 407-423.* Relates the history of the Grand Opera House in Kansas City, Missouri. Built in 1891 by Abraham Judah and a partner, the Grand earned a national reputation, attracted great stars, and maintained popular prices. In 1916 it was sold and became a movie house until 1926, when it was turned into a parking garage. Based on contemporary newspaper reports and secondary sources; 9 illus., 3 photos, 48 notes.   N. J. Street

970. Cook, Sylvia. GASTONIA: THE LITERARY REVERBERATIONS OF THE STRIKE. *Southern Literary J. 1974 7(1): 49-66.* Poor whites and communism are combined in six novels about the 1929 strike of textile workers in Gastonia, North Carolina.   S

971. Couch, Stephen R. CLASS, POLITICS, AND SYMPHONY ORCHESTRAS. *Society 1976 14(1): 24-29.* Examines the evolution of European and American orchestras as elite institutions during the 19th and 20th centuries; discusses the class bases and political nature of symphonies as exemplified by the New York Philharmonic and the London Philharmonic orchestras.

972. Craven, Wayne. THE ORIGINS OF SCULPTURE IN AMERICA: PHILADELPHIA, 1785-1830. *Am. Art J. 1977 9(2): 4-33.* Discusses sculpture in the United States that originated in Philadelphia.

973. Cuba, Stanley L. POLES IN THE EARLY MUSICAL AND THEATRICAL LIFE OF COLORADO. *Colorado Mag. 1977 54(3): 240-276.* Many internationally known actors and musicians who performed in Denver and other Colorado cities during the 19th and early 20th centuries were of Polish background, such as Helena Modjeska, Ignace Paderewski, and Marcella Sembrich. Coloradans' enthusiasm for the arts was demonstrated by creation of local societies and patronage of grand theaters. Mainly primary sources; 14 illus., 93 notes.
D. A. Hartford

974. Curtis, Julia. AUGUSTA'S FIRST THEATRE SEASON, 1790-91. *Southern Speech Communication J. 1978 43(3): 283-295.* Sketches plays and dramatic presentations by Augusta's first legitimate theater, 1790-91, which was started by actresses Mrs. Robinson and Miss Susannah Wall.

975. Davis, Ronald L.   EARLY JAZZ: ANOTHER LOOK. *Southwest R. 1973 58(1): 1-13, (2): 144-154.* Part I. Traces the three main elements in the New Orleans jazz scene after the Civil War. One element was the Creole blacks who had access "to musical instruments early, had learned to read music, and played in a style essentially derived from Europe." A second group was the uptown blacks who obtained instruments much later and played a "rougher, blues-colored music." The Creole black preferred the clarinet, but the uptown black used the cornet. The third unit was the white jazz tradition known as Dixieland. Among the individual musicians mentioned were John Robichaux, Charles (Buddy) Bolden, Manuel Perez, and George V. (Papa Jack) Laine. Another facet to New Orleans music was the development separately but parallel to the early jazz bands of the barrelhouse piano, a movement strongly influenced by the blues. The star of New Orleans pianists was Ferdinand "Jelly Roll" Morton. Part II. Traces the spread of jazz from the South (especially New Orleans) northward in the early 20th century. The first jazz band to play in the North was Tom Brown with his five-piece Dixieland combination in Chicago in 1914, not the Original Dixieland Jazz Band which played first in New York in 1917. Surprisingly, the music played in New Orleans had never been called jazz; the name was first used in Chicago. Many other groups quickly followed Brown into the North, especially after the closing of Storyville during World War I. The movement to the North prompted many changes—unionization, new instruments, commercialization. Based on taped interviews in the Jazz Archives at Tulane University.   D. F. Henderson

976. Duke, Maurice.   CABELL'S AND GLASGOW'S RICHMOND: THE INTELLECTUAL BACKGROUND OF THE CITY. *Mississippi Q. 1974 27(4): 375-392.* One of a series of three papers on Richmond, Virginia, and southern writing.   S

977. Durrell, Jane.   UPSTAIRS AT MRS. AMELUNG'S. *Cincinnati Hist. Soc. Bull. 1977 35(1): 33-42.* The artists John James Audubon and Aaron H. Corwine were associated with a group which met in the upstairs parlor of Sophia Amelung's boarding house in Cincinnati, Ohio, 1819-24, to discuss and promote the arts in that city.

978. Edmiston, Susan and Cirino, Linda D.   LITERARY HARLEM. *New York Affairs 1976 3(3): 71-90.* In the twenties and thirties, Harlem became a Mecca for talented Negroes, among them an outstanding group of writers and artists. Even now that urban decay has dealt its devastating blows, Harlem remains at the center of black literary consciousness.   J

979. Esbin, Martha.   OLD CAPITOL LIBRARY: ITS HISTORY, CONTENTS, AND RESTORATION. *Ann. of Iowa 1975 42(7): 523-540.* Describes the 1838 acquisitions of Iowa's first library, the Old Capitol Library in Iowa City, made by the first territorial librarian, Theodore S. Parvin. Also discusses recent efforts to restore the collection. 42 notes.   C. W. Olson

980. Finkelman, Paul.   CLASS AND CULTURE IN LATE NINETEENTH-CENTURY CHICAGO: THE FOUNDING OF THE NEWBERRY LIBRARY. *Am. Studies [Lawrence, KS] 1975 16(1): 5-22.* The Newberry Library was founded in the 1880's. Nominally public, the library remained a bastion for upper class values in the genteel tradition. Its collections reflected these interests and largely ignored the city's ethnic minorities. Primary and secondary sources; 64 notes.   J. Andrew

981. Gifford, James P.   THE CELEBRATED WORLD OF CURRIER & IVES: IN WHICH HEROIC FIRE LADDIES RACED TO BATTLE CONFLAGRATIONS WHILE THE POLICE DISAPPEARED IN THE MOST AMAZING WAY. *New-York Hist. Soc. Q. 1975 59(4): 348-365.* The famed Currier & Ives prints originated in New York City in 1835 when Nathaniel Currier began a lithography company. Joined in 1852 by James Merritt Ives (who became a partner five years later), Currier's name soon became well known nationwide. The concern was successful from the start and produced hundreds of prints which became an integral part of Americana. Two interesting conclusions can be reached from a study of the prints. In the first place, the artists saw it as a commercial venture and produced what the general public wanted to buy. They concentrated on firemen as well as pastoral and religious scenes. Secondly, the police as subject matter are noticeable by their absence. The police were probably ignored because of their relatively low

status in the thinking of most citizens, based on unsavory politics and undoubted corruption. On the other hand, the firemen were volunteers who appeared to be identified with the romantic views of the day. At any rate, most American ideas of the mid-19th-century United States are based in part on the Currier & Ives prints. Based on the prints and secondary sources; 6 illus., 24 notes.   C. L. Grant

982. Goldman, Arnold.   THE CULTURE OF THE PROVINCETOWN PLAYERS. *J. of Am. Studies [Great Britain] 1978 12(3): 291-310.* In 1914, Hutchins Hapgood (1869-1944), his Progressive friends, radicals, and New York City salon intellectuals such as Mabel Dodge established a theater group at Provincetown, Massachusetts. The group planned drama productions critical of contemporary American culture. Then George Cram Cook influenced the group to focus on productions which were artistically superior and social reformist in content. By 1917, the Provincetown Players were producing the works of noted playwrights such as Eugene O'Neill (1888-1953). Based on memoirs by the participants in Provincetown Players and archival source materials; 25 notes.   H. T. Lovin

983. Goode, James M.   OUTDOOR SCULPTURE: WASHINGTON'S OVERLOOKED MONUMENTS. *Historic Preservation 1973 25(1): 4-14.* Drawing on his book, *Open-Air Sculpture of Washington, D.C.: An Historical Guide* (1974), the author discusses many examples of Washington's 600 open-air sculptures. They range from the 1809 Lenthall Monument, the city's oldest, to the large abstract sculpture collection recently acquired by the Smithsonian Institution. Types represented include statues, equestrian statues, relief panels, aluminum and bronze doors, fountains, architectural sculpture, pediments, and animal, cemetery, and abstract sculpture. 13 photos.   R. M. Frame III

984. Graham, Don.   FRANK NORRIS AND "LES JEUNES": ARCHITECTURAL CRITICISM AND AESTHETIC VALUES. *Am. Literary Realism, 1870-1910 1978 11(2): 235-242.* Describes Frank Norris's relationship with "Les Jeunes" in the late 19th century during San Francisco's cultural renaissance; "Les Jeunes" were five young men who published the *Lark* from 1895 to 1897 in one of many activities to enliven San Francisco culture.

985. Grosch, Anthony R.   SOCIAL ISSUES IN EARLY CHICAGO NOVELS. *Chicago Hist. 1975 4(2): 68-77.* Discusses novels written during 1890-1910 by such men as Hamlin Garlin, Theodore Dreiser, Frank Norris, and Upton Sinclair.   S

986. Hawks, Graham P.   A NINETEENTH-CENTURY SCHOOL LIBRARY: EARLY YEARS IN MILWAUKEE. *J. of Lib. Hist. 1977 12(4): 359-363.* Provides a history of Milwaukee's first public school library, founded by Increase A. Lapham in 1851. The nature of the collection is discussed, and some specific titles mentioned. Primary and secondary sources; 9 notes.   A. C. Dewees

987. Head, Faye E.   THE BIRTH AND DEATH OF THE TULANE AND THE CRESCENT: TWIN-THEATRES OF NEW ORLEANS, LOUISIANA. *Louisiana Studies 1976 15(3): 294-303.* In 1896 Marc Klaw (1858-1936) and Abraham Lincoln Erlanger (1860-1930) formed a Theatrical Syndicate to facilitate scheduling of touring shows by combining theaters and shows under the control of a single agent. In New Orleans in 1898 they built opulent twin theaters, the Tulane and the Crescent, to put on the shows they controlled. The theaters were created to monopolize theatrical productions in New Orleans and also to house the large touring companies of the day. Seating about 1,500 each and designed in Louis XV style, they were eminently successful for 20 years. They succumbed to changing fashions in entertainment and were demolished in 1937. Based on contemporary newspaper accounts and secondary sources; 46 notes.   J. Buschen

988. Hedges, William L.   BENJAMIN RUSH, CHARLES BROCKDEN BROWN, AND THE AMERICAN PLAGUE YEAR. *Early Am. Lit. 1973 7(3): 295-311.* Compares the letters of Benjamin Rush (1745?-1813) to his wife Julia during the plague of 1793 in Philadelphia with the two plague novels of Charles Brockden Brown (1771-1810), *Ormond* and *Arthur Mervyn.* These writings reveal contrasts in character, personality, ideas, and attitudes. Rush leaves a record of heroic fortitude which his friend J. C. Lettsom, the English Quaker physician,

compared to that of Hippocrates during the plague of Athens. Where Rush's conception of virtue was clear, at least to himself, Brown's was infinitely complicated. They had radically contrasting ways of thinking about human behavior and its susceptibility to understanding and interpretation by science, religion, and literature. Sharpened by the common factor of the yellow fever, the contrast shows the precarious cultural unity of late-18th-century American intellectual life and the power of the forces that were beginning to rend it. Based on primary and secondary sources; 43 notes. D. P. Wharton

989. Hendrickson, Walter B. JACKSONVILLE ARTISTS OF THE 1870'S. *J. of the Illinois State Hist. Soc. 1977 70(4): 258-275.* Discusses the careers of Bohemian artist Ebenezer Mason, portraitist-turned-banker William S. Woodman, artist-photographer George W. Clark, and painter-sculptor Robert Campbell Smith. Considers their works and assesses the influence of Jacksonville, Illinois, a small town that is unusually rich in colleges, private academies, and cultural and literary associations. 17 illus., 82 notes. J

990. Hendrickson, Walter B. SCIENCE AND CULTURE IN NINETEENTH CENTURY MICHIGAN. *Michigan Hist. 1973 57(2): 140-150.* Traces the histories of the Flint Scientific Institute, 1853-77, and the Lyceum of Natural History in Grand Rapids which evolved into the Kent Scientific Institute, 1854-ca. 1917. The latter became the basis for the Grand Rapids Public Museum. They made important contributions to the cultural and intellectual life of their communities. 3 illus., 24 notes. D. L. Smith

991. Hennessey, Gregg R. JUNÍPERO SERRA MUSEUM: ARCHITECTURAL, CULTURAL, AND URBAN LANDMARK. *J. of San Diego Hist. 1979 25(3): 221-241.* Gives the history of the construction and accomplishments of the Junípero Serra Museum in Presidio Park in San Diego, which is celebrating its 50th birthday in 1979, dating to 1907 when the land where the museum was built was purchased.

992. Hennessey, Thomas J. THE BLACK CHICAGO ESTABLISHMENT 1919-1930. *J. of Jazz Studies 1975 2(1): 15-45.* Discusses the conflict in Chicago black jazz of the 1920's between "small groups playing improvised music and large groups with ties to the European classical tradition . . . developing a hot, big band, arranged jazz style. . . ." S

993. Henstell, Bruce. CHORDS AND DISCORDS. *Westways 1977 69(9): 28-31, 75.* The Los Angeles Philharmonic Orchestra began in 1862 under the direction of Adolf Willhartitz, and grew successively to its present status under conductors A. J. Stamm, Harley Hamilton, L. E. (Len) Behymer, and William Andrews Clark.

994. Hibbs, Jack Eugene. A HISTORY OF THE TOLEDO PUBLIC LIBRARY, 1873-1964. *Northwest Ohio Q. 1974 46(3): 72-116.*

995. Holcomb, Grant. THE FORGOTTEN LEGACY OF JEROME MYERS (1867-1940): PAINTER OF NEW YORK'S LOWER EAST SIDE. *Am. Art J. 1977 9(1): 78-91.* Jerome Myers was a "city realist" whose "early paintings of unglamorous city scenes directly defied the doctrines of academic art, while his active participation in several progressive art organizations helped challenge the narrow exhibition policies of the National Academy of Design." Discusses his involvement with the Armory Show of 1913. Based on the Myers Papers, paintings, and other primary and secondary sources; 15 fig., 56 notes. R. M. Frame, III

996. Holliday, Joseph E. STUART WALKER'S CINCINNATI THEATER. *Cincinnati Hist. Soc. Bull. 1977 35(3): 151-172.* Examines the Stuart Walker Theater in Cincinnati during 1922-31, including a biographical sketch of Stuart Walker (1880-1941), as representative of the successful integration of high quality performances with active community support at a time when most legitimate theater was expiring.

997. Hollingsworth, Gerelyn. LEGITIMATE THEATER IN ST. LOUIS, 1870-1879. *Missouri Hist. Rev. 1975 69(3): 260-281.* St. Louisans who went to DeBar's Grand Opera House and the Olympic Theatre during 1870-79 were fortunate, since they witnessed the simultaneous decline of one theatrical system and the rise of another. The great Shakespearean actors who delighted in tragic roles were replaced with large

companies of actors who traveled with all the scenery and costumes needed for a given play. The change is attributed to the development of the box set and the railroad. The box set called for realistic acting. This meant that the grand gestures and violent pacing had to be scaled down to fit the set. The railroads made it possible for a New York producer to take a successful play into the provinces with a large troupe, realistic sets and costumes. Based on primary and secondary sources; illus., 48 notes. W. F. Zornow

998. Horowitz, Helen Lefkowitz. VARIETIES OF CULTURAL EXPERIENCE OF JANE ADDAMS' CHICAGO. *Hist. of Educ. Q. 1974 14(1): 69-86.* Analyzes the attitudes toward and the definitions of art in Chicago and compares them with Jane Addams' ideas. Discusses the roots of her ideas first in Ruskinian idealism and elitism. Later Addams differed with her art patron supporters over politics and reform and her belief that the establishment of city-wide cultural institutions could be achieved in the political arena. Based on primary and secondary sources; 69 notes. L. C. Smith

999. Horowitz, Helen Lefkowitz. THE ART INSTITUTE OF CHICAGO: THE FIRST FORTY YEARS. *Chicago Hist. 1979 8(1): 2-15.* Covers 1879-1909.

1000. Howe, Barbara J. UNITING THE USEFUL AND BEAUTIFUL: THE ARTS IN CINCINNATI. *Old Northwest 1978 4(4): 319-336.* In the late 19th century industrialists, desiring to control behavior and values of workers, established and supported cultural institutions. The Cincinnati Art Museum and Art Academy were established under the assumption that workers who acquired artistic knowledge would be better disciplined, produce better designed work, and thus more profits for employers. Thus the museum received very strong upper-class male support but no support from tax funds. The Art Academy was founded in 1884, and the museum was dedicated in 1886. Based on annual reports of the museum and secondary works; 31 notes. J. N. Dickinson

1001. Hume, Paul and Hume, Ruth. OSCAR AND THE OPERA. *Am. Heritage 1973 24(2): 60-69, 87-88.* Oscar Hammerstein (1848?-1919) ran away from his affluent home in Berlin in rebellion against his classical and musical training. At age 15 he pawned his violin for steerage passage to America and found employment in a cigar factory. He invented and patented superior cigar manufacturing machinery. He put his new-found capital into uptown New York real estate. He then indulged in his true ambition; he tirelessly built theaters on a grand scale, sometimes for his own plays and music. In 1906 Hammerstein challenged the venerable Metropolitan Opera with his own Manhattan Opera House, but the battle lasted only a few seasons. Other attempts to "bull" his way back into the opera business failed. 10 illus. D. L. Smith

1002. Inge, M. Thomas. RICHMOND, VIRGINIA, AND SOUTHERN WRITING: INTRODUCTION. *Mississippi Q. 1974 27(4): 371-373.* Introduces three papers on the importance of Richmond, Virginia, in the careers of Ellen Glasgow and James Branch Cabell, and their relationship to the Southern Literary Renaissance. S

1003. Inkster, Ian. ROBERT GOODACRE'S ASTRONOMY LECTURES (1823-1825), AND THE STRUCTURE OF SCIENTIFIC CULTURE IN PHILADELPHIA. *Ann. of Sci. [Great Britain] 1978 35(4): 353-364.* Notes popular scientific culture and its significance in the city of Philadelphia during the 1820's. The impact of the public lecturer Robert Goodacre was at least some function of the difference between the demand for popular science and the provision of associational science in a city on the brink of fundamental social change. J

1004. Johnson, Claudia D. THAT GUILTY THIRD TIER: PROSTITUTION IN NINETEENTH-CENTURY AMERICAN THEATERS. *Am. Q. 1975 27(5): 575-584.* The assignment of prostitutes to the third tier in 19th-century theaters was a serious problem to those working for the survival of the theatrical institution. Not only was the issue one of continual controversy between moralists and artists, but it also had an impact on theater design, theatrical economics, and the acceptance and support of the theater in American life. The theater gradually achieved respectability only through a dissociation from prostitution. Based on primary and secondary sources. N. Lederer

1005. King, Richard L. THE BOOK COLLECTIONS OF THE NEW YORK AND SAN FRANCISCO MERCANTILE LIBRARIES. *Business Hist. [Great Britain] 1978 20(1): 37-62.* The mercantile library flourished in the mid-19th century. Discusses New York City's (founded 1820) and San Francisco's (founded 1853). Discusses the nature of the book collection, circulating statistics, and other activities as part of the 19th-century educational movement. 6 appendixes.

B. L. Crapster

1006. Kingsbury, Martha. SARGENT'S MURALS IN THE BOSTON PUBLIC LIBRARY. *Winterthur Portfolio 1976 11: 153-172.* Analyzes John Singer Sargent's (1856-1925) mural commission and resulting pieces of art for the Boston Public Library. Recent scholarship on the artist recognizes the symbolic quality of Sargent's work at the Library. Based on primary and secondary sources; 27 illus., 17 notes.

N. A. Kuntz

1007. Kwiat, Joseph J. THE "ASH-CAN" SCHOOL: THE MAGAZINE AS MATRIX. *Can. Rev. of Am. Studies 1976 7(2): 163-175.* Describes the revolt against the Genteel Tradition and the origins of the realism of the "Ashcan School" of painters. While employed in the 1890's as illustrators by newspaper and magazine publishers, John Sloan (1871-1952), Everett Shinn (1876-1953), William Glackens (1870-1938), and George Luks (1867-1933) refined their artistic values, ideas, and goals. Robert Henri (1865-1929) greatly encouraged them to do so. Thus, they were prepared to plunge headlong into the new realism when they abandoned commercial art after the turn of the century. Based on primary and secondary sources; 4 photos, 35 notes.

H. T. Lovin

1008. Laurence, Anya. THE WATERSIDE MUSEUM. *New-England Galaxy 1977 19(1): 52-58.* Recounts the life of Annie Adams (1834-1913), who married James T. Fields in November 1854 in Boston, where her home became a literary "museum." Her roles as author and consultant to authors are noted. Her friendships with Sarah Orme Jewett, Oliver Wendell Holmes, and Julia Ward Howe are also described. 3 illus.

P. C. Marshall

1009. Lax, John. CHICAGO'S BLACK JAZZ MUSICIANS IN THE TWENTIES: PORTRAIT OF AN ERA. *J. of Jazz Studies 1974 1(2): 107-127.*

1010. Luckingham, Bradford. AGENTS OF CULTURE IN THE URBAN WEST: MERCHANTS AND MERCANTILE LIBRARIES IN MID-NINETEENTH CENTURY ST. LOUIS AND SAN FRANCISCO. *J. of the West 1978 17(2): 28-35.* A desire for the moral and intellectual development of their profession prompted western merchants to establish libraries in St. Louis, Missouri, (1846) and in San Francisco, California, (1853) modeled on the mercantile libraries of eastern cities. Members of the Mercantile Library Association were also concerned about the cultural and educational development of immigrant and rural youth; teachers at the libraries provided training in business skills and the liberal arts. To counter the temptations of city life, the libraries provided chess, draughts, and backgammon games, lectures, art galleries, and natural history exhibits. Primary sources; 4 photos, 22 notes.

B. S. Porter

1011. Luckingham, Bradford. LIBRARIES AND MUSEUMS IN EMERGENT SAN FRANCISCO: A NOTE ON THE PURSUIT OF CULTURE IN THE URBAN FAR WEST. *Pacific Historian 1973 17(3): 4-11.* Discusses San Francisco in the 1850's. S

1012. Lynes, Russell. COUNTRYMAN-POET LET SOME FRESH AIR INTO OLD NEW YORK. *Smithsonian 1974 4(12): 80-87.* An account of the life and career of William Cullen Bryant (1794-1875). Bryant's first collection of poems appeared in 1821, including "Thanatopsis." In 1825 he came to New York and was editor of the New York *Evening Post* from 1829 until he died in 1878. Bryant strongly advocated preserving New York greenery. "Can we have no fresh air, no green trees, no agreeable walks and drives," Bryant wrote, "that Smith may have more houses to let, and Brown and Co. have less distance to go to their warehouses and ships?" Bryant became a man of affairs in New York City, and "a promoter of the arts, a patron and a preservationist at a time when all three were rare." 4 illus., 2 photos.

D. D. Cameron

1013. Mann, Maybelle. THE NEW YORK GALLERY OF FINE ARTS: "A SOURCE OF REFINEMENT." *Am. Art J. 1979 11(1): 76-86.* The first art gallery in New York City was the New York Gallery of Fine Arts, established in 1844. Based primarily on the collection of Luman Reed (1787-1836), the collection was shown in several locations over the next decade. Little expansion of the collection took place and it was absorbed by the New York Historical Society in 1858. The Gallery failed because it charged high admission, because other galleries with more modern works opened, and because the Luman collection, while progressive for its day, stopped in 1836. Primary and secondary sources; 11 illus., 50 notes.

J. J. Buschen

1014. Marzio, Peter C. A MUSEUM AND A SCHOOL: AN UNEASY BUT CREATIVE UNION. *Chicago Hist. 1979 8(1): 20-23, 44-52.* Traces the history of the Art Institute of Chicago, an art museum and school, from its founding in 1879 as the Chicago Academy of Fine Arts.

1015. Mattern, Carolyn J. MARY MAC LANE: A FEMINIST OPINION. *Montana 1977 27(4): 54-63.* Mary MacLane (1881-1929) wrote three books—*The Story of Mary MacLane* (1902), *My Friend Annabel Lee* (1903), and *I, Mary MacLane* (1917)—authored numerous articles, then wrote and starred in a movie, *Men Who Have Made Love To Me* (1917). Her activities created a sensation in her hometown of Butte, Montana, and nationwide. Although atypical, she was not an eccentric woman. Her ideas arose and developed from her environment, reflected the mainstream of feminist thought, and represented ideas or feelings of educated, middle class women during that era. An unhappy, self-centered young woman, MacLane craved understanding and self-expression, believing all women should be free to live fully expressive lives. During 1902-10, MacLane found happiness in the intellectual bohemia of New York City's Greenwich Village and had several affairs with men, viewing the associations dispassionately. After her return to Butte in 1910, and a near fatal bout with scarlet fever, MacLane's writing evidenced a sense of life's fragility and her own mortality; she died lonely and forgotten in Chicago. Based on writings of Mary MacLane, contemporary newspapers and journals; 3 illus., 28 notes.

R. C. Myers

1016. Maurer, Joyce C. FEDERAL THEATRE IN CINCINNATI. *Cincinnati Hist. Soc. Bull. 1974 32(1-2): 29-45.* Discusses plays staged by the Federal Theater Project in conjunction with the Works Progress Administration in Cincinnati 1935-39, including the employment of actors.

1017. McGinty, Brian. THE TROUBLE BEGAN IN SAN FRANCISCO. *Am. Hist. Illus. 1975 9(10): 10-15.* Describes Samuel L. Clemens's (1835-1910) transformation from silver speculator to the gifted writer Mark Twain. Clemens came to San Francisco in 1864 to make a fortune in silver stocks from Nevada where he had tired of working as a newspaper reporter. His speculating failed, and he got a job as a newspaper reporter in the city. During this time he met Bret Harte, who advised him on writing style and technique. Clemens lost his job in December 1864, and went to Sonora, California. When he returned to San Francisco in 1865, he wrote free-lance for various newspapers and journals about San Francisco and his experiences in the Mother Lode country. He quickly became a writer of recognition, giving lectures as well. His *Innocents Abroad*, published in 1868, was an instant success. Clemens returned to the East, but never forgot San Francisco. Partially based on Twain's autobiography and other writings; 3 illus., 4 photos.

N. J. Street

1018. Meadows, Eddie S. JAZZ ANTECEDENTS. *Freedomways 1977 17(2): 93-99.* The West African influence on the music of New Orleans contributed to the formation of modern jazz through the Congo Square ceremonies, where slaves could participate without inhibition, and through the fusion of West African and Catholic religious ceremonies in secret societies employing black bands. Later the close of the Civil War was significant to the development of jazz, as disbanding military units sold their band instruments cheaply or abandoned them on the battle fields.

1019. Metcalfe, Ralph, Jr. THE BLUES, CHICAGO STYLE. *Chicago Hist. 1974 3(1): 4-13.* Covers the history of Negro blues musicians in Chicago, 1920-74. S

1020. Moran, Irene E. BROOKLYN PUBLIC LIBRARY: 75 YEARS YOUNG. *Lib. Hist. Rev. [India] 1974 1(1): 55-82.*

1021. Moure, Nancy. FIVE LOS ANGELES ARTISTS IN THE COLLECTIONS OF THE LOS ANGELES COUNTY MUSEUM OF ART. *Southern California Q. 1975 57(1): 27-51.* Describes five artists who lived in and painted themes of southern California at various points in their careers in the early 20th century. William V. Cahill (d.1924), Norman Chamberlain (b.1887), Henri Gilbert De Kruif (1882-1944), Arthur H. Gilbert (1894?-1970), and Granville Redmond (1871-1935) were all professionally trained artists in the Los Angeles area. Their relative prominence ranged from little-known to regional acclaim. Calls for further study on early artists in southern California in order to create a better understanding of the history of art in this region. Primary and secondary sources; reproductions, 83 notes.   A. Hoffman

1022. Newberger, Eli H. THE DEVELOPMENT OF NEW OR-LEANS AND STRIDE PIANO STYLES. *J. of Jazz Studies 1977 4(2): 43-71.* Discusses piano playing styles of New Orleans jazz artists Jelly Roll Morton, Dink Johnson, Lil Hardin, Frank Melrose, Paul Lingle, Clarence Williams, James P. Johnson, Luckey Roberts, Eubie Blake, Fats Waller, Art Tatum, Willie "The Lion" Smith, Wally Rose, and Ralph Sutton, 1920's-40's.

1023. Noe, Marcia. "A ROMANTIC AND MIRACULOUS CITY" SHAPES THREE MIDWESTERN WRITERS. *Western Illinois Regional Studies 1978 1(2): 176-198.* Supporters of progressivism, socialism, and feminism, Floyd Dell, George Cram Cook, and Susan Glaspell, all spent formative years in Davenport, Iowa, where their writing styles and social attitudes were formed, 1903-11.

1024. Over, William. NEW YORK'S AFRICAN THEATRE: THE VICISSITUDES OF THE BLACK ACTOR. *Afro-Americans in New York Life and Hist. 1979 3(2): 7-13.* The African Theatre in New York City, in existence during 1820-23, was the first black acting company in America.

1025. Quimby, Ian M. G. SILVER. *Am. Art J. 1975 7(1): 68-81.* Discusses silversmithing during the 18th century, focusing on artisans (including Paul Revere) primarily from the northern colonial cities of Boston, Baltimore, New York, and Philadelphia.

1026. Regnery, Henry. STONE, KIMBALL, AND *THE CHAP-BOOK*. *Chicago Hist. 1975 4(2): 87-95.* Describes the cultural contribution of Herbert Stuart Stone and Hannibal Ingalls Kimball to Chicago, 1893-1906, with their literary journal, *The Chap-Book.*   S

1027. Rhoades, Elizabeth Adams THE FURNISHING OF PORTS-MOUTH HOUSES, 1750-1775. *Hist. New Hampshire 1973 28(1): 1-19.* Although few identifiable pieces have survived, the New England furniture of Revolutionary War days is known from inventories in probate records. Analysis of 31 room-by-room lists reveals family life as well as décor. The parlors had the best furniture, including a dining table, six to eight chairs, ceramics, glass and looking glass, and sometimes a desk, clock, or candlesticks. Few houses had dining rooms. Bedrooms contained one or two beds, chairs, and sometimes a chest of drawers and table. Pewter, candlesticks, earthenware, and "old" furniture—perhaps flagbottomed chairs and a pine table—stayed in the utilitarian kitchen. Some houses had retail shops and a few had craftsmen's workshops. Wood paneling was popular, but both wood and plaster walls were painted or papered. 8 illus., 26 notes.   T. D. S. Bassett

1028. Riedy, James L. SCULPTURE AT THE COLUMBIAN EX-POSITION. *Chicago Hist. 1975 4(2): 99-107.* Describes Chicago's public sculpture at the 1893 Exposition.   S

1029. Ritchey, David. THE PHILADELPHIA COMPANY PER-FORMS IN BALTIMORE. *Maryland Hist. Mag. 1976 71(1): 80-85.* Reviews the founding of the Philadelphia company of the Chestnut Street Theatre by Thomas Wignell in 1792, and the manner in which he used Baltimore as an adjunct center for his troupe between 1794 and 1802. Examines existing theater conditions and highlights of three seasons of activity in Baltimore—1795, 1797, and 1798. With his comanager, Alexander Reinagle, Wignell built the Holliday Street Theatre by selling

shares. The repertoire consisted mostly of 18th-century English comedies, with occasional melodramas using elaborate settings and devices. Local drama critics infuriated the actors during the 1795 season by describing mainly their weaknesses, and the City Council continually forbade performances between June and October each year, while taxing the company heavily. The 1797 season was highly successful despite these handicaps, but the fall of 1798 brought illness, death, financial difficulties, and resignations from the troupe. Nevertheless, the Baltimore atmosphere was generally receptive, and this support enabled Wignell to keep his large company together. Primary sources; 34 notes.   G. J. Bobango

1030. Ritchey, David. ROBERT DE LAPOUYADE: THE LAST OF THE LOUISIANA SCENE PAINTERS. *Louisiana Hist. 1973 14(1): 5-20.* Robert de Lapouyade was the leading set designer and scene painter for the most popular theaters in New Orleans, 1902-27. With the decline of the legitimate theater his profession became obsolete and he turned to designing department store windows and Mardi Gras floats. Based on newspapers, interviews, and the Robert de Lapouyade Collection at Louisiana State University; 9 photos, 25 notes.

R. L. Woodward

1031. Saloman, Ora Frishberg. VICTOR PELISSIER, COMPOSER IN FEDERAL NEW YORK AND PHILADELPHIA. *Pennsylvania Mag. of Hist. and Biog. 1978 102(1): 93-102.* French composer Victor Pelissier left France during the Revolution. He gave concerts in Philadelphia in 1792, when he arrived via the West Indies. The traveling Old American Company, finding in New York City a permanent home in 1798, engaged him as hornist and composer. In Philadelphia after 1811, he published *Pelissier's Columbian Melodies.* A leading composer, he spent his last years in or near New York. Based on published sources and secondary works; 24 notes.   T. H. Wendel

1032. Samuels, Peggy and Samuels, Harold. FREDERIC REMING-TON'S STIRRINGS IN KANSAS CITY. *Missouri Hist. Soc. Bull. 1978 35(1): 36-46.* Best remembered as a noted artist of western military and Indian life, Frederic Remington (1861-1909) sold his sheep ranch at Plum Grove, Kansas, in 1883 and moved to Kansas City, Missouri. There he engaged in various enterprises ranging from hardware storekeeping to a silent partnership in a saloon business. The enterprises failed and Remington solved his financial problems by selling his art work. Later Remington judged unsatisfactory his artistic productions during his years in Kansas City. Archival and newspaper sources; sketch by Remington; 49 notes.   H. T. Lovin

1033. Sanders, John. LOS ANGELES GRAND OPERA ASSOCIA-TION: THE FORMATIVE YEARS, 1924-1926. *Southern California Q. 1973 55(3): 261-302.* An account of the first three seasons of the Los Angeles Grand Opera Association. Much of the success of the association's early years was due to the dozens of women in Los Angeles society who dedicated themselves to making opera a successful cultural venture in the city, holding social functions, encouraging block ticket sales, and going to the opera in grand style. Critics generally received the operas favorably, though with some comment about shoddy scenery and production values. The major stars, however, received generous praise for the performances. Despite the early successes, Los Angeles never developed into a major opera center. Based on contemporary published materials and secondary studies; photos, 145 notes, appendices.   A. Hoffman

1034. Schlereth, Thomas J. A ROBIN'S EGG RENAISSANCE: CHICAGO CULTURE, 1893-1933. *Chicago Hist. 1979 8(3): 144-155.* Art, literature, music, radio, theater, the movies, and opera in Chicago from 1893 to 1933 were characterized as a "Robin's Egg Renaissance" by author Sherwood Anderson.

1035. Schumacher, Alan T. NEWPORT: LITERATURE AND PRINTING. *Newport Hist. 1977 50(3): 45-64.* Examines printing and publishing and the absence of literature 1700-1850 in Newport, Rhode Island.

1036. Scott, Elizabeth S. "IN FAME, NOT SPECIE": *THE RE-VIEWER*, RICHMOND'S OASIS IN "THE SAHARA OF THE BO-ZART." *Virginia Cavalcade 1978 27(3): 128-143. The Reviewer*, a small literary journal in Richmond, Virginia, during the 1920's, made Richmond the literary center of the South.

1037. Sears, Donald A. MUSIC IN EARLY PORTLAND. *Maine Hist. Soc. Q. 1977 16(3): 131-160*. Traces church influence upon Portland's post-Revolutionary music. Describes the contributions of Supply Belcher (1751-1836), John Merrick (1766-1862) and Dr. Benjamin Vaughan (1751-1838). Notes the development of musical societies, the musical contributions of the Ostinellis, the organization of the Portland Band in 1820, and the opening of a singing school by Francis L. Ilsley in 1833.   P. C. Marshall

1038. Spraul, Judith. CULTURAL BOOSTERISM: THE CONSTRUCTION OF MUSIC HALL. *Cincinnati Hist. Soc. Bull. 1976 34(3): 189-203*. Civic boosting in Cincinnati, promotion of local art and industry, and cultivation of civic pride and national reputation all converged in the construction of a permanent Music Hall in 1877.

1039. Stewart, David Marshall. WILLIAM T. BERRY AND HIS FABULOUS BOOKSTORE: NASHVILLE'S LITERARY EMPORIUM WITHOUT PARALLEL. *Tennessee Hist. Q. 1978 37(1): 36-48*. Berry's Bookstore, the best west of the Allegheny Mountains, existed from 1835 to 1876. It was the general meeting place of leading politicians. Its reading room served primarily as a gentleman's club for years. Berry's strong Union stand at the outbreak of the Civil War, however, heralded the beginning of the decline of his bookstore. Secondary material; 3 notes.   M. B. Lucas

1040. Story, Ronald. CLASS AND CULTURE IN BOSTON: THE ATHENAEUM, 1807-1860. *Am. Q. 1975 27(2): 178-199*. The founding of the library, The Athenaeum, provided a private gathering place for the Bostonian elite patterned after the British (especially the Liverpool) model. Business and cultural influences were combined in its exclusive, hereditary membership, shaping a durable elite within the capitalist order in Boston. The Athenaeum assisted in building civic pride, fostering learning, and providing stability, consolidation, and career enhancement for the Bostonian upper class.   N. Lederer

1041. Street, Douglas O. BANDS'S OPERA HOUSE, IN THE CULTURAL HUB OF CRETE, 1877-1900. *Nebraska Hist. 1979 60(1): 58-76*. Delineates the history of the three story opera house constructed by Dr. Charles W. Band in the winter of 1877. It was the first brick building in Crete and it still stands. The emphasis is on the uses to which the opera house was put in the last years of the 19th century, commenting on local and visiting performers.   R. Lowitt

1042. Swift, Mary Grace. ST. LOUIS'S RESIDENT BALLET COMPANY: 1852. *Missouri Hist. Rev. 1978 72(2): 121-135*. Ballet generally supplemented other productions, but in 1852 Joseph M. Field decided that his new Varieties Theatre in St. Louis would include a regular ballet troupe. The venture lasted only one year. Provides valuable information on the careers of the performers before and after their stay in St. Louis and on the other dance troupes with which they were associated. Primary and secondary sources; 5 illus., 29 notes.   W. F. Zornow

1043. Swift, Mary Grace. TERPSICHORE IN THE WESTERN ATHENS: ANTE-BELLUM BALLET IN THE QUEEN CITY. *Cincinnati Hist. Soc. Bull. 1977 35(2): 79-97*. Traces the history of dance performances in Cincinnati from 1787 to the Civil War, utilizing local newspaper reviews to indicate the public's reaction to this form of entertainment.

1044. Tauranac, John ART AND THE I.R.T.: THE FIRST SUBWAY ART. *Historic Preservation 1973 25(4): 26-31*. From 1914 to 1917 handsome mosaics and bas-reliefs depicting local and national history were mounted on the walls of New York City subway stations. Gives 15 examples of decorative motifs for which the history has been researched. Illus.   E. P. Stickney

1045. Thompson, Roger. WORTHINGTON CHAUNCEY FORD'S *BOSTON BOOK MARKET, 1679-1700*: SOME CORRECTIONS AND ADDITIONS. *Massachusetts Hist. Soc. Pro. 1974 86: 67-78*. Returns to the original documents to correct several mistranscriptions, ambiguities, and identifications of titles and editions included in the appendixes to Ford's book, published in Boston in 1917. Ford's argument that London booksellers misjudged the reading tastes of Bostonians is regarded as a weak one; most consignments of books sent to Boston

contained goodly numbers of so-called light literature. Based on the Jeffries Family Papers, Massachusetts Historical Society; 11 notes, index.   G. W. R. Ward

1046. Trachtenberg, Marvin. THE STATUE OF LIBERTY: TRANSPARENT BANALITY OR AVANT-GARDE CONUNDRUM? *Art in Am. 1974 62(3): 36-43*.

1047. Trent, Robert F. THE JOINERS AND JOINERY OF MIDDLESEX COUNTY, MASSACHUSETTS, 1630-1730. Quimby, Ian M. G., ed. *Winterthur Conference Report, 20th, 1974: Arts of the Anglo-American Community in the Seventeenth Century* (Charlottesville: U. Pr. of Virginia, 1975), pp. 123-148. Studies woodworkers and their pieces of 17th-century Middlesex County, principally Charlestown and Cambridge.   S

1048. Unsigned. AUGUSTUS KÖLLNER'S STATEN ISLAND DRAWINGS. *Staten Island Hist. 1971 31(6): 45-48*. Reproduces four 19th-century drawings of Staten Island from the W. C. Arnold Collection at the Metropolitan Museum of Art. Köllner was born in Dusseldorf in 1813, came to the United States in 1839 or 1840, and settled in Philadelphia. Additional Köllner drawings are believed to be extant, but as yet are undiscovered. Illus.   G. Kurland

1049. Unsigned. WHEN BRIDGEPORT WAS BEAUTIFUL. *Am. Heritage 1974 25(4): 16-31*. Collection of paintings of Bridgeport, Connecticut, by the 19th-century artist, J. F. Huge.   S

1050. Vacha, J. E. BLACK MAN ON THE GREAT WHITE WAY. *J. of Popular Culture 1973 7(2): 288-301*. Discusses the flowering of American drama during the 1920's in the context of Negro dramatists working and writing on Broadway and off-Broadway productions in New York City.   S

1051. Wall, Cheryl A. PARIS AND HARLEM: TWO CULTURE CAPITALS. *Phylon 1974 35(1): 64-73*. "What both white American and Afro-American writers actually sought during the twenties was a literature that would be their own unique voice.... In attempting to achieve their goals, they gravitated toward two cities—Paris and Harlem—which they felt would provide creative stimuli." Both overromanticized their new settings. Harlem became, to a larger extent than Paris, a rich source of material for the authors. 19 notes.   E. P. Stickney

1052. Ward, Kathryn Painter. THE FIRST PROFESSIONAL THEATER IN MARYLAND IN ITS COLONIAL SETTING. *Maryland Hist. Mag. 1975 70(1): 29-44*. Analyzes the movements and repertoire of The Company of Comedians from Virginia who began performances at the New Theater in Annapolis 22 June 1752 with John Gay's *Beggar's Opera* and David Garrick's *The Lying Valet* as the afterpiece. Headed by Walter Murray and Thomas Kean, the company performed plays which had "already proved popular in England." Restrictive ordinances against the theater such as those in Boston or Philadelphia were missing in Annapolis, and the troop enjoyed an excellent reception. The general cultural milieu of Marlyand is discussed, and summaries given of major plays which dominated the company's offerings, largely works by Susannah Centlivre, Henry Fielding, George Farquhar, and George Lillo. While comedy prevailed, *King Richard III* was given at the end of the season in December. The company also performed in Upper Marlborough, "where the first employment of an orchestra" in America is recorded, and in Chester-Town and possibly other port cities. While perhaps "not a great troupe," it served to whet appetites for the great Hallam-Douglass Company eight years later. Based on the *Maryland Gazette*, playbills, and secondary sources; illus., 22 notes.
                                                         G. J. Bobango

1053. Ward, Kathryn Painter. THE MARYLAND THEATRICAL SEASON OF 1760. *Maryland Hist. Mag. 1977 72(3): 335-345*. Records the performances, afterpieces, roles, and newspaper reception of David Douglass's Company of Comedians in Annapolis and Upper Marlborough from 3 March to 1 July 1760, "the longest stand of an acting company so far in the colonies." Thomas Otway's *The Orphan* was the opener. Nicholas Rowe's tragedy *The Fair Penitent*, Farquhar's *Beaux Strategem* and Shakespeare's *Richard III* were performed several times during a season filled with some 35 productions. Announcements and short comments on the plays in the *Maryland Gazette* were "the first theatrical criticism to appear in Maryland." Primary and secondary material; 16 notes.   G. J. Bobango

1054. Weinberg, Helene Barbara. JOHN LA FARGE AND THE DECORATION OF TRINITY CHURCH, BOSTON. *J. of the Soc. of Architectural Historians 1974 33(4): 323-353.* Details John La Farge's decoration (1876) of Trinity Church, a Gothic work of Henry Hobson Richardson.

1055. Weinberg, Helene Barbara. LA FARGE'S ECLECTIC IDEALISM IN THREE NEW YORK CITY CHURCHES. *Winterthur Portfolio 1975 (10): 199-228.* Analyzes John La Farge's (1835-1910) design and painting in three New York City churches; St. Thomas, Church of the Incarnation, and Church of the Ascension. His work suggests the fusion of the ideal and the real, two streams visible in earlier American art. Based on primary and secondary sources; 26 illus., 67 notes.   N. A. Kuntz

1056. Weinberg, Helene Barbara. THE WORK OF JOHN LA FARGE IN THE CHURCH OF ST. PAUL THE APOSTLE. *Am. Art J. 1974 6(1): 18-34.* Traces the involvement of John La Farge (1835-1910) with the Church of St. Paul the Apostle, New York City, particularly his work on church architecture and decoration between 1876 and 1899. Discusses also his relationship with Isaac Thomas Hecker, Paulist Fathers founder. Letters provide possible evidence of La Farge's early architectural training. Based on documents in Paulist Fathers' Archives, La Farge Family Papers, and other primary and secondary sources; 18 fig., 80 notes, addendum.   R. M. Frame III

1057. Weisert, John J. AN END AND SEVERAL BEGINNINGS: THE PASSING OF DRAKE'S CITY THEATRE. *Filson Club Hist. 1976 50(1): 5-28.* Traces the history of the Louisville, Kentucky, City Theatre from 1833 to 1842. The director of the program was Sam Drake, who booked a wide variety of dramatic entertainment. Actors ranged from local amateurs to famous contemporary actors like Edwin Forrest and Junius Brutus Booth. Plays written by local authors and those of William Shakespeare were often produced in the same week. Based on contemporary Louisville newspapers. 84 notes.   G. B. McKinney

1058. Wheeler, Leslie A. MONTANA'S SHOCKING "LIT'RY LADY." *Montana 1977 27(3): 20-33.* Mary MacLane (1881-1929) began her literary career at age 21 with the publication of *The Story of Mary MacLane,* a provocative, intimate diary of her unhappy life in Butte, Montana. It shocked the nation. Taking her inspiration from the confessions of Russian artist Marie Bashkirtseff, Mary MacLane kept her own journal from January through April 1901. Published in 1902, the diary reflected the author's romanticism, frustrations, and contempt for Butte and its society. It provoked mixed reactions but brought financial success to the author, who soon left Montana for Chicago, Boston, and New York. Mary MacLane wrote for the *New York World,* and published a second book, *My Friend Annabel Lee,* in 1903. This work proved less passionate, profane, and successful than her first. She returned to Butte in 1910. While there she published a third volume, *I, Mary MacLane* (1917), in which she appeared dejected and disillusioned with life as a literary eccentric. She soon left Butte to write and star in a silent movie, *Men Who Have Made Love To Me.* The movie was sensational for a short time. Thereafter, MacLane's career began to slide, and she died in poverty in 1929. Based on MacLane's writings and on contemporary newspapers and journals; 9 illus., 34 notes.   R. C. Myers

1059. Whitehill, Walter Muir. BOSTON ARTISTS AND CRAFTSMEN AT THE OPENING OF THE TWENTIETH CENTURY. *New England Q. 1977 50(3): 387-408.* Surveys Boston's fine arts institutions of the late 19th century and their contacts with the Art Workers Guild of London, focusing on the careers of architect Ralph Adams Cram (1863-1942), printer Daniel Berkeley Updike (1860-1941), typographer Bruce Rogers (1870-1957), and printer Carl Rollins (1880-1960). Secondary sources; 23 notes.   J. C. Bradford

1060. Wilbers, Steve. THE IOWA CITY WRITERS' CLUBS. *Palimpsest 1978 59(2): 44-57.* Writers' clubs, which first appeared in the 1890's, evolved from literary societies which had existed since the 1860's. Unlike the societies, which emphasized rhetorical and oratorical skills, the writers' clubs sought to create literature. Three successive generations of clubs flourished in Iowa City, the first emphasizing practical experience, the second cultivating interest in regional themes and publication, and the third serving to culminate the process by inviting out-of-town writers to give public readings. By the mid-1930's the last of the clubs had disbanded, having been pressured to do so by the more official, but less successful, university clubs. Illus., 9 photos, ref.   D. W. Johnson

1061. Will, J. Robert. LATE NINETEENTH CENTURY THEATER IN THE LEBANON OPERA HOUSE. *Cincinnati Hist. Soc. Bull. 1975 33(2): 120-135.* Chronicles drama presentations in the Lebanon Opera House in Cincinnati, Ohio, 1878-1900.

1062. Williams, Ellen. HARRIET MONROE AND *POETRY* MAGAZINE. *Chicago Hist. 1975/76 4(4): 204-213.* Retraces the life and career of art critic, writer, and editor of *Poetry* magazine Harriet Monroe, and her ties with various literary personalities in Chicago in the late 19th and early 20th centuries.

1063. Wisse, Ruth R. *DI YUNGE* AND THE PROBLEM OF JEWISH AESTHETICISM. *Jewish Social Studies 1976 38(3-4): 265-276.* The group of working class Jewish immigrant writers known as *Di Yunge* emerged on the Yiddish literary scene, mainly in New York City, during 1902-13. Their goal of striving toward an aesthetic ideal by emphasizing mood and feeling was at variance with the dominant Yiddish literary tradition of homily, practicalism, and didacticism. To the young men of *Di Yunge,* beauty was the highest ideal; and the means to achieve its actuality were to be sought not only in the Jewish milieu but also within the literary traditions of other cultures.   N. Lederer

1064. Zornow, William Frank. THE THEATRE IN TOPEKA, KANSAS, 1858-1883. *J. of the West 1978 17(2): 63-71.* The first play in Topeka, Kansas, was a morality piece offered by a local civic group in 1858. Professional performances were not available until 1867; and not until 1869 was there an adequate facility with a stage, curtains, and scenery. Lester M. Crawford established the first real theater building in 1880, Crawford's Music Hall. He earned a reputation for producing clean family shows and eventually became the owner of 100 theaters from Kansas to California. The Topeka Opera House competed with Crawford's. Both theaters presented touring troupes, but Crawford also had his own stock company of performers. Published sources; 6 photos, 30 notes.   B. S. Porter

Schooling

1065. Andrews, Andrea R. THE BALTIMORE SCHOOL BUILDING PROGRAM, 1870 TO 1900: A STUDY OF URBAN REFORM. *Maryland Hist. Mag. 1975 70(3): 260-274.* The "one-sided Progressive picture of the ward-based machine as totally corrupt and evil" needs redressing, yet the rapidly growing late-19th-century city was developing serious needs which the locally oriented city government was not equipped to meet. Analyzes the problem of providing a growing school population with buildings and equipment, describing Baltimore city and the government politically dependent school board. School commissioners were primarily ward politicians appointed by council and bound to the dictates of the machine hierarchy. Inordinate stress on budgetary economy and property tax evasion resulted in chronic deficits and lack of funds. Lack of expertise and coordination produced a shortsighted, haphazard program, with overcrowded and hazardous makeshift buildings. The reformed City Charter of 1898 created the mechanism for "centralization, independence, objectivity, and expertise" with a new Board of Estimates and a mayor-appointed board for schools, but the reform system was no guarantee that partisanship and self-interest were dead. Moreover, the popular, local control of the ward system was removed while the potential for a machine still existed. Primary and secondary works; 2 tables, 55 notes.   G. J. Bobango

1066. Calkins, David L. BLACK EDUCATION AND THE 19TH CENTURY CITY: AN INSTITUTIONAL ANALYSIS OF CINCINNATI'S COLORED SCHOOLS, 1850-1887. *Cincinnati Hist. Soc. Bull. 1975 33(3): 161-171.* Discusses socioeconomic aspects of public schools for Negroes in Cincinnati, Ohio, 1850-87.

1067. Candeloro, Dominic. THE CHICAGO SCHOOL BOARD CRISIS OF 1907. *J. of the Illinois State Hist. Soc. 1975 68(5): 396-406.* The election of reform Democrat Edward F. Dunne as mayor of Chicago in 1905 led to the appointment of Progressives such as Louis F. Post and Jane Addams to the School Board. The Board's reform element endeavored to implement staff and curriculum reforms in the school system and also to raise revenue through renegotiating private leases on downtown school land. Intense criticism from newspapers and business interests and the defeat for reelection of Dunne led to the removal of the reformers from the Board. Many of their reforms were implemented, however, following the appointment of Ella Flagg Young as school superintendent in 1910.
N. Lederer

1068. Cohen, Ronald D. SCHOOLING IN EARLY NINETEENTH CENTURY BOSTON AND NEW YORK. *J. of Urban Hist. 1974 1(1): 116-118.* Reviews of Stanley K. Schultz's *The Culture Factory: Boston Public Schools, 1789-1860* (New York: Oxford U. Pr., 1973), and Carl F. Kaestle's *Evolution of an Urban School System: New York City, 1750-1850* (Cambridge: Harvard U. Pr., 1973). 10 notes.
S. S. Sprague

1069. Cohen, Ronald D. URBAN SCHOOLING IN THE GILDED AGE AND AFTER. *J. of Urban Hist. 1976 2(4): 499-506.* Discusses recent scholarship on American urban education. Covers three general works on American education, Walter Feinberg and Henry Rosemont, Jr., eds., *Work, Technology, and Education: Dissenting Essays in the Intellectual Foundations of American Education,* Clarence J. Karier, ed., *Shaping the American Educational State: 1900 to the Present,* and Gillian Sutherland, *Policy-Making in Elementary Education, 1870-1895;* two general works on urban education, William A. Bullough, *Cities and Schools in the Gilded Age: The Revolution of an Urban Institution* and David B. Tyack, *The One Best System: A History of American Urban Education;* and one case study, Selwyn K. Troen, *The Public and the Schools: Shaping the St. Louis System, 1838-1920.* The review takes a historiographic approach.
T. W. Smith

1070. Courchesne, Gary L. PUBLIC EDUCATION IN HOLYOKE, 1850-1873. *Hist. J. of Western Massachusetts 1979 7(2): 15-24.* During 1850-63, Holyoke's school system consisted of a series of one-room district schools that had serious problems recruiting teachers and enforcing attendance. Then a superintendent was appointed and a municipal school system replaced the districts. The curriculum and calendar were expanded and reorganized. Based on School Committee and town reports; 2 illus., 41 notes.
W. H. Mulligan, Jr.

1071. Curran, Patrick J. EDUCATION IN NEW AMSTERDAM. *Halve Maen 1975 50(2): 5-6.* Based on a system long in effect in Holland, elementary schools began in New Amsterdam in 1638 and secondary education in the 1650's.
S

1072. Curry, Thomas J. ETHNIC PAROCHIAL SCHOOLS: DIVERSITY OF ISOLATION? *Rev. in Am. Hist. 1977 5(3): 354-359.* Review article prompted by James W. Sanders's *The Education of an Urban Minority: Catholics in Chicago, 1833-1965* (New York: Oxford U. Pr., 1977).

1073. Cutler, William W., III. THE SYSTEMIZATION OF AMERICAN EDUCATION. *Hist. of Educ. Q. 1976 16(1): 79-92.* Reviews William A. Bullough's *Cities and Schools in the Gilded Age: The Evolution of an Urban Institution* (New York: Kennikat Pr., 1974) and David B. Tyack's *The One Best System: A History of American Urban Education* (Cambridge, Massachusetts: Harvard U. Pr., 1974).

1074. Danbom, David B. RURAL EDUCATION REFORM AND THE COUNTRY LIFE MOVEMENT, 1900-1920. *Agric. Hist. 1979 53(2): 462-474.* The Country Life Movement wanted to improve rural life through the reform of primary education. Looking at the problem from an urban perspective, they thought that consolidating schools and broadening the curriculum to include music, art, physical education, and nature study would produce more efficient farmers and ultimately lower food costs to the cities. Rural people were slow to change and often suspicious of the motives of Country Lifers. 36 notes.
D. E. Bowers

1075. Darling, Arthur Burr. PRIOR TO LITTLE ROCK IN AMERICAN EDUCATION: THE *ROBERTS* CASE OF 1849-1850. *Massachusetts Hist. Soc. Pro. 1957-60 72: 126-142.* Discusses the controversy surrounding school segregation in the late 1950's by examining the case *Sarah C. Roberts* v. *The City of Boston* (1850) which dealt with the concept of "equal protection of the laws," in 1849-50.

1076. Dye, Charles M. CALVIN WOODWARD, MANUAL TRAINING AND THE SAINT LOUIS PUBLIC SCHOOLS. *Missouri Hist. Soc. Bull. 1975 31(2): 111-135.* Calvin Woodward (1837-1914) and a slate of reformers won control of the St. Louis Board of Education in 1897. The reformers introduced manual training into the curricula, but financial exigencies and the philosophies of the entrenched professional educationists ultimately modified Woodward's reform programs in ways of which Woodward and his reformers disapproved. Based on official Board of Education documents and on secondary sources; 97 notes.
H. T. Lovin

1077. Fishbane, Richard B. "THE SHALLOW BOAST OF CHEAPNESS": PUBLIC SCHOOL TEACHING AS A PROFESSION IN PHILADELPHIA, 1865-1890. *Pennsylvania Mag. of Hist. and Biog. 1979 103(1): 66-84.* Census manuscript data reveal the teachers' age (young), socioeconomic background (advantaged), household composition (lived with familes), training and recruitment (poor), remuneration (inadequate), feminization, and persistence (12 years). Based on 1870 census manuscripts, official records, newspapers, and secondary works; 33 notes.
T. H. Wendel

1078. Fisher, Minnie. THE YIDDISHE ARBEITEN UNIVERSITETT: AN ORAL HISTORY. *Urban Rev. 1976 9(3): 201-204.* Presents the narrative of a 76 year old former garment worker from the young immigrant Jewish community in New York City's Lower East Side during the 1920's. Through the Universitett the eager new citizens learned English, studied modern political and economic systems, debated, and developed socially.
D. L. Smith

1079. Foley, Fred J., Jr. COMMUNITY CONTROL: THE POLITICS OF URBAN SCHOOL REFORM. *Polity 1976 8(3): 463-474.* Reviews five books on the history of attempts by urban communities to gain control of their local schools between 1805 and 1973.

1080. Gardner, Bettye. ANTE-BELLUM BLACK EDUCATION IN BALTIMORE. *Maryland Hist. Mag. 1976 71(3): 360-366.* "On the eve of the Civil War Baltimore had the largest free black community in the nation." About 15 schools for blacks were operating. From Sabbath schools operated by Methodists, Presbyterians, and Quakers, black education expanded through the efforts of the African Methodist Episcopal Church under Daniel Coker, and the Oblates' Academy "for young girls of color." William Watkins's Academy was perhaps the most prestigious private school for blacks, while the school run by William Lively offered a comprehensive curriculum and "showed the seriousness with which . . . blacks pursued the education of the whole person." All black schools were self-sustaining, receiving no state or local government funds, and whites in Baltimore generally opposed educating the black population, continuing to tax black property holders to maintain schools from which black children were excluded by law. Baltimore's black community, nevertheless, was one of the largest and most cohesive in America due to this experience. From Baltimore City Records, and secondary materials; 25 notes.
G. J. Bobango

1081. Gonzales, Gilbert C. EDUCATIONAL REFORM AND THE MEXICAN COMMUNITY IN LOS ANGELES. *Southwest Econ. and Soc. 1978 3(3): 24-51.* Examines the curricula of the Los Angeles public schools as it served and affected the Mexican Americans in the community during the 1920's-30's.

1082. Grob, Gerald N. THE ILLUSION OF EDUCATIONAL OMNIPOTENCE. *Rev. in Am. Hist. 1975 3(2): 169-173.* Diane Ravitch's *The Great School Wars: New York City, 1805-1973, A History of the Public Schools as Battlefield of Social Change* (New York: Basic Books, 1974) shows the political, social, and economic conflicts between minorities and "the emerging bureaucratic and professional apparatus."

1083. Heilbron, Robert F. STUDENT PROTEST AT ITS BEST, SAN DIEGO, 1918. *J. of San Diego Hist. 1975 20(1): 15-25.* Examines student boycott of San Diego High School in 1918 following a decision by the high school board to fire 19 teachers because they were considered friends of Superintendent of Schools Duncan MacKinnon.   S

1084. Hobson, Julius, Jr. EDUCATIONAL POLICY AND THE COURTS: THE CASE OF WASHINGTON, D.C. *Urban Rev. 1978 10(1): 5-19.* Agencies conducting Washington, D.C.'s public schools, 1804-1974, failed to provide equal education for black students despite studies which provided information on discrimination. Since 1910, D.C. residents have sought judicial relief from the "malpractice and negligence" of school officials. Although the courts have corrected many educational abuses, Washington furnishes a case study of the courts' inability to formulate and execute nondiscriminatory educational policy throughout the United States. Equal education depends upon educational agencies' fulfillment of their responsibilities. Based on published government documents and secondary studies; biblio.   R. G. Sherer

1085. Hogan, David. EDUCATION AND THE MAKING OF THE CHICAGO WORKING CLASS, 1880-1930. *Hist. of Educ. Q. 1978 18(3): 227-270.* Examines why children enrolled in Chicago schools between 1880 and 1930 stayed in school for a longer time, particularly those over the age of 14, regardless of ethnic background.

1086. Homel, Michael W. THE POLITICS OF PUBLIC EDUCATION IN BLACK CHICAGO, 1910-1941. *J. of Negro Educ. 1976 45(2): 179-191.* As the black population of Chicago increased after 1910, their dissatisfaction with the public schools also increased. They worked for the next 30 years for improved facilities, integration, and representation on the Board of Education. Methods used were: white assistance, political influence, legal cases, direct action, and public verbal protest. 27 notes.   B. D. Johnson

1087. Humphrey, David C. URBAN MANNERS AND RURAL MORALS: THE CONTROVERSY OVER THE LOCATION OF KING'S COLLEGE. *New York Hist. 1973 54(1): 4-23.* In the "Grand Debate" (1747-53) over the location of a college for the province of New York, Cadwallader Colden (1688-1776), who was afraid that the vices of New York City would corrupt the students, favored Newburgh, New York. William Smith, Sr. (1697-1769), argued that students should be in the city where they would meet men of refinement and learning daily. Because eight of the 10 trustees were New York City men, King's College was built there. Attended mostly by the sons of wealthy New York families, the college insured the city's national preeminence by providing an educated elite. Primary and secondary sources; 8 illus., 56 notes.   G. Kurland

1088. Hunt, Thomas C. PUBLIC SCHOOLS, "AMERICANISM," AND THE IMMIGRANT AT THE TURN OF THE CENTURY. *J. of General Educ. 1974 26(2): 147-155.* Examines both sides of the assimilation problems of the many immigrant children in urban schools and city life circa 1890's-1920.   S

1089. Hunt, Thomas C. THE SCHOOLING OF IMMIGRANTS AND BLACK AMERICANS: SOME SIMILARITIES AND DIFFERENCES. *J. of Negro Educ. 1976 45(4): 423-431.* Lists similarities and differences between the effects of education on the Eastern and Southern European immigrant children of 1890-1920 who successfully assimilated into the American middle class, and the black children who migrated to northern cities during 1940-66 and were not upwardly mobile. The major difference is that education cannot easily offset the long history of oppression and frustration experience by blacks, who, unlike European immigrants, did not come willingly to this country in the hope of a better future. 26 notes.   B. D. Johnson

1090. Hurst, Marsha. INTEGRATION, FREEDOM OF CHOICE AND COMMUNITY CONTROL IN NINETEENTH CENTURY BROOKLYN. *J. of Ethnic Studies 1975 3(3): 33-55.* Educational politics in Brooklyn in the last decades of the 19th century was characterized by conflict between educational professionals "under the banner of progressivism," and those opposing centralization in favor of retaining the community-oriented, traditional, local committee system. The outcome meant either integration and phasing out of the "colored schools" which would reduce black political input to nothing on the Board of Education, or retaining the segregated schools with only token recognition on the board anyway. Little meaningful choice remained for Brooklyn's Negroes. The struggle carried into the black community as the small black bourgeoisie sided with the integrationists. School Board politics of the 1890's were closely related, and the Consolidation Bill of 1896 failed to eliminate borough autonomy for Brooklyn or the local committees. Progressives and reformers finally won out, which meant a significant loss of political and educational input for blacks, who were seen by the progressive centralizers as poor tenement folk deserving sympathy but not political influence, and tokenism remained the rule for black appointments. Based on Board Proceedings, newspapers, and secondary works; 58 notes.   G. J. Bobango

1091. Issel, William. AMERICANIZATION, ACCULTURATION AND SOCIAL CONTROL: SCHOOL REFORM IDEOLOGY IN INDUSTRIAL PENNSYLVANIA, 1880-1910. *J. of Social Hist. 1979 12(4): 569-590.* Analyzes school reform efforts as a consequence of dislocations caused by industrialization in Pennsylvania. It is true that elites initiated reform efforts, however, Marxists and revisionists are incorrect in asserting that economics was the motivating force. Strikes, riots, and hordes of immigrants had to be dealt with. Reformers acted to unite state, school, and community, arguing that what was good for one was good for all. The schools, therefore, stressed social control themes. Some allowance was made for the new values of immigrants as well as for those of poor native laborers. Control was designed to benefit state and society rather than industry or the individual. 54 notes.   V. L. Human

1092. Ives, Richard. COMPULSORY EDUCATION AND THE ST. LOUIS PUBLIC SCHOOL SYSTEM: 1905-1907. *Missouri Hist. Rev. 1977 71(3): 315-329.* Missouri enacted compulsory education laws in 1905 and 1907. Discusses what groups supported or opposed the laws, whether the laws were equally enforced or were immigrants discriminated against, and whether the laws attracted new students. Newspapers, legislative voting records, and state publications reveal that the laws enjoyed wide support. Most truancy cases were settled out of court, but school administrators often were influenced by an ethnic racism. Truancy was not a serious problem. Immigrants left school at a lower percentage rate than natives because they were aware of educational values. Illus., 42 notes.   W. F. Zornow

1093. Johnson, Ronald M. POLITICS AND PEDAGOGY: THE 1892 CLEVELAND SCHOOL REFORM. *Ohio Hist. 1975 84(4): 196-206.* The 1892 Cleveland School reform occurred as part of the sustained political battle between the business-dominated Republican Party and an increasingly immigrant-oriented Democratic organization. In 1892 the Republicans won control of a highly centralized school system. The new superintendent was Andrew S. Draper, whose primary objective was a revitalized educational process. Despite many improvements, the reform was only partially successful. Illus., 40 notes.   E. P. Stickney

1094. Kaestle, Carl F. and Vinovskis, Maris A. QUANTIFICATION, URBANIZATION, AND THE HISTORY OF EDUCATION: AN ANALYSIS OF THE DETERMINANTS OF SCHOOL ATTENDANCE IN NEW YORK STATE, 1845. *Hist. Methods Newsletter 1974 8(1): 1-9.* Using a regression analysis, the authors conclude that historians are overestimating the importance of the urban setting or industrialization per se. Under controlled conditions the degree of "urbanization or industrialization was not very useful in accounting for differentials in the level of school attendance." Tables.   D. K. Pickens

1095. Katz, Michael B. THE ORIGINS OF URBAN EDUCATION. *Rev. in Am. Hist. 1974 2(2): 186-192.* Review article prompted by Carl F. Kaestle's *The Education of An Urban School System: New York City, 1750-1850* (Cambridge: Harvard U. Pr., 1973) and Stanley K. Schultz's *The Culture Factory: Boston Public Schools, 1789-1860* (New York: Oxford U. Pr., 1973). Boston and New York City schools shifted from instructing the elite to moral "enculturation" of the unassimilated masses.   W. D. Piersen

1096. Kuznicki, Ellen Marie. A HISTORICAL PERSPECTIVE ON THE POLISH AMERICAN PAROCHIAL SCHOOL. *Polish Am. Studies 1978 35(1-2): 5-12.* Covers this school system from its beginning in the 1870's to the phasing-out era in the 1960's. Lists successes and failures of the system and concludes that, above all, "it was an effective Americanizer easing its pupils into English without depriving them of their ethnic heritage." 16 notes.   S. R. Pliska

1097. Lazerson, Marvin. CONFLICT AND CONSENSUS IN UR-BAN EDUCATION. *Rev. in Am. Hist. 1976 4(3): 421-427.* Review article prompted by Selwyn K. Troen's *The Public Schools: Shaping the St. Louis System, 1838-1920* (Columbia: U. of Missouri Pr., 1975); takes into account conflict and consensus in the religious, political, educational, ethnic, and economic ideologies of those in the public schools of St. Louis.

1098. Lazerson, Marvin. UNDERSTANDING AMERICAN CATHOLIC EDUCATIONAL HISTORY. *Hist. of Educ. Q. 1977 17(3): 297-317.* The development of the American Catholic parochial school system can be divided into three phases. During the first (1750-1870), parochial schools appeared as ad hoc efforts by parishes, and most Catholic children attended public schools. During the second period (1870-1910), the Catholic hierarhcy made a basic commitment to a separate Catholic school system. These parochial schools, like the big-city parishes around them, tended to be ethnically homogeneous; a German child would not be sent to an Irish school, nor vice-versa, nor a Lithuanian pupil to either. Instruction in the language of the old country was common. In the third period (1910-1945), Catholic education was modernized and modelled after the public school systems, and ethnicity was deemphasized in many areas. In cities with large Catholic populations (such as Chicago and Boston) there was a flow of teachers, administrators, and students from one system to the other. 46 notes.
                                                              J. C. Billigmeier

1099. Mabee, Carleton. EARLY BLACK PUBLIC SCHOOLS. *Long Island Forum 1973 36(12): 234-236.* Concluded from a previous article. Deals with the education of Negroes in Brooklyn.   S

1100. Mohl, Raymond A. SCHOOLS, POLITICS, AND RIOTS: THE GARY PLAN IN NEW YORK CITY, 1914-1917. *Paedagogica Hist. [Belgium] 1975 15(1): 39-72.* An archetypal experiment in progressive educational change occurred in New York City 1914-17 when reform mayor John Purroy Mitchel sought to introduce the much-discussed duplicate school plan first developed in Gary, Indiana. The struggle illustrates many of the tendencies revealed by the new educational historiography. 69 notes.   J. M. McCarthy

1101. Nagy, J. Emerick. THE SOUTH NASHVILLE INSTITUTE. *Tennessee Hist. Q. 1977 36(2): 180-196.* The first organized system of public schools in Nashville, Tennessee, came as a result of the efforts of the incorporated town of South Nashville. After an election on the feasibility of public schools for the hamlet, South Nashville Institute was established in 1851 for the 544 children in the six to 18 age category. With enrollment at 208 in four classrooms in 1853, a branch school was opened in a nearby church. In 1854, however, the two towns merged and the South Nashville Institute became part of the Nashville public schools. Primary and secondary sources; 5 notes.   M. B. Lucas

1102. Nelms, Jack. THE DALLAS ACADEMY: BACKBONE OF THE PERMANENT SCHOOL SYSTEM IN SELMA. *Alabama Rev. 1976 29(2): 113-123.* Provides a brief history of the Dallas Academy in Selma from its inception in 1836 until its closing in 1961. The school thrived during 1839-53, closed during the Civil War, and reopened in 1868, partly with aid from the George Peabody fund. Growth of a tax-supported school system, notably after 1913, and changing residential patterns eventually rendered the institution unnecessary. Based on primary and secondary sources; 27 notes.   J. F. Vivian

1103. Polos, Nicholas C. JOHN SWETT: THE RINCON PERIOD 1853-1862. *Pacific Historian 1975 19(2): 133-149.* Discusses the career of John Swett as principal of Rincon School, San Francisco. Swett was an early advocate of publicly supported education and other progressive ideas such as physical education, coeducation, better methods of teacher certification, and higher teacher salaries. He served as California's State Superintendent of Education during 1863-67. Primary sources; 32 notes.
                                                              G. L. Olson

1104. Provenzo, Eugene F., Jr. THE EDUCATIONAL MUSEUM OF THE ST. LOUIS PUBLIC SCHOOLS. *Missouri Hist. Soc. Bull. 1979 35(3): 147-153.* The St. Louis public schools have maintained an educational museum since 1901. To expand the museum, the school system acquired many of the Louisiana Purchase Exposition exhibits in 1904 and has since supplemented the collection. After 1943, the museum has mostly supplied film services to the public schools. 5 photos, 28 notes.
                                                              H. T. Lovin

1105. Putney, Martha S. THE BALTIMORE NORMAL SCHOOL FOR THE EDUCATION OF COLORED TEACHERS: ITS FOUNDERS AND ITS FOUNDING. *Maryland Hist. Mag. 1977 72(2): 238-252.* Shows that, contrary to statements in present and past school catalogues, today's Bowie State College was not the result of a legacy of Nelson Wells of Baltimore, a black man who died in 1843. Some of the Wells Fund, which had supported the Nelson Wells Free School during 1845-69, was used to help establish the Baltimore Normal School in 1871; and one of Wells's trustees, John Needles, was a founding officer of this body. Surveys the history of the Normal School and reports on the first three anniversary meetings of its directors, the Baltimore Association for the Moral and Educational Improvement of Colored People. Instrumental in the school's existence were the New England Freedmen's Aid Society, the Philadelphia Friends Association, and the Federal Freedmen's Bureau, along with the efforts of such individuals as Joseph M. Cushing and Libertus Van Bokkelen to gain state support for black education. Clarifies certain problems about where the first school building was located and when the first classes convened. Primary sources; 43 notes.
                                                              G. J. Bobango

1106. Rabinowitz, Howard N. HALF A LOAF: THE SHIFT FROM WHITE TO BLACK TEACHERS IN THE NEGRO SCHOOLS OF THE URBAN SOUTH, 1865-1890. *J. of Southern Hist. 1974 40(4): 565-594.* Examines the transformation from white to black teachers in southern schools in the post-Civil War years, using the experiences of five southern cities to provide a cross-section: Atlanta, Georgia; Raleigh, North Carolina; Nashville, Tennessee; Montgomery, Alabama; and Richmond, Virginia. Among the problems the Redeemers confronted were such matters as the removal of northern missionary ties and teachers in order to reassert southern control of the school system, the black demand for black teachers which was often accepted since it meant cheaper teachers, and the resultant black demand for equal salary for equal work, a demand usually denied. Negroes tried to obtain better quality instruction for their children, more administrative positions, and positions on the school board, but were usually unsuccessful. Ironically, since some schools became entirely black, insistence upon black instructors made it easier for the whites to discriminate. Based on manuscripts and published primary and secondary sources; 118 notes.   T. D. Schoonover

1107. Racine, Philip N. A PROGRESSIVE FIGHTS EFFICIENCY: THE SURVIVAL OF WILLIS SUTTON, SCHOOL SUPERINTENDENT. *South Atlantic Q. 1977 76(1): 103-116.* While Superintendent of Atlanta Public Schools during 1921-43, Willis Sutton fought City Hall and big business to save public education. Confronted with a financial crisis, the city tried to eliminate "frills" such as free textbooks, teachers' benefits, public elections to the School Board, Negro night schools, and music, art, and physical education courses. Sutton had initiated or improved most of these programs. Atlanta businessmen offered to bail out the schools if these programs were cut and Sutton fired. However, Sutton's allies, which included organized labor, Atlanta teachers, and the National Education Association, kept him and his programs working. 29 notes.
                                                              W. L. Olbrich

1108. Raichle, Donald. STEPHEN CONGAR AND THE ESTAB-LISHMENT OF THE NEWARK PUBLIC SCHOOL SYSTEM. *J. of the Rutgers U. Lib. 1976 38(2): 57-84.* Physicians played a leading role in the establishment of public schools in New Jersey. Administrative posts, such as school superintendent, were then part-time jobs, which physicians could fill and still practice. No physician-educator in New Jersey contributed more than Dr. Stephen Congar (1810-97), superintendent of the Newark school system during 1853-59. Congar also served in the New Jersey legislature as an assemblyman and later as a senator; he was responsible for introducing legislation that strengthened public education in the state.   R. Van Benthuysen

1109. Reese, William J. PROGRESSIVE SCHOOL REFORM IN TOLEDO, 1898-1921. *Northwest Ohio Q. 1975 47(2): 44-59.* Sketches the events which led to reform, despite conservative tenacity, in the Toledo school system; highlights work of local newspapers and the fights between school board member J. Kent Hamilton and Progressive Toledo school administrator William B. Gitteau. 5 photos, 64 notes.

1110. Russo, Francis X. JOHN HOWLAND: PIONEER IN THE FREE SCHOOL MOVEMENT. *Rhode Island Hist. 1978 37(4): 111-122.* John Howland was a hairdresser and self-educated. He became active in the Rhode Island free school movement in 1795, played a major role in securing legislation in 1800, and was active in Providence school affairs for the next several decades. Based on school records, recollections, and secondary accounts; 3 illus., 47 notes.   P. J. Coleman

1111. Scott, Osborne. PRE- AND POST-EMANCIPATION SCHOOLS. *Urban Rev. 1976 9(4): 234-241.* The slave's education typically was limited to matters of religious salvation and perhaps reading and writing. New York City's Africa Free Schools were an exception. The day schools and black colleges which emerged after the war emphasized vocational education and black history. 6 photos.   L. D. Smith

1112. Segal, Beryl. JEWISH SCHOOLS AND TEACHERS IN METROPOLITAN PROVIDENCE: THE FIRST CENTURY. *Rhode Island Jewish Hist. Notes 1977 7(3): 410-419.* Covers 1854-1946.

1113. Seller, Maxine. THE EDUCATION OF IMMIGRANT CHILDREN IN BUFFALO, NEW YORK 1890-1916. *New York Hist. 1976 57(2): 183-199.* Examines the efforts to reform the public school education of immigrant children in Buffalo, New York during 1890-1916. School reformers, mostly of old Protestant Anglo-Saxon stock, understood little about immigrants, and thought of educational reform as part of municipal reform, and as a method of Americanizing immigrant workers and discouraging radicalism. Illus., 36 notes.
                    R. N. Lokken

1114. Seller, Maxine. THE EDUCATION OF THE IMMIGRANT WOMAN, 1900-1935. *J. of Urban Hist. 1978 4(3): 307-330.* Progressive educational reformers at the turn of the century underestimated the extent of the immigrant woman's interest in education. Heavy use was made of educational facilities maintained by the ethnic communities themselves. While learning English and improving homemaking skills were the most common goals, the educational interests of immigrant women went far beyond those basic areas. 81 notes.   T. W. Smith

1115. Shade, William G. THE "WORKING CLASS" AND EDUCATIONAL REFORM IN EARLY AMERICA: THE CASE OF PROVIDENCE, RHODE ISLAND. *Historian 1976 39(1): 1-23.* According to this case study, educational reform after 1820 was not the product of a Jeffersonian Republican elite. Providence tradesmen and artisans, organized in the Providence Association of Mechanics and Manufacturers, were active in the school reform movement. These middle class tradesmen and artisans knew that they had obtained few educational benefits. In its memorials the association stressed public morality, citizenship, and the state's social duty to provide schools. 3 charts, 84 notes.
                    M. J. Wentworth

1116. Silcox, Harry C. PHILADELPHIA NEGRO EDUCATOR: JACOB C. WHITE, JR., 1837-1902. *Pennsylvania Mag. of Hist. and Biog. 1973 97(1): 75-98.* White began his career as a teacher at the Institute for Colored Youth in 1857, and was appointed principal of the Roberts Vaux Consolidated School seven years later. He held that post for the next 30 years. White was a broker between Philadelphia's white school board and the black community, and his influence and prestige grew with both groups, thus enabling him to secure acceptance of Negro teachers in black schools. White was also instrumental in easing the strain of integrating Philadelphia's schools during the 1870's and 1880's. Improvements in educational opportunity were purchased at a high price, for only by accommodating white racial prejudice and discrimination was White able to forward the cause of the Negro. Based on primary sources; 90 notes.   E. W. Carp

1117. Strober, Myra H. and Best, Laura. THE FEMALE/MALE SALARY DIFFERENTIAL IN PUBLIC SCHOOLS: SOME LES-

SONS FROM SAN FRANCISCO, 1879. *Econ. Inquiry 1979 17(2): 218-236.* Seeks to explain the differences between men's and women's salaries in San Francisco public schools, 1879.

1118. Thomas, Bettye C. PUBLIC EDUCATION AND BLACK PROTEST IN BALTIMORE, 1865-1900. *Maryland Hist. Mag. 1976 71(3): 381-391.* Reviews the efforts of the Baltimore Association for the Moral and Educational Improvement of the Colored People led by such as Isaac Myers, and Brotherhood of Liberty formed by Harvey Johnson and other Baptist ministers, to acquire public schools, have black teachers hired, secure additional school facilities, and initiate industrial education for black children. Blacks found themselves forced to support Jim Crow legislation and urge all black teachers for the colored schools because the Board of School Commissioners would not allow blacks and whites to teach in the same schools. From 1867 to 1900 black schools grew from 10 to 27 and enrollment from 901 to 9,383. The Mechanical and Industrial Association achieved success only in 1892 with the opening of the Colored Manual Training School. Black leaders were convinced by the Rev. William Alexander and his paper, the *Afro American*, that economic advancement and first-class citizenship depended on equal access to schools, and thus zealously pursued their goals in the face of a white city commission which yielded step-by-step and only very reluctantly. Primary and secondary works; 45 notes.   G. J. Bobango

1119. Tyack, David B. and Berkowitz, Michael. THE MAN NOBODY LIKED: TOWARD A SOCIAL HISTORY OF THE TRUANT OFFICER, 1840-1940. *Am. Q. 1977 29(1): 31-54.* For a long time truant officers worked on a part-time basis and faced a rather negative public. The coincidence of compulsory public school attendance and the Progressive Era led to an effort to upgrade the image of the truant officer and to professionalize the occupation. Like many other occupational groupings during the Progressive Era, the truant officers formed national associations, employed the vocabulary of social science, and bureaucratized the attendance service. However, in many rural and small-town areas, the truant officer remained a part-time amateur, upholding the community status quo and retaining a rather negative public image.
                    N. Lederer

1120. Tyack, David B. SCHOOL AND SOCIETY IN ST. LOUIS. *Hist. of Educ. Q. 1976 16(2): 195-202.* Review article prompted by Selwyn K. Troen's *The Public and the Schools: Shaping the St. Louis System, 1838-1920* (Columbia, Missouri: U. of Missouri Pr., 1975).

1121. Urban, Wayne. ORGANIZED TEACHERS AND EDUCATIONAL REFORM DURING THE PROGRESSIVE ERA: 1890-1920. *Hist. of Educ. Q. 1976 16(1): 35-52.* Examines attitudes of teachers' organizations toward educational reform in Atlanta, Georgia, New York City, and Chicago, Illinois, during 1890-1920.

1122. Walch, Timothy. CATHOLIC EDUCATION IN CHICAGO: THE FORMATIVE YEARS, 1840-1890. *Chicago Hist. 1978 7(2): 87-97.* Unable to secure state tax funds for parochial education, Chicago's Catholic community sustained itself on donations and fund raising, an enterprise led by Father Arnold Damen, 1840-90.

1123. Weiss, Michael. EDUCATION, LITERACY AND THE COMMUNITY OF LOS ANGELES IN 1850. *Southern California Q. 1978 60(2): 117-142.* A quantitative survey of literacy in Los Angeles in 1850. The federal census of 1850 made such an analysis possible because a question was included regarding ability to read and write in English or any other language. Statistical analyses can be made revealing literacy by ethnicity, sex, age, and other factors. The results show that few women or Indians were literate; Caucasian males were the most literate; and literacy depended greatly on one's status, occupation, wealth, sex, and age. The American concept of public education brought to Los Angeles a much greater opportunity for learning than the pueblo had experienced in the Spanish and Mexican periods. Includes a profile of John R. Evertsen, the deputy census marshal who compiled the census. Based on the 1850 federal census and contemporary and secondary published works; 11 tables, 49 notes.   A. Hoffman

1124. White, Arthur O. ANTEBELLUM SCHOOL REFORM IN BOSTON: INTEGRATIONISTS AND SEPARATISTS. *Phylon 1973 34(2): 203-218.* Thomas Paul Smith led black separatists in their attempt to control the Boston "African" school mastership and undermined a movement by black and white abolitionists to integrate Boston's schools, 1848-49.   S

1125.   Wilkie, Jane Riblett.   SOCIAL STATUS, ACCULTURATION AND SCHOOL ATTENDANCE IN 1850 BOSTON.   *J. of Social Hist. 1977 11(2): 179-192.* An examination of race, origin, and class differences in Boston in 1850 indicates that the "equal access to educational opportunity" appears to have preceded class mobility for much of the white immigrant population. For northern blacks, however, "formal schooling had no counter effect on the deterioration of their economic position." 6 tables, 33 notes.   L. E. Ziewacz

Social Welfare and Reform

1126.   Abel, Emily K.   MIDDLE-CLASS CULTURE FOR THE URBAN POOR: THE EDUCATIONAL THOUGHT OF SAMUEL BARNETT.   *Social Service Rev. 1978 52(4): 596-620.* Compares the ideas and activities of Samuel Augustus Barnett, founder of the first English settlement house in 1884, with American progressives, 1880's-1913.

1127.   Anderson, Eric.   PROSTITUTION AND SOCIAL JUSTICE: CHICAGO, 1910-15.   *Social Service Rev. 1974 48(2): 203-228.*

1128.   Austin, Michael J. and Betten, Neil.   INTELLECTUAL ORIGINS OF COMMUNITY ORGANIZING, 1920-1939.   *Social Service Rev. 1977 51(1): 155-170.* The roots of contemporary community organization practice can be traced to the settlement house workers and organizers of the councils of social agencies of the early 1900's. However, the education of future organizers should include the "practice wisdom" found in the writings of the organizers and educators who wrote in the 1920's and 1930's, including Hart, Lindeman, McClenahan, Pettit, and Steiner. Students of community organizing can be guided by the insights found in the first textbooks and thereby gain a perspective similar to the well-documented history of casework practice. The early manuals on community organizing represent an important dimension of the history of social work practice.   J

1129.   Bauer, Anne.   THE CHARLESTOWN STATE PRISON. *Hist. J. of Western Massachusetts 1973 2(2): 22-29.* The institution's early years were unsatisfactory; escapes, homosexuality, and overcrowding were three main problems. The Boston Prison Discipline Society, however, emphasized the ideas of penal reformers of the time and was able to transform the prison's image. The society claimed that no other prison had superior moral or religious instruction. In the 1840's prisoners had their own gardens. As the buildings grew older and reform interests were drawn elsewhere, conditions deteriorated. In the 1870's a new prison was built. Based on contemporary and secondary sources; 3 illus., 17 notes.
S. S. Sprague

1130.   Bauman, John F.   BLACK SLUMS/BLACK PROJECTS: THE NEW DEAL AND NEGRO HOUSING IN PHILADELPHIA. *Pennsylvania Hist. 1974 41(3): 311-338.* The first two New Deal housing projects in Philadelphia were restricted to whites despite the fact that black housing conditions in the city were deplorable. The Philadelphia chapter of the National Negro Congress and the Tenants League led efforts to assure that future federal housing would be used to help Philadelphia Negroes. The fact that black votes had contributed to Democratic victories in Philadelphia was not lost upon New Deal policymakers, and federal funds made available through the Wagner-Steagall Act of 1938, built two housing projects for blacks. Notes that the projects were developed in such a way as to limit the expansion of black neighborhoods and reinforce segregation patterns. Based on Housing Division Records, Housing Association Papers, government reports and other materials; 2 illus., 31 notes.   D. C. Swift

1131.   Benson, Susan Porter.   BUSINESS HEADS & SYMPATHIZING HEARTS: THE WOMEN OF THE PROVIDENCE EMPLOYMENT SOCIETY.   *J. of Social Hist. 1978 12(2): 302-312.* Recent work on women's history has led to new questions regarding "the warp of affectional and kin ties on which the fabric of daily life was woven." To answer these questions the author focuses upon the 52 women managers

of the Providence (Rhode Island) Employment Society (PES) from 1837 to 1858, which was a typical meliorist urban reform organization devoted to aiding self-supporting seamstresses. Most of the managers were members of the social and economic elite of Providence. Concludes that there emerged a sex-based culture among the women on the PES, which was an amalgam of their class and gender position. Their female culture distanced them from men with whom they lived and their class-based style of life distanced them from their working-class sisters. The society in which they lived, however, did not exacerbate these contradictions. Primary and secondary sources; 34 notes.   R. S. Sliwoski

1132.   Bolin, Winifred D. Wandersee.   HEATING UP THE MELTING POT: SETTLEMENT WORK AND AMERICANIZATION IN NORTHEAST MINNEAPOLIS.   *Minnesota Hist. 1976 45(2): 58-70.* Since the turn of the century northeast Minneapolis has remained an Eastern European ethnic enclave. Middle class Progressive reformers were concerned about the slow assimilation of these mainly Roman and Eastern Catholic groups. From a survey of the neighborhood emerged in January 1915 the North East Neighborhood House, headed by Robbins Gilman and his wife, Catheryne Cooke Gilman. The venture offered social, civic, and economic opportunities to adults and children. Initial projects such as job search aid and a day nursery were supplemented during World War I by help for men registering for the draft, Red Cross courses in a variety of subjects, recreation facilities for servicemen, and coordinating the sale of thrift stamps and war bonds to the people of the neighborhood. By 1918, the neighborhood was a scene of ethnic cooperation rather than antagonism. In the 1920's the settlement house became a center of Americanization and moral uplift efforts in the neighborhood.
N. Lederer

1133.   Brenzel, Barbara.   LANCASTER INDUSTRIAL SCHOOL FOR GIRLS: A SOCIAL PORTRAIT OF A NINETEENTH CENTURY REFORM SCHOOL FOR GIRLS.   *Feminist Studies 1975 3(1-2): 40-53.* The mid-19th-century conviction that changes in environment could encourage rehabilitation influenced early efforts to reform children. In 1856 the first reform school for girls was established in Lancaster, Massachusetts. It included girls who were merely poor, not actually delinquent. The majority of the girls were adolescents, between 12 and 16, with no mother at home. The school served to protect them from the possibilities of promiscuity and the life of vice which tempted the poverty stricken young woman on her own. The school provided some minimal education and attempted Protestant religious training, but was in the main a shelter for girls, rather than an educational or vocational center. Based on primary and secondary sources; 29 notes.
S. R. Herstein

1134.   Campbell, George Duncan.   THE SAILORS' HOME.   *Am. Neptune 1977 37(3): 179-184.* Discusses the origins of the American Seaman's Friend Society in the 1820's and its early efforts to establish and influence the development of sailors' homes or boarding houses in New York City. Describes the 19th-century system by which sailors procured their lodgings before the establishment of sailors' homes and how they could be exploited by taverners and innkeepers. Published sources; sketches, biblio.   G. H. Curtis

1135.   Cavallo, Dom.   SOCIAL REFORM AND THE MOVEMENT TO ORGANIZE CHILDREN'S PLAY DURING THE PROGRESSIVE ERA.   *Hist. of Childhood Q. 1976 3(4): 509-522.* Efforts to supervise children's play and to create formal playgrounds, exemplified by the Playground Association of America and the activity of major Progressive reformers, arose from a new view of the role of play in children's lives. As a result of the work of G. Stanley Hall and his followers, play came to be conceptualized as each child's recreation of phases of man's social evolution. By directing play the positive aspects of that evolution could be more fully inculcated. Further, associated physiological theory assumed that physical conditioning was linked to moral development. Together these ideas promised Progressives a means of dealing with the social problems of urban-industrial life. Primary and secondary sources; 40 notes.   R. E. Butchart

1136.   Clark, Roger W.   CINCINNATI CRUSADERS FOR TEMPERANCE: 1874.   *Cincinnati Hist. Soc. Bull. 1974 32(4): 185-199.* Discusses activities and demonstrations of the Women's National Christian Temperance Union in Cincinnati, Ohio, including the role of Wesley Chapel (Methodist Church) and the Ninth Street Baptist Church.

1137. Clayton, John. THE SCOURGE OF SINNERS: ARTHUR BURRAGE FARWELL. *Chicago Hist. 1974 3(2): 68-77.* Social reformer and opponent of political corruption in Chicago, Arthur Burrage Farwell, was a major force within the Hyde Park Protective Association's fight for Prohibition.   S

1138. Clement, Priscilla Ferguson. FAMILIES AND FOSTER CARE: PHILADELPHIA IN THE LATE NINETEENTH CENTURY. *Social Service Rev. 1979 53(3): 406-420.* The Home Missionary Society of Philadelphia and the Children's Aid Society of Pennsylvania placed poor, urban, usually white Protestant children in country homes as servants or farm laborers, 1880-1905.

1139. Cleveland, Mary L. A BAPTIST PASTOR AND SOCIAL JUSTICE IN CLINTON, TENNESSEE. *Baptist Hist. and Heritage 1979 14(2): 15-19.* Describes the efforts of Baptist pastor Paul Turner in dealing with the violence resulting from forced desegregation in the community of Clinton, Tennessee, in 1956.

1140. Culton, Donald R. LOS ANGELES' "CITIZEN FIXIT": CHARLES DWIGHT WILLARD, CITY BOOSTER AND PROGRESSIVE REFORMER. *California History 1978 57(2): 158-171.* Charles Dwight Willard (1860-1914) arrived in Los Angeles in 1888. Never particularly successful in business, Willard found his talents in newspaper work, promotion of the city's commercial potential, and moderate civic improvements. He was on the staff of several Los Angeles newspapers, secretary of the Chamber of Commerce in the 1890's, founder of the influential Sunset Club in 1895, and founder of several civic improvement groups. He started and contributed to several magazines. Because of his presence and involvement in City Council affairs, he was known as the "councilman from the 10th ward" in a nine-ward city. The *Times* uncharitably called him "Citizen Fixit." Despite declining health, Willard used his pen to urge such civic reforms as civil service, municipal ownership of services, and an end to bossism. His career delineates the "ties between promotion and reform in the progressive era." Primary and secondary sources; illus., 46 notes.   A. Hoffman

1141. Davis, Allen F. JACOB RIIS AND URBAN REFORM. *J. of Urban Hist. 1976 2(3): 377-379.* Jacob Riis, one of the leading urban reformers of the Progressive Era, was not the subject of a successful comprehensive scholarly investigation until James B. Lane's *Jacob A. Riis and the American City* (Port Washington, N. Y.: Kennikat Pr., 1974). Lane argues that Riis was a moral reformer whose goal was social justice, not social control and efficiency. He shows, however, that Riis, like many other reformers, could not see through prevailing racial and ethnic stereotypes.   T. W. Smith

1142. Eversole, Theodore W. THE CINCINNATI UNION BETHEL: THE COMING OF AGE OF THE SETTLEMENT IDEA IN CINCINNATI. *Cincinnati Hist. Soc. Bull. 1974 32(1-2): 47-59.* Outlines the history of social reform settlement houses in Cincinnati, Ohio, specifically the Jewish Cincinnati Union Bethel settlement house, 1838-1903.

1143. Farnam, Anne. UNCLE VENNER'S FARM: REFUGE OR WORKHOUSE FOR SALEM'S POOR? *Essex Inst. Hist. Collections 1973 109(1): 60-86.* Discusses the sociological and historical significance of Uncle Venner's farm in Nathaniel Hawthorne's *The House of the Seven Gables* (1851), and the reality of Salem's workhouse for the poor.   S

1144. Felt, Jeremy P. VICE REFORM AS A POLITICAL TECHNIQUE: THE COMMITTEE OF FIFTEEN IN NEW YORK, 1900-1901. *New York Hist. 1973 54(1): 24-51.* History of the Committee of Fifteen, an upper-middle-class reform organization dedicated to the eradication of police-protected vice and gambling in New York City. To committee members, the antivice crusade was the most effective tactic in the political war against Tammany Hall. Defeat of Tammany, rather than moral reform, was their primary objective. Primary and secondary sources; 11 illus., 36 notes.   G. Kurland

1145. Fisher, Robert. COMMUNITY ORGANIZING AND CITIZEN PARTICIPATION: THE EFFORTS OF THE PEOPLE'S INSTITUTE IN NEW YORK CITY, 1910-1920. *Social Service Rev. 1977 51(3): 474-490.* Analyzes the goals, methods, and organizational structure of the People's Institute of New York City, an urban reform group which sought, 1910-20, to organize working class immigrants on the neighborhood level as part of a larger national organization seeking to employ public schools as community centers.

1146. Frazier, Arthur H. HENRY SEYBERT AND THE CENTENNIAL CLOCK AND BELL AT INDEPENDENCE HALL. *Pennsylvania Mag. of Hist. and Biog. 1978 102(1): 40-58.* Following his admired father's death, Henry Seybert almost gave up mineralogy, to which he had significantly contributed, and turned to spiritualism. He wandered for 20 years. After 1846 he became involved in Philadelphia civic affairs. The clock and bell, first projected as a public project in 1860, were personally consummated in 1876. Believing he could obtain heaven by helping the poor, he broadly bequeathed his benificence, including the founding of Seybert Institute. Based on manuscript and printed sources, and on secondary works; 49 notes.   T. H. Wendel

1147. Fry, Annette Riley. THE CHILDREN'S MIGRATION. *Am. Heritage 1974 26(1): 4-10, 79-81.* As an alternative to the institutionalizing of New York's orphan children, Charles Loring Brace founded the Children's Aid Society in 1853. For 75 years the society sent unwanted city children into the farming communities of America to live with families who wanted and needed them. The society's failures were few, and many of the children became very successful as adults: governors, mayors, teachers, ministers, and doctors. 13 illus.   B. J. Paul

1148. George, Paul S. A CYCLONE HITS MIAMI: CARRIE NATION'S VISIT TO "THE WICKED CITY." *Florida Hist. Q. 1979 58(2): 150-159.* Carrie Nation visited Miami in 1908, attempting to establish another dry city. Her visit did not succeed. Prohibition was accomplished in 1913, but Miami flouted the law and earned a reputation as an "open city." Based on newspaper accounts and other primary sources; 57 notes.   N. A. Kuntz

1149. Gettleman, Marvin E. PHILANTHROPY AS SOCIAL CONTROL IN LATE NINETEENTH-CENTURY AMERICA: SOME HYPOTHESES AND DATA ON THE RISE OF SOCIAL WORK. *Societas 1975 5(1): 49-59.* The leaders of the New York Charity Organization Society achieved an ideology in harmony with contemporary academic theories of social organization. This led to closer cooperation with the emerging new universities and a higher degree of professionalism in the new field of social work. Notes.   W. H. Mulligan, Jr.

1150. Goren, Arthur A. MOTHER ROSIE HERTZ, THE SOCIAL EVIL, AND THE NEW YORK KEHILLAH. *Michael: On the Hist. of the Jews in the Diaspora [Israel] 1975 3: 188-210.* In 1912 the Jewish community of New York City launched its own anti-crime campaign, setting up a Bureau of Social Morals to gather eivdence and present it to the city's law-enforcement agencies for action. Presents documents written by the Bureau's chief investigator, 21-year-old Abe Shoenfeld, concerning a Hungarian Jewish immigrant family, headed by Mrs. Rosie Hertz, who owned and managed a string of brothels on the Lower East Side for more than 30 years. Convicted on 4 February 1913 of running a disorderly resort, Mrs. Hertz was committed to prison two months later. Primary and secondary sources; 15 notes.   T. Sassoon

1151. Grabowski, John J. FROM PROGRESSIVE TO PATRICIAN: GEORGE BELLAMY AND HIRAM HOUSE SOCIAL SETTLEMENT, 1896-1914. *Ohio Hist. 1978 87(1): 37-52.* Discusses the early history of Hiram House, the first social settlement in Cleveland, and how the attitudes and changing lifestyle of its founder and director, George Bellamy, affected its operations. Originally, dedicated to reform-oriented programs, Hiram House's success came only after it was transformed into an orderly operation by a group of businessmen which narrowed dramatically the range of programs the settlement could offer. Bellamy and the programs eventually focused on the proper development of individual character, which enabled him to avoid the progressive schemes of environmental alteration and social change. Based on archives, contemporary comments, and secondary sources; 2 illus., 47 notes.   N. Summers

1152. Grinder, Robert Dale. FROM INSURGENCY TO EFFICIENCY: THE SMOKE ABATEMENT CAMPAIGN IN PITTSBURGH BEFORE WORLD WAR I. *Western Pennsylvania Hist.*

Mag. 1978 61(3): 187-202. Pittsburgh's smoke abatement movement, 1890's-1918, attracted a reform and engineering elite and gained impetus after the defeat of Corwin D. Tilbury's proposal to create the post of city smoke inspector in 1906.

1153. Haber, Carole. THE OLD FOLKS AT HOME: THE DEVELOPMENT OF INSTITUTIONALIZED CARE FOR THE AGED IN NINETEENTH-CENTURY PHILADELPHIA. *Pennsylvania Mag. of Hist. and Biog. 1977 101(2): 240-257.* Philadelphia began the 19th century with not one home for the aged, and ended it with 24. The first, formed in 1817 for elderly ladies, was followed by others for women, as well as homes for men and for Negroes. None of these offered much in the way of work or recreation, as sanitation, warmth, and food were the dominant concerns. Medical aid and religious services were added. The homes endeavored to be substitutes for the real homes of days gone by. 62 notes. V. L. Human

1154. Hall, Peter Dobkin. THE MODEL OF BOSTON CHARITY: A THEORY OF CHARITABLE BENEVOLENCE AND CLASS DEVELOPMENT. *Sci. and Soc. 1974-75 38(4): 464-477.* Studies the relationship among upper class families, the development of industrial capitalism, and the privately endowed cultural institutions in the 18th and 19th centuries.

1155. Heale, M. J. FROM CITY FATHERS TO SOCIAL CRITICS: HUMANITARIANISM AND GOVERNMENT IN NEW YORK, 1790-1860. *J. of Am. Hist. 1976 63(1): 21-41.* The humanitarian role played by the affluent of New York City altered dramatically 1790-1860. As the "well-ordered community of the early republic gave way to the sprawling and overcrowded metropolis of the mid-nineteenth century," the benevolent city fathers were forced from their political positions, based on their "natural" right to govern, and were replaced by party politics based on patronage. Philanthropic associations were formed; their activities presaging the social worker. 39 notes. V. P. Rilee

1156. Heale, M. J. HARBINGERS OF PROGRESSIVISM: RESPONSES TO THE URBAN CRISIS IN NEW YORK, C. 1845-1860. *J. of Am. Studies [Great Britain] 1976 10(1): 17-36.* Analyzes the reform programs and social service work of five humanitarian organizations in New York City during the 1840's and 1850's. The groups attacked poor municipal government, crime, prostitution, gambling, and soaring death and disease rates in New York slums. In the end, the groups provided many social services which afforded relief to individuals, but their crusades failed to alter laws and make publicly controlled relief agencies more responsive. Based on publications of reform organizations and on secondary sources; 35 notes. H. T. Lovin

1157. Heale, M. J. PATTERNS OF BENEVOLENCE: ASSOCIATED PHILANTHROPY IN THE CITIES OF NEW YORK, 1830-1860. *New York Hist. 1976 57(1): 53-79.* The growth of associated philanthropy in New York during 1830-60 was a response to urbanization, immigration, increasing social distance between rich and poor, and mounting urban social problems. Describes the work of philanthropic associations in New York City, Albany, Brooklyn, Buffalo, and Rochester. 6 illus., 30 notes. R. N. Lokken

1158. Heale, M. J. PATTERNS OF BENEVOLENCE: CHARITY AND MORALITY IN RURAL AND URBAN NEW YORK, 1783-1830. *Societas 1973 3(4): 337-359.* "Increasingly, benevolence was designed not merely to aid the needy but also to strengthen or reform their characters." In the rural areas a sense of community prevailed, but in an urban setting benevolence became almost indistinguishable from moral reform, though all Americans were worried about anarchic tendencies. 65 notes. E. P. Stickney

1159. Jackson, Philip. BLACK CHARITY IN PROGRESSIVE ERA CHICAGO. *Social Service Rev. 1978 52(3): 400-417.* Black charities were formed in response to increasing social problems Negroes faced due, in part, to their exclusion from organized charity; covers 1890-1917.

1160. Kadzielski, Mark A. "AS A FLOWER NEEDS SUNSHINE": THE ORIGINS OF ORGANIZED CHILDREN'S RECREATION IN PHILADELPHIA, 1886-1911. *J. of Sport Hist. 1977 4(2): 169-188.* The play movement was the progressive response to urbanized society. Orga-

nized recreation for children supplied old values with new meanings at the turn of the 20th century. Boston began the play movement in 1886, and Philadelphia soon followed. Philanthropists and subsequently municipal authorities provided the impetus. 43 notes. M. Kaufman

1161. Kusmer, Kenneth L. THE FUNCTIONS OF ORGANIZED CHARITY IN THE PROGRESSIVE ERA: CHICAGO AS A CASE STUDY. *J. of Am. Hist. 1973 60(3): 657-678.* A study of the Charities Organization Society Movement in Chicago in the 1880's and 1890's demonstrates that in the beginning the society was concerned with transmitting the values of small-town rural America to the urban context. Values of community, country life, and the middle class were stressed by upwardly mobile charity workers from small midwestern towns whose cultural values were threatened by the many immigrant poor. The movement employed as "friendly visitors" middle-class women who applied values of the "home" to the city, and was financed by wealthy merchants, bankers, and lawyers who thought broadly of the need to avoid growing social conflict. Increasing economic dislocation and unemployment after 1890 led toward a more modern welfare system. Table, 90 notes.
K. B. West

1162. Lane, James B. FOR GOOD GOVERNMENT: JACOB A. RIIS' URBAN REFORM ACTIVITIES IN NEW YORK CITY, 1895-1897. *Societas 1973 3(2): 143-157.* Between 1895 and 1897 Riis worked along three political paths: as general agent for the New York Council of Good-Government Clubs, as secretary to Mayor Strong's Advisory Committee on Small Parks, and as a close advisor of Theodore Roosevelt, the president of the Board of Police Commissioners. Riis was unhappy with the continuing abuses of child labor. He wanted the clubs to demand better enforcement of the law and to draw up plans for proposed reforms. He achieved some results in action against tenement-housing abuses. "His practical, humanitarian deeds established him as one of the most useful allies of the slum dweller." 40 notes. E. P. Stickney

1163. Leonard, Henry B. THE IMMIGRANTS' PROTECTIVE LEAGUE OF CHICAGO, 1908-1921. *J. of the Illinois State Hist. Soc. 1973 66(3): 271-284.* The unprecedented numbers of immigrants from Southern and Eastern Europe were called racially inferior by people descended from Northwestern Europeans. The Immigrants' Protective League, founded in Chicago in 1908 by Jane Addams and other reformers, helped the new immigrants in urban-industrial American life. The league sought broad government intervention to protect the immigrants in employment, education, and the courts. Despite some failures, the league guided immigrants in an imaginative, enlightened, and humane way that acquainted the public with their problems. Based on the league's annual reports and papers in the manuscript division of the Library of the University of Illinois, Chicago Circle; 2 photos, 34 notes.
A. C. Aimone

1164. Lubove, Roy. FREDERIC C. HOWE AND THE QUEST FOR COMMUNITY. *Historian 1977 39(2): 270-291.* Frederic Clemson Howe (1867-1940) embodied liberal ideals and experience. The evolution of his thought reveals much about 20th-century American liberalism, especially the progressivism. It was inspired by the "values of agrarian equalitarianism and small-town evangelical Protestantism," but nonetheless was very complex in its origins and manifestations. Yet, through it all, there was a measure of unity: a quest for community and the restoration of social cohesion in the cities. "Howe ultimately embraced the ideal of cooperative democracy because he recognized that as the administrative and judicial prerogatives of the state expand, administrative-judicial fiat tends to supersede family and local autonomy." 66 notes.
R. V. Ritter

1165. Mabee, Carleton. CHARITY IN TRAVAIL: TWO ORPHAN ASYLUMS FOR BLACKS. *New York Hist. 1974 55(1): 55-77.* The New York Colored Orphan Asylum (now the Riverdale Children's Association) was the first orphan home established for Negro children in the New York City area. Founded in 1836 by a group of Quaker women led by Anna M. Shotwell, the asylum was controlled and staffed predominantly by whites. On the other hand, the Brooklyn Howard Colored Orphan Asylum, established in 1866 by Southern black women who had fled their native region, was controlled and staffed (until 1902) predominantly by blacks. As a result of severe financial problems, the Brooklyn home selected a predominantly white board of governors in 1902. The home went bankrupt during World War I and was forced to close its doors, but the white-controlled New York home escaped these difficulties. The Brooklyn home had deeper roots to the black community than did the New York home and was of far greater service to the Negro people of the New York area. The Brooklyn home failed because white America would not permit success to a black institution, independent of white control. Based on papers of the asylums; 7 illus., 53 notes.

G. Kurland

1166. MacPhail, Elizabeth C. WHEN THE RED LIGHTS WENT OUT IN SAN DIEGO: THE LITTLE KNOWN STORY OF SAN DIEGO'S "RESTRICTED" DISTRICT. *J. of San Diego Hist. 1975 20(2): 1-28.* Describes San Diego's Stingaree and Redlight Districts, 1870's-1917, and the efforts of Walter Bellon, City Health Inspector, to clean up the waterfront slums.

S

1167. McArthur, Benjamin. THE CHICAGO PLAYGROUND MOVEMENT: A NEGLECTED FEATURE OF SOCIAL JUSTICE. *Social Service Rev. 1975 49(3): 376-395.* Discusses the movement in American cities, begun in Chicago in 1894, to develop playgrounds for urban children as "part of the Progressive's quest for social justice."

S

1168. McClymer, John F. THE PITTSBURGH SURVEY, 1907-1914: FORGING AN IDEOLOGY IN THE STEEL DISTRICT. *Pennsylvania Hist. 1974 41(2): 169-186.* The *Pittsburgh Survey*, first published in 1909 in three issues of *Charities and the Commons*, was undertaken in 1907 by professors, social workers, charitable societies, and ethnic associations. It reflects the essentially moderate attitudes of a new class of social engineers who thought it possible to accurately measure the social effects of industrialization and to suggest viable remedies. Surveys of other industrial cities were modelled on this effort. Illus., 52 notes.

D. C. Swift

1169. McElroy, James L. SOCIAL CONTROL AND ROMANTIC REFORM IN ANTEBELLUM AMERICA: THE CASE OF ROCHESTER, NEW YORK. *New York Hist. 1977 58(1): 17-46.* Examines reform studies of antebellum Rochester, New York, to test the paradoxical association between radical reform and conservative religious benevolence. Religious revivalism led converts first to religious benevolence and then to radical reform. The divisive anti-slavery issue, secularizaton of social control, and lessened interest in religious revivalism resulted with the decline of conservative religious benevolence. These reform movements were supported mostly by white collar groups. Younger people were attracted to radical reform. 5 illus., table, 69 notes.

R. N. Lokken

1170. Mohl, Raymond and Betten, Neil. PATERNALISM AND PLURALISM: IMMIGRANTS AND SOCIAL WELFARE IN GARY, INDIANA, 1906-1940. *Am. Studies [Lawrence, KS] 1974 15(1): 5-30.* Examines social welfare in Gary and substantiates the theme that public welfare programs manipulate the poor, keep them under social control, and drive them into low income, menial jobs. Settlement house work served "the interests of American society more than those of the immigrants themselves." The houses exhibited a nativist paternalism, and tried to Americanize all immigrants. A few exceptions, such as the International Institute, fostered a sense of ethnic identification. Based on primary and secondary sources; 56 notes.

J. Andrew

1171. Monroe, Alden N. EFFECTS TO CAUSES: THE EVOLUTION OF A SOCIAL AGENCY. *Cincinnati Hist. Soc. Bull. 1979 37(3): 191-216.* Traces the evolution of charitable organizations in the United States beginning in the 1870's, particularly the Associated Charities of Cincinnati, founded in 1870 as an umbrella group for Cincinnati's charities and assistance groups; it became known as Family Service of the Cincinnati Area in 1960.

1172. Moore, Deborah Dash. FROM KEHILLAH TO FEDERATION: THE COMMUNAL FUNCTIONS OF FEDERATED PHILANTHROPY IN NEW YORK CITY, 1917-1933. *Am. Jewish Hist. 1978 68(2): 131-146.* The Federation for the Support of Jewish Philanthropic Societies as an alternative communal structure to that of the Kehillah with its religious and almost obligatory nuances began in New York City in 1917. A fund raising apparatus that recognized class differ-

ences but stressed mass participation and emphasized nonsectarianism remained the framework for a minimal community into the 1930's. Samson Benderly and other Federation leaders recognized early that potentially it could be transformed into a viable, broad, and truly Jewish community. 24 notes.

F. Rosenthal

1173. Mulder, John M. THE HEAVENLY CITY AND HUMAN CITIES: WASHINGTON GLADDEN AND URBAN REFORM. *Ohio Hist. 1978 87(2): 151-174.* Examines the relationship between the social gospel and urbanization and the social gospel's influence in urban reform through the preaching and reform efforts of Washington Gladden, one of the earliest influential social gospel leaders. Gladden's activity spanned six decades and ranged from the antislavery movement of the 1850's to the New Freedom of Woodrow Wilson. His constant theme was the need for social reform. In 1882 Gladden moved to Columbus, Ohio, where he held the pulpit of the First Congregational Church for more than 30 years. The capital provided an excellent forum for Gladden's proclamations and spurred the development of ideas on urban, social, and economic reform. He became active in Columbus politics and the progressive movement until his death. Based on primary and secondary sources; 3 illus., 72 notes.

N. Summers

1174. Nash, Gary B. POVERTY AND POOR RELIEF IN PRE-REVOLUTIONARY PHILADELPHIA. *William and Mary Q. 1976 33(1): 3-30.* Discusses the growth of private and public responsibility for the care of the increasing poor in Philadelphia in the 18th century. Emphasizes the role of the Pennsylvania Hospital for the Sick Poor. The relocation of Acadian neutrals in Philadelphia during the French and Indian War and the revival of Irish and German immigration in the 1760's added to the burden of poor relief. Quakers contributed much private philanthrophy. Also notes the new ideology regarding the poor, with some comparison to ideas in England. Based on manuscript records and secondary sources; 3 tables, 79 notes.

H. M. Ward

1175. Naylor, Timothy J. RESPONDING TO THE FIRE: THE WORK OF THE CHICAGO RELIEF AND AID SOCIETY. *Sci. & Soc. 1975/76 39(4): 450-464.* Traces the efficiency and achievements of the Chicago Relief and Aid Society in the administration and disbursement to all levels of society of five million dollars given to the city after the great fire of 1871.

1176. Nye, Ronald L. THE CHALLENGE TO PHILANTHROPY: UNEMPLOYMENT RELIEF IN SANTA BARBARA, 1930-1932. *California Hist. Q. 1977-78 56(4): 310-327.* Santa Barbara met the challenge of unemployment relief during the first two years of the Great Depression. Led by philanthropist Max Fleischmann, the community attempted to provide work relief, create jobs, and solicit private funds to subsidize public works projects. These goals were implemented through citizens' committees, especially the Emergency Unemployment Fund Committee, created in December 1930. Wealthy residents were urged to contribute. With conditions worsening by fall 1931, a second campaign raised almost $115,000. Santa Barbarans endorsed job creation, work relief, and priority aid to the city's jobless residents, including singles and Mexican Americans. Transients were encouraged to move on, and Mexican noncitizens were advised to return to Mexico. By mid-1932 the magnitude of the problem was recognized, and funding shifted to public agencies. Primary sources and secondary studies; illus., 59 notes.

A. Hoffman

1177. Parker, Peter J. RICH AND POOR IN PHILADELPHIA, 1709. *Pennsylvania Mag. of Hist. and Biog. 1975 99(1): 3-19.* The working of the 1705-06 Philadelphia Poor Law has remained misunderstood in its inner machinations. Three recently discovered papers shed some light on how the money to finance it was collected and spent in 1709. Recipients were primarily women, some having dependent children. Payment rates varied, although no formula exists to explain why. Records were meticulously kept and monies were collected by taxation. 2 tables, 4 notes.

V. L. Human

1178. Patterson, R. S. and Rooke, Patricia. THE DELICATE DUTY OF CHILD SAVING: COLDWATER, MICHIGAN, 1871-1896. *Michigan Hist. 1977 61(3): 194-219.* The Coldwater State Public School, founded in 1874, was an example of the 19th-century humanitarian effort to save dependent children from lives of crime by teaching them Protes-

tant, middle-class virtues. Social uplift at Coldwater focused on those from the "perishing class" of the potentially criminal. Whether the reformers were more interested in social control or social improvement remains an issue. Primary and secondary sources; 8 illus., 9 photos, 47 notes.
　　　　　　　　　　　　　　　　　　　　　　　　　　　D. W. Johnson

1179. Rammelkamp, Julian S. ST. LOUIS: BOOSTERS AND BOODLERS. *Missouri Hist. Soc. Bull. 1978 34(4): 200-210.* With nearly 600,000 residents in 1900 and continuing economic expansion, St. Louis encountered major urban troubles that were worsened by fast-spreading tenement districts, unresponsive and tradition-bound power and class structures in the city, and growing social ferment against the elites. Finally, out of self-interest, St. Louis business and civic leaders joined hands with Progressive reformers. Between 1900 and 1915, they made St. Louis a showplace for reforms designed to ameliorate municipal woes that were ignored during the 19th century. Based on secondary and newspaper sources; 3 photos, 36 notes.
　　　　　　　　　　　　　　　　　　　　　　　　　　　H. T. Lovin

1180. Raphael, Marc Lee. FEDERATED PHILANTHROPY IN AN AMERICAN JEWISH COMMUNITY: 1904-1948. *Am. Jewish Hist. 1978 68(2): 147-162.* The story and development of the Federation movement in one American Jewish community, that of Columbus, Ohio, illustrates the paths taken during those decades throughout the country. The shift from local to national and overseas allocations and the increase in contributors and contributions, especially after 1937-38, were accompanied by gradual democratization of the board, even though the bulk of the money continued to be contributed by a tiny minority. Yet the Federation, because of its control of philanthropy, brought secular and religious, traditional and non-traditional, Zionist and non-Zionist Jews together, the only true forum in the community. 28 notes.
　　　　　　　　　　　　　　　　　　　　　　　　　　　F. Rosenthal

1181. Rauch, Julia B. QUAKERS AND THE FOUNDING OF THE PHILADELPHIA SOCIETY FOR ORGANIZING CHARITY RELIEF AND REPRESSING MENDICANCY. *Pennsylvania Mag. of Hist. and Bio. 1974 98(4): 438-455.* Blaming poverty on pauperism and insisting on the necessity for character reformation, 19th-century charities failed to meet the needs of the urban poor. The activities of the Philadelphia Society for Organizing Charitable Relief and Repressing Mendicancy (SOC), founded in 1879 by Quakers, reflected the upper-class, moralistic, and repressive nature of charity relief. Since Philadelphia "Quakers did not recognize that an urban, industrialized society required social insurance and other economic security programs," they "ended up supporting a conservative, backward-looking program, one which was repressive toward the poor." Based on primary and secondary sources; 46 notes.
　　　　　　　　　　　　　　　　　　　　　　　　　　　E. W. Carp

1182. Rauch, Julia B. WOMEN IN SOCIAL WORK: FRIENDLY VISITORS IN PHILADELPHIA, 1880. *Social Service Rev. 1975 49(2): 241-259.* Examines the characteristics of the women involved in the Philadelphia Society for Organizing Charitable Relief and Repressing Mendicancy during the years 1864-1909, using data obtained from schedules of the 1880 US Census.
　　　　　　　　　　　　　　　　　　　　　　　　　　　S

1183. Ringenbach, Paul T. DISCARDING RURAL NOSTRUMS FOR CITY PROBLEMS: MOVING TOWARDS URBAN REFORM. *Rocky Mountain Social Sci. J. 1973 10(1): 33-42.* Only after social reformers attempted futile rural solutions did they try to improve urban life.
　　　　　　　　　　　　　　　　　　　　　　　　　　　S

1184. Rivers, Larry E. THE PITTSBURGH WORKSHOP FOR THE BLIND, 1910-1939: A CASE STUDY OF THE BLINDED SYSTEM IN AMERICA. *Western Pennsylvania Hist. Mag. 1978 61(2): 135-150.* Surveys historical attitudes toward blind persons during the 19th century, the movement toward education of the blind, and a specific case, the Pittsburgh Workshop for the Blind in western Pennsylvania which sought, 1910-39, to provide employment for the blind.

1185. Romanofsky, Peter. SAVING THE LIVES OF THE CITY'S FOUNDLINGS: THE JOINT COMMITTEE AND NEW YORK CITY CHILD CARE METHODS, 1860-1907. *New-York Hist. Soc. Q. 1977 61(1-2): 49-68.* At the turn of the century, the Joint Committee on the Care of Motherless Infants in New York City made considerable progress in attempting to solve the problem of the growing number of babies (orphans and the offspring of the poor) who needed care. Unfortu-

nately its efforts, largely directed at farming out the babies to private homes, were thwarted by politics, religious differences, and by those who believed institutionalization was the proper method of care. By 1907 adherents of the "New York System" (public money given to private institutions—largely favored by Catholics) had won out and the committee ceased to function. Such progress as had been made came to an end, and public care of the children became again regressive. Primary sources; 45 notes, 3 illus.
　　　　　　　　　　　　　　　　　　　　　　　　　　　C. L. Grant

1186. Romanofsky, Peter. "TO SAVE ... THEIR SOULS": THE CARE OF DEPENDENT CHILDREN IN NEW YORK CITY, 1900-1905. *Jewish Social Studies 1974 36(3/4): 253-261.* During 1903-05 a small number of dependent children were placed in foster homes of working class families rather than families of middle class background. The program was initiated by the United Hebrew Charities of New York City in order to cope with the increasing number of orphans and other children that needed help as Jewish immigration from Eastern Europe increased. Ideological opposition and lack of financial support terminated the program but its pioneering prepared the way for a change in the general American approach. Primary and secondary sources; 27 notes.
　　　　　　　　　　　　　　　　　　　　　　　　　　　P. E. Schoenberg

1187. Ross, Edyth L. BLACK HERITAGE IN SOCIAL WELFARE: A CASE STUDY OF ATLANTA. *Phylon 1976 37(4): 297-307.* "An examination of the social welfare heritage of black Americans demonstrates their pioneer role in devising many forms of social intervention for promoting the social welfare of the group." The First Congregational Church, the first institutional church of the country, the largest and most progressive Negro church, developed a social welfare program the effectiveness of which is shown by the fact that the death rate in the church was one-third lower than that among the white population. The program played a large part in the restoration of the city's Negro community after the terrible race riot of 1906. Describes the development of the School of Social Service which became affiliated with Atlanta University. 20 notes.
　　　　　　　　　　　　　　　　　　　　　　　　　　　E. P. Stickney

1188. Rubinoff, Michael W. RABBI IN A PROGRESSIVE ERA: C.E.H. KAUVAR OF DENVER. *Colorado Mag. 1977 54(3): 220-239.* Russian-born (1879) and New York-educated, Rabbi Charles Eliezer Hillel Kauvar served Denver's orthodox Beth Ha Medrosh Hagodol synagogue during 1902-71. A leading progressive reformer, Kauvar founded the Jewish Consumptives' Relief Society and an orphanage, worked closely with Judge Benjamin Barr Lindsey in attacking juvenile delinquency, and was a long-time leader of Denver's Community Chest. He was a Zionist, urged ecumenism, and vigorously opposed the Ku Klux Klan in the 1920's. Primary and secondary sources; 10 illus., 51 notes.
　　　　　　　　　　　　　　　　　　　　　　　　　　　O. H. Zabel

1189. Ryan, Mary P. THE POWER OF WOMEN'S NETWORKS: A CASE STUDY OF FEMALE MORAL REFORM IN ANTEBELLUM AMERICA. *Feminist Studies 1979 5(1): 66-86.* Examines the activities and influence of the Female Moral Reform Society of Utica, New York, in the 1830's and 1840's as an example of the exercise of power by women to shape history. The social climate of Utica, a small commercial city, was ideal for the development of influence by organized women, in the transitional area betwen public and private organizaiton. But the ultimate result was the development of more repressive sexual standards for women. Concludes that women's power is not always an unqualified good and draws a parallel with the New Right of the 1970's. 23 notes.
　　　　　　　　　　　　　　　　　　　　　　　　　　　L. M. Maloney

1190. Schallhorn, Cathlyn. CHEATING THE STREETS. *Chicago Hist. 1977-78 6(4): 229-241.* Describes the life of street children in Chicago in the late 19th century and efforts by the city and private reform groups, specifically the Off-the-Street Club, founded in 1898, which was run by amateurs and operated under the philosophy that the children could best be helped by dealing with them on their own level.

1191. Scharnau, Ralph. ELIZABETH MORGAN, CRUSADER FOR LABOR REFORM. *Labor Hist. 1973 14(3): 340-351.* Elizabeth Chambers Morgan (b. 1850), Chicago trade unionist and social reformer, rose from unskilled labor to prominence in Chicago reform and union circles. With a power base in the Ladies' Federal Labor Union and the Illinois Women's Alliance, Mrs. Morgan was partly instrumental in extending compulsory education for children, updating child labor laws, and the attack on sweatshops which resulted in the Factory and Workshop Inspection Act of 1893 in Illinois. Working with Hull House reformers and others, Mrs. Morgan helped explore detrimental health and labor conditions—for which exploration she has not received due credit. Based on the Thomas J. Morgan collection, Chicago newspapers, government reports, and secondary sources; 63 notes.   L. L. Athey

1192. Schlossman, Steven L. and Cohen, Ronald D. THE MUSIC MAN IN GARY: WILLIS BROWN AND CHILD-SAVING IN THE PROGRESSIVE ERA. *Societas 1977 7(1): 1-17.* Traces the checkered career of the juvenile reformer Willis Brown, concentrating on 1910-12 in the growing industrial city of Gary, Indiana. Immigration and technological advances created concern about juvenile delinquency. Brown's controversial, and not very successful, solutions "highlighted dangers implict in Progressive child-saving ideology in general." Based on collections at the Library of Congress, Indiana University, and Cornell University. Primary and secondary sources; 43 notes.   J. D. Hunley

1193. Shapiro, Edward S. ROBERT A. WOODS AND THE SETTLEMENT HOUSE IMPULSE. *Social Service Rev. 1978 52(2): 215-226.* Initially suspected by Catholics as an agency of Protestant proselytization, Boston's South End House, founded by Robert A. Woods, was intended to slow the city's growing religious, ethnic, and social heterogeneity by providing a sense of community; covers 1891-1900's.

1194. Smilor, Raymond W. CACOPHONY AT 34TH AND 6TH: THE NOISE PROBLEM IN AMERICA, 1900-1930. *Am. Studies [Lawrence, KS] 1977 18(1): 23-38.* The antinoise campaign was central to Progressive efforts at environmental reform, and provides a blueprint for early consumer activism. Led by the middle class, especially women, it represented a challenge to an industrialized society and a belief in progress. Noise was primitive and inefficient, and a danger to public health. Solutions included the establishment of "quiet zones," the formation of societies, and legislative relief. Primary and secondary sources; 58 notes.   J. Andrew

1195. Sobczak, John N. THE POLITICS OF RELIEF: PUBLIC AID IN TOLEDO, 1933-1937. *Northwest Ohio Q. 1976 48(4): 134-142.*

1196. Spatz, Marshall. CHILD ABUSE IN THE NINETEENTH CENTURY. *New York Affairs 1977 4(2): 80-90.* Discusses child abuse in New York City 1820's-80's and the establishment of the Society for the Prevention of Cruelty to Children.

1197. Sutherland, John F. THE ORIGINS OF PHILADELPHIA'S OCTAVIA HILL ASSOCIATION: SOCIAL REFORM IN THE "CONTENTED" CITY. *Pennsylvania Mag. of Hist. and Biog. 1975 99(1): 20-44.* An analysis of the philosophy, works, and influence of the Octavia Hill Association, a private reform group in Philadelphia dedicated to the improvement of the lot of the urban poor. The association purchased and improved homes, introduced strict sanitation measures, and meticulously avoided disrupting established neighborhoods. Its members lived in the affected neighborhoods but were socially not part of them. Their efforts were handicapped by the philosophy of the time but eventually led to governmental reform programs which enjoyed some success. 46 notes.   V. L. Human

1198. Sutherland, John F. RABBI JOSEPH KRAUSKOPF OF PHILADELPHIA: THE URBAN REFORMER RETURNS TO THE LAND. *Am. Jewish Hist. Q. 1978 67(4): 342-362.* Joseph Krauskopf (1858-1923) came to the United States as a 14-year-old. He graduated with the first class of four at Hebrew Union College in 1883 and was Philadelphia's foremost reform rabbi during 1887-1922. He introduced English into both services and the religious school, popularized the Jewish Sundry Services, and drafted the Pittsburgh Platform of 1885. His great concern with social reform led him into close cooperation with Jacob Riis. After a visit with Leo Tolstoy at Yasnaya Polyana, Krauskopf became the driving spirit of the Jewish "back-to-the land" movement and of the National Farm School, today known as the Delaware Valley College of Science and Agriculture, today the only private agricultural school in the country. Thoroughly part of America's urban milieu, Krauskopf nevertheless sought to modify it with the agrarian myth, an urban-agrarian ambivalence which still influences American thought and action.
                    F. Rosenthal

1199. Tobin, Eugene M. THE PROGRESSIVE AS HUMANITARIAN: JERSEY CITY'S SEARCH FOR SOCIAL JUSTICE, 1890-1917. *New Jersey Hist. 1975 93(3-4): 77-98.* Social reformers in Jersey City are classified into three groups: private, religious, and public. The Whittier House social settlement tackled problems associated with tenement slums, crime, infant mortality, and juvenile delinquency. Protestants campaigned for broad social welfare reform, while less affluent Catholics opted for assistance on an individual basis for its immigrant communicants. A separate juvenile court was established. World War I changed the priorities of reformers. A typical Jersey City reformer was "a native-stock, middle-class Protestant who resided in the Eighth or Ninth Ward and had some college training." Based on primary and secondary sources; 7 illus., 44 notes.   E. R. McKinstry

1200. Tselos, George. SELF-HELP AND SAUERKRAUT: THE ORGANIZED UNEMPLOYED, INC., OF MINNEAPOLIS. *Minnesota Hist. 1977 45(8): 306-320.* The Reverend George H. Mecklenburg founded the Organized Unemployed, Inc., in 1932. In this organization, individuals, through self-help, could lift themselves out of economic adversity. Headquartered in an old girls' high school in Minneapolis, the organization harvested, processed, and canned produce, operated a cafeteria and stores, cut wood for fuel, made clothing, and provided housing and employment services. It lasted until 1935 when superseded by government efforts. Scrip money was used as a medium of exchange, awarded in return for services to the organization. The organization's slogan, "Work Not Dole," indicated that its efforts represented a backward attempt to alleviate poverty through private endeavors rather than through organizing the poor to exert pressure on the government to provide jobs and sustenance. Primary sources.   N. Lederer

1201. Weiner, Lynn. "OUR SISTERS' KEEPERS": THE MINNEAPOLIS WOMAN'S CHRISTIAN ASSOCIATION AND HOUSING FOR WORKING WOMEN. *Minnesota Hist. 1979 46(5): 189-200.* In the late 19th century, many young women made their way to Minneapolis to find work, coming from rural areas and from Europe. The paucity of inexpensive boardinghouses available to these women and the consequent fear that poverty would drive the women into prostitution and other forms of criminal behavior, generated an effort on the part of middle and upper class Minneapolis women to provide suitable, safe and cheap housing for women. Various buildings were donated to the Women's Christian Association (WCA) for this purpose, and both long-term and temporary housing arrangements were made available. The boardinghouses sponsored by the WCA were run along rather puritanical lines but seemed to fill the needs of generations of female sojourners in the city. The WCA also sponsored Travelers' Aid efforts in which young women arriving by train were met by agents and were given advice and assistance. By the end of World War I large-scale migration into Minneapolis had ended and the efforts of the WCA tapered off but did not die out.   N. Lederer

1202. Williams, Marilyn Thornton. PHILANTHROPY IN THE PROGRESSIVE ERA: THE PUBLIC BATHS OF BALTIMORE. *Maryland Hist. Mag. 1977 72(1): 118-131.* In Baltimore the public bath system was not a clear-cut result of urban progressive reform or of simple private philanthropy. They had a semiprivate, semipublic character. Describes the long struggle of the city's Free Public Bath Commission, led by Rev. Thomas Beadenkopf and Eugene Levering, to gain support from the municipal government and the public for public baths. Only when railroad magnate Henry Walters agreed to build four baths at his own expense if the city would then maintain them, did the movement succeed. By 1912 there were five permanent baths, but the era of their greatest use was brief. Increasing numbers of urban families got their own facilities in their homes, and it was not evident that the poor had their morals significantly changed or converted to standards of middle-class cleanliness. As maintenance costs rose and patronage fell, Baltimore closed its baths in 1960. Primary sources; 50 notes.   G. J. Bobango

1203. Zainaldin, James S. and Tyor, Peter L. ASYLUM AND SOCIETY: AN APPROACH TO INSTITUTIONAL CHANGE. *J. of Social Hist. 1979 13(1): 23-48.* Studies two 19th-century asylums in Boston, one for the poor and the other for the feeble-minded. Covers the history of the institutions, discussing the sources of institutional policy and its reformulation, institutional operation, external perception and internal fact, and the social functions which the institution provides. Closes with an examination of the conclusions of other authors and a possibly fruitful path for additional studies. 7 tables, 57 notes.   V. L. Human

Law, Police, Crime, and Violence

1204. Alexander, John K. THE FORT WILSON INCIDENT OF 1779: A CASE STUDY OF THE REVOLUTIONARY CROWD. *William and Mary Q. 1974 31(4): 589-612.* On 4 October 1779 a crowd consisting mostly of militiamen rioted in Philadelphia looking for Tories and protesting the lack of price regulation. A confrontation at James Wilson's house led to a half dozen persons being killed and others wounded. Examines social and political conditions in Philadelphia as background for the actions of the Committee of 120, town meetings, Committee of Privates, and the Republican Society. Generally agrees with current generalizations of other writers, except that the disorder should be described as a crowd instead of a mob action. Based on primary and secondary sources; map, 80 notes.   H. M. Ward

1205. Aptheker, Bettina. THE SUPPRESSION OF THE *FREE SPEECH*: IDA B. WELLS AND THE MEMPHIS LYNCHING, 1892. *San José Studies 1977 3(3): 34-40.* Discusses the violent suppression of the *Free Speech,* a black newspaper in Memphis, Tennessee, whose condemnation in editorials by its publisher, Ida B. Wells, of race-related lynchings in 1892, resulted in the closure of the paper by members of the white community.

1206. Barnes, Merritt. "FOUNTAINHEAD OF CORRUPTION": PETER P. MCDONOUGH, BOSS OF SAN FRANCISCO'S UNDERWORLD. *California History 1979 58(2): 142-153.* For more than 25 years Peter P. McDonough and his brother Tom controlled San Francisco's vice operations. Outwardly a successful businessman, having established the first bail bonds business in the United States in 1896, McDonough became a millionaire through his connections to gambling, prostitution, graft, bootlegging, and political contacts. Without his approval, vice operations could not operate. For almost three decades San Franciscans tolerated the situation. McDonough's control of vice prevented the gang wars that occurred in other cities during this period. McDonough's fall from power is attributed to a change in public attitude caused by the Great Depression. People objected to the millions gained by vice when their own economic prospects were dim. When the Atherton Investigation of 1935 uncovered clear evidence of police graft, politicians abandoned McDonough. He lost his bail bond license in 1937. Despite repeated efforts, he never regained the license or his power. Photos, 70 notes.   A. Hoffman

1207. Bittner, Egon. THE RISE AND FALL OF THE THIN BLUE LINE. *Rev. in Am. Hist. 1978 6(3): 421-428.* Review article prompted by Robert M. Fogelson's *Big-City Police* (Cambridge, Mass.: Harvard U. Pr., 1977), which traces the history of graft, city politics and big-city police beginning at the turn of the century.

1208. Boyer, Lee R. LOBSTER BACKS, LIBERTY BOYS, AND LABORERS IN THE STREETS: NEW YORK'S GOLDEN HILL AND NASSAU STREET RIOTS. *New-York Hist. Soc. Q. 1973 57(4): 280-308.* Numerous clashes between British troops and colonials took place earlier than the well-publicized Boston Massacre in 1770. One of these was a bloody, two-day confrontation in New York City in January 1770 known as the Battle of Golden Hill. No deaths occurred there nor in a riot on Nassau Street a short time later. In both, merchant seamen were prominent, both money and labor problems were involved, and the outbreak was apparently spontaneous. Both were indications of deeper problems which would culminate in Lexington and Concord five years later. Based on contemporary correspondence, newspapers, and other primary sources; 9 illus., 44 notes.   C. L. Grant

1209. Cameron, Diane Maher. HISTORICAL PERSPECTIVE ON URBAN POLICE. *J. of Urban Hist. 1978 5(1): 125-132.* Until the last half dozen years, the police were an almost unexamined area of history. This has now begun to change with such books as George L. Mosse, ed., *Police Forces in History* with its cross-national comparisons and James F. Richardson, *Urban Police in the United States* with its interurban comparisons. Perhaps the chief value to both books is that they place the police in social, historical, and political context rather than treating it as an isolated topic. 12 notes.   T. W. Smith

1210. Cassell, Frank A. THE GREAT BALTIMORE RIOT OF 1812. *Maryland Hist. Mag. 1975 70(3): 241-259.* Uncontrolled armed warfare between a Republican mob and a group of Federalist zealots barricaded in a Baltimore house during 26-29 July 1812 "demonstrated profound political and social divisions in Maryland" and showed "flaws in the American . . . character" such as intolerance, "uncompromising ideological confrontation, and . . . acceptance of violence as a substitute for constitutional process." Alexander Contee Hanson, editor of the *Federal Republican*, led in opposing war with Britain, blaming war fever on Irish immigrants and the "European rabble" which made up the Republican ultrapatriots, who destroyed his press late in June. Hanson organized a little band of partisans, including "Light-Horse Harry" Lee and General James Lingan, to secretly reenter the city and defy their opponents. The ensuing armed battles at the Charles Street House and the jail saw several killed and maimed and others ruthlessly beaten and tortured, while the authorities did almost nothing. Sympathy turned "almost overnight" against the Republicans, and Federalists won massive majorities later that year, ending a decade of state control by the Jeffersonians. Primary and secondary sources; 52 notes.   G. J. Bobango

1211. Chudacoff, Nancy Fisher. THE REVOLUTION AND THE TOWN: PROVIDENCE, 1775-1783. *Rhode Island Hist. 1976 35(3): 71-89.* The American Revolution disrupted normal activities, enlarged old problems, and created new ones, but had no lasting impact on Providence. Based on records and manuscripts at Brown University, the National Archives, the Providence Public Library, and the Rhode Island Historical Society, on newspapers, and on secondary sources.   P. J. Coleman

1212. Cook, Adrian. "ASHES AND BLOOD." *Am. Hist. Illus. 1977 12(5): 30-35, 38-40.* Chronicles the riots in New York City July 1963, sparked by anti-draft sentiment during the Civil War.

1213. Crowe, Charles. SOUTHERN REPRESSION AND BLACK RESISTANCE: 1900, 1917 AND 1932. *Rev. in Am. Hist. 1977 5(3): 379-390.* Review article prompted by William Ivy Hair's *Carnival of Fury: Robert Charles and the New Orleans Race Riot of 1900* (Baton Rouge: Louisiana State U. Pr., 1976), Robert V. Haynes's *A Night of Violence: The Houston Riot of 1917* (Baton Rouge: Louisiana State U. Pr., 1976), and Charles H. Martin's *The Angelo Herndon Case and Southern Justice* (Baton Rouge: Louisiana State U. Pr., 1976).

1214. Daugherty, Robert L. PROBLEMS IN PEACEKEEPING: THE 1924 NILES RIOT. *Ohio Hist. 1976 85(4): 280-292.* A riot on 1 November 1924 in Niles, Ohio, involved the Ohio Knights of the Ku Klux Klan and the Knights of the Flaming Circle. The riot, terminated by the Ohio National Guard, was a prime example of a state government's hesitation to become involved in local law enforcement problems. Based on archival, MS., contemporary comments, and secondary sources; 5 illus., 31 notes.   N. Summers

1215. DeWitt, Howard A. THE WATSONVILLE ANTI-FILIPINO RIOT OF 1930: A CASE STUDY OF THE GREAT DEPRESSION AND ETHNIC CONFLICT IN CALIFORNIA. *Southern California Q. 1979 61(3): 291-302.* Examines the anti-Filipino riot in Watsonville, California, 19-23 January 1930. Hostility to Filipino Americans, most of whom lived in California, had been building for several years in the Watsonville area. Filipinos were victims of discrimination, exploitation, and stereotyping. Politicians and newspapers issued overtly racist statements concerning alleged Filipino threats in health, social relations, and vice. Following public anti-Filipino pronouncements by local political and business leaders, mobs of young men prowled Watsonville streets looking for Filipinos to beat up. One Filipino was shot dead. After five days the riots subsided as the public reacted negatively to the excessive violence. Police and sheriff's deputies acted impartially in protecting Filipinos but arrested few rioters. The California Filipino community failed to unite against the assault, its leaders divided on how to approach the problem. Onset of the Great Depression thus culminated years of anti-Filipino sentiment in the Watsonville riot. 33 notes.

A. Hoffman

1216. Dorffi, Christine. SAN FRANCISCO'S HIRED GUNS. *Reason 1979 11(4): 26-29, 33.* Describes the "patrol special" officers of San Francisco, private police regulated by the Police Commission, and provides a history of private policing in San Francisco since the Gold Rush.

1217.   Douthit, Nathan.   AUGUST VOLLMER, BERKELEY'S FIRST CHIEF OF POLICE, AND THE EMERGENCE OF POLICE PROFESSIONALISM. *California Hist. Q. 1975 54(2): 101-124.* A study of the career and contributions of August Vollmer (1876-1955), chief of police of Berkeley 1905-32. A progressive who believed that police work could be made more scientific and less vulnerable to political corruption, Vollmer pioneered in use of bicycles, automobiles, call boxes and radios, and attempted to recruit better educated officers, including college graduates. Vollmer wrote books and articles about police professionalism, served as a consultant for other cities, and held offices in police chiefs' associations. During his tenure in Berkeley the city's crime rate remained low, with Berkeley achieving a reputation as a leader in police innovation. In later years Vollmer served as a professor of police administration at the University of California and helped organize the first training program for police officers on the college level. Based on unpublished manuscript materials and other primary sources, and secondary books; illus., 13 photos, 95 notes.   A. Hoffman

1218.   Edwards, John Carver.   RADICAL RECONSTRUCTION AND THE NEW ORLEANS RIOT OF 1866. *Int. Rev. of Hist. and Pol. Sci. [India] 1973 10(3): 48-64.* The attempt of a few radicals to reassemble the Louisiana Constitutional Convention (1864) sparked the New Orleans Riot (1866). Indiscriminate slaughter of Negroes and white conventionists occurred on 30 July 1866. The northern public, convinced that rebel groups planned to maintain control through violence, elected a Radical Reconstruction Congress. All officials, national, military, state, and local, were partly responsible for the riot through neglect or through provocation. Based on government documents and secondary sources; 68 notes.   E. McCarthy

1219.   Ehrlich, Jessica Kross.   'TO HEAR AND TRY ALL CAUSES BETWIXT MAN AND MAN': THE TOWN COURT OF NEWTOWN, 1659-1690. *New York Hist. 1978 59(3): 277-305.* Studies of the Newtown, New York, town court records reveal social history and court functions before the abolition of town courts in 1691. The town court's principal responsibility was adjudication, but it performed numerous administrative tasks and, to a lesser extent, a legislative function. The court passed through the transition from the Dutch period to the English with little difficulty. Analyzes court cases during the English period, court procedure, and personalities involved as litigants. While the court tried to be fair, justice appeared to favor the more affluent members of society. 2 maps, 2 tables, 2 graphs, 47 notes.   R. N. Lokken

1220.   Feldberg, Michael.   THE CROWD IN PHILADELPHIA HISTORY: A COMPARATIVE PERSPECTIVE. *Labor Hist. 1974 15(3): 323-336.* Assesses Philadelphia history during 1830-50 in the context of the model of crowd behavior advanced by European historians and sociologists to explain pre-industrial collective violence. Philadelphia violence was clearly goal-oriented and dominated by economic and political power objectives. American exceptions to the model constituted collective violence against both Negroes and abolitionists. Local government forces tended to stand aside in ethnic and racial conflicts while violence became a part of politics, utilized to win jobs and political power and enforce an ideology. Based on the Philadelphia *Public Ledger* and unpublished doctoral dissertations; 30 notes.   L. L. Athey

1221.   Franklin, Vincent P.   THE PHILADELPHIA RACE RIOT OF 1918. *Pennsylvania Mag. of Hist. and Biog. 1975 99(3): 336-350.* During 1910-20 there was a 58% increase in the Negro population of Philadelphia, resulting in racial tension and riots in 1918. The city police were ineffectual in curbing the violence and the black community accused some policemen of joining the mob. The Colored Protective Association was formed to look after black interests. This and other citizens' committees "were well aware of the connection between the overt brutality of the mob, and the more subtle discriminations to which blacks were subjected in the schools, theaters, and other public places. And though many of the committees and associations were short-lived, they did have the effect of pushing the lethargic N.A.A.C.P. branch in Philadelphia into action on behalf of civil rights for blacks." 48 notes.   C. W. Olson

1222.   Friedman, Lawrence M.   THE LONG ARM OF THE LAW. *Rev. in Am. Hist. 1978 6(2): 223-228.* Review article prompted by Wilbur R. Miller's *Cops and Bobbies: Police Authority in New York and London, 1830-1870* (Chicago: U. of Chicago Pr., 1977).

1223.   Friedman, Lawrence M. and Percival, Robert V.   A TALE OF TWO COURTS: LITIGATION IN ALAMEDA AND SAN BENITO COUNTIES. *Law and Soc. Rev. 1976 10(2): 267-301.* A comparison of two trial courts in California between 1890 and 1970, one of which served the urban county of Alameda and the other the rural county of San Benito. The data show surprisingly little variation in types of cases handled, disposed of, costs of litigation, and the like. Increasingly, too, both courts handled routine settlements rather than bona fide disputes.   H. R. Mahood

1224.   George, Paul S.   THE EVOLUTION OF MIAMI AND DADE COUNTY'S JUDICIARY, 1896-1930. *Tequesta 1976 36: 28-42.* The development of Miami 1896-1930 was reflected in the development of city and county courts. From the original city court (Municipal Court) and the county court (Circuit Court), a number of courts were created to carry out special functions. Two of the more important and successful were the Criminal Court of Record (county) and the Juvenile Court. Based on primary sources, mainly newspapers and statutes; 80 notes.   H. S. Marks

1225.   George, Paul S.   POLICING MIAMI'S BLACK COMMUNITY, 1896-1930. *Florida Hist. Q. 1979 57(4): 434-450.* A double standard of justice endured in Miami, Florida, caused by racism. The police department accepted and promoted the white standard by the strict enforcement of Negro codes and by semi-official toleration of white terrorism. Such activities were designed to keep blacks in their place: Colored Town. Primary and secondary sources; 68 notes.   N. A. Kuntz

1226.   Gilbert, Daniel R.   BETHLEHEM AND THE AMERICAN REVOLUTION. *Tr. of the Moravian Hist. Soc. 1977 23(1): 17-40.* The Moravians in Bethlehem, Pennsylvania, rendered considerable voluntary and semicoerced support to the American Revolution through the provision of foodstuffs and supplies to the armies, prisoners of war, and the wounded, shelter to troops, and the extension of high quality medical services. Some damage to the town resulted from undisciplined troops, especially in the militia, although the community was never the scene of actual fighting. The prewar isolation of the town was only temporarily affected by the war. Following the shifting of combat to the South, Bethlehem rapidly returned to its prewar state, with the Moravian leaders reestablishing "rigid community control of thought and behavior." Primary and secondary sources.   N. Lederer

1227.   Goldman, Marion.   SEXUAL COMMERCE ON THE COMSTOCK LODE. *Nevada Hist. Soc. Q. 1978 21(2): 98-129.* Lured to Nevada's Comstock Lode by prospects of wealth, prostitutes created three vice districts at Gold Hill and Virginia City. By 1875, they comprised 8.6% of the female population in those mining towns, and another 5% of the townswomen had established "permanent liaisons" with miners or those within the business and professional sector. For economic reasons, members of the towns' power structure encouraged the lively sexual commerce that accompanied the opening of the mines. Based on government documents, newspaper and secondary sources, and sociological writings; 2 photos, 4 tables, 78 notes.   H. T. Lovin

1228.   Grinde, Donald A., Jr.   ERIE'S RAILROAD WAR: A CASE STUDY OF PURPOSIVE VIOLENCE FOR A COMMUNITY'S ECONOMIC ADVANCEMENT. *Western Pennsylvania Hist. Mag. 1974 57(1): 15-23.*

1229.   Hallberg, Gerald N.   BELLINGHAM, WASHINGTON'S ANTI-HINDU RIOT. *J. of the West 1973 12(1): 163-175.* An account of the anti-Hindu riot which began on 4 September 1907 in Bellingham, Washington. "Although friction between the community and the Hindu colony had been growing for months, statements of those implicated in the riots revealed that the immediate cause was the ill-feeling against Hindu employees at the Whatcom Falls Mill Company's plant.... On 9 September 1907 the city council passed a resolution which censured the mill owners of Bellingham for the alleged introduction of the Hindus into the city, a class undesirable and unwanted." 43 notes.   D. D. Cameron

1230. Haller, Mark H. HISTORICAL ROOTS OF POLICE BE-HAVIOR: CHICAGO, 1890-1925. *Law and Soc. Rev. 1976 10(2): 303-323.* The Chicago police in the early 20th century were not primarily oriented toward legality in their law enforcement activities. The local police actually allowed illegal activities. The police and their various activities were reflecting the mores of their leaders and the public at large.
H. R. Mahood

1231. Haller, Mark H. PLEA BARGAINING: THE NINE-TEENTH CENTURY CONTEXT. *Law and Soc. Rev. 1979 13(2): 273-279.* Plea bargaining apparently arose independently in a number of urban criminal courts in the nineteenth century. These simultaneous developments were presumably related to a number of broad structural changes that characterized American criminal justice at the time. Chief among them were the creation of urban police departments for the arrest of criminals and the development of a prison system for punishment or rehabilitation. Other developments included the reduced role of the victim, the relative independence of criminal justice from legal norms, and the corruption and political manipulation of the criminal justice system. The paper explores ways that such developments may have provided the context for the institutionalization of plea bargaining as a method of case disposition.
J

1232. Hammett, Theodore M. TWO MOBS OF JACKSONIAN BOSTON: IDEOLOGY AND INTEREST. *J. of Am. Hist. 1976 62(4): 845-868.* Using two dissimilar mob actions occurring in Boston, discusses the interaction of ideas and interests as the main basis for ideological development. Compares the burning of an Ursuline Convent by a mob of poor, Protestant laborers on 11 August 1834 with the Massachusetts Anti-Slavery Society riot of 24 October 1835 (by "wealthier," establishment types). Contemporaries saw one as a danger to society, the latter as righteous action against society's disrupters. These two views represent society's bipartiality in developing ideological responses to events affecting it. Economics and class structure determine "rightness." 5 tables, 70 notes.
V. P. Rilee

1233. Hansen, James E., II MOONSHINE AND MURDER: PRO-HIBITION IN DENVER. *Colorado Mag. 1973 50(1): 1-23.* Studies the prohibition experience of Denver, Colorado, in relation to the report of the Wickersham Committee of 1931. The Denver situation exemplified the committee's conclusions that prohibition was not living up to expectations. There was general resistance in the city; "undermanned, poorly organized and sometimes corrupt law enforcement; congested courts; conflicts between temperance and civil liberties; and failure to educate the public to the reform's merits." 7 illus., 85 notes.
O. H. Zabel

1234. Haynes, Robert V. THE HOUSTON MUTINY AND RIOT OF 1917. *Southwestern Hist. Q. 1973 76(4): 418-439.* A black infantry battalion was sent to Houston, Texas, in July 1917 to assume guard duty at a new training cantonment. The fighting soldiers were not happy at this reduction to guard detail, and Texas was a rigidly segregated state with a reputation of violence against nonwhites. Black troopers and white civilians anticipated trouble—which soon came. A series of physical assaults on blacks by the Houston police escalated into a sizable mutiny and riot, 23 August. The largest court-martial in American military history sentenced several soldiers to death and more to life in prison. 79 notes.
D. L. Smith

1235. Hennesey, Melinda Meek. RACE AND VIOLENCE IN RE-CONSTRUCTION NEW ORLEANS: THE 1868 RIOT. *Louisiana Hist. 1979 20(1): 77-92.* The New Orleans race riot, September-October 1868, grew out of efforts by white Democrats to reduce the Republican vote in New Orleans in the upcoming presidential election and to emasculate the recently created Metropolitan Police Force, one-third of whom were black. The worst phase of the violence began on the evening of 24 October 1868 in a clash between white Democratic and black Republican marching clubs, during their processions on Canal Street. During the next few nights Negroes indiscriminately attacked whites on the streets, and whites retaliated by ransacking the homes and businesses of black political leaders and relieving black citizens of their registration certificates. The crisis was defused when General Jame Steedman agreed to assume command of the Metropolitan Police Force. The result was 6-7 white deaths, at least 13 black deaths, and an overwhelming Democratic majority in the November election. Primary and secondary sources; 43 notes.
L. N. Powell

1236. Hickey, Donald R. THE DARKER SIDE OF DEMOCRACY: THE BALTIMORE RIOTS OF 1812. *Maryland Hist. 1976 7(2): 1-19.* Summarizes the anti-Federalist riots in Baltimore. This mob violence represented the ugly side of Jeffersonian Democracy which placed its faith in the force of public opinion in contrast to the legalistic Federalist approach to the suppression of dissent. Primary and secondary sources; 52 notes.
G. O. Gagnon

1237. Hoerder, Dirk. "MOBS, A SORT OF THEM AT LEAST, ARE CONSTITUTIONAL": THE AMERICAN REVOLUTION, POPULAR PARTICIPATION, AND SOCIAL CHANGE. *Ameri-kastudien/Am. Studies [West Germany] 1976 21(2): 289-306.* The essay deals with eighteenth-century colonial crowd action on which the intensified direct action against the British imperial government in the years from 1765 to 1780 was based. Crowd action ranged from enforcement of community norms to response to economic conflict within the community or province. Particularly the opposition to unresponsive or oppressive magistrates had a major impact on the opposition to British "placemen." At the time of the Stamp Act crowd action became necessary because no concept of, or experience with, slowly escalating institutional resistance existed. But the crowds acted not merely on the question of home rule, they immediately addressed themselves to the question of who should rule at home, too. In consequence, direct action soon met with strong repression from the socio-economic and political elites. The essay then attempts to explain the ideology of crowds on the basis of unpublished research in progress of a number of scholars. In a final section, the development of rioting from the revolutionary period to the urban disorders of the 1830's is traced.
J

1238. Howington, Arthur F. VIOLENCE IN ALABAMA: A STUDY OF LATE ANTE-BELLUM MONTGOMERY. *Alabama R. 1974 27(3): 213-231.* Reviews the incidence of violence in Montgomery 1830-60. It was notoriously high, and violence regularly took interpersonal, intergroup, and interracial forms. Efforts to control and suppress it were generally few and unavailing. A combination of frontier individualism, social and cultural anxieties, and racial animosity accounted for the pervasive tension. Based on primary and secondary sources; 102 notes.
J. F. Vivian

1239. Hudson, James J. THE CALIFORNIA NATIONAL GUARD IN THE SAN FRANCISCO EARTHQUAKE AND FIRE OF 1906. *California Hist. Q. 1976 55(2): 137-149.* Describes the work of the California National Guard in maintaining order and rendering aid to the victims of the San Francisco earthquake and fire. Governor George C. Pardee called out the guard on hearing of the disaster, but many units of the state militia and regular army were already on the scene. Coordination between civil and military authorities was marred by friction owing to political differences between Pardee and Mayor Eugene Schmitz. Schmitz and most of the San Francisco newspapers wanted the guard recalled, but thousands of people hailed the guard's maintenance of law and order. Improper conduct from guardsmen was at a bare minimum. One of five organizations charged with keeping order, the guard was withdrawn by the end of May 1906. Despite some criticism which was probably politically motivated, the guard performed its duties in a creditable manner. Based on primary and secondary sources; photos, 82 notes.
A. Hoffman

1240. Inciardi, James A. THE CHANGING LIFE OF MICKEY FINN: SOME NOTES ON CHLORAL HYDRATE DOWN THROUGH THE AGES. *J. of Popular Culture 1977 11(3): 591-596.* Explores several versions of the nature, origins, and myths surrounding the illegal use of "knockout drops," of the "Mickey Finn." The evidence suggests that the widespread use of the "Mickey" may be more popular myth than reality, but also that its notoriety was coincident with the emergence of urban vice areas about the middle of the 19th century and their decline during the early years of the 20th century. Primary and secondary sources; 24 notes.
D. G. Nielson

1241. Ingalls, Robert P. THE TAMPA FLOGGING CASE: UR-BAN VIGILANTISM. *Florida Hist. Q. 1977 56(1): 13-27.* In November 1935, three members of the Modern Democrats, a party opposed to municipal corruption, were kidnapped and flogged. One victim died. Although there was strong evidence of official complicity in the crime, the floggings and murder went unpunished. Discusses this case as an

example of urban vigilantism, a violent, illegal means of preserving the status quo against any perceived threat. In this instance, the threat was political reform. Based on newspaper and manuscript sources; 54 notes.
P. A. Beaber

1242. Jackson, Joy J. PROHIBITION IN NEW ORLEANS: THE UNLIKELIEST CRUSADE. *Louisiana Hist. 1978 19(3): 261-284.* Presidential address, 20th Annual Meeting of the Louisiana Historical Association, Alexandria, Louisiana, 10 March 1978. The Louisiana legislature ratified the 18th Amendment in August 1918 by a narrow margin, as north and central Louisiana "dry" interests defeated the "wet" votes of southern Louisiana and New Orleans. New Orleans opposed prohibition and was a center for bootlegging to dry regions throughout the Gulf South. Many establishments in the city secretly and openly defied the ban on alcoholic beverages. Despite heavy enforcement efforts, wine, beer, and liquor remained widely available throughout the period, and prohibition violation contributed to the rise of organized crime, gangsterism and bribery of public officials in New Orleans as in other large cities. Details enforcement efforts as well as popular opposition and flaunting of prohibition. Primary sources; 86 notes.
R. L. Woodward, Jr.

1243. Jones, Walter R. CASPER'S PROHIBITION YEARS. *Ann. of Wyoming 1976 48(2): 264-273.* Attempts to enforce national Prohibition in Casper, Wyoming, produced 14 troubled years, 1919-33, as many citizens refused to abide by the law. Bootlegging led to arrests and the death of a deputy sheriff, but high profits kept the illicit trade alive. Charges of corruption reached a peak by early 1933 when the sheriff and mayor were indicted along with 34 other persons. Though the trials produced no convictions, disrespect for these public officials continued even after the repeal of Prohibition at the end of 1933. Based on primary sources; 3 photos, 21 notes.
M. L. Tate

1244. Jordan, Philip D. THE CAPITAL OF CRIME. *Civil War Times Illus. 1975 13(10): 4-9, 44-47.* Crime and police activity in Washington, D. C., during the Civil War.
S

1245. Kocolowski, Gary P. EXPANDING POLICE SERVICES IN LATE-NINETEENTH-CENTURY CINCINNATI. *Cincinnati Hist. Soc. Bull. 1973 31(2): 115-126.* Between 1875 and 1900 the police of Cincinnati performed many services, including aid to victims of natural disaster, ambulance services, care for the needy, and locating lost and runaway children. The period 1884-94 was difficult because of unrest, too few officers, and politics. Based on local police reports, manuals, and regulations; 7 photos, 34 notes.
H. S. Marks

1246. Kogan, Herman. WILLIAM PERKINS BLACK: HAYMARKET LAWYER. *Chicago Hist. 1976 5(2): 85-94.* William Perkins Black, a young Chicago lawyer, earned the animosity of his fellow Chicagoans and sacrificed his career when he became the defense attorney for the eight men accused of inciting the Haymarket riot in 1886-87.

1247. Lane, Roger. CAN YOU COUNT ON THE DOWN AND OUT TO STAY DOWN FOR THE COUNT IN COLUMBUS? *Rev. in Am. Hist. 1976 4(2): 212-217.* Review article prompted by Eric H. Monkkonen's *The Dangerous Class: Crime and Poverty in Columbus, Ohio, 1860-1885* (Cambridge, Massachusetts: Harvard U. Pr., 1975); discusses data usage and interpretation in determining connections among urbanization, industrialism, and crime.

1248. Lane, Roger. CRIMINAL VIOLENCE IN AMERICA: THE FIRST HUNDRED YEARS. *Ann. of the Am. Acad. of Pol. and Social Sci. 1976 (423): 1-13.* America has long been notorious for its violence, but illegitimate criminal violence has received relatively little attention. Vigilantism is the best known of the specifically American forms of social violence. Woven deeply into our history, bound up in the westward movement, the gun culture, and slavery, vigilantism in its wider sense was an important form of political expression. Mob violence reached its apogee in the North before the Civil War, but continued to flourish in the South and West through 1876 and gave the whole nation a heritage of direct action in the name of justice. Gunfighting has been less important in our actual history, but very significant in our national imagination. The gunfighting mystique, and our fascination with it, has contributed heavily to our tradition of violence. Urban riot and crime are new fields of study, drawing heavily on interdisciplinary methods. Recent work on the city of

Philadelphia, for example, may be used in several ways. The nature of collective violence reveals something about the city's own polity and, in connection with other studies of individual violence, something about social and economic stages of development. In brief, all sorts of street violence decreased with the Industrial Revolution, and the Centennial City was quieter than any earlier.
J

1249. Lax, John and Pencak, William. THE KNOWLES RIOT AND THE CRISIS OF THE 1740'S IN MASSACHUSETTS. *Perspectives in Am. Hist. 1976 10: 163-214.* The three general schools of thought about the Knowles Riot—imperial conflict, class antagonism, and consensual communalism—do not reflect reality. The mob activity exhibited in the riot was a manifestation of Boston's new unified consciousness. Seamen who protested impressment had the support of and shared sentiment with the Boston community. This new, unified community consciousness sparked Samuel Adams to cloak his ideology of resistance in terms of the natural rights of man. 147 notes.
W. A. Wiegand

1250. Lernack, Paul. PEACE BONDS AND CRIMINAL JUSTICE IN COLONIAL PHILADELPHIA. *Pennsylvania Mag. of Hist. and Biog. 1976 100(2): 173-190.* In reaction to persecution at the hands of English authorities, the Pennsylvania Quakers established a mild criminal code. The peace bond, a legal device aimed at diverting troublemakers from the criminal justice system, was one manifestation of this lenient code. The peace bond was a form of civil or criminal bail which judges could order without criminally charging the accused. In the close-knit Quaker community, the peace bond was a flexible alternative to criminal prosecution, but by 1780, the growing anonymity of city dwellers and the inflation of the cash value of the bail nullified its flexibility and thereafter it was used infrequently. Based on primary and secondary sources; 64 notes.
E. W. Carp

1251. Levi, Steven C. THE TRIAL OF WILLIAM MC DEVITT. *Southern California Q. 1977 59(3): 289-312.* The San Francisco Chamber of Commerce created the Law and Order Committee (LAOC) to support the open shop and to oppose labor unions, Socialists, and radicals. The committee attempted to force the dismissal of Socialist William McDevitt from the Board of Election Commissioners. McDevitt had delivered an indiscreet speech at a public meeting two days before the 22 July 1916 Preparedness Day Parade and its tragic bombing; the Law and Order Committee insisted the speech had been inflammatory. The "trial" was actually a hearing before Mayor James J. Rolph, who tried to remain neutral. The proceeding was marred by numerous irregularities, not the least of which was confusion over whether it was a judicial trial or a civil hearing. After hearing evidence, much of which was verbose and irrelevant, Rolph refused to dismiss McDevitt. The limits of LAOC influence were thus shown. 51 notes.
A. Hoffman

1252. Liebman, Robert and Polen, Michael. PERSPECTIVES IN POLICING IN NINETEENTH-CENTURY AMERICA. *Social Sci. Hist. 1978 2(3): 346-360.* Records changes in the character of American policing during the 100 years starting around 1820. Reveals three main perspectives on the rise and reform of urban police: social disorganization, political process, and class conflict. Examines the redistribution of policing actions and describes some political conflicts during the expansion of industrial capitalism. 39 notes.
G. E. Pergl

1253. Light, Ivan. THE ETHNIC VICE INDUSTRY, 1880-1944. *Am. Sociol. Rev. 1977 42(3): 464-479.* Sociologists have explained the association of ethnic minorities and illegal enterprise in terms of structural blockages and opportunities, emphatically denying any ethnic contribution. A comparison of blacks and Chinese in the vice industry, 1880-1940, confirms the guiding role of American society which rewarded ethnics' participation in prostitution but restricted legal earning opportunities. Nonetheless, divergent demographic and cultural characteristics of Chinese and blacks differentially affected the internal organization of each group's vice industry as well as the process of industrial succession. This finding supports a view of illegal enterprise as a synthesis of illegal work that consumers want to buy and what disadvantaged ethnics have to offer. In general, socio-cultural characteristics of provider subgroups define the manner in which they respond to consumer demand for illegal products and services.
J

1254. Lovett, Bobby L. MEMPHIS RIOTS: WHITE REACTION TO BLACKS IN MEMPHIS, MAY 1865-JULY 1866. *Tennessee Hist. Q. 1979 38(1): 9-33.* The bloody racial riots in Memphis, Tennessee, on 1-2 May 1866, were the result of demographic changes caused by the influx of large numbers of black refugees, thus creating an urban black community and new race relationships. The claim that the presence of black troops caused the riots is a myth. The results of the riot were the opposite of what the white instigators desired since the riot helped convince national and state Republicans to pass protective civil rights legislation for blacks. Primary and secondary sources; 2 illus., 49 notes.
                                                M. B. Lucas

1255. McGinty, Brian. SHADOWS IN ST. JAMES PARK. *California History 1978-79 57(4): 290-307.* An account of mob violence in San Jose, California, in November 1933. Brooke Hart, son of a prominent local department store family, was kidnapped and brutally murdered on 9 November 1933. Within a week, Thomas Thurmond and John Holmes were taken into custody. When Hart's body was recovered from San Francisco Bay on 26 November many San Jose citizens urged the lynching of the suspects. That evening thousands of people surrounded the jail, broke down the door, took out the two suspects, and hanged them. Governor James Rolph aroused national controversy by endorsing the mob's action. Evidence against the suspects was persuasive but not conclusive, and a trial would have provided answers to important questions. The incident is remembered as "San Jose's shame" since law enforcement had been effective in capturing the suspects, the community was a prosperous middle-class one, and the violence seemed inexcusable. Primary and secondary sources; 7 photos, 102 notes.   A. Hoffman

1256. McGovern, James R. "SPORTING LIFE ON THE LINE": PROSTITUTION IN PROGRESSIVE ERA PENSACOLA. *Florida Hist. Q. 1975 54(2): 131-144.* In the first few decades of the 20th century, in Pensacola, Florida, police and city officials succeeded in confining prostitution and saloons to a restricted area of the city rather than trying to eliminate the problems entirely. Confining prostitution to a specific area afforded both safety and economy to the rest of the city. In addition, the city received revenue in fines from occasional crackdowns. Changing morals and attitudes brought an end to the district of brothels by the beginning of World War II. Based on primary and secondary works; illus., 73 notes.   P. A. Beaber

1257. Miller, W. R. POLICE AUTHORITY IN LONDON AND NEW YORK CITY, 1830-1870. *J. of Social Hist. 1976 8(2): 81-101.* "The London policeman represented the 'public good' as defined by the governing classes' concern to maintain an unequal social order with a minimum of violence and oppression. The result was impersonal authority. The New York policeman represented a 'self-governing people' as a product of that self-government's conceptions of power and the ethnic conflicts which divided that people. The result was personal authority." 95 notes.   L. Ziewacz

1258. Mitchell, John G. SAID CHICAGO'S AL CAPONE: "I GIVE THE PUBLIC WHAT THE PUBLIC WANTS..." *Am. Heritage 1979 30(2): 82-93.* Al Capone, who considered himself a pleasurable benefactor, arrived in Chicago in 1919 and gained control of most of that city's underworld prior to his demise in 1931 when found guilty of tax evasion. After eight years in prison, Capone was released. Syphillis had nearly destroyed his nervous system and he died in Miami in 1947. 18 illus.   J. F. Paul

1259. Monkkonen, Eric. TOWARD A DYNAMIC THEORY OF CRIME AND THE POLICE: A CRIMINAL JUSTICE SYSTEM PERSPECTIVE. *Hist. Methods Newsletter 1977 10(4): 157-165.* Reviews the major approaches to the history of urban police. The approach is bureaucratic. During the 19th century symbolic order increased with the increased visibility of the police. Actual arrest decreased. Tramps and other elements of the "dangerous class" need to be more closely studied to understand this process. Attempts to link criminal statistics to the behavior and structure of criminal justice institutions. Table, 3 fig., 16 notes.   D. K. Pickens

1260. Monti, Daniel J. MOB ACTION AND CIVIL RESPONSIBILITY: THE NEW YORK CASE. *New York Affairs 1977 4(3): 34-47.* Examines mass violence, rioting, and civil disobedience in New York City, 1690-1976, covering unrest over the draft, labor, and race relations; discusses civil responsibility of city officials as well as citizens.

1261. Moody, Thurman Dean. NAUVOO'S WHISTLING AND WHITTLING BRIGADE. *Brigham Young U. Studies 1975 15(4): 480-490.* Discusses the adaptation of the Whistling and Whittling Brigade, a form of police consisting of the small boys of the community. Following the loss of city government and subsequently the loss of police protection in Nauvoo, Illinois, the Mormon community found it necessary (1845) to provide themselves with this protection, the young boys seemed the safest, because they were harassing rather than threatening.

1262. Murphy, Patrick V. THE DEVELOPMENT OF THE URBAN POLICE. *Current Hist. 1976 70(417): 245-248, 272.* Glances at the history of policing in metropolitan areas since the first police department was founded in New York in 1854, and concentrates on the role of this branch of the criminal justice system and efforts to reform it in the 1960's.

1263. Murrah, Bill. THE KNOXVILLE RACE RIOT: "TO MAKE PEOPLE PROUD." *Southern Exposure 1974 1(3-4): 105-111.* Racial conflict was breaking out across the country in 1919. The riot in Knoxville was precipitated by the murder of a white woman, allegedly by a Negro. It is generally agreed that the riot contributed to better race relations, but there are differing opinions why. Whites say that blacks were put in their place; blacks say that they demonstrated to whites that they would not tolerate violent racism. 3 illus.   G. A. Bolton

1264. Myers, Rex C. AN INNING FOR SIN: CHICAGO JOE AND HER HURDY-GURDY GIRLS. *Montana 1977 27(2): 24-33.* Mary Josephine Welch (1844-1899) immigrated from Ireland in 1858, learned the business of running bordellos and dance halls in Chicago, then moved to Helena, Montana, in 1867. With the exception of the years 1869-72 spent in White Pine, Nevada, Josephine Welch operated saloons, hurdy-gurdy houses, brothels, and variety theaters in Helena. She married gambler James T. Hensley in 1878, but was known locally as Chicago Joe because she imported young ladies, principally from Chicago, to staff her businesses. Using legal technicalities, she evaded restrictive laws and became a successful business figure and one of Helena's major property owners. Changing social values and the economic depression of 1893 depleted revenues from her investments until she died in poverty. Based on contemporary newspapers and materials in the Montana Historical Society; 20 illus., 2 notes.   R. C. Myers

1265. Nash, June. THE COST OF VIOLENCE. *J. of Black Studies 1973 4(2): 153-183.* The 1898 race riot in Wilmington, North Carolina, resulted in extensive property damage and more than 20 blacks being killed. Describes the riot and the reactions of both whites and blacks and compares it with the 1971 race riots in Wilmington. Primary sources; 2 notes, biblio.   K. Butcher

1266. Nelli, Humbert S. THE HENNESSY MURDER AND THE MAFIA IN NEW ORLEANS. *Italian Q. 1975 19(75-76): 77-95.* The assassination of police chief David C. Hennessy in October 1890 marked an important point in the development of Italian crime in the United States because of the national and worldwide publicity it received, the mob killings of 11 acquitted Italians, and the confrontation between the United States and Italy. The killers' actions "indicate either non-professional perpetrators or a carefully planned frameup." Italian immigrants would henceforth avoid New Orleans. One base of boss power in the city, namely the Italian immigrant vote, was not destroyed. "If the matrangas were responsible for Hennessy's murder, the killing was part of a vendetta involving the two feuding factions and did not represent an effort to establish *Mafia* control over the city." Nevertheless, the newspapers had disseminated the belief that acquittal of the accused "represented part of a *coup d'état* that necessitated a swift unequivocal response." 17 notes.
                                                L. S. Frey

1267. Olson, James S. and Phair, Sharon. THE ANATOMY OF A RACE RIOT: BEAUMONT, TEXAS, 1943. *Texana 1973 11(1): 64-72.* Describes the events of 15-16 March 1943 in which rioting broke out between Negroes and white workers in the Pennsylvania Shipyard in Beaumont, after one of the workers' wives was allegedly raped by a black man. 48 notes.

1268. Poteet, James M. UNREST IN THE "LAND OF STEADY HABITS": THE HARTFORD RIOT OF 1722. *Pro. of the Am. Phil. Soc. 1975 119(3): 223-232.* Details the event that led up to the Hartford riot of 1722. A mob of his tenants freed Jeremiah Fitch from jail on 22 October 1722. Fitch had refused to vacate disputed lands awarded by the courts to Major John Clark. Fitch and the mob held their lands through purchase from the Indians, while Clark had received his from the colonial government. The government was hard pressed to restore order after this riot. For Connecticut, it was a period of social change. Population growth, disagreement on the validity of land sales by Indians, and an impotent legislature torn between a rigid governor and a populistic lower house caused such examples of social instability. Based on primary and secondary sources; 85 notes.
W. L. Olbrich

1269. Preston, William. COPS AND BOSSES: THE ORIGINS OF AMERICAN POLICE WORK. *Civil Liberties Rev. 1978 5(1): 23-26.* Analyzes 19th-century police behavior in the framework of the social conditions and machine politics of the period.

1270. Rabinowitz, Howard N. THE CONFLICT BETWEEN BLACKS AND THE POLICE IN THE URBAN SOUTH, 1865-1900. *Historian 1976 39(1): 62-76.* Although historians have studied post-Civil War police conflict in the urban North, they have neglected to apply their studies to the urban South. In cities such as Raleigh, Nashville, Richmond, and Atlanta there were large black populations. To Southern whites the police force was their first line of defense against blacks who lived in the cities. Whites did not want any black policemen especially because they might arrest whites. The handful of black policemen during Radical Reconstruction were limited to keeping peace among blacks. The period was marked by incidents, arrests, and hostility between urban blacks and the police force in major southern cities. 69 notes.
M. J. Wentworth

1271. Renner, Richard Wilson. IN A PERFECT FERMENT: CHICAGO, THE KNOW-NOTHINGS, AND THE RIOT FOR LAGER BEER. *Chicago Hist. 1976 5(3): 161-169.* Discusses Chicago's Know-Nothing government of 1855 which alienated German supporters with a temperance law that provoked a major riot.

1272. Richardson, James F. THE VIOLENT CITY. *J. of Urban Hist. 1975 1(4): 498-501.* Review article prompted by Adrian Cook's *The Armies of the Streets: The New York City Draft Riots of 1863* (Lexington: U. of Kentucky Pr., 1974).

1273. Rudwick, Elliott. A TALE OF TWO RIOTS. *J. of Urban Hist. 1978 4(2): 239-246.* Compares William I. Hair's *Carnival of Fury: Robert Charles and the New Orleans Race Riot of 1900* with Robert V. Haynes's *A Night of Violence: The Houston Riot of 1900.* Hair's monograph is more of a biography than a case study of the New Orleans riot, and not fully successful at either endeavor. Haynes's work is a good example of the type of research that is needed on interracial violence.
T. W. Smith

1274. Ryan, James Gilbert. THE MEMPHIS RIOTS OF 1866: TERROR IN A BLACK COMMUNITY DURING RECONSTRUCTION. *J. of Negro Hist. 1977 62(3): 243-257.* During 1-3 May 1866, race rioting in downtown Memphis resulted in nearly 50 deaths, mostly of Negroes, and widespread destruction of property, mostly Negroes'. Earlier accounts blamed black ex-soldiers but ignored the responsibility of white policemen for the onset of the rioting. Previous historical treatment also failed to examine the aggravation of the rioting by white civilian politicians and the refusal of federal General George Stoneman to declare martial law until 3 May when the black community had been ravaged. Primary and secondary materials; 95 notes.
N. G. Sapper/S

1275. Saunders, Robert M. CRIME AND PUNISHMENT IN EARLY NATIONAL AMERICA: RICHMOND, VIRGINIA, 1784-1820. *Virginia Mag. of Hist. and Biog. 1978 86(1): 33-44.* Analysis of early 19th-century court records in Richmond, Virginia, reveals not only that the city was already a comparatively violent community, but also that whites used the courts to help perpetuate slavery. Based on City of Richmond Hustings Court Order Books and Minute Books; 30 notes.
R. F. Oaks

1276. Schneider, John C. COMMUNITY AND ORDER IN PHILADELPHIA, 1834-1844. *Maryland Historian 1974 5(1): 15-26.* Examines Philadelphia's resistance to the creation of a professional police force despite riots and violence during the 1830's-40's. Concludes that Philadelphia's sense of community tolerated violence against and by outsiders but as violence was directed against the community itself professional police were soon to follow. Based on primary and secondary sources; illus., 33 notes.
G. O. Gagnon

1277. Schneider, John C. DETROIT AND THE PROBLEM OF DISORDER: THE RIOT OF 1863. *Michigan Hist. 1974 58(1): 4-24.* Detroit's response to the 1863 race riot illustrates not only the complexities of 19th-century urban institutional development, but the persistence in Detroit of an outmoded perception of community. The disturbance overwhelmed officials, who had no traditional commitment to maintain order. Despite the obvious failure of informal policing arrangements, the city did not subsequently establish a regular force on its own initiative, persisting in the belief that private arrangements were sufficient to protect and control the city. Primary and secondary sources; 7 illus., map, 32 notes.
D. W. Johnson

1278. Schneider, John C. PUBLIC ORDER AND THE GEOGRAPHY OF THE CITY: CRIME, VIOLENCE, AND THE POLICE IN DETROIT, 1845-1875. *J. of Urban Hist. 1978 4(2): 183-208.* This spatial analysis of Detroit examines the location of vice areas, boarding houses, saloons, billiard halls, businesses and residences of the Board of Trade, residences of policemen and sheriff's deputies, and "suspicious places" reported to police. Studies the spatial interrelationship of these businesses and residences and considers how Detroit's geographic expansion led to changes in the type of police force, the crime rate, and related matters. 6 fig., 57 notes.
T. W. Smith

1279. Schneider, John C. RIOT AND REACTION IN ST. LOUIS, 1854-1856. *Missouri Hist. Rev. 1974 68(2): 171-185.* Discusses the buildup, culmination, and aftermath of local political tension in St. Louis in the 1850's. Central to the conflict was a growing nativism and the emergence of the Know-Nothing Party which caused alarm among the Democrats. This resulted in rioting on election day, 7 August 1854, with a counterattack led by members of the Irish community. As a result of the conflict, the regular police force was reorganized and professionalized, the state passed a stronger riot law effective only in St. Louis County, and election procedures were restructured. The elections of 1855 and 1856 were again emotional races between the Know-Nothing Party and the Democrats, but order was kept during both, although the above changes were actually partisan in nature. Based on contemporary newspaper reports, St. Louis city documents, primary and secondary sources; 7 illus., 22 notes.
N. J. Street

1280. Schneider, John C. URBANIZATION AND THE MAINTENANCE OF ORDER: DETROIT, 1824-1847. *Michigan Hist. 1976 60(3): 260-281.* Detroit, as a transitional urban community during the second quarter of the 19th century, offers instructive comparison with existing historical studies of law and order in that era's villages and cities. Paralleling experiences elsewhere, citizens of Detroit were devoted to the American ideal of individualism and to public order and had allowed crime to become an acute problem by the early 1830's. Refusing to admit the need for a permanent police force, residents preferred temporary expedients, and countenanced them until the late 1840's, when a second period of rapid growth forced the idea of a professional approach to come into its own. Primary sources; 7 illus., map, 56 notes.
D. W. Johnson

1281. Short, John C., Jr. THE PHILADELPHIA CONNECTION. *Marine Corps Gazette 1978 62(11): 57-63.* Chronicles Marine General Smedley D. Butler's stint, 1923-24, as Director of Public Safety in Philadelphia, his battle against Prohibition violations, and his ongoing disagreements with Mayor W. Freeland Kendrick.

1282. Silliman, Lee. 1870: TO THE HANGMAN'S TREE: HELENA'S LAST VIGILANTE EXECUTION. *Montana 1978 28(4): 50-57.* Vigilantes hanged George Wilson and Arthur Compton in Helena, Montana, on 30 April 1870. They were executed for the robbery and beating of an elderly man named George Lenharth. Even though the machinery for administering official justice existed, public outrage and tradition combined to overwhelm the law for the last time in Helena. It was a final convulsive action on the part of citizens who were unconvinced that legal justice deterred violent crime. Discusses the specific incident and the history of vigilante activities in Helena. Based on contemporary newspapers, secondary works, and original materials in the Montana Historical Society, Helena; 6 illus., 10 notes.   R. C. Myers

1283. Sugimoto, Howard H. THE VANCOUVER RIOT AND ITS INTERNATIONAL SIGNIFICANCE. *Pacific Northwest Q. 1973 64(4): 163-174.* The Vancouver branch of the Asiatic Exclusion League put on a parade and public meeting on 7 September 1907 to convince officials of the seriousness of anti-Japanese sentiment in British Columbia during a time of depression and high job competition. A riot broke out involving heavy property loss to much of the Japanese community. Despite recriminations from all involved, the occasion became a landmark in Canadian diplomatic history because Britain allowed Canada to enter into direct discussions with foreign powers on questions of Asiatic immigration. Japanese claims were settled and ultimately the and the situation resulted in a spirit of cooperation between the United States and Canada abrogation of the Anglo-Japanese Treaty of Alliance (1902) in 1922. 65 notes.   R. V. Ritter

1284. Surrency, Erwin C. THE EVOLUTION OF AN URBAN JUDICIAL SYSTEM: THE PHILADELPHIA STORY, 1683 TO 1968. *Am. J. of Legal Hist. 1974 18(2): 95-123.* Surveys the historical development of the courts and judicial system of Philadelphia since the 17th century.   S

1285. Swan, Bradford F. FRONTIER JUSTICE IN NEWPORT— 1652. *Rhode Island Hist. 1974 33(1): 3-7.* Suggests that the illegal trial and execution of Captain Alexander Partridge may have delayed the reunion of the mainland towns (Providence and Warwick) with the island towns (Newport and Portsmouth) to reestablish a unified colony of Rhode Island. Based on published documents, papers, and secondary accounts.   P. J. Coleman

1286. Tracy, Charles Abbot, III. POLICE FUNCTION IN PORTLAND, 1851-1874. *Oregon Hist. Q. 1979 80(1): 5-29, (2): 134-169, (3): 287-322.* Part I. Shortly after incorporation, Portland's city council elected Hiram Wilbur as the city's first marshall. Wilbur's function, however, was limited to the execution of judicial and administrative actions of the mayor, in whom all authority was vested. The city charter of 1853 stripped the mayor of judicial authority, distributed police power between the mayor and city council, and provided for election of the marshall by a vote of the populace. In October 1857 a resolution was passed requiring voters to 'think' about supporting a permanent police force. Nothing came of the resolution; however, passage of the resolution marked the first official consideration of such a force. Based on documents in the Portland City Archives, newspaper accounts, and published secondary sources; 6 illus., 2 maps, 79 notes. Part II. The election of James H. Lappeus as city marshall in April 1859 marked the beginning of a sense of stability for the Portland police. Each year Portland's mayor called for the organization of a sense of stabiliy for the Portland police. Each year Portland's mayor called for the organization of a permanent police force and each year the city council failed to take any action on the matter. The city charter of 1864 made the city council responsible, once again, for election of the marshall. Two deputy marshalls were officially appointed in November 1864, thereby increasing the police force to a total of three full time employees. In early 1867 the city council passed two ordinances, one establishing a day police and the other establishing a night police. However, it was not until September 1870 that Portland's police department was officially established. Fall of 1870, however, saw passage in the state legislature of a bill which would establish a Portland Board of Police Commissioners whose members would be appointed by the governor. Based on documents in the Portland City Archives, newspaper accounts, and published secondary sources; 10 illus., map, 195 notes. Part III. The board abolished local control over the police, but by 1874, a new law provided for the public election of board commissioners, thus returning the police to local control. 13 illus., 285 notes.   D. R. McDonald

1287. Turnbaugh, Roy. ETHNICITY, CIVIC PRIDE, AND COMMITMENT: THE EVOLUTION OF THE CHICAGO MILITIA. *J. of the Illinois State Hist. Soc. 1979 72(2): 111-127.* By the early 1870's,

only a few militia companies remained in Illinois. They received no state funds. Under Adjutant General Edwin L. Higgins's measures, the condition of the Illinois militia improved. In 1877, in fear of the radical labor movement, the general assembly enacted a comprehensive military code and the militia was renamed the Illinois National Guard. The guardsmen were exempt during service from jury duty and from road and poll taxes. In 1877 a railroad strike occurred. The success of the First Brigade in dealing with the strike differed from the Second Regiment. The strike proved the need of a permanent Chicago militia. Official reports; illus., 51 notes.   E. P. Stickney

1288. Unsigned. THE POLICE DEPARTMENTS OF STATEN ISLAND. *Staten Island Historian 1973 31(14): 113-124.* Describes the police of Staten Island, 1780-1898. County records, newspapers, histories, and photograph collections were used to study individual policemen, uniforms, locations of precinct houses, important cases, and growth. Includes a partial roster of policemen 1870-97. Compiled by the Museum Studies class, Susan E. Wagner High School, Staten Island. 16 illus., biblio.   D. Ricciard-O'Beirne

1289. Walker, Samuel. THE POLICE AND THE COMMUNITY: SCRANTON, PENNSYLVANIA, 1866-1884: A TEST CASE. *Am. Studies [Lawrence, KS] 1978 19(1): 79-90.* Seeks to explain police operations "in the midst of extreme industrial conflict and ethnic tensions" and uses Scranton, Pennsylvania, as a microcosm of American society. Development of the anthracite coal fields, economic uncertainty, and ethnic immigration frequently produced mob violence after the Civil War, and led to insurgent working-class political activity. These events led Scranton to create a police department. Surveys the development and problems of this department, focusing on political activism and public concern with curbing the cost of government. Primary and secondary sources; 12 notes.   J. Andrew

1290. Watts, Eugene J. THE POLICE IN ATLANTA, 1890-1905. *J. of Southern Hist. 1973 39(2): 165-182.* Reviews the structure and operation of the Atlanta police department during 1890-1905. Atlanta had a centralized system; substations were requested, but not granted. Policemen were generally selected from the lower middle class. The Board of Police Commissioners had power to reelect or reject each policeman every two years. This system heavily involved the police in politics. The effectiveness of the department in controlling crime cannot be ascertained. Reform efforts near the end of the period revealed considerable corruption. 37 notes.   V. L. Human

1291. Weinbaum, Paul O. TEMPERANCE, POLITICS, AND THE NEW YORK CITY RIOTS OF 1857. *New-York Hist. Soc. Q. 1975 59(3): 246-270.* During the 1850's there was much violence in urban areas of the United States. Investigates the connection between the New York City riots of 1857, ostensibly caused by the activities of temperance forces, and local politics, particularly of the Irish and German factions. Although the temperance campaign was the chief incitement to Irish and German rioting, it was only incidental to political violence with political action that led to larger participation in city politics. Primary sources; 7 illus., 45 notes.   C. L. Grant

1292. Wilentz, Sean. CRIME, POVERTY AND THE STREETS OF NEW YORK CITY: THE DIARY OF WILLIAM H. BELL (1850-51). *Hist. Workshop J. [Great Britain] 1979 7(6): 126-131.* Provides an annotated selection of entries from the diary of the New York policeman, William H. Bell, preceded by an introduction describing the nature of Bell's work and characterizing the locale of his employment, within the context of contemporary crime in New York City. While mapping the New York City underworld of crime, poverty and politics, the diary also gives insights into the culture, mentality, and daily lives of the poorer classes in the city. It is in the manuscript collection of the New York Historical Society. 3 illus., 90 notes.   A. Fenn

1293. Willson, John. ONE HUNDRED YEARS OF THE SAINT LOUIS BAR. *Am. Bar Assoc. J. 1974 60(4): 457-460.* The St. Louis bar, celebrating its centennial has played a unique role in the growth of the American bar.   S

1294. Woolsey, Ronald C. CRIME AND PUNISHMENT: LOS ANGELES COUNTY, 1850-1856. *Southern California Q. 1979 61(1): 79-*

98. Describes the administration of justice in Los Angeles city and county at the beginning of the American period. Southern California experienced rapid growth, a high rate of transiency, and an increasing number of violent crimes. Indians were generally believed to be the cause of crime and were immediately suspected when a crime was committed. It soon became obvious that crime in Los Angeles was due to more complex factors. Local elected officials often lacked training to enforce proper legal procedure. To reduce crime the Board of Supervisors created a force of Los Angeles Rangers which often failed to observe the letter of the law. Failure to create nighttime law enforcement, belief in Indian culpability, and frustration at the failure of the legal system led citizens to endorse violent extra-legal action, including vigilantism and lynching. Los Angeles provided opportunity for all immigrants, but the criminal element overwhelmed the legal system in the years immediately following statehood. Primary and secondary sources; 86 notes.   A. Hoffman

Minorities and Ethnic Relations

General

1295. Achenbaum, W. Andrew. TOWARD PLURALISM AND AS-SIMILATION: THE RELIGIOUS CRISIS OF ANN ARBOR'S WÜRTTEMBERG COMMUNITY. *Michigan Hist. 1974 58(3): 195-218.* The evolution of Ann Arbor's Württemberg community illustrates a point often obscured in the assimilationist-pluralist controversy among historians of American immigration: that in adjusting to American society, most ethnic groups have altered some cultural patterns while preserving others. Ann Arbor Württembergers quickly accommodated themselves politically and economically but maintained their social customs and religious traditions. Following a congregational schism in 1875, one faction endeavored to preserve the pietism and ethnic solidarity of the Württemberg heritage, while the other moved into the mainstream of American Protestantism. Primary and secondary sources; 2 illus., 8 photos, 54 notes.   D. W. Johnson

1296. Berrol, Selma C. SCHOOL DAYS ON THE OLD EAST SIDE: THE ITALIAN AND JEWISH EXPERIENCE. *New York Hist. 1976 57(2): 201-213.* Compares the educational progress of Italian and Jewish immigrant children in New York City's Lower East Side during the early 1900's. Old world backgrounds and traditional attitudes explain why Jewish immigrant children were more successful academically than Italian children. In later generations the academic performance of Italian and Jewish children approached equality. 3 illus., 19 notes.
          R. N. Lokken

1297. Bodnar, John E. THE IMMIGRANT AND THE AMERICAN CITY. *J. of Urban Hist. 1977 3(2): 241-249.* Review article prompted by four recent works in ethnic history: Josef J. Barton, *Peasants and Strangers, Italians, Rumanians, and Slovaks in an American City, 1890-1950,* Leonard Dinnerstein and David M. Reimers, *Ethnic Americans: A History of Immigration and Assimilation,* Dean R. Esslinger, *Immigrants and the City: Ethnicity and Mobility in a Nineteenth Century Midwestern City,* and Kristian Hvidt, *Flight to America: The Social Background of 300,000 Danish Emmigrants.* Each work approaches immigrants from a different angle. Hvidt looks at them from the mother country, Barton examines their experience in both the old and the new world, Esslinger picks up the story deep in the heartland of the New World, and Dinnerstein and Reimers overview the entire process. 12 notes.   T. W. Smith

1298. Bodnar, John E. IMMIGRATION AND MODERNIZA-TION: THE CASE OF SLAVIC PEASANTS IN INDUSTRIAL AMERICA. *J. of Social Hist. 1976 10(1): 44-71.* Studies the impact of modernization on immigrant peasants from southern Poland, eastern Slovakia, the Ukraine, Croatia, Bosnia, Slovenia, and Serbia. Urban, industrial society can elicit behavioral patterns similar to peasant culture. "The dialectical process of modernization involves the interplay between tradition and working class necessity, producing a new working-class consciousness." This consciousness was a synthesis forged by immigrants within the structural context of a new socioeconomic milieu. "Moderniza-tion involved a clash of peasant culture and working-class pragmatism

which resulted in a reinforcement of traditional behavior and percep-tions." 6 tables, 88 notes.   R. V. Ritter

1299. Bodnar, John; Weber, Michael P.; and Simon, Roger. MIGRA-TION, KINSHIP, AND URBAN ADJUSTMENT: BLACKS AND POLES IN PITTSBURGH, 1900-1930. *J. of Am. Hist. 1979 66(3): 548-565.* Analyzes the adaptation of Poles and blacks to Pittsburgh, 1900-30, by comparing their migration experiences, socialization prac-tices, and occupational mobility patterns. The analysis relies heavily on 94 oral history interviews of Polish immigrants and black migrants. For both groups, adaptation involved strategic reactions to specific conditions in Pittsburgh. Adjustment to the new urban setting was a product of the interaction of premigration culture and urban racism. 4 tables, 42 notes..
          T. P. Linkfield

1300. Bodnar, John E. THE IMPACT OF THE "NEW IMMIGRA-TION" ON THE BLACK WORKER: STEELTON, PENNSYLVA-NIA, 1880-1920. *Labor Hist. 1976 17(2): 214-229.* Black workers in Steelton entered unskilled and semiskilled trades during 1880-1905, but with the rapid influx of Slavic and Italian immigrants Negroes suffered a devastating decline in occupational mobility until after World War I. Based on interviews and local records; 8 tables, 16 notes.
          L. L. Athey

1301. Bodnar, John E. SOCIALIZATION AND ADAPTATION: IMMIGRANT FAMILIES IN SCRANTON, 1880-1890. *Pennsylva-nia Hist. 1976 43(2): 147-162.* Studies the social mobility of the Irish and Welsh in Scranton during 1880-90 in order to test hypotheses advanced by Talcott Parsons, Philippe Aries, and Richard Sennett regarding the role of family structure in preparing children for adulthood in industrial society. Children from Irish and Welsh nuclear families enjoyed greater economic success than those reared in extended families. The sons of Welsh parents were more successful than those of Irish background be-cause they were exposed to industrial life at an earlier age. The Welsh were somewhat more inclined to live in nuclear families than were the Irish. Based on census data and other sources; illus., 7 tables, 30 notes.
          D. C. Swift

1302. Buenker, John D. DYNAMICS OF CHICAGO ETHNIC POLITICS, 1900-1930. *J. of the Illinois State Hist. Soc. 1974 67(2): 175-199.* Reviews Chicago's Italian, Irish, Swedish, Bohemian, German, Polish, and black city wards and why they supported the more effective Democratic Party. Native-stock politicians were to lose out to ethnic-orienated politicians despite financial, educational, and social advantages. The Chicago Irish took particular advantage of their numbers and group cohesiveness, and were successful on such issues as the repeal of Prohibi-tion. Based on political biographies and recent political studies; 37 notes.
          A. C. Aimone

1303. Chudacoff, Howard P. THE NEW IMMIGRATION HIS-TORY. *Rev. in Am. Hist. 1976 4(1): 99-104.* Review article prompted by Josef J. Barton's *Peasants and Strangers: Italians, Rumanians, and Slovaks in an American City, 1890-1950* (Cambridge, Massachusetts: Harvard U. Pr., 1975) and Edward R. Kantowicz's *Polish-American Politics in Chicago, 1888-1940* (Chicago: U. of Chicago Pr., 1975).

1304. Chudacoff, Howard P. A NEW LOOK AT ETHNIC NEIGH-BORHOODS: RESIDENTIAL DISPERSION AND THE CONCEPT OF VISIBILITY IN A MEDIUM-SIZED CITY. *J. of Am. Hist. 1973 60(1): 76-93.* Compares foreign-born and native residential patterns in Omaha 1880-1920. Contrary to popular belief, there was no significant concentration of foreign-born residents in particular districts. Like native Americans, few foreign-born residents remained at the same address for 20 years. The same percentages of foreign-born and native residents tended to emigrate from the city, and those remaining made about the same number of moves. Moreover, the same volatility was found among upper and middle classes as among the poor, and among the "new immi-grants" as among the old. Certain areas were still designated as "Bohemi-antown" and the "Jewish section," not because of residential concentration but because of the visibility of ethnic churches, businesses, and social institutions. 8 tables, 28 notes.   K. B. West

1305. Conzen, Kathleen Neils. IMMIGRANTS, IMMIGRANT NEIGHBORHOODS, AND ETHNIC IDENTITY: HISTORICAL IS-

SUES. *J. of Am. Hist. 1979 66(3): 603-615.* Analyzes various interpretations attempting to explain the relationship between ethnic identity, neighborhood residence, and acculturation for immigrants, especially Germans, in eastern and midwestern American cities. Although scholars must abandon old assumptions about straight-line relationships between residence, assimilation, and cultural maintenance, they cannot afford to discount the potential role of the immigrant neighborhood itself in the process of immigrant adaptation. 37 notes.   T. P. Linkfield

1306. Dannenbaum, Jed. IMMIGRANTS AND TEMPERANCE: ETHNOCULTURAL CONFLICT IN CINCINNATI, 1845-1860. *Ohio Hist. 1978 87(2): 125-139.* Ethnocultural issues, primarily anti-Catholicism, nativism, and temperance, sparked the breakdown of electoral politics and the realignment of contemporary cultural mores during the 1850's in Cincinnati, Ohio. As German and Irish immigrants grew in political power, native-born Cincinnatians increasingly associated them with rapidly worsening social problems. The issues severely disrupted the local party system and led to the virtual demise of the Whig Party in Cincinnati. Based on newspapers, contemporary comments, and secondary sources; illus., 47 notes.   N. Summers

1307. Droker, Howard A. SEATTLE RACE RELATIONS DURING THE SECOND WORLD WAR. *Pacific Northwest Q. 1976 67(4): 163-174.* Seattle's relatively small black population doubled during World War II as thousands of people came for jobs in defense industries. Jim Crowism became more prevalent and racial tension increased. To combat the possibility of race riots, Mayor William Devin created the Civic Unity Committee in February 1944. This multiracial group, dominated by conservatives, avoided conflict as it worked to defuse potential problems. Its quiet, behind-the-scenes efforts achieved limited success for black employment opportunities, but it never solved the discriminatory housing practices. The committee's efforts in behalf of displaced Japanese Americans in 1945 insured its credibility as a broad-based race relations organization which could effectively accomplish its goals. Primary and secondary sources; 6 photos, 51 notes.   M. L. Tate

1308. Gallaway, Lowell E.; Vedder, Richard K.; and Shukla, Vishwa. THE DISTRIBUTION OF THE IMMIGRANT POPULATION IN THE UNITED STATES, AN ECONOMIC ANALYSIS. *Explorations in Econ. Hist. 1974 11(3): 213-226.* Immigrant settlement patterns of 1900 show that immigrants entered the country with relatively accurate information about economic conditions in various parts of the United States. As a result they generally settled in urbanized rather than sparsely populated areas. This was consistent with an optimal allocation of labor resources. Based on published statistics and secondary accounts.   P. J. Coleman

1309. Garofalo, Charles. BLACK-WHITE OCCUPATIONAL DISTRIBUTION IN MIAMI DURING WORLD WAR I. *Prologue 1973 5(2): 98-101.* Selective Service registration records for the three registrations of 1917-18 provide data on white and black registrants with each group further divided into categories of native and foreign-born. The 6,429 subjects are grouped in the four classes by seven occupational categories from "unskilled" to "professional." Perceived patterns may be compared with other urban center records. Based on primary sources; 2 tables, 14 notes.   D. G. Davis, Jr.

1310. Garonzik, Joseph. THE RACIAL AND ETHNIC MAKE-UP OF BALTIMORE NEIGHBORHOODS, 1850-1870. *Maryland Hist. Mag. 1976 71(3): 392-402.* Analyzes the significant changes in Baltimore's economy and population and the effects on spatial patterns. Along with a great influx of immigrants after 1865, mainly of German stock, Baltimore had more blacks than any northern city, proximity according to ethnicity apparently having little to do with choice of residence. Occupational proximity was more important, and with the increasing differentiation of the city into a central industrial district and areas of specialized production, working class, commercial, and professional people grouped themselves accordingly. Residential analysis shows that by 1870 a householder's residence, occupation, and ethnic origin were more closely related than origin and residence alone. Baltimore remained a patchwork of nationalities with white natives, Germans, Irish, and blacks scattered throughout the "social quilt" in heterogeneous neighborhoods. Not until the "new immigration" arrived did the city lose this integrated character. From the author's 1974 thesis at SUNY, Stony Brook, and secondary works; 2 tables, 20 notes.   G. J. Bobango

1311. Glasco, Laurence A. THE LIFE CYCLES AND HOUSEHOLD STRUCTURE OF AMERICAN ETHNIC GROUPS: IRISH, GERMANS, AND NATIVE-BORN WHITES IN BUFFALO, NEW YORK 1855. *J. of Urban Hist. 1975 1(3): 339-364.* A study of the household structure of different ethnic groups produced evidence that the following trends existed: foreign-born women often became domestics, thus reducing the size of the family living at home; German girls remained domestics for shorter periods of time and married earlier; native-born women were the last to leave home, and German males left earliest; the Irish were the least apt to be homeowners; and the native-born population most frequently boarded with family. 6 fig., 11 notes.   S. S. Sprague

1312. Greeley, Andrew M. AN IRISH-ITALIAN? *Italian Americana 1975 1(2): 239-245.* An Irish American priest who grew up on the West Side of Chicago during the 1920's reminisces about the coming of Italian Americans to his neighborhood, discusses negative ethnic stereotypes, and offers a corrective sociological profile of these immigrants.   S

1313. Griswold del Castillo, Richard. A PRELIMINARY COMPARISON OF CHICANO, IMMIGRANT AND NATIVE BORN FAMILY STRUCTURES 1850-1880. *Aztlán 1975 6(1): 87-95.* Compares European immigrants and native born Anglo Americans in Detroit, Michigan, with Mexican Americans in Los Angeles during 1850-80. The urban Chicano family was more drastically affected by economic changes and economic opportunities were more restricted for Chicano household heads. Chicano family structure resembled that of the native born Anglo American. 14 notes.   A

1314. Hershberg, Theodore; Burstein, Alan N.; Ericksen, Eugene P.; Greenberg, Stephanie; and Yancey, William L. A TALE OF THREE CITIES: BLACKS AND IMMIGRANTS IN PHILADELPHIA: 1850-1880, 1930 AND 1970. *Ann. of the Am. Acad. of Pol. and Social Sci. 1979 441: 55-81.* Determining whether the black experience was unique, or similar to that of earlier white immigrant groups, is central to the debate over whether blacks should be the beneficiaries of special compensatory legislation in the present. Observes the experience of three waves of immigrants to Philadelphia: the Irish and Germans who settled in the "Industrializing City" of the mid-to-late 19th century; the Italians, Poles and Russian Jews who came to the "Industrial City" at the turn of the 20th century; and blacks who arrived in the "Post-Industrial City" in their greatest numbers after World War II. Analysis of the city's changing opportunity structure and ecological form, and the racial discrimination encountered shows the black experience to be unique in kind and degree. Significant changes in the structures that characterized each of the "three cities" call into question our standing notion of the assimilation process.   J

1315. Janis, Ralph. FLIRTATION AND FLIGHT: ALTERNATIVES TO ETHNIC CONFRONTATION IN WHITE ANGLO-AMERICAN PROTESTANT DETROIT, 1880-1940. *J. of Ethnic Studies 1978 6(2): 1-17.* Examines a large sampling of marriage and baptismal registers, membership rosters, and officer lists of Detroit churches to demonstrate the changing class, cultural, and spatial composition of church-related social organizations over two generations. Solid social interdicts existed against ethnic mixture in 1880. Ethnic uniformity in marriage and membership had declined by 1906, but was resurrected after this by the impact of the auto boom. Ethnocentrism, however, represented a rational 19th-century-rooted search for order by the large majority, who sought viable "acts of adjustment to urban change." Vigilantism, Klanism, and demagoguery were the exception, not the rule, of Detroit Protestants, in their search for "the creative use of social distance, not confrontation," in making the transition to new and modified social boundaries. Primary and secondary research; 2 tables, 26 notes.   G. J. Bobango

1316. Kantrowitz, Nathan. RACIAL AND ETHNIC RESIDENTIAL SEGREGATION: BOSTON, 1830-1970. *Ann. of the Am. Acad. of Pol. and Social Sci. 1979 441: 41-54.* Residential segregation in Boston between European ethnic population has declined little during the 20th century. Racial segregation rose during the 19th and early 20th century, but has remained stable since about 1940, prior to the expansion of the city's Negro population. These conclusions indicate that racial segregation is but an extension of the pattern of ethnic separation, especially since Asian and Latin ethnics show similar patterns in the contemporary city. Moreover, segregation levels are only slightly lower in the 1970 SMSA suburban ring than they are in the central city. We suggest that this demographic record is relevant to issues of Boston's public school deseg-regation controversy.   J

1317. Kessner, Thomas and Caroli, Betty Boyd. NEW IMMI-GRANT WOMEN AT WORK: ITALIANS AND JEWS IN NEW YORK CITY, 1880-1905. *J. of Ethnic Studies 1978 5(4): 19-31.* Statisti-cal analysis of first and second generation Italian and Jewish women shows that "gender proved less significant than ethnicity in shaping the occupational distribution of wives" in lower Manhattan, Brooklyn, and Harlem. Upward mobility is demonstrable from unskilled blue-collar to skilled blue-collar jobs outside the home for Italian daughters, but none reached professional status. Jewish women started at higher status levels and continued to move up rapidly. Attitudes toward education among the two groups, willingness to defer to brothers, familial values as to suitable work for women, and Italian girls' acceptance of homework on garments and artificial flowers, which Jewish girls by 1905 had abandoned, explain the divergent occupational priorities and objectives flowing from different cultural and historical perspectives. Primary and secondary data; 4 tables, 23 notes.   G. J. Bobango

1318. Klaczynska, Barbara. WHY WOMEN WORK: A COMPARI-SON OF VARIOUS GROUPS—PHILADELPHIA, 1910-1930. *Labor Hist. 1976 17(1): 73-87.* Analyzes the reasons for women working by comparing patterns of Italian, Polish, Irish, Jewish, black, and native-born white women. Central determinants were strong ethnic familial traditions, the lack of strong familial ties, and class consciousness. Italian and Polish women worked least often, and blacks, native-born whites, and Irish most often. Jewish women tended to move from a work tradition to a nonwork position as they moved into the middle class. Based on govern-ment publications and periodicals; 20 notes.   L. L. Athey

1319. Korman, Gerd. HISTORY FOR SOCIAL SCIENCE. *Rev. in Am. Hist. 1978 6(1): 68-71.* Review article prompted by Kathleen Neils Conzen's *Immigrant Milwaukee, 1836-1860: Accommodation and Community in a Frontier City* (Cambridge, Mass.: Harvard U. Pr., 1976).

1320. Krause, Corinne Azen. ITALIAN, JEWISH, AND SLAVIC GRANDMOTHERS IN PITTSBURGH: THEIR ECONOMIC ROLES. *Frontiers 1977 2(2): 18-27.* Interview 75 women in the Pitts-burgh area challenging the notion that immigrants' wives rarely worked outside the home during the early 1900's; part of a special issue on women's oral history.

1321. Krause, Corinne Azen. URBANIZATION WITHOUT BREAKDOWN: ITALIAN, JEWISH, AND SLAVIC IMMIGRANT WOMEN IN PITTSBURGH, 1900-1945. *J. of Urban Hist. 1978 4(3): 291-306.* Most immigrant women adjusted to the cultural shock of immi-gration without serious or lasting problems. In part this was due to general human resiliency, but in Pittsburgh it was also due to the exis-tence of immigrant neighborhoods and other bridges to the old world. Based on oral histories; fig., 41 notes.   T. W. Smith

1322. Laurie, Bruce; Hershberg, Theodore; and Alter, George. IMMIGRANTS AND INDUSTRY: THE PHILADELPHIA EXPE-RIENCE, 1850-1880. *J. of Social Hist. 1975 9(2): 219-248.* Attempts to provide more secure categories of occupational status for 19th-century activities beyond the ahistorical reach of sociological studies in this cen-tury. Examines 14 manufacturing industries in Philadelphia, 1850-80, and attempts to explain changes in the job status, and how the changes affected the distribution to different ethnic groups. Little change is seen in the ethnic distribution because of disadvantages different groups brought with them, and because industrialization did not necessarily equal mechanization. 11 tables, 5 figs., 30 notes.   M. Hough

1323. Leonard, Stephen J. THE IRISH, ENGLISH AND GER-MANS IN DENVER, 1860-1890. *Colorado Mag. 1977 54(2): 126-153.* During 1860-90, Irish, English, and German Americans were consistently among Denver's larger nationality groups. The Germans had both com-munity solidarity and skills the other nationalities lacked. Denver was

faster than larger American cities in acculturation, possibly because of small numbers of immigrants and their familiarity with English. Tolera-tion persisted through the 1880's. Primary sources; 12 illus., 121 notes.
O. H. Zabel

1324. Luckingham, Bradford. IMMIGRANT LIFE IN EMER-GENT SAN FRANCISCO. *J. of the West 1973 12(4): 600-617.* San Francisco was unrivalled in its attraction of immigrant groups during the gold rush era. Religious, racial, ethnic, and regional groups tended to settle in clusters in the city. Each group attempted to be self-contained, united, and more or less unfriendly to everyone else. The strength of unity often determined the success or failure of the group. Group policies gradually coalesced under one of the major political parties. The Vigi-lance Committees were in part politically oriented. The establishment of a city government was inspired by the desire to contain the growing power of immigrant groups. 31 notes.   V. L. Human

1325. McTigue, Geraldine. PATTERNS OF RESIDENCE: HOUS-ING DISTRIBUTION BY COLOR IN TWO LOUISIANA TOWNS, 1860-1880. *Louisiana Studies 1976 15(4): 345-388.* Examines housing patterns in Opelousas, the parish (county) seat, and Washington, the main port, of St. Landry Parish. Each had a population of about 600 persons. No strict dichotomy of integration-segregation existed in either town. Foreign-born Caucasians were much more apt to live in integrated areas than were native-born whites. Both towns were somewhat integrated in 1860; by 1880 all integration had disappeared in Washington and the percentage had declined in Opelousas. Economics was not the determin-ing factor; rather it was the rate at which blacks entered the community. Concludes that integration was possible though status was fixed; with growing numbers and fuller freedom, integration declined. Based on US Census Reports and secondary sources; 24 tables, 32 notes.
J. Buschen

1326. Passi, Michael M. IMMIGRANTS AND THE CITY: PROB-LEMS OF INTERPRETATION AND SYNTHESIS IN RECENT WHITE ETHNIC HISTORY. *J. of Ethnic Studies 1976 4(2): 61-72.* A review essay prompted by three ethnic studies: Dean R. Esslinger's *Immigrants and the City: Ethnicity and Mobility in a Nineteenth Century Midwestern City*; Edward R. Kantowicz's *Polish-American Politics in Chicago, 1880-1940*; and Josef J. Barton's *Peasants and Strangers: Ital-ians, Rumanians, and Slovaks in an American City, 1890-1950*. All are products of the academic trends and ferment in ethnic history since 1960. Esslinger's study is "new urban history" on social mobility in South Bend, Indiana, with "no surprises in its methodology or in its findings," but with "an excessive faith in quantitative methods" and some serious flaws in conceptual design. Kantowicz's book "demonstrates the limits of old-fashioned narrative history in writing about ethnicity," and offers at bottom only the standard chronicle of leaders and elections. Barton's work is the most genuine accomplishment, although an ultimately disap-pointing book by its leap to the triple-melting pot notion as a conclusion and its sparse attention to second-generation family formation. All of the studies show the need to get beyond the unilinear theories of cultural change and recognize the dialectical relationship between the immigrant and American society.   G. J. Bobango

1327. Radzialowski, Thaddeus. THE COMPETITION FOR JOBS AND RACIAL STEREOTYPE: POLES AND BLACKS IN CHICAGO. *Polish Am. Studies 1976 33(2): 5-18.* The struggle for jobs, not hunger for status, produced Polish prejudice against blacks in Chicago, ca. 1890-1919. Blacks from the South threatened the jobs of the settled Polish immigrants. In no time, blacks found themselves serving as strikebreakers and even killing Polish workers. For these prejudices and racial antagonisms much blame rests with American industry. Based on newspaper accounts and Polish and English secondary sources; 28 notes.
S. R. Pliska

1328. Rolle, Andrew. UPROOTED OR UPRAISED? IMMI-GRANTS IN AMERICA. *Rev. in Am. Hist. 1978 6(1): 95-98.* Review article prompted by Thomas Kessner's *The Golden Door: Italian and Jewish Immigrant Mobility in New York City, 1880-1915* (New York: Oxford U. Pr., 1977).

1329. Shover, John L. ETHNICITY AND RELIGION IN PHILA-DELPHIA POLITICS, 1924-40. *Am. Q. 1973 25(5): 499-515.* When

Philadelphia's ethnic and religious groups confronted vital political choices in 1928, they responded as blacks, Jews, Germans, or Catholics, not as assimilated Americans grouped cross-culturally by occupation, class, or neighborhood. Ethno-religious political consciousness continued to flourish in the 1930's leaving sparse evidence to sustain interpretations of voting behavior predicated on social classes. Based on primary and secondary sources; 6 tables, 40 notes.   W. D. Piersen

1330. Silvia, Philip T., Jr. THE POSITION OF "NEW" IMMI-GRANTS IN THE FALL RIVER TEXTILE INDUSTRY. *Int. Migration Rev. 1976 10(2): 221-232.* Discusses the reception of Portuguese and Polish immigrants by French Canadians in textile industries and trade unions in Fall River, Massachusetts, 1890-1905.

1331. Sullivan, Margaret Lo Piccolo. ST. LOUIS ETHNIC NEIGH-BORHOODS, 1850-1930: AN INTRODUCTION. *Missouri Hist. Soc. Bull. 1977 33(2): 64-76.* Traces the development of ethnic neighborhoods, in St. Louis, Missouri, in which persons of French, German, Irish, and South and East European origins lived. German and Irish immigrants to St. Louis predominated during 1820-60. Substantial migrations of South and East Europeans occurred during 1900-30 and were followed by major Negro migrations after 1930. Formation of Black ghettos was hastened by the passage of a segregation ordinance in 1916. Based on secondary works and government documents; 3 photos, 40 notes.
                                        H. T. Lovin

1332. Vecoli, Rudolph J. THE IMMIGRANT EXPERIENCE: NEW PERSPECTIVES AND OLD PREJUDICES. *Rev. in Am. Hist. 1979 7(1): 43-50.* Review article prompted by John W. Briggs's *An Italian Passage: Immigrants to Three American Cities, 1890-1930* (New Haven, Conn.: Yale U. Pr., 1978) and Caroline Golab's *Immigrant Destinations* (Philadelphia: Temple U. Pr., 1977).

1333. Vinyard, Jo Ellen McNergney. ON THE FRINGE IN PHILA-DELPHIA. *J. of Urban Hist. 1975 1(4): 492-498.* Review article prompted by Dennis Clark's *The Irish in Philadelphia: Ten Generations of Urban Experience* (Philadelphia: Temple U. Pr., 1973) and Allen F. Davis and Mark H. Haller's *The Peoples of Philadelphia: History of Ethnic Groups and Lower-Class Life* 1790-1940 (Philadelphia: Temple U. Pr., 1973).

1334. Waltzer, Kenneth. URBAN AMERICA: BOILING POT AND MELTING POT. *Rev. in Am. Hist. 1979 7(2): 241-246.* Review article prompted by Ronald H. Bayor's *Neighbors in Conflict: The Irish, Germans, Jews, and Italians of New York City, 1929-1941* (Baltimore, Md.: The Johns Hopkins U. Pr., 1978).

1335. Weber, Michael P. RESIDENTIAL AND OCCUPATIONAL PATTERNS OF ETHNIC MINORITIES IN NINETEENTH CEN-TURY PITTSBURGH. *Pennsylvania Hist. 1977 44(4): 317-334.* Focuses on occupational and residential patterns of ethnic groups in four Pittsburgh industrial wards during 1880-1920. In comparison to native-born workers, Irish and German immigrants were not disadvantaged in occupational mobility. Blue-collar workers who remained in Pittsburgh experienced considerable upward mobility. Age had little influence on transiency or persistence, but place of birth and occupation did influence residential persistence. Based on census data; 3 illus., map, 3 tables, 16 notes.   D. C. Swift

1336. Zunz, Olivier. THE ORGANIZATION OF THE AMERI-CAN CITY IN THE LATE NINETEENTH CENTURY: ETHNIC STRUCTURE AND SPATIAL ARRANGEMENT IN DETROIT. *J. of Urban Hist. 1977 3(4): 443-466.* Examines a sample of blocks from the 1880 census of Detroit, Michigan, and analyzes the spatial organiza-tion of the city. Finds that there was strong ethnic-racial and occupational clustering. This clustering was weakest both in the center and at the periphery. A factoral analysis of the data revealed five cluster types: central area, residential center, east side, west sides, and peripheral area. 6 maps, 6 tables, 20 notes.   T. W. Smith

Blacks

1337. Akin, Edward N. WHEN A MINORITY BECOMES THE MAJORITY: BLACKS IN JACKSONVILLE POLITICS, 1887-1907. *Florida Hist. Q. 1974 53(2): 123-145.* Develops the thesis that the dynam-ics of the urban setting allowed Negroes to exercise political power and rights on a broader scale than the state's rural black population, illus-trated by a case study of Jacksonville politics during the late 1880's. "When given proper latitude, black leaders were just as effective in the political arena as whites." It must, however, be acknowledged that Jack-sonville blacks' political success could be a unique situation. 2 illus., 2 tables, 104 notes.   R. V. Ritter

1338. Barnes, Annie S. THE BLACK BEAUTY PARLOR COM-PLEX IN A SOUTHERN CITY. *Phylon 1975 36(2): 149-154.* In New-port News, Virginia, beauty parlors serve as important social centers for the lower, middle, and upper class women of the black community. Not only are the parlors used as a means of enhancing personal appearance, they also act as centers of communication. Basically, an inverse relation-ship exists between social class of customers and significance of hair grooming services, frequency of visits, disposition of customers, and infor-mality of communication. The lower class beauty parlor is the more important for its customers because of the limited number of social gath-ering places for them and because enhancing personal appearance also enhances self-esteem.   B. A. Glasrud

1339. Beasley, Jonathan. BLACKS—SLAVE AND FREE: VICKS-BURG, 1850-1860. *J. of Mississippi Hist. 1976 38(1): 1-32.* Using Vicksburg 1850-60, the author questions Richard Wade's chief conclu-sions in *Slavery in the Cities: The South, 1820-1860* (New York, 1964), especially Wade's mian thesis "that slavery as an institution was disinte-grating in the cities" by the 1850's, a decade during which Vicksburg's slave population increased from 1,176 to 1,402. Based on primary and secondary sources; 110 notes.   J. W. Hillje

1340. Betten, Neil and Mohl, Raymond A. THE EVOLUTION OF RACISM IN AN INDUSTRIAL CITY, 1906-1940: A CASE STUDY OF GARY, INDIANA. *J. of Negro Hist. 1974 59(1): 51-64.* Racial discrimination and segregation in education, housing, employment, pub-lic services, and recreation came with the birth and growth of Gary. By World War II, Gary had a clearly defined black ghetto and discrimination was a way of life. Based on primary and secondary sources; 32 notes.
                                        N. G. Sapper

1341. Blackett, R. J. M. "... FREEDOM, OR THE MARTYR'S GRAVE": BLACK PITTSBURGH'S AID TO THE FUGITIVE SLAVE. *Western Pennsylvania Hist. Mag. 1978 61(2): 117-134.* Dis-cusses Pittsburgh's Philanthropic Society, a benevolent society to aid Negroes in the community as well as a secret society of black and white abolitionists who sought to abduct slaves from southern plantations and secure their safe passage along the underground railroad, 1830's-60's.

1342. Blassingame, John W. BEFORE THE GHETTO: THE MAK-ING OF THE BLACK COMMUNITY IN SAVANNAH, GEORGIA, 1865-1880. *J. of Social Hist. 1973 6(4): 463-488.* The strong black community which developed gave members a political, economic, social, and intellectual base from which to fight discrimination, but white migra-tion within the city supported by real estate agents, soon led to the existence of mainly black areas of town.

1343. Bodnar, John E. PETER C. BLACKWELL AND THE NE-GRO COMMUNITY OF STEELTON, 1880-1920. *Pennsylvania Mag. of Hist. and Biog. 1973 97(2): 199-209.* During 1880-1920, the segregated black community of Steelton developed community organizations mod-eled on their white counterparts. Thus the Douglass Association, com-posed of black graduates of Steelton High School, was organized in 1902 as a counterpart to the all-white Steelton High Alumni Association. Peter C. Blackwell, the most articulate spokesman for these black organiza-tions, failed to criticize the white power structure. Instead, as the first black Republican councilman in Steelton, he defended the Pennsylvania Steel Company. As publisher of the *Steelton Press,* he failed to bring the plight of the blacks to the public attention. Based on primary and second-ary sources; 36 notes.   E. W. Carp

1344. Bragaw, Donald H. STATUS OF NEGROES IN A SOUTHERN PORT CITY IN THE PROGRESSIVE ERA. *Florida Hist. Q. 1973 51(3): 281-302.* Traces the growth, leveling off, and decline of proportionate Negro population in Pensacola between 1896 and the 1920's. Discusses occupational groups and residential patterns. The decline in the employment and economic status of Negroes began around 1906 with the exhaustion of nearby forests and resultant slacking of the lumber industry. Negro fortunes received another blow in 1910 with the temporary closing of the naval base. Its reopening as a naval air station in 1916 did not bring recovery. Based on census records, city directories, newspapers, interviews, and secondary sources; 59 notes.
J. E. Findling

1345. Brownlee, W. Elliot. THE ECONOMICS OF URBAN SLAVERY. *Rev. in Am. Hist. 1977 5(2): 230-235.* Review article prompted by Claudia Dale Goldin's *Urban Slavery in the American South 1820-1860: A Quantitative History* (Chicago: U. of Chicago Pr., 1976).

1346. Camerota, Michael. WESTFIELD'S BLACK COMMUNITY, 1755-1905. *Hist. J. of Western Massachusetts 1976 5(1): 17-27.* Describes the growth of the black community in Westfield until the 20th century and its decline since then. Examines the lives of a number of black Westfielders. Illus.
W. H. Mulligan, Jr.

1347. Clarke, John Henrik. MARCUS GARVEY: THE HARLEM YEARS. *Black Scholar 1973/74 5(4): 17-24.* Marcus Garvey's Universal Negro Improvement Association centered in Harlem 1919-26. S

1348. Contee, Clarence G. BUTLER R. WILSON AND THE BOSTON NAACP BRANCH. *Crisis 1974 81(10): 346-348.* Biography of Butler R. Wilson, 1860-1939, and his work in the National Association for the Advancement of Colored People. S

1349. Cottrol, Robert J. COMPARATIVE SLAVE STUDIES: URBAN SLAVERY AS A MODEL, TRAVELERS' ACCOUNTS AS A SOURCE—BIBLIOGRAPHIC ESSAY. *J. of Black Studies 1977 8(1): 3-12.* Attempts to compare slave systems in the United States and in Latin America confront many variables, including different settings and different definitions of treatment. Travelers' accounts of urban slavery in Brazil reveal a variety of slave systems, so these accounts must be used with care. Covers ca. 1817-68. Biblio.
D. C. Neal

1350. Crosthwait, D. N., Jr. THE FIRST BLACK HIGH SCHOOL IN NASHVILLE. *Negro Hist. Bull. 1974 37(4): 266-268.* Describes the organization of Meigs High School (1886) for Negroes under its first principal, D. N. Crosthwait.

1351. Daniels, Douglas H. LOOKING FOR A HOME: THE TRAVELCRAFT SKILLS OF SAN FRANCISCO'S PIONEER BLACK RESIDENTS. *Umoja 1977 1(2): 49-70.* Travelcraft, the possession of skills which allow the possessor to adapt to different geographical areas, were important for blacks moving to San Francisco during the gold rush as well as for those who remained there to form the black community, 1850's-80's.

1352. Day, Judy and Kedro, M. James. FREE BLACKS IN ST. LOUIS: ANTEBELLUM CONDITIONS, EMANCIPATION, AND THE POSTWAR ERA. *Missouri Hist. Soc. Bull. 1974 30(2): 117-135.* Surveys the persecution and inequalities imposed upon the "free blacks" of St. Louis before the Civil War. Prewar social and economic inequalities persisted after the war. Equality was preached at St. Louis, but little racial integration developed. Based on secondary sources; 85 notes.
H. T. Lovin

1353. Foner, Philip S. THE BATTLE TO END DISCRIMINATION AGAINST NEGROES ON PHILADELPHIA STREETCARS: BACKGROUND AND BEGINNING OF THE BATTLE. *Pennsylvania Hist. 1973 40(3): 261-292, (4): 355-379.* Part I. Discusses the first stages of the efforts to end discrimination on Philadelphia streetcars. Of the 19 street railways, 11 refused to permit blacks to enter their cars; the others permitted them to ride on the front platforms of the cars. Court challenges and petitions signed by blacks and whites led some companies to run separate cars for blacks. Two companies ended discrimination in 1864. William Still, a black merchant and abolitionist, led efforts to force

other companies to do the same. Based on newspapers; 2 illus., 58 notes. Part II. In 1865 Senator Morrow B. Lowry of Erie and Crawford Counties led the fight to end segregation on Philadelphia streetcars. After two years his measure passed because the legislators knew that blacks would soon have the vote. Black organizations, particularly the State Equal Rights League, played decisive roles in winning passage of the law. Discusses the hostile attitude of most Philadelphians and the divisions within black ranks. Based largely on newspapers; illus., 51 notes.
D. C. Swift

1354. Fordham, Monroe. THE BUFFALO COOPERATIVE ECONOMIC SOCIETY, INC., 1928-1961: A BLACK SELF-HELP ORGANIZATION. *Niagara Frontier 1976 23(2): 41-49.* Discusses the Negro-owned Buffalo Cooperative Economic Society, Inc., in Buffalo, New York, 1928-61, emphasizing the role of founder Dr. Ezekiel E. Nelson.

1355. Franklin, Vincent P. GHETTO ON THEIR MINDS: AFRO-AMERICAN HISTORIOGRAPHY AND THE CITY. *Afro-Americans in New York Life and Hist. 1977 1(1): 111-119.* Review article prompted by Kenneth Kusmer's *A Ghetto Takes Shape: Black Cleveland, 1870-1930* (Urbana: U. of Illinois Pr., 1976).

1356. Furstenberg, Frank F., Jr.; Hershberg, Theodore; and Modell, John. THE ORIGINS OF THE FEMALE-HEADED BLACK FAMILY: THE IMPACT OF THE URBAN EXPERIENCE. *J. of Interdisciplinary Hist. 1975 6(2): 211-233.* Much of the speculation about the origins of the matrifocal black family in the 19th century has been lacking in specific historical data. The female-headed family emerged not so much as a legacy of slavery as a result of the destructive conditions of northern urban life. The matrifocal black family is the product of economic discrimination, poverty, and disease. 12 tables, 22 notes.
R. Howell

1357. George, Paul S. COLORED TOWN: MIAMI'S BLACK COMMUNITY, 1896-1930. *Florida Hist. Q. 1978 56(4): 432-447.* The early 20th century race relations in Florida and especially Colored Town, the northwest section of Miami. Blacks were subject to Jim Crow legislation, inadequate municipal services, cramped housing, a dual system of justice, and white terrorism. Nevertheless, black citizens formed church and fraternal organizations, established a business and professional community, and played a vital role in the economic growth of Miami. The black community's troubles worsened in later decades. Based mainly on newspapers, government records, and secondary sources; 3 illus., map, 58 notes.
P. A. Beaber

1358. Gerlach, Don R. BLACK ARSON IN ALBANY, NEW YORK: NOVEMBER 1793. *J. of Black Studies 1977 7(3): 301-312.* A 1793 arson incident in Albany, New York, suggests that the slave rebelliousness of this period was spontaneous and involved only a few slaves. The three slaves involved, however, did not act out of a grudge against their master and perhaps were hired by white men to set the fire. A period of uneasiness followed the fire. Restrictions on slaves were tightened, but the reaction was mild, although the perpetrators were speedily arrested, tried, convicted, and hanged. Whether or not this incident influenced the state legislature's position on slavery can only be conjectured. Primary and secondary sources; 9 notes, biblio.
D. C. Neal

1359. Goldstein, Michael L. PREFACE TO THE RISE OF BOOKER T. WASHINGTON: A VIEW FROM NEW YORK CITY OF THE DEMISE OF INDEPENDENT BLACK POLITICS, 1889-1902. *J. of Negro Hist. 1977 62(1): 81-99.* The failure of independent activity on national and local levels as exemplified by the Afro-American League, the Afro-American Council, and the Citizen's Protective League reveals the limited political alternatives presented to blacks at the turn of the 19th century, since the choice lay between participating in segregated party structures or nonparticipation. Their failure to mobilize resources aimed at destroying or circumventing these structures exposed the extent to which their status in national and local politics depended not on their own bargaining power but on the good will of sympathetic whites. Mainly periodical sources; 108 notes.
P. J. Taylorson

1360. Goodfriend, Joyce D. BURGHERS AND BLACKS: THE EVOLUTION OF A SLAVE SOCIETY AT NEW AMSTERDAM. *New York Hist. 1978 59(2): 125-144.* The development of a slave popula-

tion in New Netherland was prompted by the Dutch West India Company to deal with the perpetual problem of underpopulation in the Dutch settlements, and to assure prosperity by increasing agricultural production. At first slavery in New Netherland was institutionalized on a corporate basis, an unusual case in American colonial experience. By 1664, as the result of company practices, slavery had become a widespread mode of labor exploitation among the settlers in the colony. 4 illus., 44 notes.
                                                                          R. N. Lokken

1361. Grenz, Suzanna M.   THE EXODUSTERS OF 1879: ST. LOUIS AND KANSAS CITY RESPONSES. *Missouri Hist. Rev. 1978 73(1): 54-70.* Beginning in 1879, many blacks who found life in the South intolerable came north to St. Louis and Kansas City and then into Kansas where they found permanent homes. Private citizens in both cities soon formed aid programs, but public officials responded differently. St. Louis Mayor Henry Overstolz and his aides offered only medical assistance. They did not wish to encourage more immigrants, but they were anxious to avoid an epidemic. Kansas City Mayor George M. Shelley and other civic leaders supplemented the private aid program with public resources. Primary and secondary sources; illus., 61 notes.   W. F. Zornow

1362. Griffin, James S.   BLACKS IN THE ST. PAUL POLICE DEPARTMENT: AN EIGHTY-YEAR SURVEY. *Minnesota Hist. 1975 44(7): 255-265.* Since the 1880's there have been a total of 32 black policemen in St. Paul. In 1925 Blacks on the force numbered eight, the largest number per capita in the country, but between 1921 and 1937 no blacks were hired so that by 1945 only one black was on the force. Discrimination in hiring, assignments, and service ratings were typical. More recently the number of blacks has increased: 7 of 525 (1972) and 14 of 640 (1975). Based on newspapers and other sources; 13 illus., 26 notes.   S. S. Sprague

1363. Grossman, Lawrence.   IN HIS VEINS COURSED NO BOOT-LICKING BLOOD: THE CAREER OF PETER H. CLARK. *Ohio Hist. 1977 86(2): 79-95.* Nineteenth-century black history in Cincinnati, Ohio, is illuminated in this biographical sketch of one of Ohio's most prominent black men. Peter H. Clark, schoolteacher and champion of antebellum Cincinnati black rights, became a figure of national importance in racial matters by the 1880's. His childhood, education, jobs, and appointment as the first black member of the Board of Trustees of The Ohio State University are discussed. Emphasizes Clark's intense involvement in politics. Based on manuscript, newspaper, contemporary, and secondary sources; illus., 55 notes.   J

1364. Harris, William.   WORK AND THE FAMILY IN BLACK ATLANTA, 1880. *J. of Social Hist. 1976 9(3): 319-330.* Investigates whether slavery or conditions in the post civil war environment affected the opportunities of blacks and the nature of the black family. Lack of advancement was not as much a result of a poverty of skills, which could be blamed on slavery, as the lack of political opportunities in the post civil war situation. Limitations in the census information make analysis of the slight differences in fatherless families difficult. Attempts are made to enlighten the subject with comparisons with other data and conclusions about different ethnic groups in urban situations in the late 19th century. Based on a sample of 400-500 blacks and the same number of whites in Atlanta from the censuses of 1870 and 1880.   M. Hough

1365. Harvey, Diane.   THE TERRI, AUGUSTA'S BLACK ENCLAVE. *Richmond County Hist. 1973 5(2): 60-75.* Known as "The Terri" (short for "The Territory"), this all-black section of Augusta dates from the post-Civil War era. Discusses, *inter alia,* residents' work and housing. One of six articles in this issue on Augusta. Based on newspapers and secondary sources; 46 notes.   H. R. Grant

1366. Hawkins, Homer C.   TRENDS IN BLACK MIGRATION FROM 1863 TO 1960. *Phylon 1973 34(2): 140-152.* An account of Negro migration, first to the southwest, then westward to Oklahoma Territory where blacks such as Edward Preston McCabe founded Langston, an all-black community, and finally moved northward to the larger metropolitan areas.   S

1367. Hellwig, David J.   BLACK MEETS BLACK: AFRO-AMERICAN REACTIONS TO WEST INDIAN IMMIGRANTS IN THE 1920'S. *South Atlantic Q. 1978 77(2): 206-224.* During 1916-24 many

black immigrants from the West Indies arrived in the United States. Their concentration in a few cities compounded difficulties of older black residents and newly-arrived blacks from southern states who also sought urban economic opportunities. They increased competition for jobs and housing while seemingly adding little to the resources of the native blacks. They were easy targets for frustration and resentment. Depicts the numerous social, economic, and ethnic bases for hostilities between the two groups, as well as attempts to bring them together. Possible hostilities failed to materialize in the late 1920's when the West Indian black returned to his home. Based on the author's PhD dissertation, other academic studies, newspapers, and secondary materials; 44 notes.
                                                                          H. M. Parker, Jr.

1368. Henry, Keith S.   LANGUAGE, CULTURE, AND SOCIETY IN THE COMMONWEALTH CARIBBEAN. *J. of Black Studies 1976 7(1): 79-94.* The preeminence of English-speaking West Indian immigrants in New York City's public oratory after 1910 can be attributed to many factors, especially a strong interest in international affairs, but the very character of West Indian oratory also had important effects on the use of language. In the Caribbean, Standard English was expected in oratory; political discourse appealed to a story-telling tradition; and the very way of life encouraged a verbal style of loudness and aggressiveness that may have helped the West Indians to win a hearing on New York City street corners. Primary and secondary sources; notes, biblio.   D. C. Neal

1369. Hine, William C.   THE 1867 CHARLESTON STREETCAR SIT-INS, A CASE OF SUCCESSFUL BLACK PROTEST. *South Carolina Hist. Mag. 1976 77(2): 110-114.* Passage of the Military Reconstruction Act of 1867, fostered rising expectations among Negroes. In 1867, Blacks used sit-ins to protest their exclusion from the Charleston City Railway Company. While white Republicans cautioned against violence, the demonstrations and federal pressure forced the company to back down and open its cars to blacks. The policy did not change until the 20th century. Primary sources; 25 notes.   R. H. Tomlinson

1370. Hines, Linda O. and Jones, Allen W.   A VOICE OF BLACK PROTEST: THE SAVANNAH MEN'S SUNDAY CLUB, 1905-1911. *Phylon 1974 35(2): 193-202.* The Savannah Men's Sunday Club was a Negro organization established in Savannah, Georgia for the dual purposes of elevating Negroes and protesting unequal treatment. The club enjoyed wide support until 1908, when a Negro boycott and subsequent white backlash caused it to gradually wither and die. Members of the club had diverse objectives; protest seemed to worsen rather than to better conditions, and a new organization had sprung up to usurp the club's more radical functions. The Sunday Club did serve to focus and crystallize discontent. 38 notes.   V. L. Human

1371. Hoey, Edwin.   TERROR IN NEW YORK—1741. *Am. Heritage 1974 25(4): 72-77.* The great New York City slave conspiracy and its aftermath.   S

1372. Hoffecker, Carol E.   THE POLITICS OF EXCLUSION: BLACKS IN LATE NINETEENTH-CENTURY WILMINGTON, DELAWARE. *Delaware Hist. 1974 16(1): 60-72.* "Wilmington seemed to offer several major prerequisites for the success of blacks in the political system. Not only was there a large black community but Republicans and Democrats fought a see-saw battle for control of city elections throughout the late 19th century. Politicians were forced to seek out every potential vote. The Republicans in particular recognized their dependence upon the support of black voters." Blacks, however, were ill-served in their loyalty to the GOP. Black voters sided with but received few benefits from Republicans, who remained "complacent about their relations with blacks and were unable to accommodate black men into the framework of economic issues that dominated late 19th-century politics." Based largely on newspaper sources; 46 notes.   R. M. Miller

1373. Homel, Michael W.   THE LILYDALE SCHOOL CAMPAIGN OF 1936: DIRECT ACTION IN THE VERBAL PROTEST ERA. *J. of Negro Hist. 1974 59(3): 228-241.* During the 1960's black people marched, boycotted, sat-in, and took other forms of direct action to implement public school integration and to assure improved education for their children. Among earlier precedents for such direct action was an effort by black Chicagoans in 1936, at a time when most civil rights activity was verbal. Based on secondary sources; 33 notes.
                                                                          N. G. Sapper

1374. Horton, James Oliver. GENERATIONS OF PROTEST: BLACK FAMILIES AND SOCIAL REFORM IN ANTE-BELLUM BOSTON. *New England Q. 1976 49(2): 242-256.* Traces the roles of the Hall, Paul, Dalton, Neit, Snowden, Bayley, and Lewis families in Boston reform movements. Early leaders established and developed entirely black educational, religious, and masonic organizations. With William Lloyd Garrison's (1805-79) establishment of the New England Anti-Slavery Society during the 1830's they changed to integrated organizations advocating abolitionism and racial integration. Following the passage of the Fugitive Slave Act of 1850 black leaders became willing to take illegal action to assist runaways. Based on the records of black organizations and on secondary sources; 29 notes.

J. C. Bradford

1375. Hunter, Lloyd A. SLAVERY IN ST. LOUIS 1804-1860. *Missouri Hist. Soc. Bull. 1974 30(4): 233-265.* Analyzes economic and political-cultural forces that shaped the "slave system" in St. Louis. Relatively few slaves were held in St. Louis. Because the hiring out of slaves was common practice, little disruption of slave families occurred. Evils common to Southern slavery did, however, prevail in St. Louis. Based on manuscripts at the Missouri Historical Society and on secondary sources; 100 notes.

H. T. Lovin

1376. January, Alan F. THE SOUTH CAROLINA ASSOCIATION: AN AGENCY FOR RACE CONTROL IN ANTEBELLUM CHARLESTON. *South Carolina Hist. Mag. 1977 78(3): 191-201.* A small vigilance group in Charleston, 1823-50's, sought to control the actions of abolitionists, slaves, and liberal whites.

1377. Kellogg, John. NEGRO URBAN CLUSTERS IN THE POST-BELLUM SOUTH. *Geographical Rev. 1977 67(3): 310-321.* Small Negro enclaves termed "urban clusters" formed on the periphery of southern cities immediately after the Civil War. This development was precipitated by the migration of Negroes to Southern cities between 1865 and 1870. By the 1880's these newly formed enclaves had replaced the long-established antebellum urban Negro areas as the predominant Negro residential areas in the urban South. In the study cities of Lexington, Kentucky; Atlanta, Georgia; Richmond, Virginia; and Durham, North Carolina, urban clusters formed in poorly drained bottomlands, along railroads, and in other peripheral areas where residential land values were low. Subsequent to urban cluster formation a second stage of Negro community development began, characterized by the outward growth of a single, large Negro sector. Negro housing in urban clusters is substandard, but housing quality is higher in more recent additions to the Negro community, whether these additions were originally Negro or white.

J

1378. Lamon, Lester C. THE BLACK COMMUNITY IN NASHVILLE AND THE FISK UNIVERSITY STUDENT STRIKE OF 1924-1925. *J. of Southern Hist. 1974 40(2): 225-244.* Discusses Fisk University students' struggle to obtain freedom from paternalistic control of their clubs, publications, and dress codes and to secure student participation in school administration through a student council, student publications, and an athletic association. With the white administration unwilling to make any appreciable concessions, the resultant friction and confrontation moved the struggle into the community. The administration sought support from the whites in Nashville, while the students sought support from the black community in Nashville. With solid local and national black support, Fisk President Fayette Avery McKenzie was forced to resign in 1925. Although not replaced with a black, the new president granted most of the students' previous demands. Based on manuscripts and printed primary and secondary sources; 46 notes.

T. D. Schoonover

1379. Lang, William L. THE NEARLY FORGOTTEN BLACKS ON LAST CHANCE GULCH, 1900-1912. *Pacific Northwest Q. 1979 70(2): 50-57.* Though the 1910 black population of Helena (Last Chance Gulch), Montana numbered 420, the local press created only negative stories about Negroes or neglected them altogether. Helena's black citizens, led by editor Joseph B. Bass, created their own weekly *Montana Plaindealer* which appeared during 1906-11. Initially it advocated the accommodationist philosophy of Booker T. Washington, but gradually adopted the activist position of W. E. B. DuBois. Primary and secondary sources; photo, 38 notes.

M. L. Tate

1380. Massa, Ann. BLACK WOMEN IN THE "WHITE CITY." *J. of Am. Studies [Great Britain] 1974 8(3): 319-337.* Describes efforts by Negro womens' groups in Chicago to participate in the World's Columbian Exposition (1893). Despite protests from Negro groups, the exhibits in the pavilions and the proceedings of the meetings at the fair extended only token recognition to Negro achievements in America.

H. T. Lovin

1381. Matthews, Mark D. "OUR WOMEN AND WHAT THEY THINK," AMY JACQUES GARVEY AND THE *NEGRO WORLD*. *Black Scholar 1979 10(8-9): 2-13.* Discusses the ideals and motivation of women in the Universal Negro Improvement Association (UNIA) a black urban working-class movement important in the 1920's, as these were interpreted by Amy Jacques Garvey, wife of UNIA founder, Marcus Garvey, in her "Women's Page" of the UNIA newspaper, *Negro World*.

1382. Maynard, Joan BLACK URBAN CULTURE. *Historic Preservation 1973 25(1): 28-30.* Describes the discovery in the 1960's of Weeksville, a black community that existed in Brooklyn ca. 1830-70. Discusses attempts to preserve the three remaining original buildings. 3 photos.

R. M. Frame III

1383. McKee, Jesse O. A GEOGRAPHICAL ANALYSIS OF THE ORIGIN, DIFFUSION, AND SPATIAL DISTRIBUTION OF THE BLACK AMERICAN IN THE UNITED STATES. *Southern Q. 1974 12(3): 203-216.* Historical analysis of Negro migration in the United States from 1619 to the present. Data relating to the growth, distribution, and diffusion of black population are supplied. 3 Tables, 37 notes.

R. W. Dubay

1384. Meier, August and Rudwick, Elliott. NEGRO BOYCOTTS OF SEGREGATED STREETCARS IN VIRGINIA 1904-1907. *Virginia Mag. of Hist. and Biog. 1973 81(4): 479-487.* The transit boycotts of the 1950's had precedents in the late 19th and early 20th centuries, when segregation was inaugurated on southern trolley cars. In Virginia such protests against the new Jim Crow laws occurred in several cities, though they were usually short-lived and unsuccessful. Based on newspaper accounts; 39 notes.

R. F. Oaks

1385. Miller, M. Sammy. ROBERT H. TERRELL: FIRST BLACK D.C. MUNICIPAL JUDGE. *Crisis 1976 83(6): 209-210.* Robert Heberton Terrell was born in Glen Cave, Virginia, on 25 November 1857. He was reared in Washington, D.C., and graduated from Harvard in 1880, the third black to graduate from Harvard and the first to graduate *cum laude*. In 1889 he graduated from Howard University Law School where he also earned a Master of Law degree. In 1909 he was the first black to be appointed justice of the Municipal Court of D.C.

A. G. Belles

1386. Miller, M. Sammy. SLAVERY IN AN URBAN AREA—DISTRICT OF COLUMBIA. *Negro Hist. Bull. 1974 37(5): 293-295.* Describes social conditions of free blacks and slaves in the District of Columbia, 1800-60.

1387. Mitchell, J. Marcus. THE PAUL FAMILY. *Old-Time New England 1973 63(3): 73-77.* Tells of Thomas Paul, a black minister who organized the first black church in Boston, his brothers, Nathaniel and Shadrach, who were also ministers, and other members of the Paul family. Illus.

R. N. Lokken

1388. Montesano, Philip M. SAN FRANCISCO BLACK CHURCHES IN THE EARLY 1860'S: POLITICAL PRESSURE GROUP. *California Hist. Q. 1973 52(2): 145-152.* In the late 1850's and early 1860's the three black churches in San Francisco represented the interests of the city's black community, providing spiritual leadership, economic assistance, and aid to Freedmen. They also resisted attempts to deny California blacks their civil rights. Aided by a fledgling black press, the churches successfully campaigned for the repeal of laws forbidding blacks from testifying in court cases involving whites. The Emancipation Proclamation and the increasing preoccupation of nativists with the Chinese community helped the churches' campaign. The issue of voting rights was settled by the 15th Amendment, while other issues, such as school segregation, remained to be solved. Based on primary and secondary sources; illus., photos, 31 notes.

A. Hoffman

1389. Moore, N. Webster JOHN BERRY MEACHUM (1789-1854): ST. LOUIS PIONEER, BLACK ABOLITIONIST, EDUCATOR, AND PREACHER. *Missouri Hist. Soc. Bull. 1973 29(2): 96-103.* Meachum, a Virginia slave, purchased his freedom and emigrated to St. Louis in 1815, where he joined in the efforts of a white Baptist missionary, John Mason Peck, "to reclaim the Negroes through religious instruction." In 1825, Meachum was ordained and founded the First African Baptist Church in St. Louis. He initiated educational programs for Negroes in the St. Louis area and purchased and freed about 20 slaves. Secondary sources and manuscript holdings of the Missouri Historical Society; 18 notes.   H. T. Lovin

1390. Naison, Mark D. COMMUNISM AND BLACK NATIONALISM IN THE DEPRESSION: THE CASE OF HARLEM. *J. of Ethnic Studies 1974 2(2): 24-36.* "The political struggle between nationalists and communists in Harlem had its roots in the Twenties. Communists in the African Blood Brotherhood . . . waged a bitter ideological struggle with Marcus Garvey . . . over questions of race loyalty vs. class loyalty." The Garvey movement and its spinoffs were business-oriented, seeking to develop a Negro entrepreneur class. Its answer to massive black unemployment was the "Don't Buy Where You Can't Work" campaign pushed by the Harlem Business Men's Club and the *Negro World.* By 1933 a picket campaign against stores was going on. The Party insisted on black-white working class solidarity, and along with the Young Liberators and the League of Struggle for Negro Rights maintained separate picketing operations. Meanwhile a Citizen's League under Harlem ministers and the *New York Age* sought to unite diverse organizations. The March 1935 riots brought the Party new acceptance as they helped in exposing social conditions in the community during the postriot investigations. From then to 1939 the Party played a role in every major coalition of protest, but its political "victory" over Negro nationalism "was never really secure." Contemporary and secondary sources; 46 notes.   G. J. Bobango

1391. Nash, Gary B. SLAVES AND SLAVEOWNERS IN COLONIAL PHILADELPHIA. *William and Mary Q. 1973 30(2): 223-256.* Slaveholding reached a peak during the decade following the outbreak of the Seven Years War. Analyzes the slave population 1767-75. Offers reasons for the decline of the slave population after 1767. Mentions labor conditions and considers the correlation between slave ownership with wealth and religious affiliation. 8 tables, 69 notes.   H. M. Ward

1392. Nelson, H. Viscount. THE PHILADELPHIA NAACP: RACE VERSUS CLASS CONSCIOUSNESS DURING THE THIRTIES. *J. of Black Studies 1975 5(3): 255-276.* Correspondence of the Philadelphia chapter of the NAACP from the 1930's shows that its membership was made up of middle- and upper-class blacks who were almost totally unconcerned with the plight of poorer blacks. Their main concern was fund-raising and keeping on good terms with members of the white community. Though they took stands on blatantly racist issues they generally avoided taking positions which would jeopardize their social standing in the community. Notes, biblio.   K. Butcher

1393. O'Brien, John T. FACTORY, CHURCH, AND COMMUNITY: BLACKS IN ANTEBELLUM RICHMOND. *J. of Southern Hist. 1978 44(4): 509-536.* Recent studies have shed much light upon the culture of plantation slaves. Yet neglect of urban slaves have left historians with no way to explain such phenomena as the blacks of Richmond successfully organizing and petitioning President Johnson in mid-1865 to ease the US military's control on their lives. Studying and analyzing the social skills which developed from slave labor in the tobacco factories and the well-organized black Christian churches permit us to understand the surfacing of these work habits, and the revelation of firm family and community structures in the months after the Civil War. Manuscripts and printed primary and secondary sources; 99 notes.

T. D. Schoonover

1394. O'Connell, Lucille. JULIA H. SMITH: AN UNCOMMON NEW ENGLANDER. *Phylon 1978 39(3): 275-281.* Attention to black Americans has been focused largely on the rural South and urban slums, but the black middle classes are not a new phenomenon in this country, and unlike their cousins in the ghettos and on the farms, have maintained a level of achievement and education equal to that of their white neighbors. Julia H. Smith (b. 1885), a Boston aristocrat of Afro-American

descent, teacher for a time in the schools of Washington, D. C., community leader in Cambridge, and member of intellectual circles, has never known prejudice first-hand in her long and productive life. Sprung from a family long resident in Boston, distinguished by generations of accomplishment, her life shows what middle-class blacks can do when not exposed to racial discrimination. 3 notes.   J. C. Billigmeier

1395. Osthaus, Carl R. THE RISE AND FALL OF JESSE BINGA, BLACK FINANCIER. *J. of Negro Hist. 1973 58(1): 39-60.* Jesse Binga was a founding father of the black community in Chicago's South Side. Realtor, banker, and builder, Binga as he rose paralleled the growth of the black community. The onset of the depression saw the collapse of Binga's bank and his subsequent imprisonment for embezzlement. Paroled in 1938, he died in penurious obscurity 12 years later. Based on secondary sources; 106 notes.   N. G. Sapper

1396. Parker, Russell D. THE BLACK COMMUNITY IN A COMPANY TOWN: ALCOA, TENNESSEE, 1919-1939. *Tennessee Hist. Q. 1978 37(2): 203-221.* Alcoa, Tennessee, was a company town, not conducive to community leadership, black or white. Unskilled blacks were recruited to work in the Aluminum Company of America (Alcoa) plant, and blacks moved in almost as fast as whites. Blacks were allowed to purchase their homes in the Negro section. John T. Arter, a black man, was brought in as principal of the black school, and became the leader of the Negro community. His closest associates were John Brice and T. P. Marsh, but neither managed to wield influence after Arter's death. Leadership within the black community eventually fell to Hendrika Tol, a white woman, who had attended nearby Maryville College. Tol started a library for blacks and attempted to create a health plan for blacks, but without success. "Unionization in the mid-1930's reduced the vulnerability of black workers." Primary and secondary sources; 91 notes.

M. B. Lucas

1397. Pease, William H. and Pease, Jane H. WALKER'S *APPEAL* COMES TO CHARLESTON: A NOTE AND DOCUMENTS. *J. of Negro Hist. 1974 59(3): 287-292.* David Walker's pamphlet provoked fear of black insurrection throughout the South and Charleston, South Carolina, was no exception. A white sailor from Boston who distributed the *Appeal* among black Charlestonians while on shore leave was arrested by white authorities, fined $1,000, and sentenced to one year in prison. Based on primary sources in the South Carolina Archives; 8 notes.

N. G. Sapper

1398. Provine, Dorothy. THE ECONOMIC POSITION OF FREE BLACKS IN THE DISTRICT OF COLUMBIA, 1800-1860. *J. of Negro Hist. 1973 58(1): 61-72.* The black population of the District of Columbia created a viable black community during the first half of the 19th century. They overcame enormous odds to create their own business, schools, and churches. Despite legal disabilities and white prejudice, they acquired property and provided economic security for themselves and their children. Based on primary sources in the Archives of the United States; 73 notes.   N. G. Sapper

1399. Radford, John P. DELICATE SPACE: RACE AND RESIDENCE IN CHARLESTON, SOUTH CAROLINA, 1860-1880. *West Georgia Coll. Studies in the Social Sci. 1977 16: 17-37.* Antebellum residential patterns in Charleston persisted during Reconstruction despite a profound in-migration of rural freedmen; this was due to a value system begat by the plantation economy which also denied the South the postwar urban-industrial growth of cities such as Chicago.

1400. Rankin, David C. THE IMPACT OF THE CIVIL WAR ON THE FREE COLORED COMMUNITY OF NEW ORLEANS. *Perspectives in Am. Hist. 1977-78 11: 377-416.* Before the Civil War, the free black community of New Orleans enjoyed a thriving, unique culture based on French values and allegiances. They owned slaves, held property, and were commercially successful. They also took special care to separate themselves from the resident black slave population; and at the outbreak of the war, they resisted abolition and secession. Union victory brought a gradual erosion of their rights, reduced their political power, and damaged their social prestige.   W. A. Wiegand

1401. Rankin, David C. THE ORIGINS OF BLACK LEADERSHIP IN NEW ORLEANS DURING RECONSTRUCTION.

J. of Southern Hist. 1974 40(3): 417-440. While more famous black political leaders are recognized in studies of Reconstruction, the large number of secondary black politicians receive no notice. Even the major black political figures appear as people whose life begins during the Civil War. Using quantitative methodology, focuses upon the origins of 240 black leaders of New Orleans. Profiles this leadership around such characteristics as antebellum legal status, residence, birthplace, date of birth, color, occupation, wealth, and literacy. Concludes that the black politician during Reconstruction in New Orleans was already before "the Civil War a young man of unusual ancestry, uncommon wealth, and exceptional ability," and in close contact with the most sophisticated black community in mid-19th century America. Based on manuscripts and published primary and secondary sources; 9 tables, 41 notes, appendix.

T. D. Schoonover

1402. Reichard, Maximilian. BLACK AND WHITE ON THE UR-BAN FRONTIER: THE ST. LOUIS COMMUNITY IN TRANSI-TION, 1800-1830. *Missouri Hist. Soc. Bull. 1976 33(1): 3-17.* Discusses restrictions on slaves in St. Louis, 1800-30, focusing on strictures imposed through state legislation and municipal ordinances. The legislation tended also to fetter the liberties of free Negroes living in St. Louis. Social and economic tensions during the 1820's resulted in the passage of more restrictive laws. Based on archival materials, newspapers, and secondary sources; 5 photos, 69 notes.   H. T. Lovin

1403. Renshaw, Patrick. THE BLACK GHETTO 1890-1940. *J. of Am. Studies [Great Britain] 1974 8(1): 41-59.* Surveys the "ghetto experience" of Negroes to 1940. When Negroes migrated from the rural South to cities, their experiences differed markedly from the experiences of European immigrants in the same urban centers. By 1940, Blacks became "locked in" and were unable to escape urban ills in the ways that other ethnic groups had overcome the shortcomings of the urban situation. Based on secondary sources; 51 notes.   H. T. Lovin

1404. Roberson, Jere W. EDWARD P. MC CABE AND THE LANGSTON EXPERIMENT. *Chronicles of Oklahoma 1973 51(3): 343-355.* Biographical sketch of Edward P. McCabe (1850-1920), promoter of Negro migration from Kansas to Langston, Oklahoma, which he founded; emphasizes the role of frontier newspapers in the migration.

S

1405. Roff, Kenneth L. BROOKLYN'S REACTION TO BLACK SUFFRAGE IN 1860. *Afro-Americans in New York Life and Hist. 1978 2(1): 29-40.* New York City businessmen spread anti-black propaganda among poor and immigrant laborers to negate black suffrage and secure a Democratic Party victory in Brooklyn in the 1860 elections.

1406. Roof, Wade Clark. RACE AND RESIDENCE: THE SHIFT-ING BASIS OF AMERICAN RACE RELATIONS. *Ann. of the Am. Acad. of Pol. and Social Sci. 1979 441: 1-12.* Racially-segregated ghettos evolved in the early decades of this century, first in northern cities and later throughout the nation. Levels of urban residential segregation for blacks have remained high over the years and—unlike the earlier pattern for European immigrants—have not declined as blacks have made economic progress. Despite modest declines in segregation in the sixties, metropolitan decline in the seventies and structural shifts in employment conditions for blacks have resulted in growing concern for problems of de facto segregation. Mounting attention to housing discrimination and the residential basis of current black-white tensions are discussed.   J

1407. Ross, Ronald. THE ROLE OF BLACKS IN THE FEDERAL THEATRE, 1935-1939. *J. of Negro Hist. 1974 59(1): 38-50.* The Federal Theatre Project (1935-39) was designed to make drama available to the masses for the first time. Within its program, the Federal Theatre established special ethnic projects which included black theater in several cities. By the project's conclusion, 22 US cities had served as headquarters for black theater units. The success of the black writers, directors, stage designers, and actors proved that all these talented people needed was the opportunity. Secondary sources; 54 notes.   N. G. Sapper

1408. Schoenberg, Sandra and Bailey, Charles. THE SYMBOLIC MEANING OF AN ELITE BLACK COMMUNITY: THE VILLE IN ST. LOUIS. *Missouri Hist. Soc. Bull. 1977 33(2): 94-102.* Traces the development of the "Ville" in St. Louis since 1900. Originally the area was

occupied mostly by German and Irish residents; they were displaced by growing numbers of Negroes during the 20th century. Usage of restrictive covenants on the transfer of St. Louis real estate began in 1911 and hastened the influx of Blacks to the "Ville." Based on archival and secondary sources; 4 photos, 20 notes.   H. T. Lovin

1409. Schweninger, Loren. THE FREE-SLAVE PHENOMENON: JAMES P. THOMAS AND THE BLACK COMMUNITY IN ANTE-BELLUM NASHVILLE. *Civil War Hist. 1976 22(4): 293-307.* Quasi-free bondsmen comprised a significant Southern Negro group. They have received scant historical attention because of their precarious, secretive existence. Numbering perhaps many thousands throughout the South, they achieved large measures of independence. James P. Thomas, a free-slave barber, illustrates these wide possibilities, available particularly in the urban setting. Through contrivance, deception, and intelligent hard work, he and many others successfully compromised the slave system. Their condition resulted in resiliency and strength, not infantilization and demoralization. Primary and secondary sources; 71 notes.

R. E. Stack

1410. Sheldon, Marianne Buroff. BLACK-WHITE RELATIONS IN RICHMOND, VIRGINIA, 1782-1820. *J. of Southern Hist. 1979 45(1): 27-44.* Southern cities may have offered black slaves unique experiences such as lenient white behavior. Possibly cities offered blacks a life-style different from the mainstream of the slave-plantation system. Richmond's unwillingness to enforce the legal restrictionsa on slaves seems to have been characteristic of urban centers in the antebellum South. The Richmond case sustains the Genovese model of slavery as a subtle exploitive-paternalistic system. Primary and secondary materials; table, 62 notes.

T. D. Schoonover

1411. Silcox, Harry C. NINETEENTH CENTURY PHILADEL-PHIA BLACK MILITANT: OCTAVIUS V. CATTO (1839-1871). *Pennsylvania Hist. 1977 44(1): 53-76.* Octavius V. Catto (1839-71) was one of the most important spokesmen for Pennsylvania Negroes in the Civil War and Reconstruction years. The son of a minister, he taught at the Institute for Colored Youth, the Quaker-supported black high school in Philadelphia. Catto was the first black member of the Franklin Institute. Leading the effort to win places in the Pennsylvania National Guard for blacks, he became a major and inspector in the fifth brigade. A founder and corresponding secretary of the State Equal Rights League, Catto helped win passage of legislation ending segregation on street cars. As captain and star player for the Philadelphia Pythians baseball team, Catto developed a number of contacts with blacks in other states. He also assisted in the administration of the freedman schools in Washington. Catto was murdered during the antiblack election riots of 1871. "Catto's death brought to an end black militant behavior in 19th-century Philadelphia." Based on the Catto papers, the Pythian Baseball Club papers, and other sources; photo, 71 notes.   D. C. Swift

1412. Somers, Dale A. BLACK AND WHITE IN NEW ORLEANS: A STUDY IN URBAN RACE RELATIONS, 1865-1900. *J. of Southern Hist. 1974 40(1): 19-42.* Because historians have tended to confuse urban and rural racial policies and more, or to assume that antebellum urban segregation practices continued in the post-Civil War years, they have not properly assessed the role of cities in southern race relations. Southern "urban communities exerted an influence far out of proportion to the number of their inhabitants." Before the 1890's in New Orleans, manifestations of black protest and a fluctuating color line permitted flexible racial relations. The author looks at black-white relations in sports, labor organizations, education, public transportation, and other areas of urban life. In fact, before the end of the 19th century, urban New Orleans offered blacks the greatest degree of freedom from white supremacy in Louisiana. Based on published primary and secondary sources; 46 notes.   T. D. Schoonover

1413. Sowell, Thomas. BLACK EXCELLENCE: THE CASE OF DUNBAR HIGH SCHOOL. *Public Interest 1974 (35): 3-21.* An account of one of the most successful all-Negro schools, Dunbar High School in Washington, D.C., during 1870-1955. "The first black general (Benjamin O. Davis), the first black federal judge (William H. Hastie), the first black Cabinet member (Robert C. Weaver), the discoverer of blood plasma (Charles Drew), and the first black Senator (Edward W. Brooke) were all Dunbar graduates. . . . The founders of the school intended it to

be an institution solely devoted to preparing black students for college and in that special role it was unsurpassed." 8 notes.   D. D. Cameron

1414. Spain, Daphne. RACE RELATIONS AND RESIDENTIAL SEGREGATION IN NEW ORLEANS: TWO CENTURIES OF PARADOX. *Ann. of the Am. Acad. of Pol. and Social Sci. 1979 441: 82-96.* Because of its origins as one of the oldest slave trading centers in the country, New Orleans has a unique history in both race relations and residential segregation. Slavery required blacks to live in close proximity to their white owners. This created a mixed residential pattern that was characteristic of other southern cities in the nineteenth century. The rigid caste/race system defined social distance when physical distance was lacking. In the twentieth century, the advent of civil rights and equality for blacks has led to less patriarchal race relations but, paradoxically, greater residential segregation. Blacks have become more residentially isolated since the turn of the century. This essay documents the disappearance of the classic "backyard pattern" in New Orleans.   J

1415. Struhsaker, Virginia L. STOCKTON'S BLACK PIONEERS. *Pacific Hist. 1975 19(4): 341-355.* Stockton's black community included many individuals of talent, education, and dedication. Secondary sources; 2 illus.   G. L. Olson

1416. Taylor, David V. JOHN QUINCY ADAMS: ST. PAUL EDITOR AND BLACK LEADER. *Minnesota Hist. 1973 43(8): 282-296.* The *Western Appeal* (later the *Appeal*), founded after 1880, was one of the few black newspapers to achieve regional or national prominence and to survive for more than a few years. John Quincy Adams (1848-1922) was its editor for almost its entire existence. Sometime teacher, politician, and newspaper publisher, Adams published his paper simultaneously in St. Paul and Chicago. The *Appeal* conducted a "vitriolic crusade" and promoted black activism against disfranchisement, discrimination, and other injustices. 8 illus., 70 notes.   D. L. Smith

1417. Thomas, Herbert A., Jr. VICTIMS OF CIRCUMSTANCE: NEGROES IN A SOUTHERN TOWN, 1865-1880. *Register of the Kentucky Hist. Soc. 1973 71(3): 253-271.* During 1865-80 the black population of Lexington tripled. A housing shortage led to the development of black shanty towns on the fringes of the city, generally in the poorer and industrial sections. The job situation was equally discouraging. Few blacks made substantial economic progress. By 1880, blacks accounted for 45% of Lexington's population, but only 6% of its wealth. Those who did succeed were generally "free blacks" prior to 1865. Ex-slaves were thus victims of their previous lives and of a city economically unable to absorb an influx of new citizens. Based on primary and secondary sources; 42 notes.   J. F. Paul

1418. Tolbert, Emory. OUTPOST GARVEYISM AND THE UNIA RANK AND FILE. *J. of Black Studies 1975 5(3): 233-253.* Studies the appeal to blacks in Los Angeles of Marcus Garvey's Universal Negro Improvement Association. He finds that the movement appealed mainly to upwardly-mobile Negroes and that it was more conservative than some of the chapters in the East. In Los Angeles the UNIA appealed to religious family men and acted in many ways as a black fraternity. Notes, biblio.   K. Butcher

1419. Toll, William. THE GENIE OF "RACE": PROBLEMS IN CONCEPTUALIZING THE TREATMENT OF BLACK AMERICANS. *J. of Ethnic Studies 1976 4(3): 1-20.* Racial prejudice does not by itself account for the mistreatment of blacks. Proponents of internal colonization or caste project too static a relationship between blacks and whites. Blacks in 20th-century American cities have transformed themselves into an ethnic group organized to fight the consequences of having been perceived as a race. Charles Valentine's theme of voluntary ethnicity as a form of cultural revolution against white folk mythology is one of the more correct views of how blacks seek "the rewards of America's cosmopolitan culture" through this new social organization. Major studies of this black coalescence, such as W. E. B. Dubois's *The Philadelphia Negro*, Horace Cayton and St. Clair Drake's *Black Metropolis*, and Franklin Frazier's *Black Bourgeoisie* are surveyed. Secondary sources; 55 notes.   G. J. Bobango

1420. Toll, William. SOCIAL ORGANIZATION AND CULTURAL CHANGE: AN ESSAY REVIEW. *Pacific Northwest Q. 1975 66(1): 30-34.* Review article prompted by David M. Katzman, *Before the Ghetto: Black Detroit in the Nineteenth Century* (Urbana: U. of Illinois Pr., 1973) and Theodore G. Vincent, *Black Power and the Garvey Movement* (San Francisco: Ramparts Pr., 1972); discusses the importance of social structure and ideology in Afro-American history, especially in studying the organization of black urban communities, 19th-20th centuries.

1421. Watkins, Ralph. THE MARCUS GARVEY MOVEMENT IN BUFFALO, NEW YORK. *Afro-Americans in New York Life and Hist. 1977 1(1): 37-48.* A rift occurred within the black community in Buffalo between established community members and many who migrated north during the 1920's: some of the migrants decided to organize an affiliate of Marcus Garvey's United Negro Improvement Association and African Communities League, to the displeasure of local black clergy who saw their power over community affairs in danger.

1422. Watts, Eugene J. BLACK POLITICAL PROGRESS IN ATLANTA, 1868-1895. *J. of Negro Hist. 1974 59(3): 268-286.* The critical issue concerning race and politics in Atlanta, Georgia—the direct representation of blacks in city government—illustrates an important qualification of C. Vann Woodward's "forgotten alternatives" thesis. Black voters in Atlanta could vote as long as whites thought that they would benefit from it. When some blacks threatened this system, the hope of significant black political participation evaporated. Based on primary and secondary sources; 38 notes.   N. G. Sapper

1423. Weiss, Nancy J. BUILDING THE BLACK GHETTO. *Rev. in Am. Hist. 1977 5(1): 83-91.* Review article prompted by David M. Katzman's *Before the Ghetto: Black Detroit in the Nineteenth Century* (Urbana: U. of Illinois Pr., 1973, 1975) and Kenneth L. Kusmer's *A Ghetto Takes Shape: Black Cleveland, 1870-1930* (Urbana: U. of Illinois Pr., 1976).

1424. Wienker, Curtis W. MC NARY: A PREDOMINANTLY BLACK COMPANY TOWN IN ARIZONA. *Negro Hist. Bull. 1974 37(5): 282-285.* Describes social conditions and segregation of Negroes in the lumber company town of McNary, 1924-72.

1425. Wilder, Katharine A. CAPTAIN PAUL CUFFEE, MASTER MARINER OF WESTPORT, MASSACHUSETTS, 1759-1817. *Old-Time New England 1973 63(3): 78-80.* Tells of a free Negro at Westport, Massachusetts, who was the owner of ships engaged in coastwide trade. Captain Paul Cuffee was also a shipbuilder, promoter of rights of free Negroes, and builder of a schoolhouse for the education of all residents, regardless of race. After the War of 1812 he shipped free Negroes to Sierra Leone in cooperation with the British Colonization Society.   R. N. Lokken

1426. Wilkie, Jane Riblett. THE BLACK URBAN POPULATION OF THE PRE-CIVIL WAR SOUTH. *Phylon 1976 37(3): 250-262.* Examines the urbanization of blacks in the slave states, 1790-1860. Slaves and free blacks differ strikingly in the preference of blacks for cities long before the rural to urban shifts following the World Wars. "Slave labor had a significant role in early Southern industrialization, and free blacks primarily in service and trade occupations were well represented among skilled artisans," providing a major advantage for economic mobility after emancipation. Urban life during this period, however, presented severe handicaps to a stable social and economic family life. 2 tables, 4 fig., 20 notes.   E. P. Stickney

1427. Wittenberg, Clarissa K. AN INTIMATE RECORD OF HOW IT WAS IN YESTERDAY'S HARLEM. *Smithsonian 1975 6(3): 84-91.* Includes photographs by, and a biography of, James Van DerZee, who recorded the lives of Negroes from the middle class, particularly in New York City since 1900.

1428. Wright, Richard. WITH BLACK RADICALS IN CHICAGO. *Dissent 1977 24(2): 156-161.* Excerpts a chapter of the author's unpublished autobiographical work, *American Hunger;* mentions his difficulties in the Communist Party in Chicago during the 1930's.

Jews

1429. Angel, Marc D.   NOTES ON THE EARLY HISTORY OF SEATTLE'S SEPHARDIC COMMUNITY.   *Western States Jewish Hist. Q. 1974 7(1): 22-30.* The first Sephardic Jews arrived in Seattle in 1906 and by 1912 there were about 800 located there. They had many problems getting themselves organized as a religious group and locating a suitable rabbi. Their problems were similar to those faced by Sephardic Jews in other American cities who held onto the customs and traditions of their homelands. Few of the immigrants became American citizens. 15 notes.   R. A. Garfinkle

1430. Angel, Marc D.   THE SEPHARDIC THEATER OF SEATTLE.   *Am. Jewish Arch. 1973 25(2): 156-160.* An account of how the Turkish immigrant Leon Behar and others developed a theater for the Seattle Sephardic community, particularly during the 1920's and 1930's.   J

1431. Beck, Nelson R.   THE USE OF LIBRARY AND EDUCATIONAL FACILITIES BY RUSSIAN-JEWISH IMMIGRANTS IN NEW YORK CITY, 1880-1914: THE IMPACT OF CULTURE.   *J. of Lib. Hist. 1977 12(2): 129-149.* Discusses use of the public library and its services by Russian-Jewish immigrants in New York City between 1880 and 1914, and the historic and cultural influences which caused these particular immigrants not to fit Michael Harris's revisionist interpretation of American library history. Covers Hebrew educational associations and libraries, and Jewish newspapers of the period. Primary and secondary sources; 124 notes.   A. C. Dewees

1432. Berman, Myron   RABBI EDWARD NATHAN CALISH AND THE DEBATE OVER ZIONISM IN RICHMOND, VIRGINIA.   *Am. Jewish Hist. Q. 1973 62(3): 295-305.* Rabbi Calish, who served the Richmond Jewish community 1891-1945, was a consistent foe of the Zionist movement, and thus shared the position of many southern Jews of his time and generation. He was one of the original founders of the American Council for Judaism.   F. Rosenthal

1433. Bernstein, Seth.   THE ECONOMIC LIFE OF THE JEWS IN SAN FRANCISCO DURING THE 1860'S AS REFLECTED IN THE CITY DIRECTORIES.   *Am. Jewish Arch. 1975 27(1): 70-77.*

1434. Berrol, Selma C.   EDUCATION AND SOCIAL MOBILITY: THE JEWISH EXPERIENCE IN NEW YORK CITY, 1880-1920.   *Am. Jewish Hist. Q. 1976 65(3): 257-271.* The New York City public schools were totally unprepared to accommodate the large number of immigrant children pouring into the Lower East Side. Because city schools held an educational philosophy unfriendly to non-English backgrounds, most Jews until 1910 or so did not move up the economic ladder by taking advantage of New York's educational opportunities. Widespread utilization of secondary and higher education followed improvements in educational status, rather than the other way around. Primary and secondary sources; 33 notes.   F. Rosenthal

1435. Bronstein, Zelda and Kann, Kenneth.   BASHA SINGERMAN, COMRADE OF PETALUMA.   *California Hist. Q. 1977 56(1): 20-33.* Presents an interview with a resident of Petaluma, California, as part of an oral history project about the Petaluma Jewish chicken farmers. Names were changed to protect privacy. Socialist in her politics, Basha Singerman (not her real name) left Minsk, Russia, to go to South Africa, Montreal, and finally California. In 1915 Basha and her husband bought land and began operating a chicken ranch. The work was hard but Basha preferred it to the big city sweatshops. Their neighbors were mainly Jewish socialists. In the 1920's, Petaluma's Jewish population grew to 100 families. The community prospered in the 1920's but suffered in the Depression. Eventually Basha Singerman had to sell her home. Now 83, Mrs. Singerman meets socially with a declining number of old friends, and the Socialist community is fading for a conservative suburban one. Photos.   A. Hoffman

1436. Burke, John C.   THE BREAK IN.   *Rhode Island Jewish Hist. Notes 1974 6(4): 532-541.* An account of the forcible reopening of the Touro Synagogue by the Jewish community of Newport, Rhode Island, as told by Judge John C. Burke, who aided in the 1902 struggle.   S

1437. Clar, Reva.   EARLY STOCKTON JEWRY AND ITS CANTOR-RABBI HERMAN DAVIDSON.   *Western States Jewish Hist. Q. 1973 5(2): 63-86, (3): 166-187.* Part I. A biography of Herman Davidson (1846-1911) emphasizes his operatic career in Russia, his family life, and his work with Jews in Stockton, 1876-91. Part II. Chronicles the relationship between Davidson and Stockton Jews, and efforts to reform the Jewish congregation, 1893-1911.

1438. Engelbourg, Saul.   EDWARD A. FILENE: MERCHANT, CIVIC LEADER, AND JEW.   *Am. Jewish Hist. Q. 1976 66(1): 106-122.* Edward A. Filene (1860-1937), American-born son of German Jewish immigrants, became a millionaire several times over, and because of his business success he was able to obtain fame as a philanthropist and a civic leader in Boston. He is credited with the "Automatic Bargain Basement" as his most distinctive business innovation. Describes the controversy with his associate Louis Kirstein (1867-1942), his cooperation with Louis Brandeis, his share in the development of the Credit Union movement, the influence of his Twentieth Century Fund, his marginal interest in Jewish philanthropy, and the fight against Anti-Semitism. 49 notes.   F. Rosenthal

1439. Geffen, M. David.   DELAWARE JEWRY: THE FORMATIVE YEARS, 1872-1889.   *Delaware Hist. 1975 16(4): 269-297.* Although the climate in Delaware was not hostile to Jews, few settled there until the great Jewish migrations from Russia and Eastern Europe in the late 19th century. The Jewish population remained small, concentrated in Wilmington, mercantile in character. The Wilmington Jews met with a favorable reception. They worked hard, earned the respect of the community, and invested their energies in establishing worship services in the city. The Moses Montefiore Mutual Aid Society took the lead in maintaining community life and in providing social and educational services. It also worked hard to bring Jews together for religious purposes, and by its fundraising efforts helped to underwrite the building of a synagogue staffed by a resident rabbi. The Wilmington Jewish community was largely of German origin and lived in a small area near the business district. By the end of the 1880's the Wilmington Jews were receiving an increasing number of Jewish families from Eastern Europe and feeling the cultural distance separating them. Based on contemporary newspapers; 2 illus., 84 notes.   R. M. Miller

1440. Gelfand, Mitchell B.   JEWISH ECONOMIC AND RESIDENTIAL MOBILITY IN EARLY LOS ANGELES.   *Western States Jewish Hist. Q. 1979 11(4): 332-347.* Jews settled in Los Angeles as early as the final Mexican years. By 1870 they were a stable part of the commercial, social, and political life of the city. The immigration boom of the 1880's increased their numbers but reduced their relative proportion of the population. They were primarily business and professional men with a large stake in the growth of the city, which explains their tendency to remain in the area. They resided in fashionable areas on the outskirts of the business district. Their economic mobility in excess of the general population is explained by their traditional (European) commercial background; business, social, and family ties that facilitated economic opportunities; and their possession of middle-class values that inspired recent immigrants—particularly the "low status" Polish Jews—to adopt German-Jewish and American culture. Based on census records, other primary and secondary sources; 32 notes.   B. S. Porter

1441. Gendler, Carol.   THE FIRST SYNAGOGUE IN NEBRASKA: THE EARLY HISTORY OF THE CONGREGATION OF ISRAEL OF OMAHA.   *Nebraska Hist. 1977 58(3): 323-341.* Examines the beginnings of a formal Jewish community in Omaha, from 1867 through the construction of Temple Israel, dedicated in 1908. Focuses on prominent members of the community, early rabbis who served it, and the tensions between reform and traditional groups.   R. Lowitt

1442. Gendler, Carol.   THE JEWS OF OMAHA: THE FIRST SIXTY YEARS.   *Western States Jewish Hist. Q. 1973 5(3): 205-224, (4): 288-305, 6(1): 58-71, 1974 6(2): 141-154, (3): 222-233, (4): 293-304.* Part I. Discusses the role of Jews in the settlement of Omaha, 1820's-30's. Part II. Chronicles the development of the Orthodox and Reform Jewish congregations, the tenures of rabbis, and the erection of synagogues, 1854-1904. Part III. The Jews in Omaha formed several charity and mutual aid societies in the late 1800's. The main social club, the Metropolitan Club, lasted until 1911. Several Jews became leaders in Omaha.

Edward Rosewater (1841-1906) served in the state legislature and founded the Omaha *Bee*. He ran for the US Senate twice, but lost. Jonas L. Brandeis (1837-1903), a successful businessman, gave large sums of money to charities. Photo, 41 notes. Part IV. In the late 1880's, thousands of Jews fled from eastern Europe. Several Jewish organizations were set up to help the refugees find homes and jobs in America. The Jews in Omaha came to the aid of those Jews that came to Omaha and wanted to settle there. By 1880, enough Orthodox Jews had settled in Omaha to make it possible to hold orthodox prayer services. The congregations were organized according to the country of origin of the immigrants. A strong Jewish community developed in Omaha. Based on primary and secondary sources; 46 notes. Part V. Because of a depression that hit Omaha in 1890, many wealthy citizens lost their fortunes and had to move elsewhere. Although several wealthy Jews were hard hit by the bad economic conditions, the Jewish population of Omaha continued to grow. This growth necessitated the formation of new organizations to serve the community. The Jews set up their own charities, fraternal groups, and hospital. The Jewish community was a mixture of Orthodox and Reformed Jews working together to take care of their needs. Based on primary and secondary sources; 41 notes. Part VI. The Jews of Omaha became leaders in the professions and politics. Harry B. Zimman served on the city council and was acting mayor when the regular mayor died in 1906. In 1889, the first of many Jewish political groups was founded. A controversy developed over who controlled the "Hebrew vote." The Omaha Jews were planning on building a community center when in 1913 a tornado destroyed the center of the Jewish residential area. The Jewish Relief Committee was established to aid the victims. By 1915, the Jews in Omaha were well established within the larger community, and were taking an active part in its development. Based on primary and secondary sources; photo, 30 notes.   R. A. Garfinkle/S

1443. Goldberg, Arthur. THE JEW IN NORWICH, CONNECTICUT: A CENTURY OF JEWISH LIFE. *Rhode Island Jewish Hist. Notes 1975 7(1): 79-103.*

1444. Harris, Victor. HONOLULU JEWRY IN 1919. *Western States Jewish Hist. Q. 1979 11(3): 279-282.* Honolulu's Jewish community in 1919 consisted of about 13 Jewish families and an equal number of mixed marriages. There was no congregation. The old Jewish cemetery had been abandoned. The active Jews on the island were the 100 or so Jews in the US Army. These men were interested in having a Jewish center where they could meet and offer mutual encouragement in this foreign place. Reprinted from *Emanu-El*, San Francisco, 25 July 1919; 4 notes.   B. S. Porter

1445. Hasson, Aron. THE SEPHARDIC JEWS OF RHODES IN LOS ANGELES. *Western States Jewish Hist. Q. 1974 6(4): 241-254.* During 1910-30, many Jews from Rhodes came to settle in Los Angeles. Rhodesli families have remained together and continue their unique Sephardic customs and life styles. In 1917 they formed their own congregation, the Peace and Progress Society, later changed to the Sephardic Hebrew Center. The immigrants spoke Ladino, and their language barrier forced them to take lower-paying jobs. Several immigrants went into the flower business, which became the most successful occupation of the Rhodeslis. Based on interviews and secondary sources; 4 photos, 21 notes.   R. A. Garfinkle

1446. Herscher, Uri D. THE METROPOLIS OF GHETTOS. *J. of Ethnic Studies 1976 4(2): 33-47.* Portrays the "classic" and stereotypical days of the Jewish ghetto from 1890 to 1920, with its sights, smells, tenements, habitual impoverishment and insecurity, and the all-consuming task of earning a living. Despite the hardship and ugliness of life, the ghetto was a world, complete and self-sustaining, with drama, humor, and romance as well. Fever for secular schooling was high, along with an innate distrust for the public, non-Jewish charities and their agencies. Intellectual life thrived in the cafes of Canal Street, prostitutes in Allen Street, and Jewish theaters in the Bowery. The Judaism of Europe grew progressively weaker, but still coexisted with the culture of the new land. World War I saw the garment manufacturers move to 14th Street, and non-Jews begin to move into the Lower East Side; they were willing to pay the higher rents traditionally levied on non-Jews. With these changes, the good old days of the ghetto were numbered. Based largely on personal conversations by the author in 1972 with individuals of immigrant stock who grew up on New York's Lower East Side; 25 notes.   G. J. Bobango

1447. Hershkowitz, Leo. SOME ASPECTS OF THE NEW YORK JEWISH MERCHANT AND COMMUNITY, 1654-1820. *Am. Jewish Hist. Q. 1976 66(1): 10-34.* The 160-year period under discussion saw New York City grow from a village to a community of 100,000 people, and its Jewish segment from 23 to some 2,000 people. Diversity of origin and of occupation, although trade remained preeminent, were characteristic traits of the Jewish community for the entire period. The right to trade, the acquisition of citizenship, the right to worship publicly, the right to vote and to be elected, resulted in court actions producing a wealth of statistical and legal data which are provided to illustrate these points. 68 notes, 3 appendixes.   F. Rosenthal

1448. Hertzberg, Steven. THE JEWISH COMMUNITY OF ATLANTA FROM THE END OF THE CIVIL WAR UNTIL THE END OF THE FRANK CASE. *Am. Jewish Hist. Q. 1973 62(3): 250-287.* Atlanta's Jewish community was by 1913 the largest in a South transformed by urbanization, industrialization, and Negro emancipation. There were more than 1,200 Jewish immigrants from Eastern Europe by 1910. Under the leadership of Rabbi David Marx (1872-1962) the established German Jews were led into classical Reform, while the East European and Levantine settlers maintained various forms of traditional Judaism. Thus two separate communities were created. Only in philanthropic activities did the two cooperate. In Atlanta and throughout the United States during this period, discrimination against even the established community of Western European Jews was increasing, setting the stage for the Leo M. Frank tragedy of 1913. 84 notes.

      F. Rosenthal

1449. Hertzberg, Steven. MAKING IT IN ATLANTA: ECONOMIC MOBILITY IN A SOUTHERN JEWISH COMMUNITY, 1870-1911. *Yivo Ann. of Jewish Social Sci. 1978 17: 185-216.* Studies the mobility of Atlanta's Jewish population during 1870-1911. The Jews more than any other group viewed America as the Promised Land. Therefore, a study of their mobility within a major southern city is of special significance.   R. J. Wechman

1450. Hertzberg, Steven. UNSETTLED JEWS: GEOGRAPHIC MOBILITY IN A NINETEENTH CENTURY CITY. *Am. Jewish Hist. Q. 1977 67(2): 125-139.* Analyzes Jewish mobility in Atlanta, Georgia, between 1870 and 1896. Using institutional records, census schedules, city directories, and tax lists, seven tabulations are presented. Variables such as economic and marital status, and urban or rural background, are considered. It appears that Jews remained in Atlanta to a high degree (88% of Jewish immigrants v. 79% of gentile immigrants, or 71% vs. 50% as to upward social improvement) because of economic success, urban background, and advantages of living in an established center of Jewish activities. 7 tables, 16 notes.   F. Rosenthal

1451. Horvitz, Eleanor F. OLD BOTTLES, RAGS, JUNK! THE STORY OF THE JEWS IN SOUTH PROVIDENCE. *Rhode Island Jewish Hist. Notes 1976 7(2): 189-257.* Discusses the settlement of South Providence by large numbers of Jews, 1900-12; includes attention to famous local personalities, religion, and daily life.

1452. Jacobson, Daniel. LANSING'S JEWISH COMMUNITY: THE BEGINNINGS. *Michigan Jewish Hist. 1976 16(1): 5-17.* Traces the settlement of Jews from Henry Lederer in 1850 to the establishment of a formal community numbering 450 in 1918.

1453. Katz, Irving I. THE JEWISH PRESS IN DETROIT: AN HISTORICAL ACCOUNT ON THE OCCASION OF THE 150TH ANNIVERSARY OF THE JEWISH PRESS IN THE UNITED STATES. *Michigan Jewish Hist. 1974 14(1): 18-23.*

1454. Kinsey, Stephen D. THE DEVELOPMENT OF THE JEWISH COMMUNITY OF SAN JOSE, CALIFORNIA, 1850-1900. *Western States Jewish Hist. Q. 1974 7(1): 70-87, (2): 163-182, (3): 264-273.* Part I. Jews began to arrive in San Jose, California, in the 1850's. In 1861, they established Congregation Bickur Cholim, with Jacob Levy as the first president. There were 35 members in 1869 and the congregation purchased land to construct a synagogue. On 21 August 1870, the synagogue was dedicated. The first ordained rabbi to serve the congregation was Dr. Myer Sol Levy. By 1916 the congregation was a mixture of orthodox and reform Jews. Based on primary sources; 3 photos, 79 notes. Part II. The development of the Jewish community in San Jose depended upon merchants who could give their time and money for Jewish activities. Many of these individuals held offices in Jewish community organizations, Congregation Bickur Cholim, Ariel Lodge, B'nai B'rith, and other community groups. Short biographies are included in the article. Based on primary and secondary sources; 5 photos, 108 notes. Part III. Established in 1857, the Beth Olam Cemetery was the first Jewish communal organization in San Jose. Other Jewish community organizations were the Hebrew Ladies Benevolent Society (established 1869), the Hebrew Young Men's Benevolent Association of San Jose (established 1872), and Ariel Lodge No. 248 of B'nai B'rith (established 1875). Even with these few organizations, Congregation Bickur Cholim remained the center of the Jewish community in early San Jose. Based on primary sources; photo, 32 notes.   R. A. Garfinkle

1455. Kramer, William M.   THE EMERGENCE OF OAKLAND JEWRY. *Western States Jewish Hist. Q. 1978 10(2): 99-125, (3): 238-259, (4): 353-373; 11(1): 69-86; 1979 11(2): 173-186, (3): 265-278.* Part I. Jewish families were among the pioneers of Oakland, California, in the 1850's. In the early years, the Oakland Hebrew Benevolent Society, founded in 1862, was the religious, social, and charitable center of the community. Later, the first synagogue, founded in 1875, took over the religious and burial functions. Jews from Poland predominated in the community, and most of them worked in some aspect of the clothing industry. David Solis-Cohen, the noted author, was a leader in the Oakland Jewish community in the 1870's. Primary and secondary sources; 3 photos, 111 notes. Part II. In 1879 Oakland's growing Jewish community organized a second congregation, a strictly orthodox group, Poel Zedek. Women's religious organizations flourished, their charitable services extending to needy gentiles as well as Jews. Jewish participants in civic and political affairs included David S. Hirshberg, who served in several Alameda County offices, and Henry Levy, commander of the Oakland Guard militia organization. Oakland Jewry was part of the greater San Francisco community, yet maintained its own charm and character. Primary and secondary sources; 88 notes. Part III. On 6 July 1881 the First Hebrew Congregation of Oakland, California, elected Myer Solomon Levy as its rabbi. The London-born Levy practiced traditional Judaism. In 1884 the community faced the need of finding a larger, more fashionably located synagogue. The Israel Ladies Relief Society held a fair and raised $4,000 for the new building. On 17 June 1885 the First Hebrew's synagogue burned, increasing the urgency for a new building. Construction of the new synagogue began in May 1886 and was completed by September. Primary and secondary sources; 68 notes. Part IV. Oakland's Jews attended excellent schools, both secular and religious. Fannie Bernstein was the first Jewess to graduate from the University of California at Berkeley, in 1883. First Hebrew Congregation sponsored a Sabbath school which had 75 children in 1887. One of the pupils, Meyer Lissner, was a bright youngster whose letters were published in the Jewish press. The Jewish children of Oakland had an active social life with school events, birthday parties, and Bar Mitzvah. The contract of the popular Rabbi Myer S. Levy was renewed for five years, from 1888 to 1893. Primary and secondary sources; 66 notes. Part V. Oakland Jewry was active in public affairs and charitable projects in the 1880's. Rabbi Myer S. Levy was chaplain to the state legislature in 1885, and was invited several times to speak to the congregation of the Unitarian Hamiltonian Church. The Daughters of Israel Relief Society continued its good works both inside and outside the Jewish community. Beth Jacob, the traditional congregation of Old World Polish Jews, continued its separate religious practices while it maintained friendly relations with the members of the first Hebrew Congregation. Primary and secondary sources; 44 notes. Part VI. Oakland's Jewish community had able social and political leadership in David Samuel Hirshberg. Until 1886 he was an officer in the Grand Lodge of B'nai B'rith. He served as Under Sheriff of Alameda County in 1883 and was active in Democratic Party political affairs. In 1885 he was appointed Chief Clerk of the US Mint in San Francisco. As a politician, he had detractors who accused him of using his position in B'nai B'rith to foster his political career. Primary and secondary sources; 56 notes. Part VII. In 1891 Rabbi Myer S. Levy moved to a new position in San Francisco's Congregation Beth Israel, bringing to a close this era of Oakland's Jewish history. Based on published sources; 21 notes.
                                            B. S. Porter

1456. Kramer, William M. and Stern, Norton B.   A JEWISH HISTORY OF OAKLAND: A REVIEW ESSAY. *Western States Jewish*

Hist. Q. 1977 9(4): 371-377. Review article prompted by Fred Rosenbaum's book, *Free to Choose: The Making of a Jewish Community in the American West,* subtitled, "The Jews of Oakland, California, from the Gold Rush to the Present Day" (Berkeley: Judah L. Magnes Memorial Museum, 1976). The title is misleading as it mainly covers the 1920's to the present. The book has numerous errors and omissions, as Rosenbaum's research was confined primarily to personal interviews and not documented from primary sources. He selected subjects poorly, discussing several people who had little or no effect on Oakland Jewry, and one person who was a "bad example" to the community.
                                            B. S. Porter

1457. Kramer, William M.   LOS ANGELES JEWRY'S FIRST PRESIDENT. *Western States Jewish Hist. Q. 1975 7(2): 151-152.* Samuel K. Labatt served as the first president of the first Jewish organization in Los Angeles, the Hebrew Benevolent Society, which was formed in July 1854. Labatt had worked for Jewish organizations in his hometown of New Orleans before he came to California in 1853. His brother Henry J. Labatt was elected secretary of the First Hebrew Benevolent Society in San Francisco on 29 May 1853. 6 notes.   R. A. Garfinkle

1458. Kramer, William M.   THE STINGIEST MAN IN SAN FRANCISCO. *Western States Jewish Hist. Q. 1973 5(4): 257-269.* Humorous tales of the miserly attitudes and actions of one of the wealthiest Jews in San Francisco, Michael Reese, 1850-78.

1459. Lamb, Blaine.   JEWS IN EARLY PHOENIX, 1870-1920. *J. of Arizona Hist. 1977 18(3): 299-318.* Jews who came to Phoenix in the 1870's and 1880's were primarily of German and Polish extraction. By 1900 they were generally of Russian and East European origin. Though a small minority, Jews played a vital role in the maturing of Phoenix in its crucial 1870-1920 years. 5 illus., 50 notes.
                                            D. L. Smith

1460. Lapides, Abe.   HISTORY OF THE JEWISH COMMUNITY OF PONTIAC, MICHIGAN. *Michigan Jewish Hist. 1977 17(1): 3-10.* Chronicles the presence of Jews and the growth of their community in Pontiac, Michigan, 1915-77.

1461. Lease, Richard J.   EUGENE J. STERN: MERCHANT, FARMER AND PHILANTHROPIST OF LAS CRUCES, NEW MEXICO. *Western States Jewish Hist. Q. 1977 9(2): 161-166.* Eugene J. Stern emigrated from Hungary in 1903. For several years he worked in the western states of Texas and Colorado before homesteading in New Mexico in 1914. In 1917 he moved to Las Cruces and opened a general store while continuing farming in the area of the Rio Grande Valley. Stern's philanthropies included contributing to the student loan fund at New Mexico State University and the building fund of every church in Las Cruces. He also helped establish a Salvation Army unit and a chapter of the Boys' Club of America. On the 50th anniversary of his affiliation with Masonry he gave a half million dollars for the construction of a new Scottish Rite Temple in Las Cruces. Based on interviews with the subject and his family; 2 photos, note.   B. S. Porter

1462. Leibo, Steven A.   OUT THE ROAD: THE SAN BRUNO AVENUE JEWISH COMMUNITY OF SAN FRANCISCO, 1901-1968. *Western States Jewish Hist. Q. 1979 11(2): 99-110.* The first synagogue, Ahabat Achim, was formed in 1901, but the major growth of the San Bruno Avenue Jewish community took place after the 1906 earthquake. In its prime, the area comprised about 1200 Jewish residents, most of them poor, Eastern European immigrants. The Esther Hellman Settlement House, usually referred to as the "Clubhouse," was financed by wealthy "downtown" Jews, and provided for educational and social needs of the community. San Bruno Avenue, the main thoroughfare, had numerous stores and businesses operated by the local Jewish residents. Beginning in the 1930's, as they became more affluent, the younger generations moved out of the old neighborhood. Based on interviews and published sources; 3 photos, 47 notes.   B. S. Porter

1463. Lerner, Samuel and Kaplan, Rose.   A BRIEF HISTORY OF THE DETROIT JEWISH FAMILY AND CHILDREN'S SERVICE: AN OVERVIEW. *Michigan Jewish Hist. 1976 16(2): 22-26.* The Jewish Family and Children's Service is a community organization interested in the education and Americanization of Detroit's Jewish community, 1876-1976.

1464. Morgan, David T. THE SHEFTALLS OF SAVANNAH. *Am. Jewish Hist. Q. 1973 62(4): 348-361.* Benjamin Sheftall arrived in Savannah, Georgia, in 1733. The Sheftall Papers indicate that the family acquired real estate throughout the state before the Revolution. Mordecei and Levi Sheftall suffered imprisonment, banishment, and loss of livelihood for espousing the American cause when the British captured Savannah in 1778. Although the government did not reimburse the Sheftalls for losses suffered, they prospered again after 1790 and remained active in the affairs of Savannah's Jewish community. The Sheftall Papers, Keith Reid Collection, University of Georgia; 39 notes.   F. Rosenthal

1465. Papermaster, Isadore. A HISTORY OF NORTH DAKOTA JEWRY AND THEIR PIONEER RABBI. *Western States Jewish Hist. Q. 1977 10(1): 74-89; 1978 10(2): 170-184, (3): 266-283.* Part I. Rabbi Benjamin Papermaster was born in Lithuania in 1860. He agreed to come to America in 1890 to serve a party of immigrants as its religious leader and teacher. He settled in Grand Forks, North Dakota, amid a growing congregation of Jews from the Ukraine, Rumania, Poland, and Germany. Most of the Jews at that time were peddlers who mortgaged their houses and wagons to build the first synagogue. Rabbi Papermaster was enthusiastic about America; his letters to his family in Lithuania brought many relatives to join him. Grand Forks was considered a boom town because of the building of the Great Northern Railway. The influx of eastern capital helped the development of Jewish merchants. Based on personal experience and family records; 2 photos, 6 notes. Part II. Until the turn of the century, Rabbi Papermaster of Grand Forks was the only rabbi serving Jews in all of North Dakota and western Minnesota. Jewish families who started as peddlers became prosperous enough to move out to towns and villages where they opened small shops and stores. Other families followed the Great Northern Railway along its branch lines toward the Canadian border. In Grand Forks, the Jewish community established a modern Hebrew school, a Ladies' Aid Society, and a burial society. 2 photos, 11 notes. Part III. The city of Grand Forks, at the urging of Rabbi Papermaster, acquired a sanitary meat slaughtering facility with a special department for kosher beef. Rabbi Papermaster maintained an active interest in local politics, generally favoring the Republican Party but supporting Democrats when he knew them to be good men. Although a member of a Zionist organization, he worried about the antireligious character of the modern movement. During World War I he urged Jewish youths to their patriotic duty of joining the American armed forces. Rabbi Papermaster died on 24 September 1934. 3 photos, 14 notes.   B. S. Porter

1466. Pierce, Lorraine E. THE JEWISH SETTLEMENT ON ST. PAUL'S LOWER WEST SIDE. *Am. Jewish Arch. 1976 28(2): 143-161.* Much of what is known about life on the Lower West Side of St. Paul, Minn., between the late 1800's and 1920—when the neighborhood was for the most part, peopled by Jewish immigrants from Eastern Europe—"suggests parallels with New York's Lower East Side."   J

1467. Pinsky, Mark. ASSIMILATED IN MILLTOWN. *Present Tense 1978 5(3): 35-39.* Studies the socioeconomic patterns of several Jewish families in "Milltown" (not the real name), an average-sized city in the American South, from the 1890's to the present, as representative of the individual goals and attitudes of Southern Jews.

1468. Pitterman, Marvin and Schiavo, Bartholomew. HAKHAM RAPHAEL HAIM ISAAC CARIGAL: SHALIAH OF HEBRON AND RABBI OF NEWPORT, 5533 (1773). *Rhode Island Jewish Hist. Notes 1974 6(4): 587-603.* Biographical sketch of Hakham Raphael Haim Isaac Carigal's career as rabbi of Newport, Rhode Island (1773), and his contribution to the community's culture and history.   S

1469. Raphael, Marc Lee. EUROPEAN JEWISH AND NON-JEWISH MARITAL PATTERNS IN LOS ANGELES, 1910-1913: A COMPARATIVE APPROACH. *Western States Jewish Hist. Q. 1974 6(2): 100-106.* Examines more than 25,000 marriage licenses for the years 1910-1913, and concludes that European national animosities persisted when immigrants moved to Los Angeles. There were few intermarriages between people of different nationalities. Jews tended to marry Jews from the same geographic homeland areas—for instance, East Europeans married East Europeans but did not marry Jews from other parts of Europe. 7 tables.   R. A. Garfinkle

1470. Raphael, Marc Lee. THE INDUSTRIAL REMOVAL OFFICE IN COLUMBUS: A LOCAL CASE STUDY. *Ohio Hist. 1976 85(2): 100-108.* Studies an organization responsible for relocating (in Columbus, Ohio) Jewish immigrants from the East Coast (1901-16). Based on archival sources; illus., 26 notes.   T. H. Hartig

1471. Rapp, Michael G. SAMUEL N. DEINARD AND THE UNIFICATION OF JEWS IN MINNEAPOLIS. *Minnesota Hist. 1973 43(6): 213-221.* Rabbi Samuel N. Deinard (1873-1921), founder and editor of *The American Jewish World,* was the prime mover in bringing German and East European Jews together as a community in Minneapolis. His weekly newspaper is the principal source for this analysis. 5 illus., 28 notes.   D. L. Smith

1472. Reutlinger, Andrew S. REFLECTIONS ON THE ANGLO-AMERICAN JEWISH EXPERIENCE: IMMIGRANTS, WORKERS AND ENTREPRENEURS IN NEW YORK AND LONDON, 1870-1914. *Am. Jewish Hist. Q. 1977 66(4): 473-484.* Many of the factors responsible for the divergent pattern of communal development among the East European Jewish immigrants in London and New York City lay in the process of migration itself and in the differences between British and American values and institutions. For example, financial difficulties or religious predilections of an orthodox nature might be determining factors in remaining in Great Britain. Even a temporary sojourn in London made possible changes in the factory method of garment manufacture and in the men working in it to humanize the consequences of this system. Also, the Jewish labor movement benefited from the experience of many of its leaders in London's sweat shops. English models made for communal paternalism exercised by the "Cousinhood" (Rothschilds, Montefiores, etc.), but American conditions precluded national institutions or the same degree of deference to the Jewish elite.   F. Rosenthal

1473. Rockaway, Robert A. ANTISEMITISM IN AN AMERICAN CITY: DETROIT, 1850-1914. *Am. Jewish Hist. Q. 1974 64(1): 42-54.* Detroit, headquarters of the anti-Semitic activities of Henry Ford and Charles E. Coughlin in the 1920's and 1930's, was the site of many earlier instances produced by party politics in the 1850's and the emotionalism of the Civil War. After the great migration of Jews from eastern Europe to the city anti-Semitism became increasingly apparent and led to the formation of the Jewish Peddlers Protective Association in 1892. This decade also witnessed the first explicit act of social discrimination involving the Detroit Athletic Club. Overt anti-Semitism in the city created anxiety and apprehension among Detroit's Jewish citizens and led some of them to reevaluate their position as Americans and as Jews. 36 notes.   F. Rosenthal

1474. Rockaway, Robert A. THE EASTERN EUROPEAN JEWISH COMMUNITY OF DETROIT, 1881-1914. *Yivo Ann. of Jewish Social Sci. 1974 (15): 82-105.* Most East European Jews coming to Detroit in this period lived in the crowded downtown sections of the city. The author discusses the religious, economic, social and cultural life of the community, its religious identification, reaction to cultural change, and relations with non-Jews. "Although the Eastern European Jews made great strides in coming to terms with their American environment by 1914, they were still viewed with hostility and suspicion by native-born and foreign-born Detroiters." 83 notes.   R. J. Wechman

1475. Rockaway, Robert A. THE PROGRESS OF REFORM JUDAISM IN LATE 19TH AND EARLY 20TH CENTURY DETROIT. *Michigan Jewish Hist. 1974 14(1): 8-17.*

1476. Romanofsky, Peter. " ... TO RID OURSELVES OF THE BURDEN ..." NEW YORK JEWISH CHARITIES AND THE ORIGINS OF THE INDUSTRIAL REMOVAL OFFICE, 1890-1901. *Am. Jewish Hist. Q. 1975 64(4): 331-343.* Various motives combined to induce the primarily German-Jewish leadership of New York Jewish charities to actively support removal of new immigrants to other parts of the country. Overcrowding, the possibility of political radicalism, and the fear of renewed antisemitism led to various programs for job training, agricultural settlements, and resettlement outside New York. Both the Industrial Removal Office of 1901 and the Galveston Plan of 1907 were created to prevent limitation of Jewish immigration to the United States. By 1914 some 70,000 men and their families had been placed outside New York City, allowing Jewish charities to expand and develop their services

to the children, widows, and the sick of the Jewish community. 31 notes.
F. Rosenthal

1477. Rosenshine, Jay. HISTORY OF THE SHOLOM ALEICHEM INSTITUTE OF DETROIT, 1926-1971. *Michigan Jewish Hist. 1974 14(2): 9-20.*

1478. Rosenwaike, Ira. THE FIRST JEWISH SETTLERS IN LOUISVILLE. *Filson Club Hist. Q. 1979 53(1): 37-44.* By 1832 the Jewish population of Louisville was large enough to support the establishment of the Israelite Benevolent Society. Most of the community was highly mobile at this time; few of the early Jewish settlers remained in the city for more than a decade. Based on local government records and the federal census. 38 notes.
G. B. McKinney

1479. Rosenwaike, Ira. THE JEWS OF BALTIMORE: 1820 TO 1830. *Am. Jewish Hist. Q. 1978 67(3): 246-259.* Provides biographical surveys of most of the 30 individuals whose families constituted the Jewish community of Baltimore, Maryland. One-fourth were native-born by 1830. Dutch Jews predominated among European newcomers. All but two of these heads of household practiced middle class occupations, and 10 of the 24 families contained one or more blacks. This small group of men founded the first congregations, led them for many years, and thus founded an enduring organizational structure. 26 notes.
F. Rosenthal

1480. Rosenwaike, Ira. THE JEWS OF BALTIMORE TO 1810. *Am. Jewish Hist. Q. 1975 64(4): 291-320.* The systematic examination of the Jewish population of Baltimore from 1770 to 1810 reveals that by 1810 a rough outline of the communal trends in the next stage of development had been shaped: differentiation had taken place between the relatively well-off older "American" Jews and the recent immigrant arrivals. Another two decades passed, however, before the first congregation was set up. Over 40 individuals and their families provide material for this study. 85 notes.
F. Rosenthal/S

1481. Rosenwaike, Ira. THE JEWS OF BALTIMORE: 1810 TO 1820. *Am. Jewish Hist. Q. 1977 67(2): 101-124.* The Jewish population of Baltimore during this period, although subject to considerable flux, remained small (less than 25 families). These individuals, nevertheless, seem to have been broadly representative of American Jewry; because of their mobility, they were also the Jews of Philadelphia and New York. Short biographical sketches are provided for both foreign-born and native-born heads of families. 2 tabulations, 74 notes.
F. Rosenthal

1482. Rothschild, Janice. PRE-1867 ATLANTA JEWRY. *Am. Jewish Hist. Q. 1973 62(3): 242-249.* The first Jewish family—Jacob and Jeanetta Hirsch Haas with their four children—came to Atlanta in 1845, soon followed by Henry Levi, Herman Haas, David Mayer, and others, mostly from southern Germany. Sketches family, business, and social activities. Mayer was instrumental in organizing the Hebrew Benevolent Society and a Jewish cemetery, and led the small community during the Civil War. Based on contemporary newspaper data and family recollections; 26 notes.
F. Rosenthal

1483. Schmier, Louis. THE FIRST JEWS OF VALDOSTA. *Georgia Hist. Q. 1978 62(1): 32-49.* Valdosta's first Jews, Abraham Ehrlich and Bernard Kaul, arrived in 1866, closely followed by some of Ehrlich's relatives. Although the number of Jews in Valdosta, Georgia, during this period was never greater than 17, they were very involved with business and town affairs. Business ventures as well as acceptance by and involvement in the gentile community, particularly by the Ehrlichs and the Engels, are detailed. Based on primary sources, mainly newspapers, legal records, and interviews; 63 notes.
G. R. Schroeder

1484. Schwartz, Henry. THE UNEASY ALLIANCE: JEWISH-ANGLO RELATIONS IN SAN DIEGO, 1850-1860. *J. of San Diego Hist. 1975 20(3): 53-60.* Describes the generally harmonious relations between Jewish and other settlers in San Diego during the 1850's.
S

1485. Selavan, Ida Cohen. THE EDUCATION OF JEWISH IMMIGRANTS IN PITTSBURGH, 1862-1932. *Yivo Ann. of Jewish Social Sci. 1974 (15): 126-144.* Looks at the education of the Jewish immigrants

in public school, night school, and adult education. Jews flocked to the public education system and did well. Hebrew, religious, and Yiddish education are also briefly covered. 85 notes.
R. J. Wechman

1486. Selavan, Ida Cohen. JEWISH WAGE EARNERS IN PITTS-BURGH, 1890-1930. *Am. Jewish Hist. Q. 1976 65(3): 272-285.* The formation of a Jewish proletariat in Pittsburgh began after the influx of a large number of Jews from Eastern Europe. During the 40 years under discussion Jewish wage earners were found in large numbers among stogy makers, the needle trades, and the bakery trade, which was unionized in 1906. These three industries, each different in conditions, wages, and work force, are described on the basis of oral interviews, contemporary journals, newspapers, etc. Attempts to unionize tailors and seamstresses were successful only in the larger shops before 1914. 39 notes.
F. Rosenthal.

1487. Shankman, Arnold. ATLANTA JEWRY—1900-1930. *Am. Jewish Arch. 1973 25(2): 131-155.* Though little research has been devoted to the subject, few ethnic groups have made as important a contribution to Atlanta history as have her Jewish citizens.
J

1488. Shook, Robert W. ABRAHAM LEVI: FATHER OF VICTORIA JEWRY. *Western States Jewish Hist. Q. 1977 9(2): 144-154.* Victoria, Texas, was a trade and cattle center serving Texas and northern Mexico since before the Civil War. Abraham Levi (1822-1902) was among the earliest Jewish settlers in Victoria, arriving in 1848 or 1849. By the 1870's the Jewish community included 15 families and had organized a Reform congregation. Levi operated a retail store, and engaged in land transactions and private banking. The Levi Bank and Trust Company (now the Victoria Bank and Trust) was franchised in 1910. Levi's activities in the community included serving as president of the Jewish congregation and as a city alderman. Primary and secondary sources; 3 photos, 26 notes.
B. S. Porter

1489. Stern, Norton B. and Kramer, William M. THE FIRST JEWISH ORGANIZATION, THE FIRST JEWISH CEMETERY AND THE FIRST KNOWN JEWISH BURIAL IN THE FAR WEST. *Western States Jewish Hist. Q. 1979 11(4): 318-324.* The first Jewish burial in the West took place in San Francisco in December 1849. The deceased was Henry D. Johnson, religious rites were performed by Lewis A. Franklin, and burial was in the Yerba Buena public cemetery. Following this burial, the Jewish community organized the First Hebrew Benevolent Society and established a Jewish cemetery so that Jewish burials could take place in consecrated ground. The Benevolent Society was founded in January 1850, and the land for the cemetery was acquired in April 1850. Johnson's remains were moved to the new cemetery. The first funeral service in the Hart (Jewish) Cemetery was in the fall of 1850 when two victims of the Sacramento cholera epidemic were buried. Newspaper accounts and other published sources; photo, 22 notes.
B. S. Porter

1490. Stern, Norton B. JEWS IN THE 1870 CENSUS OF LOS ANGELES. *Western States Jewish Hist. Q. 1976 9(1): 71-86.* The federal census taken in 1870 showed there were 330 Jews (5.76% of the population) in the city of Los Angeles. This high proportion of Jews was probably duplicated in other cities of the early West. Demographic analysis shows the Jewish population to be predominantly young, Polish or Prussian-Polish, and employed in the merchandizing of wearing apparel. Based on the Federal Census of 1870, city and county directories, cemetery records, register of voters, secondary publications, and demographic and name listings; 11 notes.
B. S. Porter

1491. Stern, Norton B. THE NAME OF LOS ANGELES' FIRST JEWISH NEWSPAPER. *Western States Jewish Hist. Q. 1975 7(2): 153-157.* Lionel L. Edwards, publisher, and Victor Harris, editor, established the first Los Angeles Jewish newspaper, the *Emanu-El*, on 10 March 1897. Rabbi Jacob Voorsanger, publisher of the well-established Jewish newspaper *Emanu-El* in San Francisco, criticized the fact that the southern paper had copied his paper's name. In 1898, the southern paper was changed to the *B'nai B'rith Messenger*, and is still published under that title. 15 notes.
R. A. Garfinkle

1492. Stern, Norton B. A SAN FRANCISCO SYNAGOGUE SCANDAL IN 1893. *Western States Jewish Hist. Q. 1974 6(3): 196-*

203. A scandal developed at Temple Sherith Israel in 1893, when a new rabbi was being installed. The cantor, Max Rubin, did not want a new rabbi who would start receiving fees for weddings and funerals, as he had been filling in as reader for over a year and liked the large sum collected for officiating at various functions. In June, 1893, Rabbi Jacob Nieto was elected Rabbi of the congregation, and the scandal soon died down. Primary and secondary sources; 14 notes.   R. A. Garfinkle

1493. Toll, William. FRATERNALISM AND COMMUNITY STRUCTURE ON THE URBAN FRONTIER: THE JEWS OF PORTLAND, OREGON: A CASE STUDY. *Pacific Hist. Rev. 1978 47(3): 369-403.* Portland's Jews were residentially dispersed according to class standing, but they clustered in occupations to which they had been confined in Germany and Russia. Extensive trading contacts with relatives and friends in San Francisco and elsewhere produced economic stability in the late 19th and early 20th centuries so that the community retained a higher proportion of its members than most ethnic enclaves and provided remunerative employment for most of its sons and many newcomers. In general, only Jews with capital, contacts, or skills migrated to Portland. Based on manuscript census, city directories, and B'nai B'rith lodge records; map, 11 tables, 51 notes.   W. K. Hobson

1494. Twersky, Rebecca. THE FOUNDING OF A JEWISH COMMUNITY: AHAVATH SHALOM OF WEST WARWICK. *Rhode Island Jewish Hist. Notes 1977 7(3): 420-429.* History of the Congregation Ahavath Shalom of West Warwick, Rhode Island, from its inception in 1912 to around 1938.

1495. Unsigned. JEWS IN EARLY SANTA MONICA: A CENTENNIAL REVIEW. *Western States Jewish Hist. Q. 1975 7(4): 327-350.* Many Los Angeles Jews spent their summers camping out at Santa Monica Canyon before the town was established in 1875. Many of these Jews were the first to purchase lots when the town was laid out by John P. Jones and R. S. Baker in 1875. The Jewish community consisted mostly of vacationers during the summer. The first Jewish religious services were held in 1912 by Los Angeles Rabbi Sigmund Hecht. In 1939, the first permanent Jewish congregation was formed. 16 photos, 56 notes.   R. A. Garfinkle

1496. Watters, Gary. THE RUSSIAN JEW IN OKLAHOMA: THE MAY BROTHERS. *Chronicles of Oklahoma 1975-76 53(4): 479-491.* Facing increased persecution in tsarist Russia, Hyman Madanic and his son Ben emigrated to the United States in 1889. After leaving Ellis Island, where their name was changed to Madansky, they took jobs in the sweatshop system of St. Louis's clothing industry. Hard work and frugality brought enough money to bring the rest of the family from Russia in 1893. Soon the family was Americanized and opened its own clothing store in Fairfield, Illinois. In 1908 they moved to the boomtown of Tulsa, Oklahoma, where their business proved successful enough to open branches in nearby towns. Following World War I, they changed their name to May and their business became widely known. The Great Depression undercut the family fortunes and closed the Tulsa store, but the branches survived. Primary and secondary sources; 3 photos, 21 notes.   M. L. Tate

1497. Wax, Bernard. "OUR TOURO SYNAGOGUE." *Rhode Island Jewish Hist. Notes 1977 7(3): 440-441.* Discusses the history and symbolism of the Touro Synagogue in Newport, Rhode Island; discusses Jews in Newport since 1654.

1498. Werner, Alfred. GHETTO GRADUATES. *Am. Art J. 1973 5(2): 71-82.* For religious and political reasons, Jewish settlements in Eastern Europe were "devoid of anything artistic." But Jewish immigrants (1880's-1920's) settling in American urban ghettos were free from tradition, and ghetto artists involved themselves fully in revolutionary art trends. Secondary sources; 12 figs., 23 notes.   R. M. Frame III

1499. Winn, Karyl. THE SEATTLE JEWISH COMMUNITY. *Pacific Northwest Q. 1979 70(2): 69-74.* Reproduces 10 photographs of Seattle's Jewish citizens and their businesses during the early 20th century. Jews constituted less than one percent of the city's population, but their influence in civic and commercial affairs surpassed their numbers.   M. L. Tate

Irish

1500. Browne, Joseph. JOHN O'HARA AND TOM MC HALE: HOW GREEN IS THEIR VALLEY? *J. of Ethnic Studies 1978 6(2): 57-64.* Analyzes the portrayal of Irish Americans in the novels of John O'Hara (d. 1970) and Tom McHale. O'Hara never seems to get beyond a contemptuous sniggering at his Irish characters, while McHale "has a delightfully irreverent sense of 'green' humor," and "doesn't insist that the Irish are more corrupt or corruptible than any other ethnic group. . . . For Tom McHale, the Irish simply are; for John O'Hara, they never should have been." When either writer departs from the scenes and people he knows best, his work deteriorates; thus O'Hara is at his finest in his Gibbsville novels and McHale the most sound when dealing with Philadelphia and Irish and Italians transplanted from his neighborhood in Scranton. Secondary sources; 10 notes.   G. J. Bobango

1501. Callahan, Helen. A STUDY OF DUBLIN: THE IRISH IN AUGUSTA. *Richmond County Hist. 1973 5(2): 5-14.* Augusta had Irish residents before the Irish immigration which occurred nationally during and immediately after the potato famine of 1845-51. A number came during the early 1830's to work as railroad laborers. Historically Augusta's Irish took an active role in community affairs. Irishmen became important local politicians and prominent businessmen. One of six articles in this issue on Augusta. Based on newspapers, business directories, and secondary sources; 42 notes.   H. R. Grant

1502. Clark, Andrienne G. WHO MURDERED MARCUS LYON? *New-England Galaxy 1977 19(2): 15-21.* In strongly anti-Catholic, anti-Irish, and anti-immigrant Northampton, Massachusetts, Irish immigrants Dominic Daley and James Halligan were convicted with little defense and on doubtful evidence in April 1806, and hanged in June, for the murder of Marcus Lyon in November 1805. Father (later Cardinal) Jean Louis Lefebvre de Cheverus, in an eloquent sermon to Protestants waiting for the hanging, attempted to diminish their prejudice.   D. J. Engler

1503. Clark, Dennis. BABES IN BONDAGE: INDENTURED IRISH CHILDREN IN PHILADELPHIA IN THE NINETEENTH CENTURY. *Pennsylvania Mag. of Hist. and Biog. 1977 101(4): 475-486.* The Irish supplied most of the workers for the 18th-century's indentured labor system, an institution noted as late as the 1920's in some juvenile court cases. The system, rife with abuse, declined with population growth and mass production. Based on Philadelphia City Archives, Urban Archives, Temple University, official records, newspapers, and secondary works; 36 notes.   T. H. Wendel

1504. Clark, Dennis. ETHNIC ENTERPRISE AND URBAN DEVELOPMENT. *Ethnicity 1978 5(2): 108-118.* Examines the role of Irish general contractors in Philadelphia from the time of the potato famine (1846-47) to the 1960's. Construction of churches, parochial schools, and homes for Irish immigrants provided much of the impetus for Irish involvement in general contracting. In the early years, little capital was needed to start as a contractor and aspiring Irish entrepreneurs had access to fellow countrymen who quickly acquired important construction skills. Irish participation in politics and in construction became closely linked. Discusses the individual careers of leading contractors, and the increasing legal and technological complexity of the business. Based on the Philadelphia *Evening Bulletin,* and secondary sources; 44 notes.   L. W. Van Wyk

1505. Cuddy, Edward. "ARE BOLSHEVIKS ANY WORSE THAN THE IRISH?" ETHNO-RELIGIOUS CONFLICT IN AMERICA DURING THE 1920'S. *Éire-Ireland 1976 11(3): 13-32.* Shattering effects of urbanization and fear of the loss of Anglo-Saxon hegemony in the United States resulted in much anti-Catholicism and anti-Irish sentiment during the 1920's.

1506. Doyle, John E. CHICOPEE'S IRISH (1830-1875). *Hist. J. of Western Massachusetts 1974 3(1): 13-23.* Nineteenth-century Irish settlers came to the Chicopee mills via Canada and other parts of Massachusetts, and by 1848 Chicopee became a predominantly immigrant company town. Irish mores encouraged nativism among Protestants, but the record of Irish participation in the Civil War led to respectability. Primary and secondary sources; 2 illus., 34 notes.   S. S. Sprague and S

1507. Erie, Steven P. POLITICS, THE PUBLIC SECTOR AND IRISH SOCIAL MOBILITY: SAN FRANCISCO, 1870-1900. *Western Pol. Q. 1978 31(2): 274-289.* The argument that the Irish used political strategies and avenues to move from working-class to middle-class status in the nation's big cities is examined by (a) a case study of Irish political and economic progress in San Francisco, 1870-1900; and (b) a national comparison of Celtic political and economic development in urban versus non-urban settings for the same time period. The case study compares the Irish social mobility rate to rates for eight major ethnic groups; analyzes the magnitudes and ethnic distributions for three types of "political" resources—public jobs, contracts and franchises, and "unofficial" patronage; and examines the relationships between "mass" and "elite" political mobilization, public job allocations, and aggregate mobility rates for the various ethnic groups. Findings: Only a small portion of the Irish used political resources and routes to move into the middle class. Public sector economic resources in the pre-New Deal era were too limited to more than marginally affect overall group economic progress.
J

1508. Funchion, Michael F. IRISH NATIONALISTS AND CHICAGO POLITICS IN THE 1880'S. *Éire-Ireland 1975 10(2): 3-18.* The Chicago branch of the Clan na Gael, an American Irish nationalist organization, was "a highly effective local political machine." Those Clan members who were mavericks or Republican Party members, however, could not sway Irish Americans from voting Democratic, especially in presidential elections. Mentions Alexander Sullivan's pragmatic leadership of the Clan, a split in the Clan by followers of New York-based John Devoy in 1885, John Finerty's congressional campaigns in 1882 and 1884, and the presidential elections of 1884 and 1888. Based on newspapers, secondary sources, and the Devoy Papers in the National Library of Ireland; 39 notes.
D. J. Engler

1509. Gitelman, H. M. NO IRISH NEED APPLY: PATTERNS OF AND RESPONSES TO ETHNIC DISCRIMINATION IN THE LABOR MARKET. *Labor Hist. 1973 14(1): 56-68.* Surveys ethnic discrimination against the Irish in the Waltham, Massachusetts, labor market 1850-90. With on-the-job training and formal education blocked, Irishmen received the lowest-paying, unskilled jobs, establishing a vicious cycle which tended to keep the Irish in unskilled positions. The experience in Waltham probably differs from large cities or one-industry towns, and generalizations are dangerous. Based on state and federal manuscript census returns, corporate records, public registers, and city directories; 2 tables, 19 notes.
L. L. Athey

1510. Good, Patricia K. IRISH ADJUSTMENT TO AMERICAN SOCIETY: INTEGRATION OR SEPARATION? *Records of the Am. Catholic Hist. Soc. of Philadelphia 1975 86(1-4): 7-23.* Offers insights concerning Irish adjustment to American society by analyzing a late 19th-century Irish Catholic immigrant community in a borough of Pittsburgh. Their St. Andrew Parish fulfilled two major adaptation functions: it operated as an enclosive society supplying the manifest functions of spiritual instruction, sustenance, and consolation as well as the latent functions of mate and friendship choice, and opportunities to express nationalistic and psychological needs. Because its parishioners were able to express basic value orientations of the dominant society, it also stood as a model and means of successful acculturation and adaptation to the American environment. 25 notes.
J. M. McCarthy

1511. Good, Patricia K. IRISH ADJUSTMENT TO AMERICAN SOCIETY: INTEGRATION OR SEPARATION? *Records of the Am. Catholic Hist. Soc. of Philadelphia 1975 86(1-4): 7-23.* Discusses Irish adjustment to American society by analyzing a late 19th-century Irish Catholic immigrant community in a borough of Pittsburgh. The parish, St. Andrew's, fulfilled two major adaptation functions: it operated as an enclosing society supplying the manifest functions of spiritual instruction, sustenance, and consolation, as well as the latent functions of mate and friendship choice and opportunities to express nationalistic and psychological needs. Because its parishioners were able through it to express basic value orientations of the dominant society, it was also a model and means of successful acculturation and adaptation to the American environment. 25 notes.
J. M. McCarthy

1512. Less, Lynn H. and Modell, John. THE IRISH COUNTRYMAN URBANIZED: A COMPARATIVE PERSPECTIVE ON THE FAMINE MIGRATION. *J. of Urban Hist. 1977 3(4): 391-408.* Urbanization for potato famine Irish people was more often than not international rather than internal. British and American cities rather than Dublin and other Irish centers drew the greatest share of Irish people who left the land. A macrolevel analysis of London and Philadelphia, two major centers of Irish emigration, shows that Irish people filled in the bottom of the urban economic and social systems. It also shows that these urban environments offered distinct advantages to Irish people, such as seasonal employment opportunities in British cities, employment for women, and better chances for marriage. 6 tables, 18 notes.
T. W. Smith

1513. MacDonagh, Oliver. THE IRISH FAMINE EMIGRATION TO THE UNITED STATES. *Perspectives in Am. Hist. 1976 10: 357-446.* In Ireland, overpopulation and the "new farming" combined to push one-third to one-half of the total work force out of agriculture. Although unemployed Irish found a scapegoat in British Protestants, they still exhibited a desire to "cling to country." Fortunately, however, an Atlantic passenger trade simultaneously developed so fast that by 1845 it was capable of transporting cheaply 75,000 people per season. Then came the potato famine during 1845-48, which weakened the peasant's desire to cling to Ireland. Once this attitude was broken, cheap passage to America became a viable option. For many Irish, emigration was the only thing that saved them from almost certain death by starvation. In their new homeland they were for a generation the urban proletariat, but thereafter they stepped up the social ladder. They retained a distinctive identity because of their religion, Irish nationalism, and the development of their political base. Although this did not rid Anglo-Saxon Americans of their prejudice against the Irish, it did force the former to reckon with the Irish as political equals.
W. A. Wiegand

1514. Morgan, John H. THE IRISH OF SOUTH BOSTON. *Worldview 1975 18(6): 24-27.* Discusses the political and cultural factors since the late 19th century which led the Irish of South Boston, Massachusetts, to resort to civil disobedience against forced school busing in 1974.

1515. O'Connor, Thomas H. THE IRISH IN BOSTON. *Urban and Social Change Rev. 1979 12(2): 19-23.* Discusses the English military and political conquest of Ireland, and persecution of Irish Catholics, since the 16th century, and the Great Famine of 1845-49, as background to the immigration of many Irish to the United States, particularly to the Boston area, and the subsequent involvement of Irish Americans in Boston politics and city government.

1516. Owen, Polly. IS IT TRUE WHAT THEY SAY ABOUT THE IRISH? *West Tennessee Hist. Soc. Papers 1978 (32): 120-132.* Examines Irish-born men over age 20 in various occupations in the first three wards of Memphis in 1850, 1860, 1870, and 1880, and denies that Irish immigrants were less valuable, less sober, or less ingenious than their German counterparts. Points out positive qualities of the Irish-born as a group and as individuals to the economic development of Memphis and the South. Based largely on US Census statistics and Memphis histories; 4 charts, 52 notes.
H. M. Parker, Jr.

1517. Vinyard, Jo Ellen. INLAND URBAN IMMIGRANTS: THE DETROIT IRISH, 1850. *Michigan Hist. 1973 57(2): 121-139.* The Irish were the largest immigrant group in Detroit in 1850. With many opportunities and with negligible religious prejudice, the assets or liabilities of their background determined their economic and social roles in the city. They succeeded, encouraged more Irish to emigrate, and contributed to the growth of Detroit. 5 illus., 3 tables, 41 notes.
D. L. Smith

1518. Walsh, James P. and Foley, Timothy. FATHER PETER C. YORKE: IRISH-AMERICAN LEADER. *Studia Hibernica [Ireland] 1974 14: 90-103.* Galway-born Father Peter Yorke (1864-1925) became champion of the Irish working class in San Francisco, advancing their unionization and education under Catholic auspices. He was ordained in 1887, became chancellor of the archdiocese of San Francisco and editor of the diocesan newspaper, *The Monitor,* where he fought the anti-Catholic American Protective Association. After losing editorship of that newspaper he established the Irish-American paper, *The Leader,* in 1902. During his defense of Father Richard Henebry he attacked the Catholic University of America as the preserve of Anglo-Irish-American Churchmen. During World War I he attacked Garret McEnerney, champion of the Home Rule Party and critic of Irish American supporters of Sinn Fein. After the war Yorke quarrelled bitterly with Mayor James Phelan. Though a bright, energetic defender of Irish Americans, he could only cooperate with subordinates, enjoyed excessively the glory attached to popular advocacy, and never accepted the legitimate differences of opponents. Based on Yorke's published writings and MSS at University of San Francisco, newspapers, and secondary sources; 40 notes.

T. F. Moriarty

1519. Walsh, James P.   PETER YORKE AND PROGRESSIVISM IN CALIFORNIA, 1908. *Éire-Ireland 1975 10(2): 73-81.* Galway-born Father Peter C. Yorke championed the Catholic Church, Irish working people, and Irish nationalism in San Francisco from the 1880's until his death in 1925. Father Yorke, in his weekly newspaper *The Leader,* was a spokesman for Irish Americans who believed in political brokerage as a way to logically and democratically reconcile conflicting views. The Irish saw Progressive attempts at municipal charter revision in San Francisco in 1908 as the attempted removal of Irish political representation —by privileged, Protestant, University of California-oriented professional and business interests who thought themselves "disinterested" but did not accept cultural pluralism or political dissent. Based on *The Leader,* secondary sources, and correspondence; 28 notes.   D. J. Engler

Latinos

1520. Betten, Neil and Mohl, Raymond A.   FROM DISCRIMINATION TO REPATRIATION: MEXICAN LIFE IN GARY, INDIANA, DURING THE GREAT DEPRESSION. *Pacific Hist. R. 1973 42(3): 370-388.* Relates the social, economic, and political discrimination faced by Mexican Americans in the 1920's-30's in Gary, Indiana, culminating in the forced exodus of a large segment of the Mexican population during the early 1930's. The economic tensions generated by the Depression produced a new wave of nativism throughout the United States, and were fostered by antiethnic sentiments expressed in the *Saturday Evening Post* aimed particularly at Mexican Americans. "Undoubtedly the Mexican's darker skin, his Catholicism, and the usual problems and vices associated with the poor affected national opinion as well." From 1931 to May 1932 repatriation was voluntary, supported by most local institutions in Gary, including US Steel Co. and the International Institute, an immigrant-oriented welfare agency. However, "after May 1932, when the township trustee's office assumed direction of repatriation, repressive measures were used to force the return of reluctant voyagers." The organized efforts in Gary against Mexicans reflected the xenophobia present throughout American society during the early 1930's. 33 notes.

B. L. Fenske

1521. Ciro, Sepulveda.   UNA COLONIA DE OBREROS: EAST CHICAGO, INDIANA. *Aztlán 1976 7(2): 327-336.* A history of the colonia in the Indiana Harbor district of East Chicago, from the first large-scale arrival of Mexicanos (as strikebreakers) in 1919 to the mass deportations of 1932. During the 1920's, Inland Steel Co. of Indiana Harbor was the largest single employer of Mexicanos in the United States, and the colonia grew up on Block and Pennsylvania Avenues near the Inland Steel plant. Living conditions here were extremely bad, while working conditions were hazardous and a worker in the blast furnaces averaged approximately 60 hours/week. Rivalry for the best jobs caused some friction within the colonia, but relations with non-Mexicano neighbors were generally good. Primary (mainly press) and secondary sources; map, 41 notes.   L. W. Van Wyk

1522. Day, Mark.   THE PERTINENCE OF THE "SLEEPY LAGOON" CASE. *J. of Mexican Am. Hist. 1974 4(1): 71-98.* Through the use of documents preserved by Carey McWilliams, then chairman of the Citizens Committee for the Defense of Mexican-American Youth, and others, discusses the trial and aftermath (including the eventual acquittal) of 22 Mexican American youths in Los Angeles in 1942. The "Sleepy Lagoon" trial marked the first time in Los Angeles that organized Mexican Americans were to win a victory in the courts.

R. T. Fulton

1523. Dysart, Jane.   MEXICAN WOMEN IN SAN ANTONIO, 1830-1860: THE ASSIMILATION PROCESS. *Western Hist. Q. 1976 7(4): 365-375.* The Anglo sense of racial and cultural superiority in the Southwest inhibited large-scale marriage with Mexicans. Since Anglo penetration of the Southwest was preponderantly male, intermarriage was almost exclusively between Anglo men and Mexican women. The Anglo male-oriented frontier society limited the wife's function to home management and child care, while the husband made the decisions which affected the family's relationship to society. Using San Antonio, Texas, as a case study, it is found that the few Mexican women who became wives of Anglos lost their distinctive ethnic identity. In many cases their children rejected their Mexican cultural legacy. 45 notes.

D. L. Smith

1524. García, Mario T.   RACIAL DUALISM IN THE EL PASO LABOR MARKET, 1880-1920. *Aztlán 1976 6(2): 197-217.* Mexicans in El Paso suffered from structural discrimination. They received less pay for the same work as Anglos and did not have opportunities for advancement. Most Mexicans tolerated their subordinate economic position, believing they would soon return to Mexico. Some Mexican *obreros* engaged in strikes and labor organization. Based on US census documents, newspapers, and secondary sources; 61 notes.

R. Griswold del Castillo

1525. Godoy, Gustavo J.   JOSÉ ALEJANDRO HUAU: A CUBAN PATRIOT IN JACKSONVILLE POLITICS. *Florida Hist. Q. 1975 54(2): 196-206.* A naturalized American citizen, José Alejandro Huah (1836-1905) was a successful Jacksonville businessman who involved himself in city politics and became a spokesman for the city's Cuban community. In the 1890's he became increasingly involved in the Cuban freedom movement. He raised money, organized supplies and equipment for expeditions to Cuba, and sponsored Florida appearances of José Martí, a leader in the Cuban freedom movement. Huau spent most of his fortune in the cause of Cuban freedom from Spain and before his death saw the establishment of the Republic of Cuba in 1902. Based on primary and secondary sources; 35 notes.   P. A. Beaber

1526. Gonzalez, Gilbert G.   RACISM, EDUCATION AND THE MEXICAN COMMUNITY IN LOS ANGELES, 1920-30. *Societas 1974 4(4): 287-301.* Between 1922 and 1932 published studies of Mexican American children strongly influenced the education offered them in Los Angeles. On the basis of I.Q. tests and projection of career goals, many Mexican Americans were placed in vocational training for menial jobs or slow-learner tracks.   W. H. Mulligan, Jr.

1527. Griswold del Castillo, Richard.   HEALTH AND THE MEXICAN AMERICANS IN LOS ANGELES, 1850-1887. *J. of Mexican Am. Hist. 1974 4(1): 19-27.* The public health of the Mexican-American community of Los Angeles, 1850-87, was inferior to that of the Anglo-American population, particularly in regard to the care of infants and the treatment of infectious disease. Once a Mexican American had passed through the dangerous years prior to age 21, his chances of surviving were relatively better than the majority of Anglo Americans. Primary and secondary sources; 2 tables, 19 notes.   R. T. Fulton

1528. Griswold del Castillo, Richard.   LA FAMILIA CHICANA: SOCIAL CHANGE IN THE CHICANO FAMILY IN LOS ANGELES, 1850-1880. *J. of Ethnic Studies 1975 3(1): 41-58.* Examines the reaction of Mexican American families in light of the impact of modernization (urbanization and industrialization) during the period 1850-80. The pre-modern family is found to be paternalistic and extended. Modernization led to a decline in the proportion of extended families, a rise in the proportion of female headed families, and an increase in common law marriages. Rather than being functional adjustments to industrialization, these are interpreted as dysfunctional since both literacy and social mobility were associated with the declining extended family structure. Based largely on manuscript censuses and other primary sources; 27 notes.   T. W. Smith

1529. Griswold del Castillo, Richard.   MYTH AND REALITY: CHICANO ECONOMIC MOBILITY IN LOS ANGELES 1850-1880. *Aztlán 1976 6(2): 151-171.* Contrary to the American myth of success, the Chicano working class in Los Angeles did not experience upward socioeconomic mobility in the late 19th century. Compared to the Anglo population, Chicanos became second-class citizens economically. All classes were reduced in socioeconomic status and persisting residents experienced the same fate. Based on manuscript census returns; 17 notes.

A

1530. Hoffman, Abraham. STIMULUS TO REPATRIATION: THE 1931 FEDERAL DEPORTATION DRIVE AND THE LOS ANGELES MEXICAN COMMUNITY. *Pacific Hist. Rev. 1973 42(2): 205-219.* Studies the main thrust of Secretary of Labor James J. Davis's promise to reduce unemployment at the height of the depression—ousting aliens holding jobs, concentrating on illegal aliens, and curtailing legal entries. Although the campaign did not single out any one ethnic group, Mexicans were most affected. Of these most lived in Southern California, specifically in Los Angeles County. Analyzes the series of developments resulting from the activities of the federal agents which led to a mass exodus of 50,000 to 75,000 people. The fear tactics used by the federal agents had been designed to bring about that deportation and emigration. 43 notes.   R. V. Ritter

1531. Kanellos, Nicolás. FIFTY YEARS OF THEATRE IN THE LATINO COMMUNITIES OF NORTHWEST INDIANA. *Aztlán 1976 7(2): 255-265.* Discusses the development of Latino theater in Gary and East Chicago. By the 1920's, five Latino theater groups were operating in this area, the most prominent being the Cuadro Dramatico del Circulo de Obreros Catholicos "San José," founded to raise funds for construction of a Catholic church and to provide "wholesome recreation" for the community. The Great Depression and its attendant repatriations caused a hiatus in local Latino theater, but beginning in the 1950's, Puerto Rican Baptists made important contributions. The 1960's saw the formation of the Club Aristico Guadalupano, militantly Catholic and anti-Communist, which provided not only drama, but also a broad range of cultural presentations. The Teatro Desengaño del Pueblo, founded by the author in 1972, continues the tradition of these earlier groups, but with a stronger political emphasis. Based largely on contemporary accounts and announcements in the local Latino press; 26 notes.

L. W. Van Wyk

1532. Pérez, Louis A., Jr. CUBANS IN TAMPA: FROM EXILES TO IMMIGRANTS, 1892-1901. *Florida Hist. Q. 1978 57(2): 129-140.* Cuban cigarworkers in Tampa supported the Cuban independence cause in the 1880's and 1890's. The end of the war in 1898 marked a major shift in the cigarworkers' energies. Most reconciled themselves to permanent residence in the United States. Based mainly on secondary sources; 34 notes.   P. A. Beaber

1533. Pierce, Lorraine Esterly. MEXICAN AMERICANS ON ST. PAUL'S LOWER WEST SIDE. *J. of Mexican Am. Hist. 1974 4(1): 1-18.* Replacing Jewish, German and Russian immigrant workers at local factories, Mexican Americans began arriving in St. Paul's lower west side during World War I. During the Depression, Mexican Americans in St. Paul occupied the lowest rung on the economic ladder, settling in the least expensive areas and building a cohesive ethnic community. Renovation of the area into an industrial park in the 1960's forced a massive relocation of the inhabitants, who moved into similar neighborhoods and succeeded in retaining the identity and cohesiveness of St. Paul's Mexican American community. Primary and secondary material; table, 51 notes.

R. T. Fulton

1534. Poyo, Gerald E. KEY WEST AND THE CUBAN TEN YEARS WAR. *Florida Hist. Q. 1979 57(3): 289-307.* Cuban exiles after 1850 located in New Orleans, New York, and Key West. The community at Key West, despite personal conflicts, jealousies, class antagonisms, and tactical disagreements, retained the drive for Cuban independence. The Ten Years' War (1868-78) was the first step toward Cuba's political separation from Spain in 1898. Primary and secondary sources; 2 photos, 62 notes.   N. A. Kuntz

1535. Reisler, Mark THE MEXICAN IMMIGRANT IN THE CHICAGO AREA DURING THE 1920'S. *J. of the Illinois State Hist. Soc. 1973 66(2): 144-158.* Mexican immigrants replaced European labor in Chicago as European immigration was restricted after World War I and more single young Mexicans worked their way to Chicago. Illinois had more Mexican immigrants than any state except Texas, California, and Arizona. They worked as track maintenance hands for the railroads

and competed with southern blacks as strikebreakers in the steel mills and packinghouses which paid more than the railroads. Mexican labor was played off against workers of other nationalities to prevent the organization of labor unions. Shifting employment patterns, poor health and housing, plus limited English slowed improved conditions for Mexican labor. Most Mexicans hoped to return to Mexico. Based on government reports, social service periodicals, and monographs; 4 illus., 52 notes.

A. C. Aimone

1536. Rosales, Francisco Arturo. THE REGIONAL ORIGINS OF MEXICANO IMMIGRANTS TO CHICAGO DURING THE 1920'S. *Aztlán 1976 7(2): 187-201.* Of the Mexicano immigrants to the colonias of South Chicago and East Chicago during the 1920's, 68% came from the bajio region in west central Mexico. Their precursors had followed the railroads, for which many of them worked, to the Midwest, and were followed by thousands of immigrants during the revolution, in 1915. The inhabitants of the bajio were less affected by the injustices and hardships that sparked the revolution than by those it occasioned, and hence were less often moved to join it, more often to flee from it, than other Mexicanos. Many of the immigrants were recruited by US steel manufacturers. Many, too, were Catholic militants in exile. Secondary sources; 2 tables, 41 notes.   L. W. Van Wyk

1537. Sanchez, Armand J. and Wagner, Roland M. CONTINUITY AND CHANGE IN THE MAYFAIR BARRIOS OF EAST SAN JOSE. *San José Studies 1979 5(2): 6-20.* Traces the development of the Mayfair barrio area of East San Jose during 1777-1975, noting the degeneration of an integral community into one of social fragmentation, ethnic intermixture, and transient population, and the concurrent growth in politicization due to the Chicanismo movement of the 1960's.

1538. Simon, Daniel T. MEXICAN REPATRIATION IN EAST CHICAGO, INDIANA. *J. of Ethnic Studies 1974 2(2): 11-23.* By the late 1920's East Chicago, Indiana, had a 10% Mexican minority, and Inland Steel in that city was "the largest single employer of Mexican labor" in the United States. White residents resented the Mexicans, who occupied the lowest socioeconomic positions. At least a third of the city's population was on relief by 1932, including half of the Mexicans. Relief agencies began programs of repatriation which involved a degree of coercion. Since Mexicans were the newest and least established immigrant group and had a poor record of seeking citizenship, they were most vulnerable. The local American Legion Post 266 took the leading role in removal, under Russell F. Robinson and Paul E. Kelly. Conditions were created to make it easier for Mexicans to accept repatriation than get relief funds. Specially scheduled nonstop trains took 1,032 Mexicans to Laredo, Texas, from East Chicago. While the people were well-treated generally, the whole movement illustrates the appeal of the simplistic solution for the Depression, the mistake that it could be solved at the local level, and the increased ethnic tensions brought by the 1930's. Based on primary and secondary works; 43 notes.   G. J. Bobango

Asians

1539. Buck, Craig. IN SPITE OF THE FENCE. *Westways 1976 68(6): 42-45.* Discusses anti-Chinese feelings in San Francisco following the building of the railroad by Charles Crocker's coolie labor gangs; examines immigration restrictions urged by Denis Kearney.

1540. Castillo, Adelaida. FILIPINO MIGRANTS IN SAN DIEGO 1900-1946. *J. of San Diego Hist. 1976 22(3): 26-35.*

1541. Chu, Yung-Deh Richard. CHINESE SECRET SOCIETIES IN AMERICA: A HISTORICAL SURVEY. *Asian Profile [Hong Kong] 1973 1(1): 21-38.* Examines the history of Chinese tong societies in the United States. These organizations had their origins in the Hung-men societies organized in China to overthrow the Manchu rulers. The first wave of Chinese immigration to America came in the 1850's and the 1860's during the Gold Rush and the building of the transcontinental railroad, and following the defeat of the Taiping rebels. The great majority of these Chinese were men who had virtually no family life and who turned to gambling, opium, and prostitution. When Irish mobs burned their residences and all levels of government imposed prejudicial laws

against them, these Chinese immigrants turned to their secret societies. In the decades following 1870 many Chinese moved from California to the metropolitan areas of America and organized new tongs. Their identification with the anti-Manchu organizations in China continued, although their activities centered on local issues in America. In the years following World War II immigration and other restrictive laws have been amended and Chinese immigration has markedly increased. In New York City the Chinese population increased from 6,000 in the pre-World War II period to 12,000 in 1954, 30,000 in 1967, and 60,000 by 1972, with more than 100,000 in the greater New York metropolitan area. This new immigration has been not of single individuals but of urban families. Tongs have continued to provide assistance and protection for numbers of newly arrived Chinese. Based on interviews and secondary sources; 70 notes.
S. H. Frank

1542. Chun-Hoon, Lowell. [HISTORY OF AN AMERICAN CHINATOWN]. *Harvard Educ. R. 1975 45(1): 119-126.* Review article on Victor G. and Brett de Bary Nee's *Longtime Californ': A Documentary History of an American Chinatown* (New York: Pantheon, 1973).
S

1543. Dillon, Richard H. LOUIS J. STELLMAN'S CHINATOWN. *Am. West 1978 15(1): 38-53.* California journalist Louis J. Stellman (d. 1961) became a gifted photographer of considerable technical skill. He was fascinated with San Francisco's Chinatown. He devoted his expertise to the preservation on film of the metamorphosis of the colorful and exotic society into one that borrowed heavily from the Caucasian in appearance. The 1906 earthquake, the 1911 Chinese revolution, and World War I hastened the transformation. Stellman's efforts constitute a pictorial documentary history. 26 illus.
D. L. Smith

1544. Estes, Donald H. BEFORE THE WAR: THE JAPANESE IN SAN DIEGO. *J. of San Diego Hist. 1978 24(4): 425-455.* Describes daily life in the Japanese community in San Diego, 1880's-1942, including its involvement in business, agriculture, and fishing, its religious practices, and its social problems until the evacuation to the Poston, Arizona, relocation center.

1545. Kingston, Maxine Hong. SAN FRANCISCO'S CHINATOWN. *Am. Heritage 1978 30(1): 36-47.* Photographs by Arnold Genthe are shown and analyzed. Genthe's photos were taken between 1895 and 1906, and reflect Chinatown on the verge of change. The author questions the assumptions behind some of the photographic captions. 15 illus.
J. F. Paul

1546. Law, Eileen and Ken, Sally. A STUDY OF THE CHINESE COMMUNITY. *Richmond County Hist. 1973 5(2): 23-43.* Chinese first arrived in Augusta in 1873 to work on a local canal construction project. After completion of the canal a number of Chinese workers remained to become the nucleus of Augusta's Chinese community. By the turn of the century a majority of the local Chinese population had entered the grocery and laundry businesses. In 1970 more than 1,500 Orientals lived in Augusta. One of six articles in this issue on Augusta. Based on interviews with the local Chinese population and on published secondary sources; 77 notes.
H. R. Grant

1547. Light, Ivan. FROM RACKETEERS TO RESTAURANTEURS. *Mankind 1976 5(10): 8-10, 52-53.* Between 1865 and 1920 American Chinatowns were centers of gambling, prostitution, and narcotics, attracting many whites as well as Chinese, especially to houses of prostitution. After 1890 middle-class white tourists began to discover Chinatown and sought vicarious pleasures through touring dens of vice. The result was that vice waned and the tourist business began to flourish in these areas.
N. Lederer

1548. Light, Ivan. FROM VICE DISTRICT TO TOURIST ATTRACTION: THE MORAL CAREER OF AMERICAN CHINATOWNS, 1880-1940. *Pacific Hist. Rev. 1974 43(3): 367-394.* A study of the steps by which the Chinatowns were able to completely change their images from centers of vice, depravity, and filth to places which are clean, orderly, and attractive to tourists. There arose a mutual incompatibility between those Chinese merchants interested in developing tourism and the underworld gangs (tongs) interested in maintaining vice resorts. The merchants were finally victorious in the contest, and the tongs ultimately lent their support to commerce. 114 notes.
R. V. Ritter

1549. Light, Ivan and Wong, Charles Choy. PROTEST OR WORK: DILEMMAS OF THE TOURIST INDUSTRY IN AMERICAN CHINATOWNS. *Am. J. of Sociol. 1975 80(6): 1342-1368.* In the competition between institutional and cultural theories of American poverty, the success of Chinese-Americans has provided telling evidence for the cultural view. However, recent events in American Chinatowns show that the cultural interpretation was overdrawn. The dependence of Chinatowns upon the tourist industry has constrained residents to suppress visible manifestations of social unrest and pathology in order to attract customers. The inability of the tourist industry to keep pace with recent immigration is now bringing these previously suppressed manifestations to the surface. The Chinatown case suggests that the industrial division of labor will prove a fruitful place to seek a synthesis of cultural and institutional theories.
J

1550. Lyman, Stanford M. CONFLICT AND THE WEB OF GROUP AFFILIATION IN SAN FRANCISCO'S CHINATOWN, 1850-1910. *Pacific Hist. Rev. 1974 43(4): 473-499.* An analysis of the structure and operation of San Francisco's 19th-century Chinatown. "It was a complex, highly organized community whose associations were not in constant harmony with one another. Most important were the activities of the secret societies, whose competition for control of vice and whose political battles were fierce.... They acted as a further barrier to contacts with the larger society, placed many individuals under cross-pressures of loyalty to the several associations whose membership overlapped, and fastened on the community a pattern of antagonistic cooperation. Thus intra-community conflict and cooperation acted together to help isolate the Chinese from the metropolis." 111 notes.
R. V. Ritter

1551. MacPhail, Elizabeth C. SAN DIEGO'S CHINESE MISSION. *J. of San Diego Hist. 1977 23(2): 8-21.* The Chinese Mission School in San Diego offered an English education to Chinese members of the community, as well as a place of recreation and religious instruction, 1885-1960.

1552. McEvoy, Arthur F. IN PLACES MEN REJECT: CHINESE FISHERMEN AT SAN DIEGO, 1870-1893. *J. of San Diego Hist. 1977 23(4): 12-24.* Discusses Chinese Americans in the fishing industry operating out of San Diego, California, 1870-93.

1553. Rossi, Jean. LEE BING: FOUNDER OF CALIFORNIA'S HISTORICAL TOWN OF LOCKE. *Pacific Hist. 1976 20(4): 351-366.* Lee Bing came from China as a teenager, settled in California and became a successful businessman. After a fire in Walnut Grove, Bing led the effort to build the Chinese town of Locke, 30 miles south of Sacramento. Based on an interview with Lee Ping about his father's life; 5 illus.
G. L. Olson

1554. Tanaka, Stefan. THE TOLEDO INCIDENT: THE DEPORTATION OF THE NIKKEI FROM AN OREGON MILL TOWN. *Pacific Northwest Q. 1978 69(3): 116-126.* During the mid-1920's the Pacific Spruce Corporation of Toledo, Oregon, began to import Japanese Americans for lumber mill work. Local white citizens established a nativist organization to stop the Oriental influx and this led to a riot during July 1925. Though the Japanese were driven from Toledo, they received financial compensation for damages a year later. Based on newspapers and interviews; map, 4 photos, 43 notes.
M. L. Tate

1555. Tipton, Gary P. MEN OUT OF CHINA: ORIGINS OF THE CHINESE COLONY IN PHOENIX. *J. of Arizona Hist. 1977 18(3): 341-356.* Chinese first came to Phoenix in 1872, to operate a laundry. The 100 who settled there after working on eastward construction of the Southern Pacific Railroad formed the nucleus of the future Chinatown. Legal restrictions and anti-Chinese prejudice kept the number low. By diligence, however, many continued to improve their economic situations and to eliminate discrimination. They wished to avoid the ghetto image of other groups, so Phoenix gradually lost its Chinatown. Today's Phoenix Chinese range from storekeepers and restaurant owners to scholars and professional men. They are still closely knit through numerous organizations. 2 illus., 27 notes.
D. L. Smith

1556. Tobier, Emanuel. THE NEW FACE OF CHINATOWN. *New York Affairs 1979 5(3): 66-76.* Gives a history of the Chinese in the United States since 1880, then discusses the current problems of New

York City's Chinatown in light of mass Chinese immigration to New York City during 1960-75.

1557. Wai-Jane, Char and Kai, Peggy. CHINESE MERCHANT-ADVENTURERS AND SUGAR MASTERS IN HAWAII: 1802-1852. *Hawaiian J. of Hist. 1974 8: 3-75*. Examines the operations of three Chinese stores in Honolulu and the settlement of Chinese in the village of Hilo before 1852. Histories of the three stores, Hungtai Co., Tyhune Store, and Samsing & Co., are given along with lists of their employees. Chronicles seven Chinese sugar merchants and growers belonging to the village of Hilo. All married Hawaiian women and remained permanently in Hawaii. Photos, maps, glossary.   R. N. Alvis

1558. Wong, Bernard. A COMPARATIVE STUDY OF ASSIMI-LATION OF THE CHINESE IN NEW YORK CITY AND LIMA, PERU. *Comparative Studies in Soc. and Hist. [Great Britain] 1978 20(3): 335-358*. Covers 1849-1976.

Others

1559. Ainsworth, Catherine Harris. POLISH-AMERICAN CHURCH LEGENDS. *New York Folklore Q. 1974 30(4): 286-294*. Church motifs are numerous in tales of immigrants from Poland who settled in Buffalo, New York.   S

1560. Anderson, Harry H. SCANDINAVIAN IMMIGRATION IN MILWAUKEE NATURALIZATION RECORDS. *Milwaukee Hist. 1978 1(1-2): 25-37*. Presents a recent survey of naturalization records of Norwegians, Swedes, and Danes in Milwaukee during 1837-1941 in a discussion of Scandinavian political involvement and community development in Milwaukee.

1561. Arndt, Karl J. R. GEORGE RAPP'S HARMONISTS AND THE BEGINNINGS OF NORWEGIAN MIGRATION TO AMER-ICA. *Western Pennsylvania Hist. Mag. 1977 60(3): 241-264*. Describes Norwegian immigrants in George Rapp's Harmony and New Harmony settlements in Pennsylvania, 1816-26, and their letters home to relatives, friends, and interested parties in Norway whom they encouraged to emigrate.

1562. Barclay, Morgan J. IMAGES OF TOLEDO'S GERMAN COMMUNITY, 1850-1890. *Northwest Ohio Q. 1973 45(4): 133-143*. Studies reactions of the local press to Germans, the largest foreign-born element in Toledo until 1920. Because Germans "Americanized" rather quickly, the local newspapers usually regarded them as praiseworthy. Germans were criticized only when they joined radical political movements and when the temperance movement was strong in Toledo. On these occasions the Germans were accused of trying to "Germanize" America and of undercutting American morals. 72 notes.
                                                                    W. F. Zornow

1563. Bardaglio, Peter W. ITALIAN IMMIGRANTS AND THE CATHOLIC CHURCH IN PROVIDENCE, 1890-1930. *Rhode Island Hist. 1975 34(2): 46-57*. The creation of national parishes was not always a success; animosities developed among Italian Americans in Providence, Rhode Island, 1890-1930, when the insensitivity of the Scalabrini order to the cultural traditions of southern Italians combined with their anti-clericalism and propensity for disorder to form a rift between northern and southern Italian immigrants in the community.

1564. Bilodeau, Therese. THE FRENCH IN HOLYOKE (1850-1900). *Hist. J. of Western Massachusetts 1974 3(1): 1-12*. Nicholas Proulx, one of the first French Canadians to migrate to Holyoke, recruited workers in Quebec. Management found them obedient, non-union workers whose life revolved around the Catholic Church. Primary and secondary sources; 3 illus., chart, 58 notes.   S. S. Sprague

1565. Blejwas, Stanislaus A. A POLISH COMMUNITY IN TRAN-SITION. *Polish Am. Studies 1977 34(1): 26-69*. This account of two parishes in New Britain, Connecticut, mirrors the development of hundreds of Polish parishes throughout the United States during 1890-1955, especially the acculturation and Americanization of the immigrant. Based on sources in English and Polish; 114 notes.   S. R. Pliska

1566. Blejwas, Stanislaus A. A POLISH COMMUNITY IN TRAN-SITION: THE EVOLUTION OF HOLY CROSS PARISH, NEW BRITAIN, CONNECTICUT. *Polish Am. Studies 1978 35(1-2): 23-53*. Discusses a Polish American parish in relation to assimilation and the pressure to Americanize. Since its beginnings in 1928, this parish has become Polish American and no longer strictly Polish. Polish and English primary and secondary sources; 69 notes.   S. R. Pliska

1567. Blow, David J. THE ESTABLISHMENT AND EROSION OF FRENCH-CANADIAN CULTURE IN WINOOSKI, VERMONT, 1867-1900. *Vermont Hist. 1975 43(1): 59-74*. In 1867, French-speaking natives of Quebec and their children comprised 49% of the 1,745 people in Winooski village, Vermont, a woolen mill town with a machine shop and 10 other small industries. Bishop Louis de Goësbriand appointed a young Canadian priest, Jean Fréderic Audet, in 1868. Supported by three lay councillors in a "fabrique" organized in 1873, he enlarged a parochial school, built the church of St. Francis Xavier, 1870-84, and presided over a francophone enclave with mutual aid societies and basically Democratic Party politics. The second generation gradually identified with anglophone Vermont rather than with Quebec. 41 notes.
                                                                T. D. S. Bassett

1568. Buczkowski, Claudia. SEVENTY YEARS OF THE PITASS DYNASTY. *Niagara Frontier 1977 24(3): 66-75*. John Pitass, a Catholic priest of Polish descent, was largely responsible for the success of Polonization in Buffalo's east side during 1890-1934.

1569. Burchell, R. A. THE GATHERING OF A COMMUNITY: THE BRITISH-BORN OF SAN FRANCISCO IN 1852 AND 1872. *J. of Am. Studies [Great Britain] 1976 10(3): 279-312*. Analyzes census and other official statistical data about the in-migration and out-migration of British-born persons to and from San Francisco during 1852-72. San Francisco tended to attract transient British-born people who soon moved elsewhere. The out-migration was partly that of persons who first entered the United States at San Francisco and then migrated to more eastward American cities. The available data disproves the view that out-migrants consisted chiefly of unskilled and poverty-ridden persons. Based on government documents and secondary sources; 12 tables, 29 notes.   H. T. Lovin

1570. Cannistraro, Philip V. FASCISM AND AMERICANS IN DE-TROIT, 1933-1935. *Int. Migration Rev. 1975 9(1): 29-40*. Explores the impact of Italian Fascism on Italian Americans in Detroit during 1933-35, including the specific questions of Fascism and anti-Fascism within the community and the more general internal dynamics of the community's sociopolitical integration.

1571. Carlsson, Sten and Barton, H. Arnold, transl. FROM MID-SWEDEN TO THE MIDWEST. *Swedish Pioneer Hist. Q. 1974 25(3-4): 193-207*. Describes rural-urban patterns of immigration by Swedes, 1850-1930. About 35% of the emigrants moved from Swedish to American farms, about one-third from rural Sweden to American cities, and another third from urban Sweden to urban America. The majority emigrated for economic reasons. Primary and secondary sources; 38 notes.
                                                                K. J. Puffer

1572. Carvalho, Joseph, III and Everett, Robert. STATISTICAL ANALYSIS OF SPRINGFIELD'S FRENCH CANADIANS (1870). *Hist. J. of Western Massachusetts 1974 3(1): 59-63*. Ninety-six percent of all Canadians in Ward 8, in Springfield, Massachusetts, worked in cotton mills. A majority were under the age of 21 and less than one-eighth of those over 21 were US citizens. They were a church centered group. Primary and secondary sources; 4 tables, 17 notes.
                                                                S. S. Sprague

1573. Chadwick, Bruce A. and White, Lynn C. CORRELATES OF LENGTH OF URBAN RESIDENCE AMONG THE SPOKANE IN-DIANS. *Human Organization 1973 32(1): 9-16*. Uses interviews with 39 Spokan Indians residing in the city of Spokane and 50 residing on a reservation to explore the relationship of length of urban residence to eight hypothesized variables. Reviews the literature related to urban adjustment by American Indians. Noneconomic factors were more important in determining length of urban residence than economic ones, in contrast to other studies, indicating that traditional variables may not be

adequate to explain Indian migration and adjustment to the city. Abstracts in English, French, and Spanish. 3 tables, 3 notes, biblio.
E. S. Johnson

1574. Christopher, Andrew Mark. ARMENIANS IN CITIES. *Armenian Rev. 1975 28(3): 272-282.* Discusses the development of Armenian culture which led the Armenians to occupy cities in the USSR and the United States, including their involvement in trade, the Christianization of Armenia, and the forced emigration since the 16th century.

1575. Corzine, Jay and Dabrowski, Irene. THE ETHNIC FACTOR AND NEIGHBORHOOD STABILITY: THE CZECHS IN SOULARD AND SOUTH ST. LOUIS. *Missouri Hist. Soc. Bull. 1977 33(2): 87-93.* Surveys the migration of Czechs to St. Louis since 1848 and traces their dispersion to various parts of the city since 1930. Although geographically dispersed, they continued to value their "ethnic identity" and have maintained it through social organizations which focused on social affairs, gymnastics, and studying European languages. Based on secondary sources; photo, 2 illus., 13 notes.
H. T. Lovin

1576. Crawford, Michael J. INDIANS, YANKEES, AND THE MEETINGHOUSE DISPUTE OF NATICK, MASSACHUSETTS, 1743-1800. *New England Hist. and Geneal. Register 1978 132(Oct): 278-292.* The Natick meetinghouse dispute refutes the "peaceable kingdoms" thesis of 18th-century Massachusetts towns. The General Court intervened to protect the rights of "praying" Indians who built the original meetinghouse and to effect a compromise between the southern faction who lived near the meetinghouse and those who wanted it relocated in the center of town. An eventual solution came three-quarters of a century later as a result of land annexation and trading, a decline in the Indian population and other population shifts. 25 notes.
A. E. Huff

1577. Davis, Susan G. OLD-FASHIONED POLISH WEDDINGS IN UTICA, NEW YORK. *New York Folklore 1978 4(1-4): 89-102.* The traditional folk rites surrounding an old-fashioned Polish wedding in Utica, New York, would last for days; describes antecedents of the wedding, the actual ceremony, and the subsequent festivities, 1900-40's.

1578. DeRose, Christine A. INSIDE "LITTLE ITALY": ITALIAN IMMIGRANTS IN DENVER. *Colorado Mag. 1977 54(3): 277-293.* Italian immigrant history in Denver is characterized by economic difficulties, discrimination, and a lack of internal cohesiveness. Mentions the establishment of numerous societies, Catholic activities, the Angelo Noce-Columbus Day and the Father Mariano Lepore controversies, crime, poverty, business, labor, neighborhoods, and the entrance of several Italian Americans into influential positions in Denver society. Primary and secondary sources; 11 illus., 43 notes.
D. A. Hartford

1579. Drzewieniecki, Walter M. and Drzewieniecki-Abugattas, Joanna E. PUBLIC LIBRARY SERVICE TO AMERICAN ETHNICS: THE POLISH COMMUNITY ON THE NIAGARA FRONTIER, NEW YORK. *J. of Lib. Hist., Phil. and Comparative Librarianship 1974 9(2): 120-137.* Chronicles the development of the Polish community around Buffalo, New York, from the latter half of the 19th century to 1974, and the parallel specific service of the Buffalo Public Library to Polish-Americans following 1901. Largely the story of the William Ives Branch (renamed for Francis E. Fronczak in 1965), the record shows that the "public libraries in Buffalo and the surrounding area have done an excellent job of responding to the needs of the Polish ethnic community and in several cases have gone out of their way to arouse interest and educate." Based on primary sources; 2 illus., 69 notes.
D. G. Davis, Jr.

1580. Early, Frances H. MOBILITY POTENTIAL AND THE QUALITY OF LIFE IN WORKING-CLASS LOWELL, MASSACHUSETTS: THE FRENCH CANADIANS CA. 1870. *Labour [Canada] 1977 2: 214-228.* Preliminary findings for a social history of French Canadians in Lowell (1870-1900) seem to indicate the "inaccuracy of the romantic portrayal of the French-Canadian experience" in New England. In 1870, at least, life for Lowell's French Canadians was "rather grim." Most were in working-class occupations; there was no Quebec-born lay *classe dirigeante;* the vast majority of children 10 and over held jobs outside the home. Evidence suggests French Canadians "would be slow to experience occupational mobility;" neither was it possible for most to

accumulate savings for a return to Quebec. Census reports, other primary and secondary sources; 44 notes.
W. A. Kearns

1581. Ekman, Ernst. WETTERMAN AND THE SCANDINAVIAN SOCIETY OF SAN FRANCISCO. *Swedish Pioneer Hist. Q. 1974 25(2): 87-102.* August Wetterman (1828-1917) came to California during the Gold Rush. His history of the Scandinavian Society now is in the state library. Karl Wilhelm Lübeck was the leader in forming *Det Scandinaviska Sällskapet i San Francisco,* a social and benevolent organization. Based on Wetterman's *History and Review of the Scandinavian Society of San Francisco* (San Francisco: 1970) and on primary and secondary sources; 34 notes.
K. J. Puffer

1582. Elder, Harris J. HENRY KAMP AND CULTURAL PLURALISM IN OKLAHOMA CITY. *Chronicles of Oklahoma 1977 55(1): 78-92.* In 1906, young Henry Kamp left Germany for St. Louis, Missouri, where his family had previously settled. Intent on setting up his own business, he found bustling Oklahoma City a promising location, and within a few years had established a lucrative grocery business. Kamp, a strong supporter of immigrants maintaining ties with their cultural heritage, helped found the Germania German Club and the German Evangelical and Reform Church in Oklahoma City. Anti-German sentiment during both world wars forced many German Americans to leave the area, but the Kamp family remained and helped strengthen the German American community. Based on primary and secondary sources; 4 photos, 49 notes.
M. L. Tate

1583. Eliopoulos, George T. GREEK IMMIGRANTS IN SPRINGFIELD, 1884-1944. *Hist. J. of Western Massachusetts 1977 5(2): 46-56.* Greeks began arriving to the Springfield, Massachusetts, area in 1884. Among the earliest arrivals was Eleftherios Pilalas, who went to work in the candy industry which was one of the earliest sources of employment for those who followed him to the area. During 1900-12, many Greek clubs and St. George's church were established. After 1912 factionalism related to Greek politics disrupted the unity of the community. Illus., notes.
W. H. Mulligan, Jr.

1584. Ellis, Ann W. THE GREEK COMMUNITY IN ATLANTA, 1900-1923. *Georgia Hist. Q. 1974 58(4): 400-408.* The Atlanta Greek community originated around the turn of the century when Greek immigrants came to the United States because of agricultural problems in Greece. They settled in northern cities primarily, but some came south to an existing small Greek community. They became involved in business and quickly became prosperous. They developed social clubs, churches, and schools. Their desire to preserve something of their cultural heritage was sometimes a source of conflict with others. Primary and secondary sources; 36 notes.
M. R. Gillam

1585. Ericson, C. George SWEDISH RADIO SERVICES IN CHICAGO. *Swedish Pioneer Hist. Q. 1973 24(3): 157-162.* Station WIBO in Chicago broadcast Swedish services each Sunday from 1926 to 1933. Professor Gustav Edwards' Swedish broadcast over WHFC continued for almost 15 years. Interdenominational services were broadcast over various stations from 1933 to 1962. Visiting ministers and singers from Sweden participated in the broadcasts. Lists ministers who served as committee members and announcers. A Swedish service sponsored by the Salvation Army started in 1964. 2 photos.
K. J. Puffer

1586. Fairbanks, Charles H. FROM MISSIONARY TO MESTIZO: CHANGING CULTURE OF EIGHTEENTH-CENTURY ST. AUGUSTINE. *Eighteenth-Century Florida and the Caribbean 1976: 88-99.* Two St. Augustine houses recently were excavated. The abundance of Indian ceramics and the study of food remains indicate the gradual absorption of Indians into Spanish society as food providers, craftsmen, or soldiers' wives. The chronic shortage of all supplies also must have stimulated the use of Indian pottery. The increased amount of British ceramics supports this view and indicates the penetrating power of British trade. Seminole artifacts and military equipment were conspicuously lacking. Biblio.
W. R. Hively

1587. Gould, Charles F. PORTLAND ITALIANS, 1880-1920. *Oregon Hist. Q. 1976 77(3): 239-260.* Discusses Italian immigration to Oregon in the late 19th and early 20th centuries. The process was gradual because the majority of immigrants settled in eastern cities. Still, a moderate trickle seeped into Oregon, especially Portland. Antiforeign feeling was high, but the Italians stayed and eventually left a mark on the communities in which they lived. They captured the truck farming and produce facets of the economy, then moved into other occupations as their means and education improved. World War I and a congressional law forbidding illiterate immigrants brought the flow to an abrupt end. 16 photos, 78 notes.   V. L. Human

1588. Gumina, Deanna Paoli. *CONNAZIONALI, STEN-TERELLO, AND FARFARIELLO*: ITALIAN VARIETY THE-ATER IN SAN FRANCISCO. *California Hist. Q. 1975 54(1): 27-36.* For two decades following 1905, San Francisco's Italian colony enjoyed the presentation of variety theater on a more or less regular basis. Antonietta Pisanelli, a theater impresario and noted singer herself, opened a succession of theaters which brought opera, comedy, arias, and character sketches to the Italian community at a reasonable price. Italian theater enjoyed its heyday in the years prior to World War I. Comic characters such as the *Stenterello*, an Italian provincial caricature, and the *Farfariello*, a caricature of the Italian immigrant, entertained the community. As assimilation increased, Italian variety theater could no longer be profitably sustained through regular performances. By 1925 the era of the Italian variety theater had ended, superseded several years later by a permanent opera house which owed its roots to the Italian community's devotion to opera. Primary and secondary sources; illus., 16 notes.
                                                        A. Hoffman

1589. Gwinn, Erna Ottl. THE LIEDERKRANZ IN LOUISVILLE, 1848-1877. *Filson Club Hist. Q. 1975 49(3): 276-290.* The Liederkranz, a German-American music society, played an important role in the integration of the German community into the life of Louisville, Kentucky. Started in 1848, the organization was strengthened by the arrival of German liberals after the failure of the revolution of that year. By the mid-1850's the Germans formed one-third of Louisville's population and faced nativist hostility organized in the Know-Nothing movement. Violent demonstrations forced the chorus to suppress publicity of its performances that included works by composer Richard Wagner. The Liederkranz suspended operations during the Civil War, but afterward grew rapidly and was able to build a large auditorium by 1873. An audience of 8,000 that attended a performance in 1877 demonstrated that the Germans were an accepted part of Louisville life. Based on German language histories and Louisville newspapers; 71 notes.
                                                        G. B. McKinney

1590. Hesse-Biber, Sharlene. THE ETHNIC GHETTO AS PRIVATE WELFARE: A CASE STUDY OF SOUTHERN ITALIAN IMMIGRATION TO THE UNITED STATES, 1880-1914. *Urban and Social Change Rev. 1979 12(2): 9-15.* Discusses the organization of immigrant communities in the United States, particularly the social and economic assistance networks, including the Padrone system, formed among southern Italian immigrants to the United States between 1880 and 1914.

1591. Janta, Alexander. TWO DOCUMENTS ON POLISH-AMERICAN ETHNIC HISTORY. *Polish R. 1974 19(2): 3-23.* THE VIRGINIA VENTURE: A PROPOSED POLISH COLONY WHICH WENT WRONG, *pp. 3-19.* Gives documents and biographical data on Joseph Smolinski, who initiated the short-lived Polish Emigration Land Company in the 1860's. THE PHILADELPHIA INQUIRY: A CHAPTER IN EARLY STUDIES OF THE POLISH IMMIGRANT IN THE USA, *pp. 20-23.* Describes a field study on Polish assimilation in Philadelphia, from a John Dewey seminar at Columbia University, 1917-18.   S

1592. Jorgensen, Joseph G. A CENTURY OF POLITICAL ECONOMIC EFFECTS ON AMERICAN INDIAN SOCIETY, 1880-1980. *J. of Ethnic Studies 1978 6(3): 1-82.* Advances the metropolis-satellite economic model to explain the domestic dependency of the Native American. The growth of the metropolis caused the expropriation and exploitation of Indian resources, the domination of Indian lives, and the development of a vast welfare bureaucracy of administer Indian affairs. The "ideological motor" driving a century of Indian-white relations has always been a desire to transform Indian culture to white culture, to integrate Indians to a white Protestant ethos. The massive benefits given to major agricultural and mining producers by the federal government clearly deprived Indians from control of natural resources, making them

inevitable wards of the state. Only by maintaining their own collectivity ethic have Indians been able to sustain themselves. Primary and secondary sources; 6 tables, 13 notes, biblio.   G. J. Bobango

1593. Kennedy, Albert J. "THE PROVINCIALS," WITH AN INTRODUCTION BY ALAN A. BROOKES. *Acadiensis [Canada] 1975 4(2): 85-101.* During the mid-1910's at Boston's South End settlement house, social worker Albert J. Kennedy wrote a description of Canadians who had fled to Boston from the Atlantic Provinces because of economic conditions. Titled "The Provincials," the description is opinionated and dated but still offers numerous insights. The provincials were largely unskilled or semi-skilled, fairly religious, and generally had high morals. Although the first generation was clannish and uninterested in politics or unions, the second generation soon became Americanized. Based on published secondary materials, United States and Canadian census reports; 9 notes.   E. A. Churchill

1594. Khungian, Toros B. ORIGINS AND DEVELOPMENT OF THE FRESNO ARMENIAN COMMUNITY TO THE 1918 YEAR. *Armenian Rev. 1979 31(2): 157-173.* Traces the development of the Armenian community of Fresno, California, from 1881, when the first Armenian came to Fresno, to 1918.

1595. Kuzniewski, Anthony J. MILWAUKEE'S POLES, 1866-1918: THE RISE AND FALL OF A MODEL COMMUNITY. *Milwaukee Hist. 1978 1(1-2): 13-24.* Discusses the Polish immigrant community in Milwaukee during 1866-1918, including economic and political successes, community pride, and optimism.

1596. Lopata, Helena Znaniecki. WIDOWHOOD IN POLONIA. *Polish Am. Studies 1977 34(2): 7-23.* Describes the lot of widows of city workers, 1880-1977.   S. R. Pliska

1597. López, Adalberto. VITO MARCANTONIO: AN ITALIAN-AMERICAN'S DEFENSE OF PUERTO RICO AND PUERTO RICANS. *Caribbean Rev. 1979 8(1): 16-21.* Recounts the political career of Vito Marcantonio (1902-54), Congressman from East Harlem, emphasizing those events that related to the radical Republican's interest in the well-being of his own Puerto Rican constituents in New York as well as to his support of independence for Puerto Rico.

1598. Lotchin, Roger W. ETHNIC CONTINUITIES IN SICILIAN BUFFALO. *Rev. in Am. Hist. 1978 6(3): 373-378.* Review article prompted by Virginia Yans-McLaughlin's *Family and Community: Italian Immigrants in Buffalo, 1880-1930* (Ithaca, N.Y.: Cornell U. Pr., 1971, 1977).

1599. Magarian, Horen Henry. THE FOUNDING AND ESTABLISHMENT OF THE ARMENIAN COMMUNITY OF RICHMOND, VIRGINIA. *Armenian Rev. 1975 28(3): 265-271.* Gives a history of the early Armenian community in Richmond, Virginia 1887-1910, based on the recollections of the author's uncle Manuel Vranian, a member of the original party.

1600. Magnaghi, Russell M. THE ROLE OF INDIAN SLAVERY IN COLONIAL ST. LOUIS. *Missouri Hist. Soc. Bull. 1975 31(4, Part 1): 264-272.* Reviews the process of enslaving Indians in Missouri during the period when the region was alternately ruled by Spain and France. After control of the area passed to the United States, Indian slavery became unpopular and finally was ruled illegal by the Missouri Supreme Court in the case of *Marguerite* v. *Chouteau* (1834). Based on archival materials and secondary sources; 42 notes.   H. T. Lovin

1601. Martinelli, Phylis Cancilla. ITALY IN PHOENIX. *J. of Arizona Hist. 1977 18(3): 319-340.* Italians began to come to Phoenix in the 1880's. Their loosely knit community was small, and in many respects unlike Little Italies in other parts of the country. There were no Italian neighborhoods of stores, restaurants, churches, and newspapers. Yet practical concerns and their need to socialize with other Italians brought them together into clubs and other organizations. Uniquely, the Phoenix Italian American community has two distinguishable groups: one established by immigrants from Italy, and the other composed of migrants from within the United States. 4 illus., 61 notes.   D. L. Smith

1602. Mormino, Gary Ross　OVER HERE: ST. LOUIS ITALO-AMERICANS AND THE FIRST WORLD WAR. *Missouri Hist. Soc. Bull. 1973 30(1): 44-53.* At the onset of World War I Italo-Americans in St. Louis mostly lived in tight ethnic pockets and adhered closely to Old World practices. Wartime seemed to demand that "hyphenate" groups accept 100% Americanization; Italo-Americans responded favorably. Wartime pressures speeded the processes of assimilation and accultura-tion to American society. However, Italo-Americans suffered an unascer-tained degree of "psychological damage" as a result of pressure to "reject the culture and values of one's parents." Based on newspaper sources and documents in the Woodrow Wilson and George Creel papers; 32 notes.
　　　　　　　　　　　　　　　　　　　　　　　　　　　H. T. Lovin

1603. O'Connell, Lucille.　TRAVELERS' AID FOR POLISH IMMI-GRANT WOMEN. *Polish Am. Studies 1974 31(1): 15-19.* The Travel-ers' Aid Society was formed in 1907 to protect rural American and immigrant girls who came to New York City alone. After immigration had peaked, and during the depression of the 1930's, the Society took care primarily of native American girls, eventually evolving into an organiza-tion to help all travelers in all major cities of the United States. Gives examples of assistance rendered Polish immigrant girls. 15 notes.
　　　　　　　　　　　　　　　　　　　　　　　　　　　S. R. Pliska

1604. Olsson, Nils William.　THE SWEDISH BROTHERS: AN EX-PERIMENT IN IMMIGRANT MUTUAL AID. *Swedish Pioneer Hist. Q. 1974 25(3-4): 220-229.* Swedish immigrants to the United States formed mutual aid societies in the 19th century. In Minneapolis, *Svenska Bröderna* was formed in 1876; its early history was recorded by Alfred Söderström, who is quoted. Recently the membership roster for 1876 to 1888 was discovered, with statistical analyses of the information given in the entries producing valuable insights. Based on primary sources; 3 tables, 2 notes.　　　　　　　　　　　　　　　　　　K. J. Puffer

1605. Parot, Joseph.　THE RACIAL DILEMMA IN CHICAGO'S POLISH NEIGHBORHOODS, 1920-1970. *Polish Am. Studies 1975 32(2): 27-37.* Analyzes the continuing conflict in the minds of Chicago's Polonia: the ideology of neighborhood maintenance versus the ideology of escape. Because the Poles are the last ethnics to be moving into the suburbs they find themselves in the area into which blacks are steadily moving. The Poles persist in the racial frontier because of a cultural concentration. They saturate their original areas of settlement with churches, schools, hospitals, clubs, and then find it difficult to disassoci-ate themselves from this heavy economic, social, and religious investment.
　　　　　　　　　　　　　　　　　　　　　　　　　　　S. R. Pliska

1606. Passi, Michael M.　MYTH AS HISTORY, HISTORY AS MYTH: FAMILY AND CHURCH AMONG ITALO-AMERICANS. *J. of Ethnic Studies 1975 3(2): 97-103.* Reviews Silvano Tomasi's *Piety and Power: The Role of the Italian Parishes in the New York Metropoli-tan Area, 1880-1930* (1975), Richard Gambino's *Blood of My Blood: The Dilemma of the Italian Americans* (1974), and Carla Bianco's *The Two Rosetos* (1974). All three attempt to explain the nature of Italian-Ameri-can society. Tomasi finds the core to be the Catholic Church and its ethnic parishes, Gambino sees the family system as the central element, and Bianco tackles the issue by comparing Rosetos, Italy, with its namesake in Pennsylvania. Of these three finds Bianco's to be the most illuminating and promising. 14 notes.　　　　　　　　　　　　　　　T. W. Smith

1607. Patterson, G. James.　GREEK MEN IN A COFFEE HOUSE IN DENVER: FIVE LIFE HISTORIES. *J. of the Hellenic Diaspora 1976 3(2): 27-37.* Presents life histories of five Greek Americans in Den-ver, Colorado, emphasizing problems in cultural assimilation in the 20th century.

1608. Penney, Sherry and Willenkin, Roberta.　DUTCH WOMEN IN COLONIAL ALBANY: LIBERATION AND RETREAT. *Halve-Maen 1977 52(1): 9-10, 14-15, (2): 7-8, 15.* Part I. Chronicles the social status and activities of Dutch women in Albany, New York, 1600's-1790. Part II. Examines their legal treatment, including criminal punishment and inheritance matters, 1648-1700.

1609. Pier, Andrew V.　A HISTORY OF SLOVAKS IN CLEVE-LAND, OHIO. *Jednota Ann. Furdek 1978 17: 32-36.* Discusses the assimilation of Slovak Americans in Cleveland, Ohio, 1930's-50's.

1610. Pozzetta, George E.　IMMIGRANTS AND RADICALS IN TAMPA, FLORIDA. *Florida Hist. Q. 1979 57(3): 337-348.* Reprints five articles from Italian-language newspapers revealing a rich cultural and intellectual life for Italian immigrants in Tampa, Florida. The immi-grant workers were influenced in Sicily by "worker leagues." Such sotial-istic or anacharistic concepts were influencial in the development of Tampa. Primary and secondary sources; 14 notes.　　　N. A. Kuntz

1611. Radzialowski, Thaddeus.　THE VIEW FROM A POLISH GHETTO. SOME OBSERVATIONS ON THE FIRST ONE HUN-DRED YEARS IN DETROIT. *Ethnicity 1974 1(2): 125-150.* In the 1870's Polish immigrants built St. Albertus Church on the east side of Detroit and later St. Casimir to the west. The parishes have each been socially self-contained and much feeling exists for them. The Poles see black advancements as threatening their jobs, homes, communities, and churches, while a symbiotic relationship exists with the Jews. Political competition with blacks has been great, but a new Polish pride and determination to fight discrimination and exclusion has recently arisen. 15 notes.　　　　　　　　　　　　　　　　　　　　　E. Barkan

1612. Seaman, William M.　THE GERMANS OF WHEELING. *Upper Ohio Valley Hist. Rev. 1979 8(2): 21-27; 9(1): 26-30.* Part I. Discusses German Americans of Wheeling, West Virginia, from the late 17th century, when the first wave of immigrants arrived from Europe, to 1917. Part II. Discusses beer brewing and families involved in that indus-try, 1840's-1910's.

1613. Sesplaukis, Alfonsas.　LITHUANIANS IN UPTON SIN-CLAIR'S *THE JUNGLE. Lituanus 1977 23(2): 24-31.* Lithuanians were chosen as the main characters in *The Jungle* because they were the major ethnic group working in the Chicago stockyards at the time the novel was written. The characters do not embody the true Lithuanian character but represent stereotypes. Sinclair sought to bring about social justice and his Lithuanian characters were a means to that end.
　　　　　　　　　　　　　　　　　　　　　　　　K. N. T. Crowther

1614. Seyersted, Per.　THE INDIAN IN KNICKERBOCKER'S NEW AMSTERDAM. *Indian Historian 1974 7(3): 14-28.* Discusses the image of Indians in New Amsterdam projected by Washington Irving in his *Knickerbocker's History of New York* (1809).　　　　　　S

1615. Siemankowski, Francis T.　THE MAKING OF THE POLISH AMERICAN COMMUNITY: SLOAN, NEW YORK AS A CASE STUDY. *Polish Am. Studies 1977 34(2): 56-67.* Discusses a small Pol-ish community on the outskirts of Buffalo, 1873-1977. Mentions immi-grant adjustment, promotion of homogeneity, the declining influence of the parish school, and inability to perpetuate the Polish language. Con-cludes that Polish Americans will continue to survive as an ethnic group because of a "pride in family, church, community and country." 10 notes.
　　　　　　　　　　　　　　　　　　　　　　　　　　　S. R. Pliska

1616. Sorrell, Richard S.　SENTINELLE AFFAIR (1924-1929)—RELIGION AND MILITANT SURVIVANCE IN WOONSOCKET, RHODE ISLAND. *Rhode Island Hist. 1977 36(3): 67-79.* Discusses French Canadians in Woonsocket; examines problems of assimilation, religion, and nationalism. Based on the author's doctoral dissertation; 8 illus., 14 notes.　　　　　　　　　　　　　　　　　　P. J. Coleman

1617. Stout, Robert Joe.　CAN'T YOU SEE THAT WE'RE HOME? *Westways 1977 69(11): 24-27.* Discusses the immigration of Italians to the San Francisco area of California, 1890-1977.

1618. Susel, Rudolph M.　ASPECTS OF THE SLOVENE COMMU-NITY IN CLEVELAND, OHIO. *Papers in Slovene Studies 1977: 64-72.* Slovene immigrants who settled in the Cleveland area during 1880-1924 were mostly of agrarian background, albeit with some degree of literacy in Slovene. By the end of the 1890's these immigrants were numerous enough to be able to support specifically Slovene economic, cultural, and religious organizations that were instrumental in easing the transitional and cultural shock problems. Eventually a hybrid culture emerged which was enormously satisfying to most of its members, al-though American-born descendants accepted Slovene cultural traits and attitudes only to a limited degree.　　　　　　　　　T. Hočevar

1619. Tolzmann, Don Henrich. THE ST. LOUIS FREE CONGRE-GATION LIBRARY: A STUDY OF GERMAN-AMERICAN READ-ING INTERESTS. *Missouri Hist. Rev. 1976 70(2): 142-161.* The St. Louis Free Congregation was typical of most congregations of free thinkers. It was formed by immigrants who desired a free society without church and state interference. Many such congregations established schools, singing societies, and libraries. The circulation records of the Free Congregation Library are still available at the Missouri Historical Society in St. Louis. These records provide a valuable guide for an understanding of German-American reading interests in the 19th century. They refute any notion that there was a cultural lag between Germans in America and Europe. Based on primary and secondary sources; illus., 40 notes.   W. F. Zornow

1620. Virtanen, Keijo. THE INFLUENCE OF THE AUTOMO-TIVE INDUSTRY ON THE ETHNIC PICTURE OF DETROIT, MICHIGAN, 1900-1940. *U. of Turku. Inst. of General Hist. Publ. [Finland] 1977 9: 71-88.* During 1910-30 the automotive industry drew the labor it needed largely from outside areas rather than from the immigrant communities already established in Detroit. The foreign-born population underwent its most vigorous increase at this time. Social activity among the Finns living in Detroit, despite its late start, developed fairly vigorously; its inception was clearly bound up with the progress of the automotive industry. Statistics show that half of the Finns who had arrived in the United States after 1916 and resided in Detroit had made the journey from Finland straight to Detroit, the others having first lived in some other locality in the United States. Map, fig., 5 tables, 36 notes.
                                                                       E. P. Stickney

1621. Webster, Janice Reiff. DOMESTICATION AND AMERI-CANIZATION: SCANDINAVIAN WOMEN IN SEATTLE, 1888 TO 1900. *J. of Urban Hist. 1978 4(3): 275-290.* Two major processes affected Scandinavian women in Seattle, domestication and Americanization. These changes were stimulated by the fact that Seattle during this period was a boom town and that most Scandinavians had already been partly acculturated during earlier eastern residences. Table, 51 notes.
                                                                       T. W. Smith

1622. Weinberg, Daniel E. ETHNIC IDENTITY IN INDUSTRIAL CLEVELAND: THE HUNGARIANS 1900-1920. *Ohio Hist. 1977 86(3): 171-186.* Studies Hungarian immigrants in Cleveland, Ohio, in the early 20th century, the social and economic values, immediate and future goals, education, job selection, and behavior of the immigrants. Interviews 43 Hungarians who lived in the original Hungarian settlements in Cleveland, and supplements findings with traditional historical resources. Primary and secondary sources; illus., 38 notes, note on methodology.
                                                                       N. Summers

1623. White, Stephen A. THE ARICHAT FRENCHMEN IN GLOUCESTER: PROBLEMS OF IDENTIFICATION AND IDEN-TITY. *New England Hist. and Genealogical Register 1977 131(April): 83-99.* Describes the settlement of the Acadians of the Arichat region of Nova Scotia in Gloucester, Massachusetts, in the late 19th century. Gloucester had always been dominated by the fishing industry, and the winter fishery of Georges Banks was just started when the Acadians, already skilled fishermen, began to arrive. Determining how many Acadians arrived and when is difficult, but a strong desire to "become American," as well as cultural and religious prejudice, caused the Frenchmen to change their names (LeBlanc to White, Fogeron to Smith) and to work diligently to banish any trace of a French accent. The high mortality on the seas encouraged intermarriage. In addition, the absence of French priests made interaction with other non-French—and later non-Catholic —groups almost inevitable, eventually contributing to the breakdown of a sense of community. Based on oral interviews and on primary and secondary sources; 3 charts, 80 notes.   S. L. Patterson

1624. Winner, Irene Portis. ETHNICITY AMONG URBAN SLO-VENE VILLAGERS IN CLEVELAND, OHIO. *Papers in Slovene Studies 1977: 51-63.* Examines social networks and informal groups that link immigrants who came to the Cleveland area from a traditional Slovene village (Zerovnica) with other Slovene Americans. Their relations to the nation of origin, Slovenia, are also discussed. Based on oral histories and written sources. Ref.   T. Hočevar

1625. Winner, Irene Portis. THE QUESTION OF CULTURAL POINT OF VIEW IN DETERMINING THE BOUNDARIES OF ETHNIC UNITS: SLOVENE VILLAGERS IN THE CLEVELAND, OHIO AREA. *Papers in Slovene Studies 1977: 73-82.* Research among Slovene Americans in Cleveland shows evidence of regional identification based on Slovene regions (e.g., Lower, Upper, Inner Carniola) or even smaller units (e.g., Lož Valley). Another approach in defining a significant minimal ethnic unit hinges on identification with distinct regions and micro-regions in the United States. There may be considerable correspondence between these units because immigrants from the same area tended to settle near each other. Based on oral history and written sources; ref.
                                                                       T. Hočevar

1626. Zellick, Anna. THE MEN FROM BRIBIR. *Montana 1978 28(1): 44-55.* Stonemasons from Bribir, Croatia, came to Lewistown, Montana, in the early 1900's to construct buildings in the growing community. The Croatian population in Lewistown grew to more than 373 by 1915, as the masons and their families became part of the community. Labor problems and ethnic prejudice occasionally marred working conditions. Major construction projects on which Croatians worked included schools, a town reservoir, the Carnegie Library, the Masonic temple, and St. Joseph's Hospital. Workmen quarried the stone locally, made mortar, operated lime kilns, and handled all facets of construction. Families which followed the first stonemasons formed the basis for an active Croatian community, unified by religious beliefs and language. The former Bribir residents adopted many American customs while retaining native traditions; most became naturalized citizens and their descendents remain in the Lewistown area. Based on secondary sources, interviews, Lewistown city records, and personal reminiscences; 7 illus., biblio.
                                                                       R. C. Myers

Religion

1627. Arndt, Karl J. R. THE STRANGE AND WONDERFUL NEW WORLD OF GEORGE RAPP AND HIS HARMONY SOCI-ETY. *Western Pennsylvania Hist. Mag. 1974 57(2): 141-166.* Examines the development of religious theory in George Rapp's collective religious settlement, the Harmony Society established in Economy, Pennsylvania.
                                                                       S

1628. Arrington, Leonard J. and Larkin, Melvin A. THE LOGAN TABERNACLE AND TEMPLE. *Utah Hist. Q. 1973 41(3): 301-314.* Each Mormon community historically underwent three stages, concluding in the construction of a mammoth temple. The temple took years to build and symbolized the unity of the Mormon community. Logan, however, underwent this process in less than three decades. Founded in 1859, Logan began the construction of its tabernacle early in 1865. The edifice was dedicated in 1891. The towers of this five-story structure soar to 165 and 170 feet, and can be seen throughout the Cache Valley, a "reminder of the omnipresence of eternity." Based on primary and secondary sources; plan, 4 photos, 17 notes.   H. S. Marks

1629. Baker, Frank. JOHN WESLEY'S LAST VISIT TO CHARLESTON. *South Carolina Hist. Mag. 1977 78(4): 265-271.* Chronicles Methodist minister John Wesley's final mission to Charleston, 1737.

1630. Baker, James T. THE BATTLE OF ELIZABETH CITY: CHRIST AND ANTICHRIST IN NORTH CAROLINA. *North Carolina Hist. Rev. 1977 54(4): 393-408.* Discusses the battle in 1924 between Elizabeth City newspaper editor William O. Saunders (1886-1940) and Kentucky evangelist Mordecai F. Ham (1877-1961). Ham, well-known for his argumentative style, was derided by Saunders during the opening weeks of a huge revival in Elizabeth City. The controversy changed from Ham's accusations against Chicago Jewish philanthropist Julius Rosenwald to Saunders's Modernism vs. Ham's Fundamentalism. Based on Saunders' editorials, Ham's published prayers, newspapers, biographies, and reminiscences; 9 illus., 49 notes.   T. L. Savitt

1631. Berenbaum, May. "THE GREATEST SHOW THAT EVER CAME TO TOWN": AN ACCOUNT OF THE BILLY SUNDAY CRUSADE IN BUFFALO, NEW YORK, JANUARY 27-MARCH 25, 1917. *Niagara Frontier 1975 22(3): 54-67.*

1632. Blumin, Stuart M. CHURCH AND COMMUNITY: A CASE STUDY OF LAY LEADERSHIP IN NINETEENTH-CENTURY AMERICA. *New York Hist. 1975 56(4): 393-408.* A statistical study of the socioeconomic status, residential tenure, and family background of the leaders of 19th-century Kingston (New York) Protestant and Jewish churches, and their secular leadership in the Kingston community. Although church leaders "comprised a significant minority of the community's secular leadership," the underlying characteristic of community leadership was "membership in a fairly wide and fairly diverse commercial class." Illus., 7 tables, 9 notes.   R. N. Lokken

1633. Bratton, Mary J. JOHN JASPER OF RICHMOND: FROM SLAVE PREACHER TO COMMUNITY LEADER. *Virginia Cavalcade 1979 29(1): 32-39.* Black minister John Jasper (1812-1901), who was born a slave on a Virginia plantation, joined the First African Baptist Church in 1842, and gained national attention in 1878 when he preached a sermon called, "The Sun Do Move."

1634. Broadbent, Charles D. A BRIEF PILGRIMAGE: PLYMOUTH CHURCH OF ROCHESTER. *Rochester Hist. 1978 40(4): 1-22.* The Congregational Plymouth Church of Rochester existed from 1853 to 1954 and significantly influenced Rochester's religious community during 1853-1904.

1635. Buczek, Daniel S. POLISH AMERICAN PRIESTS AND THE AMERICAN CATHOLIC HIERARCHY: A VIEW FROM THE TWENTIES. *Polish Am. Studies 1976 33(1): 34-43.* Discusses the conflict between Catholic Irish American bishops and the Polish American clergy during the 1920's. Treats only the dioceses of Buffalo, Brooklyn, and Pittsburgh, but states that a revolutionary attitude pervaded the minds of Polish Americans in other dioceses as well. The bishops advocated Americanization in the Polish parishes, but the Poles called this "Irishism." Irish bishops insisted upon English as the language of instruction in all parochial schools, and the Poles fought for bilingualism. The Poles won the battle during the 1920's only to lose the campaign during the 1940's because of the gradual disappearance of the Polish language among the second and third generations. Based on primary and secondary sources; 24 notes.   S. R. Pliska

1636. Campbell, George Duncan. FATHER TAYLOR, THE SEAMEN'S APOSTLE. *Methodist Hist. 1977 15(4): 251-260.* Discusses Edward Thompson Taylor (1793-1871), sailor turned Methodist preacher, who preached to thousands of seamen from the pulpit of the Seamen's Bethel in Boston (1833-68). 2 illus., 37 notes.   H. L. Calkin

1637. Christopher, Louise. HENRY WHITEFIELD, CIRCUIT RIDER. *Chicago Hist. 1976 5(1): 2-11.* Discusses the evangelism done for the Methodist Church by Henry Whitefield; presents an image of Chicago daily life, 1833-71.

1638. Clark, David L. "MIRACLES FOR A DIME": FROM CHAUTAUQUA TENT TO RADIO STATION WITH SISTER AIMEE. *California History 1978-79 57(4): 354-363.* Assesses the activities and accomplishments of Los Angeles evangelist Aimee Semple McPherson. Sister Aimee provided a transition from traditional evangelism to modern use of the media. She was the first woman to hold an FCC broadcaster's license; her station KFSG was the first religious radio station in the United States. Her services employed theatrical devices, including props and stage sets. More traditional Protestant ministers resented her style, but her Angelus Temple proved an irresistible attraction to the lonely, the newly arrived, and the poor in health, who seemed to comprise most of the Los Angeles population during 1920's-40's. Her work in Depression relief has been underrated. The success of her church was somewhat flawed by her personal foibles, but the appeal of her evangelical style deserves acknowledgement for its pioneering use of "modern methods of communication for religious purposes." 13 photos.   A. Hoffman

1639. Clarke, Erskine. AN EXPERIMENT IN PATERNALISM: PRESBYTERIANS AND SLAVES IN CHARLESTON, SOUTH CAROLINA. *J. of Presbyterian Hist. 1975 53(3): 223-238.* Discusses the attempts of the Presbyterian Church in Charleston in the mid-1840's to establish a separate congregation for Negroes under the administration

and pastoral leadership of whites. The intention was good, but the fact that the churches were white-administered and no attempt was made to alleviate the problem of slavery still kept the blacks in a state of paternalism, in spite of the black congregation's numerical success. Based on primary and secondary sources; 38 notes.   H. M. Parker, Jr.

1640. Copeland, Robert M. THE REFORMED PRESBYTERIAN THEOLOGICAL SEMINARY IN CINCINNATI, 1845-1849. *Cincinnati Hist. Soc. Bull. 1973 31(3): 151-163.* Discusses the antislavery sentiments of the Reformed Presbyterian Church and how they were reflected in the early integration of the Reformed Presbyterian Theological Seminary.

1641. Crews, Clyde F. HALLOWED GROUND: THE CATHEDRAL OF THE ASSUMPTION IN LOUISVILLE HISTORY. *Filson Club. Hist. Q. 1977 51(3): 249-261.* Sketches the role of the Cathedral of the Assumption in the life of the Louisville, Kentucky, Catholic community since 1852. Based on newspapers and church records; 50 notes.   G. B. McKinney

1642. Cunningham, Patrick. IRISH CATHOLICS IN A YANKEE TOWN: A REPORT ABOUT BRATTLEBORO, 1847-1898. *Vermont Hist. 1976 44(4): 189-197.* Provides information from Patrick Cunningham about a Catholic parish in Brattleboro, Vermont, during 1847-98. The report was summarized in Bishop John Stephen Michaud's contribution to *The history of the Catholic Church in the New England States* (1899). Gives names, numbers, and dates for arrivals, pastors, places of worship, large contributors, baptisms, marriages, schools, and cemetery. Communicants worked mostly on the railroad or in the Estey organ factory. Notes "the intolerant spirit of a dominant party. . . . old prejudices now happily dead" which made nearly all Catholics Democrats. Based on the original report in Diocesan Archives.

T. D. S. Bassett

1643. Dahl, Curtis. THREE FATHERS, THREE SONS. *Methodist Hist. 1977 15(4): 234-250.* Enoch Mudge (1776-1850) was a Methodist minister and first chaplain of the Seamen's Bethel of New Bedford, Massachusetts. He was a friend of Edward Thompson Taylor, Methodist chaplain of the Seamen's Bethel in Boston and perhaps the model for Herman Melville's Father Mapple in *Moby Dick*. Mudge was at the Bethel for 12 years and greatly influenced the seamen. 2 illus., 36 notes.   H. L. Calkin

1644. DeMille, George E. THE EPISCOPATE OF BISHOP OLDHAM. *Hist. Mag. of the Protestant Episcopal Church 1977 46(1): 37-56.* Discusses the bishopric of the Reverend George Ashton Oldham of the Episcopal Diocese of Albany, New York, during 1922-47. His tenure embraced the Great Depression and World War II. In spite of these difficult times, he developed a strong administration, enlarged program of the diocese, developed new parishes, and increased contributions to the numerous causes of the church. In addition to his administrative acumen, Oldham was a preacher of the first rank. When he retired, he left the Diocese of Albany in a very strong financial position.

H. M. Parker, Jr.

1645. Doepke, Dale K. THE WESTERN EXAMINER: A CHRONICLE OF ATHEISM IN THE WEST. *Missouri Hist. Soc. Bull. 1973 30(1): 29-43.* The *Western Examiner,* published in St. Louis 1834-35, provoked "lively and sometimes acrimonious debate." The Mechanics Benevolent Society may have sponsored this controversial magazine. John Bobb appears to have been the original promoter and editor. He and other contributors indulged their freethinking views on religious and political topics. Conservative citizens and the "Christian establishment" were outraged. Based on the *Western Examiner* and other St. Louis publications; 23 notes.   H. T. Lovin

1646. Driedger, Leo; Fretz, J. Winfred; and Smucker, Donovan E. A TALE OF TWO STRATEGIES: MENNONITES IN CHICAGO AND WINNIPEG. *Mennonite Q. Rev. 1978 52(4): 294-311.* Mennonites do not seem to survive in the large urban areas, but do well in rural settings. Studies the mission strategies used in Chicago and Winnipeg with an analysis of the results of each and a comparison of the two in detail. 20 notes.   E. E. Eminhizer

1647. Dunn, Ethel and Dunn, Stephen P. RELIGION AND ETH-NICITY: THE CASE OF THE AMERICAN MOLOKANS. *Ethnicity 1977 4(4): 370-379.* An analysis of the nature and activities of the Molokans in California, a small group of religious dissidents who emigrated from Russia around the turn of the century. The San Francisco colony remains, though it has grown but little and has not successfully protected its neighborhood from outside penetration. Certainly the Molokans are no longer peasants, but they can hardly be called an ethnic group. Rather they are simply an offshoot religious sect, whose efforts to develop an ethnicity have largely failed.   V. L. Human

1648. Edgar, Irving I. THE EARLY SITES AND BEGINNINGS OF CONGREGATION BETH EL: THE MICHIGAN GRAND AVENUE SYNAGOGUE, 1859-1861. *Michigan Jewish Hist. 1973 13(1): 13-20.* Discusses the beginnings of Congregation Beth El in Detroit.
S

1649. Flynt, Wayne. RELIGION IN THE URBAN SOUTH: THE DIVIDED RELIGIOUS MIND OF BIRMINGHAM, 1900-1930. *Alabama Rev. 1977 30(2): 108-134.* Social Gospel activism at the turn of the century brought a number of pastors, priests, and rabbis together in overcoming Birmingham's image of a violent, sin city. Considerable success attended their efforts by World War I. Social work and public welfare were advanced, crime reduced, and prostitution controlled. Latent and powerful anti-Catholic and anti-Semitic elements gained ascendancy in the 1920's. Having turned to secular morality, religious leaders opened the door to the politicization of religion and institutional affairs. Primary and secondary sources; 73 notes.   J. F. Vivian

1650. Franch, Michael S. THE CONGREGATIONAL COMMUNITY IN THE CHANGING CITY, 1840-70. *Maryland Hist. Mag. 1976 71(3): 367-380.* The relocation of white, English-language Protestant churches from Baltimore's central city area to newer outlying neighborhoods was due not only to a desire for more select surroundings, but also to urban demographic and economic changes and "the financial imperatives of the American system of voluntary support for religious institutions." Membership in Protestant congregations depended not on geographic residency but on voluntary association: churches regardless of theology were "gathered" organizations. Congregational cohesion depended on whether a church was "pewed" or free-seat, on the social and ethnic homogeneity of the neighborhood, and on members' physical proximity to the church. As economic change allowed members to buy new residences outside the core city area, the "downtown" churches faced bankruptcy and commercial encroachment on their properties. Thus "daughter" churches were founded in the new residential areas, while older core churches came to serve lower-status groups. Primary and secondary sources; 6 maps, 2 tables, 29 notes.   G. J. Bobango

1651. Gavigan, Kathleen. THE RISE AND FALL OF PARISH COHESIVENESS IN PHILADELPHIA. *Records of the Am. Catholic Hist. Soc. of Philadelphia 1975 86(1-4): 107-131.* A special characteristic of the Catholic Church in Philadelphia, Pennsylvania, traditionally has been a strong identification with parish communities. This came about as a response to fear and insecurity, and the separation it provided created both strength and weakness for the Catholic community. Because, for many Catholics, the fears and insecurities have dissipated, the result is more vigorous participation in the community at large. 62 notes.
J. M. McCarthy

1652. Gerrard, Ginny. A HISTORY OF THE PROTESTANT EPISCOPAL CHURCH IN SHREVEPORT, LOUISIANA, 1839-1916. *North Louisiana Hist. Assoc. J. 1978 9(4): 193-203.* The Episcopal Church is the oldest Protestant Church in Louisiana and has the oldest congregation in Shreveport. Following a visit to northwestern Louisiana in 1838 by the young and newly-elected Bishop of Louisiana, Leonidas Polk, the first services were conducted in 1839. St. Paul's church was formally organized in 1845; its name was changed to St. Mark's in 1850. By 1916 the church had seen the services of 10 rectors and was the largest Episcopal church in Shreveport, thus fulfilling Polk's prophecy: "The place has a promising future." Based on the Polk Papers, Jesse duPont Library archives, University of the South, the Journal of the Diocese of Louisiana, files of St. Mark's church and secondary sources; 74 notes.
H. M. Parker, Jr.

1653. Gildrie, Richard P. CONTENTION IN SALEM: THE HIGGINSON-NICHOLET CONTROVERSY, 1672-1676. *Essex Inst. Hist. Collections 1977 113(2): 117-139.* The "spirit of contention" in Massachusetts towns in the late 17th century was connected to social change. In Salem, the hiring of Charles Nicholet in 1672 as an assistant to Reverend John Higginson (1616-1708) illustrates this point. Higginson advised the town to dismiss Nicholet after his trial year, but the majority of townspeople refused. Subsequently, the question of Nicholet's retention, fired by doctrinal and financial disagreements, developed into a struggle for control over the town's religious institution. The battle spread to the Quarterly Court and the Massachusetts General Court which supported the town's leaders in retaining Nicholet but criticized their behavior. Primary and secondary sources; 49 notes.
R. S. Sliwoski

1654. Guelzo, Allen C. GLORIA DEI: OLD SWEDES' CHURCH. *Early Am. Life. 1977 8(3): 18, 64-66.* The Gloria Dei Congregation was a group of Swedish immigrants who built Old Swedes' Church in Philadelphia, Pennsylvania during 1638-98.

1655. Haebler, Peter. HOLYOKE'S FRENCH-CANADIAN COMMUNITY IN TURMOIL: THE ROLE OF THE CHURCH IN ASSIMILATION 1869-1887. *Hist. J. of Western Massachusetts 1979 7(1): 5-21.* Examines the conflict between Father Andre B. Dufresne and his Catholic parishioners in the Holyoke, Massachusetts, French-Canadian parish over his continuation of traditional practices. The extent of the conflict over Dufresne's conduct is an example of the speed with which many French Canadians had changed their outlook on the role of the curé in their lives. 2 illus., 40 notes.   W. H. Mulligan, Jr.

1656. Hall, Robert L. TALLAHASSEE'S BLACK CHURCHES, 1865-1885. *Florida Hist. Q. 1979 58(2): 185-196.* Analyzes the establishment of black Protestant churches in Tallahassee, Florida, after the Civil War. Churches aided blacks in airing social and political problems, restrained violent protest, and acted as "agencies of social control for the larger community." The churches performed an accommodating role to the expectations of the white community. Based on local and regional church records and other primary material; 53 notes.
N. A. Kuntz

1657. Hendrickson, Walter B. A CHURCH ON THE PRAIRIE: THE FOUNDING AND EARLY YEARS OF TRINITY IN JACKSONVILLE, ILLINOIS—1832-1838. *Hist. Mag. of the Protestant Episcopal Church 1975 44(1): 5-21.* Trinity Church, founded in 1832, was the first Episcopal congregation organized in Illinois. With no minister, laymen elected wardens and vestrymen. Details the first edifice, the formation of the Illinois Diocese in 1835, and the ministry of Rev. John Batchelder, Trinity Church's missionary pastor, who served 1833-38. The Episcopal Church had difficulties on a frontier largely dominated by Presbyterians, Congregationalists, Methodists, and other Protestant groups. Based largely on primary sources, including the Parish Register of Trinity Church and the Convention Journal; 56 notes.
H. M. Parker, Jr.

1658. Hewitt, John H. NEW YORK'S BLACK EPISCOPALIANS: IN THE BEGINNING, 1704-1722. *Afro-Americans in New York Life and Hist. 1979 3(1): 9-22.* Elias Neau, a lay member of the Church of England's Society for the Propagation of the Gospel, taught and preached to Negroes in New York City.

1659. Hill, Marvin S. MORMON RELIGION IN NAUVOO: SOME REFLECTIONS. *Utah Hist. Q. 1976 44(2): 170-180.* In comparison with so much that seems secular and worldly, was there much that was religious at Nauvoo, Illinois? Erwin B. Goodenough defines religion as initially a quest for security. Peace, security, the end of social conflict are religious desires. Many things traditionally thought of as secular were not, but were designed to promote social control and social stability. Everything that occurred at Nauvoo of a social or political nature was to Mormons essentially religious. Primary and secondary sources; 2 illus., 49 notes.   J. L. Hazelton

1660. Hitchcock, James. SECULAR CLERGY IN 19TH CENTURY AMERICA: A DIOCESAN PROFILE. *Records of the Am. Catholic Hist. Soc. of Philadelphia 1977 88(1-4): 31-62.* The history of the St. Louis archdiocesan clergy during 1841-99 provides a model by which comparative studies of other dioceses can be made, with a view to achieving a historical-sociological understanding of the American priesthood during the critical decades of immigration and gradual Americanization. 15 tables, 136 notes.   J. M. McCarthy

1661. Holder, Ray. METHODIST BEGINNINGS IN NEW ORLEANS 1813-1814. *Louisiana Hist. 1977 18(2): 171-187.* Under orders from the Methodist General Conferences of 1812, itinerant preacher William Winans endeavored to establish Methodism in New Orleans, Louisiana, in 1813-14 with a school and church. He faced considerable opposition in New Orleans, and he believed he did not accomplish much. Not until 1825 did "the continuous history of Methodism in New Orleans" begin. Based on Winans' unfinished autobiography and secondary sources; 80 notes.   R. L. Woodward, Jr.

1662. Hussey, M. Edmund. THE 1878 FINANCIAL FAILURE OF ARCHBISHOP PURCELL. *Cincinnati Hist. Soc. Bull. 1978 36(1): 7-41.* Discusses the final years of the tenure of John Baptist Purcell, Catholic bishop of Cincinnati, 1833-83, and the investigations and legal entanglements brought on by the failure of his brother's banking enterprise.

1663. Janis, Ralph. ETHNIC MIXTURE AND THE PERSISTENCE OF CULTURAL PLURALISM IN THE CHURCH COMMUNITIES OF DETROIT, 1880-1940. *Mid-America 1979 61(2): 99-115.* In 1880 all church officers were male and tended to come from the middle and upper classes. Church membership was homogeneous ethnically (86% to 98%). The economic growth of Detroit changed this considerably by 1940. For example, while Lutheran parishes were uniformly German in 1880, they were less than 70% German in 1940. Other social factors involved in Detroit during this period, though, did not lead to the "melting pot" that might be expected. The cultural and social changes were silent, and other melting pot barriers arose when older ones dropped. 45 notes.   J. M. Lee

1664. Jones, Ronald W. CHRISTIAN SOCIAL ACTION AND THE EPISCOPAL CHURCH IN ST. LOUIS, MO.: 1880-1920. *Hist. Mag. of the Protestant Episcopal Church 1976 45(4): 253-274.* Analyzes movements toward social reform emanating from such American Episcopalians as Henry Codman Potter, George C. Hodges, and Philo W. Sprague, and says the Episcopal Diocese of Missouri, much like the Episcopal Church across the nation, was doing little more than "nibbling at the crust of the social reform pie." Only in a few St. Louis ministries was there any activity. The church chose to minister to individuals through institutions rather than to lead actively as an agent for social change. Based on secondary materials; 78 notes, biblio.
                    H. M. Parker, Jr.

1665. Kemper, Donald J. CATHOLIC INTEGRATION IN ST. LOUIS, 1935-1947. *Missouri Hist. Rev. 1978 73(1): 1-22.* In 1947 the Archbishop of St. Louis, Joseph E. Ritter, ordered the admission of black children to local parochial schools, an order that provoked serious resistance from parents. The success of the order came in the wake of a battle going on during the latter years of Archbishop John J. Glennon. Through the Midwest Clergy Conference on Negro Matters, some young priests had set the stage by trying to desegregate Webster College and St. Louis University. It is likely that Rome arranged the liberal Ritter's assignment to speed integration. Primary and secondary sources; illus., 58 notes.
                    W. F. Zornow

1666. Kleber, John E. "PAGAN BOB" ON THE COMSTOCK: ROBERT G. INGERSOLL VISITS VIRGINIA CITY. *Nevada Hist. Soc. Q. 1979 22(4): 243-253.* A Gilded Age orator who regularly denounced ecclesiastical orthodoxy and organized religions, Robert Ingersoll (1833-99) twice lectured at Virginia City in 1877 to appreciative audiences. The orator flattered his listeners, praising them for sufficient educational attainments to appreciate ideas and the desirability of high wages in Comstock Lode mines. Moreover, these Nevadans tolerated Ingersoll's freethinking partly because they valued free speech; and they sensed the orator's basic beliefs in "God and nature" that Ingersoll's critics had not recognized. Based on newspaper and secondary sources; 31 notes.   H. T. Lovin

1667. Kramer, William M. and Clar, Reva. EMANUEL SCHREIBER: LOS ANGELES' FIRST REFORM RABBI, 1885-1889. *Western States Jewish Hist Q. 1977 9(4): 354-370; 1977 10(1): 38-55.* Part I. Emanuel Schreiber left his native Germany in 1881. After serving synagogues in Mobile (Alabama) and Denver (Colorado) he was invited to Los Angeles' Congregation B'nai B'rith in 1885. Some of the traditionalists were offended by Schreiber's radical-Reform policies but the majority of the congregation supported him. He was active in community affairs; most significant was his role in the formation of the Associated Charities which developed into the present United Crusade. San Francisco journalist Isidore N. Choynski critized Rabbi Schreiber's accumulation of wealth from astute land speculation. Based on newspapers and other published primary and secondary sources; 68 notes. Part II. Religious and social activities at Congregation B'nai B'rith were enhanced by the participation of the rabbi's wife. Reform-Orthodox tensions decreased as Rabbi Schreiber impressed the Jewish community with his considerable knowledge of religious phenomena. Schreiber's relations with the gentile community were excellent; Christian ministers appreciated his learning and invited him to speak to their congregations. Despite his esteemed position in Los Angeles, Schreiber's ambitions caused him to leave. He served at synagogues in Arkansas, Washington, Ohio, and Illinois, 1889-99. He was minister to Chicago's Congregation Emanu-El from 1899 to 1906 when he moved to the east coast. In 1920 he returned to Los Angeles, where he remained until his death in 1932. Based on newspapers and other published primary and secondary sources; illus., 65 notes.   B. S. Porter

1668. Kramer, William M. and Stern, Norton B. A SEARCH FOR THE FIRST SYNAGOGUE IN THE GOLDEN WEST. *Western States Jewish Hist. Q. 1974 7(1): 3-20.* In 1851, the rivalry between German and Polish Jews in San Francisco led to the founding of two separate synagogues within the city. The German synagogue is Temple Emanu-El and the Polish is Temple Sherith Israel. In 1900, Rabbi Jacob Voorsanger of Emanu-El tried to prove that his temple was the first, but he used a misdated lease as his main proof. Research shows that both congregations were founded on 6 April 1851. Primary and secondary sources; photo, 56 notes.   R. A. Garfinkle

1669. Kremm, Thomas W. MEASURING RELIGIOUS PREFERENCES IN NINETEENTH-CENTURY URBAN AREAS. *Hist. Methods Newsletter 1975 8(4): 137-141.* Uses the population of Cleveland, Ohio in 1860 to discover mid-19th-century religious preferences in areas that contained a large number of Catholics. 7 notes.
                    D. K. Pickens

1670. LaFontaine, Charles V. APOSTLES TO MEATPACKERS: THE ASSOCIATE MISSION OF OMAHA, NEBRASKA, 1891-1902. *Hist. Mag. of the Protestant Episcopal Church 1978 47(3): 333-353.* An associate mission was composed of a small group of unmarried Episcopal priests who, for a given time, pledged to live a community life and devote themselves to missionary work under the guidance and direction of a bishop. Describes such an associate mission in Omaha, 1891-1902. During its brief existence it ministered to 15 congregations, baptized 981, confirmed almost 700, constructed 8 churches and 2 guild halls and founded one parish and four missions. Its work was in three basic areas: working with the poor, operating a parochial school, and preaching. Mission activity died out largely because of an inability to acquire a satisfactory sense of identification. Based largely on an article by John Albert Williams and issues of *The Pulpit and the Cross;* 68 notes.
                    H. M. Parker, Jr.

1671. Leonard, Henry B. ETHNIC CONFLICT AND EPISCOPAL POWER: THE DIOCESE OF CLEVELAND, 1847-1870. *Catholic Hist. Rev. 1976 62(3): 388-407.* In the Diocese of Cleveland the competing socioreligious desires of immigrant groups were frequently divisive. Louis Amadeus Rappe, Cleveland's first bishop, was a staunch Americanizer and an authoritarian administrator who resisted the demands of German and Irish Catholics for separate parishes and schools served by priests of their own nationality, stirred ethnic antagonisms, and raised a fundamental question concerning the proper limits to episcopal authority. By 1870 the diocese had become so disrupted by the issues of ethnicity and authority that Bishop Rappe was forced to resign his office.   A

1672. Levesque, George A. INHERENT REFORMERS—INHER-ITED ORTHODOXY: BLACK BAPTISTS IN BOSTON, 1800-1873. *J. of Negro Hist. 1975 60(4): 491-519.* Describes the early development of the black Baptist movement in Boston in the 1800's, including the foundation of a separate church in 1805 under the leadership of Thomas Paul and Scipio Dalton. Overt discrimination was not the principal motive for starting a new church, inasmuch as the parent churches financed and assisted the African offshoot. The black movement grew from a religious revival and an expansion of the black community, forced increasingly to live and work in one particular area. Considers how the new church was drawn into politics and the movement for social reform. 3 tables, 36 notes.   C. A. McNeill

1673. Lewis, Theodore. TOURO SYNAGOGUE, NEWPORT, R. I. *Newport Hist. 1975 48(3): 281-320.* Offers a history of the presence of Jews in Newport, Rhode Island, 1658-1963, and the synagogue built by them, eventuating in the construction of the Touro Synagogue, 1759. 3 reproductions, 19 photos, appendix.

1674. Lucas, Paul R. THE CHURCH AND THE CITY: CONGRE-GATIONALISM IN MINNEAPOLIS, 1850-1890. *Minnesota Hist. 1974 44(2): 55-69.* Traces the history of three Congregational churches in Minneapolis, Minnesota, and their individual commitments to the social gospel. Based on primary sources; 11 illus., 56 notes.   S

1675. Luckingham, Bradford. RELIGION IN EARLY SAN FRAN-CISCO. *Pacific Historian 1973 17(4): 56-73.* Traces the development of various religious associations in San Francisco during the 1850's.   S

1676. Luebke, Frederick C. CHURCH HISTORY FROM THE BOTTOM UP. *Rev. in Am. Hist. 1976 4(1): 68-72.* Review article prompted by Jay P. Dolan's *The Immigrant Church: New York's Irish and German Catholics, 1815-1865* (Baltimore, Maryland: Johns Hopkins U. Pr., 1975) which discusses the social aspects of religious establishment among ethnic groups in New York City.

1677. Luker, Ralph E. RELIGION AND SOCIAL CONTROL IN THE NINETEENTH-CENTURY AMERICAN CITY. *J. of Urban Hist. 1976 2(3): 363-368.* In earlier years, historians assumed that clergymen and religiously aroused laypeople forged and led reform movements because it was their innate nature to do good and help their fellow man. Current literature, such as in Nathan L. Huggins's *Protestants Against Poverty: Boston's War on Poverty, 1870-1900*, David J. Pivar's *Purity Crusade: Sexual Morality and Social Control, 1868-1900*, and Carroll Smith Rosenberg's *Religion and the Rise of the American City: The New York City Mission Movement, 1812-1870*, shows the religious reformers to be conservatives interested primarily in social control and the preservation of established moral and social values. Examines this social control thesis and the scholarly merits of the works reviewed. Concludes that 19th-century religious reform was not aimed simply at social control or social liberation but at striking a new balance between the two. 8 notes.   T. W. Smith

1678. Macnab, John B. BETHLEHEM CHAPEL: PRESBYTERI-ANS AND ITALIAN AMERICANS IN NEW YORK CITY. *J. of Presbyterian Hist. 1977 55(2): 145-160.* Presents the attempts of New York City Presbyterians, particularly the University Place Church, to minister to the needs of the mass numbers of Italian immigrants who moved into the Greenwich Village area at the turn of the century. The denomination as a whole was quite tardy in responding to the challenge which immigrants presented. Various kinds of programs, both religiously and secularly oriented, were undertaken to assist in Protestantizing and Americanizing the new immigrant. Though a couple of congregations were organized for the Italians, the formal ecclesiastical control remained in the hands of Anglo officials, in spite of a prediction that a strong ethnic church could result only if the people felt they were masters of their work. The hesitancy to turn complete control over to the Italians, coupled with the "caretaker paternalism" whereby the churches were supported by the Anglos, worked to hinder much Presbyterian growth among the Italians. Based on primary sources, including the archives of the First Presbyterian Church in the City of New York; illus., 47 notes.

H. M. Parker, Jr.

1679. Martin, Roger A. JOHN J. ZUBLY COMES TO AMERICA. *Georgia Hist. Q. 1977 61(2): 125-139.* Describes the early career of John Joachim Zubly, a Swiss immigrant who became an influential Presbyterian minister in the Savannah area during the colonial period. Primary and secondary sources; 62 notes.   G. R. Schroeder

1680. McBride, Paul. THE ITALIAN-AMERICANS AND THE CATHOLIC CHURCH: OLD AND NEW PERSPECTIVES. *Italian Americana 1975 1(2): 265-279.* Reviews Enrico C. Sartorio's *Social and Religious Life of Italians in America* (Clifton, New Jersey: Augustus M. Kelley, 1974) and Silvano Tomasi's *Piety and Power: The Role of the Italian Parishes in the New York Metropolitan Area* (New York: Center for Michigan Studies, 1975), and discusses problems of historical objectivity.   S

1681. McGuckin, Michael. THE LINCOLN CITY MISSION: A. J. CUDNEY AND SEVENTH-DAY ADVENTIST BEGINNINGS IN LINCOLN, NEBRASKA. *Adventist Heritage 1975 2(1): 24-34.* The dedicated evangelism of A. J. Cudney, led to the establishment of Seventh-Day Adventism in Lincoln, Nebraska, and the construction of two missions, 1885-87.

1682. Metz, Judith. 150 YEARS OF CARING: THE SISTERS OF CHARITY IN CINCINNATI. *Cincinnati Hist. Soc. Bull. 1979 37(3): 150-174.* Traces the history of the Sisters of Charity in Cincinnati since 1829, when Fanny Jordan, Victoria Fitzgerald, Beatrice Tyler, and Albina Levy arrived from the Sisters of Charity of St. Joseph in Emmitsburg, Maryland (the first religious community of women in the United States), to devote themselves to the education of children and care for the needy in Cincinnati.

1683. Moran, Gerald F. RELIGIOUS RENEWAL, PURITAN TRIBALISM, AND THE FAMILY IN SEVENTEENTH-CENTURY MILFORD, CONNECTICUT. *William and Mary Q. 1979 36(2): 236-254.* The First Church of Milford, Connecticut, has complete records going back to the 17th century, and hence provides a model study for answering many questions, such as those raised by Edmund S. Morgan concerning the whole social and religious context of a Puritan community. Structural restrictiveness actually did not restrain admissions to any large degree. Eventually, however, admissions did decline and the church became isolated from the community at large. In attempts to recapture its earlier vitality the church became increasingly exclusive. There appears to have been an inbred membership and a tribal spirit. Based on church records; 3 tables, graph, 53 notes.   H. M. Ward

1684. Newman, Harvey K. PIETY AND SEGREGATION: WHITE PROTESTANT ATTITUDES TOWARD BLACKS IN ATLANTA, 1865-1905. *Georgia Hist. Q. 1979 63(2): 238-251.* Following the Civil War, previously integrated Atlanta Protestant churches became segregated. In the interests of maintaining a social order with blacks at the bottom, white church members refused to cooperate with anything that might result in racial equality, even when suggested and exemplified by Bishop Gilbert Haven of the Methodist Episcopal Church. This paternalism and aloofness contributed to racial tensions which led to a tragic massacre in September 1906. Primary and secondary sources; 42 notes.

G. R. Schroeder

1685. Oates, Mary J. ORGANIZED VOLUNTARISM: THE CATHOLIC SISTERS IN MASSACHUSETTS, 1870-1940. *Am. Q. 1978 30(5): 652-680.* Discusses the social and religious forces which caused a much more rapid increase in the number of women in religious work in Boston as opposed to the number of men, and the relative position achieved. A major factor was that of need as emphases in education changed, both overall, and in relation to whether teaching boys or girls. However, they were paid about half what their male counterparts were paid, despite both having taken vows of poverty. It amounted essentially to their subsidizing the schools while having no control over the running of either school or convent. Although the teachers sometimes began with inadequate training, the lifetime commitment resulted in a consistent and steady development. Economic constraints in the women's communities resulted in limited social life, education, and outside contacts, these restrictions tightening in the same period in which men's restrictions were being lifted. 8 tables, 65 notes.   R. V. Ritter

1686. Ogasapian, John. LOWELL AND OLD SAINT ANNE'S: A STUDY IN NINETEENTH-CENTURY INDUSTRIAL-CHURCH RELATIONS. *Hist. Mag. of the Protestant Episcopal Church 1977 46(4): 381-396.* Gives a sociological, economic, and ecclesiastical description of the deteriorating relations of St. Anne's Episcopal parish with the textile industry in Lowell, Massachusetts. The church was at first the only congregation recognized by the mill in a "company" town. However other denominations entered the scene, and relations between the parish and the mill owners dissipated. After years of struggle the congregation finally obtained its corporate independence and control of its property. Much of the struggle between the church and the mill was during the ministry of the Reverend Theodore Edson. Secondary sources, with emphasis on Wilson Waters, *St. Anne's Church, Lowell, Massachusetts;* 20 notes.   H. M. Parker, Jr.

1687. Poethig, Richard P. URBAN/METROPOLITAN MISSION POLICIES: AN HISTORICAL OVERVIEW. *J. of Presbyterian Hist. 1979 57(3): 313-352.* The mission policy of the Presbyterian Church touching the urban area did not begin until 1869. The reason was the church's preoccupation with the frontier. The United Presbyterian Church of North America did not initiate an urban mission policy until 1905. When the two churches united in 1958 the new united church was thus able to build upon existing foundations, and moved into new urban programs—inner city parishes, industrial evangelism, racial problems, ethnic groups, etc. In more recent years, largely as the result of ecclesiastical reorganization, the urban work on a national level has declined, but the responsibility has been picked up by the lesser church judicatories. Based on minutes of the General Assembly and reports of the Board of National Missions; illus., 27 notes.   H. M. Parker, Jr.

1688. Rahill, Peter J. NEW LANGUAGE FOR ST. LOUIS CATHEDRAL. *Missouri Hist. Rev. 1975 69(4): 449-460.* At St. Louis Cathedral in 1818 Bishop Louis William Du Bourg prescribed that the sermons after Vespers should be in English. The practice was soon discontinued to avoid a conflict between older settlers who favored French, and the rapidly increasing number of American settlers who knew only English. Eventually in 1842 Bishop Richard Kenrick complained that French services decreased attendance and collections. He then had English sermons at all the Sunday Masses and restricted French to the talk following Sunday evening vespers. Based on primary and secondary sources; illus., 18 notes.   W. F. Zornow

1689. Ralph, Raymond M. THE CITY AND THE CHURCH: CATHOLIC BEGINNINGS IN NEWARK, 1840-1870. *New Jersey Hist. 1978 96(3-4): 105-118.* By the mid-19th century, reflecting the presence of Irish and German immigrants, Newark, New Jersey's Catholics constituted one of the city's largest religious groups. The church hierarchy had to contend with tensions between these two groups as parishes were established and churches constructed. Raising sufficient money to operate, confronting hostilities from the Protestant community, and dealing with problems involving the public schools were other concerns. The typical Catholic in Newark during the mid-19th century was a blue-collar worker who consciously retained his national characteristics. Based on the archives of the Archdiocese of Newark, church records, and directories and secondary sources; 9 illus., 32 notes.
                                              E. R. McKinstry

1690. Reilly, Timothy F. PARSON CLAPP OF NEW ORLEANS: ANTEBELLUM SOCIAL CRITIC, RELIGIOUS RADICAL, AND MEMBER OF THE ESTABLISHMENT. *Louisiana Hist. 1975 16(2): 167-191.* "Unitarianism in antebellum New Orleans was among the most distinctive religious forces in the Old South. The Church was founded and shepherded by Parson Theodore Clapp, a New England native and former Presbyterian who continually challenged sacred dictums of Christian orthodoxy." Arriving in New Orleans in 1822 and remaining until 1856, Clapp opposed revivalism and theological concepts involving the Trinity, everlasting punishment, and predestination. He defended slavery "because he recognized the supremacy of the large business class in New Orleans and the rest of the South. Such a compromise . . . entitled him to a position of social respectability. Clapp valued the propagation of his radical theology above everything else." Primary and secondary sources; 3 photos, 68 notes.   R. L. Woodward

1691. Roeber, Anthony Gregg. "HER MERCHANDIZE... SHALL BE HOLINESS TO THE LORD": THE PROGRESS AND DECLINE OF PURITAN GENTILITY AT THE BRATTLE STREET CHURCH, BOSTON, 1715-1745. *New England Hist. and Geneal. Register 1977 131: 175-194.* Examines the life and thought of Benjamin Coleman, pastor of Boston's Brattle Street Church and minister to many of the town's wealthy merchants. The congregation was at the center of a number of controversies which shook Massachusetts during 1715-40, most notably the great credit debates. Coleman's special mission was to bring the "gentility" of 18th-century England to Boston and blend it with Puritan piety. The Puritan gentility had a distinct social dimension. Coleman advocated a social hierarchy with the clergy at the top assisted by a mercantile elite serving as guardians of church and society. However, Coleman never adequately defined his concept of gentility. In the end his ideas were overwhelmed by changes in Puritan thought and in America's attitude toward the mother country. Primary and secondary sources; 56 notes.   R. J. Crandall

1692. Ryan, Mary P. A WOMEN'S AWAKENING: EVANGELICAL RELIGION AND THE FAMILIES OF UTICA, N.Y., 1800-1840. *Am. Q. 1978 30(5): 602-623.* A demographic and statistical analysis and interpretation of women's place in the Second Great Awakening as seen in Oneida County, New York, and more particularly in Utica and environs. The study reveals that the Utica women, as wives and mothers and as trustees of an extensive missionary organization, were the ones "who orchestrated the domestic revivals," yet also remained true to a narrowly maternal role and image for their sex. Concludes that "women were more than the majority of the converts, more even than the private guardians of America's souls. The combination and consequence of all these roles left the imprint of a women's awakening on American society as well as on American religion." 7 tables, 29 notes.
                                                R. V. Ritter

1693. Scheidt, David L. THE LUTHERANS IN REVOLUTIONARY PHILADELPHIA. *Concordia Hist. Inst. Q. 1976 49(4): 148-159.* Lutherans settled in the Delaware Valley prior to William Penn's arrival, but not until the 18th century did Lutherans come to Philadelphia in any great numbers. They adapted well and were absorbed by the expanding economic structure of the city; however, they maintained their ethnic identity by residing in the same areas and by speaking in their native German. When the American Revolution came, the Lutherans, as a group, did not demonstrate any enthusiasm for the patriot cause. Based on printed sources; 51 notes.   W. T. Walker

1694. Schwartz, Hillel. ADOLESCENCE AND REVIVALS IN ANTE-BELLUM BOSTON. *J. of Religious Hist. [Australia] 1974 8(2): 144-158.* Psychologists and psychiatrists have linked religious revivals to adolescence. In the early 19th century Boston witnessed the impact of four revivalists on its adolescent society: Methodist John Newland Maffett, "Presbygationalist" Charles Grandison Finney, Baptist Jacob Knapp, and Congregationalist Edward Norris Kirk. These men were fully aware that their revivals were part of youthful phenomenon. Based on printed sources; 63 notes.   W. T. Walker

1695. Singleton, Gregory H. "MERE MIDDLE-CLASS INSTITUTIONS": URBAN PROTESTANTISM IN 19TH-CENTURY AMERICA. *J. of Social Hist. 1973 6(4): 489-504.* Review article prompted by Nathan Irvin Higgins's *Protestants Against Poverty: Boston's Charities, 1870-1900* (Westport, Conn.: Greenwood, 1971), Richard J. Jensen's *The Winning of the Midwest: Social and Political Conflict, 1888-1896* (Chicago: U. of Chicago Pr., 1971), Carroll Smith Rosenberg's *Religion and the Rise of the American City: The New York City Mission Movement, 1812-1870* (Ithaca: Cornell U. Pr., 1971), and Alvin W. Skardon's *Church Leader in the City: Augustus Muhlenberg* (Philadelphia: U. of Pennsylvania Pr., 1971).

1696. Sizer, Sandra. POLITICS AND APOLITICAL RELIGION: THE GREAT URBAN REVIVALS OF THE LATE NINETEENTH CENTURY. *Church Hist. 1979 48(1): 81-98.* The Northern urban revivals of 1857-58 and 1875-77 may be suggestive of the place of the revivalist tradition in American culture. Techniques and ideologies formed there were to be appropriated again by such men as Billy Sunday and Billy Graham. Mass urban revivals were designed to create a community of feeling. Under this strategy of purification from sin for the community, individuals, purified by conversion, would detach themselves from the national tendency to aggressivenss and lust for money. This strategy shows the relation to politics and social conditions of the revivalist tradition, the apolitical political religion of America.   M. Dibert

1697. Thompson, James J., Jr. SOUTHERN BAPTIST CITY AND COUNTRY CHURCHES IN THE TWENTIES. *Foundations 1974 17(4): 351-363.* In the 1920's Southern Baptists tried to combat the decline in rural church membership and the evils of urbanization in the South with evangelicalism.

1698. Tomlinson, Juliette. CHRIST CHURCH, SPRINGFIELD, MASSACHUSETTS: FROM PARISH CHURCH TO THE CATHEDRAL OF THE DIOCESE. *Hist. Mag. of the Protestant Episcopal Church 1974 43(3): 253-260.* The congregation which ultimately became Christ Church was organized in 1817 by Colonel Roswell Lee, Superintendent of Springfield's Armory, and was incorporated by the legislature in 1839. The same year a building was started, and a new stone building following this one in 1875-76. The church prospered as did the whole diocese, so that by the turn of the century division of the diocese was seriously considered. This in turn led to discussions of Christ Church becoming the Diocesan Cathedral for western Massachusetts, a change which was consummated in 1929.   R. V. Ritter

1699. Tucker, Barbara M. OUR GOOD METHODISTS: THE CHURCH, THE FACTORY AND THE WORKING CLASS IN ANTE-BELLUM WEBSTER, MASSACHUSETTS. *Maryland Hist. 1977 8(2): 26-37.* Describes the appeal of Methodism to owners and workers in Webster's textile industry. The church provided the "moral foundation of a work effort" which provided owners with a disciplined work force and allowed workers to adjust to industrialism while having their social needs met. Illus., 39 notes.   G. O. Gagnon

1700. Walch, Timothy. CATHOLIC SOCIAL INSTITUTIONS AND URBAN DEVELOPMENTS: THE VIEW FROM NINETEENTH-CENTURY CHICAGO AND MILWAUKEE. *Catholic Hist. Rev. 1978 64(1): 16-32.* The Catholic Church committed itself to the improvement of American life by establishing a variety of urban social institutions. The impact of the Church's efforts, however, varied from one city to the next. In Eastern cities, Catholic institutions served immigrants almost exclusively. But the newness of Chicago and Milwaukee and their drastic need for social institutions precipitated a different kind of experience for the Catholic church in the Midwest. The Church mobilized quickly and offered these cities needed hospitals, asylums and schools. Non-Catholic leaders in Chicago and Milwaukee accepted these institutions with gratitude because they made their cities more attractive and helped to insure future growth. The story of Catholic social institutions in Chicago and Milwaukee highlights the complexity of relations between Catholics and non-Catholics in urban areas and emphasizes the need to look at the Church in a number of regional settings to gain a balanced picture of the American Catholic experience.   A

1701. Weber, Francis J. A CATHOLIC BISHOP MEETS THE RACIAL PROBLEM. *Records of the Am. Catholic Hist. Soc. of Philadelphia 1973 84(4): 217-220.* Describes the efforts of John J. Cantwell, bishop of Monterey-Los Angeles, to design an apostolate for Negroes in the 1920's. 14 notes.   J. M. McCarthy

1702. Willingham, William F. RELIGIOUS CONVERSION IN THE SECOND SOCIETY OF WINDHAM, CONNECTICUT, 1723-43: A CASE STUDY. *Societas 1976 6(2): 109-119.* Finds in the pattern of conversion during the Great Awakening in the Second Society of Windham, Connecticut, confirmation of Philip Greven's thesis that there is a connection in the early to middle 18th century "between the changing character of the family, brought about by geographic mobility, and religious experience." Based upon records and genealogical materials in the Connecticut State Library, other primary and secondary materials; 5 tables, 32 notes.   J. D. Hunley

1703. Wright, C. M. NEWPORT QUAKERS AND THEIR GREAT MEETING HOUSE: OR HOW WE CAME TO RESTORE THE GREAT MEETING HOUSE. *Newport Hist. 1974 47(4): 197-217.* Offers a short history of Quakers in Newport, 1657-1974, the history of the construction of one of their meeting houses, 1702-1922, and the preservation of the final building, 1974. 8 reproductions, 4 photos.

1704. Yearwood, Lennox. FIRST SHILOH BAPTIST CHURCH OF BUFFALO, NEW YORK: FROM A STOREFRONT TO MAJOR RELIGIOUS INSTITUTION. *Afro-Americans in New York Life and Hist. 1977 1(1): 81-98.* Traces the Shiloh Baptist Church's growth in political and social power within the black community in Buffalo during the 1920's and 1930's.

Medicine and Public Health

1705. Antler, Joyce and Fox, Daniel M. THE MOVEMENT TOWARD A SAFE MATERNITY: PHYSICIAN ACCOUNTABILITY IN NEW YORK CITY, 1915-1940. *Bull. of the Hist. of Medicine 1976 50(4): 569-595.* Maternal mortality was the subject of much study during 1915-40. Infant mortality rates had declined dramatically by then, and epidemic disease was no longer the threat it had been in the recent past. Yet, maternal mortality rates had not declined at all. In the mid-1930's, a report on maternal mortality by the New York Academy of Medicine led to an effective strategy for its reduction. The report did not blame midwives, but instead placed the blame with the medical profession itself. The Academy chose to publicize the report. This galvanized medical opinion and led to widespread reform of obstetric care in New York City and throughout the country. 86 notes.   M. Kaufman

1706. Atwater, Edward C. THE MEDICAL PROFESSION IN A NEW SOCIETY, ROCHESTER, NEW YORK (1811-60). *Bull. of the Hist. of Medicine 1973 47(3): 221-235.* Studies the medical profession during 1811-60 when Rochester, New York, grew to a major industrial city. Paper read before the 45th annual meeting of the American Association for the History of Medicine in Montreal, Canada, 4 May 1972.
S

1707. Atwater, Edward C. THE PHYSICIANS OF ROCHESTER, 1860-1910. *Bull. of the Hist. of Medicine 1977 51(1): 93-106.* During 1860-1910, substantial improvements occurred in the medical profession of Rochester, New York. Educational requirements were reestablished and raised, and the levels of the profession improved. Economic prosperity, scientific developments, improved technology, and reorganization of professional societies promoted specialization and research. New hospitals, with professional nursing care, provided the scene for medical activities; and staff appointments to the hospitals were eagerly sought by the physicians. The contention between sectarian and orthodox physicians, which had divided the profession during the earlier period, was resolved. The physicians, the hospitals, and the medical laws are described in detail. 30 notes.   M. Kaufman

1708. Baird, Nancy D. [ASIATIC CHOLERA].
ASIATIC CHOLERA'S FIRST VISIT TO KENTUCKY: A STUDY IN PANIC AND FEAR. *Filson Club Hist. Q. 1974 48(3): 228-240.* Traces the devastating impact of cholera on Kentucky in 1832-33. In several areas more than 10% of the population was killed by the disease. General ignorance of the cause of cholera and lack of medical resources led to widespread panic and disruption of life throughout the state, particularly in Lexington. Documentation by contemporary newspapers and journals; 51 notes.
ASIATIC CHOLERA: KENTUCKY'S FIRST PUBLIC HEALTH INSTRUCTOR. *Filson Club Hist. Q. 1974 48(4): 327-341.* Cholera epidemics in Kentucky during 1848-53, 1866, and 1873 were primary factors in improved public health in the state. Louisville, Covington, and Lexington were particularly active in the campaign to clean up the streets and residential areas. Yet by 1873, scientific understanding of the disease still had not advanced to the point where the initial outbreak could be isolated and prevented from spreading. 50 notes.   G. B. McKinney

1709. Bauer, Mary. GULFPORT'S AND BILOXI'S HOSPITALS: THEIR FIRST FIFTY YEARS. *J. of Mississippi Hist. 1977 39(4): 317-337.* Describes the development of hospitals in Gulfport and Biloxi, Mississippi, during 1907-63 and focuses on a few controversies and financial problems, and especially on the gradual expansion and improvement of physical facilities. Based on newspapers, interviews, and unpublished manuscripts; 85 notes.   J. W. Hillje

1710. Bell, Whitfield J., Jr. PRACTITIONERS OF HISTORY: PHILADELPHIA MEDICAL HISTORIANS BEFORE 1925. *Bull. of the Hist. of Medicine 1976 50(1): 73-92.* During the 19th and early 20th centuries, most medical history was written by busy physicians who wrote histories, collected books and other materials, and who prepared the way for the founding of the American Association for the History of Medicine. In Philadelphia medical history started with Benjamin Rush (1746-1813), who wrote on the comparative state of medicine between the 1760's and 1805. At mid-century, Samuel D. Gross (1805-84) made the outstanding contribution, with his *Lives of Eminent American Physicians and Surgeons* (1861), and with his *History of American Medical Literature* (1876). Other works were written on the University of Pennsylvania, and on the Pennsylvania Hospital. In the early 20th century, Francis Packard wrote a series of articles on American medical history, which formed the basis for his *History of Medicine in the United States* (1901). Edward Bell Krumbhaar (1882-1966) founded the association in 1925. 48 notes.   M. Kaufman

1711. Brewer, Paul W. VOLUNTARISM ON TRIAL: ST. LOUIS' RESPONSE TO THE CHOLERA EPIDEMIC OF 1849. *Bull. of the Hist. of Medicine 1975 49(1): 102-122.* The St. Louis cholera epidemic, which victimized at least 4,557, forced reconsideration of the voluntaristic approach to urban health and sanitation problems, and created a tentative movement toward public measures. Absence of sewers and adequate water supply made an epidemic inevitable after infected immigrants arrived, while doctors and clergy administered relief without halting the disease. When the city government failed to respond to the crisis, a citizens' Committee of Public Health assumed governmental functions and enforced sanitation regulations. Primary and secondary sources; 116 notes.   W. B. Bedford

1712. Bushnell, George D. CHICAGO'S MIRACULOUS PATENT MEDICINES. *Chicago Hist. 1974 3(2): 78-87.* Describes the era of patent medicines and the passage of federal laws curbing their sales.
                                                            S

1713. Cain, Louis P. THE CREATION OF CHICAGO'S SANITARY DISTRICT AND CONSTRUCTION OF THE SANITARY AND SHIP CANAL. *Chicago Hist. 1979 8(2): 98-110.* Describes the increasing problems with sewage disposal in Chicago beginning in the early 1850's when dysentery and cholera outbreaks led the city council and state legislature to act, and traces the construction of the Sanitary and Ship Canal from 1882 until completion in 1900.

1714. Cangi, Ellen Corwin. PATRONS AND PROTEGES: CINCINNATI'S FIRST GENERATION OF WOMEN DOCTORS 1875-1910. *Cincinnati Hist. Soc. Bull. 1979 37(2): 89-114.* Briefly describes the relative absence of women in the medical profession in the United States, except for a few isolated cases beginning in 1835, and discusses reforms in the profession which included the admission of women to medical schools; in particular, covers the situation in Cincinnati between 1875 and 1910 (women were admitted to the Cincinnati College of Medicine and Surgery beginning in 1883).

1715. Cassedy, James H. THE ROOTS OF AMERICAN SANITARY REFORM, 1843-47: SEVEN LETTERS FROM JOHN H. GRISCOM TO LEMUEL SHATTUCK. *J. of the Hist. of Medicine and Allied Sci. 1975 30(2): 136-147.* Little is known of how health reformers of the middle 19th century interacted in pursuit of their goals; however, a group of newly discovered letters from John H. Griscom of New York to Lemuel Shattuck of Boston provides details about how the activities of the two reformers helped transform "personal concerns and local reforms into a coherent national movement." 28 notes.
                                                            M. Kaufman

1716. Cohen, Abby. PUBLIC HEALTH AND PREVENTIVE MEDICINE IN PROVIDENCE, 1913. *Rhode Island Hist. 1977 36(2): 55-63.* Examines the Providence milk scandal of 1913 in the context of public health history, municipal corruption, and progressive reform. Published documents and secondary accounts; 22 notes.
                                                            P. J. Coleman

1717. Corn, Jacqueline Karnell. COMMUNITY RESPONSIBILITY FOR PUBLIC HEALTH: THE IMPACT OF EPIDEMIC DISEASE

AND URBAN GROWTH ON PITTSBURGH. *Western Pennsylvania Hist. Mag. 1976 59(3): 319-339.* Discusses theories of disease during the 19th century and their effect on public programs to improve health care and sanitation in Pittsburgh; concentrates on 1851, 1872, and 1888, three years in which the city council created new health laws or made significant changes in municipal organization of public health.
                                                            G. A. Hewlett

1718. Corn, Jacqueline Karnell. SOCIAL RESPONSE TO EPIDEMIC DISEASE IN PITTSBURGH, 1872-1895. *Western Pennsylvania Hist. Mag. 1973 56(1): 59-70.*

1719. Doyle, John E. THE EPIDEMIC CHOLERA IN SPRINGFIELD 1832 AND 1849. *Hist. J. of Western Massachusetts 1974 3(2): 1-14.* Opinions varied as to causes and cures for cholera. Springfield responded to the 1832 national epidemic by appointing a medically oriented Health Committee, and no lives were lost. In 1849 a politically oriented committee attempted to fight cholera cheaply, and some deaths did occur. Primary and secondary sources; 6 illus., 52 notes.
                                                            S. S. Sprague

1720. Duffy, John. NINETEENTH CENTURY PUBLIC HEALTH IN NEW YORK AND NEW ORLEANS: A COMPARISON. *Louisiana Hist. 1974 15(4): 325-338.*

1721. Dwork, Deborah. BORN IN URBAN AMERICA: 1830-1860. *Clio Medica [Netherlands] 1977 12(4): 227-253.* The period 1830-60 was a time of social change and medical experimentation. Phrenology, homeopathy, hydropathy, and mesmerism came in vogue. In obstetrics controversy focused on whether female midwives or male doctors should deliver. Doctors were considered inappropriate, for childbirth was considered a trial rather than an illness. Dr. Ewell in *Letters to Ladies* (1817) warned that doctors in the lying-in chamber could be driven to adultery and madness. Furthermore, if doctors were to practice obstetrics, midwifery, a respectable occupation for women, would be eliminated. Technological and theoretical advances, available only to physicians, provided safer deliveries, and many doctors needed the business. Thus by the end of the 19th century objections against male physicians in the lying-in chambers were eliminated; 112 notes, biblio.   A. J. Papalas

1722. Dwork, Deborah. THE CHILD MODEL (OR THE MODEL CHILD?) OF THE LATE NINETEENTH CENTURY IN URBAN AMERICA. *Clio Medica [Netherlands] 1977 12(2-3): 111-130.* Physicians, novelists, educators, and moralists in the late 19th century wrote extensively about child-raising. Julius Uffelman's *Manual of the Domestic Hygiene of the Child* (1881) expressed the consensus view in banning rich foods, alcohol, and prescribing active games for children. Louisa May Alcott in her novels echoed the sentiments of the day in censuring the corset and recommending household chores for girls. Elizabeth Grimmell in *How John and I Brought up the Child* (1894) gave the standard advice by linking moral development with healthy growth. 89 notes, biblio.   A. J. Papalas

1723. Ellis, John H. DISEASE AND THE DESTINY OF A CITY: THE 1878 YELLOW FEVER EPIDEMIC IN MEMPHIS. *West Tennessee Hist. Soc. Papers 1974 (28): 75-89.* Supports the thesis that "political events themselves can be determined by disease." The yellow fever epidemic which struck Memphis in 1878 was part of the plague which smote the Ohio-Mississippi valleys that year. Greatest losses in Memphis were among the poor Irish, who could not leave the city, while Negro deaths were relatively light. Politically, the epidemic prompted the abolishment of the city charter, establishment of a commission form of government, and the adoption of belated health measures. The epidemic divided the history of Memphis into two parts: the old river town which died in 1878, and the new city which emerged in 1880. Primary sources; 53 notes.   H. M. Parker, Jr.

1724. Ellis, John H. THE NEW ORLEANS YELLOW FEVER EPIDEMIC IN 1878: A NOTE ON THE AFFECTIVE HISTORY OF SOCIETIES AND COMMUNITIES. *Clio Medica [Netherlands] 1977 12(2-3): 189-216.* During 1830-60 many epidemics in New Orleans ravaged primarily the immigrant communities, and provoked mainly local interest. In 1878 a yellow fever epidemic killed the rich as well as the poor. In the early days 40,000 of the 211,000 inhabitants fled the city.

That the federal government took notice led in 1879 to the establishment of the National Board of Health and the Quarantine Act. This legislation was enacted before the study of the Yellow Fever Commission was completed. 82 notes.   A. J. Papalas

1725. Engelhardt, H. Tristram, Jr. THE DISEASE OF MASTUR-BATION: VALUES AND THE CONCEPT OF DISEASE. *Bull. of the Hist. of Medicine 1974 48(2): 234-248.* Examines 19th-century medical theories of masturbation and utilizes annual reports of the Charity Hospital of Louisiana in New Orleans to show hospitalizations and diagnoses of masturbation. Read at the 46th annual meeting of the American Association for the History of Medicine, Cincinnati, Ohio, 5 May 1973.
S

1726. Estes, J. Worth. "AS HEALTHY A PLACE AS ANY IN AMERICA": REVOLUTIONARY PORTSMOUTH, N.H. *Bull. of the Hist. of Medicine 1976 50(4): 536-552.* In 1789 Dr. Hall Jackson described Portsmouth, New Hampshire, as a healthy place. Analyzes bills of mortality and Jackson's own records to determine the accuracy of his statement and develops statistics for 1801-20. Portsmouth had a death rate up to twice that of other smaller towns in New Hampshire. Infectious diseases, especially tuberculosis and cholera, were the leading cause of death. Comparison with other statistics indicates that Portsmouth was "about average in terms of healthiness as measured by life expectancies, among the cities and towns in America and Europe." Also makes comparisons with the 20th century. 6 fig., 38 notes.   M. Kaufman

1727. Farley, M. Foster THE MIGHTY MONARCH OF THE SOUTH: YELLOW FEVER IN CHARLESTON AND SAVANNAH. *Georgia R. 1973 27(1): 56-70.* Between 1800 and 1876, 27 outbreaks of yellow fever in Charleston, South Carolina, caused more than 4,000 deaths. Though record keeping in Savannah, Georgia, was less complete, it appears that Savannah suffered similarly. The cause of the disease was never confirmed, but the atmosphere, some exotic plant, the filth of the cities, and mosquitoes were all blamed. Controversies raged over whether to quarantine stricken areas. In the 19th century three physicians suggested, without proof, insect transmission of yellow fever.
M. B. Lucas

1728. Fox, Daniel M. SOCIAL POLICY AND CITY POLITICS: TUBERCULOSIS REPORTING IN NEW YORK, 1889-1900. *Bull. of the Hist. of Medicine 1975 49(2): 169-195.* The late 19th century debate over whether tuberculosis was hereditary or contagious split the medical profession. Yet, at that time, public health advocates urged compulsory notification of tuberculosis as the first step to controlling the disease. During the 1890's, when the issue climaxed in New York, it was a time of economic stress, with the depression of 1893 adversely affecting medical incomes. New York medicine was filled with factions, and the chaotic state of the profession may have played a major role in enabling the innovations of tuberculosis control to succeed. The roles of local politics and the medical profession are examined in what is really a case study of the very early progressive period. 97 notes.   M. Kaufman

1729. Fox, Richard W. THE INTOLERABLE DEFIANCE OF THE INSANE: CIVIL COMMITMENT IN SAN FRANCISCO, 1906-1929. *Am. J. of Legal Hist. 1976 20(2): 136-154.* Analyzes the cases of more than 12,000 persons charged, convicted, and committed for insanity in San Francisco 1906-29, based on the Records of Commitment for Insanity of the Superior Court of the City and County of San Francisco. Doctors and judges convicted and committed thousands of persons to Bastille-like, state hospitals with little regard for whether the accused were insane. The cases ranged from ones involving common strangers arrested on the streets for vagrancy to those of immigrants who were arrested and refused to talk. Examiners reported nearly one-third of the people as being quiet and retiring individuals and almost two-thirds as being residual deviants who had no organic or functional disabilities and no violent or destructive tendencies. Causes of arrest, physical and mental characteristics, patterns of behavior, race and ethnic origins, and social, economic, and religious background are discussed. Primary sources; 23 notes.   L. A. Knafla

1730. Galishoff, Stuart. NEWARK AND THE GREAT POLIO EPIDEMIC OF 1916. *New Jersey Hist. 1976 94(2-3): 101-111.* An epidemic of polio was carried from New York to New Jersey by commut-

ers, vacationers, and people fleeing infected areas. The Newark public health board quickly isolated cases, began a program of widespread disinfection, and instructed children not to congregate indoors. Dumps were closed because some officials believed insects carried the disease, schools opened late, and children were sent to the country. In New Jersey, Newark was hardest hit by polio and was the first community to adopt a comprehensive plan of long-range assistance to paralyzed victims of the disease. Based on primary sources, annual reports, and newspaper reports; 2 illus., map, 2 charts, 23 notes.   E. R. McKinstry

1731. Goldfield, David R. THE BUSINESS OF HEALTH PLANNING: DISEASE PREVENTION IN THE OLD SOUTH. *J. of Southern Hist. 1976 42(4): 557-570.* Natural and social features such as the lack of a germ theory of disease, rapid urbanization, and the general climatic state of southern cites—late or no frosts, hot, humid summers—made southern cities particularly susceptible to epidemic disease. However, the cost-benefit mentality of urban business-government leaders with regard to urban public services represent a major factor in making the epidemics as deadly as they were. Street cleaning contracts let on a political reward basis without concern for performance, and quarantine laws which were not enforced because of the hostility of the business community were supplemented by city governments and public news media which denied the existence of epidemics out of competitive desire to prevent other cities from taking commercial advantage of their cities' misfortunes. Only slowly did immigrants, a growing, articulate working class, and advances in medical science produce an active public health service which could use sanitation and quarantine to effectively fight disease.

T. Schoonover

1732. Goldfield, David R. DISEASE AND URBAN IMAGE: YELLOW FEVER IN NORFOLK, 1855. *Virginia Cavalcade 1973 23(2): 34-41.*

1733. Griffin, Dick. OPIUM ADDICTION IN CHICAGO: "THE NOBLEST AND THE BEST BROUGHT LOW." *Chicago Hist. 1977 6(2): 107-116.* Opium addiction, at its worst during the 1800's-1910 in Chicago, resulted largely from nonprescription patent medicines.

1734. Griffin, William. THE MERCY HOSPITAL CONTROVERSY AMONG CLEVELAND'S AFRO-AMERICAN CIVIC LEADERS, 1927. *J. of Negro Hist. 1976 61(4): 327-350.* In Cleveland, the campaign to eliminate racial discrimination in health care institutions focused attention upon the municipal hospital which excluded Negroes from its staff and training programs. Black leaders in Cleveland were divided in their support of the proposed Negro institution, Mercy Hospital. The controversy focused attention on discrimination in hospitals, and by 1930, under pressure from black civic leaders, the Cleveland City Hospital was ordered to change its racial policies. Based upon primary materials in the Western Reserve Historical Society Library and the Library of Congress Manuscript Collection; 105 notes.

N. G. Sapper

1735. Grinder, Robert Dale. THE WAR AGAINST ST. LOUIS'S SMOKE 1891-1924. *Missouri Hist. R. 1975 69(2): 191-205.* After 1891 St. Louis initiated a series of "smoke abatement crusades." The movement contained professional and bureaucratic elements. The first considered smoke an engineering problem to be solved by educating businessmen; the second felt it was a problem to be solved with time and a large staff of inspectors. The movement contained a third element composed of public-minded citizens concerned about the harmful effects of smoke. They worked through such groups as the Civic League, the Business Men's Club, the women's Wednesday Club, and the Socialist Party. Based on primary and secondary sources; 65 notes.

W. F. Zornow

1736. Grob, Gerald N. CLASS, ETHNICITY, AND RACE IN AMERICAN MENTAL HOSPITALS, 1830-75. *J. of the Hist. of Medicine and Allied Sci. 1973 28(3): 207-229.* Discusses the difference between the theory of equality of treatment for patients in mental institutions and the practice, which often was dependent upon the patient's class, ethnic origin, and color. Private patients got the best care, followed by native poor and indigent patients, ethnic poor, especially in most urban areas with large immigrant populations, and black patients. "The evolution of the mental hospital offers an unusually good illustration of how a social institution, established with the best and most honorable of intentions, was inadvertently transformed by the behavior of many individuals and groups." Based on primary sources; 51 notes.

J. L. Susskind

1737. Hall, Dick. OINTMENT OF LOVE: OLIVER E. COMSTOCK AND TUCSON'S TENT CITY. *J. of Arizona Hist. 1978 19(2): 111-130.* Describes the efforts of the Reverend Oliver E. Comstock to care for and eventually build St. Luke's-in-the-Desert Hospital for the care of poorer citizens of Tucson, Arizona. Early travelers lived in Tent City where medical facilities were scant. Comstock, originally an Alabama printer and preacher, started Baptist missionary work among the tubercular areas of Tucson. Growing population, increasing concern for the health of its citizens, and support from the Daughters of the American Revolution, Red Cross, veterans of World War I, Congressman Carl Hayden, and the Veterans Administration transformed the hospital for tubercular patients, replacing Tent City. Reverend Comstock's sermon "Ointment of Love" in the Tucson *Star* (22 February 1925) was a continuing appeal for assistance for the new Comstock Hospital (known previously as Mercy Hospital). Based on author's recollections; 4 photos, 30 notes.

K. E. Gilmont

1738. Harkins, Michael J. PUBLIC HEALTH NUISANCES IN OMAHA, 1870-1900. *Nebraska Hist. 1975 56(4): 471-493.* Examines the lack of sanitary control and oppressive living conditions that made for major health problems in Omaha between 1870 and 1900. Not until the 20th century did an effective board of health come into existence. Includes a discussion of patent medicines consumed by Omaha residents.

R. Lowitt

1739. Hildreth, Peggy Bassett. EARLY RED CROSS: THE HOWARD ASSOCIATION OF NEW ORLEANS, 1837-1878. *Louisiana Hist. 1979 20(1): 77-92.* Founded in 1837 and incorporated in 1842, the Howard Association of New Orleans was a nonsectarian, philanthropic organization that performed medical and social work for the indigent victims of yellow fever and cholera epidemics. During its active service it cared for nearly 130,000 patients, black and white, in 11 epidemics, raised and dispensed over $750,000, and fostered 29 similar organizations in 9 states. It performed its last service in 1878, and thereafter was superseded by municipal, state, and federal health agencies. The Howard Association helped engender the national public health movement and the Public Health Service. Printed reports and secondary sources; table, 159 notes.

L. N. Powell

1740. Hornbein, Marjorie. DR. CHARLES SPIVAK OF DENVER: PHYSICIAN, SOCIAL WORKER, YIDDISH AUTHOR. *Western States Jewish Hist. Q. 1979 11(3): 195-211.* Dr. Charles Spivak (1861-1927) was a founder of Denver, Colorado's, Jewish Consumptives' relief society sanatorium (JCRS) in 1904. The JCRS, in contrast with the National Jewish Hospital, accepted patients in the advanced stages of tuberculosis. Rivalry between the hospitals was part of the schism in the city's Jewish community. A specialist in gastrointestinal diseases, Dr. Spivak taught at the Medical School of the University of Denver, and also found time to write essays on medicine and Judaism. His best known literary work was a Yiddish dictionary, published in 1911. In 1920 Dr. Spivak was part of a team of medical experts, sponsored by the US Army, sent to Europe to study and report on sanitary and medical conditions in Poland. Dr. Spivak was not actively religious until late in life, but his fortitude and serenity helped him accept his fate as a victim of cancer. One of his final requests was that his body be given to a medical school. Primary and secondary sources; 2 photos, 59 notes.

B. S. Porter

1741. Humphrey, David C. THE KING'S COLLEGE MEDICAL SCHOOL AND THE PROFESSIONALIZATION OF MEDICINE IN PRE-REVOLUTIONARY NEW YORK. *Bull. of the Hist. of Medicine 1975 49(2): 206-234.* The small number of "professionals" among the numerous physicians in prerevolutionary New York City saw the rest of the physicians as unskilled and uneducated quacks. The 1760 licensing law was not enforced, and New Yorkers patronized the city's "better known empirics." There was professional scorn, social resentment, and economic rivalry between the "professionals" and the empirics. In the mid-1760's, New York's medical leaders agreed that a medical school was a feasible solution to the problem. A medical college would improve the

quality of practice, give respectability to the graduates, and a competitive advantage over the unschooled empirics. The establishment of King's College Medical School was the result. The "professionals" also founded a medical society, but "beneath the surface reforms medical practice continued to look much the same to most colonists." True professionalization "awaited the scientific breakthroughs of the 19th century." 115 notes.

M. Kaufman

1742. Jamieson, Duncan R. CITIES AND THE AMA: THE AMERICAN MEDICAL ASSOCIATION'S FIRST REPORT ON PUBLIC HYGIENE. *Maryland Hist. 1977 8(1): 23-32.* Examines an attempt by the American Medical Association to provide impetus to the effort to relieve urban squalor by reporting on its relationship to disease. "The First Report on Public Hygiene" (1849) had little impact but became ammunition for the muckrakers of the 1880's. Based on AMA and secondary sources; 21 notes.

G. O. Gagnon

1743. Jarcho, Saul. A PAPAL PHYSICIAN AND THE SANITATION OF NEW YORK CITY. *Bull. of the Hist. of Medicine 1978 52(3): 410-418.* Giovanni Maria Lancisi (1654-1720) was physician to a series of Popes, and an author on epidemiology. In 1717 he published his classic treatise *De Noxiis Paludum Effluviis* [Harmful emanations from swamps]. In 1743 when Cadwallader Colden (1688-1776) wrote his "Observations on the Fever which Prevailed in the City of New York in 1741 and 2," he began with a long excerpt from Lancisi's work, and Colden based some of his work on Lancisi's ideas. Colden concluded that New York City's drains had to be improved. 28 notes.

M. Kaufman

1744. Kohn, Lawrence A. GOITER, IODINE AND GEORGE W. GOLER: THE ROCHESTER EXPERIMENT. *Bull. of the Hist. of Medicine 1975 49(3): 389-399.* On 24 April 1923 sodium iodide was added to the water supply of Rochester, New York, "the first recorded community act against human disease other than the infections." George W. Goler, Rochester's health officer from 1896 to 1932, was primarily responsible for this attempt to reduce the incidence of goiter in the community. With the endorsement of George H. Whipple, dean of the University's medical school, and the assistance of Beekman C. Little, superintendent of the water department from 1901 to 1926, Goler proposed the plan, and put it into action. The opposition is described, including the American Medical Liberty League, the Christian Scientists, and the home-brewing industry, who complained that iodized water prevented the development of a decent "head" on their beer. When the goiter count fell, opposition disappeared. In 1933, the program was dropped. 52 notes.

M. Kaufman

1745. Kupperman, Karen Ordahl. APATHY AND DEATH IN EARLY JAMESTOWN. *J. of Am. Hist. 1979 66(1): 24-40.* Uses an analogy between prison camps during World War II and the Korean War and the early Jamestown settlement to demonstrate the connection between nutritional diseases and psychological factors such as fear and despair. In both cases, malnutrition and psychological factors interacted to produce a withdrawal from life. Because nutritional diseases produce symptoms that appear psychological, both prisoners of war and early settlers would seem to be suffering from inexplicable melancholy. This was especially true in Jamestown, where a complex interaction between environmental and psychological factors produced high death rates between 1607 and 1624. 88 notes.

T. P. Linkfield

1746. Leavitt, Judith Walzer. POLITICS AND PUBLIC HEALTH: SMALLPOX IN MILWAUKEE, 1894-1895. *Bull. of the Hist. of Medicine 1976 50(4): 553-568.* A smallpox epidemic hit Milwaukee during summer-fall 1894 and reduced the reputation and powers of the city's health department. The episode dramatizes the relationship between politics and public health, and reminds historians that medical factors "do not alone determine the course of public health events." The epidemic had a retrogressive effect on the public health movement in Milwaukee. Health Commissioner Walter Kempster reacted to the epidemic by launching a widespread vaccination campaign, moved to isolate patients by removal to the Isolation Hospital, enforced a strict quarantine on those allowed to remain at home, and carried on education campaigns. Citizens, especially in German and Polish areas, resisted. Kempster was seen as symbolizing governmental authority which was subverting immigrant culture and threatening personal rights. The Common Council voted to dismiss the health commissioner after a lengthy investigation of charges made against him. "Patronage, class and ethnic divisions were responsible" for much of the opposition to him. Illus., 4 figs., 44 notes.

M. Kaufman

1747. Leavitt, Judith Walzer. WRITING PUBLIC HEALTH HISTORY: THE NEED FOR A SOCIAL SCAFFOLDING. *Rev. in Am. Hist. 1976 4(2): 150-157.* Review article prompted by John Duffy's *A History of Public Health in New York City, (1625-1866)* (New York: Russell Sage Foundation, 1968), Duffy's *A History of Public Health in New York City, 1866-1966* (New York: Russell Sage Foundation, 1974), and Stuart Galishoff's *Safeguarding the Public Health: Newark, 1895-1918* (Westport, Connecticut: Greenwood Pr., 1975).

1748. Lee, Anne S. and Lee, Everett S. THE HEALTH OF SLAVES AND THE HEALTH OF FREEDMEN: A SAVANNAH STUDY. *Phylon 1977 38(2): 170-180.* Discusses the lack of information on black health in interpreting black history and points out a valuable source, the Tabulated Mortuary Record of the City of Savannah from 1 January 1854 to 31 December 1869, compiled by W. Duncan, M. D. The record indicates differences in black and white health before and after the Civil War and the following causes of death are listed: repeated epidemics (yellow fever, typhoid, smallpox, cholera), nonepidemic diseases (malaria, tuberculosis, dysentery, pneumonia), now forgotten diseases (dropsy, lockjaw), heart attacks, cancer, convulsions, accident, homicide, suicide, and childbirth. Primary and secondary sources; 10 notes.

P. J. Taylorson

1749. Lovejoy, David B., Jr. THE HOSPITAL AND SOCIETY: THE GROWTH OF HOSPITALS IN ROCHESTER, NEW YORK, IN THE NINETEENTH CENTURY. *Bull. of the Hist. of Medicine 1975 49(4): 536-555.* Details the history of hospital construction in Rochester, New York, from the 1820's to the turn of the century. Demonstrates the shift from the hospital as pesthouse to the palace of healing of modern days. During the 1850's, the availability of state funding brought a resurgence of hospital construction. As hospitals became more respectable, they began to accept private patients, rather than charity cases. Previously, hospitals were places where the poor were sent to die. Now, by the late 19th century, they were places of healing. 60 notes, charts, biblio.

M. Kaufman

1750. Marcus, Alan I. PROFESSIONAL REVOLUTION AND REFORM IN THE PROGRESSIVE ERA: CINCINNATI PHYSICIANS AND THE CITY ELECTIONS OF 1897 AND 1900. *J. of Urban Hist. 1979 5(2): 183-208.* Physicians in Cincinnati became "progressives" and took up the issue of public health in order to increase the power, prestige, and organization of their profession rather than out of interest in social justice or the common welfare. They received help from other professional groups that were engaged in comparable crusades for identical motives. 56 notes.

T. W. Smith

1751. Meeker, Edward. THE SOCIAL RATE OF RETURN ON INVESTMENT IN PUBLIC HEALTH, 1880-1910. *J. of Econ. Hist. 1974 34(2): 392-421.* Estimates the social rate of return of two urban public health measures undertaken in several eastern US cities during 1880-1910, based on calculations of the social benefits and capital costs of sewers and water filtration plants. The social rate of return on such public health projects was significantly above the market rate of return, indicating that the government investments were economically sound. Based on contemporary periodicals, official published documents, and secondary sources; 8 tables, 43 notes, appendix.

O. H. Reichardt

1752. Melvin, Patricia Mooney. MAKE MILWAUKEE SAFE FOR BABIES: THE CHILD WELFARE COMMISSION AND THE DEVELOPMENT OF URBAN HEALTH CENTERS 1911-1912. *J. of the West 1978 17(2): 83-93.* Under the direction of Wilbur C. Phillips and with the backing of Milwaukee's newly elected socialist administrators, an experimental baby medical care center was established in St. Cyril's Parish. With emphasis on the neighborhood as a health unit, and after obtaining the cooperation of local doctors, the experimental center demonstrated a decline in the infant mortality rate due to nutrition and hygiene factors. The city's Child Welfare Commission advocated an expansion of the program, but the 1912 election brought in a coalition of traditional political parties that promised to end socialist programs that

cost money, including the infant health care center. Primary and secondary sources; 6 photos, 2 maps, 24 notes.

B. S. Porter

1753. Mooney-Melvin, Patricia. MOHAWK-BRIGHTON: A PIONEER IN NEIGHBORHOOD HEALTH CARE. *Cincinnati Hist. Soc. Bull. 1978 36(1): 57-72.* Wilbur C. Phillips's early venture in neighborhood health care in the Mohawk-Brighton district of Cincinnati, 1917-20, was a rallying point for neighborhood social improvement.

1754. Numbers, Ronald L. THE MAKING OF AN ECLECTIC PHYSICIAN: JOSEPH M. MC ELHINNEY AND THE ECLECTIC MEDICAL INSTITUTE OF CINCINNATI. *Bull. of the Hist. of Medicine 1973 47(2): 155-166.* Examines the Eclectic Medical Institute of Cincinnati and 19th-century medical sectarianism. Read before the 45th annual meeting of the American Association for the History of Medicine in Montreal, Canada, 4 May 1972.

S

1755. Ochsner, Alton. THE HISTORY OF THORACIC AND VASCULAR SURGERY IN THE NEW ORLEANS AREA DURING THE FIRST HALF OF THE TWENTIETH CENTURY. *Bull. of the Hist. of Medicine 1977 51(2): 169-187.* Alton Ochsner and his associates built on the rich heritage of vascular surgery in the New Orleans area that developed partly because Charity Hospital provided a large amount of clinical material and principally because of Rudolph Matas, the father of vascular surgery. During 1927-52, 100 publications on thoracic and vascular surgery came out of New Orleans, 26 on venous thrombosis, 24 on cancer of the lung, 11 on bronchiectasis, 13 on diseases of the esophagus, 4 on surgical treatment of tuberculosis, 3 on the heart and pericardium, etc. In 1948 Ochsner was president of the American Association of Thoracic Surgery and appointed a committee to organize the Board of Thoracic Surgery, established a founders group, appointed an examining committee, and set up requirements for training and certification. 129 notes.

M. Kaufman

1756. Olton, Charles S. PHILADELPHIA'S FIRST ENVIRONMENTAL CRISIS. *Pennsylvania Mag. of Hist. and Biog. 1974 98(1): 90-100.* Complaints of air pollution, spoiled drinking water, and unpleasant roads led to the enactment in 1763 of Philadelphia's first comprehensive environmental law. Philadelphia's effort to clean up the environment was only temporarily successful; by 1783, the urban environment had begun to degenerate again. Based on primary and secondary sources; 48 notes.

E. W. Carp

1757. Osbourne, George E. PHARMACY IN BRITISH COLONIAL AMERICA. Bender, George A. and Parascandola, John, eds. *American Pharmacy in the Colonial and Revolutionary Periods* (Madison, Wisconsin: Am. Inst. of the Hist. of Pharmacy, 1977): 5-14. Discusses pharmacists and the practice of pharmacy in the British North American settlements of Jamestown, Virginia, and Boston and Salem, Massachusetts, 1602-90.

1758. Pearce, George F. TORMENT OF PESTILENCE: YELLOW FEVER EPIDEMICS IN PENSACOLA. *Florida Hist. Q. 1978 56(4): 448-472.* Throughout the 19th century yellow fever plagued Pensacola. The epidemics caused a high mortality rate, disrupted business and economic life, and bitterly divided the community over solutions. By 1906, shortly after the discovery of the cause and transmission of the disease, Pensacola at last reported no cases of yellow fever. Based on newspapers, government reports, and secondary sources; 4 illus., 106 notes.

P. A. Beaber

1759. Pumphrey, Ralph E. MICHAEL DAVIS AND THE TRANSFORMATION OF THE BOSTON DISPENSARY, 1910-1920. *Bull. of the Hist. of Medicine 1975 49(4): 451-465.* Michael M. Davis, Ph.D. (1879-1971), as director of the Boston Dispensary transformed that institution into "one of the pioneering medical institutions of the twentieth century." He improved the administration of the Dispensary, and he infused it with a progressive spirit, while being able to "relate constructively to pressures from within the medical and scientific communities." Describes the extensive work of the Dispensary during 1910-20. 45 notes.

M. Kaufman

1760. Radbill, Samuel X. HOSPITALS AND PEDIATRICS, 1776-1976. *Bull. of the Hist. of Medicine 1979 53(2): 286-291.* Sketches the development of foundling hospitals and identifies the leading institutions in American pediatrics. As almshouses were the antecedents of the general hospitals, so were orphanages and foundling asylums the forerunners of children's hospitals. From the early dispensaries came the first children's hospitals. The history of children's hospitals is described, focusing on New York City, Boston, and Philadelphia. 9 notes.

M. Kaufman

1761. Rogers, Barbara. TO BE OR NOT TO BE A JEWISH HOSPITAL. *Western States Jewish Hist. Q. 1978 10(3): 195-201.* On 3 November 1887, a group of San Francisco citizens agreed to establish a charitable hospital for deserving and needy Israelites and others. Rabbi M. Friedlander of Oakland openly opposed the hospital's policy and urged that it accept only Jewish patients. San Francisco's prominent rabbis, Jacob Voorsanger, Jacob Nieto, and Myer S. Levy agreed with the hospital's board of directors that it should be nonsectarian in its admissions policy. Critics today claim the hospital is no longer Jewish because many patients and doctors are not Jewish; but supporters say that a high proportion of Bay area Jews are served by Mount Zion Hospital and it will continue to grow and develop with the San Francisco Bay area. Based on Board of Directors' minutes, secondary sources; 13 notes.

B. S. Porter

1762. Rosen, George. SOCIAL SCIENCE AND HEALTH IN THE UNITED STATES IN THE TWENTIETH CENTURY. *Clio Medica [Netherlands] 1976 11(4): 245-268.* During 1860-1910 the urban population of America rose from 19 to 45% of the total population. The influx of European immigrants and Southern blacks to industrial centers caused serious health problems. Henry W. Farnam, a Yale professor (1881-1918), urged Congress to investigate industrial diseases. In 1909 the Pittsburgh survey revealed that tuberculosis and typhoid were more likely to hit the poor living in squalid tenements. Newly established sociology departments in universities studied crime, ethnic groups, prostitution, and other urban problems. Most of these studies had chapters on public health, and in the 1930's specific works on urban health appeared. This interaction between social science and the health field has led to improvements in public health. 62 notes.

A. J. Papalas

1763. Rosenberg, Charles E. SOCIAL CLASS AND MEDICAL CARE IN NINETEENTH-CENTURY AMERICA: THE RISE AND FALL OF THE DISPENSARY. *J. of the Hist. of Medicine and Allied Sci. 1974 29(1): 32-54.* The dispensary was "the primary means for providing the urban poor with medical care and a vital link in the prevailing system of medical education." Four factors explain the rise of dispensaries: 1) their functional relationship with the medical profession, 2) their agreement with available treatments, 3) their size in relationship to the needs of their clients, and 4) their founders' expectations of the roles of government and private citizens. Two parallel developments caused the decline of the dispensary: 1) the scale of the human problems the dispensaries faced, and 2) the intellectual tools and social organization of the medical profession. The dispensary "was doomed neither by policy nor conspiracy but by a steadily shifting configuration of medical perceptions and priorities." Based on primary sources; 37 notes.

J. L. Susskind

1764. Savitt, Todd L. FILARIASIS IN THE UNITED STATES. *J. of the Hist. of Medicine and Allied Sci. 1977 32(2): 140-150.* One African parasite which was transmitted to the South was the filarial roundworm, causative organism of elephantiasis. Only Charleston, South Carolina, was an endemic focus of the disease. The disease existed there until the 1920's. Not until 1914 did a study reveal the extent of the problem at Charleston, when microfilariae were discovered in the blood of 19.25% of 400 hospital and clinic patients. Another study, in Charleston's Old Folks Home, indicated that 35% of the residents had microfilariae in their blood. Most were carriers, and about 25% had symptoms of the illness. These reports led to an intensive mosquito control campaign to eradicate filariasis from Charleston. Illus., 42 notes.

M. Kaufman

1765. Scholten, Catherine M. "ON THE IMPORTANCE OF THE OBSTETRICK ART": CHANGING CUSTOMS OF CHILDBIRTH IN AMERICA, 1760 TO 1825. *William and Mary Q. 1977 34(3): 426-445.* Discusses the changing patterns of childbirth. After 1770 male physicians were supplanting midwives; and childbirth was more private and less communal. Gives a history of midwifery in early America and

comments on medical education. William Shippen was the first male to establish a continuing practice in midwifery. William Smellie of London exerted the greatest influence on the development of obstetrics. The changes in childbirth patterns took place within an urban context. Based on medical tracts, midwives' records, and diaries; 91 notes.

H. M. Ward

1766. Shumsky, Neil Larry. THE MUNICIPAL CLINIC OF SAN FRANCISCO: A STUDY IN MEDICAL STRUCTURE. *Bull. of the Hist. of Medicine 1978 52(4): 542-559.* In 1911, the Municipal Clinic of San Francisco was opened in an attempt to reduce venereal disease in the city. The San Francisco Board of Health required that every prostitute be examined twice a week, and if healthy she would be allowed to practice her profession without official harassment. If she had the disease, however, she was given free medical care and meanwhile she was forbidden to ply her trade. The St. Louis experiment of the 1870's provided precedent for this work. Analysis of the bureaucracy involved indicates that the development of the germ theory of disease, the emergence of paraprofessionals, and the coming of specialization were all factors contributing to the structuring of modern medical institutions. 38 notes.

M. Kaufman

1767. Stern, Norton B. CHOLERA IN SAN FRANCISCO IN 1850. *Western States Jewish Hist. Q. 1973 5(3): 200-204.* Notes the charity efforts of Jews led by Samuel I. Neustadt to ameliorate conditions during the cholera epidemic.

1768. Straight, William M., M.D. JAMES M. JACKSON, JR., MIAMI'S FIRST PHYSICIAN. *Tequesta 1973 33: 75-86.* Biography of the first physician to reside in Miami, for whom Jackson Memorial Hospital was named in 1924. Based on primary and secondary sources; 16 notes.

H. S. Marks

1769. Trauner, Joan B. THE CHINESE AS MEDICAL SCAPEGOATS IN SAN FRANCISCO, 1870-1905. *California Hist. 1978 57(1): 70-87.* During 1870-1905, San Francisco's Chinatown was considered a breeding ground for smallpox, bubonic plague, leprosy, and other diseases. The Caucasian community considered Chinatown a threat to public health, accusing Chinese Americans of practicing low standards of hygiene, and attempted unsuccessfully during epidemic periods to have Chinatown isolated or quarantined. At the same time, public health services were denied to Chinese residents. Chinese were blamed for a bubonic plague outbreak in 1900 while politicians denied its existence, fearing that publicity would be bad for business. By 1906, when a plague epidemic followed the earthquake, the causes of diseases such as bubonic plague were better known, and accusations against the Chinese ceased. Nevertheless, the Chinese continued to be neglected by the Caucasian community in matters of public health, and had to combat discriminatory laws and racist stereotyping in order to obtain adequate medical care. Not until the 1970's did Chinatown's medical facilities become fully integrated into the general community. Based on contemporary and secondary published works; photos, charts, 83 notes.

A. Hoffman

1770. Waring, Joseph I. CHARLESTON MEDICINE, 1800-1860. *J. of the Hist. of Medicine & Allied Sci. 1976 31(3): 320-242.* In 1789 a group of physicians established the Medical Society of South Carolina, and they began to establish a library, adopt a fee bill, and advise municipal authorities on matters of medicine and public health. In 1823-24, due to the work of the society, the Medical College of South Carolina was established; it opened in 1824. Discusses the history of medical licensing; the conflict between the Thomsonians and the orthodox physicians played a major role in events. Describes medical literature and the diseases and treatments of the period. Illus., charts, 72 notes.

M. Kaufman

1771. Zelt, Roger P. SMALLPOX INOCULATIONS IN BOSTON, 1721-1722. *Synthesis 1977 4(1): 3-14.* There was a smallpox epidemic in Boston in 1721. Cotton Mather, having heard of smallpox inoculation in Turkey and Africa, made the controversial suggestion that physicians apply this procedure in Boston. Among the 259 persons inoculated, "the overwhelming majority [were from] . . . the highly educated, politically conservative, and religiously orthodox upper segment of the colonial socio-economic strata." Primary and secondary sources; 16 notes.

M. M. Vance

Technology

1772. Klaw, Spencer. "ALL SAFE, GENTLEMEN, ALL SAFE!" *Am. Heritage 1978 29(5): 40-47.* After Elisha Otis demonstrated the crash-proof elevator in 1853, the popularity of passenger elevators changed the skylines of cities. Improvements continued and most elevators now have electrically powered traction. 22 illus.　　B. J. Paul

1773. Kleinberg, Susan J. TECHNOLOGY AND WOMEN'S WORK: THE LIVES OF WORKING CLASS WOMEN IN PITTSBURGH, 1870-1900. *Labor Hist. 1976 17(1): 58-72.* Pittsburgh's economic structure relied primarily on male labor which prevented working-class women from an industrial role, thus reinforcing the traditional segregation of men and women. Working-class women continued time-consuming housework without technological advantages well into the 20th century, because of the political priorities of the city. For example, the decision to lay only small water pipes in working-class neighborhoods meant that only the middle and upper classes and heavy industry got enough water and sewage facilities. Working-class women were forced to perform all their household cleaning chores without adequate water. Domestic, technological inventions such as washing machines and gas stoves were also beyond the means of the working class. Based upon Pittsburgh government publications and secondary sources; 35 notes.
　　L. L. Athey

1774. McGrain, John W. ENGLEHART CRUSE AND BALTIMORE'S FIRST STEAM MILL. *Maryland Hist. Mag. 1976 71(1): 65-79.* "What may well have been the first grain mill in America powered by steam," was the suction apparatus demonstrated on "Pratt Street Wharf" in Baltimore by Englehart Cruse in May 1789, based on the design of Englishman Thomas Savery, 90 years earlier. Cruse was accused by James Rumsey of having stolen plans for a water-raising machine which Rumsey had revealed to him in 1787, and much of the article reproduces the pamphlet charges and countercharges, with evidence offered by Cruse that he had developed the machine himself. Describes Cruse's efforts to secure a patent from the Maryland Assembly and later from the new Federal Patent Office, along with his solicitation of George Washington's support. Emphasizes how far Americans were behind England in steam technology, at least until Oliver Evans' system of automation helped to outdistance the mother country. Surveys the growth and domination of Baltimore's milling industry, with names and locations. Based on primary and secondary sources; 2 illus., chart, 54 notes.
　　G. J. Bobango

1775. McShane, Clay. TRANSFORMING THE USE OF URBAN SPACE: A LOOK AT THE REVOLUTION IN STREET PAVEMENTS, 1800-1924. *J. of Urban Hist. 1979 5(3): 279-307.* In 1880 more than one-half of all urban streets were unpaved, but by 1924 virtually all of these roadways were paved. In addition to a great expansion in paving, there was a major shift in the materials, from 2.5% asphalt to 47.4%. Traces these technological changes and concludes that they resulted from a desire to solve social problems with technology and give the middle classes pleasant and isolated neighborhoods. 3 tables, 60 notes.
　　T. W. Smith

1776. Rose, Mark H. and Clark, John G. LIGHT, HEAT, AND POWER: ENERGY CHOICES IN KANSAS CITY, WICHITA, AND DENVER, 1900-1935. *J. of Urban Hist. 1979 5(3): 340-364.* Public utilities, street cars, sewage disposal, and public sanitation were "part of an effort to create convenient and congenial domestic settings in the face of massive innovations—political, social, spatial, economic, and psychological." The result was the creation of energy-hungry cities. 6 tables, 28 notes.
　　T. W. Smith

1777. Szasz, Ferenc M. and Bogardus, Ralph F. THE CAMERA AND THE AMERICAN SOCIAL CONSCIENCE: THE DOCUMENTARY PHOTOGRAPHY OF JACOB A. RIIS. *New York Hist. 1974 55(4): 409-436.* The impact of Jacob Riis upon his contemporaries can be understood better through a consideration of photographic technology in his day. Riis did most of his work in the 1890's, photographing New York City street scenes and advocating social reforms, especially for the poor, through his slides and lecture tours. Photos, 66 notes.
　　A. C. Aimone

1778. Tarr, Joel A. THE SEPARATE VS. COMBINED SEWER PROBLEM: A CASE STUDY IN URBAN TECHNOLOGY DESIGN CHOICE. *J. of Urban Hist. 1979 5(3): 308-339.* As cities grew they were forced to abandon cesspool systems of sewage disposal and adopt either combined or separate sewage systems. Large cities opted for combined systems while smaller cities used "separate" systems, although the removal of storm water was usually left to natural runoff. In deciding on the proper sewer system there is a complex and continual interaction of evolving disease control theories and public health, cost differentials, and investment in existing systems. Covers 1880-1920. Table, 60 notes.
　　T. W. Smith

1779. VanTrump, James D. A TRINITY OF BRIDGES: THE SMITHFIELD STREET BRIDGE OVER THE MONONGAHELA RIVER AT PITTSBURGH. *Western Pennsylvania Hist. Mag. 1975 58(4): 439-471.* Studies the three bridges built successively at this site by Lewis Wernwag, John A. Roebling, and Gustav Lindenthal and discusses the development of bridge construction technology during the 19th century.　　S

1780. Williams, Jon M. DAGUERREOTYPISTS, AMBROTYPISTS, AND PHOTOGRAPHERS IN WILMINGTON, DELAWARE, 1842-1859. *Delaware Hist. 1979 18(3): 180-193.* Analyzes the growth of daguerreotypy in Wilmington, noting the rapid changes in technology that led to the rise and demise of daguerreotype, then ambrotype, in the 1840's, both replaced by paper photography in the 1860's. Argues that the success of early photography lay in the determined efforts of small studios in places such as Wilmington. In Wilmington, as elsewhere, local men learned the new technology from itinerant artists and by relying on their connections with the community established their own businesses. The daguerreotype artists came from a variety of backgrounds, but the successful studios were run by commercially savvy, adaptive local men who knew the interests of the community. Includes a list of daguerreotypists, ambrotypists, and photographers in Wilmington, 1842-1859. Based on newspaper accounts and advertisements; 44 notes.　　R. M. Miller

The Physical City

General

1781. Abbott, Carl. THE NEIGHBORHOODS OF NEW YORK, 1760-1775. *New York Hist. 1974 55(1): 35-54.* Challenges the view that colonial cities made little use of urban planning. The physical layout of New York City and other colonial cities reveals a definite pattern of land use based on economic and occupational stratification. Generally, the urban core area (in this case, the southern tip of Manhattan Island beginning one block inland from the East River) was the commercial center of the city, housing the most important economic activity. The wealthy mercantile class lived in the core, where housing and land were in greatest demand, and the best commercial streets coincided with the best residential streets. The abject poor occupied the slums next to the waterfront and the urban fringe areas on the northern and western outskirts of the city. The western fringe area (along the Hudson River) contained marginal and foul commercial enterprises such as slaughter-houses, ropewalks, and breweries. Between the wealthy core and the impoverished fringes lived a middle class of artisans and shopkeepers. They occupied concentric circles radiating outward from the core, the inner core representing wealth, the outer poverty. Primary and secondary sources; 6 illus., map, 53 notes.　　G. Kurland

1782. Bailey, David T. and Haulman, Bruce E. PATTERNS OF LANDHOLDING IN SANTA FE IN 1860 AND 1870. *Social Sci. J. 1976 13(3): 9-19.* One of six articles in this issue on the subject of Spanish and Mexican land grants in the Southwest.

1783. Booth, Larry and Booth, Jane. IMAGES OF OUR PAST: THE SAN DIEGO TITLE INSURANCE AND TRUST COMPANY HISTORICAL PHOTOGRAPHS COLLECTION. *J. of San Diego Hist. 1979 25(2): 83-135.* Provides 51 photographs from the San Diego Title Insurance and Trust Company Collection to recreate both historic and commonplace scenes in San Diego, 1880's-1950's.

1784. Brown, Robert F. THE AESTHETIC TRANSFORMATION OF AN INDUSTRIAL COMMUNITY. *Winterthur Portfolio 1977 12: 35-64.* Henry Hobson Richardson (1838-86) and Frederick Law Olmsted (1822-1903) transformed the architectural character of North Easton, Massachusetts, by five new buildings, 1870-90. Natural terrain and the dominant Ames family governed Richardson's and Olmsted's transformation of the town into one of coherent planning and aesthetic merit. The Oliver Ames Free Library, the Town Hall, the Frederick Lothrop Ames gate lodge, a railroad station, and shovel shops radically transformed the town. This change was based on sophisticated design that resulted in an integrated visual statement. Primary and secondary sources; 33 illus., 33 notes.   N. A. Kuntz

1785. Burnham, Mary Maud. SAN DIEGO'S HORTON PLAZA. *J. of San Diego Hist. 1975 20(4): 38-43.* Describes the development of "New San Diego" around the Horton Plaza (1870's), which was named after land developer Alonzo E. Horton.   S

1786. Cawthon, John Ardis. A BRIEF HISTORY OF SHREVE-PORT, CADDO PARISH, BASED UPON A SAMPLING OF INSCRIPTIONS ON TOMBSTONES. *North Louisiana Hist. Assoc. J. 1975 6(4): 165-173.* Although Caddo Parish came into existence on 18 January 1838, Shreveport was not incorporated until 1839. The "Valhalla" of the city is Oakland Cemetery, "across the street from the Municipal Auditorium on the south side of Milam Street." It is here that "the forefathers of Shreveport sleep . . .the pioneer bankers, doctors, lawyers, merchants and soldiers—the rich and the poor." Mary D. C. Cane, who donated land to the city for the cemetery, is buried there. Among other prominent names to be found in the cemetery are Foster, Levy, Bercher, Kimble, Kelly, Hamilton and Munson. Other cemeteries in the area are the Hebrew Rest, the Greenwood, and the Forest Park Cemetery. In these three one can find the names Goldstein, Dreyfuss, Saenger, Hardin, and Irvine, all of which were also important in the development of this "metropolis of North Louisiana." 12 photos, 4 notes.   A. N. Garland

1787. Clay, Grady. RIGHT UP OUR ALLEYS. *Hist. Preservation 1978 30(3): 18-22.* Discusses the development, meaning, and attitudes toward the American residential alley which "has been the academic, geographic, and social outcast of the built environment for at least a half-century." Excerpts from the author's book *Alleys: A Hidden Resource.* Illus.   R. M. Frame, III

1788. Falconer, Paul A. MUYBRIDGE'S WINDOW TO THE PAST: A WET-PLATE VIEW OF SAN FRANCISCO IN 1877. *California History 1978 57(2): 130-157.* Describes San Francisco in June 1877 as seen through the 360-degree panoramic view taken by photographer Eadweard Muybridge. The 11 plates taken by Muybridge reveal San Francisco's architectural styles, business enterprises, and social activities. Muybridge took a similar panorama around May 1878. Calculates the probable date of the photographs through correlation of photographic and documentary evidence; corrects inaccuracies of several writers on Muybridge. Based on newspapers and published studies; photos, 33 notes.   A. Hoffman

1789. Foster, Edward Halsey. THE STEVENS FAMILY AND THE ARTS, 1820-1860. *New Jersey Hist. 1976 94(4): 173-183.* The Stevens family of Hoboken displayed a sophisticated knowledge of contemporary aesthetic theory in landscape gardening and architecture. Members of this family commissioned some of the country's finest Greek, Gothic, and Italian Revival buildings. The grounds they landscaped at Hoboken were the most famous of their kind in the country. Describes specific buildings and places influenced by the Stevens family. Based on the Stevens family papers and secondary sources; 4 illus., 19 notes.

E. R. McKinstry

1790. Foster, Mark S. THE MODEL-T, THE HARD SELL, AND LOS ANGELES'S URBAN GROWTH: THE DECENTRALIZATION OF LOS ANGELES DURING THE 1920'S. *Pacific Hist. R. 1975 44(4): 459-484.* Three important developments in the 1920's have not been sufficiently emphasized by students of Los Angeles' decentralization. In that decade the automobile eclipsed the trolley as the preferred mode of urban transportation. The real estate boom of the 1920's confirmed this change, as developers opened up residential tracts whose only access was by car. City leaders and planners consciously and confidently

committed themselves to a decentralized pattern of development as a positive goal. Based on primary and secondary sources; 86 notes.

W. K. Hobson

1791. Geib, Susan. LANDSCAPE AND FACTION: SPATIAL TRANSFORMATION IN WILLIAM BENTLEY'S SALEM. *Essex Inst. Hist. Collections 1977 113(3): 163-180.* Examines developments and changes in the topography and buildings in the Reverend William Bentley's (1759-1819) Salem for relationships between choice of land, architectural use, social organization, and political behavior. Architectural forms changed (returned to classics and European) to reflect changing politics; at the same time there developed new organizational patterns for the use of space and new land-use types. Many times topographical alterations became embroiled in political disputes, while the construction of buildings became symbols of political prestige. Based on the diary (1784-1819) of William Bentley and on primary and secondary sources; 54 notes.   R. S. Sliwoski

1792. Griffin, John W. ST. AUGUSTINE IN 1822. *Escribano 1977 14: 45-56.* Describes the physical layout of and daily life in St. Augustine, Florida, one year after its annexation to the United States.

1793. Horowitz, Helen Lefkowitz. "THINE ALABASTER CITIES GLEAM. . . . " *Rev. in Am. Hist. 1977 5(1): 77-82.* Review article prompted by David F. Burg's *Chicago's White City of 1893* (Lexington: U. Pr. of Kentucky, 1976), which describes the World's Columbian Exposition (Chicago, 1893).

1794. Horton, Loren N. THROUGH THE EYES OF ARTISTS: IOWA TOWNS IN THE 19TH CENTURY. *Palimpsest 1978 59(5): 133-147.* Printing of lithographs of towns was common in 19th-century America for both interior decor and public relations. Lithograph artists were travelers, often with government expeditions, or entrepreneurs of panoramic exhibits, or compilers of state and county atlases whose bird's-eye view replaced the panorama. Dubuque, Davenport, Muscatine, and Burlington were favorite subjects. Photography and mass-printing replaced lithograph artists by 1900. 30 illus., note on sources, editor's background introductory note.   N. Cahill

1795. Howe, Robert T. KNOWLTON'S AT THE CORNER. *Cincinnati Hist. Soc. Bull. 1975 33(3): 189-215.* Outlines the history, topography, and street patterns of the Knowlton's Corner area of Cumminsville in Cincinnati, Ohio, from 1788-1974.

1796. Kogan, Bernard R. CHICAGO'S PIER. *Chicago Hist. 1976 5(1): 28-38.* Chronicles the development of Chicago's pier area, 1916-76.

1797. Locker, Zelma Bays. WHATEVER HAPPENED TO IZARD STREET? PACIFIC BEACH AND ITS STREET NAMES. *J. of San Diego Hist. 1976 22(2): 20-29.*

1798. Lockwood, Charles. RINCON HILL WAS SAN FRANCISCO'S MOST GENTEEL NEIGHBORHOOD. *California History 1979 58(1): 48-61.* From the 1850's to the 1870's Rincon Hill was considered an elegant residential area, with many Greek Revival and Gothic Revival mansions. As the South of Market area became industrialized, Rincon Hill was affected by commercial intrusion. The Second Street cut in 1869 facilitated traffic from South of Market factories to the docks but ran through Rincon Hill. By 1900 the neighborhood's wealthy residents had moved and homes were being torn down or converted into boarding houses. Most of Rincon Hill was destroyed in the 1906 earthquake and fire. Little remains of the area today except for a few warehouses, some rundown hotels, and South Park. Primary and secondary sources; 3 illus., 13 photos, map, 8 notes.   A. Hoffman

1799. Lytle, Rebecca. PEOPLE AND PLACES: IMAGES OF NINETEENTH CENTURY SAN DIEGO IN LITHOGRAPHS AND PAINTINGS. *J. of San Diego Hist. 1978 24(2): 153-171.* Discusses and reprints 12 landscapes and portraits of 19th-century San Diego and San Diegans in the collection of the San Diego Historical Society.

1800. Mayor, A. Hyatt. PRINTS. *Am. Art J. 1975 7(1): 43-51.* Reprints nine prints of various American cities and scenes, 1600-1775.

1801. Olmsted, Roger. THE CITY THAT WAS. *California Hist. Q. 1976 55(2): 121-136.* Presents a photographic essay by an anonymous photographer showing San Francisco before and after the earthquake and fire of 18 April 1906. The photographs, from the Muhlmann Collection of the San Francisco Maritime Museum, show San Franciscans at work and leisure. The photographs capture a bygone era as well as the event that ended it.
                                                                A. Hoffman

1802. Raiche, Stephen J. LAFAYETTE SQUARE: A BIT OF OLD ST. LOUIS. *Missouri Hist. Soc. Bull. 1973 29(2): 88-95.* A historical account and description of Lafayette Square and its environs, 1836-1926. Established by city authorities, the square attracted posh residential developments up to about 1884. After that, commercial developments encroached on Lafayette Square. In 1918, municipal authorities zoned against further extension of commercial activities into the neighborhood, but the city's efforts to preserve the area failed. By 1926, the commercial and industrial onslaught was far advanced. St. Louis municipal records, newspapers, and secondary sources; 8 photos, 21 notes.
                                                                H. T. Lovin

1803. Robinson, Willard B. MARITIME FRONTIER ENGINEERING: THE DEFENSE OF NEW ORLEANS. *Louisiana Hist. 1977 18(1): 5-62.* Discusses the objectives, planning, and construction of fortifications protecting New Orleans during 1680-1896. Beginning with Fort Crèvecoeur (1680), depicts a large number of 18th-century French and Spanish forts in the New Orleans area, including the fortifications of the city itself. The early federal period witnessed several new fortifications, notably Forts Jackson, Pike, Philip, Macomb, and Livingston, and the Battery Bienvenue. These were expanded in midcentury as part of a national system of forts. New forts were added during the Civil War at Proctor's Landing and Ship Island. Few fortifications were added until some improvements in coast artillery were made in the 1890's. The forts were abandoned in 1920 because they were obsolete. Some of the forts, examples of military architecture of the 18th and 19th centuries, have been made into state historical parks. Others are falling into ruin. Primary sources; 27 illus., 109 notes.
                                                                R. L. Woodward, Jr.

1804. Simon, Roger D. HOUSING AND SERVICES IN AN IMMIGRANT NEIGHBORHOOD: MILWAUKEE'S WARD 14. *J. of Urban Hist. 1976 2(4): 435-458.* The 14th ward in the southwest corner of Milwaukee was the center of the city's Polish Americans at the turn of the century. Although populated by immigrants employed in unskilled and factory jobs, the ward was a neighborhood not of tenements or decayed dwellings, but of small, recently constructed, single unit dwellings. More than half of the houses were owned by their occupants. This was not achieved without sacrifices. Boarders were a frequent source of added income (and added crowding), and municipal services such as water and sewers were often delayed until residents could afford their installation. Based on the Wisconsin state census of 1905 and other primary and secondary sources; 4 tables, 6 fig., 35 notes.
                                                                T. W. Smith

1805. Smith, Suzanne. AN AMERICAN PANORAMA. *Am. Heritage 1975 26(3): 44-53.* Photographs taken by the James A. Drake family depict the scenery and citizenry of Corning, New York, 1899-1910. 14 illus.
                                                                B. J. Paul

1806. Stanford, Peter. EAST RIVER: OF TIME AND TIDE. *Sea Hist. 1979 (13): 9-11.* Pictorial history of New York City's East River as a commercial waterway, 1609-1876.

1807. Starr, Roger. F. SCOTT FITZGERALD AND ROBERT MOSES. *New York Affairs 1973 1(1): 60-69.* Describes the transformation of the cinder dump on the Flushing River which F. Scott Fitzgerald called "Valley of Ashes" in *The Great Gatsby*. New York City Commissioner of Parks Robert Moses was instrumental in obtaining the construction of Flushing Meadow Park in the mid-1930's without extensive city funding of the project. His achievement illustrates the possible accomplishments of an individual leader with sufficient authority to influence change. Illus., 2 notes.
                                                                J. A. Benson

1808. Takasaki, John. KAIMUKI. *Hawaiian J. of Hist. 1976 10: 64-74.* Kaimuki is a residential community east of downtown Honolulu. Beginning with ancient times, covers such subjects as foreign influence,

ranching in the area, and the early attempts at subdivision and transportation. Photos.
                                                                R. Alvis

1809. Tinkcom, Margaret B. URBAN REFLECTIONS IN A TRANS-ATLANTIC MIRROR. *Pennsylvania Mag. of Hist. and Biog. 1976 100(3): 287-313.* Compares London and Philadelphia's designs for urban living and architecture in the 17th and 18th centuries. "Philadelphia became in many ways a trans-Atlantic mirror of post-Fire London." Primary and secondary sources; 51 notes.
                                                                E. W. Carp

1810. Unsigned. ARTISTS DRAW SOUTH DAKOTA: PANORAMIC VIEWS OF PIONEER TOWNS. *South Dakota Hist. 1978 8(3): 221-249.* Provides "bird's-eye views" of 25 South Dakota towns sketched mostly during the 1880's. Popular with various promoters, the views were designed and printed to enhance the town's appearances for prospective settlers. Most popular in the East and Midwest, those included complete the South Dakota State Historical Society's collection. They reveal the state of lithography and printmaking, and are quasiaccurate representations of South Dakota towns in the Victorian period. Primary sources; 25 photos, table, note.
                                                                A. J. Larson

1811. Unsigned. A CELEBRATION OF CITIES. *Am. Heritage 1979 30(2): 14-25.* A portfolio of panoramic views of several American cities painted during 1850's-90's. Most of the paintings were commissioned for promotional purposes. Included are views of Salt Lake City (Utah), Quincy (Mass.), Hannibal (Mo.), Sumner (Kansas), Cripple Creek (Colo.), and New York City. 9 illus.
                                                                J. F. Paul

1812. Unsigned. NATCHEZ YESTERDAYS: A TIRELESS PHOTOGRAPHER'S RECORD OF A RIVER TOWN. *Am. Heritage 1978 29(4): 18-35.* Henry C. Norman was a photographer in Natchez, Mississippi, for almost 40 years after 1870. Thousands of his negatives are being sorted and cataloged by Thomas and Joan Gandy. The examples here are from *H. C. Norman's Natchez: An Early Photographer and His Town*, (U. of Mississippi Pr., 1978). 17 illus.
                                                                B. J. Paul

1813. Wahmann, Russell, comp. FRONT STREET, FLAGSTAFF: FROM TRAIL TO THOROUGHFARE. *J. of Arizona Hist. 1973 14(1): 31-46.* A photographic essay traces the architectural and other transformations of the main street of Flagstaff. Front Street, later named Railroad Avenue, now Santa Fe Avenue, developed differently from other main streets in the Southwest. 20 photos.
                                                                D. L. Smith

1814. Wilson, William H. "MORE ALMOST THAN THE MEN": MIRA LLOYD DOCK AND THE BEAUTIFICATION OF HARRISBURG. *Pennsylvania Mag. of Hist. and Biog. 1975 99(4): 490-499.* Discusses the campaign for city beautification in Harrisburg, Pennsylvania, and the role of Mira Lloyd Dock, one of the founders of the Civic Club of Harrisburg. Miss Dock lectured successfully to inspire the city's leaders to begin a 40-year improvement program. 23 notes.
                                                                C. W. Olson

1815. Yoder, Don. PENNSYLVANIA TOWN VIEWS OF A CENTURY AGO. *Pennsylvania Folklife 1974 23(4): 31-35.* A photographic collection of several Pennsylvania towns of the 1870's and 1880's reveals a great range of architecture, including covered bridges, and several details on town planning in 19th-century Pennsylvania.
                                                                S

1816. Zelinsky, Wilbur. THE PENNSYLVANIA TOWN: AN OVERDUE GEOGRAPHICAL ACCOUNT. *Geographical Rev. 1977 67(2): 127-147.* This field survey of a hitherto unstudied settlement form, the Pennsylvania Town and 234 specific examples thereof, directs attention to the role of the seminal Pennsylvania Culture Area in the evolution of North American urban morphology and to several related, unsolved puzzles. The Pennsylvania Town, essentially a dense aggregation of spatially mixed functions in regionally distinctive structures, closely spaced, often built of brick, set along a generally rectilinear lattice of arboreal streets and well-kept alleys frequently focused on a diamond-shaped central square, is indeed regionally distinctive. Only minor diversity occurs over time, territory, or size category within a compact, rather sharply bounded tract nearly coincident with other delimitations of the PCA. What remains unclear is why this town type is spatially detached from Philadelphia, its logical progenitor, why it is so aberrant from other American town types, and why, despite its strategic historicogeographical locus, it exercised so little effect on later forms.
                                                                J

1817. Unsigned. IDAHO'S SEAPORT. *Idaho Yesterdays 1974-75 18(4): 2-3.* Pictorial essay showing Lewiston, Idaho, at the end of the 19th century and during the 1894 flood.   S

Planning

1818. Alanen, Arnold R. and Peltin, Thomas J. KOHLER, WISCONSIN: PLANNING AND PATERNALISM IN A MODEL INDUSTRIAL VILLAGE. *J. of the Am. Inst. of Planners 1978 44(2): 145-159.* Although it never achieved the infamy of Pullman, Illinois, nor the size of Gary, Indiana, the company town of Kohler, Wisconsin, stands out as an interesting example of community planning and corporate paternalism. Walter J. Kohler, Sr., the company president from 1905 to 1940 and the primary force behind the model village, hired several nationally known planners to guide the early development of the community. These activities brought a considerable amount of fame to Kohler, but two bitter strikes (1934 and 1954-1960) tarnished the image of systematic order and seeming harmony which the company sought to maintain. While the company still plays an important role in community affairs, current residents appear to be quite satisfied with village-corporate relationships and evaluate the community's physical planning features highly.
                                                                       J

1819. Archer, John. PURITAN TOWN PLANNING IN NEW HAVEN. *J. of the Soc. of Architectural Historians 1975 34(2): 140-149.*

1820. Bach, Ira J. A RECONSIDERATION OF THE 1909 "PLAN OF CHICAGO." *Chicago Hist. 1973 2(3): 132-141.* Daniel Hudson Burnham's (1846-1912) plan for the Chicago lakefront included the metropolitan area for a radius of 60 miles. The plan called for mingling the city with Lake Michigan by means of man-made islands and peninsulas. Burnham also designed numerous interior parks connected by spacious boulevards. Burnham's design was derived in part from his work with Frederick Law Olmsted (1822-1903) on the World's Columbian Exposition (1893). The plan had shortcomings, such as its failure to foresee slums and automobiles. Nonetheless, it did open up the city, making recreational facilities available and saving the waterfront. Edward Herbert Bennett (1874-1954), Burnham's partner, deserves far more attention for his contribution to the design. Based on primary and secondary sources; 5 illus.   N. A. Kuntz

1821. Brownell, Blaine A. THE COMMERCIAL-CIVIC ELITE AND CITY PLANNING IN ATLANTA, MEMPHIS, AND NEW ORLEANS IN THE 1920'S. *J. of Southern Hist. 1975 41(3): 339-368.* An analysis of the origins and development of modern urban planning as exemplified by three southern cities. The general trend was everywhere similar; a nationwide passion for planning had developed. Business and commercial interests were the prime movers. They wanted to create cities which were firstly efficient and secondarily beautiful. The movement declined by 1930, primarily because of the great depression but also because of disillusionment. The problems were enormous; time, facilities, and financing were limited. 54 notes.   V. L. Human

1822. Brunvand, Jan Harold. THE ARCHITECTURE OF ZION. *Am. West 1976 13(2): 28-35.* Joseph Smith's 1833 master plan for a "City of Zion" specified wide streets following the cardinal points of the compass, with church and civic buildings at the center, and unpainted granaries and barns within the community perimeter, surrounded by open fields. It called for houses of substantial stone or brick masonry construction. These features were adopted to the terrain and environment—elaborate irrigation ditch networks, hay derricks, Lombardy poplar windows, and the thrifty "Mormon fence"—and characterize traditional Mormon small town communities throughout the West. 13 illus.   D. L. Smith

1823. Dougherty, J. P. BAROQUE AND PICTURESQUE MOTIFS IN L'ENFANT'S DESIGN FOR THE FEDERAL CAPITAL. *Am. Q. 1974 26(1): 23-36.* L'Enfant's proposed and partially executed plan (1791) combined a gridiron design with coordinates varying in frequency and a system of radiocentric avenues derived from the two main foci of the President's House and the Capitol. His scheme derived from his concept of a strong nationally elected executive balancing a locally elected house of legislators. His emphasis on broad vistas was better suited for the capital of an empire rather than for a republic, while his awareness of scenic backdrops for his projected public buildings indicated the influence of the English cult of the picturesque.   N. Lederer

1824. Foster, Mark. CITY PLANNERS AND URBAN TRANSPORTATION: THE AMERICAN RESPONSE, 1900-1940. *J. of Urban Hist. 1979 5(3): 365-396.* Examines the role of city planners in developing America's urban transportation system during the first half of the 20th century. Inquires why planners "allowed" the abandonment of mass transit systems such as the street car in favor of an automobile-oriented system. Finds this trend regrettable but holds the planners as blameless for the change. 101 notes.   T. W. Smith

1825. Guttenberg, Albert Z. CITY ENCOUNTER AND "DESERT" ENCOUNTER: TWO SOURCES OF AMERICAN REGIONAL PLANNING THOUGHT. *J. of the Am. Inst. of Planners 1978 44(4): 399-411.* Examines the similarity-in-diversity of two regional planning experiences in American settlement, during the 1920's: establishment of neighborhoods in Eastern cities and cooperative communities and scientific family farms in the arid West.

1826. Hamburg, James F. PAPERTOWNS IN SOUTH DAKOTA. *J. of the West 1977 16(1): 40-42.* A papertown in South Dakota was a town surveyed into blocks and lots where no buildings were ever erected. Most were established during the state's two major periods of settlement: 1) the great Dakota boom during 1878-90 and, 2) during 1900-20. Describes some of the sites. Map.   R. Alvis

1827. Heidrich, Robert W. "A VILLAGE IN A PARK": RIVERSIDE, ILLINOIS. *Hist. Preservation 1973 25(2): 28-33.* The Chicago suburb of Riverside, one of the first planned suburbs in the United States, was designed ca. 1868-70 by Frederick Law Olmsted. Rejecting the grid pattern of town planning, Olmsted used the curves of the terrain and of the Des Plaines River to incorporate commons and parks into a landscaped background for the individual houses. Notable architects who designed houses for this setting include Frank Lloyd Wright, Louis Sullivan, William Le Baron Jenney, Calvert Vaux, and Frederick E. Withers. 4 illus., 9 photos.   R. M. Frame, III

1828. Henry, Jay C.; Hines, Thomas S.; Schalck, Harry G.; Draper, Joan E.; and Henry, Jean. URBAN PLANNING IN AMERICA SINCE 1776. *J. of the Soc. of Architectural Hist. 1976 35(4): 285-292.* Columbus, Ohio, expanded and grew through permissive planning which supported the initiative of private owners, in contrast to Roland Park, Maryland, where total development was strictly controlled by a private company. Traces the connection between the Progressive Movement and the concurrent City Beautiful Movement, a prime example of which was the San Francisco Civic Center. Elements of pop culture in architecture are humanizing additions to a sterile cityscape. 6 illus.   M. Zolota

1829. Hines, Thomas S. THE PARADOX OF "PROGRESSIVE" ARCHITECTURE: URBAN PLANNING AND PUBLIC BUILDING IN TOM JOHNSON'S CLEVELAND. *Am. Q. 1973 25(4): 426-448.* Eschewing the inventive originality of modern architecture, the commissioners and citizens of Cleveland designed the municipal face-lifting of their early 20th-century Cleveland Group Plan around the ambience of L'Enfant's Washington, Old World references, and the World's Columbian Exposition. In architecture, as in Progressivism itself, retreat from the complexities of industrial society coexisted with a spirit of adventure and reform. Primary and secondary sources; 33 notes.
                                                                    W. D. Piersen

1830. Holmes, Jack D. L. VIDAL AND ZONING IN SPANISH NEW ORLEANS, 1797. *Louisiana Hist. 1973 14(3): 271-282.* Discusses a petition sent to the Governor General of the Natchez District of Louisiana from Nicolás María Vidal expressing the desire to have the zoning near his house (located near the levee in the city of New Orleans) changed to prohibit business enterprises from being built, especially that of Juan Dumaine, a local blacksmith whose noisy trade disturbed Vidal; Vidal expresses his desire to remove Dumaine from the area because of the Spanish law restricting construction of homes near ramparts of the city (which he considered the levee to be), because of the problem that Dumaine's home caused in access to water supplies in case of fire, and because of his activities in smuggling, robbery, and slave trading.
                                                                    G. A. Hewlett

1831. Jackson, Richard H. THE MORMON VILLAGE: GENESIS AND ANTECEDENTS OF THE CITY OF ZION PLAN. *Brigham Young U. Studies 1977 17(2): 223-240.* In 1833 Joseph Smith sent plans for his proposed City of Zion to a group of Missouri Mormons. Many scholars have mistakenly concluded that subsequent Mormon settlements religiously adhered to Smith's plan. Examines the development of Mormon villages, towns, and cities and concludes that most urban development deviated from the Zion plat and from each other as well. However, there are similarities, such as street widths, block sizes, and lot sizes, which seemed to set the Mormon village apart from non-Mormon settlements in the West.   M. S. Legan

1832. Johnston, Norman J. THE FREDERICK LAW OLMSTED PLAN FOR TACOMA. *Pacific Northwest Q. 1975 66(3): 97-104.* After selecting Tacoma as its Puget Sound terminus in 1873, the Northern Pacific Railroad Company set about to establish a town plan. Chief Engineer James Tilton submitted a standard model based on the Melbourne, Australia, example, but within the existing American approach to urban planning. Railroad executives, however, granted a contract to the celebrated urban architect Frederick Law Olmsted who devised a plan stressing aesthetic standards over purely practical considerations. Pressures from speculators forced the cancellation of Olmsted's design and guaranteed the acceptance of Tilton's model. Based on primary and secondary sources; 3 photos, 20 notes.   M. L. Tate

1833. Johnston, Norman J. HARLAND BARTHOLOMEW: PRECEDENT FOR THE PROFESSION. *J. of the Am. Inst. of Planners 1973 39(2): 115-124.* Biographical sketch of Harland Bartholomew (b. 1889) includes discussion of his achievements in city planning, urban renewal, rural land use policy, and housing policy formation, 1910's-20's.

1834. Kantor, Harvey A. BENJAMIN MARSH AND THE FIGHT OVER POPULATION CONGESTION. *J. of the Am. Inst. of Planners 1974 40(6): 422-429.* Benjamin C. Marsh, a vigorous young social worker in the early years of the 20th century, attacked the extreme congestion of poor people in the nation's largest cities. In his analysis of the causes of congestion, Marsh identified the basic dynamics of large-scale crowding and offered some of the most radical solutions of taxation, land-use, and planning proposed during his day. As an early leader against the overcrowding of land, the author of the first book devoted entirely to city planning and the founder of the first National Conference on City Planning, Marsh's career points up the diversity of style and ideology that characterized the pioneers of the planning profession.   J

1835. Kantor, Harvey A. CHARLES DYER NORTON AND THE ORIGINS OF THE REGIONAL PLAN OF NEW YORK. *J. of the Am. Inst. of Planners 1973 39(1): 35-42.* The passage of the nation's first comprehensive zoning law in 1916 brought a great deal of attention to the urban planners of New York City. The "promising start" that zoning represented vaulted New York to the forefront of the national planning movement. The next step to be taken would be important in setting a trend for the planning profession in general. The New York planners did not abdicate their leadership role. The route chosen after 1916 was a broadened concern for regional, rather than mere city planning. The scientific techniques of surveying and data gathering employed during the zoning campaign would now be applied to the entire metropolitan area. The result of these expanded efforts—The Regional Plan and Survey of New York and Its Environs—would again be a model of comprehensive achievement. The man who singlehandedly inspired the New York Regional Plan was Charles Dyer Norton. Through influential connections in the community and a personal dynamism, Norton was successful in overcoming the timidity of his contemporaries and in converting his vision into concrete proposals. The New York Regional Plan was the boldest effort at mastering a metropolitan area yet attempted by urban planners of the day.   J

1836. Kantor, Harvey A. THE CITY BEAUTIFUL IN NEW YORK. *New-York Hist. Soc. Q. 1973 57(2): 148-171.* At the turn of the century, many American cities attempted to pattern themselves after the "White City" of the World's Columbian Exposition (1893) in Chicago. These attempts involved such adaptations as neoclassical structures, civic centers, and massive buildings. In New York City the result was an Improvement Plan of 1907. The plan failed, but the efforts to implement it are of interest. The episode indicates that such planning must take into consideration all of the economic and social factors involved in an urban setting. This was not done in the case of the 1907 New York plan. The result was continued haphazard growth for the city. Based on contemporary newspapers and periodicals; 8 illus., 44 notes.
C. L. Grant

1837. Kaplan, Barry J. ANDREW H. GREEN AND THE CREATION OF A PLANNING RATIONALE: THE FORMATION OF GREATER NEW YORK CITY, 1865-1890. *Urbanism Past and Present 1979 (8): 32-41.* Andrew Green, an early advocate of regional urban planning as a means of overcoming existing urban problems, led the fight for the consolidation of the territories surrounding the Port of New York. However, historians ignore Green's significant contributions to controlled urban growth in general. Green viewed a metropolitan complex as functionally one. He concentrated on the physical and administrative problems of consolidation, and provided the intellectual rationale. Through political positions such as the president of the Central Park Board, Green influenced the 1894 consolidation of New York City (just Manhattan in 1868) with the municipalities of Brooklyn and Westchester. Map, 52 notes.   B. P. Anderson

1838. King, Paul E. EXCLUSIONARY ZONING AND OPEN HOUSING: A BRIEF JUDICIAL HISTORY. *Geographical Rev. 1978 68(4): 459-469.* The evolution of exclusionary zoning is reviewed from the first emergence of land use controls at the local level to recent U.S. Supreme Court decisions on the issue. Early conflicts surrounded the delegation of the police power from the states to local municipalities. After 1926, however, zoning became established and was widely applied until 1945. Associated with the rapid suburbanization following World War II exclusionary devices flourished, but after 1965 a changing judicial climate led to the overthrow of numerous ordinances by state courts. This antizoning trend notwithstanding, there is legal precedent for exclusion when it is tied to comprehensive development plans and slow-growth ordinances. Federal courts have taken a very conservative stance on local land use cases, and the conclusion is reached that exclusion will continue as long as local interests outweigh metropolitan or regional concerns.
J

1839. Kruse, Rhoda E. MYSTERY MAN OF OCEAN BEACH. *J. of San Diego Hist. 1977 23(4): 58-68.* Discusses the mysterious J. M. DePuy, the first person to conceptualize the subdivision of the Ocean Beach area of San Diego, California, 1885-87; includes a copy of the original subdivision plans.

1840. Lapping, Mark B. RADBURN: PLANNING THE AMERICAN COMMUNITY. *New Jersey Hist. 1977 95(2): 85-100.* Although Radburn never fully developed as planned, it is a testament to the Regional Planning Association of America (RPAA). Radburn was planned as a town for the motor age that would be attractive to the middle class. Discusses the government designed for the town, the population and its projected economic base, and the intended quality of social life. Concludes that the RPAA was dominated by traditionalists whose concepts of housing patterns and community organization offered little that was new. Covers 1927. Primary and secondary sources; 2 illus., 28 notes.
E. R. McKinstry

1841. Lloyd, Anne. PITTSBURGH'S 1923 ZONING ORDINANCE. *Western Pennsylvania Hist. Mag. 1974 57(3): 289-305.* Discusses debates over city planning and urbanization.   S

1842. Logan, Thomas H. THE AMERICANIZATION OF GERMAN ZONING. *J. of the Am. Inst. of Planners 1976 42(4): 377-385.* Explores the origins of zoning in the reform era which also gave rise to the planning professions in both Germany and the United States. The reform objectives of the proponents are reviewed, but the early entry of social segregation practices is also traced. It is argued that the planner's tendency to underemphasize the necessary links of a planning tool such as zoning to other supporting policies reinforces the public pressures which often subvert reform objectives.   J

1843. Mullen, John R. AMERICAN PERCEPTIONS OF GERMAN CITY PLANNING AT THE TURN OF THE CENTURY. *Urbanism Past and Present 1976-77 (3): 5-15.* Late 19th-century German city planning is a key link in the roots of American city planning. By 1900, every German city and town was undertaking some form of municipal master planning at a time when great shortcomings of the American city beautiful movement were being realized. Focuses on Frankfurt. Development occurred in health improvement, traffic engineering, the psychological and physiological well-being of residents, and administrative procedures. Of greatest interest to American planners was the Zoning Act. City planning also included the Increment Tax, which discouraged land speculation and land redistribution. 3 plates, 38 notes.

B. P. Anderson

1844. Myhra, David. REXFORD GUY TUGWELL: INITIATOR OF AMERICA'S GREENBELT NEW TOWNS, 1935 TO 1936. *J. of the Am. Inst. of Planners 1974 40(3): 176-188.* Between 1935 and 1936, the United States Department of Agriculture (USDA) initiated a public housing program that resulted in the construction of planned new communities called Greenbelt Towns. The prime mover behind this effort was Rexford Tugwell. The significance of this idea was his advanced concept of resettling the rural poor in planned towns at the edge of urban areas. Tugwell recognized, earlier perhaps than many of his colleagues, the push-pull tendencies emerging in American society in the 1930's. Arguing that urban growth was inevitable, Tugwell's Greenbelt concept was to demonstrate how housing could be surrounded with a more pleasing environment in order to accommodate the expanding rural to urban migration. In less than two years Tugwell's Resettlement Administration planned and constructed three new communities and litigated a fourth. By all standards, these accomplishments demonstrate an unprecedented speed record for action by a bureaucracy.

J

1845. Osterweis, Rollin G. THE NEW HAVEN GREEN. *Yale 1976 39(6): 12-17.* Examines the early city plans for New Haven, Connecticut, the laying out of the New Haven Green, and the position which the town and its center played in local as well as national life, 1630-1775.

1846. Peterson, Jon A. THE CITY BEAUTIFUL MOVEMENT: FORGOTTEN ORIGINS AND LOST MEANINGS. *J. of Urban Hist. 1976 2(4): 415-434.* The city beautiful movement appeared during the Progressive Era, and was noted for its classic-Renaissance architecture and for favoring monumental city planning. It emphasized municipal art, civic improvement, and outdoor art. While its roots extend back before its commonly credited progenitor, the 1893 World's Columbian Exposition, the city beautiful movement actually did not blossom until the 1897-1902 period. Primary and secondary sources; 56 notes.

T. W. Smith

1847. Peterson, Jon A. THE IMPACT OF SANITARY REFORM UPON AMERICAN URBAN PLANNING, 1840-1890. *J. of Social Hist. 1979 13(1): 83-103.* Reviews the influences on city planning by sanitary engineers, impelled by the "filth theory" of disease prevalent at the time. Remarks that true urban planners had not yet appeared. Covers the development of water-carried sewage, which led to the development of an integrated city concept, and sanitary surveys, which tried to locate all sources of disease in an urban complex. Notes the rise of consciousness regarding townsite location, which led to the development of parks and suburbs. Closes with the observation that the sanitary engineers were never really city planners and that their results were always less than complete. 74 notes.

V. L. Human

1848. Ports, Uldis. GERANIUMS VS. SMOKESTACKS: SAN DIEGO'S MAYORALTY CAMPAIGN OF 1917. *J. of San Diego Hist. 1975 21(3): 50-56.* Describes the work of George Marston in the city planning and development of San Diego, 1908-17.

S

1849. Rice, Cindy. SPRING CITY: A LOOK AT A NINETEENTH-CENTURY MORMON VILLAGE. *Utah Hist. Q. 1975 43(3): 260-277.* Spring City, Utah, is a prototype of the Mormon village, with large lots, broad streets in a typical grid system oriented to the compass points, and its use of local building materials. It is unique in having so many original structures unchanged, its Scandinavian building traditions, and the absence of large commercial establishments. It has all the ingredients needed for an insight into rural life in a 19th-century Mormon village. It merits preservation. Based on primary and secondary sources; 10 illus., 40 notes.

J. L. Hazelton

1850. Robinson, Michael. THE SUBURBAN IDEAL: 19TH-CENTURY PLANNED COMMUNITIES. *Hist. Preservation 1978 30(2): 24-29.* Details the rise and development of "the first suburbanization movement of the rural suburb" from the mid-19th century to the 1920's, including the first rural suburb created in 1853 at Llewellyn Park, West Orange, New Jersey, and Frederick Law Olmsted and Calvert Vaux's 1868 plan for Riverside, Illinois. 7 photos.

R. M. Frame, III

1851. Salmon, Myrene. L'ENFANT AND THE PLANNING OF WASHINGTON, D.C. *Hist. Today [Great Britain] 1976 26(11): 699-706.* Examines the role which Pierre Charles L'Enfant played in the design and layout of Washington, D.C., 1796-1825.

1852. Sarkissian, Wendy. THE IDEA OF SOCIAL MIX IN TOWN PLANNING: AN HISTORICAL REVIEW. *Urban Studies [Great Britain] 1976 13(3): 231-246.* Discusses the idea of social mix in city planning, describes nine goals of the idea and evaluates the development and results of the social mix concept in England and the US since its inception, in 1845, with the proposed project for a mixed village at Ilford, England.

1853. Schultz, Stanley K. and McShane, Clay. TO ENGINEER THE METROPOLIS: SEWERS, SANITATION, AND CITY PLANNING IN LATE-NINETEENTH-CENTURY AMERICA. *J. of Am. Hist. 1978 65(2): 389-411.* During the half-century preceding the Progressive Era, municipal engineers became indispensable as cities began to apply new technologies to social problems. The urban problems most successfully attacked were those susceptible to the engineer's skills. Basic to the concept of comprehensive city planning was the construction of adequate water and sewer systems, because the functions of modern city planning were inherent in water and sewer technology. Engineers could apply their skills to the problem of restructuring municipal governments, and for several decades a high percentage of city managers were trained engineers. The municipal engineer became a professional who reshaped the physical landscape of urban America. 35 notes.

T. P. Linkfield

1854. Stark, Lawrence R. THE LEWISTON-CLARKSTON IMPROVEMENT COMPANY: CITY PLANNER IN SOUTHEASTERN WASHINGTON. *Record 1975 36: 59-71.* Founded by a business corporation in 1896 as an irrigation and hydro-electric power venture, the city of Clarkston was one of the few early examples of city planning in the Pacific Northwest.

S

1855. Tafuri, Manfredo. FREDERICK LAW OLMSTED (1822-1903) E LE ORIGINI DEL PLANNING NEGLI STATI UNITI [Frederick Law Olmsted (1822-1903) and the origins of planning in the United States]. *Quaderni Storici [Italy] 1974 9(3): 785-802.* Olmsted was part of that democratic environment which, influenced by Utilitarianism and Protestant radicalism, played so great a role in the second half of the 19th century. Olmsted's principal accomplishments include the urban planning of New York and Central Park, his proposals for the restructuring of urban centers and surrounding land, his concept of the suburb, and his plans for the community of Riverside. The importance of Olmsted in American culture is confirmed by his work in regional planning and preservation of the countryside; activities which complete the wide range of his interest which were however destined to leave him disappointed as too much of an idealist in the face of the increasingly dominant capitalistic reality.

J

1856. Weiss, Ellen. ROBERT MORRIS COPELAND'S PLANS FOR OAK BLUFFS. *J. of the Soc. of Architectural Historians 1975 34(1): 60-66.* Discusses two city plans (1866-67) drawn up by Robert Morris Copeland for the Massachusetts village of Oak Bluffs on Martha's Vineyard.

1857. Winpenny, Thomas R. THE NEFARIOUS PHILADELPHIA PLAN AND URBAN AMERICA: A RECONSIDERATION. *Pennsylvania Mag. of Hist. and Biog. 1977 101(1): 103-113.* Defends the block system of urban construction, first installed by the city of Philadelphia. Critics have complained that the grid pattern has a deleterious effect on urban life, destroys the sense of community and beauty, and lowers the quality of life. Careful investigation fails to verify this thesis. Philadelphia has long been at or near the top of American cities in terms of home ownership and individual family occupancy. Tenements are nonexistent. A city's beauty probably is unrelated to street patterns. Streets are important, but only as one small factor in a multitude of elements evident in urban life. 5 tables, 37 notes.　　　V. L. Human

1858. Zoll, Stephen. SUPERVILLE: NEW YORK—ASPECTS OF VERY HIGH BULK. *Massachusetts Rev. 1973 14(3): 447-538.* Residents of New York City have lived for more than a century with two contradictory ideas: the city has to continue to grow to survive; the city is too crowded. One answer to this dilemma has been incentive zoning—encouraging developers to build tall buildings yet still leaving open areas useful to the public. New York City has approved incentive zoning in theory; but in practice, as the pressures to utilize all available space increase, incentive zoning is sacrificed. Laments "American cities' self-destructive independence." Illus., 70 notes.　　　W. A. Wiegand

Architecture, Building, and Buildings

1859. Alexander, Robert L. BALTIMORE ROW HOUSES OF THE EARLY NINETEENTH CENTURY. *Am. Studies [Lawrence, KS] 1975 16(2): 65-76.* Row housing became predominant in the industrial age and characterized most major urban centers. Surveys the rise and cost of such housing throughout the early 19th century. The chaos of style reflected the sociopolitical structure and conflict of those years. Speculation led to increasing density, and builders strove primarily for profits. Primary and secondary sources; 4 illus.; 2 maps, 17 notes.
J. Andrew

1860. Andersen, Dennis A. A JOHN PARKINSON ALBUM. *Pacific Northwest Q. 1978 69(2): 71-74.* Presents eight photographs of Seattle architecture as designed by John Parkinson during the early 1890's. Due to financial reverses, Parkinson left Seattle in 1894 and established a successful architectural firm in Los Angeles.
M. L. Tate

1861. Anderson, Paul L. WILLIAM HARRISON FOLSOM: PIONEER ARCHITECT. *Utah Hist. Q. 1975 43(3): 240-259.* Pioneer architect William Harrison Folsom (1815-1901) was the son of a New Hampshire carpenter. His most important contributions to Mormonism were his accomplishments as architect and builder. As assistant church architect (and later church architect) he planned the Salt Lake Theatre, Manti Temple, and Provo Tabernacle. His name has been almost forgotten, but not his buildings, many of which are listed on the State Register or the National Register of Historic Places. Based on primary and secondary sources; 9 illus., 36 notes.　　　J. L. Hazelton

1862. Attoe, Wayne and Latus, Mark. BUILDINGS AS SIGNS: AN EXPERIMENT IN MILWAUKEE. *J. of Popular Culture 1973 7(2): 462-465.* Customers think of "Tea house" filling stations, built throughout the Midwest, as one company; one of 12 articles in this issue on popular architecture.　　　S

1863. Attoe, Wayne and Latus, Mark. THE FIRST PUBLIC HOUSING: SEWER SOCIALISM'S GARDEN CITY FOR MILWAUKEE. *J. of Popular Culture 1976 10(1): 142-149.* Garden Homes, a product of Milwaukee's applied socialist principles ("sewer socialism"), was constructed when private building failed to meet the housing crisis that followed World War I. Built equal to or exceeding private standards, this publicly supported venture of cooperatively owned housing for low income workers was based on "model workers villages" developed earlier in Germany and England. It failed in 1925 when the residents desired private ownership. Primary and secondary sources; fig., 9 notes.
D. G. Nielson

1864. Banham, Reyner. THE SERVICES OF THE LARKIN "A" BUILDING. *J. of the Soc. of Architectural Hist. 1978 37(3): 195-197.* Frank Lloyd Wright's Larkin Administration Building in Buffalo, New York, 1904, was important for the integration of environmental services into the architecture. Attempts to clarify the basic questions about the ventilation system of the Larkin "A" building through the recent discovery of drawings (heretofore unavailable) used by the management staff. Discusses Wright's methods of ventilating this building. 3 illus.
M. Zolota

1865. Barnes, Joseph W. ROCHESTER'S CITY HALLS. *Rochester Hist. 1978 40(2): 1-24.* Originally in a local tavern, 1817, Rochester's city government has been housed in stores, clerk's offices, and official court houses and city halls; article to be continued.

1866. Bastian, Robert W. ARCHITECTURE AND CLASS SEGREGATION IN LATE NINETEENTH-CENTURY TERRE HAUTE, INDIANA. *Geographical Rev. 1975 65(2): 166-179.* Studies Terre Haute, Indiana, to examine the reliability of domestic architecture as a reflector of late 19th-century occupational class segregation in Anglo-American cities. The distributions of stylistic (Italianate, Neo-Jacobean, and Romanesque Revival) houses and of nonstylistic houses and cottages were mapped. Types of dwelling structures and residential addresses of white-collar and blue-collar heads of households were compared on maps for the years 1879, 1884, 1889, 1894, and 1900. Stylistic houses tended to be clustered in areas separate from those occupied by cottages and nonstylistic houses and generally housed white-collar residents. Most nonstylistic homes and cottages housed blue-collar workers, but some were occupied by white-collar residents.　　　J

1867. Betts, Richard J.; Magaziner, Henry J.; Webster, Richard J.; Thomas, George E.; and Teitelman, Edward. PHILADELPHIA ARCHITECTURE AFTER 1776: INNOVATION WITHIN A TRADITION. *J. of the Soc. of Architectural Hist. 1976 35(4): 295-299.* Traces the variety of Philadelphia architecture which occurred within a traditional context. Philadelphia's commercial structures and warehouses combined the latest in technological developments with a sober, traditional masonry construction. William L. Price in his House of the Democrat sought for architectural forms to express the political ideology of the United States. The qualities of the row house give the Philadelphia variety the mark of true regionalism. 6 illus.　　　M. Zolota

1868. Bloomfield, Anne. THE REAL ESTATE ASSOCIATES: A LAND AND HOUSING DEVELOPER OF THE 1870'S IN SAN FRANCISCO. *J. of the Soc. of Architectural Hist. 1978 37(1): 13-33.* Chronicles land development and home building in San Francisco with emphasis on the activities of the Real Estate Associates in the 1870's. Discusses early tract housing, homestead associations, and the speculative building of the Real Estate Associates which erected more than 1000 homes during the 1870's. Delves into the planning and development of the tracts of land and type of construction and architectural details, along with a discussion of the typical plan of a 19th-century San Francisco house. Closes with a history of the company and its method of operation and selling. 17 illus., 75 notes, appendix.　　　M. Zolota

1869. Boorse, Henry A. BARRALET'S "THE DUNLAP HOUSE, 1807," AND ITS ASSOCIATIONS. *Pennsylvania Mag. of Hist. and Biog. 1975 99(2): 131-155.* Studies the obscure and largely unnoticed 1807 painting (reproduced here) of the historic Dunlap House at the southeast corner of Market and Twelfth St., Philadelphia, done by John James Barralet, Irish painter. An examination of the painting and its history would indicate that it is an accurate reproduction of the house and its setting as it was. Traces the history of the house and its successive famous tenants, including the builder and owner John Dunlap himself, printer, as well as Joseph Bonaparte. Records all that can be learned of the life and career of the largely unknown Barralet. Illus., 97 notes.
R. V. Ritter

1870. Bower, Robert K. FRONTIER STONE: THE STORY OF IOWA'S OLD CAPITOL. *Palimpsest 1976 57(4): 98-121.* Construction on Iowa's first statehouse began in 1840. Despite persistence of the legend that Fr. Samuel Mazzuchelli designed the building, official records suggest that architect John F. Rague in fact produced working plans. Chauncey Swan, Superintendent of Public Buildings, not only supervised early stages of construction, but actually designed much of the structure. His successor, William B. Snyder, also contributed to the emerging design. The building was unfinished when Des Moines succeeded Iowa City as the state capitol in 1857. 6 Illus., 16 photos, note on sources.
D. W. Johnson

1871. Breibart, Solomon. THE SYNAGOGUES OF KAHAL KADOSH BETH ELOHIM, CHARLESTON. *South Carolina Hist. Mag. 1979 80(3): 215-235.* Provides a brief history of Jews in South Carolina dating to 1695, and describes the synagogues of Kahal Kadosh Beth

Elohim (Holy Congregation House of God), from 1749 until 1978, in Charleston; includes photographs and floor plans.

1872. Broward, Robert C. JACKSONVILLE: SOUTHERN HOME FOR THE PRAIRIE SCHOOL. *Hist. Preservation 1978 30(1): 16-19.* Jacksonville, Florida, burned in 1901 and was almost totally rebuilt by 1917. Describes a number of buildings designed by Prairie School architect Henry John Klutho (1873-1964). 2 illus. R. M. Frame III

1873. Bryant, Keith L., Jr. CATHEDRALS, CASTLES, AND ROMAN BATHS: RAILWAY STATION ARCHITECTURE IN THE URBAN SOUTH. *J. of Urban Hist. 1976 2(2): 195-230.* During 1890-1920 Southern cities built railroad stations which became important economic and cultural centers. Southern cities did not lag behind their larger Northern counterparts in physical maturation or technology. 10 figs., 72 notes. T. W. Smith

1874. Bryant, Keith L., Jr. THE RAILROAD STATION AS A SYMBOL OF URBANIZATION IN THE SOUTH, 1890's-1920. *South Atlantic Q. 1976 75(4): 499-509.* The railroad station represented urban maturity to American cities. In the South, the sheer physical growth of railroad traffic alone would have justified large stations, but the civic boomers also saw in the monumental stations a tangible "symbol of corporate prosperity, urban expansion, and anticipated economic growth." All large urban centers in the South indulged in constructing huge terminals in the central business district. Even smaller cities, such as Meridian, Mississippi, built imposing edifices. Primary and secondary sources; 40 notes. W. L. Olbrich

1875. Bryant, Keith L., Jr. RAILWAY STATIONS OF TEXAS: A DISAPPEARING ARCHITECTURAL HERITAGE. *Southwestern Hist. Q. 1976 79(4): 417-440.* Texas has a large number of railway stations, of many different architectural styles. The most common small depots were wood, brick, or stucco, built to a standardized plan, but a few big stations are outstanding. Gives details on building the M-K-T station in San Antonio (1917), Union Station in Houston (1909-11), and Union Station in Dallas (1915-16). Based on primary and secondary sources; illus., 31 notes. J. H. Broussard

1876. Burg, David F. THE AESTHETICS OF BIGNESS IN LATE NINETEENTH CENTURY AMERICAN ARCHITECTURE. *J. of Popular Culture 1973 7(2): 484-492.* Discusses the penchant for largeness in design during the late 19th century, in terms of both the introduction of the skyscraper and general public architecture. One of 12 articles in this issue on popular architecture, edited by Marshall Fishwick and J. Meredith Neil. S

1877. Bushnell, George D. CHICAGO'S MAGNIFICENT MOVIE PALACES. *Chicago Hist. 1977 6(2): 99-106.* Movies spawned a number of opulent movie theaters in Chicago, most built and destroyed 1920-50, with a few surviving today.

1878. Butler, Jeanne F. COMPETITION 1792: DESIGNING A NATION'S CAPITOL. *Capitol Studies 1976 4(1): 7-96.* Presents a biography and analysis of plans for each participant in the 1792-93 competition for the architectural design of the Capitol Building.

1879. Cahan, Cathy and Cahan, Richard. THE LOST CITY OF THE DEPRESSION. *Chicago Hist. 1976-77 5(4): 233-242.* Discusses the building of the City of Progress, a building on Chicago's lakefront in celebration of Chicago's growth and economic development, whose construction was subject to extended lapses due to the lack of money during the Depression, 1933-34.

1880. Cantor, Jay E. A MONUMENT OF TRADE: A. T. STEWART AND THE RISE OF THE MILLIONAIRE'S MANSION IN NEW YORK. *Winterthur Portfolio 1975 (10): 165-197.* The mansion of Alexander Turney Stewart (1803-76), designed by John Kellum (1809-76), was the "logical conclusion of the stylistic innovations preceeding it." Stewart's individualistic vent, characteristic of millionaires, is expressed in his mansard-roofed palazzo (1864-69). A study of the house indicates that such structures existed prior to the Civil War. Based on primary and secondary sources; 26 illus., 39 notes. N. A. Kuntz

1881. Cavalier, Julian. ELEPHANTS REMEMBERED. *Hist. Preservation 1977 29(1): 39-43.* Discusses James V. Lafferty's 1882 patent for a dwelling in the form of a large elephant and three elephant houses which were built for real estate promotion. "Lucy," built in 1881 at Margate, New Jersey, has been restored since 1970. 3 illus., 2 photos. R. M. Frame III

1882. Chandler, William. SAN DIEGO INTERIORS: 1880-1930. *J. of San Diego Hist. 1979 25(4): 298-323.* Pictorial survey of San Diego homes of the wealthy accompanied by cultural and historical descriptions.

1883. Chase, Sara B. A BRIEF SURVEY OF THE ARCHITECTURAL HISTORY OF THE OLD STATE HOUSE, BOSTON, MASSACHUSETTS. *Old-Time New England 1979 68(3-4): 31-49.* Gives the architectural history of the State House in Boston, Massachusetts, built by William Payne in 1712. It replaced the first Boston Town House, which served as a marketplace, built in 1658 and destroyed by fire in 1711; covers to 1975.

1884. Clark, Clifford E., Jr. DOMESTIC ARCHITECTURE AS AN INDEX TO SOCIAL HISTORY: THE ROMANTIC REVIVAL AND THE CULT OF DOMESTICITY IN AMERICA, 1840-1870. *J. of Interdisciplinary Hist. 1976 7(1): 33-56.* Correlates changes in architectural style with social changes during 1840-70. Earlier classical styles were replaced by Early Gothic Revival which reflected a new emphasis on family, religion, and rural domesticity, by the Italianate Villa style which became popular in suburban areas, and by the Bracketed Cottage style which was inexpensive, easy to construct, and the most popular. These new architectural styles represented a reaction to hectic industrialization, the new growth of suburbs, influences from the Romantic movement, and other social factors. They emphasized the home as a safe refuge, embodying the apex of human contentment. 3 figs., 42 notes. V. L. Human

1885. Coc, Henry Bartholomew. JAMES HOBAN'S REPORT OF 1799: "THE PROGRESS AND STATE OF THE CAPITOL BUILDING." *Manuscripts 1975 27(1): 33-37.* On 5 December 1799 President John Adams transmitted to Congress a "Special Message on the Pennsylvania Insurrection." Attached to it were important documents relative to the construction of various government buildings including "a copy of the report by James Hoban, Supervisory Architect of the Capitol, which is perhaps the fullest extant record of the precise construction details of the Capitol's original, or North Wing, the only portion built in the eighteenth century." The document is reproduced at the conclusion of the article. 7 notes. D. A. Yanchisin

1886. Condit, Carl W. STRUCTURAL ANTECEDENTS OF CONTEMPORARY HIGH BUILDING DESIGN. *XIVth International Congress of the History of Science, Proceedings No. 3* (Tokyo and Kyoto: Science Council of Japan, 1975): 130-133. The evolution in framing technology, 1820's-1970's, allowed for contemporary construction of skyscrapers.

1887. Connell, Mary Ann Strong. THE FIRST PEABODY HOTEL: 1869-1923. *West Tennessee Hist. Soc. Papers 1975 29: 38-54.* Memphis' strategic location on the Mississippi and as a railroad terminus prompted Robert Campbell Brinkley to erect a luxurious hotel there, equal to any in the South. The hotel was formally opened 5 February 1869. Costing $60,000, it contained 75 rooms with private baths, ballroom, saloon and lobby. It quickly became the locale for Memphis social life. Dignitaries made it their headquarters when in Memphis. In 1906, a huge, 200-room addition was constructed, costing $350,000. The famous hotel was closed 28 August 1923 as a result of proposed city alterations. Based on primary sources; photo, 68 notes. H. M. Parker, Jr.

1888. Cote, Richard C. RETHINKING THE EARLY GREEK REVIVAL: THE SUCCESS OF INFLUENCES AND THE FAILURE OF A BUILDER. *Old-Time New England 1974 64(3-4): 61-76.* Explores the beginnings of the Greek Revival during the 1820's in the columned portico house form of domestic architecture in Northampton, Massachusetts. Thomas Pratt, a Northampton builder, failed in his early attempt at the Greek Revival portico house form because of the persistent influence of the Federal tradition. 6 illus., 43 notes, 3 appendixes. R. N. Lokken

1889. Cowan, Natalie Jahraus. CARVILLE, SAN FRANCISCO'S OCEANSIDE BOHEMIA. *California History 1978-79 57(4): 308-319.* During 1890's-1930's an oceanfront section of San Francisco, known as Carville, was named for the architectural oddity of using obsolete horse-drawn streetcars as cottages and stores. The Market Street Railway Company sold the cars for as little as ten dollars; purchasers included many artists and writers who used the cars as vacation homes. Over 100 cars were on the sand dunes by 1900. Carville became the destination of bicyclists, picnickers, and people seeking privacy. Cable cars joined the earlier cars after the 1906 earthquake. Eventually the city's development overtook Carville, and more conventional homes replaced the streetcars. Some cars were extensively remodeled and became part of larger structures; a few cars may still be so used to this day. Contemporary published works and newspapers; 3 illus., 10 photos, 22 notes.   A. Hoffman

1890. Daiker, Virginia. THE CAPITOL OF JEFFERSON AND LATROBE. *Q. J. of the Lib. of Congress 1975 32(1): 25-32.* Benjamin Henry Latrobe (1764-1820) was the only well-trained professional architect in the country. Thomas Jefferson disagreed with Latrobe over the lighting of the House of Representatives chamber. After the War of 1812, Latrobe was hired to rebuild the Capitol and, "as Jefferson was no longer President, was able to construct his cupolas on both wings." Based upon correspondence of Jefferson and Latrobe. Illus., 19 notes.
                                                                        E. P. Stickney

1891. Davis, Julia F. et al. AMERICAN EXPOSITIONS AND ARCHITECTURE. *J. of the Soc. of Architectural Hist. 1976 35(4): 272-279.* Discusses the influence of expositions on American architecture, beginning with London's Crystal Palace (1851), through the evolution of the glasshouse form, and to the World's Columbian Exposition in 1893. This was the first exposition to treat American architecture in terms of the American urban character and setting. Discusses the search for a classic urban model and the interest in urban planning reflected by the Lincoln Memorial project which emphasized collaboration between the architect and sculptor to create a unified project. The Panama-California Exposition (1915) emphasized Spanish Revival architecture. The expositions in Chicago (1933) and New York (1939) whose progressive, modern forms were influenced chiefly by the growing importance of the automobile. 7 illus.   M. Zolota

1892. Duis, Perry R. "WHERE IS ATHENS NOW?": THE FINE ARTS BUILDING 1898 TO 1918. *Chicago Hist. 1977 6(2): 66-78.* Discusses the shops and activities which took place in Chicago's Fine Arts Building, 1898-1918, considered at the time of its construction to be one of the most modern and progressive pieces of architecture the city had to offer.

1893. Fern, Alan and Kaplan, Milton. JOHN PLUMBE, JR. AND THE FIRST ARCHITECTURAL PHOTOGRAPHS OF THE NATION'S CAPITOL. *Q. J. of the Lib. of Congress 1974 31(1): 3-20.* Plumbe had the first studio of daguerreotypy in Washington (1845) and was the first professional photographer in the Capital. High praise was lavished upon his work, one critic saying that he had brought the daguerreotype to absolute perfection. Includes a checklist of daguerreotype images by John Plumbe, Jr., and reproductions. Illus., 29 notes.
                                                                        E. P. Stickney

1894. Fuerst, JoAnne. FLOATING GRAIN ELEVATORS IN NEW YORK HARBOR, 1848-1959. *Am. Neptune 1978 38(2): 131-141.* History of floating grain elevators indigenous to the New York City and New Jersey area. Describes the evolution of these vessels' construction and design, and how they were used, until they became obsolete in the 1950's. Primary and secondary sources; 12 illus., 15 notes, appendix.
                                                                        G. H. Curtis

1895. Garvin, James L. ST. JOHN'S CHURCH IN PORTSMOUTH: AN ARCHITECTURAL STUDY. *Hist. New Hampshire 1973 28(3): 153-175.* Built in 1807 after plans by Alexander Parris of Portland, Maine, St. John's Episcopal church was erected on the site of the 1732 "Queen's Chapel" burned in 1806. Documents roles of joiners, suppliers, subscribers, and building committee and agent, from church archives and local histories. Subsequent modifications record "changing religious and aesthetic attitudes" since 1807. 11 illus., 40 notes.
                                                                        T. D. S. Bassett

1896. Gayle, Margot. CAST-IRON ARCHITECTURE U.S.A. *Historic Preservation 1975 27(1): 14-19.* Iron-front buildings, built during 1848-1900, had the advantages of "great window expanses," more usable floor space, "speedy fabrication," economy, and the iron's "capacity to take on any form." Though cast-iron architecture is concentrated in New York City, significant examples exist nationwide. Architectural iron casting has become a lost craft. 7 photos.   R. M. Frame III

1897. Gayle, Margot. A HERITAGE FORGOTTEN: CHICAGO'S FIRST CAST IRON BUILDINGS. *Chicago Hist. 1978 7(2): 98-108.* Discusses Chicago's iron-front buildings, 1854-80's, taking into account architecture and native ironworks which made the construction possible.

1898. Gifford, Robert T. CINCINNATI'S MUSIC HALL: A CENTURY OF CONTINUITY AND CHANGE. *Cincinnati Hist. Soc. Bull. 1978 36(2): 79-104.* Discusses musical and dramatic presentations and architectural and structural changes in Cincinnati's Music Hall, 1878-1978.

1899. Goode, James M. VANISHED WASHINGTON AND ITS ARCHITECTURAL "CAPITAL LOSSES." *Smithsonian 1979 10(9): 58-66.* Describes significant architectural and historical edifices destroyed for progress in Washington, D.C., during the 19th and 20th centuries.

1900. Graham, Thomas. FLAGLER'S MAGNIFICENT HOTEL PONCE DE LEON. *Florida Hist. Q. 1975 54(1): 1-17.* Discusses the origins, construction, and use of the Hotel Ponce de Leon in St. Augustine, Florida. Built in 1887 by oil magnate Henry Morrison Flagler (1830-1913), the hotel was designed by architect Bernard Maybeck in Spanish Renaissance style, and decorated by Louis Tiffany. For several years, the hotel was perhaps the country's most fashionable resort. A decline set in, brought on by such diverse causes as the depression of the 1890's, bad freezes in St. Augustine, and increasing interest in South Florida. Nevertheless, the Ponce de Leon continued to operate as a hotel until 1967, and is now the campus for Flagler College. Based on manuscript, newspaper, and secondary sources, and interviews; 9 illus., 75 notes.
                                                                        J. E. Findling

1901. Grant, Francis W. GEORGE WOODLAND: MASTER BUILDER. *Nova Scotia Hist. Q. 1977 7(1): 55-67.* George Woodland (1867-1969) was born in Nova Scotia but he moved to Boston, Massachusetts when he was 19 years old, built his first house at the age of 22, and became a US citizen in 1896. He is remembered for the fine houses he built and for his wood carvings of birds and animals.   H. M. Evans

1902. Grant, H. Roger. THE COMBINATION RAILROAD STATION IN THE OLD NORTHWEST. *Old Northwest 1978 4(2): 95-118.* Describes, with photographs, many combination railroad stations in Ohio, Indiana, and Illinois. These tripartite buildings contained provisions for passenger comfort plus ticket selling and administration, provisions for rail express and baggage handling, and provisions for telegraphy and signal control. Citizens wanted their local stations to be efficient and esthetically pleasing. Covers 1880's-1920's. Based on railroad journals, the C.B.&Q. Papers, author's photographs, and secondary works; 15 photos, 14 notes.   J. N. Dickinson

1903. Grant, H. Roger. STANDARDIZATION IN ARCHITECTURE: THE CASE OF THE RAILROAD STATION. *Studies in Hist. and Society 1976 1(2): 1-21.* Photographic essay showing the standardization of small-town railway stations in the Trans-Mississippi West during 1910's-30's. Structures in the US and Canadian midwest are remarkably similar. 25 photos, 4 notes.

1904. Grider, Sylvia Ann. THE SHOTGUN HOUSE IN OIL BOOMTOWNS OF THE TEXAS PANHANDLE. *Pioneer Am. 1975 7(2): 47-55.* Singles out the shotgun house, a cheap and quickly-built form of housing associated in this instance with the oil boomtowns of the Texas Panhandle during the mid-1920's. The shotgun house as a type is one room wide with the rooms end to end and the front and back doors in the gable ends. Construction techniques were so simple that a skilled carpenter and a helper could complete one of these buildings in one and one-half to two days. The origin of this house is obscure, but evidence suggests that the shotgun house spread from western Louisiana to Texas via rig builders, gamblers, drug pushers, and other "boom chasers." Although not built for permanence, many have remained remarkably durable. Based on field research, including interviews, and secondary sources; 2 photos, fig., 23 notes.   C. R. Gunter, Jr.

1905. Harpham, Josephine Evans. JUNCTION CITY. *Pacific Historian 1975 19(2): 114-132.* Surveys the history of Junction City, Oregon, and provides a resume of significant older houses and commercial buildings.   G. L. Olson

1906. Harris, Neil. HOUSING THE RICH. *Rev. in Am. Hist. 1974 2(1): 27-33.* Review essay prompted by H. Allen Brooks' *The Prairie School: Frank Lloyd Wright and His Midwest Contemporaries* (Toronto: U. of Toronto Pr., 1972) and Charles Lockwood's *Bricks & Brownstone: The New York Row House, 1783-1929, An Architectural & Social History* (New York: McGraw-Hill, 1972). Both books demonstrate a new historical concern for social space and the way Americans organized more effective interior environments.   W. D. Piersen

1907. Harwood, Herbert H., Jr. MT. CLARE STATION, AMERICA'S OLDEST: OR IS IT? *Railroad Hist. 1978 (139): 39-53.* Baltimore's Mt. Clare station, said to be the oldest on the Baltimore and Ohio Railroad line, has been misdated at 1830 when it was actually constructed in 1851 (leaving the 1830 station at Ellicott City, Maryland, the oldest).

1908. Heinerman, Joseph. AMELIA'S PALACE: BRIGHAM YOUNG'S GRANDEST RESIDENCE. *Montana 1979 29(1): 54-63.* Brigham Young, President of the Mormon Church, married Amelia Folsom 24 January 1863. She was his 25th wife, but appeared constantly at his side and assumed all the social duties of his "first wife." In 1875, Young commissioned Joseph Ridges, architect and builder of the Mormon Tabernacle organ, to design and construct an official residence for himself and Amelia. The four-story, Italian villa-style structure was the most magnificient in Salt Lake City. After Young's death in 1877, his successor, John Taylor, had the mansion finished in 1882. Subsequently known as the Gardo House, it served officials of the Mormon church as a residence and office building until 1894. In 1899, Edwin T. Holmes purchased the structure and his wife Susanna had it beautifully redecorated. The Holmeses sold the property to the Mormon Church in 1924 and two years later the federal government purchased it, razed the house, and built a federal bank building. Secondary sources and manuscripts in the collections of the Utah State Historical Society, the University of Utah Library, and the L. D. S. Church Archives, Salt Lake City, as well as the Brigham Young University Library, Provo; 10 illus., 21 notes.   R. C. Myers

1909. Hibbard, Don J. DOMESTIC ARCHITECTURE IN BOISE, 1904-1912: A STUDY IN STYLES. *Idaho Yesterdays 1978 22(3): 2-18.* Boise, Idaho, tripled in size between 1900 and 1910. Its new homes built during that period are good examples of the styles which were becoming popular around the nation. Shows colonial revival, mission, and bungalow styles. Primary sources; 20 illus., 24 notes.   B. J. Paul

1910. Hilliard, Celia. "RENT REASONABLE TO RIGHT PARTIES": GOLD COAST APARTMENT BUILDINGS, 1906-1929. *Chicago Hist. 1979 8(2): 66-77.* Describes the layout, rent, and occupants of deluxe Chicago apartments in the Gold Coast area, from 1882 when the first mansion in the area was built by Potter Palmer on Lake Shore Drive, until 1929 when the stock market crashed.

1911. Hills, William P. WATERTOWN'S HOTEL WOODRUFF. *York State Tradition 1974 28(1): 15-20, 25.* Discusses the ownership and history of the Hotel Woodruff in Watertown, 1851-1963.   S

1912. Hoffecker, Carol E. CHURCH GOTHIC: A CASE STUDY OF REVIVAL ARCHITECTURE IN WILMINGTON, DELAWARE. *Winterthur Portfolio 1973 (8): 215-231.* Analyzes the reasoning and circumstances that led to the erection of two Gothic revival churches in Wilmington: St. John's Episcopal (1858) and Grace Methodist (1867). The construction of St. John's reflected the congregation's desire, expressed through church leaders, to adhere to the theological statement of the Camden Society of Cambridge University. Gothic revival style was not chosen for social reasons or trends, but reflected developments of the entire Anglican Communion. Grace Methodist, on the other

hand, was dressed up with Gothic trappings but lacked the symbols of sacramentalism that had provoked the Anglican Gothic revival. Grace Methodist indicates that the revival had come to symbolize "good taste." Based on primary and secondary sources; 18 illus., 34 notes.   N. A. Kuntz

1913. Holley, Vivian. THE HAY HOUSE: AN EASY SORT OF ELEGANCE. *Georgia Life 1977 4(2): 19-21.* Describes the stately Johnson-Felton-Hay House in Macon, Georgia, now open to the public under the Georgia Trust for Historic Preservation.

1914. Holmes, Nicholas H., Jr. THE CAPITOLS OF THE STATE OF ALABAMA. *Alabama Rev. 1979 32(3): 163-171.* Survey of Alabama capitol buildings constructed during 1819-1912 at Cahaba, Tuscaloosa, and Montgomery. Discusses architectural plans, completed features, and aesthetics. 22 notes.   J. F. Vivian

1915. Holt, Glen E. "WILL CHICAGO'S ITINERANT CITY HALL BE MOVED ONCE MORE?" *Chicago Hist. 1977 6(3): 155-166.* Discusses the eight buildings which housed the Chicago City Hall, 1837-96, and the events which caused the frequent locale changes.

1916. Horton, Loren N. THE ARCHITECTURAL BACKGROUND OF TRINITY EPISCOPAL CHURCH. *Ann. of Iowa 1977 43(7): 539-548.* Built in 1871-72, Trinity Episcopal Church in Iowa City, Iowa, "is significant as an example of a common design and building technique of the mid-19th century Midwest." The frame church, built with the vertical board and batten construction technique, is of Gothic Revival style. The design was based on plans taken from the 1852 book, *Upjohn's Rural Architecture,* written by the well-known church architect, Richard Upjohn. Primary and secondary sources; 5 illus., 12 notes.   P. L. Petersen

1917. Horton, Loren N. EARLY ARCHITECTURE IN DUBUQUE. *Palimpsest 1974 55(5): 130-151.* Explores the building boom in Dubuque, Iowa, in the 1850's.   S

1918. Horwitz, Richard P. ARCHITECTURE AND CULTURE: THE MEANING OF THE LOWELL BOARDING HOUSE. *Am. Q. 1973 25(1): 64-82.* The early Lowellites' image of home as a rural dwelling of permanence, comfort, and kinship mediated their perceptions of factory boarding houses. The boarding houses of Lowell, Massachusetts, were poor imitations of the rural cottages the mill girls called home. Boasts about the houses' good qualities appear less than sincere. Primary and secondary sources; 41 notes, biblio.   W. D. Piersen

1919. Ivers, Louise Harris. THE MONTEZUMA HOTEL AT LAS VEGAS HOT SPRINGS, NEW MEXICO. *J. of the Soc. of Architectural Historians 1974 33(3): 206-213.* Examines the architecture of the two Montezuma Hotels built at Las Vegas Hot Springs, the second by noted architects Daniel Hudson Burnham and John Root in 1885.

1920. Jacobs, Herbert. OUR WRIGHT HOUSES. *Hist. Preservation 1976 28(3): 9-13.* Discusses the two Madison, Wisconsin, houses designed for the author by Frank Lloyd Wright (1869-1959): the Herbert A. Jacobs House, Usonia No. 1 (1936) and the Herbert Jacobs Second House (1948). 7 photos.   R. M. Frame III

1921. Johannesen, Eric. THE ARCHITECTURAL LEGACY OF GUY TILDEN OF CANTON. *Ohio Hist. 1973 82(3-4): 124-141.* Canton grew sevenfold during the architect's career (1880's-1920's). Tilden worked in styles from Romanesque to Prairie house, and his monuments ranged from cemetery vaults and churches to public and business buildings. Based on Tilden scrapbooks, interviews with descendants, and local histories; 20 illus., 39 notes.   S. S. Sprague

1922. Johnson, Claire D. DOMESTIC ARCHITECTURE IN VICTORIAN SALEM: A LAFAYETTE STREET SAMPLING. *Essex Inst. Hist. Collections 1979 115(3): 172-182.* During 1850-1900 there appeared in Salem, Massachusetts, a distinctive architectural expression, the Victorian house. An excellent range of Victorian designs can be found in 12 houses constructed during 1845-94 on the west side of Lafayette Street, Salem. Examines each house regarding architectural form, date of construction, and ownership. Concludes that while these 12 houses are not virtuoso pieces of their era, they are impressive by their individuality, for their attention to stylistic detail and workmanship, and for the integrity of their architectural form. Primary and secondary sources; 8 photos, 7 notes.   R. S. Sliwoski

1923. Johnson, Rue C. FRONTIER THEATRE: THE CORINNE OPERA HOUSE. *Utah Hist. Q. 1974 42(3): 285-295.* Corinne, originally a railroad tie camp, became a permanent settlement because it ran the shortest route to the mines and markets of Montana and Idaho. In 1870, the year after its founding, an opera house was built. This reflected "the high optimism of those residents who saw in Corinne the future capital of Utah and the commercial hub of the Intermountain region." Notes the early traveling companies which played there. In 1913 the opera house became a Mormon meeting house; it was torn down in 1952. Illus., 43 notes.   E. P. Stickney

1924. Jones, Robert A. MR. WOOLWORTH'S TOWER: THE SKYSCRAPER AS POPULAR ICON. *J. of Popular Culture 1973 7(2): 408-424.* Discusses Cass Gilbert's architectural design for the Woolworth Tower, 1899-1913; one of 12 articles in this issue on popular architecture.
                                                                        S

1925. Jordan, Albert F. SOME EARLY MORAVIAN BUILDERS IN AMERICA. *Pennsylvania Folklife 1974 24(1): 2-18.* Discusses the early architecture of Moravian builders (1740-68) in Bethlehem and Nazareth, Pennsylvania.   S

1926. Kahn, David M. BOGARDUS, FIRE, AND THE IRON TOWER. *J. of the Soc. of Architectural Hist. 1976 35(3): 186-203.* Traces the history and discusses the construction principles of James Bogardus's iron fire towers in New York City during the 1850's, early examples of freestanding iron framed structures. Deals with the circumstances of their construction, their purpose, and the cost. Points out Bogardus' influence on Julius B. Kroehl in his construction of a still extant New York City fire tower. Primary and secondary sources; 17 illus., 52 notes.   M. Zolota

1927. Karlowicz, Titus M. NOTES ON THE COLUMBIAN EXPOSITION'S MANUFACTURES AND LIBERAL ARTS BUILDING. *J. of the Soc. of Architectural Historians 1974 33(3): 214-218.* Daniel Hudson Burnham's design for the World's Columbian Exposition (Chicago, 1893) set the style for 20th-century architectural megapractice.

1928. Klaw, Spencer. THE WORLD'S TALLEST BUILDING. *Am. Heritage 1977 28(2): 86-99.* Frank W. Woolworth, the inventor of the five-and-ten-cent store, built the world's tallest building in New York City. Completed in 1913, the Woolworth Building's Gothic beauty impressed everyone. 16 illus.   B. J. Paul

1929. Kouwenhoven, John A. DOWNTOWN ST. LOUIS AS JAMES B. EADS KNEW IT WHEN THE BRIDGE WAS OPENED A CENTURY AGO. *Missouri Hist. Soc. Bull. 1974 30(3): 181-195.* Describes the principal waterfront structures and the prominent commercial buildings in the downtown section of St. Louis in 1874. Illus., index.
                                                                        H. T. Lovin

1930. Kouwenhoven, John A. EADS BRIDGE: THE CELEBRATION. *Missouri Hist. Soc. Bull. 1974 30(3): 159-180.* Enthusiasm and ceremonies attended the opening of the Eads Bridge at St. Louis in 1874. The builder was James Buchanan Eads (1820-87). The bridge, constructed for commercial reasons, was regarded as an engineering and aesthetic marvel. Based on newspaper and secondary sources; 8 photos, 8 notes.   H. T. Lovin

1931. Landau, Sarah Bradford. THE ROW HOUSES OF NEW YORK'S WEST SIDE. *J. of the Soc. of Architectural Historians 1975 34(1): 19-36.* Examines the period 1885-1900 in the building of New York City's row houses.

1932. Langenbach, Randolph. AMOSKEAG MILLYARD REMEMBERED. *Historic Preservation 1975 27(3): 26-29.* Begun in Manchester, New Hampshire, in 1838 by the Amoskeag Manufacturing Co., the Amoskeag Millyard (mills and related structures) "achieved an extraordinary unity of design" and "was the world's largest textile plant"

before corporate liquidation in 1936. Urban renewal has destroyed much since 1968. 6 photos.   R. M. Frame III

1933. Lowe, David. GREEK REVIVAL ARCHITECTURE IN CHICAGO. *Chicago Hist. 1975 4(3): 157-166.* Describes the use of Greek architectural styles in the construction of major buildings in Chicago, 1830-50.   S

1934. Manarin, Louis H. A BUILDING FOR THE PRESERVATION OF THE PUBLIC RECORD. *Virginia Cavalcade 1974 24(1): 22-30.* Discusses the background to the 1747 decision to build the Public Records Office in Williamsburg, Virginia, "the oldest archival structure in the Western Hemisphere."   S

1935. Marsh, John L. MR. HALL'S HALL, AN UNLOVELY RELIC OF OPERA-HOUSE AMERICA. *Western Pennsylvania Hist. Mag. 1974 57(2): 167-197.* History of Orris Hall's opera house, the Keystone Block in Warren, Pennsylvania.   S

1936. McBride, Mary Ellen Leigh. FORT PITT BLOCKHOUSE: PITTSBURGH'S OLDEST LANDMARK. *Daughters of the Am. Revolution Mag. 1976 110(1): 16-21.* Outlines the history of the Fort Pitt Blockhouse in Pittsburgh, Pennsylvania, 1760-1909.

1937. McCue, George. THE OCTAGON—TOWN HOUSE THAT PRECEDED THE TOWN. *Historic Preservation 1974 26(2): 27-31.* The Octagon was built in 1800 as a town house for Colonel John Tayloe of Virginia when Washington, D.C., was still a "marshy woodland." Designed for its "sharp-cornered site" by Dr. William Thornton, it is "one of the great prototypes" of the Federal style. Since 1902 it has been the headquarters of the American Institute of Architects. 2 illus., 6 photos.   R. M. Frame III

1938. McCue, George; Overby, Osmond; and Wayman, Norbury L. STREET FRONT HERITAGE: THE BREMEN/HYDE PARK AREA OF ST. LOUIS. *Missouri Hist. Soc. Bull. 1976 32(4): 205-221.* Describes the spatial arrangements and distinctive architectural features of the Bremen and Hyde Park sections of St. Louis. Never the home of the city's most affluent, the districts were dominated by "solid and comfortable homes" with shops, churches, parks, and other amenities consistent with the middle class values of the residents. 21 photos and diagrams, 2 notes.   H. T. Lovin

1939. McGinty, Brian. THE SPLENDID CARAVANSARY: SAN FRANCISCO'S PALACE HOTEL. *Am. Hist. Illus. 1974 9(6): 10-17.* In 1872 William C. Ralston, who had taken the lead among San Francisco's coterie of promoters, announced his plans to build the Palace Hotel along New Montgomery and Market Streets. "It was to be the largest building ever built in the West, a massive edifice of marble and brick and iron that would mark San Francisco's coming of age, signify the closing of one era and the beginning of another, and—not the least—brilliantly cap the career of William Ralston." The hotel was opened for business on 2 October 1875. During the earthquake and fire of 1906, 'the splendid caravansary' was reduced to rubble." 3 illus., 3 photos.
                                                                        D. D. Cameron

1940. Morgan, William D. HENRY VAUGHAN: AN ENGLISH ARCHITECT IN NEW HAMPSHIRE. *Hist. New Hampshire 1973 28(2): 120-140.* The design of Henry Vaughan (1845-1917) for the St. Paul's School Chapel in Concord, built 1886-94, inaugurated the modern collegiate phase of the Gothic Revival. Head draughtsman for the London firm of George Frederick Bodley and Garner, he came to Boston in 1881 to design a chapel for the Sisters of St. Margaret, and remained in the United States until his death. A High Church Episcopalian, Vaughan introduced expensive church and school architecture which influenced Ralph Adams Cram (1863-1942) and other Ivy Gothic designers. He worked on both the Cathedral of St. John the Divine and the National Cathedral in Washington. For 18 years the school architect for St. Paul's, he helped shape the American image of the transplanted English public school. With unlimited funds he produced an outstanding example of the nouveau riche castle for his 1904-15 patron, Edward F. Searles, in Windham, New Hampshire. His successful shingle-style summer residence for Mary Bradford Foote in Dublin, New Hampshire (1888) was his "only truly successful domestic design." 8 illus., 24 notes.
                                                                        T. D. S. Bassett

1941. Morrow, Sara Sprott. ADOLPHUS HEIMAN'S LEGACY TO NASHVILLE. *Tennessee Hist. Q. 1974 33(1): 3-21.* Adolphus Heiman arrived in Nashville from his native Prussia in 1836 at the age of 27. Though first employed as a stone cutter, he was most successful in architecture, including college buildings, bridges, and churches. Traces the history of his most famous work, the College Building, originally designed for the University of Nashville in 1853 and subsequently used by several other colleges. Illus., 4 photos, 21 notes.   M. B. Lucas

1942. Nagel, Gunther W. MONUMENT TO ELEGANCE: LELAND STANFORD'S NOB HILL MANSION. *Am. West 1975 12(5): 18-25.* President Leland Stanford followed his railroad offices to San Francisco. The two-million-dollar mansion he constucted is best described in superlative terms. It was a center of high society and considerable influence in late 19th-century California. 12 illus.
                    D. L. Smith

1943. Newell, Dianne. THE SHORT-LIVED PHENOMENON OF RAILROAD STATION-HOTELS. *Historic Preservation 1974 26(3): 31-36.* Discusses the phenomenon of hotels built in conjunction with railroad stations, 1830's-80's.

1944. Newell, Dianne. WITH RESPECT TO BREWERIES. *Historic Preservation 1975 27(1): 24-27.* Before artificial refrigeration was introduced in the 1860's breweries were small, rural, and of "functional-traditional" architecture. Later they became larger, urban, and more decorated. Significant structures still exist—precariously—in Baltimore, Maryland; Honolulu, Hawaii; and Denver, Colorado. 5 photos.
                    R. M. Frame III

1945. Newton, James A. CROWS' NESTS OR EAGLES' AERIES? THE OCTAGON HOUSES OF E. A. BRACKETT AND H. P. WAKEFIELD. *Old-Time New England 1977 67(3-4): 67-72.* Discusses the octagon houses built by E. A. Brackett in Winchester, Massachusetts and by H. P. Wakefield in nearby Reading. Both houses were based on Orson S. Fowler's planbook, *A Home for All* (1849). Such eccentric houses reflected the strong individuality of the men who built them. 13 illus., 68 notes.   R. N. Lokken

1946. O'Gorman, James F. THE MARSHALL FIELD WHOLESALE STORE: MATERIALS TOWARD A MONOGRAPH. *J. of the Soc. of Architectural Hist. 1978 37(3): 175-194.* Subjects Henry Hobson Richardson's Marshall Field building to historical scrutiny via available information. Discusses the economic position of Chicago in the mid and latter 19th century and the rise of Marshall Field as an entrepreneur. Traces the chronology of the building's planning, its construction which began in 1885, and the decisions Field made about the construction after Richardson's death. Chronicles the evolution of the design, the materials, and the development of the elevation. Discusses problems attendant with compiling an accurate picture of the building culled from conflicting written descriptions and the lack of detailed photographs and definitive drawings. Also describes the interior layout and exterior detailing. Concludes with possible sources for the design and the position the Field store occupies in the history of architecture. 20 illus., 86 notes.   M. Zolota

1947. Onorato, Ronald J. PROVIDENCE ARCHITECTURE, 1859-1908: STONE, CARPENTER, AND WILLSON. *Rhode Island Hist. 1974 33(3-4): 87-96.* Discusses the Stone, Carpenter, and Willson firm and its impact on the architecture popular in Providence, 1859-1908.

1948. Oppenheimer, George. HOLLYWOOD'S GARDEN OF ALLAH. *Am. Heritage 1977 28(5): 82-87.* From the late 1920's to just after World War II, the Garden of Allah on Sunset Strip was "the place" to stay in Hollywood when making a movie. Built in 1920 as a private home, the building was leased to Alla Nazimova, after whom it was named. Declining fortunes forced Madame Alla out, and a corporation converted the estate into a hotel in 1927. Sold in 1959, the building was razed. 6 illus.
                    J. F. Paul

1949. Passanti, Francesco. THE DESIGN OF COLUMBIA IN THE 1890'S: MC KIM AND HIS CLIENT. *J. of the Soc. of Architectural Hist. 1977 36(2): 69-84.* Discusses Charles F. McKim's vision of the function of a university, his design for Columbia University in 1894, and the reasons it was selected over designs submitted by Charles C. Haight and Richard M. Hunt. Notes some modifications to the original plan and analyzes the design of Low Library and its influences on other contemporary buildings. 21 illus., 36 notes.   M. Zolota

1950. Patton, Helen. LUCAS BRADLEY: CARPENTER, BUILDER, ARCHITECT. *Wisconsin Mag. of Hist. 1974-75 58(2): 107-125.* Lucas Bradley, who learned his building and architectural training from his father, constructed the Second Presbyterian Church in St. Louis. Most of his work, however, is found in Wisconsin in the First Presbyterian Church, the Fourth Ward Schoolhouse, and Racine College, all in Racine, and several buildings on the Beloit College campus. Discusses in detail the composition, plans, and construction of these buildings. 15 illus., 45 notes.   N. C. Burckel

1951. Penfield, Wallace C. THE SANTA BARBARA COUNTY BOWL. *Noticias 1973 19(1): 1-9.* Chronicles the planning and construction of Santa Barbara's outdoor concert facility, the County Bowl, 1935.

1952. Pommer, Richard. THE ARCHITECTURE OF URBAN HOUSING IN THE UNITED STATES DURING THE EARLY 1930'S. *J. of the Soc. of Architectural Hist. 1978 37(4): 235-264.* Political considerations combined with the failure of US architects and critics of the 1930's to understand European modernism's principle of the inseparability of housing, planning, and architecture. The result produced the dreary urban housing developed between the late 1930's and early 1960's. During 1932-34, under the Reconstruction Finance Corporation and the Public Works Administration, there was a brief but decisive period of developmental freedom. After that, standarization killed the architectural quality of urban housing. Focuses on Philadelphia, Cleveland, and New York. Compares the US Garden City planning, Beaux-Arts design, and the European Modern Movement, particularly as seen in the Zeilenbau system and the City of Three Million by Le Corbusier. Concludes that only in the early 1960's were the European and US approaches successfully combined. Henry Wright was particularly important in bringing about the fusion.   R. J. Jirran

1953. Poulsen, Richard C. STONE BUILDINGS OF BEAVER CITY. *Utah Hist. Q. 1975 43(3): 278-285.* Beaver City, Utah, has almost as many stone buildings as all southern Utah combined. Most of the oldest stone dwellings are of black pumice. Tufa, the pink stone, was a later innovation. Beaver City is a unique blend of European folk architecture, eastern US building traditions, and Mormon utilitarianism. Its stone buildings are part of folk tradition. Study of these traditions could lead us to an understanding of the builders as well as of ourselves. Based on primary and secondary sources; 12 illus., 9 notes.
                    J. L. Hazelton

1954. Priddy, Benjamin, Jr. OLD CHURCHES OF MEMPHIS. *West Tennessee Hist. Soc. Papers 1975 29: 130-161.* Discusses three antebellum and seven postbellum churches in Memphis which reflect 19th-century church architecture. No church structures erected before 1840 survive. In 1844 the first permanent church was erected of brick— a representation of the earliest effort of Memphis congregations to create permanent religious housing. Based on primary and secondary sources; 9 photos, 92 notes.   H. M. Parker, Jr.

1955. Pushkar, R. G. HOUSES OF CONCORD'S FAMOUS. *Early Am. Life 1977 8(2): 40-43.* Discusses the historic houses of Concord's famous literary group, the Alcotts, Nathaniel Hawthorne, Henry David Thoreau, and Ralph Waldo Emerson, during 1830-72, and their present fame.

1956. Quinan, Jack. ASHER BENJAMIN AND AMERICAN ARCHITECTURE: THE BOSTON EXCHANGE COFFEE HOUSE. *J. of the Soc. of Architectural Hist. 1979 38(3): 256-262.* The Boston Exchange House, built in 1808, is significant for its influence upon Isaiah Rogers, the acknowledged pioneer of United States hotel design. Evidence for the influence is circumstantial but convincing. For example, the first major hotel of Rogers, the Tremont House of 1828, was built within two blocks of the Boston Exchange House. 8 fig., 32 notes.
                    R. J. Jirran

1957. Quinan, Jack. ASHER BENJAMIN AND AMERICAN AR-CHITECTURE: A CHRONOLOGICALLY ARRANGED LIST OF PROJECTS AND BUILDINGS BY ASHER BENJAMIN. *J. of the Soc. of Architectural Hist. 1979 38(3): 253-254.* The list begins with Ionic capitals for the Oliver Phelps house, Auddiwls, Connecticut, in 1795 and ends with the Edmund Hastings house, Medford, Massachusetts, in 1841, since demolished. The 57 item list includes 15 marked with an asterisk to signify attribution. The list includes such items as: African Meeting House, Smith's Court, Beacon Hill, Boston (1805); Benjamin House, 63 Chestnut Street, Beacon Hill, Boston (ca. 1821-1822); expanded Faneuil Hall Market, Boston (1824-1825; Benjamin served Alexander Parris in an advisory capacity); Lexington-Concord Battle Monument, Peabody, MA (1833); and William Ellery Channing house, 83 Mt. Vernon Street, Boston (1836).   R. J. Jirran

1958. Quinan, Jack. SOME ASPECTS OF THE DEVELOPMENT OF THE ARCHITECTURAL PROFESSION IN BOSTON BE-TWEEN 1800 AND 1830. *Old-Time New England 1977 68(1-2): 32-37.* The profession, once the hobby of a few wealthy educated men, became respected; mentions several books on the profession and the earliest architectural schools.

1959. Quinan, Jack. ASHER BENJAMIN AS AN ARCHITECT IN WINDSOR, VERMONT. *Vermont Hist. 1974 42(3): 181-194.* Reviews the architecture of Asher Benjamin in Windsor, Vermont. Benjamin built three large houses and a meeting house in Windsor, of which only the latter still stands. Benjamin was a prolific architectural writer. The value of his work resides in its break with standard European tradition, being classical in the Greek sense. Benjamin, a prolific architectural writer, moved from Windsor to Boston, where he became famous. 8 photos, 18 notes.   V. L. Human

1960. Rayman, Ronald. DELUXE ACCOMMODATIONS: STOCKTON'S YO SEMITE HOUSE HOTEL, 1869-1923. *California Hist. Q. 1977 56(2): 164-169.* Describes the Yo Semite House, a major hotel constructed in Stockton in 1869. Equipped with saloon, barbershop, reading room, parlor, and private suites, the hotel provided every comfort. Every room had gas, running water, and call bells. The Yo Semite for many years was a gathering point from which tourists went to see the Yosemite Valley and the Big Trees at Mariposa. Prominent visitors to the hotel included ex-President Grant, who stopped there in 1879. By the early 20th century the Yo Semite House was itself eclipsed by modern hotels, and in 1923 it was destroyed by fire. Based on newspapers and secondary studies; photos, 30 notes.   A. Hoffman

1961. Reinhardt, Elizabeth W. and Grady, Anne A. ASHER BENJA-MIN IN EAST LEXINGTON, MASSACHUSETTS. *Old-Time New England 1977 67(3-4): 23-35.* Shows the influence of Asher Benjamin's pattern books on the building of Greek Revival doorframes in East Lexington houses during the early 19th century. 13 illus., 11 notes.   R. N. Lokken

1962. Rogers, Rebecca M. RESORT ARCHITECTURE AT NA-HANT, 1815-1850. *Old-Time New England 1974 65(1-2): 13-29.* Nahant, originally a town common of Lynn, Massachusetts, was visited by picnickers and pleasure-seekers in the 18th century. Situated on a peninsula extending into the Atlantic Ocean, Nahant was a popular summer resort during 1815-50. Describes the resort architecture of that period. 5 illus., 111 notes.   R. N. Lokken

1963. Ronnie, Art. HOLLYHOCK—THE WRIGHT HOUSE. *Westways 1974 66(11): 18-22, 86.* Hollyhock, Hollywood home of heiress Aline Barnsdall, was built by Frank Lloyd Wright in his California Romanza style (1919).   S

1964. Rubin, Barbara. A CHRONOLOGY OF ARCHITECTURE IN LOS ANGELES. *Ann. of the Assoc. of Am. Geographers 1977 67(4): 521-537.* Functioning as a record of plural society, architecture in Los Angeles reflects population density, technology, affluence, cultural myths, and environmental fantasies, 1890-1970.

1965. Sande, Theodore A.; Candee, Richard M.; DeLony, Eric N.; Eaton, Leonard K.; and Hildebrand, Grant. AMERICAN INDUS-TRIAL ARCHITECTURE FROM THE LATE EIGHTEENTH TO

THE MID-TWENTIETH CENTURY. *J. of the Soc. of Architectural Hist. 1976 35(4): 265-271.* Discuss the characteristics of industrial buildings which reflect the preoccupation with "commodity" and "firmness." This is evident in the American textile factory where the influence of technology, economy, and culture contributed to the architectural style and created two types of industrial towns, the mill village and the single-company town. Linking these towns together were the railroads whose trussed roof shed typified the spirit and confidence of 19th-century technology. Also discusses the work of Oscar A. Eckerman, architect to the John Deere Co. in the 19th century, and Albert Kahn. 5 illus.   M. Zolota

1966. Schless, Nancy Halverson. PETER HARRISON, THE TOURO SYNAGOGUE, AND THE WREN CITY CHURCH. *Winterthur Portfolio 1973 (8): 187-200.* The Touro Synagogue, Newport, Rhode Island, 1759-63, demonstrates the reliance of Peter Harrison (1716-75) on English architectural books. In spite of brief mention by other authors, the existence of a specific architectural model for the Newport synagogue has been overlooked. The prototype was the Bevis Marks Synagogue in London. The London building was derived from two sources. First, the design recalls the first London synagogue of the Resettlement, the Creechurch Lane synagogue. Secondly, Bevis Marks is related to the most common type of Wren city church of the late 17th century. The Bevis Marks Synagogue marks a halfway point and a catalyst in the "amalgamation of aisled, galleried basilica into religious architecture on both sides of the Atlantic." Based on primary and secondary sources; 19 illus., 16 notes.   N. A. Kuntz

1967. Schulze, Franz. ARCHITECTURE CITY: TWO VIEWS. *Art in Am. 1976 64(2): 98-100.* Discusses the stylistic transition which Chicago's architecture and architects have undergone in the 20th century.

1968. Schwartz, Henry. THE FIRST TEMPLE BETH ISRAEL: SAN DIEGO. *Western States Jewish Hist. Q. 1979 11(2): 153-161.* A surge in population growth following rail connection with the east in 1885 helped the growth of San Diego's Jewish congregation and led to the construction of Temple Beth Israel in 1889. The facilities were expanded for another population increase after World War I, but continued growth demanded a new synagogue, built in 1926. The old building was sold at that time but was repurchased by congregation Beth Israel in 1978. The community now intends to restore the historic building and move it to Heritage Park in Old Town. Primary and secondary sources; photo, 45 notes.   B. S. Porter

1969. Schwieder, Dorothy and Swanson, Patricia. THE SIOUX CITY CORN PALACES. *Ann. of Iowa 1973 41(8): 1209-1227.* Discusses the 19th-century creation and building of the Sioux City, Iowa, corn palaces.   S

1970. Sherman, Philip. BALTIMORE'S 104TH MEDICAL REGI-MENT ARMORY. *Maryland Hist. Mag. 1975 70(3): 275-278.* The red sandstone structure originally opened in 1858 as the Western Female High School on West Fayette near Paca Street. "One of the most spacious, commodious, and beautiful edifices in the City," the building served as a school until 1896, when turrets and battlements were added and it became a Maryland National Guard Armory. Briefly chronicles the various military units which were quartered in the building, redesignated as the 104th Medical Regiment Armory after World War I. The armory served "many civic, athletic, and veteran organizations as a meeting place and was host to many of Baltimore's most lavish functions, being known locally as "The Baltimore Garden." The 104th continued to use it until 1962, when expansion plans of the University of Maryland caused its demolition. The final military formation in the 104-year-old hall was impressive and emotional. Secondary sources; 8 notes.   G. J. Bobango

1971. Skjelver, Mabel C. RANDALL'S CONGREGATIONAL CHURCH AT IOWA CITY. *Ann. of Iowa 1974 42(5): 361-370.* Describes the building of the Congregational United Church of Christ in Iowa City, 1868-69. The church was designed in the Gothic style of architecture by Gurdon Paine Randall of Chicago. 2 illus., photo, 18 notes.   C. W. Olson

1972. Smith, Kathryn. FRANK LLOYD WRIGHT, HOL-LYHOCK HOUSE, AND OLIVE HILL, 1914-1924. *J. of the Soc. of Architectural Hist. 1979 38(1): 15-33.* Frank Lloyd Wright's female companion, Mamah Borthwick Cheney, died in the summer of 1914. Wright had been living with Cheney contrary to both the wishes of his family and the standards of customary convention. After that time for a decade, Wright was in a transition stage from his earlier Prairie House and Oak Park period to his later textile block system for concrete period as developed in Broadacre City. The metamorphosis occurred at two levels. At the level of what he was designing, Wright came to see himself more clearly as an artist. At the level of the materials he was using, Wright turned more and more to mass-produced, machine-made materials. Aline Barnsdall, an oil heiress, was his chief patron for this transition. The contemporary work on the more famous Imperial Hotel in Tokyo is less revealing of Wright than is his other work for Aline Barnsdall, particularly HollyHock House in Los Angeles and the creation and design of Olive Hill, an art community in which the HollyHock House was located.
R. J. Jirran

1973. Smith, Mary Ann. JOHN SNOOK AND THE DESIGN FOR A. T. STEWART'S STORE. *New-York Hist. Soc. Q. 1974 58(1): 18-33.* A. T. Stewart's "marble palace," which opened in New York City in late 1846, was the first department store. As such it understandably attracted widespread attention, and there was continuing speculation about the identity of its architect. Now, a study of records shows that credit goes to the architectural firm of Trench and Snook; in particular, to the junior partner John B. Snook. Both the firm (later taken over by Snook) and the career of Stewart prospered greatly, in part because of the structure, which still stands. Based on primary sources; 11 illus., 26 notes.
C. L. Grant

1974. Smith, Philip Chadwick Foster. THE METAMORPHOSIS OF EAST INDIA MARINE HALL. *Historic Preservation 1975 27(4): 10-13.* Recounts the changing surroundings of East India Marine Hall (1825) in Salem, Massachusetts, and discusses its architect, Thomas Waldron Sumner (1768-1849). 7 architectural drawings.
R. M. Frame III

1975. Snell, David. "HUBBUB" OF HOUSTON, THE RICE HOTEL, GOES TO THE GREAT CONVENTION IN THE SKY. *Smithsonian 1975 6(4): 48-59.* Offers colorful anecdotes of Jesse Holman Jones and his Rice Hotel, from its use as the Texas capitol in 1837 to its demise in 1974.

1976. Sobin, Harris J. FROM VIGAS TO RAFTERS: ARCHITECTURAL EVOLUTION IN FLORENCE, ARIZONA. *J. of Arizona Hist. 1975 16(4): 357-382.* Chronicles architectural changes from the Spanish period to the present. Includes illustrations and explanations of eight styles of architecture which characterized the area 1853-1973; map, 38 photos.

1977. Somerville, Mollie. THE UNITED STATES CAPITOL. *Daughters of the Am. Revolution Mag. 1976 110(6): 893-897, 930.* Discusses the history of the Capitol Building from its design (1792) through its construction, including descriptions of the statuary and frescoes.

1978. Sprague, Paul. FRANK LLOYD WRIGHT HOME AND STUDIO: HOMEWARD BOUND. *Hist. Preservation 1976 28(3): 4-8.* Frank Lloyd Wright's (1869-1959) "rapidly maturing architectural vision" was reflected in the design and alterations of his Oak Park, Illinois, residence and studio during the years he lived and worked there (1889-1909). 6 photos.
R. M. Frame III

1979. Stanton, Phoebe B. TWO CHICAGO LIVES: BURNHAM AND WRIGHT. *Rev. in Am. Hist. 1975 3(3): 348-354.* Review article prompted by Thomas S. Hines's *Burnham of Chicago: Architect and Planner* (New York: Oxford U. Pr., 1974) and Robert C. Twombly's *Frank Lloyd Wright: An Interpretive Biography* (New York: Harper & Row, 1973); summarizes the lives and the architectural contributions of Daniel Hudson Burnham and Frank Lloyd Wright and notes other studies of the two men.

1980. Stewart, Janet Ann. THE MANSIONS OF MAIN STREET. *J. of Arizona Hist. 1979 20(2): 193-222.* Shortly after the Civil War, Main Street, south of its intersection with Alameda, became Tucson's premier residential area. Edward Nye Fish, Hiram Stevens, Sam Hughes, Leo Goldschmidt, and other leading citizens lived on Main Street. Architectural styles changed, but Main Street remained Tucson's leading residential section into the early 1900's. Based on documents in the Arizona Historical Society, University of Arizona Library, newspaper accounts, and published secondary sources; map, 18 photos, 62 notes.
D. R. McDonald

1981. Szuberla, Guy. THREE CHICAGO SETTLEMENTS: THEIR ARCHITECTURAL FORM AND SOCIAL MEANING. *J. of the Illinois State Hist. Soc. 1977 70(2): 114-129.* Examination of British and Chicago architects' and social workers' philosophies concerning the design and functions of settlement houses, 1890's-1900's. Architectural plans illustrate the modern and traditional influences in Hull House, University of Chicago Settlement, the Chicago Commons, and London's Toynbee Hall. 14 illus., 43 notes.
J/S

1982. Tager, Jack. PARTNERS IN DESIGN: CHICAGO ARCHITECTS, ENTREPRENEURS, AND THE EVOLUTION OF URBAN COMMERCIAL ARCHITECTURE. *South Atlantic Q. 1977 76(2): 204-218.* The modern steel-frame skyscrapers originated in the freewheeling, traditionless business economy of Chicago in the 1880's. Young Western architects teamed with young business firms to produce edifices pragmatic in design and grand in stature. William Le Baron Jenney was the movement's father, and the firm of Burnham and Root his most prolific offspring. The World's Columbian Exposition (Chicago, 1893) was meant to bring the Chicago School to the world, but the beaux arts movement, always popular in Europe and the American East, impressed even the utilitarian Midwesterners. Not until after the 1920's would utilitarian architecture recover from this blow. 61 notes.
W. L. Olbrich

1983. Tatum, George B. ARCHITECTURE. *Am. Art J. 1975 7(1): 4-22.* Discusses architecture in the colonies during the 18th century, contrasting types in Philadelphia, Boston, New York, New Haven, and Savannah, all of which had architecture of various foreign influences molded to a typical American pragmatism. 16 photos, 3 drawings.

1984. Taylor, John M. WILLARD'S OF WASHINGTON: AN INSIDE VIEW OF A GREAT HOTEL. *Am. Hist. Illus. 1979 14(6): 10-15.* Begun under the proprietorship of Joseph C. and Henry A. Willard in 1853, Willard's City Hotel in Washington, D.C., served as a political and social center during the Civil War.

1985. Thomas, Richard H. FROM PORCH TO PATIO. *Palimpsest 1975 56(4): 120-127.* The porch, which created opportunities for social intercourse, both facilitated and symbolized the community-oriented social relationships characteristic of the 19th century. By contrast, the patio facilitates and symbolizes the need for privacy which pervades contemporary society. Both porch and patio are therefore significant statements about the social meaning of homes. Illus., 6 photos.
D. W. Johnson

1986. Thorndike, Joseph J., Jr. MRS. JACK AND HER BACK BAY PALAZZO. *Am. Heritage 1978 29(6): 44-49.* Belle Stewart married Jack Gardner of Boston in 1860. She was a vivacious, wealthy hostess who became a patron and collector of the arts. Her life's achievement was the building of an Italian palace in Boston's Back Bay. Fenway Court, completed in 1902, housed her extensive art collection and is now open to the public.
B. J. Paul

1987. Tolles, Bryant F., Jr. THE JOHN TUCKER DALAND HOUSE. *Essex Inst. Hist. Collections 1978 114(1): 1-23.* The John Tucker Daland House is today one of the "best examples of cube-type one-family Italianate residential architecture surviving in New England." The noted Boston architect Gridley J. F. Bryant (1816-99) built the house for the prosperous Salem merchant John Tucker Daland (1795-1861) in 1850-51. The architectural and social history of the house form a chapter in the saga of Salem and the Essex Institution, which purchased the house in 1885. Renovations have not noticeably altered the exterior of the house. Includes a detailed description of the 1851 "Anglo-Palladian interior," discusses the interior renovations and alterations up to the present, and presents a walking tour of the present interior with fixtures. Primary and secondary sources; 10 photos, 52 notes.
R. S. Sliwoski

1988. Twombly, Robert C. SAVING THE FAMILY: MIDDLE CLASS ATTRACTION TO WRIGHT'S PRAIRIE HOUSE 1901-1909. *Am. Q. 1975 27(1): 57-72.* Despite the widely accepted view that Frank Lloyd Wright's prairie houses were unpopular, the upper middle class provided the architect with many commissions. The house appealed to conventional suburbanites owing to its harkening back to their rural origins, its close association with nature, and its emphasis on securing the family from the real and alleged dangers of a rapidly changing urban environment. The house stressed shelter, internal intimacy, and togetherness with motifs of strength, security, and durability.   N. Lederer

1989. Unsigned. DOCUMENTING A LEGACY: 40 YEARS OF THE HISTORICAL AMERICAN BUILDINGS SURVEY. *Q. J. of the Lib. of Congress 1973 30(4): 268-294.* The Historical American Buildings Survey was formally organized in 1933 as a cooperative effort of the National Park Service, the Library of Congress, and the American Institute of Architects. Historic district studies have recently been made of Nantucket, Coral Gables, Florida, and the Stockade area of Kingston, New York, tracing the physical development and architectural history of the places. Measured drawings are the nucleus of the collection. Public availability of the survey's records has always been stressed. Illus.
E. P. Stickney

1990. Unsigned. THE WANTON-LYMAN-HAZARD HOUSE. *Newport Hist. 1973 43(2): 43-49.* Two letters describe the Wanton-Lyman-Hazard House built before the Revolutionary War. The first, by Ann Maria Lyman, is undated. The second, from Thomas Hunter to his mother Mary Robinson Hunter, was written in 1848.
J. H. Krenkel

1991. VanMeter, Mary. ASHER BENJAMIN AND AMERICAN ARCHITECTURE: A NEW ASHER BENJAMIN CHURCH IN BOSTON. *J. of the Soc. of Architectural Hist. 1979 38(3): 262-266.* This is the only standing Greek Revival church of Asher Benjamin in Boston. The church was raised 12 feet above street level to permit the construction of two stores below. The building is now known as the Charles Playhouse. Covers 1833-40. 5 fig., 8 notes.   R. J. Jirran

1992. Viggers, Ruth. BLAIR HOUSE—WASHINGTON'S TERRACE HILL. *Ann. of Iowa 1974 42(3): 236-239.* Blair House, in Washington, Iowa, is a fine example of Victorian architecture and has been named to the National Register of Historic Places (1972). It currently serves as the city hall. The Washington County Historical Society hopes it will be restored to its original 1880 appearance. Illus., photo.
C. W. Olson

1993. Vlach, John Michael. THE SHOTGUN HOUSE: AN AFRICAN ARCHITECTURAL LEGACY. *Pioneer Am. 1976 8(1): 47-56, (2): 57-70.* Part I. Attempts to unravel previous interpretations of Afro-American material contributions to America, especially that of the shotgun house type, an Afro-American artifact that was adopted by whites and incorporated into popular building practices. Most students of folk architecture have not attempted to seek the origins of this house type. Frequent occurrences of shotgun subtypes in the New Orleans vicinity dating to the mid-1880's suggest that this house type had had time to develop and become standardized. During the first decade of the 19th century many free Negroes came to New Orleans from Haiti. Due to a housing shortage, Negroes who were financially able to do so developed their own architectural environment—the shotgun house type. Based on documents found in the New Orleans Notarial Archives and in the Tulane University Library, Special Collection Division, two unpublished Ph.D. dissertations, and secondary works; illus., 5 photos, 5 figs., 34 notes. Part II. Traces the history of the shotgun house type from West Africa (Nigeria) to Louisiana via Haiti. Fieldwork in Haiti and New Orleans indicates that their shotgun houses are similar not only in type but also in specific detail. These architectural relations are complicated by the occurrence of similar housing constructed by the Arawak Indians, who were indigenous to Haiti. The slave trade, which reached its peak in the 1780's, is responsible for bringing Yoruba-related peoples of West Africa to Haiti. The Yoruba solution to the problem of plantation housing in Haiti reflects a form and philosophy of architecture which resembles a pattern derived from their African antecedents. Based on extensive field work in New Orleans, Haiti, and West Africa, one unpublished Ph.D. dissertation, and secondary works; 2 illus., 5 photos, 14 figs., 17 notes.
C. R. Gunter, Jr.

1994. Voye, Nancy S. ASHER BENJAMIN'S WEST CHURCH: A MODEL FOR CHANGE. *Old-Time New England 1976 67(1-2): 7-15.* Sketches of Asher Benjamin's architectural design for Boston's West Church appeared in his *The American Builder's Companion* (1806) as a model for other such buildings, and they represent an early stage in his career as architect. Benjamin later changed his original truss design to strengthen the roof structure. 9 illus., 16 notes.   R. N. Lokken

1995. Waddell, Gene. ROBERT MILLS'S FIREPROOF BUILDING. *South Carolina Hist. Mag. 1979 80(2): 105-135.* Discusses Robert Mills's efforts to convince Charleston's city council to approve the construction of fireproof buildings, specifically the downtown building which housed city offices; includes excerpts from official memos, photographs, and copies of blueprints of the Fireproof Building, which was under construction during 1822-26.

1996. Wade, Louise Carroll. BURNHAM & ROOT'S STOCKYARDS CONNECTION. *Chicago Hist. 1975 4(3): 139-147.* Describes the development of the architectural firm of Burnham & Root in Chicago after the Chicago fire of 1871, and how John Wellborn Root and Daniel Hudson Burnham prospered after marrying into families that controlled Chicago's Union Stock Yard and Transit Company.   S

1997. Walton, Elisabeth. A NOTE ON WILLIAM W. PIPER AND THE ACADEMY ARCHITECTURE IN OREGON IN THE NINETEENTH CENTURY. *J. of the Soc. of Architectural Historians 1973 32(3): 231-239.* A chronological account of Oregon's academy and university architectural building program. William W. Piper, in collaboration with Elwood M. Burton, designed many Classical schools in Portland, Salem, and Eugene. One of Piper's better known works is the Sacred Heart Academy in Salem. 11 notes.   T. H. Bauhs

1998. Ward, Barbara M. and Gerald, W. R. THE JOHN WARD HOUSE: A SOCIAL AND ARCHITECTURAL HISTORY. *Essex Inst. Hist. Collections 1974 110(1): 3-32.* Examines the John Ward house, built in 17th century Salem, Massachusetts, and restored during 1910-12.   S

1999. Ward, Gerald W. R. THE ASSEMBLY HOUSE. *Essex Inst. Hist. Collections 1975 111(4): 241-266.* Discusses the history and architecture of the Assembly House in Salem, Massachusetts, 1782-1970.

2000. Ward, Gerald W. R. THE GARDINER-PINGREE HOUSE. *Essex Inst. Hist. Collections 1975 111(2): 81-98.* A historical narrative of the planning, construction, decoration, ownership, transfer, and restoration of a residence in Salem, Massachusetts. This house, built in 1804-05, is a fine example of the Federal style, and was owned until the 1930's by wealthy merchants. The last private owner, Thomas P. Pingree, was one of the richest men in Massachusetts. The author's sources include essays on architectural history, diaries, newspapers, tax lists, deeds, business ledgers and accounts, and biographies. 3 illus., 3 photos, 54 notes.
R. M. Rollins

2001. Whitwell, W. L. SAINT ANDREW'S ROMAN CATHOLIC CHURCH: ROANOKE'S HIGH VICTORIAN GOTHIC LANDMARK. *Virginia Cavalcade 1975 24(3): 124-133.* History and architectural description of Saint Andrew's Church in Roanoke, Virginia.   S

2002. Wodehouse, Lawrence. STANFORD WHITE AND THE MACKAYS: A CASE STUDY IN ARCHITECT-CLIENT RELATIONSHIPS. *Winterthur Portfolio 1976 11: 213-233.* The architectual papers and correspondence of McKim, Mead, and White reveal a client's ability to evaluate the aesthetic qualities of architecture. The correspondence between Stanford White (1853-1906) and Clarence Mackay (1874-1938) and Katherine Alexander Duer Mackay (d. 1930) give a rare picture of the architect-client relationship in building the Mackay mansion, Harbor Hill, and Trinity Episcopal Church, Roslyn, Long Island, New York. The papers also reveal White's commentary on the revival of 17th-century French architecture. Based on primary and secondary sources; 20 illus., 12 notes.   N. A. Kuntz

2003. Wright, Geneva Aldrich. PHILADELPHIA'S GREAT TREASURES: THE COLONIAL MANSIONS IN FAIRMOUNT PARK. *Daughters of the Am. Revolution Mag. 1975 109(1): 28-31, 88-89.*

Landscape Architecture and Parks

2004. Bender, Thomas. THE "RURAL" CEMETERY MOVEMENT: URBAN TRAVAIL AND THE APPEAL TO NATURE. *New England Q. 1974 47(2): 196-211.* The rural cemetery movement, starting in Lowell, Massachusetts, in 1841, was an attempt to provide easy access to nature while granting cities their essential urbanity. Mount Auburn, a cemetery outside Boston, and Lowell's cemeteries "were established on sites of natural beauty with the intention of conserving their original aspect," and providing a park-like area for tourists. This counterpoint ideology became the foundation of the American park movement. 48 notes.   E. P. Stickney

2005. Blodgett, Geoffrey. FREDERICK LAW OLMSTED: LANDSCAPE ARCHITECTURE AS CONSERVATIVE REFORM. *J. of Am. Hist. 1976 62(4): 869-889.* Frederick Law Olmsted is an example of the 19th-century cultural elite who tried to develop American society along their own static and formal philosophies without considering the "aggressive, pluralistic thrust" of the general populace. Using park landscaping to exemplify his political and social theories, Olmsted created structured, orderly, highly cultivated designs that he envisioned being used by the masses for quiet, contemplative solitude removed from the discordancies of their mundane lives. He resembled Henry Adams, Edward Atkinson, Horace White, and others in this desire to guide lesser-cultivated fellow citizens toward the higher and better things in life. His failure is mute testimonial to the determined, kaleidoscopic citizenry of his time. 68 notes.   V. P. Rilee

2006. Chase, David B. THE BEGINNINGS OF THE LANDSCAPE TRADITION IN AMERICA. *Historic Preservation 1973 25(1): 34-41.* While based on English examples, models, and publications, "the landscape tradition in America developed a separate . . . character." As it emerged in the 19th century, the trend was away from the aesthetic theories set forth by 18th-century English writers and toward an increasing concern with the natural scenery in rural America. Examples include Washington Irving's Sunnyside estate and Thomas Jefferson's Monticello. Describes the emergence of the "rural" style cemetery as a forerunner of the large urban park. An adaptation of the author's 1970 National Trust for Historic Preservation seminar paper on landscape architecture. 4 illus., 5 plans.   R. M. Frame III

2007. Clouette, Bruce. ANTEBELLUM URBAN RENEWAL: HARTFORD'S BUSHNELL PARK. *Connecticut Hist. 1976 18: 1-21.* Discusses the planning and execution of Hartford's first public park, Bushnell Park, 1850-54, and the slum area which was cleared away without regard for its occupants in order to complete the park area.

2008. Collier, Malcolm. JENS JENSEN AND COLUMBUS PARK. *Chicago Hist. 1975-76 4(4): 225-234.* Retraces the life and career as park designer and superintendent of West Parks, Chicago, of Danish immigrant Jens Jensen, who designed Columbus Park.

2009. French, Stanley. THE CEMETERY AS CULTURAL INSTITUTION: THE ESTABLISHMENT OF MOUNT AUBURN AND THE "RURAL CEMETERY" MOVEMENT. *Am. Q. 1974 26(1): 37-59.* The establishment of Mount Auburn Cemetery near Cambridge, Massachusetts in 1831 marked the start of the rural cemetery movement, intending to provide a garden atmosphere as a decent place of interment for the dead. New England reformers such as Jacob Bigelow, influenced by literary Romanticism and social reform, hoped to elevate the senses and evoke the finer emotions in a cemetery setting while eliminating the often revolting conditions of contemporary graveyards. Mount Auburn reflected the movement toward better sanitation and concern with good health as well as changing attitudes toward death.   N. Lederer

2010. Holland, Reid. THE CIVILIAN CONSERVATION CORPS IN THE CITY: TULSA AND OKLAHOMA CITY IN THE 1930S. *Chronicles of Oklahoma 1975 53(3): 367-375.* Historians have generally treated the Civilian Conservation Corps as a rural-oriented project of the Depression years, but it also embraced urban programs. The construction of municipal parks occupied much of the CCC's attention, and many cities constructed or improved their parks only by this means. A majority of CCC activities were in the South, and Oklahoma contained a large percentage of these. Workers in the camps not only received a small salary, but also benefited from free room and board, medical care, clothing, and education in academic and vocational fields. Camps in Oklahoma City and Tulsa, which contained both white and black workers, were strictly segregated and equal benefits were not always extended to the blacks. Based on the *Camp Inspection Reports*; 3 photos, 11 notes.
                                                   M. L. Tate

2011. Holt, Glen E. PRIVATE PLANS FOR PUBLIC SPACES: THE ORIGINS OF CHICAGO'S PARK SYSTEM, 1850-1875. *Chicago Hist. 1979 8(3): 173-184.* Describes the plans for Chicago's park system, commissioned and sponsored by business and civic leaders, doctors, lawyers, and real estate developers, 1850-75.

2012. Judd, Barbara. EDWARD M. BIGELOW: CREATOR OF PITTSBURGH'S ARCADIAN PARKS. *Western Pennsylvania Hist. Mag. 1975 58(1): 53-67.* After being appointed head of the Public Works Department in Pittsburgh, Pennsylvania, Edward M. Bigelow established the city's public park system.   S

2013. Levin, Alexandra Lee. COLONEL NICHOLAS ROGERS AND HIS COUNTRY SEAT, "DRUID HILL." *Maryland Hist. Mag. 1977 72(1): 78-82.* Colonel Nicholas Rogers (1753-1822), Revolutionary War officer and Baltimore city father, acquired the sizable property known as Druid Hill through his marriage to Eleanor Buchanan. About 1796, he erected a mansion "so compact and commodious as to outvie most of the buildings in the vicinity of Baltimore." The grounds were in the best English landscape gardening style. When the house burned shortly after completion, a second dwelling, two-story and square with carefully balanced windows and doors, replaced it, by 1801. The colonel's son bequeathed the property, complete with the family burial plot, to the city of Baltimore in 1860. The present Druid Hill Park still reflects the artistry of Rogers's planning. Primary and secondary sources; 8 notes.
                                                   G. J. Bobango

2014. Lockwood, Charles. AS NEAR TO PARADISE AS ONE CAN REACH IN BROOKLYN, N.Y. *Smithsonian 1976 7(1): 56-63.* Green-Wood is a 478-acre cemetery in Brooklyn's Gowanus Heights, and one of the nation's finest remaining examples of the Romantic landscape tradition with some of the best Victorian sculpture extant in America. Started in 1840, it is the burial place of some of the best-known personalities of the 19th century. Describes some individual tombs and furnishes visitor statistics which reflect to a large degree New York's relative lack of public parks and adequate burial facilities at the time. 11 illus.
                                                   K. A. Harvey

2015. Lubove, Roy. SOCIAL HISTORY AND THE HISTORY OF LANDSCAPE ARCHITECTURE. *J. of Social Hist. 1975 9(2): 268-275.* Reviews eight works on landscape architecture, most of them about Frederick Law Olmsted. In the study of the interrelationship of environment and culture, landscape architecture ought to be a key to "the urbanization process, politics and design, social theory and reform, professionalization. . . ." 6 notes.   M. Hough

2016. Miller, Ross L. THE LANDSCAPER'S UTOPIA VERSUS THE CITY: A MISMATCH. *New England Q. 1976 49(2): 179-193.* America urbanized rapidly during the 19th century, and landscape architects sought through parks to help city dwellers maintain their rural heritage. Believing American democracy to be threatened by the urban environment, they believed that parks would provide the lower classes with the opportunity to commune with nature (something the aristocracy did at a countryseat) and thereby reestablish an environment conducive to democracy. Based on the writings of Frederick Law Olmsted (1822-1903), Horace W. S. Cleveland (1814-1900), Henry W. Bellows (1814-82), Andrew Jackson Downing (1815-52), Charles S. Sargent (1841-1927), and Sylvester Baxter (1850-1927); 14 notes.   J. C. Bradford

2017. Montes, Gregory E. SAN DIEGO'S CITY PARK 1902-1910: FROM PARSONS TO BALBOA. *J. of San Diego Hist. 1979 25(1): 1-25.* San Diego's Balboa Park was comprehensively planned during 1902-10.

2018. Montes, Gregory E. SAN DIEGO'S CITY PARK, 1868-1902: AN EARLY DEBATE ON ENVIRONMENT AND PROFIT.

J. of San Diego Hist. 1977 23(2): 40-59. Examines the history of San Diego's Balboa Park, 1868-1902, and its original plans as a public park maintaining natural landscape.

2019. Neil, J. Meredith. OLMSTED: A DUBIOUS HERITAGE. *J. of Popular Culture 1974 8(1): 185-187.* The importance of Frederick Law Olmsted, Sr., has been exaggerated by historians of American parks. The principles of park planning laid down by Olmsted are no longer a reliable guide. Olmsted's parks were for the pleasure of the upper classes rather than for the benefit of everyone. E. S. Shapiro

2020. Ranney, Victoria Post. OLMSTED. *J. of Urban Hist. 1975 2(1): 130-132.* Laura Wood Roper's *F.L.O.: A Biography of Frederick Law Olmsted* (1973) provides new material on his pre-landscape architecture career which he began at age 43. His career was national (e.g. the Yosemite Commission and the first American planned forestry experiment) rather than urban, and according to the reviewer the volume provides "an excellent foundation" for further work. S. S. Sprague

2021. Rotundo, Barbara. THE RURAL CEMETERY MOVEMENT. *Essex Inst. Hist. Collections 1973 109(3): 231-240.* Discusses the rural cemetery movement in America during the early 19th century as a reform movement, and comments on cultural aesthetic significance.
S

2022. Rutundo, Barbara. MOUNT AUBURN CEMETERY: A PROPER BOSTONIAN INSTITUTION. *Harvard Lib. Bull. 1974 22(3): 268-279.* Since its founding in 1831 as the first American garden cemetery, Mount Auburn has reflected Boston's position within the fabric of American culture in its pious founding, its role as a battleground between aesthetic and commercial values, and its continuing existence as a retreat and a relatively unspoiled ecological oasis. Primary and secondary sources; 29 notes. L. D. Smith

2023. Schultz, Stanley K. PIONEER OF THE CRABGRASS FRONTIER. *Rev. in Am. Hist. 1974 2(3): 337-342.* Laura Wood Roper's *F.L.O.: A Biography of Frederick Law Olmsted* (Baltimore: Johns Hopkins U. Pr., 1973) sympathetically narrates Olmsted's contributions to 19th-century urban landscaping, public health, planned suburban development (called the crabgrass frontier), and other social reforms.

2024. Stewart, Ian R. POLITICS AND THE PARK. *New-York Hist. Soc. Q. 1977 61(3-4): 124-155.* More than 12 years of discussion and disagreement preceded the acquisition of the land in New York City which became Central Park. Led initially by William Cullen Bryant, editor of the *New York Evening Post,* sentiment for such a park gradually increased, aided by architects, politicians, and other interested citizens. It was promoted on the basis of public health, urban consciousness, and civic pride, and was supported by reform elements and conservative residents. The final six years of the struggle were especially heated. By the summer of 1856, the land for the park was in the hands of the city. The park became popular almost immediately. Primary and secondary sources; 5 illus., 62 notes. C. L. Grant

2025. Tatum, George B. THE EMERGENCE OF AN AMERICAN SCHOOL OF LANDSCAPE DESIGN. *Hist. Preservation 1973 25(2): 34-41.* Relates the contributions of Andrew Jackson Downing (1815-52) and Frederick Law Olmsted (1822-1903) to the history of American parks and gardens. "Downing's greatest achievement may have been his ability to turn the abstruse aesthetic theory developed in England during the 18th century into a system that middle-class Americans could comprehend and utilize in designing their own houses and gardens in the 19th century." As Downing's "professional heir," Olmsted continued the "picturesque or landscape tradition," designing major public parks for New York, Boston, Chicago, Montreal, etc. Adapted from the author's paper at a 1970 National Trust for Historic Preservation seminar on 19th-century landscape architecture; 6 illus., 3 photos.
R. M. Frame, III

2026. Thompson, Priscilla M. CREATION OF THE WILMINGTON PARK SYSTEM BEFORE 1896. *Delaware Hist. 1978 18(2): 75-92.* Through the vision of Frederick Law Olmsted, William P. Bancroft, and William M. Canby, a park system was developed along the Brandywine River during 1865-95. Olmsted's philosophy of parks was embraced by Wilmington businessmen and leading park commissioners and his basic outline for Wilmington was established even without his official sanction. Based on Olmsted Papers and Wilmington Park Commission Minutes; 55 notes. R. M. Miller

2027. Unsigned. THE NEW JEWISH CEMETERY IN EAST LOS ANGELES, 1902. *Western States Jewish Hist. Q. 1978 11(1): 64-68.* Congregation B'nai B'rith (now the Wilshire Boulevard Temple) established the new Home of Peace Cemetery in East Los Angeles in 1902. Oscar Willenberg, the cemetery superintendent, kept a photograph album of scenes from the cemetery, which are presented here. 6 photos, 3 notes. B. S. Porter

2028. Unsigned. THE OLD JEWISH CEMETERY IN CHAVEZ RAVINE, LOS ANGELES: A PICTURE STORY. *Western States Jewish Hist. Q. 1977 9(2): 167-175.* The Hebrew Benevolent Society of Los Angeles established the Home of Peace Jewish Cemetery in 1855. A new cemetery was established in 1902. The remains and monuments were transferred to the new location during 1902-10. Based on photos collected by cemetery superintendent Oscar Willenberg, interviews, and published material; 8 photos, 3 notes. B. S. Porter

2029. Vinci, John. GRACELAND: THE NINETEENTH-CENTURY GARDEN CEMETERY. *Chicago Hist. 1977 6(2): 86-98.* Examines Graceland Cemetery, Chicago's first major cemetery, hailed as a garden compared to those which had preceded it; describes the grounds, architecture, and lists some of its more famous occupants, 1861-1900.

Public Services and Utilities

2030. Anderson, Glenn F. THE SOCIAL EFFECTS OF THE CONSTRUCTION OF THE WACHUSETT RESERVOIR ON BOYLSTON AND WEST BOYLSTON. *Hist. J. of Western Massachusetts 1974 3(1): 51-58.* Consequences were severe—West Boylston's population was halved during 1895-1908 and Boylston lost 2761 acres of land. Industry was totally destroyed and the inhabitants (70% native Americans and 30% French Canadians) expressed a marked distaste for the Italian and Hungarian workforce. Primary and secondary sources, 2 illus., table, 28 notes. S. S. Sprague

2031. Barnes, Joseph W. THE ARSON YEARS: FIRE PROTECTION, FIRE INSURANCE, AND FIRE POLITICS, 1908-1910. *Rochester Hist. 1976 38(2-3): 1-47.* Briefly discusses the history of fires and fire fighting in Rochester, New York, during the 19th century; then focuses on strengthening of building codes and fire protection systems, 1900-10, following a rash of arson in the downtown area.

2032. Cain, Louis P. UNFOULING THE PUBLIC'S NEST: CHICAGO'S SANITARY DIVERSION OF LAKE MICHIGAN WATER. *Technology and Culture 1974 15(4): 594-613.* In the 1890's the Sanitary District of Chicago began to flush the city's sewage into the Mississippi drainage area with water diverted from the Great Lakes. This incurred "legal resistance over the next 40 years from the War Department, other Great Lakes states, and Canada." By 1930, faced with a court decree limiting the amount of water it could divert from Lake Michigan, the Sanitary District had shifted to sewage disposal by the activated sludge method. Illus., 45 notes. C. O. Smith

2033. Calhoun, Richard B. NEW YORK CITY FIRE DEPARTMENT REORGANIZATION, 1865-1870. *New-York Hist. Soc. Q. 1976 60(1-2): 6-34.* The lessons learned from the Civil War in the organization of activities and the training of men were applied to the New York City Fire Department during the postwar period. No longer could the enthusiastic, amateur volunteer do the job—a professional force using more modern equipment was needed. Thus a new structure was created, designed for more efficiency with a much smaller force. By 1871, despite some inefficiency and lack of discipline, the President of the board of fire commissioners, Civil War veteran General Alexander Shaler, made considerable improvements. These were reflected in insurance statistics. Wartime experiences had helped to solve peacetime, postwar problems. Based on primary sources; 6 illus., 36 notes. C. L. Grant

2034. Davenport, F. Gorvin THE SANITATION REVOLUTION IN ILLINOIS, 1870-1900. *J. of the Illinois State Hist. Soc. 1973 66(3): 306-326.* Sanitation facilities in urban Illinois were begun to clear muddy water rather than to eliminate bacteria. Chicago started its water system in 1861. The reversing of the Chicago River which carried away sewage made Lake Michigan water more pure. The sanitation revolution cleaned up the milk shed and the meat market and condemned outside toilets, but it failed to produce the lasting results envisioned by sociologists such as Shailer Mathews, Jane Addams, and John Dewey. Clean food and pure water did contribute to longer life. Based on the reports of the Chicago Department of Health and annual reports of the State Board of Health of Illinois; map, 10 photos, 35 notes.   A. C. Aimone

2035. Ellis, John and Galishoff, Stuart. ATLANTA'S WATER SUPPLY 1865-1918. *Maryland Hist. 1977 8(1): 5-22.* Summarizes the efforts of Atlanta, Georgia, to provide water for its expanding population and businesses. By 1918, public funds had been committed to maintaining an adequate water supply. Bond issues were passed by the public because of fear of fires and contaminated water. Primary materials; 49 notes.
G. O. Gagnon

2036. Galishoff, Stuart. DRAINAGE, DISEASE, COMFORT, AND CLASS: A HISTORY OF NEWARK'S SEWERS. *Societas 1976 6(2): 121-138.* Concludes, following a discussion of the haphazard and unplanned provision of public and private sewers in Newark during 1854-1919, that even at the end of this period thousands of the city's poor were denied sanitary facilities for the disposal of human waste because they could not afford to lay lines from their houses to the street or because their landlords were not compelled to do so. Based upon census data, municipal and state reports, newspapers, and secondary sources; table, 76 notes.
J. D. Hunley

2037. Giglierano, Geoffrey. THE CITY AND THE SYSTEM: DEVELOPING A MUNICIPAL SERVICE 1800-1915. *Cincinnati Hist. Soc. Bull. 1977 35(4): 223-247.* Traces the development of Cincinnati's sewer system during 1800-1915 as representative of the city government's changing attitudes toward the public need, as well as its own sense of municipal responsibility.

2038. Gregory, George Peter. A STUDY IN LOCAL DECISION MAKING: PITTSBURGH AND SEWAGE TREATMENT. *Western Pennsylvania Hist. Mag. 1974 57(1): 25-42.* While water filtration offered a cheaper short-term solution to public health problems (1905-45), city officials were slow to develop adequate sewage treatment facilities.   S

2039. Hearn, Carey. FIRE CONTROL IN ANTEBELLUM MISSISSIPPI. *J. of Mississippi Hist. 1978 40(4): 319-327.* After enumerating the dangers of fire in antebellum Mississippi towns, describes the growing awareness of the need for fire control as the urban population expanded. Although fire protection organizations often began as volunteer units, city authorities were assuming greater responsibility for affording citizens fire protection by the end of the antebellum period. Using contemporary newspaper accounts to discuss the incidence and severity of fires, stresses the inclination of newspapers to report arson as the suspected origin of many fires. Specific examples of the growth of fire protection in antebellum Mississippi towns are given.
M. S. Legan

2040. Henderson, William D. RAPIDS AND POWER: THE APPOMATTOX RIVER AND ELECTRICAL POWER IN PETERSBURG, VIRGINIA. *Virginia Cavalcade 1978 27(4): 148-163.* Evolution in electric power generation through use of the Appomattox River has delivered electrical power to Petersburg, Virginia, 1884-1978.

2041. Hennessey, Gregg R. THE POLITICS OF WATER IN SAN DIEGO, 1895-1897. *J. of San Diego Hist. 1978 24(3): 367-383.* Discusses the political and journalistic components of the clash between the San Diego Flume Company and the Southern California Mountain Water Company over the development and control of water in San Diego, 1895-97.

2042. Hoffman, Abraham. ORIGINS OF A CONTROVERSY: THE U.S. RECLAMATION SERVICE AND THE OWENS VALLEY-LOS ANGELES WATER DISPUTE. *Arizona and the West 1977 19(4):*
333-346. In 1905, Los Angeles acquired a new source of water, in Owens Valley, California, some 200 miles northeast of the city near the Nevada line. When the aqueduct was completed in 1913, the city launched an aggressive annexation drive and quickly became a major metropolitan area. From the initial announcement of the project in 1905 to the present, debate has involved the city, the people of the valley, and the US Reclamation Service. The prestige of the Service was tarnished and some of its leading officials were embarrassed with charges of duplicity in the handling of the project. 5 illus., map, 28 notes.   D. L. Smith

2043. Houseknecht, Lynn and Dunn, Harold. MUNCY'S MANY FIRE COMPANIES: 1848-1973. *Now and Then 1974 17(10): 434-446, 470.*

2044. Jones, William K. LOS ANGELES AQUEDUCT: A SEARCH FOR WATER. *J. of the West 1977 16(3): 5-21.* Rapid population growth in Los Angeles from 1868 to 1900 prompted city planners to seek additional water sources. William Mulholland, chief engineer and manager of the City Water Works, prepared a report in 1904 recommending that the city buy land in Owens Valley and pipe water from the Owens River to Los Angeles. Mulholland designed and supervised the construction of the Los Angeles Aqueduct, completed in 1913. After 1920 the Owens River did not provide enough water for both Los Angeles and the Owens Valley farmers. The farmers retaliated with sabotage of the aqueduct and demands that the city pay dearly for additional land and water. When owners of the Owens Valley bank, leaders of the militant farmers, were convicted of embezzlement, the farmers lost the will to fight. The city offered jobs and land leases to the financially ruined families. After 1928 the fight over water rights cooled considerably. Based on government documents and published primary and secondary sources; map, 8 photos, 88 notes.   B. S. Porter

2045. Kahrl, William L. THE POLITICS OF CALIFORNIA WATER: OWENS VALLEY AND THE LOS ANGELES AQUEDUCT, 1900-1927: THE POLITICS OF APPROPRIATION. *California Hist. Q. 1976 55(1): 2-25, (2): 98-120.* Part I. An analysis of the Owens Valley-Los Angeles water controversy of 1900-11. Business interests and municipal leaders united in the common goal of developing a water supply that would anticipate the city's future needs. US Reclamation Service officials conceded Owens Valley water to the more aggressive demands of Los Angeles. Questionable tactics and misleading arguments were employed to win citizen approval of aqueduct bonds, with key proponents of the aqueduct standing to profit from increased value in San Fernando Valley real estate holdings. *Times* publisher H. G. Otis, Pacific Electric owner H. E. Huntington, and other business leaders promoted the aqueduct; even the opposition of W. R. Hearst's *Examiner* was aimed at the methods rather than the goal. Voter approval was also a vote of confidence for William Mulholland, who headed the aqueduct construction project. A major threat to the uses of aqueduct water came in the municipal election of 1911 when Socialist Job Harriman led in the race for mayor. Progressive and business interests united against Harriman, who also met defeat as a result of his defense of the McNamara brothers in the *Times* bombing trial. Harriman's defeat was a triumph for the aqueduct's promoters, but his charges against the San Fernando syndicate and the aqueduct promoters had not been fully answered. Part II. Examines the policies of the City of Los Angeles in the disputes and litigation that followed the completion of the Owens Valley-Los Angeles Aqueduct. From 1913-27 Owens Valley residents fought a losing battle against the city's desire to control the Owens River water supply. During this same period Los Angeles population increased by 1200%, while the area of the city grew from 108 square miles in 1915 to 364 square miles in 1920. Much of this area and population growth occurred in the San Fernando Valley, which received large amounts of Owens River water for irrigation. During the 1920's the city's efforts to gain complete control over water rights resulted in Owens Valley settlers repeatedly dynamiting the Aqueduct. Eventually Los Angeles bought the land itself, paying generous prices but making no payments for reparations or business losses. While the episode is filled with high drama, including aggressive personalities and tragedy, it demonstrates that the ethic of growth was held to be more in the public interest at the time than was the preservation of an earlier concept of settlement. Based on contemporary newspapers, published records, and secondary sources; 2 illus., photos, 131 notes.   A. Hoffman

2046. Lewis, Dottie L. THE CINCINNATI BATHTUB. *Cincinnati Hist. Soc. Bull. 1975 33(1): 49-55.* Discusses historical controversy surrounding the "Cincinnati Bathtub" in Cincinnati, Ohio, in 1842, including developments in piping for bathrooms during that era.

2047. Melnick, Mimi and Melnick, Robert. MANHOLE COVERS: ARTIFACTS IN THE STREETS. *California Hist. Q. 1976 55(4): 352-363.* Traces the manufacture of manhole covers for utility and sewer systems in California cities. Use of manhole covers dates from the 1860's and 1870's in older California cities such as San Francisco, Stockton, and Sacramento. Los Angeles subsurface facilities date from the 1880's. Early manhole covers were made from scrap iron and forged by local foundries from handcrafted designs. Telephone, water, electrical, and utility companies usually had their own specific designs. Stars, circles, and illustrations enhanced the lids which were to have skid-proof surfaces for horses, automobiles, and people. Recent lids have been standardized and lack the uniqueness of the older ones. Preservation of the early covers has been difficult because of a general lack of awareness of manhole covers as examples of industrial art. Based on examination of numerous covers and primary sources; photos, 14 notes.   A. Hoffman

2048. Melosi, Martin V. "OUT OF SIGHT, OUT OF MIND": THE ENVIRONMENT AND DISPOSAL OF MUNICIPAL REFUSE. *Historian 1973 35(4): 621-640.* The social problem of refuse was exacerbated in 19th century America by the unprecedented growth of industry and the accompanying urbanization of US society. The problem was examined from varied points of view and numerous methods of collection and disposal were devised, but the prevailing and shortsighted practice was "out of sight, out of mind." Based upon contemporary journals; 72 notes.   N. W. Moen

2049. Pease, Jane H. and Pease, William H. THE BLOOD-THIRSTY TIGER: CHARLESTON AND THE PSYCHOLOGY OF FIRE. *South Carolina Hist. Mag. 1978 79(4): 281-295.* Discusses fire and fire prevention in Charleston, South Carolina, 1830's.

2050. Piehl, Frank J. CHICAGO'S EARLY FIGHT TO "SAVE OUR LAKE." *Chicago Hist. 1976-77 5(4): 223-232.* Suffering from diseases caused by the pollution of their own drinking water, Chicagoans decided to build a series of canals between Lake Michigan and the Des Plaines River which would provide proper disposal of sewage and pure drinking water as well as save Lake Michigan from water pollution, 1873-86.

2051. Piehl, Frank J. SHALL WE GATHER AT THE RIVER. *Chicago Hist. 1973 2(4): 196-205.* Examines the development of bridges across the Chicago River, and resulting problems. By 1832 increased land traffic demanded easy access to the north shore; yet shipping interests insisted on unobstructed navigation of the river. The development of the "Chicago style" trunnion bascule bridge in 1899 seemed to end the controversy between water and land vehicles; yet cars still are backed up as the *Medusa Challenger* plies the river. Based on primary and secondary sources; 6 photos.   N. A. Kuntz

2052. Smith, Roland M. THE POLITICS OF PITTSBURGH FLOOD CONTROL, 1908-1936. *Pennsylvania Hist. 1975 42(1): 5-24.* In 1908, the Pittsburgh Chamber of Commerce established a Flood Control Commission which developed a plan calling for nine reservoirs at the headwaters of the Allegheny, Monongahela, and Ohio rivers. The plan was endorsed at the national level by Progressives who wanted centralized inland waterway development under a single authority. This approach was rejected by Congress and the Army Corps of Engineers. However, in the 1920's funds were appropriated for studies of the flood problem in the upper Ohio valley and the Corps was instructed to broaden its approach to flood control to include the use of reservoirs. On the eve of the great Pittsburgh flood of 1936, a bill providing for nine reservoirs above Pittsburgh had passed the House of Representatives and was being debated in the Senate Commerce Committee. The flood provided the necessary impetus to obtain funds for the first five reservoirs. By 1942, six were completed, and three more were finished by 1965. Illus., map, chart, 44 notes.   D. C. Swift

2053. Tarr, Joel A. FROM CITY TO FARM: URBAN WASTES AND THE AMERICAN FARMER. *Agric. Hist. 1975 49(4): 598-612.* Though there is current interest in the problems of urban waste, disposal research indicates that farmers living near large urban areas in America have for nearly 200 years used such urban waste as was generated for farm and garden fertilization. Farmers moving westward tended to ignore field fertilization for a number of years or until the soil began to show signs of exhaustion, and then interest in urban waste would increase. Based on primary and secondary sources; 52 notes.   R. T. Fulton

2054. Tierno, Mark J. THE SEARCH FOR PURE WATER IN PITTSBURGH: THE URBAN RESPONSE TO WATER POLLUTION, 1893-1914. *Western Pennsylvania Hist. Mag. 1977 60(1): 23-36.* Briefly surveys the history of Pittsburgh's efforts to secure pure water and particularly examines public and private responses to the city's water problems between 1893, when an investigation was made of the relationship between the water supply and a high incidence of epidemics, and 1914 when a filtered water system extended throughout the city.

2055. Unsigned. THE FIRE FIGHTER: ALWAYS READY. *Am. Hist. Illus. 1979 14(3): 23-28.* Discusses fire fighting in the US cities beginning in 1737 with the establishment of the first volunteer fire fighting company, and includes lithographs by Nathaniel Currier and James Merritt Ives to illustrate the action and drama of 19th-century fire fighting.

2056. Unsigned. WATER FOR PHOENIX: BUILDING THE ROOSEVELT DAM. *J. of Arizona Hist. 1977 18(3): 279-294.* Diversion dams and irrigation ditches were using the waters of the Salt River in Arizona as early as 1867, attracting hundreds of families to the irrigable lands of the valley. Alternate droughts and floods made use of the land and future growth of the area uncertain. Control by storing flood waters for dry times received increased attention. The National Reclamation Act of 1902 and the formation of a water users' association revived hope. The Bureau of Reclamation agreed to supervise building a dam. The Theodore Roosevelt Dam, "an engineer's nightmare," was completed in 1911. 15 illus., 8 notes.   D. L. Smith

2057. VanValen, Nelson. A NEGLECTED ASPECT OF THE OWENS RIVER AQUEDUCT STORY: THE INCEPTION OF THE LOS ANGELES MUNICIPAL ELECTRICAL SYSTEM. *Southern California Q. 1977 59(1): 85-109.* Assesses the importance of electric power in the campaign for the construction of the Owens Valley-Los Angeles Aqueduct. Generation of electricity for light and power was seen as an important adjunct of the Owens Valley Aqueduct. William Mulholland and other aqueduct proponents estimated that the revenue from electricity use could pay for the construction of the aqueduct, a point that contributed to voter endorsement of the aqueduct project bonds in 1907. Although three electric utility companies operated in the Los Angeles area, voters in April 1910 overwhelmingly approved municipal development of aqueduct power. This sentiment arose from several factors, including the failure of the Los Angeles City Council to regulate local utility rates, dissatisfaction with the quality of service from utility companies, and a tradition dating to Spanish times of municipally controlled water. Municipal electricity became "a corollary of municipal water." Primary and secondary sources; 60 notes.   A. Hoffman

2058. White, Harry. FOLKLORE OF THE NASHVILLE FIRE DEPARTMENT. *Tennessee Folklore Soc. Bull. 1975 41(4): 153-169.* Discusses the social life, behavior, and humor of Nashville, Tennessee's fire department during the early 20th century.

Transportation

2059. Barnes, Joseph W. BRIDGING THE LOWER FALLS. *Rochester Hist. 1974 36(1): 1-24.* Discusses Rochester, New York at the time of its incorporation in 1817, its rival across the Genesee River, Carthage, and the bridges which spanned the lower rapids between the two, beginning with the wooden Carthage Bridge in 1819 and ending with the erection (through the design and direction of John A. Roebling) of the Genesee Suspension Bridge in 1856.

2060. Barnes, Joseph W. HISTORIC BROAD STREET BRIDGE AND THE ERIE CANAL SESQUICENTENNIAL, 1825-1975.

Rochester Hist. 1975 37(3): 1-20. Discusses the two aqueducts which carried the Erie Canal across the Genesee River at Rochester, New York; the second aqueduct was converted into Rochester's Broad Street Bridge.

2061.   Barrett, Paul.   PUBLIC POLICY AND PRIVATE CHOICE: MASS TRANSIT AND THE AUTOMOBILE IN CHICAGO BETWEEN THE WARS.   *Business Hist. Rev. 1975 49(4): 473-497.* Traces the decline of mass transit riding and the growing reliance on automobile transportation during the first half of the 20th century. Attributes the alteration in riding habits to a number of factors including outmoded public policies that discouraged both new private investment in and also public ownership of transit systems. Based on primary and secondary sources; 68 notes.   C. J. Pusateri

2062.   Brown, Alexander Crosby.   COLONIAL WILLIAMSBURG'S CANAL SCHEME.   *Virginia Mag. of Hist. and Biog. 1978 86(1): 26-32.* In 1772, the Virginia House of Burgesses passed an act to build a canal from the James to the York Rivers, through Williamsburg, to make the capital a port city. The turmoil of the American Revolution prevented construction, and the government's move to Richmond in 1780 put an end to this ambitious scheme. Primary sources; 10 notes.
                                                                R. F. Oaks

2063.   Burkhardt, Sue Pope.   THE PORT OF PALM BEACH: THE BREAKERS PIER.   *Tequesta 1973 33: 69-74.* A history of the Breakers Pier at Palm Beach, used to embark passengers from Palm Beach to south Florida, Nassau, and Cuba. Based on primary and secondary sources; 3 notes.   H. S. Marks

2064.   Bushnell, George D.   WHEN CHICAGO WAS WHEEL CRAZY.   *Chicago Hist. 1975 4(3): 167-175.* Describes Chicago's bicycling craze, which lasted from the 1870's until the turn of the century, when automobiles became popular.   S

2065.   Dauer, David E.   COLONIAL PHILADELPHIA'S INTRAREGIONAL TRANSPORTATION SYSTEM: AN OVERVIEW.   *Working Papers from the Regional Econ. Hist. Res. Center 1979 2(3): 1-16.* Examines the forms of transportation used in business and trade in colonial Philadelphia during the 18th century.

2066.   Dornfeld, A. A.   THE FREIGHT TUNNEL UNDER CHICAGO.   *Chicago Hist. 1975 4(1): 23-31.* Discusses the diverse uses of the tunnel system under Chicago's Loop from its inception in 1898 to the present.   S

2067.   Dornfeld, A. A.   STEAMSHIPS: A HUNDRED YEARS AGO.   *Chicago Hist. 1975 4(3): 148-156.* Discusses the importance of steamship travel to the development of Chicago and some of the famous steamships in its history, 1821-1949.   S

2068.   Falkner, Murry C.   THE COMING OF THE MOTOR CAR.   *Southern Rev. 1974 10(1): 170-180.* Nostalgic recollections of the first opportunities to see automobiles in Oxford during the early 20th century. Records both positive and negative reactions from local citizens and describes the vehicles and the behavior patterns of Oxford residents.   R. W. Dubay

2069.   Fink, Paul M.   THE RAILROAD COMES TO JONESBORO.   *Tennessee Hist. Q. 1977 36(2): 161-179.* Talk of a railroad in east Tennessee in the early 1830's elicited great support from regional leaders, but early attempts to secure a line failed. It was not until the late 1840's that a charter was secured for a railroad into Jonesboro, and then only after 30 citizens, led by Dr. Samuel B. Cunningham, pledged their personal fortunes to purchase unsold stock. In 1857 the line was completed to Jonesboro, linking east Tennessee with the Atlantic Ocean. Primary and secondary sources; 34 notes.   M. B. Lucas

2070.   Friedman, Paul D.   BIRTH OF AN AIRPORT.   *Am. Aviation Hist. Soc. J. 1978 23(4): 285-295.* Los Angeles International Airport is 50 years old in 1978.

2071.   George, Paul S.   TRAFFIC CONTROL IN EARLY MIAMI.   *Tequesta 1977 (37): 3-18.* Traffic congestion in downtown Miami was not controlled until H. H. Arnold was chosen head of the Traffic Bureau in

1925. By the 1930's the Traffic Bureau, given a separate identity, compared favorably with those of other cities.   H. S. Marks

2072.   Granger, Denise, Sister   THE HORSE DISTEMPER OF 1872 AND ITS EFFECT ON URBAN TRANSPORTATION.   *Hist. J. of Western Massachusetts 1973 2(1): 43-52.* The "Horse Plague" of October 1872 disrupted horse-car railways. Some enterprising individuals substituted oxen when horse traffic dropped to near zero. The distemper encouraged the New York City Board of Aldermen to allow experiments with steam cars. The success of the elevated spelled the beginning of the end for the horse cars. Based on newspapers; 2 illus., 9 notes.
                                                                S. S. Sprague

2073.   Grant, H. Roger.   ELECTRIC TRACTION PROMOTION IN THE SOUTH IOWA COALFIELDS.   *Palimpsest 1977 58(1): 18-31.* Southern Iowa shared in the interurban electric railroad boom during the early years of the 20th century. Small communities in Appanoose, Mahaska, Marion, Monroe, and Wapello counties sought to take commercial advantage of the rapid population growth accompanying the growth of the coal industry by building lines to serve company towns. Enthusiasm waned after World War I as highway transportation improved, and during the 1920's all of the lines were abandoned. Primary and secondary sources; 10 photos, note on sources.

                                                                D. W. Johnson

2074.   Grant, H. Roger.   LAND DEVELOPMENT IN THE MIDDLE WEST: THE CASE OF THE AKRON, CANTON, & YOUNGSTOWN RAILROAD, 1913-1925.   *Old Northwest 1975 1(4): 359-373.* A case study of coordination between Ohio's Akron, Canton, and Youngstown Railroad (AC&Y), and its land firm, the East Akron Land Co. (EALC). Goodyear Tire and Rubber Co. founder Frank A. Seiberling (1859-1955) controlled the AC&Y in 1913 and created the EALC. He was then able to force Goodyear suppliers to purchase EALC land so that the AC&Y gained 20% of all Akron traffic. However, the EALC purchased land at inflated prices, and Seiberling was forced out of Goodyear in 1921 only to form the company named after him. Based on the Ohio Historical Society's Seiberling Papers, the University of Akron's AC&Y Papers, and local secondary works; 2 photos, map, 30 notes.
                                                                J. N. Dickinson

2075.   Grimes, Gordon F.   THE WINNIPISEOGEE CANAL.   *Hist. New Hampshire 1974 29(1): 1-19.* The early hope of Dover, New Hampshire, for economic growth lay in the dream of building the Winnipiseogee Canal.   S

2076.   Halma, Sidney.   RAILROAD PROMOTION AND ECONOMIC EXPANSION AT COUNCIL BLUFFS, IOWA, 1857-1869.   *Ann. of Iowa 1974 42(5): 371-389.* Describes congressional legislation and city efforts to make Council Bluffs, Iowa, a rail center. By 1869 the city had succeeded in getting five railroads to build there. Primary and secondary sources; 55 notes.   C. W. Olson

2077.   Hijiya, James A.   MAKING A RAILROAD: THE POLITICAL ECONOMY OF THE ITHACA AND OWEGO, 1828-1842.   *New York Hist. 1973 54(2): 145-173.* Intercity competition and the desire to protect or promote economic markets spurred internal improvements in small communities as well as large ones. Ithaca and Owego feared that the Chemung Canal linking Elmira on Seneca Lake with the Chemung River, a tributary of the Susquehanna, would deprive them of the Erie-Susquehanna trade. The Ithaca and Owego Railroad, opened in 1834, was designed to prevent that loss of trade. However, the I & O was never profitable and failed in 1841. It eventually became part of the Delaware and Lackawanna Railroad. Primary and secondary sources; 7 illus., 55 notes.   G. Kurland

2078.   Holt, Glen E.   THE MAIN LINE AND SIDE TRACKS: URBAN TRANSPORTATION HISTORY.   *J. of Urban Hist. 1979 5(3): 397-406.* Review article prompted by Clay McShane's *Technology and Reform: Street Railways and the Growth of Milwaukee, 1887-1900;* John P. McKay's *Tramways and Trolleys: The Rise of Urban Mass Transport in Europe;* and Carl W. Condit's *The Railroad and the City: A Technological and Urbanistic History of Cincinnati.* Finds a need in the field of urban transportation to go beyond the nuts and bolts of technology and to investigate the social forces and institutions that shaped the technological developments and in turn to study the social consequences of those changes. 15 notes.   T. W. Smith

2079. Hovinen, Gary R. LANCASTER'S STREETCAR SUBURBS, 1890-1920. *J. of the Lancaster County Hist. Soc. 1978 82(1): 49-59.* Lancaster, Pennsylvania's suburbs developed during 1890-1920 due to the popularity of streetcars as suitable transportation for commuters.

2080. Jackson, W. Turrentine. RACING FROM RENO TO VIRGINIA CITY BY WELLS FARGO AND PACIFIC UNION EXPRESSES. *Nevada Hist. Soc. Q. 1977 20(2): 74-91.* Describes the stiff economic competition between Wells, Fargo and Company and the Pacific Union Express Company for passenger, express, and mail business between Reno and Virginia City, Nevada. Each company used imaginative tactics, hoping to top the other's rapid and dependable service. The contest lasted from June 1868 until December 1869 when Wells, Fargo and Company prevailed. Based on newspaper sources; illus., 3 photos, 64 notes.   H. T. Lovin

2081. Johnson, Arthur L. THE BOSTON-HALIFAX STEAMSHIP LINES. *Am. Neptune 1977 37(4): 231-238.* Presents a history of the steamship lines (Cunard, the Yarmouth Steam Navigation Company, the Boston & Colonial Steamship Company) which operated between Boston, Massachusetts, and Halifax, Nova Scotia, 1840's-1917. Based on newspapers and monographs; 25 notes.   G. H. Curtis

2082. Johnson, Frank E. "EIGHT MINUTES TO NEW YORK": THE STORY OF THE HUDSON AND MANHATTAN TUBES. *Am. Hist. Illus. 1974 9(5): 12-23.* Examines attempts at constructing railroad tunnels under the Hudson River to connect New York City and New Jersey from 1871 until completion in 1908-10.

2083. Kuhm, Herbert W. WHEN MILWAUKEE STREETCARS WERE HORSE-DRAWN. *Milwaukee Hist. 1979 2(2): 30-37.* Begun in 1861, Milwaukee's streetcar lines were horse-drawn until 1879, when a few steam-powered cars were introduced; electric cars replaced them in 1890.

2084. LeBoeuf, Randall J., Jr. ROBERT FULTON AND THE FULTON FERRY. *J. of Long Island Hist. 1974 10(2): 6-20.* Sketches the life of Robert Fulton (1765-1814) and his inventions, particularly the submarine warfare project during the War of 1812 and a steam ferry running between Manhattan and Long Island, New York.   S

2085. Lipman, Andrew David. THE ROCHESTER SUBWAY: EXPERIMENT IN MUNICIPAL RAPID TRANSIT. *Rochester Hist. 1974 36(2): 1-24.* Examines plans for the Rochester, New York, subways, 1908-56.

2086. Locker, Zelma Bays. REMEMBER OLD NUMBER SIXTEEN? RECOLLECTIONS OF THE LA JOLLA STREET CAR LINE. *J. of San Diego Hist. 1977 23(4): 25-34.* Discusses the electric railway line built and operated by John D. Spreckels in the San Diego area between Ocean Beach, La Jolla, and Mission Bay, 1924-39.

2087. Lyle, Donald J. JERKY DAYS. *Cincinnati Hist. Soc. Bull. 1979 37(2): 115-125.* The mule-drawn form of transportation called a Jerky, defined as "a vehicle without springs, moving by jerks and starts characterized by abrupt transitions," was in operation in Cincinnati at the turn of the century.

2088. Mackler, Mark. THE RAILROAD COMES TO SPRINGFIELD. *Hist. J. of Western Massachusetts 1974 3(2): 15-24.* Springfield overcame pressure exerted by Hartford, Connecticut, to have the Western Railroad routed through their town. New York speculators failed to take over the company. After a $1.2 million loan by the state, aggressive building took place, and by October 1839 the road was open to Springfield. Primary and secondary sources; 6 illus., 33 notes.
                                                      S. S. Sprague

2089. Mallach, Stanley. THE ORIGINS OF THE DECLINE OF URBAN MASS TRANSPORTATION IN THE UNITED STATES, 1890-1930. *Urbanism Past and Present 1979 (8): 1-17.* Mass transit suffered a slow and steady decline; its fate was sealed by the 1920's.

Trolley companies suffered from unwise financial and maintenance practices. Also, all levels of governmental policies hurt streetcar companies: officials were reluctant to allow companies more than the standard five-cent fare (even public attitudes argued that five cents was too much); the award of much tax money for road construction aided automobile travel. Automobiles became a personalized transportation service which met the needs of rapidly expanding cities. Transport companies motorized and thus gave revenues a temporary boost, but could not compete in the end. Graph, 3 tables, 11 notes, ref.   B. P. Anderson

2090. Massouh, Michael. INNOVATIONS IN STREET RAILWAYS BEFORE ELECTRIC TRACTION: TOM L. JOHNSON'S CONTRIBUTIONS. *Technology and Culture 1977 18(2): 202-217.* By introducing the farebox and the single-fare transfer system in the 1870's, Tom L. Johnson (1854-1911) led the way in cutting costs, reducing fares, and increasing the ridership of street railways. In the mid-1880's he devised and introduced a less costly system of cable traction, but switched to electric traction on his Cleveland (Ohio) roads when its efficiency was demonstrated in 1888. Illus., 36 notes.   C. O. Smith

2091. McGregor, Alexander C. THE ECONOMIC IMPACT OF THE MULLAN ROAD ON WALLA WALLA, 1860-1883. *Pacific Northwest Q. 1974 65(3): 118-129.* Examines two periods when the Mullan Road from Walla Walla, Washington to Fort Benton, Montana served a worthwhile purpose: 1) 1860-70, when it served as an access route for Walla Walla trade to the newly discovered mining areas, and 2) 1870-83, when it helped the city's merchants to develop trade with eastern Washington settlers. Although the original purposes of the road failed to become a reality, Walla Walla was well served as was the mining personnel and the eastern Washington agricultural areas who thereby found Walla Walla a useful supply center. 2 maps, 61 notes.
                                                      R. V. Ritter

2092. Middleton, William D. "GEMS OF SYMMETRY AND CONVENIENCE." *Am. Heritage 1973 24(2): 22-37, 99.* The Richmond trolley system, whose electric cars were described as "gems of symmetry and convenience," was launched in 1888. It was the largest street railway in the world and the first to present a truly practical means of urban transportation. It set in motion a great electric railway construction boom. Frank Julian Sprague (1857?-1934) deserves the credit for this development of successful electric transportation. The industry peaked about 1917. Although it has since declined, there is now renewed interest in the form of modern rapid-transit systems. 22 illus.
                                                      D. L. Smith

2093. Newton, Wesley Phillips LINDBERGH COMES TO BIRMINGHAM. *Alabama Rev. 1973 26(2): 105-121.* Charles Augustus Lindbergh, Jr. (1902-74), stopped overnight in Birmingham, Alabama, on 5-6 October during his national tour of 1927. The Lindbergh mystique proved as effective there as elsewhere. The hero successfully neutralized local and regional skepticism concerning the merits of air transportation, promoted air mail service for the South, and helped persuade taxpayers to support a municipal airport project. Based on Lindbergh letters, newspapers, and secondary sources; 43 notes.   J. F. Vivian

2094. Oihus, Colleen A. STREET RAILWAYS IN GRAND FORKS, NORTH DAKOTA: 1887-1935. *North Dakota Hist. 1977 44(2): 12-21.* The development of the street railway system in Grand Forks paralleled national street car railway evolution, including periods of growth, expansion, and decline. Actual establishment of street railway service in Grand Forks came later than the national pattern, but from its inception in 1904 it flourished by meeting community needs and expanded until 1917. Plagued by expensive paving requirements and limitations on profit caused by the fixed fare, the system began a rapid decline in 1930 and was totally replaced by buses in 1934. Primary sources.
                                                      N. Lederer

2095. Piehl, Frank J. OUR FORGOTTEN STREETCAR TUNNELS. *Chicago Hist. 1975 4(3): 130-138.* Describes the development and use of streetcar tunnels under the Chicago River. The tunnels were first built in 1869, and in partial use until 1953.   S

2096. Polacsek, John F. THE TOLEDO, BOWLING GREEN, AND FREMONT RAILWAY. *Northwest Ohio Q. 1978 50(1): 3-16.* Discusses the negotiations over the establishment of an electric interurban railway to provide cheap transportation to farmers and businessmen of Wood County, Ohio, during 1896-1902.

2097.   Preston, Howard L.   THE AUTOMOBILE BUSINESS IN ATLANTA, 1909-1920: A SYMBOL OF "NEW SOUTH" PROSPERITY. *Georgia Hist. Q. 1974 58(2): 262-277.* Atlanta, Georgia, hosted the first automobile show outside of either New York or Chicago 6-13 November 1909. The South had not previously been considered a potential market for cars because of poor roads and low incomes. The automobile show was the beginning of a new era. Automobile sales agencies and related businesses sprang up in Atlanta, producing new jobs and housing. Robert W. Woodruff, later of Coca-Cola fame, left his father's ice plant to begin work with the automobile industry. Based on primary sources; 43 notes.
M. R. Gillam

2098.   Provenzo, Eugene F., Jr.   ST. PETERSBURG-TAMPA AIRBOAT LINE.   *Florida Hist. Q. 1979 58(1): 72-77.* The world's first regularly scheduled airline operated between St. Petersburg and Tampa, Florida, 1 January-31 March 1914. P. E. Fansler, Thomas W. Benoist, and pilot Antony Jannus were the men who formulated and implemented the plans. Based on newspapers and other sources; 20 notes.
N. A. Kuntz

2099.   Reier, Sharon.   SIDE STREETS.   *New York Affairs 1978 5(1): 87-92.* Excerpts from the author's book, *The Bridges of New York,* which traces the history of New York City's bridges since the turn of the century, and discusses some of the current problems in bridge maintanance.

2100.   Rhoda, Richard.   URBAN TRANSPORT AND THE EXPANSION OF CINCINNATI 1858 TO 1920.   *Cincinnati Hist. Soc. Bull. 1977 35(2): 130-143.* Traces the cause and effect relationship between intraurban transportation and the territorial expansion of the Cincinnati urban area during 1858-1920.

2101.   Rosenberg, Leon J. and Davis, Grant M.   DALLAS AND ITS FIRST RAILROAD.   *Railroad Hist. 1976 (135): 34-42.* Offers a history of railroads in Dallas, Texas, the influence. which they had on the exact placement of the city, and the political and economic events which brought the location of railroad connections about, 1843-73. 40 notes.

2102.   Saylor, Larry J.   STREET RAILROADS IN COLUMBUS, OHIO, 1862-1920.   *Old Northwest 1975 1(3): 291-315.* The growth of the city and of its street transportation system were directly related in Columbus, Ohio. The city chartered the Columbus Street Railroad Co. in 1862 and began regulation in 1863. After decades of growth, mergers, and electrification in 1890, the system abandoned the two-man streetcar for the one-man bus; routes were no longer restricted by steel rails. The location of the routes influenced the growth of the city, but at the same time the railroads responded to the city's expansion. Based on Columbus ordinances and local histories; map, 60 notes.   J. N. Dickinson

2103.   Siegert, Wilmer H.   SPOKANE'S INTERURBAN ERA. *Pacific Northwesterner 1973 17(2): 17-28.* An interurban electric railway linked Spokane with neighboring communities in Washington and Idaho, 1903-09. The system prospered under the Spokane and Inland Empire Railway Company and the Washington Water Power Company but after 1910 faced growing competition from the automobile. By 1940 the electric railway ceased to operate, although most of the track continued in service as a Great Northern freight carrier. Map, 3 photos.
G. H. Curtis

2104.   Sprague, Stuart Seely.   KENTUCKY AND THE CINCINNATI-CHARLESTON RAILROAD, 1835-1839.   *Register of the Kentucky Hist. Soc. 1975 73(2): 122-135.* Recounts the unsuccessful efforts of South Carolinians to link Charleston and Cincinnati by rail. A charter, granted by Kentucky in 1836, did not lead to the necessary financial support. Efforts to achieve a more favorable charter in 1837 failed. Primary and secondary sources; 51 notes.   J. F. Paul

2105.   Spude, Robert L.   A SHOESTRING RAILROAD: THE PRESCOTT & ARIZONA CENTRAL, 1886-1893.   *Arizona and the West 1975 17(3): 221-244.* As early as 1866 Prescott, Arizona, was interested in a railroad which would connect it with the outside world. Discussions and efforts were most active in periods when the productivity and profitability of the mines in the district seemed most promising. All efforts and schemes failed until the establishment of the Prescott & Arizona Central Railroad which ran for 73.3 miles to its junction with the transcontinental Atlantic & Pacific Railroad at Prescott Junction, near present-day Seligman. In its few years of operation, 1887-93, the railroad caused a population growth and stimulated a mining boom. The P & AC collapsed in 1893 because of poor management, rotting equipment, the national panic of 1893, and the competition of a rival line. 13 illus., map, 55 notes.
D. L. Smith

2106.   Stuhldreher, Mary and Weber, Kathy.   AUTOMOBILIOUSNESS.   *Western Pennsylvania Hist. Mag. 1974 57(3): 275-288.* The *Index to Pittsburgh Life,* a journal of daily life, in 1901 initiated a publicity campaign for Grant Boulevard by beginning a column on automobiles written by Eloise Horn.   S

2107.   Unsigned.   THE FERRIES.   *Staten Island Hist. 1971 31(7): 53-64.* A photo-essay about 19th-century ferry boats at Staten Island.
G. Kurland

2108.   Unsigned.   FROM MULES TO MOTORCARS: UTAH'S CHANGING TRANSPORTATION SCENE.   *Utah Hist. Q. 1974 42(3): 273-277.* Public transportation for Salt Lake City arrived in 1872 with mule cars. Horse-drawn vehicles were a familiar sight well into the 20th century. Automotive transport was making inroads into the urban delivery system, but most long-distance hauling was done by railroad. Describes briefly early air lines. Illus.   E. P. Stickney

2109.   White, John H., Jr.   THE STEAM RAILROAD COMES TO CINCINNATI.   *Cincinnati Hist. Soc. Bull. 1974 32(4): 177-183.* Discusses the advent of steam railroads in Cincinnati, Ohio, 1837-70, emphasizing the Little Miami Line and the construction specifications of the *Gov. Morrow* (locomotive).

2110.   Wilkstrom, Debbie.   THE HORSE-DRAWN STREET RAILWAY: THE BEGINNING OF PUBLIC TRANSPORTATION IN SHREVEPORT.   *North Louisiana Hist. Assoc. J. 1976 7(3): 83-90.* During 1870-72, different groups of Shreveport's citizens "formed three companies to build street railway lines through the downtown district and to outlying areas." Two of those companies eventually succeeded in building and operating street railway lines, although only one proved to be a profitable enterprise. The first line was built by the Shreveport City Railroad Company; the second by the Fairfield Streetcar Company; the third company, which "failed before it really began," was the Texas Avenue Railway Company. By 1876, the first-named line was the only survivor. "This small line, though perhaps insignificant in itself, began the public transportation system of Shreveport." 58 notes.
A. N. Garland

2111.   Williams, James C.   THE TROLLEY: TECHNOLOGY AND VALUES IN RETROSPECT.   *San José Studies 1977 3(3): 74-90.* Examines the urban transportation systems, especially the trolley (animal-drawn and automated), 1830's-1930's.

Preservation

2112.   Ezell, Paul.   THE EXCAVATION PROGRAM AT THE SAN DIEGO PRESIDIO.   *J. of San Diego Hist. 1976 22(4): 1-20.* Discusses the archaeological excavations of the San Diego Presidio sponsored by the Serra Museum in San Diego, California, 1964-70's, explaining the founding and early history of the mission during 1769-75.

2113.   Flannery, Toni   THE WATER TOWERS OF ST. LOUIS. *Missouri Hist. Soc. Bull. 1973 29(4 part 1): 236-242.* Five water towers, each one a distinctive example of a type of architecture, stand over several St. Louis neighborhoods. The oldest was constructed in the 1870's. Four remain in good repair and are worthy of historic preservation. After many controversies about proposed demolition, advocates of preservation prevailed and secured the requisite funds. 13 photos, 43 notes.
H. T. Lovin

2114. Keyes, Margaret N. PIECING TOGETHER IOWA'S OLD CAPITOL. *Historic Preservation 1974 26(1): 40-43.* Iowa's old state capitol building in Iowa City, built 1840-42 and since 1857 part of the University of Iowa, is being restored with the aid of extensive historical research and a coded and punched key-sort card method. Illus., 3 photos.
R. M. Frame III

2115. Moorhead, Max L. REBUILDING THE PRESIDIO OF SANTA FE, 1789-1791. *New Mexico Hist. R. 1974 49(2): 123-142.* The presidio in Santa Fe was in existence from the founding of the city in about 1610 until the Pueblo Revolt of 1680. The early compound consisted of the Palace of the Governor, some barracks, a guardhouse, a military chapel, and a surrounding wall. In 1780 Governor Juan Bautista de Anza began planning a new presidio. It was some time until money became available to begin construction. The completed presidio was never used as a fortress, but only as centralized housing for troops.
J. H. Krenkel

2116. Stern, Joseph S., Jr. THE QUEEN OF THE QUEEN CITY: MUSIC HALL. *Cincinnati Hist. Soc. Bull. 1973 31(1): 6-27.* In 1978 the Music Hall of Cincinnati, best known for its acoustically perfect 3,634-seat Springer Auditorium, celebrated its 100th anniversary. It houses the Cincinnati Symphony Orchestra, the Summer Opera, and the May Festival which was the inspiration for its construction. The hall underwent major restorations in 1895, 1927, 1955, and 1969 but the acoustic has been preserved intact. In 1970 the hall was named a National Historic Site. Based on primary and secondary sources; plan, 10 illus., 8 notes.
H. S. Marks

2117. Stotz, Charles Morse. THRESHOLD OF THE GOLDEN KINGDOM: THE VILLAGE OF ECONOMY AND ITS RESTORATION. *Winterthur Portfolio 1973 (8): 133-169.* The Harmony Society, founded by George Rapp (1757-1847), carved three cities out of the wilderness, one of which was Economy (now Ambridge, Pennsylvania), located 18 miles below Pittsburgh on the Ohio River. Restoration did not begin until 1937, although the site had been designated a historical landmark in 1915. The many difficulties in the restoration process added to the taxpayers' expense. Examination of the individual structures, such as the Harmonist Church, the Great House, and the Feast Hall, reveals the characteristic features of Harmonist architecture as well as the problems of restoration. Harmonist architecture was simple and functional. While an unmistakable German influence can be seen, the architecture is primarily American in design. Economy is the only "truly homogeneous early 19th century community remaining in western Pennsylvania, if not in the nation." Based on primary and secondary sources; 44 illus., 28 notes.
N. A. Kuntz

Disasters

2118. Black, Henry. A SPEAR OF HELL: THE TUPELO TORNADO OF 1936. *J. of Mississippi Hist. 1976 38(3): 263-278.* Describes the tornado which devastated Tupelo, Mississippi, on 5 April 1936, killing 233 people in a population of 7,200, and the ensuing rescue, relief, cleanup, and rebuilding operations. Based on primary sources, especially newspapers; 38 notes.
J. W. Hillje

2119. Brienes, Marvin. SACRAMENTO DEFIES THE RIVERS, 1850-1878. *California History 1979 58(1): 2-19.* Sacramento's citizens met the challenge of disastrous flooding from the Sacramento and American Rivers. The city's location made it vulnerable to floods, and the rivers' overflow in the early 1850's caused tremendous damage. Rather than relocate the new city, its citizens spent increasing amounts of money for the construction of levees, raised the level of several city streets, and built an all-weather road. Despite these efforts, river floods continued to inundate the city in wet periods. With spirit undimmed, Sacramento boosters raised the levees and streets and rechanneled the American River. Its last major flood occurred in February 1878. Enduring and outwitting floods became a source of civic pride to Sacramento, a city built in defiance of its surrounding environment. Primary and secondary sources; 7 illus., 4 photos, 2 maps, 39 notes.
A. Hoffman

2120. Geissinger, Dorothy. 922 OAK STREET: A PERSONAL REMEMBRANCE OF THE SAN FRANCISCO EARTHQUAKE. *Am. West 1977 14(1): 26-31.* The author experienced the San Francisco, California, earthquake at age eight. Recounts her family's experiences during the quake, evacuation of their home, and leaving the ruined city by ferry. 6 illus.
D. L. Smith

2121. Greer, Richard A. "SWEET AND CLEAN": THE CHINATOWN FIRE OF 1886. *Hawaiian J. of Hist. 1976 10: 33-51.* Details the fire of 18 April 1886, which wiped out most of Honolulu's Chinatown. Includes photos, map, and a description of the relief efforts after the fire.
R. Alvis

2122. Holmes, Jack D. L. THE 1794 NEW ORLEANS FIRE: A CASE STUDY OF SPANISH NOBLESSE OBLIGE. *Louisiana Studies 1976 15(1): 21-44.* Seeks to find relevance in historical events, contrasting recent US tornadoes to a major fire which devastated New Orleans on 8 December 1794. The governor general, Baron de Carondelet, immediately initiated a program of relief, recovery and reform. Food and supplies were requested from Cuba and Mexico; funds were secured from Mexico and Spain for loans to rebuild bridges and homes; measures were taken to prevent looting and price gouging; new building codes attempted to prevent fires in the future. Based on documents in archives in Madrid, Mexico, New Orleans, published documents, and secondary sources; map, 61 notes, 5 appendixes.
J. Buschen

2123. Levitt, Abraham H. IMPRESSIONS OF THE SAN FRANCISCO EARTHQUAKE-FIRE OF 1906. *Western States Jewish Hist. Q. 1973 5(3): 191-197.* Recounts the confusion and destruction of this natural disaster, and the effect of the attitudes and edifices of the city's Jews.

2124. McCormack, John F., Jr. HELL ON SATURDAY AFTERNOON. *Mankind 1976 5(5): 21-27.* A devastating fire which claimed the lives of 146 factory workers in the Asch Building in New York City's garment district, 1911, made public the dangerous working conditions in the city's factories.

2125. McGibeny, Ruth Thompson. THE IROQUOIS THEATRE FIRE. *Chicago Hist. 1974-75 3(3): 177-180.* Account of the Iroquois Theater fire in Chicago in 1903.
S

2126. Nurnberger, Ralph D. THE GREAT BALTIMORE DELUGE OF 1817. *Maryland Hist. Mag. 1974 69(4): 405-408.* "The most vivid description of the catastrophe" that hit Baltimore on 8-9 August 1817, was a letter by an eyewitness who signed himself "S.H.C.," written to a Mrs. Elisa Dugan in Boston. A flood, caused by the overflowing of Jones Falls in heavy rains, flowed through "Old Town," and "S.H.C." saw "water rising fifteen to twenty feet above its normal level within the city limits." All the bridges were destroyed or damaged, homes, stores, businesses by the score were ruined, "many bodies were found among the wreckage." The *Maryland Gazette* described the scene as one of desolation after a fearful battle, while the press in general performed vital public service by printing instructions, preaching against looting, and reporting lost items. "S.H.C.'s" letter meanwhile gives minute details in a house-to-house account of the damage. Based on contemporary newspapers, the *Maryland Gazette*, and the *Chronicles of Baltimore*, along with "S.H.C.'s" letter; 12 notes.
G. J. Bobango

2127. Olmsted, Roger and Olmsted, Nancy. DEATH AND REBIRTH OF A CITY: SAN FRANCISCO, 1906. *Am. West 1977 14(1): 10-25.* Ever since as a city of shacks and tents it first burned in December 1849, San Francisco, California, has been vulnerable to fire. The April 1906 earthquake there was not a record-breaker for intensity. The fires in the wake of the quake were responsible for most of the human toll and property damage. 23 photos.
D. L. Smith

2128. Patterson, Richard. FUNSTON AND THE FIRE. *Am. Hist. Illus. 1975 10(8): 34-45.* Describes the role of Brigadier General Frederick Funston in controlling the fire resulting from the San Francisco earthquake of 1906.

2129. Robbins, Peggy. GALVESTON'S "HURRICANE HELL." *Am. Hist. Illus. 1975 10(7): 4-9, 49-52.* Hurricane Hell hit Galveston,

Texas, 8 September 1900, claiming as many as 6,000 to 7,000 lives and causing property damage estimated as high as 30 million dollars.

2130. Rumore, Samuel A., Jr.   NOTEWORTHY BIRMINGHAM FIRES.   *Alabama Rev. 1978 31(1): 65-71.* Provides brief accounts of historic fires in Birmingham: Caldwell House hotel, 1894; City Hall, 1925 and 1944; Loveman's department store, 1934. Primary and secondary sources; 4 notes.   J. F. Vivian

2131. Schweitzer, Jeffrey.   IN SAN FRANCISCO, APRIL 18, 1906.   *Pacific Hist. 1977 21(1): 47-49.* Provides recollections of the 1906 San Francisco earthquake. Photo.   G. L. Olson

2132. Tarter, Brent.   "AN INFANT BOROUGH ENTIRELY SUPPORTED BY COMMERCE": THE GREAT FIRE OF 1776 AND THE REBUILDING OF NORFOLK.   *Virginia Cavalcade 1978 28(2): 52-61.* The Norfolk fire of late December 1776 and early January 1777 was started by the royal governor, John Murray, fourth Earl of Dunmore, but abetted by rioting Virginia and North Carolina soldiers; examines the rebuilding, and the city's problems with inadequate fire protection through the 1820's.

2133. Unsigned.   [AUGUSTA'S 1888 FLOOD].   *Richmond County Hist. 1975 7(2): 47-63.*
Callahan, Helen.   THE FLOOD THREATENS AUGUSTA'S EFFORTS TO BECOME "THE LOWELL OF THE SOUTH," *pp. 47-60.* A flood of the Savannah River hit Augusta in 1888; details rescue operations and the outcome of the flood, the erection of a levee in 1890, and the construction of the Clark Hill Reservoir in 1951. 60 notes.
Twiggs, Margaret.   REACTIONS, *pp. 61-62.* Expresses the lighter side of the flood, including local moneymaking schemes, newspaper ads for lost items, and swimming matches.
Swann, David.   REACTIONS, *p. 63.* Discusses the repercussions of construction of the levee and dam near Augusta for downstream areas, Hamburg (which was washed away in a flood as a result of the levee construction) and Savannah.

2134. Unsigned.   [1916 AUGUSTA FIRE].   *Richmond County Hist. 1975 7(2): 77-102.*
Billman, Calvin J.   THE 1916 AUGUSTA FIRE: AN UNNECESSARY TRAGEDY, *pp. 77-99.* The fire devastated Augusta. 2 charts, 89 notes.
Harris, Louis.   REACTION, *pp. 101-102.* Nonenforcement of the Building Code of 1909 was a reason for the destructiveness of the fire.

2135. Westerberg, Julia.   LOOKING BACKWARD: THE IROQUOIS THEATRE FIRE OF 1903.   *Chicago Hist. 1978-79 7(4): 238-244.* Account, with seven photographs, of the 1903 fire in Chicago's Iroquois Theatre which killed 600 persons.

2136. Wright, Bonnie.   THE M.A.C. FIRE IN ST. LOUIS, 1914.   *Missouri Hist. Rev. 1978 72(4): 424-433.* The Missouri Athletic Club in the Boatmen's Bank building at Fourth Street and Washington Avenue was considered a firetrap from its opening in 1903. On 9 March 1914 a fire of unknown origin destroyed the building and killed 30 lodgers. On 17 March crumbling walls killed seven workers in the adjacent St. Louis Seed Company. A coroner's jury on 23 March ruled all deaths to be accidental. A belated revision of the city's building codes in 1918 included many provisions directly reflecting the grim experience of the M.A.C. fire. Primary and secondary sources; illus., 41 notes.
                                              W. F. Zornow

Attitudes toward Urban Life and the City

2137. Bakerman, Jane S.   GENE STRATTON-PORTER: WHAT PRICE THE LIMBERLOST?   *Old Northwest 1977 3(2): 173-184.* Gene Stratton-Porter's (1863-1924) protagonists in her Limberlost novels contradicted the heroes of James Fenimore Cooper (1789-1851) and Mark Twain (1835-1910). Relying on intellect rather than on instincts, Stratton-Porter's characters learned from the wilderness while exploiting it. They struggled to escape from it to the material and social comforts of the town, and to them the wilderness was properly doomed. Based on Stratton-Porter's novels and secondary works; 7 notes.   J

2138. Bouden, Mary Weatherspoon.   KNICKERBOCKER'S *HISTORY* AND THE "ENLIGHTENED" MEN OF NEW YORK CITY.   *American Literature 1975 47(2): 159-172.* In Knickerbocker's *A History of New York* (1809) Washington Irving satirized the older men of the Enlightenment who ruled New York City and dominated society. Discusses the satire under four headings: *The Picture of New-York,* which provided the original inspiration; the activities of the New-York Historical Society; Irving's depiction of an enlightened, philosophic ruler; and the nature of city politics. 26 notes.   E. P. Stickney

2139. Bray, Robert.   ROBERT HERRICK: A CHICAGO TRIO.   *Old Northwest 1975 1(1): 63-84.* Three of Robert Herrick's (1868-1938) Chicago novels, *The Web of Life* (1900), *The Common Lot* (1904), and *The Memoirs of an American Citizen* (1905), are the best examples of Midwest Progressive fiction. Conceived and executed in error, Chicago was still led by moral cripples rendered infirm without mitigation by the city. Protagonists lived in the "systematic ugliness" of Chicago's social history: Haymarket bombing, Pullman Strike, Columbian Exposition, and the rise of the meatpacking industry. In his later Chicago novels Herrick was more apocalyptic. 18 notes.   J. N. Dickinson

2140. Bullough, William A.   "IT IS BETTER TO BE A COUNTRY BOY": THE LURE OF THE COUNTRY IN URBAN EDUCATION IN THE GILDED AGE.   *Historian 1973 35(2): 183-195.* Some educators at the turn of the century viewed industrialization as a threat to the virtues of earlier and more pastoral days. Because of this antagonism toward urban growth, they preached antiurban doctrines which had their greatest effect in elementary and secondary education. These doctrines failed to provide useful models or effective solutions for city children's problems. Based on collections of addresses and proceedings of the National Education Association; 41 notes.   N. W. Moen

2141. Cox, Richard.   CONEY ISLAND, URBAN SYMBOL IN AMERICAN ART.   *New-York Hist. Soc. Q. 1976 60(1-2): 35-52.* Of the many amusement parks in 20th-century America, no doubt Coney Island was the best known. For almost half a century prior to World War II it attracted millions of visitors and was celebrated in song, story, and film. However, the artists, in particular Joseph Stella, Louis Lozowick, Art Young, and Reginald Marsh, seem to have been most successful in capturing its significance. To them, Coney Island seemed to be the symbol of modern urbanization. The approach of each artist was different, yet each was influenced by the park, and in turn each contributed toward an appreciation of Coney Island. Based on primary sources; 8 illus., 21 notes.
                                              C. L. Grant

2142. Crepeau, Richard C.   URBAN AND RURAL IMAGES IN BASEBALL.   *J. of Popular Culture 1975 9(2): 315-324.* Baseball during the 1920's-30's stressed its rural origins and bound itself to the agrarian myth in American culture. *The Sporting News* reiterated baseball's connection with rural life and values and expressed resentment of the city. The concern with rural-urban issues declined in the 1930's and even more so in the 1940's. 28 notes.   J. D. Falk

2143. Crider, Gregory L.   HOWELLS' ALTRURIA: THE AMBIVALENT UTOPIA.   *Old Northwest 1975 1(4): 405-418.* Compares William Dean Howells's (1837-1920) utopian *A Traveler from Altruria* (1894) with his later utopian *Through the Eye of the Needle* (1906) to illustrate Howells' persistent ambivalence. Howells honored modern technology and regretted the demise of handicraft; he loved rural simplicity and enjoyed urban culture; and he preached democratic socialism and lived as an aristocrat. Howells' dichotomies made him a controversial, ambivalent social critic. Based on Howells's works and secondary works; 17 notes.   J. N. Dickinson

2144.   Crider, Gregory L.   WILLIAM DEAN HOWELLS AND THE ANTIURBAN TRADITION: A RECONSIDERATION.   Am. Studies [Lawrence, KS] 1978 19(1): 55-64. Reviews the literature criticizing William Dean Howells as antiurban, and then analyzes Howells's vision of the city within the context of recent urban history. Although he disliked some aspects of American cities, Howells thought they could be corrected, and spent most of his adult life in Boston and New York. Howells directed his main criticism at capitalism, not urbanism, and lamented the inability of urban social institutions to keep pace with the rapid physical and economic changes. The lack of community also bothered him. Primary and secondary sources; 41 notes.   J. Andrew

2145.   Dow, Eddy.   LEWIS MUMFORD'S PASSAGE TO INDIA: FROM THE FIRST TO THE LATER PHASE.   South Atlantic Q. 1977 76(1): 31-43. From 1922 to 1931, Lewis Mumford concentrated his writing on American literature, history, and art, as seen in relation to life in America. Beginning with Technics and Civilization (1934), Mumford expanded his thinking to include urban life, intellectual history, and cultural history seen in relation to life anywhere on earth. This shift in interest existed only in his literary works; Mumford always had a universal outlook, but concentrated on American civilization until convinced his recovery of America's usable past could be left to other competent thinkers. 19 notes.   W. L. Olbrich

2146.   Edmonds, Anthony O.   MYTHS AND MIGRANTS: IMAGES OF RURAL AND URBAN LIFE IN COUNTRY MUSIC.   Indiana Social Studies Q. 1975/76 28(3): 67-72. Examines the content of country music since the 1920's as it pertains to the urban migration of whites from the rural South.

2147.   Ekman, Ernst.   A SWEDISH VIEW OF CHICAGO IN THE 1890'S: HENNING BERGER.   Swedish Pioneer Hist. Q. 1974 25(3-4): 230-240. Discusses account of Chicago in the 1890's by Swedish author Henning Berger (1872-1924), who established his literary reputation with writings based on his experiences there. He viewed Chicago as the essence of America, and Chicago fascinated and dismayed him. He criticized Swedish immigrants who adjusted too well to America. Based on primary sources; 31 notes.   K. J. Puffer

2148.   Fanning, Charles and Skerrett, Ellen.   JAMES T. FARRELL AND WASHINGTON PARK: THE NOVEL AS SOCIAL HISTORY. Chicago Hist. 1979 8(2): 80-91. Gives a biography of author James T. Farrell, born in Chicago in 1904, and focuses on eight novels, of the 22 novels and 250 short stories he has written, set around Chicago's Washington Park and the people in its neighborhood, on the occasion of Farrell's 75th birthday in 1979.

2149.   Fanning, Michael.   NEW ORLEANS AND SHERWOOD ANDERSON.   Southern Studies 1978 17(2): 199-207. Sherwood Anderson (1876-1941), a Midwestern writer, traveled to the South on several trips during 1920-26. He found New Orleans especially significant as offering an alternative style of life to the American values of materialism, Puritanism, and industrialization, which Anderson had come to criticize. His view of New Orleans was romantic; he found the people "civilized," openly sensual, leisurely, frank, and having a mixture of commendable European and black attitudes. The metaphor of the river, based on the Mississippi, became a favored motif; it was dark, ruthless, invigorating, powerful, spontaneous. Based on Letters of Sherwood Anderson and secondary sources; 22 notes.   J. Buschen

2150.   Fine, David M.   ABRAHAM CAHAN, STEPHEN CRANE AND THE ROMANTIC TENEMENT TALE OF THE NINETIES. Am. Studies [Lawrence, KS] 1973 14(1): 95-108. By the 1890's city slums had a proven marketability in American fiction. Reform journalism became fiction, which offered a radical departure from the genteel, Victorian drawing room. The result was a mixture of cynicism and sentimentality, with all the attention devoted to the moral implications of slum conditions. For Crane and Cahan, however, poverty was not ennobling —a defiance of the romantic tenement tale. This proved uncomfortable

to genteel audiences. Based on primary and secondary sources; 21 notes.
J. Andrew

2151.   Fine, David M.   JAMES M. CAIN AND THE LOS ANGELES NOVEL.   Am. Studies [Lawrence, KS] 1979 20(1): 25-34. Surveys James M. Cain's Los Angeles novels of the 1930's and 1940's, which have now been revived amid the rediscovery of thirties Los Angeles in text and film. The gangster and the tough guy pervade these works, reflecting the fantasies and nightmares of the depression years. Cain presented us with the major metaphors for the literary identity of Los Angeles—the road, the landscape, and the commonplace. Primary and secondary sources; 11 notes.   J. A. Andrew

2152.   Frisch, Michael.   A USEFUL BLEND OF MARX AND CLIO/BUT SHORT ON KARL AND LONG ON LEO.   Rev. in Am. Hist. 1975 3(4): 425-428. Examining American attitudes on industrialization and urbanization, Thomas Bender in Toward an Urban Vision: Ideas and Institutions in Nineteenth-Century America (Lexington: U. Pr. of Kentucky, 1975) feels that Americans thought they could democratize industrial capitalism "by introducing within the city a 'counterpoint' of rural forms and values."

2153.   Garofalo, Charles.   THE ATLANTA SPIRIT: A STUDY IN URBAN IDEOLOGY.   South Atlantic Q. 1975 74(1): 34-44. The Chamber of Commerce's monthly The City Builder (1916-35) published attempts of local boosters to define Atlanta's unique characteristics and to apply them to daily city life. Money, morality, idealism, and sanctification of the city became known collectively as "the Atlanta Spirit," which, it was felt, united all citizens in a religious fervor of boosterism. Local businessmen hoped to attract new industries and populations by these zealous appeals to civic pride, which included the black community. No effort was ever made, however, to assess realistically the impact of these efforts on the local populace. Based on primary and secondary sources; 27 notes.   W. L. Olbrich

2154.   Gillette, Howard.   FILM AS ARTIFACT: THE CITY (1939). Am. Studies (Lawrence, KS) 1977 18(2): 71-85. Argues for the intelligent use of films to explore patterns in American culture, focusing on the documentary tradition. The City was an effort to draw attention to America's urban crisis in the 1930's—for exposure at the 1939 New York World's Fair. The film emphasized the need for city planning, and sought to recreate a semipastoral environment in an urban setting—the garden city. Planners tried to recast existing congested urban forms to decentralized suburban sectors and into regional frameworks. Primary and secondary sources; 6 illus., 38 notes.   J. A. Andrew

2155.   Goist, Park Dixon.   TOWN, CITY AND "COMMUNITY" 1890-1920'S.   Am. Studies [Lawrence, KS] 1973 14(1): 15-28. Notes the long-standing concern for community in the American experience. Page Smith and Malcolm Cowley have both addressed the question, along with many other intellectuals at the inception of the 20th century. Like Jane Addams, each one tried to discover a new basis and definition for community. Based on primary and secondary sources; 30 notes.
J. Andrew

2156.   Goldfield, David R.   URBAN-RURAL RELATIONS IN THE OLD SOUTH: THE EXAMPLE OF VIRGINIA.   J. of Urban Hist. 1976 2(2): 146-168. Historians frequently have emphasized the conflicts between urban and rural interests. An investigation of the city-country relations in mid-19th century Virginia reveals a high degree of mutual interdependence and binding economic advantage which centered around commercial activities, real estate investments, and slaveholding and trading. Some urban-rural disputes developed but were less pronounced than contemporary conflicts between rival cities, sections, and intraurban interests. Primary and secondary sources; 94 notes.   T. W. Smith

2157.   Hammack, David C.   ELITE PERCEPTIONS OF POWER IN THE CITIES OF THE UNITED STATES, 1880-1900: THE EVIDENCE OF JAMES BRYCE, MOISEI OSTROGORSKI, AND THEIR AMERICAN INFORMANTS.   J. of Urban Hist. 1978 4(4): 363-396. When Bryce and Ostrogorski toured the United States in the late 19th century they discussed and corresponded with a number of American informants about the political system. Bryce concluded that the country was ruled by two elites—the "best men" and a new elite of emerging capitalists. The capitalists had self-interest as their motivation and economic topics as their area of interest, while the "best men" were public-spirited and concerned about all social aspects. These groups often contended for power with machines, immigrants, and others not forming independent power bases. Ostrogorski, however, found the capitalist elite firmly in control, with the bosses holding an important subordinate role as power mediators. 123 notes.   T. W. Smith

2158.   Henderson, Floyd M.   THE IMAGE OF NEW YORK CITY IN AMERICAN POPULAR MUSIC: 1890-1970.   *New York Folklore Q. 1974 30(4): 267-278.*

2159.   Hodges, Margaret.   PITTSBURGH: SEVEN AUTHORS, SEVEN VIEWS.   *Western Pennsylvania Hist. Mag. 1973 56(3): 253-279.* Writings of Hervey Allen, Margaret Deland, Marcia Davenport, Willa Cather, Mary Roberts Rinehart, Gladys Schmitt, and Haniel Long.   S

2160.   Holt, Glen E.   ST. LOUIS OBSERVED "FROM TWO DIFFERENT WORLDS": AN EXPLORATION OF THE CITY THROUGH FRENCH AND ENGLISH TRAVELERS' ACCOUNTS, 1874-1889.   *Missouri Hist. Soc. Bull. 1973 29(2): 63-87.* Analyzes the impressions of French and English visitors to St. Louis. British and French visitors alike were favorably impressed by the Eads Bridge and other engineering achievements, and by the city's burgeoning commerce and its "many fine residential sections." French and English visitors responded differently to the social and cultural *milieu.* British visitors tended to accept the city "on its own terms," while the French probed more deeply and critically into ethnic, racial, and religious matters. 104 notes.   H. T. Lovin

2161.   Kane, Patricia.   F. SCOTT FITZGERALD'S ST. PAUL: A WRITER'S USE OF MATERIAL.   *Minnesota Hist. 1976 45(4): 141-148.* F. Scott Fitzgerald's use of St. Paul locales in *The Great Gatsby* and some of his short stories centered geographically on a one-square-mile-area focusing on Summit Avenue. His perception of the neighborhood and its people was altered to fit the fictional imperatives of his work. Generally speaking, Fitzgerald's view of St. Paul, as he recaptured his memories in fictional form, emphasized stability of residence and of social status, and described the middle and upper middle classes. His written nostalgia for a stable past is somewhat ironic, because he and his family moved frequently during their residence in the city.   N. Lederer

2162.   Langdon, Thomas C.   HAROLD BELL WRIGHT: CITIZEN OF TUCSON.   *J. of Arizona Hist. 1975 16(1): 77-98.* Harold Bell Wright's (1872?-1944) most productive years were spent in Arizona. His 1915-36 residence in and near Tucson inspired nine of his best selling novels, while his civic and philanthropic activities made him a leading citizen. Wright's story of the salubrious climate which healed his tuberculosis-stricken body, published in a national magazine, brought fame to Tucson as a health resort. 2 illus., 43 notes.   D. L. Smith

2163.   Love, Glen A.   FRANK NORRIS'S WESTERN METROPOLITANS.   *Western Am. Literature 1976 11(1): 3-22.* Withdrawal from the city to an outlying area is a typical activity of the central characters in Frank Norris's San Francisco novels. The total design of these novels shows a gradual shift from characters not fitted to modern urban life, to those who prefer adventure and finally to those who get along equally well in either setting.   M. Genung

2164.   MacDonald, Edgar.   GLASGOW, CABELL, AND RICHMOND.   *Mississippi Q. 1974 27(4): 393-414.* Examines the importance of Richmond in the writing of Ellen Glasgow and James Branch Cabell and asserts that "art is preeminently provincial." One of a series of three papers.   S

2165.   Margolies, Edward.   CITY, NATURE, HIGHWAY: CHANGING IMAGES IN AMERICAN FILM AND THEATER.   *J. of Popular Culture 1975 9(1): 14-19.* Contrasts the image of cities in pre-World War II drama and films with postwar productions. In the earlier period the city was depicted as bad but as a carrier of civilization while in the postwar period the civilizing capacities of the city are displaced by its bleakness, depersonalization, and alienation. There is a disenchantment with nature, which has disappeared as an escape from cities. Roads, like

cities, are now bound up with savage wilderness in the imagery of film and drama.   J. D. Falk

2166.   Margon, Arthur.   URBANIZATION IN FICTION: CHANGING MODELS OF HEROISM IN POPULAR AMERICAN NOVELS, 1880-1920.   *Am. Studies [Lawrence, KS] 1976 17(2): 71-86.* Social and urban change severed the ties between individualism and benevolence, thus forcing the emergence of a new kind of hero. Ignatius Donnelly and other utopians noted the "impossibility of heroism in urban culture." Novelists of all persuasions found that individualism and public welfare were not compatible in an urban age. Primary and secondary sources; 38 notes.   J. Andrew

2167.   McCarthy, Kevin M.   HISTORICAL ST. AUGUSTINE IN FICTION.   *Escribano 1978 15: 61-72.* Discusses 20th-century fiction which uses St. Augustine, Florida, as a locale.

2168.   McLear, Patrick E.   JOHN STEPHEN WRIGHT AND URBAN AND REGIONAL PROMOTION IN THE NINETEENTH CENTURY.   *J. of the Illinois State Hist. Soc. 1975 68(5): 407-420.* A real estate speculator whose credit was ruined through debt default during the Panic of 1837, John Stephen Wright founded and edited the *Union Agriculturalist and Western Prairie Farmer* in 1840 to promote the Middle West and to act as an informational exchange for prairie farmers. He continued his real estate ventures, founded a wool exchange in Chicago and established a reaper factory. His book, *Chicago: Past, Present, Future* , emphasized that the "Great Interior" of America would become the most important region on the continent and that Chicago would become the leading commercial center in the United States.   N. Lederer

2169.   Morris, R. A.   CLASSICAL VISION AND THE AMERICAN CITY: HENRY JAMES'S *THE BOSTONIANS.*   *New England Q. 1973 46(4): 543-557.* A critical look at urban-rural, classical-modern conflicts in Henry James's novel *The Bostonians.* James never felt at home in the noisy, brutal, anomic, industrial city. He fought back by utilizing classical pastoral descriptions of city life and events. The compromise never worked very well: fleeting impressions of classical harmony and beauty were quickly beaten down by the harsh facts of reality. 9 notes.   V. L. Human

2170.   Murray, Robert K.   THE DEMOCRATS VS. FRUSTRATION CITY: IT WAS NO MIX.   *Smithsonian 1976 7(1): 48-55.* Reviews a chapter in Robert K. Murray's *The 103rd Ballot: The Democrats and the Disaster in Madison Square Garden* (Harper-Row, 1976), concerning the Democratic convention in New York City in 1924, a convention which reflected American social cleavage, e.g. urban vs. agricultural, wet vs. dry, and featured the candidacy of William Gibbs McAdoo (1863-1941) and Alfred E. Smith (1873-1944). Many favorite sons were antagonistic about the convention location, and this, plus misunderstanding, influenced the candidates and the convention results. By 10 July (the convention began 24 June) the delegates, after voting for 59 different persons on 103 Presidential ballots (both records), reached a compromise with the selection of John W. Parker. 6 illus., 20 photos.   K. A. Harvey

2171.   Penna, Anthony N.   CHANGING IMAGES OF TWENTIETH CENTURY PITTSBURGH.   *Pennsylvania Hist. 1976 43(1): 49-63.* In the early 20th century Pittsburgh's business elite proclaimed the city the "Workshop of the World" and equated industrial smoke with economic progress. Despite the *Pittsburgh Survey* (1914), the Olmstead report (1911), and the Pittsburgh plan, which pointed out the gradual decay of the city, little was done to solve the mounting problems. In 1946, the business leaders, working through the Allegheny Conference on Community Development and in cooperation with Mayor David L. Lawrence, attempted to promote the city as America's Renaissance City. Their efforts included redevelopment of the central business district, smoke abatement, a new sewage treatment plant, and a highway linking the business district with the airport. Efforts have been made to improve housing conditions, but they have been subordinated to the business leadership's goals of retaining existing industries and attracting new enterprises to Pittsburgh. Illus., 53 notes.   D. C. Swift

2172.   Perkins, George.   *A MODERN INSTANCE*: HOWELLS' TRANSITION TO ARTISTIC MATURITY.   *New England Q. 1974 47(3): 427-439.* Analyzes the social thought of William Dean Howells in the 1882 novel, *A Modern Instance*. The work is transitional; Howells was moving from rural concerns of a personal nature to the problems of the new and burgeoning industrial cities. The move was incomplete; his characters succeed or fail primarily because of individual characteristics. Thus the social structure of the cities does not produce scoundrelism; rather scoundrels are likely to take up residence in the cities. The transition was nonetheless remarkable, and Howells refined the trend in later works. 14 notes.   V. L. Human

2173. Rao, Vimala. THE REGIONALISM OF RICHARD WRIGHT'S *NATIVE SON*. *Indian J. of Am. Studies [India] 1977 7(1): 94-102.* Regionalism is the social reality that has survived in a geographical background. Chicago has left its imprint on many major writers and its South Side has come to stand as the symbol of defeat for black migrants seeking the American dream. For Richard Wright (1908-60), Chicago merely externalizes the negativism Negroes develop when they discover that Chicago mirrors the racism of the South. For Wright, the Negro in Chicago is always the outsider, always alienated and rootless. 5 notes.
L. V. Eid

2174. Ronald, Ann. THE TONOPAH LADIES. *Nevada Hist. Soc. Q. 1977 20(2): 92-100.* Analyzes fiction, reminiscences, and other writings by female residents of the boom towns of Tonopah and Goldfield, Nevada, after 1900. The writers mostly idealized the 19th-century view of what constituted a lady, described the ladylike activities of the women, and romanticized about the quality of life in the desert mining towns. The main exception was Anne Ellis, author of *The Life of an Ordinary Woman*, who described graphically the unpleasantness of life on the "other side of the tracks" in those mining towns. 2 photos, note.
H. T. Lovin

2175. Ross, John R. BENTON MAC KAYE: THE APPALA-CHIAN TRAIL. *J. of the Am. Inst. of Planners 1975 41(2): 110-114.* In 1921 Benton MacKaye, a lover of wilderness, a conservationist, and a regional planner, proposed the Appalachian Trail. He projected a wilderness footpath as the backbone of an Appalachian domain consisting of camp, recreational, and industrial communities. The Appalachian Trail developed solely as a footpath, but MacKaye viewed it as a primeval barrier to the spread of metropolitanism. The Appalachian Trail became a psychological resource for the hiker and an essential part of what MacKaye called the indigenous environment: the urban, the rural, and the primeval.   J

2176. Rowland, Beryl. GRACE CHURCH AND MELVILLE'S STORY OF "THE TWO TEMPLES." *Nineteenth-Century Fiction 1973 28(3): 339-346.* The action in Herman Melville's short story "The Two Temples," although eventually placed in London, actually took place in New York City; his use of Grace Church and Trinity Church afforded him the opportunity to assail the ostentation and superficial Christianity of two new and fashionable churches, 1845-50.

2177. Schlereth, Thomas J. AMERICA, 1871-1919: A VIEW OF CHICAGO. *Am. Studies [Lawrence, KS] 1976 17(2): 87-100.* Examines Chicago as a symbol of modern American cultural history. It reflected American economic growth, industrialism, the coming of the railroad, labor problems, black migration into the North, literary and architectural changes, and the self-celebration evident in the 1893 Exposition. Primary and secondary sources; 26 notes.   J. Andrew

2178. Shideler, James H. FLAPPERS AND PHILOSOPHERS, AND FARMERS: RURAL-URBAN TENSIONS OF THE TWEN-TIES. *Agric. Hist. 1973 47(4): 283-299.* Census bureau statistics of 1920 indicate that for the first time the urban population outnumbered that of rural areas. Spokesmen for both sides were apprehensive about changing life-styles in America. To rural dwellers the city was a lair for gunmen, bootleggers, killers like Leopold and Loeb, jazz bands, aimless wastrels, and gum-chewing flapper stenographers of easy virtue. Urban residents scorned farmers as a rabble army of defectives holding clusters of civilized intellectuals under siege in a few walled towns. In the competition between polarized rural and urban worlds, the rural was fated to lose because it was economically and socially disadvantaged. Based on primary and secondary sources; 48 notes.   R. T. Fulton

2179. Siegel, Adrienne. WHEN CITIES WERE FUN: THE IMAGE OF THE AMERICAN CITY IN POPULAR BOOKS, 1840-1870. *J. of Popular Culture 1975 9(3): 573-582.* The study of the alienated intellectual elite has fostered the view of America as having a tradition of antiurbanism, but examination of the works of leaders of popular culture reveals quite different and positive attitudes toward cities. Novels about city life flooded the market in the 1840's-60's and depicted it as full of vitality, excitement, variety, and freedom from meddlers. They portrayed fancy balls, sumptuous feasts, elegant dress, gay, beautiful women, and fascinating entertainment from opera to freak shows, from art galleries to cockfights. The city was a "place of never-ending pageantry," enticing readers from the humdrum farms and villages to a life of freedom and fun. 58 notes.   J. D. Falk

2180. Smith, Carl S. FEARSOME FICTION AND THE WINDY CITY: OR, CHICAGO IN THE DIME NOVEL. *Chicago Hist. 1978 7(1): 2-11.* Discusses the appearance and format of dime novels in Chicago as a source of information on that city, 1870's-90's.

2181. Stout, Janis P. CHARITY AND THE REDEMPTION OF URBAN SOCIETY IN AMERICAN POPULAR FICTION BEFORE 1860. *Res. Studies 1975 43(3): 162-174.* Popular fiction during the first half of the 19th century reflects an ineffectual and confused American social conscience torn by conflicting values when confronted with urban problems.   S

2182. Szuberla, Guy. MAKING THE SUBLIME MECHANICAL: HENRY BLAKE FULLER'S CHICAGO. *Am. Studies [Lawrence, KS] 1973 14(1): 83-93.* Fuller reversed Emersonian notions of freedom and nature, arguing that the city, not nature, gave freedom to human senses. Fuller's cityscape, expressed in his Chicago novels, contradicted the agrarian myth of Jefferson, Emerson, and Turner, and modern architecture in the 1890's created a new sense of urban space. Based on primary and secondary sources; 16 notes.   J. Andrew

2183. Tavernier-Courbin, Jacqueline. THE VILLAGE AND AF-TER: SOCIAL EVOLUTION THROUGH CHARACTER IN *A MODERN INSTANCE*. *Am. Literary Realism, 1870-1910 1979 12(1): 127-142.* Analyzes William Dean Howells's *A Modern Instance*, stressing the inherent conflicts in the change from rural to urban living.

2184. Toth, Emily. ST. LOUIS AND THE FICTION OF KATE CHOPIN. *Missouri Hist. Soc. Bull. 1975 32(1): 33-50.* Analyzes the fiction of Kate Chopin (1851-1904). In numerous short stories and two novels, *At Fault* (1891) and *The Awakening* (1899), her descriptions of the sordid side of life and social criticism of the city enraged most of her St. Louis readers. Based on Chopin's writings and secondary sources; 61 notes.   H. T. Lovin

2185. Twombly, Robert C. DOUBTS ABOUT THE CITY. *Rev. in Am. Hist. 1978 6(4): 453-458.* Review article prompted by Sylvia Doughty Fries's *The Urban Idea in Colonial America* (Philadelphia: Temple U. Pr., 1977).

2186. Vance, James E., Jr. THE CLASSICAL REVIVAL AND UR-BAN-RURAL CONFLICT IN NINETEENTH CENTURY AMER-ICA. *Can. Rev. of Am. Studies 1973 4(2): 149-168.* Surveys the development of conflicts during the early 19th century between the exponents of an idyllic rural America and those who found many virtues in urban centers, praised the merchants and considered the city the "real, productive world." Similar conflicts erupted earlier in Europe and were brought to America during New World colonization. Early in the 1800's, antiurban views were popular in the United States. Thomas Jefferson (1743-1826) was the most able upholder of the virtues of rural life. Ultimately, the South adopted Roman models for maintaining urban-rural distinctions. Urban-rural conflicts in the North devolved into social divisions between the "responsible, propertied class and the [urban] mob." The Classical Revival in the North thus evoked classical Greek solutions to town and country hostilities.   H. T. Lovin

2187. Whitridge, Arnold. PETER STUYVESANT: DIRECTOR GENERAL OF NEW NETHERLAND. *Hist. Today [Great Britain] 1960 10(5): 324-332.* Analyzes the significance of Peter Stuyvesant's (1592-1672) vision that New Amsterdam, now New York City, would be the most important city on the Atlantic seaboard.

2188. Wolf, Edwin, II. THE ORIGINS OF PHILADELPHIA'S
SELF-DEPRECIATION, 1820-1920. *Pennsylvania Mag. of Hist. and
Biog. 1980 104(1): 58-73.* The origins include failure to become a capital
city, yellow fever epidemics, the Erie Canal, financial failures, exacer-
bated urban problems, and the abdication of descendants of old families.
Published sources and secondary works; 57 notes.   T. H. Wendel

2189. Wood, W. K. A NOTE ON PRO-URBANISM AND UR-
BANIZATION IN THE ANTEBELLUM SOUTH: AUGUSTA,
GEORGIA, 1820-1860. *Richmond County Hist. 1974 6(1): 23-31.*
Though usually considered antiurbanist as a whole, the South in isolated
areas proved actually to be prourban; this holds true for Augusta,
Georgia, where a class of planter-aristocrats favored the establishment of
cities and enjoyed the advantages which cities had to offer. 2 tables, 30
notes.   G. A. Hewlett

2. CONTEMPORARY AMERICAN URBAN LIFE (1945 TO THE PRESENT)

General

2190. Abrahamson, Mark. THE SOCIAL DIMENSIONS OF URBANISM. *Social Forces 1974 52(3): 376-383.* Examines the social dimensions of urbanism in the contemporary United States. A central thesis is that a rural-urban distinction is no substitute for an assessment of the basic dimensions of interurban variation. Toward this end, eight factors are compared and interpreted as to total variation explained and mean interrelationship holding other factors constant. The results indicate a slight predominance for the demographic factor, but a relatively small range of difference among the dimensions. The demographic aspect of urbanism has been exaggerated, and tentatively considers whether historical and cultural forces influence the structure of urbanism.   J

2191. Adams, James Ring. WHY NEW YORK WENT BROKE. *Commentary 1976 61(5): 31-37.* The external conditions creating difficulty for New York City—the declining national economy, the black and Puerto Rican migration, the illegal immigrants, and the increase in the welfare rolls—cannot be blamed for the city's bankruptcy. Its crisis results from its own political behavior. The city attempted to subsidize, not only the poor, but substantial portions of the middle class as well. New York's credit collapsed because the financial community stopped ignoring the "creative accounting" that allowed the city to hide its steadily accumulating deficits.   S. R. Herstein

2192. Adrian, Charles R. NARROW CLASS CONCERNS AND URBAN UNREST. *Am. Pol. Q. 1973 1(3): 397-404.* Review essay of Daniel J. Elazar's *The Politics of Belleville: A Profile of the Civil Community* (Philadelphia: Temple U. Pr., 1971); John J. Gargan and James G. Coke's *Political Behavior and Public Issues in Ohio* (Kent, Ohio: Kent State U. Pr., 1972); Frederick M. Wirt, Benjamin Walter, Francine F. Rabinovitz, and Deborah R. Hensler's *On the City's Rim: Politics and Policy in Suburbia* (Lexington, Massachusetts: D.C. Heath, 1972); and Robert C. Wood's *The Necessary Majority: Middle America and the Urban Crisis* (New York: Columbia U. Pr., 1972).

2193. Aldrich, Howard and Reiss, Albert J., Jr. CONTINUITIES IN THE STUDY OF ECOLOGICAL SUCCESSION: CHANGES IN THE RACE COMPOSITION OF NEIGHBORHOODS AND THEIR BUSINESSES. *Am. J. of Sociol. 1976 81(4): 846-866.* This paper concerns the problem of how residential succession affects the character of one set of local organizations: small businesses in racially changing neighborhoods. A key issue examined is the extent to which the causes and consequences of residential succession account also for the succession of small-business organizations. Only one type of succession is examined in this paper: the movement of blacks into areas previously occupied by whites. The impact of the transition in residential population on the abandonment of business sites and/or the turnover of business from white to black or Puerto Rican ownership is the particular focus of inquiry. Results of the analysis indicate that the residential succession model fits our data on business succession quite well.   J

2194. Aldrich, Howard. ECOLOGICAL SUCCESSION IN RACIALLY CHANGING NEIGHBORHOODS: A REVIEW OF THE LITERATURE. *Urban Affairs Q. 1975 10(3): 327-348.* Ecological succession occurs when the established residential group in an area does not replace itself. Once begun, succession seldom reverses, but rates of social units in succession vary. Public schools change rapidly; small businesses, voluntary associations, and churches less so. The end of cheap energy may make the central city more attractive than heretofore. 8 notes, biblio.
P. J. Woehrmann

2195. Alonso, William. URBAN DISAMENITIES. *Society 1976 13(4): 51-53.* Discusses income and migration in terms of the questionable urban disamenities premium theory which states that "people prefer to live and work in small places."

2196. Appelbaum, Richard P. and Follet, Ross. SIZE, GROWTH AND URBAN LIFE: A STUDY OF MEDIUM-SIZED AMERICAN CITIES. *Urban Affairs Q. 1978 14(2): 139-168.* Studies the effects of size and growth rates on the quality of city life in 115 geographically self-contained American cities with populations between 50,000-400,000. Found that the variance explained by size and growth in median income was comparatively small. They were even less important in explaining the extent of poverty and income concentration. The effects on unemployment and public sector services were ambiguous while health quality did not vary. Growth rate, but not size, produced systematic changes in housing costs. Growth had no impact on either murder or automobile theft rates although both varied significantly with city size. Robberies and burglaries were weakly related to size and growth. 4 tables, 12 notes, biblio.   L. N. Beecher

2197. Atwater, Elton. PHILADELPHIA'S QUEST TO BECOME THE PERMANENT HEADQUARTERS OF THE UNITED NATIONS. *Pennsylvania Mag. of Hist. of Biog. 1976 100(2): 243-257.* In 1945, Philadelphia was one of several cities under consideration for the future site of the U.N. However, John D. Rockefeller's offer in 1946 to donate the East River site in New York City destroyed Philadelphia's almost certain nomination. Based on primary and secondary sources; 54 notes.   E. W. Carp

2198. Ball, Rex M. PUBLIC-PRIVATE ENTERPRISE BRINGS NEW HELP TO CITIES. *Natl. Civic Rev. 1976 65(6): 290-291, 298.* Private enterprise techniques, working in conjunction with public initiative, provide the most viable solution—sometimes the only one—for the job of rebuilding cities. But it is necessary to provide for corporate profits to make the combination successful. Several cities have tried it.   J

2199. Barton, Bonnie. THE CREATION OF CENTRALITY. *Ann. of the Assoc. of Am. Geographers 1978 68(1): 34-44.* Received theory has departed considerably from Christaller's original conception of centrality and is an inadequate account of the achievement of centrality. A new framework is similar to a classical economic perspective rather than the neoclassical structure typical of received central place theory. Crucial elements of the alternative include the importance of exchange to the creation of centrality, the pivotal role of the entrepreneur, and the addition of a source of economic value related directly to this agent's role. The alternative portrays economic transactions institutionally; it is a technologically and historically sensitive interpretation of the achievement of centrality. Data on the economic activities and growth of colonial New England towns show that empirical interpretation within the preconceptions of standard theory is problematic. The modified classical framework is both conceptually and empirically more adequate to understanding these data as well as to answer questions raised by other selected studies of past and present urban patterns.   J

2200. Beauregard, Robert A. and Holcomb, Briavel. DOMINANT ENTERPRISES AND ACQUIESCENT COMMUNITIES: THE PRIVATE SECTOR AND URBAN REVITALIZATION. *Urbanism Past and Present 1979 (8): 18-31.* Explores the role of the private sector in urban revitalization. Private sector interests are influential and publically upheld as being compatible with those of the community. This bias causes the neglect of residential neighborhoods and central city renovation. Attempts to create a better understanding between business interest and community welfare. Explores past and present urban communities dominated by a manufacturing operation or by the administrative headquarters of a corporation. Concludes by comparing similar and dissimilar impacts of these firms and headquarters on the social relations and physical form of communities in which they are located. Ref.
B. P. Anderson

2201. Birch, David L. FROM SUBURB TO URBAN PLACE. *Ann. of the Am. Acad. of Pol. and Social Sci. 1975 422: 25-35.* The relationship of the suburbs to each other and to the central city is chang-

ing. Initially sub-urban in an urban hierarchy, suburbs are gradually gaining full urban status as nodes in a series of networks. In the process, they are inheriting many of the functions and problems previously reserved for the central city. One major result will be an increasing tension between the "old-timers" and the "newcomers." In a hierarchical, fractionated region, old-timers have always constituted a majority and have thereby resisted change. As the urban hierarchy breaks down, it may be more difficult for the parts to maintain differences, and it may seem more logical to balance what is good for people against what is good for places.
J

2202. Bradley, Tom. NO PEACE DIVIDEND. *Center Mag. 1976 9(2): 3-5.* The end of the Vietnam War did not provide a federal financial "peace dividend" for social and economic reform necessary for stability in the cities.

2203. Bruce-Briggs, B. ABOLISH NEW YORK. *New York Affairs 1979 5(3): 5-9.* New York City has been too large and unwieldy to be an effective city politically, economically, and socially, since its consolidation in the 1890's; thus it should be uncentralized.

2204. Clark, Terry Nichols. HOW MANY MORE NEW YORKS? *New York Affairs 1976 3(4): 18-27.* New York may be the first, but not the only city to suffer severe financial strain. But disaster is not the inevitable result for all American cities.
J

2205. Clawson, Marion. THE FUTURE OF NONMETROPOLITAN AMERICA. *Am. Scholar 1972-73 42(1): 102-109.* A solution for the disadvantages of rural towns and large metropolitan areas is population redistribution.
F. F. Harling

2206. Colman, William G. SCHOOLS, HOUSING, JOBS, TRANSPORTATION: INTERLOCKING METROPOLITAN PROBLEMS. *Urban Rev. 1978 10(2): 92-107.* The indissoluble linkage among income, health, education, employment, and crime in metropolitan areas must be broken to begin solving the inner cities' problems. Two possible solutions are "central city revitalization" and "central city depopulation and disinvestment." The latter strategy, providing housing or jobs in and transportation to the suburbs for inner city residents, seems to be more politically feasible. Primary and secondary sources; 2 tables, 8 notes, biblio.
R. G. Sherer

2207. Curtis, Lynn A. THE POLITICS OF CONSENSUS. *Social Policy 1977 7(4): 22-27.* Polls urban experts and politicians to determine whether there is consensus on problem solving techniques to urban problems; includes discussions of negative income tax, civil rights, and transportation as well as education and federal programs, 1970's.

2208. DeJong, Gordon F. and Donnelly, William L. PUBLIC WELFARE AND MIGRATION. *Social Sci. Q. 1973 54(2): 329-344.* Investigate the thesis that differential welfare payment levels (AFDC Program) is an important factor in explaining nonwhite migration to cities. The data suggest that AFDC payment level is a statistically significant factor in nonwhite migration to larger but not smaller northern and western cities, and not important in migration to southern cities. A participant-observation study of three newly-formed groups of welfare recipients provides a test of the applicability of the theory of democratic pluralism to American society.
J

2209. Ebner, Michael. THE FUTURE OF *RIVER CITY:* PASSAIC, NEW JERSEY'S CONTEMPORARY URBAN POLITICAL HISTORY. *Urbanism Past and Present 1976-77 (3): 16-20.* Passaic, New Jersey, fits into a constellation of "mill towns" in the Northeast which are in economic decline. Since 1960, minorities have greatly increased and industry decreased. State and federal government intervention programs have failed. In the future non-whites must assume responsibility in civic affairs. Power must be transferred from the current all-white municipal council. 19 notes.
B. P. Anderson

2210. Ellis, James R. ENVIRONMENT AND GROWTH: INCREASING INTERDEPENDENCE. *Natl. Civic Rev. 1976 65(5): 236-240.* Most observers agree that some control conditions have changed for people who live in cities but few agree on the way systems and institutions should respond. And future decisions are going to be even

harder to make as the many dimensions of economic growth and its effects are understood. With increasing interdependence, insular perspective on policy could be fatal.
J

2211. Epps, Edgar G. CITY AND SUBURBS: PERSPECTIVE ON INTERDISTRICT DESEGREGATION EFFORTS. *Urban Rev. 1978 10(2): 82-89.* Suburban fear of inner city problems; desire to keep local autonomy; racism; and black, inner city residents' fear of losing leaders, bright students, power, and cultural identity, all hinder establishment of metropolitan governments. But "consideration of historical socioeconomic and demographic trends" and federal and state financial inducements may persuade suburban and inner city leaders to cooperate in metropolitan planning to meet common problems, including desegregation. Secondary sources; 14 notes.
R. G. Sherer

2212. Ernst, Robert T. and Hugg, Lawrence. INSTITUTIONAL GROWTH AND COMMUNITY FRAGMENTATION: AN INNER CITY EXAMPLE. *Michigan Academician 1973 6(2): 179-191.*

2213. Fava, Sylvia F. BEYOND SUBURBIA. *Ann. of the Am. Acad. of Pol. and Social Sci. 1975 422: 10-24.* The next stage of suburbanization is taking place at the edges of metropolitan areas as these areas merge into the megalopolis. The United States is already a nation in which suburbanites constitute the largest portion, but not yet the majority, of Americans. Many of these suburbanites will be suburban-born and bred, rather than having decentralized from the center city. Their moves will be from suburb to suburb to suburb to exurb, and they will thus have little direct life experience with high density living and central city problems. The questions this poses for social science theory are examined in detail in this article. Early studies of life style and attitudes beyond suburbia suggest that they differ considerably from those of the earlier generation of suburbanites. The implications of megalopolitan structure for racial minorities and for women are also examined, with little evidence that racist or sexist patterns have been changed. Brief consideration of these and other public policy questions indicates that the political structures to meet the various needs of a megalopolitan constituency have not been developed and remain a major question.
J

2214. Fischer, Claude S. URBAN-TO-RURAL DIFFUSION OF OPINIONS IN CONTEMPORARY AMERICA. *Am. J. of Sociol. 1978 84(1): 151-159.* An ongoing gap in public opinion between urban and rural areas results from slow diffusion of innovation from urban to rural areas.

2215. Gallup, George. THE CITIES: UNSOLVED PROBLEMS AND UNUSED TALENTS. *Antioch Rev. 1979 37(2): 148-161.* Presents evidence for the willingness of citizen volunteer effort as a resource in effectively solving urban problems and implementing urban improvement plans, 1949-79.

2216. Ginzberg, Eli. NEW YORK: A VIEW FROM THE SEINE. *New York Affairs 1979 5(3): 53-62.* Compares New York City and Paris, based on discussions at the Two World Cities Conference in May 1978 sponsored by the French American Foundation.

2217. Goetze, Rolf. URBAN NEIGHBORHOODS IN TRANSITION. *Social Policy 1979 10(2): 53-57.* Discusses housing demands and availability, and changes in urban neighborhoods since 1890, and their relationship to population demography, using this information to predict trends and the role of public policy in city planning.

2218. Goist, Park Dixon. POLITICAL CAMPAIGNING AND PLURALISM IN A CLEVELAND SUBURB. *Indiana Social Studies Q. 1975 28(2): 103-113.* Discusses the growth of community consciousness and political and ethnic pluralism in Cleveland Heights, Ohio, during the 1960's and 70's.

2219. Goldstein, Gerald S. and Moses, Leon N. A SURVEY OF URBAN ECONOMICS. *J. of Econ. Literature 1973 11(2): 471-515.* Discusses recent models of urban growth, land use, and efforts to simulate effects of governmental policy on urban development.
S

2220. Gottmann, Jean. THE MUTATION OF THE AMERICAN CITY: A REVIEW OF THE COMPARATIVE METROPOLITAN

ANALYSIS PROJECT. *Geographical Rev. 1978 68(2): 201-208.* Deals with 20 major metropolitan areas emphasizing the underprivileged, ethnic diversity, segregation, and the social problems of the metropolis. Differences among cities are striking. "There is definitely more pessimism about northeastern cities...specially New York and Pittsburgh, than about southern and western cities...he general tone is one of lament about each metropolis... notable exception is the Twin Cities of Minnesota where satisfaction seems to reign."   E. P. Stickney

2221. Guest, Avery M. and Nelson, George H. CENTRAL CITY/ SUBURBAN STATUS DIFFERENCES: FIFTY YEARS OF CHANGE. *Sociol. Q. 1978 19(1): 7-23.* Changes in the relative status of central cities compared to their suburban rings are investigated for the periods 1920 to 1950, and 1950 to 1970. Longitudinal alterations in the relative statuses of the two components across metropolitan areas have primarily involved the suburban ring.   J

2222. Guest, Avery M. SUBURBAN SOCIAL STATUS: PERSISTENCE OR EVOLUTION? *Am. Sociol. Rev. 1978 43(2): 251-263.* Focuses on changes in socioeconomic structure of US suburbs between 1920, 1950, and 1970. Persistence in suburban socioeconomic structure has been important in both time periods, but particularly so in the post-World War II period. Moderate evidence of suburban status evolution is found in the period between World War I and 1950. In the earlier time period, evolution was explained by characteristics of both the metropolitan area and the individual community; in the most recent time period, it related primarily to characteristics of the individual community. In both time periods, evolution in suburban socioeconomic structure has been related most strongly to community population growth.   J

2223. Hamilton, Edward K. ARE BIG CITIES UNGOVERNABLE? *World Today [Great Britain] 1973 29(7): 307-316.* Examines financial, social, and psychological aspects of the problem.   J/S

2224. Hansen, Niles. DOES THE SOUTH HAVE A STAKE IN NORTHERN URBAN POVERTY? *Southern Econ. J. 1979 45(4): 1220-1224.* Studies of poverty rates, education, and migration from 1959-70's show that migration from the South has not caused urban poverty in the North, as traditionally believed.

2225. Hauser, Philip M. CHICAGO: URBAN CRISIS EXEMPLAR. *Urbanism Past and Present 1975-76 (1): 15-23.* Explores urban crises through "the social morphological revolution" which contains four elements: the population explosion, the population implosion, the displosion, and accelerated technological change. Concentrates on situations in Chicago, Illinois, concluding that urban crises in the United States will worsen.   B. P. Anderson

2226. Heiskell, Andrew. THE BUSINESS-POLITICS PARTNERSHIP FOR REBUILDING CITIES. *Natl. Civic Rev. 1974 63(5): 237-241.*

2227. Hennessey, Timothy M. and Feen, Richard H. SOCIAL SCIENCE AS SOCIAL PHILOSOPHY: EDWARD C. BANFIELD AND THE "NEW REALISM" IN URBAN POLITICS. *Am. Behavioral Scientist 1973 17(2): 171-204.* Attacks Banfield's thesis that urban problems are a natural outgrowth of social classes and therefore beyond solution by liberal, humanist reformers.   S

2228. Jolley, Clyde W. POLK COUNTY: A TALE OF TWO CITIES. *Georgia Life 1978 4(4): 12-15.* Describes Cedartown and Rockmart in Polk County, Georgia: their economic conditions, people, and points of interest.

2229. Lineberry, Robert L. SUBURBIA AND THE METROPOLITAN TURF. *Ann. of the Am. Acad. of Pol. and Social Sci. 1975 422: 1-9.* As the nation suburbanizes, the definition of suburbia becomes ever more confused. There is a useful distinction, however, between a cultural or life-style approach and a demographic-legal approach to suburbs and suburbia. From a political perspective, the most critical element of metropolitan conflict is its sociospatial character, and suburban politics epitomizes this tendency. There are useful parallels between metropolitan conflict and international relations, because both involve competition for dominance of space. In both, a common concern is that the rich grow

richer at the expense of the poor; this article examines that process within the metropolis. The question of how to deal with this "immiseration" of the central cities is answered differently by metropolitan reformers and by public choice theorists.   J

2230. Long, Norton E. THE CITY AS POLITICAL ECONOMY. *Natl. Civic Rev. 1974 63(4): 189-191.* The conceptualization of the city as a political economy is fundamental to improving performance. We know too little of the city as an interactive social system generating specifiable outcomes, which may in some measure be the fault of the political scientists who have 'studied' it. The reason: we have not set as a purpose the use of the city as a collective instrumentality for the deliberate, sustained and systematic improvement of the human condition.   J

2231. Long, Norton E. A MARSHALL PLAN FOR CITIES? *Public Interest 1977 (46): 48-58.* A Marshall Plan for American cities is only a catchy slogan, because the problems in the cities are different and more difficult than those of Europe after World War II. US foreign aid experience shows that we are able to help only those who can help themselves. The European countries, in contrast to American cities, were aiming for the restoration of self-sufficiency and were themselves responsible for the integration of recovery plans. The American cities required the solving of such complex problems as social disintegration and disinvestment due to lack of profitability, while Europe required only physical rebuilding. Rather than a brick and mortar approach, what American cities need is a kind of self-help that resists and overcomes social disorganization. Such programs are practiced by the Italian Hill and St. Ambrose Church in St. Louis, by the Muslims, and by the Puerto Rican evangelicals.   S. Harrow

2232. Luks, Allan and Feldman, Elane. WE ARE THE FORGOTTEN AMERICANS. *Antioch Rev. 1979 37(2): 170-181.* Discusses the current decay of US cities as a problem of the middle class.

2233. Mandelker, Daniel R. LEGAL AND POLITICAL FORUMS FOR URBAN CHANGE. *Ann. of the Am. Acad. of Pol. and Social Sci. 1973 (405): 41-46.* American legal institutions, and especially the judicial process, have been accustomed to dealing with an urban economic order characterized primarily by small units of economic power. As our economy has been increasingly dominated by larger aggregates of economic concentration, however, the judicial process has found it increasingly difficult to deal with the policy issues in urban resource management which these larger aggregates of economic power have raised. Policy issues of this kind are best resolved in the political rather than in the judicial forum. The law can assist the political decision-maker who must deal with these issues, but it cannot do so without redefining its traditional role.   J

2234. Mikhailov, E. CRISIS OF AMERICAN CITIES. *Int. Affairs [USSR] 1976 (5): 72-80.* The crisis of the American city is a clear reflection of the breakdown of the capitalist system. Evidence of this crisis is abundant: the spector of financial collapse facing many major cities, the rigidification of class divisions through the bifurcation of the cities into neglected metropolitan centers and affluent suburbs, increasing unemployment and alienation among the minority and working populace, and an increasing crime problem. Given the continued aggravation of these conditions, cities will become an integral part of the struggle for progressive reform. 15 notes.   D. K. McQuilkin

2235. Mitchell, Louis D. THE URBAN DILEMMA: ITS PRESENT AND FUTURE. *Crisis 1975 82(8): 304-311.* Our nation's cities seem to be suffering from troubles even while continuing to grow. It is difficult to define the "urban problem" in a way that will promote rapid and easy solution. Public housing, ugliness, high cost of living, loss of tax base, bankruptcy, citizen demands, and crime defy the liberal fantasy of logical remedy. Cities will have to be reconstructed to meet the needs of the future. A new look at old myths will be required.   A. G. Belles

2236. Mott, George Fox. COMMUNICATIVE TURBULENCE IN URBAN DYNAMICS—MEDIA, EDUCATION, AND PLANNING. *Ann. of the Am. Acad. of Pol. and Social Sci. 1973 (405): 114-130.* Examines the three most pervasive mechanisms causing communicative turbulence and thus affecting decisionmaking: media, education, and planning. The media are forsaking their objectivity and their public service responsibility for an interpretative role which deprives society of a sound information source. Television in its present aspects is an active deterrent to successful public education. Public education is foundering from a complex of nonfused programs and interpolations from the various special interest groups and the interpositioning of the courts between the citizens and their elected local school boards. Solutions suggested are both new and old. Higher education is suffering from the effects of the student population explosion, further complicated by special interest pressures and by unwise quasi-dictation from certain federal agencies. The planning process, as prerequisite to improved management in all areas of social activity, is beginning to show advances in effectiveness owing to accumulated experience, increased and assimilated data, and growing public acceptance, particularly in the field of urban planning.   J/S

2237. Mouriño Mosquera, Juan José. A VIDA URBANA: SEU PREÇO, SEU FUTURO [Urban life: its price and future]. *Veritas* [Brazil] 1976 21(82): 116-125. The enormous increase in world population since the 18th century has been accompanied by rapid urbanization which has had profound social, psychological, cultural, and economic effects that may eventually have disastrous consequences for mankind.

2238. Nathan, Richard P. IS THERE A NATIONAL URBAN CRISIS? *New York Affairs* 1976 3(4): 9-17. The existence of a national urban crisis has been taken for granted for the last ten years. Even President Nixon's declaration that the crisis was over failed to dispel the gloom and doom. But the future of many cities may not be as grim as had all supposed.   J

2239. Nathan, Richard P. and Adams, Charles. UNDERSTANDING CENTRAL CITY HARDSHIP. *Pol. Sci. Q.* 1976 91(1): 47-62. Present a comparative analysis of the degree of 'hardship' being experienced by fifty-five of the nation's largest central cities. The authors conclude that the urban crisis in America is highly differentiated and that census data are valuable tools for studying the differences that exist among cities.   J

2240. Newton, Kenneth. AMERICAN URBAN POLITICS, SOCIAL CLASS, POLITICAL STRUCTURE AND PUBLIC GOODS. *Urban Affairs Q.* 1975 11(2): 241-264. Criticizes concentration on the individual in recent political science to the neglect of historical development and social structure, and the seemingly uncritical acceptance of fragmentation in city government. Contrary to conventional wisdom, many governmental units do not provide democratic rule for all, but tend to ineffectiveness or domination by special interest groups. Table, notes, biblio.   P. J. Woehrmann

2241. Preston, Michael B. AUTHORITY STRUCTURES AND URBAN CONFLICTS: LESSONS FOR THE 1970S. *Urban Affairs Q.* 1975 11(3): 391-405. Review article on urban politics and violence in the 1960's and 1970's. In *The Politics of Turmoil: Essays on Poverty, Race and the Urban Crises* (New York: Random House, 1974), Richard A. Cloward and Francis Fox Piven in 1968 essays discuss mainly Great Society programs; in *Urban Political Movements: The Search for Power by Minority Groups in American Cities* (Englewood Cliffs, N.J.: Prentice-Hall, 1974), Norman I. and Susan I. Fainstein see modern urban political movements as new institutions; Joe R. Feagin and Harlan Hahn in *Ghetto Revolts: The Politics of Violence in American Cities* (New York: Macmillan, 1973) examine several theories of urban collective violence; J. David Greenstone and Paul E. Peterson in *Race and Authority in Urban Politics: Community Participation and the War on Poverty* (New York: Russell Sage Foundation, 1973) tell how the poverty programs have challenged political structure; and Peter H. Rossi, Richard A. Berk, and Betty K. Edison in *The Roots of Urban Discontent: Public Policy, Municipal Institutions, and the Ghetto* (New York: John Wiley and Sons, 1974) largely fail to answer why riots occur in some cities and not others. Concludes by these volumes that gains of blacks in the conflict process have been minimal.   P. J. Woehrmann

2242. Quinn, Michael A. DISPERSING THE URBAN CORE: RECENT STUDIES ON THE CITY IN SUBURBIA. *Urban Affairs Q.* 1976 11(4): 545-554. A renewed interest in suburbia exists, but Louis H. Masotti and Jeffrey K. Hadden's *The Urbanization of the Suburbs* (Beverly Hills, Calif.: Sage, 1973) and Frederick M. Wirt, Benjamin Walter, Francine F. Rabinowitz, and Deborah Hensler's *On the City's Rim: Politics and Policy in Suburbia* (Lexington, Mass.: D. C. Heath, 1972) suggest that suburbia is in danger of losing its explanatory power, that suburbinology is rudimentary, and that there is suburban political, social, and economic heterogeneity. While not arguing with the conclusion of Anthony Downs's *Opening Up the Suburbs: An Urban Strategy for America* (New Haven, Conn.: Yale U. Pr., 1973) that the suburbs are implicated in the urban crises, the reviewer feels Downs should assess both the political feasibility and the cost to core residents of suburban dispersal. Charles M. Haar and Demetrius S. Iatridis's *Housing the Poor in Suburbia: Public Policy at the Grass Roots* (Cambridge, Mass.: Ballinger, 1974) provides a didactic exposition of five dispersal case studies. Mario Matthew Cuomo's *Forest Hills Diary: The Crisis of Low-Income Housing* (New York: Random House, 1974) is a useful personal narrative of dispersal politics. Secondary sources; biblio.   L. N. Beecher

2243. Sales, William W., Jr. NEW YORK CITY: PROTOTYPE OF THE URBAN CRISIS. *Black Scholar* 1975 7(3): 20-30, 35-39. Discusses the current fiscal crisis of New York City and its impact on Negroes and the nation.

2244. Salins, Peter D. NEW YORK IN THE YEAR 2000. *New York Affairs* 1974 1(4): 6-21. By the year 2000, New York City's population will be largely black and Puerto Rican, mostly living in middle-class circumstances, while much of Manhattan and a broad swath of Brooklyn will be dominated—even more than today—by luxury apartments and restored brownstones, continents of affluence in a middle-class sea.   J

2245. Schmidt, Charles G. and Lee, Yuk. IMPACTS OF CHANGING RACIAL COMPOSITION UPON COMMERCIAL LAND USE AND COMMERCIAL STRUCTURE: A COMPARATIVE NEIGHBORHOOD ANALYSIS. *Urban Affairs Q.* 1978 13(3): 341-354. Analyzes three Denver areas, 1960-70, testing the hypothesis that the economic status of the succeeding population, not race, determines the commercial characteristics of transitional neighborhoods. Suggests that the transformation of a white into a black neighborhood has more impact on business mobility and the structure of commercial activity than changes in neighborhood income or population size. Assumes all three neighborhoods were equally influenced by external forces. 5 tables, biblio.   L. N. Beecher

2246. Serrin, William. THE DETROIT DISEASE: AN AMERICAN INFECTION. *Urban Rev.* 1975 8(2): 153-154. Social problems—racism, unemployment, crime—are rife in Detroit as in most American cities, and will be solved only with democratization of wealth and power, 1974.

2247. Sternlieb, George and Lake, Robert W. AGING SUBURBS AND BLACK HOMEOWNERSHIP. *Ann. of the Am. Acad. of Pol. and Social Sci.* 1975 422: 105-117. The 30 years since rapid post-World War II suburban residential development began have seen an increasing diversification in the characteristics of the suburbs. The principal dimensions of diversification include the age of housing, age of the population, and distance from the central city. Since suburbanization proceeded outward from the central city, the signs of this aging process are most pronounced in the inner suburbs, with densities and an aging population. As first-round suburbanites progress through the life cycle, their housing preferences can be expected to change, resulting in a large supply of older housing on the market. The primary source of demand for these units in the inner suburbs appears to be the upwardly mobile black middle class seeking to leave the central city. While black suburbanization is increasing in some localities, however, black demand appears to be below the level expected based on income. In suburban home purchase, the availability of equity associated with previous homeownership may be a better index of buying power than current income. Historical limitations on black homeownership thus continue to limit black suburban home purchases.   J

2248. Sternlieb, George and Hughes, James W. NEW YORK: FUTURE WITHOUT A FUTURE? *Society* 1976 13(4): 18-23. Examines the population growth and decline, the decline in industrial and business employment, and the increase in public employment in New York City, 1950's-70's, which have influenced that city's fiscal problems.

2249. Sussman, Carl. MOVING THE CITY SLICKERS OUT. *Southern Exposure 1974 2(2-3): 99-107.* Discusses socioeconomic aspects of urbanization in the South in the 1960's and 70's, emphasizing implications for local government and property values.

2250. Sutton, Richard J.; Korey, John; Bryant, Steve; and Dodson, Richard. AMERICAN CITY TYPES: TOWARD A MORE SYSTEMATIC URBAN STUDY. *Urban Affairs Q. 1974 9(3): 369-401.*

2251. Unsigned. NATIONAL URBAN GROWTH POLICY: 1973 CONGRESSIONAL AND EXECUTIVE ACTION. *J. of the Am. Inst. of Planners 1974 40(4): 226-242.*
Beckman, Norman, ed. [INTRODUCTION], *pp. 226-227.*
Beckman, Norman. AREAWIDE PLANNING AND DELIVERY, *pp. 227-230.*
Mitrisin, John. URBAN-RURAL BALANCE, *pp. 230-231.*
Wellborn, Clay and Schlefer, Marion. OLD AND NEW COMMUNITIES, *pp. 231-233.*
Parente, Frank. GOOD HOUSING FOR ALL AMERICANS, *pp. 233-235.*
Lane, Robert and March, Jean. LAND USE AND ENVIRONMENTAL PROTECTION, *pp. 235-238.*
Harding, Susan. IMPROVING HOUSING CAPABILITY, *pp. 238-240.*
Beckman, Norman. LOOKING TO THE FUTURE, *pp. 240-242.*
Reviews new and modified federal programs in 1973 as designed and implemented by Congress and the Executive Branch. S

2252. Unsigned. A REPORT BY THE METROPOLITAN AFFAIRS NON-PROFIT CORPORATIONS. *Natl. Civic Rev. 1975 64(10): 505-525.* The Metropolitan Affairs Nonprofit Corporations is a group of private urban affairs organizations which, under a grant from the National Science Foundation, explored means for improving productivity and technology utilization in the nonfederal public sector. The major conclusion is that the most basic step in improving regional productivity lies in public institution building, without replacing existing governmental levels and agencies. J

2253. Unsigned. [THE URBAN CRISIS AS A FAILURE OF COMMUNITY]. *Urban Affairs Q. 1974 9(4): 437-465.*
Eisinger, Peter K. SOME DATA, pp. 437-461.
Wilson, James Q. A COMMENT ON EISINGER, pp. 462-465.
Examines the current "urban crisis" in political, sociological, economic, and racial terms. S

2254. Wade, Richard C. AMERICA'S CITIES ARE (MOSTLY) BETTER THAN EVER. *Am. Heritage 1979 30(2): 4-13.* Compares status of American cities of the 1970's with that of about 1900 and concludes that the present city is cleaner, less crowded, safer, and more livable. He sees racial tensions and the urban-suburban split as the chief sources of modern tension. 14 photos. J. F. Paul

2255. Welch, Susan. THE IMPACT OF URBAN RIOTS ON URBAN EXPENDITURES. *Am. J. of Pol. Sci. 1975 19(4): 741-760.* Using as a data base US cities over 50,000, the relationship between riot incidence and changes in urban expenditures and revenue was examined. Changes in expenditures considered relevant to the demands of blacks and whites, as well as four fiscal areas thought largely unrelated to either black or white demands, were compared in cities that did and did not have riots. Greater increments in expenditures related to black and white demands were found in cities having riots as compared with those that did not, but the same difference did not appear in the other four expenditure areas. When structural variables were controlled, differences in police and fire expenditure increments remained, while differences in social welfare benefits were greatly reduced. This pattern of difference between riot and nonriot cities was not found to hold prior to 1965. Finally, comparisons in expenditure gains were made among riot and nonriot cities having a variety of political characteristics (such as political competitiveness and the presence of "reformed" political institutions) to ascertain the possible influence of political characteristics of the city on responsiveness to riots. J

2256. Wellman, Barry and Leighton, Barry. NETWORKS, NEIGHBORHOODS AND COMMUNITIES: APPROACHES TO THE STUDY OF COMMUNITY QUESTION. *Urban Affairs Q. 1979 14(3): 363-390.* Urges that the study of community be separated from any analytic framework that assumes that a community must exist within the geographic confines of a neighborhood. Proposes that the search for community center on a study of social linkages and flows of resources-networks. Describes and evaluates the policy implications of the standard theories that communities are "lost" or "saved" or "liberated." Contends that these theories should be thought of not as competing models or stages in community evolution but as representative of different network patterns: sparse (lost), dense (saved), and ramified (liberated). Concludes that while neighborhoods persist, they are subordinated to primary networks—ties to distant parents, friends, and coworkers.
L. N. Beecher

2257. Williams, Richard L. OUR OLDER CITIES ARE SHOWING AGE BUT ALSO SHOWING SIGNS OF FIGHT. *Smithsonian 1979 9(10): 66-75.* Examines the degrading situation in finances and in housing of great American cities, some of them surviving through the help of well-to-do and active citizens. Cincinnati and Philadelphia have suffered in shifting from manufacturing to service industries, but are improving with housing projects, while New York is struggling to regain its former respectability. In many cities central areas, prosperous shopping centers have been established, thus making suburbs gradually obsolete. 13 illus.
G. P. Cleyet

2258. Wittcoff, Raymond H. THE FUTURE OF CITIES. *Center Mag. 1973 6(6): 67-73.*

2259. Wood, Robert. NATIONAL URBAN POLICY—WHAT SHOULD HAPPEN NEXT? *New York Affairs 1976 3(4): 42-51.* The urban crisis involves more than money. Racial violence and union power have disturbed the peace in some of America's "dream" cities. Without a national urban policy, dark days lie ahead even for the country's healthiest cities. J

2260. Wood, Robert. SUBURBAN POLITICS AND POLICIES: RETROSPECT AND PROSPECT. *Publius 1975 5(1): 45-52.* Discusses the impact of suburban growth 1945-60's on the social problems faced by American cities, in a special issue of *Publius*, "The Suburban Reshaping of American Politics."

2261. Wood, Robert. A MATTER OF NATIONAL URGENCY. *Natl. Civic Rev. 1977 66(1): 15-18.* It is clear that in the absence of a defined national policy for housing, planning, finance, transportation, health and social services, and education the cities are carrying much more than their share of the national burden. The ad hoc policies have led inexorably to a battle between the haves and the have-mores. J

2262. Yanitsky, O. N. "EDINYI POSTGORODSKOI OBRAZ ZHIZNI"—MODEL' I REAL'NOST' [The single posturban way of life: the model and reality]. *Voprosy Filosofii [USSR] 1974 (10): 94-105.* The doctrine under analysis is a variety of the concept of "post-industrial society" whose theorists consider the American suburb and its way of life as a form of eliminating rural-urban antagonism and as a display of converging trends in the mode of living of capitalism and socialism. The suburban community and its way of life are regarded either as a continuation of present-day technological changes, or as a refuge from the world they have brought about. The idea of "unity" of the urban way of life is closely associated with the widespread theoretical-methodological orientation of bourgeois sociology—rural-urban dichotomy. The ideological substantiation of "suburban society" in bourgeois thought dates back to the 19th century as a reaction to problems of a big city and subsequently provided a basis for desurbanism—the policy of making these problems less acute and using them in class interests of the bourgeoisie. Actually, the scientific and technological revolution does not resolve the contradictions of capitalist urbanization, but reproduces them in a new form: the megalopolis and the confrontation of its cities and suburbs. The article shows deep contradictions in the life of suburban communities of the United States and the dependence of the person's mode of life on his class and value orientations. J

The Growth and Decline of Cities and Suburbs

2263. Alonso, William. THE NEW SECTIONALISM: I: METROP-OLIS WITHOUT GROWTH. *Public Interest 1978 (53): 68-86.* Until 1970 the trend in population was toward the metropolitan areas. Since 1970 the trend has been reversed, creating a new problem in sectionalism: the relationship between the city and the countryside. The principal sources of metropolitan population decline are: 1) the declining birth rate, 2) the reversal of the net migration with nonmetropolitan areas, and 3) inter-metropolitan migration, which redistributes population among losers and winners. The questions are: how these reversals should be interpreted and what images will influence economics and politics in relation to sectionalist concerns?
R. V. Ritter

2264. Appelbaum, Richard P. CITY SIZE AND URBAN LIFE: A PRELIMINARY INQUIRY INTO SOME CONSEQUENCES OF GROWTH IN AMERICAN CITIES. *Urban Affairs Q. 1976 12(2): 139-170.* Provides a general analysis of city size and urban life to facilitate development of urban policies derived from a comparative analysis of growth's costs and benefits. Available scholarship demonstrates that "speculation" about its consequences "far exceeds" the evidence. When correlates of size or growth are observed they show that the physical environment and public safety suffer but reveal little concerning economic well-being, unemployment, or occupational structures. Even the greater per capita cost of government in large cities might reflect intervening nongrowth variables. Thus, despite the empirical, atheoretical nature of the scholarship, it is valid to conclude that only an analysis of city-specific characteristics can determine relevant growth policies and optimal city size. Secondary sources; 2 tables, 12 notes, biblio.
L. N. Beecher

2265. Beeler, Park L. THE MERGER URGERS OF JACKSON-VILLE ARE WINNING A QUIET REVOLUTION. *Urban Rev. 1973 6(5-6): 57-61.* In 1967 the citizens of Jacksonville and Duval County, Florida voted to merge and thus have enjoyed renewed growth from their combined revenues, easing crime and unemployment.

2266. Berry, Brian J. L. COUNTER-URBANIZATION AND SEPARATION BY AVOIDANCE. *New York Affairs 1977 4(3): 3-13.* Discusses the current trend within older suburbs and central cities toward counter-urbanization (the fleeing of the middle and upper middle classes to newer residential suburban areas) and the incursion of minorities into these areas; details urbanization and counter-urbanization 1940's-70's.

2267. Cassity, Michael J. THE PAST FORSAKEN: THE CRISIS OF AN OKLAHOMA COMMUNITY. *Southwest Rev. 1976 61(4): 396-408.* Examines the submersion and death of the town of Kaw City, Oklahoma, 1962-76, because of the construction of a reservoir.

2268. Chan, Carole. LOCAL GROWTH CONTROL: A HUMAN RIGHTS ISSUE. *J. of Intergroup Relations 1977 6(1): 54-59.* Focusing on Petaluma, California, discusses the efforts of various suburban areas to limit population growth, 1972-76.

2269. Dye, Thomas R. and Garcia, John A. THE POLITICAL ECONOMY OF GROWTH POLICIES IN CITIES. *Policy Studies J. 1977 6(2): 175-184.* Per capita costs of city government are minimally related to city size; because growing cities have relatively inexpensive governmental costs, limited growth would be regressive by causing a greater separation of needs from resources.

2270. Glennon, Wink. SANTA BARBARA: LIMITS TO GROWTH? *Working Papers for a New Soc. 1976 4(1): 36-43.* Discusses the present situation in Santa Barbara concerning growth and local politics, focusing on the activities of environmental coalitions which are questioning indiscriminate development, especially in the face of the limited water supply.

2271. Guest, Avery M. THE FUNCTIONAL REORGANIZATION OF THE METROPOLIS. *Pacific Sociol. Rev. 1977 20(4): 553-567.* Studies the changing distribution of employment and residential activities between central cities and the suburbs, 1939-75.

2272. Guest, Avery M. NEIGHBORHOOD LIFE CYCLES AND SOCIAL STATUS. *Econ. Geography 1974 50(3): 228-243.* Examines the growth of metropolitan areas and the tendency for the suburbs to grow in outer concentric circles around the inner city, gaining income and prestige with outward progression.
S

2273. Hart, John. PETALUMA: THE LITTLE CITY THAT COULD. *Cry California 1976 11(3): 40-43.* Evaluates the possible consequences of the City of Petaluma's decision to limit its growth to 500 new units a year. The US Supreme Court upheld the legality of this move. City planners and the building trade industry are concerned over the precedent set by Petaluma. If other communities on the fringes of metropolitan areas follow Petaluma's example, then housing costs will increase, as will rent and mortgages, and housing will become an ever-acute problem. One alternative would be to revitalize the central city areas. The Petaluma decision does not solve the problem of growth; it does indicate how serious the problem is. Photos.
A. Hoffman

2274. Hughes, James W. DILEMMAS OF SUBURBANIZATION AND GROWTH CONTROLS. *Ann. of the Am. Acad. of Pol. and Social Sci. 1975 422: 61-76.* The decentralization of every facet of American life and the shifting age contours of its population structure have increased the pressures for residential diversity in suburbia. As a reaction to these geographic and demographic forces, new attitudes toward community growth are synthesizing in the form of "growth controls"—attempts by suburban communities to limit the numbers and types of residents allowed within their borders. These reactions run counter to the new responsibilities that have accompanied the benefits of suburbanization. While their justification is embedded in a matrix of environmental and "quality of life" arguments, the complex set of motivations includes a powerful socioeconomic dimension having clear implications for the metropolitan region as a whole. Moreover, the myth of suburbia—of isolated family-raising environments—is being increasingly challenged by the reality of its participation in an urbanizing region, and growth controls may be interpreted as an attempt to preserve the older ideals. The overall issues emerging are not going to fade away quietly, and since they involve so many diverse and competing interest groups, they will not be resolved easily.
J

2275. Humphrey, Craig R. and Sell, Ralph R. THE IMPACT OF CONTROLLED ACCESS HIGHWAYS ON POPULATION GROWTH IN PENNSYLVANIA NONMETROPOLITAN COMMUNITIES, 1940-1970. *Rural Sociol. 1975 40(3): 332-343.* Controlled-access highways influenced population redistribution toward suburbs in Pennsylvania, 1940-70.

2276. Johansen, Harley E. and Fuguitt, Glenn V. POPULATION GROWTH AND RETAIL DECLINE: CONFLICTING EFFECTS OF URBAN ACCESSIBILITY IN AMERICAN VILLAGES. *Rural Sociol. 1979 44(1): 24-38.* Discusses the relationship between retail trade in rural villages, increased urban accessibility, and the growth of nonurban areas which, based on a study done during 1950-70, shows conflicting results due to these interrelated factors.

2277. Kaufmann, Perry. CITY BOOSTERS, LAS VEGAS STYLE. *J. of the West 1974 13(3): 46-60.* Examines the role of modern city boosters in the development of Las Vegas, Nevada, as a major tourist center. The boosters were public relations men who "carried on a slick publicity and advertising campaign" to promote the city. Major selling points were the lack of moral restrictions and lack of tax encumberments. The early 1940's were pivotal to promotion because the first resort hotels and casinos were built then. World War II was a stimulus to growth because a gunnery school and magnesium plant were established in the vicinity. After the war, promotion was enlarged to a full-scale advertising campaign with funds raised from the community and businesses. This was successful beyond expectation but as Las Vegas increased in size and fame, the community spirit declined. Based on contemporary newspaper reports, articles from advertising and other journals, promotional pamphlets, interviews, and secondary sources; 25 notes.
N. J. Street

2278. Lyford, Joseph P. BREAKDOWN OF COMMUNITY. *Center Mag. 1975 8(6): 38-51.* Discusses how population size and density are breaking down the cities and analyzes movement to the suburbs during the 1970's.

2279. Murphy, Thomas P. RACE-BASE ACCOUNTING: AS-SIGNING THE COSTS AND BENEFITS OF A RACIALLY MOTI-VATED ANNEXATION. *Urban Affairs Q. 1978 14(2): 169-194.* To prevent black control in 1970, Richmond's city council annexed 23 square miles. Since 97% of the area's 50,000 residents were white, the city's black population declined from 52% to 42%. Notwithstanding the charge that Richmond had violated the 15th Amendment and the 1965 Voting Rights Act, the Supreme Court only used economic criteria in ruling against deannexation petitions. Criticizes the Court for using only quantifiable factors, permitting both sides to use suspect data and ignoring the economic interests of those annexed. Notes that the annexation resulted in blacks controlling a larger city when they came to power in 1977. 3 tables, fig., biblio.   L. N. Beecher

2280. Northcross, Mark. LOS ANGELES COUNTY: BITING THE LAND THAT FEEDS US. *Cry California 1976 11(3): 36-39.* Traces the takeover of agricultural land in Los Angeles County by urbanization. Of more than 300,000 acres of farmland in the county, less than 10,000 are left. The value of farmland in the southern California coast region, if developable for housing, is much greater than undevelopable farmland. This is reflected in county assessor rates which make it uneconomical for farmers to retain their lands. County planners are defeated by county assessors. As a result, Los Angeles County has been subdivided and urbanized while agricultural production in the best farmland has declined. Photo.   A. Hoffman

2281. Parlow, Anita. MILLIONAIRES AND MOBILE HOMES. *Southern Exposure 1976 3(4): 25-30.* Urban development in Pikeville in the 1970's has been brought on by local government officials who hope to stabilize the boom-bust economy of the past; little attention has been paid to local residents upset by blasting and construction.

2282. Phillips, Phillip D. and Brunn, Stanley D. SLOW GROWTH: A NEW EPOCH OF AMERICAN METROPOLITAN EVOLUTION. *Geographical Rev. 1978 68(3): 274-292.* Since 1970 the American metropolitan system has entered an epoch of slower population growth as a result of significant technological and social changes. Increased acceptance of birth control devices and abortion have lowered natural population increase in the system while communications improvements and the growth of nonmetropolitan resort and retirement communities have produced net migration out of metropolitan areas. Public perceptions have also favored a "rural renaissance" and the growth of the "Sun Belt" at the expense of the Manufacturing Belt. A near-zero-sum game of metropolitan growth has heightened interregional competition for jobs and population. Prolonged slow growth will have serious impacts on age and employment structures, possibly producing a conservative "risk-avoidance" outlook within an aging infrastructure. The metropolitan system faces an uncertain prospect because many post-1970 trends, especially extensive exurban development and higher fuel costs, are not compatible over long periods of time.   J

2283. Pred, Allan R. DIFFUSION, ORGANIZATIONAL SPATIAL STRUCTURE, AND CITY-SYSTEM DEVELOPMENT. *Econ. Geography 1975 51(3): 252-268.* "1) Considers the role of large job-providing organizations in the diffusion of *growth-inducing* innovations, 2) outlines a preliminary model for describing how the locational patterns of major job-providing organizations and the intermetropolitan circulation of specialized information interact to influence the process of city-system development . . ., and 3) presents empirical evidence supporting the diffusion component of that model."   S

2284. Redburn, Steve. RESPONDING TO THE DECLINE OF INDUSTRIAL AMERICA. *Urbanism Past and Present 1977-78 (5): 37-42.* Economic decline provides an opportunity for urban renewal by taking advantage of federal grant programs and revenue transfers. Suggests a model for managing nongrowth of cities. This includes economic self-sufficiency and lessening the impact of departing industries by creating worker relocation assistance and incentives. Advises creative use of leisure, overcoming institutional rigidity, loss of leadership, and accenting the region's unique strengths. 13 notes.   B. P. Anderson

2285. Smith, T. Lynn. SOCIOCULTURAL CHANGES IN 12 MIDWESTERN COMMUNITIES, 1930-1970. *Social Sci. 1974 49(4): 195-207.* In 1930, the author did field work in 12 villages. In 1970, he revisited all of these places for the purpose of determining and interpreting changes during the period 1930 to 1970. Contrary to what many people think, the changes in the towns and villages (five in Indiana, five in Minnesota, and two in North Dakota) are in the direction of growth, greater social differentiation and development, and not in that of decline. There has been severe depopulation in the trade zones of the respective villages and towns, or to a degree of about 50 per cent, so that the trade and service centers are serving less people than once was the case. However, they are serving them in many more ways than was the case in 1930. The homogenization of society is going on very rapidly in the 12 communities, social differentiation is becoming much more pronounced than it once was, and various levels of ecological integration—at the neighborhood level, into hamlet-centered little sub-communities, and into rural communities—are becoming much more sharply defined. The rural communities themselves more and more are being drawn into the orbits of small cities and even the metropolitan centers in the regions studied.   J/S

2286. Strickler, Carolyn J. LOS ANGELES, PROFILE OF A SUPER CITY. *Mankind 1974 4(5): 10-15, 60-64.*

2287. The Senses Bureau. SAN DIEGO-TIJUANA: PLANS ACROSS THE BORDER. *Cry California 1976 11(3): 29-35.* Both San Diego and Tijuana are among the fastest-growing areas in their respective countries. Separated by a political boundary, the cities share common problems of water supply, air pollution, and sewage disposal. San Diego planners have been successful in programs to reduce pollution, but Tijuana's growth rate and city service needs present problems for the future. Residents of both cities are beginning to realize that their common problems require unified solutions. Photo, charts.   A. Hoffman

2288. Unsigned. [ST. LOUIS AND URBAN GROWTH]. *Focus/Midwest 1974 9(61): 19-47.*
Williams, Barbara R. ST. LOUIS: A CITY AND ITS SUBURBS, pp. 20-47.
Unsigned. ST. LOUIS RESPONDS TO RAND REPORT: "BOOH," p. 19.
Reprint of the RAND Corporation report (1973) on St. Louis and local citizens' response to the report.   S

2289. Wardwell, John M. EQUILIBRIUM AND CHANGE IN NONMETROPOLITAN GROWTH. *Rural Sociol. 1977 42(2): 156-179.* The reversal of relative growth rates of metropolitan and nonmetropolitan counties in the United States during 1970-75 has implications for theories of urbanization as well as for internal population redistribution. This reversal is analyzed in the context of metropolitan expansion, changing demographic composition, and preferences for residential location. With a possible temporary equilibrium in the exchange of metropolitan and nonmetropolitan populations, demographic trends and expressed residential preferences suggest the continued growth through inmigration of nonmetropolitan counties which are adjacent to metropolitan centers. Nonmetropolitan counties more remote from metropolitan areas may also experience continued growth as a consequence of earlier and more widely diffused retirement and death benefits, the growth of recreational communities, and the increasing locational flexibility of other services-related industries.   J

2290. Watkins, Alfred J. INTERMETROPOLITAN MIGRATION AND THE RISE OF THE SUNBELT. *Social Sci. Q. 1978 59(3): 553-561.* Notes that indicators of inter-metropolitan migration and the rise of the Sunbelt were evident as early as 1940. Yet, despite their obviously beneficial impact on the sunbelt's economy, . . . if left unchecked these demographic trends may seriously disrupt the political and economic stability of the region.   J

2291. Webb, Stephen D. SEGMENTAL URBAN GROWTH: SOME CROSS-NATIONAL EVIDENCE. *Sociol. and Social Res. 1974 58(4): 387-391.* Seeks to specify the segmental growth model through an examination of a size-density relationship in 23 New Zealand cities and 682 urban places in the United States. While the evidence suggests the model is valid for both nations, it appears to have greater salience in the New Zealand case as well as operating differentially by US regions.   J

2292. Wilke, Joan. TALES OF THREE CITIES. *Freeman 1974 24(12): 748-752.* Discusses what private enterprise can do in building communities such as Sun City, California, and Florida's Walt Disney World (1960's-70's). S

2293. Wilson, Andrew W. TECHNOLOGY, REGIONAL INTERDEPENDENCE, AND POPULATION GROWTH: TUCSON, ARIZONA. *Econ. Geography 1977 53(4): 388-392.* Examines why Tucson is a population center in 1977; mentions the surrounding desert, Tucson's nearness to the rest of the Southwest, lack of food production problems, and current technological resources.

Politics and Government

Politics, Policies, and Policy Formation

2294. Acock, Alan C. and Halley, Robert. ETHNIC POLITICS AND RACIAL ISSUES RECONSIDERED: COMMENTS ON AN EARLIER STUDY. *Western Pol. Q. 1975 28(4): 737-738.* Reevaluates Harlan Hahn and Timothy Almy's "Ethnic Politics and Racial Issues: Voting in Los Angeles," which concluded America was moving from ethnic politics to class politics. Due to a mistake in calculations Hahn and Almy drew the wrong conclusions. A second look at the statistics proved: first, ethnicity is a good predictor of voting for a liberal black mayor. Second, socioeconomic status measured by median income or education is not highly related to voting for a liberal black mayor when there are no controls. Third, socioeconomic status is moderately related when ethnicity is controlled, but the relationship is the opposite direction from the report by Hahn-Almy study, thus discrediting a class coalition transcending ethnicity. 3 notes. K. McElroy

2295. Alexander, James R. THE IMPACT OF ENVIRONMENTAL FORCES ON MUNICIPAL POLICIES: A REASSESSMENT. *Rocky Mountain Social Sci. J. 1975 12(1): 85-91.* Urban policy analysis of the environmental factors influencing decisionmaking by local governments and urban planning groups. S

2296. Bails, Dale. TWO MUNICIPAL REVENUE SOURCES CONTRASTED. *Am. J. of Econ. and Sociol. 1974 33(2): 187-199.* Contrasts the land value tax and the property tax with respect to their effects on land use and urban sprawl and their administrative feasibility. Three case studies are reviewed: Pittsburgh, Pennsylvania; Fairhope, Alabama; and Southfield, Michigan. Secondary sources; 33 notes. W. L. Marr

2297. Baker, Earl M. THE SUBURBAN TRANSFORMATION OF AMERICAN POLITICS: THE CONVERGENCE OF REALITY AND RESEARCH. *Publius 1975 5(1): 1-14.* Discusses social science research on the political impact of suburban growth 1950's-70's, in an introduction by the editor to a special issue of *Publius*, "The Suburban Reshaping of American Politics."

2298. BenShea, Noah. COSTS AND BENEFITS IN BOSTON. *Center Mag. 1977 10(6): 41-49.* Interview with James Young, treasurer of Boston, Massachusetts, in which he discusses his background as well as government aid, city management, and fiscal problems.

2299. Bowen, Elinor R. URBANISM AND THE SCOPE OF GOVERNMENT. *Policy Studies J. 1975 3(4): 332-340.* Explores the question of whether contextual variables, such as economic development, are useful in explaining variations in municipal public policy (1970-75). S

2300. Davis, Judith M. and Klinger, Donald E. DEVELOPING A TRAINING CAPABILITY IN METROPOLITAN GOVERNMENT. *Natl. Civic Rev. 1978 67(2): 80-83.* Unlike private industry, government can offer the public only services. Although there are quantitative measures, the public perceives quality of service as more important. A training program in Indianapolis is being developed to help employees and supervisors to solve problems encountered in serving the public. J

2301. Dickson, Paul. THINK TANK BRINGS SYSTEMS ANALYSIS TO THE CITY STREETS. *Smithsonian 1975 5(12): 42-49.* Discusses RAND Corporation's contract with New York City to modernize health care, fire fighting, housing, and law enforcement. S

2302. Doyle, Philip. MUNICIPAL PENSION PLANS: PROVISIONS AND PAYMENTS. *Monthly Labor Rev. 1977 100(11): 24-31.* Surveys pensions offered to municipal employees across the United States, including discussion of benefits, age and service requirements, pension escalators, and similar plans provided by the federal government.

2303. Duckworth, Charles E. NEW ROLES AND NEW SOLUTIONS: THE GARLAND EXPERIENCE. *Natl. Civic Rev. 1977 66(10): 502-505.* The experience of Garland, Texas, with an Urban Observatory program in cooperation with Texas A. & M. University shows that the greatest benefit is the fresh perspective the researchers can bring for city staff who are too busy with day-to-day operations to do any long-range analysis. The research experience also provides a source for further university research and publication. J

2304. Dusansky, Richard and Nordell, L. P. CITY AND SUBURB: THE ANATOMY OF FISCAL DILEMMA. *Land Econ. 1975 51(2): 133-138.* Develops a single model to describe the fiscal problems of a declining city and an expanding suburb. The model relates production and technological growth in the public and private sectors to the growth of the tax base and the demand for government services. Identifies several conditions that yield either fiscal solvency or crisis. 6 notes, diagram, biblio. E. S. Johnson

2305. Elazar, Daniel J. SUBURBANIZATION: REVIVING THE TOWN ON THE METROPOLITAN FRONTIER. *Publius 1975 5(1): 53-79.* Argues, in a special issue of *Publius*, "The Suburban Reshaping of American Politics," that evidence 1920-70 indicates that suburban governments are efficient political systems for solving social problems.

2306. Eulau, Heinz and Prewitt, Kenneth. ECO-POLICY ENVIRONMENT AND POLITICAL PROCESSES IN 76 CITIES OF A METROPOLITAN REGION. *Publius 1975 5(1): 81-96.* Analyzes the impact of various political systems and ecological problems on the environmental policies adopted by San Francisco Bay area suburban governments during the late 1960's or early 1970's, in a special issue of *Publius*, "The Suburban Reshaping of American Politics." S

2307. Feller, Irwin and Menzel, Donald C. THE ADOPTION OF TECHNOLOGICAL INNOVATIONS BY MUNICIPAL GOVERNMENTS. *Urban Affairs Q. 1978 13(4): 469-490.* There is little empirical basis for the belief that the public sector is less receptive to technological innovation than the private sector. Analysis by mail survey of 1,635 agencies in four categories (with a high response rate of 92.1% and a low of 85.3%) in more than 800 cities of 25,000 or more demonstrates that in three areas—fire-fighting, traffic control and air pollution control—many technological adoption paths replicate traditional s-shaped diffusion curves. The fourth, solid waste disposal, was more resistant to technological change. Discusses various explanations for the different adoption curves of the various technologies within each of the four service areas. Table, 4 fig., biblio., appendix. L. N. Beecher

2308. Fitch, Lyle C. THE WAYWARD WAYS OF THE NEW YORK CITY ADMINISTRATION. *New York Affairs 1977 4(2): 42-57.* Discusses the financial difficulties experienced by New York City government, 1975-77; examines two similar crises, 1930's-50's, and examines fiscal management policies, 1954-76.

2309. Friedman, Lewis and Marlin, John T. RATING CITIES' PERFORMANCE. *Natl. Civic Rev. 1976 65(1): 1219.* The American passion for measuring—the Top Ten, the Best—can be harnessed to improve public service and enhance the quality of city life. Municipal governments' striving to be Number One can be used to encourage more economic, efficient and effective local government, and to help decide what should be done. J

2310. Gerard, Karen. THE LOCALLY INSPIRED FISCAL CRISIS. *Society 1976 13(4): 33-35.* Finds the causes of New York City's fiscal crisis in expanding expenditures, particularly in public welfare, and in the tax structure.

2311. Gitelson, Alan R. THE TOCKS ISLAND PROJECT: A CASE STUDY OF PARTICIPATION AND INTERACTION PATTERNS IN AN INTERGOVERNMENTAL DECISION-MAKING SYSTEM. *Publius 1976 6(1): 21-48.* Examines the participation and interaction of officials involved in urbanization, offering as a case study the Tocks Island Project which sought to provide water management, recreation, and hydroelectric power for New York City, Philadelphia, Washington, D.C., Newark, and Trenton, 1962-75.

2312. Greer, Edward. RACIAL BIASES IN THE PROPERTY TAX SYSTEM. *Rev. of Radical Pol. Econ. 1975 7(3): 22-31.* Regressive property taxation, 1950's-70's, works to the detriment of Negroes and city dwellers, while giving preferential treatment to industry; cites examples from the system in Gary, Indiana.

2313. Harris, Marlys J. "THE FLOATING OPERA." *New York Affairs 1976 3(2): 3-7.* Notes obstacles and recommends solutions to the 1975-76 problems in city planning and city government in New York City.

2314. Harris, Marlys. THE TWIN CITIES: REGIONAL GOVERN-MENT AT WORK. *New York Affairs 1976 3(3): 15-33.* Minneapolis and St. Paul used to be distinguished nationally only by their icy climate and a farcical game of one-upmanship. Metropolitan government hasn't changed the winter weather, but it has pushed cities and suburbs to grow up and plan for the future. J

2315. Hill, Richard Child. AT THE CROSS ROADS: THE POLITI-CAL ECONOMY OF POSTWAR DETROIT. *Urbanism Past and Present 1978 6: 1-21.* Discusses the regional distribution of physical and social space in the Midwest and Detroit region as determined by succes-sive waves of expansion in the automobile industry. This distribution establishes important ecological contexts for the political dynamics of the Detroit region. Centers on postwar governing coalitions between indus-trial magnates and United Automobile Workers of America leadership, bent on reviving Detroit's inner city though possessing a weak link in the exclusion of the black community. This exclusion caused the 1967 riots, the election of Detroit's first black mayor, and a current black socialist challenge to the city's crisis-ridden governing coalition. 3 maps, 45 notes.
B. P. Anderson

2316. Hill, Richard Child. SEPARATE AND UNEQUAL: GOV-ERNMENTAL INEQUALITY IN THE METROPOLIS. *Am. Pol. Sci. Rev. 1974 68(4): 1557-1568.* The political incorporation and munici-pal segregation of classes and status groups in the metropolis tend to divorce fiscal resources from public needs and to create and perpetuate inequality among urban residents in the United States. Investigation of data collected for a large number of metropolitan areas in 1960 reveals a number of variables associated with inequality in the distribution of fiscal resources among municipalities in metropolitan areas. The level of income inequality among municipal governments in metropolitan areas varies directly with: location in the South; age, size and density of the metropolis; nonwhite concentration; family income inequality; residential segregation among social classes; housing segregation by quality; and governmental fragmentation. The data provide support for the argument that governmental inequality occupies a central position in the urban stratification system. J

2317. Howard, John R. A FRAMEWORK FOR THE ANALYSIS OF URBAN BLACK POLITICS. *Ann. of the Am. Acad. of Pol. and Social Sci. 1978 (439): 1-15.* The analysis of urban black politics requires examining both the magnitude of the problems confronting black office holders at the municipal level and the politico-social context within which black leadership seeks to confront these problems. With regard to the former, typically cities with black leadership are older, poorer, and blacker than most in the United States. Problems of poverty long predate black political ascendancy and are usually not mitigated by federal or state income transfer policies. These problems have a ripple effect, hurting ghetto business, black and white, and diminishing choice with regard to housing, education, and health care. With regard to understanding the socio-political context within which urban black leadership is exercised, the important factors are : (a) the political and moral inaccessibility of certain policies theoretically available to white leadership (for example, the "planned shrinkage" of low income communities via cuts in service

as an alternative to citywide cuts in services); (b) the fiscal strain of varying degrees of severity; (c) the apportioning of power among city offices as reflected in the structure of city government; (d) the character of state and federal initiatives; and (e) racism as it is manifested in institu-tional and affective forms. J

2318. Hulcher, Wendell E. ELECTED LOCAL LEADERSHIP IN MUNICIPAL GOVERNMENT. *Ann. of the Am. Acad. of Pol. and Social Sci. 1973 (405): 137-144.* Though it is assumed by some that local governments are having a constantly decreasing role, the evidence is not conclusive. The manner in which local elective officials exercise leader-ship will be determining. Changing demands on the traditional functions of local government and changing complexities of the technological age result in unprecedented responsibility for local elective officials. The lead-ership role, including planning which encompasses all activity of local government, demands new, additional personal characteristics to cope with new technology and lifestyles. J

2319. James, Franklin J., Jr. THE CITY: SANDBOX, RESERVA-TION, OR DYNAMO?: A REPLY. *Public Policy 1974 22(1): 39-51.* Criticizes argument by Alexander Ganz and Thomas O'Brien (*Public Policy*, 1973 21(1): 107-123) that claims revenue-sharing is a viable urban policy. S

2320. Jones, E. Terrence. MASS MEDIA AND THE URBAN POL-ICY PROCESS. *Policy Studies J. 1975 3(4): 359-363.* Evaluates the transmitting of urban policy through the mass media, and the impact and implications of this procedure. S

2321. Karnig, Albert K. "PRIVATE-REGARDING" POLICY, CIVIL RIGHTS GROUPS, AND THE MEDIATING IMPACT OF MUNICIPAL REFORMS. *Am. J. of Pol. Sci. 1975 19(1): 91-106.* Based on data from the 417 American cities over 25,000 in population containing at least 1000 nonwhites in 1960, this report provides a test of the proposition that municipal reforms tend to blunt the impact of pri-vate-regarding demands for public policy. With controls established for region and community socioeconomic characteristics, the analysis focuses on the relationship between civil rights group mobilization and various private-regarding policies in reformed and in unreformed cities. The prin-cipal findings of the study are 1) civil rights group mobilization is strongly and positively related to the development of local private-regarding pro-grams, and 2) reforms, singularly and additively, diminish the influence of private-regarding policy demands. J

2322. Kaufman, Clifford. POLITICAL URBANISM: URBAN SPA-TIAL ORGANIZATION, POLICY, AND POLITICS. *Urban Affairs Q. 1974 9(4): 421-436.*

2323. Keil, Thomas J. and Ekstrom, Charles A. MUNICIPAL DIF-FERENTIATION AND PUBLIC POLICY: FISCAL SUPPORT LEV-ELS IN VARYING ENVIRONMENTS. *Social Forces 1974 52(3): 384-395.* Using variables derived from several conceptualizations of the urban environment, this study assesses the predictability of levels of fiscal support (as measured by per capita property tax revenue) among 21 municipal governments at two points in time. The data bear out the notion that it is useful to consider revenue level as a function of social variables differing in time and space. The results also suggest that current views of environmental impact on municipal government make the urban system excessively static. Findings indicate that over time one can expect marked changes in the influence of various environmental features.
J

2324. Keller, Edmond J. THE IMPACT OF BLACK MAYORS ON URBAN POLICY. *Ann. of the Am. Acad. of Pol. and Social Sci. 1978 (439): 40-52.* This article is an exploratory assessment of whether or not black mayors, as compared to white mayors, demonstrate patterned dif-ferences in their policy preferences and expenditures. As a rule, black mayors do not differ greatly from white mayors in the way they spend money for welfare related projects. However, their preferences do seem to differ. Black mayors, even when they would like to, are constrained from spending according to their preferences. It is Differences in expendi-tures patterns are highly conditioned by environmental and structural factors. Suggestions are made for further research. J

2325. Kennedy, R. Evan. BALTIMORE DOWNTOWN REVIVED THROUGH PRIVATE/PUBLIC COOPERATION. *Natl. Civic Rev. 1976 65(10): 503-505.* Born in the 1950's out of a realization by a few individuals that something was going badly wrong, a reconstruction effort has been taking place in downtown Baltimore—the city everybody tried to avoid. And, thanks to the Beltway, it was possible. Its success is in large measure due to local government support.   J

2326. Lamott, Kenneth. THE BERKELEY CLOCK. *Horizon 1973 15(1): 16-23.* The liberal-conservative split on the Berkeley city council mirrors the rifts which threaten the city.   S

2327. Lehne, Richard and Fisk, Donald. THE IMPACT OF URBAN POLICY ANALYSIS. *Urban Affairs Q. 1974 10(2): 115-138.* Examines the effect of 10 factors of urban policy analysis on local government decisionmaking in 10 case studies. Despite exceptions, study timing, consideration of how to implement decisions, decisionmaking interest, and the need for an immediate decision appeared most important in influencing decisionmaking. Proposed changes in funding seemed little related. Table, note, biblio.   P. J. Woehrmann

2328. Long, Norton E. THE CITY AS A SYSTEM OF PERVERSE INCENTIVES. *Urbanism Past and Present 1976 (2): 1-8.* Argues that cities lack a reasoned assessment of their role in an effective economy. City politicians concern themselves with standards which are too high for the poor. For instance, building codes prevent the poor from doing what they can on their homes so their homes deteriorate. The minimum wage prevents the poor from working at what they can do and they go on welfare instead. The city is stuck with enormous expenditures and blight. 11 notes.   B. P. Anderson

2329. Long, Norton E. ETHOS AND THE CITY: THE PROBLEM OF LOCAL LEGITIMACY. *Ethnicity 1975 2(1): 43-51.* Speculates on the importance of ethos and ethical structure in local government, asserting that shared ethos is necessary for harmonious governing and successful promotion of shared lifestyles.

2330. MacManus, Susan A. TAX STRUCTURES IN AMERICAN CITIES: LEVELS, RELIANCE, AND RATES. *Western Pol. Q. 1977 30(2): 263-287.* Based on statistics from 1962, 1967, and 1972, tax levels, reliance, and property tax rates are greatest among central cities of the Northeast with: 1) populations more than one million, 2) industry or manufacturing as an economic base, 3) and financial responsibility for education, welfare, and hospitals.

2331. Maier, Henry W. CONFLICT IN METROPOLITAN AREAS. *Ann. of the Am. Acad. of Pol. and Social Sci. 1974 416: 148-157.* The dichotomy between the central city and its suburbs is more pronounced than the more traditional conflict between rural and urban areas. Central cities contain the concentrations of the poor in the metropolitan area because of the lack of low income housing outside the city. The basic conflict arises from the contention for resources between the "have" suburban communities and the "have-not" central cities. Conflict arises as suburbs fight to maintain the housing status quo, as cities fight to prevent expressways from destroying additional housing and tax base and to attain greater emphasis on adequate transportation, as heavy reliance on the property tax leads central city and suburb to compete for the same industry. In general, voluntary intergovernmental groups have not been responsive to central city needs in the metropolitan area.   J

2332. Martin, William C. and Hopkins, Karin. ATLANTA: POLITICAL TRANSFER AND SUCCESSION IN A SOUTHERN METROPOLIS. *J. of Intergroup Relations 1975 4(3): 22-32.* Traces the growing influence of Negroes on politics in Atlanta, Georgia, during the 1940's-74, and discusses the problems faced by Mayor Maynard Jackson.   S

2333. Masotti, Louis H. PRIVATE/PUBLIC PARTNERSHIPS: THE ONLY GAME IN TOWN? *Natl. Civic Rev. 1975 64(11): 568-571, 590.* The decentralization of traditional urban functions to suburbia and the retreat from the urban crisis by the national government have placed considerable strain on local governments in trying to cope with their problems. But there are some encouraging signs: a new sense of commitment to the urban purpose by state government leaders, minority group leaders, and private corporate leadership.   J

2334. Mercer, John and Barnett, J. Ross. SPATIAL MODIFICATIONS TO MODELS OF THE URBAN POLICY PROCESS. *Policy Studies J. 1975 3(4): 320-325.* Examines locational aspects of income redistribution in urban governmental policies.   S

2335. Mogulof, Melvin. WHO DOES WHAT? A PERFORMANCE COMPARISON OF METROPOLITAN GOVERNMENTS. *Urban and Social Change Rev. 1973 6(2): 59-63.*

2336. Mollenkopf, John H. THE POST-WAR POLITICS OF URBAN DEVELOPMENT. *Pol. and Soc. 1975 5(3): 247-295.* Finds that conventional explanations of the crises in local governments in the 1960's are inadequate, and provides as an alternative a "class-based" thesis grounded in conflicts concerning urban planning and development. Provides a model for analysis of the city and its institutions based on this thesis that sees city politics as the most important moderator between the economic and the communal aspects of city life. Applies the model in case studies of four cities (Boston, Cambridge, San Francisco, and Berkeley). Based on primary and secondary sources; 7 tables, 89 notes.   D. G. Nielson

2337. Morris, Robert B. PROFESSIONAL LOCAL ADMINISTRATION IN MUNICIPAL GOVERNMENT. *Ann. of the Am. Acad. of Pol. and Social Sci. 1973 (405): 145-150.* Urban areas are no longer sharply defined, and local administrators cannot ignore neighboring areas. Trained professionals are necessary. They are employed by half of all cities in the United States with populations between 10,000 and 50,000. The professional's functions include planning and coordination of city and intergovernment agencies. His characteristics must include sound training, tact, patience, self-confidence, and communicative skill; also imagination and courage.   J

2338. Neuner, Edward J.; Popp, Dean O.; and Sebold, Frederick D. THE IMPACT OF A TRANSITION TO SITE-VALUE TAXATION ON VARIOUS CLASSES OF PROPERTY IN SAN DIEGO. *Land Econ. 1974 50(2): 181-184.*

2339. O'Dell, Doyal D. THE STRUCTURE OF METROPOLITAN POLITICAL SYSTEMS: A CONCEPTUAL MODEL. *Western Pol. Q. 1973 26(1): 64-82.* Presents a city classification scheme which can be used to compare decisionmaking capabilities of urban political systems and applies the scheme to Denver, Colorado, and Minneapolis-St. Paul, Minnesota.   S

2340. Piven, Frances Fox and Cloward, Richard A. THE URBAN CRISIS AS AN ARENA FOR CLASS MOBILIZATION. *Radical Am. 1977 11(1): 9-17.* The fiscal crisis in New York and other large cities has provided the government structure with a rationale for reducing public sector expenditures as a part of a national economic policy. The impact of these spending cuts has been especially heavy on the working class and the nonwhite urban populations. A possible effective means of reaction against these new directions of policy would be civil disobedience on the part of the groups affected.   N. Lederer

2341. Rahe, Charles P. PLANNING FOR TAX BASE CHANGES IN AN URBAN CORE AREA: THE CASE OF DENVER. *Social Sci. J. 1977 14(1): 83-95.* Examines the potential for tax base erosion in Denver City and County, Colorado, due to changes in demographic and economic trends in the 1970's; discusses the need for planning the creation of alternative methods for dealing with tax base changes in Denver and other urban core areas.

2342. Rondinelli, Dennis A. POLICY COORDINATION IN METROPOLITAN AREAS: AN ECOLOGICAL PERSPECTIVE. *Administration and Soc. 1978 10(2): 203-234.* Reviews major ecological variables influencing political interaction in city government in metropolitan areas, and suggests a framework for assessing potential policy coordination, 1960's-78.

2343. Ruchelman, Leonard and Brownstein, Charles. PUBLIC NEEDS AND PRIVATE DECISIONS IN HIGH-RISE BUILDING DEVELOPMENT: A POLICY-MAKING MODEL. *Urban Affairs Q. 1974 10(2): 139-157.* Studies the interaction of public and private values and practices in the construction of high-rise buildings in cities. Decisions on where and how to build are largely private, as public forces, which bear most of the concern for societal needs, react slowly to private decisions. Bargaining between private and public forces is little studied. If social costs are to be put in the political decisionmaking process, they must be identified and measured. Diagram, notes, biblio.

P. J. Woehrmann

2344. Rybeck, Walter. CAN THE PROPERTY TAX BE MADE TO WORK FOR RATHER THAN AGAINST URBAN DEVELOPMENT? *Am. J. of Econ. and Sociol. 1974 33(3): 259-271.* The property tax can serve good development if it is a tax on property value, assessed on market value, has few exemptions, does not fall on buildings or improvements, raises money for local government, and is integrated with planning. Secondary sources; 8 notes. W. L. Marr

2345. Schoolman, Mary McCormack and Rogoff, Edward G. "HOMETOWN JOBS FOR HOMETOWN BOYS." *New York Affairs 1974 2(2): 50-59.* The proposed revival of the Lyons Law, requiring that New York City government employees be city residents, offered few benefits. J/S

2346. Schuler, Richard E. THE INTERACTION BETWEEN LOCAL GOVERNMENT AND URBAN RESIDENTIAL LOCATION. *Am. Econ. Rev. 1974 64(4): 682-696.* Theoretical analysis concerning the optimum allocation of public services in urban areas for alleviating social problems caused by high population density.

2347. Schumaker, Paul D. POLICY RESPONSIVENESS TO PROTEST-GROUP DEMANDS. *J. of Pol. 1975 37(2): 488-521.* The responsiveness of urban politics to protest-group demands is a function of two kinds of variables: 1) protest-group characteristics and behavior, and 2) the attitudes of various sectors of the community toward protest groups and their demands. Protest groups can enhance social support for their demands—and thereby increase policy-responsiveness—by adopting behavior which can be characterized as nonmilitant. J

2348. Shefter, Martin. NEW YORK CITY'S FISCAL CRISIS: THE POLITICS OF INFLATION AND RETRENCHMENT. *Public Interest 1977 (48): 98-127.* The origins of the current New York City fiscal crisis lie in the political changes of the 1960's which saw the rise of three new political groups: the Democratic reform movement, the blacks, and the municipal employee unions. The efforts of politicians to gain power through alliances with these groups lead to budgetary inflation, indebtedness, and financial collapse. The balance of political power has shifted to New York's financial and business community, which owns the public debt. At the expense of the blacks and unions, budgetary retrenchment has started, but this retrenchment program is threatened by the lack of discipline of some of the municipal unions, by political campaigns, and elections. There are similarities between the financial and political developments in New York City since the fiscal crisis of 1975 and those in the aftermath of Boss Tweed's downfall in 1871. 2 notes. S. Harrow

2349. Sigel, Roberta S. and Pindur, Wolfgang. ROLE CONGRUENCE AND ROLE STRAIN AMONG URBAN LEGISLATORS. *Social Sci. Q. 1973 54(1): 54-65.* Interviews with elected urban school board members and councilmen demonstrate that their customary way of making policy decisions sharply contrasts with their definition of the representational role, except in the case of trustees, whose role behavior and role definition are generally congruent. Decisionmaking is not viewed by representatives as the most important aspect of their relation with the public, and that the trustee role seems more functional than that of politico or delegate in urban legislative systems. J

2350. Smith, Michael P. ELITE THEORY AND POLICY ANALYSIS: THE POLITICS OF EDUCATION IN SUBURBIA. *J. of Pol. 1974 36(4): 1006-1032.* Concerns the extent to which the technocratic-managerial role expectations of suburban educational policy-makers influence their fiscal policy choices. Analyzes public spending decisions in a ring of primarily "managerial" suburbs in Massachusetts to assess the relative impact on fiscal policy of policy-makers' social status, political ideology, and role expectations. The analysis provides little support for hypotheses linking social background and conventional ideological measures to elite fiscal choices. J

2351. Smith, Robert C. THE CHANGING SHAPE OF URBAN BLACK POLITICS: 1960-1970. *Ann. of the Am. Acad. of Pol. and Social Sci. 1978 (439): 16-28.* The years between 1960 and 1970 constitute the critical period in the emergence of a mature urban black politics. Prior to this time, blacks in the American city were, through a variety of devices, excluded from full and equal participation in the urban political process. The developments of the 1960's represent the beginnings of the incorporatin and institutionalization of blacks as constituent elements of the urban polity. This paper considers some of the changes of the last decade in city politics and black life that may account for this transformation. J

2352. Spiegel, S. Arthur. AFFIRMATIVE ACTION IN CINCINNATI. *Cincinnati Hist. Soc. Bull. 1979 37(2): 78-88.* Describes action by Cincinnati's city council and mayor's office to end employment discrimination against Negroes, starting in 1963, which culminated in the concept of affirmative action in 1965, then known as fair employment practices, and follows Cincinnati's affirmative action programs 1967.

2353. Unsigned. THE CAUSES OF NEW YORK CITY'S FISCAL CRISIS. *Pol. Sci. Q. 1975-76 90(4): 659-674.* The Congressional Budget Office analyzes long- and short-term causes of New York City's fiscal crisis, discusses the extent to which New York City's problems are unique or shared by other large cities, and concludes that the underlying causes of the crisis cannot be remedied by city action alone, but only with the help of the state and federal government. J

2354. Unsigned. [COMPETITION, MONOPOLY, AND THE ORGANIZATION OF GOVERNMENT IN METROPOLITAN AREAS]. *J. of Law & Econ. 1975 18(3): 661-694.*
Wagner, Richard E. and Weber, Warren E. COMPETITION, MONOPOLY, AND ORGANIZATION OF GOVERNMENT IN METROPOLITAN AREAS, *pp. 661-684.* Examines government as competitive suppliers of public output and as monopolistic suppliers of public output; uses budgetary consequences of governmental change in metropolitan areas to examine these two perspectives of government.
Rothenberg, Jerome. COMMENT, *pp. 685-690.*
Ostrom, Vincent. COMMENT, *pp. 691-694.*

2355. Weissman, Stephen R. WHITE ETHNICS & URBAN POLITICS IN THE SEVENTIES: THE CASE OF JERSEY CITY. *Polity 1976 9(2): 182-207.* Although the social rise of the "white ethnic" working class and the concomitant decline of the urban political machine has long been common knowledge, there is little systematic knowledge of the emerging patterns of urban politics. The author provides a better understanding of contemporary white ethnic politics and policy through his case study of "reform" in Jersey City. J

2356. Wilcox, Allen R. POPULATION AND URBAN SYSTEMS: THE BLURRING OF BOUNDARIES. *Policy Studies J. 1975 3(4): 340-345.* Examines the inadequacy of some contemporary techniques to determine the relation between population and urban politics, and explores more fruitful avenues for research in the future. S

2357. Williams, Oliver P. THE POLITICS OF URBAN SPACE. *Publius 1975 5(1): 15-26.* Discusses the relationships between ecology, urban locations, and the political impact of suburbs 1950-70, in a special issue of *Publius*, "The Suburban Reshaping of American Politics."

2358. Wirt, Frederick M. SUBURBS AND POLITICS IN AMERICA. *Publius 1975 5(1): 121-144.* Discusses the impact of suburbs on US politics primarily from 1948 to 1973, in a special issue of *Publius*, "The Suburban Reshaping of American Politics."

2359. Yates, Douglas. THE FUTURE OF URBAN GOVERNMENT. *New York Affairs 1976 3(2): 8-19.* The fragmented and unstable nature of city government and its tenuous ability to implement any policy have aggravated the "urban crisis." J

2360. Zikmund, Joseph, II. A THEORETICAL STRUCTURE FOR THE STUDY OF SUBURBAN POLITICS. *Ann. of the Am. Acad. of Pol. and Social Sci. 1975 422: 45-60.* Suburban politics, while being subjected to more and more empirical research, often is studied in a theoretical void. This article attempts to provide a general theoretical structure for the study of suburban politics which focuses on three inherent developmental factors: the developmental stage of the surrounding metropolitan area; the circumstances of origin of the suburb; and the developmental phase of the particular suburb. Also related are a number of descriptive factors pertaining to the character of the suburban community. These independent variables are used to predict three elements of suburban politics: political style, kinds of issues, and kinds of relations with neighboring communities.   J

Institutional Structure and Governmental Organization

2361.   Aleshire, Frank and Aleshire, Fran.   THE AMERICAN CITY MANAGER: NEW STYLE, NEW "GAME."   *Natl. Civic Rev. 1977 66(5): 235-239.*   Government administrators at all levels are not on the public's "most admired" list. City managers are among the most endangered species due to the recent stress on intergovernmental relations. It has created a changed role for city managers which they must recognize.
                                                                                    J/S

2362.   Almy, Timothy R.   LOCAL-COSMOPOLITANISM AND U.S. CITY MANAGERS.   *Urban Affairs Q. 1975 10(3): 243-272.*   Surveys value orientations and policy viewpoints of city managers in the San Francisco Bay area. Cosmopolitans are greater initiators of policy than locals, who themselves are more politically active. Differences also exist in education, tenure, and childhood experiences. Local control of city managers perhaps is increasing in conflict with cosmopolitan beliefs. 11 tables, 3 notes, biblio.   P. J. Woehrmann

2363.   Aram, John D. and Stratton, William E.   THE DEVELOPMENT OF INTERAGENCY COOPERATION.   *Social Service Rev. 1974 48(3): 412-421.*   Describes and analyzes a successful planning effort involving 20 local agencies which attempted to coordinate their services to the aged in a public planning project.   J

2364.   Aron, Joan.   EPITAPH FOR A SUPER SUPERAGENCY.   *New York Affairs 1975 2(3): 80-89.*   "In the last three years of the Lindsay administration, an Interdepartmental Committee on Public Utilities made an effort to have the city government speak with one voice on increasingly difficult energy problems, sometimes successfully. Although the energy situation has worsened, the committee is in limbo and the city government's attention once again unfocused."   J

2365.   Berman, David R. and Merrill, Bruce D.   CITIZEN ATTITUDES TOWARD MUNICIPAL REFORM INSTITUTIONS: A TESTING OF SOME ASSUMPTIONS.   *Western Pol. Q. 1976 29(2): 274-283.*   The reform model of municipal government calls for a council-manager plan and municipal elections that are nonpartisan, held at-large and scheduled separately from state and national elections. Survey data drawn upon in this study suggests that people: do not view reform institutions and practices in terms of a consistent cognitive model; tend to view the components of the model in relation to two separate factors or dimensions, one concerning the operation of city government and the other of the nature of its election system; and do not necessarily view reform institutions as previous studies suggest.   J

2366.   Breckinridge, John B.   THE DISTRICT OF COLUMBIA HOME RULE ACT.   *Judicature 1974 57(8): 360-363.*

2367.   Cunningham, James V.   DRAFTING THE PITTSBURGH CHARTER: HOW CITIZENS PARTICIPATED.   *Natl. Civic Rev. 1974 63(8): 410-415.*   Examines the work of the Pittsburgh Government Study Commission.   J

2368.   Cunningham, James V.; Ahlbrandt, Roger S., Jr.; Jewell, Rose; and Hendrickson, Robert.   THE PITTSBURGH ATLAS PROGRAM: TEST PROJECT FOR NEIGHBORHOODS.   *Natl. Civic Rev. 1976 65(6): 284-289.*   In November 1974 Pittsburgh voters approved a new charter with a provision for embryo neighborhood governments. A team of researchers, planners, and citizens, under the label "Pittsburgh Neighborhood Atlas," has completed a demonstration project to find a method

for boundary determination, a computerized neighborhood information system and improved communication techniques.   J

2369.   Dye, Thomas R. and Garcia, John A.   STRUCTURE, FUNCTION, AND POLICY IN AMERICAN CITIES.   *Urban Affairs Q. 1978 14(1): 103-122.*   Compared to suburban governments, city governments are functionally more diversified. Older, eastern, larger, and unreformed cities were more diversified than newer, western, smaller, and reformed cities. Moreover, the extent of functional diversification was more important than any single socioeconomic variable in determining the per capita taxation and expenditure rates. Diversification as well as reformism negatively affects policy responsiveness. Based on data drawn from the 1972 *Census of Government* relevant to all 243 cities and 340 of 1,200 suburban municipalities of 10,000 or more identified in the standard metropolitan statistical areas. 4 tables, 2 notes, biblio.
                                                                        L. N. Beecher

2370.   Fainstein, Susan and Fainstein, Norman I.   FROM THE FOLKS WHO BROUGHT YOU OCEAN HILL-BROWNSVILLE.   *New York Affairs 1974 2(2): 104-115.*   The last Lindsay administration experiment in decentralization was the creation of neighborhood government in eight communities. Modest in objectives and rhetoric, the program was reasonably successful, in large part because of the extreme moderation shown by all participants.   J

2371.   Finkelstein, Philip.   IN MEMORIAM: THE CITY ADMINISTRATOR.   *New York Affairs 1974 2(1): 62-75.*   In 1954, Mayor Wagner established the office of the city administrator in the hope of imparting a new professionalism to management of city government. In 1974, the office was quietly abolished, after some successes and some failures.
                                                                                    J

2372.   Gamm, Larry.   PA. LOCAL GOVERNMENT STUDY: OBSERVATIONS BY COMMISSIONERS.   *Natl. Civic Rev. 1975 64(8): 400-403.*   Those who have served in Pennsylvania municipalities, as provided by the 1972 Home Rule Charter and Optional Plans Law, were interviewed as part of a statewide community education program as to their experiences on local government study commissions. The biggest disappointment was the lack of public involvement and interest.   J

2373.   Ginsburg, Sigmund G.   THE NEW YORK CITY ADMINISTRATOR: A CRITICAL EULOGY.   *Natl. Civic Rev. 1975 64(9): 451-458.*   The office of city administrator in New York City was born in 1954, led a short and unhealthy life, and passed away at the age of 20. In spite of executive orders outlining its functions and mayoral pronouncements as to its significant role, the office had very little power, mixed talents, a history of frustration, poor morale and an identity crisis.
                                                                                    J

2374.   Hamilton, David K.   POLITICAL OFFICIALS AND AREA-WIDE GOVERNMENT REFORM.   *Urbanism Past and Present 1979 (8): 42-45.*   Consolidating municipal facilities through areawide government reform saves local taxpayer money, yet most efforts in this direction have failed. There are many reasons for this, but "the single most important and overriding cause for success or failure of areawide government reform is the ability of the locally elected government officials to influence voters." The influence of elected local officials, in turn, is dependent on the politicians' credibility, the degree of knowledge of the voters on reorganization proposals, and the power relationships of the officials to the voter. 2 tables, 14 notes.   B. P. Anderson

2375.   Harris, Marlys.   BUDGET BUREAU IN A BUDGET CRISIS.   *New York Affairs 1974 2(2): 20-37.*   The traditional center of power in New York City government, the Bureau of the Budget, flourished in the Lindsay era. As the city's fiscal situation worsens, Budget—like the city government—is adrift and demoralized.   J

2376.   Heiss, F. William and McKenna, Jacqueline.   DENVER'S CHARTER CHANGES: THE WORK OF SCHOLARS AND PRACTITIONERS.   *Natl. Civic Rev. 1976 65(2): 83-86.*   Denver used an innovative method to revise its charter—university scholars and researchers, through the Denver Urban Observatory, joined city policymakers in a unique, successful approach to winning citizen approval of five charter amendments, the first comprehensive review of the charter since 1948.
                                                                                    J

2377. Hetland, James L., Jr. PART WAY: PROGRESS TOWARD REGIONAL GOVERNMENT. *Cry California 1973 8(3): 14-16.* Reviews the successes and problems of the Twin Cities Metropolitan Council, 1967-73.   S

2378. Hill, Dilys M. AMERICAN METROPOLITANISM AND THE AMBIGUITY OF 'MILD CHAOS.' *Urban Studies [Great Britain] 1976 13(3): 285-293.* Analyzes the metropolitan problems of the United States since the 1930's, discusses governmental responses to these problems and the resulting growth of institutionalized intergovernmental relations at the regional-metropolitan level, and assesses the relationships between metropolitan reform, governmental structures, political structures, democratic values, and authoritative management as effective power shifts increasingly away from local control.

2379. Howe, Elizabeth. WHERE THE LINDSAY REORGANIZATION WORKED. *New York Affairs 1979 5(3): 43-52.* Discusses the positive effects of Mayor John V. Lindsay's administrative reorganization in 1966-67, which resulted in the creation of superagencies, on the city administration of Mayor Abraham Beame.

2380. Howitt, Arnold M. THE EXPANDING ROLE OF MAYORAL STAFF. *Policy Studies J. 1975 3(4): 363-370.* Analyzes the patterns of mayoral staff changes over the years and the factors that account for these changes.   S

2381. Johnson, William and Harrigan, John J. INNOVATION BY INCREMENTS: THE TWIN CITIES AS A CASE STUDY IN METROPOLITAN REFORM. *Western Pol. Q. 1978 31(2): 206-218.* Combines a non-incremental with an incremental interpretation to explain the evolution of metropolitan governmental reform in the Minneapolis-St. Paul metropolitan area. The decision to create the Minneapolis-St. Paul Metropolitan Council had characteristics of a non-incremental decision. But, the original Metropolitan Council had very limited powers. Its subsequent development into a powerful political decision-making actor came through a series of incremental changes over a ten-year period. This combination of non-incremental with incremental change enabled the achievement of metropolitan reforms that have eluded most metropolitan areas.   J

2382. Kaplan, Samuel. REGIONAL GOVERNMENT—PRO AND CON REGIONALISM—A POLEMIC. *New York Affairs 1976 3(3): 66-68.* While Richard Hatcher fears that central-city minorities will lose out with the adoption of regional government, the author believes that things are so bad now, that all of us would be winners.   J

2383. Kolderie, Ted. RECONCILING METROPOLIS AND NEIGHBORHOOD: THE TWIN CITIES. *Natl. Civic Rev. 1973 62(4): 184-188.* The Twin Cities metropolitan area is not explicitly implementing a two-tier setup for its governmental system. Yet some fairly clear outlines of this concept can be seen in the incremental decisions made in the continuing reorganization under way since 1957.   J

2384. Krefetz, Sharon Perlman and Sharaf, Alan B. CITY-COUNTY MERGER ATTEMPTS: THE ROLE OF POLITICAL FACTORS. *Natl. Civic Rev. 1977 66(4): 175-181.* To date there has been only a small number of major metropolitan government reorganizations. Five political factors seem to be of greatest potential significance in the outcomes of referenda on consolidation: taxes, blacks' positions, political leaders' roles, corruption scandals, and annexation threats.   J

2385. Krinsky, Edward B. MUNICIPAL GRIEVANCE ARBITRATION IN WISCONSIN. *Arbitration J. 1973 28(1): 50-67.* The Wisconsin municipal grievance arbitration experience shows great similarities to private sector arbitration experience both procedurally and in terms of the issues arbitrated.   J

2386. Lugar, Richard L. UNIGOV: FINDING THE BOUNDARIES OF THE REAL CITY. *Urban R. 1973 6(4): 32-34.* Political and administrative aspects of integration of urban areas.   S

2387. Lyons, W. E. and Engstrom, Richard E. SOCIO-POLITICAL CROSS PRESSURES AND ATTITUDES TOWARD POLITICAL INTEGRATION OF URBAN GOVERNMENTS. *J. of Pol. 1973*

35(3): 682-711. A study of voter attitudes toward government consolidation proposals in Lexington, Kentucky, and Augusta, Georgia, in 1969 which failed at the polls. Challenges the usual approach to studies of consolidation by testing three dimensions of voter reaction: social-distance, tax-benefit, and regime-government. These sociopolitical orientations come under heavy "cross-pressures" when integrative proposals are before the electorate and are most significantly affected by the type of proposal under consideration. Only when all three factors are considered does the picture become clear. 5 tables, fig., 43 notes.
A. R. Stoesen

2388. Marando, Vincent L. THE POLITICS OF CITY-COUNTY CONSOLIDATION. *Natl. Civic Rev. 1975 64(2): 76-81.* City-county consolidation has been relied on as one of the major forms of local government reorganization. It is relatively difficult to obtain politically and the search for methods continues. Questions of political feasibility are of central interest if this form is to be a realistic option.   J

2389. Marando, Vincent L. THE POLITICS OF METROPOLITAN REFORM. *Administration and Soc. 1974 6(2): 229-260.* "Political factors represent the major obstacles to governmental reorganization in metropolitan areas."   S

2390. Marchione, William P., Jr. THE 1949 BOSTON CHARTER REFORM. *New England Q. 1976 49(3): 373-398.* Traces the structural changes in Boston's city government 1880-1945 as background to an examination of the 1949 substitution of a nine-man council, elected at-large, for the old ward-council system. This reform was sparked by a bribery scandal involving the old council and the imprisonment of Mayor James M. Curley (1874-1958) for mail fraud, but it reflected a change in the Boston electorate, the type of services it sought from government, and its concept of what constituted good government. Based on newspaper articles and interviews; 80 notes.   J. C. Bradford

2391. Morris, Julie. DETROIT—ON THE ROAD TO REGIONALISM. *New York Affairs 1976 3(3): 45-52.* Detroit's voluntary metropolitan government can point to a few accomplishments. But its failure to effect change has brought forth a new and controversial proposal for true regional government.   J

2392. Pratt, Henry J. and Straley, Mark K. DETROIT CHARTER REFORM: INNOVATORS V. TRADITIONALISTS. *Natl. Civic Rev. 1973 62(3): 130-133, 149.* In 1972, Detroit voters defeated a charter proposed by a charter revision commission. The proposal embodied several innovative concepts and proposals; it also had two controversial issues—retention of the city's nonpartisan electoral system, and whether to retain the small council elected at large.   J

2393. Rehfuss, John. SYMBOLISM, STERILITY AND REORGANIZATION: THE U.S. EXPERIENCE IN ADMINISTRATIVE AND URBAN CONSOLIDATION. *Philippine J. of Public Administration 1974 18(3): 208-214.* An evaluation of the actual impact of political or administrative change, specifically, on human behavior, remains a neglected area. The United States' experience in urban consolidation and administrative reorganization seems to typify a situation whereby the amorphism "the more things change, the more they stay the same" holds true. Apparently, failure to effect long-term behavior change within the organization renders reorganization a politically sterile venture and often, a mere symbolic victory.   J

2394. Reschovsky, Andrew and Knaff, Eugene. TAX BASE SHARING: AN ASSESSMENT OF THE MINNESOTA EXPERIENCE. *J. of the Am. Inst. of Planners 1977 43(4): 361-370.* In 1971 Minnesota enacted tax base sharing legislation designed to share a proportion of all commercial-industrial growth occurring within the Twin Cities metropolitan area among all local governments in the area. In addition to reducing the inequities caused by the existing distribution of resources within the metropolitan area, the tax base sharing plan is designed to stimulate a more efficient and rational pattern of metropolitan area development. The article describes how the plan works and assesses its first years of operation.   J

2395. Salins, Peter D. IS THERE A METRO GOVERNMENT IN NEW YORK'S FUTURE? *New York Affairs 1976 3(3): 53-65.* Metropolitan government promises to correct fiscal disparities, remove government inefficiency and promote racial balance. But a metro system might not be able to accomplish very much in the New York region.   J

2396.   Savas, E. S.   THE BUDGET AND THE PERFORMANCE GAP.   *New York Affairs 1975 3(1): 112-119.* Discusses how New York City can use its current fiscal crisis to reform shortcomings in the management of city government.   S

2397.   Savitch, H. V.   NEW YORK'S CRISES AND THE POLITICS OF CHARTER REVISION.   *New York Affairs 1976 3(2): 68-79.* The proposals revising the city charter, voted on in 1975, addressed traditional problems of city government structure and offered traditional solutions, barely touching the grave crises that produce daily headlines.   J

2398.   Schneider, Mark.   GOVERNMENTAL ORGANIZATION: REGIONAL EVOLUTION.   *New York Affairs 1978 5(2): 206-222.* Regional government cooperation (most often between city and county governments) in the New York City area, 1970's, while presently confined to special functions will develop only through slow evolution.

2399.   Scott, Thomas M.   IMPLICATIONS OF SUBURBANIZATION FOR METROPOLITAN POLITICAL ORGANIZATION. *Ann. of the Am. Acad. of Pol. and Social Sci. 1975 422: 36-44.* The development of politically independent suburbs began in earnest at the turn of the 20th century, but their role in the metropolitan governmental complex is still being established. Efforts to consolidate and otherwise integrate fragmented local governments through massive political reorganization in the 1950's and early 1960's were essentially unsuccessful. In the meantime, other less grandiose devices for achieving a measure of metropolitan governmental coordination have flourished: special districts, shifting particular functions from municipalities to other larger scale governments, and inter-local agreements. The evidence is increasingly clear that suburbs persist because they provide life-style opportunities that are important to a large part of the populace but are not otherwise available through urban political institutions. Suburbs are increasingly beset, however, by the same kinds of local governmental problems that have long afflicted central cities, and their political independence does make long-term metropolitan planning and coordination very difficult. Major governmental reorganization of the metropolis does not seem likely, and recent changes in federal and state policies are modifying suburban political autonomy.   J

2400.   Stewart, D. Michael.   LOCAL GOVERNMENT MODERNIZATION: REFLECTIONS ON SALT LAKE CITY-COUNTY. *Natl. Civic Rev. 1977 66(6): 291-299.* The recent proposal to consolidate the governments of Salt Lake City and County was defeated by the voters . . . Lack of funding to inform the electorate of the wide-ranging proposals, as well as a fairly complex plan, were among the major reasons for the defeat .   J

2401.   Tropp, Peter.   GOVERNORS' AND MAYORS' OFFICES: THE ROLE OF THE STAFF.   *Natl. Civic Rev. 1974 63(5): 242-249.* The inadequacies and failure of state and local governments are usually attributed to many forces within and some outside the control of the individual unit. These are important, but the working structure and personality of the staff in the chief executive's office are also major factors affecting the performance of the government.   J

2402.   Unsigned.   TWO SKEPTICS VIEW POLITICAL DECENTRALIZATION.   *New York Affairs 1974 1(4): 102-124.*
Ravitch, Diane.   THE RHETORIC OF DECENTRALIZATION, pp. 103-110.
Macchiarola, Frank J.   DECENTRALIZATION—THE RIGHT ANSWER TO THE WRONG QUESTIONS?, pp. 111-124.   Decentralization of New York City government has been widely touted as the solution to the city's problems. Decentralization is likely to make things worse, not better.   J

2403.   Villanueva, A. B.   POLITICS AND REFORM IN THE TWIN CITIES METROPOLITAN AREA.   *Am. Pol. Q. 1976 4(2): 247-256.* In regions in the United States where urban sprawl has created a megalopolis (New York City to Washington, D. C.) the Twin Cities Metropolitan Council form of government will be inapplicable. Even

though some feel that such metropolitan reform is reproducible in urban areas, a consensus to reorganize must exist. The problems of the megalopolis are unique and therefore the governmental mechanism dealing with these problems needs to be similarly unique.   P. Travis

2404.   Walker, David B. and Stenberg, Carl W.   A SUBSTATE DISTRICTING STRATEGY.   *Natl. Civic Rev. 1974 63(1): 5-9.* Rising needs and expectations accompanying urbanization and rapid technological change have produced major challenges to the viability of local government. Many functions are now performed wholly or partially on a multijurisdictional basis. Effective solutions to public service problems require a geographic base, organizational structure and fiscal capacity surpassing that of many cities and towns.   J

2405.   Warren, Charles R. and Campbell, Alan K.   NEW HOPE FOR METROPOLITAN GOVERNMENT.   *New York Affairs 1976 3(3): 3-14.* Regional government has long been peddled unsuccessfully by good-government groups as the solution to local government inefficiency and unresponsiveness. But new perceptions of urban problems have brought the idea into the broader arena of public discourse.   J

2406.   Weise, R. Eric.   MUNICIPAL GOVERNMENT AND PUBLIC SERVICE.   *Natl. Civic Rev. 1974 63(8): 416-420.* Municipal voters need to be resold on the merits, accomplishments, and processes of local government as an effective servant of the community.   J

2407.   White, Allen L. and Mercer, James L.   ENDING THE SERVICE IMPASSE: DELIVERY IN ATLANTA/FULTON COUNTY. *Natl. Civic Rev. 1978 67(8): 362-367.* In 1977 a blue-ribbon study commission was appointed by the governor of Georgia to study the provision of government services in Atlanta/Fulton County. The county emerged as a full-service urban government by 1976. Atlanta charged fiscal inequities through double taxation; the county made counter-accusations. The commission found some workable solutions.   J

2408.   White, Anthony G.   DIFFERENTIAL PROPERTY TAXATION IN CONSOLIDATED CITY-COUNTIES.   *Natl. Civic Rev. 1974 63(6): 301-305.* Differential property taxation emphasizes a swing away from ability to pay as measured by property wealth and is an adequate transition until uniform services can be developed. City-county consolidation has been the vehicle through which such taxation has gained a measure of experience and legitimacy.   J

2409.   Wilbern, York.   INDIANAPOLIS: CITY AND COUNTY TOGETHER.   *New York Affairs 1976 3(3): 34-44.* Indianapolis had been moving toward metropolitan reorganization long before the 1969 adoption of Unigov. Government is now more rational (and Republican), but many basic problems are yet to be resolved.   J

2410.   Wise, Jeremy A.   THE ROLES OF THE CITY MANAGER. *Natl. Civic Rev. 1973 62(6): 306-310.* Much of the literature on the council-manager plan is devoted to the manager's relations with the council on program and policy issues. But often his greatest and most undisputed power lies in his direct and indirect involvement in routine program decisions, and in his interaction with other employees, the media, the general public and other governments in addition to the council.   J

2411.   Yates, Douglas.   THE MAYOR'S EIGHT-RING CIRCUS. *New York Affairs 1979 5(3): 10-28.* Analyzes the past and possible strategies and programs of New York City mayors to decentralize urban services, 1960's-79.

2412.   Young, Dennis R.   CONSOLIDATION OR DIVERSITY: CHOICES IN THE STRUCTURE OF URBAN GOVERNANCE. *Am. Econ. Rev. 1976 66(2): 378-385.* It is possible that for a core of public services and other economic activities no satisfactory organizational solutions exist. In certain areas, economic activity is necessarily organized in an imperfect manner. Notes.   D. K. Pickens

2413.   Zarychta, Ronald M.   MUNICIPAL REORGANIZATION: THE PITTSBURGH FIRE DEPARTMENT AS A CASE STUDY. *Western Pennsylvania Hist. Mag. 1975 58(4): 471-487.* Examines the reorganization of local government brought by increasing urbanization

that resulted in the formation of a professional fire department in 1970.
S

2414. Zimmerman, Joseph F. THE METROPOLITAN AREA PROBLEM. *Ann. of the Am. Acad. of Pol. and Social Sci. 1974 416: 133-147.* Intergovernmental service agreements, transfer of functional responsibility to the county and state levels, establishment of regional special districts and state-controlled public authorities, and federal pre-emption during the past fifteen years have combined to effect major changes in the metropolitan governance system. The failure of charters creating area-wide governments to win voter approval and the growing seriousness of metropolitan problems have been responsible for state and federal initiatives seeking solutions for the problems. The most important state initiatives have been the establishment of the Twin Cities Metropolitan Council and the creation of state-controlled public authorities in New York. The federal initiative has taken the form of promotion of interlocal cooperation and exercise of preemptive powers. Whereas interlocal cooperation has failed to solve the major problems of the metropolis, partial federal preemption of the right to regulate air and water pollution abatement has enhanced the quality of the environment.
J

2415. Zimmerman, Joseph F. MUNICIPAL CODES OF ETHICS: A COMMENTARY. *Natl. Civic Rev. 1975 64(11): 577-580, 611.* A relatively large number of statutes has been enacted over the years to promote public integrity by ensuring that private interests do not benefit unfairly from the operations of government. In recent years emphasis has been placed on legislatively enacted codes. Since 1970 in New York State every city, county, school district, village and town has been required to adopt and file such a code with the state Department of Audit and Control.
J

Parties and Politicians

2416. Borowiec, Walter A. PERCEPTIONS OF ETHNIC VOTERS BY ETHNIC POLITICIANS. *Ethnicity 1974 1(3): 267-278.* Investigates attitudes of ethnic political leaders, their perception of the responsiveness of group members to ethnic stimuli, and the effect of class and generation on those perceptions. Employed a sample of 83 in Buffalo, New York. Findings revealed their stress on a candidate's nationality and party label. Controlling for education and generation still showed that the assimilation of political leaders did not lead them to view voters in non-ethnic terms, thus affecting the political choices presented to voters. 4 tables, 21 notes.
E. Barkan

2417. Busch, Ronald J. and Abravanel, Martin D. THE URBAN PARTY ORGANIZATION AS AN OPPORTUNITY STRUCTURE: RACE AND PARTY DIFFERENCES AMONG CLEVELAND WARD LEADERS. *Western Pol. Q. 1976 29(1): 59-85.* Viewing the political party as an opportunity structure, this study examines race and party differences among ward leaders in a major American city. When communications patterns, recruitment incentives, and retention incentives are examined, race and party differences in basic political orientations emerge. The findings suggest that black ward leaders tend to be more constituency oriented while white ward leaders tend to be more leader oriented. Moreover, the party differences indicate that minority party durability may be influenced by incentives originating in other political jurisdictions. These findings further suggest that black ward leaders, like their white ethnic predecessors, may use the party as a vehicle for upward mobility, especially when the opportunities in the private sector are limited. In addition to the party differences, so often identified in this genre of literature, then, race of the ward leader furthers our understanding of the incentives underlying partisan involvement in an urban setting.
J

2418. Clark, Cal; Clark, Janet; and Karnig, Albert K. VOTING BEHAVIOR OF CHICAGO DEMOCRATS AT THE ILLINOIS CONSTITUTIONAL CONVENTION: MACHINE UNITY AND DISUNITY. *Am. Pol. Q. 1978 6(3): 325-344.* Most urban political machines have run aground due to improved economic conditions, reduced immigration, expansion of state-federal welfare programs, and the adoption of municipal reforms. One model of urban machine is the retention of power by a fairly small group of politicians; this model pictures

the relationship between machine politician and city dweller as one of more manipulation than representation. In contrast a second model "argues that the representation role of machine has generally been understated." These competing models are tested by data from the 1970 Illinois Constitutional Convention. The Chicago machine constituted a distinct voting group at the Convention. The Chicago delegation exhibited the highest degree of roll-call voting solidarity, but was marked by the greatest heterogeneity in ethnic composition. 3 tables, 6 notes, ref.
E. P. Stickney

2419. Dutton, William H. and Northrop, Alana. MUNICIPAL REFORM AND THE CHANGING PATTERN OF URBAN PARTY POLITICS. *Am. Pol. Q. 1978 6(4): 429-452.* Discusses the contribution of municipal reform structure to the decline of old-style party politics and to the rise of group politics. Explanations for the historical coincidence of municipal reform and trends in party politics are: 1) municipal reform, 2) national reform, 3) ethos, and 4) socioeconomic and regional hypotheses; the fifth reform offers the counterargument that the old-style party politics has been maintained in many local governments. Evaluates the different positions in the above debates. Of US cities with more than 50,000 people, 50% are reformed governments, 39% mixed, and 11% unreformed. One or both parties remain influential in more than one-third of reformed cities. Northeastern cities are the most likely to be characterized by party politics. 4 tables, 11 notes. ref.
E. P. Stickney

2420. Elliot, Jeffrey M. THE DYNAMICS OF BLACK LOCAL POLITICS: AN INTERVIEW WITH GILBERT LINDSAY. *Negro Hist. Bull. 1977 40(4): 718-720.* Los Angeles's first black councilman, now a 15-year veteran on the council, discusses his youth in Mississippi and the Army, how he worked his way into politics, and his career as a councilman. By making other councilmen come to him when they needed his vote, by working hard for his district and keeping himself visible to his voters, and by acting not as a black councilman, but as a representative of all his constituents, Gilbert Lindsay has attained a powerful position in Los Angeles politics. Photo.
R. E. Noble

2421. Friedman, Robert. PIRATES AND POLITICIANS: SINKING ON THE SAME SHIP. *Working Papers for a New Soc. 1976 4(1): 45, 52-56.* Presents personal experiences of Barry Feinstein, a union boss, and policemen Richie Galgano and Frank Bruno during New York City's fiscal crisis of 1975.

2422. Giroux, Henry A. THE STRUGGLE TO SAVE THE CITIES. *Massachusetts Rev. 1977 18(2): 325-332.* Basically prompted by *The Mayor's Man* by Barry Gottehrer, an example of the "new liberalism" among politicians in large cities in the 1960's. Gottehrer was executive assistant to Mayor John V. Lindsay of New York City, 1966-71. The story is a paradigm of the ambivalence of liberal politics. Lindsay and Gottehrer realize and are appalled by the problems of the poor and minorities, but they cannot bring themselves to antagonize their upper-class supporters by enforcing solutions to injustice. Note.
E. R. Campbell

2423. Green, Kenneth R. RACE, PARTY, AND CONSTITUENCY IN A LOCAL LEGISLATURE. *Social Sci. Q. 1975 56(3): 492-501.* A bloc analysis was undertaken of split votes on the Cleveland City Council during 1970-71. The data indicate that the most important determinant of black council members' votes was pressure for racial solidarity and that on issues on which the black mayor, Carl Stokes, took a strong public stand, racial divisions on the council intensified.
J

2424. Jeansonne, Glen. DE LESSEPS MORRISON: WHY HE COULDN'T BECOME GOVERNOR OF LOUISIANA. *Louisiana Hist. 1973 14(3): 255-270.* Through personal shortcomings and political misorganization, deLesseps S. Morrison, though a successful and strong mayor of New Orleans for four terms, was unable to parlay himself into the governor's mansion, 1955-61.

2425. Johnston, Michael. PATRONS AND CLIENTS, JOBS AND MACHINES: A CASE STUDY OF THE USES OF PATRONAGE. *Am. Pol. Sci. Rev. 1979 73(2): 385-398.* Studies the distribution of 675 CETA Title I jobs within a New Haven machine. Data suggest that the jobs were used as patronage, but that patronage allocations did not follow conventionally assumed patterns of organization maintenance. Ethnic particularism overshadowed, and in fact redefined, considerations of vote-maximization and recruitment of workers. Questionnaire data suggest that those hired were not highly active politically, either before or after hiring, a finding contrary to normal suppositions about patronage recipients. The seemingly anomalous (and perhaps even counterproductive) patronage allocations become understandable, however, viewed in light of some problems and contradictions inherent in patron-client politics. These involve the inflexibility of job-based incentive systems, qualifications on assumptions of reciprocity, and the "aging" of the organization.   J

2426. Kaufman, Herbert. ROBERT MOSES: CHARISMATIC BUREAUCRAT. *Pol. Sci. Q. 1975 90(3): 521-538.* Critically reviews Robert Caro's huge Pulitzer Prize winning biography of Robert Moses, *The Power Broker: Robert Moses and the fall of New York.* Speculates that if Robert Moses was as power hungry a bureaucratic politician as he is painted, he may well be pleased with the book despite the many harsh things it says about him. Caro overestimates Moses's influence, attributing to him developments that might have taken place in any event and discounting some of Moses's major defeats.   J/S

2427. Lee, Robert D., Jr. DIFFERENCES BETWEEN SUBURBAN REPUBLICANS AND DEMOCRATS. *Policy and Pol. [Great Britain] 1974 3(1): 51-59.* Analyzes the political attitudes of whites (particularly those living in suburbs) belonging to the Republican and Democratic Parties in 1972 in Bucks County, Pennsylvania.

2428. Lemon, J. T. OF POWER AND CONTEMPTUOUSNESS. *Can. Rev. of Am. Studies 1976 7(1): 88-92.* Review article prompted by Robert A. Caro's *The Power Broker: Robert Moses and the Fall of New York* (New York: Alfred A. Knopf, 1974). Caro portrays Moses (b. 1888) as a ruthless Tammany Hall leader who lusted for power; he achieved his ends but ultimately did New York City a grave disservice by losing control of the "hidden power" of the city's great bankers.
                                                          H. T. Lovin

2429. Levine, Charles H. and Kaufman, Clifford. URBAN CONFLICT AS A CONSTRAINT ON MAYORAL LEADERSHIP: LESSONS FROM GARY AND CLEVELAND. *Am. Pol. Q. 1974 2(1): 78-106.*

2430. Nelson, William E., Jr. BLACK MAYORS AS URBAN MANAGERS. *Ann. of the Am. Acad. of Pol. and Social Sci. 1978 (439): 53-67.* Black mayors face problems that are fundamentally different from those faced by white mayors because they must contend with constraints on their capacity for leadership not common to big city majors generally. The heart of their dilemma is that they are, on the one hand, pressured by expectations of high performance, but on the other, handicapped in their ability to live up to these expectations by social, economic, and political factors that rob them of the resources and power they need to be successful in their roles. This paper examines the implications of this dilemma for effective black mayoral leadership. Suggestions are made for steps that might be taken to strengthen the leadership role of black mayors.

2431. Perkins, Jerry. BASES OF PARTISAN CLEAVAGE IN A SOUTHERN URBAN COUNTY. *J. of Pol. 1974 36(1): 208-214.* Confirms the view that high status and conservatism lead to loyalty to the Republican Party among urban white southerners. In making this identity, the southerners are following a national trend. Based on data from DeKalb County, Georgia, in 1970; 5 tables, 12 notes.
                                                          A. R. Stoesen

2432. Porter, Jack Nusan. A NAZI RUNS FOR MAYOR: DANGEROUS BROWNSHIRTS OR MEDIA FREAKS? *Present Tense 1977 4(4): 27-31.* Discusses the resurgence of Matt Koehl's National Socialist White People's Party. Traces the Party's activities during 1974-76 in Milwaukee, Wisconsin. Examines the political repercussions and the split in the Jewish community. Analyzes Jewish reactions: the activist-confrontationists vs. the minimalists. Primary and secondary sources; 4 photos.   R. B. Mendel

2433. Protess, David L. BANFIELD'S CHICAGO REVISITED: THE CONDITIONS FOR AND SOCIAL POLICY IMPLICATIONS

OF THE TRANSFORMATION OF A POLITICAL MACHINE. *Social Service Rev. 1974 48(2): 184-202.*

2434. Unsigned. ECONOMIC ANALYSIS AND METROPOLITAN ORGANIZATION. *J. of the Am. Inst. of Planners 1973 39(6): 402-412.*
Heikoff, Joseph M. ECONOMIC ANALYSIS AND METROPOLITAN ORGANIZATION, *pp. 402-407.*
Bish, Robert L. COMMENTARY, *pp. 403, 407-412.* Offers two viewpoints on fiscal policy at the local government levels (1970's).
                                                          S

2435. Villanueva, A. B. LEGISLATIVE BEHAVIOR AND GOVERNMENTAL STRUCTURE: A ROLL CALL VOTE ANALYSIS OF THE FARGO CITY COMMISSION. *North Dakota Q. 1976 44(4): 86-91.* Discusses a methodological procedure, roll-call vote analysis, for analyzing the issues which divide local voting bodies; uses Fargo, North Dakota, City Commission roll-call votes, 1964-67, as a case study.

2436. Weinberg, Lee S. STABILITY AND CHANGE AMONG PITTSBURGH PRECINCT POLITICIANS, 1954-1970. *Social Sci. 1975 50(1): 10-16.* A 1970 statistical survey reveals the only significant change since 1954 in precinct politicians is their rising age; therefore, political parties must attract young political activists.   S

2437. Welch, Susan and Karnig, Albert K. CORRELATES OF FEMALE OFFICE HOLDING IN CITY POLITICS. *J. of Pol. 1979 41(2): 478-491.* City councils and mayoral seats in 264 American cities with populations over 25,000 were examined in 1978 to determine characteristics promoting female office holding. There has been a modest advance in female election to city councils since 1975. There remained no councilwomen in 104 of the cities, and only 6% had a female mayor. (Blacks, while also underrepresented in their communities, had obtained three times as equitable a numerical representation as had women). In contrast to ethnic minorities, women are less apt to become mayors under elective than appointive systems. Women were more successful in competing for less desirable council seats and offices where the salary is lower. Larger, wealthier communities with smaller proportions of homeowners were most prone to elect female council members. Still larger communities were more prone to elect female mayors as well. 3 tables, 23 notes.
                                                          A. W. Novitsky

2438. Whitehead, Ralph, Jr. THE ORGANIZATION MAN. *Am. Scholar 1977 46(3): 351-357.* Studies Richard J. Daley as big-city Democratic Party machine boss; investigates his methods and his values. The Chicago Democratic machine, under his leadership, became a powerful instrument not only in politics, but also in the economic development of the city. All of this came, not by promoting his own self-image, but by unflagging attention to the Organization, its personnel, patronage, and loyalty at every level. Although this was sometimes at the price of moral values, there was a grass roots immediacy about his presence.
                                                          R. V. Ritter

2439. Yates, Douglas. THE URBAN JIGSAW PUZZLE: NEW YORK UNDER LINDSAY. *New York Affairs 1974 2(2): 3-19.* John Lindsay's political reform policies while mayor of New York City damaged his political future, for when his hopes for the city collapsed so did his political authority.   S

Citizen Participation, Community Control, and the Distribution of Power

2440. Crenson, Matthew. ORGANIZATIONAL FACTORS IN CITIZEN PARTICIPATION. *J. of Pol. 1974 36(2): 356-378.* Examines seven citizen participatory groups in Baltimore 1969-70 to determine the effectiveness of political activity by the poor under public and private efforts to create "maximum feasible participation." While most of the difficulties that would afflict these programs were anticipated, their short life span was not. Mobilization of the poor by government for political action was "illogical." The government organized an assault on itself. This study also demonstrates that social isolation and political nonparticipation of the poor are not significant disabilities. The major organizational problems in Baltimore came from "intense organizational conflict" symptomatic of conditions existing prior to the effort to stimulate political activity among the poor. 4 tables, 17 notes. A. R. Stoesen

2441. Downs, Anthony. CITIZEN PARTICIPATION IN COMMUNITY DEVELOPMENT: WHY SOME CHANGES ARE NEEDED. *Natl. Civic Rev. 1975 64(5): 238-248.* Every community seeking funds under the Housing and Community Development Act of 1974 has created some type of "citizen participation" arrangements. Most of these will be adequate to help gain approval of first-year applications, but many will probably prove ineffective in the long run for accomplishing certain key goals of the program. J

2442. Eisinger, Peter K. SUPPORT FOR URBAN CONTROL-SHARING AT THE MASS LEVEL. *Am. J. of Pol. Sci. 1973 17(4): 669-694.* Observers of the movement for community control, or more properly, control-sharing reforms, in American cities have assumed that the demand for such arrangements is primarily a black demand and that support within the black community is high. Using survey data collected in the city of Milwaukee, this article attempts to determine the degree to which blacks and whites at the mass level understand the notion of control-sharing; the extent to which there exists mass demand and support for such arrangements and the nature and focus of that support; and finally the degree to which variation exists in these areas along class and racial lines. Standard expectations about the level of support in the black community are not borne out. The evidence suggests that the demand for control-sharing is primarily an elite demand without a significant mass base. J

2443. Fainstein, Norman I. and Fainstein, Susan S. THE FUTURE OF COMMUNITY CONTROL. *Am. Pol. Sci. Rev. 1976 70(3): 905-923.* The nature of community control ideology, its relation to more general political consciousness, and its social correlates are explored. The primary data are drawn from a survey of the attitudes of 362 civil and political leaders in seven districts of New York City conducted in 1972, intensive participant observation in three of these districts during 1973-74, and interviews with individuals in district-level voluntary organizations, interest groups, political parties, poverty boards and agencies, and "street-level" bureaucratic roles. The great majority of leaders subscribes to a democratic rather than a race-conflict rationale for community control, but that there is a strong independent relationship between minority group status and operational support for community control. Possible explanations for this finding include the present interests of minority groups in American cities, the functional inadequacies of the political party structure, and the developmental history of the civil rights movement and its ideology. The relationship between race and community control may fade, however, if community control ceases to be a useful vehicle for advancing the interests of minority groups. The data point to a continuing attachment to the community control ideology but also a recasting of it in a more qualified and complex form. J/S

2444. Fainstein, Norman I. and Martin, Mark. SUPPORT FOR COMMUNITY CONTROL AMONG LOCAL URBAN ELITES. *Urban Affairs 1978 13(4): 443-468.* Several distinctive, even contradictory motivations are used to justify administrative decentralization. Because of its political structure and ethnic characteristics New York City is an ideal locale for the study of local elites' community control attitudes. Based on surveys and intensive interviews with 201 individuals in 1974, of whom 151 had been analyzed in 1972, the authors conclude that local elites favor administrative devolution. Furthermore, decentralization has become increasingly popular among both minority groups and whites. The data suggest that the minority group liberation motivation for community control is waning while the conservative desire to protect the community from outside intrusion, including racial, is growing. 2 tables, 2 notes, biblio., appendix. L. N. Beecher

2445. Fischer, Claude S. THE CITY AND POLITICAL PSYCHOLOGY. *Am. Pol. Sci. Rev. 1975 69(2): 559-571.* Alternative theories—"social mobilization" and "urban anomie"—predict different relationships between urbanism and political involvement, i.e., that urbanism stimulates, or that urbanism alienates individuals. This study examines these theories using the 1968 Michigan Survey Research Center election survey. Overall, the results show little independent association between the urban variables and involvement. Trends indicate that large-

ness may have slight mobilizing effects even though it also slightly reduces sense of political efficacy, and that the mobilization is a shift in involvement from local to national politics. J

2446. Geist, Richard. THE WRECK OF THE ROCKAWAYS. *New York Affairs 1974 2(2): 90-103.* Politicians, administrators and journalists throughout the United States have questioned why it is that people feel so 'alienated' from government. A review of the city's misdeeds and inaction in a New York City resort community makes the answers obvious. J

2447. Hamilton, Charles V. THE PATRON-RECIPIENT RELATIONSHIP AND MINORITY POLITICS IN NEW YORK CITY. *Pol. Sci. Q. 1979 94(2): 211-227.* Suggests that the antipoverty programs of the 1960's in New York City rather than politicizing the black poor, actually produced a patron-recipient relationship that kept them depoliticized. J

2448. Heiss, F. William. THE DENVER REGIONAL STUDY: AN EXPERIMENT IN REORGANIZATION. *Natl. Civic. Rev. 1978 67(9): 407-413.* Governmental responsiveness requires participation in decisionmaking. Neighborhood decentralization is intended to grant greater resource power to citizens and to recognize differing local needs in delivering public services. J

2449. Jones, Mack H. BLACK POLITICAL EMPOWERMENT IN ATLANTA: MYTH AND REALITY. *Ann. of the Am. Acad. of Pol. and Social Sci. 1978 (439): 90-117.* Develops a theoretical framework for understanding black politics and assessing black power in America. The distinguishing characteristic of black political life in the subordination of blacks by whites and the concomitant institutionalized belief that white domination is a function of the inherent superiority of whites. Given this as a frame of reference, the evolution of black political power in Atlanta is traced. The discussion is divided into two periods, the first beginning in 1965 and extending to 1973, when Atlanta elected its first black mayor, Maynard Jackson, and the second covering the first four years of the latter's incumbency. J

2450. Levi, Margaret. POOR PEOPLE AGAINST THE STATE. *Rev. of Radical Pol. Econ. 1974 6(1): 76-98.* In the 1960's political organizations of the urban poor proliferated. The history of groups such as JOIN Community Union in Chicago, the South End Tenants Council in Boston, the National Welfare Rights Organization, and prisoners' associations, challenged bourgeois notions that the poor are incapable of sustained collective action. The state response to such pressure, ranging from minor concession to violent repression, teaches the poor the value of organization and reveals to them the social control practiced by state agencies. 22 notes. P. R. Shergold

2451. McManus, Michael J. CREATING 20TH CENTURY TOWN MEETINGS. *Natl. Civic Rev. 1975 64(1): 9-13.* Town meetings on specific issues have successfully operated in several large cities. S

2452. Miller, Michael V. and Preston, James D. VERTICAL TIES AND THE REDISTRIBUTION OF POWER IN CRYSTAL CITY. *Social Sci. Q. 1973 53(4): 772-784.* Notes how the introduction of extra-community resources and sanctions tended to disrupt the prevailing power structure, offering support for the proposition that the impingement of vertical ties contributes to a more pluralistic power structure. J

2453. Moberg, David. CHICAGO'S ORGANIZERS LEARN THE LESSONS OF CAP. *Working Papers for a New Soc. 1977 5(2): 14-19.* Discusses the failure of Chicago's Citizens Action Program (CAP), 1975-76, the first citywide coalition of neighborhood groups.

2454. Penn, Robert C. CENTRAL CITIES IN CRISIS. *Afro-Americans in New York Life and Hist. 1977 1(1): 93-98.* Discusses the rising political consciousness of central city residents throughout New York state, 1970's.

2455. Perrotta, John A. MACHINE INFLUENCE ON A COMMUNITY ACTION PROGRAM: THE CASE OF PROVIDENCE, RHODE ISLAND. *Polity 1977 9(4): 481-502.* The alleged absence of participation by low-income groups and minorities in the decisionmaking process has been a major argument against community power studies of the pluralist variety. Perrotta examines the theses of the pluralists and their critics through his case study of the Community Action Program in Providence from 1965 to 1969. He finds that members of minority groups, particularly blacks, were able to broaden their power base through the federally sponsored CAP against the centralized political structure of the city. His study provides no evidence that deprived groups are excluded from the decisionmaking process in Providence.   J

2456. Protess, David L. and Gitelson, Alan R. POLITICAL STABILITY AND URBAN REFORM CLUB ACTIVISM. *Polity 1978 10(4): 524-541.* Few political constructs have evoked more widespread discussion and application than James Q. Wilson's concept of the "Amateur Democrat." Using a sample of reform club activists in Chicago, the authors critically examine the validity of the concept itself as well as the means by which Chicago's reform club movement has managed to maintain and enhance its organizational interests in an environment of increasingly entrenched machine politics. Wilson's criteria are in need of modification. As for organizational motivations and development, they conclude that the best explanation for people's joining reform clubs can be provided in terms of the "logic of utility."   J

2457. Shore, William B. *CHOICES FOR '76*: THE RESULTS AND THE LESSONS. *Natl. Civic Rev. 1975 64(1): 6-8, 20.* Choices for '76, televised town meetings in New York, proved that such meetings create feasible means for involving citizens in urban decisionmaking.   S

2458. Singer, Grace L. CITIZENS DEFEND THE URBAN COAST. *Bull. of the Atomic Scientists 1979 35(6): 47-52.* Alarmed at growing unemployment coupled with urban and environmental degeneration, citizens' groups in Hudson County, New Jersey, formed a coalition which successfully fought the installation of proposed energy and industrial facilities, 1972-78.

2459. Stowe, Mary E. AN INTEGRATIVE FORCE: ARLINGTON'S COMMITTEE OF 100. *Natl. Civic Rev. 1976 65(5): 229-235.* Every month since 1954, the Committee of 100, an influential organization of businessmen, civic leaders and government officials representing all the principal points of view in urban-suburban Arlington County, has been proving that there can be a constructive approach to controversial issues. And it does it without taking stands, introducing motions or seeking votes.   J

2460. Unsigned. ADMINISTRATIVE DECENTRALIZATION AND NEIGHBORHOOD GOVERNMENT: THE NEW YORK CITY EXPERIENCE. *Publius 1976 6(4): 111-152.*
Mudd, John. BEYOND COMMUNITY CONTROL: A NEIGHBORHOOD STRATEGY FOR CITY GOVERNMENT, *pp. 113-135.* Discusses New York City's attempts at urban decentralization through the Office of Neighborhood Government, 1970-76, and analyzes prospects for other cities.
Walker, David. THE PROSPECTS FOR ADMINISTRATIVE DECENTRALIZATION IN OUR CITIES, *pp. 137-139.* Civil service systems, professionalization, merit systems and technical factors, and the awareness of local political history are centralizing factors which must be overcome.
Green, Gerson. ADMINISTRATIVE DECENTRALIZATION: A PREMATURE STEP BEYOND COMMUNITY CONTROL, *pp. 141-143.* Citizen participation in decentralization movements is necessary.
Hawkins, Robert B. ADMINISTRATION MUST NOT SUPPLANT POLITICS IN NEIGHBORHOOD GOVERNMENT, *pp. 145-147.* Administrative rather than political reforms are inherently dangerous.
Mudd, John. A RESPONSE TO WALKER, GREEN AND HAWKINS, *pp. 149-152.* Discusses charges that community control was undervalued in his essay, and the political, economic, and technological forces which hamper political and administrative decentralization.

2461. Unsigned. ALL-AMERICA CITIES IN DENVER: WHAT'S ON PEOPLES' MINDS? *Natl. Civic Rev. 1978 67(1): 4-9, 18.* Discusses issues and opinions expressed at the National Municipal League's

National Conference on Government held in Denver in 1977 with more than 200 representatives from finalist communities in the All-America Cities award program. Covers general conference sessions and workshops. The conference made clear "the value of understanding the interlocking elements in the community problem solving process." Workshops probed questions regarding the most effective structure and organization to achieve city goals, the problems apparent in achieving satisfactory media coverage, how to evaluate effectiveness of citizen involvement processes, and how to improve citizenship training in the schools.
R. V. Ritter

2462. Unsigned. THE CITIZENS LEAGUE: REPORT ON ITS ACHIEVEMENT OF A RECORD OF CUMULATIVE EFFECTIVENESS IN THE TWIN CITIES AREA. *Natl. Civic Rev. 1976 65(7): 322-342.* Summarizes the briefing session on the history, organization, methods and programs of the Citizens League, held in Minneapolis last spring. Citizens from 18 urban regions heard how the league, a private-sector institution, performs the critically important role of helping the metropolitan community understand what its problems are and what ought to be done about them.   J

2463. Unsigned. [DILEMMAS OF COMMUNITY ORGANIZING: MISSION HILLS IN BOSTON]. *Social Policy 1978 9(1): 41-52.*
Hartman, Chester. THE CONTEXT, *pp. 41-42.* Introduces the main points in two previous articles, Howard Waitzkin's "What to Do When Your Local Medical Center Tries to Tear Down Your Home" in *Science for the People,* March-April 1977, and Waitzkin and John A. Sharratt's "Controlling Medical Expansion" in *Society,* January-February 1977.
Grady, John and Ploss, Charlotte. THE COMPROMISE, *pp. 43-48.* Community groups during 1964-77 within Boston's Mission Hill working class neighborhood fought the expansion of the Harvard University Affiliated Hospitals Center at the expense of local housing. Though understanding was reached, further political action based on community mobilization (in the form of industrial unionism) would transgress the understanding between the community and the university.
Waitzkin, Howard. A REPLY, *pp. 49-52.* Disputes certain statements and assessments, especially pertaining to current attitudes within the Roxbury Tenants of Harvard Association and the general atmosphere of "demoralization" described.

2464. Wellstone, Paul D. NOTES ON COMMUNITY ORGANIZING. *J. of Ethnic Studies 1976 4(2): 73-89.* Review article prompted by John Hall Fish's *Black Power/White Control: The Struggle of the Woodlawn Organization in Chicago,* which is called "an important work," although with several weaknesses. While focusing on TWO (Temporary Woodlawn Organization) and its work, we are not given details of its people and their goals, either personal or political. Secondly, in supporting the Alinsky critique of the "medical" approach to ghetto problems, Fish remains ambivalent on the relationships between the TWO organizers and the rank-and-file membership, and we are not sure how, for what, and by whom decisions are made. Wellstone previews his own forthcoming book, *Organization for a Better Rice County* (OBRC) detailing his work with this poor people's group in Minnesota and the "dramatic change in political consciousness among the poor," which disproves the notion that the poor can be motivated only by material incentives. Concludes that successful organizing is "not built on self-interest but rather on expectations," and OBRC's history proves the poor will respond to purposive incentives, if only organizers will make membership education a major priority. 29 notes.
G. J. Bobango

Elections and the Electoral Process

2465. Arrington, Theodore S. PARTISAN CAMPAIGNS, BALLOTS AND VOTING PATTERNS: THE CASE OF CHARLOTTE. *Urban Affairs Q. 1978 14(2): 253-261.* During 1971-75 Charlotte, North Carolina, had a nonpartisan campaign with nonpartisan ballots (1971), a partisan campaign with nonpartisan ballots (1973), and a partisan campaign with partisan ballots (1975). Although the 1973 election revealed intensified racial voting patterns, the partisan campaign failed to change nonpartisan voting patterns. The latter phenomenon occurred only when a partisan campaign was supplemented with partisan ballots. Suggests that the Charlotte experience, not the partisan voting of Chicago, is typical of American municipal elections. 3 tables, biblio.

L. N. Beecher

2466. Blume, Norman. CHOOSING MAYORS IN OHIO: SOME DETERMINING FACTORS. *Natl. Civic Rev. 1977 66(8): 402-404, 423.* A survey focusing on mayoral selection and behavior was taken in five northwest Ohio counties. Community size was the major independent variable. Results: the larger the community the more politicized and the more likely to fit the "middle class" model of success the person chosen as mayor.

J

2467. Cho, Yong Hyo. CITY POLITICS AND RACIAL POLARIZATION: BLOC VOTING IN CLEVELAND ELECTIONS. *J. of Black Studies 1974 4(4): 396-417.* Studies racial voting blocs of 33 wards in Cleveland during 1964-71 and their influence in local elections. Though senatorial elections were influenced by racial bloc voting, gubernatorial and presidential elections were not. When elections are about issues, bloc voting, though in evidence, tends to divide. 20 notes, biblio.

K. Butcher

2468. Cole, Leonard A. ELECTING BLACKS TO MUNICIPAL OFFICE: STRUCTURAL AND SOCIAL DETERMINANTS. *Urban Affairs Q. 1974 10(1): 17-39.* Analyzes relationships between population characteristics and types of municipal government and electability of Negroes in 16 New Jersey cities. One means of analysis is equitability, the differential between percentage of black population and percentage of black elected officials. Apparently, neither a majority black electorate nor the type of government figures significantly in electing blacks. Provides political biographical sketches of four New Jersey mayors. 2 tables, 3 graphs, notes, biblio.

P. J. Woehrmann

2469. Cunningham, Robert B. and Winham, Gilbert R. COMPARATIVE URBAN VOTING BEHAVIOR: CANADA AND THE UNITED STATES. *Am. Rev. of Can. Studies 1973 3(2): 76-100.* Compares the roles of social classes, ethnicity, religion, and political party identification in the voting behavior of urban residents of Canada and the United States in elections 1952-68.

2470. Dauer, Manning J. and Maggiotto, Michael A. THE STATUS OF MULTI-MEMBER DISTRICTS IN STATE AND LOCAL GOVERNMENT. *Natl. Civic Rev. 1979 68(1): 24-27.* Multi-member or at-large districting is a common phenomenon in the United States, used to allocate seats in one or both houses of the legislature in 23 states, in half of cities over 5,000 population and in 70% of cities with the council-manager plan. Yet there is much debate over its desirability and in some cases its constitutionality.

J

2471. Gamm, Larry. VOTER EDUCATION AND PARTICIPATION: PENNSYLVANIA LOCAL REFERENDA. *Natl. Civic Rev. 1976 65(2): 75-82.* In a study of seven municipalities with local government study commissions, which voted on recommendations at a referendum, there is some evidence that in those with relatively better educated and well-to-do citizens, increasing numbers of voters over time were likely to pick up at least some very general information on the referenda issues and that they were more likely to vote on such items.

J

2472. Greeley, Andrew M. A SCRAPYARD FOR THE DALEY ORGANIZATION? *Sci. and Public Affairs 1973 29(2): 9-14.* Election "setbacks" to Chicago mayor Richard J. Daley's political organization in 1972 were overrated by liberals.

2473. Hahn, Harlan; Klingman, David; and Pachon, Harry. CLEAVAGES, COALITIONS AND THE BLACK CANDIDATE: THE LOS ANGELES MAYORALTY ELECTIONS OF 1969 AND 1973. *Western Pol. Q. 1976 29(4): 507-520.* The increasing success of black candidacies for mayor can mostly be attributed to the growth of the urban black population. In 1973, however, the election of Tom Bradley as mayor of Los Angeles raised hope for cross-racial urban coalitions. Simple and partial correlation analysis of socioeconomic data on census tracts with 1969 precinct voting data aggregated to the tract level showed that Bradley drew relatively undifferentiated support, only marginally related to

social status, from white areas. Analysis of the 1973 election revealed that the direct association between status and vote for Bradley, controlling for the effects of race, increased markedly as he became an increasingly legitimate and viable challenger to the incumbent mayor. Bradley's support was inversely associated with the percentage of Spanish ethnicity, even more so in upper-class areas. These results reassert the instability and fragility of cross-racial coalitions.

J

2474. Hain, Paul L. HOW AN ENDORSEMENT AFFECTED A NON-PARTISAN MAYORAL VOTE. *Journalism Q. 1975 52(2): 337-340.* Albuquerque adopted a nonpartisan, mayor-council form of government. In the first-round mayoral election in 1974 there were 33 candidates. Endorsement by both local daily newspapers for Mike Alarid persuaded some citizens to vote for him. The impact was primarily among the undecided. Based on telephone interviews. Primary sources; table, 12 notes.

K. J. Puffer

2475. Halley, Robert M.; Acock, Alan C.; and Greene, Thomas H. ETHNICITY AND SOCIAL CLASS: VOTING IN THE 1973 LOS ANGELES ELECTIONS. *Western Pol. Q. 1976 29(4): 521-530.* Discusses how race and social status affect voting in city elections. Confirms the importance of race in biracial elections and suggests the importance of distinguishing between ethnic groups in theories of acculturation.

J/S

2476. Hamilton, Charles V. BLACKS AND ELECTORAL POLITICS. *Social Policy 1978 9(1): 21-27.* Using examples from mayoral elections in Georgia, Michigan, California, Louisiana, New York, and Illinois, examines the black community's election of black officials to enforce their opinions and needs locally, 1970-77.

2477. Hunter, Deborah Atwater. THE AFTERMATH OF CARL STOKES: AN ANALYSIS OF POLITICAL DRAMA IN THE 1971 CLEVELAND MAYORAL CAMPAIGN. *J. of Black Studies 1978 8(3): 337-354.* Carl B. Stokes was not a candidate in the mayoral race in Cleveland, Ohio, 28 September-2 November 1971, but he was the major issue. Stokes confused his supporters by endorsing James Carney during the Democratic primary, then abruptly turning to the independent Arnold R. Pinkney, who entered the race after the primary. Although registered Democrats outnumbered Republicans 10 to one in Cleveland, Republican Ralph Perk won with an emotional campaign of personal attacks on Carney and Pinkney as being controlled by Stokes. The three major candidates' campaign styles and strategies, organizations, and positions on other issues only reemphasize Stokes' centrality. Based on newspapers and personal interviews; biblio.

R. G. Sherer

2478. Jamieson, Duncan R. MAYNARD JACKSON'S 1973 ELECTION AS MAYOR OF ATLANTA. *Midwest Q. 1976 18(1): 7-26.* The transracial voting patterns apparent in the 1973 city elections of Atlanta, Georgia, provide a model for similar urban areas. Atlanta's coalition of black and white voters dates back to the late 1940's. Maynard Jackson, unlike his main opponent Sam Massell, tried to avoid racial overtones in his campaign and concentrated instead on people-oriented issues such as crime, housing, and unemployment. An examination of the local newspapers, both black and white, showed that they mirrored the transracial support of the candidates. With the election of Maynard Jackson, Atlanta has shown the way to avoid city politics characterized by alienation and polarization. Newspapers, interviews and secondary sources; biblio.

S. J. Quinlan

2479. Jones, Clinton B. THE IMPACT OF LOCAL ELECTION SYSTEMS ON BLACK POLITICAL REPRESENTATION. *Urban Affairs Q. 1975 11(3): 345-356.* Assumes that Black Americans given the chance will vote for blacks. Concludes on the basis of a survey of 272 cities that blacks are underrepresented on city councils and that at-large elections are barriers to black representation. 4 tables, notes, biblio.

P. J. Woehrmann

2480. Karnig, Albert K. BLACK RESOURCES AND CITY COUNCIL REPRESENTATION. *J. of Pol. 1979 41(1): 134-149.* Since 1964, the black civil rights movement led to significant national victories and to state and local fair employment practices and open housing laws. In the past decade, emphasis has shifted to electoral politics. Blacks remain underrepresented on all city councils, especially in cities with at-large rather than district constituencies. The major factor is the inability of blacks to mobilize necessary resources and to compete with white ethnic groups. Table, 2 fig., 31 notes.   A. W. Novitsky

2481. Karnig, Albert K. and Walter, B. Oliver. ELECTIONS OF WOMEN TO CITY COUNCILS. *Social Sci. Q. 1976 56(4): 605-613.* Examines the candidacy, candidate success, and overall election rates for women in city council races.   J

2482. Karnig, Albert K. and Walter, B. Oliver. ELECTORAL TURNOUT IN MUNICIPAL ELECTIONS: A MULTIVARIATE ANALYSIS. *Rocky Mountain Social Sci. J. 1974 11(2): 55-71.*

2483. Karnig, Albert K. and Walter, B. Oliver. REGISTRATION AND VOTING: PUTTING FIRST THINGS SECOND. *Social Sci. Q. 1974 55(1): 159-166.* Compares the relationship between registration rates and voter turnout in presidential and in municipal elections, finding that the influence of registration on turnout is substantially greater in the former type of election, and then discusses two sets of factors—election specific and structural and environmental conditions—to help explain the differential impact of registration.   J

2484. Keller, Edmund J. ELECTORAL POLITICS IN GARY: MAYORAL PERFORMANCE, ORGANIZATION, AND THE POLITICAL ECONOMY OF THE BLACK VOTE. *Urban Affairs Q. 1979 15(1): 43-64.* Argues that most studies of black voters are based on "race voting" assumptions rather than the "rational black voter" model which underpins this study of Richard Hatcher's three consecutive election bids. Although the first depended on race voting, the others reflected superior political organization and favorable black evaluation of his performance in office. Hence organizational atrophy or a reversal of the perception of his official conduct could lead to his defeat. The sample of black voters, city officials, Hatcher, and anti-Hatcher political activists was not random and this should be considered a pilot study. 5 tables, 14 notes, biblio.   L. N. Beecher

2485. Kirlin, John J. ELECTORAL CONFLICT AND DEMOCRACY IN CITIES. *J. of Pol. 1975 37(1): 262-269.* Analysis of the city councils of 66 cities in Los Angeles County demonstrates that 73 percent of the incumbent city council candidates who sought reelection were re-elected. While the evidence relating to the defeated candidates is partial, it indicates that they were defeated on a group rather than an individual basis. 3 tables, 9 notes.   A. R. Stoesen

2486. Knoke, David and Lane, Angela. SIZE OF PLACE, MIGRATION, AND VOTING TURNOUT. *J. of Pol. and Military Sociol. 1975 3(2): 127-139.* The effects of size of place of origin, destination and year of election upon voter turnout in presidential elections were estimated on survey data from 1952-1972 using log-linear methods. A relatively simple model of additive effects of each of the three independent variables was supported. Persons raised on farms turned out less frequently than those with metropolitan backgrounds. Current central city residents and rural persons voted less often than those in intermediate-sized places. The temporal effects were not systematic, but a decline in voting rates from a peak in 1960 was observed. Neither an hypothesized "mobilization" nor "decline of community" model was supported, but speculation is offered that an "homogenization" process is at work tending to produce uniform rates of voting across communities of different size.   J

2487. Latimer, Margaret K. BLACK POLITICAL REPRESENTATION IN SOUTHERN CITIES: ELECTION SYSTEMS AND OTHER CAUSAL VARIABLES. *Urban Affairs Q. 1979 15(1): 65-86.* Notes that after consistently having large numbers of blacks and an equally consistent pattern of political discrimination, change since the Voting Rights Act (US, 1965) has been impressive. Seeks to identify and measure the variables that account for the unevenness of black representation in Alabama, Louisiana, and South Carolina city governments. Evaluates competing hypotheses and concludes that direct elections facilitates while at-large elections hamper, minority political participation; that larger governing bodies and higher percentages of black population also increase black electoral possibilities. Finally, socioeconomic variables are less important than the preceding systemic variables. 3 tables, 11 notes, biblio.   L. N. Beecher

2488. Lee, Eugene C. and Rothman, Jonathan S. SAN FRANCISCO'S DISTRICT SYSTEM ALTERS ELECTORAL POLITICS. *Natl. Civic Rev. 1978 67(4): 173-178.* In November, for the first time in this century, San Francisco voters elected their legislators by a district system. The most dramatic differences appear to be in campaigning and the role of various political groups. The implications remain a matter of speculation, and it is up to the new board to determine whether government will be more effective, representative and accountable.   J

2489. Maller, Allen S. CLASS FACTORS IN THE JEWISH VOTE. *Jewish Social Studies 1977 39(1-2): 159-162.* A study of the mayoral campaign in Los Angeles, California, in 1969 between liberal black candidate Tom Bradley and conservative Sam Yorty indicates the extent to which class factors amid the Jewish voting population are beginning to divide Jews into ascertainable subgroups. Reform rabbis and spokesmen supported Bradley in public meetings as part of their liberal commitment, while Orthodox rabbis threw their allegiance to the far more conservative Yorty. Although a majority of Los Angeles Jewish voters supported Bradley, the percentage of Bradley supporters in the most highly affluent Jewish neighborhoods was significantly higher than that in less prosperous Jewish areas. The influence of changing neighborhoods and the school desegregation issue suggests that although Jewish voting patterns are still unique, various issues affecting the well-being and personal status of Jews are having their effect on voting behavior.   N. Lederer

2490. Marando, Vincent L. VOTING IN CITY-COUNTY CONSOLIDATION REFERENDA. *Western Pol. Q. 1973 26(1): 90-96.* Analyzes the 24 city-county consolidation elections which took place during 1945-70 to determine the impact of selected economic and political factors on voter support for consolidation.   S

2491. Monroe, Alan D. URBANISM AND VOTER TURNOUT: A NOTE ON SOME UNEXPECTED FINDINGS. *Am. J. of Pol. Sci. 1977 21(1): 71-78.* Past literature has been unclear as to the relationship between urban/rural residence and voting turnout. Aggregate analysis of turnout within Illinois reveals a strong tendency for rural areas to have much higher turnout than urban. Furthermore, these rural areas have lower levels of education, income, and industrialization, so that these variables cannot account for higher turnout levels, nor can the observed patterns by accounted for by the historical pattern of political culture. Several theoretical arguments which might explain the findings are examined.   J

2492. Murray, Richard and Vedlitz, Arnold. RACE, SOCIOECONOMIC STATUS, AND VOTING PARTICIPATION IN LARGE SOUTHERN CITIES. *J. of Pol. 1977 39(4): 1064-1072.* Comparison of the voting behavior of black and white populations in Atlanta, New Orleans, Memphis, Dallas, and Houston in 73 major elections during 1960-74 reveals that blacks have now achieved near parity with whites in participation. Voting participation is strongly related to socioeconomic status among whites, but for blacks there is only an extremely modest positive relationship between the two factors. The strong black participation appears to be related to organizing campaigns during the struggle for civil rights. Primary and secondary sources; 2 tables, 10 notes.   A. W. Novitsky

2493. Murray, Richard and Vedlitz, Arnold. RACIAL VOTING PATTERNS IN THE SOUTH: AN ANALYSIS OF MAJOR ELECTIONS FROM 1960 TO 1977 IN FIVE CITIES. *Ann. of the Am. Acad. of Pol. and Social Sci. 1978 (439): 29-39.* Conflicting views have been advanced about racial voting patterns in the South. Findings indicate no consistent pattern of biracial voting exists because several factors influence voting alignments in given elections. These include the traditional patterns of racial politics in given localities; the type of election that is being contested; and the race of the candidates themselves. With regard to the latter two points: it is clear, for example, that in partisan contests black-backed candidates do best with low income whites, unless the candidates are black, in which case it is most difficult to get poor whites to vote for any black office seeker. In light of these findings, the simple models of racial voting are deficient because they fail to specify the factors that influence voting patterns in particular contexts.   J

2494. Nelson, Dalmas H.; Francis, John G.; and Lubomudrov, Slava. PRECINCT STRADDLING OF CITY BOUNDARIES. *Natl. Civic*

Rev. 1978 67(7): 317-320. In a large part of the western United States the city vote in non-city elections is considerably obscured by county practices of using precincts that straddle city boundaries. The inability to identify the city vote may have undesirable consequences for the visibility of political preferences, for the reliability and validity of the elections administration process, and the ability to analyze the city's political history.
J

2495. Newcomer, Owen E.   NONPARTISAN ELECTIONS: A LOOK AT THEIR EFFECT. *Natl. Civic Rev. 1977 66(9): 453-455, 468.* The type of city government structure, and the size and diversity of population, may have a more important impact on elections than does the type of ballot.

2496. O'Loughlin, John and Berg, Dale A.   THE ELECTION OF BLACK MAYORS, 1969 AND 1973. *Ann. of the Assoc. of Am. Geographers 1977 67(2): 223-238.* Examines initial defeat (1969) and eventual success (1973) in blacks' candidacy for mayor in Detroit, Atlanta, and Los Angeles due to bloc-voting behavior along racial lines as well as residential change, candidate choice, voting age, and social status.

2497. Price, David E. and Lupfer, Michael   VOLUNTEERS FOR GORE: THE IMPACT OF A PRECINCT-LEVEL CANVASS IN THREE TENNESSEE CITIES. *J. of Pol. 1973 35(2): 410-438.* In 1970 Senator Albert Arnold Gore of Tennessee lost to a Republican opponent who had the benefit of modern voter-organizing techniques. Gore suffered a "serious liability" from shunning modern procedures and from too great a reliance on friendships and personal contact. Examines the "belated effort" of some of his supporters to organize voters in Nashville, Knoxville, and Memphis. The device used, the voter canvass, would have, it was hoped, the "greatest potential impact . . . on voter turnout." A systematic effort was made to cover evenly-balanced precincts and areas of prior low voter turnout. Old party loyalties are eroding, the returns for canvassing are high, and canvassing will thus become a more important device for "relating to and influencing an increasingly volatile electorate." 2 figs., 2 tables, 41 notes.
A. R. Stoesen

2498. Reath, Henry T.   GOOD JUDGES FOR PHILADELPHIA: AN EXPERIMENT IN POLITICAL ACTION. *Judicature 1974 57(6): 232-236.* A citizen's action group, Good Judges for Philadelphia, unsuccessfully attempted to elect a bipartisan slate of candidates.   S

2499. Rushton, Bill.   NEW ORLEANS ELECTS BLACK MAYOR (DUTCH MORIAL). *Southern Exposure 1978 6(1): 5-7.* The election of Democrat Ernest N. Morial as the first black mayor of New Orleans in 1977 marked the rise to importance and political maturity of New Orleans and Louisiana blacks. Morial is a Creole who became the first black graduate of the Louisiana State University Law School and the first black member of the Louisiana House of Representatives since Reconstruction. He has been an important figure in legal actions by the NAACP against segregation in New Orleans. His political victory was achieved against a background of corruption and ineptness amassed by his predecessor, Major Maurice Landrieu. Morial's triumph was due at least partly to the disunity and vicious infighting of his white opponents, coupled with his electoral strength among the black community and New Orleans' influential Jewish population. Based mainly on personal observation.
N. Lederer

2500. Salces, Luis M.   SPANISH AMERICANS' SEARCH FOR POLITICAL REPRESENTATION: THE 1975 ALDERMANIC ELECTION IN CHICAGO. *J. of Pol. and Military Sociol. 1978 6(2): 175-187.* Spanish Americans' search for political representation in Chicago has not been very successful. In the 1975 aldermanic election, an unusual event took place when four Spanish surnamed politicians challenged four incumbent aldermen backed by Mayor Daley's Democratic Organization. Using official election returns for each of the precincts included in the four wards, this study attempts to determine to what extent ethnic solidarity had a greater effect than party identification on the voting behavior of Spanish Americans. The results of the analysis using ecological regression indicates that in two of the four wards under study, Spanish surnamed registrants voted for the Spanish American candidate, while in another ward they showed a preference for the candidate of the Democratic organization. Moreover, with only one exception the participation of Spanish Americans had a negligible or negative effect

on the election's turnout. Overall, the findings suggest that in 1975 the presence of a Spanish American candidate is not sufficient to produce a political mobilization on the part of the Spanish American collectivity.
J

2501. Svara, James H.   UNWRAPPING INSTITUTIONAL PACKAGES IN URBAN GOVERNMENT: THE COMBINATION OF ELECTION INSTITUTIONS IN AMERICAN CITIES. *J. of Pol. 1977 39(1): 166-175.* A common contrast in urban political theory compares reform models (nonpartisan, at-large elections, and council-mayor forms) with the traditional model (partisan, district elections, and mayor-council forms). Such models explain government in 64% of American cities, but other urban governmental structures exist which have not been effectively studied. Based on primary and secondary sources; 4 tables, 11 notes.
A. W. Novitsky

2502. Unsigned.   [BLACKS IN MUNICIPAL GOVERNMENT: STRUCTURAL VS. SOCIOECONOMIC VARIABLES]. *Urban Affairs Q. 1976 12(2): 223-256.*
Karnig, Albert K.   BLACK REPRESENTATION ON CITY COUNCILS: THE IMPACT OF DISTRICT ELECTIONS AND SOCIOECONOMIC FACTORS, *pp. 223-242.* Leonard A. Cole challenged the contention that urban political reforms—at-large elections, nonpartisan and city manager governments—decrease ethnic group access to decisionmaking. Using 1972 New Jersey data he found that socioeconomic variables such as community education and wealth levels and occupational structures were the chief correlates of black municipal representation. Based on 1972 data drawn from 139 cities, Karnig argues that even with regional variations, blacks did better in district elected systems than in at-large systems. Furthermore, black political success varied most directly with levels of black wealth, not community or white wealth levels. The evidence is mixed, but it is likely that the election of blacks may give the appearance, but not the substance, of social change. 4 tables, 5 notes, biblio.
Cole, Leonard A.   COMMENT ON "BLACK REPRESENTATION," *pp. 243-250.* Questions Karnig's failure to evaluate the impact of black socioeconomic variables other than levels of wealth and argues that methodological weaknesses distort the impact of reform on black representation. Furthermore, by limiting his analysis to 1972, Karnig ignores increasing black representation in government. Conjectures that white Americans have become politically tolerant and that black problems today, though rooted in racism, are economic. 2 notes, biblio.
Karnig, Albert K.   PUZZLES, DATA LIMITS AND PERSPECTIVES: A RESPONSE TO COLE, *pp. 251-256.* Of Cole's socioeconomic variables, only economic levels correlated significantly with black representation on city councils. Defends his methodology, adding that he used only 1972 data because he wished to replicate Cole's New Jersey data on a national scale. The election of an increasing number of blacks reflects the new voting strength of blacks in small Southern towns, not white tolerance. Argues that his original conclusions are unaffected by Cole's commentary. Biblio.
L. N. Beecher

2503. Zikmund, Joseph, II.   VOTING PATTERNS IN DETROIT SUBURBS: 1972. *Michigan Academician 1974 6(4): 399-407.*

2504. Zimmer, Troy A.   URBANIZATION, SOCIAL DIVERSITY, VOTER TURNOUT, AND POLITICAL COMPETITION IN U.S. ELECTIONS: ANALYSIS OF CONGRESSIONAL DISTRICTS FOR 1972. *Social Sci. Q. 1976 56(4): 689-697.* Using data on US congressional districts, employs multiple regression analysis to test hypotheses. Diversity was found to be significantly related to competition in a positive direction, urbanization was unrelated, and turnout was related in both positive and negative directions depending on the office involved.   J

2505. Zimmerman, Joseph F.   A PROPORTIONAL REPRESENTATION SYSTEM AND THE NEW YORK CITY SCHOOL BOARDS. *Natl. Civic Rev. 1974 63(9): 472-474, 493.* The proportional representation system used in the election of members of New York City's community school boards generally has accomplished its objective of providing representation for minority groups on the boards in proportion to their voting strength. The system appears to be accepted and no one is agitating for its replacement.
J

City-State Relations

2506. Bresnick, David A.   DECENTRALIZING THE CITY: WHO GETS CONTROL?   *Natl. Civic Rev. 1973 62(9): 486-490*. Decentralization for New York City and other large cities may soon be a reality. If the strengthening of the role of the states continues a considerable revision in the traditional autonomy of cities is predictable. More incorporation into state political systems should destroy any illusions that complete metropolitan autonomy is possible.   J

2507. Bresnick, David A.   THE OTHER SIDE OF DECENTRALIZATION: HOME RULE FOR NEW YORK CITY.   *Natl. Civic R. 1975 64(2): 71-75*. Efforts at governmental reorganization affecting New York City concentrated on the possibilities of decentralization. The other side has been the demand that external relationships, i.e., city-state relationships, be remolded. The conflicts between New York City and state go back almost a century.   J

2508. Dill, Forrest.   CRIMINAL JUSTICE: THE LOCAL TRADITION.   *New York Affairs 1978 5(2): 198-205*. Examines the expenditures of New York metropolitan region local and state governments for criminal justice, assessing the impact of increased state financing on the quality and nature of law enforcement, 1961-77.

2509. Feig, Douglas C.   EXPENDITURES IN THE AMERICAN STATES: THE IMPACT OF COURT-ORDERED LEGISLATIVE REAPPORTIONMENT.   *Am. Pol. Q. 1978 6(3): 309-326*. Uses statistical tests to show that reapportionment had an impact on state aid to education in about one-half of the states and on state expenditures for public welfare in nearly all of the states. "All but one of the states gave evidence of being affected by reapportionment in one or more of the two ways examined." This results from the fact that reapportionment decisions increased considerably urban representation; accordingly state expenditures increased in categories especially favored by urbanites. 3 tables, 4 fig., 13 notes, ref.   E. P. Stickney

2510. Firestine, Robert E.   THE IMPACT OF REAPPORTIONMENT UPON LOCAL GOVERNMENT AID RECEIPTS WITHIN LARGE METROPOLITAN AREAS.   *Social Sci. Q. 1973 54(2): 394-402*. Tests *The Impact of Reapportionment upon Local Government Aid Receipts within Large Metropolitan Areas*. Most of the tests revealed no meaningful links between reapportionment and changes in the intergovernmental aid flows from states to their local governments, although a few positive relationships were defined.   J

2511. Furniss, Susan W.   THE RESPONSE OF THE COLORADO GENERAL ASSEMBLY TO PROPOSALS FOR METROPOLITAN REFORM.   *Western Pol. Q. 1973 26(4): 747-765*. Examines the relationship between legislative politics in Colorado to prospects for metropolitan reform in Denver, its largest urban center, 1961-70.

2512. LeMay, Michael.   EXPENDITURE AND NONEXPENDITURE MEASURES OF STATE URBAN POLICY OUTPUT: A RESEARCH NOTE.   *Am. Pol. Q. 1973 1(4): 511-528*. Discusses the usefulness of expenditure measures of output in state government urban policies, 1968-70's, emphasizing the factors of population distribution, per capita income and influence of the federal government.

2513. Loewenstein, Louis K.   THE NEW YORK STATE URBAN DEVELOPMENT CORPORATION: A FORGOTTEN FAILURE OR A PRECURSOR OF THE FUTURE?   *J. of the Am. Inst. of Planners 1978 44(3): 261-273*. This article details the rapid rise and fast fall of the boldest effort of any public agency to build housing in the United States. This was the New York State Urban Development Corporation which built more than 30,000 housing units as well as commercial, industrial, and civic projects and started three brand new communities in six years before defaulting on its financial obligations and virtually going bankrupt. Discussses how and why this near bankruptcy occurred.   J

2514. McIntire, Michael V.   URBAN RECONSTRUCTION COULD BE AS CLOSE AS THE STATEHOUSE.   *Am. Bar Assoc. J. 1974 60(5): 578-582*. The task of reviving our cities should be shouldered by state government, for it alone has the resources and immediacy to do the job.   J

2515. Morgan, Daniel C., Jr.   FISCAL NEGLECT OF URBAN AREAS BY A STATE GOVERNMENT.   *Land Econ. 1974 50(2): 137-144*. "The state government of Texas neglects its urban areas."   S

2516. Newton, Robert E.   RELOCATING ALASKA'S STATE CAPITAL.   *State Government 1977 50(3): 165-169*. Examines attempts to secure the relocation of Alaska's state capital (Juneau), 1955-74, including the petition drive which resulted in voter approval for relocation, and studies, 1974-77.

2517. Unsigned.   [FISCAL NEGLECT OF URBAN AREAS BY A STATE GOVERNMENT].   *Land Econ. 1975 51(2): 186-190*.
Bowman, John H.   FISCAL NEGLECT OF URBAN AREAS BY A STATE GOVERNMENT: A COMMENT,   *pp. 186-188*. Discusses Daniel C. Morgan Jr.'s article, focusing on where expenditures were made and not on who benefited. 6 notes, biblio.
Morgan, Daniel C., Jr.   FISCAL NEGLECT OF URBAN AREAS BY A STATE GOVERNMENT: A REPLY,   *pp. 189-190*. Agrees with Bowman's criticism and examines the government policy implications of the study. Note, biblio.   E. S. Johnson

City-Federal Relations

2518. Altshuler, Alan A.   CHANGING PATTERNS OF POLICY: THE DECISION MAKING ENVIRONMENT OF URBAN TRANSPORTATION.   *Public Policy 1977 25(2): 171-203*. Traces the evaluation of federal policy on urban transportation. Recognizing the strength of the private market which accounts for nearly 90% of urban transportation spending, federal urban transportation policy has usually tried to accommodate the demands of the private sector. Rapid post-World War II expansion of motor vehicle use and concomitant urban sprawl were not products of a conscious urban development policy. Organized pressure groups, conventional wisdom, and widespread public aspirations were accommodated by government actions which reinforced public demand for low-density living and automobility. From 1945 to 1960, major government policy focused on housing, but without widespread regional land-use planning. In the 1950's and 1960's, the highway lobby promoted federal policy initiatives which accommodated public demand for massive highway construction with virtually no dissent. Recent urban transportation policy, particularly mass transit, is analyzed against the background of public concerns. Primary and secondary sources; 7 notes, appendix.
                J. M. Herrick

2519. Bach, Victor.   THE NEW FEDERALISM IN COMMUNITY DEVELOPMENT.   *Social Policy 1977 7(4): 32-38*. Examines the federal legislation governing Model Cities programs and community development block grant programs maintaining that the new federalism which they represent needs to be better balanced by allowing for more federal initiatives to complement locally organized efforts, 1970's.

2520. Beckman, Norman.   FEDERAL POLICY FOR METROPOLITAN GOVERNANCE.   *Natl. Civic Rev. 1974 63(3): 128-132, 150*. In most ways cities have given way to metropolitan areas as the centers of American life. Most activities, and the public and private institutions that serve them are areawide. But local governments show little willingness by themselves to develop an areawide capacity to deal with their problems.   J

2521. Bradford, Calvin.   FINANCING HOME OWNERSHIP: THE FEDERAL ROLE IN NEIGHBORHOOD DECLINE.   *Urban Affairs Q. 1979 14(3): 313-336*. Neighborhoods, like corporations, need credit to develop. Analyzes federal loan policy for single-family housing since 1932. Federal acceptance of dual credit and housing markets insured mortgages shortages in older, nonwhite neighborhoods. Under pressure from the civil rights movement, loan policy toward these areas has changed radically since the early 1960's. However, inadequate regulation encourages realtors to push these federally guaranteed loans without regard for their soundness. The result is a high level of foreclosures and abandonments and continued neighborhood decline. Future programs should encourage the influx of conventional mortgage credit. 12 notes, biblio.   L. N. Beecher

2522. Brintnall, Michael A. FEDERAL INFLUENCE AND UR-
BAN POLICY ENTREPRENEURSHIP IN THE LOCAL PROSECU-
TION OF ECONOMIC CRIME. *Policy Studies J. 1979 7(3): 577-591.*
Assesses programs instituted by local government prosecutors to deal
with white-collar crime and consumer fraud, 1970's, focusing on sources,
character, and consequences of this type of policy entrepreneurship and
assessing the character of federal influence.

2523. Buell, Emmett H., Jr. URBAN PUBLIC POLICY: CALIFOR-
NIA LABYRINTHS AND OHIO PLEBISCITES. *Polity 1975 7(4):
530-541.* A review of three books concerned with urban policies: Heinz
Eulau and Kenneth Prewitt, *Labyrinths of Democracy: Adaptations,
Linkages, Representation, and Policies in Urban Politics* (Minneapolis:
Bobbs-Merrill, 1973), Jeffrey L. Pressman and Aaron Wildavsky, *Implementation: How Great Expectations in Washington are Dashed in Oakland* (Berkeley: U. of California Pr., 1973), and John J. Gargan and James
G. Coke, eds. *Political Behavior and Public Issues in Ohio* (Kent, Ohio:
Kent State U. Pr., 1972). These books mark the decay of the once-rosy
hopes of federally financed urban renewal, and decry the confusion between the ease of establishing policy and the difficulty of implementing
it. 32 notes.   V. L. Human

2524. Bunce, Harold L. THE COMMUNITY DEVELOPMENT
BLOCK GRANT FORMULA: AN EVALUATION. *Urban Affairs
Q. 1979 14(4): 443-464.* The formula for dispersing funds under the
Housing and Community Development Act (US, 1974) was the heart of
a new economic relationship between the federal government and local
governments—it assured that a disproportionate share of federal dollars
earmarked for low and moderate income related problems did not go to
grantmanship-wise larger cities. The Carter Administration proposes a
second formula driven by different variables. Each grantee could choose
that which generated the greater number of dollars. Analyzes these as
well as 6 alternative formulae. 4 tables, 21 notes, biblio.
                                                              L. N. Beecher

2525. Caraley, Demetrios. CONGRESSIONAL POLITICS AND
URBAN AID. *Pol. Sci. Q. 1976 91(1): 19-45.* Analyzes the patterns of
support and opposition that have evidenced themselves in congressional
voting on federal financial assistance to large cities.   J

2526. Caraley, Demetrios. CONGRESSIONAL POLITICS AND
URBAN AID: A 1978 POSTSCRIPT. *Pol. Sci. Q. 1978 93(3): 411-419.*
Examines congressional voting on urban aid issues in 1977 and concludes
that, contrary to what some policy makers have claimed, support for
pro-urban programs did exist in the 95th Congress and was primarily
dependent not on the number of "urban" constituencies, but on the size
of the Democratic majority and the willingness of President Carter to
mobilize it. Also shows the extent to which snowbelt versus sunbelt voting
cleavages replaced more traditional ones.   J/S

2527. Chandler, Cleveland A. and David, Wilfred L. ALTERNA-
TIVE ECONOMIC POLICIES FOR THE REVITALIZATION OF
U.S. CENTRAL CITIES. *Am. Econ. Rev. 1979 69(2): 288-292.* Taking
increased federal investment as an exogenous policy change, suggests that
future federal programs be restricted to the funding of capacity building
programs. 11 ref.   D. K. Pickens

2528. Chollar, Robert G. PUBLIC-PRIVATE PARTNERSHIPS.
Antioch Rev. 1979 37(2): 162-169. Describes the growing financial crisis
of US cities and outlines ways the federal government and private business
can help, 1960's-1979.

2529. Demuth, Christopher C. DEREGULATING THE CITIES.
Public Interest 1976 (44): 115-128. Reviews two recent books, *The Poli-
tics of Neglect: Urban Aid from Model Cities to Revenue Sharing,* by
Bernard J. Frieden and Marshall Kaplan, and Charles M. Haar's *Between
the Idea and the Reality: A Study in the Origin, Fate and Legacy of the
Model Cities Program,* concerning the Model Cities program of the
Johnson administration, the most unequivocal failure of the Great Soci-
ety. Also includes the author's own experiences as a staff assistant in the
White House during the early days of the Nixon Administration. The
Model Cities program attempted to rationalize and redirect federal urban
policy. A principle reason for its failure was that the legislation drafted
to implement it was based on little more than hope and ideas on how to

improve existing programs were highly speculative. Institutional barriers
to program coordination were underestimated, and the required participation of citizen groups delayed or halted the flow of funds to model
neighborhoods for years. Haar views the arrival of the Nixon Administration as a calamity for the program, while Frieden and Kaplan rightly view
Nixon as giving less support than Johnson but nevertheless keeping the
basic commitment.   S. Harrow

2530. Dommel, Paul R. DISTRIBUTIVE POLITICS AND URBAN
POLICY. *Policy Studies J. 1975 3(4): 370-375.* Examines issues of
revenue sharing in systems designed to allocate aid to state and local
governments.   S

2531. Downs, Anthony. THE SUCCESSES AND FAILURES OF
FEDERAL HOUSING POLICY. *Public Interest 1974 (34): 124-145.*
Evaluates government aid and urban development during the: "1. low
priority period (1960 through 1965); 2. reassessment period (1966
through 1968); 3. high-production period (1968 through 1972)."

2532. Evans, Hugh and Rodwin, Lloyd. THE NEW TOWNS PRO-
GRAM AND WHY IT FAILED. *Public Interest 1979 (56): 90-107.*
The New Communities program was authorized in 1968 and dismantled
in 1978. Grand objectives, such as accommodating US population increases from 1970 to 2000, encouraging efficient use of resources and
design, and improving opportunities for the disadvantaged, were not
realized. "The New Communities program was a disaster whose magnitude surprised even the program's harshest critics." Studies of the falter-
ing program reveal: 1) defective financial arrangements, 2) major
strategy aims or an appeal to special interest groups were lacking, 3) i-
nadequate backing by state and local governments, 4) naive assumptions
concerning political support, 5) unfounded beliefs in economic stability,
and if that failed, government monies, and 6) major social aims were
jeopardized by the important role of the private sector. Table.
                                                              S. Harrow

2533. Franklin, Herbert M. A NEW METRO APPROACH.
Center Mag. 1976 9(5): 30-35, 37. Advocates greater federal government
legislative and economic control of urban development in the 1970's,
emphasizing issues in city planning, land conservation, and the role of
private enterprise.

2534. Ganz, Alexander and O'Brien, Thomas. THE CITY: SAND-
BOX, RESERVATION OR DYNAMO? *Public Policy 1973 21(1):
107-123.* Revenue sharing is a viable urban policy.   S

2535. Gifford, Bernard R. NEW YORK CITY AND COSMOPOLI-
TAN LIBERALISM. *Pol. Sci. Q. 1978-79 93(4): 559-584.* Traces the
economic decline of New York City vis-à-vis the rest of the nation to the
economic and social policies of the New Deal, the quintessential expression of New York's liberal political ideology. The recent economic difficulties of New York, coupled with increasing attention to computations
on revenue flows between New York and Washington, may lead to a
"new" New York political ideology.   J

2536. Gramlich, Edward M. THE NEW YORK CITY FISCAL
CRISIS: WHAT HAPPENED AND WHAT IS TO BE DONE?
Am. Econ. Rev. 1976 66(2): 415-429. Many of New York City's economic problems rest within the federal system, while pensions and social
services are the responsibility of local governments. Income redistribution
—the object of the New York City budget—can not be effectively
achieved since key elements of policy rest with the state and national
constitutional authorities. Tables, notes.   D. K. Pickens

2537. Greer, Edward. AIR POLLUTION AND CORPORATE
POWER: MUNICIPAL REFORM LIMITS IN A BLACK CITY.
Pol. and Soc. 1974 4(4): 483-510. Presents a case study of Gary, Indiana,
considered a prototypical industrial city. Outlines the city's political im-
potency before and since the election of black reform mayor Richard
Hatcher in face of US Steel's resistance to implementing air pollution
controls at its Gary Works. The corporation's strategy did not change
until the federal government provided the means of passing the costs for
pollution abatement along to the consumer. Based on primary and secondary sources; 136 notes.   D. G. Nielson

2538. Harrison, Bennett. THE PARTICIPATION OF GHETTO RESIDENTS IN THE MODEL CITIES PROGRAM. *J. of the Am. Inst. of Planners 1973 39(1): 43-55.* The Model Cities Program of HUD is mandated by its enabling legislation to provide "maximum opportunity for jobs in the projects and activities of the program" to residents of the target model neighborhoods (MN). Yet, by the spring of 1969, fewer than half of the salaried employees in a sample of the first-round projects across the country were actually MN residents. Moreover, MN residents earned $800-$1,300 less per year than nonresidents for roughly equivalent work. This paper, through the use of multivariate regression analysis, investigates the causes of variation in the rates of employment of ghetto residents and in the salaries of all Model Cities employees during the program's start-up period. Particular attention is addressed to political structure variables, including the extent of bureaucratization of the city personnel system and the growth of actual or potential black power. Brief attention is also given to a lower-order form of community participation: the activities of the advisory Citizens' Boards.   J

2539. Henderson, Lenneal J. THE IMPACT OF THE EQUAL EMPLOYMENT OPPORTUNITY ACT OF 1972 ON EMPLOYMENT OPPORTUNITIES FOR WOMEN AND MINORITIES IN MUNICIPAL GOVERNMENT. *Policy Studies J. 1978 7(2): 234-239.* Examines the effect of agencies which attempt to assess the position of women and minorities in city government following implementation of the Equal Employment Opportunity Act (US, 1972).

2540. Houstoun, L. O., Jr. THE CARTER URBAN POLICY A YEAR LATER. *Antioch Rev. 1979 37(2): 134-147.* Reviews the origins of the federal policy which affected President Carter's Urban and Regional Policy Group of 1978, which consists of three elements: 1) increased financial aid to cities, 2) a set of improvements designed to be more sensitive to city revitalization, 3) a new set of financial incentives.

2541. Howard, John R. A NATIONAL URBAN POLICY: SOME CLOSING OBSERVATIONS. *Ann. of the Am. Acad. of Pol. and Social Sci. 1978 (439): 147-150.* This paper reflects the perspective that the initial objective in the formulation of urban policy should be melioration of the condition of the urban black poor. Four major strategies are being considered by the Carter Administration in its effort to formulate a national urban policy. The paper discusses them briefly and then considers the role of urban black leadership in the development of an effective national urban policy.   J

2542. Jackson, Charles O. and Johnson, Charles W. THE URBANE FRONTIER: THE ARMY AND THE COMMUNITY OF OAK RIDGE, TENNESSEE, 1942-1947. *Military Affairs 1977 41(1): 8-14.* Studies the Army Corps of Engineers as the town developer and administrator of Oak Ridge, Tennessee, a creation without precedent. The Corps had a community vision, made quality of life a major concern, and insisted on a sizable civilian role in the community. This role was substantial but could be subordinated to project efficiency and security. The military dealt with problems and concerns such as housing, education, and spiritual and social needs. The military was justly proud of its accomplishments. Based on primary sources from the records of the Manhattan Engineer District.   A. M. Osur

2543. Janssen, Peter A. LESSON FROM NEW YORK. *Compact 1976 10(1): 7-9.* Discusses urban problems of New York City in the 1970's, emphasizing federal aid to education and the City University of New York.

2544. Kepler, Edwin C. THE PUSH TO GIVE MUNICIPAL OFFICIALS MAXIMUM CONTROL OVER HUMAN SERVICES. *Urban and Social Change Rev. 1976 9(1): 9-17.* Discusses the implications of the Nixon administration's New Federalism for municipal officials and human services programs in the 1970's.

2545. Kopkind, Andrew. WHY NOT THE BEST? CARTER TO CITIES: PLAY DEAD. *Working Papers for a New Soc. 1978 6(1): 6-9.* Surveys Jimmy Carter's new urban policy which is characterized by few new social programs, little increase in spending, tax incentives in the private sector, little relief for public enterprise and community corporations, use of present tools to solve urban ills, and avoidance of tax redistribution, 1977-78.

2546. Kramer, Douglas J. PROTECTING THE URBAN ENVIRONMENT FROM THE FEDERAL GOVERNMENT. *Urban Affairs Q. 1974 9(3): 359-368.*

2547. Kurtzweg, Jerry A. URBAN PLANNING AND AIR POLLUTION CONTROL: A REVIEW OF SELECTED RECENT RESEARCH. *J. of the Am. Inst. of Planners 1973 39(2): 82-92.* Examines federal government policy, legislation, and research relating to air pollution, its prevention, and its consideration in the city planning process, 1970's.

2548. Lehne, Richard. SUBURBAN FOUNDATIONS OF THE NEW CONGRESS. *Ann. of the Am. Acad. of Pol. and Social Sci. 1975 422: 141-151.* Both Congress and the American suburbs are undergoing major reformations. The election of large and increasing numbers of suburban representatives to Congress means that, today and in the future, Congress must deal with the policy positions and reform preferences of suburbanites. This article examines the behavior of suburban legislators in the House of Representatives as a reflection of political changes taking place in the suburbs which will influence current and future congressional policy making. Competing interpretations of the political significance of the emerging American suburbs are discussed and evaluated.   J

2549. Lyons, William and Morgan, David R. THE IMPACT OF INTERGOVERNMENTAL REVENUE ON CITY EXPENDITURES: AN ANALYSIS OVER TIME. *J. of Pol. 1977 39(4): 1088-1097.* Spending patterns of the 285 American cities with a minimum population of 50,000 from 1950 to 1970 were analyzed in relation to median family income, percent employed in manufacturing, population, percent nonwhite, median age, percent of owner-occupied dwellings, reform structures, operation of schools, and intergovernmental revenue. Of these nine independent variables, federal aid was the fourth most significant in 1950 and the fifth in 1960, but became by 1970 the most important influence on spending. This aid appears to stimulate greater per capita municipal spending rather than simply substitute for locally raised funds. Primary and secondary sources; 3 tables, 11 notes.
    A. W. Novitsky

2550. Marx, Wesley. LOS ANGELES AND ITS MISTRESS MACHINE. *Sci. and Public Affairs 1973 29(4): 4-6, 44-45.* Examines the confrontation between adherence to the Air Quality Act (US, 1970) to meet Environmental Protection Agency specifications and dependence on automobiles with internal combustion engines, 1970-73.

2551. Morlan, Robert L. LOCAL SELF-GOVERNMENT VS. NATIONAL RESPONSIBILITY. *Natl. Civic Rev. 1973 62(6): 294-300.* Controversy continues in democratic countries over the extent to which municipal home rule is compatible with concerns for nationwide equality of services.   J

2552. Muchnick, David M. CITIES. *Dissent 1977 24(2): 117-120.* Examines programs and attitudes of the Carter administration on urban problems; mentions appointments, federal loans, and housing programs planned.

2553. Muchnick, David M. DEATH WARRANT FOR THE CITIES: THE NATIONAL URBAN POLICY. *Dissent 1975 23(1): 21-32.* The financial crisis of New York City in 1975 reveals the federal government's punitive and irrational urban policies, notably in the Office of Management and Budget and in the Housing and Urban Development Department.

2554. Napier, John H., III. THE MILITARY, MONTGOMERY AND MAXWELL. *Aerospace Hist. 1977 24(4): 189-195.* The military development of the Montgomery area goes back to the Hernando de Soto expedition of 1540. Aviation came to Montgomery in the early 1900's, and the War Department chose the area during World War I for a flying field because of the good flying weather, open terrain, and the importuning of local businessmen. After various names, it became Maxwell Field on 8 November 1922 and received special status with the moving of the Air Corps Tactical School from Langley to Maxwell. After World War II, Air Force planners selected Maxwell as the professional military education center and that status continues to today. Also, the warm relationship between Maxwell and Montgomery has continued. Primary and secondary sources; 27 notes.   A. M. Osur

2555. Nathan, Richard P.; Dommel, Paul R.; Liebschutz, Sarah F.; and Morris, Milton D.　MONITORING THE BLOCK GRANT PROGRAM FOR COMMUNITY DEVELOPMENT.　*Pol. Sci. Q. 1977 92(2): 219-244.* Reports the highlights of an ongoing monitoring study by the Brookings Institution of the block grant program for community development (CDBG) enacted in 1974. The basic idea of the block grant appears to be working, and citizen participation has been higher than expected. The predominant approach to community development during the first year of operation involved neighborhood conservation and growth studies designed primarily to prevent urban blight. The legislative goal of encouraging "spatial deconcentration" of lower income housing has not been emphasized by applicants. The allocation system favors small suburban jurisdictions over older, distressed central cities. Based on Brookings Institution field research data; 10 tables, 7 notes, appendix.
　　　　　　　　　　　　　　　　　　　　　　W. R. Hively

2556. Nelson, William E., Jr.　FEDERAL-CITY RELATIONS: THE FAILURE OF URBAN REFORM.　*Urban Affairs Q. 1977 13(1): 117-126.* Review article prompted by four studies of federal-city relations. Mark I. Gelfand's *A Nation of Cities: The Federal Government and Urban America, 1933-1965* (New York: Oxford U. Pr., 1975), is rich in detail but preoccupied with federal policy. Bernard J. Frieden and Marshall Kaplan's *The Politics of Neglect: Urban Aid From Model Cities to Revenue Sharing* (Cambridge: MIT Pr., 1975) and Charles M. Haar's *Between the Idea and the Reality: A Study in the Origin, Fate, and Legacy of the Model Cities Program* (Boston: Little, Brown and Company, 1975) explain the failures of the Model Cities program and of the Department of Housing and Urban Development. Jeffrey L. Pressman's *Federal Programs and City Politics: The Dynamics of Aid Process in Oakland* (Berkeley and Los Angeles: U. of California Pr., 1975) argues that the Oakland experience shows that without upgrading local political leadership, money alone cannot solve urban problems. None of the studies provides a comprehensive explanation for urban reform's failure, and any successful effort must envision the political empowerment of the poor. Biblio.
　　　　　　　　　　　　　　　　　　　　　　L. Beecher

2557. Peters, Charles.　WE COULD HAVE SAVED NEW YORK.　*Washington Monthly 1975 7(10): 41-46.* Outlines steps the federal government could have taken during the 1970's to prevent New York City's current fiscal crisis, particularly in higher education.　　　　S

2558. Rondinelli, Dennis A.　REVENUE SHARING AND AMERICAN CITIES: ANALYSIS OF THE FEDERAL EXPERIMENT IN LOCAL ASSISTANCE.　*J. of the Am. Inst. of Planners 1975 41(5): 319-333.* Examines the goals and impact of the State and Local Assistance Act (1972), recommending changes in the legislation to make the act more effective.

2559. Rutledge, Philip J.　FEDERAL-LOCAL RELATIONS AND THE MISSION OF THE CITY.　*Ann. of the Am. Acad. of Pol. and Social Sci. 1974 416: 77-90.* Traditionally, municipal government has been the level of government closest to the people and responsible for answering their needs. With the advent of World War II, however, the traditional roles reversed themselves to the point where, in 1944, federal government accounted for 89% of total government expenditures, whereas local governments expended only 6.4% of that total. The modern inclination to create 'paragovernments' for special purposes has compounded the imbalance of the intergovernmental system. The current dilemma is to find a suitable split for governmental services, supported by a more equitable financial split.　　　　　　　　　　J

2560. Smookler, Helene V.　ADMINISTRATION HARA-KIRI: IMPLEMENTATION OF THE URBAN GROWTH AND NEW COMMUNITY DEVELOPMENT ACT.　*Ann. of the Am. Acad. of Pol. and Social Sci. 1975 422: 129-140.* New communities have been offered as an alternative to suburban sprawl. Through economies of scale and a "clean-slate" development approach, a more attractive and innovative environment can be produced. The federal government became involved through the 1968 Housing Act. In order to insure the attainment of social goals, loan guarantees and grants were made available to developers. In 1970 the act was strengthened by making public developers eligible and increasing the number of grants. Seven years after the passage of the original act, the program appeared to be a failure. Despite promises of 10 federally guaranteed new communities a year, only 14 received commitments. All of these communities fell behind in their development schedules, and most were close to financial collapse. While the federally guaranteed new communities were hard hit by the economic recession, most of the blame for the crisis could be placed on the Republican administration's implementation of the program. Categorical grants were suspended, other funds were impounded by the Office of Management and Budget, and there was little intra- or inter-agency cooperation or coordination.　　　　J

2561. Stafford, Walter W.　DILEMMAS OF CIVIL RIGHTS GROUPS IN DEVELOPING URBAN STRATEGIES AND CHANGES IN AMERICAN FEDERALISM, 1933-1970.　*Phylon 1976 37(1): 59-72.* Chronicles interaction of black civil rights groups in assuring urban development and in establishing viable relations with local and federal governments.

2562. Starr, Roger.　NEW YORK'S CRISIS - AND WASHINGTON'S.　*Commentary 1978 66(6): 49-57.* Questions the belief that New York City's financial crisis can be ameliorated by federal assistance.

2563. Teaford, Jon C.　SALVAGING THE CITY: FEDERAL STYLE.　*Rev. in Am. Hist. 1976 4(2): 272-276.* Review article prompted by Mark I. Gelfand's *A Nation of Cities: The Federal Government and Urban America, 1933-1965* (New York: Oxford U. Pr., 1975), which chronicles the history of federal spending in urban redevelopment programs.

2564. Thurow, Lester C.　NEW YORK, A DECLINING ACTIVITY.　*New York Affairs 1977 4(3): 14-23.* Discusses New York City's current fiscal problems, detailing possible remedies including federal government subsidization, 1975-76.

2565. Unsigned.　THE NEW POLITICS OF LESS.　*New York Affairs 1975 3(1): 3-55.* Presents the text of a 1975 conference on decreasing federal aid to New York City and its implications, including the question of what the purpose or goal of a large metropolis should be.　　　S

2566. Wade, Richard.　THE END OF THE SELF-SUFFICIENT CITY.　*New York Affairs 1976 3(4): 3-8.* New York's fiscal crisis is not unique, but marks the beginning of a threat to all large urban centers. Throughout US history, cities were self-sufficient, and the wealthiest and best-educated lived within their boundaries. After World War II suburban development led to a residential exodus, followed by an industrial move to the suburbs. The middle class left the poor and elderly behind in the cities to be joined by a migration from the South and Latin America. Racial tensions were added and the 1960's saw violence and rioting. When the era of the self-sufficient city ended the Johnson administration poured money into the urban centers; however, no consistent policy emerged. The Nixon-Ford strategy was to ignore the problem and claim the crisis was over. The Ford administration persisted in seeing New York as an exception rather than an example of the forces at work in urban America.
　　　　　　　　　　　　　　　　　　　　　　K. McElroy

2567. Wade, Richard.　THE END OF THE SELF-SUFFICIENT CITY: NEW YORK'S FISCAL CRISIS IN HISTORY.　*Urbanism Past and Present 1976-77 (3): 1-4.* The New York City fiscal crisis was not exceptional and more than a mere fiscal problem. Defines the crisis as beginning a new era in America's urban experience. Discusses urban abandonment and suburban development.　　　　B. P. Anderson

2568. Weissman, Stephen R.　THE LIMITS OF CITIZEN PARTICIPATION: LESSONS FROM SAN FRANCISCO'S MODEL CITIES PROGRAM.　*Western Pol. Q. 1978 31(1): 32-47.* Comparative analysis of San Francisco's Alinsky-style Model Cities Manpower Program in the Mission District indicates that its community mobilization approach was more successful than a community representation in service-delivery one in opening up additional and better quality jobs for the poor. Both strategies of citizen participation were severely constrained by the urban market structure, the political weakness of the poor, institutional barriers in the labor market, and institutional racism in general. Another constraint was the urban interorganizational system or neighborhood subgovernment that interacted with the Alinsky group. This system included private corporations, traditional public social service bureaucracies, and new community-based agencies.　　　　J

2569. Wengert, Norman I. THE ENERGY BOOM TOWN: AN ANALYSIS OF THE POLITICS OF GETTING. *Policy Studies J. 1978 7(1): 17-23.* Explores methods of applying for and receiving federal aid designed to ease transition for small towns experiencing population growth as a result of increased energy production.

2570. Williams, Eddie N. GENERAL REVENUE SHARING AND THE CITIES. *J. of Intergroup Relations 1974 3(3): 3-13.* Analyzes the failure of federal revenue sharing to solve urban problems and suggests reforms to make the policy more effective.   S

2571. Yates, Douglas. THE FEDERAL GOVERNMENT AND THE URBAN CRISIS. *New York Affairs 1976 3(4): 28-41.* The federal government's role in solving the urban crisis can better be determined after the crisis is defined.   S

The Economy

General

2572. Burns, Allen F. CARGO CULT IN A WESTERN TOWN: A CULTURAL APPROACH TO EPISODIC CHANGE. *Rural Sociol. 1978 43(2): 164-177.* Cargo cults in Papua New Guinea hope to procure outside economic resources for their area; Willcox, Arizona, whose geographical location necessitates similar exploitations of outside resources, has "cargo cults" including (1951-76) the "Rex Allen Days" festival.

2573. Danziger, Sheldon. DETERMINANTS OF THE LEVEL AND DISTRIBUTION OF FAMILY INCOME IN METROPOLITAN AREAS, 1969. *Land Econ. 1976 52(4): 467-478.* Constructs a model, emphasizing industrial structure, that predicts the median value and distribution of family income. Indicates those industries that bring an increase in income, and the structural elements that affect their distribution. Findings may be of value to local industrial development efforts. 5 tables, 13 notes.   E. S. Johnson

2574. Drennan, Matthew. HEADQUARTERS CITY: NEW YORK AND THE CORPORATE COMPLEX. *New York Affairs 1978 5(1): 72-81.* Discusses the decline of New York City and other older American cities caused by relocation of corporate headquarters to the suburbs, and points out the benefits of attempts to encourage corporate headquarters to locate in cities.

2575. Guest, Avery M. SUBURBAN TERRITORIAL DIFFERENTIATION. *Sociol. and Social Res. 1978 62(4): 523-536.* The theory of functional differentiation predicts an increasing specialization of residential and employment activities among communities, but data on suburban community growth in the post-World War II period suggest, if anything, that activities are increasingly becoming intermixed. Contrary to trends suggested in previous research, communities with a strong orientation to employment activities are actually suffering, on average, absolute losses in employment while continuing to grow in residential population.   J

2576. Harrison, Bennett. GHETTO ECONOMIC DEVELOPMENT: A SURVEY. *J. of Econ. Literature 1974 12(1): 1-37.*

2577. Lemann, Nicholas. THE OTHER WASHINGTON: ATTORNEYS, ACCOUNTANTS, AND ASSOCIATIONS. *Washington Monthly 1977 9(3): 10-20.* Examines the growth of law firms, accounting operations, and all forms of associations, in Washington, D.C., 1960-77.

2578. Levine, Judith. DO-IT-YOURSELF IN THE SOUTH BRONX. *Working Papers for a New Soc. 1979 6(6): 20-23.* Describes the black and Latin South Bronx community of Morrisania and the efforts on the part of the People's Development Corporation (PDC), a community group, to rehabilitate buildings and revitalize businesses since 1974.

2579. Muller, Thomas. ECONOMIC DEVELOPMENT: DEALING WITH CONTRACTION. *New York Affairs 1978 5(2): 23-36.* Discusses development, economic growth, population increase, and city

government in New York City, 1840's-1930's, to develop a structure for dealing with economic contraction in the 1960's and 70's.

2580. Netzer, Dick. THE CLOUDY PROSPECTS FOR THE CITY'S ECONOMY. *New York Affairs 1974 1(4): 22-35.* There is more reason for concern about New York City's economic future now than at any time since the opening of the Erie Canal.   J

2581. Rosentraub, Mark S. and Nunn, Samuel R. SUBURBAN CITY INVESTMENT IN PROFESSIONAL SPORTS: ESTIMATING THE FISCAL RETURNS OF THE DALLAS COWBOYS AND TEXAS RANGERS TO INVESTOR COMMUNITIES. *Am. Behavioral Scientist 1978 21(3): 393-414.* Explores the extent to which suburbs (as compared with central cities) can hope to recapture original investments used to attract professional teams; uses Arlington and Irving, Texas, discussing history, economic activity, policymaking implications for local government; covers 1968-75.

2582. Russel, Raymond; Hochner, Art; and Perry, Stewart E. SAN FRANCISCO'S "SCAVENGERS" RUN THEIR OWN FIRM. *Working Papers for a New Soc. 1977 5(2): 30-36.* Discusses the experiences of workers in San Francisco's Sunset Scavenger Company, who since 1965 have run their own garbage collection service, one of the nation's few worker-controlled firms.

2583. Savage, V. Howard. THE INTERDEPENDENCE OF THE SAN ANTONIO ECONOMIC STRUCTURE AND THE DEFENSE ESTABLISHMENT. *Land Econ. 1974 50(4): 374-379.* Discusses the impact defense contracts had on income and unemployment in San Antonio, Texas, for the decade 1959-69.   S

2584. Sveikauskas, Leo. THE PRODUCTIVITY OF CITIES. *Q. J. of Econ. 1975 89(3): 393-413.* Indicates that one reason for the existence of large population centers during 1958-70 is their high productivity rates.   S

2585. Wang, John. BEHIND THE BOOM: POWER AND ECONOMICS IN CHINATOWN. *New York Affairs 1979 5(3): 77-81.* Describes the economic developments in New York's Chinatown as a result of foreign investments from China, Hong Kong, Taiwan, and Southeast Asia from 1970 to the present.

2586. Winfield, Gerald F. THE IMPACT OF URBANIZATION ON AGRICULTURAL PROCESSES. *Ann. of the Am. Acad. of Pol. and Social Sci. 1973 (405): 65-74.* The relationship between urbanization and agriculture is examined. With heavy migrations from rural to urban areas in the United States, there have been significant changes in land utilization. Land converted to urban uses is increasing, though it has little effect on total crop production. The technological transformation of agriculture has had much larger effects and has operated as a push-pull on the cityward movement of people as farm functions have moved to the city. Energy and chemical fertilizers now come from urban bases, with large numbers of urban people working for farmers. Yields per acre and per farm worker have risen sharply so that needs for agricultural products are fully met. Urbanization and rising buying power have moved Americans up the food chain. The demand for expansive animal products grows. These forces have resulted in a dramatic escalation of solid waste production in cities and on farms. Urbanization and transformed agriculture have exploded the organic matter cycle. The nitrogen thrown away in farm and urban organic wastes in the United States each year equals 137 percent of the nitrogen in all chemical fertilizers.   J

Trade, Commerce, and Merchandising

2587. Bernstein, Shalmon. THE STREET ECONOMY. *New York Affairs 1975 3(1): 56-71.* Presents personality profiles of current New York City sidewalk vendors and tells how and why these individuals became involved in their occupations.   S

2588. Clements, Donald W. UTILITY OF LINEAR MODELS IN RETAIL GEOGRAPHY. *Econ. Geography 1978 54(1): 17-25.* Tests variables which prove to be predictive elements in retail trade functioning in both rural and urban areas in Illinois, concluding that population, traffic, and distance from metropolis all are such elements, 1960's.

2589. Donaldson, Loraine and Strangways, Raymond S. CAN GHETTO GROCERIES PRICE COMPETITIVELY AND MAKE A PROFIT? *J. of Business 1973 46(1): 61-65.* An examination of the "question of whether or not the low income section of an urban area can be provided with competitively priced grocery stores that can operate profitably." The sales volume, cost, markup, and sales mix are summarized for stores in Atlanta, Georgia. It is concluded that one cannot compare poor and higher income purchasing on the basis of a standard market basket. Even though the ghetto grocers' costs may be higher than those of larger chains, the "product mix effect" enables them to price competitively and make a profit. Based on secondary sources; 7 notes.
C. A. Gallacci

2590. Gaventa, John. CASE STUDY: PROPERTY FOR PROPHET. *Southern Exposure 1976 4(3): 101-103.* Nashville, Tennessee, known as the Religious Capital of the South, is the center of several religious publishing houses, Bible distributorships, and hawkers of religious what-nots which comprise a $100 million-a-year business.

2591. Powell, Lawrence Clark. MR. BOOKSELLER. *Westways 1974 66(7): 26-31, 67.* Biography of bookseller Jacob (Jake) Zeitlin, noting his contributions to his profession and the Los Angeles community.
S

2592. Sexton, Donald E., Jr. FOOD SALES MIX AND PROFITABILITY: GHETTO SUPERMARKETS REVISITED. *J. of Business 1974 47(4): 538-542.* Different food and nonfood product classes contribute disproportionately to gross margins for supermarkets located in different types of neighborhoods. Finds that poverty area chain groceries achieved a gross margin 3.3% greater than all supermarkets. Two other independent studies suggest a range from 1.1 to 1.5%, according to the relative amounts of different meats sold. Secondary sources; 5 tables, 6 notes.
J. W. Williams

2593. Swartz, Robert D. REGIONAL SHOPPING MALLS: STRENGTHS AND WEAKNESSES AS SUBURBAN FOCI. *Michigan Academician 1979 11(4): 363-370.* Though fulfilling retail needs and serving as a focus of activity in urban centers, shopping malls fail to meet the objectives of city centers due to their lack of a significant unit of government, inability to encourage pedestrian traffic, and their preemption of components which might encourage growth elsewhere.

2594. Unsigned. [GHETTO MERCHANTS]. *Social Sci. Q. 1973 54(2): 375-383.*
Williams, Walter E. WHY THE POOR PAY MORE: AN ALTERNATIVE EXPLANATION, pp. 375-379. Examines aspects of merchant behavior usually viewed as socially insidious in light of the context of costly information. In this context, merchants will economize on information costs by employing physical attributes as proxies for relevant data unobserved, and behavior characterization will not produce compassionate policy.
Sturdivant, Frederick D. RATIONALITY AND RACISM IN THE GHETTO MARKETPLACE, pp. 380-383. The economic model employed by Williams is outdated and inappropriate and his behavioral model encourages racist stereotyping. Public policy recommendations as offered by Williams are naive.
J

Manufacturing and Industry

2595. Beckham, Barry. SOME TEMPORAL AND SPATIAL ASPECTS OF INTER-URBAN INDUSTRIAL DIFFERENTIATION. *Social Forces 1973 51(4): 462-470.* Examines the differences between industrial employment profiles among a set of 65 urban communities in the East North Central region. Communities tended to become more alike over time, and those closer together tended to be more alike than communities farther apart. These results lead to a discussion of convergence. It is urged that functional convergence be included as a dimension in the conceptualization of systems of cities.
J

2596. Bronitsky, Leonard and Wallace, William A. THE ECONOMIC IMPACT OF URBANIZATION ON THE MINERAL AGGREGATE INDUSTRY. *Econ. Geography 1974 50(2): 130-140.*

2597. Christian, Charles M. and Bennett, Sari J. THE RECLAMATION OF INDUSTRIAL BUILDING VACANCIES: CHICAGO'S BLACK COMMUNITY. *Urban Affairs Q. 1977 13(1): 109-116.* Evaluates the use of building space vacated by relocating industries in Southside and Westside Chicago. Industrial reclamations were geared toward unskilled labor. In both communities, the majority of reclamations were nonindustrial. The extent and economic nature of reclamation varied significantly in the two areas. Biblio., 2 notes.
L. Beecher

2598. Comanor, William S. RACIAL DISCRIMINATION IN AMERICAN INDUSTRY. *Economica [Great Britain] 1973 40(160): 363-378.* Analyzes statistically the pattern of racial discrimination in employment in US metropolitan areas and investigates the relationship between discrimination and industry profit rates.

2599. Erickson, Rodney A. THE REGIONAL IMPACT OF GROWTH FIRMS: THE CASE OF BOEING, 1963-1968. *Land Econ. 1974 50(2): 127-136.*

2600. Holli, Melvin G. DETROIT TODAY: LOCKED INTO THE PAST. *Midwest Q. 1978 19(3): 251-259.* Detroit's reliance on the automobile industry has produced an exaggerated boom and bust economy for the city. The industry has attempted to maintain the status quo at the expense of research and development with the result that it has failed to diversify and has limited its ability to respond to changing technologies. Consequently the city now faces accelerated out-migration of the middle class, business, and industry resulting in inadequate school financing and increasing segregation. Significant action to renew the city can be accomplished only by a coalition of organized labor, major automobile companies, and business, but previous attempts to do this have failed. Secondary sources; biblio.
S. J. Quinlan

2601. Lee, Lance R. PRESERVATION OF A TRADITION. *US Naval Inst. Pro. 1978 104(9): 62-75.* Tells how the Maine Maritime Museum in Bath, Maine, operates its apprenticeship program. Discusses the progress of the program in teaching young adults oldtime wooden boatbuilding skills and workmanship. 25 photos.
A. N. Garland

2602. Levin, Sharon G. SUBURBAN-CENTRAL CITY PROPERTY TAX DIFFERENTIALS AND THE LOCATION OF INDUSTRY: SOME EVIDENCE. *Land Econ. 1974 50(4): 380-386.*

2603. Rees, John. MANUFACTURING HEADQUARTERS IN A POST-INDUSTRIAL URBAN CONTEXT. *Econ. Geography 1978 54(4): 337-354.* Assesses placement of manufacturing headquarters in urban areas, specifically the Dallas-Fort Worth, Texas, area, including necessary indigenous characteristics, intrametropolitan location patterns, and environmental impact, 1967-75.

2604. Rogers, David L.; Pendleton, Brian F.; Goudy, Willis J.; and Richards, Robert O. INDUSTRIALIZATION, INCOME BENEFITS, AND THE RURAL COMMUNITY. *Rural Sociol. 1978 43(2): 250-264.* Examines the impact (1960-70) of industrialization on income levels and distributions in Iowa towns with populations of 2,500-10,000.

2605. Schoeplein, Robert N. SECULAR CHANGES IN THE SKILL DIFFERENTIAL IN MANUFACTURING, 1952-1973. *Industrial and Labor Relations Rev. 1977 30(3): 314-324.* Shows that the skill differential in manufacturing, when measured on the national level, has remained surprisingly stable over the 1952-73 period, in spite of its history of narrowing throughout the first half of the century and the severe pressures of inflation during the years since 1965. At the level of individual cities, however, this skill differential is shown to be moving toward convergence at one of two points, with differentials tending to be considerably wider in less unionized cities than in more unionized cities.
J

2606. Unsigned. [THE LOCATION OF THE HEADQUARTERS OF INDUSTRIAL COMPANIES].

Evans, Alan W. THE LOCATION OF THE HEADQUARTERS OF INDUSTRIAL COMPANIES. *Urban Studies [Great Britain] 1973 10(3): 387-395.* Focuses on London, but makes comparisons with New York City. Finds no evidence of increased centralization of head offices in London, 1965-72; the same holds true for New York City, and over a longer period. Based mainly on lists of leading British industrial companies from *The Times* of London, and on US data; 8 tables, fig., biblio.

Burns, Leland S. THE LOCATION OF THE HEADQUARTERS OF INDUSTRIAL COMPANIES: A COMMENT. *Urban Studies [Great Britain] 1977 14(2): 211-214.* Statistics are based on data from *Fortune Magazine* Directory of the Largest US Corporations. During 1960-70 about 10% of the largest retail companies and 5% of the industrial firms relocated from central cities to those having no manufacturing-based economies. "Suburbanizing firms were attracted by . . . lower . . . rents and taxes." Moves from one central city to another involved such factors as access to consultants, laboratories, capital sources, and cultural facilities. The pattern of changing locations is different in the United States and Great Britain. 5 tables, biblio.   S/E. P. Stickney

Finance

2607. Bradford, Calvin P. and Rubinowitz, Leonard S. THE URBAN-SUBURBAN INVESTMENT-DISINVESTMENT PROCESS: CONSEQUENCES FOR OLDER NEIGHBORHOODS. *Ann. of the Am. Acad. of Pol. and Social Sci. 1975 422: 77-86.* The pattern of suburban growth and decline of older neighborhoods within metropolitan areas is often seen as inevitable. However, these processes are shaped, in a significant way, by a relatively small number of private sector actors, including institutional investors, developers and mortgage bankers. Because of their ideologies and their perception of the economic realities, these interests invest increasingly in large scale developments on the suburban fringe and choose not to invest in older urban and suburban neighborhoods. These investment decisions have significant negative impacts on these older, middle class neighborhoods which are struggling to remain viable. With the withdrawal of these traditional sources of real estate investment capital, such neighborhoods face a concentration of foreclosures and abandonment of housing.   J

2608. Bradford, William D. and Bates, Timothy M. LOAN DEFAULT AMONG BLACK ENTREPRENEURS FORMING NEW CENTRAL CITY BUSINESS. *Q. Rev. of Econ. and Business 1977 17(3): 25-32.* Analyzes financial characteristics and differences in failure rates for 1) black-owned ongoing firms, 2) black-owned de novo firms, and 3) white-owned de novo businesses. The major concern is the effect of the de novo status on the delinquency characteristic of black borrowers. Black ongoing firms are less likely to fail than black de novo firms, even when the financial attributes of the borrowers are controlled.   J

2609. Dingemans, Dennis. REDLINING AND MORTGAGE LENDING IN SACRAMENTO. *Ann. of the Assoc. of Am. Geographers 1979 69(2): 225-239.* Survey of mortgage lending patterns by banks and savings and loan institutions in Sacramento, California, indicates that loans vary according to social status, ethnicity, and age of neighborhoods, 1976.

2610. Dorfman, Ron. GREENLINING CHICAGO: THE CITIZEN'S ACTION PROGRAM. *Working Papers for a New Soc. 1975 3(2): 32-36.* Describes the actions taken by Chicago's Citizen's Action Program (CAP) to stop lending institutions from refusing to offer loans in inner-city areas by removing a community's savings from companies that practice redlining.   S

2611. Johnson, Lane J. NEW YORK'S PRIMACY WITHIN THE AMERICAN BANKING SYSTEM: MEGALOPOLIS AND THE ORGANIZATION OF AMERICAN SPACE. *Michigan Academician 1974 6(3): 281-289.* Considers the influence of the northeastern megalopolis on the American socioeconomic system, using banking as an index of spatial influence.   S

Employment and the Work Force

2612. Aldrich, Howard E. EMPLOYMENT OPPORTUNITIES FOR BLACKS IN THE BLACK GHETTO: THE ROLE OF WHITE-OWNED BUSINESSES. *Am. J. of Sociol. 1973 78(6): 1403-1425.* Black-white relations in economic institutions are important determinants of the life chances of blacks. Black leaders and civil rights groups argue that white ownership of businesses in black communities retards the economic and political achievement of blacks. This paper explores the empirical basis for such arguments using a panel study of small businesses in Boston, Chicago, and Washington, D.C. The following propositions are supported: (1) white-owned businesses are much larger than black businesses and dominate the labor market of the ghetto, (2) white owners are more likely than black owners to hire 'outsiders,' and (3) white owners hire white employees in greater proportions than the racial composition of the ghetto population would imply. Ghetto economic development is often seen as a solution to the problems of the black community, but this research points out several important limitations of a development strategy.   J

2613. Blackwell, James E. and Haug, Marie. RELATIONS BETWEEN BLACK BOSSES AND BLACK WORKERS. *Black Scholar 1973 4(4): 36-43.* There is a need to update theories of intraracial group and intraethnic group relations in light of developments during the 1960's-70's of the black liberation movement; uses a case study of black workers and their relations with black bosses in Cleveland, Ohio, as the basis for such a model.

2614. Buckley, John E. DO AREA WAGES REFLECT AREA LIVING COSTS? *Monthly Labor Rev. 1979 102(11): 24-29.* Compares data on 1977 wage and living-cost ratios in US metropolitan areas to results of a 1966-67 survey, and shows no significant change in the ratio.

2615. Hamburger, Robert. A STRANGER IN THE HOUSE. *Southern Exposure 1977 5(1): 22-31.* While domestic service by black women in northern cities has declined rapidly in recent years, this occupation as late as 1965 was engaged in by nearly one million black workers, about one-third of all black working women. Oral interviews with two black women, Roena Bethune and Rose Marie Hairston, reveal the poor working conditions of domestic servants.   N. Lederer

2616. Haworth, C. T. and Rasmussen, D. W. DETERMINANTS OF METROPOLITAN COST OF LIVING VARIATIONS. *Southern Econ. J. 1973 40(2): 183-192.*

2617. Jeffrey, D. REGIONAL FLUCTUATIONS IN UNEMPLOYMENT WITHIN THE U.S. URBAN ECONOMIC SYSTEM: A STUDY OF THE SPATIAL IMPACT OF SHORT TERM ECONOMIC CHANGE. *Econ. Geography 1974 50(2): 111-123.*

2618. Leigh, Duane E. and Rawlins, V. Lane. RACIAL DIFFERENTIALS IN MALE UNEMPLOYMENT RATES: EVIDENCE FROM LOW-INCOME URBAN AREAS. *Rev. of Econ. and Statistics 1974 56(2): 150-157.*

2619. Manners, Gerald. THE OFFICE IN METROPOLIS: AN OPPORTUNITY FOR SHAPING METROPOLITAN AMERICA. *Econ. Geography 1974 50(2): 92-110.* Examines the boom in white-collar workers and the resultant increase in downtown office locations.   S

2620. Rubin, Marilyn. DEBUNKING THE MYTH: WORKING WOMEN IN SUBURBIA. *New York Affairs 1979 5(4): 78-83.* Briefly traces the rise of American suburbs since the 1920's, describes the typical suburban family consisting of working-supporting husband and father, and stay-at-home housewife-mother, and debunks the myth of the non-working suburban woman based on data since the 1950's on female labor force participation.

2621. Salins, Peter D. CAN ECONOMIC DEVELOPMENT HELP NEW YORK CITY's UNEMPLOYED? *New York Affairs 1976 3(2): 80-93.* Recession or no, there is a long-term problem of finding jobs for the less-skilled residents of large, central cities. Efforts to create new jobs for them within New York City or to "export" them to suburban jobs have not had encouraging results.   J

Labor Organizations, Unions, and Strikes

2622. Conforti, Joseph M. RACIAL CONFLICT IN CENTRAL CITIES: THE NEWARK TEACHERS' STRIKES. *Society 1974 12(1): 22-33.*

2623. Egleson, Nick. SCAPEGOATING CITY WORKERS: WHAT CAN THE UNIONS DO? *Working Papers for a New Soc. 1976 4(1): 45-51.* In the New York City Workers' Strike (1975) the workers' demands were reasonable; the workers, however, have borne the major share of blame for the city's fiscal crisis.

2624. Ehrenberg, Ronald G. MUNICIPAL GOVERNMENT STRUCTURE, UNIONIZATION, AND THE WAGES OF FIRE FIGHTERS. *Industrial and Labor Relations Rev. 1973 27(1): 36-48.* This study tests the hypothesis that labor costs in municipal government are influenced by the structure of "management"—whether the chief operating officer is a professional manager or elected official—as well as by the strength of organization among employees. Using fire fighters as a test group, the author constructs a model to explain the variation among cities in the demand for and supply of firemen and applies this model to data for 1969 and a sample of 270 cities. He concludes that unionism does have a significant wage effect in cities that have agreed to a formal labor contract, but the structure of city government appears to have only a minor impact on wages. J

2625. Foster, Howard G. THE LABOR MARKET IN NONUNION CONSTRUCTION. *Industrial and Labor Relations Rev. 1973 26(4): 1071-1085.* Studies the labor market in nonunion construction. Relying primarily on interviews with 143 nonunion builders in the Buffalo area, the author examines hiring practices, worker training, wages and benefits, and seasonality of employment. The nonunion market does perform well in several aspects of wage setting and manpower utilization, but it probably does not function as effectively as the union sector in the hiring and training of workers. J

2626. Georgakas, Dan and Surkin, Marvin. NIGGERMATION IN AUTO: COMPANY POLICY AND THE RISE OF BLACK CAUCUSES. *Radical Am. 1975 9(1): 31-57.* Since 1968 several cases of company policy in the automobile industry have been challenged by ELRUM, the Detroit unit of the League of Revolutionary Black Workers.

2627. Geschwender, James A. THE LEAGUE OF REVOLUTIONARY BLACK WORKERS: PROBLEMS OF CONFRONTING BLACK MARXIST-LENINIST ORGANIZATIONS. *J. of Ethnic Studies 1974 2(3): 1-23.* Analyzes the five-year career of the Detroit-based League of Revolutionary Black Workers, formed by the integration of the Dodge Revolutionary Union Movement at the Hamtramck Assembly Plant with the component Ford and Eldon Avenue Movements in 1968; it was designed to fight racism and the oppression of Negroes in the automobile industry. Led by John Watson, General G. Baker, Jr., Luke S. Tripp, Jr., and using their periodical, *The Inner City Voice*, they called wildcat strikes, sought to raise black worker consciousness of their economic power, and organized the Detroit Branch of the Black Panther Party. Control of the Wayne State University student paper, and cooperation with the National Black Economic Development Conference followed. Ideological disagreements between adherents of a capitalist exploitation model, with socialist revolution as its goal, and the colonial model favoring a black separatist state led to the League's demise, but the stimulus it provided has not been lost. Based largely on first-hand newspaper accounts, interviews with participants; 70 notes.
G. J. Bobango

2628. Glaberman, Martin. BLACK CATS, WHITE CATS, WILDCATS: AUTO WORKERS IN DETROIT. *Radical Am. 1975 9(1): 25-29.* Gives a short history of auto workers in Detroit 1941 to present, including the influx of new workers during the war years, the years of Walter Reuther's career, and the Detroit rebellion of 1967.

2629. Haynes, John Earl. THE "RANK AND FILE" MOVEMENT IN PRIVATE SOCIAL WORK. *Labor Hist. 1975 16(1): 78-98.* In New York City the downward pressures on wages and the increase in case loads in private social work agencies stimulated a "Rank and File" movement among social workers. Three goals emerged: unionization of social workers, reformation of social work practices, and radical political action. Although resistance by the private agencies was important, the decline of the movement began with its shifts in political action caused by the influence of Communists among rank and filers. Based on papers in the Social Welfare History Archives and on *Social Work Today*; 44 notes.
L. L. Athey

2630. Levine, Charles H. and Perry, James L. PUBLIC SECTOR UNIONISM: THEORY AND METHODOLOGY. *Am. Pol. Q. 1975 3(2): 209-214.* Discusses recent writings dealing with the political theory of public sector unionism and strikes in relation to city government, 1971.

2631. Lewin, David. LOCAL GOVERNMENT LABOR RELATIONS IN TRANSITION: THE CASE OF LOS ANGELES. *Labor Hist. 1976 17(2): 191-213.* Provides a case study in public sector labor relations. During 1966-71 labor relations became more formal, but multiple sources of authority and bargaining continued. The civil service system was not reduced, public employee unions remained diverse in character and impact, government was spurred by unions into consideration of management functions, and "longitudinal methodology" as a model for study of the public sector proved important. Based on Los Angeles city and county records and publications; 38 notes.
L. L. Athey

2632. May, James W., Jr. ATLANTA TRANSIT STRIKE, 1949-1950, PRELUDE TO SALE. Fink, Gary M. and Reed, Merl E., eds. *Essays in Southern Labor History: Selected Papers, Southern Labor History Conference, 1976.* (Westport, Conn.; London, England: Greenwood Pr., 1977): 208-219. Studies the years of disagreements and negotiations between labor and management which preceded the Atlanta transit strike, longest in the city's history. Unable to break the deadlock with Division 732 of the Amalgamated Association of Street, Electric Railway and Motor Coach Employees of America, the Georgia Power Company sold its recently modernized Atlanta transit properties to the locally controlled Atlanta Transit Company. In forcing this sale Division 732 had "successfully challenged Atlanta's traditionally impervious power structure." 42 notes.
R. V. Ritter

2633. Nash, Al. THE LOCAL UNION: CENTER OF LIFE IN THE UAW. *Dissent 1978 25(4): 398-408.* Relates the history of Local 7, the representative of the Detroit Chrysler Kercheval-Jefferson plant workers in the United Auto Workers since 1937.

2634. Nigro, Felix A. URBAN GOVERNMENTS AND THE UNIONS. *Urban Affairs Q. 1974 9(4): 529-536.* Reviews Harry H. Wellington and Ralph K. Winter, Jr.'s *The Unions and the Cities* (Washington, D.C.: Brookings Inst., 1971), David T. Stanley's *Managing Local Government Under Union Pressure* (Washington, D.C.: Brookings Inst., 1971), Jack Steiber's *Public Employee Unionism: Structure, Growth, Policy* (Washington, D.C.: Brookings Inst., 1973), Robert H. Connery and William V. Farr, eds. *Unionization of Municipal Employees* (New York: Acad. of Pol. Sci., 1970), Sam Zagoria's *Public Workers and Public Unions* (Englewood Cliffs, New Jersey: Prentice-Hall, 1972), and Sterling Spero and John M. Cappozzola's *The Urban Community and Its Unionized Bureaucracies, Pressure Politics in Local Government Labor Relations* (New York: Dunellen, 1973). S

2635. Paulson, Darryl and Stiff, Janet. AN EMPTY VICTORY: THE ST. PETERSBURG SANITATION STRIKE, 1968. *Florida Hist. Q. 1979 57(4): 421-433.* A sanitation workers' strike in May 1968 began as a nonviolent movement but became violent by midsummer. After four months the workers returned to their jobs without pay raises and with a loss of seniority. The city suffered some $400,000 worth of damage plus the cost of overtime wages. It did gain with the promotion of integration, a fair housing ordinance, and redistricting. Primary and secondary sources; 2 photos, 42 notes.
N. A. Kuntz

2636. Russell, Michael B. GREENVILLE'S EXPERIMENT: THE NON-UNION CULTURE. *Southern Exposure 1979 7(1): 94-97, 100.* The business elite and the Chamber of Commerce in Greenville, South Carolina, prevent unionizing efforts and convince Greenville's citizens that nonorganization is best; 1970's.

2637. Sloan, Cliff and Hall, Bob. "IT'S GOOD TO BE HOME IN GREENVILLE" . . . BUT IT'S BETTER IF YOU HATE UNIONS. *Southern Exposure 1979 7(1): 82-93.* Describes the efforts of labor organizers in the antiunion city of Greenville, South Carolina, in the 1970's, home of Michelin Tire Corporation and J.P. Stevens & Company, among others, and gives a brief history of the area's industry since 1873.

2638. Witney, Fred. FINAL-OFFER ARBITRATION: THE INDIANAPOLIS EXPERIENCE. *Monthly Labor Rev. 1973 96(5): 20-25.* Discusses and evaluates the use of final-offer arbitration in a public sector labor dispute, specifically referring to the case of the city of Indianapolis and the American Federation of State, County, and Municipal Employees, with negotiations lasting from September 1971 through February 1972.

2639. Unsigned. PHILADELPHIA, 1973: WHY THE SPECTER OF A GENERAL STRIKE LOOMED FROM THE TEACHERS' FIGHT. *Progressive Labor 1973 9(2): 17-25.* Describes the eight-week strike waged by the Philadelphia Federation of Teachers. The general strike which was threatened and planned by almost every major union in the city overwhelmed at that moment every enemy.   J

Society and Culture

General

2640. Baldassare, Mark. THE EFFECTS OF DENSITY ON SOCIAL BEHAVIOR AND ATTITUDES. *Am. Behavioral Scientist 1975 18(6): 815-825.* Analyzes Detroit area data collected in 1965-66 in order to explore the relationships between urban crowding, crowded conditions in homes, and individual attitudes and needs for human affiliation.   S

2641. Banfield, Edward C. A CRITICAL VIEW OF THE URBAN CRISIS. *Ann. of the Am. Acad. of Pol. and Social Sci. 1973 (405): 7-14.* The accounts usually given of the causes of the "urban crisis" are not satisfactory: congestion is decreasing, not increasing; the flight to the suburbs has not left the central cities on the verge of bankruptcy; the urban housing supply is on the whole much better than ever; white racism has long been on the wane, and blacks are making rapid income and other gains; and the fragmentation of local government does not account for its ineffectiveness. Changes in the state of the public mind are the main cause of the crisis. Set in motion mainly by the ideas of philosophers, these are reflected in the attitudes of elites and of the middle class with respect to authority, the self, rational egotism, hedonism, egalitarianism, and consumerism. It follows that the crisis will not be ended by either government programs or by exhortation.   J

2642. Beck, Jane C. A TRADITIONAL WITCH OF THE TWENTIETH CENTURY. *New York Folklore Q. 1974 30(2): 101-116.* Study of Dolorez Amelia Gomez of Philadelphia, Pennsylvania, who practices traditional witchcraft.   S

2643. Brandunas, Elena. AN URBAN HERMIT. *Indiana Folklore 1977 10(2): 159-164.* Analyzes the unusual social acceptance accorded Martin Piniak, a hermit living in East Chicago, Indiana, 1942-76.

2644. Brooks, Paul. NEW ENGLAND'S OLD WAY OF LIFE SHAPES LINCOLN. *Smithsonian 1976 7(5): 74-81.* Discusses the old-fashioned flavor of Lincoln, Massachusetts, a small town which has decided to maintain its image of colonial and rural New England, 1784-1976.

2645. Coughlin, Robert E. ATTAINMENT ALONG GOAL DIMENSIONS IN 101 METROPOLITAN AREAS. *J. of the Am. Inst. of Planners 1973 39(6): 413-425.* Sixty goals grouped into 17 general categories are defined. Data on attainment are analyzed for 101 Metropolitan Areas in 1960. Between goals within a general category, intercorrelations are relatively high; but fewer significant correlations are found between goals from different categories. Income indicators are the best single measure of overall goal attainment, but are unrelated to a number of other goal attainment indicators, especially indicators of physical goals. Few negative associations are found, implying that attainment along one goal is rarely associated with decreased attainment along another goal. Factor analysis resulted in the identification of a small number of generalized variables which explain the pattern of common variation among the original goal attainment variables. These generalized variables are interpreted and metropolitan areas, which are strongly characterized by them, are identified.   J

2646. Cybriwsky, Roman A. SOCIAL ASPECTS OF NEIGHBORHOOD CHANGE. *Ann. of the Assoc. of Am. Geographers 1978 68(1): 17-33.* During the last decade, Fairmount, a small area in Philadelphia's inner city, has changed from a working-class neighborhood with a strong European-ethnic flavor to a revitalized, "fashionable" area with many young professionals. One step in the transition was the exclusion of blacks from the neighborhood. The influx of newcomers to Fairmount has altered traditional social patterns, and for some residents resulted in a declining quality of neighborhood life.   J

2647. Dorson, Richard M. HUNTING FOLKLORE IN THE ARMPIT OF AMERICA. *Indiana Folklore 1977 10(2): 97-106.* Results of a folklore project in northwestern Indiana, an area of heavy industrialization and urbanization, yielded local geographical and cultural, steelworker, ethnic, black, and crime folklore, 1976.

2648. Glazer, Nathan. ON SUBWAY GRAFFITI IN NEW YORK. *Public Interest 1979 54: 3-11.* On the outside of New York City subway cars, graffiti makers spray paint large representations of their names, while inside they obscure maps, signs, and windows. To the subway rider the graffiti is part of the story of "crime in the subways," and it contributes to the feeling that New York City is menacing and uncontrollable. At any given time there are about 500 graffiti makers, ranging in age from around 11 to 16. Various means of stopping them, from arrest to attempts to get them to paint on canvas, have failed. A new approach that might succeed involves education and therapy programs for the offenders run by youth workers and social agencies.   S. Harrow

2649. Hacker, Andrew. A CITY OF COMMUNITIES. *New York Affairs 1975 2(4): 8-27.* New York's neighborhoods are no longer quiescent places of inward-looking, undemanding locals, if they ever were. They are insistent upon their "rights," often without recognizing their obligations in the struggle for self-improvement.   J

2650. Hochschild, Arlie Russell. COMMUNAL LIFE-STYLES FOR THE OLD. *Society 1973 10(5): 50-57.* Analyzes communal bonds of aged widows who live in apartments near San Francisco Bay.   S

2651. Holstein, Constance B.; Stroud, Janice; and Haan, Norma. ALIENATED AND NONALIENATED YOUTH: PERCEPTIONS OF PARENTS, SELF-EVALUATIONS, AND MORAL REASONING OF HIPPIES AND COLLEGE YOUTH. *Youth & Soc. 1974 5(3): 279-302.* Compares data from samples of hippies and activist and nonactivist college students living in the San Francisco area during 1968-70 to determine how the youths relate to society.   S

2652. Hunter, Albert. THE LOSS OF COMMUNITY: AN EMPIRICAL TEST THROUGH REPLICATION. *Am. Sociol. Rev. 1975 40(5): 537-552.* This survey and field observation study replicates Donald Foley's *Neighbors or Urbanites?* (1952) in the same urban neighborhood [Rochester, New York] twenty-five years later to test the dynamic hypothesized "loss of community" in urban life. Three indexes reflecting three dimensions of community were explored. "Local facility use" declined, "informal neighboring" showed no change, while "sense of community" increased. The latter two did not decline because the area has attracted residents who economically and ideologically "value" the changes which have occurred in the area and the resulting "ecological niche" which the area has come to occupy. It is middle-class, racially integrated and urban. Residents have consciously sought out this area because of these characteristics and have consciously attempted to create community in part through an active local community organization. Drawing upon Mannheim's distinction between utopia and ideology, the area is defined as a consciously created "ideological community."   J

2653. Irving, Henry W. SOCIAL NETWORKS IN THE MODERN CITY. *Social Forces 1977 55(4): 867-880.* Social network concept has suffered through difficulties in developing from it any operational devices suitable for use in ordinary social survey research. Here, one such device is presented, and its utility is examined in the contrasting urban contexts of Hull, England, and Los Angeles. Existing theories about the correlates of network density are partially confirmed and partially contradicted by the findings. In particular there is an attempt to reevaluate the part played by kinship in the social networks of modern urban society.   J

2654. Morris, Jan. LETTER FROM CHATTANOOGA: VIEWS FROM LOOKOUT MOUNTAIN. *Encounter [Great Britain] 1975 44(6): 42-48.* Discusses the daily life and culture of Chattanooga, Tennessee, in 1975, including the historical heritage of Lookout Mountain.

2655. Orfield, Gary. FEDERAL POLICY, LOCAL POWER, AND METROPOLITAN SEGREGATION. *Pol. Sci. Q. 1974-75 89(4): 777-802.* Describes the spreading patterns of residential and educational segregation in urban and suburban areas and discusses the efforts of the judiciary to devise remedies for such segregation, showing the reach and limitations of existing decisions and the importance of developing metropolitanwide approaches.   J

2656. Parkin, Michael. SUICIDE AND CULTURE IN FAIRBANKS: A COMPARISON OF THREE CULTURAL GROUPS IN A SMALL CITY OF INTERIOR ALASKA. *Psychiatry 1974 37(1): 60-67.*

2657. Strickland, Donald E. BOOK REVIEW ESSAY: THE SOCIAL STRUCTURE OF URBAN NEIGHBORHOODS. *Urban Affairs Q. 1979 14(3): 391-400.* The congruence of the theoretical frameworks of the five studies under review suggests a promising new direction for neighborhoods studies. Claude S. Fischer in *The Urban Experience* (New York: Harcourt, Brace, Jovanovich, 1976) assays the effect of urban scale on the social psychology and social relations of urban residents. He rejects both the "determinist" and "compositional" schools of thought and concludes that urban life is integrated by nonplace-specific subcultural groups. Claude S. Fischer, Robert Max Jackson, C. Ann Stueve, Kathleen Gerson, and Lynne McCallister Jones, with Mark Baldassare, in *Networks and Places: Social Relations in the Urban Setting* (New York: Free Pr., 1977), extend this analysis by arguing that the urban environment provides both opportunities for and constraints on the formation of social ties. William Michelson in *Environmental Choice: Human Behavior and Residential Satisfaction* (New York: Oxford U. Pr., 1977) urges that the residential environment be seen as an "opportunity field" in which individuals engage in rationally motivated behavior. David J. O'Brien in *Neighborhood Organization and Interest Group Process* (Princeton, N.J.: Princeton U. Pr., 1976) finds some of the same constraints on political organization that Michelson found inhibiting social relations and friendship networks. David C. Thorn's *The Quest for Community: Social Aspects of Residential Growth* (New York: Halsted, 1976) is marred by theoretically unintegrated aspects of community development.   L. N. Beecher

2658. Tremblay, Kenneth R., Jr. and Dunlap, Riley E. RURAL-URBAN RESIDENCE AND CONCERN WITH ENVIRONMENTAL QUALITY: A REPLICATION AND EXTENSION. *Rural Sociol. 1978 43(3): 474-491.* Refers to earlier articles—by Frederick H. Buttel and William L. Flinn and by Buttel in *Journal of Environmental Education* 1975 7(Fall): 53-65.

2659. vanEs, J. C. and Brown, Jack E., Jr. THE RURAL-URBAN VARIABLE ONCE MORE: SOME INDIVIDUAL LEVEL OBSERVATIONS. *Rural Sociol. 1974 39(3): 373-391.* The status of 'rural-urban differences' is examined for a sample of western Illinois heads of households. Findings indicate that: 1) socioeconomic status generally accounted for more of the variation in the dependent variables than either occupation or residence; and 2) when the effect of socioeconomic status is removed, behavioral items were more often related to either occupation or residence than were attitudinal items.   J/S

2660. Viney, Wayne; Loomis, Ross; Hautaluoma, Jacob; and Wagner, Stanley. A COMPARISON OF PERCEIVED ORGANIZATIONAL INFLUENCE IN TWO METROPOLITAN COMMUNITIES.

Rocky Mountain Social Sci. J. 1974 11(1): 81-86. Compares community influence between Denver (Colorado) and Oklahoma City (Oklahoma).   S

2661. Willits, Fern K.; Bealer, Robert C.; and Crider, Donald M. THE ECOLOGY OF SOCIAL TRADITIONALISM IN A RURAL HINTERLAND. *Rural Sociol. 1974 39(3): 334-349.* Examines the utility of metropolitan and urban dominance constructs for dealing with patterning of noneconomic and nondemographic factors in hinterland areas by examining attitudes toward selected aspects of traditional morality within a large sample of Pennsylvania adolescents living in farm, open country, and small town residence categories. In general, as miles from city centers increased, the degree of adherence to traditional attitudes also increased. The patterning in correlation terms was equal to that shown in others' research for economic and demographic variables. The dominance measures compared favorably to place of residence as explanatory factors.   J

Demography, Population, and the Family

2662. Alonso, William. URBAN ZERO POPULATION GROWTH. *Daedalus 1974 102(4): 191-206.* Discusses the demographic implications of zero population growth in cities.   S

2663. Carnahan, Douglas; Gove, Walter; and Galle, Omer R. URBANIZATION, POPULATION DENSITY, AND OVERCROWDING: TRENDS IN THE QUALITY OF LIFE IN AMERICA. *Social Forces 1974 53(1): 62-72.* Explores changes in the quality of life as reflected in household density, and the possible association of household density with rates of pathological behavior. Data were drawn from the 1940-70 Housing Censuses to analyze changes at the national level, and by region, race, and setting (central city, standard metropolitan area, and farm) in median number of persons per room and percent of households with more than one person per room. Results indicated that crowding is, for the nation as a whole, on the decline; that households in central cities and SMSAs are no more crowded than the national average; that serious overcrowding is greater on farms than in other locations; that regional differences in household densities are diminishing; and that a majority of black households, though they have higher densities than whites, are gaining ground relative to whites, although a minority of black households are falling behind the density declines of both groups. The fact that household densities in central cities are not especially high compared to other locations combined with the marked improvements in household densities since 1940, suggests that this form of density does not account for increases in pathological behavior.   J

2664. Choldin, Harvey M. INTRODUCTION: URBAN DENSITY AND CROWDING. *Am. Behavioral Scientist 1975 18(6): 733-735.* Introduces a special issue of *American Behavioral Scientist* devoted to the effects of urban population density on people.   S

2665. DeVise, Pierre THE WASTING OF CHICAGO. *Focus Midwest 1973 9(58): 7-9.* A comparison of the 1960 and 1970 censuses shows that Chicago's middle-class white population is shrinking and that its proportion of black and Spanish-speaking people is growing. The metropolis is losing factories, stores, jobs, and housing to the suburbs. Fear of blacks and the overbuilding of suburban housing combined with the shortage of city housing to push whites to the suburbs.

L. H. Grothaus

2666. Dye, Thomas R. POPULATION DENSITY AND SOCIAL PATHOLOGY. *Urban Affairs Q. 1975 11(2): 265-275.* Attempts to determine if population density is an independent contributing factor to urban social pathology. Defines social pathology and concludes through use of statistical analysis that there is little to confirm a population density-social pathology relationship. 3 tables, note, biblio.

P. J. Woehrmann

2667. Glazer, Nathan. SOCIAL AND POLITICAL AGING IN NEW YORK. *Society 1976 13(4): 45-47.* Examines the impact of no-growth demography on social conditions, minorities, employment, fiscal policy, etc., in metropolitan areas in the 1970's.

2668. Graber, Edith E.   NEWCOMERS AND OLDTIMERS: GROWTH AND CHANGE IN A MOUNTAIN TOWN. *Rural Sociol. 1974 39(4): 504-513.* Demographic study from the 1970 census focusing on Georgetown, Colorado.   S

2669. Hawkes, Roland K.   SPATIAL PATTERNING OF URBAN POPULATION CHARACTERISTICS. *Am. J. of Sociol. 1973 78(5): 1216-1235.* Develops a mathematical expression of the classic zone and sector phenomena in the distribution of residential neighborhood characteristics in urban areas. Problems of evaluation are discussed, and the use of the model is illustrated with the 1960 census tract statistics for Baltimore, Maryland.   J

2670. Kale, Steven.   SMALL TOWN POPULATION CHANGE IN THE CENTRAL GREAT PLAINS: AN INVESTIGATION OF RECENT TRENDS. *Rocky Mountain Social Sci. J. 1975 12(1): 29-43.*

2671. Kanter, Rosabeth Moss.   ROOTS VERSUS RESTLESSNESS: COOPERATIVE HOUSEHOLDS, THE CITY, AND RECURRENT ISSUES IN AMERICAN FAMILY LIFE. *Massachusetts Rev. 1976 17(2): 331-351.* Roots and restlessness have been for years the dominant warring factions in American family life: the small-town extended family of nostalgia versus the big-city cooperative "families." Cooperative households in cities are as valid a part of the American tradition as town picket fences. The early cooperatives were boarding and rooming houses, and residential hotels. In the 20th century the urban communes have come to the fore. A cooperative house is more task-sharing and more public. Their fragility makes it unlikely that they will achieve an ever-increasing popularity, but they reflect a trend away from biological imperatives in households. Secondary sources; 18 notes, biblio.
                                    E. R. Campbell

2672. Kenyon, James B.   SPATIAL ASSOCIATIONS IN THE INTEGRATION OF THE AMERICAN CITY. *Econ. Geography 1976 52(4): 287-303.* Analyzes the distribution, extent, and morphological position of bicultural neighborhoods in Atlanta, Honolulu, and San Antonio, 1960's-70's.

2673. Long, Larry H.   HOW THE RACIAL COMPOSITION OF CITIES CHANGES. *Land Econ. 1975 51(3): 260-267.* Compares the population of 11 cities in 1950, 1960, and 1970. Finds the changing racial composition of the cities is due more to the out-migration of whites of child-bearing age than any other factor. 3 tables, 4 notes, biblio.
                                    E. S. Johnson

2674. Masnick, George S. and McFalls, Joseph A.   A NEW PERSPECTIVE ON THE TWENTIETH-CENTURY AMERICAN FERTILITY SWING. *J. of Family Hist. 1976 1(2): 216-243.* Using data from a fertility survey of 718 black women living in Philadelphia in 1975, the authors examine the reasons for the sharp drop in fertility until the Great Depression, the postwar baby boom that peaked in 1957, and the drop in fertility from then to the mid-70's. Traditional hypotheses for this swing, the "Demographic Transition," the "New Household Economic perspective," and the "VD hypothesis," are considered and rejected. A new theory is advanced and tested which emphasizes the critical role of early socialization to family limitation techniques. Secondary and survey data; 9 tables, 10 notes, biblio.   T. W. Smith

2675. Pampel, Fred C. and Choldin, Harvey M.   URBAN LOCATION AND SEGREGATION OF THE AGED: A BLOCK-LEVEL ANALYSIS. *Social Forces 1978 56(4): 1121-1139.* Sociological treatment of the aged as a minority group and ecological theories of urban structure suggest that the urban aged should be segregated from other age life-cycle groups and be concentrated near city centers. This study examines intraurban location and segregation of the aged in two cities, Cleveland and San Diego. Although the two cities differ in ecological structure, the aged in both tend to be located on blocks near the city center, with multi-unit structures, high value housing, low population potential, low crowding, and a high proportion of primary individuals. The relationships, however, are generally weak and the variance explained small, indicating dispersion of the aged throughout the cities. Dissimilarity indices also show a moderate degree of segregation between the aged and the non-aged. These results suggest that conceptions of the aged as segregated into centralized, undesirable urban areas are overstated.   J

2676. Pearson, Ralph L.   INTERRACIAL CONFLICT IN TWENTIETH CENTURY CONNECTICUT CITIES: THE DEMOGRAPHIC FACTOR. *Connecticut Hist. 1976 (17): 1-14.* Discusses demographic aspects of racial unrest in the cities of Bridgeport, Hartford, New Haven, and Waterbury, Connecticut, 1967-69.

2677. Polgar, S. and Hiday, Virginia A.   THE EFFECT OF ADDITIONAL BIRTH ON LOW-INCOME URBAN FAMILIES. *Population Studies [Great Britain] 1974 28(3): 463-472.* Examines effects of the birth of an additional child to families living in poverty areas of New York City using data collected in 1965 and 1967 from surveys given to parous or married women of childbearing age. Controlling for the number of children in the family in 1965, the non-occurrence of an additional birth in the following two years was found to have a significant effect on current income, savings, reliance on public assistance, general ability to plan and organize one's household, and wife's employment. No significant effects were found with respect to possession of consumer durables or attending a school or training course.   J/S

2678. Power, Mary G.   ETHNIC CONCENTRATION AND SOCIOECONOMIC STATUS IN METROPOLITAN AREAS. *Ethnicity 1978 5(3): 266-273.* Examination of data derived from standard metropolitan statistical areas (SMSA) indicates confirmation of R. Breton's findings that the institutional completeness of large ethnic communities attracts and holds those ethnic group members with the lowest education levels and skills. Those SMSA's having the lowest concentration of foreign stock residents are also those in which the latter hold the highest socioeconomic status. On the other hand, in all SMSA's the socioeconomic status of native whites of native parentage and nonwhites was highest in areas having the largest foreign stock concentration. 5 tables.   N. Lederer

2679. Ritchey, P. Neal   EFFECTS OF MARITAL STATUS ON THE FERTILITY OF RURAL-URBAN AND URBAN-RURAL MIGRANTS. *Rural Sociol. 1973 38(1): 26-35.* Determines the intervening effects of marital status on the relation between migration and fertility. Among white, married women 20 to 44 years of age, rural-urban migrants have only slightly higher fertility than that of indigenous urban women, which slightly increases the rate of population growth in urban areas. Urban-rural migrants, on the other hand, have lower fertility than indigenous rural women and consequently serve to lower the growth rate in rural areas. The relative effect upon the growth rates at place of destination is greater for urban-rural than for rural-urban migrants. In general, migrants were more likely than indigenous sending and receiving populations to have been ever-married and be married and living with spouse —including being in a sustained first marriage and being remarried. Proportionately more migrants and less indigenous women bear children. Therefore, when we examine fertility of all women, irrespective of marital status, the childbearing of rural-urban migrants makes a moderate contribution to increasing the population growth rate in urban areas. In rural areas, when women's marital status is ignored, the presence of urban-rural migrants sustains the rate of population growth— partially offsetting the lowering effect of the fertility of the rural indigenous women.
                                    J

2680. Rose, Harold M.   METROPOLITAN MIAMI'S CHANGING NEGRO POPULATION, 1950-60. *Econ. Geography 1964 40(3): 221-239.* Changes in the distribution of Miami, Florida's, black population, 1950-60, was a function of proximity to place of employment.

2681. Savitch, H. V.   BLACK CITIES/WHITE SUBURBS: DOMESTIC COLONIALISM AS AN INTERPRETIVE IDEA. *Ann. of the Am. Acad. of Pol. and Social Sci. 1978 (439): 118-134.* This essay analyzes race relations in America from the perspective of changing demographic trends between cities and suburbs. Essentially, it treats cities and suburbs as territorially distinct units through which social processes between racial or ethnic groups are carried out. Central cities are fast becoming reservations for the poor and unwanted; suburbs are increasingly exclusive and enjoy a privileged status for those who can afford to reside in them. Using data on racial/ethnic concentration, welfare and unemployment, this essay applies the analogue of colonies and colonizing societies to examine the dynamics between black central cities and white suburbs. A final section of the essay discusses the political and legal mechanisms which work to make "domestic colonialism" possible.   J

2682. Schafer, Robert. METROPOLITAN FORM AND DEMOGRAPHIC CHANGE. *Urban Studies [Great Britain] 1978 15(1): 23-33.* Variations in urban form and development depend on the distribution of population characteristics, such as age and marital status, as well as commuting costs and family income. The structure type choices of households vary substantially with stage in the family life cycle. For example, the large number of young and single households entering the housing market in the 1960's were a primary force behind the apartment boom. A stock adjustment model incorporating demographic information, income, and workplace location suggests that the addition of demographic data will lead to major improvements in housing market studies.
J

2683. Schultz, Marilyn Spigel. THE GRAYING OF WESTCHESTER. *New York Affairs 1979 5(4): 103-110.* Examines the population of Westchester since the 1950's, particularly the increasing percentage of Westchester's older residents and their needs and problems.

2684. Shaw, R. Paul. A CONCEPTUAL MODEL OF RURAL-URBAN TRANSITION AND REPRODUCTIVE BEHAVIOR. *Rural Sociol. 1974 39(1): 70-91.* Studies effects of economic conditions and social change on family size among rural to urban migrants for 1960-71.
S

2685. Simkus, Albert A. RESIDENTIAL SEGREGATION BY OCCUPATION AND RACE IN TEN URBANIZED AREAS, 1950-1970. *Am. Sociol. Rev. 1978 43(1): 81-93.* Earlier studies by Duncan and Duncan (1955), Wilkins (1956), and Uyeki (1964) examined occupational residential segregation in a total of ten US urbanized areas in 1950. The present study is a partial replication of these previous investigations, directed at measuring the changes in residential segregation in these same urbanized areas during the 1950's and 1960's. Changes in the relationship between racial segregation and occupational residential segregation are also examined. Occupational residential segregation between most occupational categories was found to have slightly increased during the 1950's. During the 1960's the degree of residential segregation between service workers and laborers vis-à-vis those in the higher occupational categories decreased, while segregation between persons in the higher categories remained much the same. Indexes of occupational residential dissimilarity calculated within and between racial groups reveal the degree to which gross occupational residential segregation was due to racial residential segregation and differentials between occupational categories in racial composition. These indexes also show that the degree of racial residential segregation depended somewhat upon the respective occupations of the whites and nonwhites whose residential distributions were compared. In 1960, the degree of racial residential segregation was slightly lower between whites and nonwhites in the lower categories. Between 1960 and 1970 nonwhites in the highest occupational categories became slightly less segregated from whites, while whites and nonwhites in the lowest occupational categories become slightly more segregated.
J

2686. Slesinger, Doris P. THE RELATIONSHIP OF FERTILITY TO MEASURES OF METROPOLITAN DOMINANCE: A NEW LOOK. *Rural Sociol. 1974 39(3): 350-361.* Examines the relationship of fertility to three measures of metropolitan dominance: size of place, distance from central city, and the Stoeckel-Beegle size-distance index. Using data from the 1965 National Fertility Study, the number of children ever born to married women under 45 is examined. Fertility differentials exist within all three dominance measures, with rural farm areas having high fertility and central city residents low fertility. However, when duration of marriage, religion, work experience, and education are controlled in a multiple regression model, very little additional variance was explained by metropolitan dominance measures. It is suggested that fertility differentials are due to the characteristics of the women living in these areas rather than to the influence of the city on the hinterland.
J

2687. Stinner, William F. and Mader, Paul D. METROPOLITAN DOMINANCE AND FERTILITY CHANGE IN PUERTO RICO 1950-1970. *Social and Econ. Studies [Jamaica] 1975 24(4): 433-444.* Relates change in fertility by municipo to distance from and degree of connectivity to a metropolitan center. Finds that a real decline in the closer, better-connected municipos occurred earlier than in the more

remote ones, but that by 1970 the fertility patterns were similar. 4 tables, 5 notes, biblio.
E. S. Johnson

2688. Woodrow, Karen; Hastings, Donald W.; and Tu, Edward J. RURAL-URBAN PATTERNS OF MARRIAGE, DIVORCE, AND MORTALITY: TENNESSEE, 1970. *Rural Sociol. 1978 43(1): 70-84.* Assesses differences in rural and urban patterns of marriage, divorce, remarriage, and mortality, according to age and sex.

2689. —. [URBAN MORTALITY RATES]. *Social Sci. Q. 1974 55(1): 182-94.*
Poston, Dudley L., Jr. AN EXAMINATION OF URBAN MORTALITY USING AGE-ADJUSTED DEATH RATES, pp. 182-188. Critique of a study by Kent Schwirian and Anthony LaGreca on the ecological causes of urban mortality. Schwirian and LaGreca failed to use an age adjusted death rate, which not only significantly alters their findings in degree, but suggests the possibility of outright error and wholly incorrect conclusions. Based on secondary sources; table, 2 figs., 25 notes.
Schwirian, Kent P. and LaGreca, Anthony J. THE EFFECT OF ALTERNATIVE AGE ADJUSTMENT PROCEDURES ON THE ANALYSIS OF URBAN MORTALITY PATTERNS, pp. 189-194. A reply to Dudley Poston's critique. Age adjusted rates were not used because the data was not readily available and not directly relevant to the problem under investigation. Reanalysis on the basis of age adjusted rates does significantly alter certain conclusions, although age adjusted rates are not the whole answer. Based on secondary sources; table, 13 notes.
V. L. Human

Voluntary Associations

2690. Brightman, Carol. THE WOMEN OF WILLIAMSBURG. *Working Papers for a New Soc. 1978 6(1): 50-57.* The work of the National Congress of Neighborhood Women, originally a neighborhood association organized in the Williamsburg section of Brooklyn, New York, 1966, includes urban and neighborhood renewal, support for abortions and contraception, and a nationally active information organization for those interested in local community action.

2691. Cohen, Steve Martin and Kapsis, Robert E. PARTICIPATION OF BLACKS, PUERTO RICANS AND WHITES IN VOLUNTARY ASSOCIATIONS: A TEST OF CURRENT THEORIES. *Social Forces 1978 56(4): 1053-1071.* To interpret the relatively high rates of voluntary organization participation among blacks, theorists have developed deprivation and normative explanations. Both interpretations suggest that oppressed minority groups will develop group coherence and salience to their members. However, unlike the deprivation argument, the normative conception does not view the development of activist norms as an inevitable outcome of this process. By examining the organizational behavior of Puerto Ricans, blacks, and whites in New York City, we test several key postulates from each interpretation. None of the postulates is consistently supported. Most damaging to both arguments is that black ethnic identifiers do not exhibit higher participatory rates than their more assimilated peers. That lower-class black women manifest an unusually active pattern of organizational membership as compared with their male counterparts is shown also to be incompatible with both the deprivation and normative conceptions. Further inquiries into the mechanisms which predispose a particular subgroup within a minority population to be more involved in voluntary organizations than another are recommended.
J

2692. Dorsey, Herbert W. THE CLEVELAND SEAMEN'S SERVICE. *Inland Seas 1977 33(1): 33-36.* The need for a seamen's aid organization at Cleveland, Ohio became evident when the opening of the St. Lawrence Seaway brought large numbers of foreign sailors to the port. The Cleveland Seamen's Service, formed in 1972, filled that need. It operated from the East Ninth Street Pier and Burke Lakefront Airport until moving into new quarters on West Third Street in 1975. Describes the facilities available and lists the officers for 1977.
K. J. Bauer

2693. Edwards, John N.; Klemmack, David L.; and Hatos, Louis, Jr. SOCIAL PARTICIPATION PATTERNS AMONG MOBILE-HOME AND SINGLE-FAMILY DWELLERS. *Social Forces 1973 51(4): 485-*

489. The central concern of this article is the differences in participation patterns between mobile-home and single-family dwellers residing in contiguous suburban areas. Based on a random sample of 60 mobile-home and 55 single-family dwellers, our findings indicate that when sociodemographic characteristics are controlled, mobile-home residents participate more in some forms of informal activities and less in voluntary associations. Type of residence appears to have a greater impact upon associational participation than do sociodemographic characteristics, indicating the need to consider this variable when examining participation patterns.   J

2694. Engel, Steven M. and Andersen, William G., Jr. THE ALL-AMERICA CITIES AWARDS: DEMONSTRATION OF INTERDE-PENDENCE. *Natl. Civic Rev. 1975 64(4): 172-187, 191.* Winners of All-America Cities Awards demonstrate how citizen's groups can make a positive contribution to cities.   S

2695. Garrett, Franklin M. A SHORT ACCOUNT OF THE AT-LANTA HISTORICAL SOCIETY. *Georgia Hist. Q. 1979 63(1): 100-108.* Describes the development and facilities of the Atlanta Historical Society, 1926-79. 3 illus., 13 notes.   G. R. Schroeder

2696. Huang, Jui-Cheng and Gould, Peter. DIFFUSION IN AN UR-BAN HIERARCHY: THE CASE OF ROTARY CLUBS. *Econ. Geography 1974 50(4): 333-340.* Discusses the growth of Rotary International in the United States.   S

2697. Matthews, Mark S. THE EXPANDING ROLE OF CIVIC ORGANIZATIONS. *Natl. Civic R. 1975 64(4): 192-194.* Volunteer civic organizations are effectively combatting urban problems while retaining their independent character.   S

2698. Miller, Walter B. THE MOLLS. *Society 1973 11(1): 32-35.* Analyzes a girls' corner gang.   S

2699. Palmer, Earl. THE UNITED WAY AND THE BLACK COMMUNITY IN ATLANTA, GEORGIA. *Black Scholar 1977 9(4): 50-61.* Covers 1960-77.

2700. Pickvance, C. G. ON THE STUDY OF URBAN SOCIAL MOVEMENTS. *Sociol. Rev. [Great Britain] 1975 23(1): 29-49.* Discusses the growth of community organizations in dealing with local social problems in Great Britain and the United States in the 1960's-70's.

2701. Sassen-Koob, Saskia. FORMAL AND INFORMAL ASSOCI-ATIONS: DOMINICANS AND COLOMBIANS IN NEW YORK. *Int. Migration Rev. 1979 13(2): 314-332.* Examines Dominican and Colombian social organizations in New York City from approximately 1972 to 1976 and concludes that the greater incidence of voluntary associations in the Dominican community and their less instrumental character is rooted in the nature of the gap between place of origin and the receiving society, a gap which is much larger in the case of the Dominican than the Colombian community.

2702. Williams, J. Allen, Jr.; Babchuk, Nicholas; and Johnson, David R. VOLUNTARY ASSOCIATIONS AND MINORITY STATUS: A COMPARATIVE ANALYSIS OF ANGLO, BLACK, AND MEXI-CAN AMERICANS. *Am. Sociol. Rev. 1973 38(5): 637-646.* Focuses on the voluntary associations of Anglos, Negroes, and Mexican Americans in Austin, Texas. A sample of 380 respondents provided the data. Ethnicity proved to be an important variable in predicting social participation, with blacks having the highest and Mexican Americans having the lowest participation rate. Using multiple classification analysis, a number of structural variables were introduced as controls; and these variables, particularly education, were found to be responsible for the difference between Anglo and Mexican Americans. Blacks continued to have significantly higher rates of participation in voluntary associations after controlling on other variables. Both isolation and cultural inhibition theories can be found in previous literature to account for low participation rates among people having a subordinate status, and compensatory and ethnic community theories have been used to account for high rates of affiliation among these same groups. The findings from this study tend to cast doubt on isolation and cultural inhibition theories and to support compensatory and ethnic community theories.   J

Social Stratification and Class Culture

2703. Abbott, Carl. SUBURB AND CITY: CHANGING PAT-TERNS OF SOCIOECONOMIC STATUS IN METROPOLITAN DENVER SINCE 1940. *Social Sci. Hist. 1977 2(1): 53-71.* Assesses population redistribution trends among ethnic and socioeconomic groups in Denver, Colorado, 1940-77.

2704. Brown, Charles and Medoff, James. REVENUE SHARING: THE SHARE OF THE POOR. *Public Policy 1974 22(2): 169-188.* Discusses the effect of revenue sharing on the poor in the cities (1974).   S

2705. Bullamore, Henry W. THREE TYPES OF POVERTY IN METROPOLITAN INDIANAPOLIS. *Geographical Rev. 1974 64(4): 536-556.* The breakdown of poor families in the Indianapolis, Indiana, SMSA by source of income (earnings, social security, and public assistance) was expected to reveal sharp differences in the spatial distribution of residence. Instead, all three types of poverty families are similarly distributed in space, with similar ecological correlates. Consideration of poverty types in relation to housing types failed to identify any differences, but it was established that poor families with income from public assistance tend to live in areas with a high proportion of very poor families. Policy implications of the study were identified in terms of welfare-office location, community centers, and welfare reform.   J

2706. Davidson, Chandler and Gaitz, Charles M. "ARE THE POOR DIFFERENT?" A COMPARISON OF WORK BEHAVIOR AND ATTITUDES AMONG THE URBAN POOR AND NONPOOR. *Social Problems 1974 22(2): 229-245.* Analysis of interview responses collected in Houston, Texas. Contrary to a popular view, the minority poor were found to be as work-oriented as the Anglo nonpoor. Poverty among minorities is less the result of attitudes toward work than such factors as discriminatory pay and large households. Notes, bibliography.   A. M. Osur

2707. Eklund, Kent E. and Williams, Oliver P. THE CHANGING SPATIAL DISTRIBUTION OF SOCIAL CLASSES IN A METRO-POLITAN AREA. *Urban Affairs Q. 1978 13(3): 313-341.* Analysis of Philadelphia-area census data (1950-70) suggests an urban growth model predicated upon increasing diversity of both the core city and the surrounding areas rather than a lower class core enveloped in increasingly differentiated middle and upper middle class municipalities. The municipalities' share of the highest income category increased disproportionately, reflecting the availability of high cost rentals in the core city, but this category also made up an increasing percentage of core city residents. There has been "slight" dispersal of core city poor, but low-cost housing has been increasingly concentrated in the area. The middle class was "ubiquitous" in the suburbs. However, except at the extremes in housing and income, the municipalities are not homogenous and cannot be mapped into any cirular geometric socioeconomic pattern. 13 tables, 2 notes, biblio.   L. N. Beecher

2708. Fallows, James. THE SEDUCTIONS OF WASHINGTON SOCIETY. *Washington Monthly 1976 8(7): 18-24.* Discusses the entrenched position of the Washington, D.C., elite, whose strength is based on, among other things, the attractions of class and snobbery, and which has withstood many reformers before Jimmy Carter.

2709. Garrett, Gerald R. and Bahr, Howard M. THE FAMILY BACKGROUNDS OF SKID ROW WOMEN. *Signs 1976 2(2): 369-381.* A sociological investigation of women's alcoholism, homelessness, and family background, 1966-69. Women end up on skid row because of failures in social relationships, whereas men become disaffiliated because of occupational failures. Family instability during childhood and marriage failure, often attributed to spousal infidelity, appear as key variables in explaining "skid behavior" in women. Based on life-history interviews in New York City; 2 tables, 17 notes.   J. Gammage

2710. Harrison, Bennett and Osterman, Paul. PUBLIC EMPLOY-MENT AND URBAN POVERTY: SOME NEW FACTS AND A POLICY ANALYSIS. *Urban Affairs Q. 1974 9(3): 303-336.*

2711. Kunreuther, Howard WHY THE POOR MAY PAY MORE FOR FOOD: THEORETICAL AND EMPIRICAL EVIDENCE. *J. of Business 1973 46(3): 368-383.* A survey of households in the New Haven area verified Kunreuther's thesis that price differentials for the same items in various-sized stores and the unit price relative to size of item affect food purchasing decisions. Tests assumed that a certain amount is budgeted for food and that purchase size did not affect consumption rate. Suggests further research on the value of time, cost of searching for a desirable store, unit pricing, and availability of brands. Based on secondary sources; 2 figs., 4 tables, 16 notes, appendixes.

C. A. Gallacci

2712. Kutner, Nancy G. THE POOR VS. THE NON-POOR: AN ETHNIC AND METROPOLITAN-NONMETROPOLITAN COMPARISON. *Sociol. Q. 1975 16(2): 250-263.* Indicators of 29 of Oscar Lewis' poverty traits were examined to see if poor and non-poor families differed significantly in frequency of demonstrating the traits. Families representing six ethnic/residence population types were considered: metropolitan white, nonmetropolitan white, metropolitan black, nonmetropolitan black, metropolitan Spanish-speaking, and nonmetropolitan Spanish-speaking. Of the 29 traits investigated, for 24 traits a significant difference was found between poor and non-poor in at least one ethnic residence group. Significant differences between poor and non-poor in the two Spanish-speaking groups existed on considerably fewer traits than in the case of the two black or the two white groups, suggesting that the traits examined may be more broadly based in Spanish culture. J

2713. Long, Larry H. POVERTY STATUS AND RECEIPT OF WELFARE AMONG MIGRANTS AND NONMIGRANTS IN LARGE CITIES. *Am. Sociol. Rev. 1974 39(1): 46-56.* Data from the 1970 census show that black migrants to six of the nation's largest cities were less likely to be poor or on welfare in 1970 than blacks born and raised in these cities. The cross-sectional pattern suggests that black migrants from the South may initially experience fairly high rates of poverty and welfare dependence, but after a few years the Southern migrants are more successful in escaping from poverty and welfare dependence than blacks native to large cities in the North. Among whites in the six cities there is no consistent relationship between migration status and being poor and on welfare, except for slightly higher than average rates of poverty and receipt of welfare among the Southern born. These findings are placed in the context of previous research on differences between first-generation black Northerners and second-(and later) generation black Northerners. J

2714. Mann, Arthur J. and Ocasio, William C. THE DETERMINANTS OF INCOME CONCENTRATION IN PUERTO RICAN MUNICIPALITIES. *Rev. Interamericana [Puerto Rico] 1977 7(2): 309-319.* Income distribution in Puerto Rico over the last two decades has moved toward greater income equality. Based on the US Censuses of 1950, 1960, and 1970; 3 tables, 7 notes.

J. A. Lewis

2715. Molotch, Harvey. CAPITAL AND NEIGHBORHOOD IN THE UNITED STATES: SOME CONCEPTUAL LINKS. *Urban Affairs Q. 1979 14(3): 289-312.* The author writing from a Marxist perspective, seeks to show that an active rentier class, controlling access to space for production, accumulation, and exploitation, insures the integration of local land use and the needs of the macro-oligarchy. Neighborhoods, therefore, should be regarded as the residuals of the needs of production. 7 notes, biblio.

L. N. Beecher

2716. Philipsen, Gerry. SPEAKING "LIKE A MAN" IN TEAMSTERVILLE: CULTURE PATTERNS OF ROLE ENACTMENT IN AN URBAN NEIGHBORHOOD. *Q. J. of Speech 1975 61(1): 13-22.* Discusses the "place of speaking in male role enactment" among blue-collar whites in Chicago. S

2717. Pines, David. ON THE SPATIAL DISTRIBUTION OF HOUSEHOLDS ACCORDING TO INCOME. *Econ. Geography 1975 51(2): 142-149.* Uses mathematical models to show that richer households live farther away from the center of the city. S

2718. Rooney, James F. EMPLOYMENT AND SOCIAL INTEGRATION AMONG THE SKID ROW POPULATION. *Sociol. Inquiry [Canada] 1977 47(2): 109-118.* Employment among skid row

residents had no significant independent association with measures of social integration: number of friends, frequency of visiting, basic conceptions of friendship, helping friends, or to any reference group measure, but retained significance with the percentage of friends in skid row, and intimacy to close friends. The lack of association with reference group measures indicates that working patterns and group identification have become independent phenomena, constituting a partial shift from the former economic functions of skid row. The theory of the disaffiliating effects of skid row living was upheld only for loss of friends outside the area, and acceptance of skid row as one's place of permanent residence. There was no association of residence in skid row and change in the qualitative components of friendship. J

2719. Salins, Peter D. THE LIMITS OF GENTRIFICATION. *New York Affairs 1979 5(4): 3-12.* Discusses the process of gentrification, or the moving of the affluent professional upper middle class to areas previously inhabited by the lower and working classes, in New York City, based on statistics collected from 1950 to 1979.

2720. Smolensky, Eugene. POVERTY, PROPINQUITY AND POLICY. *Ann. of the Am. Acad. of Pol. and Social Sci. 1973 (409): 120-124.* There is no necessary connection between poverty and income distribution. When poverty is defined by relative measures, the proportion of impoverished families is the same as it was in 1950. As a result, the urban problems of the United States have been exacerbated. While tastes vary greatly, differences in consumption patterns, in human capital investments, in political demands and in propensity or willingness to steal depend importantly on income. Furthermore, if people of very different income levels live close to one another—as they do in cities—these different choices exacerbate class conflict. To escape, those with the means to do so seek to segregate themselves and to surround themselves with moats. They also turn to government for relief. The Great Society programs constituted a use of the political process to ameliorate class conflict by lowering the cost of goods to the poor which the nonpoor wanted them to buy. Nevertheless, the poor did not become acceptable neighbors for the rest of the nation. The Nixon administration sought to terminate a good part of the effort. J

2721. Stahura, John M. THE EVOLUTION OF SUBURBAN FUNCTIONAL ROLES. *Pacific Sociol. Rev. 1978 21(4): 423-440.* Persisting stable socioeconomic characteristics (housing, employment opportunities, incomes) differentially select out suitable replacement populations for suburban areas, and maintain a constant socioeconomic atmosphere.

2722. Tobier, Emanuel. GENTRIFICATION: THE MANHATTAN STORY. *New York Affairs 1979 5(4): 13-25.* Describes the process of gentrification in Manhattan, particularly examining who the new gentry are, where they are moving from, and the changes they have made in Manhattan in the past year; also traces the roots of gentrification in Manhatten since the 1820's.

2723. Unsigned. HOW FAR DO LITTLE APPLES FALL FROM THE TREE? *New York Affairs 1979 5(4): 39-54.* Provides brief signed comments on eight towns surrounding New York City by city planners and community leaders discussing gentrification trends in their cities and what to expect in the way of development in the future; 1950's-79.

2724. Vander Kooi, Ronald. THE MAIN STEM: SKID ROW REVISITED. *Society 1973 10(6): 64-71.*

2725. Western, John SOCIAL GROUPS AND ACTIVITY PATTERNS IN HOUMA, LOUISIANA. *Geographical Rev. 1973 63(3): 301-321.* The city of Houma, in the bayou country of southern Louisiana, was once a sequestered fishing, trapping, and sugarcane- and oyster-producing area where Cajun French was the dominant language. Since World War II, however, a surge in oilfield activity has almost tripled the population of Houma. The growth has brought the superimposition of a third social group, immigrant anglophone Texans, on the two principal local groups, the blacks and the Cajun whites. Cajuns are found to be acculturated into the exogenous white system more rapidly than blacks are, and several intermediate social groups emerge. J

2726. Williamson, John B. BELIEFS ABOUT THE WELFARE POOR. *Sociol. and Social Res. 1974 58(2): 163-175.* A number of factual and subjective beliefs about the welfare poor are examined in a survey of 375 respondents living in the Greater Boston Area during the Spring of 1972. On such issues as idleness, dishonesty, and fertility there is evidence that misconceptions about the welfare poor exist at all socioeconomic levels and that these misconceptions are consistently in the anti-welfare direction; however, there is only a weak relationship between such beliefs and opposition to increases in welfare benefits. Beliefs about the motivation of the poor and such ideological predictors as self-reported liberalism and work ethic account for more variance in opposition to increased welfare benefits than do social class or factual beliefs.   J

Social and Geographic Mobility

2727. Alperovich, Gershon; Bergsman, Joel; and Ehemann, Christian. AN ECONOMETRIC MODEL OF MIGRATION BETWEEN US METROPOLITAN AREAS. *Urban Studies [Great Britain] 1977 14(2): 135-145.* We test a model of inter-metropolitan migration using 1965-70 data for 284 metropolitan areas from the 1970 Census of Population. Innovations in model specification permit us to derive estimatable equations for gross in- and out-migration from a point-to-point hypothesis. Measures of economic conditions (the unemployment rate, the growth rate in employment, and the wage rate) are shown to affect migration behaviour both at origins and destinations, as economic theory predicts. Expected effects of past migration on both subsequent in-migration and out-migration are confirmed. In addition, migrants are shown to prefer destination cities that have moderate climates, that are relatively small in size, and that are close to larger cities. The research reported in this paper is part of a larger study of the joint determination of growth in employment in US metropolitan areas and of migration flows between them.

A

2728. Berghorn, Forrest J. and Steere, Geoffrey H. RESIDENTIAL MOBILITY IN URBAN LIFE: A STUDY OF KANSAS CITY, KANSAS. *Am. Studies [Lawrence, KS] 1973 14(1): 67-82.* An analytical and statistical study of mobility and its consequences in the late 1960's. Frequent residential movement tended to be economically disadvantageous and correlated with "a disproportionate need for social services." The results of this study hold implications for urban planning, to the extent that planning can affect residential mobility. Based on primary and secondary sources; 16 notes.   J. Andrew

2729. Biggar, Jeanne C. and Martin, Julia H. ECOLOGICAL DETERMINANTS OF WHITE AND BLACK INMIGRATION TO SMALL AREAS IN CENTRAL CITIES, 1965 TO 1970. *Social Forces 1976 55(1): 72-84.* White and Negro inmigration rates into central city census tracts of five Virginia metropolitan areas were analyzed in terms of ecological characteristics—socioeconomic, demographic, and housing quality characteristics and the heterogeneity of these characteristics. As hypothesized, white inmigration rates exceeded Negro rates. Both white and Negro rates were higher in tracts with higher socioeconomic levels and better housing quality, and with smaller shares of Negro population but larger shares of families in child-rearing stages. Diversity of ecological characteristics proved to be less important than the tract characteristics, themselves, in the analysis of net relationships. Although the explained variance in Negro inmigration rates was much lower than that for whites, comparisons of the pattern of ecological determinants for the two races showed more similarities than differences.   J

2730. Bradford, David F. and Kelejian, Harry H. AN ECONOMETRIC MODEL OF THE FLIGHT TO THE SUBURBS. *J. of Pol. Econ. 1973 81(3): 566-589.* Estimates interrelated city-suburbs residential-location equations for middle- and upper-income-class families and for poor families using cross-sectional data on 87 large metropolitan areas in 1960. Residential-location decisions of middle- and upper-income-class families are determined, among other things, by the city-suburbs rent differentials, by fiscal surplus differentials, and (negatively) by the location of poor families; additional hypotheses concerning interactions with family income were suggested and statistically accepted. The location equations for the poor families involved cost and fiscal differentials and a proxy variable for employment opportunities.   J

2731. Brown, H. James. CHANGES IN WORKPLACE AND RESIDENTIAL LOCATIONS. *J. of the Am. Inst. of Planners 1975 41(1): 32-39.* Analysis of the determinants of intrametropolitan moving behavior indicates a significant association between workplace changes and residence changes, and supports the importance of the workplace in determining residence location. Workplace change operates along with the more traditional life cycle variables in explaining residential mobility.

J

2732. Clark, W. A. V. MIGRATION IN MILWAUKEE. *Econ. Geography 1976 52(1): 48-60.* Analyzes the migration of Milwaukee households, mostly due to housing costs and needs in the 1960's and 1970's.

2733. DeJong, Gordon F. and Sell, Ralph R. POPULATION REDISTRIBUTION, MIGRATION, AND RESIDENTIAL PREFERENCES. *Ann. of the Am. Acad. of Pol. and Social Sci. 1977 (429): 130-144.* Census Bureau population estimates for metropolitan and nonmetropolitan areas in the 1970's reveal for the first time in over 50 years, higher population growth and net in-migration for nonmetropolitan areas than metropolitan areas. This dramatic and largely unanticipated reversal in the traditional population growth pattern is not limited to nonmetropolitan areas adjacent to metropolitan centers, but is also happening in many of the remote nonmetropolitan counties. In this article, the impact of residential preferences on population dispersal migration behavior is analyzed by means of data from a longitudinal migration survey. The widespread preference for small cities, villages, and the countryside identified in public opinion polls is not the significant factor in nonmetropolitan migration. Rather, population dispersal migrants are characterized by the willingness and apparently better ability to give up the urban-based conveniences to shopping, work, and public transportation to live in nonmetropolitan environments.   J

2734. DeJong, Gordon F. and Humphrey, Craig R. SELECTED CHARACTERISTICS OF METROPOLITAN-TO-NONMETROPOLITAN AREA MIGRANTS: A STUDY OF POPULATION REDISTRIBUTION IN PENNSYLVANIA. *Rural Sociol. 1976 41(4): 526-538.* Using census data, 1955-70, indicates that urban to rural internal migration occurs among young, relatively high socioeconomic, small-sized households.

2735. Goering, John M. and Rogowsky, Edward T. THE MYTH OF NEIGHBORHOODS. *New York Affairs 1978 5(1): 82-86.* Questions the concept of neighborhoods as traditional sources of stability in the United States, and suggests that instead they are often characterized by constant turnover and social mobility.

2736. Jung, L. Shannon. THE SHAPE OF AMERICAN SPACE. *Religion in Life 1975 44(1): 36-46.* An exploration of the white exodus to suburbia.   S

2737. Newman, Sandra J. and Duncan, Greg J. RESIDENTIAL PROBLEMS, DISSATISFACTION, AND MOBILITY. *J. of the Am. Planning Assoc. 1979 45(2): 154-166.* Explores three facets of residential change and mobility: the incidence of perceived housing and neighborhood problems, the relationships between these problems and satisfaction with house and neighborhood, and the impact of these problems on actual mobility. Blacks and those on welfare reported a disproportionate share of serious housing and neighborhood problems, even after the effects of income level were taken into account. Links between problems and reports of discontent with housing and neighborhood were found, but specific problems in the residential environment appear to have no strong or direct effects on actual moves.   J

2738. Obermiller, Phillip. APPALACHIANS AS AN URBAN ETHNIC GROUP: ROMANTICISM, RENAISSANCE, OR REVOLUTION? AND A BRIEF BIBLIOGRAPHICAL ESSAY ON URBAN APPALACHIANS. *Appalachian J. 1978 5(1): 145-152.* Examines current research on groups migrating from Appalachia to urbanized areas; Appalachians are best studied when considered as an ethnic group.

2739. Ritchey, P. Neal. URBAN POVERTY AND RURAL TO URBAN MIGRATION. *Rural Sociol. 1974 39(1): 12-27.*

2740. Schexnider, Alvin J. BLACKS, CITIES AND THE ENERGY CRISIS. *Urban Affairs Q. 1974 10(1): 5-16.* Summarizes past population shifts affecting the central city and their relationship to present and projected fuel-induced transportation crises. Current energy shortages may check white flight to the suburbs and black central city dominance as suburban mobility becomes more costly. Extensive racially integrated housing around suburban industrial and commercial enterprises is unlikely. A severe recession will hurt central city Negroes more than other groups. 2 tables, notes, biblio.   P. J. Woehrmann

2741. Zikmund, Joseph, II. SOURCES OF THE SUBURBAN POPULATION: 1955-1960 AND 1965-1970. *Publius 1975 5(1): 27-43.* Discusses the political impact of population flows to the suburbs from 1955-60 and 1965-70, in a special issue of *Publius*, "The Suburban Reshaping of American Politics."

Leisure, Entertainment, and Recreation

2742. Barbeau, Arthur E. A MOMENT OF GLORY: THE WHEELING IRONMEN. *Upper Ohio Valley Hist. Rev. 1979 9(1): 15-25.* Discusses the establishment of the United Football League in 1960, and the subsequent founding of the Wheeling Ironmen in 1962, and traces the history of sports teams to 1963 in Wheeling since the founding of the Wheeling Nailers, a professional baseball team, in 1925.

2743. Baron, Robert. SYNCRETISM AND IDEOLOGY: LATIN NEW YORK SALSA MUSICIANS. *Western Folklore 1977 36(3): 209-225.* Analyzes the "symbolic expression of cultural and social psychological strain" and "the tendency to identify those elements in the new culture with similar elements in the old one" of Salsa music in New York City. Discusses the Cuban, African, European, Latin American and modern US elements of Salsa in both its traditional folkloric and modern commercial aspects. Primary and secondary sources; interviews, 38 notes.   S. L. Myres

2744. Bell, Michael J. TENDING BAR AT BROWN'S: OCCUPATIONAL ROLE AS ARTISTIC PERFORMANCE. *Western Folklore 1976 35(2): 93-107.* Interviews employees and patrons at a bar in a middle-class black section of Philadelphia to show how bartenders use "artistic performance" in order to construct and maintain social order. Contends that bartending, in this context, may best be understood as an artful profession in Afro-American culture. Based on primary and secondary sources; 15 notes.   S. L. Myres

2745. Boles, Jacqueline and Garbin, Albeno P. THE STRIP CLUB AND STRIPPER-CUSTOMER PATTERNS OF INTERACTION. *Sociol. and Social Res. 1974 58(2): 136-144.* Investigates the social organization of the strip club by relating the effects of environmental and spatial factors on stripper-customer relationships. The data were derived from observations at nine strip clubs in a large southeastern city, and interviews with 51 strippers at these clubs. Interactions between strippers and customers are characterized by a counterfeiting of intimacy based upon inauthentic relations.   J

2746. Clark, R. Milton. THE DANCE PARTY AS A SOCIALIZATION MECHANISM FOR BLACK URBAN PREADOLESCENTS AND ADOLESCENTS. *Sociol. and Social Res. 1974 58(2): 145-154.* The dance party is an influential element in the lives of most urban ghetto youth, but its effect on black youth has not heretofore been meaningfully recognized by students of black culture. The dance party is described and analyzed as a mechanism for the socialization of urban black youth, and in relation to the interpretation of ceremonies and rituals by Van Gennep.   J

2747. Deyak, T. A. and Parliment, T. J. AN ANALYSIS OF YOUTH PARTICIPATION AT URBAN RECREATION FACILITIES. *Land Econ. 1975 51(2): 172-176.* Analyzes the effect of several socio-economic variables on children's use of private clubs and public park recreational facilities. Private club use is related to income, but public park use is not, though the rates of use of public parks are higher for blacks than whites. 2 tables, 6 notes, biblio.   E. S. Johnson

2748. Dresser, Norine. "THE BOYS IN THE BAND IS NOT ANOTHER MUSICAL": MALE HOMOSEXUALS AND THEIR FOLKLORE. *Western Folklore 1974 33(3): 205-218.* Uses Mart Crowley's 1968 play, *Boys in the Band*, as a vehicle to "focus on the folklore generated inside the gay bar, the stories told there, and . . . the stereotype of the homosexual as communicated and perpetuated by his folklore." Based on secondary sources and research and interviews in a Los Angeles "gay bar"; 12 notes, glossary.   S. L. Myres

2749. Gluck, Leonard Jay. THE TEAM THAT COULDN'T 'WAIT 'TIL NEXT YEAR,' THE BURLINGTON ATHLETICS. *Vermont Hist. 1977 45(3): 145-154.* The Burlington Athletics, a Class C Kansas City franchise, joined the Provincial League and played a winning, 129 game season before 51,267 fans during 1954-55. It was New England's only minor league team that year. Its support came from the Burlington Baseball Club, which had operated the semiprofessional Cardinals, during 1936-52, in night games at the University of Vermont. Behind the troubles which disbanded the Provincial League in April 1956 was the general decline in minor league attendance as major league games reached expanding television audiences. Based on newspapers; 4 illus., 33 notes.   T. D. S. Bassett

2750. Hong, Lawrence K. and Duff, Robert W. GENTLEMEN'S SOCIAL CLUB: REVIVAL OF TAXI DANCING IN LOS ANGELES. *J. of Popular Culture 1976 9(4): 827-832.* Taxi dance halls, where men pay for a female dance partner, are enjoying a resurgence of popularity in Los Angeles. Relaxed moral standards have made taxi dancing a respectable form of recreation. Women employed at taxi dance parlors enjoy the attention they get. Half of the clientele is white, and the remainder is Chicano, Chinese, and Filippino, in an equal mix. Most of the minority customers are foreign-born, and the halls provide an important avenue for contact with women. Among the Asians, taxi dancing resembles arrangements at many clubs in their home countries. The white customers are almost all native-born, older, and seeking teenaged dance partners. Especially for the minorities, taxi dance halls have become places where men of similar ethnic background can meet; and so the halls will flourish with continued Asian immigration. Secondary sources; 4 notes.   J. W. Leedom

2751. Kaminsky, Stuart M. KUNG FU FILM AS GHETTO MYTH. *J. of Popular Film 1974 3(2): 129-138.* Discusses the Kung Fu motif used in cinema and the hero role it provides for ghetto youth.   S

2752. Licht, M. SOME AUTOMOTIVE PLAY ACTIVITIES OF SUBURBAN TEENAGERS. *New York Folklore Q. 1974 30(1): 44-65.*

2753. Lowenfish, Lee Elihu. A TALE OF MANY CITIES: THE WESTWARD EXPANSION OF MAJOR LEAGUE BASEBALL IN THE 1950's. *J. of the West 1978 17(3): 71-82.* In 1903 the two major leagues reached an agreement to limit the number of teams and respect each other's territories. None of the major teams was located in the West. After World War II, Los Angeles demanded major league status but was ignored. The movement of the Boston Braves to Milwaukee in 1953 was the beginning of a transfer of major league franchises to the West. Los Angeles got its team when the Brooklyn Dodgers moved there from New York in 1957. The movement of teams from one city to another reflected not the needs of desires of the cities, but the concern for profits by the franchise owners. Primary and secondary sources; 6 photos, 73 notes.   B. S. Porter

2754. March, Richard. THE TAMBURITZA TRADITION IN THE CALUMET REGION. *Indiana Folklore 1977 10(2): 127-138.* Relates findings of a 1976 folklore project pertaining to oral tradition, customs, ceremonies, music, and dance among Slavic Americans (Croats, Serbs, and Macedonians) in urban northwestern Indiana.

2755. Moskowitz, Milton R. EXPO '74: SPOKANE. *Cry California 1974 9(3): 28-32.* Discusses the environmental theme of Expo '74 and questions whether it will successfully provide an in-depth assessment of environmental issues for the public.   S

2756. Reynolds, Anthony M. URBAN NEGRO TOASTS: A HUSTLER'S VIEW FROM L.A. *Western Folklore 1974 33(4): 267-300.* Discusses the origin, development, and genre of contemporary Negro "toasts," showing their relationship to "traditional hobo . . . and cowboy lore." Defines the differences between "society," "bad-men," and "contest" toasts. Based on primary and secondary sources and interviews, with texts of 17 toasts; 16 notes.   S. L. Myres

2757.   Slade, Joseph.   PORNOGRAPHIC THEATERS OFF TIMES SQUARE.   *Trans-action 1971 9(1/2): 35-43, 79.*

2758.   Stopp, G. Harry, Jr.   THE DISTRIBUTION OF MASSAGE PARLORS IN THE NATION'S CAPITAL.   *J. of Popular Culture 1978 11(4): 989-997.* Massage parlors in Washington, D.C., have become an accepted part of the business community; if proper licensing channels are followed, these parlors receive little harassment from local law enforcement even though generally they remain centers of prostitution.

2759.   Velarde, Albert J. and Warlick, Mark.   MASSAGE PARLORS: THE SENSUALITY BUSINESS.   *Society 1973 11(1): 63-74.*

2760.   Weinberg, Martin S. and Williams, Colin J.   GAY BATHS AND THE SOCIAL ORGANIZATION OF IMPERSONAL SEX. *Social Problems 1975 23(2): 124-136.* Examines gay baths to determine if they fit the ideal conditions described by males for impersonal sex. Gay baths fairly well provide protection. They provide a fine opportunity structure; a known, shared, and organized reality; a bounding of the sexual experience; relatively congenial interaction; and a clean, relaxing physical setting.   A. M. Osur

2761.   Welsch, Roger L.   CRAP TRAPS AND DONKEY BASKET-BALL: ON THE STATUS OF URBAN AND RURAL COMPETI-TIONS.   *J. of Popular Culture 1976 10(1): 96-101.* Examination of the characteristics that differentiate urban and rural sports competitions reveals that parody of urban competitions (e.g., donkey baseball and basketball) in the rural community provides some of the best examples of laconic American folk humor. Primary sources (observation); note.
                                                              D. G. Nielson

2762.   Wepman, Dennis; Newman, Ronald B.; and Binderman, Murry B.   TOASTS: THE BLACK URBAN FOLK POETRY.   *J. of Am. Folklore 1974 87(345): 208-224.* Toasts, a folk recitative poetry depicting an urban black subculture known as "the life," are most frequently composed and performed in prisons or drug treatment centers. Their perspective is male, coupled with a cool bravado tinged with fatalism, and based on the activities of pimps. Based on 36 toasts collected in New York state prisons; 30 notes.   W. D. Piersen

2763.   Wojtowicz, Carol.   PLAY IN PHILADELPHIA.   *Pennsylvania Folklife 1975 24(3): 17-23.* Compares three generations of Philadelphians, tracing the evolution of recreation habits—specifically, what games were played and what locations were used—and assesses the impact of environmental planning on these habits.   S

Communications

2764.   Chisholm, Shirley.   THE WHITE PRESS: RACIST AND SEX-IST.   *Black Scholar 1973 5(1): 20-22.* In her refusal to attend a dinner at the all-male, all-white Gridiron Club, Shirley Chisholm states her firm intolerance of "tokenism" and reveals statistical findings which confirm discriminatory hiring practices of women and minorities by the press in several large US cities.

2765.   Cohen, Shari.   A COMPARISON OF CRIME COVERAGE IN DETROIT AND ATLANTA NEWSPAPERS.   *Journalism Q. 1975 52(4): 726-730.* Compares the crime coverage of Detroit and Atlanta newspapers to determine if such coverage is a factor in Detroit's poor image. Atlanta newspapers devoted more coverage to crime in proportion to the incidence of crime, and gave crime articles more prominent coverage. However, Detroit newspapers used banner headlines and more photographs and specific details. Such coverage is not the only reason for Detroit's negative image. The study was done by the organization New Detroit; it was based on content analysis of the major newspapers in Detroit and Atlanta for a two-week period. Based on primary sources; table, 5 notes.   K. J. Puffer

2766.   Dominick, Joseph R.   GEOGRAPHIC BIAS IN NATIONAL TV NEWS.   *J. of Communication 1977 27(4): 94-99.* Discusses the tendency of national news coverage on television to concentrate on large cities—New York, Washington, Los Angeles—and the accompanying intellectual and political biases.

2767.   Gordon, Douglas E.   *THE GREAT SPECKLED BIRD:* HA-RASSMENT OF AN UNDERGROUND NEWSPAPER.   *Journalism Q. 1979 56(2): 289-295.* This small offset newspaper that began publishing in Atlanta, Georgia, in March 1968, outlasted its liberal, hippie constituency. Despite local and state legal harassment and the dissolution of the hippie community in 1970, the paper won federal court suits and maintained its advocacy of socialism until it ceased publication in 1976. Based on articles in the newspaper, on interviews, and on federal court papers; 46 notes.   R. P. Sindermann, Jr.

2768.   Jones, E. Terrence and Saunders, Joan.   PERSUADING AN URBAN PUBLIC: THE ST. LOUIS PRIVACY CAMPAIGN. *Journalism Q. 1977 54(4): 669-673.* From February to March 1976 the American Civil Liberties Union of eastern Missouri conducted a mass media campaign in St. Louis to alert citizens of threats to their right to privacy. Telephone surveys before and after the campaign showed a statistically significant increase in the number of respondents who believed that government agencies often wiretap the phones of private citizens and who favored the regulation of information collection by the Missouri government. Television was the most effective medium used in the campaign. Documented from the surveys and from secondary sources; table, 12 notes.   R. P. Sindermann, Jr.

2769.   Jones, E. Terrence.   THE PRESS AS METROPOLITAN MONITOR.   *Public Opinion Q. 1976 40(2): 239-244.* An analysis of the coverage by two St. Louis newspapers of local crime occurrences between 1969 and 1972 finds that (1) how much various types of crime increase or decrease from year to year is unrelated to how much more or less attention is given them by the press; and (2) the type of crime and its location within the city affect the amount of coverage it receives.   J

2770.   López, Ronald W. and Enos, Darryl D.   SPANISH-LAN-GUAGE-ONLY TELEVISION IN LOS ANGELES COUNTY. *Aztlán 1973 4(2): 283-313.* Analyzes media use, attitudes, and demographic characteristics of Spanish-Language-Only Television audiences in Los Angeles during 1971-72.   S

2771.   Lyford, Joseph P.   CITY JOURNALISM.   *Center Mag. 1977 10(6): 37-40.* Discusses urban areas, particularly Oakland, California, and the urban character of individual cities; discusses the need for a responsible and responsive press in cities, 1970's.

2772.   Manheim, Jarol B.   URBANIZATION AND DIFFEREN-TIAL PRESS COVERAGE OF THE CONGRESSIONAL CAM-PAIGN.   *Journalism Q. 1974 51(4): 649-653, 669.* "Analysis of coverage by 26 papers in five midwestern districts in 1970 campaign shows quantity and quality vary systematically with degree of urbanization."   S

2773.   Martin, Harold.   ABOUT RALPH MC GILL.   *New South 1973 28(2): 24-33.* McGill (1898-1969) was editor-in-chief of the Atlanta *Constitution.*   S

2774.   McCue, Andy.   EVOLVING CHINESE LANGUAGE DAI-LIES SERVE IMMIGRANTS IN NEW YORK.   *Journalism Q. 1975 52(2): 272-276.* The new Chinese immigrants in New York City are urbanized and better educated. Older Chinese newspapers in New York focused on China. New style newspapers such as the *China Post*, contain more factual features, and more news about Chinatown and New York. They try to be politically independent of the two Chinese governments. Changes in the relations between China and the United States are reflected in Chinatown. Based on a master's project at Columbia's Graduate School of Journalism; 3 tables.   K. J. Puffer

2775.   Mulder, Ronald.   THE EFFECTS OF TELEVISED POLITI-CAL ADS IN THE 1975 CHICAGO MAYORAL ELECTION. *Journalism Q. 1979 56(2): 336-340.* The influence of the announcements appears to have been as significant among politically active viewers as among the less active. Changes of views on specific issues were more influenced by advertising than were overall evaluations of the candidates for office. Based on telephone interviews conducted before the candidates' advertising began and on the night before the election; 3 tables, 9 notes.

R. P. Sindermann, Jr.

2776. Olien, C. N.; Donohue, G. A.; and Tichenor, P. J. COMMUNITY STRUCTURE AND MEDIA USE. *Journalism Q. 1978 55(3): 445-455.* A survey of 19 Minnesota communities shows that, in the larger cities (population above 50,000) with daily newspapers, respondents tended to prefer newspapers over television as their primary source of news. In small towns with weekly and semi-weekly newspapers, respondents turned to television more than newspapers for news. The median level of education in the cities and towns was not as strong a factor in the results as was the combination of the size of the communities and the frequency of the newspapers. 13 notes, table, 5 graphs.

R. P. Sindermann, Jr.

2777. Rosenbloom, David L. THE PRESS AND THE LOCAL CANDIDATE. *Ann. of the Am. Acad. of Pol. and Social Sci. 1976 427: 12-22.* The 1975 mayoral election in Boston was waged by—as well as through—the press. This article examines the role of the press in local politics. Two principal hypotheses are proposed. The press is a major political force that seeks to amass and use its own political power; and the press is an important but selective means of communication between candidates and their voters. The elements of these hypotheses combine to suggest why the press so often opposes the development of strong and continuing political organizations. If they do not have their own organizations, candidates must either rely on the news organizations or buy their own time and space from the media.

J

2778. Shapiro, Walter. VIEWS OF THE PRESS: KAY, OTIS, AND NEWBY: THEY SELL OUT TOO. *Washington Monthly 1973 5(10): 51-60.* Exchanging favors for positive press coverage or advertisements has become commonplace in many metropolitan newspapers.

S

2779. Tipton, Leonard; Haney, Roger D.; and Baseheart, John R. MEDIA AGENDA-SETTING IN CITY AND STATE ELECTION CAMPAIGNS. *Journalism Q. 1975 52(1): 15-22.* Presents media influence on public information concerning salient issues in the Kentucky governor's race and the Lexington mayoral race in 1971. Public consensus on important issues was high; the main concern was taxes. Newspapers generally emphasized one set of issues and broadcast media another. There was no consistent evidence that media had a causal effect on public perception of important campaign issues. Primary sources; table, 5 figs., 13 notes.

K. J. Puffer

2780. Topper, Martin D. and Wilson, W. Leigh. CABLE TELEVISION: APPLIED ANTHROPOLOGY IN A NEW TOWN. *Human Organization 1976 35(2): 135-146.* Discusses the involvement of anthropologists in studying the impact of cable television on a community, focusing specifically on the town of Reston, Virginia, with data gathered in a 1972 survey.

2781. Ward, Jean and Gaziano, Cecilie. A NEW VARIETY OF URBAN PRESS: NEIGHBORHOOD PUBLIC-AFFAIRS PUBLICATIONS. *Journalism Q. 1976 53(1): 61-67, 116.* The neighborhood newspapers and newsletters in the St. Paul-Minneapolis area are a distinctive new form of urban communication. The largest number were started by neighborhood associations; most were begun since 1969. Relying on volunteers and financial subsidies, they emphasize public affairs, and are circulated to all residents. They promote community identity and information. Based on primary sources; 3 tables, 13 notes.

K. J. Puffer

2782. Warthman, Forrest. TELECOMMUNICATION AND THE CITY. *Ann. of the Am. Acad. of Pol. and Social Sci. 1974 (412): 127-137.* Telecommunication has historically been interrelated with transportation. Since railroads first used the telegraph as a scheduling aid, this interrelationship has affected almost every mode of point-to-point and broadcast telecommunication. For example, commercial radio and television depend on advertising which, in turn, is dependent on the transportation of goods to and from urban market centers. Telecommunication also serves as a substitute for travel, greatly increasing the speed of information consumption and processing and greatly broadening the

availability of information and entertainment to individual homes and moving vehicles. As long distance communication continues to decrease in cost, major urban centers will become more international, since they are the focal points of travel. Telecommunication will also assist the outward spread of metropolitan areas, but social and transportation factors will constrain this outward movement.

J

2783. Wilbur, Susan K. THE HISTORY OF TELEVISION IN LOS ANGELES, 1931-1952.
PART I: THE INFANT YEARS. *Southern California Q. 1978 60(1): 59-76.* Television experimentation in Los Angeles was led by Don Lee, who began W6XAO-TV in 1931, and by the Paramount Picture Corporation, which started W6XYZ-TV in 1942. Both stations utilized technical experts who developed equipment to improve television transmissions. Operational expenses were carried by station owners, because there were no commercial programs. W6XAO-TV achieved a number of TV firsts in Los Angeles, including showing the first feature-length motion picture on TV in 1933 and the first broadcasting of the Rose Parade in 1940. By 1939 X6XAO-TV had a regular weekly schedule of programs. W6XYZ-TV commenced regular programing in 1943. World War II delayed TV program development but contributed to electronic innovations and development. After the war the Federal Communications Commission reserved Channel 1 as a national emergency channel and in 1946 granted licenses to eight applicants for commercial operations. Whereas in the early years, Los Angeles television concentrated on technical experimentation, in the period after 1946 television focused on the social implications of TV broadcasting. Primary and secondary sources; 49 notes.
PART II: THE BOOM YEARS. *Southern California Q. 1978 60(2): 183-205.* In January 1947 W6XYZ-TV became KTLA-TV, the first commercial television station in Los Angeles and in fact in the western United States. KTLA-TV began its commercial life with sports coverage, especially wrestling, live coverage of news events, and commercially sponsored shows, of which musical variety programs were most popular. By 1948 some 16,000 television sets were in use in Los Angeles. Television set manufacturers sponsored programs to attract viewers at neighbors' homes and in public places to buy their own TV sets. Court test cases made it possible for television coverage of sports events. Local newspapers signed pacts with the new TV stations to share information on news and sports coverage. By 1948 KTLA-TV was joined by KTSL-TV (formerly Don Lee's W6XAO-TV); KLAC-TV, owned by Dorothy Schiff Thackrey; and KFI-TV, owned by Earle C. Anthony. Because the stations needed to fill air time, new companies entered the field to provide stations with programs. With KTLA-TV as the city's leader, the new TV stations continued to progress through 1948. Primary and secondary sources; photos, 40 notes.
PART III: TELEVISION DURING THE FREEZE. *Southern California Q. 1978 60(3): 255-285.* In 1949 three new Los Angeles TV stations were established: KTTV *(Times-Mirror)*, KNBH (NBC), and KEGA (ABC). Events in 1949-52 included the FCC freeze on construction of new TV stations, the beginning of the Emmy awards, several changes of ownership and call letters among the city's seven stations, and construction of new broadcasting facilities by the major networks. The number of TV sets in Los Angeles quadrupled in 1949. By October 1951 there were more than a million. Until development of the coaxial cable made instantaneous national programming possible, local stations relied on their own programming or on kinescopes. One notable achievement by KTLA was the live telecast of an atom bomb test in 1952. Questions surfaced over such issues as pay TV, an educational TV channel, and coverage of sports events. Introduction of the coaxial cable and the lifting of the FCC freeze marked an end to the first phase of Los Angeles TV history, once new stations soon were started on the UHF channels and network programming achieved a nationwide audience. Based mainly on contemporary published sources; 72 notes.

A. Hoffman

2784. Windhauser, John W. REPORTING OF CAMPAIGN ISSUES IN OHIO MUNICIPAL ELECTION RACES. *Journalism Q. 1977 54(2): 332-340.* Examines campaign items in 12 Ohio metropolitan dailies from 1 September to 1 November 1971, and concludes that editors tended to publish issues concerning the qualifications, experiences, abilities, endorsements, and testimonials of the candidates and their support-ers rather than the candidates' views on community problems and actions, and as a result issue coverage was directed toward identification and image-building of the candidates and their parties, and thus was some-what consistent with the patterns of political advertising published in newspapers.

Artistic and Intellectual Life

2785.   Byler, Robert H., Jr. JAZZ IS BACK. *Hist. Preservation 1976 28(4): 24-29.* Discusses jazz's "vast resurgence of interest during the past decade," relating a brief history from the 19th century to date, and lists locations of current jazz revival interest: San Antonio, (Texas), Washing-ton, D.C., Chester, (New Jersey), Florida, Denver (Colorado), Peninsula (Ohio), and Sacramento (California). 10 photos.

R. M. Frame, III

2786.   Castellanos, Leonard. CHICANO CENTROS, MURALS, AND ART. *Arts in Soc. 1975 12(1): 38-43.* Examines the work of the Mechicano Art Center in East Los Angeles in the 1970's.   S

2787.   Cockcroft, James D. and Cockcroft, Eva S. PEOPLE'S ART & SOCIAL CHANGE: THE COMMUNITY MURAL MOVEMENT. *Radical Am. 1978 12(2): 7-13.* The proliferation of community murals in various urban and rural areas of the United States over the last decade reflects social change in that they tend to express the values, problems, and goals of the community. Also, they are produced by artists usually having the active cooperation and volunteered involvement of members of the community in the project. The artists act as leaders of the expres-sion of the community spirit or as mediums or facilitators of that expres-sion. Community murals play a role in the politics of the Left insofar as they display the fact that art is a weapon if it is rooted in the daily lives and struggles of the community.   N. Lederer

2788.   Daley, Mary. ETHNIC CRAFTS IN CLEVELAND. *Historic Preservation 1974 26(1): 19-23.* Peoples and Cultures, Inc. was formed in 1971 to celebrate the diverse heritage of the approximately 90 ethnic groups in Cleveland, Ohio. A major project is the preservation of ethnic craft traditions and skills, and the selling of local craft products. 4 photos.   R. M. Frame III

2789.   Daniels, William G. THE EPWORTH JUBILEE COMMU-NITY ARTS CENTER OF KNOXVILLE, TENNESSEE: COMMU-NITY ARTS IN AN URBAN APPALACHIAN CENTER. *Arts in Soc. 1975 12(1): 24-31.* The primary purposes of the Epworth Jubilee Community Arts Center is to encourage appreciation of the Appalachian heritage by those who have moved to the city, away from their cultural roots, and to encourage emerging artists who represent Appalachian culture to remain in the area and develop their art.   S

2790.   Davis, Gene. STARTING OUT IN THE 50'S. *Art in Am. 1978 66(4): 88-94.* Reminisces about the work of young artists in Wash-ington, D.C., during the 1950's; assesses the growth of Washington's art scene, especially galleries and museums which began exhibiting local artists during 1961-66.

2791.   Drescher, Tim and Garcia, Rupert. RECENT RAZA MU-RALS IN THE U.S. *Radical Am. 1978 12(2): 15-31.* The last 10 years have witnessed the creation in many urban and rural Chicano and Latino communities of murals that relate on several levels to community involve-ment and support. These murals contain various motifs but generally portray in realistic fashion the contemporary plight and the historical oppression of Hispanic peoples. Artistically, the murals draw upon vari-ous sources for inspiration, commonly including the earlier work of the Mexican muralists Diego Rivera, Jose Clemente Orozco, and David Al-faro Siqueiros. Many Raza muralists are as much concerned with obtain-ing community participation in the creation of their murals as they are in the results of their labors.   N. Lederer

2792.   Furst, Alan. FANCY FOOTWORK IN SEATTLE. *New York Affairs 1978 4(4): 23-26.* Though they were severely in debt in 1969, cooperation among the various fine arts in Seattle, Washington, called

that city to the attention of the National Endowment for the Arts and the National Council on the Arts, which helped fund the refurbishment of the Seattle arts community, 1975.

2793.   Gabrielson, Walter. WHY SUCK THE MAINSTREAM IF YOU DON'T LIVE IN NEW YORK. *Art in Am. 1974 62(1): 37-38.* Attacks national imitation of New York art trends as destructive of regional, individualistic art styles.   S

2794.   Grausam, Anne Boynton. A CITY MUSEUM EXPERI-MENTS WITH THE FINE ARTS OF READING AND LIVING. *Urban Rev. 1973 6(4): 23-27.*

2795.   Harris, Neil. MUSEUMS, MERCHANDISING, AND POPU-LAR TASTE: THE STRUGGLE FOR INFLUENCE. Quimby, Ian M. G., ed. *Material Culture and the Study of American Life* (New York: W. W. Norton, 1978): 140-174. The museum has become an institution for preservation and not merely a reflection of popular taste; discusses six elements influencing the development of museums: decline of the central city, modernization, publicity, exhibitions of current interest, merchan-dising of museum reproductions, and the public's nostalgia, 1930's-70's.

2796.   Kauffmann, Stanley. THE THEATER IN NEW YORK. *New York Affairs 1978 4(4): 27-39.* Discusses various modes of theater in New York City: Broadway, Off-Broadway, and Off-Off-Broadway, 1960's-70's, and their management, financial backing, and supporting institutions.

2797.   O'Doherty, Brian. THE GRAND RAPIDS CHALLENGE. *Art in Am. 1974 62(1): 78-79.* Cooperation among civic groups was the key to social acceptance of modern sculpture in public places.   S

2798.   O'Toole, Patricia. CITY LIGHTS IN MODERN TIMES. *Change 1979 11(2): 36-39.* History of San Francisco's City Lights bookstore, famed for its role in publishing leading voices of mod-ern American literary movements: Allen Ginsberg, Lawrence Ferling-hetti, and Jack Kerouac, 1953-79.

2799.   Palles, Leon L. URBAN GATEWAYS. *Arts in Soc. 1975 12(1): 44-49.* Shows the work of Urban Gateways, a program begun in Chicago in 1961 to expose disadvantaged children to the arts.   S

2800.   Patton, Phil. OTHER VOICES, OTHER ROOMS: THE RISE OF THE ALTERNATIVE SPACE. *Art in Am. 1977 65(4): 80-89.* The emergence in the 1970's of alternative spaces, exhibition halls unaffiliated with museums, was a solution to the tight New York City museums and art galleries, and gave recognition to new or less-established artists.

2801.   Pessino, Catherine. CITY ECOLOGY FOR CITY CHIL-DREN. *Curator 1975 18(1): 47-54.* Describes the programs of the American Museum of Natural History's Alexander M. White Natural Science Center in New York City.   S

2802.   Ratcliff, Carter. ART AND SOCIAL CLASS: THE PHO-TOGRAPHY OF HARE AND ESTRIN. *Art in Am. 1979 67(8): 13, 15-16.* Review essay of Chauncey Hare's *Interior America* (Millerton, N.Y.: Aperture, 1978) and Mary Lloyd Estrin's *To the Manor Born* (Boston: New York Graphic Society, 1979), contrasting the work of Hare, whose photographs are of the poor, with Estrin's, who photographed the wealthy of Lake Forest, Illinois, a suburb of Chicago.

2803.   Ratcliff, Carter. ROUTE 66 REVISITED: THE NEW LAND-SCAPE PHOTOGRAPHY. *Art in Am. 1976 64(1): 88-91.* Discusses photography of the American landscape which focuses on industrializa-tion and suburbanization, 1970's.

2804.   Ratcliff, Carter. SOHO: DISNEYLAND OF THE AES-THETE? *New York Affairs 1978 4(4): 64-72.* Originally, conversion of the industrial SoHo district of New York City to an artists' community allowed for flourishing of the visual arts, but the growing chicness of the area threatens to trivialize the endeavors of serious artists residing there, 1970's.

2805. Romotsky, Jerry and Romotsky, Sally R.   L.A. HUMAN SCALE: STREET ART OF LOS ANGELES.   *J. of Popular Culture 1976 10(3): 653-666.* Discusses various kinds of street art in Los Angeles, assessing it as folk art and expression of urban life in the 1970's.

2806. Schiff, Bennett.   IN A TOBACCO CITY THE ARTS ARE PUT IN PLACE—OUT FRONT.   *Smithsonian 1979 9(10): 88-95.* Deals with the development of Winston-Salem, North Carolina, the "Tobacco City," as an artistic center, thanks to the Southeastern Center for Contemporary Art (SECCA), which allows presentation of works by regional young artists in a professional gallery. The SECCA brings these artists into contact with the public and helps them promote their talents. It also plans to establish a network with other regions of the country and organize an exchange program for better sharing of their artistic pursuits. 9 illus.
G. P. Cleyet

2807. Simon, Leonard.   THE SOUND OF PEOPLE.   *Arts in Soc. 1975 12(1): 18-23.* Discusses the development of a 1974 community arts project in Watts, Los Angeles.
S

2808. Tannous, David.   CAPITAL ART: IN THE MAJOR LEAGUES?   *Art in Am. 1978 66(4): 70-77.* Examines the art scene in Washington, D.C., touching on public and private galleries and the works of local artists, 1975-78.

2809. Tannous, David.   THOSE WHO STAY.   *Art in Am. 1978 66(4): 78-87.* Seventeen artists discuss living and working in the Washington, D.C., area in 1978.

2810. Titon, Jeff Todd.   THEMATIC PATTERN IN DOWNHOME BLUES LYRICS: THE EVIDENCE ON COMMERICAL PHONOGRAPH RECORDS SINCE WORLD WAR II.   *J. of Am. Folklore 1977 90(357): 316-330.* After World War II the blues songs of the black tenant farming South moved to northern cities. The lyrics continued to reflect black life in their narrative of mistreatment by bosses and lovers, and journeys in search of freedom and better times. Based on transcriptions from more than four thousand recordings and secondary sources; 49 notes.
W. D. Piersen

2811. Unsigned.   URBAN ART IN NEW YORK.   *Art in Am. 1977 65(5): 66-85.*
Kuspit, Donald B.   INDIVIDUAL AND MASS IDENTITY IN URBAN ART: THE NEW YORK CASE, *pp. 66-77.* Examines reactions of artists to the environment of New York City and the effect which the city has had on the course of 20th-century art.
Unsigned.   NEW YORK TODAY: SOME ARTISTS COMMENT, *pp. 78-85.* Interviews 15 contemporary artists in New York City who relate feelings about the city and their art and how the two combine.

2812. White, Chappell.   THE ARTS ARE ALIVE AND REASONABLY WELL UNDER ATLANTA'S BUSINESS-BRED ALLIANCE. *Southern Voices 1974 1(1): 71-74.* Activities of the Atlanta Memorial Arts Center since its opening in October 1968. The Atlanta Arts Alliance is now composed of four institutions: the Atlanta Symphony, the High Museum of Art, the Atlanta College of Art, and the Alliance Theatre Company. The alliance has concentrated power, administrative skill, and a staff of professionals.
D. D. Cameron

2813. Winkleman, Michael.   THE NEW FRONTIER: HOUSING FOR THE ARTIST-INDUSTRIALIST.   *New York Affairs 1978 4(4): 49-57.* In need of inexpensive, large space for living and working, New York City artists turned to rental of industrial space, but growing friction with industries and the possibilities of the area becoming chic (thus causing rents to rise) threaten these artistic enclaves, 1970's.

2814. Winter, Lumen Martin.   MURAL PAINTING; NOTES ON A PROJECT.   *Kansas Q. 1977 9(4): 13-22.*
MURAL PAINTING: A PEOPLE'S ART, *pp. 13-20.* Sketches and describes eight commissioned murals on Kansas history planned by the author for the Kansas state capitol building, 1977.
SOME NOTES PREPARATORY TO UNDERTAKING THE COMMISSION, *pp. 21-22.* Brief notes on the architecture, history, and present internal visual design of the Kansas state capitol building.

2815. Zeigler, Joseph Wesley.   CENTRALITY WITHOUT PHILOSOPHY: THE CRISIS IN THE ARTS.   *New York Affairs 1978 4(4): 12-22.* Emphasizes the need for responsible and lucrative management in the arts in New York City, which have gained popularity and a greater following but now face extinction due to lack of financial backing.

2816. Zucker, Martin.   WALLS OF BARRIO ARE BROUGHT TO LIFE BY STREET GANG ART.   *Smithsonian 1978 9(7): 105-111.* Discusses the recent mural paintings in East Los Angeles which "plead for the traditional values of family, religion and education, and an end to violence, and for preservation of culture, history, hope." Artists such as Manuel Cruz and Judy Baca, following the traditions of Orozco, Rivera, and Siqueiros, have attempted to rehabilitate neighborhoods and provide jobs for young Mexican Americans from the violent barrio gangs in Los Angeles. Although these projects do not solve the street gang problem, participating in mural painting at least provides "one positive experience in a life that is largely negative." 8 illus.
S. R. Quéripel

Schooling

2817. Abrams, Roger I.   NOT ONE JUDGE'S OPINION: MORGAN V. HENNIGAN AND THE BOSTON SCHOOLS.   *Harvard Educ. Rev. 1975 45(1): 5-16.* Discusses the 1974 ruling (*Morgan v. Hennigan*) on desegregation of Boston schools.
S

2818. Benavent, José A. and Sirvent, María Teresa.   LA PARTICIPACÍON ESCOLAR DEL HISPANOPARLANTE EN LA CIUDAD DE NUEVA YORK [Hispanic school paticipation in New York City]. *Perspectivas Pedagógicas [Spain] 1974 9(34): 223-246.* Forms part of a study of the Hispanic Americans of Washington Heights, New York City, and focuses on the attitudes and reactions to the school decentralization being undertaken by the local administration, 1969-74.

2819. Berlowitz, Marvin J.   INSTITUTIONAL RACISM AND SCHOOL STAFFING IN AN URBAN AREA.   *J. of Negro Educ. 1974 43(1): 25-29.* A study of the staffing of the Buffalo, New York, public schools 1956-63 shows that black schools were assigned a larger proportion of teachers who were male, young, inexperienced, or unlicensed than were white schools. This institutionalized racism is the cause of the high turnover among teachers in ghetto schools. Table, 15 notes.
B. D. Johnson

2820. Boyd, William L. and Seldin, Florence.   THE POLITICS OF SCHOOL REFORM IN ROCHESTER, NEW YORK.   *Educ. and Urban Soc. 1975 7(4): 439-463.* School decentralization in Rochester is low because urban governments and school systems are undemocratic. Concludes the true impediment to reform is the failure of the white middle-class majority to support change for the minority's benefit. Justice will not come from political bargaining but from the law and the Constitution. 18 notes.
C. D'Aniello

2821. Camejo, Peter.   BUSING—WHAT ARE THE ISSUES? THE RACIST OFFENSIVE IN BOSTON.   *Internat. Socialist Rev. 1974 35(11): 8-11.* Discusses the opposition to busing Negroes to white schools in Boston.
S

2822. Castro, Barry.   HOSTOS: REPORT FROM A GHETTO COLLEGE.   *Harvard Educ. Rev. 1974 44(2): 270-294.* Analyzes the educational and social problems which arose during the first two years at Hostos Community College in the South Bronx.
S

2823. Cataldo, Everett F.; Giles, Michael; and Gatlin, Douglas S. METROPOLITAN SCHOOL DESEGREGATION: PRACTICAL REMEDY OR IMPRACTICAL IDEAL?   *Ann. of the Am. Acad. of Pol. and Social Sci. 1975 422: 97-104.* School desegregation has become an increasingly important issue in non-Southern metropolitan areas. The absence of significant residential desegregation in the suburbs and the concentration of the black population in central cities make effective school desegregation difficult, if not impossible, without consolidated planning for the entire metropolitan region. Cross-busing between central cities and suburbs may raise stiff resistance among white parents whose children would be transferred to city schools. An analysis of areawide desegregation in Duval County, Florida, suggests that suburban diffusion of the white population does not in itself constitute a barrier to consolidated planning. A judicious application of desegregation plan features for the entire metropolitan region can produce satisfactory and equitable results.   J

2824. Chancy, Joette and Franklin, Brenda. REPORT FROM BOSTON: THE STRUGGLE FOR DESEGREGATION. *Black Scholar 1975 7(4): 19-27.* Discusses the struggle for school integration in Boston in the 1960's and 70's, and the violent reaction of whites to busing.

2825. Chow, Christopher and Leong, Russell. A PIONEER CHINATOWN TEACHER: AN INTERVIEW WITH ALICE FONG YU. *Amerasia J. 1978 5(1): 75-86.* Alice Fong Yu (b. 1905), the first Chinese American public school teacher in San Francisco, taught at Commodore Stockton Elementary School in Chinatown from 1926 to 1957. Her remarks concentrate on the history of education for Chinese American young people, including such issues as segregation, busing, and the *Bakke* decision. The interview took place on 5 February 1978.
J. C. Billigmeier

2826. Clark, Kenneth B. SEGREGATION—THE ROAD TO INTEGRATION? *Crisis 1974 81(5): 157-163.* Examines racial segregation sanctioned by school boards as a form of institutionalized discrimination, particularly in New York City in 1973.   S

2827. Colton, David and Frelich, Alan. ENROLLMENT DECLINE AND SCHOOL CLOSINGS IN A LARGE CITY. *Educ. and Urban Soc. 1979 11(3): 396-417.* Discusses the reasons for and the effects of school closures in St. Louis in the 1970's.

2828. Cuban, Larry. SHRINKING ENROLLMENT AND CONSOLIDATION: POLITICAL AND ORGANIZATIONAL IMPACTS IN ARLINGTON, VIRGINIA 1973-78. *Educ. and Urban Soc. 1979 11(3): 367-395.* Discusses the effects of school consolidation and declining enrollments on the politics and organization of public schools in Arlington, Virginia, 1973-78.

2829. Dougherty, Laurie et al. "RACISM AND BUSING IN BOSTON": COMMENTS AND CRITICISM. *Radical Am. 1975 9(3): 65-92.* Responses to "Racism and Busing in Boston," *Radical America* 1974 8(6): 1-11, which dealt with school integration and the racism of the white working class, 1974-75.

2830. Efthim, Helen. PONTIAC DESEGREGATION: MYTH AND REALITY. *Urban Rev. 1975 8(2): 155-159.* Since Pontiac, Michigan's public schools were desegregated by busing in 1971, there has been an improvement in race relations and attitudes.

2831. Elazar, Daniel J. SCHOOL DECENTRALIZATION IN THE CONTEXT OF COMMUNITY CONTROL: SOME NEGLECTED CONSIDERATIONS. *Phylon 1975 36(4): 385-394.* Examines the problem of community control of schools in a broad context beyond the prominent racial and political struggles taking place within big city schools. In an age in which centralization is not only taken for granted but is considered right and proper by governmental agencies and those who fear that the diffusion of power will interfere with the attainment of goals they have set forth, school decentralization is an issue which both brings into focus American assumptions concerning local self-government and challenges the public to decide whether or not continued centralization is politically appropriate or desirable. Based on secondary sources; 14 notes.   K. C. Snow

2832. Erber, Ernest. WHITE FLIGHT AND POLITICAL RETREAT. *Dissent 1979 26(1): 53-58.* Criticizes James S. Coleman's argument in 1975 that court-ordered desegregation drove white pupils out of city schools, a repudiation of his 1966 study, "Equality of Educational Opportunity," the major factual basis of the prointegration movement. Similarly reviews a supportive article by Diane Ravitch in 1978. Economic and demographic factors ignored by Coleman and Ravitch also affect the decreasing white enrollment in city schools since 1968.

2833. Farley, Reynolds and Taeuber, Alma F. RACIAL SEGREGATION IN THE PUBLIC SCHOOLS. *Am. J. of Sociol. 1974 79(4):*

888-905. Presents data on racial segregation in public elementary schools in 60 cities for the 1967-68 school year. The percentage Negro among students varied from less than 5 to more than 90. Among instructional staffs the percentage Negro ranges from a low of 2 to a high of 84. Levels of racial segregation were typically high. The index ranged from a low of 39 in Sacramento to a high of 97 in Tulsa and Oklahoma City. The average level of school segregation among the 60 cities was 79.   J

2834. Fitzgerald, Michael R. and Morgan, David R. CHANGING PATTERNS OF URBAN SCHOOL DESEGREGATION. *Am. Pol. Q. 1977 5(4): 437-464.* That desegregation has worked better in certain places indicates the operation of forces other than federal pressure. Analyzes forces in many Northern and Southern cities. In the North, cities with segregated housing, large school districts, and more black students proved most resistant. In the South, factors are more complex. School district size proved to be negative, but "southern desegregation engulfed the whole community." 3 tables, 11 notes, ref.   R. V. Ritter

2835. Foster, Gordon DESEGREGATING URBAN SCHOOLS: A REVIEW OF TECHNIQUES. *Harvard Educ. Rev. 1973 43(1): 5-36.* Desegregation is proceeding in at least half of the nation's urban school districts. Methods include redrawing of attendance zones, pairing and grouping of schools within a zone, establishment of feeder patterns from lower to higher schools, skip zoning (grouping or pairing by skipping over schools in sequential order), and deliberate location of new schools. Voluntary plans have proved less satisfactory. Costs, the mystique of the neighborhood school, and fears of decreased academic achievement and of busing have slowed desegregation. Recommends the metropolitan approach. Tables, notes.   J. Herbst

2836. Franklin, Vincent P. THE PERSISTENCE OF SCHOOL SEGREGATION IN THE URBAN NORTH: AN HISTORICAL PERSPECTIVE. *J. of Ethnic Studies 1974 1(4): 51-68.* Persistence of school segregation in the urban North is often attributed to the post-World War II shift of whites to the suburbs and the influx of southern blacks into the central cities. Demographic redistribution plays an important role, but it is only the latest act in the long drama of northern urban school segregation. Using Philadelphia as a prime example, shows that segregated education prevailed since the beginning of public education in northern cities. As a result the problem is not merely a product of recent housing patterns, but rather an established tradition with over 150 years of roots. Based on primary and secondary sources; 68 notes.
T. W. Smith

2837. Freeman, Ruges R. EDUCATIONAL DESEGREGATION IN ST. LOUIS. *Negro Hist. Bull. 1975 38(3): 364-369.* Summarizes the author's doctoral dissertation on the 1954-55 St. Louis desegregation plan. School desegregation in St. Louis was significant because planning for orderly integration was underway before the May 1954 Supreme Court decision.   M. J. Wentworth

2838. Fuerst, J. S. REPORT FROM CHICAGO: A PROGRAM THAT WORKS. *Public Interest 1976 (43): 59-69.* Recent achievement test scores of black children in some Chicago public schools have risen dramatically because of a concentrated reading program requiring rigid repetitive patterns, called DISTAR (Direct Instructional Systems in Training for Arithmetic and Reading). This program is used most extensively in deteriorated areas, especially in District 10, which covers Lawndale, and in five "Child/Parent Centers" (CPC's). With DISTAR, reading scores in 1974 and 1975 rose above the inner city, citywide, and, for five CPC's, national mean scores. The most immediate obstacle to the extensive use of DISTAR is its high cost, but this varies and is not always extremely expensive. The results achieved through the use of DISTAR prove that black children from slum areas can be taught to read and communicate as well as white children, and that this can be accomplished in a segregated school system.   S. Harrow

2839. Giles, Michael W. RACIAL STABILITY AND URBAN SCHOOL DESEGREGATION. *Urban Affairs Q. 1976 12(4): 499-510.* Studies Florida's Jacksonville area to test the assumption that school desegregation produces white withdrawal and resegregation. Desegregation was ordered in 1963 and began in 1972, when a court ordered plan was implemented. Initial white withdrawal was evident in previously all black public schools, but was not apparent when blacks were integrated into previously all white schools. An increased but stable percentage of students are sent to private schools. Expansion of the ghetto explains why some schools have shown a five percent or more increase in black students since 1972. Desegregation can be attained without substantial resegregation. Primary and secondary sources; 2 tables, 7 notes, biblio.

L. N. Beecher

2840. Goldberg, Gertrude S. CLASS ACTION, COMMUNITY ORGANIZATION AND SCHOOL REFORM. *Freedomways 1977 17(4): 224-238; 1978 18(1): 28-35.* Part I. Three self-help organizations, Aspira in New York City, the Philadelphia Welfare Rights Organization, and the Harlem Parents Union, have worked since 1973 to assure quality education for underprivileged children from minority backgrounds. Part II. Deals with alternative and integrated education for minority children; emphasizes community organization and neighborhood associations which become responsible for local education standards; delineates legal recourse for parents, 1970's.

2841. Grant, William R. LETTER FROM DETROIT: THE COURTS AND THE SCHOOLS. *Urban Rev. 1975 8(2): 145-152.* Although in 1970 federal courts ruled that northern urban public schools must desegregate, the Supreme Court in 1974, prohibited Detroit from involving the white suburbs in the desegregation.

2842. Graubard, Allen. ALTERNATIVE SCHOOLS. *Working Papers for a New Soc. 1976 4(3): 24-29.* Discusses the advent of free schools and their impact on the public schools in Cambridge, Massachusetts, 1969-70's.

2843. Havighurst, Robert J. EDUCATIONAL POLICY FOR THE LARGE CITIES. *Social Problems 1976 24(2): 271-281.* To save inner cities, education of inner city children is important, and all children can master the basic public school curriculum; covers 1960's-75.

2844. Henderson, Ronald D. and von Euler, Mary. METROPOLITAN SCHOOL DESEGREGATION: EMERGING RESEARCH ISSUES. *Urban Rev. 1978 10(2): 67-70.* The National Institute of Education's conference, School Desegregation in Metropolitan Areas: Choices and Prospects, in March 1977 encouraged interaction among educational scholars and practitioners. Legal authorities' papers examined "whether there is a constitutional right to a desegregated education, what may be expected from the courts, and what solutions must be supplied by the legislatures." Since 1971 the Supreme Court has recognized the mutual influence of public policies on school and housing segregation. To furnish courts with evidence of segregation by public policy, scholars should focus on "the metropolitanization concept." One secondary source, government documents, and one newspaper; 11 notes.

R. G. Sherer

2845. Hoffman, Nancy. TEACHING CHANGE: EDUCATION TO REFORM THE CITIES. *Working Papers For a New Soc. 1975 3(1): 37-43.* Describes the efforts of urban human service colleges to promote educational reform while educating low-income reformers and radicals.

S

2846. Hooyman, Nancy and Musick, John. PONTIAC: HOW PEOPLE RESPOND TO BUSING. *Dissent 1973 20(2): 210-216.*

2847. Hornburger, Jane M. DEEP ARE THE ROOTS: BUSING IN BOSTON. *J. of Negro Educ. 1976 45(3): 235-245.* Court-ordered busing in Boston in 1974 to end unequal educational opportunity through true integration led to violence in South Boston. Further busing to integrate the rest of the schools in Boston will hopefully be more peaceful. 36 notes.

B. D. Johnson

2848. Jenkins, Martin D. and Ross, Bernard H. THE URBAN INVOLVEMENT OF HIGHER EDUCATION: AN ANALYSIS OF SELECTED TRENDS AND ISSUES. *J. of Higher Educ. 1975 46(4): 399-408.* During the 1960s, in response to growing unrest in urban areas and on college campuses, colleges and universities began expanding their urban involvement activities. This article utilizes data from a nationwide survey to analyze selected trends and issues in higher education urban involvement by focusing on the current status and future direction of urban affairs activities on college and university campuses.

J

2849. Kapel, David E. and Pink, William T. THE SCHOOLBOARD: PARTICIPATORY DEMOCRACY REVISITED. *Urban Rev. 1978 10(1): 20-34.* Many scholars and citizens have noted and expressed dissatisfaction with urban schools. Decentralization, citizen participation, and community control are commonly proposed solutions. New York City and Detroit have implemented the first two reforms, but failure to include community control limited their success. Based on published secondary sources, unpublished papers, and a dissertation; table, biblio.

R. G. Sherer

2850. King, Charles E.; Mayer, Robin R.; and Borders-Patterson, Anne. DIFFERENTIAL RESPONSES TO BLACK AND WHITE MALES BY FEMALE TEACHERS IN A SOUTHERN CITY. *Sociol. and Social Res. 1973 57(4): 482-494.* This article discusses the impact of a rather far-reaching school desegregation plan on teacher-pupil interaction at the classroom level. White males were most skillful in teacher-interaction and black males were least skillful of the four race-sex groups. All students interacted more with teachers in an integrated than in the all-black school.

J

2851. Kirby, David J. and Crain, Robert L. THE FUNCTIONS OF CONFLICT: SCHOOL DESEGREGATION IN 91 CITIES. *Social Sci. Q. 1974 55(2): 478-492.* Presents five hypotheses about the effects of conflict in obtaining desegregation, drawn from the general findings that cities with militant black populations are more likely to have the issue of school desegregation come up and desegregation is more likely to occur if the school board has a high level of internal conflict; while at the same time both civil rights demonstrations and grass roots anti-integration activity by whites seem self-defeating.

J

2852. Koppelman, Lee E. and Kunz, Arthur H. EMPTY DESKS: THE SUBURBAN SCHOOL DILEMMA. *New York Affairs 1979 5(4): 88-94.* Discusses the rapid growth of Nassau and Suffolk Counties' suburbs from the 1940's to 1970 and the accompanying expansion of school facilities Examines the problems in the counties during the 1970's and in the future, as the population slowdown results in fewer students and less need for school facilities.

2853. Lalli, Michael and Savitz, Leonard D. THE FEAR OF CRIME IN THE SCHOOL ENTERPRISE AND ITS CONSEQUENCES. *Educ. and Urban Soc. 1976 8(4): 401-416.* Summarizes a multiyear study begun in 1970 among a large cohort of young Philadelphia males and their mothers. In the study group a significant number of truancies and dropouts may be explained by actual fear of physical danger in the school setting. Four tables, 3 notes, biblio.

C. A. D'Aniello

2854. Lavin, David E.; Alba, Richard D.; and Silberstein, Richard A. OPEN ADMISSIONS AND EQUAL ACCESS: A STUDY OF ETHNIC GROUPS IN THE CITY UNIVERSITY OF NEW YORK. *Harvard Educ. Rev. 1979 49(1): 53-92.* Analyzes the effects of the City University of New York's open admissions policy, adopted in 1970, on academic standards and educational equality.

2855. Levine, Daniel U. EDUCATING ALIENATED INNER-CITY YOUTH: LESSONS FROM THE STREET ACADEMIES. *J. of Negro Educ. 1975 44(2): 139-148.* Street academies are nontraditional secondary schools available to innercity youth and have been relatively successful in educating students who have done poorly in public schools. Their success depends on their small size, community ties, innovative structure, individual attention, and clear, obtainable objectives. Discusses possible lessons for the reform of public schools. Secondary sources; 20 notes.

R. E. Butchart

2856. Levine, Daniel U. and Meyer, Jeanie Keeny. LEVEL AND RATE OF DESEGREGATION AND WHITE ENROLLMENT DECLINE IN A BIG CITY SCHOOL SYSTEM. *Social Problems 1977 24(4): 451-462.* Declining enrollment of whites occurred in public schools where black populations were high; refers to Kansas City, Missouri, 1956-74.

2857. Lord, J. Dennis and Catau, John C. SCHOOL DESEGREGATION POLICY AND INTRA-SCHOOL DISTRICT MIGRATION. *Social Sci. Q. 1977 57(4): 784-796.* Examines the migration of white households with elementary school children in the Charlotte-Mecklenburg, North Carolina, school district during two years of desegregation activity. The relationship of migration to the black ratio of the assigned school, the school's racial status prior to desegregation, and whether or not the students were bused are analyzed. Migration increased 12.8% during desegregation and reflected the national pattern of white movement from central cities to suburbs. A multiple-regression model illustrates the possible relationship of this migration with factors other than school desegregation. Based on data from the Charlotte-Mecklenburg School System; 2 tables, 3 fig., 2 notes, biblio.   W. R. Hively

2858.   Lum, Philip A.   THE CREATION AND DEMISE OF SAN FRANCISCO CHINATOWN FREEDOM SCHOOLS: ONE RESPONSE TO DESEGREGATION.   *Amerasia J. 1978 5(1): 57-73.* In the fall of 1971, some Chinatown residents created a separate, private, school system as an alternative to court-ordered busing. These schools were ironically dubbed Freedom Schools. The concern of the Chinese community was mainly that the quality of education given Chinese American pupils would suffer; they also disliked the idea of their children spending hours on buses. The desire to preserve Chinese language and culture was secondary; the Freedom schools operated half-day sessions for lack of funds and the basic curriculum dominated these hours, not Chinese studies. The Freedom Schools eventually collapsed due to internal dissension, and Chinese children went back to the public schools. Fig., 21 notes.   J. C. Billigmeier

2859.   Mackler, Bernard.   CHILDREN HAVE RIGHTS, TOO! *Crisis 1974 81(7): 235-238.* Discusses the education of emotionally disturbed children in New York City during the 1960's.   S

2860.   Mann, Dale.   POLITICAL REPRESENTATION AND URBAN SCHOOL ADVISORY COUNCILS.   *Teachers Coll. Record 1974 75(3): 279-307.* "Community involvement and participation in school policy decisionmaking is, among other things, a political movement."   S

2861.   Massey, Grace Carroll; Scott, Mona Vaughn; and Dornbusch, Sanford M.   RACISM WITHOUT RACISTS: INSTITUTIONAL RACISM IN URBAN SCHOOLS.   *Black Scholar 1975 7(3): 10-19.* Argues that schools use forms of covert racism which encourage Negro students to develop unrealistic conceptions of themselves and their abilities in the 1970's.

2862.   Menatian, Steve and Lynch, Patrick D.   ETHNIC POLITICS IN A NORTHEASTERN URBAN SCHOOL SYSTEM.   *Educ. and Urban Soc. 1974 6(3): 318-332.*

2863.   Mills, Nicolaus.   COMMUNITY SCHOOLS: IRISH, ITALIANS AND JEWS.   *Society 1974 11(3): 76-84.* Reviews the long-standing issue of community-controlled schools in New York City's ethnic neighborhoods.   S

2864.   Mitchell, Maurice.   THE DESEGREGATION OF DENVER'S PUBLIC SCHOOLS.   *Center Mag. 1978 11(6): 67-76.* Offers a history of the desegregation of the public schools in Denver, Colorado, 1974-77 under federal court order.

2865.   Muller, Mary Lee.   NEW ORLEANS PUBLIC SCHOOL DESEGREGATION.   *Louisiana Hist. 1976 17(1): 69-88.* The *Brown* decision of 1954 prohibiting school segregation was a much resented intrusion of federal authority in local New Orleans affairs. The integration issue divided the white community into two opposing camps. The city's leadership sanctioned the fight against court-ordered desegregation by shunning acceptance of the order. When finally compelled to implement desegregation, the school board chose to limit racial mixing through pupil placement in the ninth ward, seemingly the course of least liability—politically, economically, and socially. 88 notes.   E. P. Stickney

2866.   Murphy, Joseph F.   FISCAL PROBLEMS OF BIG CITY SCHOOL SYSTEMS: CHANGING PATTERNS OF STATE AND FEDERAL AID.   *Urban Rev. 1978 10(4): 251-265.* Big city school systems need more money than suburban systems to furnish more vocational, compensatory, special, and language education. Cities' salary, site acquisition-construction, security, and other costs are higher than are the suburbs'. But city revenue sources are declining and non-educational

expenses consume a higher percentage of city revenue. State and federal aid has helped cities but is not equalizing city-suburban educational expenditures. Primary and secondary sources; 16 tables, 4 notes.
          R. G. Sherer

2867.   Nelson, Joel I.   PARTICIPATION AND COLLEGE ASPIRATIONS: COMPLEX EFFECTS OF COMMUNITY SIZE.   *Rural Sociol. 1973 38(1): 7-16.* Urban adolescents are more likely to plan on attending college than rural adolescents. Previous research has suggested explanations of this difference as the advantages associated with large communities and large schools. Some theoretical considerations suggest, however, that large size may not always favor the development of college aspirations. Small schools, for example, foster higher rates of participation in extra-curricular activities than do large schools. Since participation is also related to aspirations, the smaller school works to the advantage of rural students. Data from a sample of Minnesota high school juniors suggest that attending small schools appears to lower values on one variable related to aspirations (i.e., rural-urban residence) but simultaneously increases values on a different variable related to aspirations (i.e., participation in extra-curricular activities). The implications of these data are discussed regarding how simple community size differences in aspirations obscure complex and confounding pressures towards further education.   J

2868.   Niemi, Albert W., Jr.   RACIAL DIFFERENCES IN RETURNS TO EDUCATIONAL INVESTMENT IN THE SOUTH.   *Am. J. of Econ. and Sociol. 1975 34(1): 87-94.* Examines the rate of return from educational investment in the South and in the metropolitan areas of Atlanta, New Orleans, and Washington, D. C., on the basis of 1970 earnings data. There has been a relative increase in the returns to Negroes' education by 1970. Secondary sources; 2 tables, 23 notes.
          W. L. Marr

2869.   Noblit, George W. and Collins, Thomas W.   SCHOOL FLIGHT AND SCHOOL POLICY: DESEGREGATION AND RESEGREGATION IN THE MEMPHIS CITY SCHOOLS.   *Urban Rev. 1978 10(3): 203-212.* Current debate on "white flight" after desegregation of public schools is based on quantitative studies of city school systems, such as O. Z. Stephens's 1976 report on Memphis schools. Ethnographic case studies of specific schools are also needed to understand the impact of desegregation. For white parents who removed their children from one Memphis public school the main "pull" factor was the establishment of white, private academies, usually in congregational Protestant churches. The main "push" factors were the parents' desires for "quality" education, i.e. discipline and a flexible curriculum offering advanced or honors courses, and for control of the schools' student organizations. Primary and secondary sources; 3 notes, biblio.
          R. G. Sherer

2870.   Orfield, Gary.   IF WISHES WERE HOUSES THEN BUSING COULD STOP: DEMOGRAPHIC TRENDS AND DESEGREGATION POLICY.   *Urban Rev. 1978 10(2): 108-124.* For the past decade the American "national policy on urban school desegregation" was based on three erroneous assumptions—that ghettos arose because of private choices, that housing discrimination is declining, and that "school busing on any scale will only be counterproductive." Effective school integration must include entire metropolitan areas. Such desegregation often causes stable housing desegregation, not vice versa, and can occur only through positive government action. Primary and secondary sources; 56 notes.
          R. G. Sherer

2871.   O'Shea, David W.   SUBURBAN SCHOOL DISTRICT GOVERNMENT: A COMPARATIVE PERSPECTIVE.   *Educ. and Urban Soc. 1973 5(4): 405-436.* Examines the results and implications of a field study of 15 elementary districts within the urbanized area surrounding Chicago regarding the management of suburban schools.   S

2872.   O'Shea, David W.   SCHOOL DISTRICT DECENTRALIZATION: THE CASE OF LOS ANGELES.   *Educ. and Urban Soc. 1975 7(4): 377-392.* Because of Governor Reagan's veto of the Harmer-Greene legislation, the district has been allowed time to develop an organizational response to demands for decentralization and community control. This has been in the form of compensatory education, administrative decentralization, and new boundary spanning units at both the central and local school levels. 2 notes.   C. D'Aniello

2873. Pettigrew, Thomas F. and Green, Robert L. SCHOOL DESEG-REGATION IN LARGE CITIES: A CRITIQUE OF THE COLE-MAN "WHITE FLIGHT" THESIS. *Harvard Educ. Rev. 1976 46(1): 1-53.* Disagrees with the thesis of sociologist James S. Coleman that urban school integration leads to massive "white flight."

2874. Pilo, Marvin R. A TALE OF TWO CITIES: THE APPLICA-TION OF MODELS OF SCHOOL DECENTRALIZATION TO THE CASES OF NEW YORK CITY AND DETROIT. *Educ. and Urban Soc. 1975 7(4): 393-411.* Discusses the history of decentralization in these cities and predicts further change in this direction. Notes the usefulness of the political bargaining framework for understanding decentralization demands as well as for explaining the sequence of events once it has taken place. The organizational process model provides insight into the re-sponse of professional educators.   C. D'Aniello

2875. Priddy, Laurance L. "SAVE OUR NEIGHBORHOOD SCHOOLS!!" *Crisis 1975 82(4): 115-117.* A community group of par-ents met to discuss busing. The pastor of the church in which they were meeting prayed that busing was an "unworkable, immoral, and satanic scheme" to destroy neighborhood schools. Some parents called for a boycott of the schools, while others advocated impromptu private schools. Everyone supported a Constitutional amendment against busing. All of these tactics were considered justified in order to preserve the neighborhood school. The parents involved denied that they were racist.
                                                        A. G. Belles

2876. Ravitch, Diane. CANARSIE AND FUENTES: THE LIMITS OF SCHOOL DECENTRALIZATION. *New York Affairs 1973 1(1): 88-97.* Describes two episodes in school governance which illustrate a major dilemma of New York City school decentralization: how power should be divided between local school boards and the central board. Both controversies illustrate the dangers of local control: in the Luis Fuentes case a minority gained control of the board through a majority of none-lected members, and in the Canarsie schools dispute the problem of busing black children masked the real issue: the assertion of central board authority. Local control implies that each community may set its own racial and ethnic standards, but decentralization can be effective only if laws and regulations are uniform and well enforced. Illus., note.
                                                        J. A. Benson

2877. Rist, Ray C. and Orfield, Gary. SCHOOL DESEGREGA-TION AND WHITE FLIGHT. *Social Policy 1976 6(4): 6-8.* Discusses the attempt of whites in northern cities to evade the problem of school desegregation in the 1970's.

2878. Ritterband, Paul. ETHNIC POWER AND THE PUBLIC SCHOOLS: THE NEW YORK CITY SCHOOL STRIKE OF 1968. *Sociol. of Educ. 1974 47(2): 251-267.* "The 1968 New York City school strike was more a struggle between ethnic communities than a labor-management dispute."   S

2879. Ritterband, Paul. ETHNICITY AND SCHOOL DISORDER. *Educ. and Urban Soc. 1976 8(4): 383-400.* Summarizes a study conducted by means of a mail questionaire distributed to high school principals in major cities 1967-69. The most significant conclusions drawn from the data are: political disorders are more likely to reside in ethnicity than in other characteristics of students and staff; both political and nonpolitical disorders are more common in the North than the South, regardless of race; political disorders are more determinate in the North; and ethnicity is a better predictor of disorder in the North than in the South. 8 tables, note, biblio.   C. A. D'Aniello

2880. Rohn, David. 1954 DAWNS IN INDIANAPOLIS. *J. of In-tergroup Relations 1974 3(2): 3-24.* Describes the legal efforts establish-ing school integration in Indianapolis, 1971-73, and reprints Judge S. Hugh Dillin's Memorandum of Decision.   S

2881. Roomkin, Myron. ECONOMIC EFFECTS OF BASIC EDU-CATION FOR ADULTS: THE MILWAUKEE MDTA EXPERI-ENCE. *Q. Rev. of Econ. and Business 1973 13(1): 87-96.* Reports an evaluation of a remedial education program for disadvantaged adults in Milwaukee financed under the Manpower Development and Training Act of 1963. Econometric techniques are applied to data from the 1967

Survey of Economic Opportunity to estimate the expected earnings gain to trainees as a result of improvements in their level of educational achievement. The actual economic gain to trainees is determined by com-paring the posttraining earnings of trainees with those of a comparable group of nontrainees. Both the expected and actual benefit levels were found to be unimpressive.   J

2882. Rosenwaike, Ira. INTERETHNIC COMPARISONS OF ED-UCATIONAL ATTAINMENT: AN ANALYSIS BASED ON CEN-SUS DATA FOR NEW YORK CITY. *Am. J. of Sociol. 1973 79(1): 68-77.* Further studies of educational attainment among white ethnic groups are necessary to deemphasize studies about white-nonwhite differ-ences; 1960-73.

2883. Rossell, Christine. WHITE FLIGHT: PROS AND CONS. *Social Policy 1978 9(3): 46-51.* Examines the pros and cons of the current white flight debate, particularly analyzing studies on school desegregation and white flight done in the late 1960's and early 1970's.

2884. Rothstein, Stanley William. JOURNAL OF A GHETTO SCHOOL. *Crisis 1975 82(3): 84-88.* Noise, bells, spitballs, and fights characterize the disorder in ghetto schools where teachers and adminis-trators ignore the purpose of education. The schools are structured to fail.
                                                        A. G. Belles

2885. Sakolsky, R. THE MYTH OF GOVERNMENT-SPON-SORED REVOLUTION: A CASE STUDY OF INSTITUTIONAL SAFETY VALVES. *Educ. and Urban Soc. 1973 5(3): 321-344.* Presents a case study on the Ocean Hill-Brownsville school decentralization con-troversy in New York City.   S

2886. Sanchez, Ramón. SCENARIO FOR A GHETTO SCHOOL SYSTEM. *Urban Rev. 1973 6(4): 8-11.*

2887. Schneider, E. Joseph and Burton, Mary Kennedy. INNER-CITY TEACHING: A SUCCESS STORY. *Urban Rev. 1973 6(4): 28-31.*

2888. Scott, David W. METROPOLITAN TRANSACTION PAT-TERNS IN SUBURBAN CHICAGO: THE CASE OF SCHOOL DIS-TRICT COLLABORATION. *Publius 1975 5(1): 97-119.* Analyzes the variables affecting the political cooperation of Chicago suburban high school districts attempting to create junior colleges 1963-68, in a special issue of *Publius*, "The Suburban Reshaping of American Politics."

2889. Shanas, Bert. NEW YORK SCHOOL DECENTRALIZA-TION—A MIXED BAG. *New York Affairs 1976 3(4): 69-82.* School decentralization in New York City has made administration easier. It has increased parent involvement. But it has also unleashed a torrent of political power plays, racial sloganeering and misspent funds.   J

2890. Slawski, Edward J. PONTIAC PARENTS: FOR BUSING OR INTEGRATION? *Educ. and Urban Soc. 1976 8(4): 477-498.* Summa-rizes a study conducted in 1972-75 in Pontiac, Michigan, a medium-size industrial city on the fringe of the Detroit metropolitan area, to determine parental attitudes toward busing and integration in that city. Ostensibly, the data lead to the conclusion that there may be less reluctance to having children attend school with black children as long as they stay close to home. That is, class prejudice may be more operative than race prejudice. This may be merely a response given to mask race prejudice. 5 tables, 2 notes, biblio.   C. A. D'Aniello

2891. Sly, David F. and Pol, Louis G. THE DEMOGRAPHIC CON-TEXT OF SCHOOL SEGREGATION AND DESEGREGATION. *Social Forces 1978 56(4): 1072-1086.* The political perils of social re-search are salient in arguments over white-flight. Some investigators feel large city school system integration accelerates white migration to sub-urbs creating additional segregation and the need for still additional busing. Research supporting the white-flight thesis suffers methodologi-cal and substantive pitfalls. It fails to recognize the historical contribution of the various components of population change to growth of the white and black populations in cities, and the structural implications of these differences. It also fails to incorporate measures of white-flight which accurately depict the volume of white migration; and instead relies on proportional measures which are influenced by a number of factors in addition to white city-to-suburban migration. Rather than inferring white-flight from measures of school segregation, the authors relate the latter to white city-to-ring migration. The analytical factors contributing to changes in the proportion black in city public schools are given attention, particularly black-white differences in natural increase.   J

2892.   Smith, Earl.   RACISM AND THE BOSTON SCHOOLS CRISIS.   *Black Scholar 1975 6(6): 37-41.* Discusses violence over desegregation of Boston's public schools in 1974-75.

2893.   Stockton, Ronald R. and Wayman, Francis W.   THE BUSING ISSUE: RACE AND SOCIAL CHANGE.   *Michigan Academician 1976 8(4): 441-455.* Examines the volatile busing issue in Detroit and Dearborn, Michigan, finding little correlation between attitude toward busing and attitudes on racism based on a 1974 interview of 451 heads of households in the Dearborn area.

2894.   Strickman, Leonard P.   BUSING IN BOSTON.   *Civil Liberties Rev. 1977 4(2): 75-79.* Thomas J. Cottle's *Busing* (Boston: Beacon Pr., 1976) chronicles the antibusing campaign in Boston, 1974-76, brought about by strict school integration.

2895.   Stuart, Reginald.   BUSING AND THE MEDIA IN NASHVILLE.   *New South 1973 28(2): 79-87.*

2896.   Syrkin, Marie.   AGAIN: THE BUSING BLUES.   *Midstream 1977 23(7): 63-66.* Discusses the busing issue in Los Angeles, maintaining that busing is not the remedy to generations of oppression.

2897.   Taeuber, Karl E.   DEMOGRAPHIC PERSPECTIVES ON METROPOLITAN SCHOOL DESEGREGATION.   *Urban Rev. 1978 10(2): 71-81.* Meaningful desegregation is possible only in entire metropolitan areas. Legislatures and executives can effect change better than courts. The concentration of minorities in central cities, which may be slowing, is less noticeable if all urban areas are studied. Increasing suburbanization of jobs and housing necessitates metropolitan planning. School segregation is part of both the cause and the effect of the metropolitan racial crises. Metropolitan policy planning should lead to "a national agenda for social and economic change." Primary and secondary sources; biblio.   R. G. Sherer

2898.   Taylor, William L.   METROPOLITAN REMEDIES FOR PUBLIC SCHOOL DISCRIMINATION: THE NEGLECTED OPTION.   *Urban Rev. 1978 10(2): 184-192.* Intradistrict desegregation policies offer no real hope for improving the condition of urban minority students. Metropolitan desegregation plans "are administratively feasible, need not impair local control, do not require excessive busing, provide for stability and maximize prospects for educational gains beyond those of integration." The Supreme Court's decision against interdistrict plans showed their perception of public opinion and a "misunderstanding of urban reality."   R. G. Sherer

2899.   Thomson, Scott D.   SECONDARY SCHOOLS AND THE URBAN CLIMATE.   *Educ. and Urban Soc. 1976 8(3): 355-374.* Places the secondary school in the context of historical and contemporary events. The goals and achievements of educational reformers in curriculum development, administration, personnel, and public relations as they relate to minority students are discussed. 1 case, 7 references.   C. A. D'Aniello

2900.   Tractenberg, Paul L.   THE BLEAK PLIGHT OF THE URBAN TEACHER.   *Urban Rev. 1973 6(5-6): 51-56.* The findings of the Kerner Commission, Coleman Report, and Riles Report, 1966-70, show that the quality of education, from the teacher's to the classroom, are deficient in urban environments.

2901.   Treacy, John J. and Harris, Russell L.   CONTEMPORARY SUBURBAN SCHOOLS—THE NEEDY?   *Southern Econ. J. 1974 40(4): 640-646.* Questions traditional hypothesis that suburban schools are likely to need less financial assistance than urban schools.   S

2902.   Trent, Richard D.   THE PLIGHT OF THE URBAN COLLEGE AND MINORITY STUDENTS.   *Crisis 1976 83(2): 43-47.* New York recently adopted several programs to increase economic and educational opportunities for minorities. But inflation, reduced federal and state support, less income, and lower values of investments have made survival the main issue for colleges and minority student programs have been the first to suffer. Open access is an important innovation in American education and must be maintained to advance the nation's basic resource—people.   A. G. Belles

2903.   Unsigned.   [MANDATORY BUSING AND "WHITE FLIGHT"].
Ravitch, Diane.   THE "WHITE FLIGHT" CONTROVERSY.   *Public Interest 1978 (51): 135-149.* In 1975 James S. Coleman declared that court-ordered school desegregation contributed to "white flight" from the big cities and thus was causing resegregation. His findings were attacked by activist desegregationists, including scholars such as Christine Rossell of Boston University. In 1975 Rossell concluded that mandatory school-wide desegregation was the best means of insuring racial stability, and might be a "remedy" for whatever little "white flight" occurs. Her study is inadequate. By using percentages, which can mask substantial changes in enrollments, rather than absolute figures, she chose a statistical method which showed small declines when large movements occurred. Coleman's conclusions concerning the diminishing number of whites in urban schools remain valid. A city that may avoid this "white flight" is Atlanta, where the local NAACP exchanged busing for jobs and black control of the school system. 6 tables.
Rossell, Christine H.; Ravitch, Diane; and Armor, David J.   BUSING AND "WHITE FLIGHT."   *Public Interest 1978 (53): 109-115.* A three-way exchange triggered by the above article. The controversy is about the best methodology for measurement, computation, and interpretation. "White flight" is particularly serious now, when urban experts are urgently trying to attract whites back into cities. Those desiring more integration should be disturbed that court-ordered busing might cause "resegregation."
          S. Harrow/R. V. Ritter

2904.   Unsigned.   RACISM AND BUSING IN BOSTON.   *Radical America 1974 8(6): 1-11.*

2905.   Unsigned.   [SCHOOL DESEGREGATION IN THE CITIES].   *Social Policy 1976 6(4): 9-29.*
Coleman, James S.   LIBERTY AND EQUALITY IN SCHOOL DESEGREGATION,   *pp. 9-13.*
Farley, Reynolds.   IS COLEMAN RIGHT?,   *pp. 14-23.*
Orfield, Gary.   [IS COLEMAN RIGHT?],   *pp. 24-29.*
Discusses trends in school desegregation in US cities in the 1960's and 70's, and analyzes the arguments of sociology professor James S. Coleman.

2906.   Unsigned.   SELECTED BIBLIOGRAPHY ON URBAN SCHOOL DECENTRALIZATION.   *Educ. and Urban Soc. 1975 7(4): 480-484.* Lists a wide assortment of materials including government documents, serials, books, and dissertations.   C. D'Aniello

2907.   Useem, Elizabeth.   CORRELATES OF WHITE STUDENTS' ATTITUDES TOWARD A VOLUNTARY BUSING PROGRAM.   *Educ. and Urban Soc. 1976 8(4): 441-476.* Summarizes a study conducted among students in the Metropolitan Council for Educational Opportunity (METCO) busing program in Boston in 1968-69. The program transports low- and middle-class blacks to the more affluent suburbs. Findings argue that certain types of interracial contact are associated with the expression of tolerant racial attitudes while others produce insignificant positive correlations with unprejudiced views. The social stratification system omnipresent in schools fosters prejudice and encourages those not favored in it to seek scapegoats. Curriculum should be designed to encourage group effort. Unprejudiced attitudes will grow out of the cooperative interdependence of students. 8 tables, 14 notes, biblio.
          C. A. D'Aniello

2908.   Watson, Denton L.   THE DETROIT SCHOOL CHALLENGE.   *Crisis 1974 81(6): 188-198.* Describes the racial situation in Detroit and legal efforts from 1969 to 1973 to end school segregation.   S

2909. Welch, Susan and Karnig, Albert K. THE IMPACT OF BLACK ELECTED OFFICIALS ON URBAN SCHOOL EXPENDITURES. *Policy Studies J. 1979 7(4): 707-713.* Finds that the presence of black mayors in cities over 50,000 promotes an increase in public welfare and social services spending, however black city council members do not have any marked effect, 1968-75.

2910. Wiles, David K. COMMUNITY PARTICIPATION DEMANDS AND LOCAL SCHOOL RESPONSE IN THE URBAN ENVIRONMENT. *Educ. and Urban Soc. 1974 6(4): 451-468.* Discusses the level and relevance of community participation in educational decisionmaking.   S

2911. Winokur, Herbert S. EXPENDITURE EQUALIZATION IN THE WASHINGTON, D.C. ELEMENTARY SCHOOLS. *Public Policy 1976 24(3): 309-335.* Analyzes the impact of a US District Court-ordered expenditure equalization plan in Washington, D.C. as a result of the *Hobson* v. *Hansen* case (1967). Equalization was meant to insure equality of educational opportunity for Washington, D.C., pupils. Administrative problems of complying with the court order are studied. The decision to transfer teachers within the school district rather than attempt mandatory busing, the difficulty of assessing individual school needs, and the issue of compensatory education are analyzed. Time constraints imposed by the court-ordered compliance date complicated implementation. Mathematical models used to project the effects of educational resource reallocation are used. Conclusions about the short-term and long-term compliance are detailed. Based on original research and secondary sources; tables, 9 notes, biblio.   J. M. Herrick

Social Welfare and Reform

2912. Bibby, Reginald W. and Mauss, Armand L. SKIDDERS AND THEIR SERVANTS: VARIABLE GOALS AND FUNCTIONS OF THE SKID ROAD RESCUE MISSION. *J. for the Sci. Study of Religion 1974 13(4): 421-436.* Studies Seattle's skid road missions and concludes that although the official objectives of the missions are not achieved, the missions live on because they realize the personal goals of their leaders and the men who attend.

2913. Christensen, Terry. THE URBAN BIAS OF THE POVERTY PROGRAM. *Policy Studies J. 1974 2(3): 162-165.*

2914. Cox, Steven R. WHY ERADICATING URBAN POVERTY REQUIRES A LONG TERM MULTI-PROGRAM "WAR." *Am. J. of Econ. and Sociol. 1975 34(3): 249-266.* Identifying who are the urban poor may help determine why poverty exists in our cities; and, of course, knowing why people are poor is a prerequisite for designing effective policies to eradicate the problem. As the statistics presented in this paper demonstrate, poverty has many causes and, therefore, a successful 'war' on poverty will necessarily have to be long term and multi-programmed. One essential part of that 'war,' of course, will be attack on racial and sexual discrimination in labor markets; but, as this paper's analysis of the possible underlying causes of such discrimination points out, economic progress alone may be insufficient—racial and sexual prejudice itself will have to be eradicated.   J

2915. Fischer, Paul B. THE "WAR ON POVERTY" AND THE "BLACKENING" OF URBAN BUREAUCRACIES. *Policy Studies J. 1974 2(3): 179-186.* Discusses how the War on Poverty has most benefited the Negro middle class by providing them access to jobs in municipal bureaucracies.   S

2916. Gelb, Joyce and Sardell, Alice. STRATEGIES FOR THE POWERLESS: THE WELFARE RIGHTS MOVEMENT IN NEW YORK CITY. *Am. Behavioral Scientist 1974 17(4): 507-530.* Neither protest nor community organization gave the poor access to decisionmaking processes when the issue threatened the societal values of the policymakers.   S

2917. Ginzberg, Eli. FULL EMPLOYMENT: THE NEW YORK PERSPECTIVE. *New York Affairs 1977 4(1): 55-63.* Advocates a national youth employment program in New York City.

2918. Hartman, Chester W. and Thomas, Lynn. SWEET CHARITY GONE SOUR: SAN FRANCISCO'S UNITED FUND. *Society 1974 12(1): 54-58.* The United Bay Area Crusade is unresponsive to the needs of the poor while benefitting contributing corporations.   S

2919. Hill-Scott, Karen. CHILD CARE IN THE BLACK COMMUNITY. *J. of Black Studies 1979 10(1): 78-97.* A survey of child care facilities in South Central Los Angeles and interviews with parents seeking such care at a referral center show that many child care needs are unmet. Licensed day care programs could provide only 4,882 of 13,208 places needed. The problem is most severe for infant care. Sufficient child care would require expanding a voucher system for private programs, more completely subsidized public programs, and "continuous community input in needs assessment and planning." 9 tables, note, biblio.
                                                        R. G. Sherer

2920. Howe, Elizabeth. LEGISLATIVE OUTCOMES IN HUMAN SERVICES. *Social Service Rev. 1978 52(2): 173-188.* The defeat in the state legislature of many proposals by New York City's Human Resources Administration, 1970-73, is an example of the way poor people are neglected within the social order.

2921. Krisberg, Barry. THE POLITICS OF DELINQUENCY PREVENTION: THE URBAN LEADERSHIP TRAINING PROGRAM. *Social Policy 1974 5(2): 53-56.* Discusses methods for preventing and dealing with juvenile delinquency employed by the now-defunct Urban Leadership Training Program during the 1960's.

2922. Mitchell, Ruth Bryant. CHANGES IN BEDFORD-STUYVESANT. *Crisis 1977 84(1): 12-16.* The Bedford-Stuyvesant community was once a white, upper-middle class neighborhood. After World War II the black population swelled. By the mid-1960's physical and economic neglect left the 400,000 residents frustrated and disappointed despite countless programs. Senators Robert Kennedy and Jacob Javits, and mayor John Lindsay, supported the Special Impact Program which facilitated significant improvement (through the Bedford-Stuyvesant Restoration Corporation and the Development and Services Corporation) in homes, business development, employment, recreation, and culture.
                                                        A. G. Belles

2923. Musselman, Thomas H. A CRUSADE FOR LOCAL OPTION: SHREVEPORT, 1951-1952. *North Louisiana Hist. Assoc. J. 1975 6(2): 59-73.* During the early 1950's, an active political campaign was waged "for the purpose of 'drying up' Shreveport" by members and supporters of the Shreveport Ministerial Association. "Both supporters and opponents of prohibition resorted to unsavory campaign tactics," and the "local option campaign of 1951 and 1952 was bitterly fought and roughly contested." At the end, on election day, 16 July 1952, "voters turned out in near record numbers to defeat prohibition in Shreveport with a total of 28,806 going to the polls." 77 notes.
                                                        A. N. Garland

2924. O'Neill, Hugh. WILDER V. SUGARMAN: THE CRISIS IN CHILD CARE. *New York Affairs 1974 1(4): 36-47.* In May 1973, the ACLU and the Legal Aid Society filed a class-action suit alleging that racial and religious discrimination practiced by public and private child-care agencies denies the city's neediest children.   J

2925. Rodgers, Harrell R., Jr. PRELUDE TO CONFLICT: THE EVOLUTION OF CENSORSHIP CAMPAIGNS. *Pacific Sociol. Rev. 1975 18(2): 194-205.* Investigates the causes and effects of censorship movements in the United States which have many characteristics of social movements; based on studies in 18 American cities and previous 1960's studies.

2926. Rubin, Victor and Medrich, Elliott A. CHILD CARE, RECREATION AND THE FISCAL CRISIS. *Urban and Social Change Rev. 1979 12(1): 22-28.* Discusses the effects of local government cutbacks on the after-school services that function as day-care for children nine-12 years old, with a brief history of these services in American cities.

2927. Solomon, Arthur P. and Fenton, Chester G. THE NATION'S FIRST EXPERIENCE WITH HOUSING ALLOWANCES: THE KANSAS CITY DEMONSTRATION. *Urban and Social Change Rev.*

1975 8(1): 3-8. Discusses housing allowances as an alternative to existing federal housing subsidy programs.   S

2928. Sullivan, Donald G. ALL THINGS ARE POSSIBLE. *New York Affairs 1975 2(4): 60-71.* A semisatirical photographic essay proposing "solutions" to some of New York City's more pressing problems.   S

2929. Turk, Herman. COMPARATIVE URBAN STRUCTURE FROM AN INTERORGANIZATIONAL PERSPECTIVE. *Administrative Sci. Q. 1973 18(1): 37-55.* Influence of municipal government and community volunteer organizations on formation of hospital councils in 130 cities revealed wide variances in social welfare programs.   S

2930. Warren, Roland L.; Rose, Stephen M.; and Bergunder, Ann F. COMMUNITY DECISION ORGANIZATIONS AND URBAN REFORM. *Urban and Social Change Rev. 1974 7(2): 42-47.* Discusses the role of community decision organizations in deciding what is to be done about the social problems of the cities.   S

Law, Police, Crime, and Violence

2931. Aaronson, David E.; Dienes, C. Thomas; and Musheno, Michael C. CHANGING THE PUBLIC DRUNKENNESS LAWS: THE IMPACT OF DECRIMINALIZATION. *Law and Soc. Rev. 1978 12(3): 405-436.* Laws that decriminalize public drunkenness continue to use the police as the major intake agent for public inebriates under the "new" public health model of detoxification and treatment. Assuming that decriminalization introduces many disincentives to police intervention using legally sanctioned procedures, the authors hypothesize that it will be followed by a statistically significant decline in the number of public inebriates formally handled by the police in the manner designated by the "law in the books," and examine data for Washington, D.C., and Minneapolis, Minnesota. Minneapolis, in responding to strong business pressure, developed several alternative means of keeping the streets clear of transient public inebriates while Washington, D.C., treated decriminalization as an opportunity to shift police priorities and relied on informal "safe zones" to handle the inebriate population.   J

2932. Anderson, William A.; Dynes, Russell R.; and Quarantelli, E. L. URBAN COUNTERRIOTERS. *Society 1974 11(3): 50-55.* Analyzes the role of black counterrioters, or peacemakers, in urban racial disturbances.   S

2933. Berkowitz, William R. SOCIOECONOMIC INDICATOR CHANGES OF GHETTO RIOT TRACTS. *Urban Affairs Q. 1974 10(1): 69-94.* Studies socioeconomic effects of the Detroit, Washington, Newark, and Los Angeles riots of the mid- and late 1960's. Available data indicates that the riots neither speeded nor retarded socioeconomic changes in the riot areas. 3 tables, notes, biblio., appendix on procedures.
                                                                                   P. J. Woehrmann

2934. Broach, Glen. DISSONANCE THEORY AND RECEPTIVITY TO STRUCTURAL PERCEPTIONS OF THE CAUSES OF URBAN CRIME. *Western Pol. Q. 1974 27(3): 491-499.* Presents a description and test of a set of propositions attempting to specify the conditions of unfavorable and favorable reception of alternative perceptions used upon the public by advocates of change in poverty and civil rights policies.   J

2935. Brown, Don W. ADOLESCENT ATTITUDES AND LAWFUL BEHAVIOR. *Public Opinion Q. 1974 38(1): 98-106.* Traces "the development of orientations toward law and of patterns of noncompliance with law in a sample of 261 adolescents in Racine, Wisconsin." Evidence suggests that "constraint between reported noncompliance with laws and affective-evaluative orientations toward law, legal authorities, and legal institutions tend to be greater among those to whom law is more salient . . . . Public policies affecting the salience of law among various populations also affect the level of compliance with laws." 2 tables, 18 notes.   J

2936. Chadwick, Bruce; Strauss, Joseph; Bahr, Howard M.; and Halverson, Lowell K. CONFRONTATION WITH THE LAW: THE CASE OF THE AMERICAN INDIANS IN SEATTLE. *Phylon 1976 37(2): 163-171.* A serious adjustment for American Indians migrating to cities is learning how to conform to metropolitan legal norms. For the nation as a whole Indians are arrested at a rate three times higher than blacks and 10 times higher than whites. Few Indian migrants "have the sophistication to obtain assistance from helping agencies." Proposes "an intensive informational campaign designed to acquaint the urban Indian population with the existing opportunities for legal assistance." Based on a survey of Indians in Seattle; 4 tables, 6 notes.   E. P. Stickney

2937. Chambliss, William J. THE BUSINESS OF CRIME. *Working Papers for a New Soc. 1978 6(5): 59-67.* Examines organized crime in Seattle, Washington, 1960-78.

2938. Clarke, Stevens H. and Koch, Gary G. THE INFLUENCE OF INCOME AND OTHER FACTORS ON WHETHER CRIMINAL DEFENDANTS GO TO PRISON. *Law and Soc. Rev. 1976 11(1): 57-92.* Investigates 798 burglary and larceny defendants in Charlotte, North Carolina. Such variables as income, age, race, and employment were measured as having influence on sentencing. Severity of offense, prior arrest record, and strength of case also are analyzed. Race, age and employment had little or no impact on sentence.   H. R. Mahood

2939. Coates, Joseph F. URBAN VIOLENCE—THE PATTERN OF DISORDER. *Ann. of the Am. Acad. of Pol. and Social Sci. 1973 (405): 25-40.* Presents some general background information on the present status of violence and its impacts on the criminal justice system, giving particular emphasis to day-to-day crime and mass behavior. The paper emphasizes structural factors in our society with regard to the generation and control of violence and the implications they have for structural rather than short-term palliative or counterforce solutions. Among the long-term structural changes in the US society influencing urban crime are the homogenization of US society; the pervasiveness of inexpensive transportation and communication facilities; continuing urbanization; and the general trend toward middle-class status and attitudes for all citizens. Economic prosperity and the related growth of knowledge-based industries have strong implications for long-term patterns of crime and disorder. Institutional barriers to effective change within and outside the criminal justice community are touched on. Responses within that system are discussed.   J

2940. Cohen, Fay G. THE INDIAN PATROL IN MINNEAPOLIS: SOCIAL CONTROL AND SOCIAL CHANGE IN AN URBAN CONTEXT. *Law and Soc. Rev. 1973 7(4): 779-786.* A field study of an Indian patrol in the city of Minneapolis, Minnesota, conducted during 1969-70. A combination of foot and car patrols conducted by the Chippewa Indians, the patrols largely observed police squad car activity in their area and sought to be on hand in the case of a police-Indian confrontation and/or arrest. The Indian patrols had a symbolic function and replaced overt social control.   H. R. Mahood

2941. Croyle, James L. THE CRIMINAL JUSTICE SYSTEM IN AMERICAN CITIES. *Urban Affairs Q. 1977 12(4): 545-554.* Criminal justice research has been influenced by the cost effective, deterrent Crime Control Model and the expensive civil liberties oriented Due Process Model. Isaac D. Balbus's *The Dialectics of Legal Repression: Black Rebels Before the American Criminal Courts,* (Russell Sage Foundation, 1973) argues that while the formal neutrality of due process enables the strong to oppress the weak, it can thwart crime control. Martin A. Levin's *Urban Politics and the Criminal Courts* (Chicago: Univ. of Chicago Pr., 1977) argues that pre-judicial careers determine sentencing behavior. The political regime indirectly influences sentencing behavior by judicial selection. James Eisenstein and Herbert Jacob, in *Felony Justice: An Organizational Analysis of Criminal Courts* (Boston: Little, Brown, 1977), argue that sentencing variation is determined by working group cohesion and stability in the court system. Lynn M. Mather's book, *Plea Bargaining or Trial: The Dynamics of Criminal Case Disposition* (Lexington, Mass.: Lexington Books, 1977), concludes that the disposition of cases is significantly influenced by the substantive effects of conviction. It also identifies the defendant as an independent actor in the disposition of cases. Secondary sources; biblio.   L. N. Beecher

2942. Curvin, Robert and Porter, Bruce. BLACKOUT LOOTING! *Society 1979 16(4): 68-76.* The looting during the blackout of New York City, 13 July 1977, resulted from declining legitimacy, criminality, material aspirations accented by the media, and ghetto poverty, but not from the social upheavals of the 1960's.

2943. David, Pam and Helmbold, Lois. SAN FRANCISCO: COURTS AND COPS VS. GAYS. *Radical Am. 1979 13(4): 27-32.* The riot in San Francisco on 21 May 1979 in protest of the voluntary manslaughter conviction given to Daniel White, the slayer of Mayor George Moscone and City Supervisor Harvey Milk, was a reflection, in part, of the growing tension and apprehension in the city's gay community over a growing trend among the city's police and government toward conservatism and repression of homosexuals as well as a reaction to national trends. Along with being on the defensive, the homosexual community in the city is divided along male and female, conservative and radical, and class lines; gay businesspeople exploit the labor of nonunionized gay employees. The gay community is opposed by working class persons living in neighborhoods being rehabilitated by gays with resulting high rents for the renovated areas. Based on participant observation by members of Lesbians against Police Violence.   N. Lederer

2944. Decter, Midge. LOOTING AND LIBERAL RACISM. *Commentary 1977 64(3): 48-54.* Liberal spokesmen explained the looting during the July 1977 New York City blackout as another manifestation of minority youth's rage and desperation over the failure of society to respond to the needs of socially and economically disadvantaged individuals. This familiar line overlooks the billions of dollars spent on aid for the urban poor, and fails to recognize that the liberal consensus had, ironically, sanctioned the looting. Liberal racism, which refuses to hold certain individuals morally responsible for their actions and thus encourages social deviance, does the disadvantaged no favor.   D. W. Johnson

2945. Dotson, A. Bruce. SOCIAL PLANNING AND URBAN VIOLENCE: AN EXTENSION OF MC ELROY AND SINGELL. *Urban Affairs Q. 1974 9(3): 283-302.* Examines the findings of James L. McElroy's and Larry D. Singell's 1973 study of urban violence and riot behavior.   S

2946. Dynes, Russell R. and Quarantelli, E. L. URBAN CIVIL DISTURBANCES: ORGANIZATIONAL CHANGE AND GROUP EMERGENCE. *Am. Behavioral Scientist 1973 16(3): 305-311.* Introduction to ten articles dealing with civil disturbance in cities during the 1960's and 70's.   S

2947. Feinman, Clarice. AN AFRO-AMERICAN EXPERIENCE: THE WOMEN IN NEW YORK CITY'S JAIL. *Afro-Am. in New York Life and Hist. 1977 1(2): 201-210.* Discusses the House of Detention for Women and its successor, the New York City Correctional Institution for Women, 1932-75, where because of a mainly black staff, problems of race relations do not exist for Negroes there.

2948. Furstenberg, Frank F., Jr. and Wellford, Charles F. CALLING THE POLICE: THE EVALUATION OF POLICE SERVICE. *Law & Soc. Rev. 1973 7(3): 393-406.* Citizens evaluated various police services in Baltimore in 1967. Through a system of interview evaluations, public confidence in the police can be enhanced and policemen themselves can become more responsive to the community. Most persons interviewed were satisfied with the quality of police work, but blacks tended to be somewhat more critical. Generally blacks hold a lower opinion of police, but future surveys would enable the police to concentrate on this problem.   H. R. Mahood

2949. Georgakas, Dan and Surkin, Marvin. WHAT CAN ONE JUDGE DO? *Social Policy 1975 5(6): 48-52.* Reports on the election of the radical Justin Ravitz as judge in Detroit in 1972 and on his courtroom conduct.   S

2950. Gibbs, Jack P. and Erickson, Maynard L. CRIME RATES OF AMERICAN CITIES IN AN ECOLOGICAL CONTEXT. *Am. J. of Sociol. 1976 82(3): 605-620.* Given a city that contains only a small proportion of the residents in the larger ecological community, the conventional crime rate for that city could be high merely because the denominator of the rate underestimates the potential number of victims

or offenders. Accordingly, there is a basis for anticipating a direct relationship among cities between (1) community/city population size ratios and (2) rates for particular types of crimes. The relationship does hold for many American cities when Urbanized Areas (UAs) or Standard Metropolitan Statistical Areas (SMSAs) are taken as approximations of communities; but it holds only for singular cities, each of which is the only central city in a SMSA. Singular cities are much more homogeneous as regards dominance within the community than are other types of cities, and that dominance determines the extent to which a city will attract nonresident participants in crimes. In any case, the findings cast doubts on the use of conventional crime rates for cities in testing theories.   J

2951. Gross, Solomon. THE POLICE OF THE TWENTY-THIRD PRECINCT AND THE EAST HARLEM COMMUNITY. *J. of Social Issues 1975 31(1): 145-161.* Recounts an intergroup situation in New York City between October of 1966 and November of 1967 and describes the efforts made in a ghetto community to develop some appreciation between the minority inhabitants and the police. The underlying pathologies of group internalization and isolation were attacked on a day-to-day basis in an effort to dissolve some of the tensions and bitterness. The premise was the belief that a police force cannot operate effectively without the wholehearted support and cooperation of the community.   J

2952. Halpern, Stephen C. POLICE EMPLOYEE ORGANIZATIONS AND ACCOUNTABILITY PROCEDURES IN THREE CITIES: SOME REFLECTIONS ON POLICE POLICY-MAKING. *Law & Soc. R. 1974 8(4): 561-582.* Examines the impact of police employee organizations in Buffalo, Philadelphia, and Baltimore on the regulation of police through internal review procedures and civilian review boards, 1958-74.   S

2953. Hayes, Frederick O'R. PATRICK MURPHY—ON POLICE CORRUPTION. *New York Affairs 1974 2(1): 88-111.* Patrick Murphy was Police Commissioner of the City of New York from October 1970 until May 1973.   J

2954. Ivins, Molly. YO-YOS AND SHITKICKERS. *Civil Liberties Rev. 1974 1(4): 117-121.* Discusses current civil liberties problems and shortcomings in Texas, focusing on Dallas.   S

2955. Jacob, Herbert and Eisenstein, James. SENTENCES AND OTHER SANCTIONS IN THE CRIMINAL COURTS OF BALTIMORE, CHICAGO, AND DETROIT. *Pol. Sci. Q. 1975-76 90(4): 617-635.* Most persons accused of felonies in Baltimore, Chicago, and Detroit are not convicted, but nevertheless suffer significant punishment. Although convictions and prison sentences are the result of complex patterns, length of sentence seems to be much more the result of the seriousness of the original charge than of the identity of the judge or race of the defendant.   J

2956. Jacobson, Alvin L. CRIME TRENDS IN SOUTHERN AND NONSOUTHERN CITIES: A TWENTY-YEAR PERSPECTIVE. *Social Forces 1975 54(1): 226-242.* Using annual data from 1951-70, for 467 US cities, reexamines the extent to which reported crime offenses between the South and non-South continue to manifest regional differences. Alternative structuralist and normative hypotheses are evaluated with respect to both property and personal crimes. The data generally support a structural interpretation of converging crime trends with some lag among selected person crime categories. The effects of census regions and states are also examined, and here the data tentatively indicate a small but potentially increasing state effect.   J

2957. Jennings, Edward T., Jr. STATE WELFARE PROGRAMS AND URBAN RIOTING. *Policy Studies J. 1979 7(4): 739-744.* Analysis of the effects of urban riots, community action agencies, and unemployment levels on relief rolls indicates that the level of urban rioting was related to increased recipient rolls but that spending for community action was not, 1960's-72.

2958. Jensen, Gary F.; Stauss, Joseph H.; and Harris, V. William. CRIME, DELINQUENCY, AND THE AMERICAN INDIAN. *Human Organization 1977 36(3): 252-257.* Examines the disproportionately high arrest rate for Indians as compared to blacks and whites in urban and nonurban situations; discusses tribal variation in rule-breaking and how this is reflected in three different boarding schools among Navajo, Apache, and Hopi, 1976.

2959. Jiobu, Robert M. CITY CHARACTERISTICS AND RACIAL VIOLENCE. *Social Sci. Q. 1974 55(1): 52-64.* Analyzes six independent variables (city centrality, regional location, city size, black population size, black poverty and black occupational status) for the analysis of 74 cities. City centrality—assumed to reflect the impact of black protest—is positively related to racial violence, while black deprivation has a negative impact.   J

2960. Kobler, Arthur L. FIGURES (AND PERHAPS SOME FACTS) ON POLICE KILLINGS OF CIVILIANS IN THE UNITED STATES, 1965-1969. *J. of Social Issues 1975 31(1): 185-191.* Official reports for a 20-year period show that the police killed about five civilians for every officer killed. A study of newspaper reports from 1965-1969 shows that about half of the police and of their victims were young male minorities in urban areas. About a third of the civilians killed were committing misdemeanors when stopped; they tended to have weapons and to use them. The police who killed civilians tended to be on duty, in uniform, and reported that they killed the civilians to defend themselves or to prevent escape.   J

2961. Kreps, Gary A. CHANGE IN CRISIS-RELEVANT ORGANIZATIONS: POLICE DEPARTMENTS AND CIVIL DISTURBANCES. *Am. Behavioral Scientist 1973 16(3): 356-367.* Discusses the way police departments have responded to civil disturbances in the cities during the 1960's and 70's.   S

2962. Kronstadt, Sylvia. THE PRISON GUARDS: AN UNHAPPY LOT. *New York Affairs 1974 2(2): 60-77.* Poorly selected, poorly trained and poorly led, New York City's correction officers serve out their two decades of tension, boredom and demoralization awaiting retirement. Their state is yet another failure of the "criminal injustice" system.   J

2963. Kurtz, Henry I. RIOT AT ASTOR PLACE. *Am. Hist. Illus. 1974 9(7): 32-42.* The riot which took place on 10 May 1849 during a performance of *Macbeth* at the Astor Place Opera House, "which left in its wake some 30 persons dead and scores of others injured, was sparked by a petty rivalry between two vain actors—a rivalry, however, that brought to the surface the xenophobia of American nativists as well as simmering antagonism." The two actors involved in this dispute were the English actor William Charles Macready and Edwin Forrest, "the first truly outstanding native-born American actor ..." 5 illus., 2 photos.
D. D. Cameron

2964. Latané, Bibb and Darley, John M. BYSTANDER "APATHY." *New York Affairs 1975 2(4): 28-49.* Jane Jacobs and her disciples have argued that "eyes on the street" and activity on the sidewalk will insure the city dweller's safety from crime. Bystanders will deter an assault because of their supposed readiness to intervene or call police. Research, however, casts doubt on the cliché that "there's safety in numbers."   J

2965. Levine, James P. THE INEFFECTIVENESS OF ADDING POLICE TO PREVENT CRIME. *Public Policy 1975 23(4): 523-545.* A survey of 10 American cities reveals that increasing the size of police forces neither reduces nor prevents crime; rather crimes often increase proportionately. The unwillingness of courts to imprison arrested criminals is the main cause of crime. A criminal is not deterred by additional police if he knows he is unlikely to be imprisoned even if arrested. Other causes of crime are intolerable conditions in the cities and the large number of young people whose lives are without hope. Until these conditions are corrected, adding police will not reduce crime. 4 tables, fig., 50 notes.   V. L. Human

2966. Ley, David and Cybriwsky, Roman. URBAN GRAFFITI AS TERRITORIAL MARKERS. *Ann. of the Assoc. of Am. Geographers 1974 64(4): 491-505.* Graffiti mark the territories of street gangs in Philadelphia.   S

2967. Lieske, Joel A. THE CONDITIONS OF RACIAL VIOLENCE IN AMERICAN CITIES: A DEVELOPMENTAL SYNTHE-

SIS. *Am. Pol. Sci. Rev. 1978 72(4): 1324-1340.* Analyzes the social and political conditions associated with the incidence of racial violence in a sample of 119 American cities. Data on the incidence of racial disorders are drawn from newspaper accounts compiled by the Lemberg Center for the Study of Violence during the period 1967-1969. A total of 334 disorders are analyzed. Two alternative hypotheses are examined. The first assumes that the causes of the black urban riots are rooted largly in the disorganized environment of socially marginal individuals. The second attempts to locate the outbreak of rioting primarily within a closed and unresponsive political system. Paradoxically, the results tend to provide empirical support for both theoretical perspectives. At the same time, the data suggest the need to reformulate and revise conventional interpretations of the black urban riots. This is done by synthesizing and testing a developmental model which implies a curvilinear relationship between the incidence of racial violence on the one hand, and black political development on the other.   J

2968. Lovrich, Nicholas P., Jr. REDUCING CRIME THROUGH POLICE-COMMUNITY RELATIONS: EVIDENCE OF THE EFFECTIVENESS OF POLICE-COMMUNITY RELATIONS TRAINING FROM A STUDY OF 161 CITIES. *Policy Studies J. 1978 7(special issue): 505-511.* Cities with greatest commitment have a lower crime rate and a higher reportage of crime, 1960-75.

2969. Marino, Ralph J. and McKenna, Jeremiah B. THE NEW AND DANGEROUS JUVENILE DELINQUENT. *New York Affairs 1975 2(3): 3-11.* A 1975 survey of juvenile crime and a description of juvenile justice in New York City.   S

2970. Mather, Lynn M. SOME DETERMINANTS OF THE METHOD OF CASE DISPOSITION: DECISION-MAKING BY PUBLIC DEFENDERS IN LOS ANGELES. *Law & Soc. Rev. 1974 8(2): 187-216.* Analyzes 1970 Los Angeles Superior Court data in order to identify the factors which determine whether a case is settled by plea bargaining or by trial.   S

2971. McCarthy, John D.; Galle, Omer R.; and Zimmern, William. POPULATION DENSITY, SOCIAL STRUCTURE, AND INTERPERSONAL VIOLENCE: AN INTERMETROPOLITAN TEST OF COMPETING MODELS. *Am. Behavioral Scientist 1975 18(6): 771-791.* Statistical analysis of the relationship between population density variations and rates of murder and aggravated assault in American cities, 1940-70.   S

2972. McDavid, James C. INTERJURISDICTIONAL COOPERATION AMONG POLICE DEPARTMENTS IN THE ST. LOUIS METROPOLITAN AREA. *Publius 1974 4(4): 35-58.* Reports the findings of a survey of cooperative arrangements among 28 independent police departments in the St. Louis metropolitan area. Through interviews and questionnaires, focuses on the number and variety of cooperative arrangements in the area and finds that hypotheses positing the ineffectual functioning of small independent police forces were not substantiated. Claims that arguments for greater consolidation of police services are not supported by the data. Based on the survey, government studies, and secondary sources; 9 tables, 34 notes.   J. B. Street

2973. McIver, John P. THE RELATIONSHIP BETWEEN METROPOLITAN POLICE INDUSTRY STRUCTURE AND INTERAGENCY ASSISTANCE: A PRELIMINARY ASSESSMENT. *Policy Studies J. 1978 7(special issue): 406-412.* While reformers claim that fragmentation of metropolitan areas and multiplicity of police services result in reduced quality of police service for residents, studies show that informal cooperative arrangements occur in such areas and in fact improve overall police service.

2974. McKenna, Jeremiah B. CRIME IN THE SCHOOLS. *New York Affairs 1974 1(3): 3-13.* The police in 1973 arrested 219 school age children for murder, 353 for rape, 8056 for robbery and 252 for arson. Many of these children were back in class after only a month, effectively transforming the city's schools into sanctuaries for criminals who prey upon their fellow students.   J

2975. Mehay, Stephen L. INTERGOVERNMENTAL CONTRACTING FOR MUNICIPAL POLICE SERVICE: AN EMPIRI-

CAL ANALYSIS. *Land Econ. 1979 55(1): 59-72.* Investigates the cost and quality of police service provided communities during 1971-72 in Los Angeles County, California, via the Lakewood Plan. Discusses problems of measuring quality of police service and constructs a regression model to compare service in contract and noncontract communities. Finds that contract cities have lower police cost and apparently less effective service. Based on state and federal statistics; 3 tables, 17 notes.

　　　　　　　　　　　　　　　　　　　　　　　E. S. Johnson

2976. Midlarsky, Manus I. ANALYZING DIFFUSION AND CONTAGION EFFECTS: THE URBAN DISORDERS OF THE 1960'S. *Am. Pol. Sci. Rev. 1978 72(3): 996-1008.* This study concerns the analysis of diffusion and contagion processes using a lognormal model of overdispersion phenomena. The urban disorders of the past decade are examined and two processes are found to exist in the 1966-67 period. One is a classic diffusion effect in which disorders are precipitated by events which are independent of each other, but lead to outcomes such as numbers of arrests which are proportional to previous disorders. The second process is a contagious one in which disturbances occur as a consequence of smaller cities imitating the behavior of large ones experiencing a disorder. The explanatory power of the interaction effect between police and black city residents tended to increase as city size increased. Concomitantly, the effects of environmental variables tended to decrease in explanatory power as city size decreased.

　　　　　　　　　　　　　　　　　　　　　　　J

2977. Milton, Catherine Higgs et al. "IF I WERE CHIEF OF POLICE OF GOTHAM CITY . . ." *Civil Liberties Rev. 1975 2(2): 8-38.* Civil libertarians propose how they would behave as police chiefs of troubled cities to both protect civil liberties and fight crime.　　　S

2978. Monti, Daniel J. INTERGROUP CONFLICT AND COLLECTIVE VIOLENCE: THE CASE OF NEW YORK CITY, 1960-JULY 1964. *J. of Pol. and Military Sociol. 1978 6(2): 147-162.* Data on racial controversies involving New York's black and Puerto Rican population between 1960 and July 1964 were obtained from an analysis of *New York Times* articles. These data deal with "events" or exchanges between representatives of the city's minority populations and public officials or non-minority actors. Rifts among minority and government actors appear to have grown more than among non-minority actors before the outbreak of rioting in July 1964. Government representatives made some small effort to realign themselves with non-minority actors as racial controversies intensified, but the latter did not respond in that fashion. The role of non-minority and moderate minority actors as potential allies or antagonists of civil rights activists and government parties helps to clarify why violence occurred when it did, and it is suggested on the strength of these findings that such conflicts may be a necessary precondition for violent outbursts.

　　　　　　　　　　　　　　　　　　　　　　　J

2979. Monti, Daniel J. PATTERNS OF CONFLICT PRECEDING THE 1964 RIOTS: HARLEM AND BEDFORD-STUYVESANT. *J. of Conflict Resolution 1979 23(1): 41-69.* Examines racial conflict, 1960-64, between the blacks and Puerto Ricans of New York City, and analyzes the patterns of conflict in the four years preceding the Harlem and Bedford-Stuyvesant riots of 1964.

2980. Morgan, David R. and Swanson, Cheryl. ANALYZING POLICE POLICIES: THE IMPACT OF ENVIRONMENT, POLITICS, AND CRIME. *Urban Affairs Q. 1976 11(4): 489-510.* Uses data collected by the Kansas City Chief of Police (1972), the *Municipal Year Book* (1970,1971), and 1970 census data to argue that while specific city characteristics influence four police policy factors considered indicative of innovation, the strength of the influence varies from indicator to indicator. For indicators involving recruitment and technology, demographic factors were more influential than political and crime factors. But demography had less impact than either of the latter two on indicators involving manpower expenditure and community relations factors. Neither the extent of governmental reform nor the degree of police professionalism explained adoption of innovative police policies. Primary and secondary sources; 6 tables, 3 figs., 8 notes, biblio.

　　　　　　　　　　　　　　　　　　　　　　　L. N. Beecher

2981. Morgan, William R. and Clark, Terry Nichols. THE CAUSES OF RACIAL DISORDERS: A GRIEVANCE-LEVEL EXPLANATION. *Am. Sociol. Rev. 1973 38(5): 611-624.* Presents three basic arguments that draw on data from a sample of 42 American cities. First,

the data reveal that three separate factors—frequency, precipitation conditions, and severity—are important to the structure of racial disorders. Much earlier work, especially that of Spilerman, focused only on frequency. Considers disorder frequency, replicating and extending Spilerman's findings. Shows that certain city-specific differences (nonwhite population size and police force size) have strong effects on disorder frequency. Third, consideration of disorder severity shows the need for a model quite different from that used for frequency. The conditions critical to the dynamics of initial confrontation are not those critical to the dynamics of escalation. City-specific grievance variables, especially black-white differences in jobs and housing, are particularly important.

　　　　　　　　　　　　　　　　　　　　　　　J

2982. Neubauer, David W. AFTER THE ARREST: THE CHARGING DECISION IN PRAIRIE CITY. *Law & Soc. Rev. 1974 8(3): 495-517.* Examines the process of charging suspects with crimes in a medium-size Illinois city from the 1960's until 1971.　　　S

2983. Ostrom, Elinor. ON RIGHTEOUSNESS, EVIDENCE, AND REFORM: THE POLICE STORY. *Urban Affairs Q. 1975 10(4): 464-486.* Many recent conclusions regarding police effectiveness made in nationally influential literature have been compromised by local studies with contrary conclusions representing more methodologically sound research. Includes for criticism the *Task Force Report: The Police* (1967) of the President's Commission on Law Enforcement and Administration of Justice. Notes, biblio.　　　P. J. Woehrmann

2984. Palmer, Edward. BLACK POLICE IN AMERICA. *Black Scholar 1973 5(2): 19-27.* The author, a one-time policeman, and co-founder of the Afro-American's Patrolman's League in Chicago, delves into the complex process through which blacks must pass to become policemen and exposes the dynamics operating in the police department to use black police against black people.　　　M. T. Wilson

2985. Ponting, J. Rick. RUMOR CONTROL CENTERS: THEIR EMERGENCE AND OPERATIONS. *Am. Behavioral Scientist 1973 16(3): 391-401.* Discusses the emergence of Rumor Control Centers throughout the country in the 1960's, their social control and mediation functions during civil disturbances, and their possible future role in more peaceful times.　　　S

2986. Quarantelli, E. L.; Ponting, J. Rick; and Fitzpatrick, John. POLICE DEPARTMENT PERCEPTIONS OF THE OCCURRENCE OF CIVIL DISTURBANCES. *Sociol. and Social Res. 1974 59(1): 30-38.* A study of police department perceptions of four different civil disturbances in American cities, through interviews with key organizational personnel, yields five general propositions about organizational perceptions of riot participants and dynamics. In general, social control agencies saw specific events and particular types of people rather than sequential happenings and social conditions as being responsible for the occurrence of the disturbances, although they did not perceive the disorders as being organized or planned.

　　　　　　　　　　　　　　　　　　　　　　　J

2987. Reddy, W. Brendan and Lansky, Leonard M. NOTHING BUT THE FACTS—AND SOME OBSERVATIONS ON NORMS AND VALUES: THE HISTORY OF A CONSULTATION WITH A METROPOLITAN POLICE DIVISION. *J. of Social Issues 1975 31(1): 123-138.* Case study of an initial intervention in a large municipal police division. A community group/police confrontation led to the development of an 80-hour community relations training program for 39 police recruits. The program, designed and conducted by a biracial staff, followed an experience-based learning format in sharp contrast to the quasi-military traditional learning format of the police division. Focus is placed on the value and norm conflicts between change agent and the power structure of the urban police system.

　　　　　　　　　　　　　　　　　　　　　　　J

2988. Reed, John P. LAW VIEWS AND LAW WAYS OF BLACK AND WHITES IN SUNSHINE CITY. *Phylon 1974 35(4): 359-367.* Examines the opinions and experiences of blacks and whites concerning the law, and the real or imagined legal problems they have had by obtaining an area sample in 1967-68 from a medium-sized southern city. By investigating black and white ways and views of the legal system in 1) kind and variety of contacts, 2) problem recognition and disposition, and 3) experience with the lawyer-client relationship, it was found that differences existed between white and black. For example, in contacts with the system, the black experience was more likely to be restricted, and where restricted more likely to involve stigma; blacks were less likely than whites to recognize when they had a legal problem and more likely to rely on others as sources of information in ascertaining their problems; blacks were more likely to want to wait and see what happens in problem resolution; and blacks were differently treated in the initiation and maintenance of lawyer-client relationships. Based on interviews and secondary sources; 5 tables, 6 notes.   B. A. Glasrud

2989. Robertson, Leon S.; Rich, Robert F.; and Ross, H. Laurence. JAIL SENTENCES FOR DRIVING WHILE INTOXICATED IN CHICAGO: A JUDICIAL POLICY THAT FAILED. *Law and Soc. R. 1973 8(1): 55-67.* Sentencing motorists to seven-day jail terms for drunken driving failed to lower motor-vehicle-related fatality rates in Chicago in 1971.   S

2990. Robins, Lee N. and Wish, Eric. CHILDHOOD DEVIANCE AS A DEVELOPMENTAL PROCESS: A STUDY OF 223 URBAN BLACK MEN FROM BIRTH TO 18. *Social Forces 1977 56(2): 448-473.* Can one view deviance as a developmental process in which one type of deviant act leads to another? This paper proposes a number of criteria that would need to be met if there is such a process and applies them to data from records and retrospective interviews about the ages at which 13 kinds of childhood behaviors began. Results appear consistent with both a quantitative developmental process, i.e., one in which the probability of committing a new type of deviance is in part a function of the variety of acts previously committed, and a qualitative one, i.e., one in which having committed one particular type of deviant act makes more probable initiating another particular type of deviance thereafter.   J

2991. Rodgers, Harrell R., Jr. CENSORSHIP CAMPAIGNS IN EIGHTEEN CITIES: AN IMPACT ANALYSIS. *Am. Pol. Q. 1974 2(4): 371-392.* Primarily examines the impact of urban censorship campaigns during 1967-68 on the effectiveness of US Supreme Court decisions on obscenity laws which protected the "right of newsdealers to sell and the public to buy certain types of publications."   S

2992. Rose, Harold M. THE GEOGRAPHY OF DESPAIR. *Ann. of the Assoc. of Am. Geographers 1978 68(4): 453-464.* Focuses on the spatial factor in the disproportionate incidence of lethal violence in black communities in US cities since the early 1960's, when violent behavior increased.

2993. Saunders, Lonnie. EFFECTIVE CONTROL OF URBAN CRIME: MISSION IMPOSSIBLE? *Crisis 1974 81(3): 79-81.*

2994. Seidman, David and Couzens, Michael. GETTING THE CRIME RATE DOWN: POLITICAL PRESSURE AND CRIME REPORTING. *Law & Soc. Rev. 1974 8(3): 457-493.* Analyzes the impact during 1965-73 of political pressures on the Federal Bureau of Investigation's Uniform Crime Reporting Program and crime statistics reported by city police departments.   S

2995. Singer, Henry A. POLICE ACTION-COMMUNITY ACTION. *J. of Social Issues 1975 31(1): 99-106.* An experimental model was used in two cities in Connecticut to bring about improved police-community relations. Participants in the program were 300 police officers up through the grade of captain and 150 civilians representing militant, conservative, and community organizations. Questionnaires given to the police before and after the six-week program indicated dramatic favorable change in the policeman's attitudes toward himself, youth, and Puerto Ricans. However, attitudes toward blacks did not improve and in some cases regressed.   J

2996. Skogan, Wesley G. THE CHANGING DISTRIBUTION OF BIG CITY CRIME: A MULTI-CITY TIME SERIES ANALYSIS. *Urban Affairs Q. 1977 13(1): 33-48.* Analyzes the nation's 32 largest cities' crime statistics during 1946-70. Louis Wirth's 1938 model of urbanism predicted positive correlations for 1) density and crime, 2) size and crime, and 3) racial heterogeneity and crime. It is accurate for the 1970 data, but not for the 1946 data. However, the orderly changes in the time series data in a positive direction probably reflect fundamental change in the urban system. Suburbanization is the most likely causative

systemic change, and is most advanced around high-crime cities. Biblio., 8 notes.   L. Beecher

2997. Skogan, Wesley G. GROUPS IN THE POLICY PROCESS: THE POLICE AND URBAN CRIME. *Policy Studies J. 1975 3(4): 354-359.* Examines the validity of describing urban policy-making in group terms.   S

2998. Skogan, Wesley G. POLICY-MAKING AND POLICE TAKING: CONTROLLING BEHAVIOR ON THE BEAT. *Urban Affairs Q. 1974 9(4): 520-528.* Reviews Jonathan Rubinstein's *City Police* (New York: Farrar, Strauss, and Giroux, 1973). *The Knapp Commission Report on Police Corruption* (New York: George Braziller, 1973), Hervey A. Juris and Peter Feuille's *Police Unionism* (Lexington, Massachusetts: D. C. Heath, 1973), Albert J. Reiss, Jr.'s *The Police and the Public* (New Haven: Yale U. Pr., 1971), and Richard N. Harris' *The Police Academy: An Inside View* (New York: John Wiley and Sons, 1973).   S

2999. Skogan, Wesley G. THE VALIDITY OF OFFICIAL CRIME STATISTICS: AN EMPIRICAL INVESTIGATION. *Social Sci. Q. 1974 55(1): 25-38.* Comparison of official FBI "crimes known" totals with sample survey estimates of city crime rates reveals considerable overlap between the two. Both measures are related in similar fashion to independent and dependent variables commonly used in quantitative studies. Official crime statistics may be valid indicators of inter-city variations in crime.   J/S

3000. Spilerman, Seymour. STRUCTURAL CHARACTERISTICS OF CITIES AND THE SEVERITY OF RACIAL DISORDERS. *Am. Sociol. Rev. 1976 41(5): 771-793.* This study attempts to ascertain whether particular structural arrangements and demographic features of a community were responsible for especially severe disturbances during the 1960's. Preliminary to addressing this question, consideration is given to the manner of measuring severity and to the volatile components of this phenomenon. With respect to the latter, it is found that (1) disorder severity declined as a function of the number of prior outbreaks in a city and (2) there is evidence for a temporal effect, with the post-Martin Luther King-assassination disturbances having been unusually destructive. Regarding the more stable (community) determinants of disorder severity, only Negro population size and a dummy term for South were found to be related to severity. Net of these variables, various indicators of Negro disadvantage in a community failed to reveal significant associations with severity. This result is interpreted as further evidence for the distinctly national character of the disturbances in the 1960s.   J

3001. Stotland, Ezra and Guppy, William. COMMUNITY RELATIONS TRAINING IN THE SEATTLE POLICE ACADEMY. *J. of Social Issues 1975 31(3): 139-144.* Community relations training by social and behavioral scientists was incorporated into the Seattle Police Academy during the 1960's. Initially all of the training was of the stand-up-and-lecture type. But in the late sixties, role playing of difficult interracial and other police situations was conducted. The role-playing procedures and situations were planned and carried out in a collaborative effort between the police and the role-playing experts from the behavioral science community.   J

3002. Swanson, Cheryl. THE INFLUENCE OF ORGANIZATION AND ENVIRONMENT ON ARREST POLICIES IN MAJOR U.S. CITIES. *Policy Studies J. 1979 7(special issue): 390-397.* Examination of factors influencing discretionary decisionmaking by police indicates that criminal activity, citizen's preferences, and values of the community rank highest.

3003. Unsigned. CIVIL RIGHTS PROTESTS IN TAMPA: ORAL MEMOIRS OF CONFLICT AND ACCOMMODATION. *Tampa Bay Hist. 1979 1(1): 37-54.* Presents two interviews, one with Clarence Fort, a civil rights activist, the other with Julian Lane, a former mayor of Tampa, Florida, in which both discuss civil rights in general and protests in Tampa which resulted (because of peaceful demonstrations led by Fort and the work of Tampa's Biracial Committee, led by Lane) in desegregation of lunch counters, municipal facilities, and theaters, 1960.

3004.   Unsigned.   [CROWDING AND URBAN CRIME RATES]. *Urban Affairs Q. 1975 11(3): 291-322.*
Booth, Alan; Welch, Susan; and Johnson, David Richard. CROWDING AND URBAN CRIME RATES, *pp. 291-308.* Attempts to establish connections between city crime and crowding. 4 tables, notes, biblio.
Higgins, Paul C.; Richards, Pamela J.; and Swan, James H. CROWDING AND URBAN CRIME RATES: A COMMENT, *pp. 309-316.* Questions the research, mainly on methodological grounds. Table, notes, biblio.
Booth, Alan; Welch, Susan; and Johnson, David Richard. A REPLY TO HIGGINS, RICHARDS, AND SWAN, *pp. 317-322.* The criticism is insignificant and irrelevant. Note, biblio.
P. J. Woehrmann

3005.   Wanner, Craig.   THE PUBLIC ORDERING OF PRIVATE RELATIONS. *Law & Soc. Rev. 1974 8(3): 421-440; 1975 9(2): 293-306.* Part I: INITIATING CIVIL CASES IN URBAN TRIAL COURTS. Surveys cases in Baltimore, Cleveland, and Milwaukee during 1965-70 to determine "the principal users of the civil court system and the matters these users want adjudicated." Part II: WINNING CIVIL COURT CASES. An inquiry into who wins and loses civil court cases in Baltimore, Cleveland, and Milwaukee during 1965-70, based on a random selection of cases. General conclusions drawn are: organizations are more successful litigants than individuals, organizational plaintiffs resolve cases quicker than individuals, and the government is a more successful litigant than either individuals or business organizations.
H. R. Mahood/S

3006.   Warheit, George J. and Waxman, Jerry.   OPERATIONAL AND ORGANIZATIONAL ADAPTATIONS OF FIRE DEPARTMENTS TO CIVIL DISTURBANCES. *Am. Behavioral Scientist 1973 16(3): 343-355.* Discusses the way fire departments have responded to civil disturbances in cities during the 1960's and 70's.   S

3007.   Welch, Susan and Booth, Alan.   CROWDING AND CIVIL DISORDER: AN EXAMINATION OF COMPARATIVE NATIONAL AND CITY DATA. *Comparative Pol. Studies 1975 8(1): 58-74.* Examines attitudes toward violence and crowding in the cities during the 1960's.   S

3008.   Weller, Jack M.   THE INVOLUNTARY PARTISANS: FIRE DEPARTMENTS AND THE THREAT OF CONFLICT. *Am. Behavioral Scientist 1973 16(3): 368-377.* Discusses the organizational changes adopted by 16 urban fire departments in the 1960's to handle fire-fighting during civil disturbances.   S

3009.   Wenger, Dennis.   THE RELUCTANT ARMY: THE FUNCTIONING OF POLICE DEPARTMENTS DURING CIVIL DISTURBANCES. *Am. Behavioral Scientist 1973 16(3): 326-342.* Discusses the way police departments have responded to civil disturbances in the cities during the 1960's and 70's.   S

3010.   Wilson, James Q. and Boland, Barbara.   THE EFFECT OF THE POLICE ON CRIME. *Law and Soc. Rev. 1978 12(3): 367-390.* The effect of police practices on the rate of robbery in 35 large American cities is estimated by a set of simultaneous equations. The measures of police resources (patrol units on the street) and police activity on the street (moving citations issued) are more precise than anything thus far available in studies of this kind and permit the use of identification restrictions that allow stronger inferences about the causal effect of arrests on crime rates than has heretofore been possible. Police resources and police activity independently affect the robbery rate after controlling for various socioeconomic factors. The political arrangements that lead to the use of aggressive patrol strategies are discussed and their effect estimated. The implications for, and limitations upon, policy are also discussed.   J

3011.   Wolf, Eleanor P.   SOCIAL SCIENCE AND THE COURTS: THE DETROIT SCHOOLS CASE. *Public Interest 1976 42: 102-120.* Evaluates the quality and comprehensiveness of the social science materials introduced in the 1971 Detroit school segregation case, *Milliken* v. *Bradley*, which resulted in an order for interdistrict busing. Material analyzed comes from the verbatim transcript of the trial, exhibits offered

in evidence, and the transcript of the court hearing conducted in 1972 on alternative plans for desegregation. Findings show that the judge lacked a basic understanding of scientific inquiry, that presentations in the courtroom often had the form but not the substance of "social science," and that there were numerous violations of serious scientific inquiry. The 6th Circuit Court of Appeals upheld the decision, but the US Supreme Court reversed it in 1974. Concludes that with the involvement of scholars and professional academic societies, social science testimony in school cases can be of higher quality than in the Detroit case. 51 notes.
S. Harrow

Minorities and Ethnic Relations

General

3012.   Alberts, William E.   THE WHITE MAGIC OF SYSTEMIC RACISM. *Crisis 1978 85(9): 295-308.* The cause of racial violence in Boston, 1976, is covert, subtle, pervasive, sophisticated, and traditional systemic racism. Problems are redefined to mask the real issues. White magic transforms segregated neighborhoods, discriminatory election laws, unemployment, poverty, and low self-esteem into arguments about busing. Rhetoric about equality replaces analysis of racism. Institutionalized religion provides a ritualistic cathartic cop-out replacing folded hands for action. White magic is based on white persons, politically powerful and rich, who use their office and institution and the influence of their affluence to perpetuate their power, profit, and privilege at the expense of the common good. Mayor Kevin H. White and his "Committee for Boston" are excellent examples of the practitioners of white magic.
A. G. Belles

3013.   Alexander, Kelly M., Jr.   IS BOSTON BURNING? *Crisis 1976 82(3): 90-92.* The citizens of Boston will gradually go through several phases to comply with the law of the land requiring desegregation. Student and parent disruptions will characterize several of the stages, but eventually the situation will stabilize. Students, teachers, and administrators could learn from other experiences that desegregation could come without trouble, but measures to bring about calm must be taken early. An important ingredient is intelligent leadership.   A. G. Belles

3014.   Baraka, Imamu Amiri.   NEWARK SEVEN YEARS LATER: UNIDA Y LUCHA! *Monthly Rev. 1975 26(8): 16-24.* Seven years after the election of black mayor Kenneth Gibson (1967) in Newark, the rising black middle class is discriminating against Puerto Ricans the way the whites did with Negroes before the 1960's.

3015.   Blume, Norman.   UNION WORKER ATTITUDES TOWARD OPEN HOUSING: THE CASE OF THE UAW IN THE TOLEDO METROPOLITAN AREA. *Phylon 1973 34(1): 63-72.* United Auto Workers approve of open housing for Negroes in theory but balk at it in practice (1967-73).   S

3016.   Brown, David L.   RACIAL DISPARITY AND URBANIZATION, 1960 AND 1970. *Rural Sociol. 1978 43(3): 403-425.* Analyzes the residential differences in the socioeconomic position of whites and minorities in the United States, using 1960 and 1970 US Census data.

3017.   Buenker, John D.   CHICAGO'S ETHNICS AND THE POLITICS OF ACCOMMODATION. *Chicago Hist. 1974 3(2): 92-100.*

3018.   Caditz, Judith.   AMBIVALENCE TOWARD INTEGRATION: THE SEQUENCE OF RESPONSE TO SIX INTERRACIAL SITUATIONS. *Sociol. Q. 1975 16(1): 16-32.* White liberals believing in integration and living in Los Angeles County expressed their attitudes toward six interracial situations: 1) busing in the schools for the purpose of ending de facto segregation; 2) the entrance of blacks into the respondents' occupational fields; 3) blacks moving into the respondents' neighborhoods; 4) the quota system as the basis for college admission for minorities; 5) rentals to blacks in white-occupied apartment buildings; and 6) hiring of blacks. Cultural definitions of the situations and the degree of clarity of emergent norms were primary factors determining attitudinal expressions which were consistent or inconsistent with a general belief in integration.   J

3019.   Cagle, Laurence T.   INTERRACIAL HOUSING: A REAS-SESSMENT OF THE EQUAL-STATUS CONTACT HYPOTHESIS. *Sociol. and Social Res. 1973 57(3): 342-355.* Hovever much prejudice was reduced, interracial (and intraracial) contacts were not very intimate in urban society.   J/S

3020.   Carlson, Alvar W.   THE ORIGINS AND CHARACTERIS-TICS OF FOREIGN IMMIGRANTS SETTLING IN TOLEDO AND NORTHWESTERN OHIO, 1965-76. *Northwest Ohio Q. 1978 50(1): 17-28.* Discusses the settlement patterns and characteristics of the many South and East Asians, Latin Americans, and Middle Easterners who have immigrated to Toledo since 1965, based on petitions for naturaliza-tion.

3021.   Circarelli, James.   ON INCOME, RACE, AND CONSUMER BEHAVIOR. *Am. J. of Econ. and Sociol. 1974 33(3): 343-347.* Whites and Negroes in Chicago are compared on the basis of the relative income hypothesis for differences in consuming habits. Differences in consumer behavior of blacks and whites are evident among all relative income classes. Therefore the differences are a by-product of cultural factors. Secondary sources; 2 tables, 10 notes.   W. L. Marr

3022.   Corner, George W.   THE BLACK COALITION: AN EXPER-IMENT IN RACIAL COOPERATION, PHILADELPHIA, 1968. *Pro. of the Am. Phil. Soc. 1976 120(3): 178-186.* During April 1968-March 1969 32 black and white community leaders in Philadelphia at-tempted to prevent race riots. The white businessmen produced over one million dollars for the blacks—who called themselves the "Black Coali-tion"—to run 25 prototype business and social programs. The majority of the programs which were well run, received adequate funds, and pro-duced admirable results. Some of the programs failed for the lack of funds, and three—which received over half the available funds—failed because of total mismanagement. Developing interracial trust and identi-fying black community leaders proved the most durable result.
                                                                  W. L. Olbrich

3023.   Davidson, Chandler and Gaitz, Charles M.   ETHNIC ATTI-TUDES AS A BASIS FOR MINORITY COOPERATION IN A SOUTHWESTERN METROPOLIS. *Social Sci. Q. 1973 53(4): 738-748.* Using a stratified sample of Anglos, Mexican Americans and blacks in the city of Houston, it was found that Mexican Americans generally were more tolerant of and sympathetic with blacks than were Anglos in matters of equality, civil rights and social interaction. However, consis-tent with previous findings, Mexican American attitudes were in several respects closer to those of Anglos than of blacks.   J

3024.   Davison, Victoria F. and Shannon, Lyle W.   CHANGE IN THE ECONOMIC ABSORPTION OF A COHORT OF IMMIGRANT MEXICAN AMERICANS AND NEGROES BEFORE 1960 AND 1971. *Int. Migration Rev. 1977 11(2): 190-214.* Examines data from 280 Mexican Americans, 280 Negroes, and 413 Anglos in Racine, Wisconsin, discovering that during 1960-71 economic differences between Anglos, Mexicans, and Negroes remained essentially the same in occupation and income measures, while level of living and home conditions were slightly decreased.

3025.   Erbe, Brigitte Mach.   RACE AND SOCIOECONOMIC SEG-REGATION. *Am. Sociol. Rev. 1975 40(6): 801-812.* An investigation of the residential contiguity of socioeconomic status groups in the white and black population of the Chicago SMSA in 1970 shows that although segregation indices between socioeconomic groups were comparable for whites and blacks, residential propinquity between high status and low status persons differed dramatically between racial groups. Black profes-sionals and managers lived in tracts with an occupational composition comparable, on the average, to that of tracts where unskilled white work-ers lived. The neighbors of white high school drop-outs had educational backgrounds similar to those of black college graduates. Black families with incomes over $25,000 lived in poorer tracts than white families with incomes below $3,000. In comparisons of whites and blacks on any vari-able affected by neighborhood composition, therefore, control for individ-ual characteristics does not eliminate the effects of differential neighborhood characteristics.   J

3026.   Ford, W. Scott   INTERRACIAL PUBLIC HOUSING IN A BORDER CITY: ANOTHER LOOK AT THE CONTACT HYPOTH-ESIS. *Am. J. of Sociol. 1973 78(6): 1426-1447.* The contact hypothesis is reexamined within the context of public housing in a border-state city. Black and white housewives were interviewed in racially segregated and desegregated projects to determine the extent to which engaging in equal-status interracial contacts was related to racially tolerant attitudes. Whereas the findings clearly support the contact hypothesis for lower-income white housewives, in contrast to some earlier studies, the hypothe-sis as it applies to black women residing in the same environment is not supported. Discussion and suggested explanations of the seemingly dis-crepant findings emphasize the necessity of gaining a thorough under-standing of the specific conditions under which interracial contact occurs and examining the meaning such contact has for blacks in contrast to their white counterparts.   J

3027.   Greeley, Andrew M.   ETHNICITY AND RACIAL ATTI-TUDES: THE CASE OF THE JEWS AND THE POLES. *Am. J. of Sociol. 1975 80(4): 909-933.* Data from a 1968 survey drawn from the population of 15 US cities that had experienced racial unrest revealed that Polish Americans were the least sympathetic to black militancy, the Jews the most sympathetic.   S

3028.   Guest, Avery M. and Weed, James A.   ETHNIC RESIDEN-TIAL SEGREGATION: PATTERNS OF CHANGE. *Am. J. of Sociol. 1976 81(5): 1088-1111.* This study traces changes in patterns of ethnic residential segregation for Cleveland from 1930 to 1970 and for Boston and Seattle from 1960 to 1970. For Cleveland the data indicate some clear declines in residential segregation since 1930 for "new" south-ern and eastern European ethnic groups; "old" groups, however, actually increased in segregation. Between 1960 and 1970, few changes in patterns of ethnic segregation for Boston, Cleveland, and Seattle took place. On the whole, differences in residential segregation among ethnic groups, both cross-sectionally and over time, were highly related to differences in social status. It is clear, nevertheless, that ethnic segregation would con-tinue to exist even if social status differences among ethnic groups disap-peared.   J

3029.   Hall, Grace and Saltzstein, Alan.   EQUAL EMPLOYMENT OPPORTUNITY FOR MINORITIES IN MUNICIPAL GOVERN-MENT. *Social Sci. Q. 1977 57(4): 864-872.* Data from 26 Texas cities reveal unexpectedly complex employment patterns for blacks and Mexi-can Americans in municipal government. Indices which consider both a minority group's representation and its distribution across salary levels demonstrate that blacks are more disadvantaged than Spanish surnamed individuals. Mexican American employment is related more strongly to the professional and educational characteristics of that population than is the case for blacks. Urbanization has not affected the hiring of both groups equally; black employment potential seems to increase in rapidly growing central cities. Based on Equal Employment Opportunity statis-tics and secondary sources; 3 tables, 3 notes, biblio.
                                                                  W. R. Hively

3030.   Hamilton, David L. and Bishop, George D.   ATTITUDINAL AND BEHAVIORAL EFFECTS OF INITIAL INTEGRATION OF WHITE SUBURBAN NEIGHBORHOODS. *J. of Social Issues 1976 32(2): 47-67.* Interviews in 18 white suburban neighborhoods into which a new family had recently moved—in 8 neighborhoods a new black family, in the other 10 a white. Prior interviews in some neighborhoods indicated a high degree of compatibility between residents of the two sets of neighborhoods. Interviews conducted one month, three months, and one year after the families had moved in assessed a variety of attitudinal and behavioral indicators of residents' reactions to new neighbors. Results not only showed marked differences in how black and white families are received by white residents but also revealed patterns of change over time which reflect the processes inherent in the integration experience.   J

3031.   Hasse, John.   "THE WHITES RUNNIN' BECAUSE THE BLACKS ARE MOVIN' IN": AN INTERVIEW WITH REV. ROOSEVELT ROBINSON. *Indiana Folklore 1977 10(2): 183-190.* The Reverend Roosevelt Robinson, minister of the Centennial United Meth-odist Church in Gary, Indiana, discusses white flight in Gary, in-tradenominational differences in black churches, and the history of his church.

3032. Hermalin, Albert I. and Farley, Reynolds. THE POTENTIAL FOR RESIDENTIAL INTEGRATION IN CITIES AND SUBURBS: IMPLICATIONS FOR THE BUSING CONTROVERSY. *Am. Sociol. Rev. 1973 38(5): 595-610.* Controversies over busing to achieve racial integration of schools result from the intersection of social trends and prevailing values. The movement to expand the civil rights of blacks conflicts with the tradition of neighborhood schools and the residential segregation of neighborhoods. Examines the receptiveness of whites to school and neighborhood integration and explores the economic potential for residential integration. We find the receptiveness of whites to having black neighbors or having their children attend schools with Negroes has increased, and now a majority of whites endorse such integration. Data from the Census of 1970 reveal that economic factors account for little of the concentration of blacks within central cities, their absence from suburbia or the residential segregation of blacks from whites in either cities or suburbs. The attitudinal receptivity and economic potential exist for extensive residential integration, and these can achieve the dual goals of integrated schools and neighborhood schools. J

3033. Hertz, Edwin. IDEOLOGICAL LIBERALS IN REFORM POLITICS: A NOTE ON THE BACKGROUND AND MOVEMENT OF POLITICAL OUTSIDERS INTO MAJOR PARTY POLITICS. *Int. J. of Contemporary Sociol. 1974 11(1): 1-11.* Discusses the political participation of working class Jews, Negroes, and Puerto Rican Americans as pressure groups in social reform and civil rights issues in New York City, 1963-70's.

3034. Kerr, Louise A. CHICANO SETTLEMENTS IN CHICAGO: A BRIEF HISTORY. *J. of Ethnic Studies 1975 2(4): 22-32.* Describes the adaptation to and participation in political, economic, and social life of Chicago Chicanos in their three major neighborhoods: the Near West Side, Back of the Yards, and South Chicago. Distinctive neighborhood patterns "have at least partially determined the variable development of Chicano identity." The greatest obstacle to the progress has been lack of Chicano unity, especially in the face of the most significant recent problem, large-scale Puerto Rican immigration. This, combined with the antagonisms of Poles and Italians, and domination of housing by the Irish, produced varying degrees of development, parallel but different, in Chicano gains in employment, housing, social organization, interethnic relationships, and parish organization. By the 1960's the growing Black and other "Latino" populations, the closing of the stockyards, and urban renewal produced major internal changes in two of the neighborhoods. Worsened social conditions along with a new dynamism continue to coexist. Primary and secondary sources; 38 notes.

G. J. Bobango

3035. King, A. Thomas and Mieszkowski, Peter. RACIAL DISCRIMINATION, SEGREGATION, AND THE PRICE OF HOUSING. *J. of Pol. Econ. 1973 81(3): 590-606.* Estimates racial discrimination in the New Haven, Connecticut, housing market based on data from over 200 rental units for which there is comprehensive information on the characteristics of the dwellings. Blacks and whites do pay different amounts for equivalent units. For black female-headed households the markup relative to white males is 16 percent; for black male-headed households, 7.5 percent. Rents for whites in boundary (integrated) areas are about 7 percent lower than for black households in these areas. J

3036. Levine, Daniel U. and Levine, Rayna F. THE SOCIAL AND INSTRUCTIONAL SETTING FOR METROPOLITAN INTEGRATION. *Urban Rev. 1978 10(2): 157-183.* Socioeconomic integration does more to improve the opportunities and achievement of minority students than does just racial integration. Desegregation is socioeconomically possible and geographically and administratively feasible only when implemented on a metropolitan or regional basis. Successful metropolitan desegregation requires comprehensive and long-range planning and action. The best federal desegregation was the National Educational Opportunities Act of 1977. Primary and secondary sources; table, 11 fig., 18 notes.

R. G. Sherer

3037. Lovrich, Nicholas P., Jr. and Marenin, Otwin. A COMPARISON OF BLACK AND MEXICAN AMERICAN VOTERS IN DENVER: ASSERTIVE VERSUS ACQUIESCENT POLITICAL ORIENTATIONS AND VOTING BEHAVIOR IN AN URBAN ELECTORATE. *Western Pol. Q. 1976 29(2): 284-294.* The voting behavior and political attitudes of black and Mexican American voters in Denver are analyzed. The major conclusion is that the comparative weakness of Mexican American political forces, as typified by their failure to win an ethnically salient pair of elections wherein conditions were favorable to them, stems from their comparative weakness of political consciousness. The Denver Urban Observatory attitude survey of 1972, which sampled Mexican American and black citizens in the City Council districts under study, included only citizens who had voted in these 1971 elections. A comparison of responses given by these voter groups to questions regarding political interest, evaluation of public policy, self-identification (e.g., black vs. Negro, Chicano vs. Spanish American), shows that blacks are much more highly unified and politicized in this urban electorate. An attempt is made to generalize from these Denver findings to the broader area of American ethnic political behavior. J

3038. Milutinovich, Jugoslav S. EFFECTS OF GHETTO LIFE ON EMPLOYEES. *Urban and Social Change Rev. 1973 6(2): 69-72.*

3039. Moynihan, Daniel Patrick. PATTERNS OF ETHNIC SUCCESSION: BLACKS AND HISPANICS IN NEW YORK CITY. *Pol. Sci. Q. 1979 94(1): 1-14.* Reviews the gains achieved by blacks and Hispanics in New York City over the past decade and relates those gains to general patterns of ethnic succession. J

3040. Nelsen, Hart M. and Allen, H. David. ETHNICITY, AMERICANIZATION, AND RELIGIOUS ATTENDANCE. *Am. J. of Sociol. 1974 79(4): 906-922.* Two trends in the pattern of Americanization of immigrant groups are noted, one involving decreased second-generation religious interest due to alienation from the ethnic tradition and the other showing an increase in attendance at worship services from first to second generation due to the prominence of religion in American culture. The pattern of second-generation attendance depends on the extent of difference between the ethnic culture and the dominant American culture. In a secondary analysis of data on New York City Catholics, the respondents are grouped into western, eastern, and southern European categories based on country of origin. There are no meaningful differences in religious attendance among first-generation Catholics; among second-generation respondents there are substantial differences. Western Europeans show an increase in attendance from first to second generation, while southern Europeans show a decrease. It is concluded that the meltingpot concept of assimilation fails to take into account interethnic variations in patterns of Americanization. J

3041. Niemi, Albert W., Jr. WAGE DISCRIMINATION AGAINST NEGROES AND PUERTO RICANS IN THE NEW YORK SMSA: AN ASSESSMENT OF EDUCATIONAL AND OCCUPATIONAL DIFFERENCES. *Social Sci. Q. 1974 55(1): 112-120.* Assesses the impact of those differences on 1970 earnings levels of white, Negro, and Puerto Rican males, concluding that racial earnings differences largely reflect real skill differences rather than color-based employer discrimination. J

3042. Pavlak, Thomas J. SOCIAL CLASS, ETHNICITY, AND RACIAL PREJUDICE. *Public Opinion Q. 1973 37(2): 225-231.* Results of a survey in 1969 of racial attitudes in Chicago among white ethnics (mostly lower-middle-class manual workers). Those tested showed a significant degree of hostility toward Negroes and especially toward interracial marriage. Hostility was weakest toward integrated work teams. Racial hostility may simply reflect economic and social competition and not inherent racial prejudice. 3 tables, 11 notes. V. L. Human

3043. Peabody, Malcolm E., Jr. CUSTOM CHANGING. *J. of Intergroup Relations 1973 2(4): 46-58.* Text of a speech given by the author on race relations in cities, focusing on housing and unemployment during the 1970's. S

3044. Roberts, Shirley J. MINORITY-GROUP POVERTY IN PHOENIX: A SOCIO-ECONOMIC SURVEY. *J. of Arizona Hist. 1973 14(4): 347-362.* The southern part of Phoenix has always been the residence of the poverty level minority groups, principally Mexican, Indian, black, Chinese, health seekers, and migrant agricultural workers. Anglo-American hostility and indifference have changed toward a sense of responsibility. In the last few decades this change has been manifested in welfare projects and government housing. The combination of poverty and ethnic and racial barriers makes it difficult for these groups to leave this section of the city, with the exception of the Chinese, who have overcome these difficulties and have dispersed throughout the city. 2 maps, 53 notes.   D. L. Smith

3045. Roof, Wade Clark; Van Valey, Thomas L.; and Spain, Daphne. RESIDENTIAL SEGREGATION IN SOUTHERN CITIES: 1970. *Social Forces 1976 55(1): 59-71.* The authors construct a regional model of residential segregation in the South, using demographic and socioeconomic variables. Based on an analysis of the age, size, percent black, and occupational and income differentials in 32 southern cities, the findings show that: (1) age is still the strongest predictor of residential segregation; (2) socioeconomic factors need to be examined in their traditional southern context as indicators of residential segregation; (3) occupational—not income—differences have the greater effect on levels of residential segregation; and (4) changes in socioeconomic status for blacks in the South have not been accompanied by concomitant changes in residential segregation. Problems of developing and testing causal models of segregation are discussed, combined with specific suggestions for future research.   J

3046. Schatt, Stanley. THE GHETTO IN RECENT AMERICAN LITERATURE. *J. of Ethnic Studies 1973 1(1): 44-54.* Concludes from an extensive examination of recent black and Jewish literature, that an understanding of Jewish and black ghetto culture is necessary in order to understand ethnic literature. This literature can in turn provide deep insights into the nature of Jewish and black culture. Based on contemporary literature and related scholarship; 37 notes.   T. W. Smith

3047. Shannon, Lyle W. and McKim, Judith L. ATTITUDES TOWARD EDUCATION AND THE ABSORPTION OF IMMIGRANT MEXICAN-AMERICANS AND NEGROES IN RACINE. *Educ. and Urban Soc. 1974 6(4): 333-354.*

3048. Shannon, Lyle W. FALSE ASSUMPTIONS ABOUT THE DETERMINANTS OF MEXICAN-AMERICAN AND NEGRO ECONOMIC ABSORPTION. *Sociol. Q. 1975 16(1): 3-15.* It generally is believed that with age and time in the urban industrial community, differences between rural-reared and urban-reared persons decline or disappear. This longitudinal study of Mexican American, Negro, and Anglo families in Racine, Wisconsin, finds little significant change (1960-1971) in the relative position of Mexican Americans and Negroes on occupational level, income, and level of living. Race/ethnicity remains the most powerful determinant of a family's position in the community.   J

3049. Siembieda, William J. SUBURBANIZATION OF ETHNICS OF COLOR. *Ann. of the Am. Acad. of Pol. and Social Sci. 1975 422: 118-128.* The suburbanization of ethnics of color made slow progress during the 1960's. The nation continued its long term toward dual societies. Only one major metropolitan area, Los Angeles, was able to double the number of ethnics of color (black and Mexican-Americans) living outside the central city. However, the central city still became blacker, browner, and poorer. The ethnics of color who migrated to the suburbs were middle class and had a high propensity toward homeownership. Rises in real income, an available housing supply, a lessening of discrimination practices and an economically differentiated metropolitan area are variables that help explain the Los Angeles experience. Ethnics of color did not suburbanize in a random manner. They tended to locate in selected suburban communities, forming flows to the southern and eastern sections of Los Angeles County. Most lived in segregated suburban neighborhoods.   J

3050. Silverman, Irwin and Shaw, Marvin E. EFFECTS OF SUDDEN MASS DESEGREGATION ON INTERRACIAL INTERACTION AND ATTITUDES IN ONE SOUTHERN CITY. *J. of Social Issues 1973 29(4): 133-142.* The extent to which blacks and whites interacted socially on school grounds and their attitudes toward each other were ascertained across time during the first semester of an integration program in three southern secondary schools. Interracial interactions remained sparse throughout the semester and over time showed no increases approaching significance though attitudes did become more tolerant. Several effects on both variables related to race, sex, and grade level are reported.   J

3051. Stevens, A. Jay. THE ACQUISITION OF PARTICIPATORY NORMS: THE CASE OF JAPANESE AND MEXICAN AMERICAN CHILDREN IN A SUBURBAN ENVIRONMENT. *Western Pol. Q. 1975 28(2): 281-295.* Describes variations found among Japanese American, Chicano, and Anglo children on measures of political efficacy, civic duty, and personal competence. The observed variations are explained in terms of cultural patterns transmitted by the family. Japanese American children manifest the most idealized orientations, while the Mexican American children's orientations do not encourage political participation. Controls for socioeconomic status, political interest, and the children's perception of how easily laws may be changed are introduced. Socioeconomic status has the greatest effect upon the orientations of the Japanese American children; political interest primarily differentiates the orientations manifest by the Mexican American children; and the children's perception of the ease with which laws may be changed affects only the Anglo children. Socioeconomic status and political interest encourage positive participatory orientations, but the Anglo children who feel it is easy to change the laws manifest considerably more negative orientations toward political participation than the children from the other groups studied.   J

3052. Thompson, Frank J. BUREAUCRATIC RESPONSIVENESS IN THE CITIES: THE PROBLEM OF MINORITY HIRING. *Urban Affairs Q. 1974 10(1): 40-68.* Summarizes minority hiring practices of the Oakland, California, city government. Department and personnel officials faced federal and minority pressures to hire more minority workers. Job opportunity publicity was altered to attract more minority applicants. More minority candidates responded than before, but did not gain employment, because they failed written tests. 2 tables, notes, biblio.   P. J. Woehrmann

3053. Van Valey, Thomas L.; Roof, Wade Clark; and Wilcox, Jerome E. TRENDS IN RESIDENTIAL SEGREGATION: 1960-70. *Am. J. of Sociol. 1977 82(4): 826-844.* The literature on racial residential segregation in American metropolitan areas reports contradictory findings on the decade of the sixties. Some researchers have concluded that average scores declined between 1960 and 1970, while others point to evidence of increases. This paper presents tract-based indexes for all 237 SMSAs (and their central cities) in 1970 and a comparable set of indexes for 1960. These are also cross-tabulated against region, population size, and minority proportion. Several conclusions are drawn: (1) overall, the data indicate a general decline in the average level of segregation between 1960 and 1970; (2) much of that decline is due to the relatively low scores among SMSAs added during the decade; (3) contradictory findings reported in the literature are likely to be due to sampling or other methodological inconsistencies; and (4) clear variations in levels of segregation persist with regard to region, population size, and minority proportion. The importance of these findings for future research is discussed.   J

3054. Varady, David P. WHITE MOVING PLANS IN A RACIALLY CHANGING MIDDLE-CLASS COMMUNITY. *J. of the Am. Inst. of Planners 1974 40(5): 360-370.* Tests two assumptions commonly held by planners regarding racially changing communities: 1) that racial changes are accompanied by a speed-up in white outmigration, and 2) that these areas are most likely to retain the highly educated household heads. Telephone interviews were conducted in an area in Philadelphia encompassing a racially changing community and a stable, predominantly white community. White residents accelerated their moving plans in response to racial changes; education was not a significant factor in holding families to the changing community.   J/S

3055. Williams, John A. THE BOYS FROM SYRACUSE: BLACKS AND JEWS IN THE OLD NEIGHBORHOOD. *Present Tense 1977 4(3): 34-38.* Examines the historical and contemporary relationship between American Jews and Afro-Americans in Syracuse, New York. Cites author's experiences and those of other residents. Primary and secondary sources; photo, note.   R. B. Mendel

3056. Wojniusz, Helen K. RACIAL HOSTILITY AMONG BLACKS IN CHICAGO. *J. of Black Studies 1979 10(1): 40-59.* A 17-question poll of 71 black adults in Chicago revealed that the respondents were hostile toward whites. The blacks believed that whites were hypocritical about racial equality and that whites had a better chance of getting a good public school education and professional jobs. The only personal factor significant in lessening this hostility was the extent to which the black adults lived in integrated areas; residential integration promoted toleration. 4 tables, fig., 14 notes, biblio.   R. G. Sherer

Blacks

3057. Adams, John S. and Brauer, Mary. USEFUL GOAL ACHIEVEMENT MEASURES: ZELDER'S SEGREGATION INDICES. *J. of the Am. Inst. of Planners 1974 40(6): 430-438.* Raymond E. Zelder's indices describe how black populations would be geographically distributed if the housing market operated in a color-blind fashion and families were matched up with housing opportunities solely according to their incomes. The study confirms the usefulness and accuracy of Zelder's indices. The indices are applied to the Minneapolis-St. Paul area to illustrate how a city can specify an unambiguous integration goal for the 1970's given the city's existing distribution of housing opportunities and its prevailing income distribution of white and nonwhite families. Yet even a color-blind market will yield racially segregated housing patterns until metropolitan housing policy makes economic integration a reality at every neighborhood level.   J

3058. Barger, Harold M. IMAGES OF POLITICAL AUTHORITY IN FOUR TYPES OF BLACK NEWSPAPERS. *Journalism Q. 1973 50(4): 645-651, 672.* Studies political attitudes reflected in community, organizational, militant, and urban black press (1969-70).   S

3059. Bennett, Don C. SEGREGATION AND RACIAL INTERACTION. *Ann. of the Assoc. of Am. Geographers 1973 63(1): 48-57.* Black school age children of Indianapolis have far greater possibilities for interracial contact than whites in their neighborhoods or schools. Confirmation is provided by the pre-university experiences of students. Black university students reported a far higher incidence of having lived near whites, of having white friends, and of having engaged in activities with whites than vice versa.   J

3060. Bernstein, Shalmon. HARLEM'S MIDDLE-CLASS ENCLAVES. *New York Affairs 1976 3(3): 91-96.* Harlem is more than littered streets and broken-down buildings. Elegant brownstones and modern architecture offer proof of Harlem's continuing vitality.   J

3061. Braden, Anne. BIRMINGHAM, 1956-1979: THE HISTORY THAT WE MADE. *Southern Exposure 1979 7(2): 48-54.* The Reverend Fred L. Shuttlesworth, a black minister active in the southern civil rights movement, participated in integration attempts and sit-ins on buses and joined Martin Luther King, Jr., and Ralph Abernathy in organizing protests in Birmingham, Alabama.

3062. Bryce-Laporte, Roy Simón. NEW YORK CITY AND THE NEW CARIBBEAN IMMIGRATION: A CONTEXTUAL STATEMENT. *Int. Migration Rev. 1979 13(2): 214-234.* Focuses on the distinctive features of Caribbean migration from 1965 to 1979, noting that the period coincides with financial problems in New York City, a situation which has engendered considerable anti-migrant sentiment, and the public at large often does not differentiate between native-born blacks with long histories of residency in the continental US and newly arrived Caribbean blacks.

3063. Buchanan, Susan Huelsebusch. LANGUAGE AND IDENTITY: HAITIANS IN NEW YORK CITY. *Int. Migration Rev. 1979 13(2): 298-313.* Examines the dispute between two Haitian factions— those wishing to retain French as the language for masses in a Brooklyn church and those wishing to replace French with Haitian Creole—perceiving the clash (which ended more or less as a defeat for the Creole-speaking proponents) as a social dilemma inherited from the colonial slave past of Haiti transported to New York.

3064. Cahill, Edward E. MIGRATION AND THE DECLINE OF THE BLACK POPULATION IN RURAL AND NON-METROPOLITAN AREAS. *Phylon 1974 35(3): 284-292.* Discusses rural to urban, nonmetropolitan to metropolitan migration of Negroes and the implications of recent migration trends. The precipitous decline in the rural

population of the black South during the 1950's and 1960's means that the number of migrants leaving the rural South is likely to be reduced. There is some evidence to indicate black movement from the northern metropolitan areas to metropolitan areas of the South and the West. Based on primary and secondary sources; 5 tables, 11 notes.
          B. A. Glasrud

3065. Campbell, Dick. BLACK MUSICIANS IN SYMPHONY ORCHESTRAS: A BAD SCENE. *Crisis 1975 82(1): 12-17.* A survey of 60 symphony orchestras (30 with budgets over $1 million) shows that the young black mucisian will have a difficult time getting a position in the music establishment. Of the nearly 5,000 musicians playing in the 56 symphonies that responded to the questionnaire, only 70 were black. The integrated Symphony of the New World is creating a pool of musicians qualified to play in orchestras   A. G. Belles

3066. Chafe, William. THE GREENSBORO SIT-INS. *Southern Exposure 1978 6(3): 78-87.* The sit-ins were based on a long tradition in the Greensboro, North Carolina, black community of overt and covert opposition to segregation and discrimination. Black leaders either openly opposed violations of civil rights before 1960 or worked within the system to change conditions. The issue of school desegregation in the late 1950's and resultant white procrastination and hypocrisy on this issue prepared the way for the sit-ins which rapidly united and at times divided the black community. The sit-ins also resulted in white concessions in the area of segregation, but black community actions were of far greater significance than were white reactions.   N. Lederer

3067. Ciccone, James. A TRIBUTE TO EVERETT HOLMES: NEW YORK STATE'S FIRST BLACK MAYOR. *Afro-Americans in New York Life and Hist. 1978 2(1): 11-16.* Everett Holmes became New York's first black mayor when he was elected to that office in his home town of Bridgewater in 1974.

3068. Clarke, James W. FAMILY STRUCTURE AND POLITICAL SOCIALIZATION AMONG URBAN BLACK CHILDREN. *Am. J. of Pol. Sci. 1973 17(2): 302-315.* The results of this study of 94 urban black children suggest that father absence is an important variable in their political socialization. Father-absent children tend to be more cynical and also express much stronger preferences for a racially segregated environment. Beyond this, the results underscore the importance of intra-family relationships in the political socialization process.   J

3069. Clay, Phillip L. THE PROCESS OF BLACK SUBURBANIZATION. *Urban Affairs Q. 1979 14(4): 405-424.* While it has been assumed that suburbanization would enhance housing opportunities for blacks, there has been no comprehensive analysis of the phenomenon. Argues that although recent suburban migrants are younger, better educated, and more affluent than their predecessors, except for the top 15%, suburbanization had resulted in resegregation. Further, blacks are concentrated in isolated sectors of metropolitan areas that deny the popular "spillover" model of black suburbanization. Finally, attitudinal surveys show blacks have serious criticism of their suburban environments. 7 tables, 17 notes, biblio.   L. N. Beecher

3070. Conyus. IMAGES OF THE FILLMORE. *Black Scholar 1974 6(4): 24-31.* Describes the Negro ghetto in San Francisco's Fillmore district, 1974.   S

3071. Cooley, Gilbert E. ROOT DOCTORS AND PSYCHICS IN THE REGION. *Indiana Folklore 1977 10(2): 191-200.* Folklore study of hoodoo beliefs among immigrant blacks in Gary, East Chicago, and Hammond, Indiana, indicates that strong retention of beliefs among urban blacks serves as a filter for conflict, antagonism, and frustration encountered in modern city life, 1976.

3072. Cottingham, Phoebe H. BLACK INCOME AND METROPOLITAN RESIDENTIAL DISPERSION. *Urban Affairs Q. 1975 10(3): 273-296.* Analyzes black population shifts in Philadelphia. Apparently blacks there as elsewhere are reluctant to move outside the central city black neighborhoods, regardless of moderate to high income levels. Educational levels of blacks are seemingly indeterminate in suburban selection rates also. 8 tables, 20 notes, biblio.   P. J. Woehrmann

3073. Cottle, Thomas J. WE'RE ALL PRISONERS. *Urban Rev.*
1973 6(3): 26-30. Attitudes of children in a Boston ghetto.   S

3074. Darden, Joe T. THE RESIDENTIAL SEGREGATION OF
BLACKS IN DETROIT, 1960-1970. *Int. J. of Comparative Sociol.*
[Canada] 1976 17(1-2): 84-91. Determines the magnitude of racial residential segregation in Detroit (central city, suburbs, and SMSA) in 1960,
the changes 1960-70, and the degree to which segregation could be explained by housing cost inequality between blacks and whites. A high
level of black residential segregation existed in 1960 but only 14-20 percent of this could be explained by housing cost inequality between blacks
and whites. During the 1960's there were decreases in the level of segregation in the central city and SMSA but increases in the suburbs. Only 25-48
percent of segregation could be explained by housing cost inequality in
1970. This factor explained much more of the segregation in 1970 than
in 1960, but the bulk of the black residential segregation remained unex-
plained. Low-cost housing, although a necessity in some areas, is not the
answer to reducing the bulk of the residential segregation that exists. The
answer lies in reducing racial discrimination in housing. Primary and
secondary sources; 2 notes, biblio.   R. G. Neville

3075. Davis, Lenwood G. and Van Horne, Winston. THE CITY RE-
NEWED: WHITE DREAM—BLACK NIGHTMARE? *Black*
Scholar 1975 7(3): 2-9. Discusses the economic dependence of Negroes
to whites in the cities in the 1970's, and examines the benefits of Black
capitalism.

3076. Dent, Tom. NEW ORLEANS VERSUS ATLANTA: POWER
TO THE PARADE. *Southern Exposure 1979 7(1): 64-68.* Contrasts
the economic power of blacks in New Orleans (Louisiana) and Atlanta
(Georgia) since the late 1960's; blacks in New Orleans have little economic power and thus no political representation, while blacks in Atlanta
have a strong economic community and political clout.

3077. De Vise, Peter. THE SUBURBANIZATION OF JOBS AND
MINORITY EMPLOYMENT. *Econ. Geography 1976 52(4): 348-362.*
Analyzes journey-to-work data among black workers in Chicago, Illinois,
1960-70.

3078. Edwards, Ozzie L. SKIN COLOR AS A VARIABLE IN RA-
CIAL ATTITUDES OF BLACK URBANITES. *J. of Black Studies*
1973 3(4): 473-483. A 1968 survey of racial attitudes of 2,809 blacks, aged
16-19, living in 15 American cities showed that social and economic
attitudes differed among blacks of different skin color. Blacks of darker
complexion have a greater awareness of discrimination and a greater sense
of racial identification. 2 notes, biblio.   K. Butcher

3079. Elifson, Kirk W. and Irwin, Joseph. BLACK MINISTERS'
ATTITUDES TOWARD POPULATION SIZE AND BIRTH CON-
TROL. *Sociol. Analysis 1977 38(3): 252-257.* Attitudes toward ideal
black population size and genocidal efforts by whites were assessed in
conjunction with a larger study of 154 black ministers in Nashville,
Tennessee. A variety of demographic and experiential indicators which
hypothetically should serve as predictors of the stance taken by the ministers were considered. While the demographic variables did not show any
consistent relationship with the ministers' overall orientation to the issue
of minority status, both attitudinal and experiential variables were of
predictive value.   J

3080. Foner, Nancy. WEST INDIANS IN NEW YORK CITY AND
LONDON: A COMPARATIVE ANALYSIS. *Int. Migration Rev.*
1979 13(2): 284-297. While thousands of West Indians have come to the
United States since the beginning of the century, they have been admitted
to Britain in large numbers only since the 1950's. West Indians in New
York City have taken advantage of their relatively high economic and
professional status and the availability of a large business and professional
clientele among American Negroes to achieve a social status that has not
been achieved by West Indians in Britain or by American blacks.

3081. Foster, Loren S. BLACK PERCEPTIONS OF THE MAYOR:
AN EMPIRICAL TEST. *Urban Affairs Q. 1978 14(2): 242-252.* Based
on a survey of 751 grade and high school students in Peoria and East St.
Louis, explores the formation of black political attitudes. Despite the
economic disparities (a 3.9% unemployment rate in Peoria as opposed to

10.3% in East St. Louis), blacks from both cities had the same disapproval rate (77%) of then President Nixon. However, 67% of East St.
Louis' blacks rated their black mayor as very or fairly good while only
47% of their counterparts in Peoria would so rate that city's white mayor.
The findings suggest that political reality, not extent of social deprivation,
may be the most potent predictor of black attitudes. 3 tables, 2 notes,
biblio.   L. N. Beecher

3082. Goldsmith, William W. THE GHETTO AS A RESOURCE
FOR BLACK AMERICA. *J. of the Am. Inst. of Planners 1974 40(1):*
17-30. None of the four major proposals for improving conditions in
black America—suburbanization, augmented employment, ghetto capitalism, or separatism—resolves the real issue, which is the creation of
cohesive black political and economic power. Suburbanization tends directly to reduce the potential for concentrated black power. Neither
national employment programs nor local control over particular trades
or businesses will be implemented except in response to concentrated
power. New investments in ghetto private enterprise are not viable without strong grass-roots political participation. And though separatist proposals recognize the need to gather power, their faulty analogies to
international colonial situations ignore the enormous existing power and
proximity of white America.   J

3083. Guest, Avery M. THE CHANGING RACIAL COMPOSI-
TION OF SUBURBS: 1950-1970. *Urban Affairs Q. 1978 14(2): 195-*
206. A study of 1,363 southern and nonsouthern suburbs. Although the
black population grew absolutely, there was little percentage change in
the racial composition of all suburbs. The percentage of blacks in southern
suburbs actually declined. Black increases were greatest in growing suburbs rather than in the classicial central city "invasion-succession" models in established areas. The growing number of blacks in the suburbs has
not generated integration or significantly altered suburban characteristics. 3 tables, fig., note, biblio.   L. N. Beecher

3084. Hannerz, Ulf. RESEARCH IN THE BLACK GHETTO: A
REVIEW OF THE SIXTIES. *J. of Asian and African Studies [Nether-*
lands] 1974 9(3/4): 139-159. Surveys approaches to and literature of
social research on the American black community. 12 notes, biblio.
                    R. T. Brown

3085. Harris, Charles W. BLACKS AND REGIONALISM: COUN-
CILS OF GOVERNMENTS. *Natl. Civic Rev. 1973 62(5): 254-258.*
Rapid increase in the number of black mayors and vice mayors in the
United States reflects growing involvement by blacks in all aspects of the
political process. The racial character of migration and population patterns in most metropolitan areas has created a situation where the black
position on metropolitan regionalism is quite different from two or three
decades ago.   J

3086. Hatcher, Richard D. MINORITY OBJECTION. *New York*
Affairs 1976 3(3): 68-70. Maintains that "breakthroughs" in electing
black politicians to mayoral ties are merely the result of demographic
shifts which put blacks in the majority in cities; contends that further
integration in the political arena is necessary to connect blacks with the
centers of power.

3087. Henderson, Lenneal J., Jr. ADMINISTRATIVE AD-
VOCACY AND BLACK URBAN ADMINISTRATORS. *Ann. of the*
Am. Acad. of Pol. and Social Sci. 1978 (439): 68-79. Examines the extent
to which black administrators can and do advocate the interests of black
communities through civic, community, and professional organizations.
The concept of advocacy is discussed and distinguished from concepts of
representation, in order to focus more on the advocacy behavior of black
urban administrators. Advocacy behaviors are also identified and organized into a civic/community advocacy index and a professional advocacy index. Administrators from Washington, St. Louis, New Orleans,
and San Francisco participated in the study. Survey research was used not
only to examine the advocacy behavior of administrators but also to
generate social and occupational data which could be related to advocacy
scores. Although black urban administrators appeared more inclined to
advocate civic, community, and professinal interests than white administrators, the majority of both black and white administrators are generally
not advocacy prone.   J

3088. Henderson, Lenneal J., Jr. PUBLIC TECHNOLOGY AND THE METROPOLITAN GHETTO. *Black Scholar 1974 5(6): 9-18.* There should be more analysis of and more black participation in technological decisionmaking and technology assessment in the metropolis. Both harmful and helpful aspects and consequences of technology affect current black economic and political conditions, strategies, and goals. The appropriate starting point for the analysis of technology and its relationship to urban blacks is the institutional and organizational setting in which technology is housed. This includes: public utilities; large-scale corporate organizations providing contract services to governmental agencies and decisionmakers, and district governments responsible for public services requiring substantial investments of technology. Based on primary and secondary sources; 4 tables, 24 notes.

M. M. McCarthy

3089. Henry, Keith S. THE BLACK POLITICAL TRADITION IN NEW YORK: A CONJUNCTION OF POLITICAL CULTURES. *J. of Black Studies 1977 7(4): 455-484.* The political experiences of West Indian immigrants to New York City differed from those of native blacks. West Indians quickly adopted street oratory. This traces to Caribbean influences but became well developed in New York. Native black females achieved participation in political life relatively early. Caribbean women had few comparable stimuli until they arrived in New York where they made rapid advances. West Indians, particularly by observing white politicians, made progress in their sense of political community. By the 1960's, blacks of both groups shared a sense of organization and leadership in New York. Primary and secondary sources; 44 notes, biblio.

D. C. Neal

3090. Holmes, Robert A. THE AFRO-AMERICAN IN THE URBAN AGE. *J. of Black Studies 1974 4(4): 441-456.* Examines the economic and social conditions of blacks in cities. Shows that life is getting increasingly harder for blacks, who should become more self-reliant. Blacks should achieve liberation through violence, cultural unity, and political and economic power. Biblio.

K. Butcher

3091. Hunt, Larry L. and Hunt, Janet G. RELIGIOUS AFFILIATION AND MILITANCY AMONG URBAN BLACKS: SOME CATHOLIC/PROTESTANT COMPARISONS. *Social Sci. Q. 1977 57(4): 821-833.* Uses Gary Marx's "conventional civil rights militancy" and "black self-image" indices to test whether black Catholics are maintaining their distinctive secular orientation or converging into a common black urban culture. The analysis corroborates the notion that black Catholics attain higher secular status than most black Protestants. However, attitudes toward race relations and social change are complex, and reflect socioeconomic as well as religious backgrounds. Middle class black Catholics tend to display the most distinctive attitudes; they demonstrate racial pride and "structural awareness" but do not favor collective civil rights militancy. Primary and secondary sources; 3 tables, 5 notes, biblio.

W. R. Hively

3092. Kaplan, Samuel. *"THEM"*—BLACKS IN SUBURBIA. *New York Affairs 1976 3(2): 20-41.* Blacks never have been welcome in suburbia, and despite all the antidiscrimination laws and public-housing programs of recent years, the white noose around the black central city is as tight as ever.

J

3093. Kapsis, Robert E. BLACK GHETTO DIVERSITY AND ANOMIE: A SOCIOPOLITICAL VIEW. *Am. J. of Sociol. 1978 83(5): 1132-1153.* The variety of subculturally distinct residential areas in black ghettos is based on neighborhood relationship to political power structures rather than the extent of racial turnover, as viewed in two San Francisco areas, 1950-65.

3094. Kapsis, Robert E. POWERLESSNESS IN RACIALLY CHANGING NEIGHBORHOODS. *Urban Affairs Q. 1979 14(4): 425-442.* Explains the theoretical issues involved and discusses his deprivation-integration model—blacks living in integrated neighborhoods, although deprived of stabilizing social ties, will nevertheless produce lower powerlessness scores than blacks remaining in the ghetto. Based on an analysis of two San Francisco Bay Area neighborhoods, he found that blacks in transitional neighborhoods did have the lower powerlessness scores. The hypothesis that strong ghetto social ties would mitigate the sense of powerlessness proved invalid. 4 tables, 6 notes, biblio.

L. N. Beecher

3095. Kuvlesky, William and Dietrich, Katheryn SOUTHERN BLACK YOUTHS' PERCEPTIONS OF MILITARY SERVICE: A NONMETROPOLITAN-METROPOLITAN COMPARISON OF ATTITUDES, ASPIRATIONS AND EXPECTATIONS. *J. of Pol. and Military Sociol. 1973 1(1): 105-120.* Identical instruments and procedures were used to collect data on military orientations of 98 black high school sophomores in selected nonmetropolitan East Texas counties and 111 black sophomores from a Houston, Texas high school. In general, all of the nonmetropolitan and metropolitan boys were favorably inclined towards military service, and lower-class black youth with high aspirations were not more favorably inclined toward participation in the military than other black youth.

J

3096. Larson, Calvin J. LEADERSHIP IN THREE BLACK NEIGHBORHOODS. *Phylon 1975 36(3): 260-268.* A comparative study of perceptions of leadership in three black neighborhoods in a northwest Indiana city. The study was conducted at the request of the city's school system which needed to know more about the character of the neighborhood social organization and the major problems which confronted the several neighborhoods. Concludes that men of leadership quality are readily apparent in all three neighborhoods. However, none can be said to command a position of influence to effect major changes on behalf of his constituency. 3 tables, 6 notes.

R. V. Ritter

3097. Lee, Anne S. and Bowles, Gladys K. POLICY IMPLICATIONS OF THE MOVEMENT OF BLACKS OUT OF THE RURAL SOUTH. *Phylon 1974 35(3): 332-339.* As a result of the movement of a considerable number of Negroes out of the rural South into urban areas, the out-migration effected compositional changes both in the remaining population in the rural areas, and in the urban populations which the migrants joined. The service needs of rural blacks in the cities are already very much like those of other urban blacks, but improvements are needed in services, especially education, for the remaining rural blacks. If improvements are forthcoming, then the service needs of rural blacks can be reduced so that they more closely approximate those of other Americans. Based on primary and secondary sources; 4 notes.

B. A. Glasrud

3098. Marshall, Harvey and Meyer, Deborah. ASSIMILATION AND THE ELECTION OF MINORITY CANDIDATES: THE CASE OF BLACK MAYORS. *Sociol. and Social Res. 1975 60(1): 1-21.* This study examines some of the factors which affect the probability that large US cities have a black mayor, vice mayor, or mayor pro tem. The hypothesized interrelations among variables are analyzed with path analysis. The data are highly consistent with the argument that socioeconomic differentiation is inversely related to the dependent variable, calling into question the so-called "assimilationist" hypothesis, an important perspective in the analysis of minority political participation. Percent black also has a major effect, although residential segregation does not.

J

3099. Mattox, Joe L. BLACK FOLK AND DOWNTOWN. *Crisis 1974 81(7): 232-234.* Discusses the relationship between Negroes and metropolitan areas.

S

3100. Meyer, David R. BLACKS IN SLUM HOUSING: A DISTORTED THEME. *J. of Black Studies 1973 4(2): 139-152.* Though many Negroes occupy substandard housing, it is an error to equate slum housing with black housing. Yet, a survey of literature concerning blacks shows that this is often done. Examines the attitudes of both blacks and whites on this issue, shows the inaccuracies of these attitudes, and suggests ways for changing them. Secondary sources; 9 notes, biblio.

K. Butcher

3101. Miller, Abraham H. and Bolce, Louis H. THE NEW URBAN BLACKS. *Ethnicity 1976 3(4): 338-367.* Data from the Kerner Commission report as well as studies of Watts activists offered a profile of urban Negroes as products of northern socialization and relative economic prosperity. Reanalysis of the material points to deficiencies, especially in failure to differentiate between violent and nonviolent protesters. Data collected by Angus Campbell and Howard Schumann (1973) support this assertion and point to a profile of urban blacks as militant, nonviolent, and middle-aged, with tendencies toward social integration rather than alienation.

G. A. Hewlett

3102. Myers, Samuel L., Jr. and Phillips, Kenneth E. HOUSING SEGREGATION AND BLACK EMPLOYMENT: ANOTHER LOOK AT THE GHETTO STRATEGY. *Am. Econ. Rev. 1979 69(2): 298-302.* The empirical evidence is unclear in the 10-year-old debate over ghetto dispersal vs. ghetto development policy. Both techniques have contributed to the massive dislocation of poor blacks. Pocket ghettos in the suburban communities are developing. Ref.   D. K. Pickens

3103. Nathanson, Constance A. MOVING PREFERENCES AND PLANS AMONG URBAN BLACK FAMILIES. *J. of the Am. Inst. of Planners 1974 40(5): 353-359.* Provides data from a random sample survey of residents in an average income [Baltimore, Maryland] inner-city black neighborhood. Respondents' moving preferences and moving plans were equally associated with housing and neighborhood dissatisfaction, and weakly related to family composition or demographic characteristics. The physical condition of the neighborhood and respondents' social ties to the area were most important in their moving preferences and plans. J

3104. Painter, Diann Holland. THE BLACK WOMAN IN AMERICAN SOCIETY. *Current Hist. 1976 70(416): 224-227, 234.* Discusses the economic role of women in black family structure in cities 1950's-70's, emphasizing their double burden of racism and sex discrimination in the employment market.

3105. Parker, Kallis E. BLACK GHETTO HOUSING: SERVING THE UNSERVED. *Current Hist. 1974 67(399): 214-221.* Surveys legislation designed to prevent racial discrimination in housing. From an issue on "Changing Black America." S

3106. Perry, Marvin E. THE COLONIAL ANALOGY AND ECONOMIC DEVELOPMENT. *Black Scholar 1974 5(5): 37-42.* Discusses the black ghetto economy and its development apart from the mainstream of white investment. S

3107. Pettigrew, Thomas F. RACIAL CHANGE AND SOCIAL POLICY. *Ann. of Am. Acad. of Pol. and Social Sci. 1979 441: 114-131.* Five major trends in contemporary American race relations are 1) the discontinuities of social change, with uneven progress within and across institutions; 2) two contrasting processes, one benefitting the black middle class and the other restraining the black poor; 3) the altered nature of racial discrimination, from blatantly exclusionary practices to more subtle, procedural, ostensibly "non-racial" forms centered upon demographic trends, housing patterns, and spatial arrangements; 4) racial attitude changes, with greater rejection of racial injustice among whites combined with continued resistance to the measures needed to correct the injustice; and 5) the shifting demographic base of American race relations, from the national era of 1915-1945, through the metropolitan era of 1945-1970, to the present era of movement away from large cities, the Northeast, and the Midwest. Each of these trends are shown to intersect in important ways with the structural linchpin of modern race relations: the maldistribution of blacks and whites throughout metropolitan areas. J

3108. Pfautz, Harold W.; Huguley, Harry C.; and McClain, John W. CHANGES IN REPUTED BLACK COMMUNITY LEADERSHIP, 1962-72: A CASE STUDY. *Social Forces 1975 53(3): 460-467.* A comparison of data from reputational studies of black community leadership in Providence, R. I., conducted in 1962, 1970, and 1972 revealed a high turnover in personnel, a decrease in average age, more local origin, more orientation to the black community, more employment in administrative positions related to race relations, more residence in the black working-class area, and a decline in community consensus as to reputed leadership. The implications of these findings for the structure and functioning of the black community and for the future of race relations are discussed in the context of the history of blacks in Providence together with data on changes in the demographic, ecological, and socioeconomic characteristics of the city and its black population during the past 20 years. J

3109. Pierce, John C.; Avery, William P.; and Addison, Carey, Jr. SEX DIFFERENCES IN BLACK POLITICAL BELIEFS AND BEHAVIOR. *Am. J. of Pol. Sci. 1973 17(2): 422-430.* Women traditionally are less interested in politics than men. Argues that black women more often head families and assume other male roles, suggesting that their political beliefs and behavior may not mimic that of women generally. Analysis of 300 black men and women living in New Orleans reveals that their political participation levels are virtually identical. Black women, like other women, believe their political efforts to be inefficacious. The sample is small and from a single city, but it serves to cast doubt on the concept of male political dominance. 4 tables, 13 notes.

V. L. Human

3110. Reid, John D. BLACK URBANIZATION IN THE SOUTH. *Phylon 1974 35(3): 259-267.* The black population of southern urban centers, whose total populations in 1960 numbered more than 250,000, increased by 22% during the 1960's. Outlines some of the redistribution trends of the black settlement from rural to urban areas during this decade. Finds that many Negroes who remain in the rural areas of the South are faced with declining services for menial employment. On the other hand, fewer of the blacks who leave the rural areas are leaving the southern region; rather, an increasing number (though certainly not a majority) are relocating in large southern cities. Additionally, more blacks from outside the region are coming back to the South to reside in the cities. Based on primary sources; 9 tables, 2 notes.

B. A. Glasrud

3111. Roof, Wade Clark and Spain, Daphne. A RESEARCH NOTE ON CITY-SUBURBAN SOCIOECONOMIC DIFFERENCES AMONG AMERICAN BLACKS. *Social Forces 1977 56(1): 15-20.* Central city blacks in the southern metropolitan areas have higher socioeconomic levels than do those in the suburbs, whereas the reverse is true elsewhere; in northern and western SMSAs, suburban blacks have the higher status levels. There is a 10-point percentage spread, indeed striking. Blacks are becoming more like whites in their residential distribution, becoming more decentralized throughout the metropolitan region. Based on a sample of 228 Standard Metropolitan Statistical Areas (SMSA) for 1970, constituting 97% of all American metropolitan areas; 3 tables, note.

E. P. Stickney

3112. Rossi, Peter H. and Berk, Richard A. LOCAL ROOTS OF BLACK ALIENATION. *Social Sci. Q. 1974 54(4): 741-758.* A study of black assessment of urban administration in 15 large American cities, based on local police performance, welfare policies, employment, retail merchandising, and public education. Assessments vary, but the striking finding is that blacks tend to be either much more enthusiastic or much more despondent than whites, possibly because blacks, due to low income and racial prejudice, cannot readily move from the city, so that its activities are more important to them. 6 tables, 2 figs., 15 notes.

V. L. Human

3113. Sampson, William A. and Milam, Vera. THE INTERRACIAL ATTITUDES OF THE BLACK MIDDLE CLASS: HAVE THEY CHANGED? *Social Problems 1975 23(2): 153-165.* A 1974 study of middle-class Negroes from the "Pill Hill" area of Chicago and Evanston, Illinois, tries to determine their attitudes in light of the social and psychological gains of the civil rights and Black Power movements. Middle-class blacks had a positive attitude toward themselves, a strong sense of group consciousness and solidarity, and did not try to separate themselves from lower-class blacks. 4 tables; biblio.   A. M. Osur

3114. Smith, Riley B. RESEARCH PERSPECTIVES ON AMERICAN BLACK ENGLISH: A BRIEF HISTORICAL SKETCH. *Am. Speech 1974 49(1/2): 24-39.* New techniques of research and description are needed if the complex problems surrounding urban language (and specifically black English) are to be adequately studied. It is also important that data continue to be collected on dialects of the rural South. Based on secondary sources; 7 notes, biblio.   P. A. Beaber

3115. Staples, Robert. LAND OF PROMISE, CITIES OF DESPAIR: BLACKS IN URBAN AMERICA. *Black Scholar 1978 10(2): 2-11.* Discusses social problems experienced by Negroes in urban areas, 1970's.

3116. Taeuber, Karl E. RACIAL SEGREGATION: THE PERSISTING DILEMMA. *Ann. of the Am. Acad. of Pol. and Social Sci. 1975 422: 87-96.* Although moderate to high social and economic heterogeneity are typical of suburbs as well as central cities, the black population has become highly segregated residentially. This segregation has little economic base, but is based primarily on racial on racial discrimination. The military images used to describe black "invasion" of neighborhoods and white "flight" from central cities express racial conflict and distort our perception of metropolitan trends. As a one-in-eight minority nationally, blacks are not numerous enough to "take over" many central cities. The high concentration of blacks in a couple dozen cities ensures that blacks will remain a small minority in 200 other metropolitan areas. Demographic data since 1970 indicate a reversal of the centuries-long process of increasing metropolitan concentration and a sharp diminution in the flow of black migrants to large cities. There is no evidence of sharp shifts in the residential isolation of blacks. Black suburbanization in some metropolitan areas has followed the central city pattern of segregation.

J

3117. Tryman, Mfanya D.   BLACK MAYORALTY CAMPAIGNS: RUNNING THE "RACE." *Phylon 1974 35(4): 346-358.* The elections of Carl Stokes as mayor of Cleveland, Ohio (1967), Richard Hatcher as mayor of Gary, Indiana (1967), and Kenneth Gibson as mayor of Newark, New Jersey (1970), indicate a number of important features about black politics and politicians in the United States. These were the first blacks to become the political leaders of large cities in the United States, and during the elections blacks mobilized solidly behind their black candidates while white racism played an important role in the campaigns of their respective white opponents. Furthermore, in these elections, smear campaigns were directed against the black mayoral candidates, and they were charged with extremism. The elections also pointed out that none of the black candidates conformed to traditional black political styles; the elections instead portrayed a new politics in the urban areas of the United States. Based on primary and secondary sources; 39 notes.

B. A. Glasrud

3118. Tucker, C. Jack and Reid, John D.   BLACK URBANIZATION AND ECONOMIC OPPORTUNITY: A LOOK AT THE NATION'S LARGE CITIES. *Phylon 1977 38(1): 55-64.* Since World War II a major trend among black migrants has been the movement from smaller to larger metropolitan areas. Whites have moved in reverse directions. As a result the nation's largest metropolitan centers have a growing percentage of blacks. Blacks are moving to these larger centers for economic reasons and are more likely to hold a white-collar job than blacks in a smaller community. Primary and secondary sources; 5 tables, 17 notes.

B. A. Glasrud

3119. Turner, Castellano B. and Wilson, William J.   DIMENSIONS OF RACIAL IDEOLOGY: A STUDY OF URBAN BLACK ATTITUDES. *J. of Social Issues 1976 32(2): 139-152.* Six dimensions of racial ideology were analyzed based on interview data from 1934 blacks in a northern city and a southern city. Blacks who favor separatism tend to be more alienated, fearful of race genocide, race conscious, and supportive of racial violence than those who endorse interracial cooperation. An orientation of suspiciousness, distrust, and estrangement toward white society was particularly evident in the sentiments of blacks who reside in a northern city, are under age 30, and have low socioeconomic status. Moreover, younger persons and males are substantially more in favor of racial violence than older persons and females. The view that less privileged blacks are more conservative in their assessment of race relations and the view that the depressed ghetto experience restricts their knowledge about and responses to racial subjugation are not upheld in this study.

J

3120. Unsigned.   [LITTLE ROCK]. *Southern Exposure 1979 7(2): 38-47.*
Eckford, Elizabeth.   LITTLE ROCK, 1957: THE FIRST DAY, *pp. 38-39.* Elizabeth Eckford recalls the events of 3 September 1957, when, following a desegregation decree, she attempted to attend Central High School in Little Rock, Arkansas.
Mayfield, Chris.   LITTLE ROCK, 1957-1960: "THE MIDDLE GROUND TURNS TO QUICKSAND," *pp. 40-44.* Public opinion in Little Rock swung between reactionary to moderate during attempted integration of the public schools and resulted in the closure of all public schools by Governor Faubus rather than accepting submission to desegregation, 1957-60.
Egerton, John.   LITTLE ROCK, 1976: "GOING BACK WOULD BE UNTHINKABLE," *pp. 45-46.* Traces changes occurring since integration in the areas of enrollment, discipline, parental participation, and in-school segregation, 1976.

Masterson, Mike.   LITTLE ROCK, 1979: "THERE HAVE BEEN CHANGES," *pp. 46-47.* Contrasts attitudes on desegregation within the community, the school administration, and the student body 1957 and 1979.

3121. Unsigned.   [NEW ORLEANS]. *Southern Exposure 1979 7(2): 55-63.*
—.   NEW ORLEANS, 1960-1979, *pp. 55-56.* Though known as an oasis of racial tolerance in the South, New Orleans, Louisiana, reacted violently against federally-ordered integration in 1960.
Coles, Robert.   NEW ORLEANS, 1960: "AS BAD AS THEY MAKE IT, THE STRONGER I'LL GET," *pp. 57-60.* Relates the reactions of the mother and grandmother of Tessie Provost, one of three black children picked to be "integrated" into New Orleans all-white public schools, 1960.
Jupiter, Clare.   NEW ORLEANS, 1979: "IT WAS WORTH IT," *pp. 61-62.* Interview with Tessie Provost, her mother Dorothy Provost, and her grandmother, Dora Provost, recalls what the initial integration period, 1961-63 was like for all three.
—.   NEW ORLEANS, 1960: "THE VILEST SORT OF ABUSE," *p. 63.* Psychological and physical threats were used against the three white families which persisted in allowing their children to attend integrated schools in New Orleans, 1960.

3122. Unsigned.   [RESIDENTIAL SEGREGATION IN US CITIES].
Marshall, Harvey and Jiobu, Robert.   RESIDENTIAL SEGREGATION IN UNITED STATES CITIES: A CAUSAL ANALYSIS. *Social Forces 1975 53(3): 449-460.* Investigates causes of black residential segregation. The units of analysis are cities. The relative status of blacks and black population size are important determinants of segregation; these findings are especially interesting given the general belief that black socioeconomic progress is unrelated to changes in segregation, as well as the tendency to ignore absolute size of the black population in analyses of segregation. Also important are the percent black and the relative growth rates of the white and black populations; however, the impact of the latter variable was smaller than anticipated in view of the emphasis often given to it.
Macdonald, K. I.   RESIDENTIAL SEGREGATION IN UNITED STATES CITIES: A COMMENT. *Social Forces 1976 55(1): 85-88.* Discusses quantitative analysis used in the earlier article in determining the extent of residential segregation.
Marshall, Harvey and Jiobu, Robert   RESIDENTIAL SEGREGATION IN UNITED STATES CITIES: A REJOINDER. *Social Forces 1976 55(1): 89-92.*

J/S

3123. Unsigned.   REVITALIZING INNER-CITY MINORITY COMMUNITIES: THE BLACK NEIGHBORHOOD-BASED BUSINESS ENVIRONMENT IN HOUSTON. *Urbanism Past and Present 1977 (4): 11-20.*
Ikemma, William N.   REVITALIZING INNER-CITY MINORITY COMMUNITIES: THE BLACK NEIGHBORHOOD-BASED BUSINESS ENVIRONMENT IN HOUSTON, *pp. 11-18.* A lasting socioeconomic revitalization of Houston's black community depends on both the psychological disposition and managerial skills of the potential black entrepreneur, and the increased support of black-owned products and enterprises.
Manning, David.   COMMENTARY, *pp. 19-20.*

3124. Vaughan, Philip H.   THE CITY AND THE AMERICAN CREED: A LIBERAL AWAKENING DURING THE EARLY TRUMAN PERIOD, 1946-48. *Phylon 1973 34(1): 51-62.* Discusses urban problems and the Negro during the Truman years after World War II.

S

3125. Williams, John A.   THE BLACK ARTIST IN NEW YORK: AN INTERVIEW WITH JOHN A. WILLIAMS. *Centerpoint 1975 1(3): 71-76.* Discusses his feelings on black artists in New York City, compares the outpouring of black writing in the 1960's to the Harlem Renaissance of the 1920's, examines racism and the Pan-African movement as they have affected the black artist, and assesses the relationship of cities and artistic output.

3126. Wilson, Hugh. GETTING IT ON WITH THE DREAM. *New York Affairs 1979 5(4): 66-77.* Traces the experiences, problems, and opportunities of blacks in American suburbs since the mid-1940's, but particularly during the 1970's, and briefly discusses the future of black suburbanites.

Jews

3127. Glaser, Richard. THE GREEK JEWS IN BALTIMORE. *Jewish Social Studies 1976 38(3-4): 321-336.* A study of the 28 Greek Jews in Baltimore indicates that they constitute a unique entity in the Baltimore Jewish population. Some of their traditional holidays have been eliminated in order to conform with Ashkenazim customs of celebration, while others have been modified in their observance because of economic circumstances or a general lack of emphasis within the general Jewish community. Those holidays that have been retained from their Greek origins include a large amount of the traditional modes of celebration. The ethnic solidarity of the Baltimore Greek Jews is declining in strength because of the propensity of the young to marry within the Ashkenazim community and the exposure to other customs.   N. Lederer

3128. Mayer, Egon. GAPS BETWEEN GENERATIONS OF OR-THODOX JEWS IN BORO PARK, BROOKLYN, N.Y. *Jewish Social Studies 1977 39(1-2): 93-104.* The generation gap between Jewish parents and children takes on a unique form in the Orthodox Jewish neighbor-hood of Boro Park. The generations in Boro Park exhibit definite con-tinuities in economic and cultural success from parents to children. However, while the children of Orthodox parents have continued the successful patterns of their parents and have been dependent in their success on that of their elders, tensions generated by status conflict have evolved. Children claim to be more Orthodox than their parents by assert-ing more sophisticated and deeper understanding of Orthodox ritual and practice. The economic successes of the parents are countered by their children's claims to academic and professional gains. Although both parents and children surround themselves with material evidences of success, the generations display different tastes in the acquisition of such objects. Largely based on survey research.   N. Lederer

3129. Mesmer, Joseph. SOME OF MY LOS ANGELES JEWISH NEIGHBORS. *Western States Jewish Hist. Q. 1975 7(3): 191-199.* Personal accounts by the author (1855-1947), written in the 1930's about several of his close friends in Los Angeles. He wrote about his relation-ships with Maurice Kremer (1824-1907) and his wife Matilda, the daugh-ter of Rabbi Joseph Newmark; Eugene Meyer (1842-1925) and his wife Harriet, youngest daughter of Rabbi Newmark; Ephraim Greenbaum; and Isaiah M. Hellman. In the 1870's, Rabbi and Mrs. Newmark lived next door to the author. 18 notes.   R. A. Garfinkle

3130. Petrusak, Frank and Steinert, Steven. THE JEWS OF CHAR-LESTON: SOME OLD WINE IN NEW BOTTLES. *Jewish Social Studies 1976 38(3-4): 337-346.* An analysis of survey data indicates that Jewry in Charleston, South Carolina, constitutes a well-defined, highly structured, nonassimilated ethnic group. The Jewish community retains its distinctiveness as a separate entity from the majority population de-spite great pressures to assimilate. The community has considerable self-identification, and the synagogue and the state of Israel play important roles as ethnic referents. Politically the Charleston Jews are strongly Democratic and have a social welfare and liberal orientation. Primary sources.   N. Lederer

3131. Rosenwaike, Ira. ESTIMATING JEWISH POPULATION DISTRIBUTION IN U.S. METROPOLITAN AREAS IN 1970. *Jewish Social Studies 1974 36(2): 106-117.* Uses the Yiddish mother tongue data of the 1970 US census to determine the Jewish population and pattern of settlement in major metropolitan centers, concentrating on four Standard Metropolitan Statistical Areas: Baltimore, Cleveland, St. Louis, and Washington, D. C. The data implies that a high degree of geographical concentration still exists among Jews in most metropolitan areas, despite the transition to predominantly suburban residence. Yid-dish mother tongue data of the 1970 US census is highly reliable and useful for similar studies of other cities. Primary and secondary sources are in English; 25 notes.   P. E. Schoenberg

3132. Rothchild, Sylvia. A GREAT HAPPENING IN BOSTON: REVOLT OF THE YOUNG. *Present Tense 1976 3(3): 21-26.* Traces the development of the Jewish Student Movement, a renaissance born in 1960 radicalism, from Jewish Boston establishment antipathy to uneasy acceptance by urban and suburban Jewish and Gentile Boston. Describes the establishment and the impact of the student quarterlies *Response* and *Genesis 2*, the Jewish Student Projects, the communal Havurat Shalom, and the *Jewish Catalogue* on the educational and administrative policies of such religious and educational institutions as the Hillel Foundation(s), Boston University, Harvard-Radcliffe, and suburban synagogues. Quotes such movement notables as Alan Mintz, first editor of *Response*; writers Elie Wiesel and Bill Novak; activists Hillel Levine and Rav Kuk; rabbis Arthur Green, Zalman Schachter, Joseph Polak, Ben-Zion Gold, and Lawrence Kushner; professors Bernard Reisman and Leonard Fein. 4 photos.   R. B. Mendel

3133. Silverberg, David. THE "OLD" POOR—AND THE "NEW": WHAT'S HAPPENING TO THEM? *Present Tense 1977 4(3): 59-64.* Examines the plight of American urban Jewish poor. Presents case stud-ies, and quotes Ann G. Wolfe, Misha Avramoff, Yisroel Rosenfeld, Yaa-kov Tzimman, Rose Fefelman, Leonard Haber, Eugene Weiss, Jack Simcha Cohen, Max Friedson, Alfred P. Miller, and Steven Robbins. Cites official government, local community, and Hassidic sources. Pri-mary and secondary sources; 4 photos.   R. B. Mendel

Irish

3134. Casey, Daniel J. HERESY IN THE DIOCESE OF BROOK-LYN: AN UNHOLY TRINITY. *New York Affairs 1978 4(4): 73-86.* Discusses three journalist-novelists, Jimmy Breslin, Pete Hamill, and Joe Flaherty, and their criticism of Catholic Irish Americans in Brooklyn, 1960's-70's.

3135. Monahan, Kathleen. THE IRISH HOUR: AN EXPRESSION OF THE MUSICAL TASTE AND THE CULTURAL VALUES OF THE PITTSBURGH IRISH COMMUNITY. *Ethnicity 1977 4(3): 201-215.* By monitoring the types of Irish music played and requested on a two-hour radio program of Irish music in Pittsburgh, assesses the elements of traditional culture, new culture, and external culture which combine to form present perceptions of Irishness and ethnicity in the Irish community. Though Irish music in America reflects influences from modern society and other ethnic types of music, adherence to and popu-larity of traditional modes and lyrics indicate a strong tie with traditional Irish culture. Further, though Irish music from 1900 to 1970 seemed to be blending into American music, recent trends show growing interest in ballads, anti-English lyrics, and learning Gaelic.   G. A. Hewlett

3136. Morgan, John H. ETHNOCONSCIOUSNESS AND POLITI-CAL POWERLESSNESS: BOSTON'S IRISH. *Social Sci. 1978 53(3): 159-167.* A history of the city of Boston is in a real sense a history of ethnic enclaves and ethnic migratory patterns. As with the early English settlers, so with the later Irish, Italians, and Jews, each group entered at the bottom rung of the socioeconomic ladder gradually to climb up socio-economically and out geographically into the suburbs. However, with each ethnic enclave, some did not middle-classify nor de-ethnicize. The Irish of South Boston are a living example of an intentional ethnic blue-collar community within the megalopolis.   J

Latinos

3137. Chandler, Charles R. VALUE ORIENTATIONS AMONG MEXICAN AMERICANS IN A SOUTHWESTERN CITY. *Sociol. and Social Res. 1974 58(3): 262-271.* Value orientation questions related to activity, integration with kin, trust, and occupational primacy were asked of a random sample of 300 Mexican American men and women in Lubbock, Texas. As hypothesized, "modern" orientations were expressed by younger respondents with more formal schooling and higher-status occupations. Others, and in fact the majority, gave 'traditional' responses. The results are discussed in relation to other studies and in light of modernism theory.   J

3138. Chaney, Elsa M. COLOMBIAN OUTPOST IN NEW YORK CITY. *Society 1977 14(6): 60-64.* Examines the Colombian population settling in Jackson Heights and Queens, New York, including questions of illegal entry, employment, cultural and social assimilation, and politics.

3139. Cohen, Lucy M. THE FEMALE FACTOR IN RESETTLE-MENT. *Society 1977 14(6): 27-30.* Examines the resettlement patterns (especially in urban areas) of Latin American female immigrants to the United States, touching on employment, family obligations, and family ties in native countries; discusses the impact which the Immigration Act of 1965 has had on immigrants of Latin origin.

3140. Comer, John C. "STREET-LEVEL BUREAUCRACY AND POLITICAL SUPPORT": SOME FINDINGS ON MEXICAN AMERICANS. *Urban Affairs Q. 1978 14(2): 207-228.* Attempts to relate service satisfaction with agencies that help, protect, and control with Omaha's Mexican American community's support for the political structure. Consistent with the notion that Mexican Americans "cope" without government, this sample had less contact with government than blacks, or white working and middle classes in Milwaukee. Respondents tended to initiate contacts and were highly satisfied with results at roughly the same rate as the Milwaukee group. Because the data suggests that the firm dispositions developed toward the system are little effected by its short-term performance, the relation between system output and system support may vary from situation to situation. Discusses possible local explanations for these findings. 5 tables, 9 notes, biblio.
L. N. Beecher

3141. Cooney, Rosemary Santana and Contreras, Maria Alina. RESIDENCE PATTERNS OF SOCIAL REGISTER CUBANS: A STUDY OF MIAMI, SAN JUAN, AND NEW YORK SMSAS. *Cuban Studies 1978 8(2): 33-50.* The Social Register that was started in Havana before the revolution of 1959 has been continued by Cuban exiles. This list provides a useful tool to study the exile community and measure change. Cubans who migrated to Puerto Rico have maintained a much higher degree of class segregation than those living in the continental United States. Primary and secondary sources; 5 tables, 11 notes, biblio.
J. Lewis

3142. Cortés, Felix; Falcón, Angel; and Flores, Juan. THE CUL-TURAL EXPRESSION OF PUERTO RICANS IN NEW YORK: A THEORETICAL PERSPECTIVE AND CRITICAL REVIEW. *Latin Am. Perspectives 1976 3(3): 117-152.* Analyzes Puerto Rican culture in New York City. Formulates a set of seven theses about culture and class, using a Marxist framework. Analyzes aspects of proletarian culture emerging in the music, poetry, and drama of New York Puerto Ricans and the contradictions that surround its commercialization.
J. L. Dietz

3143. Domínguez, Virginia R. SPANISH-SPEAKING CARIB-BEANS IN NEW YORK: "THE MIDDLE RACE." *Rev. Interamericana Rev. [Puerto Rico] 1973 3(2): 135-142.* Although American society traditionally classifies its races as either black or white, such racial distinctions produce bewildering complications among Spanish-speaking communities in New York City. These communities bring their own racial prejudices and perceptions with them from the West Indies and are forced to live in a larger society which maintains different criteria. The result is behavior that often is unpredictable by either native American or West Indian standards. Based on research in Washington Heights, N.Y.
J. A. Lewis

3144. Faught, Jim D. CHICANOS IN A MEDIUM-SIZED CITY: DEMOGRAPHIC AND SOCIOECONOMIC CHARACTERISTICS. *Aztlán 1976 7(2): 307-326.* A study of the Chicano population of South Bend, Indiana, based on 1974 interviews with 136 respondents. Examines age and occupational structure of the population, education, income, and economic mobility. Finds evidence that the 1970 US Census heavily overrepresents the more highly educated Chicanos, and that it seriously underestimates the number of persons living at very low income levels. Enlightened action to alleviate the chronically tenuous economic position of such persons as many of those surveyed requires first a general agreement on the facts involved. 8 tables, fig., 14 notes.
L. W. Van Wyk

3145. Garcia, Juan R. HISTORY OF CHICANOS IN CHICAGO HEIGHTS. *Aztlán 1976 7(2): 291-306.* A large number of Mexicans and Chicanos came to Chicago Heights during 1910's-20's. They were recruited by the railroads, steel companies, sugar beet concerns; some job-hopped north gradually; and others came and found work on the advice and with the help of relatives. Chicago Heights Mexican nationals were apparently spared during the forced repatriations of the 1930's, but a great many left for economic reasons. World War II and the succeeding prosperity brought a new influx of immigrants, who arrived as agricultural laborers but soon shifted to year-round jobs in other sectors. The present Mexican and Chicano population represents mostly this second group of immigrants and their children. Reviews recent organizational efforts in the local Chicano community. Secondary sources; 55 notes.
L. W. Van Wyk

3146. Garza, Rudolph O. de la. VOTING PATTERNS IN "BI-CUL-TURAL EL PASO": A CONTEXTUAL ANALYSIS OF CHICANO VOTING BEHAVIOR. *Aztlán 1974 5(1-2): 235-260.*

3147. Gelber, David. CRYSTAL CITY'S CRACKED PROMISE. *Working Papers for a New Soc. 1976 4(1): 30-35.* Discusses Chicano political activity in Crystal City, Texas, since the 1970 town elections in which Chicanos ousted Anglos from the school board and city hall; also discusses the political division within the Chicano community.

3148. George, Philip Brandt. REAFFIRMATION OF IDENTITY: A LATINO CASE IN EAST CHICAGO. *Indiana Folklore 1977 10(2): 139-148.* The author's folklore project in urbanized East Chicago, Indiana, 1976, among Cuban Americans and Puerto Ricans, which included assessment of ethnic oral tradition, found that rather than being detrimental to folklore culture, urban areas often strengthened folk beliefs and were responsible for affirmation of ethnicity.

3149. Gonzalez, Rosalinda Mendez. MEXICAN WOMEN AND FAMILIES: RURAL-TO-URBAN, AND INTERNATIONAL MI-GRATION. *Southwest Econ. and Soc. 1978-79 4(2): 14-27.* Discusses the labor activities of Mexican women and their families after immigration to the United States from Mexico, specifically the ability of immigrants to fit into the American capitalist system from a rural labor system, 1970's.

3150. Gray, Lois S. THE JOBS PUERTO RICANS HOLD IN NEW YORK CITY. *Monthly Labor Rev. 1975 98(10): 12-16.* Examines white- and blue-collar occupations of Puerto Ricans in New York City in 1970 and the high rate of unemployment Puerto Ricans experienced that year.
S

3151. Grider, Sylvia Ann. *CON SAFOS*: MEXICAN-AMERI-CANS, NAMES AND GRAFFITI. *J. of Am. Folklore 1975 88(348): 132-142.* Graffiti in Mexican-American districts in the United States reflect the high value attached to personal names in Mexican culture. The term *con safos* (roughly, "the same to you") is used to protect name graffiti from defacement by suggesting that any slurs added pertain to the vandal alone. The graffiti are intended for people who will recognize the names. Interviews from Dallas, Texas, and secondary sources; 16 illus., 26 notes.
W. D. Piersen

3152. Gutierrez, Armando G. and Hirsch, Herbert. POLITICAL MATURATION AND POLITICAL AWARENESS: THE CASE OF THE CRYSTAL CITY CHICANO. *Aztlán 1974 5(1-2): 295-312.* Examines the case of Crystal City, Texas, where Mexican Americans were elected to a majority of seats on the school board.
S

3153. Holscher, Louis M. TIENE ARTE VALOR AFUERA DEL BARRIO: THE MURALS OF EAST LOS ANGELES AND BOYLE HEIGHTS. *J. of Ethnic Studies 1976 4(3): 43-52.* Discusses the murals painted by young Chicano artists during the late 1960's-70's, their colors, line, depth, and the meaning they hold both for the barrio inhabitant and the non-Chicano. They are newspapers on walls presenting the attitudes, feelings, and life styles of the Chicano community, and can greatly enlighten those unaware of Chicano history and culture. They represent a search for identity, an affirmation of Chicano culture, a concern for poverty and racism, and a joy in brotherhood, in "Chicanismo." They continue the tradition fostered by David Siqueiros and Diego Rivera. 6 illus., map.
G. J. Bobango

3154. Holtz, Janicemarie Allard. THE "LOW-RIDERS": POR-TRAIT OF A YOUTH SUBCULTURE. *Youth and Soc. 1975 6(4): 495-512.* Describes a mostly Mexican American subculture in East Los Angeles based on the possession of an elaborately modified and decorated automobile. The subculture emphasizes a media-based image of leisure. Based on 1974 interviews and observations, secondary works; 9 notes, biblio.   J. H. Sweetland

3155. Kahn, David. CHICANO STREET MURALS: PEOPLE'S ART IN THE EAST LOS ANGELES BARRIO. *Aztlán 1975 6(1): 117-121.* Chicano mural art is a reflection of a social, cultural, and political reality in which Mexican Americans find themselves in the barrio. The murals give a visible identity to those who have been denied recognition. The themes of frustration, despair, hope, and creativity find symbolic expression in this art form. 9 notes.
                                          R. Griswold del Castillo

3156. Lampe, Philip E. THE ACCULTURATION OF MEXICAN AMERICANS IN PUBLIC AND PAROCHIAL SCHOOLS. *Sociol. Analysis 1975 36(1): 57-66.* Studies the influence of the school system on the acculturation of Mexican American students in San Antonio, Texas, during 1973, by conducting a survey of eighth-grade minority students from nine public and nine parochial schools to discover the extent to which their feelings, attitudes, and values were similar to those of a group of White Anglo-Saxon Protestant respondents. The school system attended made a greater difference than did socioeconomic status or sex. Parochial school respondents were significantly more acculturated than their public school counterparts, and the difference remained even when other variables were controlled.   J

3157. Lopez, David E. CHICANO LANGUAGE LOYALTY IN AN URBAN SETTING. *Sociol. and Social Res. 1978 62(2): 267-278.* Previous investigators have concluded that the use of Spanish is stable among Chicanos in the Southwest. But most Chicanos are bilingual and bilingualism involving socially dominant and subordinate languages usually signals language shift to the dominant language. Data from Los Angeles indicate that in this urban environment the intragenerational loyalty to and intergenerational transmission of Spanish among Chicanos is only moderately greater than ethnic language maintenance among European immigrant groups earlier in this century. Chicanos who grew up in Mexico continue to use Spanish but second and especially subsequent generations are shifting to English and not passing Spanish on to their children. The persistence of Spanish is accounted for by continuing immigration, a model that fits the Chicano language experience better than wave immigration, colonialism or ethnic enclave models developed to describe the experiences of other groups. Loyalty to Spanish in Los Angeles is related to low educational attainment, but not necessarily to other aspects of social status. Nor is it clearly related to continuing ethnic social ties, suggesting that language shift does not necessarily mean a decline in ethnic integration.   J

3158. Martínez, Oscar J. CHICANOS AND THE BORDER CI-TIES: AN INTERPRETIVE ESSAY. *Pacific Hist. Rev. 1977 46(1): 85-106.* A distinctive lifestyle syncretizing Anglo-Saxon and Mexican cultures has developed in border cities along the United States-Mexican border. As a result, border Chicanos have less ambivalent bicultural social patterns than Chicanos isolated in enclaves in the US interior. Mexico's border cities have historically served three major economic functions: as springboards for workers coming to the United States, as receptacles for economically displaced Mexicans who formerly resided in the United States, and as a locus for cheap labor in assembly factories. One result of these economic functions has been widespread poverty in Mexican border cities. Based on documents and on published primary and secondary sources; 68 notes.   W. K. Hobson

3159. Muñoz, Carlos, Jr. THE POLITICS OF PROTEST AND CHI-CANO LIBERATION: A CASE STUDY OR REPRESSION AND COOPTATION. *Aztlán 1974 5(1-2): 119-141.* Reviews a case study of Mexican American political protest involving a 1968 school walk-out staged in East Los Angeles, as an example of the overall failure to institute positive social change.   S

3160. Percal, Raul Moncarz. THE GOLDEN CAGE: CUBANS IN MIAMI. *Int. Migration [Netherlands] 1978 16(3-4): 160-173.* Evidence

indicates that mobility of Cuban Americans in Miami has been minimal. "In terms of educational mobility . . . the loss of human capital has been very significant." Short-term measures of geographic mobility out of Florida through the Cuban Refugee Center and returning to Florida were very ineffective. The high rate of neutralization among Cubans since 1970 "may enhance their political leverage to economic and political power, but the political power would have come late to the original waves of refugees." As far as income mobility is concerned the study shows that the great percentage of Cuban women in the labor force makes the family income sufficient to own their own homes. 8 tables, 23 notes, biblio.
                                              E. P. Stickney

3161. Romo, Ricardo. THE URBANIZATION OF SOUTHWEST-ERN CHICANO IN THE EARLY 20TH CENTURY. *New Scholar 1977 6: 183-208.* Covers urbanization by means of three major compo-nents—structural, demographic, and behavioral—which show that Mexi-can Americans are joining urban society with significant effects on their ethnic identity. Stereotypes are increasingly dated. Part of a special issue, "New Directions In Chicano Scholarship." Table, 72 notes.
                                              D. K. Pickens

3162. Rosen, Gerald. THE DEVELOPMENT OF THE CHICANO MOVEMENT IN LOS ANGELES FROM 1967 TO 1969. *Aztlán 1973 4(1): 155-183.*

3163. Rosenberg, Terry J. and Lake, Robert W. TOWARD A RE-VISED MODEL OF RESIDENTIAL SEGREGATION AND SUC-CESSION: PUERTO RICANS IN NEW YORK, 1960-1970. *Am. J. of Sociol. 1976 81(5): 1142-1150.* Generally accepted models of ethnic assimilation outline a pattern of decreasing residential segregation asso-ciated with increasing similarity to native whites. Similar models for the black population posit continuing residential concentration combined with rapid turnover and succession. Analysis of data on recent settlement patterns of Puerto Ricans in New York City indicates that this group is conforming to neither type of previously accepted model. Competition between the Puerto Rican minority and the larger, more economically advantaged black minority, a new set of public housing opportunities, and the return migration of successful Puerto Ricans are factors that were not considered in previously developed models. A new model of residential segregation and succession must incorporate these realities of contempo-rary urbanization.   J

3164. Simson, Eve. CHICANO STREET MURALS. *J. of Popular Culture 1976 10(3): 642-652.* Discusses the sociocultural significance of Los Angeles Chicano street murals, assessing them as assertions of eth-nicity and artistic expressions.

3165. Stoddard, Ellwyn R. THE ADJUSTMENT OF MEXICAN AMERICAN BARRIO FAMILIES TO FORCED HOUSING RELO-CATION. *Social Sci. Q. 1973 53(4): 749-759.* Self-evaluations of adjust-ment success were compared with ten spatial and social factors. A serendipitous discovery was that more crucial to barrio happiness than extended or nuclear family relationships was the mini-neighborhood so-cial unit (an intimate visiting clique of five to seven families).   J

3166. Torres, Esteban E. NEW SPIRIT IN THE BARRIOS. *Cry California 1973 8(4): 9-12.* Discusses a new spirit of political aware-ness in the Mexican-American barrios of East Los Angeles and elsewhere in California during the 1970's.   S

Asians

3167. Bonacich, Edna; Light, Ivan H.; and Wong, Charles Choy. KOREANS IN BUSINESS. *Society 1977 14(6): 54-59.* Discusses the recent (1973-77) growth in the Korean population of Los Angeles, Cali-fornia, and their success in small businesses.

3168. Cha, Marn J. AN ETHNIC POLITICAL ORIENTATION AS A FUNCTION OF ASSIMILATION: WITH REFERENCE TO KO-REANS IN LOS ANGELES. *J. of Korean Affairs 1975 5(3): 14-25.* Measures the degree of assimilation and its relation to minority politics and political behavior of Korean Americans in 1970.

3169. Hartman, Chester W. SAN FRANCISCO'S INTERNATIONAL HOTEL: CASE STUDY OF A TURF STRUGGLE. *Radical Am. 1978 12(3): 47-58.* The local land-use issue embodied in the effort to prevent the expulsion of elderly Filipino and Chinese men from the International Hotel in Chinatown and its planned razing by foreign property interests reveals the limitations of liberal city government when challenged by property interests and shows the failure of involved left-wing groups to present a successful unified opposition. The failure of adequate preparation and the use of flawed oppositional strategy was revealed through the unsuccessful effort by demonstrators to prevent the eviction of the tenants of the hotel on 4 August 1977. The International Hotel question remains unresolved. The author was a participant-observer during the International Hotel activities.   N. Lederer

3170. Hessler, Richard M.; Nolan, Michael F.; Ogbru, Benjamin; and New, Peter Kong-Ming. INTRAETHNIC DIVERSITY: HEALTH CARE OF THE CHINESE-AMERICANS. *Human Organization 1975 34(3): 253-262.* The results of a survey of 200 households in Boston's Chinatown, suggesting a wide diversity of use between Chinese and Western medicine.   S

3171. Hirati, Lucie C. TOWARD A POLITICAL ECONOMY OF CHINESE AMERICA: A STUDY OF PROPERTY OWNERSHIP IN LOS ANGELES CHINATOWN. *Amerasia J. 1975 3(1): 76-95.* Discusses the employment, income, age, sex, and racial distribution of the Chinatown area of Los Angeles, California, in the 1970's, alleging internal colonialism in property ownership patterns.

3172. Johnson, Colleen Leahy and Johnson, Frank Arvid. INTERACTION RULES AND ETHNICITY—THE JAPANESE AND CAUCASIANS IN HONOLULU. *Social Forces 1975 54(2): 452-466.* The concept of ethnicity has traditionally embraced varying customs, structures, languages, attitudes, histories, and ideologies. More recently, ethnic identification has been studied as it sets boundaries between diverse subcultures. This report examines ethnicity as a function of distinctive interaction rules in encounters both within and outside the Japanese American community in Hawaii. Cost and reward criteria derived from exchange theory are related to interaction rules in an effort to account for dissonance in interethnic communication.   J

3173. Kuo, Wen H. and Lin, Nan. ASSIMILATION OF CHINESE-AMERICANS IN WASHINGTON, D.C. *Sociol. Q. 1977 18(3): 340-352.* Chinese-Americans in Washington, D.C., were studied to show their present assimilation into American society. We found that higher socioeconomic attainment had an insignificant effect on the Chinese-American's centrifugal tendencies when the effects of education were controlled. Education exerted sizable effects on the absorbing of Chinese-Americans, while the Chinese friendship tie served to sustain the Chinese subculture. Overall, most Chinese-Americans have preserved their key cultural values. The relatively slow pace of assimilation among Chinese-Americans was attributed to their subsocietal structure, which is a consequence of the difference in racial and cultural distinction from American whites, as Warner and Srole (1945) hypothesized.   J

3174. Kuroda, Yasumasa; Suzuki, Tatsuzo; and Hayashi, Chikio. A CROSS-NATIONAL ANALYSIS OF THE JAPANESE CHARACTER AMONG JAPANESE-AMERICANS IN HONOLULU. *Ethnicity 1978 5(1): 42-59.* The Institute of Statistical Mathematics has conducted, at five-year intervals since 1953, statistical studies of Japanese national characteristics. The authors conducted a similar study among Japanese Americans in Honolulu in 1971, for purposes of comparison with Japanese data. Japanese Americans, while often responding similarly, differed from Japanese in attributing less importance to money, in more strongly insisting on the value of popular government, and in emphasizing the importance of religion. Interesting geometric relationships, which however are difficult to interpret precisely, were found in the area of attitudes toward the traditional values of *giri* and *ninjo,* respectively and, very roughly, reciprocity and loyalty. 4 tables, 5 fig., 5 notes, ref.   L. W. Van Wyk

3175. Li, Peter S. OCCUPATIONAL ACHIEVEMENT AND KINSHIP ASSISTANCE AMONG CHINESE IMMIGRANTS IN CHICAGO. *Sociol. Q. 1977 18(4): 478-489.* Explores the process of stratification among Chinese immigrants in Chicago, and examines the

effects of kinship assistance on the career cycle. While kinship assistance is an important resource to some immigrants during and after migration, it frequently obligates the immigrants to remain in the ethnic business, and thereby hinders their upward mobility. This study suggests the usefulness as well as the limitations of kinship assistance in the stratification process of ethnic minorities.   J

3176. Maykovich, Minako K. TO STAY OR NOT TO STAY: DIMENSIONS OF ETHNIC ASSIMILATION. *Int. Migration Rev. 1976 10(3): 377-387.* Assesses the assimilation and social organization of Asian American immigrants, specifically Japanese, Chinese, and Filipinos, in San Francisco, California, in the 1970's; evaluates their degree of social alienation.

3177. Nishi, Setsuko Matsunaga. THE NEW WAVE OF ASIAN AMERICANS. *New York Affairs 1979 5(3): 82-96.* Discusses problems and concerns facing Asian Americans as of 1970 and the progress New York City has made in providing needed services to its Asian population, which will almost double by 1980.

3178. Tinker, John N. INTERMARRIAGE AND ETHNIC BOUNDARIES: THE JAPANESE AMERICAN CASE. *J. of Social Issues 1973 29(2): 49-66.* Intermarriage is an especially sensitive indicator of the permeability of ethnic boundaries: The rate can tell us something about how rigid the boundaries are, while the patterns can suggest the forces that maintain or reduce them. A survey of the marriage records of Japanese Americans in Fresno, California indicates that both the pattern of intermarriage (that is, whether the minority group partners are male or female) and the rate of intermarriage changed during the 1960's. Explains these changes and discusses implications for the boundary surrounding the Japanese Americans.   J

3179. Yuan, D. Y. SOCIAL CONSEQUENCES OF RECENT CHANGES IN THE DEMOGRAPHIC STRUCTURE OF NEW YORK CHINATOWN. *Phylon 1974 35(2): 156-164.* The 1955 federal law permitting increased immigration of Chinese nationals has resulted in a new social structure in New York's Chinatown. Families began to arrive, replacing the aged, single men of the past. Taiwanese immigrants are usually well educated and employable; those from Hong Kong are considerably less so. Tension between the two groups, low salaries, and lack of facilities for growing numbers of teenagers are primary problems. Existing social structures are poorly equipped to deal with these new problems. Table, 27 notes.   V. L. Human

Others

3180. Baran, Alina. DISTRIBUTION OF THE POLISH ORIGIN POPULATION IN THE USA. *Polish Western Affairs [Poland] 1976 17(1-2): 139-144.* According to US census data, Polish Americans are one of the seven largest ethnic groups. First-generation Poles still live in central cities, but second-generation Poles live in suburbs and enjoy a higher socioeconomic status. Polish immigrants during 1950-70 settled principally in New York, New Jersey, and Illinois; their children usually remained in these states.   M. Swiecicka-Ziemianek

3181. Bee, Robert and Gingerich, Ronald. COLONIALISM, CLASSES, AND ETHNIC IDENTITY: NATIVE AMERICANS AND THE NATIONAL POLITICAL ECONOMY. *Studies in Comparative Int. Development 1977 12(2): 70-93.* Traces constantly changing federal policy which has caused Indian society to become an internal colonial system. Domination and exploitation hinder the reservation Indian and the urban Indian in a fashion similar to other racial and ethnic groups. However, the urban Indian seems better situated than his reservation counterpart. Evidence also indicates that immersion in urban culture may tend to preserve ethnic identity. Complex circumstances render the internal colonial model inaccurate in measuring Indian status. Primary and secondary sources; 48 refs., 13 notes.   S. A. Farmerie

3182. Carlson, Alvar W. A MAP ANALYSIS OF MIDDLE EAST IMMIGRANTS IN DETROIT AND SUBURBS, 1961-1974. *Int. Migration [Netherlands] 1976 14(4): 283-298.* Analysis of major Middle Eastern immigrant groups located in the Detroit metropolitan area. Uses data derived from Petitions of Naturalization to determine some of the characteristics of residential clusterings among Middle Easterners. This source could be useful for "studies of migrations and settling of immigrant ethnic groups in the United States, especially on a micro scale." Based on Petitions of Naturalization (Form N-405), interviews, official statistics, and secondary works; 9 maps, 2 tables, 2 graphs, 12 notes.

R. C. Alltmont

3183. Chadwick, Bruce A. and Stauss, Joseph H. THE ASSIMILATION OF AMERICAN INDIANS INTO URBAN SOCIETY: THE SEATTLE CASE. *Human Organization 1975 34(4): 359-370.* Shows that American Indians who lived all their life in a city kept their traditions as much as those who recently left the reservation.

3184. Clinton, Lawrence; Chadwick, Bruce A.; and Bahr, Howard M. URBAN RELOCATION RECONSIDERED: ANTECEDENTS OF EMPLOYMENT AMONG INDIAN MALES. *Rural Sociol. 1975 40(2): 117-133.* Examines the results of a 1966 follow-up study of economic consequences of urban relocation of 202 American Indian males who had been relocated by the Bureau of Indian Affairs in 1963, detailing analytical procedures, variables, and findings.

3185. Dobyns, Henry F.; Stoffle, Richard W.; and Jones, Kristine. NATIVE AMERICAN URBANIZATION AND SOCIO-ECONOMIC INTEGRATION IN THE SOUTHWESTERN UNITED STATES. *Ethnohistory 1975 22(2): 155-179.* Comparison of settlement patterns on the San Carlos, Ft. Apache, Cocopah, Walapai, Havasupai and Kaibab Paiute Indian reservations reveals that lumbering, cattle husbandry and other business—not only federal payrolls—generate "agency town" nucleation and growth. The timing of federal protection of natural resources for Indian entrepreneurs to exploit has proved to be a crucial factor in urbanization.

J

3186. Gavelis, Vytautas. A DESCRIPTIVE STUDY OF THE EDUCATIONAL ATTAINMENT, OCCUPATION, AND GEOGRAPHICAL LOCATION OF THE CHILDREN OF LITHUANIAN DISPLACED PERSONS AND OF AMERICAN BORN PARENTS WHO ATTENDED IMMACULATE CONCEPTION PRIMARY SCHOOL IN EAST ST. LOUIS FROM 1948 TO 1968. *Lituanus 1976 22(1): 72-75.* Discusses the summary results of a Ph.D. dissertation comparing the educational and occupational attainment of two groups of children of Lithuanian family background. The parents of one group were American born and English speaking, the other Lithuanian born and non-English speaking. Recommendations for further research based on the results of the study are made.

K. N. T. Crowther

3187. Hartman, Peter and McIntosh, Karyl. EVIL EYE BELIEFS COLLECTED IN UTICA, NEW YORK. *New York Folklore 1978 4(1-4): 60-69.* Discusses evil eye, or malocchio, folklore collected among Italian Americans in Utica, New York, and describes perceptions of the power of the evil eye.

3188. Hartman, Peter and Tull, Marc. PHOTOGRAPHIC DOCUMENTATION OF A POLISH-AMERICAN COMMUNITY. *New York Folklore 1978 4(1-4): 21-34.* Discusses a study of Polish Americans in East and West Utica and New York Mills, New York, based on their discussion of photographs by the article authors to evoke memories of growing up in an ethnic community.

3189. Jacoby, Susan. THE ROOTS OF IMMIGRATION. *New York Affairs 1976 3(2): 54-67.* Unemployment and lack of opportunity at home force many young Italians to emigrate to the United States. More realistic and educated than their predecessors, these newcomers are providing New York City's neighborhoods with a steady flow of solid citizens.

J

3190. Kerri, James Nwannukwu. "PUSH" AND "PULL" FACTORS: REASONS FOR MIGRATION AS A FACTOR IN AMERINDIAN URBAN ADJUSTMENT. *Human Organization 1976 35(2): 215-220.* Discusses reasons for migration of Indians in the United States and Canada, based on research conducted in 1972.

3191. Kotchek, Lydia. ETHNIC VISIBILITY AND ADAPTIVE STRATEGIES: SAMOANS IN THE SEATTLE AREA. *J. of Ethnic Studies 1977 4(4): 29-38.* Any identified migrant population may be heterogenous and may use a variety of adaptive strategies in its new environment. Stresses the importance of the relative visibility of the group among the host population as one factor affecting both adaptation in general and the availability of various strategies. The Samoans in Seattle are a colony of some 700 people having almost no visibility. They use three main adaptive alternatives: *Fa'aSamoa,* or maintaining the signal native culture of kinship ties and religious affiliation; *PanSamoa,* or institutional organization to tap into available funds for ethnic political power and cultural maintenance; and *Individual isolation,* or voluntary departure from "Samoan-ness." Concludes by comparing Seattle to Hawaii where Samoans have relatively high visibility and are much less free to choose methods of adaptation and more likely to conform to stereotypical behavior. Primary and secondary references; 11 notes.

G. J. Bobango

3192. Lynch, Lawrence. IN THE URBAN SPIRIT. *Westways 1975 67(3): 22-25, 70.* Three Los Angeles American Indians assess current Indian problems and relate how each has come to terms with his heritage.

S

3193. Margavio, Anthony V. and Molyneaux, J. Lambert. RESIDENTIAL SEGREGATION OF ITALIANS IN NEW ORLEANS AND SELECTED AMERICAN CITIES. *Louisiana Studies 1973 12(4): 639-648.*

3194. Margon, Arthur. INDIANS AND IMMIGRANTS: A COMPARISON OF GROUPS NEW TO THE CITY. *J. of Ethnic Studies 1977 4(4): 17-28.* Questions the widespread view that "Native Americans are beset with special, nearly insurmountable difficulties because of the dissonance between their traditional cultures and the demands and patterns of modern urban living." At issue is how much group experience is the special provenance of the group and how much an aspect of the process of moving to and coping with an alien environment. Federally assisted Indian relocatees make up, at best, only one-third of urban Indians, so research efforts must be redirected. "There is evidence that many Native Americans migrate . . . and adapt quite successfully to urban life." This is because migration is not directly from reservation to city, but involves a set of "intermediate steps" to small town, small city, and large city. A 50% return rate to the reservation is no more extreme than that of many other immigrant groups. The whites' labeling of all Indians as "Indians" regardless of tribal differences is the same process of ignoring intragroup differences that Italians or Jews experienced. Native Americans face a situation no different from that faced before World War II by the still unhomogenized members of European ethnic groups. Secondary sources; 21 notes.

G. J. Bobango

3195. Mathias, Elizabeth. THE GAME AS CREATOR OF THE GROUP IN AN ITALIAN-AMERICAN COMMUNITY. *Pennsylvania Folklife 1974 23(4): 22-31.* Discusses the locale and mechanics of the Italian game *bocce ball,* and reveals how it has preserved cultural identity through its formation of group ties among male Italian immigrants in Philadelphia.

S

3196. Mathias, Elizabeth. THE ITALIAN-AMERICAN FUNERAL: PERSISTENCE THROUGH CHANGE. *Western Folklore 1974 33(1): 35-50.* Discusses retention and modification of the social and ritual elements in southern Italian funeral practices by Italian-American immigrants living in Philadelphia. Based on primary and secondary sources and on oral interviews; 11 illus., graph, 2 charts, 23 notes.

S. L. Myres

3197. Melendy, Patrick. TAX EXEMPTION: THE RIGHT OF URBAN INDIANS. *Indian Hist. 1978 11(3): 29-31, 59.* Almost half of the Native Americans in the United States live off the reservations, and most of these live in cities. The property they own off the reservation is taxed by state and local authorities, but since much of this property has been acquired with aid from the US Government, it should be considered tribal property and not taxed by local governments. 3 notes.

E. D. Johnson

3198. Obidinski, Eugene. THE LOS ANGELES POLONIA. *Polish Am. Studies 1974 31(2): 43-47.* Reviews Neil C. Sandberg's *Ethnic Identity and Assimilation: The Polish-American Community Case Study*

of Metropolitan Los Angeles (New York: Praeger, 1974). Discusses the use of "survey research rather than content analysis of documents and symbols," and the delineation of ethnicity in terms of cultural, religious, and national aspects. However, the detailed analysis of methodology with emphasis on the group cohesiveness scale will interest only the sociologist.
S. R. Pliska

3199. O'Leary, Timothy and Schoenberg, Sandra. ETHNICITY AND SOCIAL CLASS CONVERGENCE IN AN ITALIAN COMMUNITY: THE HILL IN ST. LOUIS. *Missouri Hist. Soc. Bull. 1977 33(2): 77-86.* Describes the economic and cultural forces that created and maintained "The Hill" as a distinctive Italian community. Since 1950 residents of "The Hill" have stressed their ethnicity, tried to develop pride in their community, and battled to prevent their area from falling victim to commercial blight and economic deterioration. Based on secondary and newspaper sources; 2 illus., photo, 26 notes.   H. T. Lovin

3200. Paučo, Joseph. TWENTY YEARS OF THE SLOVAK INSTITUTE IN CLEVELAND. *Slovakia 1973 23(46): 16-23.* Traces the history of the Slovak Institute of Cleveland during 1952-72. Founded at St. Andrew Svorad Abbey in Cleveland, Ohio, 15 September 1952, the purpose of the Institute was to give support to Slovak writers and artists. The Institute publishes the Slovak cultural quarterly *Most*, has a library of 70,000 items, and has established a branch in Rome.
J. Williams

3201. Pienkos, Donald E. DIMENSIONS OF ETHNICITY: A PRELIMINARY REPORT ON THE MILWAUKEE POLISH AMERICAN POPULATION. *Polish Am. Studies 1973 30(1): 5-19.* There still is a strong contemporary ethnicity among the descendents of the 20th-century immigrants. In an in-person study based on interviews with 1) leading members of Milwaukee's Polish population, 2) randomly selected individuals, 3) students of Polish ancestry, and 4) non-Polish college students, the author concludes that ethnic consciousness will be bolstered only with an energetic effort by the Polish government itself to present a more positive image of contemporary Poland. 12 notes.
S. R. Pliska

3202. Pienkos, Donald E. FOREIGN AFFAIRS PERCEPTIONS OF ETHNICS. THE POLISH AMERICANS OF MILWAUKEE. *Ethnicity 1974 1(3): 223-236.* Concerns attitudes toward homeland, related American foreign policies, and the continuing interest in homeland problems of American-born ethnic group members. A study of Milwaukee Poles reveals ideological and generational differences; active Polish Americans retain a stronger sense of ethnic identification, family ties in Poland, and language usage than other Polish Americans. They know more about Polish organizations and issues related to Poland. Analysis also controlled for occupational, educational, age, residential, and ideological variables. 4 tables, 23 notes.   E. Barkan

3203. Pier, Andrew V. VISIBLE SIGNS OF SLOVAK CULTURE IN CLEVELAND, OHIO. *Slovakia 1975 25(48): 73-79.*

3204. Price, John A. THE DEVELOPMENT OF URBAN ETHNIC INSTITUTIONS BY U.S. AND CANADIAN INDIANS. *Ethnic Groups 1976 1(2): 107-131.* An account of the growth of institutions (welfare agencies, bars, churches, social clubs, cultural activities, newsletters, etc.) catering solely or largely for Indians in US and Canadian cities, with special reference to Los Angeles and Toronto.   M. J. Clark

3205. Roberts, Alden E. MIGRATION, LABOR MOBILITY, AND RELOCATION ASSISTANCE: THE CASE OF THE AMERICAN INDIAN. *Social Service Rev. 1977 51(3): 464-473.* Of nonmigrant Indian families, those in areas not receiving assistance from the Bureau of Indian Affairs and those in urban areas where BIA funds are available, the latter group has a better relative and absolute standard of living; assistance needs a broader base.

3206. Simon, Andrea J. ETHNICITY AS A COGNITIVE MODEL: IDENTITY VARIATIONS IN A GREEK IMMIGRANT COMMUNITY. *Ethnic Groups 1979 2(2): 133-154.* Studies Greek Americans in New York City, discerning types of adaptation to the question of ethnic identity versus assimilation. The orientations are organized around two Greek Orthodox churches, St. Demetrios, which has adopted modern

architectural styles and dress patterns, and St. Markela, which clings to traditional and Old World ways. 5 notes, ref.   T. W. Smith

3207. Sorkin, Alan L. THE ECONOMIC AND SOCIAL STATUS OF THE AMERICAN INDIAN, 1940-1970. *J. of Negro Educ. 1976 45(4): 432-447.* Compares the economic and social progress of American Indians with that of white and black Americans, and notes that despite a great deal of progress among Indians now in urban areas, many reservation Indians are functionally illiterate and unemployed. 5 tables, 41 notes.
B. D. Johnson

3208. Stanbury, W. T. RESERVE AND URBAN INDIANS IN BRITISH COLUMBIA: A SOCIAL AND ECONOMIC PROFILE. *BC Studies [Canada] 1975 Summer (26): 39-64.* In 1971, a survey of Indians living off reserves in British Columbia was undertaken. The sample is used to develop socioeconomic characteristics such as age-sex composition, birth rates, dependency ratios, marital status, and housing. Comparisons are made with on reserve Indians. Primary and secondary sources; 63 notes.   W. L. Marr

3209. Tax, Sol. THE IMPACT OF URBANIZATION ON AMERICAN INDIANS. *Ann. of the Am. Acad. of Pol. and Social Sci. 1978 436: 121-136.* Native Americans are among the few peoples who maintain kinship and sharing cultures which contrast greatly with our large, economically oriented, individualized, impersonal, urbanizing society. Purely material requirements lead to rapidly increasing involvements. The question is "with what effect?" This paper suggests that Indians somehow frustrate attempts even to research the question by methods which suit the impersonal society. Answers will come from them when Indian people are given the means to find their own ways in the new environment.   J

3210. Thuma, Linnie H. IMAGE AND IMAGINATION: HOW AN ETHNIC COMMUNITY SEES ITSELF. *New York Folklore 1978 4(1-4): 7-19.* Discusses the perceptions of the 4,000 Polish Americans in the former textile milling village, New York Mills, toward their ethnicity, history, and important traditions, based on a three-month study. Traces the town's beginnings, 1800's-40's, when it was predominantly Scottish and Welsh, through the time it became mostly Polish in the early 20th century, until the closure of the mills in 1951.

3211. Unsigned. [SPOKANE'S INDIAN CENTER]. *Pacific Northwesterner 1974 18(1): 11-20.*
Unsigned. NEW INDIAN CENTER ASTOUNDING, pp. 11-14.
Bond, Rowland J. CENTER'S BIRTH WAS PAINFUL, pp. 14-20.
    Recounts the establishment and development of the Pacific Northwest Indian Center in Spokane, Washington, 1966-74.   S

3212. Vecoli, Rudolph J. THE COMING OF AGE OF ITALIAN AMERICANS: 1945-1974. *Ethnicity 1978 5(2): 119-147.* About two thirds of America's Italian immigrants arrived during 1900-20. Having little education or training, most of them became unskilled laborers heavily concentrated in the cities. The 1970 census revealed, however, that the second generation under 45 had achieved a level of education approaching the national average. Urban "Little Italies," strongholds of the Italian-American working class, have nonetheless shown exceptional vitality, although they have retreated in places before the advance of blacks and Puerto Ricans. Italian Americans have tended strongly to emphasize the family at the expense of the Church, fraternal societies, and politics. Discusses anti-Italian prejudice and the prospects for the survival of Italian-American consciousness. Based on US census data and secondary sources; graph, 2 fig., 31 notes.   L. W. Van Wyk

3213. Westerman, Joann. THE URBAN INDIAN. *Current Hist. 1974 67(400): 259-262, 275.* From an issue on the American Indian.
S

Religion

3214. Birchard, Roy. METROPOLITAN COMMUNITY CHURCH: ITS DEVELOPMENT AND SIGNIFICANCE. *Foundations 1977 20(2): 127-132.* The first denomination organized to serve the homosexual community established a church in Los Angeles in 1970. In 1976 there were 90 gay community churches. 8 notes.
E. E. Eminhizer

3215. Boggs, Beverly. SOME ASPECTS OF WORSHIP IN A HOLINESS CHURCH. *New York Folklore 1977 3(1-4): 29-44.* Describes beliefs of the mainly black congregation of, and music and services at, the Mt. Nebo Church of God in Christ in Binghamton, New York, a Holiness Church, based on the author's visits there between 1971 and 1974.

3216. Boling, T. Edwin. BLACK AND WHITE RELIGION: A COMPARISON IN THE LOWER CLASS. *Sociol. Analysis 1975 36(1): 73-80.* Examines the relationship of religion and social class by comparing similarities and differences between blacks and whites within the lower class in a small midwestern city. Departing from expected patterns, lower class white religious group members are just as likely to be members of church type organizations as they are to be members of sects. Whites also demonstrated a strong incongruity between organizational membership and religious attitudes. Blacks are largely sect members. By organizational membership and religious attitudes, the blacks are highly congruous. Although the study confirms that lower class blacks and whites share an ideological orientation to sectarianism as measured by religious beliefs, other measures of religiosity (e.g., private prayer and worship attendance) indicate a difference for blacks and whites in the lower class.
J

3217. Clelland, Donald A.; Hood, Thomas C.; Lipsey, C. M.; and Wimberley, Ronald. IN THE COMPANY OF THE CONVERTED: CHARACTERISTICS OF A BILLY GRAHAM CRUSADE AUDIENCE. *Sociol. Analysis 1974 35(1): 45-56.* Examination of the social characteristics of a Billy Graham Crusade audience in Knoxville, Tennessee. Basic data sources are 1) a short questionnaire administered to persons in randomly selected seats, 2) a larger follow-up mail questionnaire, and 3) a comparison survey of area residents. Crusade attenders are more educated and of higher income and occupational prestige than area residents. They attend church more frequently and are more conservative on religious beliefs than comparable samples. The thesis of the middle-class respectability of the Graham movement is substantiated by these data. The persistence of revivalism is interpreted as a functional reaffirmation of a threatened life style.
J

3218. Elifson, Kirk W. RELIGIOUS BEHAVIOR AMONG URBAN SOUTHERN BAPTISTS: A CAUSAL INQUIRY. *Sociol. Analysis 1976 37(1): 32-44.* Separate male and female causal models of religious behavior were developed in accordance with relevant literature and were tested using a 1968 sample of 1014 urban Southern Baptists. Incorporated in the models were demographic, contextual, attitudinal and behavioral measures. The latter two measures were developed via factor analysis, and path analysis was used to assess the respective models. Women were found to be more 'predictable' than men, intergenerational transmission of religious values was minimal for both, and the factor analysis revealed that the content of the attitudinal and behavioral dimensions of religiosity varies slightly by sex.
J

3219. Fish, Lydia Marie. ROMAN CATHOLICISM AS FOLK RELIGION IN BUFFALO. *Indiana Folklore 1976 9(2): 165-174.* Folk religion practiced by ethnic groups within the Catholic Church in Buffalo, New York, stems from its import from tradition-oriented rural Europe and basic ignorance of Church tenets.

3220. Gephart, Jerry C.; Siegel, Martin A.; and Fletcher, James E. A NOTE ON LIBERALISM AND ALIENATION IN JEWISH LIFE. *Jewish Social Studies 1974 36(3-4): 327-329.* A 1971 survey of the entire Jewish community of Salt Lake City indicated the willingness of the people to submerge their ideological differences in order to have one synagogue to serve the entire community instead of maintaining two separate synagogues, Reform and Conservative. Both groups saw a strengthening of a common Jewish identity but feared that the differences between Reform and Conservative Judaism would be lost through the union of the two synagogues. Primary and secondary sources; 5 notes.
P. E. Schoenberg

3221. Gizelis, Gregory. THE FUNCTION OF THE VISION IN GREEK-AMERICAN CULTURE. *Western Folklore 1974 33(1): 65-76.* Discusses both the background and nature of religious visions and their relation to folklife and folk religion, focusing on the Greek Americans in Philadelphia. Visions are "cultural phenomena with a recurrency which characterizes the folklore and folklife phenomena." Based on secondary sources and on oral interviews; 26 notes.
S. L. Myres

3222. Hasse, John. THE GARY BLACK RELIGIOUS EXPERIENCE: A PHOTO ESSAY. *Indiana Folklore 1977 10(2): 165-181.* Photo essay and extended description covers evangelical aspects of black churches in Gary, Indiana: gospel music, faith healing, possessing the Holy Spirit, and laying on of hands, 1976.

3223. Hunt, Larry L. and Hunt, Janet G. BLACK CATHOLICISM AND OCCUPATIONAL STATUS IN NORTHERN CITIES. *Social Sci. Q. 1978 58(4): 657-670.* The relationship between black Catholicism and occupational status in northern cities is examined using 1968 data for 15 cities. Multiple regression analysis shows that a modest nationwide Catholic advantage in occupational attainment is attributable to opposite trends in eastern and midwestern cities. Suggests that Catholic affiliation implies a status advantage only where it facilitates contact with whites and/or is a minority affiliation that can symbolize a distinctive lifestyle.
J

3224. Lauer, Robert H. OCCUPATIONAL AND RELIGIOUS MOBILITY IN A SMALL CITY. *Sociol. Q. 1975 16(3): 380-392.* Previous studies have suggested a relationship between occupational and religious mobility, namely, that the latter should follow upon the former in order to provide the mobile individual with a more socially congruent context. The greater the distance of occupational mobility, therefore, the more likely is religious mobility to occur. Analysis of data from a telephone survey of a small Midwestern city reveals that occupational and religious mobility are not related per se; there is, however, a significant relationship between occupational mobility distance and religious mobility. Education is also significantly and positively related to occupational mobility. Highly educated individuals who are occupationally mobile across a great distance are the most religiously mobile group of all. There is also a tendency for the religiously mobile to move into high status Protestant denominations or out of the Christian religion altogether; this pattern is intensified among those who are highly mobile occupationally. The results suggest that religious mobility is a coping mechanism rather than a search for a more socially congruent context.
J

3225. Mauss, Armand L. SHALL THE YOUTH OF ZION FALTER? MORMON YOUTH AND SEX: A TWO-CITY COMPARISON. *Dialogue 1976 10(2): 82-84.* Compares statistics from two surveys during 1967-69 in Salt Lake City and a northern California coastal city which question Mormons' attitudes toward morality, sex, and marriage.

3226. Mohs, Mayo. HEAVENLY VISIONS IN THE INNER CITY. *Horizon 1978 21(2): 22-27.* Discusses attempts of three New York City Protestant churches, Saint Peter's, Riverside, and Saint John the Divine, to combat social problems, 1970's.

Medicine and Public Health

3227. Agar, Michael H. and Stephens, Richard C. THE METHADONE STREET SCENE: THE ADDICT'S VIEW. *Psychiatry 1975 38(4): 381-387.* A New York City (1974) study evaluates the use and marketing of methadone on the streets.

3228. Bailey, Gil. STOP DRIVING OR STOP BREATHING. *Cry California 1973 8(4): 21-25.* Discusses the issues and implications of the air pollution crisis in Los Angeles in the 1970's.
S

3229. Bellin, Lowell E. SHOULD WE GET OUT OF THE MUNICIPAL HOSPITAL BUSINESS? *New York Affairs 1977 4(3): 48-58.*

Discusses medical care in New York City, private and municipal hospitals, asserting that dissolution of the municipal facilities is recommended with the advent of national health insurance, 1964-74.

3230. Bellush, Jewel. INDISPENSABLE FACILITIES: IN DEFENSE OF MUNICIPAL HOSPITALS. *New York Affairs 1979 5(4): 111-119.* Describes recent attacks on the public hospital system in New York City and dispels several myths saying that municipal hospitals are a hindrance, are physically inferior to private hospitals, and are unnecessary, 1970's.

3231. Brienes, Marvin. SMOG COMES TO LOS ANGELES. *Southern California Q. 1976 58(4): 515-532.* Describes the appearance of smog in Los Angeles. Except for some localized incidents, the first major attack of air pollution occurred in July 1943. An immediate culprit was the Southern California Gas Company's Aliso Street gas works where butadiene was produced. Mayor Fletcher Bowron and other city officials demanded that control devices be installed to prevent the spread of noxious fumes. After delays and continued complaints, complicated by the needs of the war effort, the facility installed control devices in December 1943. However, health officials warned that Los Angeles' temperature inversions, combined with the massive increase in wartime industry, meant that no one plant could be blamed for air pollution. Nevertheless, long after the control devices were in operation and even after the plant was closed, people blamed smog on butadiene. The lesson that smog was a complex problem for which there were no easy solutions had yet to be learned. Based on primary and secondary sources; 39 notes.
A. Hoffman

3232. Brown, David L. THE REDISTRIBUTION OF PHYSICIANS AND DENTISTS IN INCORPORATED PLACES OF THE UPPER MIDWEST, 1950-1970. *Rural Sociol. 1974 39(2): 205-223.* This research is concerned with the spatial distribution of physicians and dentists among population size classes of incorporated places in the upper Midwest. Specialists were more concentrated in metropolitan places than general practitioners or dentists, but the degree of centralization for all groups has decreased from its level 20 years ago. The trend for specialists is not one of uniform decentralization in which the smallest places gain but, rather, a reordering in which suburban and larger nonmetropolitan cities are emerging as the providers of specialty medical care for the rural population. These hinterland centers contain the facilities and resources to support specialty medicine and are a focus of social and economic life in rural America.
J

3233. Dammann, Grace and Soler, Esta. PRESCRIPTION DRUG ABUSE: A SAN FRANCISCO STUDY. *Frontiers 1979 4(2): 5-10.* Details the findings of the 1973-77 San Francisco Polydrug Project, a study done on the extent of prescription drug abuse and treatment, which revealed women as the primary abusers, largely neglected by the drug treatment industry.

3234. Dorsch, G. and Talley, Ruth. RESPONSES TO ALCOHOLICS BY THE HELPING PROFESSIONS IN DENVER: A THREE-YEAR FOLLOW-UP. *Q. J. of Studies on Alcohol 1973 34(1A): 165-172.* As a part of a five-year project in which three different alcoholism treatment programs were established in the Denver metropolitan area, four annual surveys of professionals and agencies were made. The data were analyzed to determine if the educational efforts to publicize the programs had increased professional awareness of and concern for persons with drinking problems, but no such trends were found.
J

3235. Feldman, Harvey. STREET STATUS AND DRUG USERS. *Society 1973 10(4): 32-38.*

3236. Fottler, Myron D. and Rock, William K. SOME CORRELATES OF HOSPITAL COSTS IN PUBLIC AND PRIVATE HOSPITAL SYSTEMS: NEW YORK CITY. *Q. R. of Econ. and Business 1974 14(1): 39-53.* Examines how the correlates of hospital costs differ between public and private institutions. Moreover, previous studies have used cross-section analysis to explain changes over time and have neglected certain variables which may be important. This article analyzes correlates of hospital costs both at a point in time and over time in the New York City voluntary and municipal hospital systems. No evidence of economies of scale was found in either system, indicating that the

average hospital size in New York City may be too large in terms of economic efficiency. The work-force skill mix and employee work load were significantly related to hospital costs in both hospital systems.
J

3237. Gordon, Diana R. THE RISE AND FALL OF THE LEAD POISONING CONTROVERSY. *New York Affairs 1974 1(3): 38-63.* Lead poisoning is a preventable disease that affects thousands of ghetto children. But its prevention in New York City remains a dream.   J

3238. Griffin, Robert M., Jr. SOCIAL STRUCTURE AND URBAN DISEASE: NEED FOR A BROADER BASE FOR HEALTH PLANNING AND RESEARCH. *Urban and Social Change Rev. 1975 8(1): 15-20.*

3239. Harvey, Milton E.; Frazier, John W.; and Matulionis, Mindaugas. CONDITIONS OF A HAZARDOUS ENVIRONMENT: REACTIONS TO BUFFALO AIRPORT NOISE. *Econ. Geography 1979 55(4): 263-286.* Develops a conceptual framework for examining the behavior of people living near the Buffalo Airport, with respect to household cognition of the effects of noise and the causal linkage path of cognition of noise and behavior.

3240. Harvey, William M. SPECIAL PROBLEMS OF FREE CLINICS SERVING MINORITY COMMUNITIES. *J. of Social Issues 1974 30(1): 61-66.* Black clinics face special problems in "getting themselves together." Black and minority clinics tend to be less oriented toward serving the needs of the young drug abuser and are much more concerned with meeting the basic health needs of a particular minority community.
J

3241. Hessler, Richard M. CITIZEN PARTICIPATION, SOCIAL ORGANIZATION, AND CULTURE: A NEIGHBORHOOD HEALTH CENTER FOR CHICANOS. *Human Organization 1977 36(2): 124-134.* This paper reports on the relationship between the organization of a comprehensive neighborhood health center and the cultural dynamics of several Chicano barrios. The paper focuses on consumer participation in health care decisionmaking as a way to include cultural factors in the organization of health services. Principles related to social organization and public policy are discussed.
J

3242. Lewis, David L. COLOR IT BLACK: THE FAILURE OF DRUG ABUSE POLICY. *Social Policy 1976 6(5): 26-32.* Discusses inadequacies of federal programs to combat drug abuse for Negroes and youths in cities in the 1960's and 70's.

3243. Liu, Ben-chieh. THE COSTS OF AIR QUALITY DETERIORATION AND BENEFITS OF AIR POLLUTION CONTROL: ESTIMATES OF MORTALITY COSTS FOR TWO POLLUTANTS IN 40 U.S. METROPOLITAN AREAS. *Am. J. of Econ. and Sociol. 1979 38(2): 187-195.* Although it is still impossible to place a dollar value on human lives and on the total health effects of air pollution, the excessive mortality costs of two air pollutants—sulfur dioxide and total suspended particulates (TSP)—have been quantified for most of the 40 Standard Metropolitan Statistical Areas in the United States. Based on 1970 data, total mortality damage for sulfur dioxide was estimated at $887 million and for TSP at $1.044 billion. The benefit from reducing these pollutants could exceed $1.328 billion annually, a figure useful in evaluating control costs.
J

3244. McIntosh, Karyl. FOLK OBSTETRICS, GYNECOLOGY, AND PEDIATRICS IN UTICA, NEW YORK. *New York Folklore 1978 4(1-4): 49-59.* Discusses a study (in 1978) of Italian and Polish women in Utica, New York, regarding folk beliefs and practices concerning childbirth, pregnancy, and early childhood, which are transmitted by the family and the group.

3245. McNamara, John J. MATERNAL AND CHILD HEALTH. *Pro. of the Acad. of Pol. Sci. 1977 32(3): 79-88.* Studies maternal and child health in New York City from birth through the reproductive period including preventive and curative services, but restricted to services provided under local government auspices. The problem has been exacerbated by the changing demography of the city, and accompanying life-style changes.
R. V. Ritter

3246. Molica, Gregory J. and Winn, Neal E. HISTORY OF THE WAIKIKI CLINIC. *J. of Social Issues 1974 30(1): 53-60.* Presents the philosophy of a free clinic. Describes setting up of an advisory board, the miscalculations made in anticipating the type of clients who would use the clinic, and the inability to foresee the lack of cooperation from the local medical facilities and counseling centers. Notes the struggles that ensued among the board and the staff, struggles that almost led to closing down the Waikiki clinic. There is then a discussion of reorganization, the definition of the executive director's job, the opening of a halfway house, and the consequent good utilization of the community.   J/S

3247. Owen, John E. NOISE: AMERICA'S NEW POLLUTION. *Int. J. of Contemporary Sociol. 1974 11(4): 245-252.* Discusses the problem of noise pollution in causing nervous disorders in city dwellers in the 1960's and 70's, including litigation involving automobiles, industry, and airplanes.

3248. Pearson, Roger W. and Smith, Daniel W. FAIRBANKS: A STUDY OF ENVIRONMENTAL QUALITY. *Arctic [Canada] 1975 28(2): 99-109.* Uses Fairbanks, Alaska, as a case study of the environmental quality of rapidly expanding northern settlements; discusses housing, crowding, and waste disposal and measures to improve environmental quality, 1970-75.

3249. Pyle, Gerald F. and Lauer, Bruce M. COMPARING SPATIAL CONFIGURATIONS: HOSPITAL SERVICE AREAS AND DISEASE RATES. *Econ. Geography 1975 51(1): 50-68.* Survey of the spatial variability of health conditions within metropolitan areas.   S

3250. Reskin, Barbara and Campbell, Frederick L. PHYSICIAN DISTRIBUTION ACROSS METROPOLITAN AREAS. *Am. J. of Sociol. 1974 79(4): 981-998.* Examines the effects of demographic and ecological variables on the distribution of physicians in greater American metropolises. The physicians considered are those in full-time, nonfederal private practice in 1966. The communities considered are those 22 SMSAs with a population of over 1 million. Indicators of medical need, access to medical care, and the presence of alternative sources of medical care are shown to be associated with the distribution of physician categories considered.   J/S

3251. Schmitt, Robert C.; Zane, Lynn Y. S.; and Nishi, Sharon. DENSITY, HEALTH, AND SOCIAL DISORGANIZATION REVISITED. *J. of the Am. Inst. of Planners 1978 44(2): 209-211.* A 1966 article by the senior author, based on 1948-1952 census tract data for the Honolulu SMSA, reported a close correlation between resident population densities and various health and social disorganization rates, even when persons per room, educational level, and income were controlled. The present study, based largely on 1974 tract data for the same SMSA, finds that the simple, multiple, and partial correlations previously reported have declined sharply in the intervening years. Census tract data on daytime and de facto population densities proved little better as indicators of health and welfare levels.   J

3252. Siassi, I.; Crocetti, G.; and Spiro, H. R. DRINKING PATTERNS AND ALCOHOLISM IN A BLUE COLLAR POPULATION. *Q. J. of Studies on Alcohol 1973 34(3-Part A): 917-926.* Interviews with 937 members (429 women) of the Baltimore United Auto Workers Union and their spouses as part of a larger survey on mental illness included questions related to drinking. Of the respondents, 377 (97 women) were drinkers (average age 41.1) and of these, 67% of the men and 38% of the women were heavy drinkers (6 or more drinks of any alcoholic beverage a week), and 10% of the men and 3% of the women were heavy-escape drinkers (heavy drinkers who frequently drank for psychological reasons). The average ages of the heavy and the heavy-escape drinkers were 41.4 and 38.9. Of the drinkers, 25% and 26% drank to be sociable or when others were drinking, 32% drank as part of an important occasion, 5% drank when nervous or tense, 4% to forget troubles. Of the drinkers, 44% had less than 9 years of education and 33% more than 12 years; 48% earned less than $6000, and 51%, over $10,000; 49% were Catholic and 40% Protestants. The findings are compared with those of a national sample reported by Cahalan [*Q. J. Stud. Alc.* 29: 130-151, 1968].
                J/S

3253. Stephens, Richard C. and McBride, Duane C. BECOMING A STREET ADDICT. *Human Organization 1976 35(1): 87-93.* Discusses social processes whereby Negro youth in slum areas become addicted to narcotics, specifically heroin, in the 1960's and 70's.

3254. Unsigned. [HOSPITAL COSTS IN NEW YORK CITY]. *Q. R. of Econ. & Business 1975 15(4): 99-105.*
Worthington, Paul N. SOME CORRELATES OF HOSPITAL COSTS IN PUBLIC AND PRIVATE HOSPITAL SYSTEMS, NEW YORK CITY: COMMENT, *pp. 99-101.*
Fottler, Myron D. SOME CORRELATES OF HOSPITAL COSTS IN PUBLIC AND PRIVATE HOSPITAL SYSTEMS, NEW YORK CITY: REPLY, *pp. 101-105.* Discusses an article by Myron D. Fottler and William K. Rock, "Some Correlates of Hospital Costs in Public and Private Hospital Systems: New York City" concerning the costs of hospitals in New York City during the 1960's.

3255. Unsigned. SMELLS LIKE MONEY. *Southern Exposure 1978 6(2): 59-65.* Serious health problems exist in Kingsport, Tennessee, due to extensive industrial pollution generated by chemical and other plants. Water and air pollution is considerable and is not being adequately coped with by state or federal agencies. Effective eradication of pollution is also thwarted by the feeling of segments of the population that full employment is more important than pure water and air.
                N. Lederer

3256. Waitzkin, Howard, and Sharratt, John A. CONTROLLING MEDICAL EXPANSION. *Society 1977 14(2): 30-35.* The proliferation of medical centers in urban areas has threatened local neighborhoods in these centers, 1960's-76.

3257. Walsh, John P. and Adelson, Richard. HEALTH CARE: NO TIME FOR PLACEBOS. *New York Affairs 1978 5(2): 151-161.* Assesses health care in New York City, 1965-75.

3258. Weaver, Jerry L. HEALTH CARE COSTS AS A POLITICAL ISSUE: COMPARATIVE RESPONSES OF CHICANOS AND ANGLOS. *Social Sci. Q. 1973 53(4): 846-854.* Based on information gathered from a sample of 484 Orange County, California residents. The data suggest that the economic burden of health care is a focal concern of a sizable portion of the Chicano community. Compared with Anglos, there was significantly more support for four health cost reduction schemes, even after controls were introduced. Speculates that concern about rising health care costs offers a focus for widespread political mobilization among Chicanos.   J

3259. Webb, Bruce J. IMPACT OF REVENUE SHARING ON LOCAL HEALTH CENTERS. *Black Scholar 1974 5(8): 10-15.* Discusses the idea of revenue sharing, implementation of the Revenue Sharing Act of 1972, and its implications for neighborhood health care centers. Secondary sources; 10 notes.   M. M. McCarthy

3260. Wepper, Robert S. AN ANTHROPOLOGICAL VIEW OF THE STREET ADDICT'S WORLD. *Human Organization 1973 32(2): 111-121.* Examines the role of anthropologists in drug-abuse treatment programs. Emphasizes the role of the drug culture in the abuse problem and suggests that the anthropologist may contribute to understanding of the subculture and possible reacculturation of the addict. 17 notes, biblio.   E. S. Johnson

The Physical City

General

3261. Babcock, Richard F. THE DEPLORABLE STATES. *Center Mag. 1976 9(5): 23-27.* Discusses inadequacies in local government management of land use regulations, zoning, and housing in cities and states in the 1970's.

3262. Baerwald, Thomas J. THE EMERGENCE OF A NEW "DOWNTOWN." *Geographical Rev. 1978 68(3): 308-318.* The suburban freeway corridor has emerged since World War II as a new "down-town" in large American metropolises. Analysis of the Minneapolis-St. Paul SFC indicated a four-stage development related to the times at which specific types of land use entered the corridor and to the vacant land available at those times. Residential and commercial uses occupied central corridor locations during the early stages. Office buildings and motor hotels were constructed later as speculative ventures. Industry developed throughout the corridor's history and was dispersed. The future of the corridor is related to the metropolitan circulation system and the ease with which the corridor may be redeveloped.   J

3263. Blumenfeld, Hans. CONTINUITY AND CHANGE IN URBAN FORM. *J. of Urban Hist. 1975 1(2): 131-147.* Using examples chiefly from Europe, propounds the belief that the natural site of a city is "fairly permanent." In case after case, characteristics of individual cities have been heightened rather than destroyed by time. Concludes that in the United States concern for urban form is as important as concern for individual landmarks.   S. S. Sprague

3264. Brodsky, Harold. LAND DEVELOPMENT AND THE EXPANDING CITY. *Ann. of the Assoc. of Am. Geographers 1973 63(2): 159-166.* Land development decisions in the rural-urban fringe are primarily made by small-scale merchant builders who have little economic incentive to adhere to metropolitan plans. Local governments have little power to regulate land use, and as a result American cities have uncoordinated sprawling suburbs. A shift from small-scale development to large-scale new community development might eliminate some of the problems caused by sprawl, but it is difficult and expensive to assemble large holdings of land adjacent to a city. Prince Georges County, a suburb of Washington, D.C., had fragmented land ownership and high land values adjacent to the urbanized area in 1970.   J

3265. Brown, Joseph E. A CITY THAT SITS ON THE PROBABILITY OF MORE QUAKES. *Smithsonian 1973 4(9): 26-33.* Hollister, California, sits on the Calaveras fault line and is subject to many earthquakes.   S

3266. Carey, George W. LAND TENURE, SPECULATION, AND THE STATE OF THE AGING METROPOLIS. *Geographical Rev. 1976 66(3): 253-265.* American urban scholars, in their unwillingness to recommend policy that will make structural changes in our land tenure system for urban areas, are locked into a passive and fatalistic role with respect to the decay of America's older urban centers. This article raises the question of whether the age of a city needs to be related to its ability to support humane life. Compares approaches to land tenure and planning in Amsterdam with the effects of the nonsystem which prevails in the greater New York area.   J

3267. Casetti, Emilio. URBAN LAND FUNCTIONS: EQUILIBRIUM VERSUS OPTIMALITY. *Econ. Geography 1973 49(4): 357-365.* Compares two models for urban land values, one based on total public welfare profit through city planning, the other based on competitive bidding for corporate profit.   S

3268. Choldin, Harvey M. RETROSPECTIVE REVIEW ESSAY: NEIGHBORHOOD LIFE AND URBAN ENVIRONMENT. *Am. J. of Sociol. 1978 84(2): 457-463.* Review article prompted by Jane Jacobs's *Death and Life of Great American Cities* (New York: Random House, Vintage Books, 1961).

3269. Cool, Robert A.; Kielbaso, J. James; and Myers, Wayne L. A SURVEY OF FORESTRY ACTIVITIES OF MICHIGAN CITIES: TREE CARE IN OUR CITIES. *Michigan Academician 1973 6(2): 223-232.* Results of a questionnaire sent to Michigan municipalities.   S

3270. Deyak, Timothy A. and Smith, V. Kerry. RESIDENTIAL PROPERTY VALUES AND AIR POLLUTION: SOME NEW EVIDENCE. *Q. Rev. of Econ. and Business 1974 14(4): 93-100.* Reports estimates of the relationship between air pollution and property values for the representative SMSA [Standard Metropolitan Statistical Area], using 1970 census data on 100 SMSAs and recent pollution data. Although the empirical findings indicate that air pollution does not affect residential property values, the results do not provide the means to measure the marginal benefits from pollution abatement.   J

3271. Ericksen, Eugene P. and Yancey, William L. WORK AND RESIDENCE IN INDUSTRIAL PHILADELPHIA. *J. of Urban Hist. 1978 5(2): 147-182.* The Burgess zonal model of spatial organization for cities does not represent the general pattern of modern cities but rather characterizes cities during only a brief and bygone era of urban development. The major force ordering the residential pattern of cities is the location of work places. The Central Business District (CBD) is seen as nothing more than "a particularly large workplace concentration." With the subsequent decline of the CBD as a primary work place the zonal model has increasingly become an inadequate description of urban spatial organization. 8 tables, 4 fig., 46 notes.   T. W. Smith

3272. Greer-Wooten, Bryn and Gilmour, G. M. LE MODÈLE DE LA STRUCTURE INTERNE DES VILLES NORD-AMÉRICAINES: UNE APPROCHE COMPLÉMENTAIRE [The model of the internal structure of North American cities: a complementary approach]. *Ann. de Géographie [France] 1973 82 (454): 675-694.* Presents the "process" modelling used by American urban scholars to understand internal urban spatial structure, thus complementing a recent review by Racine. The shortcomings of the three descriptive schemes of Burgess, Hoyt and Harris and Ullman are revealed, and one approach to the study of process —that of the urban economists—is exemplified, together with some empirical studies based on land rent theory. Criticisms of this method are then made, followed by an overview of some more recent attempts to understand decisionmaking elements of both the demand and supply sides of the residential development equation. Concluding remarks center on the continuing gap between such theoretical models of process and real-world urban dynamics, supporting Racine's more general conclusions.   J

3273. Guest, Avery M. JOURNEY TO WORK, 1960-70. *Social Forces 1975 54(1): 220-225.* In general, most metropolitan dwellers continue both to work and live within either central city or suburban rings of metropolian areas. Nevertheless, travel across central city boundaries, inward and outward, was increasing slightly in the 1960-70 decade. And tendencies to live and work in central city or suburban rings vary clearly by the age and population size of the metropolitan area.   J

3274. Guest, Avery M. OCCUPATION AND THE JOURNEY TO WORK. *Social Forces 1976 55(1): 166-181.* This paper investigates the accuracy of theory and research suggesting that higher-status workers are more likely than other workers to maximize travel distance because of disagreeable features of the area around worksites. Our evidence suggests that higher-status white, male workers have relatively long commuting distances in old metropolitan areas while this is less true of new metropolitan areas. Journey to work patterns thus seem to explain some of the differences in residential structure between new and old metropolitan areas.   J

3275. Hammer, Thomas R.; Coughlin, Robert E.; and Horn, Edward T., IV. THE EFFECT OF A LARGE URBAN PARK ON REAL ESTATE VALUE. *J. of the Am. Inst. of Planners 1974 40(4): 274-277.* Analysis of property sales in the vicinity of 1,294-acre Pennypack Park in Philadelphia indicates a statistically significant rise in land value with closeness to park, when allowance is made for effect of type of house, year of sale, and special characteristics such as location on corner of block.   J

3276. Hayden, Dolores and Wright, Gwendolyn. ARCHITECTURE AND URBAN PLANNING. *Signs 1976 1(4): 923-933.* Research on women in architecture and city planning is scant and provides a field ripe for feminist study. A few works focus on women as designers, but most examine the impact of environmental design on women's lives and work. Advances in technology and standardized housing raised the standards expected of women and increased the tasks assigned to them. Contemporary housing studies emphasize and idealize the mother-child relationship instead of contributing to shared parenting. Utopian communities were an attempt to find an alternative to the nuclear family. Some attention has been given to women's working conditions, especially offices and factory sweatshops. Based on manuscripts, research studies, and secondary works; 48 notes.   J. Gammage

3277. Hunter, Albert. THE URBAN NEIGHBORHOOD: ITS ANALYTICAL AND SOCIAL CONTEXTS. *Urban Affairs Q. 1979*

14(3): 267-288. Each of the articles in this issue of *Urban Affairs Quarterly* devoted to neighborhoods casts them as unique spatial/social links between people and the larger forces of society. Concludes that the importance of each of the neighborhood typologies may be their academic and policy utility. The author's analysis of the stages of neighborhood evolution suggests that they are residues of urban macroforces, but he finds that they still function independently in such areas as political organization, socialization, and sociability. Suspects that future scholarship will focus on neighborhoods as a component in national political federations and as an emotional base in an increasingly narrow unrooted society. Biblio.

L. N. Beecher

3278. Hushak, Leroy J. THE URBAN DEMAND FOR URBAN-RURAL FRINGE LAND. *Land Econ. 1975 51(2): 112-123.* Constructs a model using actual land transactions to estimate the demand for underdeveloped land around Columbus, Ohio. Finds that the demand for urban fringe land, as reflected by price, is directly related to commercial zoning and inversely related to the size of the parcel, and its distance from Columbus and a major highway. Discusses some policy implications of the findings. 2 tables, 4 notes, biblio.

E. S. Johnson

3279. Koppelman, Lee E. LAND USE: CHANGING THE GROUND RULES. *New York Affairs 1978 5(2): 62-74.* Examines present land use in New York City, speculates on formulation of relations between settlement patterns and environmental quality, and applies basic principles of land use and human settlement patterns to regional quality expectations.

3280. Lipton, S. Gregory. EVIDENCE OF CENTRAL CITY REVIVAL. *J. of the Am. Inst. of Planners 1977 43(2): 136-147.* Twenty of the largest United States cities were studied to see if there was any positive change in the number of census tracts with middle- and upper-income families living within two miles of the central business district during the 1960's. A number of the cities did show an increase in the number of such tracts. An analysis of the causal factors follows. The centers of the nation's largest cities are not destined for decay but in fact hold potential as the sites of middle- and upper-income neighborhoods.

J

3281. Moore, Winston; Livermore, Charles P.; and Galland, George F., Jr. WOODLAWN: THE ZONE OF DESTRUCTION. *Public Interest 1973 (30): 41-59.* An exodus of Negroes, a collapsing housing market, and an increasing crime rate led to the rapid deterioration of Chicago's Woodlawn area during 1930-71.

S

3282. Moss, Mitchell L. THE URBAN WATERFRONT: OPPORTUNITIES FOR RENEWAL. *Natl. Civic Rev. 1976 65(5): 241-244.* A complex set of forces has emerged which compels planners to consider the urban waterfront, traditionally not a major focus of attention by municipal governments, as a fundamental element in planning and managing cities. These forces are state and local coastal zone management programs, the decline of the urban port areas and a wide range of redevelopment projects currently under consideration.

J

3283. Mushkatel, Alvin H. REGULATING LAND-USE: PUBLIC VERSUS PRIVATE INTERVENTION, A BOOK REVIEW ESSAY. *Urban Affairs Q. 1979 15(1): 111-120.* Reviews the following books: Michael N. Danielson, *The Politics of Exclusion* (New York: Columbia U. Pr., 1976), Richard P. Fishman, ed., *Housing for All Under Law: New Directions in Housing, Land Use and Planning Law* (Cambridge, Mass.: Ballinger Publishing Co., 1978), Jerome G. Rose and Robert E. Rothman, eds., *After Mount Laurel: The New Suburban Zoning* (New Brunswick, New Jersey: The Center for Urban Policy Research, 1977), Robert H. Nelson, *Zoning and Property Rights: An Analysis of the American System of Land-Use Regulation* (Cambridge, Mass: MIT Pr., 1977), Franklin J. James and Denis E. Gale, *Zoning for Sale: A Critical Analysis of Transferable Development Rights Programs* (Washington, D.C.: The Urban Institute, 1977). These studies intensify the traditional criticism of past land-use planning and propose remedies ranging from increased government regulation at all levels to the elaboration of marketable, transferable development rights.

L. N. Beecher

3284. Park, Ki Suh CITY BEAUTIFICATION PROGRAMS: ARE THEY STILL NECESSARY? *Natl. Civic Rev. 1973 62(7): 362-365.*

There are positive advantages to a beautification program if it is viewed realistically in relation to basic city problems and a limited budget.

J

3285. Parvin, Manocher and Finch, Stephen J. AIR QUALITY: A POLICY MODEL. *New York Affairs 1978 5(2): 138-150.* Examines air quality in New York City, 1970-77, presenting a model for further improvement which incorporates reasonable energy demands, stable employment, and division of residential and industrial locations.

3286. Rubin, Barbara. AESTHETIC IDEOLOGY AND URBAN DESIGN. *Ann. of the Assoc. of Am. Geographers 1979 69(3): 339-361.* Contemporary urban commerce, represented by chaotically designed and decorated urban centers, although considered by some to represent cultural anarchy, has its roots in the elaboration and evolution of late 19th-century World's Fair amusement zones.

3287. Schwieder, Dorothy. HISTORIC SITES IN COUNCIL BLUFFS. *Ann. of Iowa 1973 41(7): 1148-1152.* Discusses the historical sites and legends of Council Bluffs, Iowa.

S

3288. Sexton, Thomas R. and Carroll, T. Owen. ENERGY: TAKING THE WHEEL. *New York Affairs 1978 5(2): 104-113.* Assesses energy use efficiency in New York City, 1960-75; urges greater responsibility in regional planning for future housing and public transportation.

3289. Unsigned. [PRIVATISM AND URBAN DEVELOPMENT: PROBLEM OR SOLUTION?]. *Urban Affairs Q. 1977 12(4): 431-474.*
Barnekov, Timothy K. and Rich, Daniel. PRIVATISM AND URBAN DEVELOPMENT: AN ANALYSIS OF THE ORGANIZED INFLUENCE OF LOCAL BUSINESS ELITES, *pp. 431-460.* Based on the notion that private interests can promote public welfare, businessmen's committees have influenced urban development for 30 years. In the 33 cities studied, these committees emerged because established associations were concerned with promotional, not developmental, activities. Committee influence in the community is based on the power of its elite, locally based membership. Since 1967, they have shown increasing concern for social and economic problems; but they center on the physical condition of the downtown area. Thus, even when results are spectacular, citywide benefits are not obvious. Committees influence public life in both formal and informal ways. Privatism is responsible for the conditions of urban America and restricts urban renewal. Primary and secondary sources; 13 notes, biblio.
MacGregor, Robert W. PRIVATISM AND URBAN DEVELOPMENT: A RESPONSE, *pp. 461-468.* Asserts that committee influence is balanced or overcome by competing groups. The downtown emphasis needs to be broadened but the redevelopment of the central business district benefits the whole city. The few bright spots in American cities are the result of privatism, and it is unfortunate "that privatism is waning."
Barnekov, Timothy K. and Rich, Daniel. BEYOND PRIVATISM: A REJOINDER, *pp. 469-474.* To argue that privatism can solve urban problems is to mistake their nature. Businessmen's expertise is of limited value when the definition of the problem is unclear and the criteria for evaluating success is uncertain. The committees do not have monopoly influence, but redevelopment disproportionately favors the interest of local business elites. Privatism prevents the generation of "more equitable and responsive modes of urban development." Biblio.

L. N. Beecher

3290. Waldo, Robert D. URBAN LAND: VALUES AND ACCESSIBILITY. *Land Econ. 1974 50(2): 196-200.* An empirical study (1950-60) of the time value of commuting as a position rent increment in northeastern Los Angeles.

S

3291. Witte, Ann D. and Bachman, James E. VACANT URBAN HOLDINGS: PORTFOLIO CONSIDERATIONS AND OWNER CHARACTERISTICS. *Southern Econ. J. 1978 45(2): 543-558.* Estimates the parameter of portfolio theory for vacant urban land and examines the characteristics of individuals owning such land in medium-sized cities; concludes that nondevelopment is basically rational, but not efficiently diversified, 1968-74.

Planning

3292. Adams, Gerald D. YOUR MONEY *AND* YOUR LIFE. *Cry California 1975 10(2): 2-12.* Describes the potential risk from natural dangers and the inadequate enforcement of safeguards against hazardous construction. Despite legislation regulating airport construction, private construction in fault and slide areas, and the recommendations of government agencies, people continue to live in potentially dangerous situations. Conflicting interpretations in engineering reports, economic pressure for increased employment and profits, and lax enforcement of regulations have resulted in compromises in regional and city planning. Calls for stricter scientific and engineering standards in planning and enforcement of those standards. 6 photos, 5 drawings.   A. Hoffman

3293. Alves, William R. and Morrill, Richard L. DIFFUSION THEORY AND PLANNING. *Econ. Geography 1975 51(3): 290-304.* Examines the usefulness in applying diffusion theory to city planning.   S

3294. Bauer, Rudolph. [REGIONAL AND CITY PLANNING]. STADT- UND REGIONALPLANUNG [City and regional planning]. *Neue Politische Literatur [West Germany] 1976 21(1): 58-88.* Reviews new international literature on urban problems, city and regional planning and urban reform in Europe and the United States since 1945. PLANUNGSTHEORIE POLITISCHER ZEITFINDUNGS- UND ENTSCHEIDUNGSPROZESSE: STADT- UND REGIONAL-PLANUNG [Theory of planning of political periodization and decision processes: city and regional planning]. *Neue Politische Literatur [West Germany] 1976 21(3): 315-355.* Analyzes the social and economic background of the interest groups dominating urban and regional planning in West Germany since World War II.

3295. Bjornseth, Dick. HOUSTON DEFIES THE PLANNERS . . . AND THRIVES. *Reason 1978 9(10): 16-22.* Economic stability, lower costs, aesthetics, individual incentives, and cost breaks for small businessmen all have resulted from Houston's lack of zoning ordinances, 1962-77.

3296. Bowman, David. MEMPHIS, TENNESSEE: HOW TO STOP DEVELOPERS. *Southern Exposure 1976 3(4): 18-24.* Examines a fight between Memphis citizens and local planning agencies over the plan of James Rouse, Boyle Investments, and the First Tennessee National Corporation to develop 5,000 acres of public lands into a city-within-a-city, 1971-76.

3297. Brown, Lawrence A.; Williams, Forrest B.; Youngmann, Carl E.; Holmes, John; and Walby, Karen. THE LOCATION OF URBAN POPULATION SERVICE FACILITIES: A STRATEGY AND ITS APPLICATION. *Social Sci. Q. 1974 54(4): 784-799.* Proposes a general four step strategy for locating new population planning and service facilities and illustrates it with locational options for a system of public day care centers in Columbus, Ohio.   J

3298. Cohen, Rick. NEIGHBORHOOD PLANNING AND POLITICAL CAPACITY. *Urban Affairs Q. 1979 14(3): 337-362.* The standard model of neighborhood change planners use assumes that the process is fueled by householders making individual economic decisions. Although alternate models focus on public and private institutions outside the household, both generate economic and technical programs that ultimately result in richer families replacing poorer families. Contends that the interests of the latter can be protected by politicizing and decentralizing the planning process for neighborhood reconstruction. Concludes that Pennsylvania's Neighborhood Preservation Support System evidences the superiority of this approach to traditional technical-economic fixes. Biblio.   L. N. Beecher

3299. Contini, Edgardo. PROBLEM-SOLVING IN THE REALM OF URBAN PLANNING. *Am. Behavioral Scientist 1974 18(2): 201-210.* Faced with a unique set of problems, urban planners need to formulate clear objectives, consider multiple points of view, and cultivate a certain moral perspective.   S

3300. Danielson, Michael N. THE POLITICS OF EXCLUSIONARY ZONING IN SUBURBIA. *Pol. Sci. Q. 1976 91(1): 1-18.* Discusses the factors that account for local resistance to opening the suburbs to subsidized housing. Argues that lack of incentives for local officials and residents, combined with the weak articulation of latent sources of support for open housing, tend to preclude significant policy change from within suburbia.   J

3301. Fleming, Ronald Lee. IMAGES OF A TOWN. *Hist. Preservation 1978 30(4): 26-31.* Townscape historic preservation planning should incorporate the arts, such as sculpture and mural painting, to help interpret to a community its own sense of place. Illus.   R. M. Frame III

3302. Fowler, E. P. and White, David. BIG CITY DOWNTOWNS: THE NON-IMPACT OF ZONING. *Policy Studies J. 1979 7(4): 690-700.* Maintains that land prices and zoning policies, while affecting one another, vary in extent and direction depending on the political climate in the city government, 1970's.

3303. Frieden, Bernard J. THE NEW REGULATION COMES TO SUBURBIA. *Public Interest 1979 55: 15-27.* New environmental and growth controls on the homebuilding industry in northern California have financially burdened homebuyers, especially young families trying to buy their first home. These regulations have inflated the prices of individual projects and have eliminated the construction of many housing units developers originally intended to build. The new regulation has not benefited the public at large. Instead, it has given such influential groups as environmental ideologues, and established suburbanites, who are seeking to maintain the status quo, what they want.   S. Harrow

3304. Friedlander, Stephen. NEW TOWNS AND CITIES. *Colorado Q. 1973 22(2): 203-214.* Explores the possibilities of new metropolitan satellite towns and cities and new non-metropolitan towns and cities as one way to absorb population growth in the United States. Considers such problems as land values, taxes, land costs, and development costs. Discusses the advantages and disadvantages of metropolitan satellites and nonmetropolitan creations. While such developments are a pleasant possibility, and while such new towns and cities will continue to be developed, they will not absorb major portions of the expected population growth.   B. A. Storey

3305. Gans, Herbert J. PLANNING FOR DECLINING AND POOR CITIES. *J. of the Am. Inst. of Planners 1975 41(5): 305-307.* Lists six ways in which the *Cleveland Policy Planning Report* (1970) is a new approach to planning, and shows the significance of this new approach in view of the decline of contemporary American cities.

3306. Gaskell, S. M. FIRST INTERNATIONAL CONFERENCE ON THE HISTORY OF URBAN AND REGIONAL PLANNING: A REPORT. *Urban Hist. Rev. [Canada] 1978 (1): 48-56.* Reports on the papers presented at the conference held 14-18 September 1977 at Bedford College, University of London. The dominant theme turned out to be the comparative analysis of international similarities and differences.   C. A. Watson

3307. Getreu, Sanford. DO YOU KNOW YOUR LAFCO? *Cry California 1975 10(4): 26-31.* Describes the work of the Local Agency Formation Commissions (LAFCO), created for the counties of California in 1963 to encourage planned growth and the wise use of resources. Although the use of the LAFCO's varies greatly, some have worked out important programs to stop urban sprawl and local annexation wars between cities. The LAFCO of Santa Clara County has guided cities in the region toward better planning of municipal services, negotiated boundary agreements, and prezoned areas scheduled prior to annexation. Recommends the adoption of similar programs by other LAFCO agencies.   A. Hoffman

3308. Goldfield, David R. HISTORIC PLANNING AND REDEVELOPMENT IN MINNEAPOLIS. *J. of the Am. Inst. of Planners 1976 42(1): 76-86.* The redevelopment process in Minneapolis involves an attempt to recreate the positive aspects of life that existed in the 19th-century city, an era when the city was a dynamic and positive environment. Redevelopment has focused on recovering the importance of downtown, restoring the industrial base lost to the suburbs, and revitalizing neighborhood life—all characteristic aspects of the historic city. The city's public planning efforts, well documented by Altshuler and others, have involved significant cooperation among city agencies and private organizations. This paper focuses on the role of the private sector in this partnership to encourage redevelopment. Nicollet Mall and the industrial development program are two of the major accomplishments of the recovery efforts. Where success has eluded the city, as in the Cedar-Riverside neighborhood revitalization project, more attention to the historic and social needs of residents might contribute to fulfillment of project goals. The Minneapolis recovery effort has demonstrated that the benefits of a civic-conscious business elite, a local government willing to innovate with and for private enterprise, a desire in both public and private sectors for quality planning, and the presence of historical perspective in the planning process.   J

3309. Goodenough, Richard. AN APPROACH TO LAND-USE CONTROL: THE CALIFORNIA LAND CONSERVATION ACT. *Urban Studies [Great Britain] 1978 15(3): 289-297.* Recognition of the nature of problems caused by urban growth in California has led to new legislation to cope with some of the operational difficulties faced by farmers in the urban fringe. Within this environment the California Land Conservation Act (Williamson Act) is intended to have its greatest impact. The aim of the legislation is accomplished by a voluntary contract between the farmer and local government which restricts the land to agricultural use. In return land is taxed on its agricultural value rather than its urban potential. This article represents a contribution to the appraisal of a significant initiative in public policy making which currently involves land-use control over some 5.5 million hectares of agricultural and open space land.   J

3310. Grabow, Stephen. FRANK LLOYD WRIGHT AND THE AMERICAN CITY: THE BROADACRES DEBATE. *J. of The Am. Inst. of Planners 1977 43(2): 115-124.* Frank Lloyd Wright's principal attempt at urban planning—Broadacre City—constitutes an enigma. On one hand it has often been dismissed as an example of impractical utopianism; but on the other hand it seems to have foreshadowed 40 years of suburbanization in the United States. To account for the paradox, several attempts to reassess the significance of Broadacre City have appeared in the last two decades. Combined with the original reactions to Wright's proposal in the thirties and forties, these discussions provide a timely debate which, upon examination, reveals part of the sociology of knowledge in architecture and planning. The first part of this article briefly summarizes Wright's proposal, including the philosophical background of Broadacre City, the spatial influences, and the reinforcement and support at the time of its publication. The second part analyzes the ensuing debate over questions of procedure and content between 1933 and the present. And the third part examines the disagreement in terms of the professional and philosophical orientations of the critics.   J

3311. Grant, Richard A., Jr. SAN DIEGO'S GROWTH PROBLEM —MANY QUESTIONS, SOME ANSWERS. *Cry California 1976 11(2): 12-15.* Summarizes the fifth and final session of the Town Meeting series sponsored by California Tomorrow. The meeting, held in San Diego on 24 January 1976, discussed such problems as population growth, air quality, water resources, and coordination of government agencies at several levels. San Diego attracts large numbers of people, resulting in a strain on the area's resources to meet the demands of the increasing population. Limitations on population were suggested, along with enforcement of air-quality and environmental regulations. What is most needed is a comprehensive, statewide program of resource allocation and careful city planning.   A. Hoffman

3312. Greenbie, Barrie B. SOCIAL TERRITORY, COMMUNITY HEALTH AND URBAN PLANNING. *J. of the Am. Inst. of Planners 1974 40(2): 74-82.* Sociological research has established the harmful effects of disrupting ethnic and other social structures in the central city. Proposals to redistribute urban poor in middle class suburbs may repeat these errors. Physical and social stress are least harmful to classes when familiar group support is present; also the effects are most severe on individuals with lowest social status.   J

3313. Gustafson, Gregory C. and Wallace, L. T. DIFFERENTIAL ASSESSMENT AS LAND USE POLICY: THE CALIFORNIA CASE.

J. of the Am. Inst. of Planners 1975 41(6): 379-389. The California Land Conservation Act of 1965 is enabling legislation designed to maintain the agricultural economy of the state, prevent discontiguous patterns of urban/suburban development, and assist in the preservation of prime agricultural and open space lands. The program in California is among the largest in the states that have enacted legislation to maintain land in agricultural and open space uses. This legislation has generally been ineffective as a land use management technique to stimulate orderly growth. Not only are the incentives inadequate to induce landowners in the rural-urban fringe to participate, but its unsystematic implementation by local governments has also diminished its effect on the allocation of land between uses. However, the program probably has enhanced the economic viability of agriculture by providing for taxation consistent with sustained agricultural use in rural areas affected by land speculation but not by the prospect of urbanization in the relevant future.   J

3314. Hart, John. CAN URBAN BOUNDARY LINES MANAGE GROWTH? TOWN MEETING IV: SANTA CLARA COUNTY. *Cry California 1975-76 11(1): 4-8.* Reports on the fourth Town Meeting sponsored by California Tomorrow, held at De Anza College in Cupertino in September 1975. Santa Clara County has 15 cities and an amalgam of local governmental boundaries and jurisdictions. The region now has more than a million people. Problems include how to determine the amount of development the area can logically sustain, how to save prime agricultural land, and how to make government bureaucracies respond to the needs of the people. Zoning, water, transportation, housing, and agriculture continue to challenge regional planners. Those attending the meeting expressed frustration at the limited achievements so far and the continuing problems.   A. Hoffman

3315. Hart, John. THE PETALUMA CASE. *Cry California 1974 9(2): 6-15.* Discusses a judicial decision against the city of Petaluma, California, ruling that a city cannot control its own numerical growth.   S

3316. Hart, John. SACRAMENTO TOWN MEETING. *Cry California 1975 10(2): 25-29.* Reports on the first of a series of town meetings discussing California ecological problems. The main topic was the American River and the demands made on it by a variety of federal, state, local, and private users. The demands, including recreation, fisheries, floodplain development, and sewage disposal, far exceed the river's capacity. Single-purpose agencies lack the scope to deal with the numerous issues involved; comprehensive planning along clear jurisdictional lines is needed. Based on the Sacramento town meeting hosted by California Tomorrow in January 1975. 8 photos.   A. Hoffman

3317. Houghteling, Joseph C. "IT'S TUESDAY, SO IT MUST BE PLANNING!" *Cry California 1974 9(4): 22-29.* California Tomorrow sponsored a city planning and restoration study tour of Europe in 1974.   S

3318. Johnson, Margaret. GROWTH AND CHANGE IN MANTECA. *Pacific Hist. 1977 21(1, supplement): 27-28.* Discusses the question of preservation and planning in a city, such as Manteca, which has a transient population and lack of unifying factors.   G. L. Olson

3319. Johnson, William C. and Harrigan, John J. PLANNING FOR GROWTH: THE TWIN CITIES APPROACH. *Natl. Civic Rev. 1979 68(4): 189-193, 198.* The results of efforts to limit growth in American urban areas since the 1960s have varied widely, but their impacts have not been measured with any consistency. The Minneapolis-St. Paul metropolitan land planning process may suggest some measurement criteria. All offer important lessons on how policy goals, legal tools and government structures interact.   J

3320. Johnston, Michael. PUBLIC POLICIES, PRIVATE CHOICES: NEW TOWN PLANNING AND LIFE STYLES IN THREE NATIONS. *Urban Affairs Q. 1977 13(1): 3-32.* Analyzes new towns in Great Britain, the United States, and the USSR. The Soviet Union's new towns developed remote areas, Britain redistributed population with them, and in the United States they were satellites of large metropolitan areas. Each case shows that comprehensive planning influenced physical environment more than social life. Planners in Britain and the United States failed to create a uniquely middle-class culture. The randomly formed Soviet neighborhoods did not generate a classless society. Suggests that instead of physical determinism, politics and the power to allocate neighborhood resources be used to build a sense of community. Secondary sources; 6 notes, biblio.   L. Beecher

3321. Kalba, Kas. POSTINDUSTRIAL PLANNING: A REVIEW FORWARD. *J. of the Am. Inst. of Planners 1974 40(3): 147-155.* Reviews Daniel Bell's *The Coming of Post-Industrial Society* (New York: Basic Books, 1973).   S

3322. Knittel, Robert E. NEW TOWN KNOWLEDGE, EXPERIENCE, AND THEORY: AN OVERVIEW. *Human Organization 1973 32(1): 37-48.* Reviews the theoretical and practical literature concerning new towns. Most new towns have been essentially conventional in design. There is still a lack of understanding of the human reaction to planned urban centers. Microenvironmental factors may be more important than macro factors in human adjustment. Calls for cooperative research among social scientists, planners, and developers. Abstracts in English, French, and Spanish. 4 notes, biblio.   E. S. Johnson

3323. Krumholz, Norman; Cogger, Janice M.; and Linner, John H. THE CLEVELAND POLICY PLANNING REPORT. *J. of the Am. Inst. of Planners 1975 41(5): 298-304.* Analyzes the *Cleveland Policy Planning Report* (1970), showing how the city of Cleveland has chosen a new type of planning and pointing out the implications of the Cleveland report for other major American cities.

3324. Loewenstein, Louis K. and McGrath, Dorn C., Jr. THE PLANNING IMPERATIVE IN AMERICA'S FUTURE. *Ann. of the Am. Acad. of Pol. and Social Sci. 1973 (405): 15-24.* City planning in the United States has gone through a number of changes in the past six decades and is likely to continue to change in the forthcoming years. This movement began with an interest in the City Beautiful, went on to be concerned with the City Efficient, and then with the City Social in the thirties. The postwar era produced a period of interest in the city as a system, while the sixties saw a spate of federal legislation which both institutionalized the city planning process and broadened its scope. In the future, planning should become concerned with matters of pollution, population distribution through a forceful urban growth policy, and enhancement of the quality of urban life.   J

3325. Long, Norton E. ANOTHER VIEW OF RESPONSIBLE PLANNING. *J. of the Am. Inst. of Planners 1975 41(5): 311-316.* Breaks down the *Cleveland Policy Planning Report* (1970) by topics such as subsidies, disinvestment, and the erosion of the primary labor market, briefly discussing the Report's approach to each topic.

3326. Long, Norton E. MAKING URBAN POLICY USEFUL AND CORRIGIBLE. *Urban Affairs Q. 1975 10(4): 379-397.* Analyzes reasons for rigidities in urban policies and advocates means of making them more flexible, beneficial, and practical. Suggests the use of rational thought and action, good municipal statistics for city planning, and citizen self-awareness.   P. J. Woehrmann

3327. Mader, George G. EARTHQUAKES, LANDSLIDES AND PUBLIC PLANNING. *Cry California 1974 9(3): 16-22.* Describes the leadership of the town of Portola Valley in developing land-use controls related to seismic and geological hazards, and discusses the need for instigation of similar public policy on the state level.   S

3328. Mayer, Harold M. URBAN GEOGRAPHY AND CHICAGO IN RETROSPECT. *Ann. of the Assoc. of Am. Geographers 1979 69(1): 114-118.* Chronicles the adaptation of city planning to the Geography Department and to the social sciences at the University of Chicago, 1950's-60's; from a special issue celebrating the 75th anniversary of the Association of American Geographers.

3329. Mogulof, Melvin B. A MODEST PROPOSAL FOR THE GOVERNANCE OF AMERICA'S METROPOLITAN AREAS. *J. of the Am. Inst. of Planners 1975 41(4): 250-257.* Four elements are suggested as necessary to a restructured metro government: authority, multifunctional capacity, a geographic scope approximating the urban area, and taxing powers. These four elements are seen as present to some degree in a small number of restructured metro areas. The experience of

these areas is seen as leading to a model of metro governance which would be based on the following building blocks: local units of government able to make those decisions concerning the character and responsiveness of public services; areawide special purpose districts; metropolitan governing councils having authority to constrain local governments and special districts, with policy makers responsive to state government; and state government able to serve as an arbiter between local government and areawide governments.   J

3330. Nieburg, H. L. CRIME PREVENTION BY URBAN DESIGN. *Society 1974 12(1): 41-47.* Reviews crime problems in parks and other open places and suggests the design of "defensible space" in city planning.   S

3331. Northcross, Mark. CAN THE HOUSING MARKET DO THE PLANNER'S JOB? *Cry California 1974 9(4): 32-37.* Examines recent private marketing developments in Orange County, California, that illustrate how only comprehensive public interest planning will solve land conservation problems.   S

3332. Pack, Janet Rothenberg. THE USE OF URBAN MODELS: REPORT ON A SURVEY OF PLANNING ORGANIZATIONS. *J. of the Am. Inst. of Planners 1975 41(3): 191-199.* A survey of nearly 1500 planning agencies indicates that about 25% of them have used or developed "urban models." About half of these agencies are using either land use or transportation models, or both, with the transportation planning agencies much more likely to be using models than are the other planning agencies. Among those currently developing models a wider variety of "other" types of models are included.   J

3333. Redding, Martin J. and Haefner, Lonnie E. MODELING LOCATIONAL PREFERENCES IN URBAN PLANNING. *Human Organization 1973 32(2): 163-175.* Suggests a technique to measure people's locational preferences for urban services. Presents and discusses tests of two measures: iso-disutility curves and joint probability of acceptance curves. Table, 12 fig., notes.   E. S. Johnson

3334. Reuter, Frederick H. EXTERNALITIES IN URBAN PROPERTY MARKETS: AN EMPIRICAL TEST OF THE ZONING ORDINANCE OF PITTSBURGH. *J. of Law and Econ. 1973 16(2): 313-349.* "The zoning ordinance of Pittsburgh should be revised to permit greater reliance upon the pricing mechanism in the allocation of urban property." 7 tables, 14 notes, appendix.   C. A. Gallacci

3335. Rickert, Thomas E. CAN YOU FIGHT CITY HALL. *Cry California 1974 9(2): 26-31.* Discusses attempts on the part of neighborhood improvement groups, e.g., San Francisco's Mission Coalition Organization, to maintain high standards within local neighborhoods despite city zoning ordinances.   S

3336. Rivers, David E. ATLANTA'S PLANNING PROCESS: COMPREHENSIVE, COORDINATED. *Natl. Civic Rev. 1979 68(3): 136-141.* A new charter for Atlanta, Georgia, 1974, has resulted in commitment to comprehensive and continuous city planning with extensive citizen input.

3337. Rondinelli, Dennis A. URBAN PLANNING AS POLICY ANALYSIS: MANAGEMENT OF URBAN CHANGE. *J. of the Am. Inst. of Planners 1973 39(1): 13-22.* Current approaches to and methods of urban planning are inadequate for effective urban policy analysis. Planners emerging from existing planning education programs have not been provided with the skills, knowledge, and experience required to plan for and guide urban change. Policy planning is a complex process of analyzing, intervening in, and managing the political conflict that is inextricably related to urban change.   J

3338. Roper, James H. AH, VENICE! *Am. Preservation 1979 2(4): 26-37.* Chronicles the fight to resist land developers, high rent, and high land prices in Venice, California, 1970's.

3339. Rose, Jerome G. THE COURTS AND THE BALANCED COMMUNITY: RECENT TRENDS IN NEW JERSEY ZONING LAW. *J. of the Am. Inst. of Planners 1973 39(3): 265-276.* Recent New Jersey judicial decisions have propounded the "balanced community" as a standard of validity of zoning ordinances. The "balanced community" standard is appealing to many planners in spite of the danger of ambiguity arising out of the diverse range of its meanings: (e.g., socioeconomic balance, fiscal balance, ecological balance, regional balance, and temporal balance). Judicial acceptance of the "balanced community" standard for zoning law validity would emphasize the need to evaluate the importance of the planning process because the validity of zoning laws would depend on the process by which the merits of competing land uses are evaluated. Adoption of the "community balance" standard would constitute judicial acceptance of planning principles of rational land-use allocation as criteria by which this evaluation is to be made.   J

3340. Sale, Kirkpatrick. THE POLIS PERPLEXITY: AN INQUIRY INTO THE SIZE OF CITIES. *Working Papers for a New Soc. 1978 6(1): 64-77.* Discusses city planners' views of the positive aspects of limiting growth in urban areas for purposes of healthy living environments, 1970's.

3341. Schneider, Kenneth R. THE COMMUNITY'S ROLE IN URBAN PLANNING. *Cry California 1973 8(4): 26-34.* Discusses the preparation of a community plan for West Fresno, California, in the 1970's.   S

3342. Siegan, Bernard H. COMPETITION: KEY TO CONSUMER DOMINANCE. *Freeman 1974 24(5): 298-300.* Zoning is anathema to the consumer because it destroys competition and free choice.   S

3343. Siegan, Bernard H. LAND USE REGULATION—A TOOL OF POLITICS, NOT OF PLANNING. *Freeman 1974 24(3): 138-141.*

3344. Singell, Larry D. OPTIMUM CITY SIZE: SOME THOUGHTS ON THEORY AND POLICY. *Land Econ. 1974 50(3): 207-212.*

3345. Stanfield, J. R. SLUM CLASSIFICATION AND THE URBAN PLANNER. *Rocky Mountain Social Sci. J. 1973 10(1): 86-92.* Reviews ideas on slum classification and their influence on urban planners.   S

3346. Sternlieb, George and Hughes, James W. NEW REGIONAL AND METROPOLITAN REALITIES OF AMERICA. *J. of the Am. Inst. of Planners 1977 43(3): 227-240.* Three major socioeconomic phenomena will increasingly structure and constrain the basic environment of planning activity for the next decade—the accelerating regional shift, the emerging metropolitan-nonmetropolitan dynamic, and expanding intrametropolitan differentials. These events are documented, causal processes are suggested, and their basic implications explored. A new reference framework for evaluating a host of economic and social issues has synthesized, superceding the conventions of the past decade.   J

3347. Straub, Robert W. URBAN AND RURAL DEVELOPMENT. *State Government 1978 51(3): 162-164.* Oregon's Land Conservation and Development Commission, formed in 1973, promotes the coordination of land use planning and seeks to guarantee public access to coastal areas, preserve agricultural lands, establish urban boundaries, and develop long-range growth management. One of eight articles in this issue on the West during the 1970's.

3348. Thompson, Charles W. N. and Rath, Gustave J. PLANNING SOLUTIONS AIDED BY MANAGEMENT AND SYSTEMS TECHNOLOGY. *Ann. of the Am. Acad. of Pol. and Social Sci. 1973 (405): 151-162.* Urban change is an extreme example of the proverbial product of a committee—most of the changes cannot be attributed to formal or organized planning. It is unfortunate that planners are divided, in C. P. Snow's sense, into two cultures which little understand one another. The contribution of technology to planning solutions has its greatest potential and its severest limitations in the emphasis upon formal models, and analysis and evaluation based largely on quantitative techniques. The understanding of these methods, and the combining of them with other methods of planning, will provide the optimal solution.   J

3349. Thorwaldson, Jay. THE PALO ALTO EXPERIENCE. *Cry California 1973 8(2): 4-17.* In February 1971 a rather remarkable document, "Foothills Environmental Design Study," on the question of

open space versus development in Palo Alto, California, argued the economic feasibility of retaining open space. The city has followed the study's recommendations, but there is tremendous pressure for development.
                                    R. W. Righter

3350. Unsigned. [THE URBAN PROSPECT]. *Center Mag. 1977 10(6): 20-36.*
Moore, Victor. LAND FOR THE PUBLIC GOOD, *pp. 21-28.* Discusses land use planning, in terms of legal methods of securing restricted use of certain lands for the public good; generally a comparative analysis of Great Britain and the US, 20th century.
Unsigned. DISCUSSION, *pp. 29-36.* Discussion is led by Moore (author of previous article), centering on crises which he perceives in present-day urban environments; discussion and response is provided by members of the Center for the Study of Democratic Institutions.

3351. Unsigned. [A WILLIAMSON ACT CONTROVERSY].
Dean, John B. A PANACEA THAT WASN'T: THE WILLIAMSON CONSERVATION ACT NEEDS REPAIR. *Cry California 1975 10(3): 18-23.* Examines the effect of the California Land Conservation Act of 1965, usually called the Williamson Act, on preventing the conversion of farmland into urban developments. The act intended to provide tax incentives to lands in order to prevent the sale of such land to developers when the land's fair market value exceeded its agricultural profitability. Unfortunately, certain provisions in the act have resulted in problems of interpretation and definition. Some counties have applied the act generally, while others have given the act restricted application. Only a small amount of prime agricultural land has been enrolled under the act, and at best it has proved to be only a temporary solution to the open space and agricultural problem. Recommends modification of the act and a comprehensive state plan for land use.
Lefaver, Scott. THE WILLIAMSON ACT: A VIEWPOINT FROM GILROY. *Cry California 1975 10(4): 32-33.* Disagrees with part of the above article concerning the preservation of agricultural land. Whereas the earlier article praised the Santa Clara County Urban Development and Open Space Plan, the intentions of the plan have not been realized in the southern part of the county. The county board of supervisors has rejected efforts to preserve agricultural areas there, broadly defining "rural" as including 2.5-acre landholdings. As a result, thousands of applications for subdivision of lots have been made in recent years. Calls for a planning mechanism to coordinate programs at local, regional, and state levels, and effective legislation.   A. Hoffman

3352. Whisler, Marilyn W. GROWTH MANAGEMENT STRATEGIES: POPULATION POLICY IMPLEMENTATION BY LOCAL GOVERNMENTS. *Policy Studies J. 1977 6(2): 208-215.* Discusses federal and state population growth strategies and policies; local governments need to formulate local and regional plans to meet the needs of urban and metropolitan areas.

3353. Woodbury, Steven R. TRANSFER OF DEVELOPMENT RIGHTS: A NEW TOOL FOR PLANNERS. *J. of the Am. Inst. of Planners 1975 41(1): 3-14.* Transfer of Development Rights is a tool for guiding growth and protecting low-density uses of land. Several proposals are discussed which deal in some fashion with the central problem: insuring that a market in fact exists for the development rights, to give them a value, and to provide an incentive for their transfer.   J

3354. Wrigley, Robert L., Jr. SMALL CITIES CAN HELP TO REVITALIZE RURAL AREAS. *Ann. of the Am. Acad. of Pol. and Social Sci. 1973 (405): 55-64.* In recent decades the United States increasingly has experienced an unbalanced pattern of settlement. The nation's population has become proportionally more and more concentrated into a relatively few large metropolitan areas. Rural areas have lost population as the number of jobs in farming and other activities declined. Thus, at the same time that urban congestion has aggravated big-city problems, many rural areas are stagnating with high unemployment. Several federal agencies have used the multi-county district approach, in cooperation with the states, after finding smaller—county—units too limited in scope to promote balanced growth.   J/S

3355. Zehner, Robert B. and Marans, Robert W. RESIDENTIAL DENSITY, PLANNING OBJECTIVES, AND LIFE IN PLANNED COMMUNITIES. *J. of the Am. Inst. of Planners 1973 39(5): 337-345.* In the context of a trend toward increasing moderate density townhouse construction in suburban areas, this report makes use of survey research data to explore differences in the quality of residents' lives in new-town townhouse areas compared to more conventional neighborhoods of lower density single family detached housing. Results indicate that while townhouse neighborhoods were associated with relatively less expensive housing (at a ratio of housing cost to income) and better access to selected facilities and services, they were also perceived as less attractive, less well maintained, more noisy, and less well provided with play areas for children. Overall, however, the ratings of new-town townhouse neighborhoods were as high or higher than those of traditional single family neighborhoods in the less planned control communities.   J

3356. Zikmund, Joseph. IMPACT OF THE USE OF MODELS ON URBAN PLANNING. *Policy Studies J. 1975 3(4): 325-332.* Discusses the problems, limitations, and implications of the use of computer models in city planning from 1950 to 1975.   S

Housing and Urban Renewal

3357. Abbott, Carl. NORFOLK, VIRGINIA: FROM HONKY TONK TO HONKY GLITTER. *Southern Exposure 1976 3(4): 31-34.* Urban renewal in Norfolk has progressed at the expense of leadership and community strength in the 1970's.

3358. Barbour, Kirol. SLUM CLEARANCE IN SHREVEPORT DURING THE GARDNER ADMINISTRATION: 1954-1958. *North Louisiana Hist. Assoc. J. 1979 10(2): 1-6.* Mayor Jim Gardner unsuccessfully attempted urban renewal for Shreveport as local property owners resisted "federal intervention." 20 notes.   J. F. Paul

3359. Barnes, William R. A NATIONAL CONTROVERSY IN MINIATURE: THE DISTRICT OF COLUMBIA STRUGGLE OVER PUBLIC HOUSING AND REDEVELOPMENT, 1943-46. *Prologue 1977 9(2): 91-104.* The conflict over public housing in the District of Columbia, although generated by local needs resulting from a wartime boom and consequent housing shortage, had a much broader significance than that of reconciling black and white interests and of inaugurating planning in the nation's capital. National pro- and antipublic housing advocates used the issue as a forum on which to discuss and bitterly fight over the postwar nature of the role of public housing in meeting national needs. Knowing that this issue would be an important one after the war, social reformers and representatives of private real estate interests were keenly concerned over the fate of public housing in the capital and fully participated in debates regarding the issue. The resultant clash of ideologies was revealing of the role which private interests play in the development of a city and of their employment of the device of redevelopment as a reform measure to avoid more public oriented legislation.   N. Lederer

3360. Barton, Stephen E. THE URBAN HOUSING PROBLEM: MARXIST THEORY AND COMMUNITY ORGANIZING. *Rev. of Radical Pol. Econ. 1977 9(4): 16-30.* Housing does not necessarily deteriorate in living quality as it ages. Rather, housing deterioration is a profitable consequence of the rental housing market. Housing repairs can prevent real deterioration. Yet without repairs, buildings lose exchange value though their use value remains the same. Shows the strength of a Marxist analysis of the housing problem in comparison with the explanations of both liberal and conservative bourgeois economists. Table, 46 notes.   C. Handleman

3361. Bauman, John F. SAFE AND SANITARY WITHOUT THE COSTLY FRILLS: THE EVOLUTION OF PUBLIC HOUSING IN PHILADELPHIA, 1929-1941. *Pennsylvania Mag. of Hist. and Biog. 1977 101(1): 114-128.* Traces the development of public housing in Philadelphia. The early impetus split between practical bureaucrats and persons who envisioned revivification of the community. The latter group weakened as money poured in from Washington, D.C. The bureaucrats had their way, constructed unimaginative structures, and were concerned

only with minimum standards of health and sanitation. What finally developed was new slums inhabited by persons not really in need of them. Eliminating frills also eliminated pride and character. 37 notes.   V. L. Human

3362. Berry, Brian J. L. and Bednarz, Robert S. A HEDONIC MODEL OF PRICES AND ASSESSMENTS FOR SINGLE-FAMILY HOMES: DOES THE ASSESSOR FOLLOW THE MARKET OR THE MARKET FOLLOW THE ASSESSOR? *Land Econ. 1975 51(1): 21-40.* Attempts to analyze the effect of a change in the property assessment system in Chicago. Constructs nine models that relate the price, land assessment value, improvement assessed value, and the assessment: price ratio to a number of variables reflecting building, location, and neighborhood characteristics. Finds there has been bias in past assessments and that the new system will benefit the black and large homeowners. Map, 8 tables, notes, references.   E. S. Johnson

3363. Better, Shirley. THE URBAN HOUSING CRISIS: OPPORTUNITY AND CHALLENGE. *Black Scholar 1974 6(4): 2-8.* Discusses the need for government aid to cities to improve housing (1974).   S

3364. Bingham, Richard D. and Kirkpatrick, Samuel A. PROVIDING SOCIAL SERVICES FOR THE URBAN POOR: AN ANALYSIS OF PUBLIC HOUSING AUTHORITIES IN LARGE AMERICAN CITIES. *Social Service Rev. 1975 49(1): 64-78.* Analyzes the social services provided for low-income home buyers and factors that deter or encourage the offering of these services.   S

3365. Brodsky, Barry. TENANTS FIRST: FHA TENANTS ORGANIZE IN MASSACHUSETTS. *Radical Am. 1975 9(2): 37-48.* Discusses the Tenants First Coalition organized in 1970 to obtain better public housing.   S

3366. Bryce, Herrington J.; Cousar, Gloria J.; and McCoy, William. HOUSING PROBLEMS OF BLACK MAYOR CITIES. *Ann. of the Am. Acad. of Pol. and Social Sci. 1978 (439): 80-89.* A common concern of black mayors is the housing condition in their cities. While housing is a common problem of all mayors, a disproportionately high percentage of black mayors see this factor as most critical in reversing their declining cities. This paper reviews specific policies undertaken by cities with black mayors. The success of these policies is dependent upon other policies taken by surrounding jurisdictions and by state and federal governments.   J

3367. Capeci, Dominic J., Jr. FIORELLO H. LA GUARDIA AND THE STUYVESANT TOWN CONTROVERSY OF 1943. *New-York Hist. Soc. Q. 1978 62(4): 289-310.* When Mayor La Guardia announced plans in 1943 for the Metropolitan Life Insurance Company to build a housing project on the east side of lower Manhattan, he aroused a storm of opposition. The project was designed for middle-class tenants and the company was to be given tax and other benefits to assist construction. Unfortunately for La Guardia, the company let it be known that the housing would be for whites, only. Thus, the mayor was forced to choose between public housing with private money or civil rights. He went with the public housing although he later signed a municipal law to prohibit discrimination in future projects. Stuyvesant Town would later be desegregated under a future mayor, but there would remain a blot on the liberal reputation of Fiorello La Guardia. Based on correspondence and newspapers, 5 illus., 34 notes.   C. L. Grant

3368. Chapman, Edgar L. ABANDONING THE BULLDOZER APPROACH. *Focus Midwest 1973 9(58): 16-20.* The old urban renewal practice of moving the poor out, bulldozing, and rebuilding office buildings or low-rent housing is gone. That system simply moved slums to new locations, and did not solve basic problems of unemployment, low-income employment, segregated housing, or integration of minorities in the community. In Peoria, Illinois, Gerald Osborne, redevelopment director, has sought to use an old incomplete redevelopment program to upgrade housing and restore inner city institutions.   L. H. Grothaus

3369. Cord, Steven. URBAN RENEWAL: BOON OR BOONDOGGLE? *Am. J. of Econ. and Sociol. 1974 33(2): 184-186.* Mentions some problems of urban renewal in the United States such as subsidies to the rich, destroyed housing, poverty, and relocation injustice.

W. L. Marr

3370. Corell, M. R.; Lilydahl, Jane H.; and Singell, L. D. THE EFFECTS OF GREENBELTS ON RESIDENTIAL PROPERTY VALUES: SOME FINDINGS ON THE POLITICAL ECONOMY OF OPEN SPACE. *Land Econ. 1978 54(2): 207-217.* With data from Boulder, Colorado, in 1975, uses a multiple-linear regression model to determine the effect of greenbelts on housing values. There is a $4.20 decrease in the property value with each one foot of distance from a greenbelt. If the increase in housing value due to greenbelts was adequately reflected in the tax rolls, the increase in taxes would more than return the cost of greenbelt acquisition. 4 tables, 12 notes, 19 ref.   E. S. Johnson

3371. Danielson, Michael N. OPENING THE SUBURBS TO THE POOR. *New York Affairs 1976 3(4): 83-105.* The open-housing movement has relied heavily upon litigation in the courts as a strategy, with some notable successes and a few significant setbacks. But a court order, by itself, cannot produce suburban housing for low-income minority groups.   J

3372. Davis, Otto A.; Eastman, Charles M.; and Hua, Chan-I. THE SHRINKAGE IN THE STOCK OF LOW-QUALITY HOUSING IN THE CENTRAL CITY: AN EMPIRICAL STUDY OF THE U.S. EXPERIENCE OVER THE LAST TEN YEARS. *Urban Studies [Great Britain] 1974 11(1): 13-26.* Comparison of housing data in the 1960 and 1970 U.S. Censuses show a significant decrease in substandard housing in all areas, particularly in central cities of large SMSAs. Though the classifications for substandard housing are not parallel, it can be shown that the improvement in these Central Cities was between 57 and 74 per cent. The largest improvement has been in the "dilapidated" category and the variation in the rate of improvement among different cities is statistically explained by the original stock of dilapidated housing and new construction of low cost housing. The improvement in housing "lacking facilities" has been more modest and its variation can be attributed to market demand pressures. The rate of change in poor households, non-poor households and employment are modelled along with housing in a simultaneous equation model. Tentative results show that the relative rate of improvement in housing lacking facilities is inversely related to the level of welfare payments and the rate of increase in poor families. The results also suggest the positive influence of low cost housing in retaining non-poor households in Central Cities. No evidence was found to suggest that low cost housing attracts poor families to a particular city.   J

3373. DeSalvo, Joseph S. BENEFITS AND COSTS OF NEW YORK CITY'S MIDDLE-INCOME HOUSING PROGRAM. *J. of Pol. Econ. 1975 83(4): 791-805.* A method for evaluating publicly subsidized housing is presented and applied to New York City's Mitchell-Lama middle-income housing program. Households in the 57,000 subsidized dwelling units received net benefits of $25.6 million, or $450 per household, in 1968. The public subsidy required to provide these benefits was $46.9 million, or $824 per unit. Hence, rather substantial nontenant benefits of $21.3 million, or $374 per unit, would have had to be generated by the program for it to be considered an efficient use of resources. Net benefits to participants were found to rise with age of household head and family size, to be lower for female-headed households, and to show little relation to income level. However, net benefits varied considerably for otherwise similar households. Finally, program participants were found to differ little on average from those occupying private, unsubsidized rental housing in New York City in 1968.   J

3374. Dolbeare, Cushing N. THE HOUSING STALEMATE. *Dissent 1974 21(4): 534-541.* Questions whether public housing has met the needs of the poor in the 1970's.   S

3375. Doll, Tussell C. THE ELEPHANT AND THE DAY OF THE PYGMIES. *Focus Midwest 1973 9(58): 10-15.* A community association of blue-collar and white-collar people of moderate income successfully blocked an attempt by a redevelopment corporation in Kansas City, Missouri, to designate their area as blighted. The plan had been publicly announced at election time and the area contained people with expertise

in dealing with power structures and with time to work for the association.   L. H. Grothaus

3376. Dreier, Peter. THE POLITICS OF RENT CONTROL. *Working Papers for a New Soc. 1979 6(6): 55-63.* Provides a short background of rent control in the United States since 1942 and describes current efforts for rent control in cities.

3377. Edelstein, Robert. THE DETERMINANTS OF VALUE IN THE PHILADELPHIA HOUSING MARKET: A CASE STUDY OF THE MAIN LINE 1967-1969. *Rev. of Econ. and Statistics 1974 56(3): 319-328.* Study of the housing market in the Philadelphia suburban area known as the Main Line.   S

3378. Friedman, Judith J. CENTRAL BUSINESS DISTRICT AND RESIDENTIAL URBAN RENEWAL: RESPONSE TO UNDESIRED CHANGE? *Social Sci. Q. 1977 58(1): 45-59.* Analysis shows that central business district renewal decreases with retail sales, while residential renewal increases with the percent nonwhite and the decline in the socioeconomic status of the population. Housing conditions are found to be unimportant.   J

3379. Fuerst, J. S. and Petty, Roy. BLEAK HOUSING IN CHICAGO. *Public Interest 1978 (52): 103-110.* Reviews *Hills* v. *Gautreaux* (US, 1976) and its effect on housing in Chicago. Begun in 1966, this class-action suit against the Chicago Housing Authority initially sought to provide new, integrated housing for urban blacks. However, because its lawyers broadened its scope to include the Chicago suburbs, neither objective has been obtained. Decent housing within Chicago has been sacrificed to the intention to integrate housing in the entire area around the city.   J. Tull

3380. Garvey, Timothy J. THE DULUTH HOMESTEADS: A SUCCESSFUL EXPERIMENT IN COMMUNITY HOUSING. *Minnesota Hist. 1978 46(1): 2-16.* Duluth's suburban federal subsistence homestead program started in 1936 and remained under various forms of government control until the homesteads were turned over to private interests in 1947. In mid-March 1938 84 homesteads were occupied by persons contracting to buy their government-built homes and adjacent land on an installment basis and to live in accordance with the rules of a community-based association of home owners. The residents appear to have been carefully selected for the venture and represented a group of "achievers" who maintained and improved their property. Most of the residents worked as part-time farmers and held other jobs whenever they could to pay off the considerable amounts charged by the government for the properties involved. The Duluth homestead project was among the most successful ventures of its type inaugurated by the New Deal, initially under the Interior Department and later by the Resettlement Administration. Primary research and oral interviews.   N. Lederer

3381. Guntermann, Karl L. and Cooper, James R. CAN LOCAL HOUSING PRODUCTION AND MARKET ANALYSIS BE AN INTERACTIVE PROCESS? *Urban and Social Change Rev. 1975 8(1): 9-14.* Results of a Champaign-Urbana area experiment suggest that housing market analysis, producers' surveys, and vacancy studies can help control housing construction.   S

3382. Hartman, Chester W.; Kessler, Robert P.; and LeGates, Richard T. MUNICIPAL HOUSING CODE ENFORCEMENT AND LOW-INCOME TENANTS. *J. of the Am. Inst. of Planners 1974 40(2): 90-104.* Municipal housing code enforcement often leads to rent increases, tenant moves to lower cost housing, evictions, and reduction in the low-rent housing stock, and thus may harm low-income tenants more than it helps them.   J

3383. Hartman, Chester W. and Levi, Margaret. PUBLIC HOUSING MANAGERS: AN APPRAISAL. *J. of the Am. Inst. of Planners 1973 39(2): 125-137.* Data collected through questionnaires given to managers of public housing projects, 1968, provide profiles of their characteristics and attitudes.

3384. Hawkins, Homer C. URBAN HOUSING AND THE BLACK FAMILY. *Phylon 1976 37(1): 73-84.* Compares housing conditions among blacks, especially problems with overcrowding, substandard housing, and federal programs, 1960's, with conditions faced by whites.

3385. Hendon, William S. PARK SERVICE AREAS AND RESIDENTIAL PROPERTY VALUES. *Am. J. of Econ. and Sociol. 1974 33(2): 175-183.* The use or availability of use of the park as studied in Dallas, Texas, for 1966 has some significant impact upon property values. The economic value of a park is a proxy for the broader notion of total social value. Secondary sources; 3 tables, 2 notes. W. L. Marr

3386. Holleb, Doris B. A DECENT HOME AND SUITABLE LIVING ENVIRONMENT. *Ann. of the Am. Acad of Pol. and Social Sci. 1978 (435): 102-116. Social Indicators, 1976* documents the success of the nation in solving the housing problems of the 1950's, in eliminating both a severe housing shortage and large numbers of substandard dwellings. Housing has improved greatly for all income classes, for all races, and by all standards of measurement, but wide disparities remain. This suggests great relative deprivation in a society with such universally high standards. A massive upsurge in housing construction, greater than rising demand, brought changes not only in the quality of the housing stock but in its location as well. The transformation of residential settlement patterns and the growth of extensive metropolitan cities have had profound effects on housing and community life. Because of racial and social barriers in local housing markets, polarities among metropolitan neighborhoods have increased. None of these pervasive changes emerge in the indicators. Nor do they address such contemporary concerns as rising housing costs, deteriorating neighborhood conditions in poverty areas, and the environmental and energy implications of emerging low density housing patterns. Thus, readers are likely to underestimate the scale and nature of housing deprivation and misread the direction of future trends. J

3387. Jeffery Green, R. and Von Furstenberg, George M. THE EFFECT OF RACE AND AGE OF HOUSING ON MORTGAGE DELINQUENCY RISK IN THE PITTSBURGH METROPOLITAN AREA. *Urban Studies [Great Britain] 1975 12(1): 85-89.* One of the factors contributing to the vicious cycle of neighborhood deterioration is the withdrawal of home mortgage lending once a neighborhood reaches a certain racial 'tipping point.' Examines the extent to which a high and rising percentage of blacks in the 160 wards of the Pittsburgh Metropolitan area are associated with mortgage delinquency risk and compares this model to an alternative which focuses on the age of the structure. The age of housing model does at least as well as the racial characteristics model. J

3388. Jones, Malcolm. PEOPLE, PLACE, PERSISTENCE: A VICTORY FOR NEIGHBORHOODS. *Southern Exposure 1977 5(1): 66-74.* In the early 1970's, the Redevelopment Commission of Winston-Salem, North Carolina, under the domination of James Haley, tried to clear the rundown neighborhood of Crystal Towers. It was successfully thwarted by Jon DeVries and a handful of allies. Beginning with a 1975 victory in the city government for rehabilitation rather than urban renewal through clearance, DeVries and others held neighborhood meetings to explain available loan programs, fight redlining, and begin the rejuvenation of the area. The neighborhood today has been considerably upgraded with residents of diverse incomes and mixed race. N. Lederer

3389. Keller, Frank V.; Bederman, Sanford H.; and Hartshorn, Truman A. MIGRATION PATTERNS OF ATLANTA'S INNER CITY DISPLACED RESIDENTS. *West Georgia Coll. Studies in the Social Sci. 1977 16: 49-58.* Aggressive urban renewal in early 1960's Atlanta under the Model Neighborhood Area program resulted in a gross loss of 19,000 housing units; displaced residents—95% black—relocated "within the territory of black ghetto space."

3390. Kristof, Frank S. HOUSING. *Pro. of the Acad. of Pol. Sci. 1974 31(3): 188-199.* Examines the lack of adequate housing which confronted New York in the 1960's, the establishment of the New York State Urban Development Corporation (UDC), and the resolution of housing problems. S

3391. Krumholz, Norman and Hoffmann, Susan. REVITALIZING URBAN CENTERS: BUSINESS AND NEIGHBORHOODS. *Natl. Civic Rev. 1979 68(3): 130-135.* Examines Cleveland, Ohio's, attempts at urban revitalization through active programs to provide employment for residents and to alleviate neighborhood problems, 1959-79.

3392. Lake, Robert W. RACIAL TRANSITION AND BLACK HOMEOWNERSHIP IN AMERICAN SUBURBS. *Ann. of the Am. Acad. of Pol. and Social Sci. 1979 441: 142-156.* Home ownership has traditionally served as an efficient wealth generating mechanism for the American middle class. Recent data indicating an increase in the metropolitan area black population living in the suburbs raise two questions: is black suburbanization equivalent to home ownership, and does black suburban homeownership lead to equity accumulation and the generation of wealth? These questions are addressed through analysis of a national sample of suburban housing units surveyed in 1974, and again in 1975, as part of the Census Bureau's *Annual Housing Survey.* As of the mid-1970's, black suburbanization has not been entirely synonymous with homeownership nor has homeownership automatically served the wealth generating function for blacks that it has provided for earlier suburbanizing aspirants to the middle class. J

3393. Lazin, Frederick A. FEDERAL LAW—INCOME HOUSING ASSISTANCE PROGRAMS AND RACIAL SEGREGATION: LEASED PUBLIC HOUSING. *Public Policy 1976 24(3): 337-360.* Study of the implementation of Section 23 of the Housing and Urban Development Act of 1965 which authorized the Federal Public Housing Authority to make funds available to local housing authorities, to lease privately owned dwelling units for public housing. Using the Chicago Housing Authority operation of Section 23 during 1965-73, finds racial "segregation was furthered." Negroes were unable to obtain housing in white communities in Chicago. Analysis of the ability of local constituencies to coopt federal agencies in the implementation of federal programs reveals the strength of federalism. Administrative regulations governing Section 23's operation which encouraged continued patterns of segregation in leased housing are criticized and solutions are offered. Black community response to the program is detailed. Based on original research, interviews, primary and secondary material; table, 86 notes. J. M. Herrick

3394. Levy, John M. THE POLITICS OF HOUSING IN WESTCHESTER. *New York Affairs 1979 5(4): 95-102.* Traces the trends in the housing situation in Westchester since the 1950's, particularly the housing market there during the 1970's, characterized by low vacancy rates, high prices, land restrictions, and an aging rental stock.

3395. Little, Charles E. ATLANTA RENEWAL GIVES POWER TO THE COMMUNITIES. *Smithsonian 1974 7(4): 100-107.* Discusses the urban renewal carried on by Cabbagetown, a neighborhood in Atlanta, Georgia, 1971-76.

3396. Lowry, Ira S. HOW TO RESCUE NEW YORK'S VANISHING HOUSING STOCK. *New York Affairs 1973 1(1): 20-45.* Describes the deterioration of housing in New York City in the 1960's. Rental housing is undermaintenanced because costs of operation and maintenance increased more rapidly than the rents prospective tenants were willing to pay. Proposes that a housing assistance agency in each community issue rent certificates to low-income families to supplement the monthly amount they could afford to pay for appropriate housing. Experimental programs are utilizing this concept. Condensation of a paper prepared for the Subcommittee on Housing, Committee on Banking and Currency, U.S. House of Representatives, 92nd Congress; 8 illus., 2 tables, 13 notes. J. A. Benson

3397. Marando, Vincent L. A METROPOLITAN LOWER INCOME HOUSING ALLOCATION POLICY. *Am. Behavioral Scientist 1975 19(1): 75-103.* Discusses the development 1970-75 by urban government councils and the Housing and Urban Development Department of location plans for low-income housing, in a special issue entitled "Policy Content and the Regulatory Process."

3398. Meehan, Eugene J. LOOKING THE GIFT HORSE IN THE MOUTH: THE CONVENTIONAL PUBLIC HOUSING PROGRAM IN ST. LOUIS. *Urban Affairs Q. 1975 10(4): 423-463.* Relates the development and failures of public housing in St. Louis, and concludes that little has been learned by those responsible for public housing projects. The needs of the public housing occupier receive low priority from planners and administrators, who are caught between long-term obligations and short-term funding. Concludes that society has not defined its responsibility to the poor and disadvantaged. 4 tables, notes, biblio. P. J. Woehrmann

3399. Meyer, David R. INTERURBAN DIFFERENCES IN BLACK HOUSING QUALITY. *Ann. of the Assoc. of Am. Geographers 1973 63(3): 347-352.* Racial discrimination distorts the supply of housing available to blacks.

3400. Mithun, Jacqueline S. COOPERATIVE COMMUNITY SOLIDARITY AGAINST URBAN RENEWAL. *Human Organization 1975 34(1): 79-86.* "This case study documents the initial intrusion of an urban renewal program (1971-73), designated as the Neighborhood Development Program," into a black community in Buffalo, New York.   S

3401. Newsom, Robert T. LIMITED-PROFIT HOUSING—WHAT WENT WRONG? *New York Affairs 1975 2(4): 80-91.* New York City's Mitchell-Lama housing program developed financial trouble. Inept management, poorly conceived legislation and high interest rates combined to impose serious burdens on the city's already troubled budget.   J

3402. O'Loughlin, John and Munski, Douglas C. HOUSING REHABILITATION IN THE INNER CITY: A COMPARISON OF TWO NEIGHBORHOODS IN NEW ORLEANS. *Econ. Geography 1979 55(1): 52-70.* Housing rehabilitation and restoration of historic homes in the Lower Marigny and Algiers Point neighborhoods of New Orleans, 1950-70, was influenced by the attraction of historic buildings and the proximity of urban services.

3403. Pearson, John E. URBAN HOUSING AND POPULATION CHANGES IN THE SOUTHWEST, 1940-1960. *Southwestern Social Sci. Q. 1964 44(4): 357-366.* Despite population shifts, increased fertility, and economic disturbances, housing adequacy in the Southwest (based on national persons-per-room aggregates), 1940-60, improved continually and neared the national average in 1960.

3404. Pfeiffer, Sophie Douglas. "GO URBAN, YOUNG MAN!": AMERICAN HOMESTEADING, 1862-1974. *Historic Preservation 1974 26(3): 16-22.* Discusses homesteading, various homesteading and land grant acts, and present day urban homesteading.

3405. Quigley, John M. HOUSING: PROVIDING APPROPRIATE INCENTIVES. *New York Affairs 1978 5(2): 91-103.* Assesses the effects of rent control and property tax assessment on the housing situation in New York City during 1960-75 and recommends public funding subsidies to increase low income housing.

3406. Richards, Carol and Rowe, Jonathan. RESTORING A CITY: WHO PAYS THE PRICE? *Working Papers for a New Soc. 1977 4(4): 54-61.* Examines how the middle class's move back to the District of Columbia from the suburbs has increased housing prices for Negroes and caused rampant land speculation in the 1970's.

3407. Schorr, Philip. TENANT RELOCATION: ALL LOSERS, NO WINNERS. *New York Affairs 1975 2(4): 92-101.* Ad hoc, highly politicized regulation of tenant relocation for institutional and private development has made things hard for tenants and developers alike.   J

3408. Solomon, Arthur P. and Fenton, Chester G. THE NATION'S FIRST EXPERIENCE WITH HOUSING ALLOWANCES: THE KANSAS CITY EXPERIENCE. *Land Econ. 1974 50(3): 212-223.* "The program demonstrated the feasibility of using housing allowances to improve the shelter and neighborhood conditions of low-income families within the existing housing stock, in a short period of time, at relatively low subsidy costs."   S

3409. Starr, Roger. STAGNANT METROPOLIS. *Society 1976 13(4): 42-44.* Considers the inadequacy of New York City's housing and its public housing programs, and recommends reforms.

3410. Sternlieb, George; Burchell, Robert W.; Hughes, James W.; and James, Franklin J. HOUSING ABANDONMENT IN THE URBAN CORE. *J. of the Am. Inst. of Planners 1974 40(5): 321-332.* The essential act of residential abandonment is the owner's decision to minimize expenditures in the expectation, conscious or otherwise, of ultimately giving up claim to his property. This may result from the immediacies of

current cash flow or from negative expectations of future value, or both. Study of a sample of Newark landlords suggests that abandonment is more a function of owner-tenant interplay, and neighborhood change than of the physical characteristics of the building itself.   J

3411. Thomas, Emma Wormley. BLACK HOUSING: A GAME OF FRUSTRATION. *Crisis 1979 86(5): 169-171.* Washington, D.C., is a good example of a housing dilemma for blacks. At one point, white Americans abandoned the central city, allowing the area to deteriorate into slums for low-income blacks. The year 1975 signaled a reversing trend; whites showed an increased interest in rehabilitating buildings and moving back. This caused prices to soar out of the reach of blacks, who now cannot find any place to live in the District of Columbia.
                                                                                                      A. G. Belles

3412. Unsigned. [HOUSING AND INTEGRATION]. *Center Mag. 1979 12(4): 45-49.*
Milgram, Morris. REWARDING INTEGRATION, *pp. 45-47, 49.*
    Discusses the author's experiences as the developer of an integrated housing tract in Philadelphia, Pennsylvania, 1947-79.
Mitchell, Maurice. HOUSING ALONE WILL NOT DO IT, *p. 48.* Considers integrated housing inadequate to end racial discrimination, and calls for wider social and economic planning.

3413. Unsigned. [PUBLIC HOUSING AND THE POOR]. *Public Interest 1973 (31): 126-134.*
Scobie, Richard S. "PROBLEM FAMILIES" AND PUBLIC HOUSING, *pp. 126-129.*
Starr, Roger. A REPLY, *pp. 130-134.*
Discusses data from Boston and New York City concerning Roger Starr's article "Which of the Poor Shall Live in Public Housing," *The Public Interest*, 1971, arguing that working poor families are leaving public housing projects because of friction with unemployed tenants.   S

3414. Walzer, Norman and Singer, Dan. HOUSING EXPENDITURES IN URBAN LOW-INCOME AREAS. *Land Econ. 1974 50(3): 224-231.* "The absence of a discriminatory price differential in poverty areas does not preclude the existence of discrimination in other markets. . . ."   S

3415. Weinberg, Steve. OLA DAVIS' ONE-DOLLAR HOUSE. *Am. Preservation 1979 2(4): 38-43.* After purchasing a house for one dollar in a section of Washington, D.C., deemed unlivable by local officials, Ola Davis renovated it and now owns a comfortable, easily resellable home; 1975-79.

3416. Welfeld, Irving. THE COURTS AND DESEGREGATED HOUSING: THE MEANING (IF ANY) OF THE GAUTREAUX CASE. *Public Interest 1976 (45): 123-135.* In *Hills* v. *Gautreaux* (1976) the Supreme Court ruled that when the federal government has been guilty of racial discrimination in regard to the siting of city public housing projects it can be ordered to adopt a plan that ignores municipal boundaries. In this case, the Department of Housing and Urban Development (HUD) was found guilty of violating the Constitution by confining Chicago families eligible for public housing to the city of Chicago rather than to the metropolis of Chicago, which includes the city's suburbs. This decision will be ineffectual because it adds to a Congressional housing program, which has neither increased the housing supply nor housed the poor, the requirement that it now also achieve racial and socioeconomic integration in residential areas.
                                                                                                      S. Harrow

Architecture, Building, and Buildings

3417. Cave, Richard S. THE MARIN COUNTY CIVIC CENTER. *Pacific Historian 1975 19(3): 241-252.* Presents the story of the Marin County Civic Center, 1952-63. The building was designed by Frank Lloyd Wright and dedicated in 1963. Discusses behind-the-scenes skirmishes, controversy, and conflict between Wright and County Supervisor William Fusselman. The center is a memorial to its proponents and the architect. Primary sources; 4 illus., 38 notes.
                                                                                                      G. L. Olson

3418. Fishwick, Marshall W. MUSHROOM MAGIK: ALICE IN IMAGELAND. *J. of Popular Culture 1973 7(2): 493-498.* Discusses the effects of architecture on the population in cities; one of 12 articles in this issue on popular architecture.   S

3419. Fowler, Sigrid H. *LEARNING FROM LAS VEGAS* BY VENTURI, BROWN AND IZENOUR: ARCHITECTURE AND THE CIVIC BODY. *J. of Popular Culture 1973 7(2): 425-433.* Discusses *Learning from Las Vegas* (Cambridge: MIT Press, 1972) and its important thesis that modern architecture must be responsive to the populace as well as the popular culture; one of 12 articles on popular architecture in this issue.   S

3420. Lapping, Mark B. VERNACULAR ENVIRONMENTS: THE SQUATTER SETTLEMENTS. *J. of Popular Culture 1973 7(2): 446-450.* Discusses social changes effected by squatter settlements, lower-income communities forming around, not in, cities; one of 12 articles in this issue on popular architecture.   S

3421. Lynes, Russell. THE ARCHITECT WAS TOLD "WORLD TRADE" SO HE PLANNED BIG. *Smithsonian 1978 8(10): 42-49.* Describes New York's World Trade Center (ca. 1970). The landmark structures designed by chief architect Minoru Yamasaki are not just a piece of architecture, but a "place." A small self-contained city, the center has towers 1,350 feet high and a five-acre plaza communicating the interplay between the personal and monumental. Housing all aspects of trade from importers and exporters to international bankers, it receives approximately 1,000 visitors a day. On request, they can be showered with the awesome statistics of the complex. Despite the critics' "hail of arrows," the public likes it, giving it a better than average chance for survival. 9 illus.   S. R. Quéripel

3422. McCue, George. AIRPORT ARCHITECTURE: THE DALLAS-FORT WORTH SOLUTION. *Art in Am. 1974 62(1): 74-77.*

3423. Meehan, Thomas. THE WORLD TRADE CENTER: DOES MEGA-ARCHITECTURE WORK? *Horizon 1976 18(4): 4-15.* Discusses the construction and architecture of skyscrapers in the World Trade Center of New York City 1966-70's, including safety problems.

3424. Miller, Nory. CHICAGO ON THE DRAWING BOARDS. *Horizon 1978 21(9): 50-57.* The designs of architects Harry Weese, Bertrand Goldberg, Walter Nesch, Helmut Jahn, Stanley Tigerman, Thomas Beeby, and Stuart Cohen, 1960's-70's, vary markedly from Chicago's tradition but maintain its standards of creativity and excellence.

3425. Neil, J. Meredith. LAS VEGAS ON MY MIND. *J. of Popular Culture 1973 7(2): 379-386.* Discusses the architecture found in Las Vegas, Nevada, during the 1960's-70's; one of 12 articles on popular architecture in this issue.   S

3426. Ruchelman, Leonard I. THE NEW YORK WORLD TRADE CENTER IN PERSPECTIVE. *Urbanism Past and Present 1978 (6): 29-38.* Elaborates on rationale behind high rise development. Delves into the pro and con arguments of this development and the problems in researching this phenomenon. Focuses on the World Trade Center, showing who benefitted and who lost. While initiated by the private sector, both the private and public sectors encountered many problems, e.g. filling vacant floor space, extension of municipal services, etc. These were generally resolved by trade-offs between the public and private sectors. Problems unresolved and facing future development include wind effects, pollution and transportation, and who bears these costs. 3 tables, 7 notes.
B. P. Anderson

Landscape Architecture and Parks

3427. Cook, Jess. LOS ANGELES LANDS A HUGE NEW PARK: IF IT CAN LAND THE LAND REQUIRED. *Smithsonian 1979 10(4): 26-35.* Discusses the efforts to create a Santa Monica Mountains National Recreation Area during the 1960's and 1970's.

3428. Galler, Michelle I. FROM OLD RAIL YARD TO NEW CITY PARK. *Smithsonian 1978 9(7): 150-152.* Discusses the 18-year struggle to transform a decayed stretch of Jersey City, New Jersey, waterfront into Liberty Park, a public space and wildlife refuge with a dramatic view of the Manhattan skyline. Inspired by city councilman Morris Pesin as early as 1958, the park was opened to the public for the Bicentennial. 5 illus.
S. R. Quéripel

3429. Lemonides, James S. and Young, April L. PROVISION OF PUBLIC OPEN SPACE IN URBAN AREAS: DETERMINANTS, OBSTACLES AND INCENTIVES. *J. of the Am. Inst. of Planners 1978 44(3): 286-296.* Problems encountered in public open space provision in the urban context are investigated through a case study of the Chicago metropolitan region. Correlation and regression analyses are utilized in an attempt to explain local public open space acreage levels in terms of readily available data. Park district directors, chief municipal executives, forest preserve and conservation district directors are surveyed and interviewed in order to gain more qualitative insights. Governmental regulations in general and funding allocation practices for the region are examined for any effect on provision levels. Basic impediments to public open land provision are identified, and several solution strategies are suggested.   J

3430. Simon, Donald E. A PROSPECT FOR PARKS. *Public Interest 1976 (44): 27-39.* New York City parks are not properly maintained, are often inhabited by undesirables, and are subject to vandalism. Examples discussed include Fort Greene Park, Rochdale Village Park, and Morningside Park. A park is likely to fall prey to blight when it is not well used because there is no immediate constituency, when the facility has been abandoned by the city administration, and when there is neighborhood social conflict. Solutions include community involvement, the placing of existing recreation and neighborhood programs in the parks, and planning which, by maintaining a balance between public needs and the facilities provided, does not overbuild the parks.   S. Harrow

3431. Unsigned. WASTELANDS. *Am. Preservation 1978 1(3): 45-49.* Surveys the accomplishments of the Trust for Public Land, founded in 1973, and its National Urban Land Program. Vacant lots have already been acquired in Oakland, California, Newark, New Jersey, and the South Bronx, New York. They have been transformed into community vegetable gardens, "tot lot" playgrounds, and recreational and sitting areas. Neighborhoods are beginning to assume responsibility for their development, maintenance, and management. Illus.   J. Tull

Public Services and Utilities

3432. Barnes, Joseph W. WATER WORKS HISTORY: A COMPARISON OF ALBANY, UTICA, SYRACUSE, AND ROCHESTER. *Rochester Hist. 1977 39(3): 1-24.* Discusses separately the histories of the public water supply systems in four major New York cities from the 19th century to the present.

3433. Dornan, Paul B. WHITHER URBAN POLICY ANALYSIS? A REVIEW ESSAY. *Polity 1977 9(4): 503-527.* Recommends the analysis of public services such as garbage collection, sewage removal, education, and police and fire protection to political scientists. Reviews the rapidly growing literature in several disciplines, presents a typology of public services relevant to political analysis, and reviews studies of service distribution and of citizen perceptions of these services. Attempts to establish a connection between citizens' perceptions and their political behavior, and compares the recent findings to Robert C. Wood's provocative conclusions. Based on secondary sources; 52 notes.
W. R. Hively

3434. Easterbrook, Gregg. DEEP TUNNEL: HOW OUR MONEY FLOWS INTO CHICAGO'S SEWERS. *Washington Monthly 1979 11(9): 30-36.* To solve a huge sewage and storm drainage problem, Chicago has been engaged since 1972 in the Tunnel and Reservoir Plan (TARP), which is expected to cost $11 billion (using federal funds from the Clean Water Act and the Environmental Protection Agency), involve the Army Corps of Engineers in a huge urban reservoir project, and still do no more than raise the water quality of Chicago's rivers to the state's lowest quality rating by the 1990's.

3435. Greenberg, Michael R. and O'Neill, Theodore F. SOLID WASTE: THE END OF THE BOTTOMLESS PIT. *New York Affairs 1978 5(2): 114-129.* Assesses New York City's problem with solid waste, 1963-77; proposes remedies designed to use reclamation and guarantee environmental quality and public safety.

3436. Greenberg, Michael R. SUGGESTIONS FOR EVALUATING RESOURCE RECOVERY PROPOSALS. *J. of The Am. Inst. of Planners 1977 43(1): 24-32.* Since 1973, resource recovery of residential solid waste has rapidly expanded in response to increasing landfill costs, increasing costs for virgin materials, and federal and state support. This article overviews resource recovery and presents suggestions for local governments for judging the suitability of resource recovery proposals.
                                                                                                            J

3437. Jones, Bryan D. and Kaufman, Clifford. THE DISTRIBUTION OF URBAN PUBLIC SERVICES: A PRELIMINARY MODEL. *Administration and Soc. 1974 6(3): 337-360.* A model of local public services distribution reveals two main systems: "those which discriminate in the distribution of services to city neighborhoods, and those which respond to the needs and demands of citizens."
                                                                                                            S

3438. Jones, Bryan D.; Greenberg, Saadia R.; Kaufman, Clifford; and Drew, Joseph. SERVICE DELIVERY RULES AND THE DISTRIBUTION OF LOCAL GOVERNMENT SERVICES: THREE DETROIT BUREAUCRACIES. *J. of Pol. 1978 40(2): 332-368.* Routine service delivery rules based on productivity criteria influence the observed distribution of local public services to citizens. Such rules may be modified in response to political pressures. In the early 1970's, in Detroit, the Sanitation Division directed greater efforts to poorer and wealthier districts at the expense of middle-class areas. The Environmental Enforcement Division allocated disproportionate resources to middle-class neighborhoods. As a result historically determined policies concerning the location of recreation areas, Detroit's major parks are more accessible to wealthier neighborhoods, while minor parks and playlots are close to poorer and black inner-city locations. Primary and secondary sources; 9 tables, 3 fig., 34 notes.
                                                                                            A. W. Novitsky

3439. Kramer, Eugene. ENERGY CONSERVATION AND WASTE RECYCLING: TAKING ADVANTAGE OF URBAN CONGESTION. *Sci. and Public Affairs 1973 29(4): 13-18.* Discusses the advantages of concentrated space, as in thickly populated cities, for energy conservation and the centralization of waste recycling, 1973.

3440. Mladenka, Kenneth R. and Hill, Kim Quaile. THE DISTRIBUTION OF BENEFITS IN AN URBAN ENVIRONMENT: PARKS AND LIBRARIES IN HOUSTON. *Urban Affairs Q. 1977 13(1): 73-94.* Upper income areas had no advantage in park quality, acreage, numbers, or spatial distribution. However, regarding library quality and resources, upper class areas were strongly favored. This distribution of library services is justified only if circulation rates are the sole test of equity. Inequalities in the distribution of these services based on wealth and race are dispersed rather than cumulative. Bureaucrats, not elected officials, determine who benefits from public policy. 11 notes, biblio.
                                                                                                   L. Beecher

3441. Primeaux, Walter J. THE DECLINE IN ELECTRIC UTILITY COMPETITION. *Land Econ. 1975 51(2): 144-148.* Describes competition between electric utility companies in The Dalles, Oregon, and Hagerstown, Maryland. Notes the differing decisions by state utility commissions and how they affected the competitive situation. 27 notes, biblio.
                                                                                              E. S. Johnson

3442. Ridgeway, James. ENERGY: STEPS TOWARD AN ALTERNATIVE. *Working Papers for a New Soc. 1975 3(3): 61-64.* Proposes steps that could be taken to control energy companies, conserve fuel, and make low-cost power widely available during the 1970's.

3443. Yang, Yung Y. TEMPORAL STABILITY OF RESIDENTIAL ELECTRICITY DEMAND IN THE UNITED STATES. *Southern Econ. J. 1978 45(1): 107-115.* Demand for electricity was stable during 1962-73 (pre-energy crisis) but not stable during 1973-75, indicating that rising cost of electrification does not necessarily lead to lower usage.

Transportation

3444. Alexander, Robert E. MASS TRANSIT: A FREE RIDE FOR WHOM? *Cry California 1975 10(2): 21-24.* Property in the area of a fixed-station transit system benefits from increased property values. With the main emphasis for revenue on sales taxes, the possibility of obtaining funds from the increased market value of property near transit systems has been overlooked. The fact that a property owner benefits from such increased value contradicts public interest in the area of mass transportation.
                                                                                              A. Hoffman

3445. Braly, Mark. USE THE STREETS FIRST! *Cry California 1975 10(2): 14-21.* Appraises the Southern California Association of Governments' (SCAG) recommendations for public transportation. Claims that projected mass transit systems, as in the SCAG plan, would make little difference in reducing traffic congestion or increasing the percentage of commuters using public transportation. Proposes several alternatives based on use of existing streets. These include jitneys, preferential lanes for buses and carpools, computerized systems of personal transit vehicles, and continuous-flow boulevards with the elimination of stop-and-go traffic. Air space can be utilized for pedestrian walkovers and parking. Estimates that to use existing streets is less expensive than proposed freeway or rail rapid transit construction. 3 photos.
                                                                                              A. Hoffman

3446. Bruce-Briggs, B. GASOLINE PRICES AND THE SUBURBAN WAY OF LIFE. *Public Interest 1974 (37): 131-136.* Statistical analysis of data for the period 1955-74 on the impact of recent gasoline price increases on the standard of living of the average family in America.
                                                                                                            S

3447. Bruce-Briggs, B. MASS TRANSPORTATION AND MINORITY TRANSPORTATION. *Public Interest 1975 (40): 43-75.* Analyzes various modes of transportation emphasizing the merits of mass transit over the automobile.
                                                                                                            S

3448. Chasan, Daniel Jack. AN ANSWER TO CITY TRAFFIC MAY BE A HORIZONTAL ELEVATOR. *Smithsonian 1973 4(4): 46-53.* Discusses rapid transit as a possible answer to commuter transportation problems in America in cities in the 1970's.
                                                                                                            S

3449. Colcord, Frank C., Jr. URBAN TRANSPORTATION AND POLITICAL IDEOLOGY: SWEDEN AND THE UNITED STATES. *Policy Studies J. 1977 6(1): 9-19.* Transportation systems in urban areas are the result of ideological disputes over the role of government and the goods and services it provides; the examples of Sweden and the United States illustrate how differences in national ideology affect public transportation decisions.

3450. Cornehls, James V. and Taebel, Delbert A. THE OUTSIDERS AND URBAN TRANSPORTATION. *Social Sci. J. 1976 13(2): 61-74.* Views neglect in meeting the modern transportation needs of the "outsiders" (suburban Americans, the elderly, the handicapped, and other minorities) and new directions by city planners in solving problems of urban segmentation and dispersion, 1960-76.

3451. Dajani, Jarir; Egan, M. Michael; and McElroy, Marjorie B. THE REDISTRIBUTIVE IMPACT OF THE ATLANTA MASS TRANSIT SYSTEM. *Southern Econ. J. 1975 42(1): 49-60.* Predicts the individual citizen's transportation costs and benefits in 1983 resulting from the mass transit system in Atlanta, Georgia.
                                                                                                            S

3452. DeVise, Pierre. SUBURBS AND EXPRESSWAYS, BARRIERS IN URBAN AMERICA: THE STATUS OF INTEGRATION IN SUBURBAN CHICAGO. *Focus/Midwest 1974 9(61): 10-12.*

3453. Dewees, Donald N. TRAVEL COSTS, TRANSIT, AND CONTROL OF URBAN MOTORING. *Public Policy 1976 24(1): 59-79.* Studies the effects of mass transit systems on private urban motoring in North America. Reduction of motoring has not been achieved and will not be achieved. Mass transit is more expensive than private motoring. A review of mass transit experience in Toronto, Canada, reveals that time is the factor that keeps people in their automobiles. Property values and population density increase near rapid transit stops. Riders return to their cars as soon as mass transit reduces surface travel; thus congestion redevelops. Private motoring can be reduced only by penalizing motorists by means of taxes on gasoline, miles driven, or freeway access. 2 tables, 15 notes.   V. L. Human

3454. Due, John F. URBAN MASS TRANSIT POLICY: A REVIEW ARTICLE. *Q. Rev. of Econ. and Business 1976 16(1): 93-105.* In the decade, the question of urban transit has become a major issue and one consequence has been a sharp increase in literature in a long neglected field. This article reviews four recent publications: George Smerk's *Urban Mass Transportation—A Dozen Years of Federal Policy* is primarily a summary of federal policy in the field, with a well-balanced evaluation. George Hilton's *Federal Transit Subsidies* is a severe criticism of the federal policies, with strong endorsement of the jitney approach. The Urban Institute's *Para-Transit* reviews various alternatives to conventional transit, in the realm between the private automobile and usual mass transit. The Senate Judiciary Committee report revives the old argument over whether General Motors sought to destroy the transit industry.   J

3455. Elliott, Ward. THE LOS ANGELES AFFLICTION: SUGGESTIONS FOR A CURE. *Public Interest 1975 (38): 119-128.* Discusses current problems of transportation and the automobile population of Los Angeles.   S

3456. Goldstein, Gerald S. and Moses, Leon N. TRANSPORT CONTROLS, TRAVEL COSTS, AND URBAN SPATIAL STRUCTURE. *Public Policy 1975 23(3): 355-380.* Explores implications of different types of transportation studies designed to reduce auto travel. Compares policies designed to: 1) increase the cost of auto travel; 2) improve the quality and reduce the cost of public transportation. Comparing short-run effects of transport control measures to their long-run effects coupled with higher fuel prices, shows evidence demonstrating the likelihood of long-run public transportation strategies contributing to further decline of economics of central cities. Utilization of an urban land-use model drawn from studies of urban economists enables the authors to speculate on long-run changing patterns of land use resulting from long-run transport controls. Based on original research and secondary materials; 19 notes.   J. M. Herrick

3457. Gordon, Bonnie. MORE AND MORE METROS. *Américas (Organization of Am. States) 1978 30(8): 2-6.* Describes subway systems in Mexico, the United States, Canada, and South America.

3458. Grava, Sigurd. THE EXPRESS BUS SAGA. *New York Affairs 1979 5(3): 111-123.* Established in 1968, the successful express bus service in New York City serves customers living in the outer boroughs.

3459. Grava, Sigurd. IMPROVING TRANSPORTATION AT THE GRASS ROOTS. *New York Affairs 1975 2(3): 12-29.* Notes the seeming inability of governments to make real improvements in urban transportation service, especially small-scale, localized improvement and discusses things that can be done by community groups.   J

3460. Herzlinger, Regina. COSTS, BENEFITS, AND THE WEST SIDE HIGHWAY. *Public Interest 1979 55: 77-98.* Discusses ambitious and costly plans to reconstruct New York City's West Side Highway. During the administration of Mayor Beame five alternatives were decided upon. Evaluates the five according to economic benefits and costs, and impact on traffic flow, land mass, and environmental pollution. The plan chosen, and later approved by Mayor Koch, would tear down the existing structure and replace it with an interstate highway, which has become known as Westway. The plan was chosen because it would bring the most federal money ($1.2 billion) to New York City. Questions of public good were not addressed and it is unclear if Westway is the best transportation alternative. 2 tables.   S. Harrow

3461. Hirten, John E. NEEDED—A NEW PERCEPTION OF TRANSPORTATION. *J. of the Am. Inst. of Planners 1973 39(4): 277-282.* Discusses the need in the 1970's for a reevaluation of national views of transportation away from auto-oriented transportation toward metropolitan rapid transit systems.   S

3462. Hughes, James W. REALTORS, BANKERS AND POLITICIANS IN THE NEW YORK/NEW JERSEY PORT AUTHORITY. *Society 1974 11(4): 63-70.* The Port Authority has refused to fund deficit-producing mass transit facilities, preferring profit-making enterprises which benefit realtors and bankers at the expense of urban commuters. One of five articles in this issue on state politics and public interests.   S

3463. Hutchinson, P. R. A RAPID TRANSIT SYSTEM FOR SAN FRANCISCO. *Geography [Great Britain] 1974 59(2): 148-150.* An account of the San Francisco Bay Area Rapid Transit Rail System (BART) which was opened September 1972 and which became fully operative a year later. "Supporters of the new system believe that growth will now be concentrated along the route of BART, clustered around the stations. . . . BART's opponents, on the other hand, say that rather than preventing sprawl BART will, in effect, encourage it. . . . The objection of many of the environmentalists is that whilst they are well pleased with the prospect of a relatively noise-free, non-polluting transport system, the high-rise blocks which it is encouraging are ruining the city's townscape. The only other forseeable danger is that if BART accelerates the movement of the city centre the demand for its own services could outstrip its capacity." Table, fig.   D. D. Cameron

3464. Kendrick, Frank J. URBAN TRANSPORTATION POLICY: POLITICS, PLANNING, AND PEOPLE. *Policy Studies J. 1975 3(4): 375-381.*

3465. Kirby, Ronald F. THE PROMISE OF PARA-TRANSIT. *New York Affairs 1975 2(4): 102-119.* Ordinary bus and subway service is not really an adequate substitute for most intraurban auto trips, even in New York; conventional transit is just too inflexible, and inconvenient for many purposes. For the first time, serious attention has been given to "in-between" forms of urban transportation and how their potential can be exploited.   J

3466. Marando, Vincent L. METROPOLITANISM, TRANSPORTATION, AND EMPLOYMENT FOR THE CENTRAL-CITY POOR. *Urban Affairs Q. 1974 10(2): 158-169.* Attempts to determine if lack of transportation is a significant factor in unemployment in metropolitan areas. Data from the 1970 Census Employment Survey indicates that less than 1% of central city interviewees felt that transportation problems kept them from seeking work; family responsibilities and poor health were the primary reasons given. Note, biblio.

P. J. Woehrmann

3467. Nelkin, Dorothy. MASSPORT VS. COMMUNITY. *Society 1974 11(4): 27-39.* East Boston residents' battle against the expansion of Logan Airport by the Massachusetts Port Authority pits "quality of life" against economic growth; one of five articles on state politics and public interests.   S

3468. Netzer, Dick. THE CASE AGAINST LOW SUBWAY FARES. *New York Affairs 1974 1(3): 14-25.* That low transit fares are a categorical imperative, essential for the economy of cities, their environmental preservation and a just distribution of worldly goods is an article of faith in New York and many other places. The dogma to the contrary notwithstanding, subsidies for urban transportation may be a bad idea whose time has persisted far too long.   J

3469. Owen, John E. A SOCIOLOGIST LOOKS AT AMERICA'S CITY TRAFFIC PROBLEM. *Social Sci. 1973 48(2): 87-92.* The US is a nation dependent on the automobile. Cars are multiplying faster than the population and one business in six is already dependent on the auto industry. The problem has been multiplied by urban crowding. But America has never had a national transport policy, though public awareness of the problem is rising.   J/S

3470. Perloff, Harvey S. and Connell, Kathleen M. SUBSIDIARY TRANSPORTATION: ITS ROLE IN REGIONAL PLANNING. *J. of the Am. Inst. of Planners 1975 41(3): 170-183.* Transportation planning in cities and metropolitan regions can contribute directly to meeting the transit needs of special groups and communities overlooked by generalized transit systems. This article suggests how an examination of existing subsidiary transit services might be organized; describes the

kinds of transit operations that might be included in such an examination; and outlines the types of information that should be obtained about them.
J

3471. Peters, A. Gerald and Wood, Donald F. HELICOPTER AIRLINES IN THE UNITED STATES 1945-75. *J. of Transport Hist. [Great Britain] 1977 4(1): 1-16.* Examines four helicopter airlines operating in New York, Chicago, Los Angeles, and San Francisco during 1945-65, and during the 10 years after the ending of subsidies in 1965. The high cost of operating helicopters, given the limited consumer market, meant that the Los Angeles Airways could only operate with subsidization. Once the San Francisco-Oakland Helicopter Airlines demonstrated, however, that it did not need government funds, Congress ceased in mid-1965 all subsidy payments to the Los Angeles, New York, and Chicago airlines. Two of the airlines ceased operations. The New York and San Francisco operations survived, largely because the areas they served contain many water barriers to conventional surface transport. Based on material from the Annual Reports of the LAA, NYA, CHA and SFO. 4 illus., 31 notes.
C. Anstey

3472. Piper, Robert R. TRANSIT STRATEGIES FOR SUBURBAN COMMUNITIES. *J. of the Am. Inst. of Planners 1977 43(4): 380-385.* Transit is asked to cure a variety of ills in modern, low-density cities: isolation of those who cannot drive, traffic congestion, air pollution, energy waste, and inner-city decay. Transit planning is difficult because of the wide dispersion of origins and destinations and the temporal rhythms of travel. The options in deploying buses are reviewed.
J

3473. Pushkarev, Boris. TRANSPORTATION: CRAWLING TOWARDS CONSOLIDATION. *New York Affairs 1978 5(2): 75-90.* Assesses New York City's progress toward consolidated public transportation, 1969-77.

3474. Rabin, Yale. HIGHWAYS AS A BARRIER TO EQUAL ACCESS. *Ann. of the Am. Acad. of Pol. and Social Sci. 1973 (407): 63-77.* There is a widening gap between growing concentrations of blacks and other minorities in the central cities, and whites and the expanding supply of employment opportunities in the suburbs. While exclusionary zoning controls have been seen by many as the most immediate barrier to suburban opportunities, transportation facilities and the lack of them play an important role. The federal highway program in particular, while a powerful stimulus to dispersed development, has, in its implementation, failed to protect equal access to the benefits of development such as housing and employment. As a result the comprehensive planning of metropolitan areas is seriously undermined, and new barriers are erected which threaten to perpetuate the burdens and disadvantages which a long history of racial discrimination has produced.
J

3475. Rosenbloom, Sandra and Altshuler, Alan. EQUITY ISSUES IN URBAN TRANSPORTATION. *Policy Studies J. 1977 6(1): 29-39.* Examines urban transportation systems in the United States, 1973-76, differentiating concepts of equity (fee charge, service distribution, and distribution according to need), allocation of public funds for transportation facilites, needs for mobility among the elderly and disabled, and the current state of controversy over cost effective modes of managing equity systems.

3476. Sale, James E. and Green, Bryan. OPERATING COSTS AND PERFORMANCE OF AMERICAN PUBLIC TRANSIT SYSTEMS. *J. of the Am. Planning Assoc. 1979 45(1): 22-27.* The escalation of operating costs is threatening the existing level of transit service in the United States. Over the last two decades, lengthening passenger trips, as a result of suburbanization and lower development densities, have been a major factor influencing increasing costs per passenger. Over the past decade, the cost of operating transit service has risen 148%. Since operating revenues have not kept pace with costs, transit subsidies have grown even more rapidly than operating costs. The following have been major factors in the rapid rise of operating costs: 1) Labor compensation has grown faster than the cost-of-living, without any increase in average productivity. Labor is the major component of transit operating cost, accounting for over 80% of the total; 2) There has been a state of inflation in the US economy; 3) Public transit activity has been concentrated in the largest and most expensive cities.
J

3477. Scheiner, James I. and Starling, Grover. THE POLITICAL ECONOMY OF FREE-FARE TRANSIT. *Urban Affairs Q. 1974 10(2): 170-184.* Examines the politics of implementing completely subsidized bus lines engaged in urban transportation. Capital intensive public transportation systems, such as rapid transit, are expensive to effect and are subject to the vicissitudes of population shifts and technical problems. A flat federal subsidy per passenger trip may preserve bus transit. There is precedent (such as Amtrak) and moderate political support for this. Advocates demonstration models. Table, notes, biblio.
P. J. Woehrmann

3478. Schwartz, Harry. MANHATTAN WITHOUT CARS? *New York Affairs 1973 1(1): 46-59.* Summarizes the Manhattan Auto Study, a private undertaking begun in October 1970 in an effort to suggest alternatives to the environmental and economic problems caused by unrestricted motor vehicle use. Describes specific recommendations of the study. Illus., 5 notes.
J. A. Benson

3479. Sheshinski, Eytan. CONGESTION AND THE OPTIMUM CITY SIZE. *Am. Econ. Rev. 1973 63(2): 61-66.* Employs an economic model to examine how transportation congestion affects the sizes of cities and suburbs.

3480. Soot, Siim. TRANSPORTATION COSTS AND URBAN LAND RENT THEORY: THE MILWAUKEE EXAMPLE: 1949-1969. *Land Econ. 1974 50(2): 193-195.*

3481. Veatch, James F. FEDERAL AND LOCAL URBAN TRANSPORTATION POLICY. *Urban Affairs Q. 1975 10(4): 398-422.* Criticizes the creation of a transit trust fund similar to the highway trust fund, and discusses local and federal government interrelationships regarding mass transit. Local government has not applied federal funds to benefit mass transit users. Advocates direct subsidies to these travelers, and better-defined purposes for and accounting of subsidy funds. Notes, biblio.
P. J. Woehrmann

3482. Vidich, Charles. UNION TAXIES AND GYPSY CABBIES. *Society 1973 10(5): 43-49.* Describes taxi service (legal and illegal) in New York City.
S

3483. Ward, J. Stedman. THE TROLLEY CAR DAYS OF NEWPORT, R. I. *Newport Hist. 1974 47(2): 129-152.* Chronicles the construction, under the aegis of the Newport Street Railway Company and the Edison Illuminating Company (eventually merged as the Newport and Fall River Street Railway Company), of Newport's electric trolley system in 1889 until the advent of motor-driven buses in 1927. 15 photos.

3484. Watson, Gerald G. THE POLITICS OF HIGHWAY VETOES IN TWO METROPOLITAN AREAS. *Social Sci. J. 1977 14(3): 93-104.* Public policy decisionmaking led to highway discontinuation in Denver (Colorado) and Portland (Oregon), 1975.

3485. Weigold, Marilyn. BRIDGING LONG ISLAND SOUND. *New York Affairs 1975 2(3): 52-65.* Proposals to bridge the Sound east of New York City date to the 1930's. They have been defeated by the vociferous protests of affluent and articulate communities on both shores of the Sound.
J

3486. Zimmerman, Joseph F. FINANCING PUBLIC TRANSPORTATION. *Natl. Civic Rev. 1973 62(6): 301-305.* Single Urban Fund, urban mass transit assistance, no fare/low fare concepts, direct and indirect aid to transit systems (both public and private) to help meet operating costs—all are part of the problems and the solutions for financing public transportation.
J

3487. Zimmerman, Joseph F. PUBLIC TRANSPORTATION. *Pro. of the Acad. of Pol. Sci. 1974 31(3): 214-224.* Discusses the transportation difficulties, both intercity and commuter, experienced by New York City from 1959 to the present.
S

Preservation

3488. Adler, Wendy J. THE COLLEGE OF CHARLESTON—AN INTERVIEW WITH THEODORE S. STERN. *Historic Preservation 1975 27(3): 30-37.* In this transcribed interview Stern, president of the college, discusses campus growth within Charleston, South Carolina, from "one square block" in 1968 to "about 21 acres" in the 1980's, via a "master plan" for adaptive use of many historic buildings instead of demolition. 8 photos.   R. M. Frame III

3489. Adler, Wendy J. CHANGE AND THE CHANGELESS IN SANTA FE—AN INTERVIEW WITH JOHN P. CONRON, AIA, FAID. *Historic Preservation 1974 26(1): 4-11.* Interview with John P. Conron (New Mexico Society of Architects) discussing the "two-dimensional facadism" of the architectural control ordinance of Santa Fe, New Mexico. Includes excerpts from the "Silver City [New Mexico] Historic District and Historic Properties Ordinance" proposal which Conron helped draft. 12 color photos.   R. M. Frame III

3490. Bacon, Mardges. AN HISTORIC DISTRICT DISCOVERED: THE ENDURING COLONIAL IMAGE IN NEWBURY, MASSACHUSETTS. *Old-Time New England 1976 66(3-4): 35-41.* Explains the factors involved in the designation in 1976 of the Newbury Historic District to the National Register of Historic Places. The Society for the Preservation of New England Antiquities conducted the research and prepared the Massachusetts Historical Commission's nomination of Newbury as an historic district. Sketch, 6 illus., map.   R. N. Lokken

3491. Bailey, Walter L. HISTORIC DISTRICTS: A NEGLECTED RESOURCE. *North Dakota Hist. 1976 43(3): 22-24.* The availability of public and private funding to convert run-down, profitless older areas of towns and cities into viable historic districts can provide one answer to urban financial problems in a time of inflation and austerity of financing. Many potential historic districts exist in abundance in the northern Great Plains states owing to the factors of structures designed to last, a contemporary reluctance to tear down still usable buildings, and a comparatively low population density allowing for flexibility in building usage.   N. Lederer

3492. Ball, Rex M.; Johnson, Nancy J.; and McGee, L. Edwin. REVITALIZING OLDER CITIES. *Natl. Civic Rev. 1978 67(5): 228-233, 240.* Dozens of older cities and suburbs, plus long-neglected downtown areas, have undergone a transformation. Investors, businesses, citizens and officials are joining together to bring life "back to the city." One noteworthy aspect of the movement is the recognition that it is not a job for government alone, but needs public/private policy initiatives and dollars.   J

3493. Beal, Stephen. FIGHT FOR SURVIVAL. *Am. Preservation 1978 1(2): 42-47.* Chicago's Pilsen neighborhood once was newly reclaimed swampland inhabited by Czechs and Poles in the 1850's. Today Pilsen is 85% Mexican-American and contains the oldest housing stock in Chicago. With badly deteriorating buildings and low-income residents, Pilsen Neighbors and the Eighteenth Street Development Corporation are attempting to renovate buildings without displacing tenants. CETA funds and federal loans have made possible the Pilsen Rehab Project, which renovates homes with local labor and sells them to area residents. However, the nearby South Loop New Town project may bring rising land values, displacements, and demolition. The future is uncertain despite impressive community solidarity and recent gains. 20 photos.
                                                       S. C. Strom

3494. Bernstein, Shalmon and Wilson, Angela. NEIGHBORHOODS IN TRANSITION. *New York Affairs 1974 1(3): 78-120.* Redemption of the city's run-down buildings and neighborhoods seemed to some a romantic venture—until they tried it. Excerpts from tape recorded interviews explore the feelings of brownstone renovators and those whom they find themselves forced to evict.   J

3495. Bowman, David. BEALE STREET BLUES. *Southern Exposure 1977 5(1): 75-79.* The effort to convert the once-bustling black business area of Beale Street, in Memphis, Tennessee, into a tourist attraction has been underway since 1963. Public and private agencies have obtained millions of federal tax dollars for that purpose. Viable businesses have been forcibly relocated, sound buildings have been condemned and torn down, and residents have been relocated. Schemes for updating Beale Street have not resulted in anything of merit and the neighborhood today is in a shambles.   N. Lederer

3496. Brown, Patricia Leigh. MAIN STREETS GET STREETWISE. *Hist. Preservation 1979 31(1): 29-34.* Discusses the Main Street Project of the Midwest Regional Office of the National Trust for Historic Preservation, "a demonstration program to explore small-town economic development within the context of historic preservation," begun in 1976. Describes the three pilot programs: Hot Springs, South Dakota; Madison, Indiana; and Galesburg, Illinois. Illus.   R. M. Frame, III

3497. Burke, Padraic. PIKE PLACE MARKET. *Am. Preservation 1978 1(6): 22-29.* The Pike Place Public Market has become a notable Seattle landmark and tourist attraction. Since 1907, farmer-merchants have sold produce in the architectural maze of the Market. A diverse working-class neighborhood grew up around the Market giving it its remarkable vitality. Despite the physical decay of the 1950's-60's, the Market continued to attract diverse customers. Recent demolition efforts have been successfully resisted by Friends of the Market. However, since 1972, redevelopment and restoration projects threaten the unique working-class flavor of the area, displacing low income residents. 7 photos.
                                                       S. C. Strom

3498. Burke, Padraic. PORT TOWNSEND. *Am. Preservation 1978 1(4): 9-18.* Discusses the history of Port Townsend, Washington, and notes the expanding interest in restoration work. Lists notable structures in their various stages of preservation. Preservation efforts are causing political conflict between proponents and city officials. 15 photos.
                                                       J. B. Street

3499. Burke, Padraic. TO MARKET, TO MARKET. *Historic Preservation 1977 29(1): 32-38.* As they developed in America, the village or urban marketplaces were egalitarian public institutions, bringing a natural seasonal rhythm into the constructed environment. Surveys current market restoration projects. 4 illus., 3 photos.
                                                       R. M. Frame III

3500. Capitman, Barbara Baer. RE-DISCOVERY OF ART DECO. *Am. Preservation 1978 6(6): 30-41.* Old Miami Beach, where 72% of the residents are defined as elderly, may become the country's youngest historic district with a preponderance of Spanish and Art Deco buildings dating 1920-35. The resurgence of Art Deco in New York design circles has led to a reappraisal of the 293 Art Deco structures of Miami Beach. The Miami Design Preservation League has worked with state and federal agencies to survey the buildings and obtain funding for rehabilitation. Designed by such young innovators as Henry Hohauser and Murray Dixon, the unique exteriors of the apartments and small hotels have survived in excellent condition. Supporters hope that the new appreciation will preserve the human scale of the area for its elderly residents and discourage large-scale resort redevelopment. 10 photos.
                                                       S. C. Strom

3501. Carroll, Julian M. RE-DEDICATION OF THE OLD CAPITOL. *Register of the Kentucky Hist. Soc. 1975 73(4): 337-339.* Speech by Governor Julian M. Carroll in Frankfort, Kentucky, on 7 June 1975, rededicating the old Kentucky capitol building. Built in 1830, it is now the site of the Old Capitol Restoration and the New Kentucky History Museum.   J. F. Paul

3502. Cawley, Peter. COMPANY TOWN WORKS ON ITS FUTURE. *Hist. Preservation 1977 29(3): 10-15.* Discusses the problems, options and controversies surrounding historic preservation in Collinsville, Connecticut, a factory town established by Samuel Collins. The Collins Company factory, founded in 1827, was the town nucleus until it closed in 1965, suddenly upsetting community relationships. Controversial preservation plans are being considered including factory building reuse. 3 photos.   R. M. Frame III

3503. Collins, John J. MARSHALL FALLS SHORT. *Am. Preservation 1978 1(6): 9-21.* Marshall, Michigan, founded in 1830, has not grown into the economic and political center envisioned by its founders, but as a consequence, remains rich in early Victorian architectural landmarks. Passed over as the state capitol, Marshall became a railroad center during 1844-72. Architects Sheldon Smith, John Mills Van Osdel, and Elijah Myers designed notable Gothic Revival, Italianate, and Greek Revival structures. After 50 years of economic and aesthetic stagnation, Mayor Harold C. Brooks initiated efforts to preserve and restore significant structures. Today, Marshall Historical Society leads the preservation movement with a variety of restoration and design improvement projects. 13 photos.   S. C. Strom

3504. Connelly, Edwin Wilmot. THE FIRST PROGRESS REPORT TO BEAUTIFY, RESTORE, CATALOGUE THE COMMON BURYING-GROUND, FAREWELL STREET. *Newport Hist. 1973 46(4): 96-101.* The 20-acre hill with its 3,000 gravestones has been neglected so that it is in a jungle-like condition with rutted roads and toppled gravestones. After restoration of the burial ground, hopefully much can be learned about Rhode Island's history. On the headstones are the names of governors, Revolutionary patriots, clergymen, bankers, journalists, physicians, merchants, slaves, and a signer of the Declaration of Independence.   J. H. Krenkel

3505. Cotter, John L. and Orr, David. HISTORICAL ARCHAEOLOGY OF PHILADELPHIA. *Hist. Archaeology 1975 9: 1-10.* Archaeological investigations in quest of evidence of 18th-century site data related to colonial Philadelphia and its part in the American Revolution point to subsequent development. Early excavation of Franklin Court led to others which are summarized. Describes the front step and sidewalk area of Independence Hall; the remnants of the waster deposit of the Bonnin and Morris Pottery factory; the Kensington Methodist Episcopal Church; Walnut Street Prison; the Philadelphia Gaswork Point Breeze Station, where a large archive of historical materials was discovered. The latter is an example of what might be accomplished throughout the nation. "Preservation proposals have been advanced which have facilitated the saving of key industrial buildings and machines in Philadelphis." 8 photos, map.   E. P. Stickney

3506. Crimmins, Timothy J. THE PAST IN THE PRESENT: AN AGENDA FOR PUBLIC HISTORY AND HISTORIC PRESERVATION. *Georgia Hist. Q. 1979 63(1): 53-59.* Presents the role of the urban historian in acquainting city dwellers with their past and in working for the preservation of historic buildings. 4 illus., 8 notes.   G. R. Schroeder

3507. Dennis, Lee. DOORWAY TO AMERICA. *Hist. Preservation 1978 30(2): 12-19.* Traces the history of Ellis Island in upper New York City Bay from mid-17th century to the present. Discusses various historic preservation efforts since 1954 when immigration processing ceased, particularly the Restore Ellis Island Committee formed in 1974. 9 photos.   R. M. Frame, III

3508. Ditmer, Joanne. CRESTED BUTTE. *Am. Preservation 1979 2(2): 28-37.* Crested Butte, a Colorado community of 1,200 dependent on recreation and tourism, is concerned about losing its natural beauty and quiet lifestyle. Founded as a mining town in 1878, Crested Butte fears AMAX, Inc. and its plans for a molybdenum mine. This boomtown prospect threatens the historic flavor of the old town where 75% of the restored frame structures are more than 50 years old. The challenge now is to develop a growth plan that will minimize the physical impact of the mine and its new employees. 8 photos.   S. C. Strom

3509. Doyle, Don H. SAVING YESTERDAY'S CITY: NASHVILLE'S WATERFRONT. *Tennessee Hist. Q. 1976 35(4): 353-364.* In April 1976 a diverse group of Nashvillians and the Metropolitan Historical Commission began a drive to save the city's Cumberland River waterfront buildings as part of the city's heritage rather than create a new tourist mall. Primary and secondary sources; 4 illus., 9 notes.   M. B. Lucas

3510. Dumanoski, Dianne. BOSTON'S ITALIAN NORTH END. *Am. Preservation 1979 2(3): 42-49.* The North End, Boston's traditionally Italian blue collar neighborhood, is changing. Once an embarassment to the urban planners of the 1960's, this crowded neighborhood of three and four storey brick tenements was discovered by "outsiders" seeking low rent, convenient location, and ethnic vitality. With the renovation of

the nearby waterfront and wholesale food district, North End has become fashionable. The facade of Italian shops remain but the blue collar jobs and residents are moving to the suburbs. Long time residents fear rising rents but little organized resistance to change has developed. 10 photos.   S. C. Strom

3511. Ellingsen, John D. GHOST TOWNS IN MONTANA. *Historic Preservation 1974 26(1): 24-27.* Since the 1950's, the once abundant western ghost towns have been rapidly disappearing, thanks to four-wheel-drive vehicles and bottle collectors. Recent government projects and private groups in Montana and elsewhere have prompted new preservation efforts. 3 photos.   R. M. Frame, III

3512. Faude, Wilson H. MARK TWAIN'S CONNECTICUT HOME. *Historic Preservation 1974 26(2): 16-20.* The Hartford, Connecticut, home of Mark Twain was designed by Edward Tuckerman Potter and built in 1874. The few years before Twain sold the house in 1903 were his most successful and productive. Meticulous restoration was begun in 1955. Illus., 10 photos.   R. M. Frame, III

3513. Faust, Patricia L. SAVANNAH: A CITY RECLAIMED. *Early Am. Life 1978 9(4): 20-23, 52.* Discusses a program of historic preservation of buildings and houses in Savannah, Georgia, dating from colonial times, through the aid of a local banker, Lee Adler, 1961-77.

3514. Fischer, LeRoy H. THE FAIRCHILD WINERY. *Chronicles of Oklahoma 1977 55(2): 135-156.* Surveys the history of Oklahoma City's Fairchild Wine Vault which in 1975 was named to the National Register of Historic Places. Built in 1893 by Edward B. Fairchild to process and store wine produced from his orchards, it served the local market until Oklahoma legislated prohibition in 1907. Its unique architectural design and distinction as one of Oklahoma City's oldest structures insured its restoration by the state. Based on interviews and primary sources; 12 photos, 33 notes.   M. L. Tate

3515. Ford, Larry and Fusch, Richard. NEIGHBORS VIEW GERMAN VILLAGE. *Hist. Preservation 1978 30(3): 37-41.* German Village is a 19th-century German neighborhood near downtown Columbus, Ohio, which has undergone historic preservation since 1948. Surveys of surrounding neighborhood attitudes indicate that people "view preservation positively and believe that their own neighborhoods are better places because of it." Illus.   R. M. Frame, III

3516. Foster, Lee. THE LIVING PAST: OLD SACRAMENTO, MOST AMBITIOUS HISTORIC RESTORATION IN THE WEST. *Am. West 1976 13(3): 20-27.* Federal, state, and city agencies are involved in a cooperative effort with commercial developers and private investors to restore and reconstruct California's Old Sacramento. Development of the 28-acre area was legislated in 1966. The 53 distinct projects, when completed in a few years, will offer a historically valid presentation of Old Sacramento for the 1850-90 years. 12 illus., map, note.   D. L. Smith

3517. Frank, Phil. VENERABLE ARKS RIDE THE TIDES. *Hist. Preservation 1978 30(3): 23-27.* Discusses houseboating on San Francisco Bay during 1880's-1930's. Details the restoration of two early houseboats, known as "arks." Illus.   R. M. Frame, III

3518. Gómez-Ibáñez, Miguel. PRESERVING THREE HUNDRED FIFTY YEARS OF CHANGE IN THE BLACKSTONE BLOCK. *Old-Time New England 1977 68(1-2): 19-31.* The Blackstone Block, 2.3 acres behind Boston City Hall, represents more than 300 years of development in Boston since 1625 when the Reverend William Blackstone built the first home within the city's modern boundaries: discusses efforts to preserve the historical landmark in recent years.

3519. Guida, Louis. POWELTON VILLAGE. *Am. Preservation 1979 2(2): 44-52.* Powelton Village located west of the Schuykill River in Philadelphia is a Victorian neighborhood experiencing an economic surge. Lagging behind other downtown areas, Powelton's restoration has proceeded slowly, remaining small scale and privately financed. Begun by the Powelton Village Development Association in 1955, the preservation movement has had to block University of Pennsylvania and Drexel University plans for demolition. With Powelton's growing prosperity, the displacement issue and racial polarization highlight diverse opinions on social economic systems. 14 photos.

S. C. Strom

3520. Gurr, Steve. THE SUMTER HISTORIC PRESERVATION SOCIETY. *Georgia Hist. Q. 1979 63(1): 180-187.* Describes the activities and preservation successes of the Sumter Historic Preservation Society (founded 1972) which focus on the Americus, Georgia area. Based on society archival material; 2 illus., 33 notes.

G. R. Schroeder

3521. Hays, Steele. BUTCHERTOWN. *Am. Preservation 1978 1(2): 58-63.* Butchertown, an older working-class German neighborhood in Louisville, Kentucky, is notable for its lively mixture of industrial, commercial, and residential buildings. Young, new residents attracted by low prices and community cohesiveness are purchasing the deteriorated "shotgun" houses and multistory brick townhouses. Since 1967, Butchertown, Inc., a nonprofit community group, has been buying and renovating endangered structures for resale to local residents. Louisville government officials have been supportive of such efforts although social tensions exist within the community. Older residents oppose establishing a preservation district in Butchertown which would subject exterior changes to architectural review. Describes specific residential and commercial renovation projects. 11 photos.

S. C. Strom

3522. Huth, Tom. CRESTED BUTTE: A TOWN FIGHTS FOR ITS HERITAGE. *Hist. Preservation 1979 31(1): 2-11.* Crested Butte, Colorado, began in the 1880's as a silver camp, was a coal mining town until the 1960's when it profited from the ski boom, and now is threatened by the nearby discovery of the world's third-largest known deposit of molybdenum. Townspeople believe that the proposed mining operation of AMAX, Inc., endangers the town's social and cultural environment, including its unique 19th-century Victorian architecture. Illus.

R. M. Frame III

3523. Kay, Jane Holtz. SALEM. *Am. Preservation 1978 1(2): 9-20.* The rich architectural heritage of Salem, Massachusetts, reflects the varied economic history of the area. Efforts to reverse the post-World War II deterioration of downtown Salem centered on demolition and rebuilding, 1966-71. When this approach failed, Mayor Samuel Zoll turned to historic preservation to revitalize a stagnant urban center. A pedestrian mall has brought new life to the downtown. Small town flavor, cultural facilities, and quality architecture have attracted new residents interested in restoring old homes along Chestnut Street. Salem now struggles to preserve its ethnic and architectural diversity while expanding the revitalization to less affluent neighborhoods. 21 photos.

S. C. Strom

3524. Keyes, Margaret N. OLD CAPITOL RESTORED. *Palimpsest 1976 57(4): 122-128.* Describes efforts to complete the original plan of the old state Capitol building at Iowa City, which remained unfinished in 1857 when the seat of government was moved to Des Moines. Limited reconstruction took place between 1921 and 1923. Beginning in 1970, complete restoration got underway. Original plans for the building could not be found, but examination of documents, photographs, and physical evidence enabled researchers to prepare an accurate and authentic picture of the building. It was dedicated on 3 July 1976. 8 photos, note.

D. W. Johnson

3525. Kinne, Ann Spencer. THE RENSSELAER RUSSELL HOUSE. *Ann. of Iowa 1974 42(4): 303-313.* Describes a surviving example of mid-Victorian architecture in Waterloo, Iowa. Built in 1858 by dry goods merchant Rensselaer Russell for a total recorded cost of $5,878.83, the house has been renovated in the style of the period, and is open for tours under the auspices of the Association for the Preservation of the Rensselaer Russell House. 5 photos, 6 notes.

C. W. Olson

3526. Krinsky, Carol Herselle. THE CHRYSLER PRESERVE. *Art in Am. 1979 67(4): 80-87.* Describes restoration of the Chrysler Building in New York City; it was designed by architect William Van Alen (1882-1954) in 1928.

3527. Lewis, Peirce F. TO REVIVE URBAN DOWNTOWNS, SHOW RESPECT FOR THE SPIRIT OF THE PLACE. *Smithsonian 1975 6(6): 33-41.* Suggests historic preservation of cities' central business districts to reverse the deterioration they have been experiencing in their geography and internal layout for the past 25 years.

3528. Lewis, Peirce F. LA RESTAURATION DU PATRIMOINE AUX ÉTATS-UNIS: ÉVALUATION CRITIQUE ET ORIENTATIONS [The restoration of heritage in the United States: critical appraisal and orientations]. *Cahiers de Géographie de Québec [Canada] 1977 21(53-54): 269-292.* Analyzes the results of the preservation or restoration of urban heritage in the United States; to remedy the present failure, suggests new concepts for an efficient policy of preservation.

3529. Limbaugh, R. H. WHAT PRICE PROGRESS. *Pacific Hist. 1977 21(1 supplement): 3-6.* Summarizes essays presented at conference in Stockton and Nevada City on cultural and historic preservation and urban growth.

G. L. Olson

3530. Lupold, John S. HISTORIC COLUMBUS FOUNDATION, 1966-1978. *Georgia Hist. Q. 1979 63(1): 129-137.* The restoration of the Springer Opera House was the impetus for the organization of the Historic Columbus Foundation. Describes the activities of this foundation which have resulted in improvements in nearly one quarter of the remaining original city buildings. Based on interviews; 3 illus., 9 notes.

G. R. Schroeder

3531. Lupold, John S. REVITALIZING FOUNDRIES, HOTELS AND GRIST MILLS IN COLUMBUS. *Georgia Hist. Q. 1979 63(1): 138-142.* Describes several specific successful restoration projects in Columbus, Georgia, during the 1970's, including Rankin Square and the Iron Works, and their commercial viability. Based on interviews and magazine articles; 2 illus., 4 notes.

G. R. Schroeder

3532. Manucy, Albert. TOWARD RE-CREATION OF 16TH CENTURY ST. AUGUSTINE. *Escribano 1977 14: 1-4.* The St. Augustine Restoration Foundation promotes historical preservation so that past architecture, history, and culture will be available to contemporary history students.

3533. Matlack, Carol. EUFAULA. *Am. Preservation 1978 2(1): 9-21.* Eufaula, once the thriving commercial center of southeastern Alabama's "Black Belt," suffered economic decline after World War I. Historic preservation efforts began in 1965 with the founding of Eufaula Heritage Association and the purchase of the neo-classic Shorter Mansion. Through privately raised funds, the Association purchases endangered structures for resale to those committed to historic preservation. The downtown business district has been renovated through voluntary restoration and construction guidelines. Today 72 Eufaula structures are listed on the National Register of Historic Places. 15 photos.

S. C. Strom

3534. Matlack, Carol. PAINTED LADIES. *Am. Preservation 1979 2(2): 62-72.* The origins of San Francisco's current Colorist Movement can be traced to 1967 when the psychodelic paint job of a gingerbread "hippie" house and the preservation efforts of the Junior League spurred renewed interest in bright colors for Victorian homes. As in the late 19th Century, vivid color schemes are being used to highlight ornate exterior details and several neglected neighborhoods have experienced spontaneous transformations and new popularity. 13 photos.

S. C. Strom

3535. Matlack, Carol. SAVANNAH. *Am. Preservation 1979 2(3): 9-25.* The rhythmic progression of squares planned by James Oglethorpe in 1733 and the subsequent cottom boom made Savannah architecturally unique. The late 19th-century economic crises led to a 100 year decline in the center city. The turning point was in 1954 when efforts to save the City Market Square and Davenport House led to the creation of Historic Savannah Foundation which buys threatened properties and resells them to preservationists. Two square miles of downtown were designated an historic district in 1966. Preservation has brought rising property values, tourism, and new business opportunities. Since 1967, the displacement problem has been addressed by Savannah Landmark which restores buildings for low income rental. 18 photos.

S. C. Strom

3536. Matlack, Carol. SMALL-TOWN AMERICA. *Am. Preservation 1978 1(5): 9-19.* Sketches the history of Hudson, Ohio, from founder David Hudson (1799), through the work of philanthropist and preserver James W. Ellsworth (1849-1925), to the efforts of the Hudson Heritage Association in the 1960's and 1970's to preserve Hudson's New England-style architecture. Hudson has been preserved as a "living community," but constant vigilance is needed to maintain a balance between preservation and progress. 11 photos.   J. B. Street

3537. Meadows, George Richard and Call, Steven T. COMBINING HOUSING MARKET TRENDS AND RESIDENT ATTITUDES IN PLANNING URBAN REVITALIZATION. *J. of the Am. Inst. of Planners 1978 44(3):297-305.* Exploration in the theory of neighborhood transition and in the presentation and evaluation of the use of trends in real estate values as an index of neighborhood socioeconomic vitality. The arbitrage model of neighborhood succession is shown to be directly connected to neighborhood property value appreciation trends. This model is useful because it moves the discussion of neighborhood transition beyond the "neighborhood life cycle"—where neighborhoods always go from stable to deteriorated—to a more general perspective where, depending on the circumstances, neighborhoods can be either upgraded or downgraded. It is concluded that monitoring property value trends may be helpful in the designs of neighborhood revitalization strategies, both for the direct information conveyed and for the assistance in gathering and interpreting other sources of information. J

3538. Mohr, Henry. DETROIT'S WOODWARD EAST. *Am. Preservation 1978 2(1): 22-29.* Since 1977, funding has been suspended for the Woodward East Project, Detroit's ill-fated neighborhood preservation/renovation effort. Begun in 1967, the Woodward East Project sought to restore 50 deteriorating Victorian homes and construct moderate cost housing in a 26 block inner city neighborhood. Restoration never progressed beyond the facades of nine structures. Unskilled labor, complex funding, and contractor disputes overwhelmed the now bankrupt community group and its president, Edith Woodberry. A rival organization, Concerned Homeowners and Residents of Woodward East, seeks control of the project but the future is uncertain. 5 photos.   S. C. Strom

3539. Mohr, Henry. "PARTNERS" AIM AT SAME GOALS. *Am. Preservation 1978 1(6): 42-48.* Despite philosophical differences, preservationists and environmentalists are uniting to promote a better quality of life through preservation and improvement of natural and built environments. Such wilderness advocates as the Sierra Club, the Nature Conservancy, and the Audubon Society are showing increased interest in the urban environment. In order to further common goals, 28 environmental and preservation groups united to form Partners for Livable Places in 1977. The US Department of the Interior has recently consolidated a variety of related programs to create the Heritage Conservation and Recreation Service. Includes a directory of Partners for Livable Places, giving names, addresses, and functions of member organizations. 7 photos.   S. C. Strom

3540. Mohr, Henry. THE REVITALIZATION OF WESTPORT. *Am. Preservation 1978 1(4): 62-72.* Offers a brief historical sketch of Westport in Kansas City, Missouri, and then describes the efforts and achievements of many organizations, businesses, the city government and individuals to conserve and restore the community and its architectural heritage. 17 photos.   J. B. Street

3541. Morrow, Sara Sprott. THE CHURCH OF THE HOLY TRINITY; ENGLISH COUNTRYSIDE TRANQUILITY IN DOWNTOWN NASHVILLE. *Tennessee Hist. Q. 1975 34(4): 333-349.* Describes the origins and development of the Holy Trinity Episcopal Church which began as a mission church in South Nashville during the 1840's. The church, an excellent example of Gothic Revival architecture, was completed in 1853, survived use as a powder magazine during the Civil War, and is being restored under direction of the Tennessee Historical Commission. Secondary sources; 2 illus., 18 notes.   M. B. Lucas

3542. Nicholson, Arnold. SOCIETY HILL: REFASHIONING A PHILADELPHIA NEIGHBORHOOD. *Early Am. Life 1977 8(5): 32-37.* Discusses the restoration, since 1957, of Society Hill, an 18th-century historic neighborhood in Philadelphia, Pennsylvania.

3543. Orr-Cahall, Christina. PALM BEACH: THE PREDICAMENT OF A RESORT. *Hist. Preservation 1978 30(1): 10-15.* The important architectural heritage of Palm Beach, Florida, from the 1920's and the 1960's, which has been preserved over the years "by its wealthy, privacy seeking residents," is now endangered "precisely because of those same residents' laissez-faire isolationist attitudes." There must be community-wide preservation organization and legal action. 5 photos.   R. M. Frame, III

3544. Ortega, Richard L. UNWANTED: HISTORIC DISTRICT DESIGNATION. *Historic Preservation 1976 28(1): 41-43.* Historic district designation imposed on relatively modern areas or neighborhoods which are still vital, growing and changing, "may make a district historic before its time." Such designation is necessary only for an area with "no means of sustenance." 2 photos.   R. M. Frame III

3545. Paraschos, Janet Nyberg. MT. AUBURN: HELPING RESIDENTS TAKE PRIDE IN THEIR CINCINNATI NEIGHBORHOOD. *Am. Preservation 1979 2(4): 7-17.* After the organization of the Mt. Auburn Good Housing Foundation in 1967, residents began buying out absentee landlords and renovating the neighborhood.

3546. Paraschos, Janet Nyberg. SARATOGA SPRINGS. *Am. Preservation 1978 2(1): 59-72.* Saratoga Springs, New York, was late 19th-century America's prime resort relying on natural mineral springs, horseracing, gambling, and luxury hotels to attract wealthy summer vacationers. The financial fortunes of the town fluctuated with the legal status of gambling and alcohol. World War II financially ruined the elegant but declining hotels and the decaying racetrack failed to draw visitors. However, in the past 10 years the city has experienced a revival. Renovation of the racetrack, a 28-day exclusive racing season, new highways, a winter sports boom, and an influx of young residents have all contributed to the economic and cultural renaissance. Today more than 350 Victorian homes, many previously owned by Skidmore College, have been restored and placed on the National Register of Historic Places. 15 photos.   S. C. Strom

3547. Pitzer, Donald E. THE HARMONIST HERITAGE OF THREE TOWNS. *Hist. Preservation 1977 29(4): 4-10.* Discusses the history, architecture, and historic preservation efforts of three communally oriented towns built by the followers of dissenter (Johann) George Rapp (1757-1847), who came to the United States from the German province of Württemberg. Harmony, Pennsylvania (built 1804), New Harmony, Indiana (1814), and Economy (now Ambridge), Pennsylvania (1825), all face the problem of the restorations and interpretation of an entire town rather than a single building. 6 photos.

R. M. Frame, III

3548. Platt, Frederick. NEW CASTLE: LIVING WITH HISTORY. *Early Am. Life 1977 8(1): 56-58.* A brief history of New Castle, Delaware, during 1655-1881 and describes its preservation of historic sites and restorations.

3549. Praschos, Janet Nyberg. "THEY BUILT THEM SOLID." *Am. Preservation 1978 1(6): 49-57.* Settled in the early 1800's by recent immigrants, German Village in Columbus, Ohio has survived years of neglect in the first half of the 20th century. In 1960 the area was declared an historic district and since 1963, the German Village Commission has coordinated and approved restoration projects. Today two-thirds of the 1,800 structures within the 233 acre Village have been restored. The small, sturdy, brick homes on tiny lots are reminiscent of 19th century Europe and the beauty of the community makes it a tourist attraction. Rising prices, noise, new residents, and inadequate parking have disenchanted many long time residents but the future of the German Village is tied to historic preservation. 9 photos.   S. C. Strom

3550. Randall, Willard S. AT SOUTHERN TIP OF NEW JERSEY, A GINGERBREAD SPA. *Smithsonian 1978 9(6): 120-131.* Discusses the history of the preservation effort to save a segment of Cape May, New Jersey, one of America's oldest seaside resorts. Considered a major eastern gathering place during the 19th century, Cape May attracted presidents and dignitaries, offering entertainment in the forms of gambling and music. Although ravaged by fires, floods, and urban renewal, the recent 15-year preservation effort, lead by Carolyn Pitts, has resulted in the preservation and restoration of about 600 structures, now a National Historic landmark of unparalled late-Victorian architecture. 12 illus.

S. R. Quéripel

3551. Reece, Ray. GALVESTON. *Am. Preservation 1977 1(1): 42-55.* Galveston, Texas, a prosperous seaport during 1840-1900, is a city of distinguished and opulent Victorian architecture. One of its notable neighborhoods is the East End which was allowed to deteriorate during 1910-60. Since 1960, the East End has been a focus of concern for preservationists. The Galveston Historical Foundation succeeded in establishing the East End Historical District in 1972. Led by a citizen's governing panel, the East End Historical District Board, residents are restoring homes and a new spirit of community pride is evident. With rising prices and fashionability, have come disputes over aesthetics, increased density, new construction, and the displacement of low-income residents which the Board is working to resolve. 14 photos.   S. C. Strom

3552.   Reiter, Beth Lattimore and Adler, Leopold, II.   RESTORATION OF SAVANNAH'S VICTORIAN DISTRICT.   *Georgia Hist. Q. 1979 63(1): 164-172.* The Savannah Landmark Rehabilitation Project, Inc. was formed in 1974 to rehabilitate the Victorian District of Savannah, not only to preserve the architecture, but also to improve living conditions for the inhabitants. The history of the area and the progress of this project are described. Primary and secondary sources; 3 illus., 19 notes.   G. R. Schroeder

3553.   Reynolds, Ann Vines.   NASHVILLE'S CUSTOM HOUSE. *Tennessee Hist. Q. 1978 37(3): 263-277.* Describes the acquisition of the land, the erection of the Pointed Gothic stone structure, the later additions to the edifice, and the many government agencies which occupied the Nashville Custom House, the cornerstone of which was laid by President Rutherford B. Hayes on 19 September 1877. In 1972 the structure was listed in the National Register of Historic Places, and in 1976 it was declared surplus property and given to the city of Nashville. It has now been restored to its original condition, both interior and exterior. Government sources and secondary works; 2 photos, 39 notes.   H. M. Parker, Jr.

3554.   Rhangos, Audrey Dunn.   HISTORIC SAVANNAH FOUNDATION.   *Georgia Hist. Q. 1979 63(1): 173-179.* Describes the activities of the Historic Savannah Foundation (formed 1955) to interest and educate citizens of Savannah, Georgia in preserving their architectural heritage. Many successes are reported and Savannah has become a national example for its preservation programs. 3 illus.   G. R. Schroeder

3555.   Roper, James H.   CAPE MAY.   *Am. Preservation 1978 1(5): 36-53.* The famous resort community of Cape May, New Jersey, was a quality "watering place" in the 19th century. More than 600 19th-century frame buildings in various styles remain. City residents are actively continuing preservation efforts. 15 photos.   J. B. Street

3556.   Rothenberg, Alan E.   IT PAYS TO PRESERVE.   *Cry California 1974-75 10(1): 6-12.* Discusses the possibilities of building recycling —the restoration and refurbishing of older buildings rather than their demolition. Cities such as Denver, Seattle, and San Francisco have revitalized older urban centers through such efforts. Although many variables exist in determining the feasibility of retaining an old building instead of constructing a new one, savings in cost and time and the preservation of esthetic values suggest that building rehabilitation can be an economically viable practice.   A. Hoffman

3557.   Sager, Leon B.   THE INTENTIONAL COMMUNITY. *Cry California 1973 8(2): 28-35.* A recent history of the fight to preserve the unique beauty of Santa Barbara, California, including environmental struggles with the California Division of Highways over U.S. 101, with oil companies, and with developers. The fundamental problem is whether unlimited growth and unplanned urbanization can be halted.   R. W. Righter

3558.   Segrest, Eileen.   INMAN PARK: A CASE STUDY IN NEIGHBORHOOD REVITALIZATION.   *Georgia Hist. Q. 1979 63(1): 109-117.* Inman Park, Atlanta's first garden suburb, was planned in the 1880's and many elegant Victorian homes were built there. The area declined until a group of preservationists bought homes there and in 1970 founded Inman Park Restoration, Inc. Projects have included court cases against the highway department, nomination of the area to the National Register of Historic Places, rezoning, and restoration of many homes. Based mainly on interviews; 3 illus., 3 notes, biblio.   G. R. Schroeder

3559.   Seligman, Ralph.   HOBOKEN REDISCOVERED YET AGAIN.   *New York Affairs 1979 5(4): 26-38.* Provides a brief history of Hoboken, New Jersey, since the Dutch arrived in the mid-17th century, particularly the rediscovery of the city by the upper middle class beginning the 1960's, the process of gentrification which followed, and the realization of the limits of Hoboken beginning in 1977.

3560.   Sheppard, Peggy and Corley, Kit.   A SALUTE TO COLUMBUS: ON THE OCCASION OF HER SESQUICENTENNIAL. *Georgia Life 1978 5(1): 12-16.* Chronicles the economic growth and population growth of Columbus, Georgia, covering 1828-1978, and discusses restoration and preservation projects, 1960's-70's.

3561.   Sowa, Cora Angier.   HOLY PLACES.   *New York Affairs 1977 4(3): 59-68.* Discusses the mythic and symbolic representations which cities and city landmarks hold for the inhabitants of urban areas; asserts that destruction of such structures should be eschewed in light of current trends of social dissolution in cities.

3562.   Spalding, Phinizy.   NEIGHBORHOOD CONSERVATION, OR, GETTING IT ALL TOGETHER IN COBBHAM.   *Georgia Hist. Q. 1979 63(1): 90-99.* Cobbham, first suburb of Athens, Georgia, was settled in 1834. Many fine Victorian homes in the area have recently been demolished. In 1972 the Cobb-Hill Street Community Association was formed in protest, succeeded by the Historic Cobbham Foundation in 1977. Actions, successes, and problems of these two groups are described. Based on the files of the Historic Cobbham Foundation; 3 illus., 29 notes.   G. R. Schroeder

3563.   Stephens, Suzanne.   TAKING TO THE WATERFRONT. *Horizon 1978 21(10): 30-37.* During the past decade US cities started to rediscover and develop their waterfronts; includes photographs of several waterfront rejuvenation projects.

3564.   Stuck, Goodloe.   HISTORICAL PRESERVATION IN SHREVEPORT: SIX YEARS OF STRUGGLING AND EDUCATING.   *North Louisiana Hist. Assoc. J. 1978 9(3): 131-133.* Because Shreveport lacked buildings 'over a hundred years old," it was difficult for the Historic Preservation of Shreveport Committee to persuade the public that there were buildings worth saving. The group thus began the task of educating groups and individuals in Shreveport about the value of historic preservation. The committee has renovated some Victorian houses of the late 19th century. Recounts how the committee established its goals for further preservation in the city. 2 photos.   H. M. Parker, Jr.

3565.   Terrell, David.   LITTLE ROCK STORY.   *Am. Preservation 1977 1(1): 62-72.* Downtown Little Rock is characterized by diverse neighborhoods with architecture from every period since 1840. Recent efforts to revive the downtown area involve several organizations. Quapaw Quarter Association addresses legal and economic problems of neighboring preservation. Neighborhood Housing Services brings together residents, government officials, and financiers to assist in the rehabilitation of downtown homes. Metrocentre Mall, a renovation of the downtown retail district, is a project of Little Rock Unlimited Progress. Old Town Properties is an investment group which buys deteriorating property and restores it for resale. Together these organizations are effectively reviving the historic central city of Little Rock, Arkansas. 18 photos.   S. C. Strom

3566.   Terrell, David.   OAKLAND CEMETERY.   *Am. Preservation 1979 2(6): 41-48.* Amid urban renewal and modern construction, the Historic Oakland Cemetery, Inc., group of Atlanta, Georgia, seeks to restore and preserve the Oakland Cemetery (begun in 1850), which has representative forms of southern architecture and is one of the few historic landmarks remaining in Atlanta; 1975-79.

3567.   Terrell, David.   THE RECYCLING TREND.   *Am. Preservation 1978 1(4): 20-29.* Discusses the adaptation of old buildings for use as shopping and art centers in Akron, Ohio; Denver, Colorado; Minneapolis, Minnesota; Norfolk, Virginia; Alexandria, Virginia; and San Francisco, California. Some projects face financial and bureaucratic difficulties. 8 photos.   J. B. Street

3568.   Thorp, Gregory.   ITS GLORY VANISHED, VAST CINCINNATI TERMINAL BOWS OUT.   *Smithsonian 1974 5(3): 64-69.* The

Cincinnati Union Terminal, a multimillion-dollar showplace completed in 1933, "has all come down except its mighty rotunda building, which may be purchased by the city of Cincinnati and used as a multipurpose transportation center or for governmental offices. The destruction of the station symbolizes the end of railroading's golden age—just at a time, ironically, when wistful thoughts of a resurrection of the rails are in everyone's mind. . . . A spirited fund-raising effort, led by Alfred Moore, saved the rotunda structure, along with the concourse mosaics (for reinstallation in the expanding airport). . . . The problem facing Cincinnati symbolizes one of the illnesses that disrupts our present society." 3 photos, 4 illus.   D. D. Cameron

3569. Todd, Evalyn E. HISTORIC HALIFAX. *Daughters of the Am. Revolution Mag. 1976 110(2): 186-191.* Discusses the history of Halifax, North Carolina, since its founding in 1759 and notes some important historical sites and restorations there.

3570. Unsigned. ANNAPOLIS. *Am. Preservation 1977 1(1): 27-33.* Provides a brief synopsis of the history of Annapolis, Maryland and the efforts of Historic Annapolis, Inc., during 1952-69, to obtain an historic district zoning law. 12 photos.   S. C. Strom

3571. Unsigned. BOHEMIA REBORN. *Horizon 1974 16(2): 64-77.* Photographic essay on the revitalization of New York City's SoHo district.   S

3572. Unsigned. DISPLACEMENT UNSOLVED. *Am. Preservation 1977 1(1): 20-26.* Discusses the revival of American urban neighborhoods and its grassroots origin. Contrasts this preservation effort to the massive and disruptive urban renewal projects of the 1960's. The displacement of low-income residents is still a major problem for neighborhood preservationists. The Urban Redevelopment Task Force conducts successful neighborhood revitalization programs through its Neighborhood Housing Services (NHS). Supported by five federal agencies, the Task Force has established NHS programs nationwide to bring together residents, local government officials, and bankers and to provide high risk loans. Describes successful programs in Little Rock, Cincinnati, and Chicago. 6 photos.   S. C. Strom

3573. Unsigned. EUREKA. *Am. Preservation 1978 1(2): 48-57.* Eureka Heritage Society is conducting a unique architectural survey to identify and describe all structures of aesthetic or historic interest in Eureka, California. Led by Dolores Vellutini, the Society is collecting information on 1,500 buildings including the Carson Mansion and other well-maintained wooden Victorian homes. Despite the general stability of its neighborhoods, the Eureka business district deteriorated badly in the 1950's and 1960's. Restoration began in 1973 with the E. Janssen Building and the Old Town Redevelopment Project. Today Old Town is a vital shopping district and tourist attraction. 16 photos.   S. C. Strom

3574. Unsigned. HELENA. *Am. Preservation 1977 1(1): 9-19.* Helena, Montana, has recently completed a successful urban renewal program to restore the exuberant Victorian buildings of its downtown. Damaged by a 1935 earthquake, downtown Helena fell victim to suburban sprawl in the 1950's. In 1969, Last Chance Urban Renewal Project began, and after a difficult start, undertook the restoration of architecturally significant downtown structures. Under the direction of Lawrence Gallagher, the Project has spent $50,000,000 since 1972 on building restorations and creating a pedestrian mall. Completed in 1977, the Project has stimulated private investment, and the preservation of fine homes throughout Helena. 15 photos.   S. C. Strom

3575. Unsigned. MANCHESTER. *Am. Preservation 1978 1(3): 9-19.* Discusses this Pittsburgh ghetto's 13-year struggle for urban restoration in the face of opposition and indifference. The Pittsburgh History and Landmarks Foundation, founded in the mid-1960's to secure public and private funding for the task, has finally begun restoration of these late-Victorian residences, with the cooperation of their inhabitants. Illus.   J. Tull

3576. Unsigned. NEW ORLEANS. *Am. Preservation 1978 1(3): 51-56.* The Coliseum Square Association was responsible for saving the historically valuable Lower Garden district of New Orleans, Louisiana, from demolition to allow a new bridge. The group's most significant contribution was establishment of the New Orleans Historic District Landmarks Committee in the face of city indifference. Illus.   J. Tull

3577. Unsigned. PORTLAND. *Am. Preservation 1978 1(2): 26-35.* Since 1968, Portland, Oregon, has had a model preservation program uniquely compatible with urban growth. To save significant structures in the changing downtown, the Portland Historic Landmarks Commission was established to advise on the designation of historical landmarks and districts. Such a designation requires a formal review prior to demolition or exterior remodeling. The Skidmore/Old Town Historic District, once sadly deteriorating, is now a fashionable business district because of heavy investment by local businessmen such as William Naito. Neighborhood preservation is encouraged by a historic conservation district zoning ordinance which provides stability for older neighborhoods not qualifying as historic districts. 27 photos.   S. C. Strom

3578. Unsigned. [PUBLIC ART]. *Art in Am. 1977 65(3): 15-20.*
Baldwin, Carl R. SHAHN'S BRONX P. O. MURALS: THE PERILS OF PUBLIC ART, *pp. 15-18.* Discusses the murals painted by Ben Shahn in the Bronx post office, 1938, the attempts to save it and to obscure or destroy it (primarily through vandalism), 1970-75.
Crawford, Tad. TAKING CARE OF THE GOVERNMENT'S PUBLIC ART, *pp. 19-20.* Examines the legal ramifications of trying to save vestiges of public art, 1966-76, especially those from the New Deal.

3579. Ward, Frank A., II. GALESBURG ORGANIZES FOR SUCCESSFUL PRESERVATION. *Hist. Preservation 1977 29(3): 38-41.* "Galesburg, Ill. . . . was recently selected as one of three communities to be studies in the National Trust Main Street Project." Describes the methods used by the Galesburg Historical Society during 1975-76 to inspire community-supported historic preservation. Illus.   R. M. Frame, III

3580. Watson, Catherine. BROWNSVILLE. *Am. Preservation 1979 2(5): 7-21.* Collaboration of preservation groups and the zoning commission in Brownsville, Texas, brought about zoning proposals which provided for historic preservation and restoration amid industrial growth, but misunderstanding of land use and owner freedom caused their defeat, 1974-76.

3581. Watson, Catherine. GALENA. *Am. Preservation 1979 2(2): 9-19.* From 1848-56, Galena was a dominant economic power in Illinois. Bypassed as a railroad center with the Galena River silting up and lead demand dropping, Galena never regained its early prosperity. However, economic stagnation resulted in the survival of architectural styles from 1820-1900's. Private investors from nearby urban areas have been restoring the fine Greek Revival, Italianate, and Second Empire homes. Mayor Frank L. Einsweiler helped obtain the city's first historic preservation code in 1965. Future projects include work on the DeSoto House, a footbridge connecting the depot-tourist center to downtown, and the abandoned Galena High School. 9 photos.   S. C. Strom

3582. Wilkins, Woodrow W. CORAL GABLES: 1920'S NEW TOWN. *Hist. Preservation 1978 30(1): 6-9.* Discusses recent historic preservation efforts in Coral Gables, Florida, a completely planned city developed in 1921 by George E. Merrick and chartered in 1925. Discusses the design roles of architects Phineas E. Paist, AIA, and George H. Fink, landscape architect Frank M. Button, and artists Denman and Robert Fink. 7 photos.   R. M. Frame, III

3583. Wiseman, Carter. RECYCLING THE CITY. *Horizon 1978 21(1): 43-49.* Examines remodelings and restorations of old buildings in cities for commercial, cultural, and residential purposes, 1970's.

3584. Woodbridge, Sally B. INDUSTRIAL METAMORPHOSIS. *Hist. Preservation 1978 30(2): 37-41.* Describes case studies of historic preservation and adaptive use of obsolete industrial structures in Seattle, Washington. Includes Ballard and Fremont historic districts; Gas Works Park created from 1906 Seattle Gas Co. machinery; 1902-03 Stewart House, a workingman's hotel; and the first building of the Boeing Airplane Co. 6 photos.   R. M. Frame, III

3585. Zolotow, Maurice. VICTORIAN DREAM. *Am. Preservation 1977 1(1): 34-41.* Describes the founding of the San Francisco Victoriana Company, the only company that manufactures and sells decorative ornamentation for the elaborate wooden houses built in San Francisco from 1850-1915. Of more than 13,000 remaining Victorian structures in San Francisco, 50 have substantially altered facades requiring renovation and complex ornamental details. After several years of studying Victorian house plans and decorative catalogs, making samples, and visiting preservation groups, San Francisco Victoriana began making custom millwork to order. Eventually the company became involved in the total restoration of Victorian homes. Describes the restoration process from initial interview to completion. 11 photos.   S. C. Strom

Disasters

3586. Anderson, David M. THE LOS ANGELES EARTHQUAKE AND THE FOLKLORE OF DISASTER. *Western Folklore 1974 33(4): 331-336.* An account of the Los Angeles earthquake of February 1971 and a recounting of many personal experiences and folktales which followed the disaster. Primary and secondary sources; 3 notes.
S. L. Myres

3587. Farhar, Barbara C. THE IMPACT OF THE RAPID CITY FLOOD ON PUBLIC OPINION ABOUT WEATHER MODIFICATION. *Pacific Sociol. Rev. 1976 19(1): 117-144.* Discusses psychological and sociological effects of a flood that struck Rapid City, South Dakota, in 1972.

3588. Francaviglia, Richard F. XENIA REBUILDS: EFFECTS OF PREDISASTER CONDITIONING ON POSTDISASTER REDEVELOPMENT. *J. of the Am. Inst. of Planners 1978 44(1): 13-24.* The devastating tornado of 3 April 1974, provided Xenia, Ohio, with an opportunity to rebuild while avoiding past mistakes in planning and zoning. A comprehensive redevelopment plan stressing downtown revitalization, housing reconstruction, and floodplain zoning, was approved. Simultaneous approval of "overlay zoning," however, permitted the reemergence of pretornado forces to affect redevelopment of the impacted area. Three years after the tornado, elements of the "old Xenia" are appearing in renewed strip development and continued downtown decline, a reaffirmation of residential discard in "undesirable" areas, and continued uncoordinated environmental development. This article focuses on the persistence of these predisaster motivations and their probable effect on Xenia's future.   J

3589. Hutslar, Donald A., ed. CROSSROADS: THE XENIA TORNADO, A RETROSPECTIVE VIEW. *Ohio Hist. 1974 83(3): 192-211.* Discusses conditions in Xenia and Wilberforce, Ohio, from the tornado of 13 April 1974 to the razing of the damaged buildings a few weeks later. Emphasizes the loss of a sense of historical continuity resulting from such a sudden catasrophe. Includes excerpts from Helen Hooven Santmyer's *Ohio Town* (1962). 33 photos.   J. B. Street

3590. Robbins, Peggy. TOWN IN FLAME. *Am. Hist. Illus. 1979 13(9): 20-29.* A small fire in the hold of the SS *Grand Camp,* docked at Texas City, Texas, 1947, ended in a masive explosion followed by a fire which destroyed the entire port area.

Attitudes toward Urban Life and the City

3591. Adams, Charles L. LAS VEGAS AS BORDER TOWN: AN INTERPRETIVE ESSAY. *Nevada Hist. Soc. Q. 1978 21(1): 51-55.* The *Yogi of Cockroach Court,* a 1947 novel (reissued in 1972) by Frank Waters, reflected on many deplorable human circumstances. The darker side of humanity is universal, but it was more visible in Waters's fictional Cockroach Court, a border town where debauchery was condoned openly much as Las Vegas, Nevada, tolerates it. Waters's fiction shows Las Vegas residents how to understand the negative aspects of their social environment and achieve a more redemptive life. 9 notes.   H. T. Lovin

3592. Amato, Peter W. WISCONSIN CITIZEN ATTITUDES TOWARD PUBLIC CONTROL OF AND INCENTIVES TO URBAN DEVELOPMENT. *Land Econ. 1975 51(2): 164-171.* Using data from a 3,500-sample questionnaire, develops a preference profile of citizen attitudes toward public incentives and controls of urban development. Finds some age, socioeconomic class, and geographic differences in the attitudes of the respondents. 4 tables, 4 notes, biblio.
E. S. Johnson

3593. Baerwald, Friedrich. DER FALL NEW YORKS [The case of New York]. *Frankfurter Hefte [West Germany] 1976 31(5): 35-41.* Discusses the history of New York's financial trouble, its roots in post-Classical Western Civilization's basic antipathy toward cities, and comments on President Gerald R. Ford's reluctance to help.

3594. Berry, Brian J. L. AGING METROPOLIS IN DECLINE. *Society 1976 13(4): 54-56.* Points out elements in our national self-image such as love of newness, desire to be near nature, individualism, competition, etc., that make Americans unable to contend with declining metropolitan areas and hasten their flight to the suburbs.

3595. Blackwood, Larry G. and Carpenter, Edwin H. THE IMPORTANCE OF ANTI-URBANISM IN DETERMINING RESIDENTIAL PREFERENCES AND MIGRATION PATTERNS. *Rural Sociol. 1978 43(1): 31-47.* Assesses antiurbanism (preference for living in less-populated areas when associated with concern for population size) in relation to expressed attitudes toward communities of lesser population and to expected services and amenities provided, 1970's.

3596. Bowles, Stephen E. *CABARET* AND *NASHVILLE*: THE MUSICAL AS SOCIAL COMMENT. *J. of Popular Culture 1978 12(3): 550-556.* Examines two films, *Cabaret* (1972) and *Nashville* (1975), as historical documents, as each reflects the values and cultural milieu of a particular historical period; the former, Berlin during the 1930's, the latter, Nashville, Tennessee, and the country-western music scene during the 1970's.

3597. Chachere, Ernest G. and Elliot, Richard J. PERCEPTUAL DISSONANCE AND INNER-CITY EDUCATION. *J. of Negro Educ. 1977 46(3): 329-333.* A study of teacher education students found that middle-class white students have a negative perception of inner-city life, while inner-city black students hold more positive perceptions. Based on original research; fig.   R. E. Butchart

3598. Fava, Sylvia F. CHANGING SUBURBAN IMAGES: IS THE BLOOM OFF THE ROSE? *New York Affairs 1979 5(4): 55-65.* Describes suburbanization in America since World War II, discussing public concern in the 1960's, and problems which became evident in the 1970's dealing with ethnicity and women.

3599. Fischer, Claude S. URBAN MALAISE. *Social Forces 1973 52(2): 221-235.* Popular imagery and various social science theories argue that urban life generates a sense of despair or malaise. While Americans tend to express preferences for small communities, secondary analysis of several American and foreign surveys fails to indicate that community size fosters personal unhappiness. If any result is substantial, it is that the effect, worldwide, is of rural malaise. American and French data do reveal, however, that, after controls for covariates, there is a small trend for the largest metropolises to be disproportionately places of malaise. Breaking down the samples by migration history suggests that this is owing to the ability of some to move to idealized communities.   J

3600. Foster, Lynn. DIMENSIONS OF "URBAN UNEASE" IN TEN CITIES. *Urban Affairs Q. 1974 10(2): 185-196.* Surveys citizen awareness of the urban crisis in 10 cities. Concludes that unrest is not centralized in particular neighborhoods but is city-wide, and that most individuals are not concerned with urban unease, but with inappropriate behavior in public places. 6 tables, notes, biblio.
P. J. Woehrmann

3601. Foster, William S. ALL-AMERICA CITIES: DEMOCRACY AT WORK. *Natl. Civic Rev. 1974 63(4): 178-188.* An All-America City is one that is able to demonstrate the calibre and quality of its people. If the people and their public officials stand ready to improve the quality of life in the community, one of the major criteria of the All-America Cities award program has been fulfilled, as shown by the achievements of the 1973-1974 winners.　　　J

3602.　George, (Walter) Eugene.　TRADITION AND PROGRESS: A CREATIVE PARTNERSHIP.　*Historic Preservation 1974 26(4): 15-17.* "We must come to terms with urbanization as our forebears came to terms with wilderness. The problems we face are social, moral, and economic. Important to solving them is an enhancement of the human experience by exposure to inspiration from the past." 5 photos.
R. M. Frame, III

3603.　Glenn, Norval D. and Hill, Lester, Jr.　RURAL-URBAN DIFFERENCES IN ATTITUDES AND BEHAVIOR IN THE UNITED STATES.　*Ann. of the Am. Acad. of Pol. and Social Sci. 1977 (429): 36-50.* Recent American data reveal moderate to substantial farm-nonfarm differences on a few kinds of attitudes and behavior, but since farm people now are only about 4% of the population, the farm-nonfarm distinction cannot account for much of the total variation of any kind of attitudes or behavior. The kinds of attitudes and behavior which differ substantially between farm and nonfarm people usually differ monotonically by community size; hence, "ruralism" seems to some extent to characterize residents of the smaller dense settlements and, to a lesser extent, those of intermediate-sized cities. Furthermore, city residents with rural backgrounds tend to retain rural attitudes and behavior characteristics, size of community of origin being a stronger predictor of some attitudes than size of community of current residence. Although the association of community size with a more or less representative list of attitudinal variables is weak, such correlates of community size as age and socioeconomic status do not largely account for the larger associations, which probably reflect a tendency for social and cultural change to occur earlier in the larger communities. The explanatory utility of size of community of origin and of residence seems less than that of age and education but at least as great as that of several other explanatory variables favored by social scientists, such as family income and occupational prestige.　　　J

3604.　Grasmick, Harold G. and Grasmick, Mary K.　THE EFFECT OF FARM FAMILY BACKGROUND ON THE VALUE ORIENTATIONS OF URBAN RESIDENTS: A STUDY OF CULTURAL LAG.　*Rural Sociol. 1978 43(3): 367-386.* Urban residents with farm family backgrounds, compared to urban residents with urban family backgrounds, tend to identify with traditional values contributing to cultural lag; discusses resistance to change in the 1970's.

3605.　Hohm, Charles F.　A HUMAN-ECOLOGICAL APPROACH TO THE REALITY AND PERCEPTION OF AIR POLLUTION: THE LOS ANGELES CASE.　*Pacific Sociol. Rev. 1976 19(1): 21-44.* Discusses the problem of air pollution as perceived by residents of Los Angeles, California, in the 1960's.

3606.　Ianitskii, O.　GORODA SSHA: EKOLOGICHESKAIA SITUATSIIA I ANTIURBANISTSKAIA IDEOLOGIIA [The cities of the United States: the ecological situation and antiurban ideology].　*Mirovaia Ekonomika i Mezhdunarodnye Otnosheniia [USSR] 1976 (9): 99-107.* Explores the antiurbanism in contemporary American ecological consciousness, showing its social and ideological origins, together with the antiecological reality of bourgeois life, 1970's.

3607.　Landreth, Elizabeth.　THERE SHALL BE NO NIGHT: LAS VEGAS.　*J. of Popular Culture 1975 9(1): 197-203.* Reviews the place of Las Vegas in the American dream and writings about it by practitioners of the new journalism.

3608.　Lane, James B.　VIOLENCE AND SEX IN THE POST-WAR POPULAR URBAN NOVEL: WITH A CONSIDERATION OF HAROLD ROBBINS' *A STONE FOR DANNY FISHER* AND HUBERT SELBY, JR.'S *LAST EXIT TO BROOKLYN*.　*J. of Popular Culture 1974 8(2): 295-308.* Reviews Harold Robbins' *A Stone for Danny Fisher* (New York: Pocket Book Edition, 1953) and Hubert Selby, Jr.'s *Last Exit to Brooklyn* (New York: Grove Paperback Edition, 1965) as forerunners of realistic urban novels. Although Harold Robbins is considered a hack writer today, his *A Stone for Danny Fisher* was seriously considered by critics and realistically portrayed the agony of urban dwell-

ers. Danny Fisher represents an urban Everyman who encounters prejudice, poverty, and corruption while desperately seeking respect and freedom from fear. Unfortunately, Robbins, like Danny, sold out, but Hubert Selby remained a serious novelist. His *Last Exit to Brooklyn* is both violent and sexually candid while portraying the hidden elements in American society. His characters are victimized by the harsh reality of poverty and tormented as punishment for a misplaced pride. Selby's vision foreshadowed the increasing violence in urban America.
K. McElroy

3609.　Levitt, Lee.　IS NEW YORK AS BAD AS PEOPLE SAY?　*New York Affairs 1974 2(1): 4-15.* Distrust and dislike of New York City pervades the rest of the country. Is it a crime-ridden sink of humanity as it is portrayed or has the city just neglected to tend to its image?　　J

3610.　Long, Norton E.　REBUILDING CITIES: BEYOND BRICKS AND MORTAR.　*Natl. Civic Rev. 1976 65(4): 187-191.* The rebuilding of cities is far more than a matter of bricks and mortar. The city is people, not buildings, and unless most of them are employed, self-respecting and respected, the towers of a renewed downtown are a delusion and a mockery. The city can be truly rebuilt and have a viable future only if its economy is made competitive and able to employ all its inhabitants.
J

3611.　Lovrich, Nicholas P., Jr.　DIFFERING PRIORITIES IN AN URBAN ELECTORATE: SERVICE PREFERENCES AMONG ANGLO, BLACK, AND MEXICAN AMERICAN VOTERS.　*Social Sci. Q. 1974 55(3): 704-717.* Examines data relating to the satisfaction or dissatisfaction of ethnic groups in Denver, Colorado, with city government services.　　S

3612.　Lovrich, Nicholas P., Jr. and Taylor, G. Thomas, Jr.　NEIGHBORHOOD EVALUATION OF LOCAL GOVERNMENT SERVICES: A CITIZEN SURVEY APPROACH.　*Urban Affairs Q. 1976 12(2): 197-222.* Demonstrates that blacks and Mexican Americans thought their neighborhoods were more poorly served than did Anglos. The former groups also evaluated the effectiveness of city government, including the police functions, less positively than did the Anglos. Within each ethnic group the evaluations varied according to the respondents' neighborhood condition. Concludes that neighborhood survey research is a politically acceptable mode of collecting policy inputs satisfactory to those demanding quantifiable evaluation of governmental programs as well as those demanding administrative responsiveness to the needs of neighborhoods. Based on sample survey of 800 Denver, Colorado, voters; 11 tables, 19 notes, biblio.　　L. N. Beecher

3613.　Lowe, George D. and Peek, Charles W.　LOCATION AND LIFESTYLE: THE COMPARATIVE EXPLANATORY ABILITY OF URBANISM AND RURALITY.　*Rural Sociol. 1974 39(3): 392-420.* Using data from three national surveys, studies rural-urban differences, determining if attitudinal differences remain among the rural and urban residents independent of differences generated by other potent variables and if any increase in the predictive utility of rurality can be generated by use of a composite definition (residence plus lifestyle). On the bases of the close and consistent behavorial and symbolic association of abstinence with rural life and consumption with urban life, drinking of alcoholic beverages was selected as the indicator of rural-urban lifestyles. Rural-metropolitan residence held its own in the company of other established predictors in explaining differences in attitudes. Further, the addition of a lifestyle indicator clearly increased the predictive utility of the rural-urban variable.　　J

3614.　Lowenthal, David.　THE BICENTENNIAL LANDSCAPE: A MIRROR HELD UP TO THE PAST.　*Geographical Rev. 1977 67(3): 253-267.* During recent years, Americans disillusioned with the present have taken increasing comfort in retreating to the past. Appalled by their urban milieus, many have sought to embrace half-remembered rural ways. The nation's 200th birthday provided an occasion for stock taking. Bicentennial celebrations—reenacting Revolutionary episodes, preserving and reproducing Revolutionary artifacts, and reaffirming early American virtues—have altered history to suit present purposes, and instances of historical revision litter the whole American landscape. A comparison between Centennial and Bicentennial modes of celebration and arenas of concern underscores the shift, over the past century, from confidence in a perfectible future to nostalgia for an idealized past.
J

3615. McDermott, John J. SPACE, TIME AND TOUCH: PHILO-
SOPHICAL DIMENSIONS OF URBAN CONSCIOUSNESS.
Soundings 1974 57(3): 253-274. Discusses certain philosophical attitudes
toward the 1973 urban environment relating to aesthetics and architecture.

3616. Netzer, Dick. LOCAL GOVERNMENT IN HEAVEN AND
HELL: LONDON VERSUS NEW YORK. *New York Affairs 1973
1(1): 98-108.* Examines the reasons for New Yorkers' dissatisfaction with
their local government and Londoners' belief in the effectiveness of theirs.
A major reason for this difference is that the London government is
limited in the number of services it performs for its citizens while New
York City has undertaken more responsibilities than the city administration can well fulfill. Additional factors influencing the differing expectations of the two governments are the structure of local government in each
country, the nature of local politics, and attitudes toward government in
general. Illus., table, 6 notes.   J. A. Benson

3617. Pavlak, Thomas J. and Stern, Mark. BLACK-WHITE PER-
CEPTIONS OF URBAN PRIORITIES. *Phylon 1978 39(2): 108-117.*
Describes black and white perceptions of urban priorities, based on a
survey of opinion in St. Louis in 1970. Blacks and whites agreed that
education and safety were the most important priorities, but blacks
stressed them even more than did whites. Whites, however, were also
extremely concerned about pollution of air and water, a problem that
ranked at the very bottom of blacks' worries. Blacks' third most frequently mentioned priority was housing, which was far down on the white
list. There is much agreement among all urban residents about high
priority problems; where disagreements occur, race is a major factor in
determining attitudes, as are socioeconomic status and area of residence
(downtown or suburbs). 4 tables, 16 notes.   J. C. Billigmeier

3618. Peden, Creighton. BEYOND THE FOLKLORE OF INDI-
VIDUALISM. *Richmond County Hist. 1973 5(2): 76-85.* Individualism is no longer relevant to conditions in 20th-century Augusta. Argues
for group, rather than individual, action on the city's economic and social
problems. "Let us constructively move beyond the folklore of individualism in Augusta by creating meaningful structures which will enable all
our citizens to participate in the resources of the American way of life."
One of six articles in this issue on Augusta. 2 notes.   H. R. Grant

3619. Reilly, John M. CHESTER HIMES' HARLEM TOUGH
GUYS. *J. of Popular Culture 1976 9(4): 935-947.* Chester Himes's
novels about black detectives in Harlem reflect his perceptions of the
American caste system. Himes shows that Harlem only indirectly ac-

knowledges the white community, that morality and right action depends
on particular situations, that what is good in Harlem isn't necessarily
good outside Harlem, and that racism and white exploitation pervade
black communities. The "Tough-Guy" detective is an inevitable product
of oppressive society, and Himes believes the decay that causes crimes will
eventually produce a violent revolution in black America. Primary and
secondary sources; 21 notes.   J. W. Leedom

3620. Rogers, Bruce D. and Lipsey, C. McCurdy. METROPOLI-
TAN REFORM: CITIZEN EVALUATIONS OF PERFORMANCES
IN NASHVILLE-DAVIDSON COUNTY, TENNESSEE. *Publius
1974 4(4): 19-34.* Analyzes a survey comparing citizen attitudes toward
the provision of public services in a large consolidated metropolitan area
and a smaller community. Results indicate that presumptions of improved services in the larger area were not supported. Citizens in the
smaller unit evaluated most public services more highly than citizens in
the metropolitan area. Based on the survey and secondary sources; map,
5 tables, 24 notes.   J. B. Street

3621. Rogers, Theresa F. and Friedman, Nathalie. DECENTRALIZ-
ING CITY GOVERNMENT: THE CITIZEN SURVEY AS A GUIDE
FOR PLANNING AND IMPLEMENTING INSTITUTIONAL
CHANGE. *Administration and Soc. 1978 10(2): 177-202.* Assesses
reactions to city government decentralization plans in New York City
according to responders' ethnicity, the sociopolitical composition of their
neighborhoods, and their appraisal of city services, 1974.

3622. Seward, Adrienne L. GARY'S BLACK SELF-IMAGE.
Indiana Folklore 1977 10(2): 217-222. Whites' images of Gary, Indiana,
are often negative, but blacks see that predominantly black city as a
growing metropolitan area where crime is no worse than in other cities
(contrary to images of the local newspaper), and where an experiment in
black city administration is seen as a slow but steady success.

3623. Stein, Benjamin. WHATEVER HAPPENED TO SMALL-
TOWN AMERICA? *Public Interest 1976 (44): 17-26.* Television and
the movies have changed the traditional view of American small towns
from bastions of everything good about America to frightening places of
evil and corruption. The mass media has promoted this inaccurate and
harmful image because writers for television and films are generally of an
ethnic background from large Eastern cities and hold liberal and anties-
tablishment views. To such people small towns have always been the
enemy. Yet, there are signs of a small town revival due to environmental
issues, unhappiness with big cities, and the real attractions of these towns.
                                                        S. Harrow

3. CANADIAN URBAN HISTORY AND LIFE

General

3624. Artibise, Alan F. J. WINNIPEG, 1874-1914. *Urban Hist. Rev. [Canada] 1975 75(1): 43-50.* During 1874-1914, economic growth and urbanization in Winnipeg, Manitoba, was based not on geographical advantage, but on the presence of able and dynamic political leaders and businessmen; one of eight articles in this issue on the Canadian city in the 19th century.

3625. Bourne, L. S. SOME MYTHS OF CANADIAN URBANIZATION: REFLECTIONS ON THE 1976 CENSUS AND BEYOND. *Urbanism Past and Present 1977-78 (5): 1-11.* Examines misconceptions derived from empirical research depending on statistics and images from past periods: emerging trends are overlooked until they are obvious. This dependence results in analyzing problems and processes of the past rather than those of the present or future. Future projections result in errors of interpretation. Critiques current thinking based on 1976 Canadian Census, including preoccupations of urban growth fixation, metropolitan concentration and growth, regional depopulation, high urban migration, peripheral growth of the industrial and financial heartland, stability of urban growth, and institutional reorganization. Concludes with policy implications and plea for future-oriented and politically-sensitive research. 5 tables, 7 notes. B. P. Anderson

3626. Careless, J. M. S. METROPOLIS AND REGION: THE INTERPLAY BETWEEN CITY AND REGION IN CANADIAN HISTORY BEFORE 1914. *Urban Hist. Rev. [Canada] 1979 78(3): 99-118.* Ties between the developing frontier and the regional city have resulted in the modern metropolis-hinterland of 20th-century Canada. C. A. Watson

3627. Forward, Charles N. PARALLELISM OF HALIFAX AND VICTORIA. *Can. Geographical J. 1975 90(3): 34-43.* Highlights some similarities between provincial capitals Halifax and Victoria (1749-1971). S

3628. Forward, Charles N. REGINA AND SASKATOON AS RETIREMENT CENTRES. *Urban Hist. Rev. [Canada] 1978 (1): 9-17.* Saskatoon, Saskatchewan, has a higher percentage of elderly than Regina, despite close similarities between the two cities. More elderly immigrate to Saskatoon and more elderly already there remain after retiring. Economic, social, and environmental factors are not significant enough to explain the greater attractiveness of Saskatoon. The latter probably has been perceived for a long time as a better place, but there is no obvious explanation. Based on census reports and secondary sources; fig., 4 tables, 8 notes. C. A. Watson

3629. Horn, Michiel. KEEPING CANADA "CANADIAN": ANTI-COMMUNISM AND CANADIANISM IN TORONTO, 1928-29. *Canada 1975 3(1): 34-47.* Discusses the role of immigration and national self-image in anti-Communist movements and anti-Semitism in Toronto, Ontario, in 1928-29, emphasizing freedom of speech issues.

3630. LaFrance, Marc and Ruddell, Thiery. ELEMENTS DE L'URBANISATION DE LA VILLE DE QUEBEC: 1790-1840 [Elements of urbanization in the city of Quebec: 1790-1840]. *Urban Hist. Rev. [Canada] 1975 75(1): 22-30.* Discusses urbanization in Quebec, Quebec, 1790-1840, examining the rapid physical expansion and the military, administrative, and commercial functions in the city; one of eight articles in this issue on the Canadian city in the 19th century.

3631. Linteau, Paul-André. MONTREAL, 1850-1914. *Urban Hist. Rev. [Canada] 1975 75(1): 31-35.* Discusses urbanization in Montreal, Quebec, 1850-1914, examining physical and economic growth, living conditions, and the beginning of administrative positions in municipal government; one of eight articles in this issue on the Canadian city in the 19th century.

3632. MacDonald, Norbert. VANCOUVER IN THE NINETEENTH CENTURY. *Urban Hist. Rev. [Canada] 1975 75(1): 51-54.* Geographical and natural resources aided in parallel growth of the economy and population in Vancouver, British Columbia, during the 19th century; one of eight articles in this issue on the Canadian city in the 19th century.

3633. Marshall, John U. CITY SIZE, ECONOMIC DIVERSITY, AND FUNCTIONAL TYPE: THE CANADIAN CASE. *Econ. Geography 1975 51(1): 37-49.*

3634. Pressman, Norman E. P. and Lauder, Kathleen. RESOURCES TOWNS AS NEW TOWNS. *Urban Hist. Rev. [Canada] 1978 (1): 78-95.* A resource town is one existing to exploit natural resources. Focuses on the Canadian north and reviews demographic, geographic, economic, and social characteristics. The early response by planners was to use plans from Great Britian and southern Canada. This ignored the different circumstances of the north, and planners have had to adapt their plans. Developers have had to raise the quality of life in order to recruit and retain skilled workers. In the beginning of resource development, the resource towns were principally company towns; greater concern for the environment and more government interest are more recent factors. Secondary sources; 3 photos, 2 maps, 22 notes. C. A. Watson

3635. Spencer, Stephen. THE GOOD QUEEN OF HOGS: TORONTO, 1850-1914. *Urban Hist. Rev. [Canada] 1975 75(1): 38-42.* Discusses the economic and governmental growth of Toronto, Ontario, concentrating on Toronto's image as a center of manufacturing, culture, and "righteousness"; one of eight articles in this issue on the Canadian city in the 19th century.

3636. Stelter, Gilbert A. INTRODUCTION. *Urban Hist. Rev. [Canada] 1975 75(1): 2-6.* Introduces eight papers in this issue on the Canadian city in the 19th century; examines economic growth, metropolitan development, population, social organization, and environment. Papers are those to be presented at the 1975 Canadian Historical Association meeting.

3637. Sutherland, David. HALIFAX, 1815-1914: "COLONY TO COLONY." *Urban Hist. Rev. [Canada] 1975 75(1): 7-11.* Discusses colonial affairs and economic and urban growth in Halifax, Nova Scotia, 1815-1914; one of eight articles in this issue on the Canadian city in the 19th century.

3638. Taylor, John. OTTAWA: THE CITY AS CONGLOMERATE. *Urban Hist. Rev. [Canada] 1975 75(1): 36-37.* The physical, economic, and political growth of Ottawa, Ontario, during the 19th century resembled that of a geological conglomerate more than that of a biological organism; one of eight articles in this issue on the Canadian city in the 19th century.

3639. Tremblay, Marc-Adelard. ESPACES GÉOGRAPHIQUES ET DISTANCE CULTURELLE: ESSAI DE DÉFINITION DU FONDEMENT DES MENTALITÉS REGIONALES AU QUEBEC [Geographical space and cultural distance: essay on the definition of the cause of regionalism in Quebec]. *Tr. of the Royal Soc. of Can. [Canada] 1976 14: 131-147.* Questions the influence of space on the Canadian and Quebecois mentalities. Canada is made up of many diverse ethnic groups each settled in its own region. The railroad changed Canadians' view of space and brought more cultural interaction. Canada is multicultural with four main geographical regions: the west coast, the Prairies, the central region, and the Atlantic region. Notes Alfred Kroeber's studies concerning ethnic groups. The spaces are too vast and culture too heterogeneous to make valid studies in all cases. Studies the effect of space on French Canadians and discusses the impact of urbanization on areas such as Quebec. 4 notes, biblio. J. D. Neville

3640. Wallace, C. M. SAINT JOHN, NEW BRUNSWICK (1800-1900). *Urban Hist. Rev. [Canada] 1975 75(1): 12-21.* Examines economic growth, urbanization, manufacturing, population, religious composition, social organization, and environment in Saint John; one of eight articles in this issue on the Canadian city in the 19th century.

The Growth and Decline of Cities and Suburbs

3641. Aiken, S. Robert and Kredl, Lawrence P. MONTREAL'S UPPER PEEL STREET: HOW FAST THE PAST HAS GONE. *Can. Geographic [Canada] 1979 98(2): 38-43.* Chronicles urbanization as shown on Montreal's Upper Peel Street, 1860's-1978.

3642. Artibise, Alan F. J. PATTERNS OF POPULATION GROWTH AND ETHNIC RELATIONSHIPS IN WINNIPEG, 1874-1974. *Social Hist. [Canada] 1976 9(18): 297-335.* Winnipeg's population growth can be divided into five major periods during 1874-1974. During the formative years, 1874-99, Anglo-Canadian migration set the enduring character and tone of Winnipeg society. During 1900-13, the population more than tripled because of an influx of Slavic and Jewish immigrants. Anglo-Canadians expressed bigotry toward the immigrants and used the schools in an attempt to Anglicize them. During 1914-20, ethnic conflict escalated and left social scars that took decades to heal. After 1921 the growth rate slowed and Winnipegers searched for ways to create more harmonious relationships between ethnic groups. After 1960, a period of stability and maintenance of earlier trends can be identified. Based on newspapers, other primary sources, and secondary sources; 2 maps, 12 tables, 96 notes. W. K. Hobson

3643. Barker, G.; Penney, J.; and Seccombe, W. THE DEVELOPERS. *Can. Dimension 1973 9(2-3): 19-50.* Discusses urbanization and housing in Toronto. Comments on demographic shifts, industrial concentration, and the role of government in financing development. Certain development corporations maintain inflated prices, evade taxes, and exploit labor. Some neighborhoods intended for development have fought back. 11 photos, 7 graphs, 3 charts, 2 tables. W. B. Whitham

3644. Bradbury, J. H. CLASS STRUCTURES AND CLASS CONFLICTS IN "INSTANT" RESOURCE TOWNS IN BRITISH COLUMBIA: 1965 TO 1972. *BC Studies [Canada] 1978 (37): 3-18.* The provincial government of British Columbia cooperated with multinational resource extraction companies, 1965-72, to create new "instant" towns to replace company towns. The promoters hoped that this would eliminate some of the class conflicts and industrial strikes present in the older towns. Such was not the case. 3 tables, graph, 27 notes. D. L. Smith

3645. Carcassonne, Marcel. LA JONQUIÈRE ET LES ORIGINES DE TORONTO [La Jonquière and the origins of Toronto]. *R. française d'hist. d'Outre-Mer [France] 1974 61(224): 366-394.* Toronto, a city with a population of more than two million, was originally established in 1750 as a fortified French fur trading station. Pierre-Jacques de Taffanel (1685-1752), the Marquis de La Jonquière, and governor of New France from 1749-52, suggested that the post be established. Based on documents in the Archives nationales de France, and secondary works; 48 notes. L. B. Chan

3646. Careless, J. M. S. URBAN DEVELOPMENT IN CANADA. *Urban Hist. Rev. [Canada] 1974 74(1): 9-13.* Examines the effect of Canadian urbanization on the hinterland and rural areas surrounding urban centers, during 1955-75.

3647. Carter, Margaret. BENNETT: TOWN OR ILLUSION? *Alaska J. 1978 8(1): 52-59.* A history of the town of Bennett, British Columbia. With the discovery of gold at Bonanza Creek, Yukon Territory, in 1896, White Pass and Chilkoot Pass became the leading routes to the Yukon interior. Both trails led from Taiya Inlet to the upper end of Lake Bennett, where the town of Bennett soon sprang up. It was prosperous because there travelers and freight exchanged land transport for water transport. At first it was a center for boat building; later, with the advent of stern-wheeler service north to Whitehorse, it became a center for warehousing. When the railroad through White Pass arrived

in 1899, Bennett's prosperity seemed assured, but the railroad continued on to Whitehorse, and the town all but disappeared. Based on contemporary newspaper accounts, archival materials, and secondary sources; 3 illus., map, 29 notes. L. W. Van Wyk

3648. Clark, S. D. CANADIAN URBAN DEVELOPMENT. *Urban Hist. Rev. [Canada] 1974 74(1): 14-19.* Urbanization in Canada during 1955-75 followed the pattern in northern Ontario and Quebec; rural persons moved into cities to find employment and gave cities a rural, conservative attitude rather than a metropolitan one.

3649. Dahms, Frederic A. HOW ONTARIO'S GUELPH DISTRICT DEVELOPED. *Can. Geographical J. [Canada] 1977 94(1): 48-55.* Discusses the urban development which waxed and waned, 1824-1971.

3650. Dechêne, Louise. LA CROISSANCE DE MONTRÉAL AU XVIIIᵉ SIÈCLE [The growth of Montreal in the 18th century]. *Rev. d'Hist. de l'Amérique Française [Canada] 1973 27(2): 163-180.* In spite of the proportionately large number of people inhabiting the cities of New France in the 18th century, the population of the cities did not tend to increase during this period at a significantly higher rate than that of the countryside.

3651. denOtter, A. A. COAL TOWN IN WHEAT COUNTRY: LETHBRIDGE, ALBERTA, 1885-1905. *Urban Hist. Rev. [Canada] 1976 76(1): 3-5.* Lethbridge's development as the first industrial city of western Canada resulted principally from the collieries and railways established during 1882-90 by Sir Alexander T. Galt (1817-93). The town grew like other prairie cities, with a youthful and energetic population, but was unique in that the transient mine workers produced an unruly society and the Galt family dominated its early life. Lists sources for the study of Lethbridge. Based on the author's dissertation; note. C. A. Watson

3652. den Otter, A. A. URBAN PIONEERS OF LETHBRIDGE. *Alberta Hist. [Canada] 1977 25(1): 15-24.* Lethbridge, founded in the early 1880's as a dreary coal mining village in Alberta, became a major urban center. The development of transportation and industry, as well as the city's educational, social, recreational, religious, and professional life are examined until 1890, when a municipal council was elected. 27 notes. 6 illus. D. Chaput

3653. Foran, Max. FOUR FACES OF CALGARY. *Alberta Hist. [Canada] 1979 27(1): 1-9.* Impressions of Calgary in 1883, 1900, 1912, and 1932. Describes key elements in the city's development, from the frontier Indian village of 1883 to the crushing impact of the Great Depression. In between, Calgary had become a small city, and in 1900 was concerned with such events as the Boer War and the Boxer Rebellion. By 1912, urbanization was in full swing, with the construction of many business blocks, theaters, and churches. 4 illus. D. Chaput

3654. Gierman, D. M. L'URBANISATION DES TERRES RURALES DU CANADA [The urbanization of rural lands in Canada]. *Cahiers de Géographie du Québec [Canada] 1978 22(55): 73-78.* Discusses the findings of a report on rural urbanization: *Urbanisation des Terres Rurales, 1966-1971,* centering on 71 Canadian urban areas, including findings on the actual quantity of urbanized lands, their past quality and use, and the rate of urban development for every 1,000 inhabitants.

3655. Inkster, Tom H. FORT LANGELEY, MAINLAND B.C.'S BIG TOWN, 1827-58. *Can. Geographical J. [Canada] 1977 95(1): 48-53.* Fort Langeley, built by Hudson's Bay Company in 1827, served as the primary city along an important trade route on the Fraser River until it became the capital of British Columbia in 1858.

3656. Johnson, Arthur L. THE TRANSPORTATION REVOLUTION ON LAKE ONTARIO, 1817-1867: KINGSTON AND OGDENSBURG. *Ontario Hist. [Canada] 1975 67(4): 199-209.* Discusses the growth of steamboating on Lake Ontario, suggests some of the causes, and indicates the impact of the changing transportation patterns on the two towns named. These were seen as comparable, and in both cases towns which did not develop as their citizens had hoped, largely due to shifts in the inland transportation patterns feeding the lake steamers. Some examples of cargoes are given, as are some generalized descriptions of selected vessels to indicate changes over the years. Based on primary sources; 43 notes.   W. B. Whitham

3657. Kerr, D. C. SASKATOON 1910-1913: IDEOLOGY OF THE BOOMTIME. *Saskatchewan Hist. [Canada] 1979 32(1): 16-28.* The classic boom and bust cycle of the American and Canadian West was repeated with a vengeance in Saskatoon during 1901-17. Started as a small colony in 1883, aided by the coming of the railroad, encouraged by the establishment of the University, the land speculation bubble burst by the time of World War I. The city has yet to fill some of the subdivisions sold in 1912. 2 photos, 73 notes.   C. Held

3658. Knight, David. 'BOOSTERISM' AND LOCATIONAL ANALYSIS: OR ONE MAN'S SWAN IS ANOTHER MAN'S GOOSE. *Urban Hist. Rev. [Canada] 1973 3: 10-16.* Discusses the role of boosterism, the exaggerated proclamation of one place over another, in the location of Ottawa as the national capital, 1857-59; offers a brief history of the development of Bytown (as Ottawa was previously known), 1822-59.

3659. Marple, David. THE UTILITY OF QUANTITATIVE SOURCES IN THE STUDY OF TRANSPORTATION AND THE GROWTH OF ONTARIO AND QUEBEC URBAN HIERARCHY, 1861-1901: AN EXAMPLE. *Urban Hist. Rev. [Canada] 1973 (2): 2-7.*

3660. McCracken, Jane. YORKTON DURING THE TERRITORIAL PERIOD, 1882-1905. *Saskatchewan Hist. [Canada] 1975 28(3): 95-110.* Discusses the importance of Canadian national policy in the settlement and economic growth of Yorkton, Saskatchewan, and specifically the effects of colonization companies and the extension of the Manitoba and North Western Railways lines. Map, 3 photos, 25 notes.

3661. McGahan, Elizabeth. THE PORT OF SAINT JOHN, NEW BRUNSWICK, 1867-1911: EXPLORATION OF AN ECOLOGICAL COMPLEX. *Urban Hist. Rev. [Canada] 1976 (3): 3-13.* Using Saint John, New Brunswick, as a model, examines how one urban community was integrated, through its transport mode, into a larger ecosystem of cities. The stimulus for the integration was the impact of the Industrial Revolution on its provincial-based prosperity. Saint John sought to expand its economic horizons in the 1880's by seeking a railroad connection with central Canada. The integration into a national transportation system caused organizational and spatial changes within the city. Secondary sources; 4 maps, table, 18 notes.   C. A. Watson

3662. Powell, T. J. D. NORTHERN SETTLEMENT, 1929-1935. *Saskatchewan Hist. [Canada] 1977 30(3): 81-98.* "Back to the land" movements have occurred several times in Canadian history, but the one which took place from 1929 to 1935 in the pioneer region of Saskatchewan had the most governmental support and perhaps the most problems. It arose naturally from the economic hard times of the period and was supported by the hard pressed city governments in the southern part of Saskatchewan as well as the Provincial and Dominion governments. The Conservative administration of J. T. M. Anderson took most of the blame for the general failure of the movement which came about mostly because of the haste and lack of supervision which allowed unsuitable lands to be opened up. This was only partially relieved by the Liberal Gardiner administration with the Land Utilization Board and the Northern Settlers' Reestablishment Branch. Map, photo, 90 notes.   C. Held

3663. Rees, R. THE "MAGIC CITY ON THE BANKS OF THE SASKATCHEWAN": THE SASKATCHEWAN REAL ESTATE BOOM 1910-1913. *Saskatchewan Hist. [Canada] 1974 27(2): 51-59.* By 1909 Saskatoon had acquired the basic functions which were to form the basis for its subsequent economic growth, the Canadian Pacific Railway, Canadian Northern, The Grand Trunk, and the University of Saskatchewan. The boom psychology was endemic throughout the prairie West and was served in Saskatoon by 257 real estate firms at its height in 1912. At its peak such things as the promotional group, the Industrial League, industrial cities named Factoria and Cordage Park, and a labor providing company with the Dickensian title of Toil Corporation Limited lent concepts to the boom, as did the adoption of Henry George's "single tax." J. C. Yorath, appointed city commissioner in 1913, gave some physical

reality to Saskatoon with his city planning and famous map. Map, 30 notes.   C. Held

3664. Robinson, J. Lewis. HOW VANCOUVER HAS GROWN AND CHANGED. *Can. Geographical J. 1974 89(4): 40-48.*

3665. Séguin, N. HERBERTVILLE AU LAC SAINT-JEAN, 1850-1900: UN EXEMPLE QUEBECOIS DE COLONISATION AU XIXᵉ SIECLE [Herbertville in the Lake St. John Region, 1850-1900: An example of 19th-century Quebec colonization]. *Can. Hist. Assoc. Hist. Papers 1973: 251-268.* Herbertville was a traditional market center for the sawmill industry founded in a remote area. It was dominated by the parish priest and a group of families who provided local functionaries: the merchants and moneylenders who throve on the indebtedness of subsistence farmers. The railway, in 1893, tightened the commercial and financial connections with larger centers, while after 1896 a paper mill marked a shift to intensified industrialization and an urban work force. Based on provincial archives, church archives, and secondary sources; 36 notes.
                                                        G. E. Panting

3666. Wallace, C. M. SAINT JOHN BOOSTERS AND THE RAILROADS IN THE MID-NINETEENTH CENTURY. *Acadiensis [Canada] 1976 6(1): 71-91.* In 1851 Saint John had 31,174 people, its population grew 2.5% annually, and it was the third largest city in British North America. It saw itself as a great trading center. Eight selected residents illustrate this. They were either Presbyterian or Low Church Anglican, were successful businessmen, entrepreneurs, or lawyers, and promoted railways for New Brunswick. They gave Saint John vitality, but by the end of the 1870's its population was declining because the railways failed to make it a metropolis. 87 notes.   D. F. Chard

3667. Wallace, Mrs. Ernest. THE HISTORY OF THE MUNICIPALITY OF EAST HANTS. *Nova Scotia Hist. Q. [Canada] 1978 8(1): 51-79.* Outlines the early history (1861-1923) of East Hants, Nova Scotia. Examines the records of the officers, councillors, and wardens of the town in relation to actions on the development of roads and bridges, establishment of a Board of Health, a system of education, fisheries industry, the effects of a railway, election procedures, and farm legislation. Lists names of justices, commissioners and wardens. Primary and secondary sources; 7 notes.   H. M. Evans

3668. Weaver, John C. EDMONTON'S PERILOUS COURSE 1904-1929. *Urban Hist. Rev. [Canada] 1977 (2): 20-32.* Describes the boom and bust years of Edmonton, Alberta. Huckster elements promoted Edmonton after its incorporation in 1904 and it gained a reputation as a progressive municipality. After the crash of 1913, however, its earlier corruption and lack of a solid financial base led to a very difficult 15 years. Based on Edmonton city records and secondary works; 38 notes.
                                                        C. A. Watson

3669. Weaver, John C. FROM LAND ASSEMBLY TO SOCIAL MATURITY: THE SUBURBAN LIFE OF WESTDALE (HAMILTON), ONTARIO, 1911-1951. *Social Hist. [Canada] 1978 11(22): 411-440.* Studies Westdale (begun in 1911) as a Canadian measure of 20th-century urban trends. It started as a 100-acre residential development, then expanded to 800 acres. Like many suburbs, new transportation links made it possible. World War I and postwar problems prevented half of its approximately 1,700 lots from being developed until 1931. Westdale by design was overwhelmingly Protestant at first, although restrictive covenants did not prohibit native-born Catholics or Jews. By 1951 racial aspects of restrictive covenants were eliminated, and the area had become more diversified. 3 illus., 11 tables, 60 notes.   D. F. Chard

3670. Youe, Christopher. EAU CLAIRE, THE COMPANY AND THE COMMUNITY. *Alberta Hist. [Canada] 1979 27(3): 1-6.* The Eau Claire district of Calgary was named after the lumber company headed by Isaac Kerr. In 1886, at the urging of K. N. MacFee of Ottawa, Kerr moved his operations from Eau Claire, Wisconsin, to Calgary. This was indeed a transplanted outfit: personnel, machinery, and the Scandinavian work force from Wisconsin moved to Alberta. Kerr was born in Ontario, and the manager of the Calgary operation, Peter Prince, was from Quebec. The company flourished, as Calgary's housing needs were taken care of by the Eau Claire Co., with mills on the Bow River, and large forests nearby. The district of Eau Claire retained its overall appearance until the early 1970's, when high-rise apartment units began to replace the common one- and two-story residential structures. Based on company records, newspapers, and printed sources; illus., map.   D. Chaput

Politics and Government

3671.   Andrew, Caroline; Blais, André; and Des Rosiers, Rachel. LE LOGEMENT PUBLIC À HULL   [Public housing in Hull]. *Can. J. of Pol. Sci. 1975 8(3): 403-430.* The authors try to explain through the use of several indices why the municipal government began the housing program enthusiastically in 1968, but later allowed its commitment to dwindle. 5 tables, 2 figs., 82 notes.   R. V. Kubicek

3672.   Artibise, Alan F. J.   MAYOR ALEXANDER LOGAN OF WINNIPEG. *Beaver [Canada] 1974 304(4): 4-12.* Relates the life and public career of Alexander Logan (1841-94) who served four terms as mayor of Winnipeg in the 1870's and 1880's.   S

3673.   Baker, Melvin.   THE POLITICS OF MUNICIPAL REFORM IN ST. JOHN'S, NEWFOUNDLAND, 1888-1892. *Urban Hist. Rev. [Canada] 1976 76(2): 12-29.* Describes the reform movement in St. John's during 1888-92. Because the Newfoundland government was slow to respond to municipal needs and was burdened by an archaic, unwieldy administration, a reform movement for responsible city government began in the 1880's. Immersed in partisan party politics and opposed by the local business and professional elite, the movement compromised with the Municipal Act (1888). Because the colonial government retained its influence in city government, reform efforts remained frustrated until 1902. Based on secondary sources, newspapers, and legislative debates; 58 notes.   C. A. Watson

3674.   Belanger, Gerard.   QUESTIONS DE BASE A TOUTE RE-FORME DU FINANCEMENT MUNICIPAL   [Basic questions of municipal financial reform]. *Can. Public Administration [Canada] 1977 20(2): 370-379.* Examines financial support given to Quebec's local governments by the provincial government; discusses the degree of autonomy granted to municipalities, 1960-73.

3675.   Bourassa, Guy.   LA CONNAISSANCE POLITIQUE DE MONTREAL: BILAN ET PERSPECTIVES   [The political consciousness of Montreal: balance and perspective]. *Recherches Sociographiques [Canada] 1965 6(2): 163-179.* Discusses Montreal politics, 1950's.

3676.   Cestre, Gilbert.   QUÉBEC: ÉVOLUTION DES LIMITES MU-NICIPALES DEPUIS 1831-1832   [The city of Québec: development of its municipal limits since 1831-32]. *Cahiers de Géographie de Québec [Canada] 1976 20(51): 561-567.* Studies and interprets the evolution of the administrative limits of the city of Québec, 1831-1972.

3677.   Day, John P.   EDMONTON CIVIC POLITICS 1891-1914. *Urban Hist. Rev. [Canada] 1978 (3): 42-68.* The coming of the Canadian Pacific Railway in 1891 stimulated the typical prairie town prewar boom in Edmonton. Describes the wide variety of political groupings which contended for political power in the prewar boom period. Primary sources; 3 tables, 3 fig., 57 notes.   C. A. Watson

3678.   Fuga, Olga.   NEW WINNIPEG GOVERNMENT IS UNIQUE URBAN EXPERIMENT. *Natl. Civic Rev. 1973 62(4): 189-192.* Winnipeg, not a large urban center by US standards, is large enough to have experienced typical urban problems. Since January 1972 it has been governed under a new law accepting the thesis that the city is one in community in the social and economic sense and should be one for the purposes of government. Poor financial power is the major drawback to the new structure and administration as it was for the old.   J

3679.   Gauvin, Michel.   THE REFORMER AND THE MACHINE: MONTREAL CIVIC POLITICS FROM RAYMOND PRÉFON-TAINE TO MÉDÉRIC MARTIN. *J. of Can. Studies [Canada] 1978 13(2): 16-26.* Focuses on machine politicians Préfontaine and Martin and on reform leader Hormisdas Laporte; reviews Montreal city politics 1894-1921. Early in the period, Alderman Préfontaine dispensed much patronage as chairman of the Roads Committee. Laporte's Reform Party came

to power in 1900, but the Roads Committee soon became a stronghold of ward politics again. Discusses the Royal Commission investigation of political corruption in Montreal (1909) and the problem of undue influence by the Montreal Light, Heat and Power Company. A watchdog Board of Control, established in 1909, itself became a center of corruption with the election of the demagogic machine politician Martin to the mayoralty (1914). Concludes that the dominant themes in Montreal politics were those prominent throughout urban North America. Primary sources; 72 notes.   L. W. Van Wyk

3680.   Grayson, J. Paul and Grayson, L. M.   THE SOCIAL BASE OF INTERWAR POLITICAL UNREST IN URBAN ALBERTA. *Can. J. of Pol. Sci. 1974 7(2): 289-313.* A statistical analysis based on census returns and reports of electoral officers. Provides a set of empirical generalizations which are used to test the conventional wisdom using different methods and sources about political protest movements. 3 tables, 41 notes.   R. V. Kubicek

3681.   Hall, Frank.   CITY OF WINNIPEG—OFFSPRING OF CON-FLICTING PASSIONS. *Manitoba Pageant [Canada] 1974 19(3): 2-9.* In 1873, recent immigrants from Ontario favored the incorporation of Winnipeg while their opponents—wealthy landowners, retired fur traders, and the Hudson's Bay Company—fought the establishment of municipal government and subsequent taxation for public works. On November 8, after months of debate and some violence, the Legislative Council and the Legislative Assembly passed a Bill of Incorporation. 2 illus.   D. M. Dean

3682.   Hare, John E.   LE COMPORTEMENT DE LA PAYSAN-NERIE RURALE ET URBAINE DE LA RÉGION DE QUÉBEC PENDANT L'OCCUPATION AMÉRICAINE, 1775-1776   [The behavior of the rural and urban peasantry of the Quebec region during the American occupation]. *Rev. de l'U. d'Ottawa [Canada] 1977 47(1-2): 145-150.* During the American occupation of the province of Quebec (1775-76), a minority of the rural, peasant militiamen responded favorably to Governor Guy Carleton's appeal to resistance; however, the majority of them remained neutral with sometimes a friendly attitude toward Americans and a small group of activists rebelled against the governor's orders. In the city of Quebec, an equal lack of enthusiasm to resistance was shown by the urban peasantry. The expulsion of the American army from the province proved for the rebels a humiliating defeat which ensured the clergy and the gentry a favorable position toward the British government. Primary and secondary sources; 2 tables, 15 notes.   G. P. Cleyet

3683.   Jacek, Henry; McDonough, John; Shimizu, Ronald; and Smith, Patrick.   SOCIAL ARTICULATION AND AGGREGATION IN POLITICAL PARTY ORGANIZATIONS IN A LARGE CANA-DIAN CITY. *Can. J. of Pol. Sci. 1975 8(2): 274-298.* Examines how three political parties in Hamilton, Ontario, relate to that city's socioeconomic groups. 18 tables, 23 notes.   R. V. Kubicek

3684.   Jarvis, Eric.   MUNICIPAL COMPENSATION CASES: TORONTO IN THE 1860'S. *Urban Hist. Rev. [Canada] 1976 (3): 14-22.* Toronto seems to stand out as an exception to the generally accepted belief that 19th-century government lacked social responsibility. The Toronto City Council compensated private citizens for injuries received from faulty sidewalks and streets while municipal employees were compensated for long-time service, injuries sustained on the job, and layoffs. Compensation was partly voluntary and partly demanded by provincial statute. Based on Toronto City Council Minutes; 20 notes.   C. A. Watson

3685.   Lightbody, James.   ELECTORAL REFORM IN LOCAL GOVERNMENT: THE CASE OF WINNIPEG. *Can. J. of Pol. Sci. [Canada] 1978 11(2): 307-332.* Reform of this city's election system, i.e., extension of the ward system, has only marginally extended working class power in local politics. 2 maps, 7 tables, 98 notes.   R. V. Kubicek

3686.   Long, J. Anthony and Slemko, Brian.   THE RECRUITMENT OF LOCAL DECISION-MAKERS IN FIVE CANADIAN CITIES: SOME PRELIMINARY FINDINGS. *Can. J. of Pol. Sci. 1974 7(3): 550-559.* Uses data from aldermen in five Alberta cities obtained through extensive interviews in 1971. Notes importance of service groups with no formalized political function in the recruitment process. 4 tables, 24 notes.

R. V. Kubicek

3687. Massam, Bryan H. FORMS OF LOCAL GOVERNMENT IN THE MONTREAL AREA, 1911-71: A DISCRIMINANT APPROACH. *Can. J. of Pol. Sci.* 1973 6(2): 243-253. Probes, with the aid of a linear discriminant function, the variables (socioeconomic and size attributes) which account for municipalities opting for city-manager or mayor-council forms of government. The calculations are made at 10-year intervals coinciding with census years. Based on census data from Statistics Canada; 3 tables, 16 notes. R. V. Kubicek

3688. Masson, Jack K. DECISION-MAKING PATTERNS AND FLOATING COALITIONS IN AN URBAN CITY COUNCIL. *Can. J. of Pol. Sci.* 1975 8(1): 128-137. Edmonton city councillors who have campaigned together as an electoral party or slate do not regularly vote together on issues before the municipal government. 4 tables, 32 notes. R. V. Kubicek

3689. McKillop, A. B. SOCIALIST AS CITIZEN: JOHN QUEEN AND THE MAYORALTY OF WINNIPEG, 1935. *Tr. of the Hist. and Sci. Soc. of Manitoba [Canada]* 1973-74 (30): 61-80. Discusses the political involvement of socialist John Queen from the time he arrived in Winnipeg in 1909 through his mayoralty of Winnipeg (1935-42), concentrating on the issues faced and reforms sought by his administration. After his initial campaign to readjust the tax base of the city, much of his time was spent in the provincial legislature or in Ottawa making known "the urgency of Constitutional adjustments and provincial and federal legislation necessary for the coming into being of a full measure of social justice." Primary and secondary works; 69 notes, appendix.

S. R. Quéripel

3690. McKillop, A. B. A COMMUNIST IN CITY HALL. *Can. Dimension* 1974 10(1): 41-50. The political battles between Ralph Webb and Jacob Pennir epitomized Winnipeg's economic, ideological, and ethnic divisions in the 1930's. S

3691. Migner, Robert Maurice. LE BOSSISME POLITIQUE À MONTRÉAL: CAMILLIEN HOUDE REMPLACE MÉDERIC MARTIN (1923-1929) [Bossism politics in Montreal: Camillien Houde replaces Méderic Martin (1923-1929)]. *Urban Hist. Rev. [Canada]* 1974 74(1): 2-8. Examines bossism in Montreal politics; rivalry between Médéric Martin and Camillien Houde led to Houde's replacement of Martin as local government "boss" in 1928.

3692. Miller, Fern. VANCOUVER CIVIC POLITICAL PARTIES: DEVELOPING A MODEL OF PARTY-SYSTEM CHANGE AND STABILIZATION. *BC Studies [Canada]* 1975 (25): 3-31. Surveys the appearance and disappearance of political groups in Vancouver elections since 1937. A model is proposed and tested to explain the dominance of one group until 1965, the appearance of new groups after 1965, and the unpopularity of political parties at higher levels of government. Secondary sources; 43 notes. W. L. Marr

3693. Nowlan, David M. TOWARDS HOME RULE FOR URBAN POLICY. *J. of Can. Studies [Canada]* 1978 13(1): 70-79. In the last quarter-century, two factors have militated for a more centralized Canadian urban policy. One is increased financial dependence of municipalities on senior governments. The other is the emphasis, especially during the 60's, on what Jay W. Forrester called the "counter-intuitive" long-run effects of social policy. Calls for a reversal of this trend, based on a greater appreciation of the importance of the short run, and of the need for an urban policy responsive to local desires. Calls for the enactment of legislation giving local government's a broader range of policy tools. 8 notes, 20 ref. L. W. Van Wyk

3694. O'Connor, D'Arcy. THE MONTREAL CITIZENS' MOVEMENT. *Working Papers for a New Soc.* 1976 4(1): 22-29. Discusses the conflict between the Montreal Citizens' Movement since 1974 and Jean Drapeau, Mayor of Montreal since 1957, showing the political and economic effects of the MCM.

3695. Piva, Michael J. WORKERS AND TORIES: THE COLLAPSE OF THE CONSERVATIVE PARTY IN URBAN ONTARIO, 1908-1919. *Urban Hist. Rev. [Canada]* 1976 (3): 23-39. Examines the Canadian election of 1919 with regard to the major losses by Conservative Party candidates in southern Ontario urban areas as compared with the prewar elections of 1908, 1911, and 1914. The analysis shows that class was more important in determining voting patterns than either ethnicity or religion and that the class patterns of voting in 1919 represent a culmination of prewar social and political trends rather than an aberration in working class voting behavior. Based on papers in the Public Archives of Canada and on secondary sources; 2 tables, 20 notes.

C. A. Watson

3696. Romney, Paul. WILLIAM LYON MACKENZIE AS MAYOR OF TORONTO. *Can. Hist. Rev.* 1975 56(4) 416-436. Reviews data relating to Mackenzie's mayoralty. Criticizes Frederick H. Armstrong's disparaging account of it in *Canadian Historical Review* 1967 48 and his conclusions as to Mackenzie's personality and historical importance. Mackenzie was not the arbitrary, corrupt and incompetent executive depicted by Armstrong. Rather, he was an honest, hard-working and reasonably effective mayor. Based on municipal records and contemporary newspapers. A

3697. Senior, Elinor. THE BRITISH GARRISON IN MONTREAL IN THE 1840'S. *J. of the Soc. for Army Hist. Res.* 1974 52 (210): 111-127. From its capitulation (1760) until 1870, "Montreal was a British garrison town" and was "never without a regiment of the line, a battery of Royal Artillery and some Royal Engineers." For those 110 years it rivalled "Quebec as the major British military station" in Canada. For much of the 1840's, in fact, "when the city was also the political capital of the united province of Canada, Montreal resembled a European metropolis, having the seat of government and military headquarters located in the most important commercial city of the country," and "it is difficult to touch any aspect of Montreal history without encountering the influence or, at least, the presence of the military." Probably the most important duty of the British garrison was aiding the civil authorities in times of disturbance—"and the forties in Montreal proved exceptionally disturbing"—and particularly during the annual municipal elections, the provincial elections in 1844 and 1848, and the troubles during the summer of 1849 "as the house of assembly debated the Rebellion Losses Bill." 110 notes. A. N. Garland

3698. Spector, David. THE 1884 FINANCIAL SCANDALS AND ESTABLISHMENT OF BUSINESS GOVERNMENT IN WINNIPEG. *Prairie Forum [Canada]* 1977 2(2): 167-178. A business-minded city government in Winnipeg, Manitoba, sought efficient bookkeeping, limited services, and low taxes to promote effective administration for urbanization during the 1880's.

3699. Stevens, Neil. THE SOLUTION? WIPE OUT THE TOWN, NOT THE POLLUTION. *Can. Dimension* 1974 10(5): 10-12. In the Falconbridge-Sudbury area (Happy Valley) of Ontario, people have been relocated with government aid to escape pollution. S

3700. Taylor, John H. FIRE, DISEASE AND WATER IN OTTAWA: AN INTRODUCTION. *Urban Hist. Rev. [Canada]* 1979 8(1): 7-37. Ottawa is investigated as an example of the relationship among fire, diseases, and water supply in 19th-century urban Canada. Disease and fire were major problems for the growing city, and the supply of pure water became an important part of the solution: an adequate water supply and modern firefighting equipment for fire, pure drinking water for better health. Ottawa politicians had to be pressured into making the necessary changes because they failed to see the connection between a safer and healthier city and their own economic interests. Based on municipal and federal records; 2 tables, 79 notes. C. A. Watson

3701. Taylor, K. W. and Wiseman, Nelson. CLASS AND ETHNIC VOTING IN WINNIPEG: THE CASE OF 1941. *Can. Rev. of Sociol. and Anthrop. [Canada]* 1977 14(2): 174-187. A unique opportunity to assess the relative strengths of class versus ethnic determinants of voting in provincial elections was offered by the historical development of class and ethnic relations in Winnipeg and the fact that the entire city was a multiple-member constituency for purposes of representation in the provincial legislature. Data analyses were carried out on areal units using census social area data, poll-by-poll voting results, and party and campaign literature. Class factors were found to be only marginally less important than ethnic factors in accounting for voting patterns despite a Liberal/Conservative/CCF party coalition and the lowest voter turnout in a provincial election historically recorded in Manitoba—factors which would tend to minimize class factors in voting. These results were corroborated by an analysis of transferable ballot data. Apart from minor differences in the relative weighting of class and ethnic factors, these results support the conclusions of an earlier similar study of Winnipeg voting patterns in the 1945 provincial election.   J

3702.   Thrall, Grant Ian.   SPATIAL INEQUITIES IN TAX ASSESSMENT: A CASE STUDY OF HAMILTON, ONTARIO.   *Econ. Geography 1979 55(2): 123-134.* Explores geographic properties of the assessment function in order to outline a procedure for determining the fairness of that method of property assessment, citing a study done in Hamilton, Ontario, as evidence.

3703.   Warfe, Chris.   THE SEARCH FOR PURE WATER IN OTTAWA: 1910-1915.   *Urban Hist. Rev. [Canada] 1979 8(1): 90-112.* As a result of concern on health matters, a search for an alternative source of purer water for Ottawa was begun in 1910. Little was achieved, however, until the water supply for fire fighting became a problem. Then, economic pressure rather than health concerns being the motivating force, a solution was immediately found. Based on municipal records and newspapers; map, 2 photos, 63 notes.   C. A. Watson

3704.   Weaver, John C.   THE MEANING OF MUNICIPAL REFORM: TORONTO, 1895.   *Ontario Hist. [Canada] 1974 66(2): 89-100.* Analyzes in detail the background to and shift from the municipal government of Toronto "by Council to that by Council and an Executive branch." The shift occurred during a depression, following exposure of serious corruption and graft in the Council. Additional exposure of financially powerful businesses and other pressure groups influencing city government to their own advantage also aided the reform movement. The final influence came from a major public health scare, stimulating sufficient public pressure to push reforms through. Briefly comments on the character and biographic data of some of the major figures involved. The role of the press is also analyzed. 67 notes.   W. B. Whitham

3705.   Weaver, John C.   ORDER AND EFFICIENCY: SAMUEL MORLEY WICKETT AND THE URBAN PROGRESSIVE MOVEMENT IN TORONTO, 1900-1915.   *Ontario Hist. [Canada] 1977 69(4): 218-234.* Wickett represented the strand of urban progressivism which pressed for professionalization of urban government through the city management approach. His father had been an alderman in Toronto, on a reform ticket, in the late 19th century. Wickett's studies at University of Toronto, and postgraduate work in Vienna and then several German centers, exposed him to other influences. He returned to teach political economy at the University of Toronto for years, with time out for the family business. Details his life and services to the city government, both before and after his election as alderman in 1913. Examines his economic ideas and sets them in a broader context than local politics and interests. He died in 1915 of a heart attack, some of his work unfinished. Mainly primary sources; 92 notes.   W. B. Whitham

3706.   Winn, Conrad and McMenemy, John.   POLITICAL ALIGNMENT IN A POLARIZED CITY: ELECTORAL CLEAVAGES IN KITCHENER, ONTARIO.   *Can. J. of Pol. Sci. 1973 6(2): 230-242.* Examines characteristics and sources of support for or rejection of redevelopment of Kitchener's downtown core through an analysis of municipal and provincial elections during 1967-71. Finds that the electorate was polarized on a left-right axis for which there was ample historical precedent. 4 tables, 33 notes, appendix.   R. V. Kubicek

3707.   Wiseman, Nelson and Taylor, K. W.   CLASS AND ETHNIC VOTING IN WINNIPEG DURING THE COLD WAR.   *Can. Rev. of Sociol. and Anthrop. [Canada] 1979 16(1): 60-76.* Using a combination of poll and census tract data, this paper examines the relative strength of ethnic and class determinants of the voting patterns of three Winnipeg multiple member constituencies in the provincial elections of 1949 and 1953. Compared to the patterns in the provincial elections of 1941 and 1945, class voting remained high in Winnipeg South and Winnipeg Centre, but ethnic voting became stronger in Winnipeg North—the strongest

base for left-wing parties in previous elections. We argue that these changes can be explained as a local effect of the larger changes in international relations between the capitalist and communist blocs during the Cold War. 4 tables, biblio.   J

3708.   Wiseman, Nelson and Taylor, K. W.   ETHNIC VS CLASS VOTING: THE CASE OF WINNIPEG, 1945.   *Can. J. of Pol. Sci. 1974 7(2): 314-328.* Based on census and electoral returns and using multiple regression analyses, shows class voting to be exceptionally high and ethnicity a confounding factor disguising class voting behavior. 6 tables, fig, 33 notes.   R. V. Kubicek

The Economy

3709.   Acheson, T. William.   THE GREAT MERCHANT AND ECONOMIC DEVELOPMENT IN ST. JOHN 1820-1850.   *Acadiensis [Canada] 1979 8(2): 3-27.* In 1840 St. John, New Brunswick, was one of the largest urban centers in British North America, with a population of 27,000. Leading merchants were involved in banking or shipping, but showed little interest in secondary manufacturing. Most merchants supported the shipowners and opposed producers' demands for economic diversification and protective tariffs. By 1871 agriculture and manufacturing became dynamic elements in the province's economic diversification, but the great merchants had delayed this for two critical decades. 104 notes.   D. F. Chard

3710.   Adam, Judith.   TORONTO GETS INTO THE "ACTE."   *Can. Labour 1973 18(3): 3-5, 24.* Labor unions work to organize white-collar employees.   S

3711.   Alexander, David and Panting, Gerry.   THE MERCANTILE FLEET AND ITS OWNERS: YARMOUTH, NOVA SCOTIA, 1840-1889.   *Acadiensis [Canada] 1978 7(2): 3-28.* Yarmouth lacked a significant hinterland, but had the resources and tradition to compete in international shipping. Yarmouth had 5,500 tons of registered shipping in 1840; but 179,400 tons in 1879, or more than one-quarter of the Maritimes' tonnage. Schooners comprised 62% of the registered tonnage in the 1840's and 40% in the 1870's. About 2,200 individuals invested in ships during 1840-89. Some 5% of investors, dominated by a 12-man elite, owned 66% of the tonnage. The elite invested extensively in nonshipping ventures in the 1860's and 1870's, but by the 1890's ceased to reinvest in shipping. 51 notes.   D. F. Chard

3712.   Armstrong, Frederick H.   CAPT. HUGH RICHARDSON: FIRST HARBOR MASTER OF TORONTO.   *Inland Seas 1975 31(1): 34-40, 42, 49-50.* Hugh Richardson (1784-1870) emigrated to York (Toronto), Upper Canada, in 1821. He became a shipowner and maintained aids to navigation around Toronto at his own expense until the city and provincial governments assumed responsibility. In 1850 he was appointed Harbor Master of Toronto and actively directed the improvement of the harbor, notably the reconstruction of Queen's Wharf. Based on materials in the Public Archives of Ontario and newspapers; 22 notes.   K. J. Bauer

3713.   Bauer, Charles and Laplante, Pierre.   TRICOFIL—WHERE WORKERS ARE MANAGERS.   *Can. Labour 1975 20(3): 2-6.* Textile workers in St. Jérôme, Quebec, organized a collective, the Société populaire Tricofil, in 1974 to reopen and operate their factory which had closed.

3714.   Bernard, Jean-Paul; Linteau, Paul-André; and Robert, Jean-Claude.   LA STRUCTURE PROFESSIONNELLE DE MONTRÉAL EN 1825   [The professional structure of Montreal in 1825]. *Rev. d'Hist. de l'Amérique Française [Canada] 1976 30(3): 383-415.* In 1825, Montreal was a mercantile city uninfluenced by the industrial revolution. Petty bourgeois merchants and artisans competed for the business of a small commercial economy. Based on published government statistics and on secondary works; 4 tables, 28 notes, appendix.

                                    L. B. Chan

3715.   Bosher, J. F.   A QUEBEC MERCHANT'S TRADING CIRCLES IN FRANCE AND CANADA: JEAN-ANDRÉ LAMALETIE

BEFORE 1763. *Social Hist. [Canada] 1977 10(19): 24-44.* The trading merchants of 18th-century Quebec depended on a particular network of associates in other ports and cities of the trading region. These trading circles were usually composed of family members and close friends. This study of the trading circle of Jean-André Lamaletie, a merchant in Quebec from 1741 to 1758, reveals the nature of these business relationships. Lamalatie was not one of the merchants arrested by the French government in 1761 for profiteering and fraud (the *affaire du Canada),* although probably he was not completely innocent. Based on documents in the Public Record Office (London), Quebec Archives, and national and department archives in France; 2 tables, 3 charts, 50 notes.
W. K. Hobson

3716. Bradbury, John H. TOWARDS AN ALTERNATIVE THEORY OF RESOURCE-BASED TOWN DEVELOPMENT IN CANADA. *Econ. Geography 1979 55(2): 147-166.* Discusses resource-based settlements in Canada within the context of capital accumulation, the internationalization of capital and the law of uneven development, using the Iron Ore Company of Canada and the mining town of Schefferville in Quebec as case studies.

3717. Breen, David H. CALGARY: THE CITY AND THE PETROLEUM INDUSTRY SINCE WORLD WAR TWO. *Urban Hist. Rev. [Canada] 1977 (2): 55-71.* Suggests that the oil economy of Calgary, Alberta, begun in 1914, but now based on the Leduc area discovered in 1947, fit nicely into the social-cultural milieu of the city's beef economy of the 19th and early 20th centuries. Calgary is compared with other prairie cities in terms of the oil industry and demographic change. Secondary works; 4 tables, 18 notes.
C. A. Watson

3718. Brooks, G. W. S. EDGAR CROW BAKER: AN ENTREPRENEUR IN EARLY BRITISH COLUMBIA. *BC Studies [Canada] 1976 (31): 23-43.* Edgar Crow Baker (d. 1920) was a representative entrepreneur in Victoria when that city was the social, business, and political center of British Columbia. Although he came to Victoria as an employee, he had ideas and ambitions, a valuable family connection, and fraternal affiliations that allowed him into the business life of the city. Baker was involved in almost every major economic activity in the province: land, lumber, railroads, coal, shipping, public utilities. He was also active in municipal, provincial, and federal politics. 51 notes.
D. L. Smith

3719. Brooks, Stanley; Gilmour, James M.; and Murricane, Kenneth. THE SPATIAL LINKAGES OF MANUFACTURING IN MONTREAL AND ITS SURROUNDINGS. *Cahiers de Géographie de Québec [Canada] 1973 17(40): 107-122.* Material linkages of manufacturing in Montreal, correlated to size and location of enterprises within the industrial complex, seem to show that overall linkage is weak and that the strength of linkage varies inversely with the size of establishments studied. There does not seem to be a diminution of linkage from the center to the edge of the industrial complex, although the opposite occurs in the case of purchase linkages. Further investigation is needed. 10 tables, 2 figs., biblio.
A. E. LeBlanc

3720. Brouillette, Normand LES FACTEURS DU DECLIN INDUSTRIEL DE SHAWINIGAN, PROVINCE DE QUEBEC [The factors underlying the industrial decline of Shawinigan, Province of Quebec]. *Cahiers de Géographie de Québec [Canada] 1973 17(40): 123-133.* After a period of phenomenal industrial growth, Shawinigan has declined since the early 1960's. Explains the decline in terms of the dynamics of industrial location. Shawinigan is no longer situated favorably to foster technological progress; as such, its industrial development is suffering. 2 figs., 14 notes, biblio.
A. E. LeBlanc

3721. Burgess, Joanne. L'INDUSTRIE DE LA CHAUSSURE À MONTRÉAL 1840-1870: LE PASSAGE DE L'ARTISANAT À LA FABRIQUE [The shoe industry in Montreal 1840-1870: The transformation from craft to factory]. *Rev. D'Hist. De L'Amérique Française [Canada] 1977 31(2): 187-210.* The production of shoes formed a central element in the economic life of 19th-century Montreal. During three decades, it evolved from a traditional craft into a highly organized industry. The division of labor, the introduction of machinery, and the advent of the factory system slowly displaced the traditional modes of production, despite strikes and disruptions. The transition from the artisan's shop to the factory was harsh, however it operated progressively over a relatively long period of time. 71 notes.
M. R. Yerburgh

3722. Cameron, James M. THE PICTOU BANK. *Nova Scotia Hist. Q. [Canada] 1976 6(2): 119-144.* The Pictou Bank, 1872-85, served the citizens of Pictou, Nova Scotia, until it went bankrupt and was taken over by the Bank of Nova Scotia.

3723. Carter, Norman M. JOHNNY HARRIS OF SANDON. *Beaver [Canada] 1976 306(4): 42-49.* Sandon, in southeast British Columbia, was an important mining zone at the turn of the century, and Harris quickly had control of the best real estate. He ran hotels, saloons, shops, and gambling houses, and for several decades was the most important of the entrepreneurs in the area. Harris was hurt by investments in wheat futures at the time of the Depression. Based on reminiscences of the author, whose father was a dentist in Sandon; 9 illus.
D. Chaput

3724. Cermakian, Jean L'INFRASTRUCTURE ET LE TRAFIC DU PORT DE TROIS-RIVIERES [The infrastructure and traffic of the port of Three Rivers]. *Cahiers de Géographie de Québec [Canada] 1973 17(40): 171-191.* Three-Rivers has always benefited in times of economic prosperity despite its midway location between the ports of Quebec City and Montreal. When the economic situation of the St. Maurice valley manufacturing plants and forest operation deteriorated, however, there was a direct impact on the port. The opening of the St. Lawrence Seaway in 1959 strengthened the transshipment side of the port, but in recent years better-equipped ports in eastern Quebec and on the Pacific coast have cut into this development. The detailed traffic analysis for 1961-70 can be used as a model for most other Canadian ports. 3 tables, 6 figs., 7 notes, biblio.
A. E. LeBlanc

3725. Chung, Joseph A. SPECULATION FONCIERE ET BANQUE DE SOL URBAIN [Speculative funding and an urban land bank]. *Actualité Econ. [Canada] 1973 49(1): 39-57.* Urban land costs are increasingly a major factor in housing costs. Examines the rate of increase of such costs in recent years for Canada, and forecasts the rate of increase up to 1981. Specific causes include speculation and realtors. A land bank will be a necessary component of any effective solution. 7 tables, 12 notes, appendix.
W. B. Whitham

3726. Chung, Joseph. LA NATURE DU DÉCLIN ÉCONOMIQUE DE LA RÉGION DE MONTRÉAL [The nature of the economic decline in the Montreal area]. *Actualité Econ. [Canada] 1974 50(3): 326-338.* Montreal's economic decline, not a new phenomenon, is caused by the competition of newer markets in the west and by the incapacity to adapt its older industrial structure to contemporary demands.
S

3727. Cross, L. Doreen. LOCATING SELECTED OCCUPATIONS: OTTAWA, 1870. *Urban Hist. Rev. [Canada] 1974 74(2): 5-14.* The city directory and a historical atlas provide the basis for an examination of the occupational structure in Ottawa, Ontario, 1870; focuses on professional and skilled labor.

3728. Cutler, Maurice. HOW FOREIGN OWNERS SHAPE OUR CITIES. *Can. Geographical J. 1975 90(6): 34-48.* Discusses foreign use and Canadian control of Canada's land and resources.
S

3729. Durand, Guy. LE TISSU URBAIN QUÉBÉCOIS, 1941-1961: ÉVOLUTION DES STRUCTURES URBAINES DE L'INDUSTRIE ET DES OCCUPATIONS [The Quebec urban fabric, 1941-61: evolution of the urban structures of industry and the work force]. *Recherches Sociographiques [Canada] 1977 18(1): 133-157.* Industrialization was crucial in the urban development of Quebec until the beginning of the 1950's. From this point on, the industrialization process lagged behind the urbanization of the province. From an occupational perspective, this resulted in the dominance of occupations related to the tertiary sector which took over as the driving force behind urban development. 16 tables, 14 notes.
A. E. Le Blanc

3730. Fingard, Judith. THE DECLINE OF THE SAILOR AS A SHIP LABOURER IN NINETEENTH CENTURY TIMBER PORTS. *Labour [Canada] 1977 2: 35-53.* Examines sailors' working conditions and the relationship between sailors and shore-based laborers and traces "the diminishing but persistent role that sailors played in working cargo" in the timber ports of Saint John, New Brunswick, and Quebec. High sailor desertion rates and other factors led to increased employment of local ship laborers which in turn led to increased militancy by labor unions and the near-exclusion of sailors from cargo handling. The end of the age of sail, however, effectively terminated competition between the two groups. Covers ca. 1820-90. Primary and secondary sources; table, 32 notes. W. A. Kearns

3731. Gidney, Norman. FROM COAL TO FOREST PRODUCTS: THE CHANGING RESOURCE BASE OF NANAIMO, B. C. *Urban Hist. Rev. [Canada] 1978 (1): 18-47.* Traces the development of Nanaimo, British Columbia, a single-enterprise community, from its dependence on coal for over 70 years to an economy based on forest products. Begun by the Hudson's Bay Company in the 1850's, coal mining reached a peak between 1880 and 1900. Gradually declining, coal mining came to an end as a major economic factor in the 1930's. At that time diversification took place by expansion of older industries such as fishing, sawmilling, and logging, and development of its central location for distribution in the region. A pulp mill, opened in 1950, was the forerunner of the increasing prosperity through the use of forest products. Based on government documents, newspapers and secondary sources; 6 photos, 2 maps, 52 notes. C. A. Watson

3732. Harvey, Jacquelin. HAVRE-SAINT-PIERRE: LE PLUS ANCIEN DES PORTS MINIERS QUEBECOIS [Saint Pierre Harbor: Quebec's oldest mining port]. *Cahiers de Géographie de Québec 1974 18(44): 357-365.*

3733. Heap, Margaret. LE GRÈVE DES CHARRETIERS À MONTRÉAL, 1864 [The teamsters' strike in Montreal, 1864]. *Rev. d'Hist. de l'Amérique Française [Canada] 1977 31(3): 371-395.* In September 1864, the Montreal teamsters launched a spectacular, highly organized strike; the commercial life of the city was completely paralyzed. The teamsters demanded a cessation of certain monopolistic practices employed by the Grand Trunk Railway Company—practices which seriously jeopardized their livelihood. Despite the solidarity of the teamsters, the courts would not consider their demands. The rising tide of industrial capitalism continued to erode the status of the working classes. 76 notes. M. R. Yerburgh

3734. House, J. Douglas. ENTREPRENEURIAL CAREER PATTERNS OF RESIDENTIAL REAL ESTATE AGENTS IN MONTREAL. *Can. Rev. of Sociol. and Anthrop. 1974 11(2): 110-124.* Real estate agents are best understood as a type of modern entrepreneur. A model of their entrepreneurial behavior is developed here which includes an explanation of strategies producing short- and long-term success. Given this model, five career patterns are distinguished: abortives, marginals, regulars, upwardly mobiles, and perennial high producers. Finally, these patterns are explained in terms of three determinants: sales success through implementing productive entrepreneurial strategies; mobility opportunities or structurally imposed barriers to mobility, which in turn depend upon ascribed ethnicity and sex status; and individual decisions at crucial career phases. J

3735. Igartua, José. A CHANGE IN CLIMATE: THE CONQUEST AND THE *MARCHANDS* OF MONTREAL. *Can. Hist. Assoc. Hist. Papers 1974: 115-134.* Discusses the change from French to British commercial ascendancy among the middle classes of Montreal, Quebec, 1750-92, emphasizing the fur trade.

3736. Igartua, José E. THE MERCHANTS OF MONTREAL AT THE CONQUEST: SOCIO-ECONOMIC PROFILE. *Social Hist. [Canada] 1975 8(16): 275-293.* Of the 200 merchants and traders who can be identified in Montreal 1750-75, 92 form a core group of those in business for an extended period of time. Examinations of the core group reveals that they were not wealthy, their social mobility was restricted, and a distinct hierarchy existed among them. Importers and wholesale merchants formed the highest group; they married within their group or one notch below. Fifty-five fur trade outfitters formed the second category. They also tended to marry within their group, but had few social or business connections with the colony's governing elite. The third category, "shopkeepers," was not a socially cohesive group. The fourth category consisted of assorted traders, artisans, and one moneylender. Based on published primary sources and documents in the Public Archives of Canada and the National Archives of Quebec. 82 notes, 2 appendixes. W. K. Hobson

3737. Kealey, Gregory S. ARTISANS RESPOND TO INDUSTRIALISM: SHOEMAKERS, SHOE FACTORIES AND THE KNIGHTS OF ST. CRISPIN IN TORONTO. *Can. Hist. Assoc. Hist. Papers 1973: 137-157.* Traces the part played by the Knights of St. Crispin in the organization of boat and shoe factory workers. The Crispins, beginning as a craft society, adapted to the industrialization of their trade in Toronto during the early 1870's. They were regarded as leading working class intellectuals and their spirit and tactics were carried into the Knights of Labor. Based on primary and secondary sources; 3 tables, 75 notes. G. E. Panting

3738. Kealey, Gregory S. "THE HONEST WORKINGMAN" AND WORKERS' CONTROL: THE EXPERIENCE OF TORONTO SKILLED WORKERS, 1860-1892. *Labour [Canada] 1976 1: 32-68.* Local coopers', iron moulders', and printers' unions in Toronto exemplified variants of "shop floor control." Adaptation to increasing industrialization and to pressures from management and government gave craftsmen greater production control than generally realized. Struggles to maintain that control brought varied results. Mechanization defeated the coopers. Organizational strength, solidarity with unskilled coworkers, and the failure of technological developments sufficient to replace their skills brought general success to the moulders. The printers "met the machine and triumphed" by increasing the degree of control. Political activity and workers' cooperatives were two effects of the unions' efforts. Primary and secondary sources; 162 notes. W. A. Kearns

3739. Kelly, Kenneth. THE DEVELOPMENT OF FARM PRODUCE MARKETING AGENCIES AND COMPETITION BETWEEN MARKET CENTERS IN EASTERN SIMCOE COUNTY, 1850-1875. Akenson, Donald H., ed. *Canadian Papers in Rural History, Vol. I* (Grananoque, Ontario: Langdale Pr., 1978): 67-86. Before 1850, agricultural marketing agencies in Simcoe County, Ontario, followed a typical, diffused pattern. With the introduction of roads, particularly those that enabled easy transport to Toronto, marketing agencies took on a linear pattern stretching along the roads. This was accentuated in the late 1860's with the introduction of railroads: marketing centers developed at railheads. Most farmers were able to take advantage of competition among marketing centers and thereby receive higher prices, except in the most rural and isolated areas of the county. This competition benefited farmers and consumers, but the towns that acted as commercial agents often suffered from drastic economic fluctuations as they undercut competitors and were later themselves undercut. 73 notes. J. W. Leedom

3740. Kojder, Apolonja Maria. THE SASKATOON WOMEN TEACHERS' ASSOCIATION: A DEMAND FOR RECOGNITION. *Saskatchewan Hist. [Canada] 1977 30(2): 63-74.* Women educators in Saskatchewan can point to 1918 as the date when they first demonstrated their professional responsibility and integrity with the founding of the Saskatoon Women Teachers' Association (SWTA). Because the status of elementary teachers was very low, a positive self-image was necessary. The leaders in this early movement were Victoria "Tory" Miners and Hattie Wolfe. Later important figures were Ethel Coppinger and Caroline Robins. Great strides in improving conditions and wages for all teachers were made and the influence of the SWTA was widespread. 12 notes. C. Held

3741. Lapointe, Michelle. LE SYNDICAT CATHOLIQUE DES ALLUMETTIÈRES DE HULL, 1919-1924 [The Catholic matchmakers' union in Hull, 1919-24]. *Rev. d'Hist. de l'Amérique Française [Canada] 1979 32(4): 603-628.* Analysis of the matchmakers' union in Hull, Quebec, enables the researcher to develop much-needed perspective on the female Catholic workers' movement. It was a vigorous union; membership was impressive. Two strike actions were conducted in a very conservative milieu. The union played an important role in raising the consciousness of its membership and in ensuring, on a modest scale, that the needs of female workers in Canada would receive additional attention in years to come. 40 notes. M. R. Yerburgh

3742. Lavigne, Marie and Stoddart, Jennifer. LES TRAVAILLEUSES MONTRÉALAISES ENTRE LES DEUX GUERRES [Women in the workforce of Montreal between the wars]. *Labour [Canada] 1977 2: 170-183.* Examines the participation of women in the Montreal workforce where they constituted at least 25% of the total throughout the period. Includes an analysis of their distribution in various occupations and the problem of wage discrimination. Comparisons are made with men workers in Montreal and with men and women in Toronto. The unique influence of large numbers of religious women, especially in teaching, is also examined. Most employed women were young (15-24), single, and most worked in jobs which did not damage their role and traditional function in the family. Census reports, primary and secondary sources; 3 tables, 34 notes.   W. A. Kearns

3743.   Martin, Fernand.   EFFETS DE LA CRISE DE L'ENERGIE SUR LA CROISSANCE ECONOMIQUE DE MONTREAL ET DU QUEBEC   [Effects of the energy crisis on the economic growth of Montreal and Quebec]. *Actualité Econ. [Canada] 1974 50(3): 351-361.*

3744.   McCalla, Douglas.   THE DECLINE OF HAMILTON AS A WHOLESALE CENTER. *Ontario History [Canada] 1973 65(4): 247-254.* Briefly discusses basic aspects of mid-19th century business practices, and analyzes shifts of business activity in Hamilton, Ontario, during 1840-70. Drawn from the records of Hamilton's largest wholesale house. Map, 2 tables, 16 notes, appendix.   W. B. Whitham

3745.   McCann, Larry D.   STAPLES AND THE NEW INDUSTRIALISM IN THE GROWTH OF POST-CONFEDERATION HALIFAX. *Acadiensis [Canada] 1979 8(2): 47-79.* Between 1871 and 1921 its population almost doubled, but Halifax, Nova Scotia, dropped from Canada's fifth leading city to its 11th. Between 1920 and 1926 manufacturing employment dropped from 7,171 to 3,287. Halifax did not engage in staple processing because little occurred in the province, except for fish and timber, and Halifax was not near their sources. Difficult communication lines and high transportation costs outweighed low labor costs. 9 tables, 5 fig., 81 notes.   D. F. Chard

3746.   Miquelon, Dale.   HAVY AND LEFEBVRE OF QUEBEC: A CASE STUDY OF METROPOLITAN PARTICIPATION IN CANADIAN TRADE, 1730-1760. *Can. Hist. Rev. 1975 56(1): 1-24.* The business papers of a French trading company, Robert Dugard et Cie of Rouen, housed in the Archives nationales, Paris, and Canadian private papers and notarial archives have been used to reconstruct the day-to-day business of these 18th-century factors, answering some questions regarding Canadian economic history while posing the larger one of the influence of French business society on Canada.   A

3747.   Racine, Jean-Bernard   LE DISPOSITIF BANCAIRE A LA PERIPHERIE DE LA METROPOLE MONTREALAISE   [Location of banks on the periphery of metropolitan Montreal]. *Cahiers de Géographie de Québec [Canada] 1973 17(40): 210-216.* A study of banking in suburban Montreal shows that the establishment of bank branches seems to favor the crystallization of the area. When branches do not emerge, on the other hand, it suggests that the area is considered a risk. The existence of bank branches is not a function of demographic demand nor of distance from the city center. List of references.   A. E. LeBlanc

3748.   Roberts, Wayne.   ARTISANS, ARISTOCRATS AND HANDYMEN: POLITICS AND UNIONISM AMONG TORONTO SKILLED BUILDING TRADES WORKERS, 1896-1914. *Labour [Canada] 1976 1: 92-121.* During the pre-World War I building boom, contracting and subcontracting methods, including use of immigrant and unskilled workers, caused marked but diverse alterations to the building trades' artisanal character and engendered varied political responses. Using Toronto carpenters, woodworkers, plumbers, ironworkers, stone and granite cutters, and bricklayers' unions to "sample this diversity," concludes that the greater the retention of artisanal character, the lesser the degree of politicization; the greater the retention of craft consciousness, the lesser the degree of class consciousness. Primary and secondary sources; 154 notes.   W. A. Kearns

3749.   Rosenthal, Star.   UNION MAIDS: ORGANIZED WOMEN WORKERS IN VANCOUVER, 1900-1915. *BC Studies [Canada] 1979 (41): 36-55.* Conventional mythology had it that women in the labor movement did not attempt to organize in the past, that women were "in fact unorganizable." Conventional attitudes held that women threatened male job security and that factory work was not helpful for women specifically. Women were viewed as "reactionary, materialistic and nonclass-conscious." There are also obvious parallels of the history of women

in the labor movement with the history of nonwhite workers. The distortions of history to the contrary and these obstacles notwithstanding, working women in Vancouver, British Columbia, did organize and carry on union activity during 1900-15. Data is scarce, but enough evidence has been discovered to warrant a reassessment of the role of women in the labor movement. 91 notes.   D. L. Smith

3750.   Scott, Bruce.   "A PLACE IN THE SUN": THE INDUSTRIAL COUNCIL AT MASSEY-HARRIS, 1919-1929. *Labour [Canada] 1976 1: 158-192.* Analysis of the industrial council at the Massey-Harris Toronto plant suggests that such organizations had greater importance than historians have acknowledged. Intended as an alternative to unions and a means to increased productivity, the council was essentially a management public relations tool. It operated, after 1922, with "smooth formality." The balance of power favored management, but worker representatives developed organizational and leadership skills. Despite general employee indifference to the council, workers made gains in control of work conditions, especially relating to safety. The council helped "achieve a decade of relative labour peace." Primary and secondary sources; 137 notes.   W. A. Kearns

3751.   Sherwood, Roland H.   THEY BUILT A FORTUNE. *Nova Scotia Hist. Q. [Canada] 1976 6(2): 109-118.* Discusses the Crerar brothers of Pictou, Nova Scotia, who built a family fortune around their shipping and shipbuilding operations, 1840's-50's.

3752.   Sprague, D. N.   THE MYTHICAL COMMERCIAL REVOLUTION. *Acadiensis [Canada] 1978 8(1): 114-120.* Review article prompted by Gerald J. J. Tulchinsky's *The River Barons: Montreal Businessmen and the Growth of Industry and Transportation, 1837-1854* (Toronto: U. of Toronto Pr., 1977).

3753.   Steed, Guy P. F.   CENTRALITY AND LOCATIONAL CHANGE: PRINTING, PUBLISHING, AND CLOTHING IN MONTREAL AND TORONTO. *Econ. Geography 1976 52(3): 193-205.* Examines locational clustering of publishing and clothing industries in metropolitan areas, centering on Montreal and Toronto, 1949-67.

3754.   Stephens, David E.   BOOMTOWN OF IRON AND STEEL. *Nova Scotia Hist. Q. [Canada] 1974 4(1): 23-30.* Traces the history of the iron and steel industry in the town of Londonderry, on the Bay of Fundy, from 1844 (when iron ore was discovered) through 1898 (when the plant ceased operations).   H. M. Evans

3755.   Stortz, Gerald J.   ARCHBISHOP LYNCH AND THE TORONTO SAVINGS BANK. *Study Sessions: Can. Catholic Hist. Assoc. [Canada] 1978 45: 5-19.* John Joseph Lynch, the first Roman Catholic archbishop of Toronto, helped set up the Toronto Savings Bank to aid the poor of the city, but was unable to prevent the bank from being used for more secular, profit-oriented aims during the 1870's.

3756.   Sutherland, David.   HALIFAX MERCHANTS AND THE PURSUIT OF DEVELOPMENT, 1783-1850. *Can. Hist. Rev. [Canada] 1978 59(1): 1-17.* The American War of Independence caused an exodus of settlers to Halifax, Nova Scotia, who were determined to convert the town into another New England. Appeals to England brought only limited assistance. The Napoleonic Wars brought great prosperity, thought to be lasting, but the following peace treaty hurt the Halifax cause. Hard times set in. A Chamber of Commerce was created to explore new avenues to prosperity. Halifax's isolation from the rest of Canada was underscored, and demands were voiced for a railroad, which was not soon in coming. Halifax's real problem was its merchants, who preferred traditional commerce and failed to establish an industrial base. 63 notes.   V. L. Human

3757.   Tunbridge, John E.   SEPARATION OF RESIDENCE FROM WORKPLACE: A KINGSTON EXAMPLE. *Urban Hist. Rev. [Canada] 1979 (3): 23-32.* Although the theory that as cities industrialize people move their homes away from their workplace is well known, much needs to be discovered about these processes and patterns. The medical profession of Kingston, Ontario, a well-defined elite group, is studied as an example. In 1857 almost all the doctors had offices in their homes; since the 1920's there has been a gradual separation of office and home until 1975 when almost all the doctors had their offices away from home.

Based on city directories and secondary sources; 2 maps, graph, 12 notes.
C. A. Watson

3758. Wong, George G. CLASS STRUGGLE AND THE WIN-NIPEG GENERAL STRIKE. *Bull. of the Soc. for the Study of Labour Hist. 1975 (30): 80-85.* Reviews David Jay Bercuson's *Confrontation at Winnipeg: Labour Industrial Relations and the General Strike* (Montreal: McGill-Queens U. Pr., 1974) and the social structure of industrial relations. 3 notes.
L. L. Athey

3759. Zerker, Sally. THE DEVELOPMENT OF COLLECTIVE BARGAINING IN THE TORONTO PRINTING INDUSTRY IN THE NINETEENTH CENTURY. *Industrial Relations [Canada] 1975 30(1): 83-97.* Analysts of collective bargaining have tended to stress predominant functional characteristics, in general classed as marketing, governmental, and managerial theories. Less emphasis has been placed on the importance of power relationships between organizations. A careful review of the development of collective bargaining in the Toronto printing industry in the 19th century suggests that the latter is the most significant factor in the historical process.
J

Society and Culture

3760. Anderson, Michael. FAMILY AND CLASS IN NINE-TEENTH-CENTURY CITIES. *J. of Family Hist. 1977 2(2): 139-149.* Reviews the first book-length product of the Canadian Social History Project at the University of Toronto, Michael B. Katz's *The People of Hamilton, Canada West: Family and Class in a Mid-Nineteenth-Century City.* Analyzes each of Katz's main themes: the distribution of wealth and power, social and geographic mobility, and the structure and role of the family. 10 notes, biblio.
T. W. Smith

3761. Bains, Yashdip Singh. THE ARTICULATE AUDIENCE AND THE FORTUNES OF THE THEATRE IN HALIFAX IN 1816-1819. *Dalhousie Rev. [Canada] 1977-78 57(4): 726-736.* Halifax critics valued the theater, but their dilemma was, should they condemn Halifax drama if it was poor, or continually aspire to London? Examines the question through the writings of pseudonymous critics. The dilemma is never clearly solved. 30 notes.
C. H. Held

3762. Baldwin, Doug. A STUDY IN SOCIAL CONTROL: THE LIFE OF THE SILVER MINER IN NORTHERN ONTARIO. *Labour [Canada] 1977 2: 79-106.* A study of working conditions and owner-miner relations in silver mining camps of Cobalt, Ontario, 1903-20. Company housing, social clubs, team sports, and an employment bureau were utilized by owners to maintain control of workers. Companies were aided by strict liquor laws and inadequate mining laws. Antiunion activities by management prevented labor solidarity, but a strike in 1919 "marked the end of Cobalt's golden era." Primary and secondary sources, including government documents and journals; 77 notes.
W. A. Kearns

3763. Bannister, Geoffrey. POPULATION CHANGE IN SOUTH-ERN ONTARIO. *Ann. of the Assoc. of Am. Geographers 1975 65(2): 177-188.* Uses autocovariance procedures to study the temporal and spatial patterns of population change in an urban system.
S

3764. Bannister, Geoffrey. SPACE-TIME COMPONENTS OF UR-BAN POPULATION CHANGE. *Econ. Geography 1976 52(3): 228-240.* Uses activity levels and spatial structure of urban systems to identify associations between population change and urban hierarchies in southern Ontario, 1941-71.

3765. Bredin, Thomas F. THE RED RIVER ACADEMY. *Beaver [Canada] 1974 305(3): 10-17.* The Red River Academy opened in 1832 in Winnipeg, but there had been earlier efforts towards education beginning with the early 1820's. Though discipline was harsh, attendance was good; it was not, however, a financial success. Most of the students were children of Hudson's Bay Company employees and the school performed essential education until the late 1850's. By that time most parents preferred to send their children to schools in eastern Canada, England, or the United States. 8 illus., map.
D. Chaput

3766. Brookes, Alan A. OUT-MIGRATION FROM THE MARI-TIME PROVINCES, 1860-1900: SOME PRELIMINARY CONSID-ERATIONS. *Acadiensis [Canada] 1976 5(2): 26-56.* Emigration from the Maritime Provinces during 1860-1900 was largely because of persistent depressions and economic dislocation. By the 1880's the exodus had spread into rural areas not previously affected, and to industrializing urban centers. Beginning with young, single people, the movement later embraced older, more stable elements and whole families. Most went to New England, especially Boston, where they "assumed a wide range of better jobs." Transportation and communication links and commercial orientation favored Boston. 78 notes.
D. F. Chard

3767. Burns, R. J. GOD'S CHOSEN PEOPLE: THE ORIGINS OF TORONTO SOCIETY, 1793-1818. *Can. Hist. Assoc. Hist. Papers 1973: 213-228.* Lieutenant-governor John Graves Simcoe (1752-1806) and the original officials of Upper Canada regarded themselves as people with a mission. They were to perpetuate and spread a type of society which provided an alternative to the American Revolution. By 1818, having established themselves and their families in Toronto, the official elite awaited a leader who could carry their ideas throughout Upper Canada. Anglican Archdeacon John Strachan (1778-1867) arrived at that point and took up the task. Based on primary and secondary sources; 59 notes.
G. E. Panting

3768. Campbell, H. C. METROPOLITAN PUBLIC LIBRARY SYSTEMS IN CANADA. *Pakistan Lib. Bull. [Pakistan] 1973 6(1-2): 1-28.* Regional quality of public library service necessitated by metropolitan growth was achievable only by consolidation. This has been hampered by municipalities clinging to control over their libraries. Secondary sources; 8 tables, 23 notes.
V. Samaraweera

3769. Cauthers, Janet, ed. A VICTORIAN TAPESTRY. *Sound Heritage [Canada] 1978 7(3): 1-5.* Provides a brief introduction to a special issue devoted to the life of the elite in Victoria, B.C., between 1880 and 1914, and provides brief biographies of the residents of Victoria whose reminiscences are excerpted in this issue.

3770. Corbet, Elise A. WOMAN'S CANADIAN CLUB OF CAL-GARY. *Alberta Hist. [Canada] 1977 25(3): 29-36.* The Woman's Canadian Club of Calgary was founded in 1911 as part of the elitism prominent at the turn of the century. Prior to World War I, the group was active in community affairs and patriotic activities. During the war, the club's efforts supported defense efforts. In postwar years, the group emphasized nationalism, integrating immigrants, and encouraging music and the arts. By the end of the 1920's, the group primarily was concerned with fostering a Canadian identity. Based on executive minutes and other organizational sources; 2 illus., 43 notes.
D. Chaput

3771. Creighton, Edith. A HALIFAX TRAGEDY. *Nova Scotia Hist. Q. 1973 3(3): 191-196.* Reconstructs the events of an 1816 Halifax murder in which John Westmacott was killed by two thieves, Michael M'Grath and Charles Devit, both of whom were brought to trial, found guilty, and publicly executed.

3772. Cuneo, Carl J. and Curtis, James E. SOCIAL ASCRIPTION IN THE EDUCATIONAL AND OCCUPATIONAL STATUS AT-TAINMENT OF URBAN CANADIANS. *Can. Rev. of Sociol. and Anthrop. 1975 12(1): 6-24.* Focuses on the nature and extent of social ascription—the effect of family background, language, and gender on the educational and occupational status attainment of francophone men and women and anglophone men and women. Social ascription is strong in that family background has rather strong and different effects on occupational attainment, through its influence on respondent's education, among women and men and among francophones and anglophones. Mother's education has, of all family background variables, the strongest effect on respondent's education among French males; family size has a greater negative impact on education among anglophones than among francophones; respondent's education has greater effects on occupation among francophones than among anglophones, and among men than among women. Previous American and Canadian data on social mobility have often shown strong ascriptive effects in stratification in contrast to the achievement interpretation which has been placed on them.
J/S

3773. Davey, Ian E. TRENDS IN FEMALE SCHOOL ATTENDANCE IN MID-NINETEENTH CENTURY ONTARIO. *Social Hist. [Canada] 1975 8(16): 238-254.* Although there was a steady increase in female attendance at schools in Ontario in the 1850's-60's, it was more spectacular in cities than in rural areas. The increase seems directly attributable to the greater availability of public schools. Despite these trends, the long-standing class and sex biases in school attendance persisted. Girls were more likely than their brothers to be withdrawn from school in times of economic hardship. Middle-class girls were far more likely to attend school than were children of the working class. Based on superintendents' annual reports, Hamilton school records, and the Hamilton manuscript census. 10 tables, 20 notes.   W. K. Hobson

3774. Delude-Clift, Camille and Champoux, Edouard. LE CONFLIT DES GÉNÉRATIONS [The generations' conflict]. *Recherches Sociographiques [Canada] 1973 14(2): 157-201.* An analysis of the perceptions of adults and adolescents with respect to family, religion, and education shows that the socioeconomic milieu of the individual determines attitudes concerning social integration, whereas age is an important factor in the quest for identity. Intergenerational tension is largely due to this emergence of a private self among members of the younger generation. Based on 196 interviews conducted in Québec City.

A. E. LeBlanc

3775. Dempsey, Hugh A. GLENBOW CENTRE: CALGARY'S NEW MUSEUM. *Can. Geographical J. [Canada] 1977 94(2): 46-53.* Traces the history of the Glenbow-Alberta Institute from its beginnings in 1954 as the Glenbow Foundation, founded by Eric L. Harvie, to the 1976 opening of Glenbow Centre which houses the institute's museum collections, art gallery, library, and archives.

3776. Denton, Frank T. and George, Peter J. SOCIO-ECONOMIC CHARACTERISTICS OF FAMILIES IN WENTWORTH COUNTY, 1871: SOME FURTHER RESULTS. *Social Hist. [Canada] 1974 7(13): 103-110.* Study of 429 urban and 671 rural families in Wentworth County, Ontario, in 1871 reveals that most occupational, religious, birthplace, and ethnic origin variables were not significantly related to number of children; only the wife's birthplace was. The observed urban-rural difference in family size was not due to the differences in socio-economic characteristics of rural and urban families. School attendance was significantly related to father's occupation, parental birthplace, and to basic urban-rural differences, but not to religion or ethnic origin. Based on manuscript census; 2 tables, 6 notes.   W. K. Hobson

3777. Dunlop, Allan C. PHARMACIST AND ENTREPRENEUR: PICTOU'S J. D. B. FRASER. *Nova Scotia Hist. Q. [Canada] 1974 4(1): 1-21.* James Daniel Bain Fraser (1807-69), pioneer pharmacist of Pictou, Nova Scotia, served the community as Justice of the Peace, dentist, Commissioner of Streets, and inventor. He is best remembered, however, for the first use of chloroform in childbirth. Based on documents in the Public Archives of Nova Scotia (W721) and secondary sources; 69 notes.

H. M. Evans

3778. Fetherling, Doug. TORONTO'S CULTURAL FERMENT, 1978-STYLE. *Can. Geographical J. [Canada] 1978 96(2): 28-35.* Discusses Toronto's cultural events and municipal encouragement of the arts programs, including, art galleries, opera, theater, public art fairs, ballet, civic orchestra, and municipal educational television, 1978.

3779. Fingard, Judith. ENGLISH HUMANITARIANISM AND THE COLONIAL MIND: WALTER BROMLEY IN NOVA SCOTIA, 1813-25. *Can. Hist. R. 1973 54(2): 123-151.* Examines the career of Walter Bromley as a social activist in Nova Scotia and as an agent of Christian imperialism in both the Maritimes and South Australia, concentrating particularly on the response in Nova Scotia to his self-help projects for relieving the urban poor and ameliorating the condition of the Micmacs. The degree of success enjoyed by Bromley's schemes depended almost entirely on his tireless energy and dedication rather than on the support of the local population which was channelled through voluntary associations. Concludes that the colonial response to Bromley's pioneering efforts at social improvement was characterized by a parasitic reliance on the benevolence and financial assistance of the mother country.   J

3780. Fingard, Judith. MASTERS AND FRIENDS, CRIMPS AND ABSTAINERS: AGENTS OF CONTROL IN 19TH CENTURY SAILORTOWN. *Acadiensis [Canada] 1978 8(1): 22-46.* During 1850's-90's three agencies competed for control of sailors in eastern Canadian ports. Boardinghouse keepers exploited them, but enhanced their wage rates. Despised by civic elites, the keepers were tolerated as agents of control. The government shipping office, intending to reduce desertion and control wage rates, lacked the means to do either. Social reformers promoted temperance and sailors' homes, but failed because of their paternalism. By the 1880's the need for control declined as working conditions improved. 87 notes.   D. F. Chard

3781. Fingard, Judith. THE RELIEF OF THE UNEMPLOYED POOR IN SAINT JOHN, HALIFAX AND ST. JOHN'S, 1815-1860. *Acadiensis [Canada] 1975 5(1): 32-53.* Overseas immigration, economic recession, and other factors forced urban poverty to the forefront of public attention in the major centers of eastern British North America after the Napoleonic Wars. Responses were influenced by "interest in economy, order, and the wider welfare of the town. . . ." Heavy outdoor labor, such as stonebreaking, and indoor factory work were seen as solutions. Generally, however, organizations dispensed charity rather than campaigning for economic reform, and capitalists exploited patterns of unemployment. 101 notes.   D. F. Chard

3782. Forward, Charles N. RELATIONSHIPS BETWEEN ELDERLY POPULATION AND INCOME SOURCES IN THE URBAN ECONOMIC BASES OF VICTORIA AND VANCOUVER. *BC Studies [Canada] 1977-78 (36): 34-46.* The British Columbia cities of Victoria and Vancouver are widely known as leading Canadian retirement centers. Of 20 Canadian metropolitan areas, Victoria has the lowest proportion of income from employment and the highest from both investments and pensions. Vancouver's proportion of people 65 and older is second only to Victoria, but its income characteristics tend to resemble those of the average Canadian city. These conclusions are derived from taxation statistics, ordinarily overlooked in studies of urban functional characteristics. 2 tables, 7 graphs, 7 notes.   D. L. Smith

3783. Fox, Richard W. "MODERNIZING" MOBILITY STUDIES. *Hist. of Educ. Q. 1977 17(2): 203-209.* Reviews Michael B. Katz's *The People of Hamilton, Canada West: Family and Class in a Mid-Nineteenth Century City* (Cambridge, Mass: Harvard U. Pr., 1975), an important work comparable to Stephen Thernstrom's *Progress and Poverty* (1964) and one that takes a major step in more fully understanding social mobility. Argues against using occupations as a surrogate for class and analyzes the social structure of mobility. Includes work on poor Irish Catholics in Hamilton. 2 notes.   L. C. Smith

3784. Gaffield, Chad and Levine, David. DEPENDENCY AND ADOLESCENCE ON THE CANADIAN FRONTIER: ORILLIA, ONTARIO IN THE MID-NINETEENTH CENTURY. *Hist. of Educ. Q. 1978 18(1): 35-47.* Using Orillia, Ontario, argues that social changes in a 19th-century community, particularly employment opportunities, affected aspects of adolescence and dependency. For example, age at time of marriage was lowered as job opportunities increased. Makes some comparison with urban studies on Hamilton. Primary and secondary sources; 4 tables, 11 notes.   L. C. Smith

3785. Gouett, Paul M. THE HALIFAX ORPHAN HOUSE, 1752-87. *Nova Scotia Hist. Q. [Canada] 1976 6(3): 281-291.* Discusses the Orphan House in Halifax, Nova Scotia, and its function as provider of food, shelter, and education for poor and orphaned children during 1752-87.

3786. Grenier, Manon; Roy, Maurice; and Bouchard, Louis. L'EVOLUTION DE LA POPULATION DES ENFANTS AU CENTRE DE LA VILLE DE QUEBEC ET EN BANLIEU, 1951-1971 [The evolution of the population of children in downtown Quebec City and the suburbs, 1951-1971]. *Cahiers de Géographie de Québec 1974 18(45): 541-552.*

3787. Hagan, John. CRIMINAL JUSTICE IN RURAL AND URBAN COMMUNITIES: A STUDY OF THE BUREAUCRATIZATION OF JUSTICE. *Social Forces 1977 55(3): 597-612.* This paper inquires into the effects of urbanization and bureaucratization on one type of institutionalized decisionmaking: judicial sentencing. Theoretical and empirical links between urbanization, bureaucratization, and sentencing are reviewed. Then, two data sets from Alberta are analyzed: (1) 507 questionnaires based on pre-sentence reports completed in all provincial probation departments, and (2) 974 offenders admitted to the five major provincial prisons. The analysis is built on comparisons of sentencing patterns for North American Indians and whites in urban and rural communities. The results reveal that probation officers in rural jurisdictions, as contrasted with those in urban communities, sentence Indians severely, without the justification of correlated legal variables. In addition, Indians are more likely to be sent to jail in default of fine payments in rural, than in urban communities. The implications of these findings for an understanding of the bureaucratization of criminal justice are discussed.   J

3788. Hall, Frederick A.   MUSICAL LIFE IN WINDSOR: 1875-1901.   *U. of Windsor Rev. [Canada] 1974 9(2): 76-92.* Traces the development of live musical performances in Windsor, Ontario. Early local efforts were concentrated in town churches and featured religious, classical, and popular pieces. Notes the establishment in the city of music education schools and programs and describes important music clubs and societies. A brief history is provided of the 1874-1901 Windsor Opera House. Emphasizes the difficulties of establishing a viable and independent Windsor musical tradition in close proximity to similar American activities in much-larger Detroit. In spite of this competition, Windsor succeeded in inaugurating and maintaining an active musical life. 25 notes.   H. S. Shields

3789. Hare, John.   LA POPULATION DE LA VILLE DE QUÉBEC, 1795-1805 [The population of the city of Queébec, 1795-1805]. *Social Hist. [Canada] 1974 7(13): 23-47.* Parish censuses of 1795 and 1805 reveal a strong pattern of religious group residential segregation and high rates of geographic mobility. The special occupational and ethnic character of each of the city's four districts is also apparent. Ethnic differences strongly influenced patterns of social stratification in 1795. Based on published census schedules; 9 maps, 17 tables, 3 graphs, 31 notes.
                                                        W. K. Hobson

3790. Howard, Victor.   THE VANCOUVER RELIEF CAMP STRIKE OF 1935: A NARRATIVE OF THE GREAT DEPRESSION. *Can.: An Hist. Mag. 1974 1(3): 9-16, 26-33.*

3791. Hynes, Gisa I.   SOME ASPECTS OF THE DEMOGRAPHY OF PORT ROYAL, 1650-1755. *Acadiensis [Canada] 1973 3(1): 3-17.* Emphasizes immigration to Port Royal, Nova Scotia, from France.

3792. Kaestle, Carl F.   MOBILITY AND ANXIETY IN A COMMERCIAL CITY. *Rev. in Am. Hist. 1976 4(4): 504-512.* Review article prompted by Michael B. Katz's *The People of Hamilton, Canada West: Family and Class in a Mid-Nineteenth-Century City* (Cambridge, Mass.: Harvard U. Pr., 1975); discusses family organization and class structure in Hamilton, 1851-61.

3793. Katz, Michael B.   THE ENTREPRENEURIAL CLASS IN A CANADIAN CITY.   *J. of Social Hist. 1975 8(2): 1-29.* Although an entrepreneurial elite ruled Hamilton, Ontario, in the mid-19th century, the individual members of the elite often varied—"the identity of its members swirled with the vicissitudes of commerce, the whims of creditors, the logic of character and the vagaries of chance." 2 tables, 42 notes.
                                                        L. Ziewacz

3794. Katz, Michael B.   THE ORIGINS OF PUBLIC EDUCATION: A REASSESSMENT. *Hist. of Educ. Q. 1976 16(4): 381-408.* Assesses the expectations for and outcomes of public schools as tools for socialization in Hamilton, Ontario, during 19th-century industrialization.

3795. Katz, Michael B.; Doucet, Michael J.; and Stern, Mark J. POPULATION PERSISTENCE AND EARLY INDUSTRIALIZATION IN A CANADIAN CITY: HAMILTON, ONTARIO, 1851-71. *Social Sci. Hist. 1978 2(2): 208-229.*

3796. Katz, Michael B. and Davey, Ian E.   SCHOOL ATTENDANCE AND EARLY INDUSTRIALIZATION IN A CANADIAN CITY: A MULTIVARIATE ANALYSIS. *Hist. of Educ. Q. 1978*

18(3): 271-293. Examines the relationship between industrialization and school attendance in Hamilton, Ontario, during the mid- and late 19th century, based on a mid-1970's study which concluded that adolescents' school attendance increased rapidly between 1851 and 1871 when jobs were difficult to find, then dropped when industrialization made more jobs available.

3797. Keane, Patrick.   A STUDY IN EARLY PROBLEMS AND POLICIES IN ADULT EDUCATION: THE HALIFAX MECHANICS' INSTITUTE.   *Social Hist. [Canada] 1975 8(16): 255-274.* The Halifax Mechanics' Institute, founded in 1831, reflected the hopes of its middle-class sponsors of molding the urban working class in its own image. The Institute failed to attract large numbers of mechanics, and soon became a center of occasional middle-class entertainment and recreation. It failed in its original purpose because its sponsors never came to grips with the needs and aspirations of Halifax workingmen. Based on documents in Public Archives of Nova Scotia, newspapers, and secondary sources. 98 notes.   W. K. Hobson

3798. Klassen, Henry C.   SOCIAL TROUBLES IN CALGARY IN THE MID-1890'S.   *Urban Hist. Rev. [Canada] 1974 74(3): 8-16.* During 1894-96 the city government of Calgary, Alberta, was forced to deal with myriad social problems: poverty, public housing, unemployment, crime, sanitation, and disease.

3799. Kutcher, Stan.   J. W. BENGOUGH AND THE MILLENNIUM IN HOGTOWN: A STUDY OF MOTIVATION IN URBAN REFORM.   *Urban Hist. Rev. [Canada] 1976 76(2): 30-49.* The career of John Wilson Bengough (1851-1923), cartoonist and author, illustrates the idealism of certain aspects of the urban reform movement. Religiously motivated, he believed in worshiping God by serving mankind. Concerned with the social conditions of Toronto, he used his weekly satirical magazine, *Grip,* to promote morality in city government. He became involved in politics by serving as an alderman for three years. Frustrated by the necessity of political compromise, he retired from office in 1909, preferring the freedom of an outside critic. Based on the Bengough Papers, secondary sources, and newspapers; 76 notes.   C. A. Watson

3800. Larocque, Paul.   APERÇU DE LA CONDITION OUVRIÈRE À QUÉBEC, 1896-1914 [A look at the condition of workers in Quebec, 1896-1914]. *Labour [Canada] 1976 1: 122-138.* Examines workers' lives in Quebec City's Lower Town when industries were diversifying, growing, and becoming mechanized. In crowded neighborhoods near the factories and commercial areas, workers lived in or close to misery and were plagued by poor working conditions and pay, disease, unemployment, fires, and monotony. In frustration, many turned to alcohol. Despite efforts by charitable organizations such as the St. Vincent de Paul Society and some feeble action by government, neither the law nor the social system provided much to alleviate conditions which produced a fundamental alienation of the working class. Primary and secondary sources; 93 notes.   W. A. Kearns

3801. Lejeunesse, Marcel.   LES CABINETS DE LECTURE À PARIS ET À MONTRÉAL AU 19ᵉ SIÈCLE [Reading rooms in Paris and Montreal in the 19th century]. *Recherches Sociographiques [Canada] 1975 16(2): 241-247.* The reading room was one of the major sociocultural forces at work in Paris during the first half of the 19th century, but its popularity only began in Montreal in the late 1850's. Its development in Montreal was closely related to the interests of the Roman Catholic Church.   A. E. LeBlanc

3802. Lunardini, Rosemary.   "TUQUE BLEUE."   *Beaver [Canada] 1976 307(3): 40-45.* Relates the history of the Montreal Snowshoe Club. Officially founded in Montreal in 1843, the club met weekly in the winters to tramp cross-country and to have annual races. Club members competed against Indian guests who usually won. The club grew, but by the turn of the century social activities and charitable works threatened to replace the snowshoe aspects, as few members kept up an interest in the rigorous sport. Today there are many snowshoe clubs in Quebec, totaling more than 5,000 members. They socialize and practice the sport, as well as emphasize the historic role of snowshoeing in discovery and exploration. Based on materials in the Public Archives of Canada; 5 illus.
                                                        D. Chaput

3803. McDonald, R. H. NOVA SCOTIA NEWSPAPERS VIEW THE UNITED STATES 1827-1840. *Nova Scotia Hist. Q. [Canada] 1976 6(1): 1-16.* Examines editorial policies of the *Colonial Patriot* and the *Yarmouth Herald* of Pictou and Yarmouth and contrasts them with the newspapers of Halifax during 1827-40. The Halifax press was more critical of US policies in foreign relations and domestic affairs. 61 notes.
H. M. Evans

3804. Metcalfe, Alan. THE EVOLUTION OF ORGANIZED PHYSICAL RECREATION IN MONTREAL, 1840-1895. *Social Hist. [Canada] 1978 11(21): 144-166.* Before 1840, organized physical recreation in Montreal was elitist. In the 1840's public concern at the lack of recreational facilities developed, but throughout the 19th century most facilities remained private. In the 1870's and 1880's the number of baseball, lacrosse, and hockey clubs grew significantly, and new sports, such as golf, swimming, and biking, emerged. Public concern about parks grew in the 1870's, but not until the 1890's did mass sports, still largely Anglophone, develop. Commercial spectator sports increased gradually after 1870. 56 notes.
D. F. Chard

3805. Mitchell, John Fletcher and Driedger, Leo. CANADIAN ETHNIC FOLK ART: AN EXPLORATORY STUDY IN WINNIPEG. *Ethnicity 1978 5(3): 252-265.* A survey of 12 Latvian and 38 Ukrainian artists working in Winnipeg seeking to ascertain sociocultural complexity employed a general schema of folk art emphasizing art forms, role of the artist, distribution and reward systems, the art consuming public, and principles of judgment. In art forms design and use of colors were indicated as important, along with employment of symbols and patterns. The role of the artist included ethnic loyalty and a general interest in other ethnic activities. Art created was used in the home with some artists entering contests and selling their creations at exhibitions and fairs. The ethnic group to which the artist adhered was the most responsive to the art created.
N. Lederer

3806. Olivier-Lecamp, Gaël and Legare, Jacques. QUELQUES CARACTERISTIQUES DES MENAGES DE LA VILLE DE QUEBEC ENTRE 1666 ET 1716 [Some characteristics of Quebec City households between 1666 and 1716]. *Social Hist. [Canada] 1979 12(23): 66-78.* Quebec City grew from a market-town of 550 people in 1666 to a small city of 2,500 inhabitants in 1716. Its households also changed in this period. In the first 20 years of the period French immigration to Canada reached a peak. In these years Quebec City differed considerably from 17th and 18th century Europe. In 1716 Quebec was closer to European norms. This is clear from studying the censuses of 1666, 1667, 1681, and 1716. 5 tables, 17 notes.
D. F. Chard

3807. O'Neill, P. B. REGINA'S GOLDEN AGE OF THEATER: HER PLAYHOUSES AND PLAYERS. *Saskatchewan Hist. [Canada] 1975 28(1): 29-37.* The "Golden Age" of theater in North America, including Regina, was 1900-14. Mentions nearly a dozen theaters and several well-known performers, including Melba, Madame Albani, Minnie Maddern Fiske, Sophie Tucker, Lewis Waller, and Sir Johnston Forbes-Robertson. 3 photos, 35 notes.
C. Held

3808. Orrell, John. EDMONTON THEATRES OF ALEXANDER W. CAMERON. *Alberta Hist. [Canada] 1978 26(2): 1-10.* In 1906, Alexander W. Cameron brought vaudeville to Edmonton at the Empire Theater. Until 1913, Cameron was the driving force in this aspect of Edmonton's cultural life. He was either the main investor, or planner, of the Edmonton Opera House, the Kevin, Orpheum, and Lyric Theaters. Cameron was innovative. When attendance dropped at the opera house, he converted the building into a roller skating rink during the weekdays. Cameron left the Edmonton area around 1913. Based on newspaper accounts and government documents. 4 illus., 16 notes.
D. Chaput

3809. Paquet, Gilles and Wallot, Jean-Pierre. LES INVENTAIRES APRÈS DÉCÈS À MONTRÉAL AU TOURNANT DU XIXᵉ SIÈCLE: PRÉLIMINAIRES À UNE ANALYSE [Inventories after death in Montreal at the turn of the 19th century: preliminaries to an analysis]. *Rev. d'Hist. de l'Am. Française [Canada] 1976 30(2): 163-221.* At the turn of the 19th century, Lower Canada's role in the trans-Atlantic commercial economy was transformed by external and internal forces. Presents research regarding wealth distribution, social stratification, and

behavioral adjustment. Based on notarial documents and secondary works; 3 tables, 96 notes, 2 appendixes.
L. B. Chan

3810. Robert, Jean-Claude. LES NOTABLES DE MONTRÉAL AU XIXᵉ SIÈCLE [Montreal's "worthies" in the 19th century]. *Social Hist. [Canada] 1975 8(15): 54-76.* In 1892 J. Douglas Bothwick (1832-1912) published the *History and Biographical Gazetteer of Montreal to the Year 1892.* It includes usable biographical sketches of 491 Montreal notables. "Intellectuals" and professionals are overrepresented and businessmen are underrepresented, but it is otherwise a good source on the social composition of the 19th century Montreal elite. Almost 50% of the notables were born outside Lower Canada, in Great Britain for the most part. The elite was proportionately more English-speaking than the population. Occupations showed ethnic specialization. British-born tended to be in business; Canadian-born tended to be doctors or lawyers. Francophones formed the majority of the political class. Anglophones formed the majority of the business class. 4 tables, 28 notes.
W. K. Hobson

3811. Roberts, David. SOCIAL STRUCTURE IN A COMMERCIAL CITY: SAINT JOHN, 1871. *Urban Hist. Rev. [Canada] 1974 74(2): 15-18.* Using the Dominion Census of 1871, effects a methodology for interpreting information provided and applies it to analysis of the social organization in Saint John, New Brunswick.

3812. Roberts, Wayne. SIX NEW WOMEN: A GUIDE TO THE MENTAL MAP OF WOMEN REFORMERS IN TORONTO. *Atlantis [Canada] 1977 3(1): 145-164.* Provides brief portraits of activists in the Toronto women's movement before World War I: Emily Stowe, Augusta Stowe-Gullen, Flora Macdonald Denison, Helen MacMurchy, Florence Gooderham Huestis, and Mrs. Constance Hamilton; 1870's-1910's.

3813. Roy, Patricia E. THE PRESERVATION OF THE PEACE IN VANCOUVER: THE AFTERMATH OF THE ANTI-CHINESE RIOT OF 1887. *BC Studies [Canada] 1976 (31): 44-59.* The Vancouver, British Columbia, riot of 1887 brought unprecedented anti-Chinese violence and a press war between that city and Victoria. It did show the determination of the provincial government to act decisively to preserve peace, justice, and the reputation of the province. The young city had not done as well for itself. 45 notes.
D. L. Smith

3814. Smith, Mary Elizabeth. THEATRE IN SAINT JOHN: THE FIRST THIRTY YEARS. *Dalhousie Rev. [Canada] 1979 59(1): 5-27.* From the first dramatic performance in Saint John, New Brunswick, in 1789 to the closing of the Saint John Theatre in 1817, examines all kinds of theatrical performances from the charity inspired *The Busy Body* presented in "Mallard's Long Room" to more professional performances at the Saint John Theatre. Most of the professional presentations were from traveling or visiting actors from Edinburgh, Halifax, Philadelphia, and other large centers of civilization. Based on newspapers, journals, and letters from participants and observers; 36 notes.
C. Held

3815. Smith, Michael D. PRECIPITANTS OF CROWD VIOLENCE. *Sociol. Inquiry [Canada] 1978 48(2): 121-132.* Using instances of sports-related crowd violence reported in the Toronto *Globe and Mail,* 1963-73, finds that in 75% of the cases, crowd action was preceded by extraordinary individual displays of violence (usually between players from opposing teams).

3816. Steck, Warren F. and Sarjeant, William A. S. A LOCAL SOCIETY IN URBAN AND PROVINCIAL AFFAIRS: THE HISTORY AND ACHIEVEMENTS OF THE SASKATOON ENVIRONMENTAL SOCIETY. *Urban Hist. Rev. [Canada] 1977 (2): 33-54.* Two members describe the formation and activities of the Saskatoon Environmental Society. As the leading private environmental group in Saskatoon, Saskatchewan, the S.E.S. became a major influence on environmental issues in and around the municipality. The S.E.S. decided to remain local in scope, urging the formation of similar groups in other Saskatchewan municipalities. 2 maps, biblio.
C. A. Watson

3817. Stewart, Catharine McArthur. QUEBEC CITY IN THE 1770'S. *Hist. Today [Great Britain] 1973 23(2): 116-121.* "Life in Quebec was considerably changed by the arrival of merchants from Britain and by the effects of the American Revolution."

3818. Tetrault, Gregory. A CARNEGIE LIBRARY FOR DAWSON CITY. *Beaver [Canada] 1974 305(3): 47-50.* A. Nicol appealed from this Yukon city of about 30,000 in 1902 to Andrew Carnegie for library funds; Nicol had family connections who were personally acquainted with Carnegie. A substantial construction and maintenance gift was provided, and the library opened in the fall of 1903. The library was crucial for Dawson's citizens during the long, cold winters. By 1920 the population of Dawson was down to 1,000, the library was soon sold to a local lodge, and the books were deposited in the public school. Includes details on community attitudes towards the Carnegie grant, along with various construction and labor information. 2 photos, diagram.
D. Chaput

3819. Unsigned. ACCROISSEMENT ET STRUCTURE DE LA POPULATION À QUÉBEC AU DÉBUT DU XIXe SIÈCLE [Growth and structure of the Quebec population at the beginning of the 19th century]. *Social Hist. [Canada] 1976 9(17): 187-196.*
Paillé, Michel P. ACCROISSEMENT ET STRUCTURE DE LA POPULATION À QUÉBEC AU DÉBUT DU XIXe SIÈCLE (À PROPOS D'UN ARTICLE DE JOHN HARE) [Growth and structure of the Quebec population at the beginning of the 19th century (with respect to an article by John Hare)], *pp. 187-193.* Reviews John Hare's article on the population of the city of Quebec during 1795-1805. Corrects several compilation errors, defines several concepts, and illustrates methodology for studying population growth and age structure. 3 tables, 33 notes.
Hare, John E. À PROPOS DES COMMENTAIRES DE MICHEL PAILLÉ [Response to Michel Paillé], *pp. 193-196.* Michel Paillé's reexamination is flawed because he relies on the published census' summary tables, which do not correspond to the census' details when examined street by street and house by house. Studying the age structure cannot be as exact as Paillé believes because it must be based on census data using the age of communicants. During 1703-1840, the age for communion was not precise; it was allowed to vary between 10 and 14 years old. 3 tables.
W. K. Hobson

3820. Wright, Jeffrey. THE HALIFAX RIOT OF APRIL, 1863. *Nova Scotia Hist. Q. [Canada] 1974 4(3): 299-310.* Recounts the circumstances leading to the difficulties, later referred to as the "riot," between the military and the civilian population of Halifax. The uprising lasted from 14-23 April 1863. 35 notes, biblio.
H. M.Evans

Minorities and Ethnic Relations

3821. Arnold, A. J. THE EARLIEST JEWS IN WINNIPEG 1874-1882. *Beaver [Canada] 1974 305(2): 4-11.* Describes the settlement of Russian Jews in Winnipeg. Disappointed at first because most failed to receive land grants or find employment, many eventually moved out of the city to find or create employment opportunities. For those who stayed, the city offered closer ties with Jewish cultural institutions. 11 illus.
D. Heermans

3822. Astrachan, Anthony. ON THE BROAD PRAIRIE: IN WINNIPEG, MANITOBA: A JEWISH PHENOMENON. *Present Tense 1975 2(4): 31-35.* History and description of the flourishing Jewish community in Winnipeg, Manitoba.
S

3823. Battistelli, Fabrizio. L'AUTONOMIA CULTURALE COME STRUMENTO DI ASSIMILAZIONE: I MASS MEDIA ITALIANI NELLA COMUNITÀ IMMIGRATA DI TORONTO, [Cultural autonomy as means of assimilation: Italian mass media in the Toronto immigrant community]. *Rassegna Italiana di Sociologia [Italy] 1975 16(3): 449-465.* A study of Italian mass media in Toronto during the 1970's shows that the media, by carrying the message of Anglo-Canadian capitalism to immigrants, tends to assimilate and thus eradicate the minority community.

3824. Baureiss, Gunter. THE CHINESE COMMUNITY IN CALGARY. *Alberta Hist. R. 1974 22(2): 1-8.* Traces the history of Calgary's Chinese community. The first Chinese came in 1886 when the coolie work force was no longer needed for railway construction in the

Rockies. Through years of prejudice and discrimination a closely knit subcommunity has been formed. Today perpetuation of ethnic cultures and communities is official policy. 3 illus., table, 16 notes.
D. L. Smith

3825. Budakowska, Elżbieta. STRUKTURA DEMOGRAFICZNA POLONII KANADYJSKIEJ [Demographic structure of the Poles in Canada]. *Kultura i Społeczeństwo [Poland] 1976 20(1): 107-116.* The largest center of the Canadian Polonia is still Toronto, followed by Winnipeg, Montreal, Edmonton, Hamilton, Vancouver, Calgary, and Ottawa. The Canadian Polonia, hindered by foreign heritage and low income, shows a considerable rise in its professional structure since World War II. The educated or partly educated pre- and postwar Polish emigration greatly influenced this because it increased the number of intellectuals and scholars. The number of Polish students at Canadian universities also has risen considerably.
M. Swiecicka-Ziemianek

3826. Burley, Kevin. OCCUPATIONAL STRUCTURE AND ETHNICITY IN LONDON, ONTARIO, 1871. *Social Hist. [Canada] 1978 11(22): 390-410.* London grew rapidly in the three decades before 1871. Its population of 15,826 made it the fourth largest town in Ontario. The foreign-born, particularly those from Great Britain, dominated London's work force. London's percentage of foreign-born (54%) was well below the national average, but typical of western Ontario towns. The Canadian-born were more active in the city's commercial sector and in some professions. Occupations apparently differed widely between ethnic groups, but the distribution by socioeconomic class was remarkably alike for all ethnic groups. Based on the 1871 census and on other primary and secondary sources; 9 tables, 45 notes.
D. F. Chard

3827. Chichekian, Garo. ARMENIAN IMMIGRANTS IN CANADA AND THEIR DISTRIBUTION IN MONTREAL. *Cahiers de Géographie de Québec [Canada] 1977 21(52): 65-82.* Using census data and information from Canada's Immigration Department, chronicles the immigration pattern of Armenians into Canada, 1900-66.

3828. Driedger, Leo. CANADIAN MENNONITE URBANISM: ETHNIC VILLAGERS OR METROPOLITAN REMNANT? *Mennonite Q. Rev. 1975 49(3): 226-241.* Presents a study of the effect of urbanization on traditional Mennonite beliefs and practices in an attempt to determine the amount of erosion, if any, on urban Mennonites in contrast to those in rural areas. Urban Mennonites are lost to other groups in lesser numbers. Institutions (colleges, etc.) are shifting to urbanized areas successfully. The study shows that Canadian Mennonites have suffered less than their American counterparts in urbanization. 3 charts, 19 notes.
E. E. Eminhizer

3829. Driedger, Leo. ETHNIC BOUNDARIES: A COMPARISON OF TWO URBAN NEIGHBORHOODS. *Sociol. and Social Res. 1978 62(2): 193-211.* This study in metropolitan Winnipeg shows that St. Boniface and the North End represent two "natural ethnic areas" with distinct urban boundaries. Territory, institutions and culture are important boundary maintenance factors. The community of the North End, originally dominated by East European Jews, Ukrainians, and Poles is experiencing the process of invasion and succession as has been demonstrated in many other urban community studies. The Jews have moved to the suburbs taking their culture and institutions with them; the Ukrainians and Poles are also changing and adjusting to newcomers. The East European ethnic boundaries are giving way to a more heterogeneous, multi-ethnic invasion by native Indian and south European newcomers. In contrast, the community of north St. Boniface has remained essentially a French urban neighborhood for 160 years. The urban French community by means of residential segregation, with limited out mobility, has maintained a French culture within a fairly complete ethnic institutional framework. The unique French St. Boniface urban community does not follow the numerous other invasion-succession patterns which have been reported. This paper explores possible reasons for the two differential community change patterns within the same metropolitan area.
J

3830. Driedger, Leo. MAINTENANCE OF URBAN ETHNIC BOUNDARIES: THE FRENCH IN ST. BONIFACE. *Sociol Q. 1979 20(1): 89-108.* Discusses the reasons for the segregation of French Canadians in St. Boniface, Manitoba, and the recent attempts to get the French to assimilate, based on studies done in the 1970's dating to 1871.

3831.　Driedger, Leo and Church, Glenn.　RESIDENTIAL SEGRE-GATION AND INSTITUTIONAL COMPLETENESS: A COMPAR-ISON OF ETHNIC MINORITIES.　*Can. Rev. of Sociol. and Anthrop. 1974 11(1): 30-52.* The importance of residential segregation for the maintenance of institutional completeness is clearly demonstrated by this study of six ethnic groups in Winnipeg. The French community maintain-ers follow Joy's Quebec core area pattern in St. Boniface with extensions of their ethnic belt adjacent to the ore and extensive intra-area mobility. On the other hand, the Scandinavians were never able to establish a very complete ethnic institutional base in a segregated ecological area, so they scattered as assimilationists would predict. Contrary to Joy's prediction, extensive Jewish mobility into their West Kildonan and River Heights suburban extended belt areas resulted in the establishment of two new segregated Jewish communities where they have created new complexes of ethnic institutions, leaving the original North End Jewish core area almost entirely.　　　　　　　　　　　　　　　　　　　　　　　　　J

3832.　Frideres, J.; Goldenberg, S.; and Reeves, W.　THE ECONOMIC ADAPTATION OF WEST INDIANS IN TORONTO.　*Can. Rev. of Sociol. and Anthrop. [Canada] 1978 15(1): 93-96.* Critiques an article by S. Ramcharan, "The Economic Adaptation of West Indians in Toronto, Canada." It falls short in both structure and content, much being doubt-ful, ambiguous, or in error. This applies to its interpretation of economic adaptation, the analysis of racial background and racial discrimination, the sampling procedures, and the choice of data analysis techniques, and their interpretation.　　　　　　　　　　　　　　　　　　　R. V. Ritter

3833.　Gutwirth, Jacques.　HASSIDIM ET JUDAÏCITÉ À MON-TRÉAL [Hasidism and Judaicity in Montreal].　*Recherches Sociogra-phiques 1973 14(3): 291-325.* The Hasidic groupings that established themselves in Montreal during 1941-52 have, through their sociocultural and religious presence, had a direct and salutary impact on the Jewish community of the city. This has become possible through common refer-ence points of Judaism where institutional collaboration takes place. In turn, Montreal's Jewish faction has permitted the Hasidic groupings to implant themselves. Based on field research and secondary sources; 87 notes.　　　　　　　　　　　　　　　　　　　　　　　　A. E. LeBlanc

3834.　Harney, Robert F.　BOARDING AND BELONGING.　*Urban Hist. Rev. [Canada] 1978 78(2): 8-37.* A recent study of immi-grants has focused on the relationship between ethnic colonies and their acculturation or lack of it. There is now a need to make comparative studies of the migration of immigrants, their sojourning, and finally their settling patterns. The boardinghouse as an institution in the acculturation process of sojourners is described with an emphasis on the Italian board-inghouse in Toronto. Interviews, published government reports, and sec-ondary sources; illus., 59 notes.　　　　　　　　　　　　C. A. Watson

3835.　Harney, Robert F.　CHIAROSCURO: ITALIANS IN TORONTO 1885-1915.　*Italian Americana 1975 1(2): 143-167.* Dis-cusses the settlement of Italian immigrants who lived and found employ-ment in Toronto.　　　　　　　　　　　　　　　　　　　　　　S

3836.　Harney, Robert F. and Troper, Harold.　INTRODUCTION [TO AN ISSUE ON IMMIGRANTS IN THE CITY].　*Can. Ethnic Studies [Canada] 1977 9(1): 1-5.* Seeking to offer broader perspectives than the Anglo-Celtic political historian's approach to urban studies, this issue analyzes 19th- and 20th-century Toronto through its immigrant communities. The eight contributors, using a variety of nontraditional sources (demotic and oral), examine tensions along ethnic boundaries. They conclude that immigrants who encountered overt hostility to their urban settlement reluctantly identified themselves, personally and eco-nomically, by their Canadian "caretakers' " stereotypes. This ethnocul-tural research provides a new and "more honest" dimension in urban history.　　　　　　　　　　　　　　　　　　　K. S. McDorman

3837.　Harney, R. F.　THE NEW CANADIANS AND THEIR LIFE IN TORONTO.　*Can. Geographical J. [Canada] 1978 96(2): 20-27.* Discusses the influx of immigrants from Spain, Portugal, Hungary, Ger-many, Greece, Yugoslavia, Korea, France, and the United Kingdom, 1950's-70's and their acculturation in Toronto.

3838.　Kardonne, Rick.　MONTREAL, QUEBEC.　*Present Tense 1975 2(2): 50-55.* Discusses the social and religious life of the Jews of Montreal, Quebec during the 1970's and the problems presented by the emigration of Jews from Morocco in the 1960's.

3839.　Li, Peter S.　THE STRATIFICATION OF ETHNIC IMMI-GRANTS: THE CASE OF TORONTO.　*Can. Rev. of Sociol. and Anthrop. [Canada] 1978 15(1): 31-40.* Recent developments in the study of ethnic stratification have placed a greater emphasis on differential opportunities by way of explanation, as opposed to the more traditional interpretation of motivational variations. Evaluates the theory of differen-tial opportunities with regard to occupational status differences among eight European immigrant groups in Toronto. It is found that a wide range of gross status differences exist among the various immigrant groups, and that inequality persists despite adjusting for intergroup differ-ences in social origin, education, and prior achieved occupational status. To the extent that immigrants with similar qualifications are received differently in the occupational structure on the basis of ethnic origin, this study gives support to the theory of differential opportunities.　　　J

3840.　Loudfoot, Raymonde.　THE NUYTTENS OF BELGIAN TOWN.　*Manitoba Pageant [Canada] 1974 19(3): 15-18.* Discusses Ed-mund and Octavia Nuytten and other Belgian immigrants who settled in the East St. Boniface area of Winnipeg. Appended is a list of over 300 Belgian families who arrived in Winnipeg, 1880-1914. Illus.

　　　　　　　　　　　　　　　　　　　　　　　　　D. M. Dean

3841.　O'Gallagher, Marianna.　CARE OF THE ORPHAN AND THE AGED BY THE IRISH COMMUNITY OF QUEBEC CITY, 1847 AND YEARS FOLLOWING.　*Study Sessions: Can. Catholic Hist. Assoc. [Canada] 1976 43: 39-56.* Indicates the history and develop-ment of St. Bridget's Home in Quebec, and the work of Father Patrick McMahon, Irish immigrants, and the Catholic Church to provide for the needy, 1847-1972.

3842.　Paupst, Kathy.　A NOTE ON ANTI-CHINESE SENTIMENT IN TORONTO.　*Can. Ethnic Studies [Canada] 1977 9(1): 54-59.* Anti-Chinese prejudice is usually associated with British Columbia, but Toronto, which lacked a large Chinese community, also feared and hated the "yellow peril." Before World War I journals such as *Jack Canuck* repeatedly hammered out racial hatred and stereotyped Orientals as de-ceitful, seductive, and morally degraded.　　　　　　　K. S. McDorman

3843.　Petroff, Lillian.　MACEDONIANS: FROM VILLAGE TO CITY.　*Can. Ethnic Studies [Canada] 1977 9(1): 29-41.* Because they believed that Slavic peoples were inferior immigrants, Canadian Protes-tants, educators, and health officials urged major programs of Canadiza-tion upon the Macedonian community in Toronto's East End. Though aided by elementary language education and nursing services, most of Toronto's first-generation Macedonian population refused to adopt Prot-estantism or surrender their unique traditions. By World War I second-generation Macedonian Canadians had begun to accept their adopted country's culture. Despite some assimilation a distinct ethnic community remains.　　　　　　　　　　　　　　　　　　　K. S. McDorman

3844.　Petroff, Lillian.　MACEDONIANS IN TORONTO: FROM ENCAMPMENT TO SETTLEMENT.　*Urban Hist. Rev. [Canada] 1978 78(2): 58-73.* Before 1914 most Macedonians in Toronto felt they were migrants expecting to return home after earning sufficient money. Conditions in Europe after 1918 led them to decide to settle permanently in Canada. The men, who normally lived in boardinghouses, then tended to marry and set up their own homes, often in slums. Bad conditions were knowingly tolerated in order to live cheaply to save to improve living conditions later. Owning a private home, however, was not quite as important a goal for Macedonians as it was for other immigrant groups: they apparently preferred to invest in commercial enterprises. Interviews, official reports, and secondary sources; 2 illus., map, 50 notes.

　　　　　　　　　　　　　　　　　　　　　　　　　C. A. Watson

3845.　Polyzoi, Eleoussa.　THE GREEK COMMUNAL SCHOOL AND CULTURAL SURVIVAL IN PRE-WAR TORONTO.　*Urban Hist. Rev. [Canada] 1978 78(2): 74-94.* Communal language schools, often ignored by historians, were established to maintain an immigrant group's cultural heritage. Toronto had a growing Greek population in the early decades of this century concerned that their children retain their ethnic and religious heritage. After one Greek school was founded and failed in the early 1920's, a permanent After-Four school was established in 1926. It grew in numbers and received strong parental and community support. The school was successful in helping Greek immigrants become an ethnic group although some former students remembered resentment at extra hours spent in school. Interviews, census reports, and secondary sources; 5 illus., diagram, 53 notes. C. A. Watson

3846. Ramcharan, Subhas. THE ECONOMIC ADAPTATION OF WEST INDIANS IN TORONTO, CANADA. *Can. Rev. of Soc. and Anthrop. 1976 13(3): 295-304.* Analyzes the economic adaptation of West Indian immigrants in Metropolitan Toronto. Two hundred and ninety heads of household were interviewed during the summer of 1972. The experiences of migrants in the economic system differed considerably, with the major explanatory variables appearing to be occupational status and length of residence in Canada. Highly educated, white-collar workers were less likely to have suffered initial status dislocation and more likely to report a fulfillment of their aspirations and a high satisfaction with their new society than blue collar workers. Skin color gradations within the West Indian group did not prove to be a variable causing differing experiences in the economic system, although comparisons between West Indians and white immigrant groups with similar educational levels and length of residence, suggest that the incidence of discrimination in employment is higher for West Indians. J

3847. Rayfield, J. R. MARIA IN MARKHAM STREET: ITALIAN IMMIGRANTS AND LANGUAGE-LEARNING IN TORONTO. *Ethnic Groups 1976 1(2): 133-150.* An account of the sociocultural and psychological problems faced by monolingual Italian working-class housewives in Toronto, Ontario, and their efforts to overcome these problems by enrolling in an English-language school for immigrants run by the Ontario Citizenship Board. M. J. Clark

3848. Regeher, Ted D. MENNONITE CHANGE: THE RISE AND DECLINE OF MENNONITE COMMUNITY ORGANIZATIONS AT COALDALE, ALBERTA. *Mennonite Life 1977 32(4): 13-22.* Russian German immigrants settled Coaldale, Alberta, 1920-30, but because they came as individuals rather than as a colony, they were subject to Canadian regulations and could not transplant distinctly Mennonite institutions and social structures. Organizations evolving from the settlement included churches, a German library, a language preservation society, and Saturday schools. Settlers founded a cooperative cheese factory, a Savings and Credit Union, and a society to provide medical care. Although prosperous, Mennonites at Coaldale had become assimilated into the larger Canadian society by 1976, largely because of the decline of the German language, economic consolidation, superiority of government welfare services, and internal divisions involving religious splits and inadequate leadership. Primary sources; 13 photos. B. Burnett

3849. Richmond, Anthony H. LANGUAGE, ETHNICITY, AND THE PROBLEM OF IDENTITY IN A CANADIAN METROPOLIS. *Ethnicity 1974 1(2): 175-206.* Discusses a central Canadian problem, cultural diversity and national identity, and determines types of self-identification among a Toronto sample from 1970. The analysis focuses on competing identifications, the influence of age at time of arrival and length of residence in Canada, the effects of status and mobility, attitudes toward Canadian society, and the relationship of language to identification. Age, language, mobility, and length of residence are critical factors. 20 tables, biblio. E. Barkan

3850. Shaffir, William. THE ORGANIZATION OF SECULAR EDUCATION IN A CHASSIDIC JEWISH COMMUNITY. *Can. Ethnic Studies [Canada] 1976 8(1): 38-51.* Examines how the religious community of Lubavitcher chassidim in Montreal, Quebec, attempts to minimize their children's exposure to contradictive materials during their secular learning; covers late 1969 to 1971.

3851. Sheriff, Peta. PREFERENCES, VALEURS ET DIFFERENTIATION INTRAPROFESSIONNELLE SELON L'ORIGINE ETHNIQUE [Preferences, values, and intraoccupational distribution according to ethnic origin]. *Can. Rev. of Sociol. and Anthrop. 1974 11(2): 125-137.* Using a sample of French- and English-speaking engineers of the city of Montreal, tests the hypothesis that their occupational values influence their distribution within the profession. The results of the study suggest that the values of the two ethnic groups are similar; however, their

occupational preferences, which reflect social constraints, are more closely linked to their professional situation. J

3852. Sturino, Franc. A CASE STUDY OF A SOUTH ITALIAN FAMILY IN TORONTO, 1935-60. *Urban Hist. Rev. [Canada] 1978 78(2): 38-57.* City directories are used to trace the occupational and residential history of one immigrant family. Part of a larger research project, the history of this one family seems typical. The family was upwardly mobile in residence, moving from a working-class to a middle-class district, and in occupation, the sons moving from factory to white collar jobs. Many of the upward moves were a result of aid given because of kinship ties. Interviews, city directories, and secondary sources; illus., 2 tables, fig., 18 notes. C. A. Watson

3853. Tandon, B. B. EARNING DIFFERENTIALS AMONG NATIVE BORN AND FOREIGN BORN RESIDENTS OF TORONTO. *Int. Migration Rev. 1978 12(3): 406-410.* Immigrants entering the Canadian labor market start with lower earnings than native born residents, but their earnings equalize within a period of five years.

3854. Thomson, Colin A. DOC SHADD. *Saskatchewan Hist. [Canada] 1977 30(2): 41-55.* Alfred Schmitz Shadd, a black man from Ontario, moved to the Carrot River Valley in 1896. His ancestors, fugitive slaves, had long been activists who strove for equality for Canadian blacks. Deals with the black community around Chatham, Ontario, from the 1850's to about 1900. Shadd attended medical school in Toronto before moving to the North-West Territories where he became a school teacher and a "practical" doctor until he returned briefly to Toronto to complete his medical studies. From 1898 until his early death in 1915, Shadd's contributions to early Saskatchewan are well documented. Photo, 51 notes. C. Held

3855. Tomasi, Lydio F. THE ITALIAN COMMUNITY IN TORONTO: A DEMOGRAPHIC PROFILE. *Int. Migration Rev. 1977 11(4): 486-513.* Examines Italian immigration during 1946-72; Italian Canadians are a cohesive, socially active group in Toronto.

3856. Weiermair, Klaus. THE ECONOMIC EFFECTS OF LANGUAGE TRAINING TO IMMIGRANTS: A CASE STUDY. *Int. Migration Rev. 1976 10(2): 205-219.* Discusses the role of English language training in the employment and economic assimilation of immigrants in Toronto, Ontario, 1968-70.

Religion

3857. Betts, E. Arthur. PLACES OF WORSHIP ON THE HALIFAX SCOTIA SQUARE SITE. *Nova Scotia Hist. Q. [Canada] 1979 9(3): 215-223.* Traces the history of nine churches in Halifax (1784-1825). The places of worship were: Lady Huntingdon's Society Meeting Place, Marchinton's Hall, Zoar Chapel, Burton's Church, Poplar Grove Presbyterian, Salem Chapel, Chalmers, Trinity Free Church, and a building which was used by Baptist, Universalist and Jewish congregations. None of the buildings are standing today. Primary sources from Public Archives of Nova Scotia and Maritime Conference Archives; map. H. M. Evans

3858. Campbell, Bertha J. EARLY HISTORY OF PRESBYTERIANS OF SPRINGHILL, NOVA SCOTIA. *Nova Scotia Hist. Q. [Canada] 1977 7(1): 1-30.* Traces the history of the Presbyterian Church and its clergy in Springhill, Nova Scotia, from 1874, when the first elders were elected, until 1925, when the congregation joined the United Church of Canada. Primary sources; 48 notes. H. M. Evans

3859. Campbell, Bertha J. EARLY HISTORY OF ST. ANDREW'S WESLEY UNITED CHURCH OF CANADA: SPRINGHILL, NOVA SCOTIA. *Nova Scotia Hist. Q. [Canada] 1976 6(2): 173-192.* Discusses St. Andrew's Presbyterian Church and the Wesley Methodist Church in Springhill, Nova Scotia, 1800-1976; originally separate congregations, the two amalgamated in 1964.

3860. Choquette, Robert. JOHN THOMAS MC NAILLY ET L'ERECTION DU DIOCÈSE DE CALGARY [John Thomas McNailly

and the establishment of the diocese of Calgary]. *Rev. de l'U. d'Ottawa [Canada] 1975 45(4): 401-416.* John Thomas McNailly (1871-1952), the first bishop of Calgary, was an anglophone who defended the interests of the Catholic anglophiles in Calgary, particularly the Irish. The Pope, in selecting McNailly, believed that western Canada was English in both language and culture. Provides brief sketch of McNailly's life and accomplishments and discusses his problems as bishop, particularly with the French Canadians. Primary and secondary sources; 84 notes.
　　　　　　　　　　　　　　　　　　　　　　M. L. Frey

3861.　Ellis, Walter E.　GILBOA TO ICHABOD: SOCIAL AND RELIGIOUS FACTORS IN THE FUNDAMENTALIST-MODERNIST SCHISMS AMONG CANADIAN BAPTISTS, 1895-1934. *Foundations 1977 20(2): 109-126.* Examines the socioeconomic makeup of the Jarvis Street Baptist Church in Toronto, and the change that occurred during the Fundamentalist-Modernist controversy. As the Fundamentalists gained control, the professional and entrepreneur class left to form churches in new upper-class areas. Contrasts the Jarvis Street Church with the Central Baptist Church and compares it to the Conventional churches and Union churches. The Fundamentalist Union churches attracted the working class (91%), while the Conventional churches attracted the professional class. This increased the social stratification of the church. 23 notes.
　　　　　　　　　　　　　　　　　　　　　E. E. Eminhizer

3862.　Emery, George N.　THE ORIGINS OF CANADIAN METHODIST INVOLVEMENT IN THE SOCIAL GOSPEL MOVEMENT 1890-1914. *J. of the Can. Church Hist. Soc. [Canada] 1977 19(1-2): 104-119.* The massive, rapid transformation of Canada in the early 20th century through urbanization, immigration, and industrialization brought about the growth of Methodism and other Christian denominations of the social gospel movement. There were a number of reasons. First was the decline of the evangelical tradition with the growing affluence of Methodists and the development of the higher criticism. Moreover, the strong belief in individual perfectionism evolved into concern about society as a whole. In their nationalism, pietism, optimism about the future of man, and desire to avoid theological controversy, many Methodists saw in the social gospel movement an opportunity to express their concern about the growing problems caused by the modern changes. All these factors helped bring Canadian Methodists into the forefront of the social gospel movement in Canada. Primary and secondary sources; table, 38 notes. This issue is *J. of the Can. Church Hist. Soc.* 1977 19(1-2) and *Bull. of the United Church of Can.* 1977 26.
　　　　　　　　　　　　　　　　　　　J. A. Kicklighter

3863.　Gruneir, Robert.　THE HEBREW MISSION IN TORONTO. *Can. Ethnic Studies [Canada] 1977 9(1): 18-28.* Focuses primarily on the Presbyterian Church and the Protestant-supported Jewish mission founded in 1912. Examines efforts to convert immigrant Jews to Protestantism. Though presented as an aid to social assimilation, conversion (even the hybrid Hebrew-Protestant variety which allowed maintenance of ethnic identity), failed to attract large numbers of Jews. The movement faded after World War I.
　　　　　　　　　　　　　　　　　　　K. S. McDorman

3864.　Hovinen, Elizabeth.　QUAKERS OF YONGE STREET. *Can. Geographical J. 1976 92(1): 52-57.* Discusses the members of the Society of Friends who lived in southern Ontario in the 19th century.

3865.　Kennedy, Estella.　IMMIGRANTS, CHOLERA, AND THE SAINT JOHN SISTERS OF CHARITY, 1854-1864. *Study Sessions: Can. Catholic Hist. Assoc. [Canada] 1977 44: 25-44.* Following a cholera epidemic in 1854, the Sisters of Charity of the Immaculate Conception, was founded in Saint John, New Brunswick, to care for orphaned children, but expanded to include education of youth and care for the elderly during 1854-64.

3866.　Masters, D. C.　THE ANGLICAN EVANGELICALS IN TORONTO 1870-1900. *J. of the Can. Church Hist. Soc. [Canada] 1978 20(3-4): 51-66.* Describes the beliefs and contributions of some 55 Anglican evangelicals in the diocese of Toronto during the late 19th century. Consisting of both clergy and laity, the group struggled successfully with the High Church party for influence within the Canadian Church, and consequently had an important role in shaping its future. Emphasizing the role of the individual in his relationship to God, the Evangelicals were also individualistic in their socioeconomic views. Almost all were com-

fortably middle-class, and advocated private charity for the poor and distressed, while they opposed government intervention to aid working people and the indigent. Like Protestant groups with whom they were on good terms, the Evangelicals advocated total abstinence from alcoholic beverages and maintained a theology centered around God's sovereignty. At the same time, they held to traditional Anglican beliefs in liturgical worship and an ecclesiastical hierarchy. Based on printed and unprinted primary and secondary sources; 36 notes.
　　　　　　　　　　　　　　　　　　　J. A. Kicklighter

3867.　Stewart, Gordon.　SOCIO-ECONOMIC FACTORS IN THE GREAT AWAKENING: THE CASE OF YARMOUTH, NOVA SCOTIA. *Acadiensis [Canada] 1973 3(1): 18-34.* Discusses social and economic tensions of colonial society in Yarmouth, Nova Scotia, during the Great Awakening of the 1760's and 70's.

3868.　Thomas, C. E.　REV. WILLIAM TUTTY, M. A.: FIRST MISSIONARY TO THE ENGLISH IN NOVA SCOTIA. *Nova Scotia Hist. Soc. Collections [Canada] 1977 39: 169-186.* Examines Anglican missionary work in Halifax by William Tutty, 1752-78.

3869.　Unsigned.　A SHORT HISTORY OF THE SLOVAK CATHOLICS OF THE BYZANTINE PARISH OF THE ASSUMPTION OF THE B.V.M. *Jednota Ann. Furdek 1977 16: 207-209.* This Uniate parish in Hamilton, Ontario, was founded in 1952, and in 1963 the Shrine of Our Lady of Klocočov was dedicated there; Father Francis J. Fuga has been pastor since 1954.

Medicine and Public Health

3870.　Andrews, Margaret W.　EPIDEMIC AND PUBLIC HEALTH: INFLUENZA IN VANCOUVER, 1918-1919. *BC Studies [Canada] 1977 (34): 21-44.* The influenza pandemic during 1918-19 struck one-fourth of the world's population and was the greatest short term killer of any kind in human history. In Vancouver, British Columbia, the threat of a breakdown in delivery of crucial public health services and the high level of public concern temporarily weakened public confidence in public health authorities. As a whole, the epidemic experience was remarkably ephemeral and the long term trends of centralization, specialization, and bureaucratization of public health matters quickly resumed. Table, 6 graphs, 76 notes.
　　　　　　　　　　　　　　　　　　　　D. L. Smith

3871.　Andrews, Margaret W.　MEDICAL ATTENDANCE IN VANCOUVER, 1886-1920. *BC Studies [Canada] 1978-79 (40): 32-56.* Studies the medical attendance on patients in Vancouver, British Columbia, as a social process. A collective investigation of 332 doctors and an analysis of the daily records of an individual doctor reveal that the character of medical attendance, still prevailing in Vancouver, was established in the city's first 34 years: the services of an adequate supply of well-trained and well-paid doctors were usually delivered in the impersonal setting of their downtown offices; the patients came from a wide spectrum of ethnic, economic, and social backgrounds; and medical care for those patients who could not pay was subsidized by those who could afford to pay for it. 3 maps, 7 tables, 4 graphs, 55 notes.
　　　　　　　　　　　　　　　　　　　　D. L. Smith

3872.　Geoffrey, Bilson.　THE CHOLERA EPIDEMIC IN SAINT JOHN, N.B., 1854. *Acadiensis [Canada] 1974 4(1): 85-99.* When St. John experienced an outbreak of cholera in 1854, efforts to counter the epidemic or eradicate its causes were half-hearted and ineffectual. Uncertain what caused the disease, townspeople were unsure how to combat it, while local politicians avoided such potentially unpopular solutions as quarantining infested neighborhoods or introducing expensive cleanup programs. Realizing by fall that the disease was probably contagious, the city bought and overhauled the polluted water system, which eased political pressure. Based on provincial archives of New Brunswick, printed government documents, private papers, newspapers, printed secondary sources; 95 notes.
　　　　　　　　　　　　　　　　　　　E. A. Churchill

3873.　Lloyd, Sheila.　THE OTTAWA TYPHOID EPIDEMICS OF 1911 AND 1912: A CASE STUDY OF DISEASE AS A CATALYST FOR URBAN REFORM. *Urban Hist. Rev. [Canada] 1979 8(1): 66-89.* The typhoid fever epidemics created a strong movement in Ottawa for urban health improvements. Reforms were resisted by politicians and the business element on the basis of expense and a lack of clear understanding of typhoid. Some changes were made while the crisis was fresh; once the crisis was perceived to be past, little concern was manifested. Based on municipal and federal documents; 2 illus., 74 notes.

C. A. Watson

3874.   McGinnis, J. P. Dickin.   A CITY FACES AN EPIDEMIC. *Alberta Hist. [Canada] 1976 24(4): 1-11.* Examines the impact of the influenza epidemic of 1918-19 on Calgary. Dr. Cecil S. Mahood, city health officer, coordinated the programs, often leading to controversies regarding school closings and quarantine regulations. Calgary lacked doctors and nurses, many of whom were still in Europe with the armed forces. Based mostly on newspaper accounts; 4 illus., 27 notes.

D. Chaput

The Physical City

3875.   Armstrong, Christopher and Nelles, H. V.   GETTING YOUR WAY IN NOVA SCOTIA: "TWEAKING" HALIFAX, 1907-1917. *Acadiensis [Canada] 1976 5(2): 105-131.* During 1909-17 Montreal-dominated interests incorporated a company in Nova Scotia to develop and distribute hydroelectric power. The syndicate then obtained control of the Halifax street railway. A new charter exempting the company from the jurisdiction of the Public Utilities Commission enabled the syndicate to issue watered stock. The syndicate then effected a merger and recapitalization, ensuring itself of large profits. It retained high electricity rates and tram fares, and neglected to develop promised hydroelectric power. 104 notes.

D. F. Chard

3876.   Armstrong, Frederick H. and Phelps, Edward C. H.   IN ALMOST PERPETUAL CIRCLES: URBAN PRESERVATION AND THE MUNICIPAL ADVISORY COMMITTEE IN LONDON, ONTARIO. *Urban Hist. Rev. [Canada] 1977 (2): 10-19.* The authors, members of the committee concerned with the urban architectural heritage of London, Ontario, describe the antecedents of a coalition of groups and individuals in the early 1970's to preserve London's architecture. Over protests, the Mutual Advisory Committee pressured the city administration to recognize preservation when dealing with city planning and development. Using their experiences as an example, they urged preservation groups to: 1) list buildings deserving of preservation, 2) have the municipality obtain the legal power to designate buildings and areas, and 3) have the city appoint an official committee.

C. A. Watson

3877.   Bernier, Jacques.   LA CONSTRUCTION DOMICILAIRE À QUÉBEC 1810-1820 [House construction in Quebec 1810-20]. *Rev. d'Hist. de l'Amérique Française [Canada] 1978 31(4): 547-561.* Examines domestic building contracts in Quebec during a period of sustained population growth. Details the geographical and architectural development of the city. Contracts, for example, reveal type, size, and location of house, name of builder, mode of payment, etc. These documents provide little information on the daily life of the construction worker, but are a valuable source of information in their own right. 12 notes.

M. R. Yerburgh

3878.   Beszedits, S.   TORONTO'S 19TH CENTURY ARCHITECTS. *Can. Geographic [Canada] 1978-79 97(3): 52-59.* Discusses architects John G. Howard, Henry B. Lane, William Thomas, F. W. Cumberland, and W. G. Storm.

3879.   Bloomfield, G. T.   MIRABEL, A GREAT AIRPORT WANTING TRAFFIC. *Can. Geographic [Canada] 1979 98(3): 8-15.* Chronicles the planning and construction of Mirabel International Airport outside of Montreal, Quebec, 1969-78.

3880.   Bohi, Charles W. and Grant, H. Roger.   THE STANDARDIZED RAILROAD STATION IN SASKATCHEWAN: THE CASE OF THE CANADIAN PACIFIC. *Saskatchewan Hist. [Canada] 1978 31(3): 81-96.* The railway depot was very much a part of the economic and social life of the communities through which the railroads passed. This was especially true for the Canadian Pacific Railway towns because so many were founded by the company. Because its lines were older and later had to develop different styles of architecture to compete with the

Canadian National Lines, a large number of styles are characteristic of the CP stations. Map, 17 photos, 10 notes.   C. H. Held

3881.   Buggey, Susan.   HALIFAX WATERFRONT BUILDINGS: AN HISTORICAL REPORT. *Can. Historic Sites 1975 (9): 119-168.* The study attempts to explain and document the historical role and associations of a complex of 19th-century Halifax waterfront buildings. It undertakes as well to distinguish their architectural features and structural alterations.

J

3882.   Cain, Louis P.   WATER AND SANITATION SERVICES IN VANCOUVER: AN HISTORICAL PERSPECTIVE. *BC Studies [Canada] 1976 (30): 27-43.* Traces the origin and development of the water supply, sewage-disposal and drainage practices of Vancouver, British Columbia. The evolution of these strategies have been analogous to those of other salt-water cities. Its relative youth enabled Vancouver to benefit from the mistakes of other cities and to adopt the best modern practices. 30 notes.

D. L. Smith

3883.   Charles, Réjane.   CHOIX D'UTILISATION DU SOL À TRAVERS LE ZONAGE: ÉVALUATION ET ÉVOLUTION DANS TROIS VILLES DE LA RIVE-SUD DE MONTRÉAL   [Land-use choice through zoning: appraisal and evolution in three Montreal South Shore cities]. *Cahiers de Géographie du Québec [Canada] 1978 22(57): 350-376.* Analyzes types of land-use groupings that have been maintained through zoning by-laws amendments between 1965 and 1973 in Boucherville, Brossard, and Longueuil.

3884.   Collins, Lewis W.   LOYAL SUBJECTS, ABLE ARTISTS AND HONEST MEN. *Nova Scotia Hist. Q. 1973 3(3): 225-244.* Presents a commentary on the growth of the profession of architecture in Halifax, 1749-1973.

3885.   Davis, Donald F.   MASS TRANSIT AND PRIVATE OWNERSHIP: AN ALTERNATIVE PERSPECTIVE ON THE CASE OF TORONTO. *Urban Hist. Rev. [Canada] 1979 (3): 60-98.* Toronto's mass transit system's good reputation over the past 30 years is partly a result of its essentially accidental maintenance of the streetcar system: when such a mode of transportation was out of favor, Toronto had too large an investment in rolling stock to scrap it. Another reason for the high reputation is that the privately owned Toronto Railway Company (TRC) (1891-1921) tried to maximize profits by keeping Toronto compact and the transit system small to avoid overexpansion; the TRC also had a monopoly, thus it avoided the bankrupting competition that occurred in US cities. The result was 1) intensive use of mass transit; 2) retardation of suburban growth; 3) the city government's own street railway system outside the TRC-served area resulted in a double-fare system forcing the suburban middle class to pay a fairer share of transportation cost without being subsidized by inner city residents. The publicly owned Toronto Transportation Commission (TTC) took it over in 1921 and was successful principally because of the TRC's policies. Since 1953 the TTC has had increasing problems. Primary and secondary sources; 3 tables, 54 notes.

C. A. Watson

3886.   Doucet, Michael J.   MASS TRANSIT AND THE FAILURE OF PRIVATE OWNERSHIP: THE CASE OF TORONTO IN THE EARLY TWENTIETH CENTURY. *Urban Hist. Rev. [Canada] 1978 (3): 3-33.* Discusses the trials and tribulations of Torontonians and the street railway system during its most important period of development. The first franchise to a private company expired in 1891 at which time Toronto, not yet ready for public ownership, gave the next 30 year franchise to the private Toronto Railway Company. The subsequent clash of interests—the TRC efforts to make profits and the city administration and civic groups' efforts to get the TRC to provide better service—led to the municipal takeover of the street railway system in 1921 as a public utility. Primary and secondary sources; 3 tables, 3 fig., 70 notes.

C. A. Watson

3887.   Fear, Jon.   "THE LUMBER PILES MUST GO": OTTAWA'S LUMBER INTERESTS AND THE GREAT FIRE OF 1900. *Urban Hist. Rev. [Canada] 1979 8(1): 38-65.* The great Ottawa fire of April 1900 created a difficult situation for the city: how to balance the need for storage space for lumber and cheap, wooden homes for the working class with the need for general public safety. The lumber interests, led by local lumber king John Rudolphus Booth (1826-1925), managed to create a political deadlock which led to no changes being made. Based on newspapers; 2 maps, photo, 83 notes.   C. A. Watson

3888. Ferguson, Ted. ERIC HARVIE'S LEGACY REVIVES ALBERTA TOWNS: SCORES OF THEM WAKE UP AND SMARTEN UP. *Can. Geographic [Canada] 1979 99(1): 60-63.* The Devonian Group of Charitable Foundations, a philanthropy set up and funded by Eric Lafferty Harvie (1892-1975), provides money for towns in Alberta to sponsor projects in historic preservation, creation of public parks, and scientific research; 1955-79.

3889. Fergusson, C. Bruce. HALIFAX HAS A WINNER: HISTORIC PROPERTIES. *Can. Geographic [Canada] 1978 97(2): 34-39.* Halifax Historic Properties, a group of seven historic buildings, dating 1825-1905, were renovated and restored, providing an authentic representation of wharf and waterfront life for tourists.

3890. Fraser, Don. WINNIPEG'S POST OFFICES. *Manitoba Pageant [Canada] 1974 19(3): 12-15.* Discusses, with physical descriptions, the evolution of Winnipeg's post office buildings from 1855 to the present. 5 illus.   D. M. Dean

3891. Holmgren, Eric J. EDMONTON'S REMARKABLE HIGH LEVEL BRIDGE. *Alberta Hist. [Canada] 1978 26(1): 1-9.* In 1891, the Calgary and Edmonton Railway reached north to the North Saskatchewan River; across the river was Edmonton, still without any rail connection to the south. Construction of a high-level bridge was begun in 1910, and the bridge first saw service on 2 June 1913. Discusses bridge-building, as well as motives of competing railway lines, attitudes of citizens of Edmonton, and workings of the city council and other city agencies, who had conflicting views about the bridge's location. Based on newspapers and legal documents; 4 illus.   D. Chaput

3892. Kilbourn, William. THE NEW TORONTO: A GREAT MODERN CITY. *Can. Geographical J. [Canada] 1978 96(2): 10-19.* Discusses city planning which has aided in the controlled growth and beautification of Toronto, Ontario; examines shopping facilities, business districts, architectural standards, historic renovation, and transportation systems, 1970's.

3893. Klassen, Henry C. BICYCLES AND AUTOMOBILES IN EARLY CALGARY. *Alberta Hist. [Canada] 1976 24(2): 1-8.* The bicycle and automobile as modes of transportation in Calgary developed in a similar fashion to other North American cities, though the impact of the bicycle was slightly less in Calgary because of the cost. Examines impact of the bicycle and automobile on social habits, law, economy, and general community life. Impact on the livery stables was particularly harsh. 5 illus.   D. Chaput

3894. Lafrance, Marc. ÉVOLUTION PHYSIQUE ET POLITIQUES URBAINES: QUÉBEC SOUS LE RÉGIME FRANÇAIS [Physical evolution and urban policies: Quebec under the French]. *Urban Hist. [Canada] 1975 (3): 3-22.* Quebec, capital of New France, grew rapidly in the century and a half between its founding and the British conquest; the French authorities did their best to plan this development according to the city planning ideas of the day.

3895. Lucas, Richard. THE CONFLICT OVER PUBLIC POWER IN HAMILTON, ONTARIO, 1906-1914. *Ontario Hist. [Canada] 1976 68(4): 236-246.* Analyzes the attitudes in Hamilton to public power in the years between the formation of Ontario Hydro and the coming of Ontario Hydro power to the city. Hamilton's private power company provided cheap power to industrial users, but not to private consumers. Analyzes divisions within the Hamilton public, the influence of the power company, various pressure groups, the "blocs" on city council, etc. 41 notes.   W. B. Whitham

3896. Lutman, John H. CONDUCTING URBAN HERITAGE SURVEYS: A CASE STUDY OF LONDON, ONTARIO. *Urban Hist. Rev. [Canada] 1977 (1): 46-54.* The Heritage Act (Ontario, 1975) empowered provincial municipalities to set up a Local Architectural Conservation Advisory Committee to recommend to its city council the designation of buildings having architectural or historical value. The

author describes the organization and procedures used by the city of London in surveying that city under the terms of the Heritage Act, in the hopes of providing a model for other cities doing the same.
                                    C. A. Watson

3897. MacDonald, Norbert. THE CANADIAN PACIFIC RAILWAY AND VANCOUVER'S DEVELOPMENT TO 1900. *BC Studies [Canada] 1977 (35): 3-35.* The Canadian Pacific Railway played a critical role in shaping the overall development of Vancouver, British Columbia, in the 19th century, especially in the late 1880's and early 1890's. Its impact was clearly evident in the city's waterfront area, residential districts, street layout, parks, real estate prices, economy, politics, and social clubs. The CPR boom ended with the depression of 1893. When Vancouver began to recover with the Klondike gold rush in the late 1890's the CPR still played an important role, but the "utter dependence" of former years was over. 4 maps, 3 tables, 81 notes.
                                    D. L. Smith

3898. MacKenzie, Robert C. PRAIRIE ELEVATORS "GO TO TOWN." *Can. Geographic [Canada] 1979 98(1): 52-57.* Though originally sprinkled throughout rural agricultural Canada, grain elevators, due to rural depopulation, use of trucks, improved roads, and railroad shipping, are disappearing from the rural landscape and reappearing in urban centers; covers 1930's-70's.

3899. Major, Marjorie. THE GREAT PONTACK INN. *Nova Scotia Hist. Q. 1973 3(3): 171-190.* Presents a history of the Great Pontack Inn, one of the waterfront inns in Halifax, 1754-1837.

3900. McKee, William C. THE VANCOUVER PARK SYSTEM, 1886-1929: A PRODUCT OF LOCAL BUSINESSMEN. *Urban Hist. Rev. [Canada] 1979 (3): 33-49.* Businessmen dominated the parks committees in early Vancouver, British Columbia. They looked on parks and green areas not primarily for their contribution to the quality of life or the good of the neighborhood but for what the parks could provide in a material way (attract tourists, improve property values, attract settlers and therefore customers) or political benefits (votes for local politicians claiming credit for a local park). The park system was not planned or coordinated but was a collection of scattered parks unfairly distributed, particularly away from the poorer sections with less political power. Primary and secondary sources; 2 maps, 17 notes.   C. A. Watson

3901. Moon, Robert. RESTORING 17TH CENTURY LOWER TOWN QUEBEC. *Can. Geographical J. 1975 91(3): 38-45.* Describes the historic restoration of 17th-century buildings in Lower Town Place Royale, Quebec.   S

3902. Newinger, Scott. THE STREET CARS OF CALGARY. *Alberta Hist. Rev. [Canada] 1974 22(3): 8-12.*

3903. Nobert, Yves. LES CHANGEMENTS DE LA PROPRIÉTÉ FONCIÉRE DANS LA FRANGE URBAINE DE TROIS-RIVIÈRES, 1964-1974 [Changes in property values on the urban fringe of Three Rivers, Quebec]. *Cahiers de Géographie du Québec [Canada] 1978 22(55): 51-72.* Studys the urban land market near transportation routes as a key to understanding urban pressures.

3904. O'Malley, Martin. HOW ONTARIO SUPPLIES WINNIPEG'S WATER. *Can. Geographical J. 1975 91(3): 28-31.* History (1912-75) of the aqueduct flowing from Ontario's Lake of the Woods to Winnipeg to supply the city with water.   S

3905. Pearce, William. RESERVATION OF LAND AT CALGARY. *Alberta Hist. [Canada] 1979 27(2): 22-28.* William Pearce, a government surveyor, arrived in Calgary in late 1883 to set aside lands and to aid in approving squatters' claims. He worked closely with the Mounted Police and other authorities. There were some quarrels with Mètis, church authorities, and citizens. In a few years, most claims were approved, considerable land was set aside for education, churches, parks, and hospitals. Based on Pearce's account in the Glenbow Archives; map, photo.   D. Chaput

3906. Phillips, Doris. NOVA SCOTIA'S AID FOR THE SUFFERERS OF THE GREAT SAINT JOHN FIRE (JUNE 20TH, 1877).

Nova Scotia Hist. Q. [Canada] 1977 7(4): 351-366. Saint John, New Brunswick, was virtually demolished by a fire which started in bales of hay in a warehouse. The 20 June 1877 fire was the 16th recorded fire in the city and the worst in its history. It burned out of control for nine hours despite efforts to contain it. The conflagration reduced two-fifths of the city to ashes and left 20,000 homeless. Food, tents, clothing, and donations of money came from all over Canada, the United States, and Great Britain; but the disaster relief from other cities in Nova Scotia was particularly appreciated by Saint John's residents. 2 notes, biblio.
H. M. Evans

3907. Rees, Ronald. CHANGING ST. JOHN: THE OLD AND THE NEW. *Can. Geographical J. 1975 90(5): 12-17.* Largely rebuilt after the 1877 fire, St. John, New Brunswick, comprises a variety of mid-Victorian architecture, now endangered by unprecedented industrial expansion.
S

3908. Rostecki, Randy R. THE EARLY HISTORY OF THE CAU-CHON BLOCK, LATER THE EMPIRE HOTEL. *Manitoba Pageant [Canada] 1976 21(3): 10-17.* Lieutenant-Governor Cauchon purchased the land in Winnipeg in late 1880, and the building opened in February 1883. It is one of only a few cast iron-fronted buildings ever built in Canada. Expected rental income did not materialize, and in 1884 the firm of Dunn and Price converted the building into apartments. In 1904 the building was converted into the Empire Hotel. Based on primary and secondary sources; illus., 54 notes.
B. J. LaBue

3909. Rostecki, R. R. SOME OLD WINNIPEG BUILDINGS. *Tr. of the Hist. and Sci. Soc. of Manitoba [Canada] 1972-73 Series 3(29): 5-22.* A chronological coverage "of some of the treasures to be found among Winnipeg's old buildings." Thirty-five buildings are described and historical sketches of each one presented. Based on printed and manuscript sources; 17 notes, biblio.
J. A. Casada

3910. Roy, Patricia. THE ILLUMINATION OF VICTORIA: LATE NINETEENTH-CENTURY TECHNOLOGY AND MUNICI-PAL ENTERPRISE. *BC Studies [Canada] 1976-77 (32): 79-92.* Following considerable debate about monopoly privileges and prices, the privately owned Victoria Gas Company was incorporated in 1863. It did not get a street lighting contract for another decade. Hostility to the policies and services of the gas company and Victoria's growth and ambition to remain the leading Canadian Pacific Coast city made Victorians receptive to a new lighting medium, electricity. By the mid-1890's Victoria had adopted electricity and made it a municipal enterprise. 32 notes.
D. L. Smith

3911. Russell, Hilary. ALL THAT GLITTERS: A MEMORIAL TO OTTAWA'S CAPITOL THEATRE AND ITS PREDECESSORS. *Can. Historic Sites 1975 (13): 5-125.* This paper is one result of the 1970 destruction of Ottawa's Capitol Theatre, a movie palace built in 1920. Movie palaces were those gigantic, extravagantly embellished theatres built between about 1914 and 1932 in which vaudeville and motion picture entertainment was presented. One movie palace, the Capitol in Ottawa, is examined in terms of its construction, decoration, equipment and ownership. The investigation includes a general discussion of the movie palace phenomenon and the major developments in the evolution of motion picture exhibition that contributed to the building of movie palaces. Certain American prototypes are considered, as many Canadian palaces were built by American-controlled theatre circuits, designed by American architects, and exhibited American movies.
J

3912. Séguin, Robert-Lionel. LE RABOT DANS LA RÉGION MONTRÉALAISE [The plane in the Montreal region]. *Rev. d'Hist. de l'Amérique Française [Canada] 1960 14(3): 378-383.* Describes nine types of planes used in construction in Montreal in the 17th century.

3913. Selwood, H. John. URBAN DEVELOPMENT AND THE STREETCAR: THE CASE OF WINNIPEG, 1881-1913. *Urban Hist. Rev. [Canada] 1978 (3): 34-41.* Traces the growth of the streetcar system in Winnipeg through a series of four maps, and concludes that the streetcar system was shaped by the developing city and not vice versa. Primary and secondary sources; 4 maps, 13 notes.
C. A. Watson

3914. Selwood, H. John and Baril, Evelyn. LAND POLICIES OF THE HUDSON'S BAY COMPANY AT UPPER FORT GARRY: 1869-1879. *Prairie Forum [Canada] 1977 2(2): 101-119.* Though precise plans were drafted for the layout of Hudson's Bay Company lands surrounding Upper Fort Garry (now Selkirk, Manitoba), tradition, environmental factors, and politics caused much compromise in the original city planning, 1869-79.

3915. Thouez, Jean-Pierre. L'UTILISATION DES CARTES HIS-TORIQUES DANS L'ANALYSE DE L'EVOLUTION DES SOLS EN MILIEU URBAIN: LE CAS DE SHERBROOKE, 1863-1951 [The use of historical maps in analyzing the evolution of land use in an urban setting: the case of Sherbrooke, 1863-1951]. *Urban Hist. Rev. [Canada] 1979 (3): 50-59.* Shows how maps from various stages of a city's growth can be used to reconstitute the progress of land occupation. Use of original maps enables one to describe the larger changes in the urban landscape and gives a basis for evaluating present and future tendencies. 3 maps, 2 tables, 2 graphs, 3 notes.
C. A. Watson

3916. Tolson, Elsie Churchill. FIRST TWO YEARS OF THE BED-FORD FIRE DEPARTMENT. *Nova Scotia Hist. Q. [Canada] 1976 6(3): 311-316.* Discusses the organization, funding, and establishment of the Fire Department in Bedford, Nova Scotia, 1921-22.

3917. VanNus, Walter. THE FATE OF CITY BEAUTIFUL THOUGHT IN CANADA, 1893-1930. *Can. Hist. Assoc. Hist. Papers [Canada] 1975: 191-210.* After the Chicago World's Fair in 1893, city planners called for curved streets, parks, parkways and civic centers in order to make cities beautiful. Advocates of better workers' housing called for suburbs in the name of health and humanity. By the 1920's, city planning meant the efficient provision of suburban housing. Therefore, orderliness from efficient zoning was all that was left of a city beautiful movement that became identified with the irresponsible use of public money. Based on government reports, proceedings of architectural associations, and secondary sources; 98 notes.
G. E. Panting

3918. van Nus, Walter. SOURCES FOR THE HISTORY OF UR-BAN PLANNING IN CANADA, 1890-1939. *Urban Hist. Rev. [Canada] 1976 76(1): 6-9.* Surveys urban planning in Canada since 1912. Reviews the sources for the history of urban planning, listing the journals and most important city planning reports of the period. Urges further historical study of urban planning and suggests possible research topics, particularly case studies of individual cities. 11 notes.
C. A. Watson

3919. White, C. O. THE HUMBOLDT MUNICIPAL ELEC-TRICAL UTILITY: A GRASSROOTS FEATURE OF THE SAS-KATCHEWAN POWER CORPORATION. *Saskatchewan Hist. [Canada] 1976 29(3): 103-113.* The electrical utility at Humboldt deserves attention because it became the first unit of the provincial electrical system on 1 November 1929, having been a small municipal system since 1907. Financial and operational problems occurred almost from the beginning, and the necessity of joining a larger system climaxed early in 1929. The choice of whether to sell out to the private Dominion Electric or join the new and untried Saskatchewan Power Corporation was finally decided in the latter's favor due to the work of such prominent local leaders as Frank H. Bence, Charles Cutting, Dr. Harry Fleming, Robert Telfer, and Father Dominic Hoffman. 58 notes.
C. Held

3920. Whitely, Albert S. COMMUNICATIONS ON THE LOWER NORTH SHORE. *Can. Geographical J. [Canada] 1977 95(1): 42-47.* Discusses the communications difficulties of the towns and remote hamlets located along the St. Lawrence Seaway's Lower North Shore during the winter months, 1850's-1950's.

Attitudes toward Urban Life and the City

3921. Jones, David C. "WE CANNOT ALLOW IT TO BE RUN BY THOSE WHO DO NOT UNDERSTAND EDUCATION": AGRICULTURAL SCHOOLING IN THE TWENTIES. *BC Studies [Canada] 1978 (39): 30-60.* Federal and provincial efforts endeavored to stem the tide toward Canadian urbanization in the 1920's with its "flight from the countryside." John Wesley Gibson was the architect and director of the program in British Columbia. Predicated on the idea that education was the best vehicle, he sought to bring the schools and communities together in their programs. Examines, in particular, the educational efforts and promotion of livestock production. The quotation in the title was made by J. C. Readey, a district supervisor of agricultural education who was afraid a local school fair might be run by administrators rather than educators. Table, 119 notes.   D. L. Smith

3922. Melnyk, George. WINNIPEG REVISITED: NOTES OF AN IMMIGRANT SON. *Can. Dimension [Canada] 1977 12(4-5): 31, 34-35.* The author discusses his impressions of Winnipeg, Manitoba; he moved there as an immigrant in 1949.

3923. Waterston, Elizabeth. HOWELLS AND THE CITY OF QUEBEC. *Can. Rev. of Am. Studies [Canada] 1978 9(2): 155-167.* Travel accounts, a flourishing literary genre of the 1800's, often covered Quebec. But accounts by Americans differed from the writings of others, because American men-of-letters mostly were impressed by Quebec's rich imperial heritage and monuments of past wars, its Catholic cultural milieu, and its quaint preindustrial setting. In *Their Wedding Journey* (1871) and *A Chance Acquaintance* (1872), William Dean Howells (1837-1920) pictured Quebec as charming for the same reasons as did other Americans. However, Howells preferred the "rawer countryside" surrounding that "antique city." Based on Howells's writings; 4 photos, 9 notes.   H. T. Lovin

4. AMERICAN INDIAN URBAN SETTLEMENTS

3924. Clarke, Steven K. A METHOD FOR THE ESTIMATION OF PREHISTORIC PUEBLO POPULATIONS. *Kiva 1974 39(3/4): 283-287.* A method for estimating the population of prehistoric pueblos is presented in the form of an equation (population equals one-third floor area in square meters) arrived at by means of extrapolating specific Pueblo ethnographic data to specific archaeological data. J

3925. Ebert, James I. and Hitchcock, Robert K. CHACO CANYON'S MYSTERIOUS HIGHWAYS. *Horizon 1975 17(4): 48-53.* Excavations in the Chaco Canyon area of New Mexico reveal multiple civilizations, including the Anasazi, who settled there from prehistoric times to 1250.

3926. Fliedner, Dietrich. PRE-SPANISH PUEBLOS IN NEW MEXICO. *Ann. of the Assoc. of Am. Geographers 1975 65(3): 363-377.* Discusses the social organization and other aspects of Indian pueblos in the Jemez Mountains, 1300-1600. S

3927. Grebinger, Paul. PREHISTORIC SOCIAL ORGANIZA-TION IN CHACO CANYON, NEW MEXICO: AN ALTERNATIVE RECONSTRUCTION. *Kiva 1973 39(1): 3-23.* It has been proposed that the social organization of the occupants of two different types of sites in Chaco Canyon, New Mexico was different. Residents of "villages" were organized according to a principle of localized corporate lineages, while residents of "towns" were organized according to a principle of dual division. As an alternative, proposes that a rank society developed under nearly pristine conditions from 850 to 1130. The basis for the rank society was differential agricultural productivity. Some local groups that were favored by a fortuitous combination of summer thundershowers and natural catchment systems became the nucleus of the "towns." Their rights through prior use to the abundant harvests of the favored zones were the basis for the emergence of status differentiation, redistribution and ultimately craft and task specialization. Water control systems developed only after the principles of the rank society had become established and probably in response to a combination of increasing population and increasingly heavy summer thundershowers. J

3928. Ivers, Louise Harris. EARLY PHOTOGRAPHS OF INDIAN PUEBLOS IN NEW MEXICO. *Masterkey 1977 51(3): 85-100.* Discusses photographers of the 19th century who, for scientific and ethnological purposes, set out to photograph the Pueblo Indians of the Southwest.

3929. Johnston, Patricia Condon. GUSTAF NORDENSKIOLD AND THE TREASURE OF THE MESA VERDE. *Am. West 1979 16(4): 34-43.* Gustaf Nordenskiold (1868-95), a young Swede, conducted the first scientific investigation of the Mesa Verde of Colorado in 1891. He incorporated his voluminous notes into *The Cliff Dwellers of the Mesa Verde,* published in 1893, and thereby set significant standards for American archaeological investigation and documentation. His representative collection of several hundred artifacts is housed in the National Museum of Finland. Mesa Verde was later set aside as a national park. 5 illus., note, biblio. D. L. Smith

3930. Kirk, Ruth and Daugherty, Richard D. A "POMPEII" BY THE NORTHWEST SEA. *Am. West 1974 11(2): 26-37.* Describes the excavation and finds of an abandoned Makah Indian village at Ozette on Washington's Olympic Peninsula. The archaeological site was occupied for perhaps 4,000 years. Pompeii-like mud slides which covered houses have saved a great variety of well-preserved material that reveals the intricacy of life of the Northwest whale hunters who practiced a high level of artistry and ritual. One 70 by 40 foot size house, occupied by 20 to 40 people, has yielded more than 20,000 artifacts. Ozette is the first archaeological discovery to show a full range of items of a pre-Columbian household. The excavation, begun in 1966, will take several more years. Based on a forthcoming book; 12 illus. D. L. Smith

3931. Morris, Don P. ARCHITECTURAL DEVELOPMENT AND MASONRY STYLE AT ANTELOPE HOUSE. *Kiva 1975 41(1): 33-37.* The developmental sequence of the Pueblo III architecture at Antelope House is described, and is related to different behavioral chains. These differing behavioral chains may indicate different, contemporaneous social units at the site. J

3932. Olguin, John Philip and Olguin, Mary T. ISLETA: THE PUE-BLO THAT ROARED. *Indian Hist. 1976 9(4): 2-13.* The Isleta Pueblo in central New Mexico is a community that has existed for hundreds of years. Since the Spanish conquest it has been nominally Catholic and many priests have served there. In the 1960's an unpopular priest was assigned there, and his attempts to end the tribal practices associated with the Church were disliked. After enduring his dictatorial methods for several years, the tribal council requested his removal. When this failed, they actually drove him out of the Pueblo. E. D. Johnson

3933. Pfeiffer, John. AMERICA'S FIRST CITY. *Horizon 1974 16(2): 58-63.* Cahokia: a Mississippi Valley Indian metropolis. S

3934. Smith, Dean. CLIFF DWELLERS OF THE MESA VERDE. *Am. Hist. Illus. 1977 12(6): 4-9, 43-45.* Richard Wetherill in December 1888 discovered, in southwestern Colorado, the largest cliff dwelling known to man. A Swedish archaeologist made the first excavation there in 1891. Most visitors were looters until Congress created the 52,073-acre Mesa Verde National Park in 1906. Since then hundreds of researchers, representing at least 30 disciplines, have examined dozens of cliff cities of the Anasazi culture. The early Pueblos, known as "Basket makers," apparently settled the Mesa Verde about the time of the birth of Christ. They lived in the cliff caves and began substantial homes there about 450 A.D. The dwellings were abandoned in the late 13th century (a drought, 1276-1300, apparently was the final blow). Many mysteries remain about the reasons for settlement, abandonment, structures, and the people. 9 illus. D. Dodd

3935. Soule, Edwin C. LOST CITY II. *Masterkey 1976 50(1): 10-18.* Discusses a 1975 archeological expedition to the Lost City in the Moapa Valley of Nevada and the Indian artifacts (ca. 530) uncovered there.

3936. Soule, Edwin C. LOST CITY REVISITED. *Masterkey 1975 49(1): 4-19.* Examines an Anasazi culture village site in Nevada. S

5. HISTORIOGRAPHY, METHODOLOGY, BIBLIOGRAPHY, TEACHING

3937. Adam, Andreas. URBAN HISTORIES: 3 FOR 25 CENTS. *Hist. Preservation 1977 29(3): 28-31.* "Every picture postcard that depicts a cityscape shows one stage in a historical process. A comparison of postcards from different times can provide clues to a city's history." US postcards were first produced in 1882 and proliferated after the 1893 World's Columbian Exposition. Discusses New York City and Chicago examples. Reproduces 7 postcards. R. M. Frame III

3938. Baldwin, Doug. PRIMARY SOURCE MATERIALS FOR THE HISTORY OF NORTHERN ONTARIO MINING TOWNS: THE CASE OF COBALT, ONTARIO. *Urban Hist. Rev. [Canada] 1978 (3): 80-85.* Details the types of sources available for historical research in Cobalt, Ontario, a northern mining town. Urges investigation in similar towns before the early records are destroyed by fire, rot, or neglect. 2 illus., 3 notes. C. A. Watson

3939. Bell, Gwen. PERIODICAL LITERATURE ON HUMAN SETTLEMENTS: EVALUATION AND RECOMMENDATIONS. *J. of the Am. Inst. of Planners 1977 43(2): 178-182.* In a survey of over 15,000 citations from articles in major urban planning journals between 1965 and 1975, more than 1,500 journals were cited. This indicates the wide range of sources used by urban planners. Yet most authors draw on only a limited number: the *Journal of the American Institute of Planners* is the most frequently cited with 10% of the citations; and the top 100 journals account for more than 80% of the citations. J

3940. Blumin, Stuart M. "THE NEW URBAN HISTORY" UPDATED. *Rev. in Am. Hist. 1975 3(3): 293-299.* Asking what is new about the new urban history and "where is the study of the urban past heading," reviews *The New Urban History: Quantitative Explorations by American Historians* (Princeton, N.J.: Princeton U. Pr., 1975) edited by Leo F. Schnore; outlines the book's content, analyzes the book within the context of urban historiography, and discusses the various methodologies used by contributors to the book.

3941. Bourne, L. S. THE CENTRE FOR URBAN AND COMMUNITY STUDIES. *Urban Hist. Rev. [Canada] 1978 78(2): 100-104.* Describes the research themes and the objectives of the Centre for Urban and Community Studies, University of Toronto, and suggests ways in which urban historians can utilize it. Urban history and urban studies can both benefit by such interdisciplinary links. C. A. Watson

3942. Brown, Richard E. DOING THE HISTORY OF A COMMUNITY: PROJECT ADVENTURE. *New England Social Studies Bull. 1976-77 34(2): 3-18.* Examines the Hamilton, Massachusetts, Hamilton-Wenham Regional high school educational project, Project Adventure, 1977, which attempted to record the town's history. Outlines class structure and administration of surveys.

3943. Brownell, Blaine A. URBAN THEMES IN THE AMERICAN SOUTH. *J. of Urban Hist. 1976 2(2): 139-145.* The journal's southern cities have been the orphans of American urban history. This neglect leads to an unbalanced view of the urban history and metropolitan growth of the United States by picturing the northeastern experience as typical of the nation. 7 notes. T. W. Smith

3944. Brownell, Blaine A. THE METROPOLIS AND THE MUSE: THE HUMANIST PERSPECTIVE IN URBAN STUDIES. *Southern Humanities Rev. 1975 9(3): 289-298.* Examines urban studies from a humanistic approach, taking into account the fragmentation of knowledge currently exhibited in most higher education institutions, the relationship between theory and practice, new methodologies, and the constant problems posed by subjectivity and objectivity.

3945. Brubaker, Robert L. THE DEVELOPMENT OF AN URBAN HISTORY RESEARCH CENTER: THE CHICAGO HISTORICAL SOCIETY'S LIBRARY. *Chicago Hist. 1978 7(1): 22-36.* Discusses the founding and aims of the Chicago Historical Society's research library over the past 120 years.

3946. Bush, Robert D. and Touchstone, Blake. A SURVEY OF MANUSCRIPT HOLDINGS IN THE HISTORIC NEW ORLEANS COLLECTION. *Louisiana Hist. 1975 16(1): 89-96.* Describes the principal manuscript holdings of the Historic New Orleans Collection, which includes many items of interest for New Orleans and Louisiana history from the colonial period to 1966. Especially notable holdings are 11 Spanish land grants and other Spanish colonial documents (particularly for the administration of Bernardo de Gálvez), numerous financial records of the early 19th century, records relating to slavery and the Civil War, papers relating to late 19th-century industrial expansion, and the papers of New Orleans composer and pianist Louis M. Gottschalk. Photo. R. L. Woodward, Jr.

3947. Carpenter, Inta Gale. COORDINATING AN URBAN TEAM PROJECT. *Indiana Folklore 1977 10(2): 107-112.* Relates problems encountered in directing a folklore project through Indiana University, 1976, including aspects of organization, project assignation, university bureaucracy, equipment acquisition, and collection, compilation, and interpretation of data.

3948. Casterline, Gail Ferr. HISTORIANS AT THE DRAWING BOARD: ORGANIZING *CHICAGO: CREATING NEW TRADITIONS. Chicago Hist. 1977 6(3): 130-142.* Discusses the collection, coordination, and presentation of an exhibition of Chicagoana by the Chicago Historical Society; exhibition includes Chicago architecture, merchandising, urban planning, reform, culture, and literature, 1860's-1970's.

3949. Clark, Stephen. GABRIEL FURMAN: BROOKLYN'S FIRST HISTORIAN. *J. of Long Island Hist. 1974 10(2): 21-32.* Discusses the life and writings of Gabriel Furman, (1800-54), lawyer and historian. S

3950. Conzen, Kathleen Neils. APPROACHES TO EARLY MILWAUKEE COMMUNITY HISTORY. *Milwaukee Hist. 1978 1(1-2): 4-12.* Several approaches to the early history of Milwaukee use earlier means of documenting community history—to explore such areas as family structure, social mobility, and prestige.

3951. Cortinovis, Irene E. DOCUMENTING AN EVENT WITH MANUSCRIPTS AND ORAL HISTORY, THE ST. LOUIS TEACHERS' STRIKE, 1973. *Oral Hist. Rev. 1974: 59-63.* Describes methodology of making oral history tapes of a specific event, the St. Louis Teachers' Strike of 1973, for use in the class "The Politics of Education" at the University of Missouri-St. Louis. 8 notes. D. A. Yanchisin

3952. Cox, Richard J. THE PLIGHT OF AMERICAN MUNICIPAL ARCHIVES: BALTIMORE, 1729-1979. *Am. Archivist 1979 42(3): 281-292.* Minimal care was given the Baltimore city archives until 1874 when they became one of several responsibilities of the city librarian. From 1874 to 1927, the attention the archives received depended largely upon the interests of each librarian and his ability to secure support from municipal officials. From 1927 to 1978, under the Bureau of Archives, the archives "disintegrated into a morass through mishandling and lack of direction." With the hiring of a professional archivist in 1978 and the strengthening of archival legislation the outlook for the Baltimore city archives is positive. 4 fig., 61 notes. G.-A. Patzwald

3953. Cox, Richard J. and Vanorny, Patricia M. THE RECORDS OF A CITY: BALTIMORE AND ITS HISTORICAL SOURCES. *Maryland Hist. Mag. 1975 70(3): 286-310.* The "slow appreciation of the significance of urban history" is reflected in the lack of care and attention paid to preserving Baltimore's historical documents. Despite progress earlier in this century, the historian of Baltimore today faces the same disorganization as 100 years ago, and still no separate records building with modern research and storage facilities has been erected. Provides a lengthy checklist, divided into private papers and public records, of Maryland depositories holding Baltimore City records. Most entries are annotated, with brief introductory comments on the history of the collections. Public Records are further subdivided. Based on diverse archival manuals, catalogs, and secondary works; 44 notes.

G. J. Bobango

3954. Dahms, Frederic A. SOME QUANTITATIVE APPROACHES TO THE STUDY OF CENTRAL PLACES IN THE GUELPH AREA, 1851-1970. *Urban Hist. Rev. [Canada] 1975 (2): 9-30.* Explores methodology available to urban geographers and urban historians, in the Guelph Central Place System of 1970.

3955. Daniels, Maygene. DISTRICT OF COLUMBIA BUILDING PERMITS. *Am. Archivist 1975 38(1): 23-30.* National Archives Record Group 351 consists of District of Columbia building permits issued during 1877-1949. The records are useful for economic, social, demographic, and architectural studies as well as for guiding restoration of historic areas. Because the procedures and forms remained unchanged during the period, uniform quantifiable data is readily available. Based on primary sources; 2 illus., 14 notes.   J. A. Benson

3956. Doucette, Laurel. FAMILY STUDIES AS AN APPROACH TO ORAL HISTORY. *Can. Oral Hist. Assoc. J. [Canada] 1976-77 2: 24-31.* Excerpts a tape-recorded collection from research on the James Kealey family in Hull, Quebec, whose history lends itself to both folklore and oral history, 1974-75.

3957. Doyle-Frenière, Murielle. LES ARCHIVES DE LA VILLE DE QUEBEC [The archives of the city of Quebec]. *Urban Hist. Rev. [Canada] 1977 (1): 33-37.* Describes the historical background and contents of the Quebec city archives and lists general information on the facilities available and their use by researchers.   C. A. Watson

3958. Duis, Perry. BESSIE LOUISE PIERCE: SYMBOL AND SCHOLAR. *Chicago Hist. 1976 5(3): 130-140.* Depicts the academic career of Bessie Louise Pierce (1888-1974) and evaluates her contribution to the urban history of Chicago.

3959. Fox, M. F. BIRD'S-EYE VIEWS OF CANADIAN CITIES: A REVIEW. *Urban Hist. Rev. [Canada] 1977 (1): 38-45.* Reviews the exhibition of bird's-eye maps of Canadian cities (ca. 1865-1905) at the Public Archives of Canada from July to November 1976, and discusses their potential and limitations for the historical researcher. The detail and design of the maps suggest some uses that could be made of them by the researcher. 3 illus.   C. A. Watson

3960. Frank, Carrolyle O. "MIDDLETOWN" REVISITED: REAPPRAISING THE LYNDS' CLASSIC STUDIES OF MUNCIE, INDIANA. *Indiana Social Studies Q. 1977 30(1): 94-100.* Examines the sociological study of Muncie, Indiana, by Robert S. Lynd and Helen M. Lynd in 1929; explores the politics discussed in the book, brings forth evidence to shed some doubt on their findings, and expresses the possibility that some of their hypotheses may be false.

3961. Funigiello, Philip J. URBAN RESEARCH. *J. of Urban Hist. 1976 2(2): 256-260.* Reviews *The National Archives and Statistical Research*, edited by Meyer H. Fishbein, and *The National Archives and Urban Research*, edited by Jerome Finster. Praises the two collections of essays but notes they hardly contain the cutting edge of research since the National Archives conferences from which they grew were held in 1968 and 1970. The books, nonetheless, alert scholars to the rich research holdings of the National Archives.   T. W. Smith

3962. Gérin-Lajoie, Henri. LES ARCHIVES MUNICIPALES DE LA VILLE DE MONTRÉAL [Municipal archives in the city of Montreal]. *Urban Hist. Rev. [Canada] 1974 74(2): 2-4.* Chronicles the Montreal city archives, 1913-74; mentions library facilities, collections, and research possibilities.

3963. Germain, Annick. HISTOIRE URBAINE ET HISTOIRE DE L'URBANISATION AU QUÉBEC: BRÈVE REVUE DES TRAVAUX RÉALISÉS AU COURS DE LA DÉCENNIE [Urban history and the history of urbanization in Québec: brief review of work accomplished in the past decade]. *Urban Hist. Rev. [Canada] 1979 (3): 3-22.* Traditional historiography of the cities of Quebec was mostly anecdotal monographs of parishes and small cities and some "urban biographies" of Montreal. A review of the literature since 1968 shows that the more recent writing examines the forgotten majorities, the working classes, the women, and the poor. Not only subjects but research practices are changing too: new groups of researchers are often interdisciplinary, work together over a long time, and use quantitative methods. Greater interest is shown in urban history by local communities and some professions, such as architects. There is a new sensitivity to the usefulness of historical research in urban studies, particularly in urban politics. Secondary sources; 68 notes.   C. A. Watson

3964. Goheen, Peter G. INTERPRETING THE AMERICAN CITY: SOME HISTORICAL PERSPECTIVES. *Geographical J. 1974 64(3): 362-384.* Social scientists have examined the historical experience of cities in the United States and in Canada from two different perspectives. They have regarded the city as a laboratory in which a new culture evolves in response to economic change and social pressure. The work of Robert E. Park has given theoretical orientation to this large body of writing, in which many themes of change have been examined. Social scientists have also thought of the city as historically significant for the impact that ideas and institutions developing there have had on the national social and political scene. Both of these approaches have proven inadequate to the task of developing an historically sensitive theory of the American city. One formulation is proposed as a way of contributing to such an understanding.   J

3965. Goldfield, David R. LIVING HISTORY: THE PHYSICAL CITY AS ARTIFACT AND TEACHING TOOL. *Hist. Teacher 1975 8(4): 535-556.* A discussion of the use of cities for research in history, including the study of urban problems such as traffic congestion and sanitation. The physical city can also be used to explore community development, including city planning and the use of open spaces. Based on primary and secondary sources; 6 illus., 25 notes.

P. W. Kennedy

3966. Grabow, Stephen. THE OUTSIDER IN RETROSPECT: E. A. GUTKIND. *J. of the Am. Inst. of Planners 1975 41(3): 200-212.* When E. A. Gutkind formally began his last project, the *International History of City Development* (New York: Free Press, 1964-72), for which he is most widely known in the United States, he was already 70 years old. What is not generally known is that at that time, his accumulated works as an urban theorist and his professional experience and accomplishments as an architect and planner had already surpassed, in sheer magnitude, the creative output of most figures in the field. The few people who were aware of his work, mostly colleagues, theoreticians, or scholars, considered him an anomaly—an outsider.   J

3967. Halvorson, Peter and Stave, Bruce M. A CONVERSATION WITH BRIAN J. L. BERRY. *J. of Urban Hist. 1978 4(2): 209-238.* Interviews Brian J. L. Berry, a leading urban geographer. Describes his family background and education in England and his academic career in America. Of special interest are the discussions of how difficult it was to get colleagues to accept his early quantitative methods as geography and his comments on Marxist geographers. 54 notes, biblio.

T. W. Smith

3968. Hamer, Collin Bradfield, Jr. RECORDS OF THE CITY OF JEFFERSON (1850-1870) IN THE CITY ARCHIVES OF THE NEW ORLEANS PUBLIC LIBRARY. *Louisiana Hist. 1976 17(1): 51-67.* Describes in some detail the group of records in 69 volumes from Jefferson City turned over to the city archives of New Orleans from 1870-1972. Several attempts at cataloging these records had been initiated by personnel of the city archives since 1870, including an inventory completed by a federal works project. 17 notes.   E. P. Stickney

3969. Hammack, David C. PROBLEMS IN THE HISTORICAL STUDY OF POWER IN THE CITIES AND TOWNS OF THE UNITED STATES, 1800-1960. *Am. Hist. Rev. 1978 83(2): 323-349.*

Historians of cities and towns in the United States have often considered the distribution of power, but with a small number of recent exceptions they have usually done so implicitly, indirectly, and incompletely. A close reading of the historical literature demonstrates that historians have long focused on the power of economic and social elites, and have offered two groups of interpretations of the history of power distributions in American cities. One group of interpretations stresses the continuing or declining power of economic and social elites; the other stresses the continuing, increasing or decreasing power of non-elite pressure groups. This historical debate parallels in many ways the "power structure" debate among social scientists. An examination of the social science literature suggests some ways to make historical research more rigorous, but it also shows that many of the interpretations offered by political scientists and sociologists rest upon untested historical assumptions. At present, our best knowledge would support the conclusion that power became significantly more widely distributed in American cities and towns between 1890 and 1960; but we have so few rigorous and comparable studies that this conclusion remains very tentative indeed.   A

3970.   Harlan, Robert D.   REVIEW ARTICLE: ORAL HISTORIES OF SAN FRANCISCO PRINTING.   *Lib. Q. 1975 45(2): 202-205.* Reviews a series of 25 interviews by the University of California, Berkeley, Regional Oral History Office.   S

3971.   Harney, Robert F.   A NOTE ON SOURCES IN URBAN AND IMMIGRANT HISTORY (INCLUDING EXCERPTS FROM PRIMARY MATERIALS ON MACEDONIANS IN TORONTO). *Can. Ethnic Studies [Canada] 1977 9(1): 60-76.* Of the three major sources on immigrants in Toronto (municipal statistics, "caretakers' " records, and immigrant literature), the last has been the most ignored and offers the greatest enrichment to urban history. Provides four types of immigrant sources: a description of the Canadian Baptist mission for Macedonians, the actual records of a Macedonian church, a community historian's depiction of the founding of a Macedonian church in Toronto, and an interview with Gina Petroff, a Macedonian immigrant. Interviews with living immigrants will better document the ethnic community's experience.   K. S. McDorman

3972.   Harris, Carl V.   THE UNDERDEVELOPED HISTORICAL DIMENSION OF THE STUDY OF COMMUNITY POWER STRUCTURE.   *Hist. Methods Newsletter 1976 9(4): 195-200.* Discusses the recent historiography of community studies. Divides it into a power-elite school which finds economic and social power resting in the hands of elites and a pluralist school which argues that no group really dominates local government. Pluralists denounce the power elitist's reputationalist method and the conspiracy theory of interest politics. The major difference between the two schools is the problem of the meaning of history and the meaning to be found in history. Neither school has a satisfactory solution. 16 notes.   D. K. Pickens

3973.   Hays, Samuel P.   THE DEVELOPMENT OF PITTSBURGH AS A SOCIAL ORDER.   *Western Pennsylvania Hist. Mag. 1974 57(4): 431-448.* Examines research problems and opportunities in the study of urbanization, especially the question of social structure, and suggests ways to apply these ideas to the study of Pittsburgh, Pennsylvania.   S

3974.   Hayward, Robert J.   SOURCES OF URBAN HISTORICAL RESEARCH: INSURANCE PLANS AND LAND USE ATLASES. *Urban Hist. Rev. [Canada] 1973 (1): 2-9.* Explores information available to urban historians through building plans of insurance agencies and land use atlases of Canada, 1696-1973.

3975.   Hershberg, Theodore; Burstein, Alan N.; and Drobis, Susan M. THE HISTORICAL STUDY OF URBAN SPACE.   *Hist. Methods Newsletter 1976 9(2&3): 99-137.* Consists of a detailed account of two methodologies on spatial distribution drawn from the Philadelphia Social History Project. Both techniques cover the general area of residential distribution and differentiation and mobility of Irish and German immigrants.   D. K. Pickens

3976.   Hershberg, Theodore.   THE NEW URBAN HISTORY: TOWARD AN INTERDISCIPLINARY HISTORY OF THE CITY. *J. of Urban Hist. 1978 5(1): 3-40.* Much that passes for urban history

whether of the old-narrative or new-quantitative form is neither the actual study of cities as active social forces or of urbanization. It is rather the study of politics, mobility, labor, etc., in which the cities are mere backdrops. What is needed is the study of cities as process. The cities can be considered as either the dependent or independent variables in the analysis (depending on its purpose), but must be considered as more than the mere geographic setting for other events. 65 notes.   T. W. Smith

3977.   Hershberg, Theodore and Dockhorn, Robert.   OCCUPATIONAL CLASSIFICATION.   *Hist. Methods Newsletter 1976 9(2&3): 59-99.* After a brief historiographic background discusses the nature of the Occupation Dictionary Codebook for The Philadelphia Social History Project and its contributions to various research projects. The Codebook is included in this article.   D. K. Pickens

3978.   Hershberg, Theodore.   THE PHILADELPHIA SOCIAL HISTORY PROJECT: AN INTRODUCTION.   *Hist. Methods Newsletter 1976 9(2-3): 43-58.* The author, Director of the Projects, describes the Philadelphia Social History Project in terms of trying to find the specific workings and consequences of industrialization and urbanization. Many research programs are underway. The main thrust of the parent project is in four areas; the nature of work, the uses of urban space, life course developments, and special group experiences.   D. K. Pickens

3979.   Hershberg, Theodore.   TOWARD THE HISTORICAL STUDY OF ETHNICITY.   *J. of Ethnic Studies 1973 1(1): 1-5.* Notes the growing interest in the study of ethnicity and urges development and expansion of ethnic study programs. The field of ethnic studies is a prime example of the need for greater interdisciplinary research and collaboration. Departmental provincialism and the emphasis on individual rather than group research hinder better scholarship in ethnic studies and other subjects. Illustrates the importance of examining population subgroups by showing that each racial-ethnic group varied in its pattern of employment and ability to acquire real property. Describes the Philadelphia Social History Project, a quantitative study of the social structure and mobility of blacks, Irish, Germans, and "native white Americans" in Philadelphia 1850-80.   T. W. Smith

3980.   Hoffman, Paul E.   ST. AUGUSTINE 1580: THE RESEARCH PROJECT.   *Escribano 1977 14: 5-19.* Discusses a project involving research into documents, maps, manuscripts, and personal journals to reconstruct daily life in St. Augustine, Florida, in 1580.

3981.   Hoover, Dwight W.   SURVEYING THE AMERICAN URBAN PAST.   *J. of Urban Hist. 1974 1(1): 111-115.* Reviews five survey textbooks on American urban history: Sam Bass Warner, Jr., *The Urban Wilderness: A History of the American City* (New York: Harper & Row, 1972); Zane L. Miller, *The Urbanization of Modern America: A Brief History* (New York: Harcourt Brace Jovanovich, 1973); Blake McKelvey, *American Urbanization: A Comparative History* (Glenview, Ill.: Scott, Foresman, 1973); Bayrd Still, *Urban America: A History with Documents* (Boston: Little, Brown, 1974); and Raymond A. Mohl and James F. Richardson, *The Urban Experience: Themes in American History* (Belmont, Calif.: Wadsworth, 1973).   S. S. Sprague

3982.   Israel, Jerry.   MIDWESTERN SMALL CITIES: BUILDING AN INTEGRATED SOCIAL SCIENCE CURRICULUM.   *AHA Newsletter 1979 17(4): 4, 6.* Development of an integrated social science curriculum at Illinois Wesleyan University focused on community and local history, the Amish community of Arthur, Illinois, and the community development of Pontiac, Illinois, 19th-20th centuries.

3983.   James, R. Scott.   THE CITY OF TORONTO ARCHIVES. *Urban Hist. Rev. [Canada] 1973 (3): 2-9.* Assesses the accessibility, archival holdings, future plans, and history of the City Archives of Toronto, Ontario, 1959-73.

3984.   Juliani, Richard J.   CHURCH RECORDS AS SOCIAL DATA: THE ITALIANS IN PHILADELPHIA IN THE NINETEENTH CENTURY.   *Records of the Am. Catholic Hist. Soc. of Philadelphia 1974 85(1-2): 3-16.* Despite problems of completeness, coverage, and availability, church records can provide fragmentary information on the size and growth of the immigrant community, its duration in the place, occupations of individuals, and their origins in the home country and intentions in the new. They can also provide clues to infant mortality rates and to relations of immigrants with the larger society, and keys to the study of other materials. 24 notes. J. M. McCarthy

3985. Kantrowitz, Nathan. THE INDEX OF DISSIMILARITY: A MEASUREMENT OF RESIDENTIAL SEGREGATION FOR HISTORICAL ANALYSIS. *Hist. Methods Newsletter 1974 7(4): 285-289.* After receiving current research projects using the index in several cities, the author concludes that Detroit's pattern of racial segregation during 1850-60 was atypical. The index, used carefully, provides historians with a technique for considering their findings in broad, comparative contexts. 3 tables, notes. D. K. Pickens

3986. Kelsey, Harry. CALIFORNIA HISTORY RESOURCES: THE LOS ANGELES COUNTY MUSEUM OF NATURAL HISTORY. *California Hist. Q. 1975 54(3): 272-276.* Describes the holdings of the Los Angeles County Museum of Natural History and its research facilities. Over 100,000 photographs, 2,500 maps, a 10,000-item manuscript collection, a reference file of notes and clippings, 12,000 color postcards, and other sources are available. Subjects include the museum displays themselves, Indians, graphic arts, California pioneers, materials on Lincoln, and local history. Illus., 2 notes. A. Hoffman

3987. Klein, Mitchell S. G. SURVEY OF THE DOMINANT TOPIC AREAS AMONG POLITICAL SCIENCE URBANISTS. *Teaching Pol. Sci. 1977 4(3): 329-340.* Through examination of course content, evaluates dominant topics as perceived by political science urbanists, 1970's.

3988. Kleinberg, Susan J. THE SYSTEMATIC STUDY OF URBAN WOMEN. *Hist. Methods Newsletter 1975 9(1): 14-25.* In focusing on the relationship between urbanization and industrialization and women's varied activities, the author first examines the nature of women's work and the determinants of female participation and then concentrates on techniques and methodology of studying urban women.
D. K. Pickens

3989. Knight, David B. and Taylor, John H. "CANADA'S URBAN PAST": A REPORT ON THE CANADIAN URBAN HISTORY CONFERENCE. *Urban Hist. Rev. [Canada] 1977 (2): 72-86.* Describes the Canadian Urban History Conference held at the University of Guelph, 12-14 May 1977. Analyzes the papers presented along with important comments from the audience. C. A. Watson

3990. Knight, David B. and Clark, John. SOME REFLECTIONS ON A CONFERENCE ON THE HISTORICAL URBANIZATION OF NORTH AMERICA. *Urban Hist. Rev. [Canada] 1973 (1): 10-14.* Discusses the proceedings and papers delivered at the Conference on the Historical Urbanization of North America; topics included sources and methodology of urban history research, role of the city in 19th-century North America, internal relationships in urban situations, urbanization in the colonial era, regional variations in urbanization, and residential change in North America.

3991. Kooij, P. STADSGESCHIEDENIS EN DE VERHOUDING STAD-PLATTELAND [Urban history and the relationship of urban and rural areas]. *Econ.- en Sociaal-Hist. Jaarboek [Netherlands] 1975 38: 124-140.* Surveys recent studies on urban histories in the United States, Great Britain, and Germany. Discusses the relationship of urban and rural areas.

3992. LaRose, Helen. THE CITY OF EDMONTON ARCHIVES. *Urban Hist. Rev. [Canada] 1974 74(3): 2-7.* Chronicles the Edmonton, Alberta, city archives, 1938-74, and discusses collection holdings and plans for the facility.

3993. LeGacy, Arthur. IMAGES OF THE CITY: TEACHING HISTORY THROUGH FILM AT SYRACUSE UNIVERSITY. *Film & Hist. 1974 4(2): 14-17.*

3994. Lemon, James T. APPROACHES TO THE STUDY OF THE URBAN PAST: GEOGRAPHY. *Urban Hist. Rev. [Canada] 1973 (2): 13-19.* Examines geographical studies concerning city planning and settlement in both the United States and Canada, 19th-20th centuries.

3995. Levitt, James H. and La Barre, Claude E. BUILDING A DATA FILE FROM HISTORICAL ARCHIVES. *Computers and the Humanities 1975 9(2): 77-82.* Computerization of New Jersey port records from the colonial period enables historians to analyze complex relationships between people, objects, and events.

3996. Lewy, Cheryl Winter. URBAN DOCUMENTS AS REFERENCE TOOLS. *Government Publ. Rev. 1974 1(3): 269-275.* The key to using municipal documents as a valuable reference tool lies in knowing the statistical and substantive information which they contain. This paper points out the problems of access, availability, and bibliographic control. It reviews the municipal documents which contain the most useful information, i.e., annual reports, statistical reports, proceedings, minutes, news releases, bulletins, budgets and appropriation ordinances, rules and regulations, and ordinances. The potential worth of municipal documents as reference tools will be increased through the use and knowledge of the indexes published with the documents themselves which provide internal bibliographic control and subject access. J

3997. Lindner, Carl M. THE INDUSTRIAL SOCIETY PROGRAM AT THE UNIVERSITY OF WISCONSIN-PARKSIDE. *Liberal Educ. 1974 60(3): 340-347.* An interdisciplinary program, "Studies in the City," encourages further curricular experimentation. S

3998. Linteau, Paul-André. LA SOCIETE MONTREALAISE AU 19ᵉ SIECLE: BILAN DES TRAVAUX [Montreal society in the 19th century: balance of workers]. *Urban Hist. Rev. [Canada] 1973 (3): 17-19.* Explores the work of the Research Group on Montreal Society of the 19th century which set about, in 1971, to write a social history of Montreal during the era when commercial capitalism was changing into industrial capitalism.

3999. Luckingham, Bradford. THE CITY IN THE WESTWARD MOVEMENT—A BIBLIOGRAPHICAL NOTE. *Western Hist. Q. 1974 5(3): 295-306.* Reviews and comments on the literature concerned with the urban dimension of the westward movement, from colonial times to the present. Suggests areas and themes that need further research. 18 notes. D. L. Smith

4000. MacDermaid, Anne. THE CITY OF KINGSTON ARCHIVES. *Urban Hist. Rev. [Canada] 1978 (1): 3-8.* Describes the city archives and their establishment as the City of Kingston [Ontario] Archives in 1972 in conjunction with the Queen's University archives where the Kingston archives are housed and administered. Available city records date back to 1838. C. A. Watson

4001. Maness, Lonnie E. A COMMENT ON LOCAL HISTORY. *West Tennessee Hist. Soc. Papers 1975 29: 162-165.* Appeals for good local history, asserting that the history of cities has been largely ignored until comparatively recent times. Argues that the study of cities is important for a proper understanding of developments on the regional, sectional, and national levels. Discusses three histories of Memphis, with particular emphasis on Judge J. P. Young's *Standard History of Memphis, Tennessee*, first published in 1912, and recently (1974) reprinted. Note. H. M. Parker, Jr.

4002. Marshall, John U. GEOGRAPHY'S CONTRIBUTION TO THE HISTORICAL STUDY OF URBAN CANADA. *Urban Hist. Rev. [Canada] 1973 (1): 15-23.* Surveys major literature in the field of Canadian urban studies, ca 1900-73.

4003. May, Dean L. THE MAKING OF SAINTS: THE MORMON TOWN AS A SETTING FOR THE STUDY OF CULTURAL CHANGE. *Utah Hist. Q. 1977 45(1): 75-92.* Mormon communities are historical specimens of a central theme of American experience: the tension between preservation of order and libertarian ideologies. Past studies of Mormon towns failed to examine the process of change over time. Techniques used for New England towns by such historians as Philip Greven, John Demos, Kenneth Lockridge, and Michael Zuckerman suggest questions to ask about Mormon communities. These scholars identified forces of disintegration. Mormon studies may show forces of reintegration. Primary and secondary sources; illus., 38 notes.
J. L. Hazelton

4004. Mays, H. J. and Manzl, H. F. LITERACY AND SOCIAL STRUCTURE IN NINETEENTH-CENTURY ONTARIO: AN EXERCISE IN HISTORICAL METHODOLOGY. *Social Hist. [Canada] 1974 7(14): 331-345.* The manuscript census has very serious limitations for students of literacy in 19th-century Canada, particularly in rural areas. Linkage of mortgage and probate records with the 1861 census in Peel County, Ontario, revealed a very significant underenumeration of illiterates by the census-takers. Inconsistencies in the census forms filled out by urban residents in three wards in Hamilton cast doubt on their accuracy as an indicator of literacy. Based on the manuscript census in the Public Archives of Canada, and mortgage and probate records in the Public Archives of Ontario; 5 tables, 33 notes. W. K. Hobson

4005. McCarthy, Michael P. TEACHING URBAN HISTORY WITH GAMES: A REVIEW ESSAY. *Hist. Teacher 1973 7(1): 62-66.* Few games are available in history as such, but there are some for the study of cities. Because games are useful in contemporary problems classes, history teachers should design their own. Based on primary and secondary sources; 6 notes. P. W. Kennedy

4006. McKee, Bill. THE RESOURCES OF THE VANCOUVER CITY ARCHIVES. *Urban Hist. Rev. [Canada] 1977 (2): 3-9.* Discusses the public and private records at the Vancouver City Archives and suggests topics that urban historians can research there.
C. A. Watson

4007. McKelvey, Blake. A CITY HISTORIAN'S REPORT. *Rochester Hist. 1973 35(3): 1-24.* The author became assistant city historian of Rochester in June 1936 when the city was in the Depression. There has since been considerable industrial development in the city. A good supply of water power contributed to the development of industries, especially flour milling and the Kodak Company.
J. H. Krenkel

4008. Meigs, Peveril. JOHN G. HALES, BOSTON GEOGRAPHER AND SURVEYOR, 1785-1832. *New England Hist. and Genealogical Register 1975 129(January): 23-29.* John Groves Hales (1785-1832) was a Boston geographer and surveyor who executed the most complete maps of Boston and the surrounding Massachusetts area that these communities had had, from about 1814 until his death 18 years later. His maps incorporated exact mileages between towns, descriptions of the towns and their mills and agriculture, their dwelling houses, and even their taverns. The original of Hales' maps for 48 Massachusetts communities are in the Archives of the Commonwealth of Massachusetts at the State House. Based on primary and secondary sources; 15 notes.
S. L. Patterson

4009. Miller, Zane L. and Shapiro, Henry D. LEARNING HISTORY BY DOING: THE LABORATORY IN AMERICAN CIVILIZATION. *Hist. Teacher 1978 11(4): 483-497.* Details the story of a local history experiment at the University of Cincinnati. Project assumes that teachers do not teach as much as students should learn and learn primarily by doing actual historical research. It is an "open learning situation" in which students are led into the process of inquiry. Uses the available historical documents from the city records of Cincinnati. 6 notes. L. C. Smith

4010. Miller, Zane L. DEFINING THE CITY—AND URBAN HISTORY. *Rev. in Am. Hist. 1976 4(3): 436-441.* Review article prompted by Blaine A. Brownell's *The Urban Ethos in the South, 1920-1930* (Baton Rouge: Louisiana State U. Pr., 1975); discusses the introduction of cultural considerations into urban history.

4011. Miller, Zane; Griffen, Clyde; and Stelter, Gilbert A. URBAN HISTORY IN NORTH AMERICA. *Urban Hist. Y. [Great Britain] 1977: 6-29.* Examines the changing concepts and definitions of the contemporary city in the United States. The 18th-century view of the city as a residential community began to wane in the late 19th century and the the idea of the city as an organic yet man-made community emerged. This ultimately led to the growth of urban history as a speciality which flourished and diversified in the 20th century. Proponents of the "new urban history" see themselves as committed to social science history and as focusing on populations and their interactions, but methodological differences are manifold. Examination of some of the more interesting develop-

ments in recent historical studies of urban occupational and residential structures, and mobility through them, together with elites and voluntary associations, indicates just a few of the directions taken. The growth of interest in the study of Canadian cities is a relatively new phenomenon involving a wide range of disciplines. A survey of research work indicates the main stream of current activity in this field. 64 notes.
A. Armstrong

4012. Montgomery, David. THE NEW URBAN HISTORY. *Rev. in Am. Hist. 1974 2(4): 498-504.* Review article prompted by Dennis Clark's *The Irish in Philadelphia: Ten Generations of Urban Experience* (Philadelphia: Temple U. Pr., 1973), Allen F. Davis and Mark H. Haller's *The Peoples of Philadelphia: A History of Ethnic Groups and Lower-Class Life, 1790-1940* (Philadelphia: Temple U. Pr., 1973), and Estelle F. Feinstein's *Stamford in the Gilded Age: The Political Life of a Connecticut Town 1868-1893* (Stamford, Conn.: The Stamford Historical Society, 1973) which outlines the books' contents, discusses the books' relation to the "new urban history," mentions the authors' methodologies, use of data, theoretical assumptions, and historical assumptions, and assesses the books' contributions to understanding the history of "ordinary people" living in American cities.

4013. Moore, Harry T. LEWIS MUMFORD: PHILOSOPHER OF HISTORY. *Mankind 1977 6(1): 21-24, 44-45.* Lewis Mumford's writings exhibit an organic wholeness derived from his bringing together technology, architecture, sociology and the humanities in an effort not only to analyze the past and present condition of humanity, but also to supply desired guidelines for future development and growth. Throughout his many books ostensibly dealing with a diversity of subjects, Mumford is concerned with effecting in civilization a balance, reunion, reaffirmation, and renewal of life to have the result of eventuating in a human condition in which all will have acquired a wholeness of being. He is deeply concerned that persons become imbued with an acute sense of history to be used as a tool in effecting a desirable social order which in political terms would be along democratic socialist lines.
N. Lederer

4014. Muhlin, Gregory L. and Milcarek, Barry I. URBAN ANALYSIS AND PLANNING A CAUTIONARY NOTE ON THE UTILIZATION OF CENSUS DATA. *Urban Affairs Q. 1974 10(2): 212-222.* Questions the effect on data reliability of substitution—assignment of a full set of characteristics for a person in a household for which there are known members but none present. Uses a New York City health survey (1961-74) as an example. Table, note, biblio. P. J. Woehrmann

4015. Norris, Darrell A. SOME COMMENTS CONCERNING A MEETING OF ONTARIO HISTORICAL GEOGRAPHERS. *Urban Hist. Rev. [Canada] 1976 76(1): 14-20.* Reports on the papers of the urban historical geography of Ontario and the prehistoric and historical geography of the native peoples of Canada, presented at a meeting at McMaster University, 20 March 1976. Summarizes the papers and calls for more interdisciplinary study and cooperation between urban historians and historical geographers. C. A. Watson

4016. Ogden, R. Lynn. VANCOUVER CITY ARCHIVES: A NEW RESOURCE. *Urban Hist. Rev. [Canada] 1974 74(1): 20-23.* Examines the facilities, staff, and collections of the Vancouver, British Columbia, city archives, 1970-74.

4017. Olson, Frederick I. MILWAUKEE AND THE NEW URBAN HISTORY. *Milwaukee Hist. 1978 1(1-2): 2-3.* Discusses recent trends in the study of urban history, specifically of Milwaukee, since the publication of Bayrd Still's *Milwaukee: The History of a City* in 1948.

4018. Orr, David G. PHILADELPHIA AS INDUSTRIAL ARCHAEOLOGICAL ARTIFACT: A CASE STUDY. *Hist. Archaeology 1977 11: 3-14.* During 1974-77, the University of Pennsylvania's Department of American Civilization used a procedure to accumulate evidence on Philadelphia industry, 1850's-1910; includes photographs, interviews, and corporate archives. Suggests linking industrial technology artifacts to social history interpretations. J/S

4019. Pessen, Edward. REFLECTIONS ON NEW YORK AND ITS RECENT HISTORIANS. *New-York Hist. Soc. Q. 1979 63(2): 145-*

156. Discusses the new kind of history that is being written about New York. Historians of the city and state are concentrating on subjects not stressed previously. Such areas as the professions, "the sociology of politics," functions of municipalities, local history, and voluntary associations have been investigated recently. Finds many of the results somewhat dull and poorly written. Suggests many other areas which need to be investigated for a better understanding of the state's past. In particular, suggests jazz and its impact on New York City and the nation as an excellent field for a social historian. The notes accompanying the article constitute an excellent bibliography of the work being done. 27 notes, mostly bibliographical.   C. L. Grant

4020. Pressman, Norman E. P.   THE BUILT ENVIRONMENT: A PLANNING APPROACH TO THE STUDY OF PAST URBAN SETTLEMENT.   *Urban Hist. Rev. [Canada] 1973 (2): 8-12.* Examines human settlement patterns in both the Old and New World from the point of view of a city planning historian, 2000 BC-20c.

4021. Price, Jacob M.   QUANTIFYING COLONIAL AMERICA: A COMMENT ON NASH AND WARDEN.   *J. of Interdisciplinary Hist. 1976 6(4): 701-709.* Comments on quantitative studies of pre-Revolutionary America by Gary B. Nash and Gerard B. Warden. Discusses the technical problems in the handling of the data and the possibilities of constructing a general model of urban development of the preindustrial port town. Suggests that a greater awareness of the comparative dimension in studies of urban structure is needed. 9 notes.   R. Howell

4022. Raphael, Marc Lee.   THE GENESIS OF A COMMUNAL HISTORY: THE COLUMBUS JEWISH HISTORY PROJECT.   *Am. Jewish Arch. 1977 29(1): 53-69.* Writes of the Columbus (Ohio) Jewish History Project as a joint undertaking of the Columbus Jewish Federation, the Ohio Historical Society, and the Ohio State University. Believes that "the writing of serious American Jewish communal history is still in its infancy," though "such studies are valuable for the insights they offer into particular historical processes, . . . the information they offer indirectly about a society, and . . . the questions they raise about similar cases."   J

4023. Raphael, Marc Lee.   ORAL HISTORY IN AN ETHNIC COMMUNITY: THE PROBLEMS AND THE PROMISE.   *Ohio Hist. 1977 86(4): 248-257.* Discusses techniques in oral history interviews. Using brief excerpts from the tapes of the Jewish History Project of Columbus, Ohio, since 1920, the author touches on the strengths and weaknesses of recording and transcribing oral history. Secondary sources; 23 notes.   N. Summers

4024. Raphael, Marc Lee.   THE UTILIZATION OF PUBLIC LOCAL AND FEDERAL SOURCES FOR RECONSTRUCTING AMERICAN JEWISH LOCAL HISTORY: THE JEWS OF COLUMBUS, OHIO.   *Am. Jewish Hist. Q. 1975 65(1): 10-35.* Using 19th-century and early 20th-century statistics from various sources, discusses the history of the majority of Jews in Columbus, Ohio, whose activities were not recorded by the local Jewish newspaper. Examines the validity of quantitative methods in history. 10 tables, 43 notes.

F. Rosenthal

4025. Reynolds, Regina and Ruwell, Mary Elizabeth.   FIRE INSURANCE RECORDS: A VERSATILE RESOURCE.   *Am. Archivist 1975 38(1): 15-21.* Fire insurance records of the Insurance Company of North America Corporation of Philadelphia contain useful data for genealogists, architects, and historians. Policy records dating from 1841 include property descriptions, changes in ownership, structural changes, and description of the contents of buildings. Fire surveys and perpetual policies include detailed descriptions, architectural drawings, and street plans. Quantitative research may benefit from the uniformity of the data. Based on primary sources; 4 illus.   J. A. Benson

4026. Rowland, A. Ray   THE AUGUSTA CITY DIRECTORY.   *Richmond County Hist. 1973 5(1): 5-28.* An overview of city directories published for Augusta since 1841. Lists facts of publication and locations of all extant Augusta directories. 3 illus., 7 notes.   H. R. Grant

4027. Schlereth, Thomas J.   THE CITY AS ARTIFACT.   *AHA Newsletter 1977 15(2): 6-9.* Examines various aspects of urban history

which are extant for history teaching today as relics of the past, including buildings, art murals, geographical layout, street plans, and photographs of cities, 20th century.

4028. Schlereth, Thomas J.   REGIONAL STUDIES IN AMERICA: THE CHICAGO MODEL.   *Am. Studies [Washington, DC] 1974 13(1): 20-34.* Bibliographical essay which cites sources and references for a systematic study of Chicago's regional culture which can also serve as the "national story." Biblio.   L. L. Athey

4029. Schmandt, Henry.   URBAN RESEARCH IN A METROPOLITAN SETTING.   *Urbanism Past and Present 1976 (2): 9-12.* Focuses on the problem of dissemination of urban research using metropolitan Milwaukee as an example. Classification of research as either action-directed (focusing on specific problems) or knowledge-directed (focusing on broad questions) impedes collaboration of potentially supportive groups. Recommends collecting and disseminating information and creating a consortium of local researchers and agencies to promote collaborative efforts. 10 notes.   B. P. Anderson

4030. Schmid, Georg E.   URBANISMUS. DIE STADT IN DER GESCHICHTE [Urbanization: The city in history].   *Zeitgeschichte [Austria] 1974 1(7): 174-179.* Describes the changing view of the city as a social scene where history unfolds to a center of growing problems and discontent. Reviews recent approaches to urban history in the United States, Great Britain, France, and Germany. A strong interdisciplinary approach to urban history has developed furthest in the United States. Secondary works; 25 notes.   J. B. Street

4031. Schneider, Gail.   DEVELOPING A SMALL RESOURCE COLLECTION ON LOCAL BLACK HISTORY: THE STATEN ISLAND PROJECT.   *Afro-Americans in New York Life and Hist. 1977 1(1): 99-104.* Discusses a project initiated in 1969 which sought to collect taped oral histories of the elder black residents of Staten Island, a project supported by the Staten Island Institute of Arts and Sciences; continues with synopses of other library holdings including genealogies, photograph and slide collections, and publications.

4032. Schnore, Leo F.   URBAN HISTORY AND THE SOCIAL SCIENCES.   *J. of Urban Hist. 1975 1(4): 395-408.* Urban historians and urban sociologists have much to learn from the social sciences; foremost among the examples are statistical analysis and the application of broad conceptual themes.

4033. Scollie, F. Brent.   EVERY SCRAP OF PAPER: ACCESS TO ONTARIO'S MUNICIPAL RECORDS.   *Can. Lib. J. 1974 31(1): 8-10, 11-16.* Gives guidelines for making Ontario's public records more accessible to historians, librarians, and city planners.   S

4034. Smith, Daniel Scott.   UNDERREGISTRATION AND BIAS IN PROBATE RECORDS: AN ANALYSIS OF DATA FROM EIGHTEENTH-CENTURY HINGHAM, MASSACHUSETTS.   *William and Mary Q. 1975 32(1): 100-110.* Determines a method for measuring the inclusiveness and bias in colonial probate records and mentions the need to correlate with alternative sources. Probate records of Hingham, Massachusetts, are correlated with a death register compiled by the Rev. Ebenezer Gay, complete for the first parish from 1718 to 1786. Shows calculation of percentage of persons leaving wills, and data on age and wealth. Argues that wealth bias in probate records should not be a deterrent in their use. 4 tables, fig., 22 notes.   H. M. Ward

4035. Somers, Dale A.; Crimmins, Timothe J.; and Reed, Merl E.   SURVEYING THE RECORDS OF A CITY: THE HISTORY OF ATLANTA PROJECT.   *Am. Archivist 1973 36(3): 353-359.* The "History of Atlanta Project" was begun in 1970 by the Department of History and the School of Urban Life at Georgia State University. The first task was finding records for businesses, industries, churches, professional societies, and service organizations. The second task was a search for municipal records. Describes the records and suggests research uses. Project participants have encouraged the establishment of records management and archives programs. 6 notes.   D. E. Horn

4036. Stave, Bruce M.   A CONVERSATION WITH SAMUEL P. HAYS.   *J. of Urban Hist. 1975 2(1): 88-123.* A transcription of a taped interview tracing the background, education, and works of Hays as well as the people and sources that had the most impact upon him. Biblio, 12 notes.   S. S. Sprague

4037. Stave, Bruce M. A CONVERSATION WITH BAYRD STILL. *J. of Urban Hist. 1977 3(3): 323-360.* Interview of urban historian Bayrd Still, Director of the New York University Archives. Still discusses his personal background, his Chicago and Milwaukee stage, and his New York stage. 55 notes, biblio.   T. W. Smith

4038. Stave, Bruce M. A CONVERSATION WITH BLAKE MC KELVEY. *J. of Urban Hist. 1976 2(4): 459-486.* Blake McKelvey, official city historian of Rochester, New York, describes his training, early career, and scholarship. This interview reveals as much about the man as about the history he writes. McKelvey's four-volume history of Rochester had a combined sales total of under 10,000—respectable by scholarly standards but less than a single week on the best sellers' list. 28 notes, biblio.   T. W. Smith

4039. Stave, Bruce M. A CONVERSATION WITH RICHARD C. WADE. *J. of Urban Hist. 1977 3(2): 211-238.* Richard C. Wade, urban, slavery, and frontier historian, describes his family background, education, historical training, studies, and writings. Mentions the role of Robert Moses in the development of New York City, the most influential works in urban history, and prospects for violence in the ghettos. 31 notes, biblio.   T. W. Smith

4040. Stave, Bruce M. A CONVERSATION WITH CONSTANCE MC LAUGHLIN GREEN. *J. of Urban Hist. 1977 4(1): 77-116.* Interviews Constance McLaughlin Green and continues the series of conversations with leading urban historians and social scientists (which have been collected in *The Making of Urban History: Historiography through Oral History*). Covers the historian's family background and education, her writings and their development, and the place of her work in urban history. 23 notes, biblio.   T. W. Smith

4041. Stave, Bruce M. A CONVERSATION WITH SAM BASS WARNER, JR. *J. of Urban Hist. 1974 1(1): 85-110.* Recounts Warner's formal college training, the books and people who influenced him, and how he came to write *Street Car Suburbs* (1969), *The Private City* (1971), and *The Urban Wilderness* (1972). Warner has moved from city planning to fieldwork and sees a need for more systematic studies.   S. S. Sprague

4042. Stelter, Gilbert A. CANADA'S URBAN PAST: CANADIAN URBAN HISTORY CONFERENCE. *Urban Hist. Rev. [Canada] 1977 (1): 3-32.* Discusses the Canadian Urban History Conference held at the University of Guelph, 12-14 May 1977, and presents abstracts of the papers presented. The program emphasized the city-building process within which these topics were discussed: 1) the factors involved in urban growth, 2) the role of planners, developers, and builders in the shaping of cities, and 3) the place of government, especially provincial and municipal, in determining urban form.   C. A. Watson

4043. Stelter, Gilbert A. CURRENT RESEARCH IN CANADIAN URBAN HISTORY. *Urban Hist. Rev. [Canada] 1975 (3): 27-36.* Discusses and presents a bibliography of recent research in Canadian urban history covering the 19th and 20th centuries.

4044. Stelter, Gilbert A. THE HISTORIAN'S APPROACH TO CANADA'S URBAN PAST. *Social Hist. [Canada] 1974 7(13): 5-22.* Two main approaches characterize Canadian urban history. The most common are studies dealing with anything that has happened in cities, without concern for what is "urban" in the subject. Less common are studies which focus on the processes of urbanization and the problems such processes generate. An increasing methodological sophistication and a genuine interest in interdisciplinary communication characterize recent work. Based on secondary sources. 58 notes.   W. K. Hobson

4045. Stelter, Gilbert. A SENSE OF TIME AND PLACE: THE HISTORIAN'S APPROACH TO THE URBAN PAST. *Urban Hist. Rev. [Canada] 1973 (2): 20-22.* Examines methodology of urban historians in studying urban history in Canada, 1960's-70's.

4046. Stephenson, Charles. TRACING THOSE WHO LEFT: MOBILITY STUDIES AND THE SOUNDEX INDEXES TO THE UNITED STATES CENSUS. *J. of Urban Hist. 1974 1(1): 73-84.* With soundex indexes for 1880 and 1900, historians have a tool with which they can trace individuals who move from cities.   S. S. Sprague

4047. Strave, Bruce M. A CONVERSATION WITH OSCAR HANDLIN. *J. of Urban Hist. 1977 3(1): 119-130.* Interviews Oscar Handlin, who brought ethnic history and local history to the mainstream of social history. 12 notes, biblio.   T. W. Smith

4048. Sullivan, James F. and Adrian, Charles R. URBAN GOVERNMENT RESEARCH: A VIEW OF THREE DECADES. *Natl. Civic Rev. 1977 66(9): 437-446.* Since World War II, the suburban movement, the population boom, the war on poverty, urban riots and new urban programs have provided added research incentives in political science.   J/S

4049. Swanson, Merwin. OWEN WISTER, CHARLES RUSSELL, AND FREDERIC REMINGTON: USING POPULAR CULTURE IN THE CLASSROOM. *Studies in Hist. and Society 1977 2(1-2): 1-22.* Uses the paintings of Russell and Remington to illustrate how Americans of the Progressive Era reacted to increased urbanization and industrialization by creating an idealized West. Also uses Owen Wister's *The Virginian* to illustrate how Americans, perhaps subconsciously, invented a West of freedom and individuality in sharp contrast to an increasingly industrial and urban world. Discusses the use of these three figures to introduce popular culture as a learning technique in the author's US history survey course. 20 illus.   S

4050. Taylor, John H. THE WESTERN CANADIAN URBAN HISTORY CONFERENCE: A REPORT. *Urban Hist. Rev. [Canada] 1974 74(2): 19-21.* Synopses of papers offered at the Western Canadian Urban History Conference held 24-26 October 1974 at the University of Winnipeg.

4051. Thernstrom, Stephan. THE NEW URBAN HISTORY. Delzell, Charles F., ed. *The Future of History: Essays in the Vanderbilt University Centennial Symposium* (Nashville: Vanderbilt U. Pr., 1977): 43-51. The term "new urban history," first employed in 1969, is misleading because it extends back to the 1930's. Major early contributions in the field included Oscar Handlin's *Boston's Immigrants* (1941) and Frank and Harriet Owsley's *Plain Folk of the Old South* (1949). During the 1950's, works of this genre often were overlooked or quickly forgotten. For the future, the geographical and temporal scopes of urban inquiries should be broadened. The blue collar-white collar delineation of stratification must be made less crude, and less emphasis should be placed on male heads of households. A greater awareness of migration is needed. In addition, the pitfalls of quantification must be avoided; the most thorough mastery of the new methods is not sufficient to make a good historian. 15 notes.   P. L. Solodkin

4052. Thorne, Tanis. THE ALMANACS OF THE SAN FRANCISCO BAY REGION, 1850-1861: A NEGLECTED HISTORICAL SOURCE. *J. of the West 1978 17(2): 36-45.* Almanacs published in the San Francisco Bay area during 1850-61 rank with newspapers and magazines as historical research sources about the daily life of the community. They also contain data on such specialized subjects as urban development, immigrant population, California architecture, medical practices, folk speech, and art. Almanacs provided accurate information on the human and material resources in the state to its residents, and to prospective immigrants. Primary and secondary sources; 6 illus., 40 notes.   B. S. Porter

4053. Troper, Harold. IMAGES OF THE "FOREIGNER" IN TORONTO, 1900-1930: A REPORT. *Urban Hist. Rev. [Canada] 1975 (2): 1-8.* Describes a 1974 archival project to assemble photographs of early immigrants in Ontario, 1900-30.

4054. Trout, Charles H. RECONSTRUCTING BOSTON IN THE 1930S: THE HISTORIAN AND THE CITY. *Massachusetts Hist. Soc. Pro. 1978 90: 58-74.* Urban history, to be both accurate and rich, needs to combine the old, elite-oriented styles of urban history with the new, quantitative methods of today's scholar. This wedding of old and new methodology was attempted by the author in his book, *Boston, the Great Depression, and the New Deal,* published in 1977. Based on the author's book, primary sources, and other secondary sources; 35 notes.

G. W. R. Ward

4055. Unsigned.   PERIODICAL LITERATURE IN URBAN STUDIES AND PLANNING.   *J. of the Am. Inst. of Planners 1976 42(2): 227-230.* Lists material published in 1975.

4056. Unsigned.   URBAN HISTORY AND URBAN SOCIETY. *Urbanism Past and Present 1975-76 (1): 1-10.*
Miller, Zane L.   URBAN HISTORY, URBAN CRISES, AND PUBLIC POLICY, *pp. 1-8.* Explores the relation between the emerging urban society and the emerging speciality of urban history. Denotes changes in the terms "city" and "urban" from colonial times to the present, and includes both positive and negative views of the city. Discusses urban problems and institutions in need of academic analysis and possible future directions for urban historians.
Greer, Scott.   COMMENTARY, *pp. 9-10.* Agrees with Miller on past views of the city. Believes that the new urban history, involving quantification, is the best approach for pragmatically dealing with the city.   B. P. Anderson

4057. Vance, James E., Jr.   GEOGRAPHY AND THE STUDY OF CITIES.   *Am. Behavioral Scientist 1979 22(1): 131-149.* Describes the evolution and changing focus of urban geography since the 1920's, with emphasis on the changes since 1954.

4058. VanValey, Thomas L. and Roof, Wade Clark.   MEASURING RESIDENTIAL SEGREGATION IN AMERICAN CITIES: PROBLEMS OF INTERCITY COMPARISON.   *Urban Affairs Q. 1976 11(4): 453-468.* Because of the utility of the tract-based segregation index, researchers need to study its comparability to the more typical block-based index. Using published census data and based on an analysis of 141 cities, the authors conclude that the differences in the indexes vary systematically according to city size and percent nonwhite population. This difference contracts with increasing city size and expands with increasing percent nonwhite population. Interchanging block and tract indexes produces the least bias when done with large cities with a small percentage of nonwhite population. Biases with reference to small cities with a large percentage of nonwhite population can be substantial. These biases as well as the impact of the two variables on both indexes have implications for a wide range of national urban policies. Primary and secondary sources; 4 tables, 4 notes, biblio.   L. N. Beecher

4059. Waddell, Louis M.   THE 1975 RESEARCH CONFERENCE AT HARRISBURG.   *Pennsylvania Hist. 1975 42(4): 316-323.* The 1975 Research Conference of the Pennsylvania Historical Association was held at Harrisburg 11 and 12 April 1975 in conjunction with the Pennsylvania Historical and Museum Commission. Topics discussed included the Philadelphia Social History Project (1850-1880), history of childhood and the aged, historical preservation and restoration, careers in history, and the status of history in the schools.   D. C. Swift

4060. Walton, John.   COMMUNITY POWER AND THE RETREAT FROM POLITICS: FULL CIRCLE AFTER TWENTY YEARS?   *Social Problems 1976 23(3): 292-303.* Traces the development of research on community politics since Floyd Hunter's classic study of Atlanta in 1953, *Community Power Structure.* Hunter was an innovative research craftsman with a bold new effort to chart the political contours of a major American city. Social science of the 1950's and early 1960's was not prepared to pursue the kinds of questions he raised. Today there are new and encouraging trends focusing on the events taking place in US cities beginning in the late 1960's. Ref.   A. M. Osur

4061. Ward, Robert Elmer.   THE CITY DIRECTORY: A KEY TO FAMILY HISTORY.   *Family Heritage 1979 2(2): 54-59.* Uses the Buschow family in Cleveland, Ohio, 1883-1900, to demonstrate the value and use of city directories as sources of local and family history.

4062. Warsen, Allen A.   THE DETROIT JEWISH DIRECTORY OF 1907 AS A RESEARCH SOURCE.   *Michigan Jewish Hist. 1978 18(2): 20-23.* The Detroit Jewish directory listed 2,470 people with their occupations and addresses, reflecting the demographic, vocational, and organizational history of Detroit Jewry.

4063. Waters, Deborah Dependahl.   PHILADELPHIA'S BOSWELL: JOHN FANNING WATSON.   *Pennsylvania Mag. of Hist. and Biog. 1974 98(1): 3-52.* Biographical sketch of John Fanning Watson (1779-1860), whose *Annals of Philadelphia* (1830) and other historical works constitute an important primary source for historians of colonial Philadelphia and New York. Watson's pioneering use of the oral history interview and the public opinion questionnaire, in conjunction with the enduring usefulness of his historical works, demands that "his reputation as an antiquarian should be joined with that of 'historian.' " Based on primary sources; 205 notes.   E. W. Carp

4064. Weaver, John C.   INTRODUCTION: APPROACHES TO THE HISTORY OF URBAN REFORM.   *Urban Hist. Rev. [Canada] 1976 76(2): 3-11.* Introduces an issue on the history of urban reform. Compares recent Canadian interest in urban reform to earlier US interest. Combines a bibliographic approach to the history of Canadian urban reform with a historical overview of the subject. Raises questions about the definition of urban reform and notes that urban changes are not necessarily urban reforms. 16 notes.   C. A. Watson

4065. Weber, Michael P.   QUANTIFICATION AND THE TEACHING OF AMERICAN URBAN HISTORY.   *Hist. Teacher 1975 8(3): 391-402.* Discusses the course, "Opportunity in 19th Century America: A Quantitative View," taught at Carnegie-Mellon University. Students read and discuss the literature relating to opportunity and social mobility in 19th-century America, then test hypotheses using quantitative data from selected communities. Data is recorded, tabulated, compared, and discussed in oral reports. Primary and secondary sources; 5 notes, biblio.   P. W. Kennedy

4066. Welch, Edwin.   THE CITY OF OTTAWA ARCHIVES. *Urban Hist. Rev. [Canada] 1976 76(1): 10-13.* The author, Ottawa city archivist, describes the status of the records of Canada's capital city. Archives have not been well maintained nor have records been available for study. Other organizations such as the Public Archives of Canada, the Provincial Archives of Ontario, and local societies hold various records concerned with Ottawa history. A professional archivist was first appointed in 1975 and a start has been made on organizing and cataloging the records. Because of the conditions of some records and lack of study space, visits are by appointment only.   C. A. Watson

4067. Woods, Joseph Gerald.   ON AMERICAN URBAN HISTORY.   *Queen's Q. [Canada] 1976 83(3): 483-487.* A review article prompted by Adrian Cook's *The Arms of the Streets: The New York City Draft Riots of 1863* (Lexington: U. Pr. of Kentucky, 1975) and Howard M. Gitelman's *The Workingmen of Waltham: Mobility in American Urban Industrial Development 1850-1890* (Baltimore: John Hopkins U. Pr., 1975), which are typical of the tendency to examine relatively small, isolated topics, in view of our inability to define urban history. Both studies make significant contributions, Cook's more traditional, Gitelman's a quantitative analysis of mobility, typifying the differences of subject matter and method which make consensus difficult.

R. V. Ritter

4068. Woodward, Francis M.   FIRE INSURANCE PLANS AND BRITISH COLUMBIA URBAN HISTORY: A UNION LIST. *BC Studies [Canada] 1979 (42): 13-26.* Fire insurance plans are among measures adopted since the early 18th century to assess and control urban fire risks. Plans have been used in British Columbia towns since 1885. They contain scaled diagrams; the size, shape, and type of construction materials; the number of floors, doors, and other features; a description of fire protection facilities; the use of the buildings; special equipment and the source of power for its operation; and much other pertinent data. Produced by underwriters' associations, the plans were an invaluable source of information by fire insurance companies. They now constitute a largely untapped body of research materials for the urban historian. 3 illus., chart, 7 notes, biblio.   D. L. Smith

SUBJECT INDEX

Subject Profile Index (ABC-SPIndex) carries both generic and specific index terms. Begin a search at the general term but also look under more specific or related terms. Cross-references are included.

Each string of index descriptors is intended to present a profile of a given article; however, no particular relationship between any two terms in the profile is implied. Terms within the profile are listed alphabetically after the leading term. The variety of punctuation and capitalization reflects production methods and has no intrinsic meaning; e.g., there is no difference in meaning between "History, study of" and "History (study of)."

Cities, towns, and counties are listed following their respective states or provinces; e.g., "Ohio (Columbus)." The chronology of the bibliographic entry follows the subject index descriptors. In the chronology, "c" stands for "century"; e.g., "19c" means "19th century."

Note that "United States" is not used as a leading index term; if no country is mentioned, the index entry refers to the United States alone. When an entry refers to both Canada and the United States, both "Canada" and "USA" appear in the string of index descriptors, but "USA" is not a leading term. When an entry refers to any other country and the United States, only the other country is indexed.

The last number in the index string, in italics, refers to the bibliographic entry number.

A

Abercrombie, Anderson. Bricks. Creary, John W. Florida (Pensacola). Manufacturing. Raiford, Phillip H. 1854-60. *487*

Abernathy, Ralph. Alabama (Birmingham). Civil rights. Demonstrations. King, Martin Luther, Jr. Shuttlesworth, Fred L. 1956-79. *3061*

Abolition Movement *See also* Antislavery Sentiments; Emancipation.

—. Censorship. South Carolina (Charleston). Walker, David *(Appeal)*. 1830. *1397*

—. Negroes. Pennsylvania (Philadelphia). Riots. 1830-50. *1220*

Abolitionists. Fugitive Slaves. Negroes. Pennsylvania (Pittsburgh). Philanthropic Society. 1830's-60. *1341*

Academies. Architecture. Colleges and Universities. Oregon. Piper, William W. 1834-83. *1997*

Acadians *See also* Cajuns; French Canadians.

—. Assimilation. Massachusetts (Gloucester). Nova Scotia (Arichat region). 1850's-1900. *1623*

Accidents *See also* specific types of accidents.

—. City Government. Compensation, municipal. Ontario (Toronto). Public Employees. 1858-70. *3684*

—. Industrial safety. Massachusetts (Lowell). 1890-1905. *563*

Accounting. City Government. 1900-35. *256*

—. District of Columbia. Lawyers. Organizations. 1960-77. *2577*

Acculturation *See also* Assimilation.

—. Bianco, Carla. Catholic Church. Gambino, Richard. Italian Americans (review article). Pennsylvania (Rosetos). Social Organization. Tomasi, Silvano. 20c. *1606*

—. Boardinghouses. Immigrants. Italian Canadians. Ontario (Toronto). 20c. *3834*

—. California (Los Angeles). City Life. Indians. 1970's. *3192*

—. California (Los Angeles). Ethnicity. Race. Social status. Voting and Voting Behavior. 1973. *2475*

—. Catholic Church. Human Relations. Irish Americans. Pennsylvania (Pittsburgh; St. Andrew's Parish). 1863-90. *1511*

—. Catholic Church. Irish Americans. Pennsylvania (Pittsburgh). St. Andrew Parish. 1863-90. *1510*

—. Church Schools. Mexican Americans. Public Schools. Texas (San Antonio). 1973. *3156*

—. City Life. Ethnic Groups. Indians. Migration, Internal. 1945-75. *3194*

—. Colorado (Denver). English Americans. German Americans. Irish Americans. 1860-90. *1323*

—. Education. Immigrants. Massachusetts (Boston). Negroes. Social status. 1850. *1125*

—. Educational Reform. Ideology. Industrialization. Pennsylvania. Social control. 1880-1910. *1091*

—. Ethnicity. German Americans. Immigrants. Neighborhoods. 1840's-1970's. *1305*

—. Garment industry. Jews (Russian). May family. Oklahoma (Tulsa). 1889-1970. *1496*

—. German Americans. Ohio (Toledo). Press. 1850-90. *1562*

—. Illinois (Chicago). Immigrants. ca 1937-74. *642*

—. Immigrants. Ontario (Toronto). 1950's-70's. *3837*

—. Immigration. Jews. New York City. Yiddishe Arbeiten Universitet. 1921-39. *1078*

—. Immigration. Pennsylvania (Pittsburgh). Women. 1900-45. *1321*

—. Samoans. Washington (Seattle). 1890-1973. *3191*

Acting. Browne, Maurice. Chicago Little Theatre. Euripides *(Trojan Women)*. Illinois. Theater Production and Direction. VanVolkenburg, Ellen. 1912-17. *950*

Actors and Actresses. African Theatre. Negroes. New York City. 1820-23. *1024*

—. Chapman family. Pennsylvania (Pittsburgh). Showboats. 1827-47. *857*

—. Chestnut Street Theatre. Maryland (Baltimore). Reinagle, Alexander. Wignell, Thomas. 1792-1802. *1029*

—. Forrest, Edwin. Macready, William Charles. Nativism. New York City (Astor Place). Riots. 1849. *2963*

—. Saskatchewan (Regina). Theater. 1900-14. *3807*

Adams, John Quincy (1848-1922). Editors and Editing. Minnesota (St. Paul). Negroes. *Western Appeal.* 1888-1922. *1416*

Addams, Jane. Art. Attitudes. Illinois (Chicago). Reform. 1889-1916. *998*

Addiction *See also* Alcoholism; Drug Abuse.

—. Illinois (Chicago). Opium. 1880's-1910. *1733*

Admissions policies. Education. Equality. Ethnic groups. New York, City University of. 1970-79. *2854*

Adolescence *See also* Youth.

—. Adulthood. Institutions. Social change. 1850-1970. *708*

—. Employment. Frontier and Pioneer Life. Ontario (Orillia). Social change. 1861-71. *3784*

—. Employment. Industrialization. Ontario (Hamilton). School (attendance). 1851-90's. *3796*

—. Massachusetts (Boston). Revivals. 1822-42. *1694*

Adolescents. Attitudes. Law. Wisconsin (Racine). 1971. *2935*

—. College and Universities. Rural-Urban Studies. 1973. *2867*

Adrian, Charles R. City Government (review article). Griffith, Ernest S. Hershkowitz, Leo. Teaford, Jon C. 1776-1876. *238*

Adult education. Halifax Mechanics' Institute. Middle Classes. Nova Scotia. Working class. 1830's-40's. *3797*

Adultery. Boardinghouses. Hungarian Americans. Illinois. Immigrants. Landlords and Tenants. 1899-1914. *815*

Adulthood. Adolescence. Institutions. Social change. 1850-1970. *708*

Adventists. Cudney, A. J. Missions and Missionaries. Nebraska (Lincoln). 1885-87. *1681*

Advertising *See also* Marketing; Propaganda; Public Relations; Publicity.

—. Agriculture. Boom towns. Colorado, southeastern. Rain and Rainfall. Speculation. 1886-94. *219*

—. Alabama. Boosterism. Economic growth. Newspapers. 1812-20. *207*

—. Architecture. Midwest. Service stations. 1917-25. *1862*

—. Federal Regulation. Illinois (Chicago). Medicine, Patent. Pure Food and Drug Act (1906). 1850-1906. *1712*

—. Illinois (Chicago). Political Campaigns (mayoral). Public Opinion. Television. 1975. *2775*

—. Medicine, patent. New York (Rochester). Warner, Hulbert Harrington. 1879-93. *414*

Advisory Bodies. Local government. Pennsylvania. 1972-74. *2372*

Advocacy. California (San Francisco). Louisiana (New Orleans). Missouri (St. Louis). Negroes. Public Administration. 1974-78. *3087*

Aeronautics, Military. Alabama (Montgomery). Maxwell Field. 1922-77. *2554*

Aestheticism. Architecture. California (San Francisco). Jeunes (group). Norris, Frank. 1890's. *984*

—. Jews. Literature. New York City. *Yunge* (group). 1902-13. *1063*

Aesthetics. Architecture. 1973. *3615*

—. Architecture. Exhibits and Expositions. 1890's-1970's. *3286*

—. Architecture. Skyscrapers. ca 1876-1900. *1876*

Affirmative action. City Government. Discrimination, employment. Negroes. Ohio (Cincinnati). 1963-67. *2352*

Africa, West. Louisiana (New Orleans; Congo Square). Music (jazz). Negroes. Religion. Rites and Ceremonies. 18c-19c. *1018*

African Baptist Church. Education. Emancipation. Meachum, John Berry. Missouri (St. Louis). Negroes. 1815-54. *1389*

African Theatre. Actors and Actresses. Negroes. New York City. 1820-23. *1024*

Afro-Americans. *See* Negroes.

Age. Environment. Methodology. Mortality. 1974. *2689*

—. Marriage. Marriage. Massachusetts (Newburyport). Men. Women. ca 1800-30. *695*

Aged *See also* Death and Dying; Pensions; Public Welfare.

—. British Columbia (Vancouver, Victoria). Income. Population. Taxation. 1951-74. *3782*

—. California. Friendship. Widows. 1973. *2650*

—. California (San Diego). Ohio (Cleveland). Segregation. 1970. *2675*

—. Catholic Church. Irish Canadians. McMahon, Patrick. Orphans. Poor. Quebec (Quebec). St. Bridget's Home. 1847-1972. *3841*

—. Migration, Internal. Retirement. Saskatchewan (Regina, Saskatoon). 1921-78. *3628*

—. New York (Westchester). 1950's-70's. *2683*

—. Pennsylvania (Philadelphia). Rest homes. 1817-1900. *1153*

—. Planning. Public Housing. Social services. 1972-74. *2363*

Agrarian myth. Illinois (Chicago). Novels. Ruller, Henry Blake. 1890's. *2182*

Agricultural Commodities. Marketing. Ontario (Simcoe County). Railroads. Roads. Towns. 1850-75. *3739*

Agricultural Cooperatives. Farms. Neighborhoods. Regional planning. 1920's. *1825*

Agricultural Labor *See also* Migrant Labor; Peasants.

—. California (El Monte). Foreign Relations. Japan. Mexico. Strikes. 1933. *600*

Aqueducts. Broad Street Bridge. Erie Canal. Genesee River. New York (Rochester). 1817-1975. *2060*

Arab Americans. Asian Americans. Hispanic Americans. Immigrants. Ohio (Toledo). Settlement. 1965-76. *3020*

—. Immigration. Michigan (Detroit). Settlement. 1961-74. *3182*

Arbitration. American Federation of State, County, and Municipal Employees. Indiana (Indianapolis). Labor Disputes. 1971-72. *2638*

—. City Government. Wisconsin. 1973. *2385*

Archaeology *See also* Anthropology; Artifacts; Cliff Dwellers; Excavations; Indians; Museums; Stone Implements.

—. Anasazi culture. Cliff dwellers. Colorado, southwestern. Indians. Mesa Verde National Park. ca 450-1300. 1888-1977. *3934*

—. Architecture. Arizona (Antelope House). Indians. Masonry style. 1070-1300. *3931*

—. Artifacts. Nevada (Lost City, Moapa Valley). ca 530. 1975. *3935*

—. Cliff dwellers. Colorado. Indians. Nordenskiold, Gustaf (*Cliff Dwellers of the Mesa Verde*). Prehistory. 1891-93. *3929*

—. Indians. Methodology. Population. Pueblo Indians. Southwest. Prehistory. *3924*

—. Pennsylvania (Philadelphia). Preservation. 18c. 1950's-75. *3505*

Archdeacon, Thomas J. (review article). Colonial Government. Dutch Americans. New York City. Social Classes. 1664-1710. 1976. *26*

Architects. California. County Government. Fusselman, William. Marin County Civic Center. 1952-63. *3417*

—. Capitols. Construction. District of Columbia. Hoban, James. 1799. *1885*

—. Churches. Folsom, William Harrison. Mormons. Utah (Provo, Salt Lake City). ca 1850's-1901. *1861*

—. City Planning. Illinois (Riverside). Olmsted, Frederick Law. Suburbs. 1868-70. *1827*

—. Department stores. New York City. Snook, John B. Stewart, Alexander Turney. 1846-84. *1973*

—. East India Marine Hall. Massachusetts (Salem). Sumner, Thomas Waldron. 1825-1975. *1974*

—. Great Britain (London). Illinois (Chicago). Settlement houses. Social workers. 1890's-1900's. *1981*

—. Nova Scotia (Halifax). 1749-1973. *3884*

—. Ontario (Toronto). 1834-90's. *3878*

Architects (review article). Burnham, Daniel Hudson. Hines, Thomas S. Twombly, Robert C. Wright, Frank Lloyd. 1867-1970. 1973-74. *1979*

Architecture *See also* Buildings; Construction.

—. 20c. *3418*

—. Academies. Colleges and Universities. Oregon. Piper, William W. 1834-83. *1997*

—. Advertising. Midwest. Service stations. 1917-25. *1862*

—. Aestheticism. California (San Francisco). Jeunes (group). Norris, Frank. 1890's. *984*

—. Aesthetics. 1973. *3615*

—. Aesthetics. Exhibits and Expositions. 1890's-1970's. *3286*

—. Aesthetics. Skyscrapers. ca 1876-1900. *1876*

—. Airports. Texas (Dallas, Fort Worth). 1974. *3422*

—. Alabama (Cahaba, Montgomery, Tuscaloosa). Capitols. 1819-1912. *1914*

—. Alleys. Attitudes. Neighborhoods. 17c-20c. *1787*

—. Apartment houses. Illinois (Chicago; Gold Coast). Landlords and Tenants. Upper Classes. 1882-1929. *1910*

—. Archaeology. Arizona (Antelope House). Indians. Masonry style. 1070-1300. *3931*

—. Arizona (Florence). 1853-1973. *1976*

—. Art. City beautiful movement. City planning. 1890-1910. *1846*

—. Assembly House. Massachusetts (Salem). 1782-1970. *1999*

—. Barnsdall, Aline. California (Los Angeles; Olive Hill). HollyHock House. Wright, Frank Lloyd. 1914-24. *1972*

—. Beaux arts movement. Illinois (Chicago). Jenney, William Le Baron. Skyscrapers. World's Columbian Exposition (Chicago, 1893). 1880-1920. *1982*

—. Beer. Breweries. 19c. *1944*

—. Benjamin, Asher. Boston Exchange House. Hotels. Massachusetts. Rogers, Isaiah. Tremont House. 1808-28. *1956*

—. Benjamin, Asher. Massachusetts (Boston). West Church. 1805-23. *1994*

—. Benjamin, Asher. New England. 1795-1841. *1957*

—. Benjamin, Asher. Vermont (Windsor). 1797-1802. *1959*

—. Boardinghouses. Massachusetts (Lowell). 1820-70. *1918*

—. Bogardus, James. Construction. Fire towers. Iron-framed structures. Kroehl, Julius B. New York City. 1850's. *1926*

—. Boom towns. Houses, shotgun. Oil Industry and Trade. Texas Panhandle. 1920-40. *1904*

—. Brackett, E. A. Fowler, Orson Squire (*A Home for All*). Houses, octagon. Massachusetts (Reading, Winchester). Wakefield, H. P. 1848-60. *1945*

—. Bradley, Lucas. Missouri (St. Louis). Wisconsin (Racine). 1840-90. *1950*

—. Bricks. German Americans. Ohio (Columbus; German Village). Preservation. 19c. 1960-78. *3549*

—. Bridges. City Planning. Pennsylvania. Photographs. 1870's-80's. *1815*

—. Broadacre City (proposed). City Planning. Wright, Frank Lloyd. 1933-76. *3310*

—. Bryant, Gridley J. F. Essex Institution. John Tucker Daland House. Massachusetts (Salem). 1850-1978. *1987*

—. Burnham, Daniel Hudson. Business. Illinois (Chicago). Root, John Wellborn. Union Stockyard. 1871-1902. *1996*

—. Burnham, Daniel Hudson. Illinois. World's Columbian Exposition (Chicago, 1893). 1891-93. 20c. *1927*

—. Burnham, Daniel Hudson. Montezuma Hotel. New Mexico (Las Vegas). Root, John Wellborn. 1879-85. *1919*

—. Calico Printing. Cotton mills. Dover Manufacturing Company Print Works. New Hampshire (Dover). 1820-25. *474*

—. California. Eureka Heritage Society. Restorations. Vellutini, Dolores. 1973-78. *3573*

—. California (Los Angeles). Insurance. Marks, David X. Marks, Joshua H. Philanthropy. 1902-77. *49*

—. California (Los Angeles). Social Change. 1890-1970. *1964*

—. Canada. Railroad stations. Standardization. USA. Western States. ca 1910-30's. *1903*

—. Canadian Pacific Railway. Railroad stations. Saskatchewan. 20c. *3880*

—. Capitol Theatre. Entertainment. Movie theaters. Ontario (Ottawa). Vaudeville. 1920-70. *3911*

—. Capitols. District of Columbia. 1792-1850. *1977*

—. Capitols. District of Columbia. 1792-93. *1878*

—. Capitols. District of Columbia. House of Representatives Chamber. Jefferson, Thomas. Latrobe, Benjamin Henry. 1803-12. *1890*

—. Capitols. Massachusetts (Boston). Payne, William. 1658-1975. *1883*

—. Cauchon, Joseph-Edouard. Empire Hotel. Iron-front buildings. Manitoba (Winnipeg). 1880-1920. *3908*

—. Charities. Daily Life. Garrett, John Work. Garrett, Mary Frick. Garrett, Robert. Maryland (Baltimore). Mount Vernon Place (residence). Upper Classes. 1872-1928. *770*

—. Chrysler Building. New York City. Restorations. VanAlen, William. 1928-79. *3526*

—. Church of St. Paul the Apostle. Decorative Arts. LaFarge, John. New York City. 1876-99. *1056*

—. Churches. Tennessee (Memphis). 19c. *1954*

—. City Life. Middle Classes. New York City (Harlem). 1976. *3060*

—. City Planning. 1776-1970's. *1828*

—. City planning. Cleveland Group Plan. Ohio. 1890-1912. *1829*

—. City Planning. Conron, John P. (interview). Government Regulation. New Mexico (Santa Fe, Silver City). 1974. *3489*

—. City Planning. District of Columbia. L'Enfant, Pierre Charles. 1791. *1823*

—. City planning. Europe. Housing. Modernism. New Deal. New York City. Ohio (Cleveland). Pennsylvania (Philadelphia). 1932-60. *1952*

—. City Planning. Florida (Coral Gables). Preservation. 1920's. 1960-70's. *3582*

—. City Planning. Gutkind, Erwin Anton. ca 1943-53. *3966*

—. City planning. Housing. Women. Working conditions. 1960's-70's. *3276*

—. City Planning. Massachusetts (North Easton). Olmsted, Frederick Law. Richardson, Henry Hobson. 1870-90. *1784*

—. City Planning. Mormons. Smith, Joseph. Western States. 1833-90. *1822*

—. City planning. Mutual Advisory Committee. Ontario (London). Politics. Preservation. 1970-77. *3876*

—. City planning. Northern Pacific Railroad Company. Olmsted, Frederick Law. Tilton, James. Washington (Tacoma). 1873. *1832*

—. College Building. Heiman, Adolphus. Tennessee (Nashville). 1836-1974. *1941*

—. Columbia University (and Low Library). McKim, Charles F. New York City. 1894-20c. *1949*

—. Connecticut (Hartford). Potter, Edward Tuckerman. Restoration. Twain, Mark (home). 1874. 1955. *3512*

—. Connecticut (New Haven). Georgia (Savannah). Massachusetts (Boston). New York City. Pennsylvania (Philadelphia). 18c. *1983*

—. Country Life. Mormons. Scandinavian Americans. Utah (Spring City). 1851-1975. *1849*

—. Daguerreotypes. District of Columbia. Photography. Plumbe, John, Jr. 1845-49. *1893*

—. Demolition. District of Columbia. 19c-20c. *1899*

—. Domesticity. Houses. Social change. 1840-70. *1884*

—. Environment. Larkin Administration Building. New York (Buffalo). Ventilation system. Wright, Frank Lloyd. 1904. *1864*

—. Episcopal Church, Protestant. New Hampshire (Portsmouth). St. John's Episcopal Church. 1807-09. *1895*

—. Exhibits and Expositions. 1851-1939. *1891*

—. Fine Arts Building. Illinois (Chicago). 1898-1918. *1892*

—. Gardiner-Pingree House. Massachusetts (Salem). 1800-1975. *2000*

—. Georgia (Atlanta). Historic Oakland Cemetery, Inc. Oakland Cemetery. Preservation. 1850-1979. *3566*

—. Gilbert, Cass. Skyscrapers. Woolworth Tower. 1899-1913. *1924*

—. Grant, Madison. New York Zoological Park. Wildlife conservation. 1894-1911. *880*

—. Great Britain (London). Pennsylvania (Philadelphia). 1619-1800. *1809*

—. Haiti. Houses, shotgun. Louisiana (New Orleans). Nigeria. Yoruba. 18c-1974. *1993*

—. Harmony Society. Pennsylvania (Economy). Restoration. 1780-1973. *2117*

—. Historical Sites and Parks. Missouri (St. Louis). Water towers. 1870-1970. *2113*

—. Historical Sites and Parks. Nova Scotia (Halifax). Waterfronts. 1815-1973. *3881*

—. Houses. Indiana (Terre Haute). Segregation. Social classes. 1879-1900. *1866*

—. Houses. Jacobs, Herbert A. Wisconsin (Madison). Wright, Frank Lloyd. 1936-48. *1920*

—. Houses. Patios. Porches. Social Change. 1860-1960. *1985*

—. Houses. Wood carving. Woodland, George. 1867-1969. *1901*

—. Houses, elephant. Lafferty, James V. New Jersey (Margate). Patents. Publicity. Real estate. 1880's. 1970-77. *1881*

—. Housing. Idaho (Boise). 1904-12. *1909*

—. Housing. Industrialization. Maryland (Baltimore). Row Houses. 1800-30. *1859*

—. Hunter, Mary Robinson. Hunter, Thomas. Letters. Lyman, Ann Maria. Rhode Island (Newport). Wanton-Lyman-Hazard House. 18c-19c. *1990*

—. Illinois. Indiana. Ohio. Railroad stations. 1880's-1920's. *1902*

—. Illinois (Chicago). 1960's-77. *3424*

—. Illinois (Chicago). 20c. *1897*

—. Illinois (Chicago). Iron-front buildings. 1854-80's. *1897*

—. Illinois (Chicago). Marshall Field building. Richardson, Henry Hobson. 1880's. *1946*

—. Illinois (Galena). Preservation. 1820's-1900's. 1965-79. *3581*

—. Illinois (Oak Park). Wright, Frank Lloyd. 1889-1909. *1978*

—. Indiana (New Harmony). Pennsylvania (Economy, Harmony). Preservation. Rapp, George. Restorations. 1804-25. 20c. *3547*

—. Iowa (Dubuque). 1850's. *1917*

—. Iron-front buildings. 1848-1900. *1896*

—. Kellum, John. Mansions. New York. Stewart, Alexander Turney. 1860-90. *1880*

—. Business. Missouri (Kansas City). Remington, Frederic. 1883-85. *1032*

—. California (East Los Angeles). Mechicano Art Center. Mexican Americans. Murals. 1970's. *2786*

—. California (East Los Angeles). Mexican Americans. Murals, street. Values. 1978. *2816*

—. California (Los Angeles). Ethnicity. Mexican Americans. Murals, street. 1970's. *3164*

—. Clark, George W. Illinois (Jacksonville). Mason, Ebenezer. Smith, Robert Campbell. Woodman, William S. 1870's. *989*

—. Cultural Imperialism. New York City. Regionalism. 1974. *2793*

—. Davis, Gene. District of Columbia. Personal Narratives. 1950-66. *2790*

—. District of Columbia. 1975-78. *2808*

—. Exhibits and Expositions. New York City. 1970's. *2800*

—. Ghettos. Immigrants. Jews. 1880-1930. *1498*

—. Interborough Rapid Transit. New York City. Subways. 1914-17. *1044*

—. Museums. New York Gallery of Fine Arts. Reed, Luman. 1844-58. *1013*

—. North Carolina (Winston-Salem). Southeastern Center for Contemporary Art. 1979. *2806*

Art and Society. Illinois (Chicago). Novels. 1890-1910. *985*

—. Planning. Preservation. 1978. *3301*

Art (criticism). Bartholdi, Auguste. New York City. Statue of Liberty. 1875-86. 1974. *1046*

Art Deco. Buildings. Florida (Miami Beach). Miami Design Preservation League. Preservation. 1920-35. 1978. *3500*

Art Galleries and Museums *See also* names of particular galleries and museums, e.g. Boston Museum of Fine Arts, etc.

—. Fenway Court (home). Gardner, Isabella Stewart. Massachusetts (Boston). 1860-1920. 1978. *1986*

Art Institute of Chicago. Illinois. 1879-1909. *999*

—. Illinois. 1879-1978. *1014*

Art, public. California (Los Angeles). City life. 1970's. *2805*

—. Law. Murals. New York City (Bronx). Post offices. Preservation. Shahn, Ben. 1938-76. *3578*

Art Workers Guild. Arts and Crafts. Great Britain (London). Massachusetts (Boston). 1890's-1940. *1059*

Artifacts *See also* Excavations.

—. Archaeology. Nevada (Lost City, Moapa Valley). ca 530. 1975. *3935*

—. Buildings. City Planning. Communes. Harmony Society. Indiana (New Harmony). Pennsylvania (Economy, Harmony). Planning. Social customs. 1820's-1905. *648*

—. Commercialism. Folk art. Greek Americans. Pennsylvania (Philadelphia; Upper Darby). Religion. 1970's. *461*

—. Florida (St. Augustine). Spain. 16c. 1972-78. *646*

Artisans. Apprenticeship. Journeymen. Maryland (Baltimore). Slavery. Wealth. 1790-1820. *514*

—. City government. Hogs and Hog Raising. New York City. Public Health. Reform. 1796-1819. *805*

—. Construction. Labor Unions and Organizations. Ontario (Toronto). Politics. 1896-1914. *3748*

—. Cotton industry. Iron industry. Rhode Island (Pawtucket). Technology. 1790's-1810's. *491*

—. Economic conditions. Industrialization. Occupations. Pennsylvania (Germantown). 1767-91. *526*

—. Industrialization. Morality. Pennsylvania (Philadelphia). Social customs. Work ethic. Working Class. 1820-50. *787*

—. Ohio (Cincinnati). Organs. 1850-1900. *494*

Artists. Appalachia. Epworth Jubilee Community Arts Center. Folk art. Tennessee (Knoxville). 1970's. *2789*

—. Business. Signboards. Virginia (Williamsburg). 1740's-70's. *959*

—. Businessmen. Cole, Thomas. Maine (Bar Harbor). Pratt, Henry. Resorts. 1840-70. *198*

—. California (East Los Angeles, Los Angeles; Boyle Heights). Ethnicity. Mexican Americans. Murals. 1965-75. *3153*

—. California, southern. Los Angeles County Museum of Art (collection). ca 1900-40. *1021*

—. Community Participation in Politics. Leftism. Murals. Social change. Social change. 1970's. *2787*

—. District of Columbia. Personal Narratives. 1978. *2809*

—. Hispanic Americans. Murals. 1970's. *2791*

—. Housing. Industry. New York City. 1970's. *2813*

—. Iowa. Lithographs. 1830's-90's. *1794*

—. Köllner, Augustus (drawings). New York City (Staten Island). 19c. *1048*

—. Literature. Negroes. New York City. Williams, John A. (interview). 1920's-70's. *3125*

—. McConaughy, David. Pennsylvania (Philadelphia). Petitions. Tariff. 1868-90. *962*

—. New York City. 20c. *2811*

—. New York City (SoHo). 1970's. *2804*

Arts. Atlanta Arts Alliance. Georgia. 1968-73. *2812*

—. California (Los Angeles; Watts). 1974. *2807*

—. Children. Illinois (Chicago). Poor. Urban Gateways program. 1961-75. *2799*

—. Ethnicity. New York City. Puerto Ricans. 1960's-70's. *3142*

—. Management. New York City. 1970's. *2815*

—. National Council on the Arts. National Endowment for the Arts. Subsidies. Washington (Seattle). 1969-75. *2792*

Arts and Crafts *See also* Decorative Arts; Folk Art; Wood Carving.

—. Art Workers Guild. Great Britain (London). Massachusetts (Boston). 1890's-1940. *1059*

—. Business. Fine Arts Building. Illinois (Chicago). 1898-1917. *423*

—. Ethnic groups. Ohio (Cleveland). Peoples and Cultures, Inc. 1974. *2788*

Arts programs. Ontario (Toronto). 1978. *3778*

Asia, Southeast. China. Chinatowns. Economic development. Foreign investments. Ghettos. New York City. 1970's. *2585*

Asian Americans. Arab Americans. Hispanic Americans. Immigrants. Ohio (Toledo). Settlement. 1965-76. *3020*

—. Assimilation. California (San Francisco). Immigrants. Social organization. 1970's. *3176*

—. City Government. New York City. Public Policy. Social Conditions. 1970's. *3177*

Asiatic Exclusion League. Anglo-Japanese Treaty of Alliance (1902). British Columbia (Vancouver). Canada. Japan. Nativism. Riots. USA. 1907-22. *1283*

Aspira (organization). Educational Reform. Harlem Parents Union. Minorities. New York City. Pennsylvania (Philadelphia). Voluntary Associations. Welfare Rights Organization. 1970's. *2840*

Assembly House. Architecture. Massachusetts (Salem). 1782-1970. *1999*

Assembly line. Automobiles. Ford Motor Company. Labor. Michigan (Highland Park). 1910-14. *509*

Assimilation *See also* Acculturation; Integration.

—. Acadians. Massachusetts (Gloucester). Nova Scotia (Arichat region). 1850's-1900. *1623*

—. Alberta (Coaldale). Germans, Russian. Mennonites. Organizations. 1920-76. *3848*

—. Aliens, Illegal. Colombian Americans. Employment. New York City (Jackson Heights, Queens). Politics. 1965-77. *3138*

—. Asian Americans. California (San Francisco). Immigrants. Social organization. 1970's. *3176*

—. Atlantic Provinces. Canadians. Economic conditions. Immigration. Kennedy, Albert J. Massachusetts (Boston). 1910's. *1593*

—. California (Los Angeles). Europe. Immigrants. Jews. Marriage. 1910-13. *1469*

—. California (Los Angeles). Korean Americans. Minorities in Politics. 1970. *3102*

—. Catholic Church. Clergy. Dufresne, Andre B. French Canadians. Massachusetts (Holyoke). 1869-87. *1655*

—. Catholic Church. Connecticut (New Britain; Holy Cross Parish). Polish Americans. 1928-76. *1566*

—. Catholic Church. Connecticut (Waterbury). Lithuanian Americans. Newspapers. *Rytas*. Zebris, Joseph. 1896-98. *948*

—. Catholic Church. French Americans. Vermont (Winooski). 1867-1900. *1567*

—. Catholic Church. Parishes. Pennsylvania (Philadelphia). 1759-1975. *1651*

—. Chinese Americans. District of Columbia. Education. Friendship. 1940's-70's. *3173*

—. Chinese Americans. New York City. Peru (Lima). 1849-1976. *1558*

—. City life. Immigrants. Public schools. 1890's-1920. *1088*

—. Colorado (Denver). Greek Americans. 20c. *1607*

—. Converts. Jews. Ontario (Toronto). Presbyterian Church. 1912-18. *3863*

—. Education. Employment. English Language. Immigrants. Ontario (Toronto). 1968-70. *3856*

—. Education. Immigrants. Negroes. Racism. Slavic Americans. Social Mobility. 1890-1966. *1089*

—. Ethnic groups. Fraternal organizations. Health. Pennsylvania (Pittsburgh). 1900-70. *729*

—. Ethnic groups. Negroes. Pennsylvania (Philadelphia). 1850-1970. *1314*

—. Ethnicity. Greek Americans. New York City. Orthodox Eastern Church. St. Demetrios Church. St. Markela Church. 1970's. *3206*

—. Ethnicity. Intermarriage. Mexican Americans. Texas (San Antonio). Women. 1830-60. *1523*

—. French Canadians. Nationalism. Religion. Rhode Island (Woonsocket). 1924-29. *1616*

—. German Americans. Immigration. Kentucky (Louisville). Liederkranz (society). Music. 1848-77. *1589*

—. German Americans. Michigan (Ann Arbor). Pluralism. Protestantism. Württembergers. 1830-1955. *1295*

—. Immigrants. Macedonian Canadians. Ontario (Toronto). 1900-20. *3843*

—. Indians. Washington (Seattle). 1975. *3183*

—. Italian Americans. Missouri (St. Louis). World War I. 1914-18. *1602*

—. Italian Canadians. Mass media, Italian. Ontario (Toronto). 1970's. *3823*

—. Mayors, black. Negroes. Political participation. 1960-71. *3098*

—. Mexican Americans. Southwest. Urbanization. 1900-30. *3161*

—. Models. New York City. Puerto Ricans. Residential segregation. 1960-70. *3163*

—. New York (Sloan). Polish Americans. 1873-1977. *1615*

—. Ohio (Cleveland). Slovak Americans. 1930's-50's. *1609*

—. Pennsylvania (Philadelphia). Polish Americans. Polish Emigration Land Company. Smolinski, Joseph. Virginia. 1860's. 1917-18. *1591*

Associated Silk Workers Union. American Civil Liberties Union. Freedom of Assembly. Freedom of Speech. New Jersey (Paterson). Strikes. 1924. *596*

Associates of the Jersey Company. City government. Land Tenure. New Jersey (Jersey City). Water rights. Waterfronts. 1845-50. *255*

Association of Commercial and Technical Employees. Canadian Labour Congress. Labor Unions and Organizations (white-collar). Ontario (Toronto). 1972. *3710*

Atheism *See also* Rationalism.

—. Bobb, John. Missouri (St. Louis). Periodicals. *Western Examiner*. 1834-35. *1645*

—. Ingersoll, Robert. Lectures. Nevada (Virginia City). Public Opinion. 1877. *1666*

Athenaeum (library). Elites. Massachusetts (Boston). Social Organizations. 1807-60. *1040*

Athletic clubs. Ethnic groups. Social status. 19c. *747*

—. New York City. Social Classes. 1866-1915. *821*

Athletics. See Sports.

Atkinson, John R. Blacksmiths. Idaho (Boise). Photographs. 1890's. *518*

Atlanta Arts Alliance. Arts. Georgia. 1968-73. *2812*

Atlanta Chamber of Commerce. Georgia. Grady, Henry. Industrialization. Urbanization. 1920's. *105*

Atlanta *Constitution*. Editors and Editing. McGill, Ralph. Political Commentary. South. 1930-69. *2773*

Atlanta Historical Society. Georgia. Historical Societies. 1926-79. *2695*

Atlanta Transit Company. Georgia Power Company. Street, Electric Railway and Motor Coach Employees of America. Strikes. 1946-50. *2632*

Atlantic Provinces *See also* Maritime Provinces; New Brunswick; Newfoundland; Nova Scotia.

—. Assimilation. Canadians. Economic conditions. Immigration. Kennedy, Albert J. Massachusetts (Boston). 1910's. *1593*

—. Boardinghouses. Government. Labor. Merchant Marine. Ports. Social reform. ca 1850's-90's. *3780*

Attitudes *See also* Political Attitudes; Public Opinion; Values.
—. Addams, Jane. Art. Illinois (Chicago). Reform. 1889-1916. *998*
—. Adolescents. Law. Wisconsin (Racine). 1971. *2935*
—. Alcohol. Rural-urban studies. 1966-68. *3613*
—. Alleys. Architecture. Neighborhoods. 17c-20c. *1787*
—. American Revolution. Carleton, Guy. Military Occupation. Peasants. Quebec. 1775-76. *3682*
—. Arkansas (Little Rock). Eckford, Elizabeth. Negroes. Personal Narratives. Public schools. School Integration. 1957-79. *3120*
—. Behavior. Crowding. Michigan (Detroit area). Social Conditions. 1965-66. *2640*
—. Behavior. Employment. Minorities. Poverty. Texas (Houston). 1974. *2706*
—. Behavior. Integration. Suburbs. 1950's-60's. *3030*
—. Behavior. Rural-Urban Studies. 1960's-70's. *3603*
—. Bigelow, Jacob. Cemeteries. Massachusetts (Cambridge). Mount Auburn Cemetery. Public Health. Rural cemetery movement. 1831. *2009*
—. Birth control. Clergy. Negroes. Population. Tennessee (Nashville). 20c. *3079*
—. Blind. Education. Employment. Pennsylvania. Pittsburgh Workshop for the Blind. 19c-1939. *1184*
—. Busing. Michigan (Pontiac). Parents. School Integration. 1972-75. *2890*
—. Butler, Benjamin Franklin. Civil War. Letters. Louisiana (New Orleans). Military Occupation. Women. 1861-62. *328*
—. California (Los Angeles County). Integration. Liberals. Negroes. Whites. 1972. *3018*
—. California (San Francisco). Earthquakes. Jews. 1906. *2123*
—. California (San Francisco). Jews. Reese, Michael. Wealth. 1850-78. *1458*
—. Canada. Migration, Internal. Rural-Urban Studies. Urbanization. 1955-75. *3648*
—. Capitalism. Howells, William Dean. 1860-1900. *2144*
—. Childbirth. Midwives. Physicians. 1830-60. *1721*
—. Child-rearing. 1880-99. *1722*
—. City government. Ohio (Cincinnati). Sanitation. 1800-1915. *2037*
—. City Life. France. 1960's-70's. *3599*
—. Civil rights. Illinois (Chicago, Evanston). Middle Classes. Negroes. 1974. *3113*
—. Colorado (Denver). Mexican Americans. Negroes. Neighborhoods. Public services. Whites. 1970's. *3612*
—. Coney Island. New York City (Brooklyn). Popular Culture. Recreation. Technology. 1829-1910. *915*
—. Country Life. Environment. 1978. *2658*
—. Death and Dying. Pennsylvania (Pittsburgh). Working class. 1890's. *786*
—. Decentralization. Educational Policy. Hispanic Americans. New York City (Washington Heights). 1969-74. *2818*
—. Economic theory. Illinois (Chicago). Indiana (Indianapolis). Occupations. Ohio (Cincinnati). 1850's. *392*
—. Education. Immigration. Mexican Americans. Negroes. Wisconsin (Racine). 1974. *3047*
—. Ethnicity. Foreign Policy. Polish Americans. Wisconsin (Milwaukee). 1970's. *3202*
—. Ethnicity. Illinois (Chicago). Negroes. Race Relations. Social Classes. 1969. *3042*
—. Ford, Gerald R. New York City. Public Finance. 1970's. *3593*
—. Georgia (Augusta). Urbanization. 1820-60. *2189*
—. Ghettos. Working Conditions. 1967-73. *3038*
—. Great Britain (London). Local Government. New York City. ca 1960-73. *3616*
—. Hawaii (Honolulu). Japanese Americans. National characteristics. 1971. *3174*
—. Historical Sites and Parks. Ohio (Columbus; German Village). Preservation. 19c-20c. *3515*
—. Housing. Migration, Internal. Population. 1970's. *3595*
—. Housing. Negroes. 1970. *3100*
—. Housing. Negroes. Ohio (Toledo). Racism. United Automobile Workers of America. 1967-73. *3015*

—. Howells, William Dean. Literature. Utopias. 1894-1906. *2143*
—. Illinois (Chicago). Negroes. Whites. 1975. *3056*
—. Illinois, western. Rural-urban studies. Social Classes. 1974. *2659*
—. Income. Metropolitan Areas. Migration. 1975. *2195*
—. Jews. Social Conditions. South. 1890-1977. *1467*
—. Ku Klux Klan. Morality. Ohio (Youngstown). Reform. 1920's. *736*
—. Local Government. Metropolitan Areas. Public services. Tennessee (Nashville-Davidson County). 1962-73. *3620*
—. Management. Public housing. 1968. *3383*
—. Metropolitan areas. Migration, Internal. National self-image. 1975. *3594*
—. Mexican Americans. Negroes. Race Relations. Texas (Houston). Whites. -1973. *3023*
—. Military service. Negroes. Rural-Urban Studies. Texas (East Texas, Houston). 1973. *3095*
—. Negroes. Race. 1968. *3078*
—. Neighborhoods. Real estate. Urban Renewal. 1970's. *3537*
—. Rural-urban studies. Stereotypes. 1920's. *2178*
—. Social Problems. -1973. *2641*
—. Social Problems. ca 1953-74. *3600*

Audience. Billy Graham Crusade. Revivals. Social classes. -1974. *3217*
Audiences. California (Los Angeles). Spanish Language. Television. 1971-72. *2770*
Audiovisual Materials. New York. Reynolds Library, Inc. Rochester Public Library. 1812-1963. *952*
Audubon, John James. Amelung, Sophia. Art. Corwine, Aaron H. Ohio (Cincinnati). 1819-24. *977*
Auerbach's Department Store. California. Jews. Retail Trade. Utah (Salt Lake City). 1857-1977. *451*
Australia (Melbourne). Boom towns. California (San Francisco). City Government. Gold Rushes. 1848-70. *144*
Authority. Great Britain (London). New York City. Police. Social organization. 1830-70. *1257*

Authors *See also* names of individual authors; Poets.
—. Arizona (Tucson). Wright, Harold Bell. 1915-36. *2162*
—. Cabell, James Branch. Glasgow, Ellen. Literature. Southern Renaissance. Virginia (Richmond). 1920's. *1002*
—. Cabell, James Branch. Glasgow, Ellen. Virginia (Richmond). 1733-1900's. *976*
—. Colorado (Denver). Jews. Physicians. Social work. Spivak, Charles. ca 1880-1927. *1740*
—. Cook, George Cram. Dell, Floyd. Feminism. Glaspell, Susan. Iowa (Davenport). Progressivism. Socialism. 1903-11. *1023*
—. Feminism. MacLane, Mary. Montana (Butte). 1902-29. *1015*
—. Fields, Annie Adams. Friendship. Massachusetts (Boston). 1834-1913. *1008*
—. France (Paris). Negroes. New York City (Harlem). Whites. 1920's. *1051*
—. MacLane, Mary. Montana (Butte). Women. 1901-29. *1058*

Autobiography *See also* Personal Narratives.
—. Civil War. Education. Friends, Society of. Hallowell, Benjamin. Science. Virginia (Alexandria). 1824-60. *672*
—. Communist Party. Illinois (Chicago). Negroes. Wright, Richard. 1930's. *1428*

Automobile Industry and Trade. City Politics. Michigan (Detroit). Negroes. United Automobile Workers of America. 1945-78. *2315*
—. Economic Conditions. Michigan (Detroit). 20c. *2600*
—. Economic Growth. Georgia (Atlanta). Woodruff, Robert W. 1909-20. *2097*
—. Finnish Americans. Michigan (Detroit). 1900-40. *1620*
—. Industrialization. League of Revolutionary Black Workers. Michigan (Detroit). Negroes. 1968-75. *2626*
—. Labor Disputes. Michigan (Detroit). Negroes. Whites. 1941-75. *2628*
—. Labor Unions and Organizations. League of Revolutionary Black Workers. Michigan (Detroit). Negroes. Radicals and Radicalism. 1968-73. *2627*
—. Michigan (Detroit). Social Conditions. 1701-1975. *32*

Automobile Workers Union. Communist Party. Labor Unions and Organizations. Michigan (Detroit). 1920's-1935. *620*
Automobiles. Air Quality Act (US, 1970). California (Los Angeles). Environmental Protection Agency. 1970-73. *2550*
—. Alberta (Calgary). Bicycles. Daily Life. 1880-1914. *3893*
—. Arnold, H. H. Florida (Miami). Traffic Bureau. 1896-1935. *2071*
—. Assembly line. Ford Motor Company. Labor. Michigan (Highland Park). 1910-14. *509*
—. California (East Los Angeles). Leisure. Low-riders. Mexican Americans. Youth. 1970's. *3154*
—. California (Los Angeles). City Planning. Development. 1920's. *1790*
—. California (Los Angeles). Transportation. 1975. *3455*
—. City Life. 1973. *3469*
—. City Life. Horn, Eloise. *Index to Pittsburgh Life* (periodical). Pennsylvania (Pittsburgh; Grant Boulevard). 1901. *2106*
—. City Planning. Mass transit. 1900-40. *1824*
—. City Planning. Pennsylvania (Pittsburgh; East End; Shadyside). Streetcars. 1852-1916. *138*
—. Ethnicity. Michigan (Detroit). Protestant Churches. Social organization. 1880-1940. *1315*
—. Illinois (Chicago). Mass transit. Public policy. 1900-50. *2061*
—. Manhattan Auto Study. New York City. 1970. *3478*
—. Mass transit. North America. 1960-75. *3453*
—. McKenzie, Roderick D. Railroads. Urbanization. Washington (Puget Sound area). 1850's-1920's. *115*
—. Mississippi (Oxford). 1900-10. *2068*
—. New York. Play. Suburbs. Youth. 1970. *2752*

Autumn. Daily Life. Eden Fair. Maine (Bar Harbor). Resorts. 1920's. *856*
Aviation. *See* Aeronautics.

B

Bail. Crime and Criminals. Friends, Society of. Peace bonds. Pennsylvania (Philadelphia). 1680-1829. *1250*
Bail bonds. California (San Francisco). City Government. McDonough, Peter P. Vice. 1896-1937. *1206*
Baker, Edgar Crow. British Columbia (Victoria). Entrepreneurs. 1872-98. *3718*
Bakeries. Economic Regulations. New York City. Strikes. 1801-13. *625*
Balboa Park. California (San Diego). City Planning. 1902-10. *2017*
—. California (San Diego). Parks. 1868-1902. *2018*
Balbus, Isaac D. Criminal justice (review article). Eisenstein, James. Jacob, Herbert. Levin, Martin A. Mather, Lynn M. 1970's. *2941*
Ballet. Field, Joseph M. Missouri (St. Louis). Varieties Theatre. 1852. *1042*
—. Ohio (Cincinnati). Public Opinion. 1787-1861. *1043*
Ballinger-Pinchot controversy. Alaska (Kennecott). Company Towns. Copper Mines and Mining. Corporations. Mining Engineering. 1906-38. *112*
Ballrooms (Trianon, Aragon). Illinois (Chicago). Karzas, Andrew. Karzas, William. 1907-71. *851*
Baltimore and Ohio Railroad. Maryland (Baltimore). Mount Clare station. Railroads. 1830. 1851-52. *1907*
—. Mathews, Henry M. Railroads. Strikes. West Virginia (Berkeley County, Martinsburg). 1877. *588*
Baltimore Normal School. Bowie State College. Education. Maryland. Negroes. Wells, Nelson. 1843-72. *1105*
Baltimore Reform League. Lawyers' Round Table. Maryland. Niles, Alfred Salem. Voluntary Associations. 1852-1972. *740*
Bancroft, William P. Canby, William M. Delaware (Wilmington). Olmsted, Frederick Law. Parks. 1865-95. *2026*
Band's Opera House. Nebraska (Crete). 1877-1900. *1041*
Banfield, Edward C. City politics. Humanism. Reform. Social classes. Social sciences. -1973. *2227*
—. Illinois (Chicago). Political Machines. Political Reform. Social policy. 1972-74. *2433*

—. Farmers. Ohio (Wood County). Railroads (electric). 1896-1902. *2096*

—. Iron Industry. Social classes. 1874-1900. *782*

—. Ownership. Ports. Progressivism. Washington (Seattle). 1911-20. *357*

Busing. Attitudes. Michigan (Pontiac). Parents. School Integration. 1972-75. *2890*

—. California (Los Angeles). 1965-77. *2896*

—. California (San Francisco). Chinese Americans. Freedom Schools. Public schools. 1971-72. *2858*

—. Civil disobedience. Irish Americans. Massachusetts (Boston). 19c-1974. *1514*

—. Cottle, Thomas J. (review article). Massachusetts (Boston). School integration. 1974-76. *2894*

—. Discrimination, Educational. Michigan (Detroit). *Milliken* v. *Bradley* (US, 1974). Social sciences. Trials. 1971-76. *3011*

—. Educational Reform. Massachusetts (Boston). Negroes. Racism. Whites. 1974. *2821*

—. Integration. Mass Media. Tennessee (Nashville). 1970-73. *2895*

—. Integration. Metropolitan Areas. Race Relations. Residential Patterns. Schools. 1970. *3032*

—. Massachusetts (Boston). Public Schools. Racism. 1974. *2904*

—. Massachusetts (Boston). Race Relations. School Integration. Violence. 1970-76. *2847*

—. Massachusetts (Boston). Race Relations. Students. 1968-69. *2907*

—. Massachusetts (Boston). Racism. Violence. 1960's-70's. *2824*

—. Massachusetts (Boston). Racism. Whites. Working class. 1974-75. *2829*

—. Michigan (Dearborn, Detroit). Racism. Social change. 1974. *2893*

—. Michigan (Pontiac). National Action Group. 1971-72. *2846*

—. Race Relations. Schools. 1975. *2875*

Butler, Benjamin Franklin. Armies. Elections (presidential). Lincoln, Abraham. New York City. 1864. *293*

—. Attitudes. Civil War. Letters. Louisiana (New Orleans). Military Occupation. Women. 1861-62. *328*

Butler, Smedley D. Kendrick, W. Freeland. Pennsylvania (Philadelphia). Prohibition. 1923-24. *1281*

C

Cabaret (film). Germany (Berlin). Music. *Nashville* (film). Social criticism. Tennessee. 1930's-70's. *3596*

Cabell, James Branch. Authors. Glasgow, Ellen. Literature. Southern Renaissance. Virginia (Richmond). 1920's. *1002*

—. Authors. Glasgow, Ellen. Virginia (Richmond). 1733-1900's. *976*

—. Glasgow, Ellen. Literature. Virginia (Richmond). 1898-1912. *2164*

Cabildo. Local government. Louisiana (New Orleans). Spain. 1769-1803. *251*

Cabinetmaking. Bentley, William. Diaries. Furniture and Furnishings. Massachusetts (Salem). 1784-1819. *478*

Cahan, Abraham. Crane, Stephen. Fiction. 1890's. *2150*

Cain, James M. California (Los Angeles). Depressions. Novels. 1925-45. *2151*

Cajuns. Louisiana (Houma). Negroes. Population. Race Relations. Social change. Texans. 1945-73. *2725*

Calgary and Edmonton Railway. Alberta (Edmonton). Bridges. City Government. Railroads. 1910-13. *3891*

Calico Printing. Architecture. Cotton mills. Dover Manufacturing Company Print Works. New Hampshire (Dover). 1820-25. *474*

California. Aged. Friendship. Widows. 1973. *2650*

—. Agriculture. Land use. Urbanization. Williamson Act (California, 1965). 1965-75. *3313*

—. Airplanes. Los Angeles International Airport. 1928-78. *2070*

—. Architects. County Government. Fusselman, William. Marin County Civic Center. 1952-63. *3417*

—. Architecture. Eureka Heritage Society. Restorations. Vellutini, Dolores. 1973-78. *3573*

—. Archives. Los Angeles County Museum of Natural History. 1975. *3986*

—. Auerbach's Department Store. Jews. Retail Trade. Utah (Salt Lake City). 1857-1977. *451*

—. Boycotts. MacKinnon, Duncan. San Diego High School. Student protest. 1918. *1083*

—. Cantwell, John J. Catholic Church. Negroes. 1920's. *1701*

—. Chinese. Labor. Reform. Workingmen's Party of California. 1877-82. *633*

—. Chinese Americans. Metropolitan areas. Tong societies. Voluntary Associations. 1850-1972. *1541*

—. City Lights (bookstore). Literature. Publishers and Publishing. 1953-79. *2798*

—. Coke, James G. Eulau, Heinz. Federal Programs. Gargan, John J. Ohio. Pressman, Jeffrey L. Prewitt, Kenneth. Public policy (review article). Wildavsky, Aaron. ca 1960-73. *2523*

—. Conductors. Los Angeles Philharmonic Orchestra. Symphony Orchestras. 1862-1977. *993*

—. Construction. Depressions. Santa Barbara County Bowl. 1935. *2951*

—. Daily Life. Photographs. San Diego Title Insurance and Trust Company Collection. 1880's-1950's. 1979. *1783*

—. Drug abuse. Medical care. Prescriptions. San Francisco Polydrug Project. Women. 1969-79. *3233*

—. Gold rushes. New York City (Brooklyn). Newspapers. Reporters and Reporting. 1848-53. *941*

—. Housing. Restorations. San Francisco Victoriana Company. Wood. 1850-1915. 1977. *3585*

—. Idealism. Los Angeles *Illustrated Daily News*. Newspapers. Vanderbilt, Cornelius, Jr. 1923-26. *934*

—. Landscape Painting. Lithographs. Portraits. 19c. *1799*

—. Los Angeles Grand Opera Association. Opera. ca 1924-30. *1033*

—. Manhole covers. Public Utilities. 1860's-1970's. *2047*

—. Military Camps and Forts. Missions and Missionaries. 1769-84. *74*

—. Politics. San Diego Flume Company. Southern California Mountain Water Company. Water Supply. 1895-97. *2041*

—. San Diego Historical Society. 1880-1979. *744*

—. San Diego Zoological Society. 1916-21. *910*

California (Alameda, San Benito counties). Courts. Lawsuits. 1890-1970. *1223*

California (Amador City). Boom towns. Daily Life. Gold mines and mining. 1907. *41*

California (American River, Sacramento). California Tomorrow (group). Ecology. Regional planning. 1975. *3316*

California (Anaheim). City Government. Ku Klux Klan. Political Participation. ca 1923-25. *742*

California (Berkeley). City government. 1971-73. *2326*

—. Colleges and Universities. Police. Professionalization. Vollmer, August. 1905-55. *1217*

California (Berkeley, San Francisco). City politics. Development. Local government. Massachusetts (Boston, Cambridge). 1960's-70's. *2336*

California (Bodie). Ghost towns. Gold Mines and Mining. 1859-88. *75*

—. Ghost towns. Gold Rushes. Historical Sites and Parks. 1860-1974. *216*

California (East Los Angeles). Art. Mechicano Art Center. Mexican Americans. Murals. 1970's. *2786*

—. Art. Mexican Americans. Murals, street. Values. 1978. *2816*

—. Automobiles. Leisure. Low-riders. Mexican Americans. Youth. 1970's. *3154*

—. Barrios. Mexican Americans. Murals. Social Conditions. 1970-75. *3155*

—. Barrios. Mexican Americans. Political activism. 1970-73. *3166*

—. Cemeteries. Congregation B'nai B'rith. Home of Peace Cemetery. Jews. 1902. *2027*

—. Ethnic Groups. Mexican Americans. Political protest. Social Change. 1968-74. *3159*

California (East Los Angeles, Los Angeles; Boyle Heights). Artists. Ethnicity. Mexican Americans. Murals. 1965-75. *3153*

California (East San Jose; Mayfair district). Ghettos. Mexican Americans. Social Change. 1777-1975. *1537*

California (El Monte). Agricultural Labor. Foreign Relations. Japan. Mexico. Strikes. 1933. *600*

California (Fresno). Armenian Americans. Settlement. 1881-1918. *1594*

—. Ethnicity. Intermarriage. Japanese Americans. 1960-73. *3178*

—. Freedom of Speech. Industrial Workers of the World. 1910-11. *594*

California (Fresno; West Fresno). City Planning. Community Participation in Politics. 1968-73. *3341*

California (Grass Valley, Nevada City). Local government. Mining towns. Political Parties. 1850-70. *250*

California (Hollister). Earthquakes. 20c. *3265*

California (Imperial Valley, San Diego). Irrigation. Local History. Smythe, William E. 1880-1910. *150*

California (Julian, San Diego, Temecula). City Life. Levi, Adolph. Levi, Simon. 1850-1943. *452*

California (Kenworthy). Gold Rushes. 1897-1900. *71*

California Land Conservation Act (1965). Agriculture and Government. Land use. Taxation. Urbanization. 1965-75. *3309*

California (Locke). Chinese Americans. Lee, Bing. 1880-1970. *1553*

California (Los Angeles). 1769-1974. *2286*

—. Acculturation. City Life. Indians. 1970's. *3192*

—. Acculturation. Ethnicity. Race. Social status. Voting and Voting Behavior. 1973. *2475*

—. Air pollution. 1970-73. *3228*

—. Air pollution. City Government. Southern California Gas Company. 1940-45. *3231*

—. Air pollution. Ecology. 1960's. *3605*

—. Air Quality Act (US, 1970). Automobiles. Environmental Protection Agency. 1970-73. *2550*

—. Alexander, George. City Government. Progressivism. Reform. ca 1909-13. *383*

—. Architecture. Insurance. Marks, David X. Marks, Joshua H. Philanthropy. 1902-77. *49*

—. Architecture. Social Change. 1890-1970. *1964*

—. Arizona (Prescott). Department of Arizona. Military Government. 1870-1902. *311*

—. Art. Ethnicity. Mexican Americans. Murals, street. 1970's. *3164*

—. Art, public. City life. 1970's. *2805*

—. Assimilation. Europe. Immigrants. Jews. Marriage. 1910-13. *1469*

—. Assimilation. Korean Americans. Minorities in Politics. 1970. *3168*

—. Audiences. Spanish Language. Television. 1971-72. *2770*

—. Automobiles. City Planning. Development. 1920's. *1790*

—. Automobiles. Transportation. 1975. *3455*

—. *B'nai B'rith Messenger*. Jews. Newspapers. 1895-1929. *1491*

—. Bookselling. Zeitlin, Jacob (Jake). ca 1920-74. *2591*

—. Boosterism. City Government. Journalism. Political Reform. Willard, Charles Dwight. 1888-1914. *1140*

—. Bradley, Tom. Coalitions. Elections (mayoral). Minorities in Politics. Social status. 1969-73. *2473*

—. Business. Housing. Jews. Middle Classes. Social Mobility. 1880's. *1440*

—. Busing. 1965-77. *2896*

—. Cain, James M. Depressions. Novels. 1925-45. *2151*

—. Census. Clothing. Jews. Retail Trade. 1870's. *1490*

—. Census. Education. Literacy. Quantitative Methods. 1850. *1123*

—. Chandler, Otis. District of Columbia. Graham, Katherine. Newspapers. Noyes, Newbold. Reporters and Reporting. 1967-72. *2778*

—. Chinatowns. Chinese Americans. Ghettos. Ownership. Property. 1970's. *3171*

—. Citizens Committee for the Defense of Mexican-American Youth. Mexican Americans. "Sleepy Lagoon" trial. Trials. 1942-44. *1522*

—. City Government. Clinton, Clifford. Political Reform. Recall. Shaw, Frank. 1938. *368*

—. City Government. Lindsay, Gilbert. Negroes. 1950's-77. *2420*

—. City Planning. 1836-49. *107*

—. Community control. Decentralization. Schools. 1975. *2872*

—. Conductors. Frankenstein, Abraham Frankum. Jews. 1897-1934. *879*

—. Census. Research. Urbanization. 1950's-78. *3625*
—. City Government. Libraries (public). Metropolitan Areas. 1950-71. *3768*
—. City Government. Political Reform. 1875-1976. *4064*
—. City planning. Environment. Housing. Suburbs. 1893-1930. *3917*
—. City planning. Geography. Settlement. USA. 19c-20c. *3994*
—. Conference on the Historical Urbanization of North America. Urban history. USA. 1973. *3990*
—. Country Life. Grain elevators. Transportation. 1930's-70's. *3898*
—. Demography. Economic conditions. 1961-73. *3633*
—. Development. Models. Residential patterns. USA. 1973. *3272*
—. Economic Development. Iron Ore Company. Natural Resources. Quebec (Schefferville). 1954-78. *3716*
—. Education. Occupations. Social mobility. 1972. *3772*
—. Ethnicity. National Self-image. Ontario (Toronto). 1970. *3849*
—. Exhibits and Expositions. Maps. Public Archives of Canada. Research. Urban history. 1865-1905. *3959*
—. Federal Policy. Local government. 1950's-78. *3693*
—. Foreign Investments. Real Estate. USA. 1960's-75. *3728*
—. Frontier and Pioneer Life. Regions. 16c-1914. *3626*
—. Geography. Urban studies. 1900-73. *4002*
—. Historiography. Urban History. USA. -1974. *3964*
—. Historiography. Urbanization. 17c-1974. *4044*
—. Housing. Land. Prices. ca 1970-81. *3725*
—. Indians. Institutions. USA. 20c. *3204*
—. Indians. Migration. USA. 1972. *3190*
—. Mennonites. Social Customs. Urbanization. USA. 1961-71. *3828*
—. Methodism. Social gospel. 1890-1914. *3862*
—. Methodology. Urban history. 1960's-70's. *4045*
—. Mexico. South America. Subways. USA. 19c-1978. *3457*
—. Polish Canadians. 1945-70's. *3825*
—. Research. Urban history. USA. 18c-20c. *4011*
—. Rural areas. Urbanization. 1966-71. *3654*
—. Rural-Urban Studies. Urbanization. 1955-75. *3646*
—. Urban history. Western Canadian Urban History Conference (papers). 1974. *4050*
—. USA. Voting and Voting Behavior. 1952-68. *2469*
Canada (northern). City Planning. Natural Resources. 1945-78. *3634*
Canadian Labour Congress. Association of Commercial and Technical Employees. Labor Unions and Organizations (white-collar). Ontario (Toronto). 1972. *3710*
Canadian Pacific Railway. Alberta (Edmonton). City Politics. Railroads. 1891-1914. *3677*
—. Architecture. Railroad stations. Saskatchewan. 20c. *3880*
—. British Columbia (Vancouver). Economic Development. 1880's-93. *3897*
Canadian Urban History Conference. City Planning. Urban history. 19c-20c. 1977. *4042*
—. Urban history. 1977. *3989*
Canadians. Assimilation. Atlantic Provinces. Economic conditions. Immigration. Kennedy, Albert J. Massachusetts (Boston). 1910's. *1593*
Canals *See also* names of canals, e.g. Panama Canal, etc.; Navigation, Inland.
—. Illinois (Chicago). Michigan, Lake. Water pollution. 1873-86. *2050*
—. Indiana Company. Kentucky. Ohio Canal Company. Ohio River (Falls). 1804-30. *208*
—. Indiana, northern. Urbanization. 1817-40's. *160*
—. New Hampshire (Dover). Winnipiseogee Canal. 1796-1834. *2075*
—. Virginia (Williamsburg). 1772-1820. *2062*
Canby, William M. Bancroft, William P. Delaware (Wilmington). Olmsted, Frederick Law. Parks. 1865-95. *2026*
Canton *Daily News*. Editors and Editing. Mellett, Donald Ring. Ohio. Political Corruption. 1926-27. *942*
Cantwell, John J. California. Catholic Church. Negroes. 1920's. *1701*

Capital *See also* Banking; Capitalism; Investments; Labor; Monopolies.
—. Great Lakes. Ports. Urbanization. Wisconsin. 1830's. *117*
—. Home ownership. Massachusetts (Boston). Social Status. 1890-1910. *791*
—. Iron Industry. Wisconsin (Milwaukee). 1840's-80's. *522*
—. Landlords and Tenants. Neighborhoods. 1979. *2715*
Capitalism *See also* Capital; Socialism.
—. Attitudes. Howells, William Dean. 1860-1900. *2144*
—. Behavior. Family. Labor. Massachusetts (Lowell). Sex roles. 1860. *562*
—. Charities. Massachusetts (Boston). Upper Classes. 18c-19c. *1154*
—. Quebec (Montreal). Research Group on Montreal Society. Social History. 19c. *3998*
—. Reform. Social Problems. 1960's-70's. *2234*
—. Suburbs. Technology. Urbanization. 19c-1970's. *2262*
Capitol Theatre. Architecture. Entertainment. Movie theaters. Ontario (Ottawa). Vaudeville. 1920-70. *3911*
Capitols. Alabama (Cahaba, Montgomery, Tuscaloosa). Architecture. 1819-1912. *1914*
—. Alaska. Location. State Government. 1955-77. *2516*
—. American Revolution. Location. State Government. Virginia (Richmond, Williamsburg). 1779. *326*
—. Architects. Construction. District of Columbia. Hoban, James. 1799. *1885*
—. Architecture. District of Columbia. 1792-1850. *1977*
—. Architecture. District of Columbia. 1792-93. *1878*
—. Architecture. District of Columbia. House of Representatives Chamber. Jefferson, Thomas. Latrobe, Benjamin Henry. 1803-12. *1890*
—. Architecture. Massachusetts (Boston). Payne, William. 1658-1975. *1883*
—. Boosterism. Location. Ontario (Ottawa). 1822-59. *3658*
—. British Columbia (Fort Langeley). Hudson's Bay Company. Trade. 1827-58. *3655*
—. Congress. Federal Government. Location. 1783. *67*
—. Federal Government. Location. Potowmack Company. Stuart, David. Virginia (Alexandria). Washington, George. 1783-91. *217*
—. Iowa (Iowa City). 1838-57. *1870*
—. Iowa (Iowa City). Iowa, University of. Restorations. 1840-1974. *2114*
—. Iowa (Iowa City). Restorations. 1840-1976. *3524*
—. Kansas. Murals. Personal Narratives. Winter, Lumen Martin. 1977. *2814*
—. Kentucky (Frankfort). Restorations. 1975. *3501*
—. Location. Minnesota (St. Paul). State Government. 1849-1905. *332*
Capone, Al. Crime and Criminals. Illinois (Chicago). 1919-47. *1258*
Carey, John R. Ainslie, Peter. Discrimination, employment. Maryland (Baltimore). National Urban League. Negroes. Social conditions. 1921-35. *746*
Cargo cults. Arizona (Willcox). Economic Conditions. Papua New Guinea. "Rex Allen Days" (festival). Towns. 1951-76. *2572*
Caribbean Region. Economic Conditions. Immigration. Negroes. New York City. Public Opinion. 1965-79. *3062*
Carigal, Hakham Raphael Haim Isaac. Jews. Rhode Island (Newport). 1771-77. *1468*
Carleton, Guy. American Revolution. Attitudes. Military Occupation. Peasants. Quebec. 1775-76. *3682*
Carnegie, Andrew. Libraries. Nicol, A. Yukon Territory (Dawson). 1902-20's. *3818*
Carnegie-Mellon University. History Teaching. Quantification. Urban history. 1975. *4065*
Carney, James. Ohio (Cleveland). Perk, Ralph. Pinkney, Arnold R. Political Campaigns (mayoral). Stokes, Carl B. 1971. *2477*
Caro, Robert A. (review article). Bureaucracies. City Politics. Moses, Robert. New York City. 20c. *2426*
—. City Government. Moses, Robert. New York City. 1924-54. *2428*
—. Moses, Robert. Mugwumps. New York. Politics. State government. 1920's-40's. 1974. *301*
Carpenter, Inta Gale. City Life. Folklore. Methodology. Personal Narratives. 1976. *3947*

Carpenter's Company. Colonial Government. Labor Unions and Organizations. Pennsylvania (Philadelphia). ca 1700-74. *616*
Carpentry. Agriculture. Business. Dunlap, John. Furniture and Furnishings. New Hampshire (Bedford, Goffstown). 1746-92. *482*
Carpetbaggers. Alden, Augustus E. Brownlow, William G. City Government. Reconstruction. Republican Party. Tennessee (Nashville). 1865-69. *295*
Carriage and wagon industry. Habakkuk, H. J. Labor. Ohio (Cincinnati). Technology. 1850-1900. *485*
Carson Pirie Scott and Co. Buildings. Illinois (Chicago). Retail Trade. 1854-1979. *462*
Carter, Jimmy (administration). Domestic Policy. 1977-78. *2545*
—. Federal Policy. 1977. *2552*
—. Federal Policy. Negroes. Political Leadership. Poor. 1978. *2541*
—. Federal policy. Urban and Regional Policy Group. 1978. *2540*
Carthage Bridge. Bridges. Genesee Suspension Bridge. New York (Rochester). 1817-57. *2059*
Cartography. *See* Maps.
Cathedral of the Assumption. Catholic Church. Kentucky (Louisville). 1852-1976. *1641*
Catholic Church *See also* religious orders by name, e.g. Franciscans, Jesuits, etc.
—. Acculturation. Bianco, Carla. Gambino, Richard. Italian Americans (review article). Pennsylvania (Rosetos). Social Organization. Tomasi, Silvano. 20c. *1606*
—. Acculturation. Human Relations. Irish Americans. Pennsylvania (Pittsburgh; St. Andrew's Parish). 1863-90. *1511*
—. Acculturation. Irish Americans. Pennsylvania (Pittsburgh). St. Andrew Parish. 1863-90. *1510*
—. Aged. Irish Canadians. McMahon, Patrick. Orphans. Poor. Quebec (Quebec). St. Bridget's Home. 1847-1972. *3841*
—. Alberta (Calgary Diocese). French Canadians. Irish Canadians. McNailly, John Thomas. 1871-1952. *3860*
—. Americanization. Clergy. Irish Americans. Polish Americans. 1920-40's. *1635*
—. Americanization. Connecticut (New Britain). Polish Americans. 1890-1955. *1565*
—. Architecture (Gothic Revival). Churches. St. Andrew's Church. Virginia (Roanoke). 1882-1975. *2001*
—. Assimilation. Clergy. Dufresne, Andre B. French Canadians. Massachusetts (Holyoke). 1869-87. *1655*
—. Assimilation. Connecticut (New Britain; Holy Cross Parish). Polish Americans. 1928-76. *1566*
—. Assimilation. Connecticut (Waterbury). Lithuanian Americans. Newspapers. *Rytas*. Zebris, Joseph. 1896-98. *948*
—. Assimilation. French Americans. Vermont (Winooski). 1867-1900. *1567*
—. Assimilation. Parishes. Pennsylvania (Philadelphia). 1759-1975. *1651*
—. Banking. Bishops. Ohio (Cincinnati). Purcell, John Baptist. 1833-83. *1662*
—. Bishops. Lynch, John Joseph. Ontario. Poor. Toronto Savings Bank. 1870's. *3755*
—. California. Cantwell, John J. Negroes. 1920's. *1701*
—. California (San Francisco). City Politics. Irish Americans. Progressivism. Yorke, Peter C. 1900's. *1519*
—. California (San Francisco). Clergy. Editors and Editing. Irish Americans. Yorke, Peter C. ca 1885-1925. *1518*
—. Cathedral of the Assumption. Kentucky (Louisville). 1852-1976. *1641*
—. Church Schools. 1750-1945. 1930D 1940D 1900H. *1098*
—. Church Schools. Damen, Arnold. Fund raising. Illinois (Chicago). 1840-90. *1122*
—. Church Schools. Ethnic Groups. Illinois (Chicago). Sanders, James W. (review article). 1833-1965. 1977. *1072*
—. Church Schools. Glennon, John J. Missouri (St. Louis). Ritter, Joseph E. School Integration. 1935-47. *1665*
—. Church Schools. Polish Americans. 1874-1960's. *1096*
—. Clergy. Indian-White Relations. New Mexico (Isleta Pueblo). 1960's. *3932*
—. Clergy. Missouri (St. Louis). 1841-99. *1660*

—. Commodore Barry Country Club. Illinois (Chicago). Irish Americans. Knights of Columbus. Wisconsin (Twin Lakes). 1907-20's. *732*

—. Conflict and Conflict Resolution. French (language). Haitian Americans. New York City. 1970's. *3063*

—. Conflict and Conflict Resolution. Italian Americans. Parishes, national. Rhode Island (Providence). 1890-1930. *1563*

—. Cunningham, Patrick (report). Irish Americans. Vermont (Brattleboro). 1847-98. *1642*

—. Dolan, Jay P. (review article). German Americans. Irish Americans. New York City. Social Conditions. 1815-65. 1975. *1676*

—. Education. Ohio (Cincinnati). Sisters of Charity of St. Joseph. Social Work. Women. 1809-1979. *1682*

—. English language. French language. Missouri. St. Louis Cathedral. 1818-42. *1688*

—. Ethnic groups. Folklore. New York (Buffalo). 1960's-75. *3219*

—. Ethnic Groups (review article). Horowitz, Helen Lefkowitz. Illinois (Chicago). Kessner, Thomas. New York City. Philanthropy. Sanders, James W. 1883-1965. 1970's. *48*

—. France (Paris). Quebec (Montreal). Reading rooms. Social Customs. 19c. *3801*

—. German Americans. Irish Americans. New Jersey (Newark). Social Problems. 1840-70. *1689*

—. German Americans. Irish Americans. Ohio (Cleveland Diocese). Rappe, Louis Amadeus. 1847-70. *1671*

—. Hispanic Americans. Indiana (East Chicago, Gary). Theater. 1920-76. *1531*

—. Illinois (Chicago). Social Work. Wisconsin (Milwaukee). 19c. *1700*

—. Irish Canadians. Katz, Michael B. (review article). Occupations. Ontario (Hamilton). Social mobility. 1850-75. 1975. *3783*

—. Italian Americans (review article). New York City. Sartorio, Enrico C. Tomasi, Silvano. 1918. 1975. *1680*

—. Massachusetts (Boston). Religious Orders. Teaching. Voluntarism. Women. 1870-1940. *1685*

—. Negroes. North. Occupations. Social Status. 1968. *3223*

—. New Brunswick (Saint John). Sisters of Charity of the Immaculate Conception. 1854-64. *3865*

—. New York (Buffalo). Pitass, John. Polish Americans. 1890-1934. *1568*

—. Ohio (Cleveland). Religion. 1860. *1669*

Catholics. Americanization. Ethnicity. New York City. Religion. -1974. *3040*

Cattle Raising. Economic conditions. Kansas (Trail City). Social customs. 1883-87. *43*

—. Economic growth. Missouri (Sedalia). 1856-66. *511*

Catto, Octavius V. Civil Rights. Negroes. Pennsylvania (Philadelphia). 1861-71. *1411*

Cauchon, Joseph-Edouard. Architecture. Empire Hotel. Iron-front buildings. Manitoba (Winnipeg). 1880-1920. *3908*

Cement industry. Ghost towns. Kansas (Le Hunt). United Kansas Portland Cement Company. 1905-18. *193*

Cemeteries. Attitudes. Bigelow, Jacob. Massachusetts (Cambridge). Mount Auburn Cemetery. Public Health. Rural cemetery movement. 1831. *2009*

—. California (East Los Angeles). Congregation B'nai B'rith. Home of Peace Cemetery. Jews. 1902. *2027*

—. California (Los Angeles; Chavez Ravine). Hebrew Benevolent Society of Los Angeles. Home of Peace Cemetery. Jews. Photographs. 1855-1910. *2028*

—. California (San Francisco). First Hebrew Benevolent Society. Funerals. Jews. Johnson, Henry D. 1849-50. *1489*

—. Graceland Cemetery. Illinois (Chicago). 1861-1900. *2029*

—. Green-Wood Cemetery. Landscaping. New York City (Brooklyn). Sculpture, Victorian. 1840-1976. *2014*

—. Historical Sites and Parks. Massachusetts (Boston). Mount Auburn Cemetery. 1831-1974. *2022*

—. Historical Sources. Louisiana (Shreveport). 1839-1975. *1786*

—. Massachusetts (Boston, Lowell). Parks. Rural cemetery movement. 1841-65. *2004*

—. Restorations. Rhode Island (Newport). 1767-1973. *3504*

—. Rural Cemetery movement. Social Reform. 1804-35. *2021*

Censorship *See also* Freedom of Speech; Freedom of the Press.

—. Abolition Movement. South Carolina (Charleston). Walker, David *(Appeal)*. 1830. *1397*

—. Behavior. Social Psychology. 1960's-70's. *2925*

—. Films. Illinois (Chicago). Nickelodeons. Progressivism. 1907-15. *892*

Census *See also* Statistics.

—. California (Los Angeles). Clothing. Jews. Retail Trade. 1870's. *1490*

—. California (Los Angeles). Education. Literacy. Quantitative Methods. 1850. *1123*

—. Canada. Research. Urbanization. 1950's-78. *3625*

—. City Life. Family. Historiography. Indiana (Vanderburgh County; Evansville). Negroes. 1865-80. *686*

—. City Life. Pennsylvania (Philadelphia). 1693-1790. *710*

—. City Planning. New York City. Social Surveys. 1961-74. *4014*

—. Geographic Mobility. Soundex indexes. 1880-1900. *4046*

—. Households. Rhode Island. Rural-Urban Studies. 1774-1800. *717*

—. Literacy. Methodology. Ontario (Peel County; Hamilton). Social classes. 19c. *4004*

—. Methodology. New Brunswick (Saint John). Social Classes. 1871. 1974. *3811*

—. Pennsylvania (Philadelphia). Public Schools. Teachers. 1865-90. *1077*

Centennial Celebrations *See also* Bicentennial Celebrations; Sesquicentennial Celebrations.

—. Boosterism. Jamestown Tercentennial Exposition. Virginia (Norfolk). 1900-10. *53*

—. City of Progress. Construction. Depressions. Economic development. Illinois (Chicago). 1933-34. *1879*

—. Illinois (Chicago). Mosher, Charles D. Philanthropy. Photography. 1870-97. *679*

—. Independence Hall. Pennsylvania (Philadelphia). Philanthropy. Seybert, Henry. 1793-1882. *1146*

—. Iowa (Des Moines). Parades. 1876. *854*

—. Louisiana Purchase Exposition. Missouri (St. Louis). 1904. *916*

Central Labor Union. Ohio (Cincinnati). Strikes. 1886. *615*

Central Park. City Politics. New York City. Parks. 1844-56. *2024*

Centrality (concept). Economic Theory. New England. 17c-18c. *2199*

Centralization. California (San Francisco). Charters. City government. Class Struggle. Ethnic Groups. Political Reform. 1898. *371*

—. Politics. Public schools. School Attendance. Virginia (Arlington). 1973-78. *2828*

Centre for Urban and Community Studies. Ontario (Toronto). Rural-Urban Studies. Urban history. 1965-78. *3941*

Centrifugal Rotary Engine Company. Engines. Hayes, Alexander L. Pennsylvania (Lancaster). Steam Power. 1870. *515*

Chamber of Commerce Law and Order Committee. California (San Francisco). Chipman, Miner. Labor disputes. 1915-19. *607*

Chambers of Commerce. Business. Labor. South Carolina (Greenville). 1970's. *2636*

Chandler, Otis. California (Los Angeles). District of Columbia. Graham, Katherine. Newspapers. Noyes, Newbold. Reporters and Reporting. 1967-72. *2778*

Chap-Book (periodical). Illinois (Chicago). Kimball, Hannibal Ingalls. Literature. Stone, Herbert Stuart. 1893-1906. *1026*

Chapman family. Actors and actresses. Pennsylvania (Pittsburgh). Showboats. 1827-47. *857*

Charities *See also* Philanthropy; Public Welfare.

—. Alienation. Government. Quebec (Quebec; Lower Town). Social Problems. Working Class. 1896-1914. *3800*

—. Architecture. Daily Life. Garrett, John Work. Garrett, Mary Frick. Garrett, Robert. Maryland (Baltimore). Mount Vernon Place (residence). Upper Classes. 1872-1928. *770*

—. Beth Ha Medrosh Hagodol synagogue. Colorado (Denver). Judaism. Kauvar, Charles E. H. 1902-71. *1188*

—. Brooklyn Howard Colored Orphan Asylum. Negroes. New York Colored Orphan Asylum. Orphan asylums. Race Relations. 1836-1902. *1165*

—. California (San Francisco). Cholera. Epidemics. Jews. Neustadt, Samuel I. 1850. *1767*

—. California (San Francisco). Corporations. Poor. United Bay Area Crusade. 1958-73. *2918*

—. California (San Francisco). Immigration. Voluntary Associations. ca 1850-60. *741*

—. Capitalism. Massachusetts (Boston). Upper Classes. 18c-19c. *1154*

—. Children. Nova Scotia (Halifax). Orphan House. 1752-87. *3785*

—. City government. New York City. Outdoor relief. Reform. Subsidies. 1870-98. *372*

—. Colleges and Universities. New York Charity Organization Society. Social Organization Theory. 1880-1910. *1149*

—. Family Service of the Cincinnati Area. Ohio (Cincinnati). 1870-1979. *1171*

—. Friends, Society of. Pennsylvania. Philadelphia Society for Organizing Charitable Relief and Repressing Mendicancy. 1800-1900. *1181*

—. Friends, Society of. Pennsylvania Hospital for the Sick Poor. Pennsylvania (Philadelphia). Poor. 18c. *1174*

—. Galveston Plan of 1907. Immigration. Industrial Removal Office. Jews. Migration, Internal. New York City. 1890-1914. *1476*

—. Georgia (Atlanta). Negroes. United Way of America. 1960-77. *2699*

—. Hannah Schloss Old Timers. Jews. Michigan (Detroit). 1903-73. *734*

—. Illinois (Chicago). Negroes. Social problems. 1890-1917. *1159*

—. Jews. Michigan (Detroit). Odessa Progressive Aid Society. 1915-18. *757*

—. Jews. Migration, Internal. Nebraska (Omaha). Political Leadership. Refugees. 1820-1937. *1442*

—. Morality. New York. Rural-Urban Studies. 1783-1830. *1158*

—. New Brunswick (Saint John). Newfoundland (St. John's). Nova Scotia (Halifax). Poverty. Unemployment. 1815-60. *1171*

—. New York (Albany). Odd Fellows, Independent Order of. Social Classes. 1845-85. *733*

—. New York City. Reform. Social Services. 1845-60. *1156*

—. Pennsylvania (Philadelphia). Social work. Society for Organizing Charitable Relief and Repressing Mendicancy. Women. 1864-1909. *1182*

—. Rescue mission. Skid rows. Washington (Seattle). 1973. *2912*

Charities Organization Society Movement. Illinois (Chicago). Values. 1880-1930. *1161*

Charity Hospital of Louisiana. Disease, concept of. Louisiana (New Orleans). Masturbation. 1848-1933. *1725*

Charleston City Railway Company. Desegregation. Negroes. Reconstruction. South Carolina. Streetcars. 1867. *1369*

Charleston, College of. Preservation. South Carolina. Stern, Theodore S. (interview). 1960-80. *3488*

Charlestown State Prison. Boston Prison Discipline Society. Massachusetts. Prison reform. 1804-78. *1129*

Charter Committee. City Councils. Elitism. Ohio (Cincinnati). 1933-36. *239*

Charters. California (San Francisco). Centralization. City government. Class Struggle. Ethnic Groups. Political Reform. 1898. *371*

—. City Government. Democratic Party. New York City. Political Reform. Whig Party. 1845-49. *248*

—. City Government. Michigan (Detroit). Political Reform. 1972. *2392*

—. City Government. New York City. Politics. Reform. 1898-1976. *2397*

—. City politics. Havemeyer, William Frederick. New York City. Reform. 1845-47. *249*

—. Colorado. Denver Urban Observatory. 1972-74. *2376*

—. Illinois (Nauvoo). Mormons. 1839-41. *142*

—. Pennsylvania. Pittsburgh Government Study Commission. Political Participation. 1972-74. *2367*

Chestnut Street Theatre. Actors and Actresses. Maryland (Baltimore). Reinagle, Alexander. Wignell, Thomas. 1792-1802. *1029*

Cheverus, Jean Louis Lefebvre de. Anti-Catholicism. Daley, Dominic. Halligan, James. Irish Americans. Lyon, Marcus. Massachusetts (Northampton). Murder. Trials. 1805-06. *1502*

—. Company towns. Economic Development. Kentucky (Lynch). US Coal and Coke Company. 1917-30. *140*

—. Elites. Migration, Internal. Pennsylvania (Wilkes-Barre). Urbanization. 1820-80. *89*

—. Iowa, south. Railroads (electric). 1895-1925. *2073*

—. Kemmerer, Mahlon S. Quealy, Patrick J. Wyoming (Kemmerer). 1897-1903. *60*

—. Labor Disputes. Pennsylvania (Scranton). Police. Violence. 1866-84. *1289*

Coalitions. Bradley, Tom. California (Los Angeles). Elections (mayoral). Minorities in Politics. Social status. 1969-73. *2473*

—. Pennsylvania (Lancaster). Political Parties. Reform. 1921-30. *363*

Coffeehouses. Industrial Revolution. Social Customs. 18c-19c. *863*

Cohan, Jerry. Gagbooks. Humor. Manuscripts. Murphy, J. C. Vaudeville. 1790's-1890's. *909*

Cohen, Octavus Roy. Alabama (Birmingham). Fiction. Loafers (literary group). 1920's. *956*

Coke, James G. California. Eulau, Heinz. Federal Programs. Gargan, John J. Ohio. Pressman, Jeffrey L. Prewitt, Kenneth. Public policy (review article). Wildavsky, Aaron. ca 1960-73. *2523*

—. City Politics (review article). Elazar, Daniel J. Gargan, John J. Hensler, Deborah R. Rabinovitz, Francine F. Social Classes. Walter, Benjamin. Wirt, Frederick M. Wood, Robert C. 1960's-72. *2192*

Cold War. Ethnic Groups. Manitoba (Winnipeg). Social Classes. Voting and Voting Behavior. 1949-53. *3707*

Colden, Cadwallader. Columbia University. Location. New York City. Smith, William, Sr. 1747-53. *1087*

—. Lancisi, Giovanni Maria. New York City. Sanitation. 1717-43. *1743*

Coldwater State Public School. Children. Michigan. Protestantism. Public Schools. Social Reform. 1874-96. *1178*

Cole, Thomas. Artists. Businessmen. Maine (Bar Harbor). Pratt, Henry. Resorts. 1840-70. *198*

Coleman, Benjamin. Brattle Street Church. Elites. Gentility (concept). Massachusetts (Boston). Puritans. 1715-45. *1691*

Coleman, James S. Courts. Methodology. School Integration. White flight. 1970's. *2903*

—. Courts. Ravitch, Diane. School Integration. White flight. 1966-78. *2832*

—. Equality. School Integration. 1960's-70's. *2905*

—. Migration, Internal. School integration. White flight. 1966-76. *2873*

Coliseum Square Association. Louisiana (New Orleans; Lower Garden). New Orleans Historic District Landmarks Committee. Preservation. 1807-1978. *3576*

Collective Bargaining See also Labor Unions and Organizations; Strikes.

—. Ontario (Toronto). Organizational Theory. Printing. 19c. *3759*

College and Universities. Adolescents. Rural-Urban Studies. 1973. *2867*

College Building. Architecture. Heiman, Adolphus. Tennessee (Nashville). 1836-1974. *1941*

Colleges and Universities See also names of individual institutions; Higher Education; Students.

—. Academies. Architecture. Oregon. Piper, William W. 1834-83. *1997*

—. California (Berkeley). Police. Professionalization. Vollmer, August. 1905-55. *1217*

—. Charities. New York Charity Organization Society. Social Organization Theory. 1880-1910. *1149*

—. Community participation. 1960's. *2848*

—. Economic Conditions. Education. Minorities. 1970's. *2902*

—. Educational reform. Poor. Radicals and Radicalism. 1960's-75. *2845*

—. Ghettos. Hostos Community College. New York City (Bronx). Social problems. 1970-72. *2822*

Collins Company. Company Towns. Connecticut (Collinsville). Industry. Preservation. 1827-1965. *3502*

Colombian Americans. Aliens, Illegal. Assimilation. Employment. New York City (Jackson Heights, Queens). Politics. 1965-77. *3138*

—. Dominican Americans. New York City. Social organizations. ca 1972-76. *2701*

Colonial Government See also Neocolonialism.

—. American Revolution. Business. City Life. Immigration. New York City. 17c-20c. *133*

—. Archdeacon, Thomas J. (review article). Dutch Americans. New York City. Social Classes. 1664-1710. 1976. *26*

—. Carpenter's Company. Labor Unions and Organizations. Pennsylvania (Philadelphia). ca 1700-74. *616*

—. Disaster Relief. Fire. Louisiana (New Orleans). Spain. 1794-95. *2122*

—. Economic Conditions. Maryland (St. Mary's City). 1634-1730. *77*

—. Louisiana (New Orleans). Spain. Vidal, Nicholás María. Zoning. 1797. *1830*

—. Partridge, Alexander. Rhode Island. Trials. 1652. *1285*

Colonization See also Settlement.

—. Apathy. Death and Dying. Malnutrition. Virginia (Jamestown). 1607-24. *1745*

Colonization companies. Economic growth. Railroads. Saskatchewan (Yorkton). 1882-1905. *3660*

Colorado See also Western States.

—. Archaeology. Cliff dwellers. Indians. Nordenskiold, Gustaf (Cliff Dwellers of the Mesa Verde). Prehistory. 1891-93. *3929*

—. Baseball. Leadville Blues (team). 1882. *913*

—. Charters. Denver Urban Observatory. 1972-74. *2376*

—. Denver Post. Newspapers. Patterson, Thomas M. Reform. Rocky Mountain News. 1906-07. *926*

—. Music. Poles. Theater. 1859-1913. *973*

Colorado (Boulder). Greenbelts. Housing. Prices. Real Estate. 1975. *3370*

Colorado (Central City). Best's Pharmacy. Gold Rushes. Miners. Pharmacy. 1861-1974. *457*

Colorado (Crested Butte). AMAX, Inc. Economic Growth. Mines. 1979. *3508*

—. AMAX, Inc. Mines. Molybdenum. Preservation. Resorts. 1880's-1978. *3522*

Colorado (Denver). Acculturation. English Americans. German Americans. Irish Americans. 1860-90. *1323*

—. Alcoholism. Social work. 1967-70. *3234*

—. Assimilation. Greek Americans. 20c. *1607*

—. Attitudes. Mexican Americans. Negroes. Neighborhoods. Public services. Whites. 1970's. *3612*

—. Authors. Jews. Physicians. Social work. Spivak, Charles. ca 1880-1927. *1740*

—. Bars. Homosexuality. 1885-1976. *895*

—. Barth, Gunther. Blumin, Stuart M. California (San Francisco). Lotchin, Roger W. Urbanization (review article). 1820's-90's. 1970's. *90*

—. Barth, Gunther (review article). California (San Francisco). Urbanization. 19c. 1975. *109*

—. Beth Ha Medrosh Hagodol synagogue. Charities. Judaism. Kauvar, Charles E. H. 1902-71. *1188*

—. Boom towns. Economic Growth. 1858-1973. *50*

—. Business. Economic Structure. Migration, Internal. Neighborhoods. Race. 1960-70. *2245*

—. California (Sacramento). District of Columbia. Music (jazz). New Jersey (Chester). Ohio (Peninsula). Texas (San Antonio). 19c-20c. *2785*

—. California (San Francisco). Restorations. Urban Renewal. Washington (Seattle). ca 1970's. *3556*

—. Cities. Decisionmaking. Minnesota (Minneapolis, St. Paul). Political systems. 1967-70. *2339*

—. City Government. Community Participation in Politics. Decisionmaking. Public services. 1975-78. *2448*

—. City government. Ethnic groups. Public Services. 1974. *3611*

—. Community Participation in Politics. Oklahoma (Oklahoma City). 1963. 1966. 1970. *2660*

—. Courts. Federal Government. School Integration. 1974-78. *2864*

—. Daily Life. Frontier and Pioneer Life. Saloons. 1858-76. *894*

—. Decisionmaking. Highways. Metropolitan areas. Oregon (Portland). Public policy. 1975. *3484*

—. Denver Pacific Railroad. Evans, John. Palmer, William Jackson. Railroads. 1850-80. *181*

—. Elections (mayoral). Londoner, Wolfe. Political reform. 1889-91. *391*

—. Employment. Geographic mobility. Social Mobility. 1870-92. *844*

—. Ethnic Groups. Residential Patterns. Social Status. 1940-77. *2703*

—. Immigrants. Saloons. 1865-1933. *893*

—. Italian Americans. 1870's-1920's. *1578*

—. Metropolitan Areas. Political Reform. State Legislatures. 1961-70. *2511*

—. Mexican Americans. Negroes. Political attitudes. Voting and Voting Behavior. 1971. *3037*

—. Prohibition. Wickersham Committee (1931). 1907-33. *1233*

Colorado (Denver County; Denver). City Planning. Demography. Economic conditions. Taxation. 1970's. *2341*

Colorado (Florence). Economic Development. Mineral Resources. Oil Industry and Trade. 1885-1910. *199*

Colorado (Georgetown). Population. Rural Development. 1950-70's. *2668*

Colorado (Gothic). Settlement. Silver Mining. 1878-80. *116*

Colorado (Leadville). Leadville Daily Chronicle (newspaper). Science fiction. Stein, Orth. 1880-82. *928*

—. Silver mining. Tabor, Elizabeth "Baby Doe". Tabor, Horace A. W. 1877-1935. *644*

Colorado River. Arizona (Yuma). Ferries. Poston, Charles D. Railroads. Trade Routes. 1854-91. *158*

Colorado, southeastern. Advertising. Agriculture. Boom towns. Rain and Rainfall. Speculation. 1886-94. *219*

Colorado, southwestern. Anasazi culture. Archaeology. Cliff dwellers. Indians. Mesa Verde National Park. ca 450-1300. 1888-1977. *3934*

Colored Protective Association. Civil Rights. NAACP. Negroes. Pennsylvania (Philadelphia). Riots. 1918. *1221*

Columbia Garden. Maryland (Baltimore). Recreation. Theater. 1805-07. *907*

Columbia Restaurant. Louisiana (Shreveport). ca 1900-69. *861*

Columbia University. Colden, Cadwallader. Location. New York City. Smith, William, Sr. 1747-53. *1087*

Columbia University (and Low Library). Architecture. McKim, Charles F. New York City. 1894-20c. *1949*

Columbia University (Medical School). Medical education. New York City. Physicians. Professionalization. 1760's. *1741*

Columbus Enquirer-Sun. Editors and Editing. Georgia. Harris, Julian LaRose. Ku Klux Klan. Racism. 1920's. *943*

Columbus Street Railroad Company. City Government. Ohio. Streetcars. 1862-1920. *2102*

Commerce See also Banking; Business; Chambers of Commerce; International Trade; Monopolies; Prices; Retail Trade; Statistics; Stocks and Bonds; Tariff; Trade; Trade Routes; Transportation.

—. Boosterism. Economic Conditions. Iowa (Sioux City). Real estate. Speculation. 1855-57. *205*

—. Brazil (Rio de Janeiro). Ports. South Carolina (Charleston). 18c. *439*

—. Economic development. Indiana (Indianapolis). Ohio (Cincinnati). Public Opinion. Railroads. 1848-57. *52*

—. Economic Development. Louisiana (New Orleans). Mississippi River. Technology. 1850-1950. *417*

—. Economic development. New Brunswick (Saint John). 1820-50. *3709*

—. Economic Development. Ports. Technology. 1900-70's. *415*

—. France. Fur trade. Great Britain. Middle classes. Quebec (Montreal). 1750-92. *3735*

—. Industrialization. Ontario (Hamilton). Population. 1851-71. *3795*

—. Industry. Wisconsin (Milwaukee). 1835-80. *408*

—. Manufacturing. Northeastern or North Atlantic States. Urbanization. 19c. *194*

—. Navigation, Inland. New York City (East River). Photographs. 1609-1876. *1806*

—. Nova Scotia (Halifax). 1783-1850. *3756*

—. Quebec (Lower Canada). Social Classes. 1792-1812. *3809*

Commercialism. Artifacts. Folk art. Greek Americans. Pennsylvania (Philadelphia; Upper Darby). Religion. 1970's. *461*

—. Industrialization. Materialism. Politics. Urbanization. 19c. *19*

Corwine, Aaron H. Amelung, Sophia. Art. Audubon, John James. Ohio (Cincinnati). 1819-24. *977*

Cosmopolitanism. American Revolution. Massachusetts. Political parties. Urbanization. 1760-1820. *70*

—. California (San Francisco Bay area). City managers. Localism. ca 1958-74. *2362*

—. Ohio (Cleveland). Pennsylvania (Philadelphia, Pittsburgh). Upper Classes. 1850-1900. *781*

Cost of Living *See also* Medical Care (costs); Prices; Wages.

—. 1970. *2616*

—. Electric Power. 1962-75. *3443*

—. Employment. Ethnic Groups. Income. Pennsylvania (Philadelphia). Poverty. 1880. *564*

—. Metropolitan areas. Wages. 1966-77. *2614*

Cotillo, Salvatore. Italian Americans. Liberalism. New York City. Politics. Reform. 1904-39. *367*

Cottle, Thomas J. (review article). Busing. Massachusetts (Boston). School integration. 1974-76. *2894*

Cotton Exchange. Economic Development. Louisiana (New Orleans). 1870-81. *534*

Cotton industry. Artisans. Iron industry. Rhode Island (Pawtucket). Technology. 1790's-1810's. *491*

—. Barnsley, Godfrey. Civil War. Gilmour, Henry S. Letters. Louisiana (New Orleans). Trade. 1861-62. *456*

—. Economic conditions. Industrialization. Manufacturing. Pennsylvania (Rockdale). Social change. 1825-65. *521*

—. Marketing. South. Urbanization. 1880-1930. *227*

Cotton mills. Architecture. Calico Printing. Dover Manufacturing Company Print Works. New Hampshire (Dover). 1820-25. *474*

—. Ethnic Groups. Michigan (Detroit). Occupations. Residential Patterns. 1880. *1336*

Cotton trade. Banking. Brown, Alexander & Sons. Foreign exchange. Great Britain (Liverpool). Maryland (Baltimore). New York City. Pennsylvania (Philadelphia). 1820-80. *437*

Country Life *See also* Rural Settlements.

—. Architecture. Mormons. Scandinavian Americans. Utah (Spring City). 1851-1975. *1849*

—. Attitudes. Environment. 1978. *2658*

—. Canada. Grain elevators. Transportation. 1930's-70's. *3898*

—. City Life. Classical Revival. Jefferson, Thomas. Values. ca 1800-40. *2186*

—. Howells, William Dean (*A Modern Instance*). Social Change. Urbanization. 19c. *2183*

Country Life Movement. Agriculture. Educational Reform. 1900-20. *1074*

County Government *See also* Local Government; State Government.

—. Alabama (Calhoun County; Anniston). Economic Conditions. Politics. 1862-1900. *108*

—. Architects. California. Fusselman, William. Marin County Civic Center. 1952-63. *3417*

—. City Government. Courts. Intergovernmental Relations. Virginia. 1776-1800. *261*

Courthouse Gang. Local Politics. Nebraska (Loup City). Political Factions. Railroad Gang. 1887-91. *246*

Courts *See also* Courts Martial and Courts of Inquiry; Judges; Judicial Process; Supreme Court.

—. California (Alameda, San Benito counties). Lawsuits. 1890-1970. *1223*

—. California (Los Angeles). Plea bargaining. Public defenders. 1970. *2970*

—. California (Petaluma). Government Regulation. Population. 1956-73. *3315*

—. California (San Francisco). City Government. Homosexuals. Police. Riots. 1979. *2943*

—. City Government. County Government. Intergovernmental Relations. Virginia. 1776-1800. *261*

—. City Life. Criminal Law. Violence. 1973. *2939*

—. City Planning. New Jersey. Zoning. 1970-73. *3339*

—. Coleman, James S. Methodology. School Integration. White flight. 1970's. *2903*

—. Coleman, James S. Ravitch, Diane. School Integration. White flight. 1966-78. *2832*

—. Colorado (Denver). Federal Government. School Integration. 1974-78. *2864*

—. Crime and Criminals. Police. Social Conditions. 1960-75. *2965*

—. Crime and Criminals. Slavery. Virginia (Richmond). 1784-1820. *1275*

—. Dillin, S. Hugh. Indiana (Indianapolis). School integration. 1971-73. *2880*

—. Discrimination, Educational. District of Columbia. Negroes. Public schools. 1804-1974. *1084*

—. Education. Federal policy. Metropolitan Areas. Residential segregation. 1974. *2655*

—. Florida (Dade County; Miami). 1896-1930. *1224*

—. Generations. Massachusetts (Ipswich, Salem). Social Classes. Values. 1636-56. *773*

—. Housing. Land use. Suburbs. Zoning. 1922-78. *1838*

—. Integration. Poor. Suburbs. 1960's-70's. *3371*

—. Juvenile delinquency. New York City. Prisons. 1975. *2969*

—. Maryland (Baltimore). Ohio (Cleveland). Wisconsin (Milwaukee). 1965-70. *3005*

—. Michigan (Detroit). Public schools. Race Relations. School Integration. 1970-74. *2841*

—. Michigan (Detroit). Public Schools. Race Relations. Segregation. 1969-73. *2908*

—. New York (Newtown). Social Classes. 1659-90. *1219*

—. Plea bargaining. Sentencing. 19c. *1231*

Courts martial and Courts of Inquiry. Illinois (Chicago). Militia. 1858-59. *748*

Cowley, Malcolm. Community (concept). Smith, Page. 1890-1930. *2155*

Crafts. *See* Arts and Crafts.

Craftsmen. *See* Artisans.

Crane, Stephen. Cahan, Abraham. Fiction. 1890's. *2150*

Crawford, Lester M. Kansas. Theater Production and Direction. Topeka Opera House. 1858-83. *1064*

Creary, John W. Abercrombie, Anderson. Bricks. Florida (Pensacola). Manufacturing. Raiford, Phillip H. 1854-60. *487*

Credit *See also* Banking; Loans.

—. Business. Maryland (Baltimore). 1757-76. *463*

—. Loan sharking. Pennsylvania (Pittsburgh). Reform. Working Class. 1900-15. *548*

Crerar family. Nova Scotia (Pictou). Shipping. 1840's-50's. *3751*

Crescent Theater. Erlanger, Abraham Lincoln. Klaw, Marc. Louisiana (New Orleans). Theater. Tulane Theater. 1896-1937. *987*

Crime and Criminals *See also* names of crimes, e.g. Murder, etc.; Criminal Law; Juvenile Delinquency; Police; Prisons; Riots; Terrorism; Trials; Violence.

—. 1951-70. *2956*

—. 1970-74. *2993*

—. Arrest rate. Boarding schools. Indians. 1976. *2958*

—. Bail. Friends, Society of. Peace bonds. Pennsylvania (Philadelphia). 1680-1829. *1250*

—. Behavior. Jacobs, Jane. 1968. *2964*

—. Blackouts. Looting. New York City. Poverty. 1977. *2942*

—. California (Los Angeles County). Law Enforcement. 1850-56. *1294*

—. Capone, Al. Illinois (Chicago). 1919-47. *1258*

—. Children. City Life. Massachusetts (Boston). 1973. *3073*

—. City planning. Parks. 1930's-60's. *3330*

—. City Politics. Demography. Missouri (Kansas City). Police policies. 1970's. *2980*

—. Civil Rights. Dissonance theory. Metropolitan Areas. Poverty. Public Opinion. 1963-72. *2934*

—. Consumers. Fraud. Local government. Public Policy. 1970's. *2522*

—. Courts. Police. Social Conditions. 1960-75. *2965*

—. Courts. Slavery. Virginia (Richmond). 1784-1820. *1275*

—. Crowding. Methodology. ca 1960-75. *3004*

—. Deneen, Charles S. Illinois (Chicago). Political Corruption. Primaries. Republican Party. Thompson, William Hale. 1928. *346*

—. District of Columbia. Police. 1861-65. *1244*

—. Dropouts. Pennsylvania (Philadelphia). School attendance. Students. 1970. *2853*

—. Economic conditions. Housing. Illinois (Chicago; Woodlawn). Negroes. 1930-71. *3281*

—. Economic Growth. Florida (Duval County; Jacksonville). Metropolitan Government. Unemployment. 1967-73. *2265*

—. Employment. Housing. Metropolitan areas. Schools. Transportation. 1970's. *2206*

—. Federal Bureau of Investigation. Statistics. 1974. *2999*

—. Federal Bureau of Investigation (Uniform Crime Reporting Program). Politics. 1965-73. *2994*

—. Gangs. Graffiti. Juvenile Delinquency. Pennsylvania (Philadelphia). Race Relations. 1970-72. *2966*

—. Geography. Michigan (Detroit). Police. 1845-75. *1278*

—. Georgia (Atlanta). Michigan (Detroit). Newspapers. Reporters and Reporting. 1974. *2765*

—. Gilmer, Elizabeth M. (pseud. Dorothy Dix). Journalism. New York *Journal*. Women. 1901-16. *931*

—. Hennessy, David. Italian Americans. Louisiana (New Orleans). Mafia. Murder. 1890. *1266*

—. Historiography. Law and Society. Michigan (Detroit). Urbanization. 1824-47. *1280*

—. Illinois (Chicago). Law enforcement. Police. Political Corruption. Social Customs. 1890-1925. *1230*

—. Illinois (Chicago). Maryland (Baltimore). Michigan (Detroit). Sentencing. 1975-76. *2955*

—. Industrialism. Monkkonen, Eric H. (review article). Ohio (Columbus). Poverty. Urbanization. 1860-85. 1975. *1247*

—. Industrialization. Pennsylvania (Philadelphia). Violence. 1820's-1976. *1248*

—. Louisiana (New Orleans). Prohibition. 1918-33. *1242*

—. Missouri (St. Louis). Newspapers. Reporters and Reporting. 1969-72. *2769*

—. New York City. Parks. 1970's. *3430*

—. New York City. Public Opinion. 1968-75. *3609*

—. North Carolina (Charlotte). Sentencing. 1970's. *2938*

—. Police. Public Opinion. 1960-75. *2968*

—. Police. Public Policy. 1970-75. *2997*

—. Population. Statistics. 1970's. *2950*

—. Suburbanization. 1946-77. *2996*

—. Washington (Seattle). 1960-78. *2937*

Criminal justice (review article). Balbus, Isaac D. Eisenstein, James. Jacob, Herbert. Levin, Martin A. Mather, Lynn M. 1970's. *2941*

Criminal Law *See also* Trials.

—. City Life. Courts. Violence. 1973. *2939*

—. Illinois. 1960's-71. *2982*

Criminology. Police. Statistics. 1840-1977. *1259*

Criticism. Breslin, Jimmy. Flaherty, Joe. Hamill, Pete. Irish Americans. New York City (Brooklyn). Novels. 1960's-70's. *3134*

Croatian Americans. Construction. Ethnic Groups. Montana (Lewistown). 1897-1920. *1626*

Crocker, Charles. California (San Francisco). Chinese. Immigration. Kearney, Denis. Racism. Railroads. 1863-82. *1539*

Croker, Richard. New York City. Political Corruption. Tammany Hall. 1886-1901. *345*

Crosswaith, Frank R. Negro Labor Committee. New York City (Harlem). 1925-39. *634*

Crosthwait, D. N. Meigs High School. Negroes. Tennessee (Nashville). 1886. *1520*

Crosthwaite, Philip. California (San Diego). City Government. 1845-74. *305*

Crowding. Attitudes. Behavior. Michigan (Detroit area). Social Conditions. 1965-66. *2640*

—. City Planning. Marsh, Benjamin C. National Conference on City Planning. Poor. Social Reform. 1900-17. *1834*

—. Crime and Criminals. Methodology. ca 1960-75. *3004*

—. Deviant behavior. Households. Quality of Life. 1940-70's. *2663*

—. Metropolitan Areas. Population. 1975. *2664*

—. Public Opinion. Violence. 1961-68. *3007*

Crowds *See also* Demonstrations; Riots; Social Psychology.

—. American Revolution. Ideology. Social change. 1765-1830's. *1237*

—. Ontario (Toronto). Sports. Violence. 1963-73. *3815*

Crowley, Mart (*Boys in the Band*). California (Los Angeles). Folklore. Homosexuals. Men. 1968-71. *2748*

Crump, Edward. Democratic Party. Elections (gubernatorial). Politics. Tennessee (Shelby County). 1932. *347*

Cruse, Englehart. Grain. Maryland (Baltimore). Milling. Rumsey, James. Steam Power. 1787-1804. *1774*

Cuba. City politics. Florida (Jacksonville). Huah, José Alejandro. Independence Movements. Martí, José. 1836-1905. *1525*

—. Exiles. Florida (Key West). Human Relations. Independence Movements. 1868-78. *1534*

Detroit Citizens League. Leland, Henry. Michigan. Progressivism. Social Classes. 1912-24. *362*

Detroit Medical Center. Michigan. Urban Renewal. 1972. *2212*

Development *See also* Economic Development.

—. Alaska (Fairbanks). Environment. 1970-75. *3248*

—. Automobiles. California (Los Angeles). City Planning. 1920's. *1790*

—. Business. Public lands. Tennessee (Memphis). 1971-76. *3296*

—. California (Berkeley, San Francisco). City politics. Local government. Massachusetts (Boston, Cambridge). 1960's-70's. *2336*

—. California (Owens Valley, San Fernando Valley). Harriman, Job. Los Angeles Aqueduct. Population. State Politics. Water Supply. 1900-74. *2045*

—. California (San Francisco). Housing. Real Estate Associates. 1846-81. *1868*

—. Canada. Models. Residential patterns. USA. 1973. *3272*

—. Cities. Fort Smith and Western Railroad Company. Negroes. Oklahoma (Boley). Railroads. Speculators. 1903-05. *119*

—. City Government. Housing. Landlords and Tenants. New York. Relocation. 1940's-74. *3407*

—. Demography. Government Regulation. Social Change. Suburbanization. 1970-75. *2274*

—. Economic Conditions. Investments. Neighborhoods. Public Policy. Suburbs. 1968-75. *2607*

—. Fisher, Carl Graham. Florida (Miami Beach). Indianapolis Speedway. ca 1880-1939. *164*

—. Historical Sites and Parks. Lafayette Square. Missouri (St. Louis). 1836-1926. *1802*

—. Kentucky (Pikeville). Local government. 1970's. *2281*

—. Land. 1968-74. *3291*

—. Land. Maryland (Prince Georges County). Suburbs. 1970-73. *3264*

—. Property tax. 1974. *2344*

Dever, William. Elections (mayoral). Ethnic groups. Illinois (Chicago). Negroes. Prohibition. 1923-27. *355*

Deviant behavior. Crowding. Households. Quality of Life. 1940-70's. *2663*

—. Liberalism. Looting. New York City. Political Attitudes. Racism. 1977. *2944*

—. Negroes. Youth. 1930's-60's. *2990*

Devit, Charles. M'Grath, Michael. Murder. Nova Scotia (Halifax). Trials. Westmacott, John. 1816. *3771*

Devonian Group of Charitable Foundations. Alberta. Harvie, Eric Lafferty. Parks. Preservation. Scientific Experiments and Research. 1955-79. *3888*

DeVries, Jon. Community Participation in Politics. Neighborhoods. North Carolina (Winston-Salem; Crystal Towers). Redevelopment Commission. Urban renewal. 1970's. *3388*

Diaries *See also* Personal Narratives.

—. Bell, William H. Law Enforcement. New York City. 1850-51. *1292*

—. Bentley, William. Cabinetmaking. Furniture and Furnishings. Massachusetts (Salem). 1784-1819. *478*

—. Bentley, William. Massachusetts (Salem). Voluntary Associations. 1784-1819. *727*

—. California (San Francisco). Immigrants. Irish Americans. Labor. Roney, Frank. 1875-76. *809*

—. City Life. West Virginia (Charleston). Wilson, Elizabeth Ruffner. 1890-92. *677*

Diet. See Food Consumption.

Diffusion. Contagion hypothesis. Negroes. Police. Riots. 1966-67. *2976*

—. Innovation. Public opinion. Rural-Urban Studies. 1953-76. *2214*

Diffusion theory. City planning. 1975. *3293*

—. City Planning. Economic Growth. Employment. 1960-73. *2283*

Dillin, S. Hugh. Courts. Indiana (Indianapolis). School integration. 1971-74. *2880*

Dinnerstein, Leonard. Barton, Josef J. Esslinger, Dean R. Ethnic groups. Hvidt, Kristian. Immigration (review article). Reimers, David M. 1850-1950. 1970's. *1297*

Disaster Relief. Armies. California (San Francisco). Earthquakes. Greeley, Adolphus. 1906. *330*

—. Chicago Relief and Aid Society. Fire. Illinois (Chicago). 1871-72. *1175*

—. Colonial Government. Fire. Louisiana (New Orleans). Spain. 1794-95. *2122*

—. Fire. New Brunswick (Saint John). Nova Scotia. 1877. *3906*

—. Mississippi (Tupelo). Tornadoes. 1936. *2118*

Disasters *See also* names of particular disasters, e.g. San Francisco Earthquake and Fire (1906); Earthquakes; Fire Prevention and Extinction; Floods.

—. Building codes. City Government. Fire. Georgia (Augusta). 1916. *2134*

—. Building codes. City planning. 1970's. *3292*

Discovery and Exploration *See also* Westward Movement.

—. Anza, Juan Bautista de. California (San Francisco). Mexico. Settlement. 1775-76. *152*

Discrimination *See also* Civil Rights; Minorities; Racism; Segregation; Sex Discrimination.

—. Banking. Citizens Action Program. Illinois (Chicago). Redlining. Urban Renewal. 1969-75. *2610*

—. Child Welfare. Lawsuits. New York. 1973-74. *2924*

—. Dancey, John C. Michigan (Detroit). Urban League. Washington, Forrester B. 1916-39. *754*

—. Economic Conditions. Immigration. Italian Americans. Oregon (Portland). 1880-1920. *1587*

—. Economic Conditions. Ontario (Toronto). West Indians. 1977. *3832*

—. Ethnic groups. Immigrants. Manitoba (Winnipeg). Population. 1874-1974. *3642*

—. Georgia (Atlanta). Jews. 1865-1915. *1448*

—. Hospitals. Mercy Hospital. Negroes. Ohio (Cleveland). 1927-30. *1734*

—. Housing. Poverty areas. Prices. 1970-72. *3414*

—. Irish Americans. Labor. Massachusetts (Waltham). 1850-90. *1509*

—. Medicine (practice of). Mental Institutions. Minorities. Social Classes. 1830-75. *1736*

—. Men. Poverty. Unemployment. 1970-72. *2618*

—. Michigan (Detroit). Residential segregation. 1960-70. *3074*

—. Middle classes. Negroes. New Jersey (Newark). Puerto Ricans. 1967-74. *3014*

—. Negroes. New York City. Puerto Ricans. Skill differential. Wages. Whites. 1970. *3041*

—. Suburbs. 1937-75. *3092*

Discrimination, Educational. 1967-68. *2833*

—. Alabama (Montgomery). Georgia (Atlanta). Negroes. North Carolina (Raleigh). Teachers. Tennessee (Nashville). Virginia (Richmond). 1865-90. *1106*

—. Busing. Michigan (Detroit). *Milliken* v. *Bradley* (US, 1974). Social sciences. Trials. 1971-76. *3011*

—. Courts. District of Columbia. Negroes. Public schools. 1804-1974. *1088*

—. Education. New York City. Segregation. 1973. *2826*

—. North. Pennsylvania (Philadelphia). 1800-1965. *2836*

—. Ontario. Social Classes. Women. 1851-71. *3773*

Discrimination, employment. Affirmative action. City Government. Negroes. Ohio (Cincinnati). 1963-67. *2352*

—. Ainslie, Peter. Carey, John R. Maryland (Baltimore). National Urban League. Negroes. Social conditions. 1921-35. *746*

—. Chinese Americans. Negroes. Vice. 1880-1940. *1253*

—. Georgia (Atlanta). Labor. Racism. Women. 1930's. *556*

—. Immigrants. Ontario (Toronto). Social Status. West Indians. 1972. *3846*

—. Industry. Metropolitan areas. Profit. Racism. 1973. *2598*

—. Labor Unions and Organizations. Mexicans. Texas (El Paso). 1880-1920. *1524*

—. Musicians. National Endowment for the Arts. Negroes. Symphony orchestras. 1974-75. *3065*

—. New Jersey (Newark). Public Schools. Race Relations. Strikes. 1950's-70's. *2622*

Discrimination, Housing. Civil rights. LaGuardia, Fiorello. Metropolitan Life Insurance Company. New York City (Stuyvesant Town). Public housing. 1943. *3367*

—. Connecticut (New Haven). Negroes. Rents. Whites. 1973. *3035*

—. Ethnic Groups. Massachusetts (Boston). 1830-1970. *1316*

—. Ghettos. Legislation. Negroes. 1970's. *3105*

—. Income. Minnesota (Minneapolis, St. Paul). Negroes. Zelder, Raymond E. 1965-73. *3057*

—. Metropolitan areas. Negroes. Suburbanization. 1970's-80's. *3116*

—. Metropolitan areas. School integration. 1945-77. *2870*

—. Negroes. 1968-72. *3399*

—. Occupations. Racism. 1950-70. *2685*

—. Race relations. 20c. *1406*

Disease, concept of. Charity Hospital of Louisiana. Louisiana (New Orleans). Masturbation. 1848-1933. *1725*

Diseases *See also* names of diseases, e.g. diphtheria, etc.; Epidemics; Medicine (practice of).

—. City Government. Fire. Ontario (Ottawa). Public Health. Reform. Water supply. 1830-90. *3700*

—. City planning. Sanitation. 1840-90. *1847*

—. Civil Engineering. Illinois (Chicago). Intergovernmental Relations. Sanitary and Ship Canal. Sewage disposal. Water Pollution. 1850's-1900. *1713*

—. Elephantiasis. Mosquito control. Public Health. Roundworms, filarial. South Carolina (Charleston). 1900-20's. *1764*

—. Georgia (Savannah). Negroes. 1850's-60's. *1748*

—. Hospitals. Location. Metropolitan Areas. 1970-74. *3249*

—. Jackson, Hall. Mortality. New Hampshire (Portsmouth). Statistics. 18c. 20c. *1726*

—. Public Health. Social Classes. 1900-75. *3238*

Dispensaries. Medical care. Social classes. 1786-1920. *1763*

Dispensary Act. Liquor trade. Manning, Richard Irvine. Monopolies. South Carolina (Charleston). 1915-18. *312*

Dissimilarity, index of. Methodology. Michigan (Detroit). Segregation. 1850-60. 1974. *3985*

Dissonance theory. Civil Rights. Crime and Criminals. Metropolitan Areas. Poverty. Public Opinion. 1963-72. *2934*

DISTAR (program). Illinois (Chicago). Negroes. Public schools. Reading. 1970's. *2838*

District of Columbia. Accounting. Lawyers. Organizations. 1960-77. *2577*

—. Alcohol. Drunkenness, public. Law Reform. Minnesota (Minneapolis). Police. 1960's-70's. *2931*

—. Architects. Capitols. Construction. Hoban, James. 1799. *1885*

—. Architecture. Capitols. 1792-1850. *1977*

—. Architecture. Capitols. 1792-93. *1878*

—. Architecture. Capitols. House of Representatives Chamber. Jefferson, Thomas. Latrobe, Benjamin Henry. 1803-12. *1890*

—. Architecture. City Planning. L'Enfant, Pierre Charles. 1791. *1823*

—. Architecture. Daguerreotypes. Photography. Plumbe, John, Jr. 1845-49. *1893*

—. Architecture. Demolition. 19c-20c. *1899*

—. Architecture (Federal style). Octagon (house). Thornton, William. 1800. *1937*

—. Archives, National. Building permits. 1877-1949. *3955*

—. Art. 1975-78. *2808*

—. Art. Davis, Gene. Personal Narratives. 1950-66. *2790*

—. Artists. Personal Narratives. 1978. *2809*

—. Assimilation. Chinese Americans. Education. Friendship. 1940's-70's. *3173*

—. California (Los Angeles). Chandler, Otis. Graham, Katherine. Newspapers. Noyes, Newbold. Reporters and Reporting. 1967-72. *2778*

—. California (Los Angeles). Economic conditions. Michigan (Detroit). Negroes. New Jersey (Newark). Riots. Social change. ca 1960-73. *2933*

—. California (Los Angeles). New York City. Reporters and Reporting. Television. 1976. *2766*

—. California (Sacramento). Colorado (Denver). Music (jazz). New Jersey (Chester). Ohio (Peninsula). Texas (San Antonio). 19c-20c. *2785*

—. City Government. Home Rule Act (US, 1973). 1780's-1973. *2366*

—. City Planning. L'Enfant, Pierre Charles. 1796-1825. *1851*

—. Congress. Emancipation. Lincoln, Abraham. Public Administration. 1862. *318*

—. Congress. Militia. 1800-1975. *316*

—. Courts. Discrimination, Educational. Negroes. Public schools. 1804-1974. *1084*

—. Crime and Criminals. Police. 1861-65. *1244*

—. Davis, Ola. Urban Renewal. 1975-79. *3415*

—. Decisionmaking. Intergovernmental relations. New Jersey (Newark, Trenton). New York City. Pennsylvania (Philadelphia). Tocks Island Project. Urbanization. Water projects. 1962-75. *2311*

—. Pennsylvania (Philadelphia). Religion. Social classes. Voting and Voting Behavior. 1924-40. *1329*

—. Pennsylvania (Philadelphia). Women. Working Class. 1910-30. *1318*

—. Population. Quebec (Quebec). Residential patterns. 1795-1805. *3789*

—. Poverty. Rural-Urban Studies. 1970-75. *2712*

—. Prohibitionists. Saloons. Values. Working Class. 1890-1920. *885*

—. Social Problems. Suburbs. Women. 1940's-70's. *3598*

Ethnic Groups (review article). Catholic Church. Horowitz, Helen Lefkowitz. Illinois (Chicago). Kessner, Thomas. New York City. Philanthropy. Sanders, James W. 1883-1965. 1970's. *48*

—. Irish Americans. Pennsylvania (Philadelphia). Working Class. 1725-1975. *1333*

Ethnic studies (review article). Barton, Josef J. Esslinger, Dean R. Immigrants. Kantowicz, Edward R. 19c-20c. 1976. *1326*

Ethnicity. Acculturation. California (Los Angeles). Race. Social status. Voting and Voting Behavior. 1973. *2475*

—. Acculturation. German Americans. Immigrants. Neighborhoods. 1840's-1970's. *1305*

—. Americanization. Catholics. New York City. Religion. -1974. *3040*

—. Art. California (Los Angeles). Mexican Americans. Murals, street. 1970's. *3164*

—. Artists. California (East Los Angeles, Los Angeles; Boyle Heights). Mexican Americans. Murals. 1965-75. *3153*

—. Arts. New York City. Puerto Ricans. 1960's-70's. *3142*

—. Assimilation. Greek Americans. New York City. Orthodox Eastern Church. St. Demetrios Church. St. Markela Church. 1970's. *3206*

—. Assimilation. Intermarriage. Mexican Americans. Texas (San Antonio). Women. 1830-60. *1523*

—. Attitudes. Foreign Policy. Polish Americans. Wisconsin (Milwaukee). 1970's. *3202*

—. Attitudes. Illinois (Chicago). Negroes. Race Relations. Social Classes. 1969. *3042*

—. Automobiles. Michigan (Detroit). Protestant Churches. Social organization. 1880-1940. *1315*

—. Birth Rate. Massachusetts (Boston; South End). Occupations. 1880. *696*

—. Black Power. Jews. Polish Americans. Racial attitudes. 1968. *3027*

—. Bocce ball. Games. Immigrants. Italian Americans. Pennsylvania (Philadelphia). 1974. *3195*

—. California (Fresno). Intermarriage. Japanese Americans. 1960-73. *3178*

—. California (San Francisco). Immigrants. Vigilance Committees. 1849-56. *1324*

—. California (San Francisco). Jews. Synagogues. 1848-1900. *1668*

—. California (San Francisco). Molokans. Sects, Religious. 1906-76. *1647*

—. Canada. National Self-image. Ontario (Toronto). 1970. *3849*

—. City Life. Cuban Americans. Folklore. Indiana (East Chicago). Puerto Ricans. 1976. *3148*

—. Civil Disturbances. High Schools. 1967-69. *2879*

—. Czech Americans. Missouri (St. Louis). Neighborhoods. Social organizations. 1848-1970. *1575*

—. Elections (mayoral). Hylan, John F. Mitchel, John Purroy. New York City. Patriotism. World War I. 1917. *284*

—. Folk art. Latvian Canadians. Manitoba (Winnipeg). Ukrainian Canadians. 1978. *3805*

—. German Americans. Kamp, Henry. Oklahoma (Oklahoma City). 1906-57. *1582*

—. Greek Canadians. Immigration. Ontario (Toronto). Private Schools. 1900-40. *3845*

—. Hawaii (Honolulu). Japanese Americans. Race relations. Whites. 1975. *3172*

—. Hungarian Americans. Immigrants. Ohio (Cleveland). 1900-20. *1622*

—. Interdisciplinary studies. Philadelphia Social History Project. 1850-80. 1973. *3979*

—. Irish Americans. Massachusetts (Boston). 19c-20c. *3136*

—. Irish Americans. Music. Pennsylvania (Pittsburgh). Radio. 1900-77. *3135*

—. Italian Americans. Missouri (St. Louis; The Hill). Social Classes. 1890-1970. *3199*

—. Italian Americans. Social Conditions. 1945-74. *3212*

—. Jews. Political Attitudes. South Carolina (Charleston). 1970's. *3130*

—. Mexican Americans. Minnesota (St. Paul, lower west side). 1914-65. *1533*

—. Michigan (Detroit). Polish Americans. 1870-1970. *1611*

—. Negroes. Race Relations. Social organization. Valentine, Charles. 1865-1975. *1419*

—. New York (Buffalo). Political Leadership. 1970. *2416*

—. New York (New York Mills). Polish Americans. Social Customs. Textile Industry. 19c-20c. *3210*

—. Ohio (Cleveland). Regionalism. Slovene Americans. 20c. *1625*

—. Ohio (Cleveland). Slovak Americans. 1975. *3203*

—. Ohio (Cleveland). Slovak Institute. 1952-72. *3200*

—. Ohio (Cleveland). Slovene Americans. Social Organization. 1880-1924. *1618*

—. Ohio (Cleveland). Slovene Americans. Social Organizations. 20c. *1624*

—. Polish Americans. Wisconsin (Milwaukee). -1973. *3201*

Ethnocentrism. Amoskeag Manufacturing Company. Family. Industrial Relations. Modernization. New Hampshire (Manchester). 1912-22. *776*

Ethnology *See also* Acculturation; Anthropology; Folklore; Language; Negroes; Race Relations.

—. California (Los Angeles). Methodology. Polish Americans. Sandberg, Neil C. (review article). 1968-74. *3198*

—. Indians. Photographers. Pueblo Indians. Southwest. 19c. *3928*

Eufaula Heritage Association. Alabama. Restorations. 1965-78. *3533*

Eulau, Heinz. California. Coke, James G. Federal Programs. Gargan, John J. Ohio. Pressman, Jeffrey L. Prewitt, Kenneth. Public policy (review article). Wildavsky, Aaron. ca 1960-73. *2523*

Eureka Heritage Society. Architecture. California. Restorations. Vellutini, Dolores. 1973-78. *3573*

Euripides *(Trojan Women)*. Acting. Browne, Maurice. Chicago Little Theatre. Illinois. Theater Production and Direction. VanVolkenburg, Ellen. 1912-17. *950*

Europe. Architecture. City planning. Housing. Modernism. New Deal. New York City. Ohio (Cleveland). Pennsylvania (Philadelphia). 1932-60. *1952*

—. Assimilation. California (Los Angeles). Immigrants. Jews. Marriage. 1910-13. *1469*

—. California Tomorrow (group). City planning. Restoration. Travel. 1960's-1974. *3317*

—. Elites. New York Philharmonic Orchestra. Symphony orchestras. 19c-20c. *971*

—. Federal Aid. Marshall Plan. Self-help. Social Problems. 1940's-70's. *2231*

Evangelicalism. Baptists, Southern. Rural Areas. South. Urbanization. 1920's. *1697*

—. Great Awakening (2d). New York (Utica). Women. 1800-40. *1692*

—. Indiana (Gary). Negroes. 1976. *3222*

Evangelicals. Church of England. Ontario (Toronto). 1870-1900. *3866*

Evangelism. California (Los Angeles). McPherson, Aimee Semple. Radio. 1920-44. *1638*

—. Daily life. Illinois (Chicago). Methodist Church. Whitefield, Henry. 1833-71. *1637*

—. New York (Buffalo). Sunday, William Ashley ("Billy"). 1917. *1631*

Evans, John. Colorado (Denver). Denver Pacific Railroad. Palmer, William Jackson. Railroads. 1850-80. *181*

Everett, Phil Marshall. Iron Industry. Jackson Iron Company. Marquette Iron Company. Michigan (Carp River Region; Marquette). 1670-1854. *192*

Evictions. California (San Francisco). Chinatowns. City government. Ethnic Groups. International Hotel. Landlords and Tenants. Leftism. 1977. *3169*

Evil eye. Folklore. Italian Americans. New York (Utica). 20c. *3187*

Excavations *See also* Artifacts.

—. Anasazi culture. Indians. New Mexico (Chaco Canyon). 6000 BC-1250 AD. *3925*

—. California (San Diego). Military Camps and Forts. Missions and Missionaries. Serra Museum. 1769-75. 1964-70's. *2112*

—. Makah Indians. Villages. Washington (Ozette). Whale hunters. Prehistory. 1966-74. *3930*

Exhibits and Expositions *See also* Art.

—. Aesthetics. Architecture. 1890's-1970's. *3286*

—. Architecture. 1851-1939. *1891*

—. Art. New York City. 1970's. *2800*

—. Canada. Maps. Public Archives of Canada. Research. Urban history. 1865-1905. *3959*

—. Chicago Historical Society. Illinois. 1860's-1970's. *3948*

Exiles. Cuba. Florida (Key West). Human Relations. Independence Movements. 1868-78. *1534*

Experimental Schools. *See* Free Schools.

Explosions. Fire. *Grand Camp* (vessel). Texas (Texas City). 1947. *3590*

Expo '74. Environmentalism. Washington (Spokane). 1960's-76. *2755*

Exports. Alabama (Mobile). Lumber and Lumbering. 1760-1860. *427*

—. Deerskins. South Carolina. 1735-75. *444*

—. Economic Conditions. Occupations. Ports. 18c. *191*

—. Furniture and Furnishings. Rhode Island. Woodenware. 1783-1800. *445*

—. Georgia (Savannah). Lumber and Lumbering. 1830's-1850's. *428*

—. Lumber and Lumbering. Ports. South Carolina (Charleston). 18c-1860. *425*

F

Factories. Christianity. Slavery. Social Organization. Tobacco workers. Virginia (Richmond). ca 1820-65. *1393*

—. Fire. Garment industry. Industrial Safety. New York City. 1911. *2124*

Fagan, Mark. City Politics. New Jersey (Jersey City). Progressivism. 1896-1907. *389*

—. New Jersey (Jersey City). Progressives. Single tax. Taxation. 1901-17. *388*

Fairchild Wine Vault. Historical Sites and Parks. Oklahoma (Oklahoma City). Winemaking. 1890-1925. *3514*

Family *See also* Divorce; Marriage; Women.

—. Alcoholism. Human relations. New York City. Skid Rows. Women. 1966-69. *2709*

—. Amoskeag Manufacturing Company. Ethnocentrism. Industrial Relations. Modernization. New Hampshire (Manchester). 1912-22. *776*

—. Amoskeag Manufacturing Company. New Hampshire (Manchester). Working Class. 1900-24. *698*

—. Barrios. Housing. Mexican Americans. Relocation. -1973. *3165*

—. Behavior. Capitalism. Labor. Massachusetts (Lowell). Sex roles. 1860. *562*

—. Budgets. Decisionmaking. Pennsylvania (Philadelphia). 1870-80. *693*

—. Business. New York (Poughkeepsie). 1850-80. *400*

—. California (Los Angeles). Demography. Economic Conditions. Methodology. Social change. 1850-75. *702*

—. California (Los Angeles). Economic Conditions. Immigrants. Mexican Americans. Michigan (Detroit). Whites. 1850-80. *1313*

—. California (Los Angeles). Economic Conditions. Population. Social change. 1850-70. *703*

—. California (Los Angeles). Mexican Americans. Modernization. Social change. 1850-80. *1528*

—. Census. City Life. Historiography. Indiana (Vanderburgh County; Evansville). Negroes. 1865-80. *686*

—. Children. City Life. Massachusetts (Boston). 1860. *694*

—. Children. Income. Pennsylvania (Philadelphia). 1880. *565*

—. Children. Negroes. Political Socialization. 1973. *3068*

—. Children's Aid Society. Foster homes. Home Missionary Society. Pennsylvania (Philadelphia). 1880-1905. *1138*

—. Cities. Social Organization. 1700-1977. *684*

—. Connecticut (Fairfield, Hartford, Norwich). Officeholding. 1700-60. *265*

—. Connecticut (Guilford). Land ownership. Social Classes. 18c. *819*

—. Connecticut (Milford). Puritans. 1639-90's. *1683*

—. Connecticut (Windsor). Geographic mobility. Social classes. 17c. *824*

—. Economic conditions. Migration, Internal. Rural-Urban Studies. Social change. 1960-71. *2684*

—. Ethnic groups. Massachusetts (Holyoke). 1880. *709*

Ferris wheel. Ferris, George W. G. Illinois. Rice, Luther V. World's Columbian Exhibition (Chicago, 1893). 1893. *852*

Fertility. Birth Control. Negroes. Pennsylvania (Philadelphia). Socialization. Women. 1901-75. *2674*

—. Marital status. Migration, Internal. Rural-Urban Studies. 1967. *2679*

—. Metropolitan areas. Rural areas. 1965. *2686*

—. Puerto Rico. 1950-70. *2687*

Fertilizers. Farmers. Sewage. 19c-1975. *2053*

Fey, Charles. California (San Francisco). Gambling. Liberty Bell slot machine. ca 1895-1906. *489*

Fiction *See also* Novels.

—. Alabama (Birmingham). Cohen, Octavus Roy. Loafers (literary group). 1920's. *956*

—. Cahan, Abraham. Crane, Stephen. 1890's. *2150*

—. Chopin, Kate. Missouri (St. Louis). Social criticism. ca 1889-1902. *2184*

—. Christianity. Churches. Melville, Herman ("The Two Temples"). New York City. 1845-50. *2176*

—. Florida (St. Augustine). History. 16c-20c. *2167*

—. Social reform. Values. 1800-60. *2181*

Field, Joseph M. Ballet. Missouri (St. Louis). Varieties Theatre. 1852. *1042*

Fields, Annie Adams. Authors. Friendship. Massachusetts (Boston). 1834-1913. *1008*

Filene, Edward A. Business. Civic leaders. Jews. Massachusetts (Boston). 1860-1937. *1438*

Filipino Americans. California (San Diego). Immigration. 1900-46. *1540*

—. California (Watsonville). Depressions. Racism. Riots. Violence. 1926-30. *1215*

Film scripts. Barnes, Joseph W. Documentaries. McKelvey, Blake. New York (Rochester). 1811-1960's. *168*

Films *See also* Acting; Actors and Actresses; Audiovisual Materials; Documentaries.

—. Business. Saxe brothers. Wisconsin (Milwaukee). 1906-25. *874*

—. Censorship. Illinois (Chicago). Nickelodeons. Progressivism. 1907-15. *892*

—. Cities, image of. Drama. 1920's-73. *2165*

—. *The City* (film). City planning. 1939. *2154*

—. Ghettos. Kung Fu motif. Youth. 1970-74. *2751*

—. History Teaching. New York. Syracuse University. 1970-74. *3993*

—. Illinois (Chicago). Movie theaters. 1920-74. *1877*

—. Louisiana Purchase Exposition. Missouri (St. Louis). Museums. Public schools. 1901-78. *1104*

—. Wisconsin (Milwaukee). 1906-47. *873*

Films, silent. American Film Manufacturing Company. Ammex Motion Picture Manufacturing Company. California (San Diego). Essanay Western Company. 1898-1912. *502*

—. Illinois (Chicago). 1893-1930. *498*

Finance *See also* Education (finance); Business; etc.

—. Banking. German Americans. Jews. New York City. 19c. *529*

—. Business. Federal government. 1960's-79. *2528*

—. Business. Negroes. Pennsylvania (Philadelphia). Race Relations. 1968. *3022*

—. California (San Francisco). Pioche, François L. A. 1849-72. *532*

—. Housing. 1979. *2257*

—. Mass transit. New Jersey. New York. Port Authority. State politics. 1921-74. *3462*

—. New York. Public Housing. Urban Development Corporation. 1968-78. *2513*

—. State government. Texas. 1970-74. *2515*

Findlay Market. Ohio (Cincinnati; Over-the-Rhine). 1852-1976. *458*

Fine Arts Building. Architecture. Illinois (Chicago). 1898-1918. *1892*

—. Arts and Crafts. Business. Illinois (Chicago). 1898-1917. *423*

Fine, Sidney (review article). City Government. Depressions. Mayors. Michigan (Detroit). Murphy, Frank. 1930-33. 1975. *286*

Finnish Americans. Automobile Industry and Trade. Michigan (Detroit). 1900-40. *1620*

Finns. Alaska Colonization and Development Company. Immigrants. Port Axel. 1903-40. *183*

Finster, Jerome. Archives, National. Fishbein, Meyer H. Research. Urban history (review article). 1968-74. *3961*

Fire *See also* Fuel.

—. Alabama (Birmingham). 1889-1950. *2130*

—. American Revolution. Dunmore, 4th Earl of. Great Britain. Virginia (Norfolk). 1776-1820's. *2132*

—. Banking. Murphey, Alonzo Miles. Washington (Spokane). 1889-1927. *547*

—. Booth, John Rudolphus. City Government. Housing. Lumber and Lumbering. Ontario (Ottawa). Working class. 1900-03. *3887*

—. Building codes. City Government. Disasters. Georgia (Augusta). 1916. *2134*

—. Building codes. City Government. Missouri Athletic Club. St. Louis Seed Company. 1903-18. *2136*

—. California (San Francisco). Earthquakes. 1906. *2127*

—. Chicago Relief and Aid Society. Disaster Relief. Illinois (Chicago). 1871-72. *1175*

—. Chinatowns. Chinese Americans. Ghettos. Hawaii (Honolulu). 1886. *2121*

—. City Government. Diseases. Ontario (Ottawa). Public Health. Reform. Water supply. 1830-90. *3700*

—. Colonial Government. Disaster Relief. Louisiana (New Orleans). Spain. 1794-95. *2122*

—. Disaster relief. New Brunswick (Saint John). Nova Scotia. 1877. *3906*

—. Economic Conditions. Massachusetts (Salem). Shoe industry. 1900-20. *483*

—. Explosions. *Grand Camp* (vessel). Texas (Texas City). 1947. *3590*

—. Factories. Garment industry. Industrial Safety. New York City. 1911. *2124*

—. Illinois (Chicago). Iroquois Theatre. 1903. *2125*

—. Illinois (Chicago). Iroquois Theatre. 1903. *2135*

Fire companies. Pennsylvania (Muncy). 1848-1973. *2043*

Fire departments. Civil disturbances. Public Administration. 1960's-70's. *3006*

—. Civil disturbances. Public Administration. 1960's-70's. *3008*

—. Folklore. Humor. Tennessee (Nashville). ca 1900-25. *2058*

—. Local government. Pennsylvania (Pittsburgh). Urbanization. 1870. *2413*

—. Missouri. Professionalization. St. Louis Firemen's Association. Violence. 1850-57. *726*

—. Modernization. New York City. Shaler, Alexander. 1865-1971. *2033*

—. Nova Scotia (Bedford). 1921-22. *3916*

Fire departments, volunteer. German Americans. Institutions. Irish Americans. New York City (South Bronx; Morrisania). 1848-87. *751*

Fire fighting. California (San Francisco). Earthquakes. Funston, Frederick. 1906. *2128*

—. City Government. Labor Unions and Organizations. Management. 1969-73. *2624*

—. Currier, Nathaniel. Ives, James Merritt. Lithographs. 19c. *2055*

—. Currier, Nathaniel. Ives, James Merritt. Lithography. New York City. Police. 1835-81. *981*

—. Illinois (Chicago). 1831-58. *723*

—. Mississippi. 1814-50's. *2039*

—. Ontario (Ottawa). Public Health. Water Supply. 1910-15. *3703*

Fire insurance. British Columbia. Buildings. Urban history. 1885-1979. *4068*

—. Documents. Insurance Company of North America Corporation. Pennsylvania (Philadelphia). 1790-1975. *4025*

—. Franklin, Benjamin. Pennsylvania. Philadelphia Contributionship for the Insurance of Houses from Loss by Fire. 1666-1792. *539*

Fire Prevention and Extinction. Arson. Building codes. New York (Rochester). 1900-10. *2031*

—. South Carolina (Charleston). 1830's. *2049*

Fire towers. Architecture. Bogardus, James. Construction. Iron-framed structures. Kroehl, Julius B. New York City. 1850's. *1926*

Fireproof Building. City Government. Construction. Mills, Robert. South Carolina (Charleston). 1822-26. *1995*

First Hebrew Benevolent Society. California (Los Angeles). Jews. Labatt, Samuel K. Voluntary Associations. 1851-54. *1457*

—. California (San Francisco). Cemeteries. Funerals. Jews. Johnson, Henry D. 1849-50. *1489*

First Shiloh Baptist Church. Baptists. Negroes. New York (Buffalo). 1920's-30's. *1704*

First Ward Ball. Illinois (Chicago). Politics. 1880's-1903. *243*

Fiscal crisis. Civil disobedience. Minorities. Working Class. 1970's. *2340*

—. Employment. New York City. Population. Public employees. 1950's-70's. *2248*

—. Federal Policy. New York City. 1950's-70's. *2567*

—. Negroes. New York City. 1975. *2243*

—. New York City. 1960-76. *2353*

—. New York City. Public welfare. Taxation. 1970's. *2310*

—. Suburbs. 1898-1976. *2566*

Fiscal Policy. Apportionment. Public welfare. State aid to education. State Legislatures. 1951-73. *2509*

—. Children. Local government. Recreation. 1970's. *2926*

—. City councils. Mayors. Negroes. Public welfare. 1968-75. *2909*

—. City government. Depressions. New Jersey (Paterson). Public Welfare. Textile industry. 1920-32. *253*

—. City government. New York City. 1975. *2396*

—. City Government. Riots. 1960's-75. *2255*

—. Decisionmaking. Educational Policy. Elites. Massachusetts. Suburbs. 1968-75. *2350*

—. Economic Conditions. Intergovernmental Relations. Liberalism. New Deal. New York City. 1930's-70's. *2535*

—. Economic Conditions. Local government. 1970's. *2434*

—. Economic Growth. Metropolitan Areas. 1975. *2304*

—. Employment. Metropolitan areas. Minorities. Population. Social conditions. 1970's. *2667*

—. Federal government. Higher education. New York City. 1970's. *2557*

—. Federal government. New York City. 1975-76. *2564*

—. Federal Programs. Gelfand, Mark I. (review article). Urban Renewal. 1933-65. 1975. *2563*

—. Mayors, black. Negroes. 1960's-70's. *2324*

—. Metropolitan Areas. Public Finance. State government. 1970's. *2517*

—. Public Welfare. Riots. State Government. 1960's-75. *2957*

Fish, John Hall. Community Participation in Politics (review article). Illinois (Chicago). Minnesota (Rice County). Organization for a Better Rice County. Poor. Temporary Woodlawn Organization. Wellstone, Paul D. 1970-76. *2464*

Fishbein, Meyer H. Archives, National. Finster, Jerome. Research. Urban history (review article). 1968-74. *3961*

Fisher, Carl Graham. Development. Florida (Miami Beach). Indianapolis Speedway. ca 1880-1939. *164*

Fisher, Walter L. City Government. Illinois (Chicago). Reform. 1880-1910. *364*

Fishermen. California (San Francisco Bay). Italian Americans. Reminiscences. Tarantino, Gaetano. 1850's-1940's. *493*

Fishing *See also* Whaling Industry and Trade.

—. Camping. City life. Hunting. New York (Adirondack Mountains). Wilderness. ca 1830's-90's. *919*

Fishing industry. California (San Diego). Chinese Americans. 1870-93. *1552*

Fishman, Richard P. Danielson, Michael N. Gale, Denis E. Government Regulation. James, Franklin J. Land Use (review article). Nelson, Robert H. Property Rights. Rose, Jerome G. Rothman, Robert E. 1970's. *3283*

Fisk, Robert E. Helena Board of Trade. Montana. Urbanization. 1864-81. *63*

Fisk University. Race Relations. Tennessee (Nashville). Youth Movements. 1909-26. *1378*

Fitch, Jeremiah. Connecticut (Hartford). Land Tenure. Riots. Social change. 1700-22. *1268*

Fitzgerald, F. Scott. Flushing Meadow Park. Moses, Robert. New York City. Parks. 1925-36. *1807*

—. Middle classes. Minnesota (St. Paul). Social status. 1900's-20's. *2161*

Flagler, Henry Morrison. Florida (St. Augustine). Hotel Ponce de Leon. Maybeck, Bernard. Tiffany, Louis. 1885-1974. *1900*

Flaherty, Joe. Breslin, Jimmy. Criticism. Hamill, Pete. Irish Americans. New York City (Brooklyn). Novels. 1960's-70's. *3134*

—. Economic Conditions. Jews. Social Mobility. 1870-1911. *1449*
—. Economic Conditions. Louisiana (New Orleans). Minorities in Politics. 1960's-79. *3076*
—. Educational reform. Illinois (Chicago). New York City. Organizations. Teachers. 1890-1920. *1121*
—. Ethnic Groups. Labor. Louisiana (New Orleans). Texas (San Antonio). Women. 1930-40. *557*
—. Family. Negroes. Social Mobility. 1870-80. *1364*
—. Federal Programs. Freedmen. Reconstruction. Religious organizations (northern). 1865-69. *755*
—. General Motors Corporation. Strikes. United Automobile Workers of America. 1936. *599*
—. Geographic mobility. Immigrants. Jews. Settlement. 1870-96. *1450*
—. Ghettos. Grocery stores. Prices. -1973. *2589*
—. Ghettos. Housing. Kentucky (Lexington). Negroes. North Carolina (Durham). Virginia (Richmond). 1850-1930. *1377*
—. Ghettos. Migration, Internal. Negroes. Urban renewal. 1960's. *3389*
—. *Great Speckled Bird* (newspaper). Hippies. Lawsuits. Press, underground. Socialism. 1968-76. *2767*
—. Greek Americans. Immigrants. 1900-23. *1584*
—. Haas, Jacob (and family). Immigration. Jews. 1845-65. *1482*
—. Haven, Gilbert. Negroes. Protestant Churches. Segregation. 1865-1906. *1684*
—. Hawaii (Honolulu). Integration. Neighborhoods. Residential Patterns. Texas (San Antonio). 1960's-70's. *2672*
—. Inman Park Restoration, Inc. Neighborhoods. Preservation. 1880's. 1970-79. *3558*
—. Jackson, Maynard. Mayors. Political Campaigns. Race Relations. Voting and Voting Behavior. 1973. *2478*
—. Jackson, Maynard. Minorities in Politics. Negroes. 1940's-74. *2332*
—. Jews. 1900-30. *1487*
—. Mass transit. 1970-71. *3451*
—. Negroes. North Carolina (Raleigh). Police. Race Relations. Reconstruction. Tennessee (Nashville). Virginia (Richmond). 1865-1900. *1270*
—. Negroes. Residential patterns. Transportation. Women. 1910-40. *228*
—. Police. Political Corruption. 1890-1905. *1290*
—. Water supply. 1865-1918. *2035*
Georgia (Atlanta; Cabbagetown). Urban renewal. 1971-76. *3395*
Georgia (Augusta). Attitudes. Urbanization. 1820-60. *2189*
—. Building codes. City Government. Disasters. Fire. 1916. *2134*
—. Chinese Americans. 1873-1970's. *1546*
—. City directories. 1841-1973. *4026*
—. City Government. Individualism. Social Reform. 1973. *3618*
—. City Government. Kentucky (Lexington). Political Attitudes. 1969. *2387*
—. City Politics. Industrial Relations. Textile Industry. ca 1865-1900. *398*
—. Deerskins. Indians. Slaves, Indian. South. South Carolina (Charleston). Trade. 1690-1715. *440*
—. Economic development. Industrialization. Reconstruction. Walsh, Patrick. 1865-99. *395*
—. Floods. Levee construction. Savannah River. 1888. 1890-1951. *2133*
—. Immigration. Irish Americans. 1830-1970. *1501*
—. Robinson, Mrs. Theater. Wall, Susannah. 1790-91. *974*
—. Strikes. Textile mills. Working conditions. 1886. *621*
Georgia (Augusta, Summerville). Suburbs. ca 1800-1911. *78*
Georgia (Augusta; The Terri). Ghettos. Negroes. 1865-1973. *1365*
Georgia (Columbus). Economic growth. Population. Preservation. 1828-1978. *3560*
—. Restorations. 1970's. *3531*
Georgia (DeKalb County). Conservatism. Political Stratification. Republican Party. Social Classes. 1970. *2431*
Georgia (Fulton County; Atlanta). Local Government. Public services. State Government. Taxation. 1976-77. *2407*

Georgia (Macon). Hay House. Houses. 1976. *1913*
—. Ku Klux Klan. Morality. Violence. Yarbrough, C. A. 1919-25. *735*
Georgia (Polk County; Cedartown, Rockmart). Daily Life. Economic conditions. 19c-1977. *2228*
Georgia Power Company. Atlanta Transit Company. Street, Electric Railway and Motor Coach Employees of America. Strikes. 1946-50. *2632*
Georgia (Rockmart). Blance, Joseph G. Parker, Charles Taylor. Slate. 1832-1978. *174*
Georgia (Rome). Economic growth. Social Conditions. 1834-1976. *137*
Georgia (Savannah). American Revolution. Jews. Sheftall, Benjamin (and family). 1730-1800. *1464*
—. Architecture. Connecticut (New Haven). Massachusetts (Boston). New York City. Pennsylvania (Philadelphia). 18c. *1983*
—. Buildings. Preservation. 1961-77. *3513*
—. Community Participation in Politics. Negroes. Residential Patterns. Whites. 1865-80. *1342*
—. Diseases. Negroes. 1850's-60's. *1748*
—. Education. Historic Savannah Foundation. Preservation. 1955-79. *3554*
—. Epidemics. South Carolina (Charleston). Yellow fever. 1800-76. *1727*
—. Exports. Lumber and Lumbering. 1830's-1850's. *428*
—. Historic Savannah Foundation. Historical Sites and Parks. Preservation. 18c-19c. 1954-79. *3535*
—. Plantations. Rice. South Carolina (Savannah River area). 1800-1933. *403*
—. Presbyterian Church. Zubly, John Joachim. 1724-58. *1679*
Georgia (Valdosta). Ehrlich, Abraham. Jews. Kaul, Bernard. 1866-90. *1483*
German Americans. Acculturation. Colorado (Denver). English Americans. Irish Americans. 1860-90. *1323*
—. Acculturation. Ethnicity. Immigrants. Neighborhoods. 1840's-1970's. *1305*
—. Acculturation. Ohio (Toledo). Press. 1850-90. *1562*
—. American Revolution. Lutherans. Pennsylvania (Philadelphia). 1776-81. *1693*
—. Architecture. Bricks. Ohio (Columbus; German Village). Preservation. 19c. 1960-78. *3549*
—. Assimilation. Immigration. Kentucky (Louisville). Liederkranz (society). Music. 1848-77. *1589*
—. Assimilation. Michigan (Ann Arbor). Pluralism. Protestantism. Württembergers. 1830-1955. *1295*
—. Banking. Finance. Jews. New York City. 19c. *529*
—. Beer. Breweries. West Virginia (Wheeling). 17c-1917. *1612*
—. Catholic Church. Dolan, Jay P. (review article). Irish Americans. New York City. Social Conditions. 1815-65. 1975. *1676*
—. Catholic Church. Irish Americans. New Jersey (Newark). Social Problems. 1840-70. *1689*
—. Catholic Church. Irish Americans. Ohio (Cleveland Diocese). Rappe, Louis Amadeus. 1847-70. *1671*
—. Ethnicity. Kamp, Henry. Oklahoma (Oklahoma City). 1906-57. *1582*
—. Fire departments, volunteer. Institutions. Irish Americans. New York City (South Bronx; Morrisania). 1848-87. *751*
—. Government Regulation. Illinois (Chicago). Know-Nothing Party. Local Politics. Riots. Temperance. 1855. *1271*
—. Illinois (Belleville). Music. Philharmonic Society. 1850-1975. *954*
—. Immigrants. Missouri. Reading. St. Louis Free Congregation Library (records). 1850-99. *1619*
—. Irish Americans. Local politics. New York City. Riots. Temperance. 1857. *1291*
—. Songfests. West Virginia (Wheeling). 1860. 1885. *922*
Germans. Immigration. Land ownership. Protestants. Spotswood, Alexander. Virginia (Germanna). 1714-21. *177*
Germans, Russian. Alberta (Coaldale). Assimilation. Mennonites. Organizations. 1920-76. *3848*
Germany *See also* component parts, e.g. Bavaria, Prussia, etc.; Germany, West.
—. City Planning. Reform. Zoning. 1860-1968. *1842*

—. Great Britain. Historiography. Rural-Urban Studies. 1975. *3991*
Germany (Berlin). *Cabaret* (film). Music. *Nashville* (film). Social criticism. Tennessee. 1930's-70's. *3596*
Germany (Frankfurt am Main). City planning. 1890-1916. *1843*
Germany, West. City planning. Interest Groups. Reform. Regional planning. Social Problems. 1945-76. *3294*
—. France. Great Britain. Urban history. 1960-74. *4030*
Ghettos. Art. Immigrants. Jews. 1880-1930. *1498*
—. Asia, Southeast. China. Chinatowns. Economic development. Foreign investments. New York City. 1970's. *2585*
—. Attitudes. Working Conditions. 1967-73. *3038*
—. Black Capitalism. Economic Growth. Neocolonialism. 1960-74. *3106*
—. Black power. 1974. *3082*
—. Business. Loans. Negroes. Whites. 1967-70. *2608*
—. California (East San Jose; Mayfair district). Mexican Americans. Social Change. 1777-1975. *1537*
—. California (Los Angeles). Chinatowns. Chinese Americans. Ownership. Property. 1970's. *3171*
—. California (San Francisco). Chinatowns. Chinese Americans. Genthe, Arnold. Photography. 1895-1906. *1545*
—. California (San Francisco). Negroes. Political power. 1950-65. *3093*
—. California (San Francisco; Fillmore district). Negroes. 1974. *3070*
—. Chinatowns. Chinese Americans. Fire. Hawaii (Honolulu). 1886. *2121*
—. Chinatowns. Chinese Americans. Immigration. New York City. 1880-1975. *1556*
—. Chinese Americans. Tourism. Vice. 1865-1920. *1547*
—. Colleges and Universities. Hostos Community College. New York City (Bronx). Social problems. 1970-72. *2822*
—. Cooperative Urban Teacher Education. Missouri (Kansas City). Teacher Training. 1964-73. *2887*
—. Discrimination, Housing. Legislation. Negroes. 1970's. *3105*
—. District of Columbia. Illinois (Chicago). Massachusetts (Boston). Race Relations. Small Business. 1973. *2612*
—. Economic Growth. Federal Programs. Minorities. 1965-73. *2576*
—. Education. Negroes. Teacher Training. Whites. 1974-75. *3597*
—. Educational Policy. Public Schools. 1973. *2886*
—. Employment. Federal Policy. Model Cities Program. Negroes. 1969-73. *2538*
—. Employment. Highways. Minorities. Segregation. Suburbs. -1973. *3474*
—. Employment. Negroes. Social Policy. Suburbs. 1969-79. *3102*
—. Ethnic Groups. Negroes. Social Problems. 1890-1940. *1403*
—. Films. Kung Fu motif. Youth. 1970-74. *2751*
—. Georgia (Atlanta). Grocery stores. Prices. -1973. *2589*
—. Georgia (Atlanta). Housing. Kentucky (Lexington). Negroes. North Carolina (Durham). Virginia (Richmond). 1850-1930. *1377*
—. Georgia (Atlanta). Migration, Internal. Negroes. Urban renewal. 1960's. *3389*
—. Georgia (Augusta; The Terri). Negroes. 1865-1973. *1365*
—. Jews. Literature. Negroes. 20c. *3046*
—. Jews. New York City (Lower East Side). 1890-1920. *1446*
—. Kusmer, Kenneth L. (review article). Negroes. Ohio (Cleveland). 1870's-1930's. *1355*
—. Marketing. Racism. -1973. *2594*
—. Negroes. Schools. 1975. *2884*
—. Negroes. Sociology. 20c. *3084*
—. Pennsylvania (Pittsburgh; Manchester). Pittsburgh History and Landmarks Foundation. Restorations. 1965-78. *3575*
Ghettos (review article). Katzman, David M. Kusmer, Kenneth L. Michigan (Detroit). Negroes. Ohio (Cleveland). 19c-1930. 1973-76. *1423*

Ghost towns. California (Bodie). Gold Mines and Mining. 1859-88. *75*

H

Hyde Park Protective Association. Farwell, Arthur Burrage. Illinois (Chicago). Prohibition. Reform. 1885-1936. *1137*

Hygiene. American Medical Association (report, 1849). Public Health. 1820-80. *1742*

Hylan, John F. Elections (mayoral). Ethnicity. Mitchel, John Purroy. New York City. Patriotism. World War I. 1917. *284*

I

Ice industry. Law. Monopolies. Nebraska. Omaha Ice Trust. 1899-1900. *438*

—. Pennsylvania (Philadelphia). Technology. 19c. *499*

Idaho (Blackfoot). 1878-1910. *64*

Idaho (Boise). Architecture. Housing. 1904-12. *1909*

—. Atkinson, John R. Blacksmiths. Photographs. 1890's. *518*

—. Banks. Depressions. Reconstruction Finance Corporation. 1932. *546*

Idaho (Idaho City). Daily life. Mining towns. 1865. *673*

Idaho (Lewiston). Floods. Rivers. 1894-1915. *1817*

Ideal States. *See* Utopias.

Idealism. California. Los Angeles *Illustrated Daily News*. Newspapers. Vanderbilt, Cornelius, Jr. 1923-26. *934*

—. Churches. LaFarge, John. New York City. Painting. 1877-88. *1055*

—. City government. Louisiana (New Orleans). Morrison, deLesseps S. Political reform. 1946-64. *373*

Identity. Behavior. Generations. Quebec (Quebec). 1968. *3774*

—. City Life. Indiana (Gary). Negroes. 1976. *3622*

—. Pennsylvania (Philadelphia). 1820-1920. *2188*

—. Racism. Schools. Students. 1970's. *2861*

Ideology. Acculturation. Educational Reform. Industrialization. Pennsylvania. Social control. 1880-1910. *1091*

—. American Revolution. Crowds. Social change. 1765-1830's. *1237*

—. Ecology. 1970's. *3606*

—. Garvey, Marcus. Katzman, David M. Michigan (Detroit). Negroes (review article). Social organization. Vincent, Theodore G. 19c-20c. *1420*

—. Massachusetts (Boston). Riots. Social Classes. 1834-35. *1232*

—. Missouri (St. Louis). Public schools. Troen, Selwyn K. (review article). 1838-1920. 1975. *1097*

—. Music (Salsa). New York City. 1976. *2743*

—. Public transportation. Sweden. 1950's-70's. *3449*

Illinois *See also* North Central States.

—. Acting. Browne, Maurice. Chicago Little Theatre. Euripides *(Trojan Women).* Theater Production and Direction. VanVolkenburg, Ellen. 1912-17. *950*

—. Adultery. Boardinghouses. Hungarian Americans. Immigrants. Landlords and Tenants. 1899-1914. *815*

—. American Federation of Labor. Chicago Newspaper Guild. Labor Unions and Organizations (white-collar). 1933-40. *604*

—. Anti-Catholicism. Chicago *Tribune.* Editors and Editing. Political Parties. 1853-61. *935*

—. Architecture. Burnham, Daniel Hudson. World's Columbian Exposition (Chicago, 1893). 1891-93. 20c. *1927*

—. Architecture. Indiana. Ohio. Railroad stations. 1880's-1920's. *1902*

—. Art Institute of Chicago. 1879-1909. *999*

—. Art Institute of Chicago. 1879-1978. *1014*

—. Baseball. Chicago Cubs. 1850's-1914. *849*

—. Bennett, Edward Herbert. Burnham, Daniel Hudson. Chicago Plan (1909). City Planning. 1895-1966. *1820*

—. Burg, David F. (review article). World's Columbian Exposition (Chicago, 1893). 1893. 1976. *1793*

—. Chicago Historical Society. Exhibits and Expositions. 1860's-1970's. *3948*

—. Chicago Historical Society. Libraries. Urban history. 1850's-1978. *3945*

—. Chicago Housing Authority. *Hills* v. *Gautreaux* (US, 1976). Integration. Negroes. Public Housing. 1966-78. *3379*

—. Chicago School of Television. Television. Vocational Education. 1930's-53. *945*

—. Chicago, University of (Geography Department). City planning. Geography. Social sciences. 1950's-60's. *3328*

—. Criminal Law. 1960's-71. *2982*

—. Ferris, George W. G. Ferris wheel. Rice, Luther V. World's Columbian Exhibition (Chicago, 1893). 1893. *852*

—. Galesburg Historical Society. National Trust Main Street Project. Preservation. 1975-76. *3579*

—. Geography. Models, linear. Retail trade. 1960's. *2588*

—. Local Government. Lochner, Louis Paul. Peace Movements. People's Council of America for Democracy and Peace. State Government. 1917. *333*

—. Rural-Urban Studies. Voting and voting behavior. 1970's. *2491*

Illinois (Arthur, Pontiac). Curricula. History Teaching. Illinois Wesleyan University. Social Sciences. 19c-20c. 1978. *3982*

Illinois (Belleville). German Americans. Music. Philharmonic Society. 1850-1895. *954*

Illinois (Blue Island). Debs, Eugene V. Federal Government. Pullman Strike. Strikes. 1894. *601*

Illinois (Cahokia). Indians. Villages. 900-1150. *3933*

Illinois (Champaign, Urbana). City Planning. Housing. 1969-72. *3381*

Illinois (Chicago). 1837-1977. *38*

—. 1871-1919. *2177*

—. Acculturation. Immigrants. ca 1937-74. *642*

—. Addams, Jane. Art. Attitudes. Reform. 1889-1916. *998*

—. Addiction. Opium. 1880's-1910. *1733*

—. Advertising. Federal Regulation. Medicine, Patent. Pure Food and Drug Act (1906). 1850-1906. *1712*

—. Advertising. Political Campaigns (mayoral). Public Opinion. Television. 1975. *2775*

—. Agrarian myth. Novels. Ruller, Henry Blake. 1890's. *2182*

—. Air Lines. California (Los Angeles, San Francisco). Federal Government. Helicopters. New York City. Subsidies. 1945-75. *3471*

—. Alcohol. Drunken drivers. Sentencing. 1971. *2989*

—. Amateur Democrat (concept). City Politics. Political participation. Reform clubs. Wilson, James Q. 1960's-70's. *2456*

—. American dream. Bowen, George S. Business. Investments. 1849-1905. *533*

—. Amusement parks. Recreation. Riverview Park. 1903-67. *877*

—. Anarchism and Anarchists. Black, William Perkins. Haymarket riot. Lawyers. Trials. 1886-87. *1246*

—. Animals. Society for the Prevention of Cruelty to Animals. 1869-99. *724*

—. Architects. Great Britain (London). Settlement houses. Social workers. 1890's-1900's. *1981*

—. Architecture. 1960's-77. *3424*

—. Architecture. 20c. *1967*

—. Architecture. Beaux arts movement. Jenney, William Le Baron. Skyscrapers. World's Columbian Exposition (Chicago, 1893). 1880-1920. *1982*

—. Architecture. Burnham, Daniel Hudson. Business. Root, John Wellborn. Union Stockyard. 1871-1902. *1996*

—. Architecture. Fine Arts Building. 1898-1918. *1892*

—. Architecture. Iron-front buildings. 1854-80's. *1897*

—. Architecture. Marshall Field building. Richardson, Henry Hobson. 1880's. *1946*

—. Architecture (Greek Revival). 1830-50. *1933*

—. Army Corps of Engineers. City Government. Reservoirs. Tunnel and Reservoir Plan. Water Pollution. 1972-79. *3434*

—. Art and Society. Novels. 1890-1910. *985*

—. Arts. Children. Poor. Urban Gateways program. 1961-75. *2799*

—. Arts and Crafts. Business. Fine Arts Building. 1898-1917. *423*

—. Attitudes. Economic theory. Indiana (Indianapolis). Occupations. Ohio (Cincinnati). 1850's. *392*

—. Attitudes. Ethnicity. Negroes. Race Relations. Social Classes. 1969. *3016*

—. Attitudes. Negroes. Whites. 1975. *3056*

—. Autobiography. Communist Party. Negroes. Wright, Richard. 1930's. *1428*

—. Automobiles. Mass transit. Public policy. 1900-50. *2061*

—. Ballrooms (Trianon, Aragon). Karzas, Andrew. Karzas, William. 1907-71. *851*

—. Banfield, Edward C. Political Machines. Political Reform. Social policy. 1972-74. *2433*

—. Banking. Citizens Action Program. Discrimination. Redlining. Urban Renewal. 1969-75. *2610*

—. Baseball. Business. City life. Social change. Values. 1865-70. *871*

—. Baseball. Georgia (Atlanta). New York City. Religion. Social change. Values. 1892-1934. *905*

—. Baseball (team owners). Bossism. City Politics. Gambling. Georgia (Atlanta). New York City. ca 1877-1916. *906*

—. Belcher, Wyatt W. Business. Leadership. Missouri (St. Louis). 1830-80. *200*

—. Bender, Thomas. Cities (review article). Community (concept). Philpott, Thomas Lee. Social Change. 1870's-1930's. 1978. *659*

—. Berger, Henning. Immigrants. Literature. Sweden. Travel Accounts. USA. 1872-1924. *2147*

—. Berry, George L. Newspapers. Strikes. 1912-14. *630*

—. Bibliographies. Regional studies. 1871-1919. *4028*

—. Bicycles. 1870's-1908. *2064*

—. Boosterism. Publicity. Regionalism. Wright, John Stephen. 1815-74. *2168*

—. Buildings. Carson Pirie Scott and Co. Retail Trade. 1854-1979. *462*

—. Buildings. City halls. 1837-96. *1915*

—. Buildings (vacant). Economic Conditions. Negroes. 1970's. *2597*

—. Business. Elites. 1830-1930. *775*

—. Business. Feminism. Philanthropy. Schmidt, Minna Moscherosch. 1886-1961. *9*

—. Business. Ogden, William Butler. 1835-77. *543*

—. Canals. Michigan, Lake. Water pollution. 1873-86. *2050*

—. Capone, Al. Crime and Criminals. 1919-47. *1258*

—. Catholic Church. Church Schools. Damen, Arnold. Fund raising. 1840-90. *1122*

—. Catholic Church. Church Schools. Ethnic Groups. Sanders, James W. (review article). 1833-1965. 1977. *1072*

—. Catholic Church. Commodore Barry Country Club. Irish Americans. Knights of Columbus. Wisconsin (Twin Lakes). 1907-20's. *732*

—. Catholic Church. Ethnic Groups (review article). Horowitz, Helen Lefkowitz. Kessner, Thomas. New York City. Philanthropy. Sanders, James W. 1883-1965. 1970's. *48*

—. Catholic Church. Social Work. Wisconsin (Milwaukee). 19c. *1700*

—. Cemeteries. Graceland Cemetery. 1861-1900. *2029*

—. Censorship. Films. Nickelodeons. Progressivism. 1907-15. *892*

—. Centennial Celebrations. City of Progress. Construction. Depressions. Economic development. 1933-34. *1879*

—. Centennial Celebrations. Mosher, Charles D. Philanthropy. Photography. 1870-97. *679*

—. *Chap-Book* (periodical). Kimball, Hannibal Ingalls. Literature. Stone, Herbert Stuart. 1893-1906. *1026*

—. Charities. Negroes. Social problems. 1890-1917. *1159*

—. Charities Organization Society Movement. Values. 1880-1930. *1161*

—. Chicago Relief and Aid Society. Disaster Relief. Fire. 1871-72. *1175*

—. Chicago *Tribune.* Marks, Nora (pseud. of Eleanora Stackhouse). Reporters and Reporting. Social Problems. 1888-90. *937*

—. Chicago Zoo. Zoological Gardens. 1874-1975. *876*

—. Child Welfare. Off-the-Street Club. 1890's. *1190*

—. Children. Playgrounds. Progressivism. Social Reform. 1894-1917. *1167*

—. Chinese Americans. Immigration. Kinship. Social Mobility. 1970's. *3175*

—. Citizens Action Program. Community Participation in Politics. 1960's-76. *2453*

—. City Government. Constitutional conventions, state. Democratic Party. Political machines. Voting and Voting Behavior. 1970. *2418*

—. City Government. Fisher, Walter L. Reform. 1880-1910. *364*

—. City News Bureau. Newspapers. 1891-1974. *932*

Illinois, western. Attitudes. Rural-urban studies. Social Classes. 1974. *2659*

Immaculate Conception Primary School. Education. Illinois (East St. Louis). Lithuanian Americans. Occupations. 1948-68. *3186*

Immigrants. Acculturation. Boardinghouses. Italian Canadians. Ontario (Toronto). 20c. *3834*

—. Acculturation. Education. Massachusetts (Boston). Negroes. Social status. 1850. *1125*

—. Acculturation. Ethnicity. German Americans. Neighborhoods. 1840's-1970's. *1305*

—. Acculturation. Illinois (Chicago). ca 1937-74. *642*

—. Acculturation. Ontario (Toronto). 1950's-70's. *3837*

—. Adultery. Boardinghouses. Hungarian Americans. Illinois. Landlords and Tenants. 1899-1914. *815*

—. Alaska Colonization and Development Company. Finns. Port Axel. 1903-40. *183*

—. Americanization. Educational Reform. New York (Buffalo). Public Schools. 1890-1916. *1113*

—. Arab Americans. Asian Americans. Hispanic Americans. Ohio (Toledo). Settlement. 1965-76. *3020*

—. Archives. Ontario (Toronto). Photographs. 1900-30. 1974. *4053*

—. Art. Ghettos. Jews. 1880-1930. *1498*

—. Asian Americans. Assimilation. California (San Francisco). Social organization. 1970's. *3176*

—. Assimilation. California (Los Angeles). Europe. Jews. Marriage. 1910-13. *1469*

—. Assimilation. City life. Public schools. 1890's-1920. *1088*

—. Assimilation. Education. Employment. English Language. Ontario (Toronto). 1968-70. *3856*

—. Assimilation. Education. Negroes. Racism. Slavic Americans. Social Mobility. 1890-1966. *1089*

—. Assimilation. Macedonian Canadians. Ontario (Toronto). 1900-20. *3843*

—. Barton, Josef J. Esslinger, Dean R. Ethnic studies (review article). Kantowicz, Edward R. 19c-20c. 1976. *1326*

—. Berger, Henning. Illinois (Chicago). Literature. Sweden. Travel Accounts. USA. 1872-1924. *2147*

—. Bocce ball. Ethnicity. Games. Italian Americans. Pennsylvania (Philadelphia). 1974. *3195*

—. Boycotts. Industry. Irish Americans. Labor. New York City. 1880-86. *597*

—. California (Los Angeles). Economic Conditions. Family. Mexican Americans. Michigan (Detroit). Whites. 1850-80. *1313*

—. California (San Francisco). Diaries. Irish Americans. Labor. Roney, Frank. 1875-76. *809*

—. California (San Francisco). Ethnicity. Vigilance Committees. 1849-56. *1324*

—. Chinese Americans. New York City. Newspapers, Chinese. 1974. *2774*

—. Church records. Italian Americans. Methodology. Pennsylvania (Philadelphia). 1789-1900. *3984*

—. City Government. Economic Conditions. Housing. Polish Americans. Wisconsin (Milwaukee; 14th ward). 1880-1910. *1804*

—. City Politics. Nativism. Ohio (Cincinnati). Temperance. 1845-60. *1306*

—. Colorado (Denver). Saloons. 1865-1933. *893*

—. Community Participation in Politics. New York City. People's Institute of New York City. Reform. Working Class. 1910-20. *1145*

—. Compulsory education. Missouri (St. Louis). Public Schools. Truancy. 1905-07. *1092*

—. Democratic Party. New York City. Prohibition. Tammany Hall. 1840-60. *350*

—. Demography. Economic conditions. 1900. *1308*

—. Discrimination. Ethnic groups. Manitoba (Winnipeg). Population. 1874-1974. *3642*

—. Discrimination, Employment. Ontario (Toronto). Social Status. West Indians. 1972. *3846*

—. Education. Jews. Pennsylvania (Pittsburgh). 1862-1932. *1485*

—. Educational associations. Jews (Russian). Libraries. New York City. Newspapers. 1880-1914. *1431*

—. Employment. Greek Americans. Massachusetts (Springfield). Political Factions. Social Conditions. 1884-1944. *1583*

—. Employment. Italians. Ontario (Toronto). 1885-1915. *3835*

—. Employment. Oral history. Pennsylvania (Pittsburgh). Women. ca 1900-20. 1976. *1320*

—. Ethnic groups. Industry. Occupations. Pennsylvania (Philadelphia). Social Status. 1850-80. *1322*

—. Ethnicity. Hungarian Americans. Ohio (Cleveland). 1900-20. *1622*

—. Geographic mobility. Georgia (Atlanta). Jews. Settlement. 1870-96. *1450*

—. Geographic Mobility. Methodology. Philadelphia Social History Project. Residential patterns. 1850-80. 1976. *3975*

—. Georgia (Atlanta). Greek Americans. 1900-23. *1584*

—. German Americans. Missouri. Reading. St. Louis Free Congregation Library (records). 1850-99. *1619*

—. Indiana (Gary). Public welfare. Settlement houses. 1906-40. *1170*

—. Irish Americans. Pennsylvania (Scranton). Social mobility. Welsh Americans. 1880-90. *1301*

—. Italian Americans. Negroes. Occupational mobility. Pennsylvania (Steelton). Slavic Americans. 1880-1920. *1300*

—. Italian Americans. Padrone system. Social Organization. 1880-1914. *1590*

—. Jews. Minnesota (St. Paul; Lower West Side). Settlement. ca 1860-1920. *1466*

—. Kentucky (Louisville). Migration, Internal. Ohio (Cincinnati). 1865-1901. *837*

—. Labor Unions and Organizations. Massachusetts (Fall River). Textile industry. 1890-1905. *1330*

—. Language. New York City. West Indians. 1910-76. *1368*

—. Latin America. Women. 1960's-77. *3139*

—. Legends. New York (Buffalo). Polish Americans. Religion. 1870-1973. *1559*

—. Letters. Norwegian Americans. Pennsylvania (Harmony, New Harmony). Rapp, George. 1816-26. *1561*

—. Macedonian Canadians. Ontario (Toronto). Urban history. 20c. *3971*

—. Massachusetts (Charlestown). Oligarchy. 1630-40. *766*

—. Michigan (Holland). Migration. Occupations. Social mobility. 1850-80. *836*

—. Negroes. New York City. Politics. West Indians. Women. 1915-70's. *3089*

—. Ontario (Toronto). Stereotypes. 19c-20c. *3836*

Immigrants' Protective League. Illinois (Chicago). Social Reform. 1908-21. *1163*

Immigration *See also* Assimilation; Demography; Deportation; Emigration; Naturalization; Population; Race Relations; Refugees; Social Problems.

—. Acculturation. Jews. New York City. Yiddishe Arbeiten Universitet. 1921-39. *1078*

—. Acculturation. Pennsylvania (Pittsburgh). Women. 1900-45. *1321*

—. American Revolution. Business. City Life. Colonial government. New York City. 17c-20c. *133*

—. Anti-Communist movements. Anti-Semitism. Freedom of speech. National self-image. Ontario (Toronto). 1928-29. *3629*

—. Arab Americans. Michigan (Detroit). Settlement. 1961-74. *3182*

—. Arizona (Phoenix). Economic Development. Jews. 1870-1920. *1459*

—. Arizona (Phoenix). Italian Americans. Migration, Internal. Social Organization. 1880's. *1601*

—. Armenian Canadians. Quebec (Montreal). 1900-66. *3827*

—. Armenians. USSR. 16c-20c. *1574*

—. Assimilation. Atlantic Provinces. Canadians. Economic conditions. Kennedy, Albert J. Massachusetts (Boston). 1910's. *1593*

—. Assimilation. German Americans. Kentucky (Louisville). Liederkranz (society). Music. 1848-77. *1589*

—. Attitudes. Education. Mexican Americans. Negroes. Wisconsin (Racine). 1974. *3047*

—. Behavior. Modernization. Peasants. Slavic Americans. Working class. 1850-1925. *1298*

—. Belgian Canadians. Manitoba (East St. Boniface, Winnipeg). Nuytten, Edmund (and Family). Nuytten, Octavia. 1880-1914. *3840*

—. Bethlehem Chapel. Italian Americans. New York City (Greenwich Village). Presbyterian Church. 1900-30. *1678*

—. Boosterism. Population. Washington (Spokane). 1905-10. *124*

—. British Americans. California (San Francisco). 1852-72. *1569*

—. Business. Great Britain (London). Jews. Labor Unions and Organizations. New York City. 19c-20c. *1472*

—. California (Los Angeles). Jews (Rhodesli). Sephardic Hebrew Center. 1900-74. *1445*

—. California (San Diego). Filipino Americans. 1900-46. *1540*

—. California (San Francisco). Charities. Voluntary Associations. ca 1850-60. *741*

—. California (San Francisco). Chinese. Crocker, Charles. Kearney, Denis. Racism. Railroads. 1863-82. *1539*

—. California (San Francisco). Italian Americans. 1890-1977. *1617*

—. California (San Jose). Ethnic Groups. Social mobility. 1860-70. *840*

—. Caribbean Region. Economic Conditions. Negroes. New York City. Public Opinion. 1965-79. *3062*

—. Charities. Galveston Plan of 1907. Industrial Removal Office. Jews. Migration, Internal. New York City. 1890-1914. *1476*

—. Chicopee Manufacturing Company. Irish Americans. Massachusetts (Chicopee). Mills. Nativism. 1830-75. *1506*

—. Child Welfare. Foster homes. Jews. New York City. Working class. 1900-05. *1186*

—. Chinatowns. Chinese Americans. Ghettos. New York City. 1880-1975. *1556*

—. Chinatowns. Chinese Americans. New York City. Social Conditions. 1950-69. *3179*

—. Chinatowns. Chinese Americans. Poverty. Tourism. 1960-74. *1549*

—. Chinese Americans. Illinois (Chicago). Kinship. Social Mobility. 1970's. *3175*

—. City government. Irish Americans. Massachusetts (Boston area). 16c-1979. *1515*

—. City Life. Jews, Russian. Manitoba (Winnipeg). 1874-82. *3821*

—. Discrimination. Economic Conditions. Italian Americans. Oregon (Portland). 1880-1920. *1587*

—. Economic Conditions. Negroes. Social Problems. West Indians. 1916-20's. *1367*

—. Economic Growth. Irish Americans. Michigan (Detroit). 1850. *1517*

—. Education. Women. 1900-35. *1114*

—. Ethnic Groups. Nebraska (Omaha). Residential patterns. 1880-1920. *1304*

—. Ethnic Groups. Occupations. Ontario (Toronto). Social Status. 1940's-70's. *3839*

—. Ethnic groups. Oregon (Portland). 1860-1910. *706*

—. Ethnicity. Greek Canadians. Ontario (Toronto). Private Schools. 1900-40. *3845*

—. Family. Italian Americans. Jews. Rhode Island. 1880-1940. *712*

—. Famines. Great Britain (London). Irish Americans. Pennsylvania (Philadelphia). Urbanization. 1840's-60. *1512*

—. France. Households. Quebec (Quebec). 1666-1716. *3806*

—. France. Nova Scotia (Port Royal). Settlement. 1650-1755. *3791*

—. French Canadians. Massachusetts (Holyoke). Proulx, Nicholas. Working Class. 1850-1900. *1564*

—. French Canadians. Massachusetts (Springfield). 1870. *1572*

—. Georgia (Atlanta). Haas, Jacob (and family). Jews. 1845-65. *1482*

—. Georgia (Augusta). Irish Americans. 1830-1970. *1501*

—. Germans. Land ownership. Protestants. Spotswood, Alexander. Virginia (Germanna). 1714-21. *177*

—. Great Britain. Localism. Massachusetts. Settlement. Towns. 1630-60. *5*

—. Great Britain (London). Negroes. New York City. Social status. West Indians. 20c. *3080*

—. Illinois (Chicago). Mexican Americans. Social Conditions. 1910's-20's. *1536*

—. Indiana (East Chicago; Indiana Harbor). Inland Steel Company. Mexican Americans. Michigan, Lake. Social Conditions. 1919-32. *1521*

—. Italian Americans. New York City. 1924-70's. *3189*

—. Italian Canadians. Ontario (Toronto). Population. 1946-72. *3855*

—. Jews, East European. Michigan (Detroit). Social Customs. 1881-1914. *1474*

—. Jews, Sephardic. Washington (Seattle). 1906-24. *1429*

—. Law. Migration, Internal. Washington (Seattle). 1970's. *2936*

—. Migration, Internal. Spokan Indians. Washington (Spokane). 1970. *1573*

—. Missions and Missionaries. New Mexico (Santa Fe). Settlement. Spaniards. 1540-1882. *157*

—. New Mexico (Chaco Canyon). Social organization. ca 850-1130. *3927*

—. New Mexico (Jemez Mountains). Pueblos. Social organization. 1300-1600. *3926*

—. Pacific Northwest Indian Center. Washington (Spokane). 1966-74. *3211*

—. Urbanization. 1930's-70's. *3209*

Indians (agencies). Missouri Fur Company. Nebraska (Bellevue). 1822-42. *135*

Indians (reservations). Ethnic groups. Federal policy. 1970's. *3181*

—. Southwest. Urbanization. 19c-20c. *3185*

Indian-White Relations. Catholic Church. Clergy. New Mexico (Isleta Pueblo). 1960's. *3932*

—. Chippewa Indians. Law Enforcement. Minnesota (Minneapolis). 1969-70. *2940*

—. Economic Conditions. Federal Policy. Natural resources. 1831-1978. *1592*

—. Local Politics. Massachusetts (Natick). Meetinghouses. 1650-18c. *1576*

—. *Marguerite* v. *Chouteau* (Missouri, 1834). Missouri (St. Louis). Slavery. 1764-1834. *1600*

Individualism. Boxing. Pennsylvania (Pittsburgh). Professionalization. Regionalism. Social mobility. 1890's-1900's. *860*

—. City Government. Georgia (Augusta). Social Reform. 1973. *3618*

—. Dance competitions. Louisiana (New Orleans). Minstrel shows. 1840's-50's. *864*

—. Massachusetts (Salem). Organicism. Political Leadership. Puritans. Social Classes. 1680's. *13*

Industrial Archaeology. Pennsylvania (Philadelphia). Social history. 1850's-1910. 1974-77. *4018*

Industrial council. Massey-Harris plant. Ontario (Toronto). Working Conditions. 1919-29. *3750*

Industrial Relations *See also* Collective Bargaining; Labor Unions and Organizations; Strikes.

— Amoskeag Manufacturing Company. Ethnocentrism. Family. Modernization. New Hampshire (Manchester). 1912-22. *776*

— Art. Business. Cincinnati Art Museum and Art Academy. Ohio. Philanthropy. 1874-90. *1000*

— Bercuson, David J. (review article). General Strikes. Manitoba (Winnipeg). Social organization. 1975. *3758*

— Christianity. Massachusetts (Lawrence). Scudder, Vida Dutton. Social reform. Socialism. Strikes. Textile Industry. Women. 1912. *585*

—. City Politics. Georgia (Augusta). Textile Industry. ca 1865-1900. *398*

—. Howard, Robert. Massachusetts (Fall River). Textile industry. 1860-85. *574*

—. Iron industry. Pennsylvania (Hopewell Village). 1800-50. *411*

—. Negroes. Ohio (Cleveland). 1960's-70's. *2613*

Industrial Removal Office. Charities. Galveston Plan of 1907. Immigration. Jews. Migration, Internal. New York City. 1890-1914. *1476*

—. Jews. Migration, Internal. Ohio (Columbus). 1901-16. *1470*

Industrial Revolution. Coffeehouses. Social Customs. 18c-19c. *863*

—. Economic Development. New Brunswick (Saint John). Ports. Railroads. Transportation. 1867-1911. *3661*

—. Massachusetts (Lynn). Social Classes. Work Ethic. 1826-60. *772*

Industrial safety. Accidents. Massachusetts (Lowell). 1890-1905. *563*

—. Factories. Fire. Garment industry. New York City. 1911. *2124*

Industrial society program. Education, Experimental Methods. Interdisciplinary studies. Marketplaces. Wisconsin, University of, Parkside. 1973. *3997*

Industrial Workers of the World. Alaska (Nome). American Federation of Labor. Labor Unions and Organizations. 1905-20. *593*

—. American Federation of Labor. Louisiana. Marine Transport Workers. Sailors' Union. Strikes. United Fruit Company. 1913. *584*

—. California (Fresno). Freedom of Speech. 1910-11. *594*

—. California (San Diego). Freedom of Speech. Mexico (Tijuana). 1911-12. *628*

—. Freedom of Speech. Political Protest. Pratt, N. S. Washington (Spokane). 1909-10. *580*

—. Freedom of Speech. Political Repression. Washington (Aberdeen). 1911-12. *609*

—. Labor Reform. New York (Little Falls). Strikes. Textile Industry. Women. 1912. *629*

Industrialism. Crime and Criminals. Monkkonen, Eric H. (review article). Ohio (Columbus). Poverty. Urbanization. 1860-85. 1975. *1247*

Industrialization *See also* Economic Growth; Modernization.

—. Acculturation. Educational Reform. Ideology. Pennsylvania. Social control. 1880-1910. *1091*

—. Adolescence. Employment. Ontario (Hamilton). School (attendance). 1851-90's. *3796*

—. Agriculture. Railroads. Rural-Urban Studies. Slavery. Virginia. 1840's-60. *14*

—. Architecture. Housing. Maryland (Baltimore). Row Houses. 1800-30. *1859*

—. Architecture, Victorian. New Brunswick (Saint John). Urban Renewal. 17c-1966. *3907*

—. Artisans. Economic conditions. Occupations. Pennsylvania (Germantown). 1767-91. *526*

—. Artisans. Morality. Pennsylvania (Philadelphia). Social customs. Work ethic. Working Class. 1820-50. *787*

—. Atlanta Chamber of Commerce. Georgia. Grady, Henry. Urbanization. 1920's. *105*

—. Automobile industry and Trade. League of Revolutionary Black Workers. Michigan (Detroit). Negroes. 1968-75. *2626*

—. Bender, Thomas (review article). Urbanization. Values. 19c. 1975. *2152*

—. Boston Manufacturing Company. Great Britain. International trade. Lowell, Francis Cabot. Massachusetts. 1807-20. *471*

—. Business. Farmers. New South. Textile Industry. 1870-1900. *401*

—. Businessmen. Education. Labor. Mechanics' institutes. Pennsylvania (Pittsburgh). 1830-40. *794*

—. California (San Francisco; Rincon Hill). Elites. 1850-1979. *1798*

—. Commerce. Ontario (Hamilton). Population. 1851-71. *3795*

—. Commercialism. Materialism. Politics. Urbanization. 19c. *19*

—. Community (concept). New York City (Greenwich Village). Reform. Urbanization. 1890-1917. *668*

—. Cotton industry. Economic conditions. Manufacturing. Pennsylvania (Rockdale). Social change. 1825-65. *521*

—. Crime and Criminals. Pennsylvania (Philadelphia). Violence. 1820's-1976. *1248*

—. Dawley, Alan (review article). Massachusetts (Lynn). Social Classes. 18c-19c. 1976. *658*

—. Economic development. Georgia (Augusta). Reconstruction. Walsh, Patrick. 1865-99. *395*

—. Economic development. Massachusetts. Modernization. Waltham-Lowell system. 1815-60. *480*

—. Elites. Pareto, Vilfredo. Pennsylvania (Duquesne). Social change. 1891-1933. *765*

—. Family. Urbanization. 1800-1977. *697*

—. History Teaching. Popular culture. Urbanization. Western States. 1890's-1910. 1970's. *4049*

—. Howells, William Dean (*A Modern Instance*). Social Theory. 1882. *2172*

—. Income. Iowa. Rural areas. Towns. 1960-70. *2604*

—. Knights of Labor. Knights of St. Crispin. Labor Unions and Organizations. Ontario (Toronto). 1856-90. *3737*

—. Knights of St. Crispin. Massachusetts (Lynn). Radicals and Radicalism. Working class. 1820-90. *559*

—. Location. Ontario (Kingston). Physicians. Residential Patterns. 1857-1975. *3757*

—. Manufactures. Nova Scotia (Halifax). 1867-1926. *3745*

—. Massachusetts (Fall River, Lynn). Social Organization. Working class. 1850-1930. *767*

—. Medicine (practice of). New York (Rochester). 1811-60. *1706*

—. Methodology. Urbanization. Women. 19c. 1975. *3988*

—. Michigan (Detroit). Railroads. Sawmills. Shipbuilding. Stoves. 1840's-90's. *527*

—. New Jersey (Hoboken). New York City. Resorts. Stevens, John. Urbanization. 1820-60. *87*

—. Oklahoma (Oklahoma City). Population. Railroads. 1889-1939. *171*

—. Ontario (Hamilton). Public schools. Socialization. 19c. *3794*

—. Pennsylvania. Philadelphia Social History Project. Research. Urbanization. 1976. *3978*

—. Pennsylvania. *Pittsburgh Survey* (1909). Social Surveys. 1907-14. *1168*

—. Pennsylvania (Rockdale). Religion. Social Classes. Technology. Wallace, Anthony F. C. (review article). 1825-65. 1978. *20*

—. Photography. Suburbanization. 1970's. *2803*

—. Politics. 1850-1974. *244*

—. Quebec. Urbanization. 1941-61. *3729*

—. Quebec (Herbertville). Settlement. 1844-1900. *3665*

—. Quebec (Montreal). Shoe industry. 1840-70. *3721*

—. Reform. Social Organization. Urban history. 1870's-90's. 1970's. *47*

—. Urbanization. 1840-1900. *110*

Industry *See also* individual industries, e.g. Iron Industry, etc.; Industrialization; Management; Manufactures.

—. Air pollution. Employment. Government. Tennessee (Kingsport). Water Pollution. 1970's. *3255*

—. Alberta (Lethbridge). Daily Life. Pioneers. Transportation. 1880's. *3652*

—. Artists. Housing. New York City. 1970's. *2813*

—. Boycotts. Immigrants. Irish Americans. Labor. New York City. 1880-86. *597*

—. Business. Quebec (Montreal). Transportation. Tulchinsky, Gerald J. J. (review article). 1837-53. 1977. *3752*

—. Collins Company. Company Towns. Connecticut (Collinsville). Preservation. 1827-1965. *3502*

—. Commerce. Wisconsin (Milwaukee). 1835-80. *408*

—. Community Participation in Politics. Energy. New Jersey (Hudson County). Pollution. 1972-78. *2458*

—. Discrimination, Employment. Metropolitan areas. Profit. Racism. 1973. *2598*

—. Economic Conditions. Geography. Quebec (Shawinigan). 1932-72. *3720*

—. Economic Conditions. Meat-packing. Midwest. Urbanization. 1835-75. *523*

—. Economic Conditions. Urban renewal. 1978. *2284*

—. Economic development. Maine (Portland). Nebraska (St. John). Poor, John. Railroads. 1850-1914. *393*

—. Employment. 1973. *2595*

—. Employment. Illinois (Chicago). Negroes. Polish Americans. Racism. Violence. 1890-1919. *1327*

—. Ethnic groups. Immigrants. Occupations. Pennsylvania (Philadelphia). Social Status. 1850-80. *1322*

—. Family. Income. Metropolitan areas. 1969. *2573*

—. Great Britain (London). Location. New York City. 1960-72. *2606*

—. Illinois (Chicago). Maryland (Baltimore). Missouri (St. Louis). Pennsylvania (Pittsburgh). Railroads. Strikes. 1877. *631*

—. Indiana (Cannelton). 1847-51. *516*

—. Labor Unions and Organizations. South Carolina (Greenville). 1873-1979. *2637*

—. Location. Texas (Dallas, Fort Worth). 1967-75. *2603*

—. Massachusetts (Assabet River, Concord). 1776-1862. *121*

—. Minnesota (Minneapolis, St. Paul). Quality of life. 1683-1976. *76*

—. Negroes. Property tax. 1950's-70's. *2312*

—. Preservation. Washington (Seattle). 19c-20c. *3584*

—. Property tax. Suburbs. 1968-74. *2602*

Inflation. Labor. Mass Transit. Prices. Public Policy. 1950's-70's. *3476*

Influenza. Alberta (Calgary). Epidemics. Mahood, Cecil S. 1918-19. *3874*

—. British Columbia (Vancouver). Epidemics. Public health. 1918-19. *3870*

Ingalls, Melville E. Business. Ohio (Cincinnati). 1871-1914. *540*

Ingersoll, Robert. Atheism. Lectures. Nevada (Virginia City). Public Opinion. 1877. *1666*

Ingraham, John N. (review article). Elites. Entrepreneurs. Iron industry. Ohio (Youngstown). Pennsylvania (Philadelphia, Pittsburgh). West Virginia (Wheeling). 1874-1965. *803*

Inheritance *See also* Land Tenure.

J

L

Lappeus, James H. City Government. Oregon (Portland). Police. Wilbur, Hiram. 1851-74. *1286*

Larkin Administration Building. Architecture. Environment. New York (Buffalo). Ventilation system. Wright, Frank Lloyd. 1904. *1864*

Last Chance Urban Renewal Project. Montana (Helena). Restorations. Urban renewal. 1972-77. *3574*

Latin America. Bibliographies. Slavery. Travel Accounts. 1817-68. *1349*

—. Economic development. Urbanization. 19c. *33*

—. Immigrants. Women. 1960's-77. *3139*

Latrobe, Benjamin Henry. Architecture. Capitols. District of Columbia. House of Representatives Chamber. Jefferson, Thomas. 1803-12. *1890*

Latvian Canadians. Ethnicity. Folk art. Manitoba (Winnipeg). Ukrainian Canadians. 1978. *3805*

Law See also Courts; Criminal Law; Judges; Judicial Process; Lawyers; Legislation; Police.

—. Adolescents. Attitudes. Wisconsin (Racine). 1971. *2935*

—. American Bar Association. Missouri (St. Louis). 1874-1974. *1293*

—. American Civil Liberties Union. Mass media campaign. Missouri (St. Louis). Privacy. 1975-76. *2768*

—. Arizona. Fraud. Government. Real estate business. Tombstone Townsite Company. 1880's. *224*

—. Art, public. Murals. New York City (Bronx). Post offices. Preservation. Shahn, Ben. 1938-76. *3578*

—. City Life. Environment. Pennsylvania (Philadelphia). 1750-84. *1756*

—. Decentralization. Educational Reform. Minorities. New York (Rochester). Whites. 1975. *2820*

—. Dutch Americans. New York (Albany). Social status. Women. 1600's-1790. *1608*

—. Elites. Florida (Palm Beach). Preservation. 1920's. 1960's-70's. *3543*

—. Epidemics. Pennsylvania (Pittsburgh). Public health. Urbanization. 19c. *1717*

—. Ethics. New York. State Government. 1970-75. *2415*

—. Historic Annapolis, Inc. Historical Sites and Parks. Maryland (Annapolis). Zoning. 1649-1845. 1952-1969. *3570*

—. Housing and Urban Development Act (US, 1965, Section 23). Illinois (Chicago). Negroes. Public Housing Authority. Segregation. 1964-75. *3393*

—. Ice industry. Monopolies. Nebraska. Omaha Ice Trust. 1899-1900. *438*

—. Indians. Migration, Internal. Washington (Seattle). 1970's. *2936*

—. Marital Status. Maryland (Baltimore). Social classes. Women. 1729-97. *701*

—. Massage parlors. Sex. 1971-73. *2759*

—. Missouri (St. Louis). Negroes, Free. Slaves. 1800-30. *1402*

—. Negroes. South. Whites. 1967-68. *2988*

—. Nervous disorders. Noise pollution. 1960's-70's. *3247*

Law and Order Committee. Business. California (San Francisco). Construction. Eight-hour day. Strikes. Working Conditions. 1916-17. *606*

—. California (San Francisco). City Government. McDevitt, William. Rolph, James J. Socialism. 1916. *1251*

—. California (San Francisco). Labor Disputes. 1916. *608*

Law and Society. Crime and Criminals. Historiography. Michigan (Detroit). Urbanization. 1824-47. *1280*

—. Desegregation. Massachusetts (Boston). *Morgan* v. *Hennigan* (Massachusetts, 1974). Negroes. Schools. 1974-75. *2817*

—. Police. Public Policy. Robbery. 1970's. *3010*

Law Enforcement. Bell, William H. Diaries. New York City. 1850-51. *1292*

—. British Columbia (Vancouver). Chinese. Provincial government. Racism. Riots. 1887. *3813*

—. Bureau of Social Morals. Hertz, Rosie. Jews. New York City. Prostitution. 1912-13. *1150*

—. California (Los Angeles County). Crime and Criminals. 1850-56. *1294*

—. Chippewa Indians. Indian-White Relations. Minnesota (Minneapolis). 1969-70. *2940*

—. City Government. Michigan (Detroit). Negroes. Riots. 1863-65. *1277*

—. Class Struggle. Migrant labor. New York (Buffalo). Tramp Act (New York, 1885). 1892-94. *777*

—. Connecticut. Local Government. New Jersey. New York. Public Finance. State government. 1961-77. *2508*

—. Crime and Criminals. Illinois (Chicago). Police. Political Corruption. Social Customs. 1890-1925. *1230*

—. District of Columbia. Massage parlors. Prostitution. 1970's. *2758*

—. Florida (Miami). Racism. Terrorism. 1896-1930. *1225*

—. Graffiti. Juvenile Delinquency. New York City. Subways. 1970's. *2648*

—. Knights of the Flaming Circle. Ku Klux Klan. Ohio (Niles). Riots. State government. 1924. *1214*

—. Metropolitan areas. 1978. *2973*

—. Race Relations. Reconstruction. Riots. Tennessee (Memphis). 1866. *1274*

—. Race Relations. Slavery. Virginia (Richmond). 1782-1820. *1410*

Law Reform. Alcohol. District of Columbia. Drunkenness, public. Minnesota (Minneapolis). Police. 1960's-70's. *2931*

—. City Politics. Landlords and Tenants. Rent control. 1942-79. *3376*

Lawsuits. California (Alameda, San Benito counties). Courts. 1890-1970. *1223*

—. Child Welfare. Discrimination. New York. 1973-74. *2924*

—. Georgia (Atlanta). *Great Speckled Bird* (newspaper). Hippies. Press, underground. Socialism. 1968-76. *2767*

Lawyers See also Judges.

—. Accounting. District of Columbia. Organizations. 1960-77. *2577*

—. Anarchism and Anarchists. Black, William Perkins. Haymarket riot. Illinois (Chicago). Trials. 1886-87. *1246*

Lawyers' Round Table. Baltimore Reform League. Maryland. Niles, Alfred Salem. Voluntary Associations. 1852-1972. *740*

Lead poisoning. New York City. -1974. *3237*

Leadership See also Political Leadership.

—. Aluminum Company of America. Company Towns. Labor. Negroes. Tennessee (Alcoa). 1919-39. *1396*

—. American Revolution (antecedents). Elites. Pennsylvania (Philadelphia). Philadelphia Resistance Committee. Political activism. 1765-76. *259*

—. Belcher, Wyatt W. Business. Illinois (Chicago). Missouri (St. Louis). 1830-80. *200*

—. Cook, Edward M., Jr. (review article). New England. Social Organization. 18c. 1976. *813*

—. Economic Development. Illinois (Chicago). Missouri (St. Louis). Ohio (Cincinnati). Wisconsin (Milwaukee). 1830-80. *149*

—. Elites. Maryland (Baltimore). 1781-1806. 1827-36. *271*

—. Indiana (northwestern). Negroes. Neighborhoods. 1975. *3096*

—. Intellectuals. Massachusetts (Boston). Middle classes. Negroes. Smith, Julia H. 1885-1978. *1394*

—. Jews. Levi, Abraham. Texas (Victoria). 1850-1902. *1488*

—. Negroes. Rhode Island (Providence). 1962-72. *3108*

Leadville Blues (team). Baseball. Colorado. 1882. *913*

Leadville Daily Chronicle (newspaper). Colorado (Leadville). Science fiction. Stein, Orth. 1880-82. *928*

League of Revolutionary Black Workers. Automobile industry and Trade. Industrialization. Michigan (Detroit). Negroes. 1968-75. *2626*

—. Automobile industry and Trade. Labor Unions and Organizations. Michigan (Detroit). Negroes. Radicals and Radicalism. 1968-73. *2627*

Leases. City Government. Indians. Iroquois Indians (Seneca). Land. New York (Salamanca). 1850-1974. *245*

Leatherworkers. Massachusetts (Lynn). Social Organization. Strikes. 1890. *586*

Lebanon Opera House. Drama. Ohio (Cincinnati). 1878-1900. *1061*

Lector (reader). Cubans. Florida (Tampa). Labor Disputes. Perez, Louis A., Jr. Reminiscences. Tobacco workers. ca 1925-35. *572*

Lectures. Atheism. Ingersoll, Robert. Nevada (Virginia City). Public Opinion. 1877. *1666*

—. Louisiana (New Orleans). 1840-50. *957*

Lederer, Henry. Jews. Michigan (Lansing). Settlement. 1850-1918. *1452*

Lee, Bing. California (Locke). Chinese Americans. 1880-1970. *1553*

Leftism See also Communism; Radicals and Radicalism; Socialism.

—. Artists. Community Participation in Politics. Murals. Social change. Social change. 1970's. *2787*

—. California (San Francisco). Chinatowns. City government. Ethnic Groups. Evictions. International Hotel. Landlords and Tenants. 1977. *3169*

Legends. Immigrants. New York (Buffalo). Polish Americans. Religion. 1870-1973. *1559*

Legislation See also Congress; Law.

—. Civil rights. Population. Race Relations. Riots. Tennessee (Memphis). 1865-66. *1254*

—. Discrimination, Housing. Ghettos. Negroes. 1970's. *3105*

—. Educational Reform. Howland, John. Public Schools. Rhode Island. 1757-1838. 1800H. *1110*

—. Federal government. Louisiana (New Orleans). Public Health. Yellow fever. 1830's-79. *1724*

—. Integration. Pennsylvania (Philadelphia). Streetcars. 1850's-70. *1353*

—. Local government. Metropolitan areas. Minnesota. Planning. Tax base sharing. 1970's. *2394*

Leisure See also Recreation.

—. Automobiles. California (East Los Angeles). Low-riders. Mexican Americans. Youth. 1970's. *3154*

—. Daily Life. Rhode Island (Newport). 1723. *875*

Leland, Henry. Detroit Citizens League. Michigan. Progressivism. Social Classes. 1912-24. *362*

L'Enfant, Pierre Charles. Architecture. City Planning. District of Columbia. 1791. *1823*

—. City Planning. District of Columbia. 1796-1825. *1851*

Letters. Architecture. Hunter, Mary Robinson. Hunter, Thomas. Lyman, Ann Maria. Rhode Island (Newport). Wanton-Lyman-Hazard House. 18c-19c. *1990*

—. Attitudes. Butler, Benjamin Franklin. Civil War. Louisiana (New Orleans). Military Occupation. Women. 1861-62. *328*

—. Barnsley, Godfrey. Civil War. Cotton industry. Gilmour, Henry S. Louisiana (New Orleans). Trade. 1861-62. *456*

—. Brown, Charles Brockden. Epidemics. Literature. Pennsylvania (Philadelphia). Rush, Benjamin. Yellow Fever. 1793-1800. *988*

—. Griscom, John H. Public Health. Reform. Sanitation. Shattuck, Lemuel. 1843-47. *1715*

—. Hodgdon, Elizabeth. Hodgdon, Sarah. Labor. Massachusetts (Lowell). New Hampshire (Rochester). Textile Industry. 1830-40. *560*

—. Immigrants. Norwegian Americans. Pennsylvania (Harmony, New Harmony). Rapp, George. 1816-26. *1561*

Levee construction. Floods. Georgia (Augusta). Savannah River. 1888. 1890-1951. *2133*

Levi, Abraham. Jews. Leadership. Texas (Victoria). 1850-1902. *1488*

Levi, Adolph. California (Julian, San Diego, Temecula). City Life. Levi, Simon. 1850-1943. *452*

Levi, Simon. California (Julian, San Diego, Temecula). City Life. Levi, Adolph. 1850-1943. *452*

Levin, Martin A. Balbus, Isaac D. Criminal justice (review article). Eisenstein, James. Jacob, Herbert. Mather, Lynn M. 1970's. *2941*

Lewis, Edward Gardner. Entrepreneurs. Government. Missouri (St. Louis, University City). Publishers and Publishing. *Woman's Magazine.* 1893-1928. *939*

Lewiston-Clarkston Improvement Company. City planning. Washington (Clarkston). 1896-1953. *1854*

Liberal Advocate. Dogberry, Obediah. New York (Rochester). Newspapers. Religious liberty. 1832-34. *925*

Liberalism. Alienation. Judaism. Utah (Salt Lake City). 1974. *3220*

—. City Politics. Civil rights. LaGuardia, Fiorello. New York City. Powell, Adam Clayton, Jr. 1941-43. *358*

—. City Politics. Gotthehrer, Barry (review article). Lindsay, John V. New York City. Social Problems. 1960's-71. *2422*

—. Community (concept). Democracy. Howe, Frederic C. Progressivism. ca 1890-1940. *1164*

—. Federal government. Grants, block. Housing and Community Development Act (US, 1974). 1974-79. *2524*

—. Federal Government. Grants, block. Model Cities program. 1970's. *2519*

—. Federal government. Mass transit. Metropolitan Areas. Trust fund. 1975. *3481*

—. Federal policy. Metropolitan areas. -1974. *2520*

—. Fire departments. Pennsylvania (Pittsburgh). Urbanization. 1870. *2413*

—. Georgia (Fulton County; Atlanta). Public services. State Government. Taxation. 1976-77. *2407*

—. Hemingway, William. Mississippi (Jackson). Mississippi, University of. 1901-37. *296*

—. Home rule. -1973. *2551*

—. Illinois. Lochner, Louis Paul. Peace Movements. People's Council of America for Democracy and Peace. State Government. 1917. *333*

—. Indiana (Indianapolis). Regional Government. 1850's-70's. *2409*

—. Intergovernmental Relations. New Netherland. Provincial Government. 1624-63. *263*

—. Intergovernmental Relations. Provincial government. Public Finance. Quebec. 1960-73. *3674*

—. Land use. States. 1970's. *3261*

—. Legislation. Metropolitan areas. Minnesota. Planning. Tax base sharing. 1970's. *2394*

—. Maryland (Baltimore). Urban Renewal. 1950's-70's. *2325*

—. Massachusetts (Boston). Political Leadership. Provincial Government. Social Status. 1692-1775. *274*

—. Metropolitan Government. 1945-74. *2388*

—. Metropolitan Government. Property tax. 1974. *2408*

—. Neighborhoods. Pennsylvania. Pittsburgh Neighborhood Atlas. 1968-70's. *2368*

—. Nova Scotia (East Hants). 1861-1923. *3667*

—. Political Ethics. 1975. *2329*

—. Political leadership. 1973. *2318*

—. Political structure. Suburbanization. ca 1950-75. *2399*

—. Population. Public Policy. 1970's. *3352*

—. Population. Public services. 1970's. *2346*

—. Public Finance. Revenue sharing. State Government. Urban policy. 1948-75. *2530*

—. Public Service Districts. -1974. *2404*

—. Quality of life. 1970's. *2309*

—. Quebec (Montreal area). 1911-71. *3687*

—. Social problems. Suburbs. 1920-70. *2305*

Local history. Archival Catalogs and Inventories. Negroes. New York City. Personal Narratives. Staten Island Institute of Arts and Sciences. 1969-76. *4031*

—. Buschow family. City directories. Ohio (Cleveland). 1883-1900. 1979. *4061*

—. California (Imperial Valley, San Diego). Irrigation. Smythe, William E. 1880-1910. *150*

—. Cincinnati, University of. History Teaching. Ohio. Students. 1974-75. *4009*

—. Gross, Robert A. (review article). Massachusetts (Concord). 1740's-1820's. 1976. *678*

—. High Schools. Massachusetts (Hamilton). 1977. *3942*

—. Historiography. Tennessee (Memphis). 1912. 1975. *4001*

Local Politics *See also* Local Government.

—. California (San Diego). City planning. Elections (municipal). Marston, George. 1908-17. *1848*

—. California (Santa Barbara). City Planning. Environmentalism. Water supply. 1976. *2270*

—. Cameron, Simon. Pennsylvania (Philadelphia). Political machines. 1867-72. *352*

—. City government. Community control. Decentralization. New York City. 1970's. *2460*

—. Committee of Fifteen. New York City. Reform. Tammany Hall. Vice. 1900-01. *1144*

—. Connecticut. Elections. Officeholding. Provincial Legislatures. 1701-90. *264*

—. Courthouse Gang. Nebraska (Loup City). Political Factions. Railroad Gang. 1887-91. *246*

—. Delaware (Wilmington). Negroes. Republican Party. 1850-1900. *1372*

—. Democratic Party. Elections. Know-Nothing Party. Missouri (St. Louis). Riots. 1844-56. *1279*

—. Elections (municipal). Louisiana (Shreveport). Prohibition. 1950-52. *2923*

—. German Americans. Government Regulation. Illinois (Chicago). Know-Nothing Party. Riots. Temperance. 1855. *1271*

—. German Americans. Irish Americans. New York City. Riots. Temperance. 1857. *1291*

—. Illinois (Chicago). Negroes. Public schools. 1910-41. *1086*

—. Illinois (Chicago area). School districts. Suburbs. 1963-68. *2888*

—. Indian-White Relations. Massachusetts (Natick). Meetinghouses. 1650-18c. *1576*

—. Metropolitan Government. Voting and Voting Behavior. 1945-70. *2490*

—. Pennsylvania (Lancaster). Stevens, Thaddeus. 1842-68. *292*

—. Pennsylvania (Reading). Socialist Party. Women. ca 1927-38. *298*

Localism. California (San Francisco Bay area). City managers. Cosmopolitanism. ca 1958-74. *2362*

—. Great Britain. Immigration. Massachusetts. Settlement. Towns. 1630-60. *5*

Location. Alaska. Capitols. State Government. 1955-E. *2516*

—. American Revolution. Capitols. State Government. Virginia (Richmond, Williamsburg). 1779. *326*

—. Banks. Quebec (Montreal). Urbanization. 1966-71. *3747*

—. Boosterism. Capitols. Ontario (Ottawa). 1822-59. *3658*

—. Business Size. Manufactures. Quebec (Montreal). 1927-71. *3719*

—. Capitols. Congress. Federal Government. 1783. *67*

—. Capitols. Federal Government. Potowmack Company. Stuart, David. Virginia (Alexandria). Washington, George. 1783-91. *217*

—. Capitols. Minnesota (St. Paul). State Government. 1849-1905. *332*

—. Churches. Economic change. Maryland (Baltimore). Protestantism. 1840-70. *1650*

—. City planning. Public services. 1970. *3333*

—. Colden, Cadwallader. Columbia University. New York City. Smith, William, Sr. 1747-53. *1087*

—. Diseases. Hospitals. Metropolitan Areas. 1970-74. *3249*

—. Downtown areas. Labor (white collar). 1950-73. *2619*

—. Employment. Garment industry. Maryland (Baltimore). 1860-1900. *505*

—. Garment industry. Ontario (Toronto). Publishers and Publishing. Quebec (Montreal). 1949-67. *3753*

—. Great Britain (London). Industry. New York City. 1960-72. *2606*

—. Illinois (Chicago). Michigan (Detroit). Ohio (Cleveland). Pennsylvania. Production. Steel Industry. 1910-72. *495*

—. Industrialization. Ontario (Kingston). Physicians. Residential Patterns. 1857-1975. *3757*

—. Industry. Texas (Dallas, Fort Worth). 1967-75. *2603*

Location theory. Economic Development. Land use. Models. 1960-73. *2219*

Lochner, Louis Paul. Illinois. Local Government. Peace Movements. People's Council of America for Democracy and Peace. State Government. 1917. *333*

Lockwood, Charles. Architecture (Prairie School). Brooks, H. Allen. Housing (review article). Interior design. Town houses. Wright, Frank Lloyd. 1783-1929. 1972. *1906*

Logan, Alexander. City Government. Manitoba (Winnipeg). Mayors. 1870's-80's. *3672*

Logan International Airport. Airports. Community Participation in Politics. Ecology. Massachusetts (Boston). Massachusetts Port Authority. 1959-74. *3467*

London, Jack. Bierce, Ambrose. California (San Francisco). Social Change. Sterling, George. Urbanization. 1880-1920. *958*

Londoner, Wolfe. Colorado (Denver). Elections (mayoral). Political reform. 1889-91. *391*

Long, Huey P. Barksdale Air Force Base. Louisiana (Shreveport). Politics. State legislatures. 1923-33. *322*

Longfellow, Henry Wadsworth. Furniture and Furnishings. Kimball, Abraham. Massachusetts (Salem). Sargent, Winthrop. 1820-45. *475*

Longshoremen. Labor Unions and Organizations. Louisiana (New Orleans). Race Relations. 1850's-1976. *637*

Looting. Blackouts. Crime and Criminals. New York City. Poverty. 1977. *2942*

—. Deviant Behavior. Liberalism. New York City. Political Attitudes. Racism. 1977. *2944*

Lopez, Aaron. Rhode Island (Newport). Slave Trade. Triangular Trade. 1761-74. *447*

Los Angeles Aqueduct. California (Owens Valley, San Fernando Valley). Development. Harriman, Job. Population. State Politics. Water Supply. 1900-74. *2045*

Los Angeles County Museum of Art (collection). Artists. California, southern. ca 1900-40. *1021*

Los Angeles County Museum of Natural History. Archives. California. 1975. *3986*

Los Angeles Grand Opera Association. California. Opera. ca 1924-30. *1033*

Los Angeles *Illustrated Daily News*. California. Idealism. Newspapers. Vanderbilt, Cornelius, Jr. 1923-26. *934*

Los Angeles International Airport. Airplanes. California. 1928-78. *2070*

Los Angeles Philharmonic Orchestra. California. Conductors. Symphony Orchestras. 1862-1977. *993*

Lotchin, Roger W. Barth, Gunther. Blumin, Stuart M. California (San Francisco). Colorado (Denver). Urbanization (review article). 1820's-90's. 1970's. *90*

Louisiana. American Federation of Labor. Industrial Workers of the World. Marine Transport Workers. Sailors' Union. Strikes. United Fruit Company. 1913. *584*

—. Historic Preservation of Shreveport Committee. Preservation. 1972-78. *3564*

—. Public transportation. Shreveport City Railroad Company. Streetcars. 1870-76. *2110*

Louisiana (Columbia). Humphries, Daniel. Ports. ca 1827-1970's. *231*

Louisiana (Houma). Cajuns. Negroes. Population. Race Relations. Social change. Texans. 1945-73. *2725*

Louisiana (Jefferson City, New Orleans). Archives. Libraries. 1850-1972. *3968*

Louisiana (New Orleans). Advocacy. California (San Francisco). Missouri (St. Louis). Negroes. Public Administration. 1974-78. *3087*

—. Anderson, Sherwood. Values. 1920-27. *2149*

—. Architecture. Haiti. Houses, shotgun. Nigeria. Yoruba. 18c-1974. *1993*

—. Archival Catalogs and Inventories. Gálvez, Bernardo de. Gottschalk, Louis M. Historic New Orleans Collection. Manuscripts. 18c-20c. *3946*

—. Attitudes. Butler, Benjamin Franklin. Civil War. Letters. Military Occupation. Women. 1861-62. *328*

—. Barnsley, Godfrey. Civil War. Cotton industry. Gilmour, Henry S. Letters. Trade. 1861-62. *456*

—. Business. Godchaux, Leon. 19c. *412*

—. Businessmen. City planning. Elites. Georgia (Atlanta). Tennessee (Memphis). 1907-30. *1821*

—. Cabildo. Local government. Spain. 1769-1803. *251*

—. Charity Hospital of Louisiana. Disease, concept of. Masturbation. 1848-1933. *1725*

—. Cholera. Howard Association. Philanthropy. Public health. Yellow fever. 1837-78. *1739*

—. City government. Idealism. Morrison, deLesseps S. Political reform. 1946-64. *373*

—. City Government. School Integration. 1952-61. *2865*

—. City Life. Jefferson, Thomas. 18c-19c. *134*

—. Civil War. Negroes (free). 1855-1900. *1400*

—. Clapp, Theodore. Slavery. Theology, radical. Unitarianism. 1822-56. *1690*

—. Colonial Government. Disaster Relief. Fire. Spain. 1794-95. *2122*

—. Colonial Government. Spain. Vidal, Nicolás María. Zoning. 1797. *1830*

—. Commerce. Economic Development. Mississippi River. Technology. 1850-1950. *417*

—. Constitutional conventions, state. Reconstruction. Riots. Violence. 1866. *1218*

—. Cotton Exchange. Economic Development. 1870-81. *534*

—. Crescent Theater. Erlanger, Abraham Lincoln. Klaw, Marc. Theater. Tulane Theater. 1896-1937. *987*

—. Crime and Criminals. Hennessy, David. Italian Americans. Mafia. Murder. 1890. *1266*

—. Crime and Criminals. Prohibition. 1918-33. *1242*

—. Dance competitions. Individualism. Minstrel shows. 1840's-50's. *864*

—. deLapouyade, Robert. Stage Setting and Scenery. 1902-27. *1030*

—. Democratic Party. Elections (municipal). Flower, Walter C. Political Reform. 1896. *377*

—. Democratic Party. Morial, Ernest N. Negroes. Political Campaigns (mayoral). 1977. *2499*

—. District of Columbia. Education. Employment. Georgia (Atlanta). Income. Negroes. South. 1970. *2868*

—. Economic Conditions. Georgia (Atlanta). Minorities in Politics. 1960's-79. *3076*

—. Economic growth. Panama Canal. 1900-14. *404*

—. Ethnic Groups. Georgia (Atlanta). Labor. Texas (San Antonio). Women. 1930-40. *557*

—. Federal government. Legislation. Public Health. Yellow fever. 1830's-79. *1724*

—. Governors. Mayors. Morrison, deLesseps S. 1955-61. *2424*

—. Hair, William Ivy. Haynes, Robert V. Herndon, Angelo. Martin, Charles H. Racism (review article). South. Texas (Houston). 1900-30's. 1976. *1213*

—. Hair, William Ivy. Haynes, Robert V. Race Relations. Riots (review article). Texas (Houston). 1900-17. 1970's. *1273*

—. Harper, William Poynot. Mardi Gras. 1866-72. *870*

—. Italian Americans. Press. Stereotypes. 1880-1920. *938*

—. Italian Americans. Residential segregation. 20c. *3193*

—. Labor Unions and Organizations. Longshoremen. Race Relations. 1850's-1976. *637*

—. Labor Unions and Organizations. Screwmen's Benevolent Association. 1850-61. *610*

—. Lectures. 1840-50. *957*

—. Mardi Gras. 1718-1978. *908*

—. Marine Engineering. Military Camps and Forts. 1680-1970's. *1803*

—. Matas, Rudolph. Medical Research. Ochsner, Alton. Reminiscences. Surgery, thoracic and vascular. 1927-52. *1755*

—. Men. Negroes. Political participation. Women. 1969-70. *3109*

—. Methodist Church. Winans, William. 1813-14. *1661*

—. Metropolitan Police Force. Negroes. Politics. Riots. Whites. 1868. *1235*

—. Music (jazz). Negroes. Voodoo. Women. ca 19c. *967*

—. Music (Jazz). North. 1890-1930. *975*

—. Music (jazz). Pianos. 1920's-40's. *1022*

—. Negroes. Political Leadership. Reconstruction. ca 1800-75. *1401*

—. Negroes. Provost, Tessie. Public schools. School Integration. 1960-79. *3121*

—. New York City. Public health. 19c. *1720*

—. Public opinion. Street, Electric Railway and Motor Coach Employees of America. Street railroads. Strikes. 1929-30. *583*

—. Race relations. 1865-1900. *1412*

—. Race relations. Residential patterns. 19c-20c. *1414*

Louisiana (New Orleans; Algiers Point, Lower Marigny). Restorations. 1950-70. *3402*

Louisiana (New Orleans; Congo Square). Africa, West. Music (jazz). Negroes. Religion. Rites and Ceremonies. 18c-19c. *1018*

Louisiana (New Orleans; Lower Garden). Coliseum Square Association. New Orleans Historic District Landmarks Committee. Preservation. 1807-1978. *3576*

Louisiana (Opelousas, Washington). Negroes. Residential Patterns. Whites. 1860-80. *1325*

Louisiana Purchase Exposition. Centennial Celebrations. Missouri (St. Louis). 1904. *916*

—. Films. Missouri (St. Louis). Museums. Public schools. 1901-78. *1104*

Louisiana (Shreveport). Barksdale Air Force Base. Long, Huey P. Politics. State legislatures. 1923-33. *322*

—. Bishops. Episcopal Church, Protestant. Polk, Leonidas. 1830-1916. *1652*

—. Cemeteries. Historical Sources. 1839-1975. *1786*

—. City Politics. Federal Government. Gardner, Jim. Urban renewal. 1954-58. *3358*

—. Civil War. Daily Life. Economic Conditions. 1861-65. *44*

—. Columbia Restaurant. ca 1900-69. *861*

—. Elections (municipal). Local politics. Prohibition. 1950-52. *2923*

—. Epidemics. Kellogg, William Pitt. Reconstruction. Secession. State Government. Texas. Yellow fever. 1873-77. *327*

—. Ku Klux Klan. Morality. 1920-29. *731*

Louisville and Portland Canal. Kentucky (Louisville). Population. Public health. Steamboats. 1800-30. *147*

Lowell, Francis Cabot. Boston Manufacturing Company. Great Britain. Industrialization. International trade. Massachusetts. 1807-20. *471*

Low-riders. Automobiles. California (East Los Angeles). Leisure. Mexican Americans. Youth. 1970's. *3154*

Loyalists. American Revolution. New England. Rural areas. 1770's. *260*

—. Militia. Pennsylvania (Philadelphia). Politics. Prices. Riots. Wilson, James. 1779. *1204*

Lucas, Stephen E. American Revolution. Cities (review article). Foner, Philip S. Maryland (Annapolis). Olton, Charles S. Papenfuse, Edward C. Pennsylvania (Philadelphia). 1763-87. 1975-76. *2*

Luks, George. Glackens, William. Henri, Robert. Painting. Realism. Shinn, Everett. Sloan, John. 1890's. *1007*

Lumber and Lumbering. Alabama (Mobile). Exports. 1760-1860. *427*

—. Alberta (Calgary; Eau Claire district). Eau Claire Company. Housing. Kerr, Isaac. Prince, Peter. 1886-1970's. *3670*

—. Arizona (McNary). Company towns. Negroes. Segregation. Social conditions. 1924-72. *1424*

—. Booth, John Rudolphus. City Government. Fire. Housing. Ontario (Ottawa). Working class. 1900-03. *3887*

—. British Columbia (Nanaimo). Coal Mines and Mining. 1850-1978. *3731*

—. Exports. Georgia (Savannah). 1830's-1850's. *428*

—. Exports. Ports. South Carolina (Charleston). 18c-1860. *425*

—. Florida (Pensacola). Trade. 1800-60. *426*

—. Japanese Americans. Oregon (Toledo). Pacific Spruce Corporation. Riots. 1925-26. *1554*

—. Labor. Merchant Marine. New Brunswick (Saint John). Ports. Quebec. Working conditions. ca 1820-90. *3730*

—. Mississippi (Laurel). 1882-1916. *496*

—. New York (Rochester). 1788-1880. *504*

—. Wisconsin (Marinette). 1850-70. *24*

Lumbermen. Community Participation in Politics. Michigan (Bay City, Saginaw). Strikes. 1880's. *603*

Lummis, Charles F. California (Los Angeles). Culture. Historic preservation. Newmark, Harris. Newmark, Marco. Newmark, Maurice. Southwest Museum. 1859-1930. *654*

Lunn, George. New York (Schenectady). Socialist Party. Voting and Voting Behavior. Working Class. 1911-16. *290*

Lutey Brothers Marketeria. Food Industry. Grocery stores. Montana. 1897-1924. *442*

Lutherans. American Revolution. German Americans. Pennsylvania (Philadelphia). 1776-81. *1693*

Lyman, Ann Maria. Architecture. Hunter, Mary Robinson. Hunter, Thomas. Letters. Rhode Island (Newport). Wanton-Lyman-Hazard House. 18c-19c. *1990*

Lynch, John Joseph. Bishops. Catholic Church. Ontario. Poor. Toronto Savings Bank. 1870's. *3755*

Lynching. California (San Jose). Hart, Brooke. Holmes, John. Murder. St. James Park. Thurmond, Thomas. 1933. *1255*

—. *Free Speech*. Negroes. Newspapers. Tennessee (Memphis). Wells, Ida B. 1892. *1205*

Lynd, Helen M. Indiana (Muncie). Lynd, Robert S. Politics. Sociology. 1929-76. *3960*

Lynd, Robert S. Indiana (Muncie). Lynd, Helen M. Politics. Sociology. 1929-76. *3960*

Lyon, Marcus. Anti-Catholicism. Cheverus, Jean Louis Lefebvre de. Daley, Dominic. Halligan, James. Irish Americans. Massachusetts (Northampton). Murder. Trials. 1805-06. *1502*

Lyons Law (1937). City Government. Employment. New York City. Reform. 1973-75. *2345*

Lyrics. Music (blues). Negroes. Phonograph records. 1945-76. *2810*

M

Macdonald, Charles Blair. Golf. Illinois (Chicago). Sports. 1870's-1975. *921*

Macedonian Canadians. Assimilation. Immigrants. Ontario (Toronto). 1900-20. *3843*

—. Immigrants. Ontario (Toronto). Urban history. 20c. *3971*

—. Immigration. Ontario (Toronto). Social Conditions. 1900-30. *3844*

Mackay, Clarence. Architecture. Mackay, Katherine Alexander Duer. New York (Long Island). White, Stanford. 1898-1906. *2002*

Mackay, Katherine Alexander Duer. Architecture. Mackay, Clarence. New York (Long Island). White, Stanford. 1898-1906. *2002*

MacKaye, Benton. Appalachian Trail. Regional Planning. Wilderness. 1921-66. *2175*

Mackenzie, William Lyon. Armstrong, Frederick H. Mayors. Ontario (Toronto). 1835-37. 1967. *3696*

MacKinnon, Duncan. Boycotts. California. San Diego High School. Student protest. 1918. *1083*

MacLane, Mary. Authors. Feminism. Montana (Butte). 1902-29. *1015*

—. Authors. Montana (Butte). Women. 1901-29. *1058*

Macready, William Charles. Actors and Actresses. Forrest, Edwin. Nativism. New York City (Astor Place). Riots. 1849. *2963*

Madison, James. Economic Planning. Ports. State Government. Virginia. 1784-88. *165*

Mafia. Crime and Criminals. Hennessy, David. Italian Americans. Louisiana (New Orleans). Murder. 1890. *1266*

Magazines. *See* Periodicals.

Mahood, Cecil S. Alberta (Calgary). Epidemics. Influenza. 1918-19. *3874*

Maine (Bar Harbor). Artists. Businessmen. Cole, Thomas. Pratt, Henry. Resorts. 1840-70. *198*

—. Autumn. Daily Life. Eden Fair. Resorts. 1920's. *856*

Maine (Bath). Apprenticeship. Maine Maritime Museum. Shipbuilding. 1978. *2601*

Maine (Gardiner). New England. Ports. Shipping. 1830's. *454*

Maine Maritime Museum. Apprenticeship. Maine (Bath). Shipbuilding. 1978. *2601*

Maine (Portland). Economic development. Industry. Nebraska (St. John). Poor, John. Railroads. 1850-1914. *393*

—. Music. 1785-1836. *1037*

Makah Indians. Excavations. Villages. Washington (Ozette). Whale hunters. Prehistory. 1966-74. *3930*

Malnutrition. Apathy. Colonization. Death and Dying. Virginia (Jamestown). 1607-24. *1745*

Management *See also* Collective Bargaining; Industrial Relations.

—. Arts. New York City. 1970's. *2815*

—. Attitudes. Public housing. 1968. *3383*

—. City Government. Fire fighting. Labor Unions and Organizations. 1969-73. *2624*

—. Department stores. Sales clerks. Women. Working Conditions. 1890-1960. *554*

—. Historiography. Massachusetts (Boston). Mental Institutions. Poor. 1847-1920. *1203*

—. Johnson, Tom L. Ohio (Cleveland). Streetcars. Technology. 1883-98. *503*

Management, scientific. Johnson Company. Pennsylvania (Johnstown). Streetcar industry. Taylor, Frederick W. 1896. *506*

Manhattan Auto Study. Automobiles. New York City. 1970. *3478*

Manhattan Opera House. Hammerstein, Oscar. New York City. Opera. 1863-1910. *1001*

Manhole covers. California. Public Utilities. 1860's-1970's. *2047*

Manion, Edward J. Banking. Brotherhood of Railway Telegraphers. Gardner, Vernon O. Labor Unions and Organizations. Missouri (St. Louis). Telegraphers National Bank. 1922-42. *537*

Manitoba (East St. Boniface, Winnipeg). Belgian Canadians. Immigration. Nuytten, Edmund (and Family). Nuytten, Octavia. 1880-1914. *3840*

Manitoba (St. Boniface). French Canadians. Integration. 1871-1971. *3830*

Manitoba (St. Boniface, Winnipeg; North End). Ethnic Groups. Neighborhoods. 19c-1978. *3829*

Manitoba (Selkirk). City planning. Hudson's Bay Company. 1869-79. *3914*

Manitoba (Winnipeg). Architecture. Cauchon, Joseph-Edouard. Empire Hotel. Iron-front buildings. 1880-1920. *3908*

—. Architecture. Post offices. 1855-1974. *3890*

—. Bercuson, David J. (review article). General Strikes. Industrial relations. Social organization. 1975. *3758*

—. Bill of Incorporation (1873). City Government. Taxation. 1873. *3681*

—. Buildings. 19c-1973. *3909*

—. Business. City government. Political Corruption. Public Administration. Urbanization. 1884-85. *3698*

—. Business. Economic growth. Political Leadership. Urbanization. 1874-1914. *3624*

—. City Government. 1972-73. *3678*

—. City Government. Logan, Alexander. Mayors. 1870's-80's. *3672*

—. City Government. Mayors. Queen, John. Socialism. Tax reform. 1909-42. *3689*

—. City government. Political Reform. Working class. 1873-1971. *3685*

—. City Life. Immigration. Jews, Russian. 1874-82. *3821*

—. City Politics. Penner, Jacob. Webb, Ralph. 1919-34. *3690*

—. Cold War. Ethnic Groups. Social Classes. Voting and Voting Behavior. 1949-53. *3707*

—. Discrimination. Ethnic groups. Immigrants. Population. 1874-1974. *3642*

—. Education. Red River Academy. 1820's-50's. *3765*

—. Ethnic Groups. Residential patterns. -1974. *3831*

—. Ethnic Groups. Social Classes. Voting and Voting Behavior. 1941. *3701*

—. Ethnic Groups. Social Classes. Voting and Voting Behavior. 1945-46. *3708*

—. Ethnicity. Folk art. Latvian Canadians. Ukrainian Canadians. 1978. *3805*

—. Illinois (Chicago). Mennonites. Missions and Missionaries. 1866-1977. *1646*

—. Immigration. Melnyk, George. Reminiscences. 1949. 1977. *3922*

—. Jews. 1860's-1975. *3822*

—. Lake of the Woods. Ontario. Water supply. 1912-75. *3904*

—. Streetcars. Urbanization. 1881-1913. *3913*

Mannaseh, Joseph Samuel. Business. California (San Diego). City Government. Jews. Schiller, Marcus. 1853-97. *436*

Manning, Richard Irvine. Dispensary Act. Liquor trade. Monopolies. South Carolina (Charleston). 1915-18. *312*

Mansions. Architecture. Kellum, John. New York. Stewart, Alexander Turney. 1860-90. *1880*

—. Architecture. Pennsylvania (Philadelphia; Fairmount Park). Restorations. 1774-99. *2003*

—. Arizona (Tucson; Main Street). Elites. 1865-1907. *1980*

—. California (San Francisco; Nob Hill). Stanford, Leland. 1870's-1906. *1942*

Manufactures *See also* names of articles manufactured, e.g. Furniture, etc.; names of industries, e.g. Steel Industry and Trade, etc.; Corporations; Patents; Prices.

—. Barney and Smith Car Company. Ohio (Dayton). Railroad cars. 1850-1926. *470*

—. Business Size. Location. Quebec (Montreal). 1927-71. *3719*

—. Industrialization. Nova Scotia (Halifax). 1867-1926. *3745*

Manufacturing. Abercrombie, Anderson. Bricks. Creary, John W. Florida (Pensacola). Raiford, Phillip H. 1854-60. *487*

—. Commerce. Northeastern or North Atlantic States. Urbanization. 19c. *194*

—. Cotton industry. Economic conditions. Industrialization. Pennsylvania (Rockdale). Social change. 1825-65. *521*

—. Economic Growth. Furniture and Furnishings. Michigan (Grand Rapids). 1876-90. *468*

—. Labor Unions and Organizations. Skill differential. 1952-73. *2605*

Manuscripts *See also* Documents.

—. Archival Catalogs and Inventories. Gálvez, Bernardo de. Gottschalk, Louis M. Historic New Orleans Collection. Louisiana (New Orleans). 18c-20c. *3946*

—. Cohan, Jerry. Gagbooks. Humor. Murphy, J. C. Vaudeville. 1790's-1890's. *909*

Maps. Arizona (Phoenix). Urbanization. 1867-1977. *72*

—. Building plans. Canada. Historical sources. Insurance agencies. Land use atlases. Urban historians. 1696-1973. *3974*

—. Canada. Exhibits and Expositions. Public Archives of Canada. Research. Urban history. 1865-1905. *3959*

—. City Planning. Land use. Quebec (Sherbrooke). 1824-1951. *3915*

—. Hales, John Groves. Massachusetts (Boston area). 1800-32. *4008*

Marcantonio, Vito. House of Representatives. New York City (East Harlem). Puerto Ricans. Republican Party. 20c. *1597*

Mardi Gras. Harper, William Poynot. Louisiana (New Orleans). 1866-72. *870*

—. Louisiana (New Orleans). 1718-1978. *908*

Marguerite v. *Chouteau* (Missouri, 1834). Indian-White Relations. Missouri (St. Louis). Slavery. 1764-1834. *1600*

Marin County Civic Center. Architects. California. County Government. Fusselman, William. 1952-63. *3417*

Marine Engineering. Harbor Masters. Ontario (Toronto). Richardson, Hugh. 1821-70. *3712*

—. Louisiana (New Orleans). Military Camps and Forts. 1680-1970's. *1803*

Marine Transport Workers. American Federation of Labor. Industrial Workers of the World. Louisiana. Sailors' Union. Strikes. United Fruit Company. 1913. *584*

Marital status. Fertility. Migration, Internal. Rural-Urban Studies. 1967. *2679*

—. Law. Maryland (Baltimore). Social classes. Women. 1729-97. *701*

Maritime Provinces *See also* Atlantic Provinces.

—. Economic Conditions. Emigration. Massachusetts (Boston). New England. 1860-1900. *3766*

Market Street Railway Company. California (San Francisco; Carville). Housing. Streetcars. Vacations. 1890's-1930's. *1889*

Marketing. Agricultural Commodities. Ontario (Simcoe County). Railroads. Roads. Towns. 1850-75. *3739*

—. Clothing. Department stores. Neiman-Marcus Company. Texas (Dallas). 1900-17. *431*

—. Cotton industry. South. Urbanization. 1880-1930. *227*

—. Drug Abuse. Methadone. New York City. 1975. *3227*

—. Fashion. Neiman-Marcus Company. Texas (Dallas). 1880-1970. *421*

—. Food. Government Regulation. Massachusetts (Boston). 18c. *652*

—. Ghettos. Racism. -1973. *2594*

—. Indentured servants. Pennsylvania (Philadelphia). 1771-73. *567*

Marketplaces. Education. Experimental Methods. Industrial society program. Interdisciplinary studies. Wisconsin, University of, Parkside. 1973. *3997*

—. Restorations. 17c-20c. *3499*

Marks, David X. Architecture. California (Los Angeles). Insurance. Marks, Joshua H. Philanthropy. 1902-77. *49*

Marks, Joshua H. Architecture. California (Los Angeles). Insurance. Marks, David X. Philanthropy. 1902-77. *49*

Marks, Nora (pseud. of Eleanora Stackhouse). Chicago *Tribune*. Illinois (Chicago). Reporters and Reporting. Social Problems. 1888-90. *937*

Marquette Iron Company. Everett, Phil Marshall. Iron Industry. Jackson Iron Company. Michigan (Carp River Region; Marquette). 1670-1854. *192*

Marriage *See also* Divorce; Family; Intermarriage; Sex.

—. Age. Marriage. Massachusetts (Newburyport). Men. Women. ca 1800-30. *695*

—. Assimilation. California (Los Angeles). Europe. Immigrants. Jews. 1910-13. *1469*

—. Divorce. Mortality. Rural-Urban Studies. Tennessee. 1970. *2688*

Marsh, Benjamin C. City Planning. Crowding. National Conference on City Planning. Poor. Social Reform. 1900-17. *1834*

Marshall Field building. Architecture. Illinois (Chicago). Richardson, Henry Hobson. 1880's. *1946*

Marshall Plan. Europe. Federal Aid. Self-help. Social Problems. 1940's-70's. *2231*

Marston, George. California (San Diego). City planning. Elections (municipal). Local Politics. 1908-17. *1848*

Martí, José. City politics. Cuba. Florida (Jacksonville). Huah, José Alejandro. Independence Movements. 1836-1905. *1525*

Martin, Charles H. Hair, William Ivy. Haynes, Robert V. Herndon, Angelo. Louisiana (New Orleans). Racism (review article). South. Texas (Houston). 1900-30's. 1976. *1213*

Martin, Médéric. Bossism. Houde, Camillien. Local government. Quebec (Montreal). 1923-29. *3691*

—. City politics. Laporte, Hormisdas. Political corruption. Préfontaine, Raymond. Quebec (Montreal). 1894-1921. *3679*

Martin, William. Nashville and Northwestern Railway. Railroads. Tennessee (Martin). 1832-93. *220*

Marxism *See also* Anarchism and Anarchists; Class Struggle; Communism; Socialism.

—. Community Participation in Politics. Economic Theory. Housing. Technology. 1870-1974. *3360*

Maryland. Baltimore Normal School. Bowie State College. Education. Negroes. Wells, Nelson. 1843-72. *1105*

—. Baltimore Reform League. Lawyers' Round Table. Niles, Alfred Salem. Voluntary Associations. 1852-1972. *740*

—. Connecticut. Massachusetts. Wealth. 1650-1890. *792*

Maryland (Annapolis). American Revolution. Cities (review article). Foner, Philip S. Lucas, Stephen E. Olton, Charles S. Papenfuse, Edward C. Pennsylvania (Philadelphia). 1763-87. 1975-76. *2*

—. Company of Comedians. Theater. 1752. *1052*

—. Hamilton, Alexander (1712-56). Satire. Tuesday Club. 1744-56. *721*

—. Historic Annapolis, Inc. Historical Sites and Parks. Law. Zoning. 1649-1845. 1952-1969. *3570*

Maryland (Annapolis, Upper Marlborough). Company of Comedians. Theater. 1752-60. *1053*

Maryland (Baltimore). Actors and Actresses. Chestnut Street Theatre. Reinagle, Alexander. Wignell, Thomas. 1792-1802. *1029*

—. Ainslie, Peter. Carey, John R. Discrimination, employment. National Urban League. Negroes. Social conditions. 1921-35. *746*

—. Alabama (Birmingham). Anderson, Alan D. City Government (review article). Harris, Carl V. 1871-1930. 1977. *11*

—. Alcoholism. Labor (blue collar). Social Classes. 1973. *3252*

—. Alexander, William. Commission merchants. George's Creek Coal and Iron Company. Retail Trade. 1837-43. *432*

—. Annexation. City Government. Suburbs. 1745-1918. *308*

—. Apprenticeship. Artisans. Journeymen. Slavery. Wealth. 1790-1820. *514*

—. Architecture. Charities. Daily Life. Garrett, John Work. Garrett, Mary Frick. Garrett, Robert. Mount Vernon Place (residence). Upper Classes. 1872-1928. *710*

—. Architecture. Housing. Industrialization. Row Houses. 1800-30. *1859*

—. Archival Catalogs and Inventories. Urban history. 1797-1975. *3953*

—. Archives. City Government. 1729-1979. *3952*

—. Armories. Buildings. National Guard. 1858-1962. *1970*

—. Baltimore and Ohio Railroad. Mount Clare station. Railroads. 1830. 1851-52. *1907*

—. Banking. Brown, Alexander. Merchants. Shipping. Social change. Trade. ca 1800-34. *419*

—. Banking. Brown, Alexander & Sons. Cotton trade. Foreign exchange. Great Britain (Liverpool). New York City. Pennsylvania (Philadelphia). 1820-80. *437*

—. Baths, public. Philanthropy. 1893-1920. *1202*

—. Bossism. City Politics. Democratic Party. 1919-47. *334*

—. Business. Credit. 1757-76. *463*

—. Churches. Economic change. Location. Protestantism. 1840-70. *1650*

—. City Government. Negroes. Political protest. Public schools. 1865-1900. *1118*

—. City government. Political reform. Public Schools. 1870-1900. *1065*

—. City Politics. Progressivism. 1895-1911. *360*

—. Civilian review boards. Labor Unions and Organizations. New York (Buffalo). Pennsylvania (Philadelphia). Police. 1958-74. *2952*

—. Columbia Garden. Recreation. Theater. 1805-07. *907*

—. Conductors. Klasmer, Benjamin. Music. 1909-49. *968*

—. Courts. Ohio (Cleveland). Wisconsin (Milwaukee). 1965-70. *3005*

—. Crime and Criminals. Illinois (Chicago). Michigan (Detroit). Sentencing. 1975-76. *2955*

—. Cruse, Englehart. Grain. Milling. Rumsey, James. Steam Power. 1787-1804. *1774*

—. Fertility. Rural areas. 1965. *2686*
—. Fiscal Policy. Public Finance. State government. 1970's. *2517*
—. Florida (Duval County). Integration. Regional Planning. Schools. 1955-75. *2823*
—. Geographic Mobility. Population. 1860-1960. *225*
—. Geographic space. Methodology. Politics. Suburbs. 1960's-75. *2229*
—. Government. Politics. 1970-74. *2389*
—. Housing. Negroes. 1960's. *3384*
—. Housing. Population. Southwest. 1940-60. *3403*
—. Intergovernmental Relations. 1947-70's. *2414*
—. Intergovernmental relations. Regional Government. Social Problems. 1930-74. *2378*
—. Intergovernmental Relations. Social Problems. Suburbs. *2331*
—. Jews. Population. 1970. *3131*
—. Law Enforcement. 1978. *2973*
—. Legislation. Local government. Minnesota. Planning. Tax base sharing. 1970's. *2394*
—. Lifestyles. Public policy. Suburbanization. 1960's-75. *2213*
—. Migration, Internal. Migration, internal. Poverty. Rural areas. 1960-67. *2739*
—. Migration, Internal. Negroes. Rural Areas. South. 1950-70. *3064*
—. Minnesota (Minneapolis, St. Paul). Regional government. Twin Cities Metropolitan Council. 1967-73. *2377*
—. Minorities. Planning. School Integration. 1960's-70's. *2897*
—. Missions and Missionaries. Presbyterian Church. 1869-1977. *1687*
—. Missouri (St. Louis). Police. Public administration. 1972-74. *2972*
—. National Institute of Education. Public policy. School Integration. Supreme Court. 1970's. *2844*
—. Negroes. 1975. *3099*
—. Negroes. New York. Political attitudes. Puerto Ricans. 1970's. *2454*
—. Neighborhoods. Social status. 1925-73. *2272*
—. Occupations. Residential patterns. Social Classes. Transportation. 1970. *3274*
—. Ohio (Cincinnati). Transportation. 1858-1920. *2100*
—. Ontario, southern. Population. 1871-1975. *3763*
—. Physicians. 1966. *3250*
—. Police. Reform. 1854-1960's. *1262*
—. Politics. Suburbs. 1965-75. *2360*
—. Population. Rural areas. 1970's. *2205*
—. Population. Sectionalism. ca 1970-78. *2263*
—. Population. Social change. Technology. 1970's. *2282*
—. Public Opinion. 1920-70. *2221*
—. Race Relations. Residential segregation. 1960-70. *3053*
—. School Integration. 1970's. *2898*
—. School Integration. Social Change. 1970's. *3036*
—. School Integration. White flight. 1955-70. *2891*
—. Social problems. 1970's. *2220*
Metropolitan Community Church. California (Los Angeles). Homosexuality. Religion. 1970-76. *3214*
Metropolitan Government. 1957-70's. *2384*
—. City Planning. Green, Andrew. New York City. 1865-90. *1837*
—. Crime and Criminals. Economic Growth. Florida (Duval County; Jacksonville). Unemployment. 1967-73. *2265*
—. Local government. 1945-74. *2388*
—. Local Government. Property tax. 1974. *2408*
—. Local Politics. Voting and Voting Behavior. 1945-70. *2490*
—. New York City. 1970's. *2398*
—. Politics. Voting and Voting Behavior. 1979. *2374*
—. Public Administration. 1965-73. *2393*
—. Utah (Salt Lake City). Voting and Voting Behavior. 1973-75. *2400*
Metropolitan Historical Commission. Cumberland River. Historical Sites and Parks. Tennessee (Nashville). Waterfront. 1976. *3509*
Metropolitan Life Insurance Company. Civil rights. Discrimination, Housing. LaGuardia, Fiorello. New York City (Stuyvesant Town). Public housing. 1943. *3367*
Metropolitan Police Force. Louisiana (New Orleans). Negroes. Politics. Riots. Whites. 1868. *1235*

Metropolitan Protective Association. New Mexico (Santa Fe). New York City. Reform. Sanitation. Spiegelberg, Flora Langermann. 1875-1943. *661*
Mexican Americans. Acculturation. Church Schools. Public Schools. Texas (San Antonio). 1973. *3156*
—. Art. California (East Los Angeles). Mechicano Art Center. Murals. 1970's. *2786*
—. Art. California (East Los Angeles). Murals, street. Values. 1978. *2816*
—. Art. California (Los Angeles). Ethnicity. Murals, street. 1970's. *3164*
—. Artists. California (East Los Angeles, Los Angeles; Boyle Heights). Ethnicity. Murals. 1965-75. *3153*
—. Assimilation. Ethnicity. Intermarriage. Texas (San Antonio). Women. 1830-60. *1523*
—. Assimilation. Southwest. Urbanization. 1900-30. *3161*
—. Attitudes. Colorado (Denver). Negroes. Neighborhoods. Public services. Whites. 1970's. *3612*
—. Attitudes. Education. Immigration. Negroes. Wisconsin (Racine). 1974. *3047*
—. Attitudes. Negroes. Race Relations. Texas (Houston). Whites. -1973. *3023*
—. Automobiles. California (East Los Angeles). Leisure. Low-riders. Youth. 1970's. *3154*
—. Barrios. California (East Los Angeles). Murals. Social Conditions. 1970-75. *3155*
—. Barrios. California (East Los Angeles). Political activism. 1970-73. *3166*
—. Barrios. Clinics. Decisionmaking. 1969-70. *3241*
—. Barrios. Family. Housing. Relocation. -1973. *3165*
—. Bureaucracies. Government. Minorities in Politics. Nebraska (Omaha). Wisconsin (Milwaukee). 1970's. *3140*
—. California (East Los Angeles). Ethnic Groups. Political protest. Social Change. 1968-74. *3159*
—. California (East San Jose; Mayfair district). Ghettos. Social Change. 1777-1975. *1537*
—. California (Los Angeles). Citizens Committee for the Defense of Mexican-American Youth. "Sleepy Lagoon" trial. Trials. 1942-44. *1522*
—. California (Los Angeles). Congress of Industrial Organizations. Labor Unions and Organizations. 1938-50. *576*
—. California (Los Angeles). Curricula. Educational reform. Public schools. 1920's-30's. *1081*
—. California (Los Angeles). Economic Conditions. Family. Immigrants. Michigan (Detroit). Whites. 1850-80. *1313*
—. California (Los Angeles). Education. Racism. 1920-32. *1526*
—. California (Los Angeles). Family. Modernization. Social change. 1850-80. *1528*
—. California (Los Angeles). Migration, Internal. Occupational mobility. 1918-28. *843*
—. California (Los Angeles). Negroes. Social Change. Suburbanization. 1960's-75. *3049*
—. California (Los Angeles). Pacific Electric Railroad. Strikes. 1900-03. *638*
—. California (Los Angeles). Public health. 1850-87. *1527*
—. California (Los Angeles). Social mobility. Working Class. 1850-80. *1529*
—. California (Los Angeles). Spanish language. 1960's-70's. *3157*
—. California (Los Angeles). United Mexican American Students. Youth Movements. 1967-69. *3162*
—. California (Monterey). Migration, Internal. Social change. Whites. 1835-50. *129*
—. California (Orange County). Medical Care (costs). Whites. -1973. *3258*
—. Children. Japanese Americans. Political participation. Whites. 1970's. *3051*
—. City Government. Employment. Negroes. Texas. Urbanization. 1973. *3029*
—. City Government. Political Factions. Texas (Crystal City). 1970-76. *3147*
—. City Life. Economic Conditions. Negroes. Social Organization. 1960-71. *3048*
—. City Politics. Power structure. Social organization. Texas (Crystal City). 1963-70. *2452*
—. Colorado (Denver). Negroes. Political attitudes. Voting and Voting Behavior. 1971. *3037*
—. Daily Life. Poverty. Social Conditions. Southwest. 1945-77. *3158*
—. Depressions. Indiana (East Chicago). Repatriation. 1919-33. *1538*

—. Depressions. Indiana (Gary). Nativism. Repatriation. 1920's-30's. *1520*
—. Economic Conditions. Negroes. Whites. Wisconsin (Racine). 1960-71. *3024*
—. Education. Income. Indiana (South Bend). Population. Social Mobility. *3144*
—. Elections. School boards. Texas (Crystal City). 1970. *3152*
—. Employment. Illinois (Chicago Heights). Politics. Social Conditions. 1910-76. *3145*
—. Ethnicity. Minnesota (St. Paul, lower west side). 1914-65. *1533*
—. Graffiti. Names. 1967-75. *3151*
—. Illinois (Chicago). Immigration. Social Conditions. 1910's-20's. *1536*
—. Illinois (Chicago). Neighborhoods. Social conditions. 1920-70. *3034*
—. Immigration. Indiana (East Chicago; Indiana Harbor). Inland Steel Company. Michigan, Lake. Social Conditions. 1919-32. *1521*
—. Immigration. Labor. Women. 1970's. *3149*
—. Negroes. Texas (Austin). Voluntary associations. Whites. 1969-70. *2702*
—. Texas (El Paso). Voting and voting behavior. 1972. *3146*
—. Texas (Lubbock). Values. 1974. *3137*
Mexicans. California (Los Angeles County). Davis, James J. Deportation. Depressions. Unemployment. 1931. *1530*
—. Discrimination, employment. Labor Unions and Organizations. Texas (El Paso). 1880-1920. *1524*
—. Illinois (Chicago). Labor. 1908-30. *1535*
Mexico. Agricultural Labor. California (El Monte). Foreign Relations. Japan. Strikes. 1933. *600*
—. Anza, Juan Bautista de. California (San Francisco). Discovery and Exploration. Settlement. 1775-76. *152*
—. Canada. South America. Subways. USA. 19c-1978. *3457*
Mexico (Tijuana). California (San Diego). City Planning. Economic Growth. 1970's. *2287*
—. California (San Diego). Freedom of Speech. Industrial Workers of the World. 1911-12. *628*
M'Grath, Michael. Devit, Charles. Murder. Nova Scotia (Halifax). Trials. Westmacott, John. 1816. *3771*
Miami Design Preservation League. Art Deco. Buildings. Florida (Miami Beach). Preservation. 1920-35. 1978. *3500*
Michigan *See also* North Central States.
—. Children. Coldwater State Public School. Protestantism. Public Schools. Social Reform. 1874-96. *1178*
—. City Government. Tree care. 1960-73. *3269*
—. Culture. Flint Scientific Institute. Grand Rapids Public Museum. Museums. Science. 1853-1917. *990*
—. Detroit Citizens League. Leland, Henry. Progressivism. Social Classes. 1912-24. *362*
—. Detroit Medical Center. Urban Renewal. 1972. *2212*
—. Labor Unions and Organizations. Politics. Reform. Saloons. Working class. 1830-1910. *869*
—. Methodology. Political Participation. Psychology. 1968. *2445*
Michigan (Ann Arbor). Assimilation. German Americans. Pluralism. Protestantism. Württembergers. 1830-1955. *1295*
Michigan (Battle Creek). Labor Disputes. Open shop movement. Post, Charles William. 1895-1920. *612*
Michigan (Bay City, Saginaw). Community Participation in Politics. Lumbermen. Strikes. 1880's. *603*
Michigan (Carp River Region; Marquette). Everett, Phil Marshall. Iron Industry. Jackson Iron Company. Marquette Iron Company. 1670-1854. *192*
Michigan (Dearborn, Detroit). Busing. Racism. Social change. 1974. *2893*
Michigan (Detroit). Americanization. Education. Jewish Family and Children's Service. Voluntary Associations. 1876-1976. *1463*
—. Anti-Semitism. 1850-1914. *1473*
—. Arab Americans. Immigration. Settlement. 1961-74. *3182*
—. Automobile Industry and Trade. City Politics. Negroes. United Automobile Workers of America. 1945-78. *2315*
—. Automobile Industry and Trade. Economic Conditions. 20c. *2600*
—. Automobile Industry and Trade. Finnish Americans. 1900-40. *1620*

—. Metropolitan Areas. Regional government. Twin Cities Metropolitan Council. 1967-73. *2377*

—. Neighborhoods. Newspapers. Public affairs. 1969-74. *2781*

—. Regional Government. 1950-70's. *2314*

Minnesota (Moorhead). Competition. Economic development. North Dakota (Fargo). Railroads. 1870's. *55*

Minnesota (Rice County). Community Participation in Politics (review article). Fish, John Hall. Illinois (Chicago). Organization for a Better Rice County. Poor. Temporary Woodlawn Organization. Wellstone, Paul D. 1970-76. *2464*

Minnesota (St. Paul). Adams, John Quincy (1848-1922). Editors and Editing. Negroes. *Western Appeal.* 1888-1922. *1416*

—. Capitols. Location. State Government. 1849-1905. *332*

—. Fitzgerald, F. Scott. Middle classes. Social status. 1900's-20's. *2161*

—. Negroes. Police. 1890-1975. *1362*

—. Winter Carnival. 1886-1979. *920*

Minnesota (St. Paul; lower west side). Ethnicity. Mexican Americans. 1914-65. *1533*

—. Immigrants. Jews. Settlement. ca 1860-1920. *1466*

Minorities *See also* Discrimination; Ethnic Groups; Nationalism; Population; Racism; Segregation.

—. Aid to Families with Dependent Children. Migration, Internal. Public Welfare. -1973. *2208*

—. Aspira (organization). Educational Reform. Harlem Parents Union. New York City. Pennsylvania (Philadelphia). Voluntary Associations. Welfare Rights Organization. 1970's. *2840*

—. Attitudes. Behavior. Employment. Poverty. Texas (Houston). 1974. *2706*

—. Bureaucracies. Community control. New York City. Political Leadership. 1972-74. *2443*

—. California (Oakland). City government. Employment. 1965-73. *3052*

—. City Government. Economic Conditions. New Jersey (Passaic). 1960's-70's. *2209*

—. City government. Equal Employment Opportunity Act (US, 1972). Federal Policy. Public Employees. Women. 1972-78. *2539*

—. City Planning. Suburbs. Transportation. 1960-76. *3450*

—. City Politics. Community Action Program. Decisionmaking. Rhode Island (Providence). 1965-69. *2455*

—. Civil disobedience. Fiscal crisis. Working Class. 1970's. *2340*

—. Clinics. Health care. 1974. *3240*

—. Colleges and Universities. Economic Conditions. Education. 1970's. *2902*

—. Decentralization. Educational Reform. Law. New York (Rochester). Whites. 1975. *2820*

—. Discrimination. Medicine (practice of). Mental Institutions. Social Classes. 1830-75. *1736*

—. Economic Change. Housing. Illinois (Chicago). Population. 1960-70. *2665*

—. Economic Conditions. Government. Population. Social Problems. 1900-70's. *2254*

—. Economic Conditions. Housing. Social Status. Urbanization. Whites. 1960. 1970. *3016*

—. Economic Growth. Federal Programs. Ghettos. 1965-73. *2576*

—. Educational achievement. New York City. Whites. 1960-73. *2882*

—. Employment. Fiscal policy. Metropolitan areas. Population. Social conditions. 1970's. *2667*

—. Employment. Ghettos. Highways. Segregation. Suburbs. -1973. *3474*

—. Metropolitan areas. Planning. School Integration. 1960's-70's. *2897*

—. Middle Classes. Migration, Internal. Suburbs. 1940's-70's. *2266*

—. New York City. Proportional representation. School Boards. 1969-74. *2505*

—. New York City. Public Schools. Ravitch, Diane (review article). Social Change. 1805-1973. *1082*

—. New York City (South Bronx; Morrisania). People's Development Corporation. Urban Renewal. 1974-79. *2578*

—. Reform. Secondary Education. ca 1970's. *2899*

Minorities in Politics. Assimilation. California (Los Angeles). Korean Americans. 1970. *3168*

—. Bradley, Tom. California (Los Angeles). Coalitions. Elections (mayoral). Social status. 1969-73. *2473*

—. Bureaucracies. Government. Mexican Americans. Nebraska (Omaha). Wisconsin (Milwaukee). 1970's. *3140*

—. City Government. Elections, mayoral. Negroes. 1970-77. *2476*

—. City Politics. Hispanic Americans. Illinois (Chicago). Voting and Voting Behavior. 1975. *2500*

—. Civil rights. Liberals. New York City. Social reform. 1963-70's. *3033*

—. Economic Conditions. Georgia (Atlanta). Louisiana (New Orleans). 1960's-79. *3076*

—. Georgia (Atlanta). Jackson, Maynard. Negroes. 1940's-74. *2332*

—. Negroes. New York City. 1889-1902. *1359*

—. New York City. Public Welfare. 1960-77. *2447*

Minstrel shows. Dance competitions. Individualism. Louisiana (New Orleans). 1840's-50's. *864*

Minuit, Peter. Indians. Land. New Netherland (New Amsterdam). Settlement. 1624-25. *232*

Mirabel International Airport. Quebec (Montreal). 1969-78. *3879*

Mission Cliff Gardens. Amusement parks. California (San Diego). 1898-1942. *902*

Missions and Missionaries. Adventists. Cudney, A. J. Nebraska (Lincoln). 1885-87. *1681*

—. California. Military Camps and Forts. 1769-84. *74*

—. California (San Diego). Excavations. Military Camps and Forts. Serra Museum. 1769-75. 1964-70's. *2112*

—. Church of England. Nova Scotia (Halifax). Tutty, William. 1752-78. *3868*

—. Episcopal Church, Protestant. Nebraska (Omaha). 1891-1902. *1670*

—. Illinois (Chicago). Manitoba (Winnipeg). Mennonites. 1866-1977. *1646*

—. Indians. New Mexico (Santa Fe). Settlement. Spaniards. 1540-1882. *157*

—. Metropolitan Areas. Presbyterian Church. 1869-1977. *1687*

Mississippi. Economic Development. Geography. 1699-1840. *54*

—. Fire Fighting. 1814-50's. *2039*

Mississippi (Biloxi, Gulfport). Hospitals. 1907-63. *1709*

Mississippi (Jackson). Hemingway, William. Local Government. Mississippi, University of. 1901-37. *296*

Mississippi (Laurel). Lumber and Lumbering. 1882-1916. *496*

Mississippi (Natchez). Norman, Henry C. Photography. 1870's-1900's. *1812*

Mississippi (Oxford). Automobiles. 1900-10. *2068*

Mississippi River. Commerce. Economic Development. Louisiana (New Orleans). Technology. 1850-1950. *417*

—. Dams. Illinois (Nauvoo). Mormons. 1830-1913. *488*

—. Economic growth. Illinois (Nauvoo). Mormons. 1839-46. *450*

—. Iowa (Davenport). Ports. 1833-50. *130*

Mississippi (Tupelo). Disaster Relief. Tornadoes. 1936. *2118*

Mississippi, University of. Hemingway, William. Local Government. Mississippi (Jackson). 1901-37. *296*

Mississippi (Vicksburg). Slavery. Wade, Richard. 1850-60. 1964. *1339*

Mississippi (Washington). City Life. 1800's-50's. *42*

Missouri *See also* North Central States.

—. Catholic Church. English language. French language. St. Louis Cathedral. 1818-42. *1688*

—. Democratic Party (Bourbons). Francis, David R. Rural-urban alliance. 1894-96. *257*

—. Fire departments. Professionalization. St. Louis Firemen's Association. Violence. 1850-57. *726*

—. German Americans. Immigrants. Reading. St. Louis Free Congregation Library (records). 1850-99. *1619*

—. Mass Transit. Modernization. Monopolies. St. Louis Transit Company. Strikes. 1900. *619*

—. St. Louis Zoological Society. Zoos. 1910-16. *884*

Missouri and North Arkansas Railroad. Arkansas (northern). Economic Growth. Railroads. Settlement. 1880-1920's. *122*

Missouri Athletic Club. Building codes. City Government. Fire. St. Louis Seed Company. 1903-18. *2136*

Missouri Fur Company. Indians (agencies). Nebraska (Bellevue). 1822-42. *135*

Missouri (Kansas City). Annexation. City Government. Kansas. 1855-84. *324*

—. Art. Business. Remington, Frederic. 1883-85. *1032*

—. Buildings. Grand Opera House. Judah, Abraham. Theater. 1883-1926. *969*

—. Business. McGee family. 1828-1918. *466*

—. City Government. Pendergast. Thomas. Progressivism. 1900-26. *378*

—. City Politics. Crime and Criminals. Demography. Police policies. 1970's. *2980*

—. Community Participation in Politics. Urban Renewal. Voluntary associations. 1971. *3375*

—. Cooperative Urban Teacher Education. Ghettos. Teacher Training. 1964-73. *2887*

—. Enrollment. Race Relations. School Integration. 1956-74. *2856*

—. Federal Government. Housing allowances. 1970-74. *3408*

—. Housing and Urban Development Department. Model Cities Program. Subsidies. 1972-75. *2927*

—. Negroes. Pendergast, Thomas. Political machines. Truman, Harry S. 1922-34. *291*

Missouri (Kansas City, St. Louis). City Government. Migration, Internal. Negroes. Philanthropy. Public Health. 1879. *1361*

Missouri (Kansas City; Westport). Architecture. Restorations. 1970-78. *3540*

Missouri (St. Louis). Advocacy. California (San Francisco). Louisiana (New Orleans). Negroes. Public Administration. 1974-78. *3087*

—. African Baptist Church. Education. Emancipation. Meachum, John Berry. Negroes. 1815-54. *1389*

—. Air Pollution. Smoke abatement. 1891-1924. *1735*

—. Aloe, Louis Patrick. Anti-Semitism. Elections (mayoral). Jews. Progressivism. 1910-25. *281*

—. American Bar Association. Law. 1874-1974. *1293*

—. American Civil Liberties Union. Law. Mass media campaign. Privacy. 1975-76. *2768*

—. Architecture. Bradley, Lucas. Wisconsin (Racine). 1840-90. *1950*

—. Architecture. Historical Sites and Parks. Water towers. 1870-1970. *2113*

—. Assimilation. Italian Americans. World War I. 1914-18. *1602*

—. Atheism. Bobb, John. Periodicals. *Western Examiner.* 1834-35. *1645*

—. Ballet. Field, Joseph M. Varieties Theatre. 1852. *1042*

—. Banking. Brotherhood of Railway Telegraphers. Gardner, Vernon O. Labor Unions and Organizations. Manion, Edward J. Telegraphers National Bank. 1922-42. *537*

—. Baseball. Civic pride. 1867-75. *855*

—. Belcher, Wyatt W. Business. Illinois (Chicago). Leadership. 1830-80. *200*

—. Bridges. Eads Bridge. Eads, James B. 1874. *1930*

—. Buildings. Downtown areas. 1874. *1929*

—. Business. Elites. Progressivism. Reform. 1900-15. *1179*

—. California (San Francisco). City life. Education. Libraries. Mercantile Library Association. 1840-56. *1010*

—. Catholic Church. Church Schools. Glennon, John J. Ritter, Joseph E. School Integration. 1935-47. *1665*

—. Catholic Church. Clergy. 1841-99. *1660*

—. Centennial Celebrations. Louisiana Purchase Exposition. 1904. *916*

—. Cholera. Epidemics. Public Health committee. 1849-67. *1711*

—. Chopin, Kate. Fiction. Social criticism. ca 1889-1902. *2184*

—. City Government. Conflict and Conflict Resolution. Frontier and Pioneer Life. 19c. *237*

—. City Government. Merry, Samuel. Political Change. Suffrage. 1833-38. *258*

—. City Government. Political Reform. Progressivism. 1893-1904. *361*

—. City Planning. Poor. Public housing. 1975. *3398*

—. Competition. Economic Growth. Illinois (Chicago). 1850-1910. *127*

—. Compulsory education. Immigrants. Public Schools. Truancy. 1905-07. *1092*

—. Crime and Criminals. Newspapers. Reporters and Reporting. 1969-72. *2769*

—. Czech Americans. Ethnicity. Neighborhoods. Social organizations. 1848-1970. *1575*

—. DeBar's Grand Opera House. Olympic Theatre. Railroads. Stage Setting and Scenery. Theater. 1870-79. *997*
—. Democratic Party. Elections. Know-Nothing Party. Local Politics. Riots. 1844-56. *1279*
—. Development. Historical Sites and Parks. Lafayette Square. 1836-1926. *1802*
—. Economic Development. Illinois (Chicago). Leadership. Ohio (Cincinnati). Wisconsin (Milwaukee). 1830-80. *149*
—. Economic Development. Urbanization. 1764-1865. *100*
—. Economic Growth. RAND Corporation (report). Suburbs. Urbanization. 1973. *2288*
—. Educational Reform. Vocational Education. Woodward, Calvin. 1897-1914. *1076*
—. English. French. Travel Accounts. 1874-89. *2160*
—. Episcopal Church, Protestant. Social reform. 1880-1920. *1664*
—. Ethnic Groups. Negroes. Residential segregation. 1850-1930. *1331*
—. Films. Louisiana Purchase Exposition. Museums. Public schools. 1901-78. *1104*
—. Ideology. Public schools. Troen, Selwyn K. (review article). 1838-1920. 1975. *1097*
—. Illinois (Chicago). Industry. Maryland (Baltimore). Pennsylvania (Pittsburgh). Railroads. Strikes. 1877. *631*
—. Indian-White Relations. *Marguerite* v. *Chouteau* (Missouri, 1834). Slavery. 1764-1834. *1600*
—. Law. Negroes, Free. Slaves. 1800-30. *1402*
—. Metropolitan areas. Police. Public administration. 1972-74. *2972*
—. Missouri, University of, St. Louis. Oral history. St. Louis Teachers Strike. Strikes. 1973. *3951*
—. Negroes. Public Opinion. Social Problems. Whites. 1970. *3617*
—. Negroes. School Integration. 1954-55. *2837*
—. Negroes. Young Men's Christian Association. 1877-1976. *743*
—. Negroes (free). Race Relations. 1830-70. *1352*
—. Neighborhood associations (private). Segregation. 1850-1930. *793*
—. Olympic Theater. Short, Patrick. Theater. 1889-1916. *965*
—. Public Schools. School Attendance. 1970's. *2827*
—. Public Schools. Social Organization. Troen, Selwyn K. (review article). 1838-1920. 1975. *1120*
—. Sesquicentennial Celebrations. 1914. *900*
—. Slavery. 1804-60. *1375*
Missouri (St. Louis; Bremen, Hyde Park districts). Architecture. Middle classes. Values. 1835-1976. *1938*
Missouri (St. Louis; The Hill). Ethnicity. Italian Americans. Social Classes. 1890-1970. *3199*
Missouri (St. Louis, University City). Entrepreneurs. Government. Lewis, Edward Gardner. Publishers and Publishing. *Woman's Magazine*. 1893-1928. *939*
Missouri (St. Louis; Ville). Ethnic Groups. Negroes. Residential segregation. 1900-70. *1408*
Missouri (Sedalia). Cattle Raising. Economic growth. 1856-66. *511*
Missouri (Springfield). City Planning. Economic Conditions. 1865-81. *187*
Missouri, University of, St. Louis. Missouri (St. Louis). Oral history. St. Louis Teachers Strike. Strikes. 1973. *3951*
Mitchel, John Purroy. Committee on Unemployment and Relief. Gary, Elbert H. New York City. Progressives. Unemployment. 1914-17. *382*
—. Educational reform. Indiana (Gary). New York City. 1914-17. *1100*
—. Elections (mayoral). Ethnicity. Hylan, John F. New York City. Patriotism. World War I. 1917. *284*
Mitchell-Lama program. City Government. Housing. Middle Classes. New York City. Subsidies. 1955-68. *3373*
—. Housing. Limited Profit Housing Law (New York City, 1955). New York City. 1955-75. *3401*
Mobile homes. Houses. Suburbs. Voluntary Associations. 1970's. *2693*
Mobility. See Geographic Mobility; Social Mobility.
Model Cities Program. California (San Francisco; Mission district). Community Participation in Politics. Employment. Poverty. 1960's-70's. *2568*

—. City Government. Federal Government. Frieden, Bernard J. Gelfand, Mark I. Haar, Charles M. Intergovernmental relations (review article). Kaplan, Marshall. Political Reform. Pressman, Jeffrey L. 1930's-70's. *2556*
—. Employment. Federal Policy. Ghettos. Negroes. 1969-73. *2538*
—. Federal Government. Grants, block. Local Government. 1970's. *2519*
—. Housing and Urban Development Department. Missouri (Kansas City). Subsidies. 1972-75. *2927*
Model Cities program (review article). Frieden, Bernard J. Haar, Charles M. Kaplan, Marshall. Urban Renewal. 1960's-70's. *2529*
Models See also Methodology.
—. Assimilation. New York City. Puerto Ricans. Residential segregation. 1960-70. *3163*
—. British Columbia (Vancouver). Elections. Political parties. 1937-74. *3692*
—. Burgess, Ernest W. Housing. Occupations. Pennsylvania (Philadelphia). 1920-60. *3271*
—. Canada. Development. Residential patterns. USA. 1973. *3272*
—. City planning. Electronic Data Processing. 1950-75. *3356*
—. City planning. Land. Prices. 1972. *3267*
—. Davis-Swanson model. Urbanization. 1890-1910. *94*
—. Decentralization. Michigan (Detroit). New York City. Schools. 1975. *2874*
—. Economic Development. Land use. Location theory. 1960-73. *2219*
—. Educational Reform. Michigan (Detroit). New York City. School boards. 1966-76. *2849*
—. Immigration. Massachusetts (Boston). North America. Pennsylvania (Philadelphia). South Carolina (Charleston). 16c-17c. *92*
—. Nash, Gary B. Quantitative Methods. Urbanization. Warden, Gerard B. 18c. *4021*
—. New Zealand. Population. Urbanization. 1970's. *2291*
—. Planning organizations. 1970's. *3332*
—. Population. Violence. 1940-70. *2971*
—. Suburbs. Traffic. 1972. *3479*
Models, linear. Geography. Illinois. Retail trade. 1960's. *2588*
Modernism. Architecture. City planning. Europe. Housing. New Deal. New York City. Ohio (Cleveland). Pennsylvania (Philadelphia). 1932-60. *1952*
Modernization See also Economic Theory; Industrialization; Social Change.
—. Amoskeag Manufacturing Company. Ethnocentrism. Family. Industrial Relations. New Hampshire (Manchester). 1912-22. *776*
—. Behavior. Immigration. Peasants. Slavic Americans. Working class. 1850-1925. *1298*
—. B'nai B'rith Lodge. Jews. Oregon (Portland). Social Change. Voluntary Associations. 1920's. *756*
—. California (Los Angeles). Family. Mexican Americans. Social change. 1850-80. *1528*
—. California (San Diego). Economic development. 1850-60. *429*
—. California (San Francisco). Reform. Social Conditions. Workingmen's Party of California. 1870-80. *810*
—. Economic development. Industrialization. Massachusetts. Waltham-Lowell system. 1815-60. *480*
—. Fire Departments. New York City. Shaler, Alexander. 1865-1971. *2033*
—. Mass Transit. Missouri. Monopolies. St. Louis Transit Company. Strikes. 1900. *619*
Mohl, Raymond A. History Teaching. McKelvey, Blake. Miller, Zane L. Richardson, James F. Still, Bayrd. Textbooks. Urban history (review article). Warner, Sam Bass, Jr. 1972-74. *3981*
Molokans. California (San Francisco). Ethnicity. Sects, Religious. 1906-76. *1647*
Molton, Flora. District of Columbia. Folk songs. Negroes. Women. 1930's-70's. *903*
Molybdenum. AMAX, Inc. Colorado (Crested Butte). Mines. Preservation. Resorts. 1880's-1978. *3522*
Monkkonen, Eric H. (review article). Crime and Criminals. Industrialism. Ohio (Columbus). Poverty. Urbanization. 1860-85. 1975. *1247*
Monopolies See also Capitalism; Railroads.
—. Company Towns. Ethnic Groups. Indiana (Gary). Middle Classes. US Steel Corporation. 1905-76. *113*
—. Competition. Local Government. Metropolitan areas. 1975. *2354*

—. Dispensary Act. Liquor trade. Manning, Richard Irvine. South Carolina (Charleston). 1915-18. *312*
—. Grand Trunk Railway Company. Quebec (Montreal). Strikes. Teamsters. 1864. *3733*
—. Ice industry. Law. Nebraska. Omaha Ice Trust. 1899-1900. *438*
—. Mass Transit. Missouri. Modernization. St. Louis Transit Company. Strikes. 1900. *619*
Monroe, Harriet. Illinois (Chicago). Periodicals. *Poetry*. 1870's-1910's. *1062*
Montana See also Western States.
—. Fisk, Robert E. Helena Board of Trade. Urbanization. 1864-81. *63*
—. Food Industry. Grocery stores. Lutey Brothers Marketeria. 1897-1924. *442*
—. Ghost towns. 1950-74. *3511*
Montana (Augusta, Gilman). Competition. Railroads. 1912-76. *84*
Montana (Butte). Authors. Feminism. MacLane, Mary. 1902-29. *1015*
—. Authors. MacLane, Mary. Women. 1901-29. *1058*
Montana Club. Montana (Helena). 1884-1976. *745*
Montana (Coburg). Agriculture. Railroads. 1880-1940. *66*
Montana (Fort Benton). Mullan Road. Trade. Washington (Walla Walla). Westward Movement. 1860-83. *2091*
Montana (Helena). Bass, Joseph B. *Montana Plaindealer*. Negroes. Press. 1900-12. *1379*
—. Compton, Arthur. Hanging. Vigilantes. Wilson, George. 1870. *1282*
—. Dance halls. Prostitution. Welch, Mary Josephine ("Chicago Joe"). 1867-99. *1264*
—. Last Chance Urban Renewal Project. Restorations. Urban renewal. 1972-77. *3574*
—. Montana Club. 1884-1976. *745*
Montana (Kendall). Ghost towns. Gold Mines and Mining. 1900-20. 1974. *102*
Montana (Lewistown). Construction. Croatian Americans. Ethnic Groups. 1897-1920. *1626*
Montana Plaindealer. Bass, Joseph B. Montana (Helena). Negroes. Press. 1900-12. *1379*
Montezuma Hotel. Architecture. Burnham, Daniel Hudson. New Mexico (Las Vegas). Root, John Wellborn. 1879-85. *1919*
Montreal Citizens' Movement. Drapeau, Jean. Pressure Groups. Quebec. 1957-76. *3694*
Montreal Snowshoe Club. Quebec. Snowshoe clubs. 1840's-1900's. *3802*
Monuments. District of Columbia. Sculpture. 1809-1974. *983*
Moore, Alfred. Cincinnati Union Terminal. Ohio. Railroads. 1933-73. *3568*
Morality See also Ethics; Values.
—. Artisans. Industrialization. Pennsylvania (Philadelphia). Social customs. Work ethic. Working Class. 1820-50. *787*
—. Attitudes. Ku Klux Klan. Ohio (Youngstown). Reform. 1920's. *736*
—. California, northern. Mormons. Sex. Utah (Salt Lake City). Youth. 1967-69. *3225*
—. Charities. New York. Rural-Urban Studies. 1783-1830. *1158*
—. Female Moral Reform Society. New York (Utica). Reform. Social Organization. 1830's-40's. *1189*
—. Georgia (Macon). Ku Klux Klan. Violence. Yarbrough, C. A. 1919-25. *735*
—. Ku Klux Klan. Louisiana (Shreveport). 1920-29. *731*
—. Lane, James B. (review article). Riis, Jacob. Social Reform. 1890's-1920. *1141*
Moravian Church. American Revolution. Pennsylvania (Bethlehem). 1775-83. *1226*
—. Architecture. Pennsylvania (Bethlehem, Nazareth). 1740-68. *1925*
Morgan, Elizabeth Chambers. Illinois (Chicago). Labor reform. 1874-97. *1191*
Morgan, Thomas John. Elections. Labor Unions and Organizations. Reform. Socialism. United Labor Party. 1886-96. *302*
Morgan v. *Hennigan* (Massachusetts, 1974). Desegregation. Law and Society. Massachusetts (Boston). Negroes. Schools. 1974-75. *2817*
Morial, Ernest N. Democratic Party. Louisiana (New Orleans). Negroes. Political Campaigns (mayoral). 1977. *2499*
Mormons. Architects. Churches. Folsom, William Harrison. Utah (Provo, Salt Lake City). ca 1850's-1901. *1861*
—. Architecture. City Planning. Smith, Joseph. Western States. 1833-90. *1822*

N

Nash, Gary B. Models. Quantitative Methods. Urbanization. Warden, Gerard B. 18c. *4021*

Nashville and Northwestern Railway. Martin, William. Railroads. Tennessee (Martin). 1832-93. *220*

Nashville (film). *Cabaret* (film). Germany (Berlin). Music. Social criticism. Tennessee. 1930's-70's. *3596*

Nassau Street Riots. Golden Hill (battle). New York City. Riots. 1770. *1208*

Nation, Carrie. Florida (Miami). Temperance Movements. 1908-13. *1148*

National Action Group. Busing. Michigan (Pontiac). 1971-72. *2846*

National Characteristics *See also* National Self-image; Nationalism.

—. Attitudes. Hawaii (Honolulu). Japanese Americans. 1971. *3174*

National Conference on City Planning. City Planning. Crowding. Marsh, Benjamin C. Poor. Social Reform. 1900-17. *1834*

National Congress of Neighborhood Women. Community action. New York City (Brooklyn; Williamsburg). Politics. Women. 1966-78. *2690*

National Council on the Arts. Arts. National Endowment for the Arts. Subsidies. Washington (Seattle). 1969-75. *2792*

National Endowment for the Arts. Arts. National Council on the Arts. Subsidies. Washington (Seattle). 1969-75. *2792*

—. Discrimination. Employment. Musicians. Negroes. Symphony orchestras. 1974-75. *3065*

National Guard *See also* Militia.

—. Armories. Buildings. Maryland (Baltimore). 1858-1962. *1970*

—. California (San Francisco). Earthquakes. Pardee, George C. Schmitz, Eugene. 1906. *1239*

National Institute of Education. Metropolitan Areas. Public policy. School Integration. Supreme Court. 1970's. *2844*

National Municipal League (Conference on Government). All-America Cities award program. 1977. *2461*

National Recreation Areas. California (Santa Monica Mountains). Real Estate. 1960's-70's. *3427*

National Register of Historic Places. Historical Sites and Parks. Massachusetts. Newbury Historic District. Society for the Preservation of New England Antiquities. 1976. *3490*

National Self-image *See also* National Characteristics.

—. Anti-Communist movements. Anti-Semitism. Freedom of speech. Immigration. Ontario (Toronto). 1928-29. *3629*

—. Attitudes. Metropolitan areas. Migration, Internal. 1975. *3594*

—. Canada. Ethnicity. Ontario (Toronto). 1970. *3849*

National Socialist White People's Party. City Politics. Jews. Koehl, Matt. Nazism. Wisconsin (Milwaukee). 1974-76. *2432*

National Textile Workers Union. North Carolina (Gastonia). Reminiscences. Strikes. Textile Industry. Weisbord, Vera Buch. 1929. *636*

National Trust for Historic Preservation. Economic development. Illinois (Galesburg). Indiana (Madison). Preservation. South Dakota (Hot Springs). Streets, main. Towns. 19c-1978. *3496*

National Trust Main Street Project. Galesburg Historical Society. Illinois. Preservation. 1975-76. *3579*

National Urban Land Program. California (Oakland). Neighborhoods. New Jersey (Newark). New York City (South Bronx). Public Lands. Real Estate. Trust for Public Land. 1973-78. *3431*

National Urban League. Ainslie, Peter. Carey, John R. Discrimination, employment. Maryland (Baltimore). Negroes. Social conditions. 1921-35. *746*

Nationalism *See also* Independence Movements; Minorities; Patriotism.

—. Assimilation. French Canadians. Religion. Rhode Island (Woonsocket). 1924-29. *1616*

—. Clan na Gael. Illinois (Chicago). Irish Americans. Politics. 1880's. *1508*

Nativism. Actors and Actresses. Forrest, Edwin. Macready, William Charles. New York City (Astor Place). Riots. 1849. *2963*

—. Anglo-Japanese Treaty of Alliance (1902). Asiatic Exclusion League. British Columbia (Vancouver). Canada. Japan. Riots. USA. 1907-22. *1283*

—. Chicopee Manufacturing Company. Immigration. Irish Americans. Massachusetts (Chicopee). Mills. 1830-75. *1506*

—. City Politics. Immigrants. Ohio (Cincinnati). Temperance. 1845-60. *1306*

—. Depressions. Indiana (Gary). Mexican Americans. Repatriation. 1920's-30's. *1520*

—. Indiana (Gary, Valparaiso). Ku Klux Klan. 1920's. *720*

Natural Gas *See also* Oil and Petroleum Products.

—. Boom towns. Indiana (Albany). 1886-1910. *99*

Natural History *See also* Geology; Museums.

—. American Museum of Natural History, Alexander M. White Natural Science Center. Children. Ecology. Museums. New York City. 1974-75. *2801*

Natural Resources *See also* Conservation of Natural Resources; Fishing; Mineral Resources; Wilderness.

—. British Columbia. Multinational Corporations. Provincial government. Settlement. Social Classes. Towns. 1965-72. *3644*

—. British Columbia (Vancouver). Economic Growth. Population. 19c. *3632*

—. Canada. Economic Development. Iron Ore Company. Quebec (Schefferville). 1954-78. *3716*

—. Canada (northern). City Planning. 1945-78. *3634*

—. City Planning. Local government. Refuse disposal. 1973-77. *3436*

—. Economic Conditions. Federal Policy. Indian-white relations. 1831-1978. *1592*

Naturalization. Community Participation in Politics. Public Records. Scandinavian Americans. Wisconsin (Milwaukee). 1837-1941. *1560*

Nature *See also* Ecology; Wilderness.

—. Landscape architecture. 18c-19c. *2006*

Naval Bases. *See* Navy-Yards and Naval Stations.

Naval Construction. *See* Shipbuilding.

Naval Engineering. *See* Marine Engineering.

Naval Recruiting and Enlistment. *See* Conscription, Military.

Navies *See also* headings beginning with the word naval; Marine Engineering; Military; Navy-yards and Naval Stations; Shipbuilding; Torpedoes.

—. California (San Francisco Bay area). 1776-1940's. *307*

Navigation, Inland *See also* Canals; Rivers.

—. Bridges. Illinois (Chicago; Chicago River). 1832-1973. *2051*

—. Commerce. New York City (East River). Photographs. 1609-1876. *1806*

Navy-yards and Naval Stations. British Columbia (Victoria). Nova Scotia (Halifax). 1749-1971. *3627*

—. California (San Diego). House of Representatives. Kettner, William. 1907-30. *314*

Nazism. City Politics. Jews. Koehl, Matt. National Socialist White People's Party. Wisconsin (Milwaukee). 1974-76. *2432*

Neau, Elias. Church of England. Laity. Negroes. New York City. Society for the Propagation of the Gospel. 1704-22. *1658*

Nebraska *See also* Western States.

—. Ice industry. Law. Monopolies. Omaha Ice Trust. 1899-1900. *438*

Nebraska (Bellevue). Indians (agencies). Missouri Fur Company. 1822-42. *135*

Nebraska (Brownsville). Economic Development. 1854-1974. *69*

Nebraska (Crete). Band's Opera House. 1877-1900. *1041*

Nebraska (Lincoln). Adventists. Cudney, A. J. Missions and Missionaries. 1885-87. *1681*

Nebraska (Loup City). Courthouse Gang. Local Politics. Political Factions. Railroad Gang. 1887-91. *246*

Nebraska (Omaha). Bossism. City Politics. Dennison, Tom. Reform. Vice. 1890's-1934. *339*

—. Bureaucracies. Government. Mexican Americans. Minorities in Politics. Wisconsin (Milwaukee). 1970's. *3140*

—. Charities. Jews. Migration, Internal. Political Leadership. Refugees. 1820-1937. *1442*

—. Economic Conditions. Race Relations. Riots. Social Conditions. 1919. *25*

—. Episcopal Church, Protestant. Missions and Missionaries. 1891-1902. *1670*

—. Ethnic Groups. Immigration. Residential patterns. 1880-1920. *1304*

—. Judaism. Temple Israel. 1867-1908. *1441*

—. Medicine, Patent. Public Health. Sanitation. 1870-1900. *1738*

Nebraska (St. John). Economic development. Industry. Maine (Portland). Poor, John. Railroads. 1850-1914. *393*

Nee, Brett de Bary. California (San Francisco). Chinatowns. Nee, Victor G. 20c. *1542*

Nee, Victor G. California (San Francisco). Chinatowns. Nee, Brett de Bary. 20c. *1542*

Negro Labor Committee. Crosswaith, Frank R. New York City (Harlem). 1925-39. *634*

Negro World. Garvey, Amy Jacques. Newspapers. Universal Negro Improvement Association. Women. 1920's-32. *1381*

Negroes *See also* Black Capitalism; Black Nationalism; Black Power; Civil War; Discrimination; Race Relations; Racism; Reconstruction; Slavery.

—. Abolition Movement. Pennsylvania (Philadelphia). Riots. 1830-50. *1220*

—. Abolitionists. Fugitive Slaves. Pennsylvania (Pittsburgh). Philanthropic Society. 1830's-60. *1341*

—. Acculturation. Education. Immigrants. Massachusetts (Boston). Social status. 1850. *1125*

—. Actors and Actresses. African Theatre. New York City. 1820-23. *1024*

—. Adams, John Quincy (1848-1922). Editors and Editing. Minnesota (St. Paul). *Western Appeal.* 1888-1922. *1416*

—. Advocacy. California (San Francisco). Louisiana (New Orleans). Missouri (St. Louis). Public Administration. 1974-78. *3087*

—. Affirmative action. City Government. Discrimination, employment. Ohio (Cincinnati). 1963-67. *2352*

—. Africa, West. Louisiana (New Orleans; Congo Square). Music (jazz). Religion. Rites and Ceremonies. 18c-19c. *1018*

—. African Baptist Church. Education. Emancipation. Meachum, John Berry. Missouri (St. Louis). 1815-54. *1389*

—. Ainslie, Peter. Carey, John R. Discrimination, employment. Maryland (Baltimore). National Urban League. Social conditions. 1921-35. *746*

—. Alabama (Montgomery). Discrimination, educational. Georgia (Atlanta). North Carolina (Raleigh). Teachers. Tennessee (Nashville). Virginia (Richmond). 1865-90. *1106*

—. Alienation. City Government. 1968-70. *3112*

—. Aluminum Company of America. Company Towns. Labor. Leadership. Tennessee (Alcoa). 1919-39. *1396*

—. Archival Catalogs and Inventories. Local history. New York City. Personal Narratives. Staten Island Institute of Arts and Sciences. 1969-76. *4031*

—. Arizona (McNary). Company towns. Lumber and Lumbering. Segregation. Social conditions. 1924-72. *1424*

—. Arkansas (Little Rock). Attitudes. Eckford, Elizabeth. Personal Narratives. Public schools. School Integration. 1957-79. *3120*

—. Artists. Literature. New York City. Williams, John A. (interview). 1920's-70's. *3125*

—. Assimilation. Education. Immigrants. Racism. Slavic Americans. Social Mobility. 1890-1966. *1089*

—. Assimilation. Ethnic groups. Pennsylvania (Philadelphia). 1850-1970. *1314*

—. Assimilation. Mayors, black. Political participation. 1960-71. *3098*

—. Attitudes. Birth control. Clergy. Population. Tennessee (Nashville). 20c. *3079*

—. Attitudes. California (Los Angeles County). Integration. Liberals. Whites. 1972. *3018*

—. Attitudes. Civil rights. Illinois (Chicago, Evanston). Middle Classes. 1974. *3113*

—. Attitudes. Colorado (Denver). Mexican Americans. Neighborhoods. Public services. Whites. 1970's. *3612*

—. Attitudes. Education. Immigration. Mexican Americans. Wisconsin (Racine). 1974. *3047*

—. Attitudes. Ethnicity. Illinois (Chicago). Race Relations. Social Classes. 1969. *3042*

—. Attitudes. Housing. 1970. *3100*

—. Attitudes. Housing. Ohio (Toledo). Racism. United Automobile Workers of America. 1967-73. *3015*

—. Attitudes. Illinois (Chicago). Whites. 1975. *3056*

—. Attitudes. Mexican Americans. Race Relations. Texas (Houston). Whites. -1973. *3023*

—. Attitudes. Military service. Rural-Urban Studies. Texas (East Texas, Houston). 1973. *3095*

—. Attitudes. Race. 1968. *3078*

—. Authors. France (Paris). New York City (Harlem). Whites. 1920's. *1051*
—. Autobiography. Communist Party. Illinois (Chicago). Wright, Richard. 1930's. *1428*
—. Automobile Industry and Trade. City Politics. Michigan (Detroit). United Automobile Workers of America. 1945-78. *2315*
—. Automobile industry and Trade. Industrialization. League of Revolutionary Black Workers. Michigan (Detroit). 1968-75. *2626*
—. Automobile Industry and Trade. Labor Disputes. Michigan (Detroit). Whites. 1941-75. *2628*
—. Automobile industry and Trade. Labor Unions and Organizations. League of Revolutionary Black Workers. Michigan (Detroit). Radicals and Radicalism. 1968-73. *2627*
—. Baltimore Normal School. Bowie State College. Education. Maryland. Wells, Nelson. 1843-72. *1105*
—. Banking. St. Luke's Penny Savings Bank. United Order of St. Luke. Virginia (Richmond). Walker, Maggie Lena. 1903-34. *549*
—. Baptists. First Shiloh Baptist Church. New York (Buffalo). 1920's-30's. *1704*
—. Baptists. Jasper, John. Sermons. Virginia (Richmond). 1812-1901. *1633*
—. Baptists. Massachusetts (Boston). Social Reform. 1800-73. *1672*
—. Bartenders. Pennsylvania (Philadelphia). Social organization. 1976. *2744*
—. Bass, Joseph B. Montana (Helena). *Montana Plaindealer*. Press. 1900-12. *1379*
—. Beauty parlors. Interpersonal Relations. Social Customs. Virginia (Newport News). Women. 1970's. *1338*
—. Birth Control. Fertility. Pennsylvania (Philadelphia). Socialization. Women. 1901-75. *2674*
—. Blackwell, Peter C. Organizations. Pennsylvania (Steelton). 1880-1920. *1343*
—. Boycotts. Segregation. Transportation. Virginia. 1904-07. *1384*
—. Brooklyn Howard Colored Orphan Asylum. Charities. New York Colored Orphan Asylum. Orphan asylums. Race Relations. 1836-1902. *1165*
—. Buffalo Cooperative Economic Society, Inc. Nelson, Ezekiel E. New York (Buffalo). 1928-61. *1354*
—. Buildings (vacant). Economic Conditions. Illinois (Chicago). 1970's. *2597*
—. Bureaucracies. City government. Employment. Public Welfare. War on Poverty. 1968-71. *2915*
—. Business. Entertainment. Tennessee (Memphis; Beale Street). 1930's-78. *923*
—. Business. Finance. Pennsylvania (Philadelphia). Race Relations. 1968. *3022*
—. Business. Ghettos. Loans. Whites. 1967-70. *2608*
—. Business. Tennessee (Memphis; Beale Street). Urban Renewal. 1963-70's. *3495*
—. Businessmen. Democratic Party. New York City (Brooklyn). Political Campaigns. Propaganda. Racism. Suffrage. 1860. *1405*
—. Busing. Educational Reform. Massachusetts (Boston). Racism. Whites. 1974. *2821*
—. Cajuns. Louisiana (Houma). Population. Race Relations. Social change. Texans. 1945-73. *2725*
—. California. Cantwell, John J. Catholic Church. 1920's. *1701*
—. California (Los Angeles). City Government. Lindsay, Gilbert. 1950's-77. *2420*
—. California (Los Angeles). Day Nurseries. 1970's. *2919*
—. California (Los Angeles). District of Columbia. Economic conditions. Michigan (Detroit). New Jersey (Newark). Riots. Social change. ca 1960-73. *2933*
—. California (Los Angeles). Folklore. Toasts. 19c-20c. *2756*
—. California (Los Angeles). Garvey, Marcus. Universal Negro Improvement Association. 1920's. *1418*
—. California (Los Angeles). Mexican Americans. Social Change. Suburbanization. 1960's-75. *3049*
—. California (San Francisco). Civil rights. Pressure groups. Religion. 1860's. *1388*
—. California (San Francisco). Ghettos. Political power. 1950-65. *3093*
—. California (San Francisco). Migration, Internal. 1850's-80's. *1351*
—. California (San Francisco). Neighborhoods. Powerlessness. 1979. *3094*

—. California (San Francisco; Fillmore district). Ghettos. 1974. *3070*
—. California (Stockton). Pioneers. 1821-75. *1415*
—. Caribbean Region. Economic Conditions. Immigration. New York City. Public Opinion. 1965-79. *3062*
—. Carter, Jimmy (administration). Federal Policy. Political Leadership. Poor. 1978. *2541*
—. Catholic Church. North. Occupations. Social Status. 1968. *3223*
—. Catto, Octavius V. Civil Rights. Pennsylvania (Philadelphia). 1861-71. *1411*
—. Census. City Life. Family. Historiography. Indiana (Vanderburgh County; Evansville). 1865-80. *686*
—. Charities. Georgia (Atlanta). United Way of America. 1960-77. *2699*
—. Charities. Illinois (Chicago). Social problems. 1890-1917. *1159*
—. Charleston City Railway Company. Desegregation. Reconstruction. South Carolina. Streetcars. 1867. *1369*
—. Chicago Housing Authority. *Hills* v. *Gautreaux* (US, 1976). Illinois. Integration. Public Housing. 1966-78. *3379*
—. Children. Family. Political Socialization. 1973. *3068*
—. Chinese Americans. Discrimination, Employment. Vice. 1880-1940. *1253*
—. Church of England. Laity. Neau, Elias. New York City. Society for the Propagation of the Gospel. 1704-22. *1658*
—. Church of God in Christ. Music. New York (Binghamton). 1971-74. *3215*
—. Cities. Development. Fort Smith and Western Railroad Company. Oklahoma (Boley). Railroads. Speculators. 1903-05. *119*
—. Cities, central. Migration, Internal. Virginia. Whites. 1965-70. *2729*
—. City councils. Decisionmaking. Economic Conditions. Political Participation. Political reform. 1970's. *2502*
—. City councils. Elections. 1964-78. *2480*
—. City councils. Elections. Officeholding. ca 1964-73. *2479*
—. City councils. Fiscal Policy. Mayors. Public welfare. 1968-75. *2909*
—. City Government. Community Participation in Politics. Decentralization. Whites. Wisconsin (Milwaukee). -1973. *2442*
—. City Government. Elections. New Jersey. ca 1950-73. *2468*
—. City Government. Elections, mayoral. Minorities in Politics. 1970-77. *2476*
—. City Government. Employment. Mexican Americans. Texas. Urbanization. 1973. *3029*
—. City government. Georgia (Atlanta). Political participation. Woodward, C. Vann. 1868-95. *1422*
—. City Government. Hatcher, Richard. Indiana (Gary). Mayors. Voting and Voting Behavior. 1979. *2484*
—. City Government. Law Enforcement. Michigan (Detroit). Riots. 1863-65. *1277*
—. City Government. Maryland (Baltimore). Political protest. Public schools. 1865-1900. *1118*
—. City Government. Metropolitan areas. Regionalism. 1973. *3085*
—. City Government. Migration, Internal. Missouri (Kansas City, St. Louis). Philanthropy. Public Health. 1879. *1361*
—. City Life. Dance parties. Socialization. Youth. -1974. *2746*
—. City Life. Economic Conditions. Mexican Americans. Social Organization. 1960-71. *3048*
—. City life. Folklore. Indiana (East Chicago, Gary, Hammond). Voodoo. 1976. *3071*
—. City Life. Identity. Indiana (Gary). 1976. *3622*
—. City Life. Migration. Occupations. Pennsylvania (Pittsburgh). Polish Americans. 1900-30. *1299*
—. City Politics. 1960-70. *2351*
—. City politics. Democratic Party. New York City (Harlem). Tammany Hall. 1920's. *342*
—. City Politics. Elections, municipal. Knights of Labor. Labor Unions and Organizations. Political Reform. Virginia (Richmond). 1886-88. *592*
—. City Politics. Georgia (Atlanta). Jackson, Maynard. Political Leadership. 1965-77. *2449*
—. City Politics. Mayors, black. Political Leadership. 1960's-70's. *2430*

—. City Politics. Political Leadership. 1970's. *2317*
—. Civic Unity Committee. Defense industries. Japanese Americans. Race relations. Washington (Seattle). World War II. 1940-45. *1307*
—. Civil Rights. Clark, Peter H. Ohio (Cincinnati). Politics. 1880's-1925. *1363*
—. Civil Rights. Colored Protective Association. NAACP. Pennsylvania (Philadelphia). Riots. 1918. *1221*
—. Civil rights. Demonstrations. Desegregation. Florida (Tampa). Fort, Clarence. Lane, Julian. 1960. *303*
—. Civil rights. Religion. Social Classes. 1960's-70's. *3091*
—. Civil rights Movement. Federal government. Local Government. 1933-70. *2561*
—. Civil rights movement. Illinois (Chicago). School integration. 1936. *1373*
—. Class consciousness. NAACP. Pennsylvania (Philadelphia). Race. 1930's. *1392*
—. Clergy. Garvey, Marcus. New York (Buffalo). Political Factions. Universal Negro Improvement Association. 1830's-1920's. *1421*
—. Clergy. Massachusetts (Boston). Paul, Thomas (and family). 1773-1973. *1387*
—. Colorado (Denver). Mexican Americans. Political attitudes. Voting and Voting Behavior. 1971. *3037*
—. Community control. Education. Integration. New York City (Brooklyn). 1882-1902. *1090*
—. Community Participation in Politics. Georgia (Savannah). Residential Patterns. Whites. 1865-80. *1342*
—. Conflict and Conflict Resolution. School Integration. 1955-73. *2851*
—. Congregationalism. Georgia (Atlanta). Social Work. 1886-1970. *1187*
—. Connecticut (New Haven). Discrimination, housing. Rents. Whites. 1973. *3035*
—. Consumers. Illinois (Chicago). Income. Whites. 1965. *3021*
—. Contagion hypothesis. Diffusion. Police. Riots. 1966-67. *2976*
—. Courts. Discrimination, Educational. District of Columbia. Public schools. 1804-1974. *1084*
—. Crime and Criminals. Economic Conditions. Housing. Illinois (Chicago; Woodlawn). 1930-71. *3281*
—. Crosthwait, D. N. Meigs High School. Tennessee (Nashville). 1886. *1350*
—. Decisionmaking. Technology. 1974. *3088*
—. Delaware (Wilmington). Local Politics. Republican Party. 1850-1900. *1372*
—. Democratic Party. Louisiana (New Orleans). Morial, Ernest N. Political Campaigns (mayoral). 1977. *2499*
—. Desegregation. Law and Society. Massachusetts (Boston). *Morgan* v. *Hennigan* (Massachusetts, 1974). Schools. 1974-75. *2817*
—. Dever, William. Elections (mayoral). Ethnic groups. Illinois (Chicago). Prohibition. 1923-27. *355*
—. Deviant Behavior. Youth. 1930's-60's. *2990*
—. Discrimination. Hospitals. Mercy Hospital. Ohio (Cleveland). 1927-30. *1734*
—. Discrimination. Middle classes. New Jersey (Newark). Puerto Ricans. 1967-74. *3014*
—. Discrimination. New York City. Puerto Ricans. Skill differential. Wages. Whites. 1970. *3041*
—. Discrimination, Employment. Musicians. National Endowment for the Arts. Symphony orchestras. 1974-75. *3065*
—. Discrimination, Housing. 1968-72. *3399*
—. Discrimination, Housing. Ghettos. Legislation. 1970's. *3105*
—. Discrimination, Housing. Income. Minnesota (Minneapolis, St. Paul). Zelder, Raymond E. 1965-73. *3057*
—. Discrimination, Housing. Metropolitan areas. Suburbanization. 1970's-80's. *3116*
—. Diseases. Georgia (Savannah). 1850's-60's. *1748*
—. DISTAR (program). Illinois (Chicago). Public schools. Reading. 1970's. *2838*
—. District of Columbia. Dunbar High School. High Schools (black). 1870-1955. *1413*
—. District of Columbia. Education. Employment. Georgia (Atlanta). Income. Louisiana (New Orleans). South. 1970. *2868*
—. District of Columbia. Folk songs. Molton, Flora. Women. 1930's-70's. *903*

—. District of Columbia. Housing. Land. Middle Classes. Migration, Internal. Prices. Speculation. Urban Renewal. 1970's. *3406*

—. District of Columbia. Housing. Prices. 1960's-79. *3411*

—. District of Columbia. Judges. Terrell, Robert Heberton. 1880-1925. *1385*

—. Domestic service. North. Women. Working conditions. 20c. *2615*

—. Drama. New York City. 1920's. *1050*

—. Drug abuse. Federal programs. Youth. 1960's-70's. *3242*

—. Drug Abuse. Youth. 1960's-70's. *3253*

—. Economic Conditions. Florida (Pensacola). 1896-1920's. *1344*

—. Economic Conditions. Immigration. Social Problems. West Indians. 1916-20's. *1367*

—. Economic Conditions. Kentucky (Lexington). Urbanization. 1865-80. *1417*

—. Economic Conditions. Metropolitan areas. Migration, Internal. Urbanization. 1945-75. *3118*

—. Economic Conditions. Metropolitan areas. Social Status. Suburbs. 1970. *3111*

—. Economic Conditions. Mexican Americans. Whites. Wisconsin (Racine). 1960-71. *3024*

—. Economic Conditions. South. 1790-1860. *1426*

—. Economic Development. Political Protest. Socialization. 1964-73. *3101*

—. Education. 1674-1917. *1111*

—. Education. Ghettos. Teacher Training. Whites. 1974-75. *3597*

—. Education. Income. Pennsylvania (Philadelphia). Residential Patterns. ca 1965-73. *3072*

—. Education. Ohio (Cincinnati). Public schools. Segregation. 1850-87. *1066*

—. Educational Reform. Massachusetts (Boston). Segregation. Smith, Thomas Paul. 1848-49. *1124*

—. Educational Reform. Pennsylvania (Philadelphia). White, Jacob C., Jr. 1857-1902. *1116*

—. Elections (mayoral). Indiana (Gary). New Jersey (Newark). Ohio (Cleveland). 1965-75. *3117*

—. Elections (mayoral). Voting and Voting Behavior. 1969-73. *2496*

—. Employment. Federal Policy. Ghettos. Model Cities Program. 1969-73. *2538*

—. Employment. Florida (Miami). Population. Residential Patterns. 1950-60. *2680*

—. Employment. Ghettos. Social Policy. Suburbs. 1969-79. *3102*

—. Employment. Illinois (Chicago). Industry. Polish Americans. Racism. Violence. 1890-1919. *1327*

—. Employment. Illinois (Chicago). Suburbanization. Transportation. 1960-70. *3077*

—. Energy. Housing. Population. Transportation. 1970's. *2740*

—. English Language (black). Linguistics. Research. 1970's. *3114*

—. Ethnic Groups. Ghettos. Social Problems. 1890-1940. *1403*

—. Ethnic Groups. Hispanic Americans. New York City. Social Change. 1960's-70's. *3039*

—. Ethnic Groups. Missouri (St. Louis). Residential segregation. 1850-1930. *1331*

—. Ethnic Groups. Missouri (St. Louis; Ville). Residential segregation. 1900-70. *1408*

—. Ethnicity. Race Relations. Social organization. Valentine, Charles. 1865-1975. *1419*

—. Evangelicalism. Indiana (Gary). 1976. *3222*

—. Family. Georgia (Atlanta). Social Mobility. 1870-80. *1364*

—. Family. Racism. Sex discrimination. Women. 1950's-70's. *3104*

—. Family. Women. 19c. *1356*

—. Federal Theatre Project. Theater. 1935-39. *1407*

—. Fiscal crisis. New York City. 1975. *2243*

—. Fiscal Policy. Mayors, black. 1960's-70's. *2324*

—. Florida (Jacksonville). Political Participation. 1887-1907. *1337*

—. Florida (Miami). Occupations. Whites. World War I. 1917-18. *1309*

—. *Free Speech.* Lynching. Newspapers. Tennessee (Memphis). Wells, Ida B. 1892. *1205*

—. Geographic space. Violence. 1960's-70's. *2992*

—. Georgia. Savannah Men's Sunday Club. Social Change. 1905-11. *1370*

—. Georgia (Atlanta). Ghettos. Housing. Kentucky (Lexington). North Carolina (Durham). Virginia (Richmond). 1850-1930. *1377*

—. Georgia (Atlanta). Ghettos. Migration, Internal. Urban renewal. 1960's. *3389*

—. Georgia (Atlanta). Haven, Gilbert. Protestant Churches. Segregation. 1865-1906. *1684*

—. Georgia (Atlanta). Jackson, Maynard. Minorities in Politics. 1940's-74. *2332*

—. Georgia (Atlanta). North Carolina (Raleigh). Police. Race Relations. Reconstruction. Tennessee (Nashville). Virginia (Richmond). 1865-1900. *1270*

—. Georgia (Atlanta). Residential patterns. Transportation. Women. 1910-40. *228*

—. Georgia (Augusta; The Terri). Ghettos. 1865-1973. *1365*

—. Ghettos. Jews. Literature. 20c. *3046*

—. Ghettos. Kusmer, Kenneth L. (review article). Ohio (Cleveland). 1870's-1930's. *1355*

—. Ghettos. Schools. 1975. *2884*

—. Ghettos. Sociology. 20c. *3084*

—. Ghettos (review article). Katzman, David M. Kusmer, Kenneth L. Michigan (Detroit). Ohio (Cleveland). 19c-1930. 1973-76. *1423*

—. Great Britain (London). Immigration. New York City. Social status. West Indians. 20c. *3080*

—. Himes, Chester. New York City (Harlem). Novels (detective). Social Conditions. 1957-76. *3619*

—. Holmes, Everett. Mayors. New York (Bridgewater). 1974-78. *3067*

—. Home ownership. Social Mobility. Suburbs. 1970's. *3392*

—. Home ownership. Suburbs. 1960-75. *2247*

—. Housing. Integration. Pennsylvania (Philadelphia). Planning. 1947-79. *3412*

—. Housing. Intergovernmental Relations. Mayors, black. 1950-76. *3366*

—. Housing. Metropolitan Areas. 1960's. *3384*

—. Housing. Mortgages. Pennsylvania (Pittsburgh). 1975. *3387*

—. Housing. New Deal. Pennsylvania (Philadelphia). 1930's. *1130*

—. Housing and Urban Development Act (US, 1965, Section 23). Illinois (Chicago). Law. Public Housing Authority. Segregation. 1964-75. *3393*

—. Illinois (Chicago). Local Politics. Public schools. 1910-41. *1086*

—. Illinois (Chicago). Music (jazz). 1919-30. *992*

—. Illinois (Chicago). Musicians, blues. 1920-74. *1019*

—. Illinois (Chicago). Musicians, jazz. 1920's. *1009*

—. Illinois (Chicago). Polish Americas. Residential Patterns. 1920-70. *1605*

—. Illinois (Chicago). Residential Patterns. Segregation. Social Classes. Whites. 1970. *3025*

—. Illinois (Chicago). Women. World's Columbian Exposition (Chicago, 1893). 1893. *1380*

—. Illinois (Chicago; South Side). Migration, Internal. Regionalism. Wright, Richard (*Native Son*). 20c. *2173*

—. Illinois (East St. Louis, Peoria). Mayors. Public Opinion. Students. 1978. *3081*

—. Immigrants. Italian Americans. Occupational mobility. Pennsylvania (Steelton). Slavic Americans. 1880-1920. *1300*

—. Immigrants. New York City. Politics. West Indians. Women. 1915-70's. *3089*

—. Indiana (Gary). Methodism. Robinson, Roosevelt (interview). White flight. 1976. *3031*

—. Indiana (Indianapolis). Race relations. Students. 1973. *3059*

—. Indiana (northwestern). Leadership. Neighborhoods. 1975. *3096*

—. Industrial relations. Ohio (Cleveland). 1960's-70's. *2613*

—. Industry. Property tax. 1950's-70's. *2312*

—. Integration. Racism. 1960's-70's. *3119*

—. Intellectuals. Leadership. Massachusetts (Boston). Middle classes. Smith, Julia H. 1885-1978. *1394*

—. Iron Industry. Migration, internal. Pennsylvania (Pittsburgh). Steel Industry. 1916-30. *830*

—. Jews. New York (Syracuse). Race Relations. 1787-1977. *3055*

—. Law. South. Whites. 1967-68. *2988*

—. Leadership. Rhode Island (Providence). 1962-72. *3108*

—. Liberalism. Social Conditions. 1946-48. *3124*

—. Literature. New York City (Harlem). 1920's-76. *978*

—. Louisiana (New Orleans). Men. Political participation. Women. 1969-70. *3109*

—. Louisiana (New Orleans). Metropolitan Police Force. Politics. Riots. Whites. 1868. *1235*

—. Louisiana (New Orleans). Music (jazz). Voodoo. Women. ca 19c. *967*

—. Louisiana (New Orleans). Political Leadership. Reconstruction. ca 1800-75. *1401*

—. Louisiana (New Orleans). Provost, Tessie. Public schools. School Integration. 1960-79. *3121*

—. Louisiana (Opelousas, Washington). Residential Patterns. Whites. 1860-80. *1325*

—. Lyrics. Music (blues). Phonograph records. 1945-76. *2810*

—. Maryland (Baltimore). Residential mobility. 1970-74. *3103*

—. Massachusetts (Boston). NAACP. Wilson, Butler R. 1860-1939. *1348*

—. Massachusetts (Boston). Social reform. Voluntary Associations. ca 1800-60. *1374*

—. Massachusetts (Springfield). Occupations. Property. Social Mobility. 1868-80. *839*

—. Massachusetts (Westfield). 1755-1905. 20c. *1346*

—. McCabe, Edward Preston. Migration, Internal. Newspapers. Oklahoma (Langston). 1850-1920. *1404*

—. McCabe, Edward Preston. Migration, Internal. Oklahoma (Langston). 1863-1960. *1366*

—. Medicine (Practice of). Ontario (Chatham). Saskatchewan. Shadd, Alfred Schmitz. 1896-1915. *3854*

—. Metropolitan areas. 1975. *3099*

—. Metropolitan areas. Migration, Internal. Rural Areas. South. 1950-70. *3064*

—. Metropolitan Areas. New York. Political attitudes. Puerto Ricans. 1970's. *2454*

—. Mexican Americans. Texas (Austin). Voluntary associations. Whites. 1969-70. *2702*

—. Middle classes. New York City (Harlem). Photography. VanDerZee, James. 1900-74. *1427*

—. Midwest. Poor. Religion. Sects, Religious. Whites. 1969. *3216*

—. Migration, Internal. 1636-1970. *1383*

—. Migration, Internal. North Carolina (Charlotte, Mecklenburg). Public Schools. School Integration. Whites. 1971-73. *2857*

—. Migration, Internal. Occupations. Texas (Dallas). 1880-1910. *828*

—. Migration, Internal. Poverty. Public Welfare. Whites. 1974. *2713*

—. Migration, Internal. Rural Areas. South. 1974. *3097*

—. Migration, Internal. South. Urbanization. 1960's. *3110*

—. Military. Mutinies. Race Relations. Texas (Houston). 1917. *1234*

—. Minnesota (St. Paul). Police. 1890-1975. *1362*

—. Minorities in Politics. New York City. 1889-1902. *1359*

—. Missouri (Kansas City). Pendergast, Thomas. Political machines. Truman, Harry S. 1922-34. *291*

—. Missouri (St. Louis). Public Opinion. Social Problems. Whites. 1970. *3617*

—. Missouri (St. Louis). School Integration. 1954-55. *2837*

—. Missouri (St. Louis). Young Men's Christian Association. 1877-1976. *743*

—. Musicians (jazz). New York City (Harlem). Waller, Fats. 1920's-30's. *953*

—. Neighborhood Development Program. New York (Buffalo). Urban renewal. 1971-73. *3400*

—. Neighborhoods. Residential Patterns. Small business. Whites. 1960-72. *2193*

—. New York. Poetry. Prisons. Toasts. 1959-74. *2762*

—. New York (Buffalo). Public schools. Racism. Teachers. 1956-63. *2819*

—. New York City. Puerto Ricans. Voluntary associations. Whites. 1963-78. *2691*

—. New York City (Bedford-Stuyvesant). Special Impact Program. Urban Renewal. 1960-77. *2922*

—. New York City (Bedford-Stuyvesant, Harlem). Puerto Ricans. Race Relations. Riots. 1960-64. *2979*

—. New York City (Brooklyn). Public schools. 1840's. *1099*

—. New York City (Brooklyn; Weeksville). 1830-70. *1382*

—. New York City Correctional Institution for Women. Prisons. Race relations. Women. 1932-75. *2947*

—. Newspapers, black. Political attitudes. 1969-70. *3058*

—. Oklahoma (Langston). Settlement. 1890-97. *118*

—. Peacemakers. Riots. 1968-69. *2932*

—. Police. 1973. *2984*

—. Political power. 1970's. *3086*

—. Politics. Public Policy. Violence (review article). 1960's-70's. *2241*

—. Population. Suburbs. 1950-70. *3083*

—. Quantitative Methods. Residential segregation. 1930's-70's. *3122*

—. School Integration. White flight. 1968-79. *2883*

—. Social problems. 1970's. *3115*

—. South. Voting and Voting Behavior. 1960-77. *2493*

—. Suburbanization. 1979. *3069*

—. Suburbs. 1940's-70's. *3126*

—. Voluntary associations. 1775-1976. *758*

Negroes, free. British Colonization Society. Cuffee, Paul. Massachusetts (Westport). Shipping. 1759-1817. *1425*

—. Civil War. Louisiana (New Orleans). 1855-1900. *1400*

—. District of Columbia. Economic conditions. 1800-60. *1398*

—. Law. Missouri (St. Louis). Slaves. 1800-30. *1402*

—. Maryland (Baltimore). Private Schools. 1794-1860. *1080*

—. Missouri (St. Louis). Race Relations. 1830-70. *1352*

Negroes (review article). Garvey, Marcus. Ideology. Katzman, David M. Michigan (Detroit). Social organization. Vincent, Theodore G. 19c-20c. *1420*

Neighborhood associations (private). Missouri (St. Louis). Segregation. 1850-1930. *793*

Neighborhood Development Program. Negroes. New York (Buffalo). Urban renewal. 1971-73. *3400*

Neighborhood Housing Services. Poor. Preservation. Relocation. Urban Redevelopment Task Force. 1970's. *3572*

Neighborhoods. 1979. *3277*

—. Acculturation. Ethnicity. German Americans. Immigrants. 1840's-1970's. *1305*

—. Agricultural Cooperatives. Farms. Regional planning. 1920's. *1825*

—. Alleys. Architecture. Attitudes. 17c-20c. *1787*

—. Annexation. New York (Buffalo; Black Rock). Urbanization. 1850-90's. *111*

—. Architecture (Victorian). California (San Francisco). Painting. Preservation. 1967-79. *3534*

—. Architecture, Victorian. East End Historical District. Preservation. Texas (Galveston). 1972-77. *3551*

—. Arkansas (Little Rock). Preservation. 1970-77. *3565*

—. Attitudes. Colorado (Denver). Mexican Americans. Negroes. Public services. Whites. 1970's. *3612*

—. Attitudes. Real estate. Urban Renewal. 1970's. *3537*

—. Brownstone buildings. New York City. Restoration. 1960-74. *3494*

—. Business. California (San Francisco; San Bruno Avenue). Esther Hellman Settlement House. Jews. 1901-68. *1462*

—. Business. Colorado (Denver). Economic Structure. Migration, Internal. Race. 1960-70. *2245*

—. California (Oakland). National Urban Land Program. New Jersey (Newark). New York City (South Bronx). Public Lands. Real Estate. Trust for Public Land. 1973-78. *3431*

—. California (San Francisco). Negroes. Powerlessness. 1979. *3094*

—. California (San Francisco Bay area). City Government. Community Participation in Politics. Zoning. 1970's. *3335*

—. Capital. Landlords and Tenants. 1979. *2715*

—. Cities, central. Middle Classes. Residential Patterns. Upper Classes. 1960's. *3280*

—. City Government. Employment. Ohio (Cleveland). Urban Renewal. 1959-79. *3391*

—. City Life. Housing. Human Relations. Migration, internal. Social Problems. 1950's-70's. *2737*

—. City life. Pennsylvania (Philadelphia; Fairmount). Residential Patterns. Social Change. 1960's-70's. *2646*

—. City planning. Housing. Population. Public policy. 1890-1979. *2217*

—. City planning. New York City. 1760-75. *1781*

—. City Planning. Politics. Urban Renewal. 1979. *3298*

—. Community (Concept). Social Networks. 1979. *2256*

—. Community Participation in Politics. DeVries, Jon. North Carolina (Winston-Salem; Crystal Towers). Redevelopment Commission. Urban renewal. 1970's. *3388*

—. Czech Americans. Ethnicity. Missouri (St. Louis). Social organizations. 1848-1970. *1575*

—. Development. Economic Conditions. Investments. Public Policy. Suburbs. 1968-75. *2607*

—. Ethnic Groups. Manitoba (St. Boniface, Winnipeg; North End). 19c-1978. *3829*

—. Ethnic groups. Maryland (Baltimore). Residential patterns. 1850-70. *1310*

—. Ethnic Groups. Michigan (Detroit). Population. Residential Patterns. 1880-85. *718*

—. Farrell, James T. Illinois (Chicago; Washington Park). Novels. 1904-79. *2148*

—. Federal Government. Housing. Mortgages. 1932-79. *2521*

—. Georgia (Athens; Cobbham). Historic Cobbham Foundation. Preservation. 1834-79. *3562*

—. Georgia (Atlanta). Hawaii (Honolulu). Integration. Residential Patterns. Texas (San Antonio). 1960's-70's. *2672*

—. Georgia (Atlanta). Inman Park Restoration, Inc. Preservation. 1880's. 1970-79. *3558*

—. Historic district designation. 1976. *3544*

—. Illinois (Chicago). Mexican Americans. Social conditions. 1920-70. *3034*

—. Indiana (northwestern). Leadership. Negroes. 1975. *3096*

—. Jacobs, Jane (review article). 1961-78. *3268*

—. Local government. Pennsylvania. Pittsburgh Neighborhood Atlas. 1968-75. *2368*

—. Massachusetts (Boston; North End). Urban Renewal. 1960's-79. *3510*

—. Medical care. Ohio (Cincinnati; Mohawk-Brighton). Phillips, Wilbur C. Social Reform. 1917-20. *1753*

—. Medical centers. 1960's-76. *3256*

—. Metropolitan areas. Social status. 1925-73. *2272*

—. Minnesota (Minneapolis, St. Paul). Newspapers. Public affairs. 1969-74. *2781*

—. Mount Auburn Good Housing Foundation. Ohio (Cincinnati; Mount Auburn). Restorations. 1967-79. *3545*

—. Negroes. Residential Patterns. Small business. Whites. 1960-72. *2193*

—. New York City. Residential patterns. 1730. *716*

—. New York City. Socialism. Working class. 1908-18. *788*

—. Pennsylvania (Philadelphia). Powelton Village Development Association. Restorations. 1955-79. *3519*

—. Race. Residential Patterns. ca 1924-74. *2194*

—. Social mobility. 1970's. *2735*

—. Social Organization (review article). 1976-79. *2657*

Neiman-Marcus Company. Clothing. Department stores. Marketing. Texas (Dallas). 1900-17. *431*

—. Fashion. Marketing. Texas (Dallas). 1880-1970. *421*

Nelson, Ezekiel E. Buffalo Cooperative Economic Society, Inc. Negroes. New York (Buffalo). 1928-61. *1354*

Nelson, Nelson O. Business. Consumer cooperative movement. Garden City Movement. Progressivism. 1890's-1918. *405*

Nelson, Robert H. Danielson, Michael N. Fishman, Richard P. Gale, Denis E. Government Regulation. James, Franklin J. Land Use (review article). Property Rights. Rose, Jerome G. Rothman, Robert E. 1970's. *3283*

Neocolonialism. Black Capitalism. Economic Growth. Ghettos. 1960-74. *3106*

Nervous disorders. Law. Noise pollution. 1960's-70's. *3247*

Netherlands (Amsterdam). City Life. Land tenure. New York City. 1960's-70's. *3266*

Neustadt, Samuel I. California (San Francisco). Charities. Cholera. Epidemics. Jews. 1850. *1767*

Nevada (Gold Hill, Virginia City). Comstock Lode. Mines. Prostitution. 1860-80. *1227*

Nevada (Goldfield, Tonopah). Daily Life. Ellis, Anne. Literature. Mining towns. Women. 1900-20. *2174*

Nevada (Las Vegas). 1905-73. *186*

—. American Dream. Reporters and Reporting. 1964-74. *3607*

—. Architecture. 1960's-70's. *3425*

—. Architecture (review article). Daily Life. 1960's-70's. *3419*

—. Boosterism. Public relations. Tourism. 1905-74. *2277*

—. Daily Life. Ranching. Stewart, Helen J. 1879-1926. *410*

—. Social Conditions. Waters, Frank *(The Yogi of Cockroach Court)*. 1947-78. *3591*

Nevada (Lost City, Moapa Valley). Archaeology. Artifacts. ca 530. 1975. *3935*

Nevada (Lovelock). Economic development. 1861-1970. *166*

Nevada (Pueblo Grande de Nevada). Anasazi Culture. Indians. Villages. 900. *3936*

Nevada (Reno, Virginia City). Competition. Pacific Union Express Company. Transportation. Wells, Fargo and Company. 1868-69. *2080*

Nevada (Virginia City). Atheism. Ingersoll, Robert. Lectures. Public Opinion. 1877. *1666*

—. Fourth of July. Great Overland Circus. 1870. *904*

Neve, Felipe de. California (Los Angeles). Historiography. Palou, Francisco. Pioneers. 1780-82. *141*

New Brunswick (Saint John). Architecture, Victorian. Industrialization. Urban Renewal. 17c-1966. *3907*

—. Boosterism. Population. Railroads. 1851-80. *3666*

—. Catholic Church. Sisters of Charity of the Immaculate Conception. 1854-64. *3865*

—. Census. Methodology. Social Classes. 1871. 1974. *3811*

—. Charities. Newfoundland (St. John's). Nova Scotia (Halifax). Poverty. Unemployment. 1815-60. *3781*

—. Cholera. City Government. Epidemics. 1854. *3872*

—. Commerce. Economic development. 1820-50. *3709*

—. Disaster relief. Fire. Nova Scotia. 1877. *3906*

—. Economic Development. Industrial Revolution. Ports. Railroads. Transportation. 1867-1911. *3661*

—. Economic Growth. Social Conditions. 19c. *3640*

—. Labor. Lumber and Lumbering. Merchant Marine. Ports. Quebec. Working conditions. ca 1820-90. *3730*

—. Theater. 1789-1817. *3814*

New Castle's Cascade Park. Pennsylvania (Pittsburgh). Railroads (electric). 1897. *858*

New Communities program. Federal Government. Housing. Social Policy. 1968-78. *2532*

New Deal. Architecture. City planning. Europe. Housing. Modernism. New York City. Ohio (Cleveland). Pennsylvania (Philadelphia). 1932-60. *1952*

—. City Politics. Depressions. Massachusetts (Boston). Roosevelt, Franklin D. (administration). Trout, Charles H. (review article). 1929-39. 1977. *315*

—. Democratic Party. Hague, Frank. New Jersey. Roosevelt, Franklin D. 1932-40. *313*

—. Depressions. Massachusetts (Boston). Methodology. Urban history. 1930's. 1977-79. *4054*

—. Economic Conditions. Fiscal Policy. Intergovernmental Relations. Liberalism. New York City. 1930's-70's. *2535*

—. Greenbelt Towns. Ohio (Cincinnati, Greenhills). Tugwell, Rexford Guy. Urban Renewal. 1935-39. *96*

—. Housing. Negroes. Pennsylvania (Philadelphia). 1930's. *1130*

—. Illinois (Chicago). Kelly, Edward J. Political machines. Roosevelt, Franklin D. 1932-40. *317*

New England *See also* individual states; Northeastern or North Atlantic States.

—. American Revolution. Loyalists. Rural areas. 1770's. *260*

—. Architecture. Benjamin, Asher. 1795-1841. *1957*

—. Centrality (concept). Economic Theory. 17c-18c. *2199*

—. Cities (review article). Connecticut (Stamford). New York. Pennsylvania (Germantown). 1660's-18c. *7*

—. City Government. 18c. *242*

—. Cook, Edward M., Jr. (review article). Leadership. Social Organization. 18c. 1976. *813*

—. Doherty, Robert. Doyle, Don Harrison. Illinois (Jacksonville). Social Organization. 1800-70. 1977-78. *671*

—. Economic Conditions. Emigration. Maritime Provinces. Massachusetts (Boston). 1860-1900. *3766*

—. Kibbutzim. Palestine. Puritans. Social Organization. Towns. 17c. 1900-50. *662*

—. Maine (Gardiner). Ports. Shipping. 1830's. *454*

New Federalism. City Government. Public services. 1970's. *2544*

New Hampshire *See also* New England; Northeastern or North Atlantic States.

—. Architecture (Gothic Revival). Vaughan, Henry. 1881-1915. *1940*

—. Migration, Internal. Population. Rural Settlements. 1765-90. *196*

—. Portsmouth Marine Society. Shipping. Social Classes. ca 1763-68. *448*

New Hampshire (Bedford, Goffstown). Agriculture. Business. Carpentry. Dunlap, John. Furniture and Furnishings. 1746-92. *482*

New Hampshire (Dover). Architecture. Calico Printing. Cotton mills. Dover Manufacturing Company Print Works. 1820-25. *474*

—. Canals. Winnipiseogee Canal. 1796-1834. *2075*

New Hampshire (Manchester). Amoskeag Manufacturing Company. Ethnocentrism. Family. Industrial Relations. Modernization. 1912-22. *776*

—. Amoskeag Manufacturing Company. Family. Working Class. 1900-24. *698*

—. Amoskeag Manufacturing Company. Textile industry. 1838-1968. *1932*

—. Amoskeag Manufacturing Company. Textile Industry. Working Conditions. 1920's-30's. *566*

New Hampshire (Portsmouth). Architecture. Episcopal Church, Protestant. St. John's Episcopal Church. 1807-09. *1895*

—. Diseases. Jackson, Hall. Mortality. Statistics. 18c. 20c. *1726*

—. Furniture and Furnishings. 1750-75. *1027*

New Hampshire (Rochester). Hodgdon, Elizabeth. Hodgdon, Sarah. Labor. Letters. Massachusetts (Lowell). Textile Industry. 1830-40. *560*

New Jersey *See also* Northeastern or North Atlantic States.

—. Archives. Computers. Documents. Ports. 18c. 1975. *3995*

—. City Government. Elections. Negroes. ca 1950-73. *2468*

—. City Planning. Courts. Zoning. 1970-73. *3339*

—. Connecticut. Law enforcement. Local Government. New York. Public Finance. State government. 1961-77. *2508*

—. Democratic Party. Hague, Frank. New Deal. Roosevelt, Franklin D. 1932-40. *313*

—. Finance. Mass transit. New York. Port Authority. State politics. 1921-74. *3462*

—. Grain elevators. New York City. Shipbuilding. 1848-1964. *1894*

—. Hudson River. New York City. Railroads. Tunnels. 1871-1910. *2082*

New Jersey (Atlantic City). Funnell, Charles E. Kasson, John F. New York City (Coney Island). Resorts (review article). Social Change. 1890-1910. 1975-78. *891*

New Jersey (Cape May). Architecture. Preservation. Resorts. 19c-1978. *3555*

—. Architecture, Victorian. Preservation. Resorts. 1700-1978. *3550*

New Jersey (Chester). California (Sacramento). Colorado (Denver). District of Columbia. Music (jazz). Ohio (Peninsula). Texas (San Antonio). 19c-20c. *2785*

New Jersey (Hoboken). Architecture. Landscaping. Stevens family. 1820-60. *1789*

—. Economic Conditions. Food. Housing. World War I. 1914-18. *12*

—. Industrialization. New York City. Resorts. Stevens, John. Urbanization. 1820-60. *87*

—. Middle Classes. Migration, internal. 17c-1979. *3559*

New Jersey (Hudson County). Community Participation in Politics. Energy. Industry. Pollution. 1972-78. *2458*

New Jersey (Jersey City). Associates of the Jersey Company. City government. Land Tenure. Water rights. Waterfronts. 1845-50. *255*

—. City Politics. Ethnic Groups. Political Reform. Social Classes. Whites. 1970's. *2355*

—. City Politics. Fagan, Mark. Progressivism. 1896-1907. *389*

—. Fagan, Mark. Progressives. Single tax. Taxation. 1901-17. *388*

—. Liberty Park. Parks. Pesin, Morris. Waterfronts. 1958-78. *3428*

—. Progressivism. Social reform. Whittier House. 1890-1917. *1199*

New Jersey (Margate). Architecture. Houses, elephant. Lafferty, James V. Patents. Publicity. Real estate. 1880's. 1970-77. *1881*

New Jersey (Newark). California (Los Angeles). District of Columbia. Economic conditions. Michigan (Detroit). Negroes. Riots. Social change. ca 1960-73. *2933*

—. California (Oakland). National Urban Land Program. Neighborhoods. New York City (South Bronx). Public Lands. Real Estate. Trust for Public Land. 1973-78. *3431*

—. Catholic Church. German Americans. Irish Americans. Social Problems. 1840-70. *1689*

—. Cities (central). Housing abandonment. Landlords and Tenants. 1960's-73. *3410*

—. Congar, Stephen. Educational Administration. Physicians. Public schools. 1838-59. *1108*

—. Discrimination. Middle classes. Negroes. Puerto Ricans. 1967-74. *3014*

—. Discrimination, Employment. Public Schools. Race Relations. Strikes. 1950's-1973. *2622*

—. Duffy, John. Galishoff, Stuart. New York City. Public Health (review article). 1625-1975. *1747*

—. Elections (mayoral). Indiana (Gary). Negroes. Ohio (Cleveland). 1965-75. *3117*

—. Epidemics. Polio. Public health. 1916. *1730*

—. Public Health. Sewers. Social Classes. 1854-1919. *2036*

New Jersey (Newark, Trenton). Decisionmaking. District of Columbia. Intergovernmental relations. New York City. Pennsylvania (Philadelphia). Tocks Island Project. Urbanization. Water projects. 1962-75. *2311*

New Jersey (Passaic). City Government. Economic Conditions. Minorities. 1960's-70's. *2209*

New Jersey (Paterson). American Civil Liberties Union. Associated Silk Workers Union. Freedom of Assembly. Freedom of Speech. Strikes. 1924. *596*

—. City government. Depressions. Fiscal Policy. Public Welfare. Textile industry. 1920-32. *253*

New Jersey (Pitman Grove). Religion. Urbanization. 1860-1975. *212*

New Jersey (Radburn). City Planning. Middle classes. Regional Planning Association of America. 1927. *1840*

New Jersey (West Orange; Llewellyn Park). City Planning. Illinois (Riverside). Olmsted, Frederick Law. Suburbs. Vaux, Calvert. 1853-1920's. *1850*

New Mexico (Albuquerque). Elections (mayoral). Newspapers. Political endorsements. 1974. *2474*

New Mexico (Chaco Canyon). Anasazi culture. Excavations. Indians. 6000 BC-1250 AD. *3925*

—. Indians. Social organization. ca 850-1130. *3927*

New Mexico (Isleta Pueblo). Catholic Church. Clergy. Indian-White Relations. 1960's. *3932*

New Mexico (Jemez Mountains). Indians. Pueblos. Social organization. 1300-1600. *3926*

New Mexico (Las Cruces). Jews. Philanthropy. Stern, Eugene J. 1903-70. *1461*

New Mexico (Las Vegas). Architecture. Burnham, Daniel Hudson. Montezuma Hotel. Root, John Wellborn. 1879-85. *1919*

New Mexico (Santa Fe). Indians. Missions and Missionaries. Settlement. Spaniards. 1540-1882. *157*

—. Landholding. 1860-70. *1782*

—. Metropolitan Protective Association. New York City. Reform. Sanitation. Spiegelberg, Flora Langermann. 1875-1943. *661*

—. Military Camps and Forts. 1610-1791. *2115*

New Mexico (Santa Fe, Silver City). Architecture. City Planning. Conron, John P. (interview). Government Regulation. 1974. *3489*

New Netherland *See also* New York.

—. Dutch West India Company. Slavery. 1646-64. *1360*

—. Intergovernmental Relations. Local Government. Provincial Government. 1624-63. *263*

—. Provincial Government. Stuyvesant, Peter. 1650-54. *287*

New Netherland (New Amsterdam). Education. 17c. *1071*

—. Indians. Irving, Washington (*Knickerbocker's History of New York*). 17c. 1809-48. *1614*

—. Indians. Land. Minuit, Peter. Settlement. 1624-25. *232*

New Order of Cincinnatus. City Government. Conservatism. Political Parties. Potts, Ralph. Washington (Seattle). ca 1933-39. *384*

New Orleans Historic District Landmarks Committee. Coliseum Square Association. Louisiana (New Orleans; Lower Garden). Preservation. 1807-1978. *3576*

New South. Business. Farmers. Industrialization. Textile Industry. 1870-1900. *401*

New towns. City Planning. -1973. *3322*

—. City Planning. Great Britain. USSR. 1945-70's. *3320*

—. Population. -1973. *3304*

New York *See also* Northeastern or North Atlantic States.

—. Airplanes. Behavior. Buffalo Airport. Noise pollution. 1970's. *3239*

—. Architecture. Kellum, John. Mansions. Stewart, Alexander Turney. 1860-90. *1880*

—. Audiovisual Materials. Reynolds Library, Inc. Rochester Public Library. 1812-1963. *952*

—. Automobiles. Play. Suburbs. Youth. 1970. *2752*

—. Banks. Social Classes. 1819-61. *544*

—. Bossism. DeSapio, Carmine. Tammany Hall. 1950's-60's. *338*

—. Brace, Charles Loring. Children's Aid Society. Orphans. 1853-1929. *1147*

—. Caro, Robert A. (review article). Moses, Robert. Mugwumps. Politics. State government. 1920's-40's. 1974. *301*

—. Charities. Morality. Rural-Urban Studies. 1783-1830. *1158*

—. Child Welfare. Discrimination. Lawsuits. 1973-74. *2924*

—. Cities (review article). Connecticut (Stamford). New England. Pennsylvania (Germantown). 1660's-18c. *7*

—. City Government. Decisionmaking. Television. Town meetings. 1973. *2457*

—. City Government. Development. Housing. Landlords and Tenants. Relocation. 1940's-74. *3407*

—. City Government. Intergovernmental Relations. State 1905-73. *321*

—. Connecticut. Law enforcement. Local Government. New Jersey. Public Finance. State government. 1961-77. *2508*

—. Ethics. Law. State Government. 1970-75. *2415*

—. Family. Great Britain. Italian Americans. Social change. ca 1850-1920. *715*

—. Films. History Teaching. Syracuse University. 1970-74. *3993*

—. Finance. Mass transit. New Jersey. Port Authority. State politics. 1921-74. *3462*

—. Finance. Public Housing. Urban Development Corporation. 1968-78. *2513*

—. Historiography. 1970's. *4019*

—. Historiography. Oral history. Pennsylvania (Philadelphia). Social Surveys. Watson, John Fanning. 1779-1860. *4063*

—. Housing. State Government. Urban Development Corporation. 1960-73. *3390*

—. Metropolitan Areas. Negroes. Political attitudes. Puerto Ricans. 1970's. *2454*

—. Negroes. Poetry. Prisons. Toasts. 1959-74. *2762*

—. Philanthropy. Social problems. Voluntary associations. 1830-60. *1157*

—. Quantitative Methods. School attendance. Urbanization. 1845. *1094*

New York (Adirondack Mountains). Camping. City life. Fishing. Hunting. Wilderness. ca 1830's-90's. *919*

New York (Albany). Arson. Slavery. 1793-99. *1358*

—. Charities. Odd Fellows, Independent Order of. Social Classes. 1845-85. *733*

—. Dutch Americans. Law. Social status. Women. 1600's-1790. *1608*

New York (Albany diocese). Episcopal Church, Protestant. Oldham, George Ashton. 1922-47. *1644*

New York (Albany, Rochester, Syracuse, Utica). Water supply. 19c-1977. *3432*

New York Athletic Club. Allegheny Athletic Association. Football. Pennsylvania (Pittsburgh). Professionalization. 1866-90's. *881*

—. Social Classes. Sports. 1865-1900. *820*

New York (Binghamton). Church of God in Christ. Music. Negroes. 1971-74. *3215*

New York (Bridgewater). Holmes, Everett. Mayors. Negroes. 1974-78. *3067*

New York (Buffalo). Americanization. Educational Reform. Immigrants. Public Schools. 1890-1916. *1113*

—. Architecture. Environment. Larkin Administration Building. Ventilation system. Wright, Frank Lloyd. 1904. *1864*

—. Baptists. First Shiloh Baptist Church. Negroes. 1920's-30's. *1704*

—. Buffalo Cooperative Economic Society, Inc. Negroes. Nelson, Ezekiel E. 1928-61. *1354*

—. Catholic Church. Ethnic groups. Folklore. 1960's-75. *3219*

—. Catholic Church. Pitass, John. Polish Americans. 1890-1934. *1568*

—. Civilian review boards. Labor Unions and Organizations. Maryland (Baltimore). Pennsylvania (Philadelphia). Police. 1958-74. *2952*

—. Class Struggle. Law Enforcement. Migrant labor. Tramp Act (New York, 1885). 1892-94. *777*

—. Clergy. Garvey, Marcus. Negroes. Political Factions. Universal Negro Improvement Association. 1830's-1920's. *1421*

—. Construction. Labor. -1973. *2625*

—. Ethnic groups. Households. Life cycles. 1855. *1311*

—. Ethnicity. Political Leadership. 1970. *2416*

—. Evangelism. Sunday, William Ashley ("Billy"). 1917. *1631*

—. Family. Italian Americans. Yans-McLaughlin, Virginia (review article). 1880-1930. 1971-77. *1598*

—. Grocery stores. Reminiscences. Wiener, Alfred D. 1947-65. *464*

—. Immigrants. Legends. Polish Americans. Religion. 1870-1973. *1559*

—. Libraries, public. Polish Americans. 1900-70. *1579*

—. Negroes. Neighborhood Development Program. Urban renewal. 1971-73. *3400*

—. Negroes. Public schools. Racism. Teachers. 1956-63. *2819*

New York (Buffalo; Black Rock). Annexation. Neighborhoods. Urbanization. 1850-90's. *111*

New York (Buffalo, Kingston, Poughkeepsie). Employment. Ethnic Groups. Ontario (Hamilton). Pennsylvania (Philadelphia). Property. Social Classes. 19c. *778*

New York Charity Organization Society. Charities. Colleges and Universities. Social Organization Theory. 1880-1910. *1149*

New York City. Acculturation. Immigration. Jews. Yiddishe Arbeiten Universitet. 1921-39. *1078*

—. Actors and Actresses. African Theatre. Negroes. 1820-23. *1024*

—. Aestheticism. Jews. Literature. *Yunge* (group). 1902-13. *1063*

—. Air Lines. California (Los Angeles, San Francisco). Federal Government. Helicopters. Illinois (Chicago). Subsidies. 1945-75. *3471*

—. Air quality. Public Policy. 1970-77. *3285*

—. Alcoholism. Family. Human relations. Skid Rows. Women. 1966-69. *2709*

—. American Museum of Natural History, Alexander M. White Natural Science Center. Children. Ecology. Museums. Natural History. 1974-75. *2801*

—. American Revolution. Business. City Life. Colonial government. Immigration. 17c-20c. *133*

—. American Revolution. Labor. Political participation. 1797-1813. *26*

—. American Seaman's Friend Society. Boardinghouses. Housing. Merchant Marine. 1825-42. *1134*

—. Americanization. Catholics. Ethnicity. Religion. -1974. *3040*

—. Amusement parks. Art. Coney Island. Urbanization. 1897-1940. *2141*

—. Archdeacon, Thomas J. (review article). Colonial Government. Dutch Americans. Social Classes. 1664-1710. 1976. *26*

—. Architects. Department stores. Snook, John B. Stewart, Alexander Turney. 1846-84. *1973*

—. Architecture. Bogardus, James. Construction. Fire towers. Iron-framed structures. Kroehl, Julius B. 1850's. *1926*

—. Architecture. Chrysler Building. Restorations. VanAlen, William. 1928-79. *3526*

—. Architecture. Church of St. Paul the Apostle. Decorative Arts. LaFarge, John. 1876-99. *1056*

—. Architecture. City planning. Europe. Housing. Modernism. New Deal. Ohio (Cleveland). Pennsylvania (Philadelphia). 1932-60. *1952*

—. Architecture. Columbia University (and Low Library). McKim, Charles F. 1894-20c. *1949*

—. Architecture. Connecticut (New Haven). Georgia (Savannah). Massachusetts (Boston). Pennsylvania (Philadelphia). 18c. *1983*

—. Architecture. Woolworth Building. 1880-1913. *1928*

—. Architecture. World Trade Center. Yamasaki, Minoru. 1970's. *3421*

—. Archival Catalogs and Inventories. Local history. Negroes. Personal Narratives. Staten Island Institute of Arts and Sciences. 1969-76. *4031*

—. Armies. Butler, Benjamin Franklin. Elections (presidential). Lincoln, Abraham. 1864. *293*

—. Art. Cultural Imperialism. Regionalism. 1974. *2793*

—. Art. Exhibits and Expositions. 1970's. *2800*

—. Art. Interborough Rapid Transit. Subways. 1914-17. *1044*

—. Art (criticism). Bartholdi, Auguste. Statue of Liberty. 1875-86. 1974. *1046*

—. Artisans. City government. Hogs and Hog Raising. Public Health. Reform. 1796-1819. *805*

—. Artists. 20c. *2811*

—. Artists. Housing. Industry. 1970's. *2813*

—. Artists. Literature. Negroes. Williams, John A. (interview). 1920's-70's. *3125*

—. Arts. Ethnicity. Puerto Ricans. 1960's-70's. *3142*

—. Arts. Management. 1970's. *2815*

—. Asia, Southeast. China. Chinatowns. Economic development. Foreign investments. Ghettos. 1970's. *2585*

—. Asian Americans. City Government. Public Policy. Social Conditions. 1970's. *3177*

—. Aspira (organization). Educational Reform. Harlem Parents Union. Minorities. Pennsylvania (Philadelphia). Voluntary Associations. Welfare Rights Organization. 1970's. *2840*

—. Assimilation. Chinese Americans. Peru (Lima). 1849-1976. *1558*

—. Assimilation. Ethnicity. Greek Americans. Orthodox Eastern Church. St. Demetrios Church. St. Markela Church. 1970's. *3206*

—. Assimilation. Models. Puerto Ricans. Residential segregation. 1960-70. *3163*

—. Athletic clubs. Social Classes. 1866-1915. *821*

—. Attitudes. Ford, Gerald R. Public Finance. 1970's. *3593*

—. Attitudes. Great Britain (London). Local Government. ca 1960-73. *3616*

—. Authority. Great Britain (London). Police. Social organization. 1830-70. *1257*

—. Automobiles. Manhattan Auto Study. 1970. *3478*

—. Bakeries. Economic Regulations. Strikes. 1801-13. *625*

—. Bank Reserves. Massachusetts (Boston). Pennsylvania (Philadelphia). 1856-58. *536*

—. Banking. Brown, Alexander & Sons. Cotton trade. Foreign exchange. Great Britain (Liverpool). Maryland (Baltimore). Pennsylvania (Philadelphia). 1820-80. *437*

—. Banking. Economic Conditions. Social Conditions. 1971. *2611*

—. Banking. Finance. German Americans. Jews. 19c. *529*

—. Bankruptcy. City Politics. Public Finance. ca 1960-76. *2191*

—. Banks. Investments. Portfolio management. Trustees. 1830-62. *545*

—. Baseball. Georgia (Atlanta). Illinois (Chicago). Religion. Social change. Values. 1892-1934. *905*

—. Baseball (team owners). Bossism. City Politics. Gambling. Georgia (Atlanta). Illinois (Chicago). ca 1877-1916. *906*

—. Bayor, Ronald H. (review article). Conflict and Conflict Resolution. Ethnic Groups. 1929-41. 1978. *1334*

—. Beame, Abraham. City Government. Lindsay, John V. Public Administration. 1966-79. *2379*

—. Bell, William H. Diaries. Law Enforcement. 1850-51. *1292*

—. Birth Rate. Poor. Public Welfare. 1965-67. *2677*

—. Blackouts. Crime and Criminals. Looting. Poverty. 1977. *2942*

—. Boycotts. Immigrants. Industry. Irish Americans. Labor. 1880-86. *597*

—. Bridges. 1900-78. *2099*

—. Brooklyn Public Library. Libraries. 1899-1974. *1020*

—. Brownstone buildings. Neighborhoods. Restoration. 1960-74. *3494*

—. Bryant, William Cullen. Environment. Journalism. Poets. 1825-78. *1012*

—. Budget Bureau. City government. Economic Conditions. 1974-75. *2375*

—. Budgets. Economic Structure. Federal Government. Income redistribution. Local government. 1970's. *2536*

—. Buildings. City Planning. 1893-1907. *1836*

—. Buildings. Zoning. 1850-1973. *1858*

—. Bureau of Social Morals. Hertz, Rosie. Jews. Law Enforcement. Prostitution. 1912-13. *1150*

—. Bureaucracies. Caro, Robert A. (review article). City Politics. Moses, Robert. 20c. *2426*

—. Bureaucracies. Community control. Minorities. Political Leadership. 1972-74. *2443*

—. Burr, Aaron. Davis, Matthew Livingston. Political change. Tammany Hall. 1790's-1850. *349*

—. Buses. 1968-79. *3458*

—. Business. California (San Francisco). Libraries. Mercantile Libararies. 19c. *1005*

—. Business. City Government. World Trade Center. 1950's-78. *3426*

—. Business. Economic development. Elites. Social organization. 1780-1850. *784*

—. Business. Great Britain (London). Immigration. Jews. Labor Unions and Organizations. 19c-20c. *1472*

—. Business. Jews. 1654-1820. *1447*

—. Business. Women. 1660-1775. *434*

—. California (Los Angeles). District of Columbia. Reporters and Reporting. Television. 1976. *2766*

—. Caribbean Region. Economic Conditions. Immigration. Negroes. Public Opinion. 1965-79. *3062*

—. Caro, Robert A. (review article). City Government. Moses, Robert. 1924-54. *2428*

—. Catholic Church. Conflict and Conflict Resolution. French (language). Haitian Americans. 1970's. *3063*

—. Catholic Church. Dolan, Jay P. (review article). German Americans. Irish Americans. Social Conditions. 1815-65. 1975. *1676*

—. Catholic Church. Ethnic Groups (review article). Horowitz, Helen Lefkowitz. Illinois (Chicago). Kessner, Thomas. Philanthropy. Sanders, James W. 1883-1965. 1970's. *48*

—. Catholic Church. Italian Americans (review article). Sartorio, Enrico C. Tomasi, Silvano. 1918. 1975. *1680*

—. Census. City Planning. Social Surveys. 1961-74. *4014*

—. Central Park. City Politics. Parks. 1844-56. *2024*

—. Charities. City government. Outdoor relief. Reform. Subsidies. 1870-98. *372*

—. Charities. Galveston Plan of 1907. Immigration. Industrial Removal Office. Jews. Migration, Internal. 1890-1914. *1476*

—. Charities. Reform. Social Services. 1845-60. *1156*

—. Charters. City Government. Democratic Party. Political Reform. Whig Party. 1845-49. *248*

—. Charters. City Government. Politics. Reform. 1898-1976. *2397*

—. Charters. City politics. Havemeyer, William Frederick. Reform. 1845-47. *249*

—. Child abuse. Society for the Prevention of Cruelty to Children. 1820's-80's. *1196*

—. Child Welfare. Foster homes. Immigration. Jews. Working class. 1900-05. *1186*

—. Child Welfare. Joint Committee on the Care of Motherless Infants. Orphans. Public Policy. 1860-1907. *1185*

—. Children. Education. Mental Illness. 1960's. *2859*

—. Children. Guggenheim Museum. Museums. Reading. 1971-73. *2794*

—. Children. Local government. Maternity. Medical care. 1950-77. *3245*

—. Chinatowns. Chinese Americans. Ghettos. Immigration. 1880-1975. *1556*

—. Chinatowns. Chinese Americans. Immigration. Social Conditions. 1950-69. *3179*

—. Chinese Americans. Immigrants. Newspapers, Chinese. 1974. *2774*

—. Industrialization. New Jersey (Hoboken). Resorts. Stevens, John. Urbanization. 1820-60. *87*

—. Intergovernmental Relations. State government. 1894-1974. *2507*

—. International Trade. Shipowners. 1715-64. *465*

—. Irish Americans. Italian Americans. Jews. Schools. 1840-1942. *2863*

—. Italian Americans. Jews. Kessner, Thomas (review article). Social Mobility. 1880-1915. 1977. *1328*

—. Jews. Labor Unions and Organizations. Social Classes. Socialism. United Hebrew Trades. 1877-1926. *627*

—. Jews. Public schools. Social mobility. 1880-1920. *1434*

—. Juvenile Delinquency. Schools. 1973. *2974*

—. Kaestle, Carl F. Massachusetts (Boston). Public Schools (review article). Schultz, Stanley K. 1750-1860. *1068*

—. Kaestle, Carl F. Massachusetts (Boston). Public Schools (review article). Schultz, Stanley K. 1750-1860. *1095*

—. Labor Unions and Organizations. Radicals and Radicalism. Social work. 1931-51. *2629*

—. Labor Unions and Organizations. Taxicabs. 1966-73. *3482*

—. LaGuardia, Fiorello. Mayors. Reform. 1933-45. *386*

—. Lead poisoning. -1974. *3237*

—. Louisiana (New Orleans). Public health. 19c. *1720*

—. Maryland (Baltimore). Pennsylvania (Philadelphia). Silversmithing. 18c. *1025*

—. Massachusetts (Boston). Midwest. Muhlenberg, Augustus. Politics. Protestantism (review article). Social Problems. 1812-1900. *1695*

—. Massachusetts (Boston). Pennsylvania (Philadelphia). Political participation. 1700-65. *252*

—. Massachusetts (Boston). Poor. Public housing. Starr, Roger. 1960's-70's. *3413*

—. Maternity. Mortality. Obstetrics. Physicians. 1915-40. *1705*

—. Medical care. 1965-75. *3257*

—. Metropolitan government. 1970's. *2398*

—. Metropolitan Protective Association. New Mexico (Santa Fe). Reform. Sanitation. Spiegelberg, Flora Langermann. 1875-1943. *661*

—. Middle Classes. Migration (internal). 1950-79. *2719*

—. Minorities. Proportional representation. School Boards. 1969-74. *2505*

—. Minorities. Public Schools. Ravitch, Diane (review article). Social Change. 1805-1973. *1082*

—. Minorities in Politics. Negroes. 1889-1902. *1359*

—. Minorities in Politics. Public Welfare. 1960-77. *2447*

—. Music, popular. 1890-1970's. *2158*

—. Negroes. Puerto Ricans. Voluntary associations. Whites. 1963-78. *2691*

—. Neighborhoods. Residential patterns. 1730. *716*

—. Neighborhoods. Socialism. Working class. 1908-18. *788*

—. Occupations. Puerto Ricans. Unemployment. 1970. *3150*

—. Pennsylvania (Philadelphia). Urbanization. 1785-1850. *82*

—. Photography. Riis, Jacob. Social reform. 1890's. *1777*

—. Photography. Social Problems. 1975. *2928*

—. Political power. Social Classes. Suffrage. 1820-60. *270*

—. Politics. Public Finance. Social Problems. 1960's-70's. *2348*

—. Prices. Subsidies. Subways. Transportation. -1974. *3468*

—. Prison guards. Public Employees. 1962-73. *2962*

—. Protestant churches. Social problems. 1970's. *3226*

—. Public Administration. 1954-74. *2373*

—. Public Employees. Strikes. 1975. *2623*

—. Public housing. Reform. 1975. *3409*

—. Public schools. Race Relations. Strikes. 1968. *2878*

—. Public Services. RAND Corporation. Systems analysis. 1968-75. *2301*

—. Public Transportation. 1959-74. *3487*

—. Public transportation. 1969-77. *3473*

—. Radio City Music Hall. Theater Production and Direction. 1932-73. *918*

—. Refuse disposal. 1963-77. *3435*

—. Regional government. 1960-70's. *2395*

—. Riis, Jacob. Social reform. 1895-97. *1162*

—. Slave conspiracy. 1741. *1371*

—. Social Conditions. 1950-74. *2244*

—. Stuyvesant, Peter. 1640's-60's. *2187*

—. Theater. 1960's-70's. *2796*

—. Transportation. 1960's-74. *3465*

New York City (Astor Place). Actors and Actresses. Forrest, Edwin. Macready, William Charles. Nativism. Riots. 1849. *2963*

New York City (Bedford-Stuyvesant). Negroes. Special Impact Program. Urban Renewal. 1960-77. *2922*

New York City (Bedford-Stuyvesant, Harlem). Negroes. Puerto Ricans. Race Relations. Riots. 1960-64. *2979*

New York City (Bronx). Art, public. Law. Murals. Post offices. Preservation. Shahn, Ben. 1938-76. *3578*

—. Colleges and Universities. Ghettos. Hostos Community College. Social problems. 1970-72. *2822*

New York City (Brooklyn). Attitudes. Coney Island. Popular Culture. Recreation. Technology. 1829-1910. *915*

—. Breslin, Jimmy. Criticism. Flaherty, Joe. Hamill, Pete. Irish Americans. Novels. 1960's-70's. *3134*

—. Businessmen. Democratic Party. Negroes. Political Campaigns. Propaganda. Racism. Suffrage. 1860. *1405*

—. California. Gold rushes. Newspapers. Reporters and Reporting. 1848-53. *941*

—. Cemeteries. Green-Wood Cemetery. Landscaping. Sculpture, Victorian. 1840-1976. *2014*

—. Community control. Education. Integration. Negroes. 1882-1902. *1090*

—. Furman, Gabriel. Historians. 1800-54. *3949*

—. Negroes. Public schools. 1840's. *801*

—. Pennsylvania (Philadelphia). Upper classes. 1825-50. *801*

New York City (Brooklyn; Boro Park). Children. Judaism (Orthodox). Parents. Social Status. 1973. *3128*

New York City (Brooklyn; Weeksville). Negroes. 1830-70. *1382*

New York City (Brooklyn; Williamsburg). Community action. National Congress of Neighborhood Women. Politics. Women. 1966-78. *2690*

New York City (Brownsville, Ocean Hill). Decentralization. Educational Policy. Public Opinion. 1962-71. *2885*

New York City (Coney Island). Amusement parks. Postcards. 1870-1950. *914*

—. Funnell, Charles E. Kasson, John F. New Jersey (Atlantic City). Resorts (review article). Social Change. 1890-1910. 1975-78. *891*

New York City Correctional Institution for Women. Negroes. Prisons. Race relations. Women. 1932-75. *2947*

New York City (East Harlem). House of Representatives. Marcantonio, Vito. Puerto Ricans. Republican Party. 20c. *1597*

New York City (East River). Commerce. Navigation, Inland. Photographs. 1609-1876. *1806*

New York City (East Village). Housing. Methodology. Social Classes. 1899. *789*

New York City (Ellis Island). Immigration. Preservation. Restore Ellis Island Committee. 17c-20c. *3507*

New York City (Greenwich Village). Bethlehem Chapel. Immigration. Italian Americans. Presbyterian Church. 1900-30. *1678*

—. Community (concept). Industrialization. Reform. Urbanization. 1890-1917. *668*

—. Social classes. 1900-20. *663*

New York City (Harlem). Architecture. City Life. Middle Classes. 1976. *3060*

—. Authors. France (Paris). Negroes. Whites. 1920's. *1051*

—. Black nationalism. Business. Communism. Garvey, Marcus. Political Protest. Race Relations. 1931-39. *1390*

—. Black Nationalism. Garvey, Marcus. Universal Negro Improvement Association. 1919-26. *1347*

—. City politics. Democratic Party. Negroes. Tammany Hall. 1920's. *342*

—. Crosswaith, Frank R. Negro Labor Committee. 1925-39. *634*

—. Himes, Chester. Negroes. Novels (detective). Social Conditions. 1957-76. *3619*

—. Literature. Negroes. 1920's-76. *978*

—. Middle classes. Negroes. Photography. VanDerZee, James. 1900-74. *1427*

—. Musicians (jazz). Negroes. Waller, Fats. 1920's-30's. *953*

—. Police. Race Relations. 1966-67. *2951*

New York City (Jackson Heights, Queens). Aliens, Illegal. Assimilation. Colombian Americans. Employment. Politics. 1965-77. *3138*

New York City (Lower East Side). Children. Education. Italian Americans. Jews. 1900-10. *1296*

—. Ghettos. Jews. 1890-1920. *1446*

—. Myers, Jerome. Painting. 1880's-1940. *995*

New York City (Manhattan). Middle Classes. Migration, internal. 1820's-1979. *2722*

New York City Mutual Savings Bank. Banks (review article). Olmstead, Alan L. Osthaus, Carl R. 1819-70's. 1976. *551*

New York City (Ocean Hill-Brownsville). City government. Decentralization. Lindsay, John V. (administration). 1972-73. *2370*

New York City (Rockaway). City Government. Resorts. Social Problems. 1950-75. *2446*

New York City (SoHo). Artists. 1970's. *2804*

—. Photographs. Urban Renewal. 1973-74. *3571*

New York City (South Bronx). California (Oakland). National Urban Land Program. Neighborhoods. New Jersey (Newark). Public Lands. Real Estate. Trust for Public Land. 1973-78. *3431*

New York City (South Bronx; Morrisania). Fire departments, volunteer. German Americans. Institutions. Irish Americans. 1848-87. *751*

—. Minorities. People's Development Corporation. Urban Renewal. 1974-79. *2578*

New York City (Staten Island). Artists. Köllner, Augustus (drawings). 19c. *1048*

—. Boats. Ferries. 19c. *2107*

—. Police. 1780-1898. *1288*

New York City (Stuyvesant Town). Civil rights. Discrimination. Housing. LaGuardia, Fiorello. Metropolitan Life Insurance Company. Public housing. 1943. *3367*

New York City (Times Square). Movie theaters. Pornography. 1971. *2757*

New York, City University of. Admissions policies. Education. Equality. Ethnic groups. 1970-79. *2854*

—. Federal aid to education. 1970's. *2543*

New York City (Washington Heights). Attitudes. Decentralization. Educational Policy. Hispanic Americans. 1969-74. *2818*

New York City (West Side). Architecture. Town houses. 1885-1900. *1931*

New York Colored Orphan Asylum. Brooklyn Howard Colored Orphan Asylum. Charities. Negroes. Orphan asylums. Race Relations. 1836-1902. *1165*

New York (Corning). Drake, James A. (family). Photographs. 1899-1910. *1805*

New York (Erie County). Economic development. Geographic Mobility. Population. Social Organization. 1855. *835*

New York Gallery of Fine Arts. Art. Museums. Reed, Luman. 1844-58. *1013*

New York Herald. Bennett, James Gordon. Newspapers. Yellow journalism. 1835-65. *930*

New York (Ithaca, Owego). Economic Growth. Ithaca and Owego Railroad. Railroads. 1828-42. *2077*

New York Journal. Crime and Criminals. Gilmer, Elizabeth M. (pseud. Dorothy Dix). Journalism. Women. 1901-16. *931*

New York (Kingston). Blumin, Stuart M. (review article). City Life. 19c. 1976. *23*

—. Blumin, Stuart M. (review article). Community (concept). Urbanization. 19c. 1976. *203*

—. Jews. Political Leadership. Protestant Churches. Social Status. 1825-60. *1632*

New York (Kingston, Marborough, Troy). Family. Households. 1800-60. *687*

New York (Little Falls). Industrial Workers of the World. Labor Reform. Strikes. Textile Industry. Women. 1912. *629*

New York (Long Island). Architecture. Mackay, Clarence. Mackay, Katherine Alexander Duer. White, Stanford. 1898-1906. *2002*

—. Ferries. Fulton, Robert. Inventions. 1765-1814. *2084*

New York (Long Island Sound). Bridges. Community Participation in Politics. 1930's-75. *3485*

New York (Nassau, Suffolk counties). Public Schools. School attendance. Suburbs. 1940's-70's. *2852*

New York (New York Mills). Company towns. Polish Americans. Sex roles. Women. 1900-51. *558*

Ohio (Dayton). Barney and Smith Car Company. Manufactures. Railroad cars. 1850-1926. *470*

Ohio (Hudson). Architecture. Preservation. 1799-1978. *3536*

Ohio (Niles). Knights of the Flaming Circle. Ku Klux Klan. Law enforcement. Riots. State government. 1924. *1214*

Ohio (Peninsula). California (Sacramento). Colorado (Denver). District of Columbia. Music (jazz). New Jersey (Chester). Texas (San Antonio). 19c-20c. *2785*

Ohio River (Falls). Canals. Indiana Company. Kentucky. Ohio Canal Company. 1804-30. *208*

Ohio (Toledo). Acculturation. German Americans. Press. 1850-90. *1562*

—. Arab Americans. Asian Americans. Hispanic Americans. Immigrants. Settlement. 1965-76. *3020*

—. Attitudes. Housing. Negroes. Racism. United Automobile Workers of America. 1967-73. *3015*

—. Educational reform. Elites. Niles Bill (Ohio, 1898). Progressive Era. School boards. 1890's. *380*

—. Gitteau, William B. Hamilton, J. Kent. Progressivism. Public Schools. Reform. 1898-1921. *1109*

—. Jews. Kraus, William. Mayors. 1869-76. *278*

—. Libraries (public). 1873-1964. *994*

—. Public Welfare. 1933-37. *1195*

Ohio (Toledo; Trilby). 1835-1919. *101*

Ohio (Toledo; Vistula). 1832-1974. *151*

Ohio Valley, middle. Economic development. Urbanization. 1800-60. *175*

Ohio (Wilberforce, Xenia). Santmyer, Helen Hooven *(Ohio Town)*. Tornadoes. 1962-74. *3589*

Ohio (Wood County). Businessmen. Farmers. Railroads (electric). 1896-1902. *2096*

Ohio (Xenia). City Planning. Tornadoes. Zoning. 1974-77. *3588*

Ohio (Youngstown). Attitudes. Ku Klux Klan. Morality. Reform. 1920's. *736*

—. Elites. Entrepreneurs. Ingraham, John N. (review article). Iron industry. Pennsylvania (Philadelphia, Pittsburgh). West Virginia (Wheeling). 1874-1965. *803*

Oil and Petroleum Products *See also* Gasoline; Oil Industry and Trade.

—. Economic growth. Energy. Quebec (Montreal). 1960-80. *3743*

Oil Industry and Trade. Alberta (Calgary). Economic Conditions. 19c-20c. *3717*

—. Architecture. Boom towns. Houses, shotgun. Texas Panhandle. 1920-40. *1904*

—. Boom towns. Depressions. Texas (Conroe). 1929-33. *182*

—. Boom towns. Railroads. Texas (Burkburnett). Wichita Falls and Northwestern Railway. 1902-40. *497*

—. Colorado (Florence). Economic Development. Mineral Resources. 1885-1910. *199*

—. Pennsylvania. Pittsburgh Stock Exchange. Stocks and Bonds. 1884-96. *550*

Oklahoma. Business. Settlement. 1890's. *81*

—. Railroads. Settlement. Texas. Wichita Falls and Northwestern Railway. 1900-20. *125*

Oklahoma (Boley). Cities. Development. Fort Smith and Western Railroad Company. Negroes. Railroads. Speculators. 1903-05. *119*

Oklahoma (Cherokee Strip; Kildare). Agriculture. Boom towns. Settlement. 1893-1975. *153*

Oklahoma (Kaw City). Floods. Reservoirs. 1962-76. *2267*

Oklahoma (Langston). McCabe, Edward Preston. Migration, Internal. Negroes. 1863-1960. *1366*

—. McCabe, Edward Preston. Migration, Internal. Negroes. Newspapers. 1850-1920. *1404*

—. Negroes. Settlement. 1890-97. *118*

Oklahoma (Oklahoma City). Colorado (Denver). Community Participation in Politics. 1963. 1966. 1970. *2660*

—. Ethnicity. German Americans. Kamp, Henry. 1906-57. *1582*

—. Fairchild Wine Vault. Historical Sites and Parks. Winemaking. 1890-1925. *3514*

—. Industrialization. Population. Railroads. 1889-1939. *171*

Oklahoma (Oklahoma City, Tulsa). Civilian Conservation Corps. Segregation. 1930's. *2010*

Oklahoma (Shawnee; Benson Park). Parks. Recreation. 1908-32. *850*

Oklahoma (Stillwater). Girl Scouts of America. 1927-79. *753*

Oklahoma (Tulsa). Acculturation. Garment industry. Jews (Russian). May family. 1889-1970. *1496*

Old Capitol Library (collections). Iowa (Iowa City). Libraries. Parvin, Theodore S. 1838. 1970's. *979*

Old Swedes' Church. Gloria Dei Congregation. Pennsylvania (Philadelphia). Swedish Americans. 1638-98. *1654*

Oldham, George Ashton. Episcopal Church, Protestant. New York (Albany diocese). 1922-47. *1644*

O'Leary, Jim. Gambling. Illinois (Chicago). 1892-1925. *878*

Oligarchy. Connecticut. Officeholding. 1700-80. *266*

—. Immigrants. Massachusetts (Charlestown). 1630-40. *766*

Olmstead, Alan L. Banks (review article). New York City Mutual Savings Bank. Osthaus, Carl R. 1819-70's. 1976. *551*

Olmsted, Frederick Law. Architects. City Planning. Illinois (Riverside). Suburbs. 1868-70. *1827*

—. Architecture. City Planning. Massachusetts (North Easton). Richardson, Henry Hobson. 1870-90. *1784*

—. Architecture. City planning. Northern Pacific Railroad Company. Tilton, James. Washington (Tacoma). 1873. *1832*

—. Bancroft, William P. Canby, William M. Delaware (Wilmington). Parks. 1865-95. *2026*

—. City Planning. Illinois (Riverside). New Jersey (West Orange; Llewellyn Park). Suburbs. Vaux, Calvert. 1853-1920's. *1850*

—. City Planning. Landscape Architecture. Roper, Laura Wood (review article). Social reform. 19c. *2023*

—. City Planning. Regional planning. 1822-1903. *1855*

—. Downing, Andrew Jackson. Landscaping. 19c. *2025*

—. Landscape architecture. Reform. Social Theory. 19c. *2005*

—. Landscape architecture. Roper, Laura Wood (review article). 1822-1903. 1973. *2020*

—. Landscape architecture. Social history. 1840-1900. *2015*

—. Parks. Upper classes. 1850's-90's. *2019*

Olson, Floyd B. Hormel, George A., and Company. Minnesota (Austin). Strikes. 1933. *591*

Olton, Charles S. American Revolution. Cities (review article). Foner, Philip S. Lucas, Stephen E. Maryland (Annapolis). Papenfuse, Edward C. Pennsylvania (Philadelphia). 1763-87. 1975-76. *2*

Olympic Theater. Missouri (St. Louis). Short, Patrick. Theater. 1889-1916. *965*

—. DeBar's Grand Opera House. Missouri (St. Louis). Railroads. Stage Setting and Scenery. Theater. 1870-79. *997*

Omaha Ice Trust. Ice industry. Law. Monopolies. Nebraska. 1899-1900. *438*

Ontario. Bishops. Catholic Church. Lynch, John Joseph. Poor. Toronto Savings Bank. 1870's. *3755*

—. City government. Mass transit. Private Enterprise. Profit. Toronto Railway Company. 1891-1976. *3885*

—. Discrimination, Educational. Social Classes. Women. 1851-71. *3773*

—. Geography, historical. Urban history. Prehistory-1976. *4015*

—. Historical sources. Quantification. Quebec. Transportation. 1861-1901. *3659*

—. Lake of the Woods. Manitoba (Winnipeg). Water supply. 1912-75. *3904*

—. Mass transit. Public Utilities. Toronto Railway Company. 1891-1921. *3886*

—. Public Records. 1974. *4033*

Ontario (Chatham). Medicine (Practice of). Negroes. Saskatchewan. Shadd, Alfred Schmitz. 1896-1915. *3854*

Ontario (Cobalt). Mining towns. Research. 20c. *3938*

—. Silver mining. Working conditions. 1903-20. *3762*

Ontario (Falconbridge-Sudbury). Pollution. 1970-74. *3699*

Ontario (Guelph area). Quantitative Methods. Urbanization. 1851-1970. *3954*

—. Urbanization. 1824-1971. *3649*

Ontario (Hamilton). Adolescence. Employment. Industrialization. School (attendance). 1851-90's. *3796*

—. Business. Wholesale Trade. 1840-75. *3744*

—. Catholic Church. Irish Canadians. Katz, Michael B. (review article). Occupations. Social mobility. 1850-75. 1975. *3783*

—. Cities (review article). Massachusetts (Lynn). Methodology. Ohio (Columbus). Pennsylvania (Warren). Wisconsin (Milwaukee). 1830's-1910's. 1970's. *37*

—. City Government. Pressure groups. Public Utilities. 1900-25. *3895*

—. Commerce. Industrialization. Population. 1851-71. *3795*

—. Elites. Entrepreneurs. 1850's. *3793*

—. Employment. Ethnic Groups. New York (Buffalo, Kingston, Poughkeepsie). Pennsylvania (Philadelphia). Property. Social Classes. 19c. *778*

—. Family. Katz, Michael B. (review article). Social Classes. 1850-80. *3760*

—. Family. Katz, Michael B. (review article). Social Mobility. 1851-61. 1975. *3792*

—. Fuga, Francis J. Shrine of Our Lady of Klocočov. Slovak Canadians. Uniates. 1952-77. *3869*

—. Industrialization. Public schools. Socialization. 19c. *3794*

—. Political parties. Social Classes. 1967-72. *3683*

—. Property Tax. 1940-78. *3702*

Ontario (Hamilton; Westdale). Suburbs. 1911-51. *3669*

Ontario (Kingston). Archives. City Government. Queen's University. 1838-1978. *4000*

—. Industrialization. Location. Physicians. Residential Patterns. 1857-1975. *3757*

—. New York (Ogdensburg). Ontario, Lake. Steamboats. Transportation. 1815-70. *3656*

Ontario (Kitchener). Elections (municipal, provincial). Urban Renewal. 1967-71. *3706*

Ontario, Lake. New York (Ogdensburg). Ontario (Kingston). Steamboats. Transportation. 1815-70. *3656*

Ontario (London). Architecture. City planning. Mutual Advisory Committee. Politics. Preservation. 1970-77. *3876*

—. Ethnic groups. Occupations. 1871. *3826*

—. Heritage Act (Ontario, 1975). Local Architectural Conservation Advisory Committee. Preservation. 1945-77. *3896*

Ontario (Orillia). Adolescence. Employment. Frontier and Pioneer Life. Social change. 1861-71. *3784*

Ontario (Ottawa). Architecture. Capitol Theatre. Entertainment. Movie theaters. Vaudeville. 1920-70. *3911*

—. Archives. City Government. 19c-1976. *4066*

—. Boosterism. Capitols. Location. 1822-59. *3658*

—. Booth, John Rudolphus. City Government. Fire. Housing. Lumber and Lumbering. Working class. 1900-03. *3887*

—. City Government. Diseases. Fire. Public Health. Reform. Water supply. 1830-90. *3700*

—. City Politics. Epidemics. Public Health. Reform. Typhoid fever. 1911-12. *3873*

—. Economic Growth. Urbanization. 19c. *3638*

—. Fire fighting. Public Health. Water Supply. 1910-15. *3703*

—. Occupations. 1870. *3727*

Ontario (Peel County; Hamilton). Census. Literacy. Methodology. Social classes. 19c. *4004*

Ontario (Simcoe County). Agricultural Commodities. Marketing. Railroads. Roads. Towns. 1850-75. *3739*

Ontario, southern. Conservative Party. Voting and Voting Behavior. Working Class. 1908-19. *3695*

—. Geographic Space. Population. Urbanization. 1941-71. *3764*

—. Metropolitan Areas. Population. 1871-1975. *3763*

Ontario (Toronto). Accidents. City Government. Compensation, municipal. Public Employees. 1858-70. *3684*

—. Acculturation. Boardinghouses. Immigrants. Italian Canadians. 20c. *3834*

—. Acculturation. Immigrants. 1950's-70's. *3837*

—. Anti-Communist movements. Anti-Semitism. Freedom of speech. Immigration. National self-image. 1928-29. *3629*

—. Architects. 1834-90's. *3878*

—. Archives. Immigrants. Photographs. 1900-30. 1974. *4053*

—. Archives, City. 1959-73. *3983*

—. Garment industry. Location. Ontario (Toronto). Publishers and Publishing. Quebec (Montreal). 1949-67. *3753*

Papertowns. City Planning. South Dakota. Speculation. 1878-1920. *1826*

Papua New Guinea. Arizona (Willcox). Cargo cults. Economic Conditions. "Rex Allen Days" (festival). Towns. 1951-76. *2572*

Parades. Centennial Celebrations. Iowa (Des Moines). 1876. *854*

Pardee, George C. California (San Francisco). Earthquakes. National Guard. Schmitz, Eugene. 1906. *1239*

Parents. Attitudes. Busing. Michigan (Pontiac). School Integration. 1972-75. *2890*

—. Children. Judaism (Orthodox). New York City (Brooklyn; Boro Park). Social Status. 1973. *3128*

Pareto, Vilfredo. Elites. Industrialization. Pennsylvania (Duquesne). Social change. 1891-1933. *765*

Parishes. Assimilation. Catholic Church. Pennsylvania (Philadelphia). 1759-1975. *1651*

Parishes, national. Catholic Church. Conflict and Conflict Resolution. Italian Americans. Rhode Island (Providence). 1890-1930. *1563*

Parker, Charles Taylor. Blance, Joseph G. Georgia (Rockmart). Slate. 1832-1978. *174*

Parkinson, John. Architecture. Washington (Seattle). 1890's. *1860*

Parks. Alberta. Devonian Group of Charitable Foundations. Harvie, Eric Lafferty. Preservation. Scientific Experiments and Research. 1955-79. *3888*

—. Balboa Park. California (San Diego). 1868-1902. *2018*

—. Bancroft, William P. Canby, William M. Delaware (Wilmington). Olmsted, Frederick Law. 1865-95. *2026*

—. Bigelow, Edward M. Pennsylvania (Pittsburgh). 1888-1916. *2012*

—. British Columbia (Vancouver). Business. Political power. 1886-1928. *3900*

—. Bureaucracies. City Government. Libraries. Race. Social Classes. Texas (Houston). 1970's. *3440*

—. Cemeteries. Massachusetts (Boston, Lowell). Rural cemetery movement. 1841-65. *2004*

—. Central Park. City Politics. New York City. 1844-56. *2024*

—. City planning. Crime and Criminals. 1930's-60's. *3330*

—. City Planning. Illinois (Chicago). Private Enterprise. 1850-75. *2011*

—. Clubs. Recreation. Youth. 1974. *2747*

—. Crime and Criminals. New York City. 1970's. *3430*

—. Democracy. Landscape architecture. Urbanization. 1850-1900. *2016*

—. Fitzgerald, F. Scott. Flushing Meadow Park. Moses, Robert. New York City. 1925-36. *1807*

—. Illinois (Chicago; Columbus Park). Jensen, Jens. 1860-1900's. *2008*

—. Liberty Park. New Jersey (Jersey City). Pesin, Morris. Waterfronts. 1958-78. *3428*

—. Oklahoma (Shawnee; Benson Park). Recreation. 1908-32. *850*

—. Olmsted, Frederick Law. Upper classes. 1850's-90's. *2019*

—. Pennsylvania (Philadelphia; Pennypack Park). Prices. Property. -1974. *3275*

—. Prices. Property. Texas (Dallas). 1966. *3385*

Parochial Schools. *See* Church Schools; Religious Education.

Parsons case. Massachusetts (Springfield). Witchcraft. 1650-55. *681*

Parties, Political. *See* Political Parties.

Partners for Livable Places. Environment. Preservation. 1977-78. *3539*

Partridge, Alexander. Colonial Government. Rhode Island. Trials. 1652. *1285*

Parvin, Theodore S. Iowa (Iowa City). Libraries. Old Capitol Library (collections). 1838. 1970's. *979*

Patents *See also* Inventions.

—. Architecture. Houses, elephant. Lafferty, James V. New Jersey (Margate). Publicity. Real estate. 1880's. 1970-77. *1881*

Patios. Architecture. Houses. Porches. Social Change. 1860-1960. *1985*

Patriotism *See also* Naturalization.

—. Elections (mayoral). Ethnicity. Hylan, John F. Mitchel, John Purroy. New York City. World War I. 1917. *284*

—. Ku Klux Klan. LaFollette, Philip. Reform. Wisconsin (Madison). 1922-27. *730*

Patronage. Comprehensive Employment and Training Act (US, 1973). Connecticut (New Haven). 1973-75. *2425*

Pattern Books. Architecture (Greek Revival). Benjamin, Asher. Doorframes. Massachusetts (East Lexington). 1833-40. *1961*

Patterson, Thomas M. Colorado. Denver *Post.* Newspapers. Reform. *Rocky Mountain News.* 1906-07. *926*

Paul, Thomas (and family). Clergy. Massachusetts (Boston). Negroes. 1773-1973. *1387*

Pavar, David J. Huggins, Nathan L. Reform (review article). Religion. Rosenberg, Carroll Smith. Social control. 1812-1900. 1970's. *1677*

Pavements. Middle classes. Roads. Social problems. Technology. 1880-1924. *1775*

Payne, William. Architecture. Capitols. Massachusetts (Boston). 1658-1975. *1883*

Peabody Hotel. Brinkley, Robert Campbell. Tennessee (Memphis). 1869-1923. *1887*

Peace bonds. Bail. Crime and Criminals. Friends, Society of. Pennsylvania (Philadelphia). 1680-1829. *1250*

Peace Movements. Illinois. Local Government. Lochner, Louis Paul. People's Council of America for Democracy and Peace. State Government. 1917. *333*

Peacemakers. Negroes. Riots. 1968-69. *2932*

Pearce, William. Alberta (Calgary). Land. Settlement. Surveying. 1883-86. *3905*

Peasants *See also* Agricultural Labor; Farmers; Land Tenure; Working Class.

—. American Revolution. Attitudes. Carleton, Guy. Military Occupation. Quebec. 1775-76. *3682*

—. Behavior. Immigration. Modernization. Slavic Americans. Working class. 1850-1925. *1298*

Pedagogy. *See* Teaching.

Peddlers. City Life. New York City. Retail Trade. 1975. *2587*

—. Folklore. Street cries. 19c-20c. *418*

Pediatrics. Folklore. Gynecology. Italian Americans. New York (Utica). Obstetrics. Polish Americans. 20c. *3244*

—. Hospitals, children's. Massachusetts (Boston). New York City. Pennsylvania (Philadelphia). 1776-1976. *1760*

Pelissier, Victor. Composers. New York City. Pennsylvania (Philadelphia). 1792-1817. *1031*

Pendergast, Thomas. City Government. Missouri (Kansas City). Progressivism. 1900-26. *378*

—. Missouri (Kansas City). Negroes. Political machines. Truman, Harry S. 1922-34. *291*

Penner, Jacob. City Politics. Manitoba (Winnipeg). Webb, Ralph. 1919-34. *3690*

Pennsylvania *See also* Northeastern or North Atlantic States.

—. Acculturation. Educational Reform. Ideology. Industrialization. Social control. 1880-1910. *1091*

—. Advisory Bodies. Local government. 1972-74. *2372*

—. Architecture. Bridges. City Planning. Photographs. 1870's-80's. *1815*

—. Attitudes. Blind. Education. Employment. Pittsburgh Workshop for the Blind. 19c-1939. *1184*

—. Baseball. Boys. Lancaster City Kid Leagues. 1911-15. *890*

—. Charities. Friends, Society of. Philadelphia Society for Organizing Charitable Relief and Repressing Mendicancy. 1800-1900. *1181*

—. Charters. Pittsburgh Government Study Commission. Political Participation. 1972-74. *2367*

—. Economic development. Elites. Philadelphia Board of Trade. 1825-61. *394*

—. Economic growth. Occupational mobility. 19c. *847*

—. Education. Referendum. Voting and Voting Behavior. 1972-74. *2471*

—. Fire insurance. Franklin, Benjamin. Philadelphia Contributionship for the Insurance of Houses from Loss by Fire. 1666-1792. *539*

—. Highways. Population. Suburbs. 1940-70. *2275*

—. Illinois (Chicago). Location. Michigan (Detroit). Ohio (Cleveland). Production. Steel Industry. 1910-72. *495*

—. Industrialization. Philadelphia Social History Project. Research. Urbanization. 1976. *3978*

—. Industrialization. *Pittsburgh Survey* (1909). Social Surveys. 1907-14. *1168*

—. Local government. Neighborhoods. Pittsburgh Neighborhood Atlas. 1968-70's. *2368*

—. Migration, internal. Rural areas. 1955-70. *2734*

—. Oil Industry and Trade. Pittsburgh Stock Exchange. Stocks and Bonds. 1884-96. *550*

—. Philadelphia Federation of Teachers. Strikes. Teachers. 1973. *2639*

—. Rural-Urban Studies. Tradition. 1970. *2661*

Pennsylvania (Bethlehem). American Revolution. Moravian Church. 1775-83. *1226*

Pennsylvania (Bethlehem, Nazareth). Architecture. Moravian Church. 1740-68. *1925*

Pennsylvania (Bucks County). Democratic Party. Republican Party. Suburbs. Whites. 1972. *2427*

Pennsylvania (Duquesne). Elites. Industrialization. Pareto, Vilfredo. Social change. 1891-1933. *765*

Pennsylvania (Economy). Architecture. Harmony Society. Restoration. 1780-1973. *2117*

—. Harmony Society. Rapp, George. Religion. Utopias. 1785-1847. *1627*

Pennsylvania (Economy, Harmony). Architecture. Indiana (New Harmony). Preservation. Rapp, George. Restorations. 1804-25. 20c. *3547*

—. Artifacts. Buildings. City Planning. Communes. Harmony Society. Indiana (New Harmony). Planning. Social customs. 1820's-1905. *648*

Pennsylvania (Erie). Economic Development. Railroads. Violence. 1852-55. *1228*

Pennsylvania (Germantown). Artisans. Economic conditions. Industrialization. Occupations. 1767-91. *526*

—. Cities (review article). Connecticut (Stamford). New England. New York. 1660's-18c. *7*

—. Family. Population. Social Organization. Wolf, Stephanie Grauman (review article). 1683-1800. 1976. *689*

Pennsylvania (Harmony, New Harmony). Immigrants. Letters. Norwegian Americans. Rapp, George. 1816-26. *1561*

Pennsylvania (Harrisburg). City beautification. Civic Club of Harrisburg. Dock, Mira Lloyd. 1900-03. *1814*

Pennsylvania Historical and Museum Commission. Historical societies. Pennsylvania Historical Association (10th annual research conference). 1975. *4059*

Pennsylvania Historical Association (10th annual research conference). Historical societies. Pennsylvania Historical and Museum Commission. 1975. *4059*

Pennsylvania (Hopewell Village). Industrial relations. Iron industry. 1800-50. *411*

Pennsylvania Hospital for the Sick Poor. Charities. Friends, Society of. Pennsylvania (Philadelphia). Poor. 18c. *1174*

Pennsylvania (Johnstown). Johnson Company. Management, scientific. Streetcar industry. Taylor, Frederick W. 1896. *506*

Pennsylvania (Lancaster). Centrifugal Rotary Engine Company. Engines. Hayes, Alexander L. Steam Power. 1870. *515*

—. Coalitions. Political Parties. Reform. 1921-30. *363*

—. Commuting. Streetcars. Suburbs. 1890-1920. *2079*

—. Local politics. Stevens, Thaddeus. 1842-68. *292*

Pennsylvania (Mauch Chunk). Boom towns. Coal Mines and Mining. 1814-25. *189*

Pennsylvania (Muncy). Fire companies. 1848-1973. *2043*

Pennsylvania (Philadelphia). Abolition Movement. Negroes. Riots. 1830-50. *1220*

—. Aged. Rest homes. 1817-1900. *1153*

—. American Association for the History of Medicine. Medical history. 1760-1925. *1710*

—. American Revolution. Cities (review article). Foner, Philip S. Lucas, Stephen E. Maryland (Annapolis). Olton, Charles S. Papenfuse, Edward C. 1763-87. 1975-76. *2*

—. American Revolution. German Americans. Lutherans. 1776-81. *1693*

—. American Revolution (antecedents). Business. 1764-76. *799*

—. American Revolution (antecedents). Elites. Leadership. Philadelphia Resistance Committee. Political activism. 1765-76. *259*

—. American Revolution (antecedents). Friends, Society of. Merchants. Radicals and Radicalsim. 1769-74. *254*

—. Archaeology. Preservation. 18c. 1950's-75. *3505*

—. Architecture. City planning. Europe. Housing. Modernism. New Deal. New York City. Ohio (Cleveland). 1932-60. *1952*

—. Architecture. Connecticut (New Haven). Georgia (Savannah). Massachusetts (Boston). New York City. 18c. *1983*

—. Architecture. Great Britain (London). 1619-1800. *1809*

—. Architecture. Regionalism. 1776-20c. *1867*

—. Artisans. Industrialization. Morality. Social customs. Work ethic. Working Class. 1820-50. *787*

—. Artists. McConaughy, David. Petitions. Tariff. 1868-90. *962*

—. Aspira (organization). Educational Reform. Harlem Parents Union. Minorities. New York City. Voluntary Associations. Welfare Rights Organization. 1970's. *2840*

—. Assimilation. Catholic Church. Parishes. 1759-1975. *1651*

—. Assimilation. Ethnic groups. Negroes. 1850-1970. *1314*

—. Assimilation. Polish Americans. Polish Emigration Land Company. Smolinski, Joseph. Virginia. 1860's. 1917-18. *1591*

—. Bail. Crime and Criminals. Friends, Society of. Peace bonds. 1680-1829. *1250*

—. Bank Reserves. Massachusetts (Boston). New York City. 1856-58. *536*

—. Banking. Brown, Alexander & Sons. Cotton trade. Foreign exchange. Great Britain (Liverpool). Maryland (Baltimore). New York City. 1820-80. *437*

—. Barralet, John James. Dunlap House. Painting. ca 1750-1815. *1869*

—. Bartenders. Negroes. Social organization. 1976. *2744*

—. Benjamin, Philip S. Feldberg, Michael. Miller, Richard G. Politics. Religion. Sinclair, Bruce. Technology. Urbanization (review article). 1790-1920. 1974-76. *8*

—. Birth Control. Fertility. Negroes. Socialization. Women. 1901-75. *2674*

—. Block system. City Planning. 1776-1977. *1857*

—. Bocce ball. Ethnicity. Games. Immigrants. Italian Americans. 1974. *3195*

—. British West Indies. Economic Conditions. International trade. 1750-75. *424*

—. Brown, Charles Brockden. Epidemics. Letters. Literature. Rush, Benjamin. Yellow Fever. 1793-1800. *988*

—. Budgets. Decisionmaking. Family. 1870-80. *693*

—. Bureaucrats. Public housing. Urban Renewal. 1929-41. *3361*

—. Burgess, Ernest W. Housing. Models. Occupations. 1920-60. *3271*

—. Business. Dreiser, Theodore. Robber barons. Yerkes, Charles Tyson. ca 1837-1905. *535*

—. Business. Finance. Negroes. Race Relations. 1968. *3022*

—. Business. Transportation. 18c. *2065*

—. Butler, Smedley D. Kendrick, W. Freeland. Prohibition. 1923-24. *1281*

—. Cameron, Simon. Local Politics. Political machines. 1867-72. *352*

—. Carpenter's Company. Colonial Government. Labor Unions and Organizations. ca 1700-74. *616*

—. Catto, Octavius V. Civil Rights. Negroes. 1861-71. *1411*

—. Census. City Life. 1693-1790. *710*

—. Census. Public Schools. Teachers. 1865-90. *1077*

—. Centennial Celebrations. Independence Hall. Philanthropy. Seybert, Henry. 1793-1882. *1146*

—. Charities. Friends, Society of. Pennsylvania Hospital for the Sick Poor. Poor. 18c. *1174*

—. Charities. Social work. Society for Organizing Charitable Relief and Repressing Mendicancy. Women. 1864-1909. *1182*

—. Children. Family. Income. 1880. *565*

—. Children. Indentured servants. Irish Americans. 1771-1920's. *1503*

—. Children. Massachusetts (Boston). Progressivism. Recreation. 1886-1911. *1160*

—. Children's Aid Society. Family. Foster homes. Home Missionary Society. 1880-1905. *1138*

—. Church records. Immigrants. Italian Americans. Methodology. 1789-1900. *3984*

—. Cities (review article). Clark, Dennis J. Klein, Milton M. New York City. Ohio (Cleveland). Porter, Philip W. 17c-1978. *82*

—. City halls. Construction. Political Corruption. Stokley, William. 1830-75. *340*

—. City life. 1681-1970's. *230*

—. City Life. Environment. Law. 1750-84. *1756*

—. City planning. Recreation. ca 1900-60's. *2763*

—. City Politics. Construction. Contractors. Entrepreneurs. Irish Americans. 1846-1960's. *1504*

—. City Politics. Economic Conditions. Social Mobility. 1681-1776. *842*

—. Civil Rights. Colored Protective Association. NAACP. Negroes. Riots. 1918. *1221*

—. Civilian review boards. Labor Unions and Organizations. Maryland (Baltimore). New York (Buffalo). Police. 1958-74. *2952*

—. Clark, Dennis J. Connecticut (Stamford). Davis, Allen F. Ethnic Groups. Feinstein, Estelle F. Haller, Mark H. Urban History (review article). 1700-1970. 1965-74. *4012*

—. Class consciousness. NAACP. Negroes. Race. 1930's. *1392*

—. Community Participation in Politics. Elections. Good Judges for Philadelphia (organization). Judges. 1973. *2498*

—. Composers. New York City. Pelissier, Victor. 1792-1817. *1031*

—. Construction. Housing. Prices. 1785-1830. *467*

—. Cost of living. Employment. Ethnic Groups. Income. Poverty. 1880. *564*

—. Crime and Criminals. Dropouts. School attendance. Students. 1970. *2853*

—. Crime and Criminals. Gangs. Graffiti. Juvenile Delinquency. Race Relations. 1970-72. *2966*

—. Crime and Criminals. Industrialization. Violence. 1820's-1976. *1248*

—. Decisionmaking. District of Columbia. Intergovernmental relations. New Jersey (Newark, Trenton). New York City. Tocks Island Project. Urbanization. Water projects. 1962-75. *2311*

—. Democratic Party. Elections (Municipal). Independent Democratic Campaign Committee. O'Donnell, John. Political Reform. Vare, William S. 1933. *366*

—. Democratic Party. Elections (presidential). Ethnic groups. 1924-36. *303*

—. Democratic Republicans. Merchants. Swanwick, John. 1790-98. *280*

—. Discrimination, educational. North. 1800-1965. *2836*

—. Documents. Fire insurance. Insurance Company of North America Corporation. 1790-1975. *4025*

—. Economic Conditions. Social Organization. 18c-19c. *4*

—. Economic Development. Lindstrom, Diane (review article). 1810-50. *407*

—. Economic Growth. Entrepreneurs. Gentry. Social Organization. 1790-99. *796*

—. Education. Income. Negroes. Residential Patterns. ca 1965-73. *3072*

—. Educational Reform. Negroes. White, Jacob C., Jr. 1857-1902. *1116*

—. Elites. Social Theory. 1820's. *823*

—. Employment. Ethnic Groups. New York (Buffalo, Kingston, Poughkeepsie). Ontario (Hamilton). Property. Social Classes. 19c. *778*

—. Enlightenment. Franklin, Benjamin. Friends, Society of. Inventions. 1727-76. *722*

—. Ethnic groups. Immigrants. Industry. Occupations. Social Status. 1850-80. *1322*

—. Ethnic Groups. Indiana (Indianapolis). Massachusetts (Boston). Occupations. Social Mobility. Texas (Houston). 1850-60. *832*

—. Ethnic Groups. Religion. Social classes. Voting and Voting Behavior. 1924-40. *1329*

—. Ethnic Groups. Women. Working Class. 1910-30. *1318*

—. Ethnic Groups (review article). Irish Americans. Working Class. 1725-1975. *1333*

—. Famines. Great Britain (London). Immigration. Irish Americans. Urbanization. 1840's-60. *1512*

—. *Favorite* (vessel). Shipping. Trade routes. *William* (vessel). 1782-86. *430*

—. Folk religion. Greek Americans. Visions. 1900-74. *3221*

—. Folklore. Gomez, Dolorez Amelia. Occult Sciences. 1974. *2642*

—. French Revolution. Genêt, Edmond-Charles. Jacobin societies. Politics. 1792-94. *737*

—. Funerals. Italian Americans. Social Change. 1800-1974. *3196*

—. Furniture and Furnishings. 1820-40. *476*

—. Gloria Dei Congregation. Old Swedes' Church. Swedish Americans. 1638-98. *1654*

—. Goodacre, Robert. Popular Culture. Science. 1823-25. *1003*

—. Historiography. New York. Oral history. Social Surveys. Watson, John Fanning. 1779-1860. *4063*

—. Hospitals, children's. Massachusetts (Boston). New York City. Pediatrics. 1776-1976. *1760*

—. Housing. Integration. Negroes. Planning. 1947-79. *3412*

—. Housing. Negroes. New Deal. 1930's. *1130*

—. Ice industry. Technology. 19c. *499*

—. Identity. 1820-1920. *2188*

—. Immigration. Massachusetts (Boston). Models. North America. South Carolina (Charleston). 16c-17c. *92*

—. Indentured servants. Marketing. 1771-73. *567*

—. Industrial Archaeology. Social history. 1850's-1910. 1974-77. *4018*

—. Institutions. Residential patterns. Social Classes. Suburbs. 1880-1900. *161*

—. Integration. Legislation. Streetcars. 1850's-70. *1353*

—. Integration. Migration. Planning. Whites. 1969. *3054*

—. Judicial system. 1683-1968. *1284*

—. Loyalists. Militia. Politics. Prices. Riots. Wilson, James. 1779. *1204*

—. Maryland (Baltimore). New York City. Silversmithing. 18c. *1025*

—. Massachusetts (Boston). New York City. Political participation. 1700-65. *252*

—. Massachusetts (Boston). New York (Poughkeepsie). Occupational mobility. 19c. *833*

—. Neighborhoods. Powelton Village Development Association. Restorations. 1955-79. *3519*

—. New York City. Urbanization. 1785-1850. *82*

—. New York City (Brooklyn). Upper classes. 1825-50. *801*

—. Octavia Hill Association. Public Welfare. Social reform. ca 1890-1909. *1197*

—. Pilots, Ship. Strikes. Wages. 1792. *602*

—. Police. Violence. 1834-44. *1276*

—. Political Factions. Proprietary gentry. Provincial government. Social Change. 1720-76. *761*

—. Political Factions. Riots. Yellow fever. 1793. *15*

—. Poor Laws. Public Welfare. 1705-09. *1177*

—. Population. 1700-90. *683*

—. Religion. Slavery. Wealth. 1684-1775. *1391*

—. Residential Patterns. Social classes. 1950-70. *2707*

—. Sculpture. 1785-1830. *972*

—. UN (headquarters site). 1945-46. *2197*

—. Vital Statistics. 1720-75. *711*

Pennsylvania (Philadelphia; Fairmount). City life. Neighborhoods. Residential Patterns. Social Change. 1960's-70's. *2646*

Pennsylvania (Philadelphia; Fairmount Park). Architecture. Mansions. Restorations. 1774-99. *2003*

Pennsylvania (Philadelphia; Main Line). Housing. Prices. Suburbs. 1967-69. *3377*

Pennsylvania (Philadelphia; Pennypack Park). Parks. Prices. Property. -1974. *3275*

Pennsylvania (Philadelphia, Pittsburgh). Cosmopolitanism. Ohio (Cleveland). Upper Classes. 1850-1900. *781*

—. Elites. Entrepreneurs. Ingraham, John N. (review article). Iron industry. Ohio (Youngstown). West Virginia (Wheeling). 1874-1965. *803*

Pennsylvania (Philadelphia, Scranton). Irish Americans. McHale, Tom. Novels. O'Hara, John. 1934-77. *1500*

Pennsylvania (Philadelphia; Society Hill). Restorations. 18c. 1957-70's. *3542*

Pennsylvania (Philadelphia; Upper Darby). Artifacts. Commercialism. Folk art. Greek Americans. Religion. 1970's. *461*

Pennsylvania (Pittsburgh). Abolitionists. Fugitive Slaves. Negroes. Philanthropic Society. 1830's-60. *1341*

—. Acculturation. Catholic Church. Irish Americans. St. Andrew Parish. 1863-90. *1510*

—. Acculturation. Immigration. Women. 1900-45. *1321*

—. Actors and actresses. Chapman family. Showboats. 1827-47. *857*

—. Air Pollution. Elites. Reform. Smoke abatement. Tilbury, Corwin D. 1890's-1918. *1152*

—. Alabama (Fairhope). City Government. Michigan (Southfield). Taxation. 1887-1973. *2296*

—. Allegheny Athletic Association. Football. New York Athletic Club. Professionalization. 1866-90's. *881*

—. Allegheny Conference on Community Development. Federal Aid. Flood control. Upper Classes. 1936-60. *329*

—. Army Corps of Engineers. Congress. Flood Control Commission. Reservoirs. 1908-65. *2052*

—. Assimilation. Ethnic groups. Fraternal organizations. Health. 1900-70. *729*

—. Attitudes. Death and Dying. Working class. 1890's. *786*

—. Bigelow, Edward M. Parks. 1888-1916. *2012*

—. Boxing. Individualism. Professionalization. Regionalism. Social mobility. 1890's-1900's. *860*

—. Bridges. Construction. Lindenthal, Gustav. Roebling, John A. Smithfield Street Bridge. Wernwag, Lewis. 19c. *1779*

—. Business. Economic Conditions. Urban Renewal. 1900-76. *2171*

—. Businessmen. Education. Industrialization. Labor. Mechanics' institutes. 1830-40. *794*

—. City Government. Consolidation. 1854-72. *197*

—. City Government. Decisionmaking. Public health. Sanitation. 1873-1945. *2038*

—. City government. Political Change. Political leadership. 1954-70. *2436*

—. City Life. Migration. Negroes. Occupations. Polish Americans. 1900-30. *1299*

—. City Planning. Zoning. 1917-23. *1841*

—. Credit. Loan sharking. Reform. Working Class. 1900-15. *548*

—. Depressions. Labor. Wages. 1908. *573*

—. Education. Immigrants. Jews. 1862-1932. *1485*

—. Employment. Immigrants. Oral history. Women. ca 1900-20. 1976. *1320*

—. Epidemics. Health Boards. 1872-95. *1718*

—. Epidemics. Law. Public health. Urbanization. 19c. *1717*

—. Epidemics. Public Policy. Water pollution. 1893-1914. *2054*

—. Ethnic groups. Occupational mobility. Residential patterns. 1880-1920. *1335*

—. Ethnicity. Irish Americans. Music. Radio. 1900-77. *3135*

—. Fire departments. Local government. Urbanization. 1870. *2413*

—. Fort Pitt Blockhouse. Military Camps and Forts. 1760-1909. *1936*

—. Housing. Mortgages. Negroes. 1975. *3387*

—. Housing. Population. Social status. 1815. *714*

—. Illinois (Chicago). Industry. Maryland (Baltimore). Missouri (St. Louis). Railroads. Strikes. 1877. *631*

—. Iron Industry. Migration, internal. Negroes. Steel Industry. 1916-30. *830*

—. Jews. Working Class. 1890-1930. *1486*

—. Literature. 18c-20c. *2159*

—. Methodology. Social Classes. Urbanization. 1974. *3973*

—. New Castle's Cascade Park. Railroads (electric). 1897. *858*

—. Prices. Property. Zoning. 1973. *3334*

—. Shipbuilding. Technology. Technology. 1790-1865. *517*

—. Social Conditions. Technology. Women. Working class. 1870-1900. *1773*

—. Steel Industry. Strikes. 1919. *577*

Pennsylvania (Pittsburgh; East End). Daily Life. Fleming, Hartley G. Reminiscences. Youth. 1898-1915. *651*

Pennsylvania (Pittsburgh; East End; Shadyside). Automobiles. City Planning. Streetcars. 1852-1916. *138*

Pennsylvania (Pittsburgh; Grant Boulevard). Automobiles. City Life. Horn, Eloise. *Index to Pittsburgh Life* (periodical). 1901. *2106*

Pennsylvania (Pittsburgh; Manchester). Ghettos. Pittsburgh History and Landmarks Foundation. Restorations. 1965-78. *3575*

Pennsylvania (Pittsburgh; St. Andrew's Parish). Acculturation. Catholic Church. Human Relations. Irish Americans. 1863-90. *1511*

Pennsylvania (Pittsburgh; 26th Ward). Labor. Population. Steel Industry. 1880-1915. *705*

Pennsylvania (Reading). Local Politics. Socialist Party. Women. ca 1927-38. *298*

Pennsylvania (Rockdale). Cotton industry. Economic conditions. Industrialization. Manufacturing. Social change. 1825-65. *521*

—. Industrialization. Religion. Social Classes. Technology. Wallace, Anthony F. C. (review article). 1825-65. 1978. *20*

Pennsylvania (Rosetos). Acculturation. Bianco, Carla. Catholic Church. Gambino, Richard. Italian Americans (review article). Social Organization. Tomasi, Silvano. 20c. *1606*

Pennsylvania (Scranton). Beamish, Frank A. City Politics. Knights of Labor. Powderly, Terence V. 1878-84. *288*

—. Coal Mines and Mining. Labor Disputes. Police. Violence. 1866-84. *1289*

—. Immigrants. Irish Americans. Social mobility. Welsh Americans. 1880-90. *1301*

Pennsylvania (Steelton). Blackwell, Peter C. Negroes. Organizations. 1880-1920. *1343*

—. Immigrants. Italian Americans. Negroes. Occupational mobility. Slavic Americans. 1880-1920. *1300*

Pennsylvania Town. Towns. 19c-20c. *1816*

Pennsylvania (Warren). Cities (review article). Massachusetts (Lynn). Methodology. Ohio (Columbus). Ontario (Hamilton). Wisconsin (Milwaukee). 1830's-1910's. 1970's. *37*

Pennsylvania (Warren; Keystone Block). Buildings. Hall, Orris. Opera house. 1869-83. *1935*

Pennsylvania (Warrensville). Daily Life. 1890's. 1900's. *31*

Pennsylvania (Wilkes-Barre). Coal Mines and Mining. Elites. Migration, Internal. Urbanization. 1820-80. *89*

Pensions *See also* Aged.

—. City Government. Federal government. Public Employees. 1977. *2302*

Peoples and Cultures, Inc. Arts and Crafts. Ethnic groups. Ohio (Cleveland). 1974. *2788*

People's Council of America for Democracy and Peace. Illinois. Local Government. Lochner, Louis Paul. Peace Movements. State Government. 1917. *333*

People's Development Corporation. Minorities. New York City (South Bronx; Morrisania). Urban Renewal. 1974-79. *2578*

People's Institute of New York City. Community Participation in Politics. Immigrants. New York City. Reform. Working Class. 1910-20. *1145*

Perez, Louis A., Jr. Cubans. Florida (Tampa). Labor Disputes. *Lector* (reader). Reminiscences. Tobacco workers. ca 1925-35. *572*

Periodicals *See also* Editors and Editing; Freedom of the Press; Newspapers; Press.

—. *American Miller.* Flour. Mills. Minnesota. Research. 1880's-1930's. 1978. *490*

—. Atheism. Bobb, John. Missouri (St. Louis). *Western Examiner.* 1834-35. *1645*

—. Bibliographies. City Planning. Urban studies. 1975. *4055*

—. City Planning. *Journal of the American Institute of Planners.* 1965-75. *3939*

—. Illinois (Chicago). Monroe, Harriet. *Poetry.* 1870's-1910's. *1062*

—. Labor. Rhode Island (Lincoln; Saylesville). Sayles Finishing Plants. Social Organization. Textile Industry. 1920's-30's. *590*

—. Literature. *Reviewer.* Virginia (Richmond). 1920's. *1036*

Perk, Ralph. Carney, James. Ohio (Cleveland). Pinkney, Arnold R. Political Campaigns (mayoral). Stokes, Carl B. 1971. *2477*

Personal Narratives *See also* Autobiography; Diaries; Memoirs; Oral history; Travel Accounts.

—. Archival Catalogs and Inventories. Local history. Negroes. New York City. Staten Island Institute of Arts and Sciences. 1969-76. *4031*

—. Arkansas (Little Rock). Attitudes. Eckford, Elizabeth. Negroes. Public schools. School Integration. 1957-79. *3120*

—. Art. Davis, Gene. District of Columbia. 1950-66. *2790*

—. Artists. District of Columbia. 1978. *2809*

—. Capitols. Kansas. Murals. Winter, Lumen Martin. 1977. *2814*

—. Carpenter, Inta Gale. City Life. Folklore. Methodology. 1978. *3947*

—. City Politics. Labor Unions and Organizations. New York City. Police. Public Finance. 1975. *2421*

Persons, Stow. Jaher, Frederick C. Pessen, Edward. Social Mobility (review article). Thernstrom, Stephan. 19c-1970. 1973. *808*

Peru (Lima). Assimilation. Chinese Americans. New York City. 1849-1976. *1558*

Pesin, Morris. Liberty Park. New Jersey (Jersey City). Parks. Waterfronts. 1958-78. *3428*

Pessen, Edward. Jaher, Frederick C. Persons, Stow. Social Mobility (review article). Thernstrom, Stephan. 19c-1970. 1973. *808*

Petitions. Artists. McConaughy, David. Pennsylvania (Philadelphia). Tariff. 1868-90. *962*

Petroleum. *See* Oil and Petroleum Products.

Pharmacy *See also* Drug Abuse.

—. Best's Pharmacy. Colorado (Central City). Gold Rushes. Miners. 1861-1974. *457*

—. Fraser, James Daniel Bain. Medicine (practice of). Nova Scotia (Pictou). 1807-69. *3777*

—. Massachusetts (Boston, Salem). Virginia (Jamestown). 1602-90. *1757*

Philadelphia Board of Trade. Economic development. Elites. Pennsylvania. 1825-61. *394*

Philadelphia Contributionship for the Insurance of Houses from Loss by Fire. Fire insurance. Franklin, Benjamin. Pennsylvania. 1666-1792. *539*

Philadelphia Federation of Teachers. Pennsylvania. Strikes. Teachers. 1973. *2639*

Philadelphia Resistance Committee. American Revolution (antecedents). Elites. Leadership. Pennsylvania (Philadelphia). Political activism. 1765-76. *259*

Philadelphia Social History Project. Ethnicity. Interdisciplinary studies. 1850-80. 1973. *3979*

—. Geographic Mobility. Immigrants. Methodology. Residential patterns. 1850-80. 1976. *3975*

—. Industrialization. Pennsylvania. Research. Urbanization. 1976. *3978*

—. Methodology. Occupation Dictionary Codebook. 1850-80. 1976. *3977*

Philadelphia Society for Organizing Charitable Relief and Repressing Mendicancy. Charities. Friends, Society of. Pennsylvania. 1800-1900. *1181*

Philanthropic Society. Abolitionists. Fugitive Slaves. Negroes. Pennsylvania (Pittsburgh). 1830's-60. *1341*

Philanthropy *See also* Charities.

—. Architecture. California (Los Angeles). Insurance. Marks, David X. Marks, Joshua H. 1902-77. *49*

—. Arizona (Phoenix). Business. Culture. Heard, Dwight Bancroft. Politics. 1895-1950's. *657*

—. Art. Business. Cincinnati Art Museum and Art Academy. Industrial Relations. Ohio. 1874-90. *1000*

—. Baths, public. Maryland (Baltimore). 1893-1920. *1202*

—. Business. Feminism. Illinois (Chicago). Schmidt, Minna Moscherosch. 1886-1961. *9*

—. California (Santa Barbara). Fleischmann, Max. Relief work. Unemployment. 1930-32. *1176*

—. Catholic Church. Ethnic Groups (review article). Horowitz, Helen Lefkowitz. Illinois (Chicago). Kessner, Thomas. New York City. Sanders, James W. 1883-1965. 1970's. *48*

—. Centennial Celebrations. Illinois (Chicago). Mosher, Charles D. Photography. 1870-97. *679*

—. Centennial Celebrations. Independence Hall. Pennsylvania (Philadelphia). Seybert, Henry. 1793-1882. 1977. *2773*

—. Cholera. Howard Association. Louisiana (New Orleans). Public health. Yellow fever. 1837-78. *1739*

—. City Government. Migration, Internal. Missouri (Kansas City, St. Louis). Negroes. Public Health. 1977. *1361*

—. Culture. Horowitz, Helen Lefkowitz (review article). Illinois (Chicago). Social Classes. 1880's-1917. 1976. *814*

—. Federation for the Support of Jewish Philanthropic Societies. Jews. New York City. 1917-33. *1172*

—. Federation movement. Jews. Ohio (Columbus). 1904-48. *1180*

—. Jews. New Mexico (Las Cruces). Stern, Eugene J. 1903-70. *1461*

—. New York. Social problems. Voluntary associations. 1830-60. *1157*

Philharmonic Society. German Americans. Illinois (Belleville). Music. 1850-1975. *954*

Philhellenism. Dawson, Moses. Greece. Independence Movements. Ohio (Cincinnati). 1821-24. *676*

Phillips, Wilbur C. Medical care. Neighborhoods. Ohio (Cincinnati; Mohawk-Brighton). Social Reform. 1917-20. *1753*

Philosophy of History *See also* Historiography.

—. Mumford, Lewis. 1896-1977. *4013*

R

—. City government. Political Attitudes. 1970's. *2365*

—. City Government. Political theory. 1972. *2501*

—. City government. Texas (Beaumont). 1902-09. *370*

—. City Planning. Germany. Zoning. 1860-1968. *1842*

—. City planning. Germany, West. Interest Groups. Regional planning. Social Problems. 1945-76. *3294*

—. City Politics. Epidemics. Ontario (Ottawa). Public Health. Typhoid fever. 1911-12. *3873*

—. Civil rights Organizations. Public Policy. 1960. *2321*

—. Coalitions. Pennsylvania (Lancaster). Political Parties. 1921-30. *363*

—. Colorado. Denver *Post*. Newspapers. Patterson, Thomas M. *Rocky Mountain News*. 1906-07. *926*

—. Committee of Fifteen. Local Politics. New York City. Tammany Hall. Vice. 1900-01. *1144*

—. Community (concept). Industrialization. New York City (Greenwich Village). Urbanization. 1890-1917. *668*

—. Community Participation in Politics. Immigrants. New York City. People's Institute of New York City. Working Class. 1910-20. *1145*

—. Community Participation in Politics. Social problems. 1974. *2930*

—. Congregationalism. Gladden, Washington. Ohio (Columbus). Social gospel. 1850's-1914. *1173*

—. Cotillo, Salvatore. Italian Americans. Liberalism. New York City. Politics. 1904-39. *367*

—. Credit. Loan sharking. Pennsylvania (Pittsburgh). Working Class. 1900-15. *548*

—. Elections. Labor Unions and Organizations. Morgan, Thomas John. Socialism. United Labor Party. 1886-96. *302*

—. Farwell, Arthur Burrage. Hyde Park Protective Association. Illinois (Chicago). Prohibition. 1885-1936. *1137*

—. Female Moral Reform Society. Morality. New York (Utica). Social Organization. 1830's-40's. *1189*

—. Gitteau, William B. Hamilton, J. Kent. Ohio (Toledo). Progressivism. Public Schools. 1898-1921. *1109*

—. Griscom, John H. Letters. Public Health. Sanitation. Shattuck, Lemuel. 1843-47. *1715*

—. Industrialization. Social Organization. Urban history. 1870's-90's. 1970's. *47*

—. Ku Klux Klan. LaFollette, Philip. Patriotism. Wisconsin (Madison). 1922-27. *730*

—. Labor Unions and Organizations. Michigan. Politics. Saloons. Working class. 1830-1910. *869*

—. LaGuardia, Fiorello. Mayors. New York City. 1933-45. *386*

—. Landscape architecture. Olmsted, Frederick Law. Social Theory. 19c. *2005*

—. Methodology. Police. 1967-75. *2983*

—. Metropolitan areas. Police. 1854-1960's. *1262*

—. Metropolitan Protective Association. New Mexico (Santa Fe). New York City. Sanitation. Spiegelberg, Flora Langermann. 1875-1943. *661*

—. Minorities. Secondary Education. ca 1970's. *2899*

—. New York City. Public housing. 1975. *3409*

—. Noise Pollution. Progressivism. 1900-30. *1194*

—. Providence Employment Society. Rhode Island. Social Classes. Women. 1837-58. *1131*

Reform clubs. Amateur Democrat (concept). City Politics. Illinois (Chicago). Political participation. Wilson, James Q. 1960's-70's. *2456*

Reform (review article). Huggins, Nathan L. Pavar, David J. Religion. Rosenberg, Carroll Smith. Social control. 1812-1900. 1970's. *1677*

Reform schools. Girls. Lancaster Industrial School for Girls. Massachusetts. ca 1850-70. *1133*

Reformed Presbyterian Theological Seminary. Antislavery sentiments. Integration. Ohio (Cincinnati). Presbyterian Church, Reformed. 1845-49. *1640*

Refugees *See also* Exiles.

—. Charities. Jews. Migration, Internal. Nebraska (Omaha). Political Leadership. 1820-1937. *1442*

Refuse Disposal *See also* Sewage Disposal.

—. California (San Francisco). Labor. Ownership. Sunset Scavenger Company. 1965-75. *2582*

—. City Planning. Local government. Natural Resources. 1973-77. *3436*

—. Environment. Urbanization. 1860-1920. *2048*

—. New York City. 1963-77. *3435*

Regional government. 1950-76. *2405*

—. City Government. Michigan (Detroit). 1970's. *2391*

—. City Government. New York City. 1976. *2382*

—. Desegregation. Metropolitan Areas. 1960's-70's. *2211*

—. Indiana (Indianapolis). Local Government. 1850's-70's. *2409*

—. Intergovernmental relations. Metropolitan Areas. Social Problems. 1930-74. *2378*

—. Megalopolis. Minnesota (Minneapolis, St. Paul). Twin Cities Metropolitan Council. 1970's. *2403*

—. Metropolitan Areas. Minnesota (Minneapolis, St. Paul). Twin Cities Metropolitan Council. 1967-73. *2377*

—. Minnesota (Minneapolis, St. Paul). 1950-70's. *2314*

—. New York City. 1960-70's. *2395*

Regional Plan and Survey of New York and Its Environs. City Planning. New York City. Norton, Charles Dyer. Zoning. 1916-20. *1835*

Regional Planning *See also* City Planning; Social Surveys.

—. Agricultural Cooperatives. Farms. Neighborhoods. 1920's. *1825*

—. Appalachian Trail. MacKaye, Benton. Wilderness. 1921-66. *2175*

—. California (American River, Sacramento). California Tomorrow (group). Ecology. 1975. *3316*

—. California (Santa Clara County). California Tomorrow (group). Economic Growth. Local government. 1975. *3314*

—. City Planning. 1960's. *3346*

—. City planning. Germany, West. Interest Groups. Reform. Social Problems. 1945-76. *3294*

—. City Planning. Olmsted, Frederick Law. 1822-1903. *1855*

—. Energy. New York City. 1960-75. *3288*

—. Florida (Duval County). Integration. Metropolitan areas. Schools. 1955-75. *2823*

—. Transportation. 1960's-70's. *3470*

Regional Planning Association of America. City Planning. Middle classes. New Jersey (Radburn). 1927. *1840*

Regional studies. Bibliographies. Illinois (Chicago). 1871-1919. *4028*

Regionalism. Architecture. Pennsylvania (Philadelphia). 1776-20c. *1867*

—. Art. Cultural Imperialism. New York City. 1974. *2793*

—. Boosterism. Illinois (Chicago). Publicity. Wright, John Stephen. 1815-74. *2168*

—. Boxing. Individualism. Pennsylvania (Pittsburgh). Professionalization. Social mobility. 1890's-1900's. *860*

—. City Government. Metropolitan areas. Negroes. 1973. *3085*

—. Ethnic groups. French Canadians. Geographic space. Quebec. Urbanization. 1930-73. *3639*

—. Ethnicity. Ohio (Cleveland). Slovene Americans. 20c. *1625*

—. Illinois (Chicago; South Side). Migration, Internal. Negroes. Wright, Richard *(Native Son)*. 20c. *2173*

Regions. Arizona (Tucson). Population. Technology. 1977. *2293*

—. Canada. Frontier and Pioneer Life. 16c-1914. *3626*

—. Economic development. Social organization. 1890. *1*

Reimers, David M. Barton, Josef J. Dinnerstein, Leonard. Esslinger, Dean R. Ethnic Groups. Hvidt, Kristian. Immigration (review article). 1850-1950. 1970's. *1297*

Reinagle, Alexander. Actors and Actresses. Chestnut Street Theatre. Maryland (Baltimore). Wignell, Thomas. 1792-1802. *1029*

Relief Camp Workers Union. British Columbia (Vancouver). Strikes. 1935. *3790*

Relief work. California (Santa Barbara). Fleischmann, Max. Philanthropy. Unemployment. 1930-32. *1176*

Religion *See also* Atheism; Christianity; Clergy; Missions and Missionaries; Rationalism; Revivals; Sects, Religious; Sermons; Theology.

—. Africa, West. Louisiana (New Orleans; Congo Square). Music (jazz). Negroes. Rites and Ceremonies. 18c-19c. *1018*

—. Americanization. Catholics. Ethnicity. New York City. -1974. *3040*

—. Artifacts. Commercialism. Folk art. Greek Americans. Pennsylvania (Philadelphia; Upper Darby). 1970's. *461*

—. Assimilation. French Canadians. Nationalism. Rhode Island (Woonsocket). 1924-29. *1616*

—. Baptists, Southern. 1968. *3218*

—. Baseball. Georgia (Atlanta). Illinois (Chicago). New York City. Social change. Values. 1892-1934. *905*

—. Benjamin, Philip S. Feldberg, Michael. Miller, Richard G. Pennsylvania (Philadelphia). Politics. Sinclair, Bruce. Technology. Urbanization (review article). 1790-1920. 1974-76. *8*

—. Business. Tennessee (Nashville). 1960's-70's. *2590*

—. California (Los Angeles). Homosexuality. Metropolitan Community Church. 1970-76. *3214*

—. California (San Francisco). 1850's. *1675*

—. California (San Francisco). Civil rights. Negroes. Pressure groups. 1860's. *1388*

—. Catholic Church. Ohio (Cleveland). 1860. *1669*

—. Civil rights. Negroes. Social Classes. 1960's-70's. *3091*

—. Education. Midwest. Occupational mobility. 1955-75. *3224*

—. Edwards, Gustav. Illinois (Chicago). Radio. Swedish Americans. 1926-73. *1585*

—. Ethnic Groups. Pennsylvania (Philadelphia). Social classes. Voting and Voting Behavior. 1924-40. *1329*

—. Harmony Society. Pennsylvania (Economy). Rapp, George. Utopias. 1785-1847. *1627*

—. Huggins, Nathan L. Pavar, David J. Reform (review article). Rosenberg, Carroll Smith. Social control. 1812-1900. 1970's. *1677*

—. Illinois (Nauvoo). Mormons. Social control. 1833-46. *1659*

—. Immigrants. Legends. New York (Buffalo). Polish Americans. 1870-1973. *1559*

—. Industrialization. Pennsylvania (Rockdale). Social Classes. Technology. Wallace, Anthony F. C. (review article). 1825-65. 1978. *20*

—. Midwest. Negroes. Poor. Sects, Religious. Whites. 1969. *3216*

—. New Jersey (Pitman Grove). Urbanization. 1860-1975. *212*

—. New York (Rochester). Radicals and Radicalism. Revivals. Social Reform. 1830-56. *1169*

—. Pennsylvania (Philadelphia). Slavery. Wealth. 1684-1775. *1391*

Religious Education *See also* Church Schools; Theology.

—. Judaism. Michigan (Detroit). Sholom Aleichem Institute. 1926-71. *1477*

Religious liberty. Dogberry, Obediah. *Liberal Advocate*. New York (Rochester). Newspapers. 1832-34. *925*

—. Jews. Rhode Island (Newport). Touro Synagogue. 1902. *1436*

Religious Orders *See also* religious orders by name.

—. Catholic Church. Massachusetts (Boston). Teaching. Voluntarism. Women. 1870-1940. *1685*

Religious organizations (northern). Federal Programs. Freedmen. Georgia (Atlanta). Reconstruction. 1865-69. *755*

Religious Revivals. See Revivals.

Relocation *See also* Migration, Internal.

—. Barrios. Family. Housing. Mexican Americans. -1965. *3165*

—. Bureau of Indian Affairs. Employment. Indians. Men. 1963-66. *3184*

—. City Government. Development. Housing. Landlords and Tenants. New York. 1940's-74. *3407*

—. Neighborhood Housing Services. Poor. Preservation. Urban Redevelopment Task Force. 1970's. *3572*

Remedial education. Wages. Wisconsin (Milwaukee). 1967-73. *2881*

Remington, Frederic. Art. Business. Missouri (Kansas City). 1883-85. *1032*

Reminiscences. Armenian Americans. Virginia (Richmond). Vranian, Manuel. 1887-1910. *1599*

—. British Columbia (Sandon). Entrepreneurs. Harris, Johnny. 1890's-1950's. *3723*

—. California (Los Angeles). Jews. Mesmer, Joseph. Newmark, Joseph. 1824-1947. *3129*

—. California (San Francisco). Earthquakes. Geissinger, Dorothy. 1906. *2120*

—. California (San Francisco Bay). Fishermen. Italian Americans. Tarantino, Gaetano. 1850's-1940's. *493*

—. Cubans. Florida (Tampa). Labor Disputes. *Lector* (reader). Perez, Louis A., Jr. Tobacco workers. ca 1925-35. *572*

—. Daily Life. Fleming, Hartley G. Pennsylvania (Pittsburgh; East End). Youth. 1898-1915. *651*

—. Greeley, Andrew M. Illinois (Chicago; West Side). Irish Americans. Italian Americans. Stereotypes. 1920's-75. *1312*

—. Grocery stores. New York (Buffalo). Wiener, Alfred D. 1947-65. *464*

—. Immigration. Manitoba (Winnipeg). Melnyk, George. 1949. 1977. *3922*

—. Louisiana (New Orleans). Matas, Rudolph. Medical Research. Ochsner, Alton. Surgery, thoracic and vascular. 1927-52. *1755*

—. National Textile Workers Union. North Carolina (Gastonia). Strikes. Textile Industry. Weisbord, Vera Buch. 1929. *636*

—. New York (Sloatsburg). Ward, Seely. 1915-73. *674*

Rensselaer Russell House. Architecture (Victorian). Iowa (Waterloo). Restorations. 1858-1974. *3525*

Rent control. City Government. Housing. New York City. Property tax. Subsidies. 1960-75. *3405*

—. City Politics. Landlords and Tenants. Law Reform. 1942-79. *3376*

—. Housing codes. Landlords and Tenants. Poor. 1949-73. *3382*

Rent theory. Land. Prices. Transportation. Wisconsin (Milwaukee). 1949-69. *3480*

Rents. Connecticut (New Haven). Discrimination, housing. Negroes. Whites. 1973. *3035*

Repatriation. Depressions. Indiana (East Chicago). Mexican Americans. 1919-33. *1538*

—. Depressions. Indiana (Gary). Mexican Americans. Nativism. 1920's-30's. *1520*

Reporters and Reporting *See also* Editors and Editing; Journalism; News; Press.

—. American Dream. Nevada (Las Vegas). 1964-74. *3607*

—. California. Gold rushes. New York City (Brooklyn). Newspapers. 1848-53. *941*

—. California (Los Angeles). Chandler, Otis. District of Columbia. Graham, Katherine. Newspapers. Noyes, Newbold. 1967-72. *2778*

—. California (Los Angeles). District of Columbia. New York City. Television. 1976. *2766*

—. Chicago *Tribune*. Illinois (Chicago). Marks, Nora (pseud. of Eleanora Stackhouse). Social Problems. 1888-90. *937*

—. Crime and Criminals. Georgia (Atlanta). Michigan (Detroit). Newspapers. 1974. *2765*

—. Crime and Criminals. Missouri (St. Louis). Newspapers. 1969-72. *2769*

—. Domestic Policy. Foreign relations. Newspapers. Nova Scotia (Halifax, Pictou, Yarmouth). USA. 1827-40. *3803*

—. Elections (municipal). Newspapers. Ohio. Political Campaigns. 1971. *2784*

—. Political Campaigns (congressional). Urbanization. 1970. *2772*

Republican Party. Alden, Augustus E. Brownlow, William G. Carpetbaggers. City Government. Reconstruction. Tennessee (Nashville). 1865-69. *295*

—. California (San Diego). City Government. Lincoln-Roosevelt Republican League. Political reform. Progressivism. 1905-10. *375*

—. City Government. Reconstruction. South. 1865-75. *299*

—. Conservatism. Georgia (DeKalb County). Political Stratification. Social Classes. 1970. *2431*

—. Crime and Criminals. Deneen, Charles S. Illinois (Chicago). Political Corruption. Primaries. Thompson, William Hale. 1928. *346*

—. Delaware (Wilmington). Local Politics. Negroes. 1850-1900. *1372*

—. Democratic Party. Pennsylvania (Bucks County). Suburbs. Whites. 1972. *2427*

—. Elections (gubernatorial). Mayors. Michigan (Detroit). Pingree, Hazen S. 1889-96. *369*

—. Elections (mayoral). Illinois (Chicago). Merriam, Charles E. Political machines. Progressivism. 1911. *374*

—. House of Representatives. Marcantonio, Vito. New York City (East Harlem). Puerto Ricans. 20c. *1597*

Rescue mission. Charities. Skid rows. Washington (Seattle). 1973. *2912*

Research *See also* Methodology.

—. *American Miller*. Flour. Mills. Minnesota. Periodicals. 1880's-1930's. 1978. *490*

—. Archives, National. Finster, Jerome. Fishbein, Meyer H. Urban history (review article). 1968-74. *3961*

—. Bibliographies. Canada. City planning. 1890-1939. *3918*

—. California (Los Angeles). Great Britain (Hull). Kinship. Social networks. 1960's-70's. *2653*

—. Canada. Census. Urbanization. 1950's-78. *3625*

—. Canada. Exhibits and Expositions. Maps. Public Archives of Canada. Urban history. 1865-1905. *3959*

—. Canada. Urban history. USA. 18c-20c. *4011*

—. City Government. Political science. 1945-74. *4048*

—. City Government. Texas A. & M. University. Texas (Garland). Urban Observatory program. 1970's. *2303*

—. Community Participation in Politics. Hunter, Floyd. Social Sciences. 1953-76. *4060*

—. Daily life. Florida (St. Augustine). Spain. 1580. 1970's. *3980*

—. English Language (black). Linguistics. Negroes. 1970's. *3114*

—. Industrialization. Pennsylvania. Philadelphia Social History Project. Urbanization. 1976. *3978*

—. Mining towns. Ontario (Cobalt). 20c. *3938*

—. Politics. Suburbs. 1950's-70's. *2297*

—. Wisconsin (Milwaukee). 1850-1900. *3950*

—. Wisconsin (Milwaukee). 1970's. *4029*

Research Group on Montreal Society. Capitalism. Quebec (Montreal). Social History. 19c. *3998*

Reservoirs *See also* Irrigation; Water Supply.

—. Army Corps of Engineers. City Government. Illinois (Chicago). Tunnel and Reservoir Plan. Water Pollution. 1972-79. *3434*

—. Army Corps of Engineers. Congress. Flood Control Commission. Pennsylvania (Pittsburgh). 1908-65. *2052*

—. Floods. Oklahoma (Kaw City). 1962-76. *2267*

—. Massachusetts (Boylston, West Boylston). Social Change. Wachusett reservoir. 1889-1902. *2030*

Resettlement Administration. City Planning. Greenbelt towns. Poor. Tugwell, Rexford Guy. 1935-36. *1844*

—. Homesteading and Homesteaders. Interior Department. Minnesota (Duluth). Public Housing. 1936-47. *3380*

Residential location. Social Classes. Suburbs. 1960. *2730*

Residential mobility. City Life. Kansas (Kansas City). 1960's. *2728*

—. Maryland (Baltimore). Negroes. 1970-74. *3103*

Residential pattern. Architecture. Social Change. Working Class. 1950's-60's. *3420*

Residential Patterns. Busing. Integration. Metropolitan Areas. Race Relations. Schools. 1970. *3032*

—. Canada. Development. Models. USA. 1973. *3272*

—. Cities, central. Middle Classes. Neighborhoods. Upper Classes. 1960's. *3280*

—. City life. Neighborhoods. Pennsylvania (Philadelphia; Fairmount). Social Change. 1960's-70's. *2646*

—. Colorado (Denver). Ethnic Groups. Social Status. 1940-77. *2703*

—. Community Participation in Politics. Georgia (Savannah). Negroes. Whites. 1865-80. *1342*

—. Cotton mills. Ethnic Groups. Michigan (Detroit). Occupations. 1880. *1336*

—. Economic Development. Income. Maryland (Baltimore). Occupations. 1800. *3*

—. Education. Income. Pennsylvania (Philadelphia). ca 1965-73. *3072*

—. Employment. Florida (Miami). Negroes. Population. 1950-60. *2080*

—. Employment. Metropolitan areas. Transportation. 1960-70. *3273*

—. Employment. Suburbs. 1939-75. *2271*

—. Ethnic Groups. Immigration. Nebraska (Omaha). 1880-1920. *1304*

—. Ethnic Groups. Manitoba (Winnipeg). -1974. *3831*

—. Ethnic groups. Maryland (Baltimore). Neighborhoods. 1850-70. *1310*

—. Ethnic Groups. Michigan (Detroit). Neighborhoods. Population. 1880-85. *718*

—. Ethnic groups. Occupational mobility. Pennsylvania (Pittsburgh). 1880-1920. *1335*

—. Ethnic groups. Population. Quebec (Quebec). 1795-1805. *3789*

—. Freedmen. Racism. Reconstruction. South Carolina (Charleston). 1860-80. *1399*

—. Geographic Mobility. Immigrants. Methodology. Philadelphia Social History Project. 1850-80. 1976. *3975*

—. Georgia (Atlanta). Hawaii (Honolulu). Integration. Neighborhoods. Texas (San Antonio). 1960's-70's. *2672*

—. Georgia (Atlanta). Negroes. Transportation. Women. 1910-40. *228*

—. Illinois (Chicago). Negroes. Polish Americas. 1920-70. *1605*

—. Illinois (Chicago). Negroes. Segregation. Social Classes. Whites. 1970. *3025*

—. Industrialization. Location. Ontario (Kingston). Physicians. 1857-1975. *3757*

—. Institutions. Pennsylvania (Philadelphia). Social Classes. Suburbs. 1880-1900. *161*

—. Louisiana (New Orleans). Race relations. 19c-20c. *1414*

—. Louisiana (Opelousas, Washington). Negroes. Whites. 1860-80. *1325*

—. Maryland (Baltimore). 1960-73. *2669*

—. Metropolitan areas. Occupations. Social Classes. Transportation. 1970. *3274*

—. Negroes. Neighborhoods. Small business. Whites. 1960-72. *2193*

—. Neighborhoods. New York City. 1730. *716*

—. Neighborhoods. Race. ca 1924-74. *2194*

—. Pennsylvania (Philadelphia). Social classes. 1950-70. *2707*

Residential segregation. Assimilation. Models. New York City. Puerto Ricans. 1960-70. *3163*

—. Courts. Education. Federal policy. Metropolitan Areas. 1974. *2655*

—. Discrimination. Michigan (Detroit). 1960-70. *3074*

—. Ethnic Groups. Massachusetts (Boston). Ohio (Cleveland). Washington (Seattle). 1930-70. *3028*

—. Ethnic Groups. Missouri (St. Louis). Negroes. 1850-1930. *1331*

—. Ethnic Groups. Missouri (St. Louis; Ville). Negroes. 1900-70. *1408*

—. Italian Americans. Louisiana (New Orleans). 20c. *3193*

—. Methodology. 1970's. *4058*

—. Metropolitan areas. Race Relations. 1960-70. *3053*

—. Negroes. Quantitative Methods. 1930's-70's. *3122*

—. South. 1970. *3045*

Resorts. AMAX, Inc. Colorado (Crested Butte). Mines. Molybdenum. Preservation. 1880's-1978. *3522*

—. Architecture. Massachusetts (Nahant). 1815-50. *1962*

—. Architecture. New Jersey (Cape May). Preservation. 19c-1978. *3555*

—. Architecture, Victorian. New Jersey (Cape May). Preservation. 1700-1978. *3550*

—. Artists. Businessmen. Cole, Thomas. Maine (Bar Harbor). Pratt, Henry. 1840-70. *198*

—. Autumn. Daily Life. Eden Fair. Maine (Bar Harbor). 1920's. *856*

—. California (Santa Monica). Jews. 1875-1939. *1495*

—. City Government. New York City (Rockaway). Social Problems. 1950-75. *2446*

—. Industrialization. New Jersey (Hoboken). New York City. Stevens, John. Urbanization. 1820-60. *87*

—. Mineral springs. Wisconsin (Waukesha). 1868-1910. *145*

—. New York (Saratoga Springs). Restorations. 1810-1978. *3546*

—. Rhode Island (Narragansett Pier). Upper classes. 1840-1920. *886*

Resorts (review article). Funnell, Charles E. Kasson, John F. New Jersey (Atlantic City). New York City (Coney Island). Social Change. 1890-1910. 1975-78. *891*

Rest homes. Aged. Pennsylvania (Philadelphia). 1817-1900. *1153*

Restoration. Architecture. Connecticut (Hartford). Potter, Edward Tuckerman. Twain, Mark (home). 1874. 1955. *3512*

—. Architecture. Harmony Society. Pennsylvania (Economy). 1780-1973. *2117*

—. Brownstone buildings. Neighborhoods. New York City. 1960-74. *3494*

—. Attitudes. Military service. Negroes. Texas (East Texas, Houston). 1973. *3095*

—. Attitudes. Stereotypes. 1920's. *2178*

—. Baseball. Newspapers. *Sporting News.* 1920's-30's. *2142*

—. Canada. Urbanization. 1955-75. *3646*

—. Census. Households. Rhode Island. 1774-1800. *717*

—. Centre for Urban and Community Studies. Ontario (Toronto). Urban history. 1965-78. *3941*

—. Charities. Morality. New York. 1783-1830. *1158*

—. Diffusion. Innovation. Public opinion. 1953-76. *2214*

—. Divorce. Marriage. Mortality. Tennessee. 1970. *2688*

—. Economic conditions. Family. Migration, Internal. Social change. 1960-71. *2684*

—. Economic Conditions. Virginia. 1840-60. *2156*

—. Ethnic Groups. Poverty. 1970-75. *2712*

—. Family. Ontario (Wentworth County). 1871. *3776*

—. Fertility. Marital status. Migration, Internal. 1967. *2679*

—. Folk humor. Sports. 20c. *2761*

—. Georgia (Athens). Social Conditions. South. 1850-80. *780*

—. Germany. Great Britain. Historiography. 1975. *3991*

—. Illinois. Voting and voting behavior. 1970's. *2491*

—. Migration, Internal. 1970's. *2733*

—. Pennsylvania. Tradition. 1970. *2661*

—. Political machines. Populism. 1860's-90's. *344*

—. Population. 1970's. *2289*

Rush, Benjamin. Brown, Charles Brockden. Epidemics. Letters. Literature. Pennsylvania (Philadelphia). Yellow Fever. 1793-1800. *988*

Russia *See also* USSR.

—. California (Stockton). Davidson, Herman. Judaism. Opera. Rabbis. 1846-1911. *1437*

Rutherfoord, Thomas. Business. Virginia (Richmond). 1784-1852. *455*

Rytas. Assimilation. Catholic Church. Connecticut (Waterbury). Lithuanian Americans. Newspapers. Zebris, Joseph. 1896-98. *948*

S

Sailors' Union. American Federation of Labor. Industrial Workers of the World. Louisiana. Marine Transport Workers. Strikes. United Fruit Company. 1913. *584*

St. Andrew Parish. Acculturation. Catholic Church. Irish Americans. Pennsylvania (Pittsburgh). 1863-90. *1510*

St. Andrew's Church. Architecture (Gothic Revival). Catholic Church. Churches. Virginia (Roanoke). 1882-1975. *2001*

St. Andrew's Wesley United Church of Canada. Methodist Church. Nova Scotia (Springhill). Presbyterian Church. 1800-1976. *3859*

St. Anne's Parish. Edson, Theodore. Episcopal Church. Protestant. Massachusetts (Lowell). Textile industry. 1800-65. *1686*

St. Augustine Library Association. Florida. Libraries. 1874-80. *955*

St. Augustine Restoration Foundation. Florida. Preservation. 1977. *3532*

St. Bridget's Home. Aged. Catholic Church. Irish Canadians. McMahon, Patrick. Orphans. Poor. Quebec (Quebec). 1847-1972. *3841*

St. Demetrios Church. Assimilation. Ethnicity. Greek Americans. New York City. Orthodox Eastern Church. St. Markela Church. 1970's. *3206*

St. James Park. California (San Jose). Hart, Brooke. Holmes, John. Lynching. Murder. Thurmond, Thomas. 1933. *1255*

St. John's Episcopal Church. Architecture. Episcopal Church. Protestant. New Hampshire (Portsmouth). 1807-09. *1895*

—. Architecture (Gothic Revival). Delaware (Wilmington). Episcopal Church. Protestant. Grace Methodist Church. Methodist Church. 1850-90. *1912*

St. Lawrence Seaway. Communications. Isolation. Quebec (Lower North Shore). 1850's-1950's. *3920*

—. Ports. Quebec (Three Rivers). Shipping. 1874-1972. *3724*

St. Louis Cathedral. Catholic Church. English language. French language. Missouri. 1818-42. *1688*

St. Louis Firemen's Association. Fire departments. Missouri. Professionalization. Violence. 1850-57. *726*

St. Louis Free Congregation Library (records). German Americans. Immigrants. Missouri. Reading. 1850-99. *1619*

St. Louis Seed Company. Building codes. City Government. Fire. Missouri Athletic Club. 1903-18. *2136*

St. Louis Teachers Strike. Missouri (St. Louis). Missouri, University of, St. Louis. Oral history. Strikes. 1973. *3951*

St. Louis Transit Company. Mass Transit. Missouri. Modernization. Monopolies. Strikes. 1900. *619*

St. Louis Zoological Society. Missouri. Zoos. 1910-16. *884*

St. Luke's Penny Savings Bank. Banking. Negroes. United Order of St. Luke. Virginia (Richmond). Walker, Maggie Lena. 1903-34. *549*

St. Luke's-in-the-Desert Hospital. Arizona (Tucson; Tent City). Baptists. Comstock, Oliver E. Medical care. 1907-37. *1737*

St. Markela Church. Assimilation. Ethnicity. Greek Americans. New York City. Orthodox Eastern Church. St. Demetrios Church. 1970's. *3206*

St. Petersburg-Tampa Airboat Line. Air Lines. Florida. 1914. *2098*

Salaries. *See* Wages.

Sales clerks. Department stores. Management. Women. Working Conditions. 1890-1960. *554*

Salmon packing industry. Alaska (Loring). 1883-1936. *508*

Saloons. Alaska. Gold Rushes. Social Conditions. 1896-1917. *865*

—. Beer. Breweries. Ohio (Cincinnati). 1840-1920. *917*

—. Colorado (Denver). Daily Life. Frontier and Pioneer Life. 1858-76. *894*

—. Colorado (Denver). Immigrants. 1865-1933. *893*

—. Ethnic groups. Prohibitionists. Values. Working Class. 1890-1920. *885*

—. Illinois (Chicago). Liquor trade. Prohibition. 1880's-1920. *868*

—. Labor Unions and Organizations. Michigan. Politics. Reform. Working class. 1830-1910. *869*

Samoans. Acculturation. Washington (Seattle). 1890-1973. *3191*

San Diego Flume Company. California. Politics. Southern California Mountain Water Company. Water Supply. 1895-97. *2041*

San Diego High School. California. Boycotts. California. MacKinnon, Duncan. Student protest. 1918. *1083*

San Diego Historical Society. California. 1880-1979. *744*

San Diego Title Insurance and Trust Company Collection. California. Daily Life. Photographs. 1880's-1950's. 1979. *1783*

San Diego Zoological Society. California. 1916-21. *910*

San Francisco Polydrug Project. California. Drug abuse. Medical care. Prescriptions. Women. 1969-79. *3233*

San Francisco Redevelopment Agency. California (San Francisco; South of Market district). Skid Rows. Urban Renewal. 1850-1969. *760*

San Francisco Victoriana Company. California. Housing. Restorations. Wood. 1850-1915. 1977. *3585*

Sanborn, Henry. Berry, J. T. Brookes, H. H. Editors and Editing. Texas (Amarillo). 1888-91. *126*

Sandberg, Neil C. (review article). California (Los Angeles). Ethnology. Methodology. Polish Americans. 1968-74. *3198*

Sanders, James W. Catholic Church. Ethnic Groups (review article). Horowitz, Helen Lefkowitz. Illinois (Chicago). Kessner, Thomas. New York City. Philanthropy. 1883-1965. 1970's. *48*

Sanders, James W. (review article). Catholic Church. Church Schools. Ethnic Groups. Illinois (Chicago). 1833-1965. 1977. *1072*

Sanitary and Ship Canal. Civil Engineering. Diseases. Illinois (Chicago). Intergovernmental Relations. Sewage disposal. Water Pollution. 1850's-1900. *1713*

Sanitation *See also* Cemeteries; Pollution; Public Health; Water Supply.

—. Attitudes. City government. Ohio (Cincinnati). 1800-1915. *2037*

—. British Columbia (Vancouver). Water supply. 1886-1976. *3882*

—. City Government. Decisionmaking. Pennsylvania (Pittsburgh). Public health. 1873-1945. *2038*

—. City Government. Florida (St. Petersburg). Public Employees. Strikes. 1968. *2635*

—. City planning. Civil engineering. Water Supply. 1880's-90's. *1853*

—. City planning. Diseases. 1840-90. *1847*

—. Colden, Cadwallader. Lancisi, Giovanni Maria. New York City. 1717-43. *1743*

—. Energy. Public utilities. Sewage disposal. Streetcars. 1870-1940. *1776*

—. Griscom, John H. Letters. Public Health. Reform. Shattuck, Lemuel. 1843-47. *1715*

—. Illinois (Chicago). 1865-1900. *2034*

—. Medicine, Patent. Nebraska (Omaha). Public Health. 1870-1900. *1738*

—. Metropolitan Protective Association. New Mexico (Santa Fe). New York City. Reform. Spiegelberg, Flora Langermann. 1875-1943. *661*

Santa Barbara County Bowl. California. Construction. Depressions. 1935. *1951*

Santmyer, Helen Hooven (*Ohio Town*). Ohio (Wilberforce, Xenia). Tornadoes. 1962-74. *3589*

Sarah C. Roberts v. *The City of Boston* (1850). Civil Rights. Massachusetts (Boston). Roberts, Sarah C. School Integration. 1849-50. 1950's. *1075*

Sargent, John Singer. Boston Public Library. Massachusetts. Murals. 1878-1976. *1006*

Sargent, Winthrop. Furniture and Furnishings. Kimball, Abraham. Longfellow, Henry Wadsworth. Massachusetts (Salem). 1820-45. *475*

Sartorio, Enrico C. Catholic Church. Italian Americans (review article). New York City. Tomasi, Silvano. 1918. 1975. *1680*

Saskatchewan. Architecture. Canadian Pacific Railway. Railroad stations. 20c. *3880*

—. Environment. Saskatoon Environmental Society. 1970-77. *3816*

—. Government. Land. Settlement. 1929-35. *3662*

—. Medicine (Practice of). Negroes. Ontario (Chatham). Shadd, Alfred Schmitz. 1896-1915. *3854*

—. Saskatoon Women Teachers' Association. Teachers. Women. 1918-70's. *3740*

Saskatchewan (Humboldt). Electric Power. Saskatchewan Power Corporation. 1907-29. *3919*

Saskatchewan Power Corporation. Electric Power. Saskatchewan (Humboldt). 1907-29. *3919*

Saskatchewan (Regina). Actors and Actresses. Theater. 1900-14. *3807*

Saskatchewan (Regina, Saskatoon). Aged. Migration, Internal. Retirement. 1921-78. *3628*

Saskatchewan (Saskatoon). Boom towns. City planning. Economic growth. Real estate. Yorath, J. C. 1909-30. *3663*

—. Boosterism. Economic Conditions. Land. Speculation. 1910-13. *3657*

Saskatchewan (Yorkton). Colonization companies. Economic growth. Railroads. 1882-1905. *3660*

Saskatoon Environmental Society. Environment. Saskatchewan. 1970-77. *3816*

Saskatoon Women Teachers' Association. Saskatchewan. Teachers. Women. 1918-70's. *3740*

Satire. Elites. Irving, Washington (Knickerbocker's *History of New York*). New York City. 1807-09. *2138*

—. Hamilton, Alexander (1712-56). Maryland (Annapolis). Tuesday Club. 1744-56. *721*

Saunders, William O. Ham, Mordecai F. Newspapers. North Carolina (Elizabeth City). Revivals. 1924. *1630*

Savannah Landmark Rehabilitation Project, Inc. Architecture (Victorian). Georgia. Housing. Restorations. 1870's-1979. *3552*

Savannah Men's Sunday Club. Georgia. Negroes. Social Change. 1905-11. *1370*

Savannah River. Floods. Georgia (Augusta). Levee construction. 1888. 1890-1951. *2133*

Sawmills. Industrialization. Michigan (Detroit). Railroads. Shipbuilding. Stoves. 1840's-90's. *527*

Saxe brothers. Business. Films. Wisconsin (Milwaukee). 1906-25. *874*

Seiberling, Frank A. Akron, Canton, and Youngstown Railroad. East Akron Land Company. Goodyear Tire and Rubber Company. Ohio. Railroads. Real Estate Business. 1913-25. *2074*

Seigniorialism, French. Michigan (Detroit). Social organization. 1701-1837. *779*

Selby, Hubert, Jr. Novels. Robbins, Harold. Sex. Violence. 1953. 1965. *3608*

Self-help. Bromley, Walter. Humanitarianism. Indians. Micmac Indians. Nova Scotia. Poor. 1813-25. *3779*

—. Depressions. Mecklenburg, George H. Minnesota (Minneapolis). Organized Unemployed, Inc. Poor. 1932-35. *1200*

—. Europe. Federal Aid. Marshall Plan. Social Problems. 1940's-70's. *2231*

Sentencing. Alberta. Bureaucratization. Indians. Rural-Urban Studies. Urbanization. 1973. *3787*

—. Alcohol. Drunken drivers. Illinois (Chicago). 1971. *2989*

—. Courts. Plea bargaining. 19c. *1231*

—. Crime and Criminals. Illinois (Chicago). Maryland (Baltimore). Michigan (Detroit). 1975-76. *2955*

—. Crime and Criminals. North Carolina (Charlotte). 1970's. *2938*

Sephardic Hebrew Center. California (Los Angeles). Immigration. Jews (Rhodesli). 1900-74. *1445*

Serials. *See* Periodicals.

Sermons. Baptists. Jasper, John. Negroes. Virginia (Richmond). 1812-1901. *1633*

Serra Museum. California (San Diego). Excavations. Military Camps and Forts. Missions and Missionaries. 1769-75. 1964-70's. *2112*

Servants. Elites. Glessner family. Human Relations. Illinois (Chicago). 1870-1907. *764*

Service stations. Advertising. Architecture. Midwest. 1917-25. *1862*

Sesquicentennial Celebrations *See also* Bicentennial Celebrations; Centennial Celebrations.

—. Missouri (St. Louis). 1914. *900*

Settlement *See also* Colonization; Frontier and Pioneer Life; Homesteading and Homesteaders; Pioneers; Rural Settlements.

—. Agriculture. Boom towns. Oklahoma (Cherokee Strip; Kildare). 1893-1975. *153*

—. Alaska (Sterling). 1937-71. *184*

—. Alberta (Calgary). Land. Pearce, William. Surveying. 1883-86. *3905*

—. American Revolution. Clark, George Rogers. Indians. Kentucky (Louisville). 1773-89. *120*

—. Anza, Juan Bautista de. California (San Francisco). Discovery and Exploration. Mexico. 1775-76. *152*

—. Arab Americans. Asian Americans. Hispanic Americans. Immigrants. Ohio (Toledo). 1965-76. *3020*

—. Arab Americans. Immigration. Michigan (Detroit). 1961-74. *3182*

—. Arizona (Florence). Ruggles, Levi. 1866-1910. *180*

—. Arkansas (northern). Economic Growth. Missouri and North Arkansas Railroad. Railroads. 1880-1920's. *122*

—. Armenian Americans. California (Fresno). 1881-1918. *1594*

—. British Columbia. Multinational Corporations. Natural Resources. Provincial government. Social Classes. Towns. 1965-72. *3644*

—. Business. Oklahoma. 1890's. *81*

—. California (San Jose). 1777-1850. *106*

—. Canada. City planning. Geography. USA. 19c-20c. *3994*

—. Chinese Americans. Hawaii (Hilo, Honolulu). Merchants. Sugar. 1802-52. *1557*

—. City Planning. Mormons. Smith, Joseph. Western States. 19c. *1831*

—. Colorado (Gothic). Silver Mining. 1878-80. *116*

—. Donelson, John. Robertson, James. Tennessee (Nashville). 1780-99. *83*

—. Environment. Land use. New York City. 1970's. *3279*

—. Folklore. Washington (Pullman). ca 1877-1922. *213*

—. France. Immigration. Nova Scotia (Port Royal). 1650-1755. *3791*

—. Geographic mobility. Georgia (Atlanta). Immigrants. Jews. 1870-96. *1450*

—. Government. Land. Saskatchewan. 1929-35. *3662*

—. Great Britain. Immigration. Localism. Massachusetts. Towns. 1630-60. *5*

—. Illinois (Chicago; Jefferson Township). Suburbs. 1870-89. *188*

—. Immigrants. Jews. Minnesota (St. Paul; Lower West Side). ca 1860-1920. *1466*

—. Immigration. Midwest. Swedish Americans. 1850-1930. *1571*

—. Indians. Land. Minuit, Peter. New Netherland (New Amsterdam). 1624-25. *232*

—. Indians. Missions and Missionaries. New Mexico (Santa Fe). Spaniards. 1540-1882. *157*

—. Industrialization. Quebec (Herbertville). 1844-1900. *3665*

—. Jews. Lederer, Henry. Michigan (Lansing). 1850-1918. *1452*

—. Kentucky (Newport). Taylor, James. 1793-1848. *223*

—. Kentucky (Owensboro, Newport, Covington). 1814-20. *209*

—. Massachusetts (Swampscott). 1629-96. *136*

—. Negroes. Oklahoma (Langston). 1890-97. *118*

—. Oklahoma. Railroads. Texas. Wichita Falls and Northwestern Railway. 1900-20. *125*

—. South. Towns. Ukraine (southern). 18c-19c. *91*

Settlement houses. Americanization. Minnesota (Minneapolis). North East Neighborhood House. Progressivism. Social Reform. 1910's-20's. *1132*

—. Architects. Great Britain (London). Illinois (Chicago). Social workers. 1890's-1900's. *1981*

—. Bellamy, George. Hiram House. Ohio (Cleveland). Social Reform. 1896-1914. *1151*

—. Cincinnati Union Bethel. Jews. Ohio. Social reform. 1838-1903. *1142*

—. Immigrants. Indiana (Gary). Public welfare. 1906-40. *1170*

—. Massachusetts (Boston). South End House. Woods, Robert A. 1891-1900's. *1193*

Seventh-day Adventists *See* Adventists.

Sewage. Farmers. Fertilizers. 19c-1975. *2053*

—. Illinois (Chicago). Michigan, Lake. Pollution. 1890-1940. *2032*

Sewage disposal. City Planning. Public health. Water Supply. 1880-1910. *1751*

—. Civil Engineering. Diseases. Illinois (Chicago). Intergovernmental Relations. Sanitary and Ship Canal. Water Pollution. 1850's-1900. *1713*

—. Energy. Public utilities. Sanitation. Streetcars. 1870-1940. *1776*

—. Public Finance. Public health. Technology. 1880-1920. *1778*

Sewers. New Jersey (Newark). Public Health. Social Classes. 1854-1919. *2036*

Sex *See also* Homosexuality; Men; Women.

—. Baths, gay. Homosexuality. Social organization. 1975. *2760*

—. California, northern. Morality. Mormons. Utah (Salt Lake City). Youth. 1967-69. *3225*

—. Law. Massage parlors. 1971-73. *2759*

—. Novels. Robbins, Harold. Selby, Hubert, Jr. Violence. 1953. 1965. *3608*

Sex Discrimination. Chisholm, Shirley. Press. Racism. 1972-73. *2764*

—. Family. Negroes. Racism. Women. 1950's-70's. *3104*

—. Poverty. Race Relations. Social Reform. 1975. *2914*

Sex roles. Behavior. Capitalism. Family. Labor. Massachusetts (Lowell). 1860. *562*

—. Company towns. New York (New York Mills). Polish Americans. Women. 1900-51. *558*

—. Illinois (Chicago). Language. Men. Whites. Working Class. 1975. *2716*

—. Illinois (Chicago). Pioneers. Social History. Women. 1833-37. *645*

—. Labor. Occupations. Quebec (Montreal). Women. 1911-41. *3742*

Seybert, Henry. Centennial Celebrations. Independence Hall. Pennsylvania (Philadelphia). Philanthropy. 1793-1882. *1146*

Shadd, Alfred Schmitz. Medicine (Practice of). Negroes. Ontario (Chatham). Saskatchewan. 1896-1915. *3854*

Shahn, Ben. Art, public. Law. Murals. New York City (Bronx). Post offices. Preservation. 1938-76. *3578*

Shaler, Alexander. Fire Departments. Modernization. New York City. 1865-1971. *2033*

Shared Cataloging and Regional Acquisitions Program. *See* National-Program for Acquisitions and Cataloging.

Shattuck, Lemuel. Griscom, John H. Letters. Public Health. Reform. Sanitation. 1843-47. *1715*

Shaw, Frank. California (Los Angeles). City Government. Clinton, Clifford. Political Reform. Recall. 1938. *368*

Sheftall, Benjamin (and family). American Revolution. Georgia (Savannah). Jews. 1730-1800. *1464*

Shew, William. California (San Francisco). Daguerreotypes. 1851-1903. *966*

Shinn, Everett. Glackens, William. Henri, Robert. Luks, George. Painting. Realism. Sloan, John. 1890's. *1007*

Shipbuilding. Apprenticeship. Maine (Bath). Maine Maritime Museum. 1978. *2601*

—. Dry Docks. Federal Aid. Florida (Tampa). Kreher, Ernest. Public Works Administration. Tampa Shipbuilding and Engineering Company. 1932-37. *320*

—. Grain elevators. New Jersey. New York City. 1848-1964. *1894*

—. Great Lakes. Wisconsin (Milwaukee). 19c. *500*

—. Industrialization. Michigan (Detroit). Railroads. Sawmills. Stoves. 1840's-90's. *527*

—. Massachusetts (Provincetown). 1900-77. *486*

—. Norwegian Americans. Wisconsin (Milwaukee). 19c. *469*

—. Pennsylvania (Pittsburgh). Technology. Technology. 1790-1865. *517*

Shipowners. International Trade. New York City. 1715-64. *465*

Shipping *See also* Merchant Marine; Navigation, Inland.

—. Banking. Brown, Alexander. Maryland (Baltimore). Merchants. Social change. Trade. ca 1800-34. *419*

—. British Colonization Society. Cuffee, Paul. Massachusetts (Westport). Negroes, free. 1759-1817. *1425*

—. Business. California (Port Costa). Tourism. Wheat. 1874-1978. *221*

—. Crerar family. Nova Scotia (Pictou). 1840's-50's. *3751*

—. *Favorite* (vessel). Pennsylvania (Philadelphia). Trade routes. *William* (vessel). 1782-86. *430*

—. Investments. Nova Scotia (Yarmouth). Ports. 1840-89. *3711*

—. Maine (Gardiner). New England. Ports. 1830's. *454*

—. New Hampshire. Portsmouth Marine Society. Social Classes. ca 1763-68. *448*

—. Politics. Rhode Island (Newport). Social Organization. 1700-70's. *806*

—. Ports. Quebec (Three Rivers). St. Lawrence Seaway. 1874-1972. *3724*

Shoe industry. Economic Conditions. Fire. Massachusetts (Salem). 1900-20. *483*

—. Industrialization. Quebec (Montreal). 1840-70. *3721*

—. Massachusetts (Marlboro). Public Opinion. Strikes. 1898-99. *587*

Sholom Aleichem Institute. Judaism. Michigan (Detroit). Religious Education. 1926-71. *1477*

Shootings. Civilians. Police. 1965-69. *2960*

Shopping centers. Art. Buildings. Restorations. 1970-78. *3567*

—. Suburbs. 1979. *2593*

Short, Patrick. Missouri (St. Louis). Olympic Theater. Theater. 1889-1916. *916*

Showboats. Actors and actresses. Chapman family. Pennsylvania (Pittsburgh). 1827-47. *857*

Shreveport City Railroad Company. Louisiana. Public transportation. Streetcars. 1870-76. *2110*

Shrine of Our Lady of Klococov. Fuga, Francis J. Ontario (Hamilton). Slovak Canadians. Uniates. 1952-77. *3869*

Shuttlesworth, Fred L. Abernathy, Ralph. Alabama (Birmingham). Civil rights. Demonstrations. King, Martin Luther, Jr. 1956-79. *3061*

Signboards. Artists. Business. Virginia (Williamsburg). 1740's-70's. *959*

Silk industry. Corticelli Company. Massachusetts (Northampton). Whitmarsh, Samuel. 1830-1930. *510*

Silver Mining. Colorado (Gothic). Settlement. 1878-80. *116*

—. Colorado (Leadville). Tabor, Elizabeth "Baby Doe". Tabor, Horace A. W. 1877-1935. *644*

—. Ontario (Cobalt). Working conditions. 1903-20. *3762*

Silversmithing. Maryland (Baltimore). New York City. Pennsylvania (Philadelphia). 18c. *1025*

—. City life. Neighborhoods. Pennsylvania (Philadelphia; Fairmount). Residential Patterns. 1960's-70's. *2646*

—. City planning. 1973. *3337*

—. Civil disturbances. 1960's-70's. *2946*

—. Clergy. Higginson, John. Massachusetts (Salem). Nicholet, Charles. Puritans. 1672-76. *1653*

—. Connecticut (Hartford). Fitch, Jeremiah. Land Tenure. Riots. 1700-22. *1268*

—. Connecticut (Windham). Converts. Great Awakening. 1723-43. *1702*

—. Cotton industry. Economic conditions. Industrialization. Manufacturing. Pennsylvania (Rockdale). 1825-65. *521*

—. Country Life. Howells, William Dean (*A Modern Instance*). Urbanization. 19c. *2183*

—. Demography. Development. Government Regulation. Suburbanization. 1970-75. *2274*

—. Domesticity. Massachusetts (Salem). Women. 1660-1770. *713*

—. Economic conditions. Family. Migration, Internal. Rural-Urban Studies. 1960-71. *2684*

—. Economic Conditions. Race Relations. Suburbanization. 1900-76. *226*

—. Elites. Industrialization. Pareto, Vilfredo. Pennsylvania (Duquesne). 1891-1933. *765*

—. Ethnic Groups. Hispanic Americans. Negroes. New York City. 1960's-70's. *3039*

—. Family. Farmers. Values. 1970's. *3604*

—. Family. Great Britain. Italian Americans. New York. ca 1850-1920. *715*

—. Family. Households. Massachusetts (Worcester). Urbanization. 1860-80. *688*

—. Funerals. Italian Americans. Pennsylvania (Philadelphia). 1800-1974. *3196*

—. Funnell, Charles E. Kasson, John F. New Jersey (Atlantic City). New York City (Coney Island). Resorts (review article). 1890-1910. 1975-78. *891*

—. Georgia. Negroes. Savannah Men's Sunday Club. 1905-11. *1370*

—. Heroes. Novels. Public welfare. Urbanization. 1880-1920. *2166*

—. Historiography. Mormons. Utah. 1849-1970's. *4003*

—. Illinois (Chicago). 1930-60. *656*

—. Illinois (Jacksonville). Social Theory. 19c. *649*

—. Jews. Massachusetts (Boston). Radicals and Radicalism. Youth Movements. 1960-75. *3132*

—. Journalism. Kansas. 1854-1970's. *929*

—. Massachusetts (Boston). Thernstrom, Stephan (review article). 1974. *829*

—. Massachusetts (Boylston, West Boylston). Reservoirs. Wachusett reservoir. 1889-1902. *2030*

—. Metropolitan areas. Population. Technology. 1970's. *2282*

—. Metropolitan Areas. School Integration. 1970's. *3036*

—. Midwest. Villages. 1930-70. *2285*

—. Minorities. New York City. Public Schools. Ravitch, Diane (review article). 1805-1973. *1082*

—. Pennsylvania (Philadelphia). Political Factions. Proprietary gentry. Provincial government. 1720-76. *761*

—. Police. 1820-1900. *1252*

—. Race relations. 1915-70. *3107*

—. Suburbs. 1900-70. *2201*

Social Classes *See also* Class Struggle; Elites; Middle Classes; Social Mobility; Social Status; Upper Classes; Working Class.

—. Alcoholism. Labor (blue collar). Maryland (Baltimore). 1973. *3252*

—. American Revolution. British North America. Great Awakening. Urbanization. 1740's-70's. *88*

—. Archdeacon, Thomas J. (review article). Colonial Government. Dutch Americans. New York City. 1664-1710. 1976. *26*

—. Architecture. Houses. Indiana (Terre Haute). Segregation. 1879-1900. *1866*

—. Athletic clubs. New York City. 1866-1915. *821*

—. Attitudes. Ethnicity. Illinois (Chicago). Negroes. Race Relations. 1969. *3042*

—. Attitudes. Illinois, western. Rural-urban studies. 1974. *2659*

—. Audience. Billy Graham Crusade. Revivals. -1974. *3217*

—. Banfield, Edward C. City politics. Humanism. Reform. Social sciences. -1973. *2227*

—. Banks. New York. 1819-61. *544*

—. Baptists. Fundamentalist-Modernist controversy. Jarvis Street Church. Ontario (Toronto). Schisms. Social Classes. 1895-1934. *3861*

—. Baptists. Fundamentalist-Modernist controversy. Jarvis Street Church. Ontario (Toronto). Schisms. Social Classes. 1895-1934. *3861*

—. British Columbia. Multinational Corporations. Natural Resources. Provincial government. Settlement. Towns. 1965-72. *3644*

—. Bureaucracies. City Government. Libraries. Parks. Race. Texas (Houston). 1970's. *3440*

—. Businessmen. Iron Industry. 1874-1900. *782*

—. California (Los Angeles). Ethnic Groups. Race. Voting and Voting Behavior. 1971. *2294*

—. California (Los Angeles). Jews. Political Campaigns (mayoral). Voting and Voting Behavior. 1969. *2489*

—. Census. Literacy. Methodology. Ontario (Peel County; Hamilton). 19c. *4004*

—. Census. Methodology. New Brunswick (Saint John). 1871. 1974. *3811*

—. Charities. New York (Albany). Odd Fellows, Independent Order of. 1845-85. *733*

—. City Government. Humanitarianism. New York City. 1790-1860. *1155*

—. City Government. Metropolitan areas. Public Finance. 1960. *2316*

—. City government. Political science. 1950-75. *2240*

—. City Politics. Ethnic Groups. New Jersey (Jersey City). Political Reform. Whites. 1970's. *2355*

—. City Politics (review article). Coke, James G. Elazar, Daniel J. Gargan, John J. Hensler, Deborah R. Rabinovitz, Francine F. Walter, Benjamin. Wirt, Frederick M. Wood, Robert C. 1960's-72. *2192*

—. Civil rights. Negroes. Religion. 1960's-70's. *3091*

—. Cold War. Ethnic Groups. Manitoba (Winnipeg). Voting and Voting Behavior. 1949-53. *3707*

—. Commerce. Quebec (Lower Canada). 1792-1812. *3809*

—. Company towns. Ohio. Steel Industry. Strikes. 1937. *578*

—. Connecticut. Wealth. 1700-76. *769*

—. Connecticut (Guilford). Family. Land ownership. 18c. *819*

—. Connecticut (Windsor). Family. Geographic mobility. 17c. *824*

—. Conservatism. Georgia (DeKalb County). Political Stratification. Republican Party. 1970. *2431*

—. Courts. Generations. Massachusetts (Ipswich, Salem). Values. 1636-56. *773*

—. Courts. New York (Newtown). 1659-90. *1219*

—. Cuban Americans. Florida (Miami). New York City. Puerto Rico (San Juan). 1950-77. *3141*

—. Culture. Horowitz, Helen Lefkowitz (review article). Illinois (Chicago). Philanthropy. 1880's-1917. 1976. *814*

—. Dawley, Alan (review article). Industrialization. Massachusetts (Lynn). 18c-19c. 1976. *658*

—. Detroit Citizens League. Leland, Henry. Michigan. Progressivism. 1912-24. *362*

—. Discrimination. Medicine (practice of). Mental Institutions. Minorities. 1830-75. *1736*

—. Discrimination, Educational. Ontario. Women. 1851-71. *3773*

—. Diseases. Public Health. 1900-75. *3238*

—. Dispensaries. Medical care. 1786-1920. *1763*

—. Divorce. Economic Conditions. 1880-1920. *704*

—. Economic Conditions. Ethnic Groups. Metropolitan areas. 1978. *2678*

—. Elections (congressional). Urbanization. Voting and Voting Behavior. 1972. *2504*

—. Employment. Ethnic Groups. New York (Buffalo, Kingston, Poughkeepsie). Ontario (Hamilton). Pennsylvania (Philadelphia). Property. 19c. *778*

—. Epidemics. Inoculation. Massachusetts (Boston). Mather, Cotton. Smallpox. 1721-22. *1771*

—. Ethnic Groups. Manitoba (Winnipeg). Voting and Voting Behavior. 1941. *3701*

—. Ethnic Groups. Manitoba (Winnipeg). Voting and Voting Behavior. 1945-46. *3708*

—. Ethnic Groups. Pennsylvania (Philadelphia). Religion. Voting and Voting Behavior. 1924-40. *1329*

—. Ethnicity. Italian Americans. Missouri (St. Louis; The Hill). 1890-1970. *3199*

—. Family. Katz, Michael B. (review article). Ontario (Hamilton). 1850-80. *3760*

—. Fur Traders. Merchants. Quebec (Montreal). 1750-75. *3736*

—. Hospitals. New York (Rochester). 19c. *1749*

—. Housing. Methodology. New York City (East Village). 1899. *789*

—. Housing patterns. Income. Suburbs. 1975. *2717*

—. Ideology. Massachusetts (Boston). Riots. 1834-35. *1232*

—. Illinois (Chicago). Negroes. Residential Patterns. Segregation. Whites. 1970. *3025*

—. Income. Massachusetts (Boston). 1880-1920. *790*

—. Individualism. Massachusetts (Salem). Organicism. Political Leadership. Puritans. 1680's. *13*

—. Industrial Revolution. Massachusetts (Lynn). Work Ethic. 1826-60. *772*

—. Industrialization. Pennsylvania (Rockdale). Religion. Technology. Wallace, Anthony F. C. (review article). 1825-65. 1978. *20*

—. Institutions. Pennsylvania (Philadelphia). Residential patterns. Suburbs. 1880-1900. *161*

—. Jews. Labor Unions and Organizations. New York City. Socialism. United Hebrew Trades. 1877-1926. *627*

—. Law. Marital Status. Maryland (Baltimore). Women. 1729-97. *701*

—. Massachusetts (Boston). Real Estate. 1692-1775. *817*

—. Methodology. Pennsylvania (Pittsburgh). Urbanization. 1974. *3973*

—. Metropolitan areas. Occupations. Residential patterns. Transportation. 1970. *3274*

—. New Hampshire. Portsmouth Marine Society. Shipping. ca 1763-68. *448*

—. New Jersey (Newark). Public Health. Sewers. 1854-1919. *2036*

—. New York Athletic Club. Sports. 1865-1900. *820*

—. New York City. Political power. Suffrage. 1820-60. *270*

—. New York City (Greenwich Village). 1900-20. *663*

—. Ontario (Hamilton). Political parties. 1967-72. *3683*

—. Pennsylvania (Philadelphia). Residential Patterns. 1950-70. *2707*

—. Political Participation. Race. South. Voting and Voting Behavior. 1960-74. *2492*

—. Providence Employment Society. Reform. Rhode Island. Women. 1837-58. *1131*

—. Residential location. Suburbs. 1960. *2730*

Social Classes (review article). Estrin, Mary Lloyd. Hare, Chauncey. Illinois (Lake Forest). Photography, Artistic. 1978-79. *2802*

Social Conditions *See also* Cost of Living; Country Life; Daily Life; Economic Conditions; Family; Labor; Marriage; Migration, Internal; Popular Culture; Social Classes; Social Mobility; Social Problems; Social Reform; Social Surveys; Standard of Living.

—. 1970's. *2190*

—. Ainslie, Peter. Carey, John R. Discrimination, employment. Maryland (Baltimore). National Urban League. Negroes. 1921-35. *746*

—. Alaska. Gold Rushes. Saloons. 1896-1917. *865*

—. Alberta. Political protest. 1918-39. *3680*

—. American Revolution. Economic Conditions. 18c. *798*

—. American Revolution. Historiography. Massachusetts (Boston). Methodology. 18c. *818*

—. Arizona (McNary). Company towns. Lumber and Lumbering. Negroes. Segregation. 1924-72. *1424*

—. Asian Americans. City Government. New York City. Public Policy. 1970's. *3177*

—. Attitudes. Behavior. Crowding. Michigan (Detroit area). 1965-66. *2640*

—. Attitudes. Jews. South. 1890-1977. *1467*

—. Automobile industry and Trade. Michigan (Detroit). 1701-1975. *32*

—. Banking. Economic Conditions. New York City. 1971. *2611*

—. Barrios. California (East Los Angeles). Mexican Americans. Murals. 1970-75. *3155*

—. Behavior. Bossism. City Politics. Police. 19c. *1269*

—. Black Power. Economic Conditions. Violence. 1970's. *3090*

—. General Motors Corporation. Georgia (Atlanta). United Automobile Workers of America. 1936. *599*
—. Georgia (Augusta). Textile mills. Working conditions. 1886. *621*
—. Grand Trunk Railway Company. Monopolies. Quebec (Montreal). Teamsters. 1864. *3733*
—. Higgins, Edwin L. Illinois (Chicago). Militia. 1870's-80's. *1287*
—. Hormel, George A., and Company. Minnesota (Austin). Olson, Floyd B. 1933. *591*
—. Illinois (Chicago). Industry. Maryland (Baltimore). Missouri (St. Louis). Pennsylvania (Pittsburgh). Railroads. 1877. *631*
—. Illinois (Chicago; Back of the Yards). Meat-packers. Polish Americans. 1921. *618*
—. Industrial Workers of the World. Labor Reform. New York (Little Falls). Textile Industry. Women. 1912. *629*
—. Labor Disputes. Washington (Seattle). World War I. 1914-19. *626*
—. Leatherworkers. Massachusetts (Lynn). Social Organization. 1890. *586*
—. Louisiana (New Orleans). Public opinion. Street, Electric Railway and Motor Coach Employees of America. Street railroads. 1929-30. *583*
—. Mass Transit. Missouri. Modernization. Monopolies. St. Louis Transit Company. 1900. *619*
—. Massachusetts (Marlboro). Public Opinion. Shoe Industry. 1898-99. *587*
—. Missouri (St. Louis). Missouri, University of, St. Louis. Oral history. St. Louis Teachers Strike. 1973. *3951*
—. National Textile Workers Union. North Carolina (Gastonia). Reminiscences. Textile Industry. Weisbord, Vera Buch. 1929. *636*
—. New York City. Public Employees. 1975. *2623*
—. New York City. Public schools. Race Relations. 1968. *2878*
—. North Carolina (Gastonia). Novels. Radicals and Radicalism. Textile Industry. 1929-30's. *622*
—. Pennsylvania. Philadelphia Federation of Teachers. Teachers. 1973. *2639*
—. Pennsylvania (Philadelphia). Pilots, Ship. Wages. 1792. *602*
—. Pennsylvania (Pittsburgh). Steel Industry. 1919. *577*
—. Rhode Island. Streetcars. 1890's-1904. *614*
—. Streetcar workers. Violence. Virginia Passenger and Power Company. Virginia (Richmond). 1903. *598*
Strippers. Behavior. Customers. -1974. *2745*
Stuart, David. Capitols. Federal Government. Location. Potowmack Company. Virginia (Alexandria). Washington, George. 1783-91. *217*
Student protest. Boycotts. California. MacKinnon, Duncan. San Diego High School. 1918. *1083*
Students *See also* Colleges and Universities; Schools.
—. Alienation. California (San Francisco). Hippies. 1968-70. *2651*
—. Busing. Massachusetts (Boston). Race Relations. 1968-69. *2907*
—. Cincinnati, University of. History Teaching. Local history. Ohio. 1974-75. *4009*
—. Crime and Criminals. Dropouts. Pennsylvania (Philadelphia). School attendance. 1970. *2853*
—. Desegregation. Florida (Jacksonville). 1960's-70's. *2839*
—. Desegregation. Race Relations. Teachers. 1973. *2850*
—. Identity. Racism. Schools. 1970's. *2861*
—. Illinois (East St. Louis, Peoria). Mayors. Negroes. Public Opinion. 1978. *3081*
—. Indiana (Indianapolis). Negroes. Race relations. 1973. *3059*
Stuyvesant, Peter. New Netherland. Provincial Government. 1650-54. *287*
—. New York City. 1640's-60's. *2187*
Subsidies. Air Lines. California (Los Angeles, San Francisco). Federal Government. Helicopters. Illinois (Chicago). New York City. 1945-75. *3471*
—. Arts. National Council on the Arts. National Endowment for the Arts. Washington (Seattle). 1969-75. *2792*
—. Charities. City government. New York City. Outdoor relief. Reform. 1870-98. *372*
—. City Government. Housing. Middle Classes. Mitchell-Lama program. New York City. 1955-68. *3373*
—. City Government. Housing. New York City. Property tax. Rent control. 1960-75. *3405*

—. Housing. Suburbs. Zoning. 1950-76. *3300*
—. Housing and Urban Development Department. Missouri (Kansas City). Model Cities Program. 1972-75. *2927*
—. New York City. Prices. Subways. Transportation. -1974. *3468*
Suburban Life *See also* Housing; Metropolitan Areas.
—. Housing. Planning. Town houses. 1973. *3355*
Suburbanization. California (Los Angeles). Mexican Americans. Negroes. Social Change. 1960's-75. *3049*
—. City Planning. Company towns. Illinois (Pullman). Pullman, George M. 1870-1972. *56*
—. City Planning. Population. Western States. 1900-70. *692*
—. Crime and Criminals. 1946-77. *2996*
—. Demography. Development. Government Regulation. Social Change. 1970-75. *2274*
—. Discrimination, Housing. Metropolitan areas. Negroes. 1970's-80's. *3116*
—. Economic Conditions. Race Relations. Social Change. 1900-76. *226*
—. Employment. Illinois (Chicago). Negroes. Transportation. 1960-70. *3077*
—. Industrialization. Photography. 1970's. *2803*
—. Lifestyles. Metropolitan areas. Public policy. 1960's-75. *2213*
—. Local government. Political structure. ca 1950-75. *2399*
—. Migration, Internal. Transportation. 1800's-1970's. *176*
—. Negroes. 1979. *3069*
Suburbs. Annexation. City Government. Maryland (Baltimore). 1745-1918. *308*
—. Annexation. Decentralization. 1900-70. *139*
—. Architects. City Planning. Illinois (Riverside). Olmsted, Frederick Law. 1868-70. *1827*
—. Attitudes. Behavior. Integration. 1950's-60's. *3030*
—. Automobiles. New York. Play. Youth. 1970. *2752*
—. Bossism. City Politics. Middle classes. Reform. 1900-77. *348*
—. Buses. Mass Transit. Planning. 1970's. *3472*
—. California, northern. Construction. Government regulation. Housing. Prices. 1970's. *3303*
—. California (Petaluma). Government Regulation. Human rights. Population. 1972-76. *2268*
—. California (San Francisco Bay area). Environment. Local Government. Politics. 1960's-70's. *2306*
—. Canada. City planning. Environment. Housing. 1893-1930. *3917*
—. Capitalism. Technology. Urbanization. 19c-1970's. *2262*
—. City Planning. Illinois (Riverside). New Jersey (West Orange; Llewellyn Park). Olmsted, Frederick Law. Vaux, Calvert. 1853-1920's. *1850*
—. City Planning. Minorities. Transportation. 1960-76. *3450*
—. Commuting. Pennsylvania (Lancaster). Streetcars. 1890-1920. *2079*
—. Congress. Political change. Public Policy. 1962-75. *2548*
—. Courts. Housing. Land use. Zoning. 1922-78. *1838*
—. Courts. Integration. Poor. 1960's-70's. *3371*
—. Dallas Cowboys (team). Investments. Sports. Texas (Arlington, Irving). Texas Rangers (team). 1968-75. *2581*
—. Decisionmaking. Educational Policy. Elites. Fiscal Policy. Massachusetts. 1968-75. *2350*
—. Democratic Party. Pennsylvania (Bucks County). Republican Party. Whites. 1972. *2427*
—. Development. Economic Conditions. Investments. Neighborhoods. Public Policy. 1968-75. *2607*
—. Development. Land. Maryland (Prince Georges County). 1970-73. *3264*
—. Discrimination. 1937-75. *3092*
—. Ecology. Politics. 1950-70. *2357*
—. Economic Conditions. Metropolitan areas. Negroes. Social Status. 1970. *3111*
—. Economic Conditions. Population. Social Organization. 1970's. *2721*
—. Economic Development. Freeway corridor. Land use. Minnesota (Minneapolis, St. Paul). Urbanization. 1950's-70's. *3262*
—. Economic Growth. Missouri (St. Louis). RAND Corporation (report). Urbanization. 1973. *2288*

—. Education, Finance. Public Schools. 1970-74. *2901*
—. Elections (presidential). Michigan (Detroit). Voting and Voting Behavior. 1972. *2503*
—. Employment. Ghettos. Highways. Minorities. Segregation. -1973. *3474*
—. Employment. Ghettos. Negroes. Social Policy. 1969-79. *3102*
—. Employment. Population. 1945-78. *2575*
—. Employment. Residential patterns. 1939-75. *2271*
—. Ethnic Groups. Social Problems. Women. 1940's-70's. *3598*
—. Fiscal crisis. 1898-1976. *2566*
—. Gasoline. Prices. Standard of living. 1955-74. *3446*
—. Geographic space. Methodology. Metropolitan areas. Politics. 1960's-75. *2229*
—. Georgia (Augusta, Summerville). ca 1800-1911. *78*
—. Highways. Pennsylvania. Population. 1940-70. *2275*
—. Home ownership. Negroes. 1960-75. *2247*
—. Home ownership. Negroes. Social Mobility. 1970's. *3392*
—. Houses. Mobile homes. Voluntary Associations. 1970's. *2693*
—. Housing. Pennsylvania (Philadelphia; Main Line). Prices. 1967-69. *3377*
—. Housing. Subsidies. Zoning. 1950-76. *3300*
—. Housing patterns. Income. Social Classes. 1975. *2717*
—. Illinois (Chicago). Integration. Urbanization. 1974. *3452*
—. Illinois (Chicago). King, Charles R., & Company. Newspapers. Publishers and Publishing. 1870-97. *944*
—. Illinois (Chicago area). Local Politics. School districts. 1963-68. *2888*
—. Illinois (Chicago; Jefferson Township). Settlement. 1870-89. *188*
—. Industry. Property tax. 1968-74. *2602*
—. Institutions. Pennsylvania (Philadelphia). Residential patterns. Social Classes. 1880-1900. *161*
—. Intergovernmental Relations. Metropolitan Areas. Social Problems. *2331*
—. Labor. Women. 1920's-70's. *2620*
—. Local Government. Social problems. 1920-70. *2305*
—. Metropolitan areas. Politics. 1965-75. *2360*
—. Middle Classes. Migration, Internal. Minorities. 1940's-70's. *2266*
—. Migration, Internal. Whites. 1975. *2736*
—. Models. Traffic. 1972. *3479*
—. Negroes. 1940's-70's. *3126*
—. Negroes. Population. 1950-70. *3083*
—. New York (Nassau, Suffolk counties). Public Schools. School attendance. 1940's-70's. *2852*
—. Ohio (Cincinnati; Kennedy Heights). 1880-1976. *79*
—. Ontario (Hamilton; Westdale). 1911-51. *3669*
—. Politics. 1948-73. *2358*
—. Politics. Population. 1955-60. 1965-70. *2741*
—. Politics. Research. 1950's-70's. *2297*
—. Politics. Social problems. 1945-60's. *2260*
—. Population. 1970's. *2278*
—. Public Opinion. 1920-70. *2222*
—. Race relations. Social Organization. 1950-70. *2681*
—. Residential location. Social Classes. 1960. *2730*
—. Shopping centers. 1979. *2593*
—. Social Change. 1900-70. *2201*
—. Tennessee (Nashville; Edgefield). 19c-1978. *195*
Suburbs (review article). Housing. Politics. Poor. Urbanization. 1970's. *2242*
Subways *See also* Mass Transit.
—. Art. Interborough Rapid Transit. New York City. 1914-17. *1044*
—. Canada. Mexico. South America. USA. 19c-1978. *3457*
—. Graffiti. Juvenile Delinquency. Law Enforcement. New York City. 1970's. *2648*
—. New York City. Prices. Subsidies. Transportation. -1974. *3468*
—. New York (Rochester). 1908-56. *2085*
Suffrage *See also* Naturalization; Voter Registration; Voting and Voting Behavior.
—. Businessmen. Democratic Party. Negroes. New York City (Brooklyn). Political Campaigns. Propaganda. Racism. 1860. *1405*
—. City Government. Merry, Samuel. Missouri (St. Louis). Political Change. 1833-38. *258*

—. Audiences. California (Los Angeles). Spanish Language. 1971-72. *2770*
—. Baseball. Burlington Athletics (team). Provincial League. Vermont (Burlington). 1954-55. *2749*
—. California (Los Angeles). 1931-52. *2783*
—. California (Los Angeles). District of Columbia. New York City. Reporters and Reporting. 1976. *2766*
—. Chicago School of Television. Illinois. Vocational Education. 1930's-53. *945*
—. City Government. Decisionmaking. New York. Town meetings. 1973. *2457*
—. Minnesota. News. Press. Towns. 1969-70's. *2776*
Television, cable. Anthropology. Virginia (Reston). 1972. *2780*
Temperance. City Politics. Immigrants. Nativism. Ohio (Cincinnati). 1845-60. *1306*
—. German Americans. Government Regulation. Illinois (Chicago). Know-Nothing Party. Local Politics. Riots. 1855. *1271*
—. German Americans. Irish Americans. Local politics. New York City. Riots. 1857. *1291*
Temperance Movements *See also* Alcoholism.
—. Demonstrations. Ohio (Cincinnati). Protestant Churches. Women's Christian Temperance Union. 1874. *1136*
—. Florida (Miami). Nation, Carrie. 1908-13. *1148*
—. Massachusetts (Boston). Social Customs. Values. Working class. 1838-40. *771*
Temple Beth Israel. California (San Diego). Jews. Population. 1889-1978. *1968*
Temple Israel. Judaism. Nebraska (Omaha). 1867-1908. *1441*
Temple Sherith Israel. California (San Francisco). Jews. Nieto, Jacob. Rubin, Max. 1893. *1492*
Temples. Mormons. Utah (Logan). 1850-1900. *1628*
Temporary Woodlawn Organization. Community Participation in Politics (review article). Fish, John Hall. Illinois (Chicago). Minnesota (Rice County). Organization for a Better Rice County. Poor. Wellstone, Paul D. 1970-76. *2464*
Tenants First Coalition. Massachusetts. Pressure Groups. Public housing. 1970-75. *3365*
Tenements. Family. Hadley Falls Company. Irish Americans. Massachusetts (Holyoke). 1860-1910. *691*
Tennessee. *Cabaret* (film). Germany (Berlin). Music. *Nashville* (film). Social criticism. 1930's-70's. *3596*
—. Divorce. Marriage. Mortality. Rural-Urban Studies. 1970. *2688*
Tennessee (Alcoa). Aluminum Company of America. Company Towns. Labor. Leadership. Negroes. 1919-39. *1396*
Tennessee (Bristol). Boundaries (disputes). Virginia (Bristol). Water Works War. 1889. *323*
Tennessee (Chattanooga). Social Customs. 1975. *2654*
Tennessee (Clinton). Baptists. Desegregation. Turner, Paul. Violence. 1956. *1139*
Tennessee (Jonesboro). Cunningham, Samuel B. Railroads. 1830-60. *2069*
Tennessee (Kingsport). Air pollution. Employment. Government. Industry. Water Pollution. 1970's. *3255*
Tennessee (Knoxville). American Federation of Labor. Armies. Police. Streetcars. Strikes. 1919-20. *582*
—. Appalachia. Artists. Epworth Jubilee Community Arts Center. Folk art. 1970's. *2789*
—. Race relations. Riots. 1919. *1263*
Tennessee (Knoxville, Memphis, Nashville). Gore, Albert Arnold. Political Campaigns. Voting and Voting Behavior. 1970. *2497*
Tennessee (Martin). Martin, William. Nashville and Northwestern Railway. Railroads. 1832-93. *220*
Tennessee (Memphis). Architecture. Churches. 19c.
—. Brinkley, Robert Campbell. Peabody Hotel. 1869-1923. *1887*
—. Business. Development. Public lands. 1971-76. *3296*
—. Businessmen. City planning. Elites. Georgia (Atlanta). Louisiana (New Orleans). 1907-30. *1821*
—. Chickasaw Indians. Civil War. deSoto, Hernando. Urbanization. Yellow fever. 16c-19c. *154*
—. City Government. Economic Conditions. Political Leadership. Reconstruction. 1873-77. *234*

—. City Government. Epidemics. Public Health. Yellow fever. 1878. *1723*
—. Civil rights. Legislation. Population. Race Relations. Riots. 1865-66. *1254*
—. Economic development. Irish Americans. 1850-80. *1516*
—. *Free Speech.* Lynching. Negroes. Newspapers. Wells, Ida B. 1892. *1205*
—. Historiography. Local history. 1912. 1975. *4001*
—. Law Enforcement. Race Relations. Reconstruction. Riots. 1866. *1274*
—. School Integration. White flight. 1963-76. *2869*
Tennessee (Memphis; Beale Street). Business. Entertainment. Negroes. 1930's-78. *923*
—. Business. Negroes. Urban Renewal. 1963-70's. *3495*
Tennessee (Nashville). Alabama (Montgomery). Discrimination, educational. Georgia (Atlanta). Negroes. North Carolina (Raleigh). Teachers. Virginia (Richmond). 1865-90. *1106*
—. Alden, Augustus E. Brownlow, William G. Carpetbaggers. City Government. Reconstruction. Republican Party. 1865-69. *295*
—. Architecture. College Building. Heiman, Adolphus. 1836-1974. *1941*
—. Architecture, Gothic Revival. Churches. Holy Trinity Episcopal Church. Restorations. 1840's-1970's. *3541*
—. Attitudes. Birth control. Clergy. Negroes. Population. 20c. *3079*
—. Berry, Harry S. Construction. Political Corruption. Works Progress Administration. 1935-43. *310*
—. Berry, William T. Bookselling. Literature. 1835-76. *1039*
—. Business. Religion. 1960's-70's. *2590*
—. Busing. Integration. Mass Media. 1970-73. *2895*
—. Civil War. Federal Government. Military Occupation. 1861-65. *6*
—. Crosthwait, D. N. Meigs High School. Negroes. 1886. *1350*
—. Cumberland River. Historical Sites and Parks. Metropolitan Historical Commission. Waterfront. 1976. *3509*
—. Custom House. Federal Government. Restorations. 1877-1977. *3553*
—. Donelson, John. Robertson, James. Settlement. 1780-99. *83*
—. Fire departments. Folklore. Humor. ca 1900-25. *2058*
—. Fisk University. Race Relations. Youth Movements. 1909-26. *1378*
—. Frontier and Pioneer Life. Political Leadership. 1780-1800. *241*
—. Georgia (Atlanta). Negroes. North Carolina (Raleigh). Police. Race Relations. Reconstruction. Virginia (Richmond). 1865-1900. *1270*
—. Public schools. South Nashville Institute. 1851-54. *1101*
—. Slavery. South. Thomas, James P. 1818-82. *1409*
Tennessee (Nashville; Edgefield). Suburbs. 19c-1978. *195*
Tennessee (Nashville-Davidson County). Attitudes. Local Government. Metropolitan Areas. Public services. 1962-73. *3620*
Tennessee (Oak Ridge). Army Corps of Engineers. City Planning. 1942-47. *2542*
Tennessee (Shelby County). Crump, Edward. Democratic Party. Elections (gubernatorial). Politics. 1932. *347*
Terrell, Robert Heberton. District of Columbia. Judges. Negroes. 1880-1925. *1385*
Terrorism *See also* Crime and Criminals.
—. Florida (Miami). Law Enforcement. Racism. 1896-1930. *1225*
Texans. Cajuns. Louisiana (Houma). Negroes. Population. Race Relations. Social change. 1945-73. *2725*
Texas. Architecture. Railroad stations. 1890-1976. *1875*
—. City Government. Employment. Mexican Americans. Negroes. Urbanization. 1973. *3029*
—. Epidemics. Kellogg, William Pitt. Louisiana (Shreveport). Reconstruction. Secession. State Government. Yellow fever. 1873-77. *327*
—. Finance. State government. 1970-74. *2515*
—. Oklahoma. Railroads. Settlement. Wichita Falls and Northwestern Railway. 1900-20. *125*

Texas A & M University. City Government. Research. Texas (Garland). Urban Observatory program. 1970's. *2303*
Texas (Amarillo). Berry, J. T. Brookes, H. H. Editors and Editing. Sanborn, Henry. 1888-91. *126*
Texas (Arlington, Irving). Dallas Cowboys (team). Investments. Sports. Suburbs. Texas Rangers (team). 1968-75. *2581*
Texas (Austin). Mexican Americans. Negroes. Voluntary associations. Whites. 1969-70. *2702*
Texas (Beaumont). City government. Reform. 1902-09. *370*
—. Race Relations. Riots. 1943. *1267*
Texas (Brownsville). Preservation. Zoning. 1974-76. *3580*
Texas (Burkburnett). Boom towns. Oil Industry and Trade. Railroads. Wichita Falls and Northwestern Railway. 1902-40. *497*
Texas (Conroe). Boom towns. Depressions. Oil Industry and Trade. 1929-33. *182*
Texas (Crystal City). City Government. Mexican Americans. Political Factions. 1970-76. *3147*
—. City Politics. Mexican Americans. Power structure. Social organization. 1963-70. *2452*
—. Elections. Mexican Americans. School boards. 1970. *3152*
Texas (Dallas). Civil Rights. ca 1960's-70's. *2954*
—. Clothing. Department stores. Marketing. Neiman-Marcus Company. 1900-17. *431*
—. Fashion. Marketing. Neiman-Marcus Company. 1880-1970. *421*
—. Migration, Internal. Negroes. Occupations. 1880-1910. *828*
—. Parks. Prices. Property. 1966. *3385*
—. Railroads. 1843-73. *2101*
Texas (Dallas, Fort Worth). Airports. Architecture. 1974. *3422*
—. Industry. Location. 1967-75. *2603*
Texas (East Texas, Houston). Attitudes. Military service. Negroes. Rural-Urban Studies. 1973. *3095*
Texas (El Paso). Discrimination, employment. Labor Unions and Organizations. Mexicans. 1880-1920. *1524*
—. Mexican Americans. Voting and voting behavior. 1972. *3146*
Texas (Galveston). Architecture, Victorian. East End Historical District. Neighborhoods. Preservation. 1972-77. *3551*
—. City government. Political Reform. Progressivism. 1890-1906. *381*
—. Federal aid. Ports. 1851-90. *185*
—. Hurricanes. 1900. *2129*
Texas (Garland). City Government. Research. Texas A & M University. Urban Observatory program. 1970's. *2303*
Texas (Houston). Amalgamated Association of Street Railway Employees. Public Opinion. Strikes. 1897-1905. *640*
—. Attitudes. Behavior. Employment. Minorities. Poverty. 1974. *2706*
—. Attitudes. Mexican Americans. Negroes. Race Relations. Whites. -1973. *3023*
—. Black Capitalism. 1976. *3123*
—. Buildings. Jones, Jesse Holman. Rice Hotel. 1837-1974. *1975*
—. Bureaucracies. City Government. Libraries. Parks. Race. Social Classes. 1970's. *3440*
—. City Planning. Economic conditions. Zoning. 1962-77. *3295*
—. Ethnic Groups. Indiana (Indianapolis). Massachusetts (Boston). Occupations. Pennsylvania (Philadelphia). Social Mobility. 1850-60. *832*
—. Geographic Mobility. 1850-60. *834*
—. Guerard, Albert J. Memoirs. 1924-72. *114*
—. Hair, William Ivy. Haynes, Robert V. Herndon, Angelo. Louisiana (New Orleans). Martin, Charles H. Racism (review article). South. 1900-30's. 1976. *1213*
—. Hair, William Ivy. Haynes, Robert V. Louisiana (New Orleans). Race Relations. Riots (review article). 1900-17. 1970's. *1273*
—. Military. Mutinies. Negroes. Race Relations. 1917. *1234*
Texas (Lubbock). Mexican Americans. Values. 1974. *3137*
Texas Panhandle. Architecture. Boom towns. Houses, shotgun. Oil Industry and Trade. 1920-40. *1904*
Texas Rangers (team). Dallas Cowboys (team). Investments. Sports. Suburbs. Texas (Arlington, Irving). 1968-75. *2581*
Texas (San Antonio). Acculturation. Church Schools. Mexican Americans. Public Schools. 1973. *3156*

—. Greenbelt Towns. New Deal. Ohio (Cincinnati, Greenhills). Urban Renewal. 1935-39. *96*

Tulane Theater. Crescent Theater. Erlanger, Abraham Lincoln. Klaw, Marc. Louisiana (New Orleans). Theater. 1896-1937. *987*

Tulchinsky, Gerald J. J. (review article). Business. Industry. Quebec (Montreal). Transportation. 1837-53. 1977. *3752*

Tunnel and Reservoir Plan. Army Corps of Engineers. City Government. Illinois (Chicago). Reservoirs. Water Pollution. 1972-79. *3434*

Tunnels. Freight and Freightage. Illinois (Chicago). 1898-1975. *2066*

—. Hudson River. New Jersey. New York City. Railroads. 1871-1910. *2082*

Turner, Frederick Jackson. Frontier thesis. Social Mobility. Wisconsin (Racine). 1850-1880. *848*

Turner, Paul. Baptists. Desegregation. Tennessee (Clinton). Violence. 1956. *1139*

Tutty, William. Church of England. Missions and Missionaries. Nova Scotia (Halifax). 1752-78. *3868*

Twain, Mark. California (San Francisco). Harte, Bret. 1864-1906. *1017*

Twain, Mark (home). Architecture. Connecticut (Hartford). Potter, Edward Tuckerman. Restoration. 1874. 1955. *3512*

Tweed, William M. Hershkowitz, Leo (review article). New York City. Political Corruption. Tammany Hall. 1869-71. 1977. *343*

Twin Cities Metropolitan Council. Megalopolis. Minnesota (Minneapolis, St. Paul). Regional Government. 1970's. *2403*

—. Metropolitan Areas. Minnesota (Minneapolis, St. Paul). Regional government. 1967-73. *2377*

Two World Cities Conference. France (Paris). French American Foundation. New York City. 1978. *2216*

Twombly, Robert C. Architects (review article). Burnham, Daniel Hudson. Hines, Thomas S. Wright, Frank Lloyd. 1867-1970. 1973-74. *1979*

Tyack, David B. Bullough, William A. Education (review article). Feinberg, Walter. Karier, Clarence J. Rosemont, Henry, Jr. Sutherland, Gillian. Troen, Selwyn K. 1830's-1976. *1069*

—. Bullough, William A. Education (review article). Public Schools. 19c. *1073*

Typhoid fever. City Politics. Epidemics. Ontario (Ottawa). Public Health. Reform. 1911-12. *3873*

Typography. *See* Printing.

U

Ukraine (southern). Settlement. South. Towns. 18c-19c. *91*

Ukrainian Canadians. Ethnicity. Folk art. Latvian Canadians. Manitoba (Winnipeg). 1978. *3805*

UN (headquarters site). Pennsylvania (Philadelphia). 1945-46. *2197*

Unemployment *See also* Employment.

—. Armaments Industry. Economic Structure. Texas (San Antonio). 1959-69. *2583*

—. California (Los Angeles County). Davis, James J. Deportation. Depressions. Mexicans. 1931. *1530*

—. California (Santa Barbara). Fleischmann, Max. Philanthropy. Relief work. 1930-32. *1176*

—. Charities. New Brunswick (Saint John). Newfoundland (St. John's). Nova Scotia (Halifax). Poverty. 1815-60. *3781*

—. Committee on Unemployment and Relief. Gary, Elbert H. Mitchel, John Purroy. New York City. Progressives. 1914-17. *382*

—. Crime and Criminals. Economic Growth. Florida (Duval County; Jacksonville). Metropolitan Government. 1967-73. *2265*

—. Discrimination. Men. Poverty. 1970-72. *2618*

—. Economic change. 1970-73. *2617*

—. Economic development. New York City. 1962-73. *2621*

—. Housing. Race relations. 1970's. *3043*

—. New York City. Occupations. Puerto Ricans. 1970. *3150*

Uniates. Fuga, Francis J. Ontario (Hamilton). Shrine of Our Lady of Klococov. Slovak Canadians. 1952-77. *3869*

Union Stockyard. Architecture. Burnham, Daniel Hudson. Business. Illinois (Chicago). Root, John Wellborn. 1871-1902. *1996*

Union (USA 1861-65). *See* Civil War; also names of US Government agencies, bureaus, and departments, e.g., Bureau of Indian Affairs, War Department.

Unionists. Constitutional Union Party. Economic Conditions. Kentucky (Louisville). Prentice, George Dennison. Secession. 1860-61. *30*

Unions. *See* Labor Unions and Organizations.

Unitarianism. Clapp, Theodore. Louisiana (New Orleans). Slavery. Theology, radical. 1822-56. *1690*

United Automobile Workers of America. Attitudes. Housing. Negroes. Ohio (Toledo). Racism. 1967-73. *3015*

—. Automobile Industry and Trade. City Politics. Michigan (Detroit). Negroes. 1945-78. *2315*

—. Chrysler Corporation (Kercheval-Jefferson plant). Labor Unions and Organizations. Michigan (Detroit). 1937-78. *2633*

—. Friedlander, Peter (review article). Michigan (Detroit). Working Class. 1936-39. 1975. *579*

—. General Motors Corporation. Georgia (Atlanta). Strikes. 1936. *599*

United Bay Area Crusade. California (San Francisco). Charities. Corporations. Poor. 1958-73. *2918*

United Football League. Football. West Virginia. Wheeling Ironmen (team). 1962-64. *2742*

United Fruit Company. American Federation of Labor. Industrial Workers of the World. Louisiana. Marine Transport Workers. Sailors' Union. Strikes. 1913. *584*

United Hebrew Trades. Jews. Labor Unions and Organizations. New York City. Social Classes. Socialism. 1877-1926. *627*

United Kansas Portland Cement Company. Cement industry. Ghost towns. Kansas (Le Hunt). 1905-18. *193*

United Labor Party. Elections. Labor Unions and Organizations. Morgan, Thomas John. Reform. Socialism. 1886-96. *302*

United Mexican American Students. California (Los Angeles). Mexican Americans. Youth Movements. 1967-69. *3162*

United Order of St. Luke. Banking. Negroes. St. Luke's Penny Savings Bank. Virginia (Richmond). Walker, Maggie Lena. 1903-34. *549*

United Society for Manufactures and Importation. Employment. Massachusetts (Boston). Poverty. Textile Industry. Women. 1735-60. *571*

United States. *See* entries beginning with the word American; US; states; regions, e.g. New England, Western States, etc.; British North America; also names of government agencies and departments, e.g., Bureau of Indian Affairs, State Department, etc.

United Way of America. Charities. Georgia (Atlanta). Negroes. 1960-77. *2699*

Universal Negro Improvement Association. Black Nationalism. Garvey, Marcus. New York City (Harlem). 1919-26. *1347*

—. California (Los Angeles). Garvey, Marcus. Negroes. 1920's. *1418*

—. Clergy. Garvey, Marcus. Negroes. New York (Buffalo). Political Factions. 1830's-1920's. *1421*

—. Garvey, Amy Jacques. *Negro World.* Newspapers. Women. 1920's-32. *1381*

Upjohn, Richard. Architecture (Gothic Revival). Churches. Iowa (Iowa City). Trinity Episcopal Church. 1871-72. *1916*

Upper Classes. Allegheny Conference on Community Development. Federal Aid. Flood control. Pennsylvania (Pittsburgh). 1936-60. *329*

—. Apartment houses. Architecture. Illinois (Chicago; Gold Coast). Landlords and Tenants. 1882-1929. *1910*

—. Architecture. Charities. Daily Life. Garrett, John Work. Garrett, Mary Frick. Garrett, Robert. Maryland (Baltimore). Mount Vernon Place (residence). 1872-1928. *770*

—. California (San Diego). Californios. Economic Conditions. Social Conditions. 1846-60. *774*

—. California (San Diego). Housing. 1880-1930. *1882*

—. Capitalism. Charities. Massachusetts (Boston). 18c-19c. *1154*

—. Cities, central. Middle Classes. Neighborhoods. Residential Patterns. 1960's. *3280*

—. Cosmopolitanism. Ohio (Cleveland). Pennsylvania (Philadelphia, Pittsburgh). 1850-1900. *781*

—. New York City (Brooklyn). Pennsylvania (Philadelphia). 1825-50. *801*

—. Harvard University. Massachusetts (Boston). 1800-65. *811*

—. Illinois (Chicago). Libraries. Newberry Library. Values. 1880's. *980*

—. Olmsted, Frederick Law. Parks. 1850's-90's. *2019*

—. Resorts. Rhode Island (Narragansett Pier). 1840-1920. *886*

Urban and Regional Policy Group. Carter, Jimmy (administration). Federal policy. 1978. *2540*

Urban development. Federal Policy. Housing. 1960-72. *2531*

Urban Development Corporation. Finance. New York. Public Housing. 1968-78. *2513*

—. Housing. New York. State Government. 1960-73. *3390*

Urban form. Prehistory-1975. *3263*

Urban fringe land. Land. Ohio (Columbus). Prices. Zoning. 1972. *3278*

Urban Gateways program. Arts. Children. Illinois (Chicago). Poor. 1961-75. *2799*

Urban Growth and New Community Development Act (US, 1970). City Planning. Federal government. Housing Act (US, 1968). 1968-75. *2560*

Urban growth policy. Environment. Federal programs. Housing. Land use. 1973. *2251*

Urban historians. Building plans. Canada. Historical sources. Insurance agencies. Land use atlases. Maps. 1696-1973. *3974*

Urban history. 1930's-70's. *4051*

—. Archival Catalogs and Inventories. Maryland (Baltimore). 1797-1975. *3953*

—. Bibliographies. Canada. 19c-20c. *4043*

—. British Columbia. Buildings. Fire insurance. 1885-1979. *4068*

—. Brownell, Blaine A. (review article). Social Conditions. South. 1920-30. 1970's. *4010*

—. Canada. Conference on the Historical Urbanization of North America. USA. 1973. *3990*

—. Canada. Exhibits and Expositions. Maps. Public Archives of Canada. Research. 1865-1905. *3959*

—. Canada. Historiography. USA. -1974. *3964*

—. Canada. Methodology. 1960's-70's. *4045*

—. Canada. Research. USA. 18c-20c. *4011*

—. Canada. Western Canadian Urban History Conference (papers). 1974. *4050*

—. Canadian Urban History Conference. 1977. *3989*

—. Canadian Urban History Conference. City Planning. 19c-20c. 1977. *4042*

—. Carnegie-Mellon University. History Teaching. Quantification. 1975. *4065*

—. Centre for Urban and Community Studies. Ontario (Toronto). Rural-Urban Studies. 1965-78. *3941*

—. Chicago Historical Society. Illinois. Libraries. 1850's-1978. *3945*

—. Depressions. Massachusetts (Boston). Methodology. New Deal. 1930's. 1977-79. *4054*

—. Education. Historical Sites and Parks. Preservation. Public History. 1966-79. *3506*

—. France. Germany, West. Great Britain. 1960-74. *4030*

—. Games. Teaching. 1970's. *4005*

—. Geography, historical. Ontario. Prehistory-1976. *4015*

—. Green, Constance McLaughlin (interview). Historians. 1928-76. *4040*

—. Historiography. Interdisciplinary Studies. Quebec. 1968-78. *3963*

—. Historiography. Methodology. Schnore, Leo F. (review article). 1969-75. *3940*

—. Historiography. Warner, Sam Bass, Jr. (interview). 1946-74. *4041*

—. History teaching. 20c. *4027*

—. Illinois (Chicago). Pierce, Bessie Louise. 1888-1974. *3958*

—. Immigrants. Macedonian Canadians. Ontario (Toronto). 20c. *3971*

—. Industrialization. Reform. Social Organization. 1870's-90's. 1970's. *47*

—. Methodology. 1960's-70's. *3976*

—. Mumford, Lewis. Technology. Western Civilization. 1900-70. *2145*

—. Public policy. Quantitative Methods. Social Conditions. 17c-1970's. *4056*

—. Social sciences. Statistics. 1945-75. *4032*

—. Wisconsin (Milwaukee). 1948-77. *4017*

Urban history (review article). Archives, National. Finster, Jerome. Fishbein, Meyer H. Research. 1968-74. *3961*

—. Hatch, Stephen D. Howard, John. Howard Opera House. Theater. 1879-1904. *963*
Vermont (Windsor). Architecture. Benjamin, Asher. 1797-1802. *1959*
Vermont (Winooski). Assimilation. Catholic Church. French Americans. 1867-1900. *1567*
Vice. Bail bonds. California (San Francisco). City Government. McDonough, Peter P. 1896-1937. *1206*
—. Bossism. City Politics. Dennison, Tom. Nebraska (Omaha). Reform. 1890's-1934. *339*
—. Chinese Americans. Discrimination, Employment. Negroes. 1880-1940. *1253*
—. Chinese Americans. Ghettos. Tourism. 1865-1920. *1547*
—. Committee of Fifteen. Local Politics. New York City. Reform. Tammany Hall. 1900-01. *1144*
Vice areas. Chloral hydrate. "Mickey Finn" (potion). 1850's-1910's. *1240*
Victoria Gas Company. British Columbia. Public Utilities. 1860's-90's. *3910*
Vidal, Nicholás María. Colonial Government. Louisiana (New Orleans). Spain. Zoning. 1797. *1830*
Vietnam War. Federal Aid. 1975. *2202*
Vigilance Committees. California (San Francisco). Ethnicity. Immigrants. 1849-56. *1324*
Vigilantes. Compton, Arthur. Hanging. Montana (Helena). Wilson, George. 1870. *1282*
—. Racism. South Carolina Association. South Carolina (Charleston). 1823-50's. *1376*
Vigilantism. City Government. Florida (Tampa). Murder. Political Corruption. 1935-38. *1241*
Villages *See also* Rural Settlements.
—. Anasazi Culture. Indians. Nevada (Pueblo Grande de Nevada). 900. *3936*
—. Excavations. Makah Indians. Washington (Ozette). Whale hunters. Prehistory. 1966-74. *3930*
—. Illinois (Cahokia). Indians. 900-1150. *3933*
—. Midwest. Social Change. 1930-70. *2285*
—. Population. Retail trade. 1950-70. *2276*
Vincent, Theodore G. Garvey, Marcus. Ideology. Katzman, David M. Michigan (Detroit). Negroes (review article). Social organization. 19c-20c. *1420*
Violence. Alabama (Montgomery). 1830-60. *1238*
—. Baptists. Desegregation. Tennessee (Clinton). Turner, Paul. 1956. *1139*
—. Black Power. Economic Conditions. Social conditions. 1970's. *3090*
—. Busing. Massachusetts (Boston). Race Relations. School Integration. 1970-76. *2847*
—. Busing. Massachusetts (Boston). Racism. 1960's-70's. *2824*
—. California (Watsonville). Depressions. Filipino Americans. Racism. Riots. 1926-30. *1215*
—. City Government. New York City. Race Relations. Riots. 1960-64. *2978*
—. City Life. Courts. Criminal Law. 1973. *2939*
—. Civil Disobedience. New York City. 1690-1976. *1260*
—. Coal Mines and Mining. Labor Disputes. Pennsylvania (Scranton). Police. 1866-84. *1289*
—. Committee for Boston. Massachusetts (Boston). Racism. White, Kevin H. 1976. *3012*
—. Constitutional conventions, state. Louisiana (New Orleans). Reconstruction. Riots. 1866. *1218*
—. Crime and Criminals. Industrialization. Pennsylvania (Philadelphia). 1820's-1976. *1248*
—. Crowding. Public Opinion. 1961-68. *3007*
—. Crowds. Ontario (Toronto). Sports. 1963-73. *3815*
—. Depressions. Kentucky (Louisville). Labor. 1877. *635*
—. Economic Development. Pennsylvania (Erie). Railroads. 1852-55. *1228*
—. Employment. Illinois (Chicago). Industry. Negroes. Polish Americans. Racism. 1890-1919. *1327*
—. Fire departments. Missouri. Professionalization. St. Louis Firemen's Association. 1850-57. *726*
—. Geographic space. Negroes. 1960's-70's. *2992*
—. Georgia (Macon). Ku Klux Klan. Morality. Yarbrough, C. A. 1919-25. *735*
—. Massachusetts (Boston). Racism. School Integration. 1974-75. *2892*

—. McElroy, James L. Planning. Riots. Singell, Larry D. Social organization. 1960's-73. *2945*
—. Models. Population. 1940-70. *2971*
—. Novels. Robbins, Harold. Selby, Hubert, Jr. Sex. 1953. 1965. *3608*
—. Pennsylvania (Philadelphia). Police. 1834-44. *1276*
—. Race Relations. 1965-69. *2959*
—. Streetcar workers. Strikes. Virginia Passenger and Power Company. Virginia (Richmond). 1903. *598*
Violence (review article). Negroes. Politics. Public Policy. 1960's-70's. *2241*
Virginia. Agriculture. Industrialization. Railroads. Rural-Urban Studies. Slavery. 1840's-60. *14*
—. Assimilation. Pennsylvania (Philadelphia). Polish Americans. Polish Emigration Land Company. Smolinski, Joseph. 1860's. 1917-18. *1591*
—. Baseball. Richmond Lawmakers (team). 1908. *912*
—. Boycotts. Negroes. Segregation. Transportation. 1904-07. *1384*
—. Cities, central. Migration, Internal. Negroes. Whites. 1965-70. *2729*
—. City Government. County Government. Courts. Intergovernmental Relations. 1776-1800. *261*
—. Economic Conditions. Rural-Urban Studies. 1840-60. *2156*
—. Economic Planning. Madison, James. Ports. State Government. 1784-88. *165*
—. Norfolk and Western Railroad. Railroad equipment. Roanoke Machine Works. 1881-1976. *472*
Virginia (Alexandria). Autobiography. Civil War. Education. Friends, Society of. Hallowell, Benjamin. Science. 1824-60. *672*
—. Capitols. Federal Government. Location. Potowmack Company. Stuart, David. Washington, George. 1783-91. *217*
Virginia (Appomattox River, Petersburg). Electric power. 1884-1978. *2040*
Virginia (Arlington). Centralization. Politics. Public schools. School Attendance. 1973-78. *2828*
Virginia (Arlington County). Committee of 100. Social Problems. 1954-76. *2459*
Virginia (Bristol). Boundaries (disputes). Tennessee (Bristol). Water Works War. 1889. *323*
Virginia (Germanna). Germans. Immigration. Land ownership. Protestants. Spotswood, Alexander. 1714-21. *177*
Virginia (Jamestown). Apathy. Colonization. Death and Dying. Malnutrition. 1607-24. *1745*
—. Massachusetts (Boston, Salem). Pharmacy. 1602-90. *1757*
Virginia (Lynchburg). Baseball. 1830's-40's. *862*
Virginia (Newport News). Beauty parlors. Interpersonal Relations. Negroes. Social Customs. Women. 1970's. *1338*
Virginia (Norfolk). American Revolution. Dunmore, 4th Earl of. Fire. Great Britain. 1776-1820's. *2132*
—. Boosterism. Centennial Celebrations. Jamestown Tercentennial Exposition. 1900-10. *53*
—. City Planning. Local Government. Urban renewal. 1970's. *3357*
—. Yellow fever. 1855. *1732*
Virginia (Norfolk, Petersburg, Richmond). Competition. Railroads. 1830's-50's. *215*
Virginia Passenger and Power Company. Streetcar workers. Strikes. Violence. Virginia (Richmond). 1903. *598*
Virginia (Reston). Anthropology. Television, cable. 1972. *2780*
Virginia (Richmond). Alabama (Montgomery). Discrimination, educational. Georgia (Atlanta). Negroes. North Carolina (Raleigh). Teachers. Tennessee (Nashville). 1865-90. *1106*
—. Annexation. City Government. Race Relations. Supreme Court. 1970-77. *2279*
—. Armenian Americans. Reminiscences. Vranian, Manuel. 1887-1910. *1599*
—. Authors. Cabell, James Branch. Glasgow, Ellen. 1733-1900's. *976*
—. Authors. Cabell, James Branch. Glasgow, Ellen. Literature. Southern Renaissance. 1920's. *1002*
—. Banking. Negroes. St. Luke's Penny Savings Bank. United Order of St. Luke. Walker, Maggie Lena. 1903-34. *549*
—. Baptists. Jasper, John. Negroes. Sermons. 1812-1901. *1633*

—. Business. City Government. Wynne, Thomas Hicks. 1840's-75. *397*
—. Business. Rutherfoord, Thomas. 1784-1852. *455*
—. Cabell, James Branch. Glasgow, Ellen. Literature. 1898-1912. *2164*
—. Calish, Edward Nathan. Zionism. 1891-1945. *1432*
—. Christianity. Factories. Slavery. Social Organization. Tobacco workers. ca 1820-65. *1393*
—. City life. Civil War. Military Occupation. 1861-65. *10*
—. City Politics. Elections, municipal. Knights of Labor. Labor Unions and Organizations. Negroes. Political Reform. 1886-88. *592*
—. Civil War. Daily Life. 1860-65. *46*
—. Courts. Crime and Criminals. Slavery. 1784-1820. *1275*
—. Georgia (Atlanta). Ghettos. Housing. Kentucky (Lexington). Negroes. North Carolina (Durham). 1850-1930. *1377*
—. Georgia (Atlanta). Negroes. North Carolina (Raleigh). Police. Race Relations. Reconstruction. Tennessee (Nashville). 1865-1900. *1270*
—. Law Enforcement. Race Relations. Slavery. 1782-1820. *1410*
—. Literature. Periodicals. *Reviewer.* 1920's. *1036*
—. Sprague, Frank Julian. Streetcars. 1888-1973. *2092*
—. Streetcar workers. Strikes. Violence. Virginia Passenger and Power Company. 1903. *598*
Virginia (Richmond, Williamsburg). American Revolution. Capitols. Location. State Government. 1779. *326*
Virginia (Roanoke). Architecture (Gothic Revival). Catholic Church. Churches. St. Andrew's Church. 1882-1975. *2001*
Virginia (Williamsburg). Archives. Public Records Office. 1747. *1934*
—. Artists. Business. Signboards. 1740's-70's. *959*
—. Canals. 1772-1820. *2062*
Visions. Folk religion. Greek Americans. Pennsylvania (Philadelphia). 1900-74. *3221*
Vital Statistics *See also* Birth Rate; Census; Mortality; Population.
—. Pennsylvania (Philadelphia). 1720-75. *711*
Vocabulary. *See* Language.
Vocational Education. Chicago School of Television. Illinois. Television. 1930's-53. *945*
—. Community relations training. Police. Seattle Police Academy. Washington. 1960's. *3001*
—. Corruption. Labor Unions and Organizations. Local Government. Police (review article). 1971-73. *2998*
—. Educational Reform. Missouri (St. Louis). Woodward, Calvin. 1897-1914. *1076*
Vogel, Donald. Conzen, Kathleen Neils. Goldbach, John C. McShane, Clay. Schmandt, Henry J. Simon, Roger D. Urbanization (review article). Wells, Robert W. Wisconsin (Milwaukee). 1836-1977. *45*
Vollmer, August. California (Berkeley). Colleges and Universities. Police. Professionalization. 1905-55. *1217*
Voluntarism. Catholic Church. Massachusetts (Boston). Religious Orders. Teaching. Women. 1870-1940. *1685*
Voluntary Associations. All-America Cities Award program. City Life. Civic Organizations. 1975. *2694*
—. Americanization. Education. Jewish Family and Children's Service. Michigan (Detroit). 1876-1976. *1463*
—. Aspira (organization). Educational Reform. Harlem Parents Union. Minorities. New York City. Pennsylvania (Philadelphia). Welfare Rights Organization. 1970's. *2840*
—. Baltimore Reform League. Lawyers' Round Table. Maryland. Niles, Alfred Salem. 1852-1972. *740*
—. Bentley, William. Diaries. Massachusetts (Salem). 1784-1819. *727*
—. B'nai B'rith Lodge. Jews. Modernization. Oregon (Portland). Social Change. 1920's. *756*
—. California. Chinese Americans. Metropolitan areas. Tong societies. 1850-1972. *1541*
—. California (Los Angeles). First Hebrew Benevolent Society. Jews. Labatt, Samuel K. 1851-54. *1457*
—. California (San Francisco). Charities. Immigration. ca 1850-60. *741*

—. Federal government. Legislation. Louisiana (New Orleans). Public Health. 1830's-79. *1724*

—. Pennsylvania (Philadelphia). Political Factions. Riots. 1793. *15*

—. Virginia (Norfolk). 1855. *1732*

Yellow journalism. Bennett, James Gordon. *New York Herald*. Newspapers. 1835-65. *930*

Yerkes, Charles Tyson. Business. Dreiser, Theodore. Pennsylvania (Philadelphia). Robber barons. ca 1837-1905. *535*

Yiddishe Arbeiten Universitet. Acculturation. Immigration. Jews. New York City. 1921-39. *1078*

Yo Semite House. California (Stockton). Hotels. 1869-1923. *1960*

Yorath, J. C. Boom towns. City planning. Economic growth. Real estate. Saskatchewan (Saskatoon). 1909-13. *3663*

Yorke, Peter C. California (San Francisco). Catholic Church. City Politics. Irish Americans. Progressivism. 1900's. *1519*

—. California (San Francisco). Catholic Church. Clergy. Editors and Editing. Irish Americans. ca 1885-1925. *1518*

Yoruba. Architecture. Haiti. Houses, shotgun. Louisiana (New Orleans). Nigeria. 18c-1974. *1993*

Young, Amelia Folsom. Houses. Mormons. Utah (Salt Lake City). Young, Brigham. 1863-1926. *1908*

Young, Brigham. Houses. Mormons. Utah (Salt Lake City). Young, Amelia Folsom. 1863-1926. *1908*

—. Utah (Salt Lake City). 1847-1973. *62*

Young, James. City Government. Massachusetts (Boston). Public Finance. 1976. *2298*

Young Men's Christian Association. Great Britain (London). Libraries. Pool, Reuben B. 1844-1974. *739*

—. Missouri (St. Louis). Negroes. 1877-1976. *743*

Youth *See also* Adolescence; Children; Youth Movements.

—. Automobiles. California (East Los Angeles). Leisure. Low-riders. Mexican Americans. 1970's. *3154*

—. Automobiles. New York. Play. Suburbs. 1970. *2752*

—. California, northern. Morality. Mormons. Sex. Utah (Salt Lake City). 1967-69. *3225*

—. City Life. Dance parties. Negroes. Socialization. -1974. *2746*

—. City Life. New York (New York Mills, Utica). Photographs. Polish Americans. 20c. *3188*

—. Clubs. Parks. Recreation. 1974. *2747*

—. Daily Life. Fleming, Hartley G. Pennsylvania (Pittsburgh; East End). Reminiscences. 1898-1915. *651*

—. Deviant Behavior. Negroes. 1930's-60's. *2990*

—. Drug abuse. Federal programs. Negroes. 1960's-70's. *3242*

—. Drug abuse. Medical care. Social Status. 1969-73. *3235*

—. Drug Abuse. Negroes. 1960's-70's. *3253*

—. Educational Reform. High Schools. Street academies. 1965-75. *2855*

—. Employment. New York City. 1974-76. *2917*

—. Films. Ghettos. Kung Fu motif. 1970-74. *2751*

Youth Movements *See also* Demonstrations.

—. California (Los Angeles). Mexican Americans. United Mexican American Students. 1967-69. *3162*

—. Fisk University. Race Relations. Tennessee (Nashville). 1909-26. *1378*

—. Jews. Massachusetts (Boston). Radicals and Radicalism. Social Change. 1960-75. *3132*

Yu, Alice Fong (interview). California (San Francisco). Chinese Americans. Elementary Education. 1926-78. *2825*

Yukon Territory. Boom towns. British Columbia (Bennett). Gold Rushes. 1896-99. *3647*

Yukon Territory (Dawson). Carnegie, Andrew. Libraries. Nicol, A. 1902-20's. *3818*

Yunge (group). Aestheticism. Jews. Literature. New York City. 1902-13. *1063*

Z

Zebris, Joseph. Assimilation. Catholic Church. Connecticut (Waterbury). Lithuanian Americans. Newspapers. *Rytas*. 1896-98. *948*

Zeh, Nellie M. Garment Industry. Illinois (Chicago). O'Reilly, Mary. Socialist Party. Strikes. Women. 1910. *581*

Zeitlin, Jacob (Jake). Bookselling. California (Los Angeles). ca 1920-74. *2591*

Zelder, Raymond E. Discrimination, Housing. Income. Minnesota (Minneapolis, St. Paul). Negroes. 1965-73. *3057*

Zionism *See also* Jews.

—. Calish, Edward Nathan. Virginia (Richmond).

1891-1945. *1432*

Zoning *See also* Building codes.

—. Agriculture. California (Santa Clara County; Gilroy). Urbanization. Williamson Act (California, 1965). 1965-75. *3351*

—. Buildings. New York City. 1850-1973. *1858*

—. California (San Francisco Bay area). City Government. Community Participation in Politics. Neighborhoods. 1970's. *3335*

—. California (Santa Clara County). City Planning. Local Agency Formation Commissions. Public services. 1963-75. *3307*

—. City government. Downtown Areas. Land. Politics. Prices. Public Policy. 1970's. *3302*

—. City Planning. Courts. New Jersey. 1970-73. *3339*

—. City Planning. Economic conditions. Texas (Houston). 1962-77. *3295*

—. City Planning. Germany. Reform. 1860-1968. *1842*

—. City Planning. New York City. Norton, Charles Dyer. Regional Plan and Survey of New York and Its Environs. 1916-20. *1835*

—. City Planning. Ohio (Xenia). Tornadoes. 1974-77. *3588*

—. City Planning. Pennsylvania (Pittsburgh). 1917-23. *1841*

—. Colonial Government. Louisiana (New Orleans). Spain. Vidal, Nicolás María. 1797. *1830*

—. Competition. 1974. *3342*

—. Courts. Housing. Land use. Suburbs. 1922-78. *1838*

—. Historic Annapolis, Inc. Historical Sites and Parks. Law. Maryland (Annapolis). 1649-1845. 1952-1969. *3580*

—. Housing. Subsidies. Suburbs. 1950-76. *3300*

—. Land. Ohio (Columbus). Prices. Urban fringe land. 1972. *3278*

—. Land. Quebec (Boucherville, Brossard, Longueuil). 1965-73. *3883*

—. Land use. Planning. Politics. 1974. *3343*

—. Pennsylvania (Pittsburgh). Prices. Property. 1973. *3334*

—. Preservation. Texas (Brownsville). 1974-76. *3580*

Zoological Gardens. Chicago Zoo. Illinois (Chicago). 1874-1975. *876*

—. Missouri. St. Louis Zoological Society. 1910-16. *884*

—. Ohio (Cincinnati). 1872-1974. *872*

Zubly, John Joachim. Georgia (Savannah). Presbyterian Church. 1724-58. *1679*

AUTHOR INDEX

Bushnell, George D. 723 1712 1877 2064
Butler, Jeanne F. 1878
Butler, Jon 7
Butler, Martin J. 420
Byford, Liz 182
Byler, Robert H., Jr. 2785

C

Caditz, Judith 3018
Cagle, Laurence T. 3019
Cahan, Cathy 1879
Cahan, Richard 1879
Cahill, Edward E. 3064
Cahill, Helen Kennedy 73
Cain, Louis P. 1713 2032 3882
Calhoun, Richard B. 2033
Calkin, Homer L. 854
Calkins, David L. 1066
Call, Steven T. 3537
Callahan, Helen 395 1501 2133
Callahan, Helen C. 764
Callahan, John M. 965
Calmenson, Wendy Cunkle 966
Camejo, Peter 2821
Cameron, Diane Maher 1209
Cameron, James M. 3722
Camerota, Michael 1346
Campbell, Alan K. 2405
Campbell, Bertha J. 3858 3859
Campbell, Dick 3065
Campbell, Frederick L. 3250
Campbell, George Duncan 1134 1636
Campbell, H. C. 3768
Campbell, Leon G. 74
Candee, Richard 474
Candee, Richard M. 1965
Candeloro, Dominic 1067
Cangi, Ellen Corwin 1714
Cannistraro, Philip V. 1570
Cantor, Jay E. 1880
Capeci, Dominic J., Jr. 358 3367
Capen, Dorothy 75
Capitman, Barbara Baer 3500
Caraley, Demetrios 2525 2526
Carcassonne, Marcel 3645
Cardona-Hine, Alvaro 76
Careless, J. M. S. 3626 3646
Carey, George W. 3266
Carlson, Alvar W. 3020 3182
Carlsson, Sten 1571
Carnahan, Douglas 2663
Caroli, Betty Boyd 1317
Carosso, Vincent P. 529
Carpenter, Edwin H. 3595
Carpenter, Gerald 583
Carpenter, Inta Gale 3947
Carr, Lois Green 77
Carroll, Julian M. 3501
Carroll, T. Owen 3288
Carson, Gerald 724
Carter, Gregg Lee 855
Carter, Margaret 3647
Carter, Norman M. 3723
Carvalho, Joseph, III 1572
Casetti, Emilio 3267
Casey, Daniel J. 3134
Cashin, Edward J. 78
Cassedy, James H. 1715
Cassell, Frank A. 1210
Cassity, Michael J. 2267
Castellanos, Leonard 2786
Casterline, Gail Ferr 3948
Castillo, Adelaida 1540
Castro, Barry 2822
Catalano, Kathleen M. 475 476
Cataldo, Everett F. 2823
Catau, John C. 2857
Cauthers, Janet 3769
Cavalier, Julian 1881
Cavallo, Dom 1135
Cave, Richard S. 3417
Cavin, Susan 967
Cawley, Peter 3502
Cawthon, John Ardis 1786
Cebula, James E. 79
Cerillo, Augustus, Jr. 359
Cermakian, Jean 3724
Cestre, Gilbert 3676

Cha, Marn J. 3168
Chachere, Ernest G. 3597
Chadwick, Bruce 2936
Chadwick, Bruce A. 1573 3183 3184
Chafe, William 3066
Chalmers, Leonard 282 283
Chambliss, William J. 2937
Champlin, Richard S. 477
Champoux, Edouard 3774
Chan, Carole 2268
Chancy, Joette 2824
Chandler, Charles R. 3137
Chandler, Cleveland A. 2527
Chandler, William 1882
Chaney, Elsa M. 3138
Chapman, Edgar L. 3368
Chaput, Donald 311
Charles, Réjane 3883
Chasan, Daniel Jack 3448
Chase, David B. 2006
Chase, Sara B. 1883
Chern, Kenneth S. 284
Chichekian, Garo 3827
Chilman, C. William 856
Chisholm, Shirley 2764
Cho, Yong Hyo 2467
Choldin, Harvey M. 2664 2675 3268
Chollar, Robert G. 2528
Choquette, Robert 3860
Chow, Christopher 2825
Christensen, Terry 2913
Christian, Charles M. 2597
Christopher, Andrew Mark 1574
Christopher, Louise 1637
Chu, Yung-Deh Richard 1541
Chudacoff, Howard P. 688 1303 1304
Chudacoff, Nancy Fisher 1211
Chung, Joseph A. 3725
Chung, Joseph A. 3726
Chun-Hoon, Lowell 1542
Church, Glenn 3831
Ciccone, James 3067
Circarelli, James 3021
Cirino, Linda D. 978
Ciro, Sepulveda 1521
Claereen, Wayne J. 857
Clar, Reva 1437 1667
Clark, Andrienne G. 1502
Clark, Cal 2418
Clark, Clifford E., Jr. 1884
Clark, David L. 1638
Clark, Dennis 8 1503 1504
Clark, Janet 2418
Clark, John 3990
Clark, John G. 1776
Clark, Kenneth B. 2826
Clark, R. Milton 2746
Clark, Roger W. 1136
Clark, S. D. 3648
Clark, Stephen 3949
Clark, Terry Nichols 2204 2981
Clark, W. A. V. 2732
Clarke, Erskine 1639
Clarke, James W. 3068
Clarke, John Henrik 1347
Clarke, Steven K. 3924
Clarke, Stevens H. 2938
Clawson, Marion 2205
Clay, Grady 1787
Clay, Phillip L. 3069
Clayton, John 1137
Clelland, Donald A. 3217
Clement, Priscilla Ferguson 1138
Clements, Donald W. 2588
Cleveland, Mary L. 1139
Clinton, Katherine 645
Clinton, Lawrence 3184
Clotfelter, Charles 234
Clouette, Bruce 2007
Cloward, Richard A. 2340
Clunie, Margaret B. 478
Coates, Joseph F. 2939
Coc, Henry Bartholomew 1885
Cockcroft, Eva S. 2787
Cockcroft, James D. 2787
Coerver, Don M. 421
Coffman, Ralph J. 766
Cogger, Janice M. 3323
Cohen, Abby 1716
Cohen, Arthur H. 858

Cohen, Blanche Klasmer 968
Cohen, Fay G. 2940
Cohen, Lucy M. 3139
Cohen, Rick 3298
Cohen, Ronald D. 1068 1069 1192
Cohen, Shari 2765
Cohen, Steve Martin 2691
Coiner, Miles W., Jr. 969
Colburn, David R. 337
Colcord, Frank C., Jr. 3449
Cole, Glyndon 479
Cole, Leonard A. 2468 2502
Coleman, Alan 312
Coleman, James S. 2905
Coles, Robert 3121
Colley, Charles C. 285
Collier, Malcolm 2008
Collins, John J. 3503
Collins, Lewis W. 3884
Collins, Thomas W. 2869
Colman, William G. 2206
Colton, David 2827
Comanor, William S. 2598
Comer, John C. 3140
Condit, Carl W. 1886
Conforti, Joseph M. 2622
Connell, Kathleen M. 3470
Connell, Mary Ann Strong 1887
Connelly, Edwin Wilmot 3504
Contee, Clarence G. 1348
Contini, Edgardo 3299
Contreras, Maria Alina 3141
Conyus 3070
Conzen, Kathleen Neils 422 689 1305 3950
Conzen, Michael P. 422 530 531 826
Cook, Adrian 1212
Cook, Bernard A. 584
Cook, Jess 3427
Cook, Nancy 80
Cook, Sylvia 970
Cookman, Aubrey O. 859
Cool, Robert A. 3269
Cooley, Gilbert E. 3071
Cooney, Rosemary Santana 3141
Cooper, James R. 3381
Copeland, Robert M. 1640
Corbet, Elise A. 3770
Corbett, Theodore G. 690
Corcoran, Theresa 585
Cord, Steven 3369
Corell, M. R. 3370
Corley, Kit 3560
Corn, Jacqueline Karnell 1717 1718
Cornehls, James V. 3450
Corner, George W. 3022
Cortés, Felix 3142
Cortinovis, Irene E. 3951
Corwin, Margaret 9
Corzine, Jay 1575
Cote, Richard C. 1888
Cotter, John L. 3505
Cottingham, Phoebe H. 3072
Cottle, Thomas J. 3073
Cottrol, Robert J. 1349
Couch, Stephen R. 971
Coughlin, Robert E. 2645 3275
Courchesne, Gary L. 1070
Cousar, Gloria J. 3366
Couzens, Michael 2994
Cowan, Natalie Jahraus 1889
Cowles, Karen 765
Cox, Richard 2141
Cox, Richard J. 3952 3953
Cox, Steven R. 2914
Crain, Robert L. 2851
Crandall, Ralph J. 766
Craven, Wayne 972
Crawford, Michael J. 1576
Crawford, Tad 3074
Creighton, Edith 3771
Crenson, Matthew 2440
Crepeau, Richard C. 2142
Crews, Clyde F. 1641
Crider, Donald M. 2661
Crider, Gregory L. 2143 2144
Crimmins, Timothy J. 228 3506 4035
Croak, Thomas M. 860
Crocetti, G. 3252
Crockett, Norman L. 81
Crooks, James B. 360

Cross, L. Doreen 3727
Crosthwait, D. N., Jr. 1350
Crouthamel, James L. 930
Crowe, Charles 1213
Crowther, Simeon J. 82
Croyle, James L. 2941
Crutchfield, James A. 83
Cuba, Stanley L. 973
Cuban, Larry 2828
Cuddy, Edward 1505
Cullen, Joseph P. 10
Culley, Margaret 931
Culton, Donald R. 1140
Cumbler, John T. 586 767 768
Cuneo, Carl J. 3772
Cunniff, Jeffrey L. 84
Cunningham, James V. 2367 2368
Cunningham, Patrick 1642
Cunningham, Robert B. 2469
Curran, Patrick J. 1071
Curry, Leonard P. 85
Curry, Thomas J. 1072
Curtis, Allan 86
Curtis, James E. 3772
Curtis, Julia 974
Curtis, Lynn A. 2207
Curvin, Robert 2942
Cutler, Maurice 3728
Cutler, William W., III 1073
Cybriwsky, Roman 2966
Cybriwsky, Roman A. 2646

D

Dabrowski, Irene 1575
Dahl, Curtis 1643
Dahms, Frederic A. 3649 3954
Daiker, Virginia 1890
Dajani, Jarir 3451
Daley, Mary 2788
Dalin, David G. 532
Dalzell, Robert F., Jr. 480
Damaris, Gypsy 861
Dammann, Grace 3233
Danbom, David B. 1074
Dancis, Bruce 827
Danforth, Brian J. 87
Daniel, W. Harrison 862
Daniels, Bruce C. 235 236 264 265 266 769
Daniels, Bruce E. 88
Daniels, Douglas H. 1351
Daniels, Maygene 3955
Daniels, Roger 286
Daniels, William G. 2789
Danielson, Michael N. 3300 3371
Dannenbaum, Jed 1306
Danziger, Sheldon 2573
Darden, Joe T. 3074
Darley, John M. 2964
Darling, Arthur Burr 1075
Darling, Sharon 423
Dauer, David E. 2065
Dauer, Manning J. 2470
Daugherty, Richard D. 3930
Daugherty, Robert L. 1214
Davenport, F. Gorvin 2034
Davenport, John F. 338
Davey, Ian E. 3773 3796
David, Pam 2943
David, Wilfred L. 2527
Davidson, Chandler 2706 3023
Davies, Edward J., II 89
Davies, Omar 692
Davis, Allen F. 1141
Davis, Donald F. 3885
Davis, Gene 2790
Davis, Grant M. 2101
Davis, James M., Jr. 863
Davis, John Kyle 339
Davis, Judith M. 2300
Davis, Julia F. 1891
Davis, Lenwood G. 3075
Davis, Otto A. 3372
Davis, Ronald L. 127 975
Davis, Ronald L. F. 237 361
Davis, Susan G. 558 1577
Davison, Victoria F. 3024
Dawley, Alan 559
Day, John P. 3677
Day, Judy 1352
Day, Mark 1522

Deagan, Kathleen A. 646
Dean, John B. 3351
Dechêne, Louise 3650
Decter, Midge 2944
Dehler, Katherine B. 770
DeJong, Gordon F. 2208 2733 2734
deKay, Drake 287
DeLony, Eric N. 1965
Delude-Clift, Camille 3774
Delzell, Charles F. 4051
deMetz, Kaye 864
DeMille, George E. 1644
Dempsey, Hugh A. 3775
Demuth, Christopher C. 2529
Dennis, Lee 3507
denOtter, A. A. 3651 3652
Dent, Tom 3076
Denton, Frank T. 3776
Derone, William E. 31
DeRose, Christine A. 1578
DeSalvo, Joseph S. 3373
DeSantis, Hugh S. 533
DesRosiers, Rachel 3671
Destler, Chester McArthur 481
Detweiler, Robert 647
DeVise, Peter 3077
DeVise, Pierre 2665 3452
Dewees, Donald N. 3453
DeWitt, Howard A. 1215
Deyak, T. A. 2747
Deyak, Timothy A. 3270
Dial, Scott 865
Dibble, Ann W. 482
Dickson, Paul 2301
Dienes, C. Thomas 2931
Dietrich, Katheryn 3095
Dill, Forrest 2508
Dillon, Richard H. 1543
Dingemans, Dennis 2609
Ditmer, Joanne 3508
Dobkin, J. B. 866
Dobyns, Henry F. 3185
Dockhorn, Robert 3977
Dodd, Jill Siegel 771
Dodd, Martin H. 587
Dodson, Richard 2250
Doepke, Dale K. 1645
Doherty, William T., Jr. 588
Dolbeare, Cushing N. 3374
Doll, Tussell C. 3375
Domínguez, Virginia R. 3143
Dominick, Joseph R. 2766
Dommel, Paul R. 2530 2555
Donaldson, Loraine 2589
Donnell, Robert F. 483
Donnelly, Gaylord 484
Donnelly, William L. 2208
Donohue, G. A. 2776
Dorffi, Christine 1216
Dorfman, Ron 2610
Dornan, Paul B. 3433
Dornbusch, Sanford M. 2861
Dornfeld, A. A. 2066 2067
Dornfield, A. A. 932
Dorsch, G. 3234
Dorsett, Lyle W. 313
Dorsey, Herbert W. 2692
Dorson, Richard M. 2647
Dotson, A. Bruce 2945
Doucet, Michael J. 835 3795 3886
Doucette, Laurel 3956
Dougherty, J. P. 1823
Dougherty, Laurie 2829
Douglas, Paul H. 648
Douthit, Nathan 1217
Dow, Eddy 2145
Downs, Anthony 2441 2531
Doyle, Don H. 725
Doyle, Don Harrison 90 649 3509
Doyle, John E. 1506 1719
Doyle, Philip 2302
Doyle-Frenière, Murielle 3957
Drachman, Mose 867
Draper, Joan E. 1828
Dreier, Peter 3376
Drennan, Matthew 2574
Drescher, Tim 2791
Dresser, Norine 2748
Drew, Joseph 3438
Driedger, Leo 1646 3805 3828 3829 3830 3831
Drobis, Susan M. 3975
Droker, Howard A. 1307
Druzhinina, E. I. 91

Johnston, Patricia Condon 3929
Jolley, Clyde W. 137 2228
Jones, Allen W. 1370
Jones, Bryan D. 3437 3438
Jones, Clinton B. 2479
Jones, David C. 3921
Jones, E. Terrence 2320 2768 2769
Jones, Gene Delon 317
Jones, John Paul 540
Jones, Kristine 3185
Jones, Mack H. 2449
Jones, Malcolm 3388
Jones, Robert A. 1924
Jones, Ronald W. 1664
Jones, Walter R. 1243
Jones, William K. 2044
Jordan, Albert F. 1925
Jordan, Jean P. 434
Jordan, Philip D. 1244
Jorgensen, Joseph G. 1592
Jucha, Robert J. 138
Judd, Barbara 2012
Juliani, Richard J. 3984
Jung, L. Shannon 2736
Jupiter, Clare 3121

K

Kadzielski, Mark A. 1160
Kaestle, Carl F. 1094 3792
Kahn, David 3155
Kahn, David M. 1926
Kahrl, William L. 2045
Kai, Peggy 1557
Kalba, Kas 3321
Kale, Steven 2670
Kaminsky, Stuart M. 2751
Kane, Patricia 2161
Kanellos, Nicolás 1531
Kann, Kenneth 1435
Kanter, Rosabeth Moss 2671
Kantor, Harvey 1834
Kantor, Harvey A. 1835 1836
Kantrowitz, Nathan 1316 3985
Kapel, David E. 2849
Kaplan, Barry J. 372 1837
Kaplan, Marilyn 435
Kaplan, Milton 1893
Kaplan, Rose 1463
Kaplan, Samuel 2382 3092
Kapsis, Robert E. 2691 3093 3094
Kardonne, Rick 3838
Karlowicz, Titus M. 1927
Karnig, Albert K. 2321 2418 2437 2480 2481 2482 2483 2502 2909
Karsarda, John D. 139
Karsh, Audrey R. 436
Karsh, Michael B. 658 835 1095 3794 3795 3796
Kauffmann, Stanley 2796
Kaufman, Burton I. 404
Kaufman, Clifford 2322 2429 3437 3438
Kaufman, Herbert 2426
Kaufmann, Perry 2277
Kay, Jane Holtz 3523
Kealey, Gregory S. 3737 3738
Keane, Patrick 3797
Kedro, M. James 1352
Keefe, Thomas M. 935
Keil, Thomas J. 2323
Kelejian, Harry H. 2730
Kelemen, Thomas A. 140
Keller, Edmond J. 2324
Keller, Edmund J. 2484
Keller, Frank V. 3389
Keller, Kenneth W. 602
Keller, Morton 344
Kellogg, John 1377
Kelly, Kenneth 3739
Kelly, Susan Croce 884
Kelsey, Harry 141 3986
Kemper, Donald J. 1665
Ken, Sally 1546
Kendrick, Frank J. 3464
Kennedy, Albert J. 1593
Kennedy, Estella 3865
Kennedy, Michael 737
Kennedy, R. Evan 2325
Kenney, Alice P. 232

Kenyon, James B. 2672
Kepler, Edwin C. 2544
Kerr, D. C. 3657
Kerr, Louise A. 3034
Kerri, James Nwannukwu 3190
Kessler, Robert P. 3382
Kessner, Thomas 1317
Keyes, Margaret N. 2114 3524
Khungian, Toros B. 1594
Kielbaso, J. James 3269
Kilar, Jeremy W. 246 603
Kilbourn, William 3892
Killick, John 437
Kimball, James L., Jr. 142
King, A. Thomas 3035
King, Charles E. 2850
King, Paul E. 1838
King, Richard L. 1005
Kingsbury, Martha 1006
Kingsdale, Jon M. 885
Kingston, Maxine Hong 1545
Kinne, Ann Spencer 3525
Kinsey, Stephen D. 1454
Kintrea, Frank 143
Kipp, Samuel M., III 785
Kirby, David J. 2851
Kirby, Ronald F. 3465
Kirk, Carolyn Tyirin 836
Kirk, Gordon W., Jr. 836
Kirk, Ruth 3930
Kirkby, Dianne 144
Kirkpatrick, Samuel A. 3364
Kirlin, John J. 2485
Kittell, Robert S. 438
Klaczynska, Barbara 1318
Klassen, Henry C. 3798 3893
Klaw, Spencer 1772 1928
Kleber, John E. 1666
Klein, Maury 886 936
Klein, Mitchell S. G. 3987
Klein, Walter E. 738
Kleinberg, S. J. 786
Kleinberg, Susan J. 1773 3988
Kleinmaier, Judith 145
Klemmack, David L. 2693
Klinger, Donald E. 2300
Klingman, David 2473
Kmet, Jeffrey 887
Knaff, Eugene 2394
Knapp, Vertie 499
Knight, David B. 3658 3989 3990
Knight, Oliver 146
Knights, Peter R. 845
Knittel, Robert E. 3322
Knoke, David 2486
Kobler, Arthur L. 2960
Koch, Gary G. 2938
Kocolowski, Gary P. 837 1245
Kogan, Bernard R. 1796
Kogan, Herman 1246
Kohn, Lawrence A. 1744
Kojder, Apolonja Maria 3740
Kolderie, Ted 2383
Kooij, P. 3991
Kopf, Edward 838
Kopkind, Andrew 2545
Koppelman, Lee E. 2852 3279
Korey, John 2250
Korman, Gerd 1319
Kotchek, Lydia 3191
Kotter, Richard E. 247
Kouwenhoven, John A. 1929 1930
Koziol, John A. 888
Kramer, Carl E. 147
Kramer, Douglas J. 2546
Kramer, Eugene 3439
Kramer, Rita 345
Kramer, William M. 889 1455 1456 1457 1458 1489 1667 1668
Krause, Corinne Azen 1320 1321
Krause, Joe W. 739
Kredl, Lawrence P. 3641
Krefetz, Sharon Perlman 2384
Kremm, Thomas W. 1669
Kreps, Gary A. 2961
Krinsky, Carol Herselle 3526
Krinsky, Edward B. 2385
Krisberg, Barry 2921
Kristof, Frank S. 3390
Kritzberg, Barry 604
Krog, Carl 24

Kronstadt, Sylvia 2962
Krumholz, Norman 3323 3391
Kruse, Rhoda E. 1839
Kuepper, Stephen L. 346
Kuhm, Herbert W. 500 2083
Kulik, Gary 605
Kulik, Gary B. 501
Kunreuther, Howard 2711
Kunz, Arthur H. 2852
Kuo, Wen H. 3173
Kupperman, Karen Ordahl 1745
Kuroda, Yasumasa 3174
Kurtz, Henry I. 2963
Kurtz, Michael J. 318
Kurtz, Michael L. 373
Kurtzweg, Jerry A. 2547
Kusmer, Kenneth L. 659 1161
Kuspit, Donald B. 2811
Kutcher, Stan 3799
Kutner, Nancy G. 2712
Kuvlesky, William 3095
Kuzniak, Ellen Marie 1096
Kuzniewski, Anthony J. 1595
Kwiat, Joseph J. 1007

L

LaBarre, Claude E. 3995
LaFontaine, Charles V. 1670
LaFrance, Marc 3893
Lafrance, Marc 3894
LaGory, Mark 148
LaGreca, Anthony J. 2689
Lahmeyer Lobo, Eulália María 439
Lake, Robert W. 2247 3163 3392
Lalli, Michael 2853
Lamb, Blaine P. 502 1459
Lamon, Lester C. 1378
Lamott, Kenneth 2326
Lampe, Philip E. 3156
Lampman, Evelyn Sibley 660
Landau, Sarah Bradford 1931
Landis, Frank W. 890
Landreth, Elizabeth 3607
Lane, Angela 2486
Lane, James B. 1162 3608
Lane, Robert 2251
Lane, Roger 1247 1248
Lang, William L. 1379
Langdon, Thomas C. 2162
Langenbach, Randolph 566 1932
Lansky, Leonard M. 2987
Lapides, Abe 1460
Laplante, Pierre 3713
Lapointe, Michelle 3741
Lapping, Mark B. 1840 3420
Larkin, Melvin A. 1628
Larocque, Paul 3800
LaRose, Helen 3992
Larsen, Lawrence H. 149
Larson, Calvin J. 3096
Laslett, Barbara 702 703
Latané, Bibb 2964
Latimer, Margaret K. 2487
Latus, Mark 1862 1863
Lauder, Kathleen 3634
Lauer, Bruce M. 3249
Lauer, Robert H. 3224
Laurence, Anya 1008
Laurie, Bruce 787 1322
Lavender, David 541
Lavigne, Marie 3742
Lavin, David E. 2854
Law, Eileen 1546
Lawson, Michael L. 25 661
Lax, John 1009 1249
Lazerson, Marvin 1097 1098
Lazin, Frederick A. 3393
Lease, Richard J. 1461
Leavitt, Judith W. 1746
Leavitt, Judith Walzer 1747
LeBoeuf, Randall J., Jr. 2084
Lederer, Francis L., II 937
Lee, Anne S. 1748 3097
Lee, David D. 347
Lee, Eugene C. 2488
Lee, Everett S. 1748
Lee, Lance R. 2601
Lee, Lawrence B. 150
Lee, Robert D., Jr. 2427
Lee, Yuk 2245

LeFave, Don 440
Lefaver, Scott 3351
LeGacy, Arthur 3993
Legare, Jacques 3806
LeGares, Richard T. 3382
Lehne, Richard 2327 2548
Leibo, Steven A. 1462
Leigh, Duane E. 2618
Leighton, Barry 2256
Leinenweber, Charles 788
Lejeunesse, Marcel 3801
Lemann, Nicholas 2577
LeMay, Michael 2512
Lemon, J. T. 2428
Lemon, James T. 3994
Lemonides, James S. 3429
Leonard, Henry B. 1163 1671
Leonard, Ira M. 248 249
Leonard, Stephen J. 1323
Leong, Russell 2825
Lernack, Paul 1250
Lerner, Samuel 1463
Less, Lynn H. 1512
Levesque, George A. 1672
Levi, Margaret 2450 3383
Levi, Steven C. 606 607 608 1251
Levin, Alexandra Lee 2013
Levin, Sharon G. 2602
Levine, Charles H. 2429 2630 3036
Levine, Daniel U. 2855 2856 3036
Levine, David 3784
Levine, James P. 2965
Levine, Judith 2578
Levine, Rayna F. 3036
Levitt, Abraham H. 2123
Levitt, James H. 3995
Levitt, Lee 3609
Levy, John M. 3394
LeWarne, Charles Pierce 609
Lewin, David 2631
Lewis, David L. 3242
Lewis, Dottie L. 2046
Lewis, H. H. Walker 740
Lewis, Peirce 3527
Lewis, Peirce F. 3528
Lewis, Theodore 1673
Lewy, Cheryl Winter 3996
Ley, David 2966
Li, Peter S. 3175 3839
Licht, M. 2752
Liebermann, Richard K. 789
Liebman, Robert 1252
Liebschutz, Sarah F. 2555
Lieske, Joel A. 2967
Light, Ivan 1253 1547 1548 1549
Light, Ivan H. 3167
Lightbody, James 3685
Ligibell, Ted J. 151
Lilydahl, Jane H. 3370
Limbaugh, R. H. 3529
Lin, Nan 3173
Lindner, Carl M. 3997
Lindsey, David 152 441
Lineberry, Robert L. 2229
Linner, John H. 3323
Linteau, Paul-André 3631 3714 3998
Lipman, Andrew David 2085
Lipsey, C. M. 3217
Lipsey, C. McCurdy 3620
Lipton, S. Gregory 3280
Little, Charles E. 3395
Littlefield, Daniel F., Jr. 153
Liu, Ben-chieh 3243
Livermore, Charles P. 3281
Lloyd, Anne 1841
Lloyd, Sheila 3873
Locke, Raymond Friday 154 155 156 157
Locker, Zelma Bays 1797 2086
Lockwood, Charles 1798 2014
Loewenstein, Louis K. 2513 3324
Logan, Thomas H. 1842
Long, J. Anthony 3686
Long, Larry H. 2673 2713
Long, Norton E. 2230 2231 2328 2329 3325 3326 3610
Loomis, Ross 2660
Lopata, Helena Znaniecki 1596
López, Adalberto 1597
Lopez, David E. 3157

López, Ronald W. 2770
Lord, J. Dennis 2857
Lotchin, Roger W. 319 1598
Loudfoot, Raymonde 3840
Love, Frank 158
Love, Glen A. 2163
Lovejoy, David B., Jr. 1749
Lovett, Bobby L. 1254
Lovrich, Nicholas P., Jr. 3037 3611 3612
Lovritch, Nicholas P., Jr. 2968
Lowe, David 1933
Lowe, George D. 3613
Lowenfish, Lee Elihu 2753
Lowenthal, David 3614
Lowry, Charles B. 320 662
Lowry, Ira S. 3396
Lubomudrov, Slava 2494
Lubove, Roy 1164 2015
Lucas, Paul R. 1674
Lucas, Richard 3895
Luckingham, Bradford 741 1010 1011 1324 1675 3999
Luebke, Frederick C. 1676
Lugar, Richard L. 2386
Luker, Ralph E. 1677
Luks, Allan 2232
Lum, Philip A. 2858
Lunardini, Rosemary 3802
Luning Prak, N. 159
Lupfer, Michael 2497
Lupold, John S. 3530 3531
Luria, Daniel 790
Luria, Daniel D. 791
Lurie, Jonathan 542
Lutey, Kent 442
Lutman, John H. 3896
Lyford, Joseph P. 2278 2771
Lyle, Donald J. 2087
Lyman, Stanford M. 1550
Lynch, Joseph P. 839
Lynch, Lawrence 3192
Lynch, Patrick D. 2862
Lynes, Russell 1012 3421
Lynn, Kenneth S. 663
Lyon, Eugene 664
Lyons, W. E. 2387
Lyons, William 2549
Lytle, Rebecca 1799

M

Mabee, Carleton 1099 1165
Macchiarola, Frank J. 321 2402
MacDermaid, Anne 4000
MacDonagh, Oliver 1513
MacDonald, Edgar 2164
Macdonald, K. I. 3122
MacDonald, Norbert 3632 3897
MacGregor, Robert W. 3289
MacKenzie, Robert C. 3898
Mackler, Bernard 2859
Mackler, Mark 2088
MacManus, Susan A. 2330
Macnab, John B. 1678
MacPhail, Elizabeth C. 1166 1551
Mader, George G. 3327
Mader, Paul D. 2687
Magarian, Horen Henry 1599
Magaziner, Henry J. 1867
Maggiotto, Michael A. 2470
Magnaghi, Russell M. 1600
Maier, Henry W. 2331
Main, Gloria L. 26 792
Major, Marjorie 3899
Maldonado, Edwin 160
Mallach, Stanley 2089
Maller, Allen S. 2489
Manarin, Louis H. 1934
Mandelker, Daniel R. 2233
Maness, Lonnie E. 4001
Manheim, Jarol B. 2772
Mann, Arthur J. 2714
Mann, Dale 2860
Mann, Maybelle 1013
Mann, Ralph 250
Manners, Gerald 2619
Manning, David 3123
Manucy, Albert 3532
Manzl, H. F. 4004
Marando, Vincent L. 2388 2389 2490 3397 3466

Palmer, Earl 2699
Palmer, Edward 2984
Pampel, Fred C. 2675
Panting, Gerry 3711
Papermaster, Isadore 1465
Paquet, Gilles 3809
Parascandola, John 1757
Paraschos, Janet Nyberg 3545 3546
Parente, Frank 2251
Park, Ki Suh 3284
Parker, Kallis E. 3105
Parker, Peter J. 1177
Parker, Russell D. 1396
Parkin, Michael 2656
Parliment, T. J. 2747
Parlow, Anita 2281
Parot, Joseph 1605
Parvin, Manocher 3285
Passanti, Francesco 1949
Passi, Michael M. 1326 1606
Patrick, Robert W. 324
Patterson, G. James 1607
Patterson, R. S. 1178
Patterson, Richard 2128
Patton, Helen 1950
Patton, Phil 2800
Paučo, Joseph 3200
Paulson, Darryl 2635
Paupst, Kathy 3842
Pavlak, Thomas J. 3042 3617
Pawson, Stella 707
Peabody, Malcolm E., Jr. 3043
Pearce, George F. 1758
Pearce, William 3905
Pearson, John E. 3403
Pearson, Ralph L. 746 2676
Pearson, Roger W. 3248
Pease, Jane H. 1397 2049
Pease, William H. 1397 2049
Peden, Creighton 3618
Pedersen, Elsa 183 184
Pedersen, Walt 184
Peebles, Robert H. 185
Peek, Charles W. 3613
Peltin, Thomas J. 1818
Pencak, William 1249
Pendergrass, Lee F. 379
Pendleton, Brian F. 2604
Penfield, Wallace C. 1951
Penn, Robert C. 2454
Penna, Anthony N. 2171
Penney, J. 3643
Penney, Sherry 1608
Percal, Raul Moncarz 3160
Percival, Robert V. 1223
Pérez, Louis A., Jr. 572 1532
Perkins, Edwin J. 407
Perkins, George 2172
Perkins, Jerry 2431
Perloff, Harvey S. 3470
Perrotta, John A. 2455
Perry, James E. 2630
Perry, Marvin E. 3106
Perry, Stewart E. 2582
Pessen, Edward 37 270 801 802 803 4019
Pessino, Catherine 2801
Peters, A. Gerald 3471
Peters, Charles 2557
Peterson, Jon A. 1846 1847
Petraitus, Paul W. 667
Petroff, Lillian 3843 3844
Petrusak, Frank 3130
Pettigrew, Thomas F. 2873 3107
Petty, Roy 3379
Pfautz, Harold W. 3108
Pfeiffer, John 3933
Pfeiffer, Sophie Douglas 3404
Pfeil, Don 186
Phair, Sharon 1267
Phelps, Edward C. H. 3876
Philipsen, Gerry 2716
Phillips, Doris 3906
Phillips, Kenneth E. 3102
Phillips, Phillip D. 2282
Phillips, Rob 850
Pickvance, C. G. 2700
Piehl, Charles K. 187
Piehl, Frank J. 2050 2051 2095
Pienkos, Donald 3201
Pienkos, Donald E. 3202
Pier, Andrew V. 1609 3203
Pierce, John C. 3109
Pierce, Lorraine E. 1466

Pierce, Lorraine Esterly 1533
Pierce, Richard A. 183
Pilo, Marvin R. 2874
Pindur, Wolfgang 2349
Pines, David 2717
Pink, William T. 2849
Pinsky, Mark 1467
Piott, Steven L. 619
Piper, Robert R. 3472
Pitterman, Marvin 1468
Pitzer, Donald E. 3547
Piva, Michael J. 3695
Piven, Frances Fox 2340
Platt, Frederick 3548
Platt, Hermann K. 255
Platt, Virginia B. 447
Ploss, Charlotte 2463
Poethig, Richard P. 1687
Pol, Louis G. 2891
Polacsek, John F. 2096
Polen, Michael 1252
Polgar, S. 2677
Polos, Nicholas C. 1103
Polyzoi, Eleoussa 3845
Pommer, Richard 1952
Ponting, J. Rick 2985 2986
Popp, Dean O. 2338
Porter, Bruce 2942
Porter, Jack Nusan 2432
Ports, Uldis 1848
Posadas, Barbara M. 188
Post, Carl 901
Poston, Dudley L., Jr. 2689
Poteet, James M. 1268
Potter, Beverly 902
Potts, James H. 256
Poulsen, Richard C. 1953
Powell, H. Benjamin 189
Powell, Lawrence Clark 190 2591
Powell, T. J. D. 3662
Power, Mary G. 2678
Poyo, Gerald E. 1534
Pozzetta, George E. 337 1610
Praschos, Janet Nyberg 3549
Pratt, Henry J. 2392
Pratt, William C. 298
Pred, Allan R. 2283
Pressman, Norman E. P. 3634 4020
Preston, Howard L. 2097
Preston, James D. 2452
Preston, Michael B. 2241
Preston, William 1269
Prewitt, Kenneth 2306
Price, David E. 2497
Price, Jacob M. 191 4021
Price, John A. 3204
Prickett, James R. 620
Priddy, Benjamin, Jr. 1954
Priddy, Laurance L. 2875
Primeaux, Walter J. 3441
Prior, Moody E. 38
Protess, David L. 2433 2456
Provenzo, Eugene F., Jr. 1104 2098
Provine, Dorothy 1398
Pumphrey, Ralph E. 1759
Pusateri, C. Joseph 257
Pushkar, R. G. 1955
Pushkarev, Boris 3473
Putney, Martha S. 1105
Pyle, Gerald F. 3249

Q

Quandt, Jean B. 668
Quarantelli, E. L. 2932 2946 2986
Quigley, John M. 3405
Quilici, R. H. 448
Quimby, Ian M. G. 416 1025 1047 2795
Quinan, Jack 1956 1957 1958
Quinan, John 1959
Quinn, Michael A. 2242
Quinney, Richard 590

R

Rabin, Yale 3474
Rabinowitz, Howard N. 299 1106 1270
Racine, Jean-Bernard 3747
Racine, Philip N. 669 1107

Radbill, Samuel X. 1760
Rader, Benjamin G. 747
Radford, John 670
Radford, John P. 1399
Radzialowski, Thaddeus 1611
Radzialowski, Thaddeus 1327
Rahe, Charles P. 2341
Rahill, Peter J. 1688
Raiche, Stephen J. 1802
Raichle, Donald 1108
Ralph, Raymond M. 1689
Ramcharan, Subhas 3846
Rammelkamp, Julian S. 1179
Randall, David C. 1400 1401
Rankin, Ernest H. 192
Ranney, Victoria Post 2020
Rao, Vimala 2173
Raphael, Marc Lee 1180 1469 1470 4022 4023 4024
Rapp, Michael G. 1471
Rasmussen, D. W. 2616
Ratcliff, Carter 2802 2803 2804
Rath, Gustave J. 3348
Ratzlaff, Robert K. 193
Rauch, Julia B. 1181 1182
Ravitch, Diane 2402 2876 2903
Rawlins, V. Lane 2618
Rayfield, J. R. 3847
Rayman, Ronald A. 1960
Raymond, Robert S. 449
Reagon, Bernice 903
Reath, Henry T. 2498
Redburn, Steve 2284
Redding, Martin J. 3333
Reddy, W. Brendan 2987
Redfearn, George V. 139
Reece, Ray 3551
Reed, John P. 2988
Reed, Merl E. 583 621 2632 4035
Rees, John 2603
Rees, R. 3663
Rees, Ronald 3907
Regeher, Ted D. 3848
Regnery, Henry 1026
Rehfuss, John 2393
Reichard, Maximilian 258 1402
Reichmann, Keith W. 457
Reid, John D. 3110 3118
Reier, Sharon 2099
Reilly, John M. 622 3619
Reilly, Timothy F. 1690
Reinhardt, Elizabeth W. 1961
Reisler, Mark 1535
Reiss, Albert J., Jr. 2193
Reiter, Beth Lattimore 3552
Renner, Richard Wilson 748 1271
Renshaw, Patrick 1403
Reschovsky, Andrew 2394
Reskin, Barbara 3250
Reuter, Frederick H. 3334
Reutlinger, Andrew S. 1472
Reverby, Susan 552
Reynolds, Ann Vines 3553
Reynolds, Anthony M. 2756
Reynolds, Regina 4025
Rhangos, Audrey Dunn 3554
Rhoades, Elizabeth Adams 1027
Rhoda, Richard 2100
Ricards, Sherman L. 904
Rice, Bradley R. 381
Rice, Cindy 1849
Rich, Daniel 3289
Rich, David 623
Rich, Robert F. 2989
Richards, Carol 3406
Richards, Pamela J. 3004
Richards, Robert O. 2604
Richardson, James F. 1272
Richmond, Anthony H. 3849
Rickert, Thomas E. 3335
Ridgeway, James 3442
Ridgway, Whitman H. 271 804
Riedy, James L. 1028
Riefler, Roger F. 194
Riess, Steven 905
Riess, Steven A. 906
Riley, Mark B. 195
Ring, Daniel F. 325

Ringenbach, Paul T. 1183
Rischin, Moses 300
Rist, Ray C. 2877
Ritchey, David 907 1029 1030
Ritchey, P. Neal 2679 2739
Ritchie, Donald A. 382
Ritterband, Paul 2878 2879
Rivers, David E. 3336
Rivers, Larry E. 1184
Robbins, Peggy 908 2129 3590
Roberson, Jere W. 1404
Robert, Jean-Claude 3714 3810
Roberts, Alden E. 3205
Roberts, David 3811
Roberts, Shirley J. 3044
Roberts, Wayne 3748 3812
Robertson, Leon S. 2989
Robins, Lee N. 2990
Robinson, J. Lewis 3664
Robinson, Michael 1850
Robinson, Willard B. 1803
Rock, Howard B. 624 625 805
Rock, William K. 3236
Rockaway, Robert A. 1473 1474 1475
Rockoff, Hugh 536
Rodgers, Harrell R., Jr. 2925 2991
Rodwin, Lloyd 2532
Roeber, Anthony Gregg 1691
Roff, Kenneth L. 1405
Roff, Sandra Schoiock 941
Rogers, Barbara 1761
Rogers, Bruce D. 3620
Rogers, David L. 2604
Rogers, Rebecca M. 1962
Rogers, Theresa F. 3621
Rogoff, Edward G. 2345
Rogowsky, Edward T. 2735
Rohn, David 2880
Rolle, Andrew 1328
Romanofsky, Peter 1185 1186 1476
Romney, Paul 3696
Romo, Ricardo 843 3161
Romotsky, Jerry 2805
Romotsky, Sally R. 2805
Ronald, Ann 2174
Rondinelli, Dennis A. 2342 2558 3337
Ronnie, Art 1963
Roof, Wade Clark 1406 3045 3053 3111 4058
Rooke, Patricia 1178
Roomkin, Myron 2881
Rooney, James F. 2718
Roper, James H. 3338 3555
Roppel, Patricia 508
Rorabaugh, William J. 350
Rosales, Francisco Arturo 1536
Rose, Harold M. 2680 2992
Rose, Jerome G. 3339
Rose, Mark H. 1776
Rose, Stephen M. 2930
Rosen, Benton H. 749
Rosen, George 1762
Rosen, Gerald 3162
Rosenberg, Charles E. 1763
Rosenberg, Leon J. 2101
Rosenberg, Terry J. 3163
Rosenbloom, David L. 2777
Rosenbloom, Sandra 3475
Rosenshine, Jay 1477
Rosenthal, Star 3749
Rosentraub, Mark S. 2581
Rosenwaike, Ira 1478 1479 1480 1481 2882 3131
Ross, Bernard H. 2848
Ross, Edyth L. 1187
Ross, H. Laurence 2989
Ross, John R. 2175
Ross, Richard L. 99
Ross, Ronald 1407
Rossell, Christine 2883 2903
Rossi, Jean 1553
Rossi, Peter H. 3112
Rostecki, Randy R. 3908 3909
Rothchild, Sylvia 3132
Rothenberg, Alan E. 3556
Rothenberg, Jerome 2354
Rothman, Jonathan S. 2488
Rothschild, Janice 1482

Rothstein, Stanley William 2884
Rotundo, Barbara 2021
Rouse, Parke, Jr. 326
Rowe, Jonathan 3406
Rowland, A. Ray 4026
Rowland, Beryl 2176
Rowley, Dennis 450
Roy, Maurice 3786
Roy, Patricia 3910
Roy, Patricia E. 3813
Rubin, Barbara 1964 3286
Rubin, Marilyn 2620
Rubin, Victor 2926
Rubinoff, Michael W. 1188
Rubinowitz, Leonard S. 2607
Ruchelman, Leonard 2343
Ruchelman, Leonard I. 3426
Rudd, Hynda 451
Ruddell, Thiery 3630
Rudolph, Richard H. 806
Rudwick, Elliott 1273 1384
Ruffin, Thomas F. 327
Rumore, Samuel A., Jr. 2130
Rushton, Bill 2499
Russel, Raymond 2582
Russell, Francis 351
Russell, Hilary 3911
Russell, Jack 509
Russell, Michael B. 2636
Russo, Francis X. 1110
Rutledge, Philip J. 2559
Rutman, Darrett B. 196
Rutundo, Barbara 2022
Ruwell, Mary Elizabeth 4025
Ryan, James Gilbert 1274
Ryan, Mary P. 1189 1692
Rybeck, Walter 2344
Ryerson, R. A. 259

S

Saalberg, Harvey 942
Sager, Leon B. 3557
Sakolsky, R. 2885
Salces, Luis M. 2500
Sale, James E. 3476
Sale, Kirkpatrick 3340
Sale, Roger 626
Sales, William W., Jr. 2243
Salins, Peter D. 2244 2395 2621 2719
Salmon, Myrene 1851
Saloman, Ora Frishberg 1031
Saltzstein, Alan 3029
Sampson, William A. 3113
Samuels, Harold 1032
Samuels, Peggy 1032
Sanchez, Armand J. 1537
Sanchez, Ramón 2886
Sandburg, Everett A. 547
Sande, Theodore Anton 1965
Sanders, John 1033
Sardell, Alice 2916
Sarjeant, William A. S. 3816
Sarkissian, Wendy 1852
Sassen-Koob, Saskia 2701
Sauers, Bernard J. 197
Saunders, Joan 2768
Saunders, Lonnie 2993
Saunders, Robert M. 1275
Savage, Richard A. 198
Savage, V. Howard 2583
Savas, E. S. 2396
Saveth, Edward N. 301
Savitch, H. V. 2397 2681
Savitt, Todd L. 1764
Savitz, Leonard D. 2853
Savoie, Ronald 510
Saylor, Larry J. 2102
Scamehorn, H. Lee 199
Schafer, Robert 2682
Schalck, Harry G. 1828
Schallhorn, Cathlyn 1190
Schappes, Morris U. 627
Scharnau, Ralph 1191
Scharnau, Ralph William 302
Schatt, Stanley 3046
Scheidt, David L. 1693
Scheiner, James I. 3477
Schexnider, Alvin J. 2740
Schiavo, Bartholomew 1468
Schiesl, Martin J. 383
Schiff, Bennett 2806
Schlefer, Marion 2251
Schlereth, Thomas J. 1034 2177 4027 4028

LIST OF PERIODICALS

A

Acadiensis: Journal of the History of the Atlantic Region [Canada]
Actualité Économique [Canada]
Administration and Society
Administrative Science Quarterly
Adventist Heritage
Aerospace Historian
Afro-Americans in New York Life and History
Agricultural History
AHA Newsletter
Alabama Historical Quarterly
Alabama Review
Alberta Historical Review (see Alberta History) [Canada]
Alberta History [Canada]
Amerasia Journal
American Archivist
American Art and Antiques (see Art and Antiques)
American Art Journal
American Aviation Historical Society. Journal
American Bar Association Journal
American Behavioral Scientist
American Economic Review
American Heritage
American Historical Review
American History Illustrated
American Jewish Archives
American Jewish Historical Quarterly (see American Jewish History)
American Jewish History
American Journal of Economics and Sociology
American Journal of Legal History
American Journal of Political Science
American Journal of Sociology
American Literary Realism, 1870-1910
American Literature
American Neptune
American Political Science Review
American Politics Quarterly
American Preservation
American Quarterly
American Review of Canadian Studies
American Scholar
American Sociological Review
American Speech
American Studies International
American Studies (Lawrence, KS)
American Studies (Washington, DC) (see American Studies International)
American West
Americas: A Quarterly Review of Inter-American Cultural History (Academy of American Franciscan History)
Américas (Organization of American States)
Amerikastudien/American Studies [German Federal Republic]
Annales de Géographie [France]
Annales: Économies, Sociétés, Civilisations [France]
Annales Historiques de la Révolution Française [France]
Annals of Iowa
Annals of Science [Great Britain]
Annals of the American Academy of Political and Social Science
Annals of the Association of American Geographers
Annals of Wyoming
Antioch Review
Appalachian Journal
Arbitration Journal
Arctic [Canada]
Arizona and the West
Arkansas Historical Quarterly
Armenian Review
Art in America
Arts in Society (ceased pub 1976)
Asian Profile [Hong Kong]
Atlantis: A Women's Studies Journal [Canada]
Audience (ceased pub 1973)
Australian Journal of Politics and History [Australia]
Aztlán

B

Baptist History and Heritage
BC Studies [Canada]
Beaver [Canada]
Black Scholar
Brigham Young University Studies
Bulletin of the Atomic Scientists (briefly known as Science and Public Affairs)

Bulletin of the History of Medicine
Bulletin of the Society for the Study of Labour History [Great Britain]
Business History [Great Britain]
Business History Review

C

Cahiers de Géographie de Québec [Canada]
California Historical Quarterly (see California History)
California History
Canada: An Historical Magazine (ceased pub 1976) [Canada]
Canadian Dimension [Canada]
Canadian Ethnic Studies = Études Ethniques au Canada [Canada]
Canadian Geographic [Canada]
Canadian Geographical Journal (see Canadian Geographic) [Canada]
Canadian Historic Sites [Canada]
Canadian Historical Association Historical Papers (see Historical Papers) [Canada]
Canadian Historical Review [Canada]
Canadian Journal of History = Annales Canadiennes d'Histoire [Canada]
Canadian Journal of History of Sport = Revue Canadienne de l'Histoire des Sports [Canada]
Canadian Journal of Political Science = Revue Canadienne de Science Politique [Canada]
Canadian Labour [Canada]
Canadian Library Journal [Canada]
Canadian Oral History Association Journal = Journal de la Société Canadienne d'Histoire Orale [Canada]
Canadian Public Administration = Administration Publique du Canada [Canada]
Canadian Review of American Studies [Canada]
Canadian Review of Sociology and Anthropology = Revue Canadienne de Sociologie et d'Anthropologie [Canada]
Capitol Studies (see Congressional Studies)
Caribbean Review
Catholic Historical Review
Center Magazine
Centerpoint
Change
Chicago History
Chronicle
Chronicles of Oklahoma
Church History
Cincinnati Historical Society Bulletin
Civil Liberties Review (ceased pub 1979)
Civil War History
Civil War Times Illustrated
Clio Medica [Netherlands]
Colorado Magazine
Colorado Quarterly
Commentary
Compact
Comparative Political Studies
Comparative Studies in Society and History [Great Britain]
Computers and the Humanities
Concordia Historical Institute Quarterly
Connecticut History
Crisis
Cry California
Cuban Studies
Curator (American Museum of Natural History)
Current History

D

Daedalus
Dalhousie Review [Canada]
Daughters of the American Revolution Magazine
Delaware History
Dialogue: A Journal of Mormon Thought
Dissent

E

Early American Life
Early American Literature
Economic Development and Cultural Change
Economic Geography
Economic Inquiry
Economica [Great Britain]
Economisch- en Sociaal-Historisch Jaarboek [Netherlands]

Education and Urban Society
Eighteenth-Century Life
Éire-Ireland
Encounter
Escribano
Essex Institute Historical Collections
Ethnic Groups
Ethnicity
Ethnohistory
Explorations in Economic History

F

Family Heritage (ceased pub 1979)
Feminist Studies
Film and History
Filson Club History Quarterly
Florida Historical Quarterly
FOCUS/Midwest
Foundations: A Baptist Journal of History and Theology
Frankfurter Hefte [German Federal Republic]
Freedomways
Frontiers

G

Gateway Heritage
Geographical Review
Geography [Great Britain]
Georgia Historical Quarterly
Georgia Life (ceased pub 1980)
Georgia Review
Government Publications Review Part A: Research Articles
Great Plains Journal

H

Halve Maen
Harvard Educational Review
Harvard Library Bulletin
Hawaiian Journal of History
Historian
Historic Preservation
Historical Archaeology
Historical Journal of Massachusetts
Historical Journal of Western Massachusetts (see Historical Journal of Massachusetts)
Historical Magazine of the Protestant Episcopal Church
Historical Methods
Historical Methods Newsletter (see Historical Methods)
Historical New Hampshire
Historical Papers = Communications Historiques [Canada]
History of Childhood Quarterly: The Journal of Psychohistory (see Journal of Psychohistory)
History of Education Quarterly
History Teacher
History Today [Great Britain]
History Workshop Journal [Great Britain]
Horizon
Human Organization

I

Idaho Heritage (ceased pub 1978)
Idaho Yesterdays
Indian Historian (see Wasseje Indian Historian)
Indian Journal of American Studies [India]
Indiana Folklore
Indiana History Bulletin
Indiana Magazine of History
Indiana Social Studies Quarterly
Industrial and Labor Relations Review
Industrial Relations = Relations Industrielles [Canada]
Inland Seas
International Affairs [Union of Soviet Socialist Republic]
International Journal of Comparative Sociology [Canada]
International Journal of Women's Studies [Canada]
International Migration = Migrations Internationales = Migraciones Internacionales [Netherlands]
International Migration Review
International Review of History and Political Science [India]

International Socialist Review
Italian Americana
Italian Quarterly (ceased pub 1977-79)

J

Jednota Annual Furdek
Jewish Social Studies
Journal for the Scientific Study of Religion
Journal of American Folklore
Journal of American History
Journal of American Studies [Great Britain]
Journal of Arizona History
Journal of Asian and African Studies [Netherlands]
Journal of Black Studies
Journal of Business
Journal of Canadian Studies = Revue d'Études
    Canadiennes [Canada]
Journal of Communication
Journal of Conflict Resolution
Journal of Economic History
Journal of Economic Literature
Journal of Ethnic Studies
Journal of Family History: Studies in Family,
    Kinship, and Demography
Journal of Forest History
Journal of General Education
Journal of Higher Education
Journal of Historical Geography
Journal of Inter-American Studies (see Journal of
    Interamerican Studies and World Affairs)
Journal of Interamerican Studies and World Affairs
Journal of Interdisciplinary History
Journal of Intergroup Relations
Journal of Jazz Studies
Journal of Korean Affairs (ceased pub 1977)
Journal of Law & Economics
Journal of Library History, Philosophy, and
    Comparative Librarianship
Journal of Long Island History
Journal of Mexican American History
Journal of Mississippi History
Journal of Negro Education
Journal of Negro History
Journal of Political and Military Sociology
Journal of Political Economy
Journal of Politics
Journal of Popular Culture
Journal of Popular Film (see Journal of Popular
    Film and Television)
Journal of Popular Film and Television
Journal of Presbyterian History
Journal of Religious History [Australia]
Journal of San Diego History
Journal of Social History
Journal of Social Issues
Journal of Southern History
Journal of Sport History
Journal of Studies on Alcohol
Journal of the American Institute of Planners (see
    Journal of the American Planning Association)
Journal of the American Planning Association
Journal of the Canadian Church Historical Society
    [Canada]
Journal of the Folklore Institute
Journal of the Hellenic Diaspora: Critical Thoughts
    on Greek and World Issues
Journal of the History of Medicine and Allied
    Sciences
Journal of the Illinois State Historical Society
Journal of the Lancaster County Historical Society
Journal of the Rutgers University Library
Journal of the Society for Army Historical Research
    [Great Britain]
Journal of the Society of Architectural Historians
Journal of the West
Journal of Transport History [Great Britain]
Journal of Urban History
Journalism Quarterly
Judicature

K

Kansas Historical Quarterly (superseded by Kansas
    History)
Kansas History
Kansas Quarterly
Kiva
Kultura i Społeczeństwo [Poland]

L

Labor History
Labour = Travailleur [Canada]
Land Economics

Latin American Perspectives
Law & Society Review
Liberal Education
Library History Review [India]
Library Quarterly
Lincoln Herald
Lituanus
Long Island Forum
Louisiana History
Louisiana Studies (see Southern Studies: An
    Interdisciplinary Journal of the South)

M

Manitoba History [Canada]
Manitoba Pageant (superseded by Manitoba History)
    [Canada]
Mankind
Manuscripts
Marine Corps Gazette
Maryland Historian
Maryland Historical Magazine
Massachusetts Historical Society Proceedings
Massachusetts Review
Masterkey
Mennonite Life
Mennonite Quarterly Review
Methodist History
Michael: On the History of the Jews in the Diaspora
    [Israel]
Michigan Academician
Michigan History
Michigan Jewish History
Mid-America
Midstream
Midwest Quarterly
Midwest Review
Military Affairs
Military Collector and Historian
Milwaukee History
Minnesota History
Mirovaia Ekonomika i Mezhdunarodnye Otnosheniia
    [Union of Soviet Socialist Republic]
Mississippi Quarterly
Missouri Historical Review
Missouri Historical Society. Bulletin (superseded by
    Gateway Heritage)
Montana Magazine of History (see Montana:
    Magazine of Western History)
Montana: Magazine of Western History
Monthly Labor Review
Monthly Review

N

National Civic Review
Nautical Research Journal
Nebraska History
Negro History Bulletin
Neue Politische Literatur [German Federal
    Republic]
Nevada Historical Society Quarterly
New England Historical and Genealogical Register
New England Quarterly
New England Social Studies Bulletin
New Jersey History
New Mexico Historical Review
New Scholar
New South (superseded by Southern Voices)
New York Affairs
New York Folklore
New York Folklore Quarterly (superseded by New
    York Folklore)
New York History
Newberry Library Bulletin (suspended pub 1979)
New-England Galaxy
Newport History
New-York Historical Society Quarterly
Niagara Frontier
Nineteenth-Century Fiction
North Carolina Historical Review
North Dakota History
North Dakota Quarterly
North Jersey Highlander
North Louisiana Historical Association Journal
Northwest Ohio Quarterly: a Journal of History and
    Civilization
Noticias
Nova Scotia Historical Quarterly [Canada]
Nova Scotia Historical Society Collections [Canada]
Novaia i Noveishaia Istoriia [Union of Soviet
    Socialist Republic]
Now and Then *

O

Ohio History
Old Northwest
Old-Time New England
Ontario History [Canada]
Oral History Review
Oregon Historical Quarterly

P

Pacific Historian
Pacific Historical Review
Pacific Northwest Quarterly
Pacific Northwesterner
Pacific Sociological Review
Paedagogica Historica [Belgium]
Pakistan Library Bulletin [Pakistan]
Palimpsest
Panhandle-Plains Historical Review
Papers in Slovene Studies (see Slovene Studies)
Past and Present [Great Britain]
Pennsylvania Folklife
Pennsylvania History
Pennsylvania Magazine of History and Biography
Perspectivas Pedagógicas (IHE) [Spain]
Perspectives in American History
Pharmacy in History
Philippine Journal of Public Administration
    [Philippines]
Phylon
Pioneer America
Policy and Politics [Great Britain]
Policy Studies Journal
Polish American Studies
Polish Review
Polish Western Affairs [Poland]
Political Science Quarterly
Political Studies [Great Britain]
Politics & Society
Polity
Population Studies [Great Britain]
Prairie Forum [Canada]
Present Tense
Proceedings of the Academy of Political Science
Proceedings of the American Antiquarian Society
Proceedings of the American Philosophical Society
Progressive Labor
Prologue: the Journal of the National Archives
Psychiatry: Journal for the Study of Interpersonal
    Processes
Public Interest
Public Opinion Quarterly
Public Policy
Publius

Q

Quaderni Storici [Italy]
Quarterly Journal of Economics
Quarterly Journal of Speech
Quarterly Journal of Studies on Alcohol (see Journal
    of Studies on Alcohol)
Quarterly Journal of the Library of Congress
Quarterly Review of Economics and Business
Queen's Quarterly [Canada]

R

Radical America
Radical History Review
Railroad History
Rassegna Italiana di Sociologia [Italy]
Reason
Recherches Sociographiques [Canada]
Record
Records of the American Catholic Historical Society
    of Philadelphia
Register of the Kentucky Historical Society
Religion in Life (ceased pub 1980)
Rendezvous
Research Studies
Review of Economics and Statistics
Review of Radical Political Economics
Reviews in American History
Revista de História [Brazil]
Revista del Instituto de Cultura Puertorriqueña
    (IHE) [Puerto Rico]
Revista/Review Interamericana [Puerto Rico]
Revue de l'Université d'Ottawa (see University of
    Ottawa Quarterly = Revue de l'Université
    d'Ottawa) [Canada]
Revue d'Histoire de l'Amérique Française [Canada]
Revue Française d'Études Américaines [France]
Revue Française d'Histoire d'Outre-mer [France]

Rhode Island History
Rhode Island Jewish Historical Notes
Richmond County History
Rochester History
Rocky Mountain Social Science Journal (see Social
    Science Journal)
Rural Sociology

S

San José Studies
Saskatchewan History [Canada]
Science and Public Affairs (see Bulletin of the
    Atomic Scientists)
Science and Society
Scottish Historical Review [Great Britain]
Sea History
Sessions d'Étude: Société Canadienne d'Histoire de
    l'Église Catholique (published simultaneously in
    one volume with Study Sessions: Canadian
    Catholic Historical Association) [Canada]
Signs: Journal of Women in Culture and Society
Slovakia
Smithsonian
Social and Economic Studies [Jamaica]
Social Education
Social Forces
Social History = Histoire Sociale [Canada]
Social Policy
Social Problems
Social Science
Social Science History
Social Science Journal
Social Science Quarterly
Social Service Review
Societas
Society
Sociological Analysis
Sociological Inquiry
Sociological Quarterly
Sociological Review [Great Britain]
Sociology and Social Research
Sociology of Education
Sound Heritage [Canada]
Soundings (Nashville, TN)
South Atlantic Quarterly
South Carolina Historical Magazine
South Dakota History
Southern California Quarterly
Southern Economic Journal
Southern Exposure
Southern Humanities Review
Southern Literary Journal
Southern Quarterly
Southern Review

Southern Speech Communication Journal
Southern Studies: An Interdisciplinary Journal of the
    South
Southern Voices (ceased pub 1974)
Southwest Economy and Society
Southwest Review
Southwestern Historical Quarterly
Southwestern Social Science Quarterly (see Social
    Science Quarterly)
Spiegel Historiael [Netherlands]
State Government
Staten Island Historian *
Studia Hibernica [Republic of Ireland]
Studies in Comparative International Development
Studies in History and Society (suspended pub 1977)
Study Sessions: Canadian Catholic Historical
    Association (published simultaneously in one
    volume with Sessions d'Étude: Société
    Canadienne d'Histoire de l'Église Catholique)
    [Canada]
Swedish Pioneer Historical Quarterly
Synthesis

T

Tampa Bay History
Teachers College Record
Teaching Political Science
Technology and Culture
Tennessee Folklore Society Bulletin
Tennessee Historical Quarterly
Tequesta
Texana (ceased pub 1974)
Theatre Survey: The American Journal of Theatre
    History
Trans-Action: Social Science and Modern Society
    (see Society)
Transactions of the Historical and Scientific Society
    of Manitoba (superseded by Manitoba History)
    [Canada]
Transactions of the Moravian Historical Society
Transactions of the Royal Society of Canada =
    Mémoires de la Société Royale du Canada
    [Canada]

U

Umoja: A Scholarly Journal of Black Studies
United States Naval Institute Proceedings
University of Ottawa Quarterly = Revue de
    l'Université d'Ottawa [Canada]
University of Turku, Institute of General History.
University of Windsor Review [Canada]
Upper Ohio Valley Historical Review
Urban Affairs Quarterly
Urban and Social Change Review

Urban History Review = Revue d'Histoire Urbaine
    [Canada]
Urban History Yearbook [Great Britain]
Urban Review
Urban Studies [Great Britain]
Urbanism Past and Present
Utah Historical Quarterly

V

Veritas [Brazil]
Vermont History
Virginia Cavalcade
Virginia Magazine of History and Biography
Voprosy Filosofii [Union of Soviet Socialist
    Republic]

W

Washington Monthly
West Georgia College Studies in the Social Sciences
West Tennessee Historical Society Papers
West Virginia History
Western American Literature
Western Folklore
Western Historical Quarterly
Western Illinois Regional Studies
Western Pennsylvania Historical Magazine
Western Political Quarterly
Western States Jewish Historical Quarterly
Westport Historical Quarterly (ceased pub 1975) *
Westways
William and Mary Quarterly
Winterthur Portfolio
Wisconsin Magazine of History
Wisconsin Then and Now (ceased pub 1979) *
Working Papers for a New Society
Working Papers from the Regional Economic
    History Center
World Affairs
World Today [Great Britain]
Worldview

Y

Yale Alumni Magazine
Yivo Annual of Jewish Social Science
York State Tradition (ceased pub 1974)
Youth and Society

Z

Zeitgeschichte [Austria]

LIST OF ABSTRACTERS

A

Aimone, A. C.
Alltmont, R. C.
Alvis, R. N.
Anderson, B. P.
Andrew, J. A.
Anstey, C.
Armstrong, A.
Athey, L. L.

B

Barkan, E.
Bassett, T. D. S.
Bauer, K. J.
Bauhs, T. H.
Baylen, J. O.
Beaber, P. A.
Bedford, W. B.
Beecher, L. N.
Belles, A. G.
Benson, J. A.
Billigmeier, J. C.
Blanc, A. E. Le
Bobango, G. J.
Bolton, G. A.
Bowers, D. E.
Bradford, J. C.
Broussard, J. H.
Brown, R. T.
Burckel, N. C.
Burnett, B.
Buschen, J. J.
Butchart, R. E.
Butcher, K.

C

Cahill, N.
Calkin, H. L.
Cameron, D. D.
Campbell, E. R.
Carp, E. W.
Casada, J. A.
Chan, L. B.
Chaput, D.
Chard, D. F.
Churchill, E. A.
Clark, M. J.
Cleyet, G. P.
Coleman, P. J.
Crandall, R. J.
Crapster, B. L.
Crowther, K. N. T.
Curtis, G. H.

D

D'Aniello, C. A.
Davis, D. G.
Davison, S. R.
Dean, D. M.
Dewees, A. C.
Dibert, M.
Dickinson, J. N.
Dietz, J. L.
Dodd, D.
Dubay, R. W.

E

Egerton, F. N.
Eid, L. V.
Eminhizer, E. E.
Engler, D. J.
Evans, H. M.

F

Falk, J. D.
Farmerie, S. A.
Fenn, A.
Fenske, B. L.
Findling, J. E.
Fox, G.
Frame, R. M., III
Frank, S. H.
Frey, L. S.
Frey, M. L.
Fulton, R. T.

G

Gagnon, G. O.
Gallacci, C. A.
Gammage, J.
Garfinkle, R. A.
Garland, A. N.
Genung, M.
Gillam, M. R.
Gilmont, K. E.
Glasrud, B. A.
Grant, C. L.
Grant, H. R.
Griswold del Castillo, R.
Grothaus, L. H.
Gunter, C. R.

H

Handleman, C.
Harling, F. F.
Harrow, S.
Hartford, D. A.
Hartig, T. H.
Harvey, K. A.
Hazelton, J. L.
Heermans, D.
Held, C. H.
Henderson, D. F.
Herbst, J.
Herrick, J. M.
Herstein, S. R.
Hewlett, G. A.
Hillje, J. W.
Hively, W. R.
Hobson, W. K.
Hočevar, T.
Hoffman, A.
Homan, G. D.
Horn, D. E.
Hough, M.
Howell, R.
Huff, A. E.
Human, V. L.
Hunley, J. D.

J

Jirran, R. J.
Johnson, B. D.
Johnson, D. W.
Johnson, E. D.
Johnson, E. S.
Johnson, L. F.

K

Kaufman, M.
Kearns, W. A.
Kennedy, P. W.
Kennedy, S. E.
Kicklighter, J. A.
Knafla, L. A.
Krenkel, J. H.
Kubicek, R. V.
Kuntz, N. A.
Kurland, G.

L

LaBue, B. J.
Larson, A. J.
LeBlanc, A. E.
Ledbetter, B. D.
Lederer, N.
Lee, J. M.
Leedom, J. W.
Legan, M. S.
Levy, D. N.
Lewis, J. A.
Linkfield, T. P.
Lokken, R. N.
Lovin, H. T.
Lowitt, R.
Lucas, M. B.

M

Mahood, H. R.
Maloney, L. M.
Marks, H. S.
Marr, W. L.
Marshall, P. C.
McCarthy, E.
McCarthy, J. M.
McCarthy, M. M.
McDonald, D. R.
McDorman, K. S.
McElroy, K.
McIntyre, W. D.
McKinney, G. B.
McKinstry, E. R.
McNeill, C. A.
McQuilkin, D. K.
Mendel, R. B.
Miller, R. M.
Moen, N. W.
Moore, J.
Moriarty, T. F.
Mulligan, W. H.
Murdock, E. C.
Myers, R. C.
Myres, S. L.

N

Neal, D. C.
Neville, J. D.
Neville, R. G.
Newton, C. A.
Newton, P. T.
Nicholls, D. J.
Nielson, D. G.
Noble, R. E.
Novitsky, A. W.

O

Oaks, R. F.
Ohrvall, C. W.
Olbrich, W. L.
Olson, C. W.
Olson, G. L.
Osur, A. M.

P

Panting, G. E.
Papalas, A. J.
Parker, H. M.
Patterson, S. L.
Patzwald, G.-A.
Paul, B. J.
Paul, J. F.
Pergl, G. E.
Petersen, P. L.
Pickens, D. K.
Piersen, W. D.
Pliska, S. R.
Porter, B. S.
Powell, L. N.
Preece, C. A.
Puffer, K. J.
Pusateri, C. J.

Q

Quéripel, S. R.
Quinlan, S. J.

R

Reichardt, O. H.
Ricciard-O'Beirne, D.
Righter, R. W.
Rilee, V. P.
Ritter, R. V.
Rollins, R. M.
Rosenthal, F.

S

Samaraweera, V.
Sapper, N. G.
Sassoon, T.
Savitt, T. L.
Schoenberg, P. E.
Schoonover, T. D.
Schroeder, G. R.
Shapiro, E. S.
Sherer, R. G.
Shergold, P. R.
Shields, H. S.
Sindermann, R. P.
Sliwoski, R. S.
Smith, C. O.

Smith, D. L.
Smith, L. C.
Smith, L. D.
Smith, T. W.
Snow, K. C.
Solodkin, P. L.
Sprague, S. S.
Stack, R. E.
Stickney, E. P.
Stoesen, A. R.
Storey, B. A.
Street, J. B.
Street, N. J.
Strom, S. C.
Summers, N.
Susskind, J. L.
Sweetland, J. H.
Swiecicka-Ziemianek, M.
Swift, D. C.

T

Tate, M. L.
Taylorson, P. J.
Thacker, J. W.
Thomas, J. R.
Tomlinson, R. H.
Travis, P.
Tull, J.

V

Van Benthuysen, R.
Van Wyck, L.
Vance, M. M.
Vivian, J. F.

W

Walker, W. T.
Ward, G. W. R.
Ward, H. M.
Watson, C. A.
Webb, R. A.
Wechman, R. J.
Wendel, T. H.
Wentworth, M. J.
West, K. B.
Wharton, D. P.
Wheeler, S.
White, J. L.
Whitehead, V. B.
Whitham, W. B.
Wiegand, W. A.
Williams, J. W.
Wilson, M. T.
Woehrmann, P. J.
Woodward, R. L.
Woolfe, L.

Y

Yanchisin, D. A.
Yerburgh, M. R.

Z

Zabel, O. H.
Ziewacz, L. E.
Zolota, M.
Zornow, W. F.